Red Hat®
Fedora™ Linux® 2 Bible

Red Hat®
Fedora™ Linux® 2 Bible

Christopher Negus

WILEY

Wiley Publishing, Inc.

Red Hat® Fedora™ Linux® 2 Bible

Published by
Wiley Publishing, Inc.
10475 Crosspoint Boulevard
Indianapolis, IN 46256
www.wiley.com

For general information on our other products and services or to obtain technical support, please contact our Customer Care Department within the U.S. at (800) 762-2974, outside the U.S. at (317) 572-3993 or fax (317) 572-4002.

Wiley also publishes its books in a variety of electronic formats. Some content that appears in print may not be available in electronic books.

CIP data available upon request.

ISBN: 0-7645-5745-9

Printed in the United States of America.

10 9 8 7 6 5 4 3 2 1

1B/QW/RX/QU/IN

About the Author

Christopher Negus has been working with UNIX systems, the Internet, and (most recently) Linux systems for more than two decades. During that time, Chris worked at AT&T Bell Laboratories, UNIX System Laboratories, and Novell, helping to develop the UNIX operating system. Features from many of the UNIX projects Chris worked on at AT&T have found their way into Red Hat, Fedora, and other Linux systems.

Most recently, Chris co-wrote the books *Linux Troubleshooting Bible* and *Linux Toys* for Wiley Publishing. During the past few years, Chris has written several books on UNIX and the Internet, including *Internet Explorer 4 Bible* and *Netscape Plug-Ins For Dummies* for Wiley Publishing. He also co-wrote several books for Que Publishing, including *The Complete Idiot's Guide to Networking* (second and third editions) and *Using UNIX* (second edition). Chris's other writings include articles for *Internet World*, *NetWare Connection*, and *Visual Developer* magazines.

At home, Chris enjoys spending time with his wife, Sheree, and his boys, Caleb and Seth. His hobbies include soccer, singing, and exercising with Sheree.

As always, I dedicate this book to my wife, Sheree. This book would never have happened without her love and support.

Credits

Acquisitions Editor
Debra Williams Cauley

Development Editor
Sara Shlaer

Technical Editors
Jesse Keating
François Caen
Eric Foster-Johnson

Production Editor
Eric Newman

Copy Editor
Michael Koch

Editorial Manager
Mary Beth Wakefield

**Vice President and
Executive Group Publisher**
Richard Swadley

Vice President and Executive Publisher
Bob Ipsen

Vice President and Publisher
Joseph B. Wikert

Executive Editorial Director
Mary Bednarek

Project Coordinator
Bill Ramsey

Indexer
Johnna VanHoose Dinse

Preface

Many Linux books resemble someone's throwing a bunch of high-performance car parts on the floor and saying, "Go ahead and build a Porsche." Although it's true that the parts you need for power computing are in Linux, you still need to know how to put them together. *Red Hat Fedora Linux 2 Bible* takes you through those steps.

Who Are You?

You don't need to be a programmer to use this book. You may be someone who just wants to use Linux (to run programs, access the Internet, and so on). Or you may simply want to know how to administer a Linux system in a workgroup or on a network.

I assume that you are somewhat computer literate but have little or no experience with Linux (or UNIX). You may be migrating from Microsoft operating systems to Linux because of its networking and multiuser features. You may be looking to start a career as a computer technician or network administrator and find that spending a few dollars for an entire operating system and book is more economical than taking those technical classes offered on late-night television. Or you might just think a "free" operating system is cool.

In any case, after you peruse this book you should have a good idea how to run applications, set up a small network, connect to the Internet, and configure a variety of server types (Web servers, print servers, file servers, and so on). This book represents a great first couple of steps toward your becoming someone who can set up a home network or a small office network and maintain a group of computers.

This Book's Learn-through-Tasks Approach

The best way to learn a computer system is to get your hands on it. To help you learn Linux, this book takes a task-oriented approach. Where possible, I step you through the process of working with a feature, such as setting up a network or configuring your desktop.

When you are done with a task, you should have a good, basic setup of the feature that it covers. After that, I often provide pointers to further information on tweaking and tuning the feature.

Instead of assuming that you already know about cryptic topics such as troff, NFS, and TCP/IP, I ease you into those features with headings such as "Publishing with Fedora," "Setting up a File Server," and "Connecting to the Internet." Heck, if you already knew what all those things were and how to get them working, you wouldn't need me, would you?

When many tools can be used to achieve the same results, I usually present one or two examples. In other words, I don't describe six different Web browsers, twelve different text editors, and three different news servers. I tell you how to get one or two similar tools really working and then note the others that are available.

What You Need

To follow along with this book, you must install the software found on the accompanying CDs. To do that, you need a PC with the following general configuration:

- An Intel Pentium or compatible CPU, 200Mhz Pentium or better (for text mode); 400Mhz Pentium II or better (for GUI mode). Fedora Core 2 has been optimized for Pentium PRO processors. (Intel 486 computers will not work with Fedora Core 2.)

- At least 64MB of RAM. To run the GNOME or KDE desktop 192MB are needed, although Red Hat recommends 256MB.

- At least 520MB of hard disk space (you have to select a minimal install). You need 1.9GB of hard disk space for a personal desktop install, 2.4GB for a typical workstation installation, or at least 870MB of space for a server installation. To install everything, you need about 6.2GB of space.

- A CD-ROM drive. This is recommended for installation, although you can install over a network or from a local hard disk instead. For those types of installs, booting installation from a 3.5-inch floppy disk drive is no longer supported (beginning with Fedora Core 2). Chapter 2 describes methods of launching installation if you don't have a bootable CD drive. Once the install is started, you need either an extra hard disk partition or another computer (that can be reached over the network) that has packages or images of the Fedora Core CDs on it. (I tell you how to do that later, in case you're interested.)

Not every piece of PC hardware works with Fedora. While there is no official hardware compatibility list as there was for Red Hat Linux (www.redhat.com/hardware), overall hardware support should be improved in Fedora Core 2.

> **CROSS-REFERENCE:** See Chapter 27 for information on improved hardware support included in the new 2.6 kernel. I also describe hardware requirements in more detail during descriptions of Fedora Core installation in Chapter 2.

Red Hat Fedora Linux 2 Bible Improvements

Red Hat Fedora Linux 2 Bible represents the continuing development of *Red Hat Linux Bible*, which I began in 1999. About every six months since Red Hat Linux 6.1, I've followed new versions of Red Hat Linux with updates of this book. That tradition continues with what Red Hat is calling Fedora Core 2.

The foundation for Fedora Core 2 and this book both rest on the tradition begun with Red Hat Linux. The enhancements included in this edition reflect that foundation, plus some bold, new cutting-edge Linux technology.

As this book, too, is meant to reflect a progression of Red Hat Linux, I have included a variety of enhancements from the previous book in this series: *Red Hat Linux Bible: Fedora and Enterprise Edition.* The following list describes enhancements that have been made to the current book, *Red Hat Fedora Linux 2 Bible*:

- **Using the 2.6 Kernel** — A new chapter, Chapter 27, explains how the new Linux 2.6 kernel affects your use of the Fedora Core system.

- **Using Security Enhanced Linux** — Another major new feature in Fedora Core 2 is Security Enhanced (SE) Linux. Most of the book describes how to use Fedora Core with SE Linux disabled. Chapter 28 describes the impact of SE Linux if it is turned on in Fedora.

- **Creating a network-shared address book with LDAP** — The Lightweight Directory Access Protocol is a popular facility for sharing information among LDAP-enabled applications. Chapter 22 describes how to use LDAP to create an address book that you can use to share e-mail addresses and other information with people using e-mail clients, such as Mozilla mail.

- **Installing Fedora Core** — With the 2.6 kernel included in Fedora Core 2 come some changes in installation opportunities. Because the 2.6 kernel no longer fits on a 3.5-inch floppy disk, I had to describe other installation types in Chapter 2 for those who don't have a bootable CD drive. Other changes to the Fedora Core installation have also been included, so you can follow along with the CDs that come with this book.

- **X.Org X Server** — The XFree86 X server that serves as the foundation for Fedora and Red Hat desktop interfaces (GNOME and KDE) has been replaced by the new X server from X.Org (www.X.org). Changes that relate to that X server have been sprinkled throughout Chapter 3.

- **GNOME 2.6 and KDE 3.2** — Chapter 3 has been enhanced to reflect minor updates to the GNOME and KDE desktops. For those using Fedora, improvements are reflected in some new applications and changes to some desktop, mouse, and keyboard behaviors.

- **Linux gaming** — I've made some enhancements to Chapter 7, to keep you up on the latest perspective on Linux gaming. That includes a brief description of the Neverwinter Nights Linux client.

- **Using yum to get software** — I think yum is so cool that I continue to tune up the section on using yum to install and update software. Yum, or apt-get for those who prefer that tool, are excellent tools for getting high-quality software that is outside of the main Fedora distribution, and for keeping your Fedora software updated.

- **ALSA sound and multimedia** — As Linux continues to improve offerings in sound, video, and other multimedia applications, so Fedora has been adding software in that area. In Chapter 8, I describe the ALSA sound system (which replaces the old OSS sound system), Rhythmbox (an excellent music player), and TVtime (a television player that has just been added to the Fedora distribution).

- **Mounting disk images** — In Chapter 10, I added a short section on mounting disk images as a loop device, so you can view and use the content of those images in your Linux file system.

- **Backups with rsync** — I asked my friends how they did their own backups. The most consistent answer I received was that they backed up their data over the network with rsync. So I added an example of how to do that in Chapter 13.

- **Virtual Private Network (VPN) with IPSEC** — With the 2.6 kernel comes the ability to create low-level VPNs with IPSEC. In Fedora Core 2, IPSEC replaces CIPE as the preferred method of doing VPNs in Fedora. Chapter 16 describes how to configure IPSEC.

- **NFS automounts** — Chapter 18 describes how to use the autofs automounter on networks where you are sharing directories using NFS.

- **Mail server overhaul** — The sendmail section was based on an older method of configuring that service. Based on some excellent help from my friend François Caen, I reworked the entire sendmail section to, I believe, greatly improve descriptions of sendmail access, relaying, virtual hosting, and other topics. To support the mail server, I also added descriptions of squirrelmail (webmail service), as well as the dovecot and cyrus-imapd POP3 and IMAP servers.

Besides new features just described, procedures throughout the book have been tested and corrected to match changes that have occurred to Fedora Core software in this version.

Conventions Used in This Book

Throughout the book, special typography indicates code and commands. Commands and code are shown in a monospaced font:

```
This is how code looks.
```

In the event that an example includes both input and output, the monospaced font is still used, but input is presented in bold type to distinguish the two. Here is an example:

```
$ ftp ftp.handsonhistory.com
Name (home:jake): jake
Password: ******
```

The following boxes are used to call your attention to points that are particularly important.

> **NOTE:** A Note box provides extra information to which you need to pay special attention.

> **TIP:** A Tip box shows a special way of performing a particular task.

> **CAUTION:** A Caution box alerts you to take special care when executing a procedure, or damage to your computer hardware or software could result.

> **CROSS-REFERENCE:** A Cross-Reference box refers you to further information on a subject that you can find outside the current chapter.

How This Book Is Organized

The book is organized into five parts.

Part I: Getting Started in Fedora

Part I consists of Chapters 1 through 4. Chapters 1 and 2 contain brief descriptions of the Linux technology and tell you what you need in order to get the operating system installed. Chapter 1 serves as an introduction to the Linux OS and to Fedora in particular. I also pay special attention to the division Red Hat, Inc., makes between the Fedora Project and Red Hat Enterprise Linux. Chapter 2 discusses what you need in order to install Fedora and how to make the decisions you'll be faced with during installation. It includes procedures for installing from CD-ROM, hard disk, or network connection (NFS, FTP, or HTTP servers).

In Chapter 3, you learn about the GNOME desktop environment, the KDE desktop environment, and the X Window system. These GUIs provide graphical means of using Fedora. Chapter 4 describes ways of exploring and understanding Fedora, primarily from the Linux shell command interpreter. You learn how to use the bash shell, the vi text editor, and the commands for moving around the Linux file system.

Part II: Using Fedora

Part II consists of Chapters 5 through 9, which include information for the average user who must use Linux to run applications and access the Internet.

Chapter 5 contains information on obtaining, installing, and running Linux applications. It also helps you run applications from other operating systems in Linux. Chapter 6 describes both old-time publishing tools and new, graphical word processors that are available with Fedora. Old tools include the troff and TeX text processing tools, whereas newer publishing software includes OpenOffice (included on the CDs) and StarOffice (commercially available).

Graphical and character-based games that run in Fedora are described in Chapter 7. This chapter also describes how to run commercial Windows games using WineX, and commercial Linux games, such as "Civilization: Call to Power" and "Myth II," some of which have demo versions available. Chapter 8 describes how to use audio and video players, as well as how to configure sound cards and CD burners. Chapter 9 describes tools for browsing the Web (such as the Mozilla browser) and related tools (such as e-mail clients and newsreaders).

Part III: Administering Fedora

Part III consists of Chapters 10 through 14, which cover general setup and system maintenance tasks, including how to set up user accounts, automate system tasks, and back up your data. Chapter 10, in which you learn what you need to know about basic system administration, describes the root login, administrative commands, configuration files, and log files. Chapter 11 describes how to set up and provide support for multiple users on your Fedora system.

In Chapter 12 you learn to create shell scripts and to use the cron facility to automate a variety of tasks on your Fedora system. Techniques for backing up your system and restoring files from backup are described in Chapter 13. Chapter 14 describes issues related to securing your computing assets in Fedora.

Part IV: Fedora Network and Server Setup

Part IV consists of Chapters 15 through 26, which describe step-by-step procedures for setting up a variety of server types. Simple configurations for what might otherwise be complex tasks are contained in each chapter. Learn to arrange, address, and connect your Linux computers to a local area network (LAN) in Chapter 15. Chapter 16 describes techniques for connecting your Linux computer and LAN to the Internet, using features such as Point-to-Point Protocol (PPP), IP forwarding, IP masquerading, routing, virtual private networks, and proxy servers.

Chapter 17 describes how to set up different types of print server interfaces, including Samba (to share with Windows systems), NetWare, and native Linux printing. Chapter 18 describes file servers, such as Network File System (NFS) servers, Samba file servers, and NetWare file servers. Chapter 19 describes how to configure sendmail or postfix e-mail servers.

Chapter 20 describes how to configure and secure an FTP server, as well as how to access the server using FTP client programs. Chapter 21 teaches you how to set up Fedora as a Web server, focusing on the popular Apache server software. Chapter 22 explains how to use LDAP to create a shared address book. Chapter 23 describes how to set up both DHCP and NIS services to distribute information to client workstations on the network.

Chapter 24 describes how to set up and use a MySQL database server in Linux. Chapter 25 takes you through the process of making the servers you configured in the other chapters available on the public Internet. Setting up a Domain Name System (DNS) server is also described in Chapter 25. Chapter 26 describes how to set up Fedora to be a Macintosh file and printer server.

Part V: New Technology

Part V contains Chapter 27, which describes the Linux 2.6 kernel, and Chapter 28, which describes Security Enhanced Linux.

Appendixes

This book contains three appendixes. Appendix A describes the contents of the companion CD-ROMs, Appendix B lists the hundreds of RPMs (software packages) that come with the Fedora Core 2 distribution, and Appendix C provides an overview of setting up and running network services.

About the Companion CD-ROMs

The Fedora Core 2 CD-ROMs that accompany this book provide the software you need for a complete, working Fedora system. With this software, you can install sets of software packages that result in personal desktop, workstation, or server configurations. This book describes how to configure and use the software for those different configurations.

About the Companion Web Site

Even in a book that pushes the 1,000-page boundary, a few topics don't seem to make the cut. After you have gone through the book, you can visit the companion Web site at www.wiley.com/compbooks/negus for some bonus material on topics such as using the X Window system, finding neat add-on software, and exploring alternative administrative interfaces.

Software moved to the Web site from previous editions of this book includes information on using legacy UNIX remote commands (rlogin, rcp, and the like), running Tripwire to manage system security, and using crack and other password protection tools. Features moved from the immediately preceding edition include descriptions of the wu-FTPd FTP server, INN news server, and the sendmail.cf file.

Reach Out

If you have any questions or comments about this book, feel free to contact me by e-mail at this address: chris@linuxtoys.net.

Acknowledgments

A special acknowledgment to the people at Red Hat, Inc., who, despite the massive shift in direction of their Red Hat Linux product line, have managed to (once again) produce a rock-solid Linux distribution. Fedora Core 2 continues their brave move to make the latest cutting-edge Linux technology available in a high-quality Linux distribution. We're proud to include that complete Linux distribution with this book. Great job!

At Wiley, I'd like to thank Debra Williams Cauley, who has continued her heroic efforts to push the latest editions of this book out to the world. Thanks to the tag team of Sara Shlaer and Eric Newman for their editing and production work on this book, coming off of our massive effort to get out *Linux Troubleshooting Bible* as well. Thanks to Margot Maley Hutchison and the others at Waterside Productions for bringing me this project.

I want to thank the very special team of people who contributed directly to improving the content of this book:

- Jesse Keating, leader of the Fedora Legacy Project, headed up the technical editing for this book. His insights on software installation and upgrades, from his work on Fedora Legacy, were invaluable to getting that critical information included in this edition.

- François Caen offered his experience gained from configuring hundreds of Red Hat Linux servers to work through how I could improve the mail and Web server chapters.

- Eric Foster-Johnson reworked some multimedia and network setup content and also picked up some of the tech editing on the tail end of the project.

- Kate Wrightson and Joe Merlino helped keep us on track by updating some chapters, per instructions from me and Jesse.

I'd also like to thank members of the Tacoma Linux User's Group for being a great resource for discussions on Linux and (occasionally) non-Linux topics. On more than one occasion, the insights from its members have helped me fix or rewrite parts of this book.

Thanks, as always, to my dear family for helping me through this project. Hopefully, I'll be able to join Sheree, Caleb, and Seth on their next rock-climbing expedition.

Finally, a special thanks to those of you who bought this and earlier editions of *Red Hat Linux Bible*. Go out and become a force for Linux in your work, home, and community. If you're looking for something fun to do with Linux, check out *Linux Toys* (Wiley Publishing), by me and Chuck Wolber. If you run into trouble, check out our new *Linux Troubleshooting Bible* (Wiley Publishing), by me and Thomas Weeks.

Contents

Part I

Getting Started in Fedora

Chapter 1: An Overview of Fedora

Chapter 2: Installing Fedora

Chapter 3: Getting Started with the Desktop

Chapter 4: Using Linux Commands

Chapter 1

An Overview of Fedora

In This Chapter

- Introducing Fedora
- What is Linux?
- Linux's roots in UNIX
- Common Linux features
- Primary advantages of Linux
- What is Fedora?
- Why choose Fedora?
- The culture of free software

Linux was a phenomenon waiting to happen. The computer industry suffered from a rift. In the 1980s and 1990s, people had to choose between inexpensive, market-driven PC operating systems from Microsoft and expensive, technology-driven operating systems such as UNIX. Free software was being created all over the world, but lacked a common platform to rally around. Linux has become that common platform.

For several years, Red Hat Linux has been the most popular commercial distribution of Linux. In 2003, Red Hat, Inc. changed the name of the distribution from Red Hat Linux to Fedora Core and moved its commercial efforts toward its Red Hat Enterprise Linux products. It then set up Fedora to be:

- Sponsored by Red Hat
- Supported by the Linux community
- Inclusive of high-quality, cutting-edge open source technology
- A proving ground for software slated for commercial Red Hat deployment and support

The complete Fedora operating system (referred to as Fedora Core 2) is included on the CDs that come with this book and is described in this book.

Introducing Fedora and Red Hat Linux

With the recent split between community (Fedora) and commercial (Red Hat Enterprise Linux) versions of Red Hat Linux, Red Hat has created a model that can suit the fast-paced changes in the open source world, while still meeting the demands for a well-supported commercial Linux distribution.

Technical people have chosen Red Hat Linux because of its reputation for solid performance. With the new Fedora Project, Red Hat has created an environment where open source developers can bring high-quality software packages to Red Hat Linux that would be beyond the resources of Red Hat, Inc. to test and maintain on its own.

Over 1,600 individual software packages (compared to just over 600 in Red Hat Linux 6.2) are included in Fedora Core 2. These packages contain features that would cost you hundreds or thousands of dollars to duplicate if you bought them as separate commercial products. These features let you:

- Connect your computers to a LAN or the Internet.
- Create documents and publish your work on paper or on the Web.
- Work with multimedia content to manipulate images, play music files, view video, and even burn your own CDs.
- Play games individually or over a network.
- Communicate over the Internet using a variety of Web tools for browsing, chatting, transferring files, participating in newsgroups, and sending and receiving e-mail.
- Protect your computing resources by having Red Hat Linux act as a firewall and/or a router to protect against intruders coming in through public networks.
- Configure a computer to act as a network server, such as a print server, Web server, file server, mail server, news server, and a database server.

This is just a partial list of what you can do with Red Hat's Fedora . Using this book as your guide, you will find that there are many more features built into Fedora as well.

Support for new video cards, printers, storage devices, and applications are being added every day. Linux programmers around the world are no longer the only ones creating hardware drivers. Every day more hardware vendors are creating their own drivers, so they can sell products to the growing Linux market. New applications are being created to cover everything from personal productivity tools to programs that access massive corporate databases.

Remember that old Pentium computer in your closet? Don't throw it away! Just because a new release of Fedora is out doesn't mean that you need all new hardware for it to run. Support for many old computer components get carried from one release to the next. There are old PCs running Fedora today as routers (to route data between your LAN and the Internet), firewalls (to protect your network from outside intrusion), and file servers (to store shared files on your LAN) — with maybe an Ethernet card or an extra hard disk added.

At this point, you may feel that Linux is something you want to try out. This brings us to the basic question: What is Linux?

What Is Linux?

Linux is a free operating system that was created by Linus Torvalds when he was a student at the University of Helsinki in 1991. Torvalds started Linux by writing a *kernel* — the heart of the operating system — partly from scratch and partly by using publicly available software. (For the definition of an operating system and a kernel, see the sidebar "What Is an Operating System?" later in this chapter.) Torvalds then released the system to his friends and to a community of "hackers" on the Internet and asked them to work with it, fix it, and enhance it. It took off.

> **CROSS-REFERENCE:** See Chapter 14 for a discussion about the difference between hackers (who just like to play with computers) and crackers (who break into computer systems and cause damage).

Today, there are hundreds of software developers around the world contributing software to the Linux effort. Because the source code for the software is freely available, anyone can work on it, change it, or enhance it. Developers are encouraged to feed their fixes and improvements back into the community so that Linux can continue to grow and improve.

On top of the Linux kernel effort, the creators of Linux also drew on a great deal of system software and applications that are now bundled with Linux distributions from the GNU software effort (GNU stands for "GNU is Not UNIX"), which is directed by the Free Software Foundation (www.gnu.org). There is a vast amount of software that can be used with Linux, making it an operating system that can compete with or surpass features available in any other operating system in the world.

If you have heard Linux described as a free version of UNIX, there is good reason for it. Although much of the code for Linux started from scratch, the blueprint for what the code would do was created to follow POSIX (Portable Operating System Interface for UNIX) standards. POSIX is a computer industry operating system standard that every major version of UNIX complied with. In other words, if your operating system was POSIX-compliant, it was UNIX.

Linux's Roots in UNIX

Linux grew within a culture of free exchange of ideas and software. Like UNIX — the operating system on which Linux is based — the focus was on keeping communications open among software developers. Getting the code to work was the goal and the Internet was the primary communications medium. Keeping the software free and redistributable was a means to that goal. What, then, were the conditions that made the world ripe for a computer system such as Linux?

What Is an Operating System?

An operating system is made up of software instructions that lie between the computer hardware (disks, memory, ports, and so on) and the application programs (word processors, Web browsers, spreadsheets, and so on). At the center is the kernel, which provides the most basic computing functions (managing system memory, sharing the processor, opening and closing devices, and so on). Besides the kernel, an operating system provides other basic services needed to operate the computer, including:

- **File systems** — The file system provides the structure in which information is stored on the computer. Information is stored in files, primarily on hard disks inside the computer. Files are organized within a hierarchy of directories. The Linux file system holds the data files that you save, the programs you run, and the configuration files that set up the system.

- **Device drivers** — These provide the interfaces to each of the hardware devices connected to your computer. A device driver enables a program to write to a device without needing to know details about how each piece of hardware is implemented. The program opens a device, sends and receives data, and closes a device.

- **User interfaces** — An operating system needs to provide a way for users to run programs and access the file system. Linux has both graphical and text-based user interfaces. GNOME and KDE provide graphical user interfaces, whereas shell command interpreters (such as bash) run programs by typing commands and options.

- **System services** — An operating system provides system services, many of which can be started automatically when the computer boots. In Linux, system services can include processes that mount file systems, start your network, and run scheduled tasks. In Linux, many services run continuously, enabling users to access printers, Web pages, files, databases, and other computing assets over a network.

Without an operating system, an application program would have to know the details of each piece of hardware, instead of just being able to say, "open that device and write a file there."

In the 1980s and 1990s, while Microsoft flooded the world with personal computers running DOS and Windows operating systems, power users demanded more from an operating system. They ached for systems that could run on networks, support many users at once (multiuser), and run many programs at once (multitasking). DOS (Disk Operating System) and Windows didn't cut it.

UNIX, on the other hand, grew out of a culture where technology was king and marketing people were, well, hard to find. Bell Laboratories in Murray Hill, New Jersey, was a think tank where ideas came first and profits were somebody else's problem. A quote from Dennis Ritchie, co-creator of UNIX and designer of the C programming language, in a 1980 lecture on the evolution of UNIX, sums up the spirit that started UNIX. He was commenting on both his hopes and those of his colleagues for the UNIX project after a similar project called Multics had just failed:

> *What we wanted to preserve was not just a good environment in which to do programming, but a system around which a fellowship could form. We knew from experience that the essence of communal computing as supplied by remote-access, time-shared machines, is not just to type programs into a terminal instead of a keypunch, but to encourage close communication.*

In that spirit, the first source code of UNIX was distributed free to universities. Like Linux, the availability of UNIX source code made it possible for a diverse population of software developers to make their own enhancements to UNIX and share them with others.

By the early 1980s, UNIX development moved from the organization in Murray Hill to a more commercially oriented development laboratory in Summit, New Jersey (a few miles down the road). During that time, UNIX began to find commercial success as the computing system of choice for applications such as AT&T's telephone switching equipment, for supercomputer applications such as modeling weather patterns, and for controlling NASA space projects.

Major computer hardware vendors licensed the UNIX source code to run on their computers. To try to create an environment of fairness and community to its OEMs (original equipment manufacturers), AT&T began standardizing what these different ports of UNIX had to be able to do to still be called UNIX. To that end, compliance with POSIX standards and the AT&T UNIX System V Interface Definition (SVID) were specifications UNIX vendors could use to create compliant UNIX systems. Those same documents also served as road maps for the creation of Linux.

Elsewhere, the UNIX source code that had been distributed to universities had taken on a life of its own. The Berkeley Software Distribution (BSD) began life in the late 1970s as patches to the AT&T UNIX source code from students and staff at the University of California at Berkeley. Over the years, the AT&T code was rewritten and BSD became freely distributed, with offshoot projects such as FreeBSD, OpenBSD, and NetBSD still available.

Linux has been described as a UNIX-like operating system that reflects a combination of SVID, POSIX, and BSD compliance. Linux continues to aim toward POSIX compliance, as well as compliance with standards set by the new owner of the UNIX trademark, The Open Group (www.unix-systems.org/). Much of the direction of Linux today comes from the Open Source Development Labs (www.osdl.org), which includes Linus Torvalds on its staff and whose members include most of the major commercial vendors.

Common Linux Features

No matter what version of Linux you use, the piece of code common to all is the Linux kernel. Although the kernel can be modified to include support for the features you want, every Linux kernel can offer the following features:

- **Multiuser** — Not only can you have many user accounts available on a Linux system, you can also have multiple users logged in and working on the system at the same time. Users can have their own environments arranged the way they want: their own home directory for storing files and their own desktop interface (with icons, menus, and applications arranged to suit them). User accounts can be password-protected, so that users can control who has access to their applications and data.

- **Multitasking** — In Linux, it is possible to have many programs running at the same time, which means that not only can you have many programs going at once, but that the Linux operating system can itself have programs running in the background. Many of these system processes make it possible for Linux to work as a server, with these background processes listening to the network for requests to log in to your system, view a Web page, print a document, or copy a file. These background processes are referred to as *daemons*.

- **Graphical User Interface (X Window System)** — The powerful framework for working with graphical applications in Linux is referred to as the X Window System (or simply X). X handles the functions of opening X-based graphical user interface (GUI) applications and displaying them on an X server process (the process that manages your screen, mouse, and keyboard).

  On top of X, you use an X-based desktop environment to provide a desktop metaphor and window manager to provide the look-and-feel of your GUI (icons, window frames, menus, and colors, or a combination of those items called *themes*). There are several desktop environments and several desktop managers to choose from. (Fedora includes a few desktop managers, but focuses on the GNOME and KDE desktop environments.)

- **Hardware support** — You can configure support for almost every type of hardware that can be connected to a computer. There is support for floppy disk drives, CD-ROMs, removable disks (such as DVDs and Zip drives), sound cards, tape devices, video cards, and most anything else you can think of. As device interfaces, such as USB and Firewire, have been added to computers, support for those devices has been added to Linux as well.

> **NOTE:** Most hardware manufacturers don't provide Linux drivers with their peripheral devices and adapter cards. Although most popular hardware will be supported eventually in Linux, it can sometimes take a while for a member of the Linux community to write a driver.

- **Networking connectivity** — To connect your Linux system to a network, Linux offers support for a variety of local area network (LAN) boards, modems, and serial devices. In addition to LAN protocols, such as Ethernet (both wired and wireless), all the most popular upper-level networking protocols can be built-in. The most popular of these protocols is TCP/IP (used to connect to the Internet). Other protocols, such as IPX (for Novell networks) and X.25 (a packet-switching network type that is popular in Europe), are also available.

- **Network servers** — Providing networking services to the client computers on the LAN or to the entire Internet is what Linux does best. A variety of software packages are available that enable you to use Linux as a print server, file server, FTP server, mail server, Web server, news server, or workgroup (DHCP or NIS) server.

- **Application support** — Because of compatibility with POSIX and several different application programming interfaces (APIs), a wide range of freeware and shareware software is available for Linux. Most GNU software from the Free Software Foundation will run in Linux (although some may take a bit of tweaking).

NOTE: Because of the popularity of the RPM Package Management (RPM) format for packaging software, many software packages are available on the Internet in RPM format. If the RPM version matches your processor type (most have i386 and or i686 versions available), you can install the package without building and compiling the package. In fact, there are major software repositories that include software packaged specifically for Fedora. See Chapters 2 and 5 for information on working with RPM packages.

Primary Advantages of Linux

When compared to different commercially available operating systems, Linux's best assets are its price and its reliability. With the latest 2.6 Linux kernel, you can also argue that scalability is one of its greatest assets.

Most people know that its initial price is free (or at least under $50 when it comes in a box or with a book). However, when people talk about Linux's affordability, they are usually thinking of its total cost, which includes no (or low) licensing fees and the capability of using inexpensive hardware and compatible free add-on applications. Although commercial operating systems tend to encourage upgrading to later hardware, Linux doesn't (although faster hardware and larger disks are nice to have).

In terms of reliability, the general consensus is that Linux is comparable to many commercial UNIX systems but more reliable than most desktop-oriented operating systems. This is especially true if you rely on your computer system to stay up because it is a Web server or a file server. (You don't have to reboot every time you change something.)

Another advantage of using Linux is that help is always available on the Internet. There is probably someone out there in a Linux newsgroup or mailing list willing to help you get around your problem. Because the source code is available, if you need something fixed you can even patch the code yourself! On the other hand, I've seen commercial operating system vendors sit on reported problems for months without fixing them. Remember that the culture of Linux is one that thrives on people helping other people.

What Are Red Hat Linux and Fedora?

Having directories of software packages floating extraneously around the Internet was not a bad way for hackers to share software. However, for Linux to be acceptable to a less technical population of computer users, it needed to be simple to install and use. Likewise, businesses that were thinking about committing their mission-critical applications to a computer system would want to know that this system had been carefully tested.

To those ends, several companies and organizations began gathering and packaging Linux software together into usable forms called *distributions*. The main goal of a Linux distribution is to make the hundreds of unrelated software packages that make up Linux work together as a cohesive whole. For the past few years, the most popular commercial distribution has been Red Hat Linux.

In September 2003, Red Hat, Inc., changed its way of doing business. That change resulted in the formation of the Red Hat–sponsored Fedora Project to take the development of Red Hat Linux technology into the future. But what does that mean to individuals and businesses that have come to rely on Red Hat Linux?

Red Hat forms the Fedora Project

The announcement of the Fedora Project by Red Hat, Inc. at first prompted more questions than answers about the future direction of the company and its flagship Red Hat Linux product. In fact, it seemed that nothing named Red Hat Linux even existed anymore. Instead, what *was* Red Hat Linux would be reflected by Linux distributions coming from two paths:

- **Fedora Project** (http://fedora.redhat.com) — An open source project, beginning from a Red Hat Linux 9 base, that produces its own Linux distribution. While the project is sponsored by Red Hat, Inc., there is no official support for the Linux distribution (called Fedora Core) that the project produces.

- **Red Hat Enterprise Linux** (www.redhat.com/software/rhel) — An official set of commercial Linux products from Red Hat, Inc. that are offered on an annual subscription basis. Red Hat backs up its Enterprise product line with technical support, training, and documentation.

The primary result of the Fedora Project are sets of binary and source code CDs containing the Linux distribution referred to as the Fedora Core. Before its name was changed to Fedora Core 1, that distribution was being tested simply as the next in the series of Red Hat Linux distributions (presumably, Red Hat Linux 10). The four binary, installation CDs included with this book are those distributed as the official second release of that software: Fedora Core 2.

The name change from Red Hat Linux to Fedora Core wasn't the only difference between Fedora and Red Hat Enterprise Linux, however. Red Hat, Inc. also changed its association with Fedora Core in the following ways:

- **No boxed sets** — Red Hat decided to not sell Fedora through retail channels. The ever-shortening release cycle was making it difficult to manage the flow of boxed sets to and from retail channels every few months, and Red Hat believed that early adopters of Linux technology were clever enough to get the software themselves.

- **No technical support offerings** — There are no technical support programs available from Red Hat for Fedora.

- **No Red Hat documentation** — The set of manuals that came with the previous Red Hat Linux product is not being brought over to Fedora. Instead, a series of small task-oriented documents will be collected for the project in article format.

By not creating a whole support industry around Fedora, that project is free to produce software release on a much shorter schedule (possibly two or three times per year). This allows Fedora users to always have the latest software features and fixes included with a recent version of the operating system.

Another potential upside to Fedora is that the Fedora Project hopes to encourage community software developers to create compatible software. By including software download and installation tools (such as the yum utility) in Fedora Core, the Fedora Project hopes to encourage people to contribute to software repositories that Fedora users can rely on to download additional software packages.

Red Hat shifts to Enterprise Linux

The major shift of attention to Red Hat Enterprise Linux as the focus of Red Hat, Inc.'s commercial efforts has been on the horizon for some time. Some characteristics of Red Hat Enterprise Linux are:

- **Longer release intervals** — Instead of offering releases every 4 to 6 months, Enterprise software will have a 12 to 18 month update cycle. Customers can be assured of a longer support cycle without having to upgrade to a later release.

- **Multiple support options** — Customers will have the choice of purchasing different levels of support. All subscriptions will include the Update Module, which allows easy access to updates for Red Hat Enterprise Linux systems. The Management Module lets customers develop custom channels and automate management of multiple systems. The Monitoring Module allows customers to monitor and maintain an entire infrastructure of systems.

- **Documentation and training** — Manuals and training courses will center on the Red Hat Enterprise Linux distribution.

Red Hat Enterprise Linux install types focus on three different types of computer systems, referred to as WS (for workstations), AS (for high-end systems), and ES (for small and mid-range servers). Red Hat has also recently released a new Red Hat Desktop product targeted for wide-scale desktop deployments. Each system in the Red Hat Enterprise Linux family is meant to be compatible with the others. There are Basic, Standard, and Premium editions of these Enterprise systems. While Basic offers only software downloads, standard and premium editions offer hard copy documentation and additional technical support.

Choosing between Fedora and Enterprise

If you bought this book to try out Linux for the first time, rest assured that what you have on the four CDs with this book is a solid, battle-tested operating system. There is still a lot of overlap between Fedora Core and Red Hat Enterprise Linux. However, the newest features of Fedora Core 2 provide a way to test out much of the software that is slated to go in later Enterprise editions.

Although Fedora may not be right for everyone, Fedora is still great for students, home users, most small businesses, and anyone just wanting to try out the latest Linux technology. Larger businesses should seriously consider the implications on support, training, and future upgrade paths before choosing whether to go the Fedora route or sign on with Red Hat Enterprise Linux. But as a way to learn and use the latest Linux technology before it makes its way to Red Hat Enterprise Linux, Fedora Core 2 is a great choice.

Why Choose Fedora or Red Hat Enterprise Linux?

To distinguish itself from other versions of Linux, each distribution adds some extra features. Because many power features included in most Linux distributions come from established open source projects (such as Apache, Samba, KDE, and so on), often enhancements for a particular distribution exist to make it easier to install, configure, and use Linux. Also, because there are different software packages available to do the same jobs (such as window managers or a particular server type), a distribution can distinguish itself by which packages it chooses to include and feature.

Fedora is continuing the Red Hat Linux by offering many features that set it apart from other Linux distributions. Those features include:

- **Cutting-edge Linux technology** — In Fedora Core 2, major new features include the Linux 2.6 kernel, Security Enhanced Linux, and a new X server from X.Org. You can get your hands on those and many other new Linux features before they go into commercial Linux products.

- **Software packaging** — Red Hat, Inc. created the RPM Package Management (RPM) method of packaging Linux. RPMs allow less technically savvy users to easily install Linux software. With RPM tools, you can install from CD, hard disk, over your LAN, or over the Internet. It's easy to track which packages are installed or to look at the contents of a package. Because RPM is available to the Linux community, it has become one of the de facto standards for packaging Linux software.

CROSS-REFERENCE: Chapter 5 describes how to install RPM packages.

- **Easy installation** — The Fedora installation process (called *anaconda*) provides easy steps for installing Linux. During installation, anaconda also helps you take the first few steps toward configuring Linux. You can choose which packages to install and how to partition your hard disk. You can even get your desktop GUI ready to go by configuring your video card, user accounts, and even your network.

CROSS-REFERENCE: Chapter 2 covers Fedora Linux installation.

- **UNIX System V–style run-level scripts** — To have your system services (daemon processes) start up and shut down in an organized way, Fedora uses the UNIX System V mechanism for starting and stopping services. Shell scripts (that are easy to read and change) are contained in subdirectories of /etc. When the run level changes, such as when the system boots up or you change to single-user mode, messages tell you whether each service started correctly or failed to execute properly. Chapter 12 describes how to use run-level scripts.

- **Desktop environments (GNOME and KDE)** — To make it easier to use Linux, Fedora comes packaged with the GNOME and KDE desktop environments. GNOME is installed by default and offers some nice features that include drag-and-drop protocols and tools for configuring the desktop look and feel. KDE is another popular desktop manager that includes a wide range of tools tailored for the KDE environment, such as the KDE Control Center for configuring the desktop.

- **Desktop look-and-feel** — With the latest Fedora and other Red Hat Linux distributions, whether you use KDE or GNOME as your desktop environment, you can expect to see many of the same icons and menus to help standardize how you use your Linux system. Tools you can launch from those environments help you configure your network, set up servers, watch log files, and manage system services.

- **GUI Administration tools** — There are some helpful configuration tools for setting up some of the trickier tasks in Linux. Several different GUI tools provide a graphical, form-driven interface for configuring networking, users, file systems, and initialization services. Instead of creating obtuse command lines or having to create tricky configuration files, these graphical tools can set up those files automatically. (Prior to Fedora Core 2, many of these GUI administration tools were launched from commands that began with redhat-config-*. Now, those commands have been renamed to start with system-config-*.)

> **NOTE:** There are advantages and disadvantages of using a GUI-based program to manipulate text-based configuration files. GUI-based configuration tools can lead you through a setup procedure and error-check the information you enter. However, some features can't be accessed through the GUI, and if something goes wrong, it can be trickier to debug. With Linux, you have the command-line options available as well as the GUI administration tools.

- **Testing** — The exact configuration that you get on the Fedora distribution has been thoroughly tested by experts around the world. The simple fact that a software package is included in Fedora or other Red Hat Linux distributions is an indication that Red Hat and the community that supports Fedora believes it has achieved a certain level of quality. By opening testing of early versions of Fedora to the open source community, many more bugs have been uncovered and fixed than might otherwise have been the case.

- **Automatic updates** — The software packages that make up Fedora are constantly being fixed in various ways. To provide a mechanism for the automatic selection, download, and installation of updated software packages, Red Hat created the up2date facility. For officially supported Red Hat Linux distributions, the Red Hat Network provides a focal point for software updates. While Fedora also supports the up2date facility to allow you to get software updates, on the back end Fedora will point up2date at community-supported yum and apt software repositories for providing those updates. Using the up2date command, as a Fedora user you can receive critical security fixes and patches very simply over the Internet.

Features in Fedora Core 2

The major components in Fedora Core 2 include (with version numbers):

- Linux kernel: version 2.6.5 — This reflects a major upgrade over the 2.4.22 kernel included in Fedora Core 1. (See Chapter 27 for information about the Linux 2.6 kernel.)
- GNOME (desktop environment): version 2.6
- KDE (desktop environment): version 3.2.2
- GCC (GNU C language compilation system): version 3.3.3
- Apache (Web server): version 2.0.49
- Samba (Windows SMB file/printer sharing): version 3.0.3
- CUPS (print services): version 1.1.20
- Sendmail (mail transport agent): version 8.12.11
- vsFTPd (secure FTP server): version 1.2.1
- INN (Usenet news server): version 2.3.5
- MySQL (database server): version 3.23.58

- BIND (Domain name system server): version 9.2.3

> **TIP:** If you want the latest features in Linux when looking at different Linux distributions, compare the version numbers shown above. Version numbers and names that Linux distributors such as Mandrake, SUSE, and Red Hat associate with their releases can be arbitrary. By comparing versions of the kernel, KDE and GNOME desktops, and GNU compiler they are using, you can tell which distribution actually has the latest features.

As Fedora continues to consolidate its distribution, some popular packages have been dropped from Fedora Core since the previous version of Fedora, such as the following:

- **cipe** — The Crypto IP Encapsulation (cipe) package was dropped because its function (virtual private networks) was replaced by IPSEC in the 2.6 kernel included with Fedora Core 2.

- **imap** — The imap package was dropped. In Fedora Core 2, you can use either the dovecot or cyrus-imapd package for providing IMAP and POP features allowing e-mail clients from remote systems to get e-mail from your mail server in Fedora.

- **ipchains** — While it has been on the way out for a while, ipchains has been officially dropped from Fedora (iptables has been the default firewall feature for some time).

- **mars-nwe** —This package for creating Netware file and print servers in Linux has been dropped from Fedora Core 2.

- **redhat-config*** — All packages providing Red Hat graphical administration utilities have been renamed to begin with system-config*.

- **sndconfig** — A popular utility for configuring your sound card was dropped, so system-config-soundcard is now the primary utility for configuring a sound card in Fedora.

- **xawtv** — This popular utility for watching television and video input was dropped and replaced by the tvtime utility.

- **XFree86*** — This entire set of packages, which provided the X server that acted as the foundation of all GUI tools in Fedora, was dropped and replaced by the X server from X.Org.

See Appendix B for information on other packages no longer included in Fedora.

> **NOTE:** Just because a package has been dropped from Fedora doesn" mean that you can't still get and use the package. In fact, in this book I tell you how to find and install packages like wine and mars-nwe that have been dropped from previous versions of Fedora and Red Hat Linux.

The following paragraphs describe many of the major features in Fedora Core 2.

Linux 2.6 Kernel

The Linux 2.6 kernel represents a major rewrite and reorganization of the Linux kernel included with the previous Fedora release (2.4.22). The 2.6 kernel could result in better performance from your Linux desktop, support for additional devices, and a kernel that can scale efficiently from hand-held devices to PCs to enterprise servers. Chapter 27 contains a more complete description of 2.6 kernel features.

ALSA Sound System

The ALSA sound system replaces the OSS sound system used in previous versions of Fedora and Red Hat Linux. See Chapter 8 for information on features in the ALSA sound system.

Security Enhanced Linux

Security Enhanced Linux (SE Linux) represents a new model for managing the security of your Linux system. If SE Linux is turned on (it is off by default), a system administrator has much better control over file and process permissions in Linux. For example, with SE Linux enabled and access control lists configured, if someone were to gain control of a particular user account (even root) or process, that person would be limited in what else he or she could control on the computer. See Chapter 28 for further information on SE Linux.

System config tools

Red Hat has renamed and continued to enhance its growing arsenal of graphical administrative tools. Since dropping the linuxconf and bypassing the Webmin graphical administrative interfaces, Red Hat has been steadily developing and adding its own administrative tools to its Fedora and Red Hat Linux distributions. As a result, a systems administrator can often skip running shell commands and editing plain-text configuration files to set up servers, manage system resources, or add users.

The following list provides an overview of GUI administration tools and what each is used to configure:

- **system-config-bind** — Domain Name System server
- **system-config-boot** — Change boot loader settings
- **system-config-date** — System time and date
- **system-config-display** — Configure the X display, monitor and video card
- **system-config-httpd** — Apache Web server
- **system-config-language** — Languages for Fedora
- **system-config-keyboard** — Keyboard selection
- **system-config-kickstart** — Kickstart files for unattended Fedora Core installations
- **system-config-mouse** — A mouse
- **system-config-network** — Network interfaces
- **system-config-nfs** — Network File System shared directories
- **system-config-packages** — Fedora software packages

- **system-config-printer** — Printers
- **system-config-printer-gui** — Printers (GUI)
- **system-config-printer-tui** — Printers (text-based)
- **system-config-proc** — Kernel tunable parameters
- **system-config-rootpassword** — Change your root password
- **system-config-samba** — Samba Windows file and printer sharing
- **system-config-securitylevel** — Iptables firewalls
- **system-config-services** — System services
- **system-config-soundcard** — Sound card
- **system-config-users** — User accounts
- **system-logviewer** — System log file viewer

You can launch the tools associated with the previous packages either from the main desktop menu or from a Terminal window. In most cases, the name of the command you run to launch the window is the same name as the package it comes in.

X and other desktop interfaces

Because of licensing issues, the XFree86 X server has been replaced by the X server from X.Org. Because most of the look-and-feel of the desktop is provided by the GNOME or KDE environment you choose (or other window manager you use with X), the new X server itself should not have much impact on how you use your desktop.

KDE and GNOME are desktop environments that provide a framework for running and developing graphical applications and offer a full range of preferences to allow users to tailor the exact desktop look-and-feel. The new GNOME version 2.6, in particular, has many look-and-feel changes over the version delivered with Fedora Core 2. For example, the Nautilus window has been streamlined, and double-clicking the title bar does a maximize behavior instead of a window scroll. Refer to Chapter 3 for descriptions of how the new GNOME behaves differently (and how to change back to some of the previous GNOME defaults, if you are so inclined).

Unlike previous releases of Fedora and Red Hat Linux, you have to work a bit to get the KDE desktop. If you choose to install Fedora Core as a Personal Desktop or Workstation system, you get the GNOME desktop by default. You must specifically ask to install additional packages to get KDE. By default, it is only included in an Everything install.

Fedora Core 2 offers new versions of the GNOME (2.6) and KDE (3.2.2) desktop environments. You can read about X, GNOME, and KDE in Chapter 3.

More software packages

By far, most of the enhancements to Fedora Core over previous versions of Red Hat Linux have come in existing packages. Nearly 200 new packages have been added, however. In particular, I noticed a lot of support tools have been added for Java development and, of course, new packages have been added to support new features described earlier (such as the X.Org X server and SE Linux). For a complete list of software packages in Fedora Core 2, refer to Appendix B.

The Culture of Free Software

I would be remiss to not say something about the culture of free software development from which Linux has thrived and will continue to thrive. The copyright for Fedora and other Red Hat Linux systems is covered under the GNU public license. That license, which most free software falls under, provides the following:

- **Author rights** — The original author retains the rights to his or her software.

- **Free distribution** — People can use the GNU software in their own software, changing and redistributing it as they please. They do, however, have to include the source code with their distribution (or make it easily available).

- **Copyright maintained** — Even if you were to repackage and resell the software, the original GNU agreement must be maintained with the software. This means that all future recipients of the software must have the opportunity to change the source code, just as you did.

It is important to remember that there is no warranty on GNU software. If something goes wrong, the original developer of the software has no obligation to fix the problem. However, the Linux culture has provided resources for that event. Experts on the Internet can help you iron out your problems, or you can access one of the many Linux newsgroups to read how others have dealt with their problems and to post your own questions about how to fix yours. Chances are that someone will know what to do — maybe even going so far as to provide the software or configuration file you need.

> **NOTE:** The GNU project uses the term *free software* to describe the software that is covered by the GNU license. On occasion, you may see the term *open-source software* being used to describe software. Though source code availability is part of the GNU license, the GNU project claims that software defined as open source is not the same as free software because it can encompass semi-free programs and even some proprietary programs. See www.opensource.org for a description of open-source software.

Summary

Linux is a free computer operating system that was created by Linus Torvalds in 1991 and has grown from contributions from software developers all over the world. Fedora Core and Red

Hat Enterprise versions of Red Hat Linux are distributions of Linux that package together the software needed to run Linux and make it easier to install and run.

This book specifically describes Fedora Core 2, a complete version of which is included on the CDs that come with this book. Fedora Core includes cutting-edge Linux technology that is slated for inclusion in commercial Red Hat Linux systems. Features in Fedora Core 2 include a simplified installation procedure, RPM Package Management (RPM) tools for managing the software, and easy-to-use GNOME and KDE desktop environments. You can get Fedora Core from the Internet or from distributions that come with books such as this one.

Linux is based on a culture of free exchange of software. Linux's roots are based in the UNIX operating system. UNIX provided most of the framework that was used to create Linux. That framework came from the POSIX standard, the System V Interface Definition, and the Berkeley Software Distribution, pieces of which have all found their way into Linux.

Chapter 2

Installing Fedora

In This Chapter

- Quick installation
- Detailed installation instructions
- Special installation procedures
- Special installation topics
- Troubleshooting installation

A simplified installation procedure is one of the best reasons for using a Linux distribution such as Fedora Linux. In many cases, for a computer dedicated to using Fedora Linux, you can just pop in the CDs (that come with this book), choose from several preset configurations, and be up and running Linux in less than an hour.

If you want to share your computer with both Linux and Microsoft Windows, Fedora offers several ways to go about doing that. If your computer doesn't have a CD drive, network and hard disk installs are available. To preconfigure Fedora Linux to install on multiple, similar computers, you can use the kickstart installation.

Quick Installation

It can be a little intimidating to see a thick chapter on installation. But the truth is, if you have a little bit of experience with computers and a computer with common hardware, you can probably install Fedora Linux pretty easily. The procedure in this section will get you going quickly if you have:

- The Fedora Linux installation CDs (Fedora Core) that come with this book.
- A Pentium-class PC (at least 200 MHz for text mode; 400 MHz Pentium II for GUI) with a built-in, bootable CD-ROM drive, at least 64MB of RAM (for text mode) or 192MB of RAM (for GUI mode). You need at least 520MB of free hard disk space for a Minimum custom install, at least 1.9GB of hard disk space for a personal desktop install, at least 2.4GB of free space for a workstation install, and at least 870MB for a server install. (The Minimum install is configured to be used as a Linux firewall and/or router.)

A custom Everything install requires at least 6.3GB of disk space. In all of these installations, you will want to have more disk space than the bare minimum.

For this quick procedure, you must either be dedicating your entire hard disk to Linux, have a preconfigured Linux partition, or have sufficient free space on your hard disk outside any existing Windows partition.

> **CAUTION:** If you are not dedicating your whole hard disk to Fedora Linux and you don't understand partitioning, skip to the "Detailed Installation Instructions" section in this chapter. That section describes choices for having both Linux and Windows on the same computer.

Here's how you get started:

1. Insert Fedora Linux (Fedora Core) installation CD #1 into your computer's CD-ROM drive.

2. Reboot your computer.

3. When you see the installation screen (with a `boot:` prompt at the bottom), press Enter to begin the installation.

During installation, you are asked questions about your computer hardware and the network connections. After you have completed each answer, click Next. The following list describes the information you will need to enter. (If you need help, all of these topics are explained later in this chapter.)

- **Media Check** — Optionally check each CD to be sure it is not damaged or corrupted.

- **Language Selection** — Choose your language.

- **Keyboard Configuration** — Choose your keyboard type.

- **Monitor Configuration** — Identify your monitor model (alternatively, select a generic LCD or CRT setting or set your own horizontal and vertical sync).

- **Upgrade** — If you have an earlier version of Fedora Linux installed, you can choose Upgrade to upgrade your system without losing data files. Otherwise, you can continue with a new installation.

- **Installation Type** — Choose a configuration, such as Personal Desktop (for laptop, home, or desktop use), Workstation (desktop plus software development), Server (file, print, Web, and other server software), or Custom (adds selected Linux packages, Minimum, or Everything installs).

- **Disk Partitioning Setup** — Either have Fedora automatically choose your partitions or manually partition yourself (with Disk Druid). With Automatic, you can choose to remove Linux partitions, all partitions, or no partitions (and use existing free space). Because repartitioning can result in lost data, I recommend that you refer to descriptions on repartitioning your hard disk later in this chapter.

- **Disk Druid** — Whether you choose Automatic or Manual partitioning, Disk Druid appears onscreen to let you review or change the partitions.

- **Boot Loader Configuration** — Add the GRUB boot manager to control the boot process. (GRUB is described later in this chapter.) With multiple operating systems on the computer, select which one to boot by default.

- **Network Configuration** — Set up your LAN connection (not dial-up). You can simply choose to get addresses using DHCP, or you can manually enter your computer's IP address, netmask, host name, default gateway, and DNS servers. You can also indicate whether to activate your network when Linux boots.

- **Firewall Configuration** — Choose a default firewall configuration. Select Enable firewall if you want to block access to most services to your computer from outside computers. If you do enable the firewall, you can select to open particular services to computers on the network or choose to allow all computers on a selected network interface (such as eth0 for your first Ethernet card) to connect to any service on your computer. Select No Firewall only if you are connected to a trusted network, with no connection to a public network.

- **Additional Language Support** — Choose to install support for additional languages.

- **Time Zone Selection** — Identify the time zone in which you are located.

- **Set Root Password** — Add the root user account password.

- **Package Installation Defaults** — Select to install the current package list (for the install type you chose) or customize it. For custom installations, choose groups of software packages to install, choose Everything, or Mimimum. (You can also choose separate packages if you like.)

CAUTION: If your computer is connected to the Internet, you should be more selective about which server packages you install because they may pose potential security risks. A misconfigured server can be like an open window to your computer. In a safe environment, however, an Everything install (if you have enough disk space) allows you to follow the procedures in this book without continuously going back and installing new packages from the CD.

- **About to Install** — To this point, you can quit the install process without having written anything to disk. When you select Next, the disk is formatted (as you chose) and selected packages are installed.

NOTE: After answering the questions, the actual installation of packages takes between 20 and 60 minutes, depending on the number of packages and the speed of the computer hardware. During this time, you will be asked to insert the other Fedora installation CDs.

- **Monitor Configuration** — You may be asked to configure your Monitor at this point. If it was probed properly, you should be able to just continue.

When installation is done, remove the Fedora Linux CD and click Exit to reboot your computer. When you see the boot screen, use up and down arrows to select a partition. Linux should boot by default. After Linux boots for the first time, the Fedora Setup Agent runs to let you read the license agreement, set system date and time, configure your display, add a user account, configure your sound card, and install additional CDs. On subsequent reboots, you will see a login prompt. If you need more information than this procedure provides, go to the detailed installation instructions just ahead.

> **NOTE:** If you did a Server or Minimum install where no graphical interface is installed, the Fedora Setup Agent does not run.

Detailed Installation Instructions

This section provides more detail on installation. Besides expanding on the installation procedure, this section also provides information on different installation types and on choosing computer hardware.

> **TIP:** If anything goes wrong during installation and you get stuck, go to the "Troubleshooting Your Installation" section at the end of this chapter. It gives suggestions for solving common installation problems.

> **CAUTION:** If you are installing a dual-boot system that includes a Windows operating system, try to install the Windows system first and the Fedora Linux system later. Some Windows systems blow away the Master Boot Record (MBR), making the Fedora Linux partition inaccessible.
>
> If, when installing Windows or Fedora Linux, you find that the other operating system is no longer available on your boot screen, don't panic and don't immediately reinstall. You can usually recover from the problem by booting with the Fedora Linux emergency boot disk, and then using either the `grub-install` or `lilo` commands to reinsert the proper MBR. If you are uncomfortable working in emergency mode, seek out an expert to help you.

Installing Fedora Linux 2

This chapter details how to install Fedora Linux 2 from the CDs that come with this book. If you are installing Fedora Linux from those CDs, you can simply follow the instructions in this chapter.

Installing Other Red Hat Linux Systems

Much of the installation procedure described here is the same as you will find when you install a Red Hat Enterprise Linux system. However, here are a few issues you should be aware of if you are using the installation procedure in this chapter to install

Red Hat Enterprise Linux.

- Instead of having a 4-CD installation set, Red Hat Enterprise Linux consists of a different boot CD for AS and WS installs. After starting installation with the appropriate boot CD, both install types use the same set of additional CDs (marked disc2, disc3, and disc4).

- Installation classes for Fedora and Enterprise are different.

- The names and logos used for Fedora and Enterprise are different.

- Unlike the Fedora installation, which installs all CDs in order, Red Hat Enterprise Linux requires that you insert the boot CD again near the end of the install process.

Besides those differences, an installation of Fedora Enterprise Linux should match the instructions in this chapter. There are differences in which packages are included with the Fedora and Enterprise distributions, however. (See Appendix B for Fedora package descriptions.)

Choosing an installation method

Fedora Linux offers very flexible ways of installing the operating system. Of course, I recommend installing Fedora Linux from the CDs that come with this book. However, if you don't have the Fedora CDs or if you don't have a working CD-ROM drive, you can install Fedora Linux from any of several different types of media. There are also several special types of installation. The installation types noted here are described fully in the "Special Installation Procedures" section.

Install or upgrade?

First you should determine if you are doing a new install or an upgrade. If you are upgrading an existing Red Hat Linux or Fedora Linux system to the latest version, the installation process will try to leave your data files and configuration files intact as much as possible. This type of installation takes longer than a new install. A new install will simply erase all data on the Linux partitions (or whole hard disk) that you choose.

> **NOTE:** While you can upgrade to Fedora Linux 2 from previous Fedora or Red Hat Linux systems (such as Red Hat Linux 8 or 9), you cannot upgrade to Fedora Linux 2 from a Red Hat Enterprise Linux system.

From CD, network, or hard disk?

When you install Fedora Linux, the distribution doesn't have to come from the installation CDs. After booting the installation CD and typing **linux askmethod** at the boot prompt, you are offered the choice of installing Fedora from the following locations:

- **Local CDROM** — This is the most common method of installing Fedora and the one you get by simply pressing Enter from the installation boot prompt. All packages needed to complete the installation are on the set of CDs that come with this book.

- **HTTP**— Lets you install from a Web page address (http://).

- **FTP** — Lets you install from an FTP site (ftp://).

- **NFS image** — Allows you to install from any shared directory on another computer on your network using the Network File System (NFS) facility.

- **Hard drive** — If you can place a copy of the Fedora Linux distribution on your hard drive, you can install it from there. (Presumably, the distribution is on a hard drive partition to which you are *not* installing.)

If you don't have a bootable CD drive, there are other ways to start the Fedora installation. Unlike earlier Fedora and Red Hat Linux versions, Fedora Core 2 doesn't support floppy disk boot images (the Linux 2.6 kernel is too large to fit on a floppy disk). Therefore, if you don't have a bootable CD drive, you need to start the install process from some other medium (such as a PXE server or hard drive, as described later in this chapter.)

The following specialty installation type also may be of interest to you:

- **Kickstart installation** — Lets you create a set of answers to the questions Fedora Linux asks you during installation. This can be a time-saving method if you are installing Fedora Linux on many computers with similar configurations.

There is no specific installation guide provided with the Fedora Project. However, the Red Hat Linux Installation Guide is available from any Red Hat FTP site (such as ftp.redhat.com). The location on the ftp.redhat.com server of the Red Hat Linux 9 Installation Guide is:

```
pub/redhat/linux/9/en/doc/RH-DOCS/rhl-ig-x86-en-9/index.html
```

Another document you may find useful before installing is the Fedora Linux Reference Guide (also listed in the RH-DOCS directory, as rhl-rg-en-9.0). You'll need to check for yourself to find out whether the Fedora Project eventually updates the reference guides for Fedora Core.

Choosing computer hardware

This may not really be a choice. You may just have an old PC lying around that you want to try Fedora Linux on. Or you may have a killer workstation with some extra disk space and want to try out Fedora Linux on a separate partition or whole disk. To install the PC version of Fedora Linux successfully (that is, the version on the accompanying CDs), the computer must have the following:

- **x86 processor** — Your computer needs an Intel-compatible CPU. With the latest version, Fedora recommends that you at least have a Pentium-class processor to run

Fedora Linux. For a text-only installation, a 200 MHz Pentium is the minimum, while a 400 MHz Pentium II is the minimum for a GUI installation. Although some 486 machines will work, they cannot be counted on.

- **CD-ROM** drive— You need to be able to boot up the installation process from a CD-ROM. If you don't have a CD-ROM drive, you need a LAN connection to install Fedora Linux from a server on the network or figure out a way to copy the contents of the CD to a hard disk.

- **Hard disk** — The minimum amount of space you need varies depending on the installation type and packages you select. If you are an inexperienced user, you want at least1.9GB of space so you can get the GUI with a Personal Desktop or Workstation install:

  - **Personal Desktop** — Requires 1.9GB of disk space.

  - **Workstation** — Requires 2.4GB of disk space.

  - **Server** — Requires 870MB of disk space.

  - **Everything** (Custom) — Requires about 5.3 GB.

  - **Mimimum** (Custom) — Requires at least 520MB of disk space.

- **RAM** — You should have at least 64MB of RAM to install Fedora Linux. If you are running in graphical mode, you will probably need at least 192MB. The recommended RAM for GUI mode is 256MB.

- **Keyboard and monitor** — Although this seems obvious, the truth is that you only need a keyboard and monitor during installation. You can operate Fedora Linux quite well over a LAN using either a shell interface from a network login or an X terminal.

Fedora Linux versions, not included with this book, are available for the AMD64 architecture. For other hardware, such as Intel Itanium, IBM PowerPC, and IBM mainframe, there are versions of Red Hat Enterprise Linux available (which you have to purchase from Red Hat, Inc.). The CDs that come with this book and the installation procedures presented here, however, are specific to PCs. Most of the software described in this book will work the same in any of those hardware environments. (Check out `http://redhat.com/mirrors` for sites that offer Fedora Linux for different computer hardware architectures.)

> **NOTE:** The list of hardware supported by previous versions of Red Hat Linux is available on the Internet at `www.redhat.com/hardware`.

Installing Fedora Linux on a Laptop

Because laptops can contain non-standard equipment, before you begin installing on a laptop you should find out about other people's experiences installing Linux on your model. Do that by visiting the Linux on Laptops site (`www.linux-on-laptops.com`).

Most modern laptops contain bootable CD-ROM drives, If yours doesn't, you probably need to install from a device connected to a USB or PCMCIA slot on your laptop. PCMCIA slots let you connect a variety of devices to your laptop using credit card–sized cards (sometimes called PC Cards). Linux supports hundreds of PCMCIA devices. You can use your laptop's PCMCIA slot to install Fedora Linux from several different types of PCMCIA devices, including:

- A CD-ROM drive
- A LAN adapter

If you would like to know which PCMCIA devices are supported in Linux, see the SUPPORTED.CARDS file (located in the /usr/share/doc/kernel-pcmcia-cs* directory). In any of these cases, you need the PCMCIA support disk to use the device as an installation medium. The section on creating install disks describes how to create these installation floppy disks. (See Chapter 10 for further information on using Linux on laptops.)

Beginning the installation

If you feel you have chosen the right type of installation for your needs, you can begin the installation procedure. Throughout most of the procedure, you can click Back to make changes to earlier screens. However, once you are warned that packages are about to be written to hard disk, there's no turning back. Most items that you configure can be changed after Fedora Linux is installed.

CAUTION: It is quite possible that your entire hard disk is devoted to a Windows 95, 98, 2000, ME, NT, or XP operating system and you may want to keep much of that information after Fedora Linux is installed. Personal Desktop, Workstation, and Custom install classes retain existing partitions (by default), but they don't let you take space from existing DOS partitions without destroying them. See the section on reclaiming free disk space called "Using the FIPS Utility" for information on how to assign your extra disk space to a different partition before you start this installation process.

TIP: If you are upgrading an existing Fedora Linux system to this release, you should consider first removing any unwanted packages from your old Fedora Linux system. Fewer packages that have to be checked during an upgrade can mean a significantly faster upgrade installation, as well as the consumption of less space.

1. **Insert the first CD-ROM in the CD-ROM drive.** This procedure assumes you are booting installation and installing from the CD set that comes with this book. (If you are not able to boot from CD, refer to the "Alternatives for Starting Installation" section. If you are booting installation from CD, but installing from a network or hard disk, refer to the "Installing from Other Media" section.)

2. **Start your computer.** If you see the Fedora Linux installation screen, continue to the
    next step.

TIP: If you don't see the installation screen, your CD-ROM drive may not be bootable. Creating a bootable
floppy is no longer an option because the 2.6 kernel doesn't fit on a floppy. However, you may have the
choice of making your CD-ROM drive bootable. Here's how: Restart the computer. Immediately, you should
see a message telling you how to go into setup, such as by pressing the F1, F2, or Del key. Enter setup and
look for an option such as "Boot Options" or "Boot from." If the value is "A: First, Then C:" change it to "CD-
ROM First, Then C:" or something similar. Save the changes and try to install again.

If installation succeeds, you may want to restore the boot settings. If your CD drive still won't boot, you may
need to use an alternative method to boot Fedora installation (described in "Alternatives for Starting
Installation" later in this chapter).

---

3. **Start the boot procedure.** At the boot prompt, press Enter to start the boot procedure
    in graphical mode. If for some reason your computer will not let you install in graphical
    mode (16-bit color, 800 x 600 resolution, framebuffer), refer to the "Choosing Different
    Install Modes" sidebar. Different modes let you start network installs and nongraphical
    installs (in case, for example, your video card can't be detected). There are also options
    for turning off certain features that may be causing installation to fail.

4. **Media check.** At this point, you may be asked to check your installation media. If so,
    press Enter to check that the CD is in working order. If one of the CDs is damaged, this
    step saves you the trouble of getting deep into the install before failing. Repeat this step
    for each CD in the set; then reinsert CD #1 and select Skip to continue.

5. **Continue.** When the welcome screen appears, click Release Notes to see information
    about this version of Fedora Linux. Click Next when you're ready to continue.

6. **Choose a language.** When prompted, indicate the language that you would like to use
    during the installation procedure by moving the arrow keys and selecting Next. (Later,
    you will be able to add additional languages.) You are asked to choose a keyboard.

7. **Choose a keyboard.** Select the correct keyboard layout (U.S. English, with Generic 101-
    key PC keyboard by default). Some layouts enable dead keys (on by default). Dead keys
    let you use characters with special markings (such as circumflexes and umlauts).

8. **Select Monitor Configuration.** Scroll down the list to find your monitor's manufacturer;
    then click the plus sign to choose the model. When you select the model, the correct
    horizontal and vertical sync rates are added, or you can type your own values. If your
    model is not found, consult the monitor's manual. Then try a Generic CRT or Generic
    LCD (depending on the type of monitor you have) or type the monitor's horizontal and
    vertical sync rates into the appropriate box. Click Next to continue.

9. **Choose install type.** Select either "Install Fedora Core" for a new install or "Upgrade an
    existing installation" to upgrade an existing version of Fedora.

Choosing Different Install Modes

Although most computers will enable you to install Fedora Linux in the default mode (graphical), there may be times when your video card does not support that mode. Also, though the install process will detect most computer hardware, there may be times when your hard disk, Ethernet card, or other critical piece of hardware cannot be detected and will require you to enter special information at boot time.

The following is a list of different installation modes you can use to start the Fedora Linux install process. You would typically only try these modes if the default mode failed (that is, if the screen was garbled or installation failed at some point). For a list of other supported modes, refer to the `/usr/share/doc/anaconda*/command-line.txt` file or press F2 to see short descriptions of some of these types.

- **linux text:** Type **linux text** to run installation in a text-based mode. Do this if installation doesn't seem to recognize your graphics card. The installation screens aren't as pretty, but they work just as well.

- **linux lowres:** Type **linux lowres** to run installation in 640x480 screen resolution for graphics cards that can't support the higher resolution.

- **linux nofb:** Type **linux nofb** to turn off frame buffer.

- **linux noprobe:** Normally, the installation process will try to determine what hardware you have on your computer. In `noprobe` mode, installation will not probe to determine your hardware; you will be asked to load any special drivers that might be needed to install it.

- **linux mediacheck:** Type **linux mediacheck** to check your CDs before installing. Because media checking is done next in the normal installation process, you should do this only to test the media on a computer you are not installing on.

- **linux rescue:** The **linux rescue** mode is not really an installation mode. This mode boots from CD, mounts your hard disk, and lets you access useful utilities to correct problems preventing your Linux system from operating properly.

- **linux vnc vncpassword=******:** Run your computer as a vnc server to allow other computers to install Fedora Linux from your computer. The password (represented by asterisks) must be at least six characters. The client must connect to display :1 and supply the password to be able to install.

- **linux dd:** Type **linux dd** if you have a driver disk you want to use to install.

- **linux expert:** Type **linux expert** if you believe that the installation process is not properly auto-probing your hardware. This mode bypasses probing so you can choose your mouse, video memory, and other values that would otherwise be chosen for you.

- **linux askmethod:** Type **linux askmethod** to have the installation process ask where to install from (local CD, NFS image, FTP, HTTP, or hard disk).

- **linux updates:** Type **linux updates** to install from an update disk.

You can add other options to the linux boot command to identify particular hardware that is not being detected properly. For example, to specify the number of cylinders, heads, and sectors for your hard disk (if you believe the boot process is not detecting these values properly), you could pass the information to the kernel as follows: `linux hd=720,32,64`. In this example, the kernel is told that the hard disk has 720 cylinders, 32 heads, and 64 sectors. You can find this information in the documentation that comes with your hard disk (or stamped on the hard disk itself on a sticker near the serial number).

NOTE: To upgrade, you must have at least a Linux 2.0 kernel installed. With an upgrade, all of your configuration files are saved as `filename.rpmsave` (for example, the hosts file is saved as `hosts.rpmsave`). The locations of those files, as well as other upgrade information, is written to `/tmp/upgrade.log`. The upgrade installs the new kernel, any changed software packages, and any packages that the installed packages depend on being there. Your data files and configuration information should remain intact. By clicking the "Customize" box, you can choose which packages to upgrade.

WARNING: The personal desktop and workstation installation types do not install server packages or many system administration tools. To use most of the administration and server features described in this book (especially from Part IV), you must either 1) select to add additional packages to those install types, or 2) add extra packages as you need them with the system-config-packages tool described later in this chapter or `yum` command described in Chapter 5.

For a new install, you must choose one of the following types (also referred to as classes) of installation. For any of these installation types, you will have the opportunity to install a set of preset packages or customize that set.

- **Personal Desktop** — Installs software appropriate for a home or office personal computer or laptop computer. This includes the GNOME desktop (no KDE) and various desktop-related tools (word processors, Internet tools, and so on). Server tools, software development tools, and many system administration tools are not installed.

- **Workstation** — Similar to a Personal Desktop installation but adds tools for system administration and software development. (Server software is not installed.)

> **CAUTION:** Any Linux partitions or free space on your hard disk(s) will be assigned to the new installation with the Personal Desktop or Workstation types of installation. Any Windows partitions (VFAT or FAT32 file system types) will not be touched by this install. After installation, you will be able to boot Linux or Windows. If there is no free space outside of your Windows partition, you must run Partition Magic, the parted utility, the FIPS program (described later) or other disk-resizing software before proceeding, or you will lose your Windows installation.

- **Server** — Server installs the software packages that you would typically need for a Linux server (in particular, Web server, file server, and print server). It does not include many other server types (DHCP, mail, DNS, FTP, SQL, or news servers). The default server install does not include a GUI (so you'd better know how to use the shell). This install type also erases all hard disks and assigns them to Linux by default.

> **CAUTION:** This is a big one. In case you didn't catch the previous paragraph, Server installs erase the whole hard disk by default! If you have an existing Windows partition that you want to keep, change the Automatic Partitioning option that appears next either to only remove the Linux Partitions or to only use existing free space.

- **Custom System** — You are given the choice of configuring your own partitions and selecting your own software packages.

> **NOTE:** If you are just trying out Linux, an Everything custom install gives you all the desktop, server, and development tools that come with Fedora Linux. If you have the disk space, an Everything install saves you the trouble of installing packages you need later. If you plan to use the computer as an Internet server, you should be more selective in which packages you install.

At this point, the procedure will continue through a Custom System installation. Even though different install classes choose different partitioning methods by default, in all cases you have the choice to see and change the partitioning that was chosen for you.

10. **Choose your partitioning strategy.** You have two choices related to how your disk is partitioned for a Fedora installation:

- **Automatically partition** — With this selection, all Linux partitions on all hard disks are erased and used for the installation. The installation process automatically handles the partitioning. (It does give you a chance to review your partitioning, however.)
- **Manually partition with Disk Druid** — With this selection, the Disk Druid utility is run to let you partition your hard disk.

Click Next to continue.

11. **Choose partitioning.** If you selected to have the installer automatically partition for you, you can choose from the following options:

> **NOTE:** If you selected to use Disk Druid for partitioning, refer to the section on partitioning your hard disk later in this chapter for details on using those tools.

- **Remove all Linux partitions on this system** — Windows and other non-Linux partitions remain intact with this selection.

- **Remove all partitions on this system** — This erases the entire hard disk.

- **Keep all partitions and use existing free space** — This only works if you have enough free space on your hard disk that is not currently assigned to any partition.

If you have multiple hard disks, you can select which of those disks should be used for your Fedora Linux installation. Turn the Review check box on to see how Linux is choosing to partition your hard disk. Click Next to continue.

After reviewing the Partitions screen, you can change any of the partitions you choose, providing you have at least one root (/) partition that can hold the entire installation and one swap partition. A small /boot partition (about 100MB) is also recommended.

The swap partition is often set to twice the size of the amount of RAM on your computer (for example, for 128MB RAM you could use 256MB of swap). Linux uses swap space when active processes have filled up your system's RAM. At that point, an inactive process is moved to swap space. You get a performance hit when the inactive process is moved to swap and another hit when that process restarts (moves back to RAM). For example, you might notice a delay on a busy system when you reopen a Window that has been minimized for a long time.

The reason you need to have enough swap space is that when RAM and swap fill up, no other processes can start until something closes. Bottom line: add RAM to get better performance; add swap space if processes are failing to start. Red Hat suggests a minimum of 32MB and maximum of 2GB of swap space.

Click the Next button (and select OK to accept any changes) to continue.

12. **Configure boot loader.** All bootable partitions and default boot loader options are displayed. By default, the install process will use the GRUB boot loader, install the boot loader in the master boot record of the computer, and choose Fedora Linux as your default operating system to boot.

> **NOTE:** If you keep the GRUB boot loader, you have the option of adding a GRUB password. The password protects your system from having potentially dangerous kernel options sent to the kernel by someone without that password. GRUB and LILO boot loaders are described later in this chapter.

The names shown for each bootable partition will appear on the boot loader screen when the system starts. Change a partition name by clicking it and selecting Edit. To change the location of the boot loader, click "Configure advanced boot loader options" and continue to the next step. If you do not want to install a boot loader (because you don't want to change the current boot loader), click "Change boot loader" and select "Do not install a boot loader." (If the defaults are okay, skip the next step.)

13. **Configure advanced boot loader.** To choose where to store the boot loader, select one of the following:

- **Master Boot Record (MBR)** — This is the preferred place for GRUB. It causes GRUB to control the boot process for all operating systems installed on the hard disk.

- **First Sector of Boot Partition** — If another boot loader is being used on your computer, you can have GRUB installed on your Linux partition (first sector). This lets you have the other boot loader refer to your GRUB boot loader to boot Fedora Linux.

You can choose to add Kernel Parameters (which may be needed if your computer can't detect certain hardware). You can select to use linear mode (which was once required to boot from a partition on the disk that is above cylinder 1024, but is now rarely needed).

> **NOTE:** For more information on GRUB, refer to the section on boot loaders later in this chapter.

14. **Configure networking.** At this point, you are asked to configure your networking. This applies only to configuring a local area network. If you will use only dial-up networking, skip this section by clicking Next. If your computer is not yet connected to a LAN, you should skip this section.

    Network address information is assigned to your computer in two basic ways: statically (you type it) or dynamically (a DHCP server provides that information from the network at boot time). One Network Device appears for each network card you have installed on your computer. The first Ethernet interface is eth0, the second is eth1, and so on. Repeat the setup for each card by selecting each card and clicking Edit.

> **CROSS-REFERENCE:** Refer to Chapter 15 for descriptions of IP addresses, netmasks, and other information you need to set up your LAN and to Chapter 16 for information related to domain names.

    With the Edit Interface eth0 dialog box displayed, add the following:

    - **Configure using DHCP** — If your IP address is assigned automatically from a DHCP server, a checkmark should appear here. With DHCP checked, you don't have to set other values on this page. Remove the checkmark to set your own IP address.

    - **IP Address** — If you set your own IP address, this is the four-part, dot-separated number that represents your computer to the network. How IP addresses are formed and how you choose them is more than can be said in a few sentences (see Chapter 15 for a more complete description). An example of a private IP address is 192.168.0.1.

    - **Netmask** — The netmask is used to determine what part of an IP address represents the network and what part represents a particular host computer. An example of a netmask for a Class C network is 255.255.255.0.

    - **Activate on boot** —You should indicate also whether you want the network to start at boot time (you probably do if you have a LAN).

    Click OK. Then add the following information on the main screen:

- **Set the hostname** — This is the name identifying your computer within your domain. For example, if your computer were named "baskets" in the `handsonhistory.com` domain, your full hostname may be `baskets.handsonhistory.com`. You can either set the domain name yourself (manually) or have it assigned automatically, if that information is being assigned by a DHCP server (automatically via DHCP).

- **Gateway** — This is the IP number of the computer that acts as a gateway to networks outside your LAN. This typically represents a host computer or router that routes packets between your LAN and the Internet.

- **Primary DNS** — This is the IP address of the host that translates computer names you request into IP addresses. It is referred to as a Domain Name System (DNS) server. You may also have Secondary and Tertiary name servers in case the first one can't be reached. (Most ISPs will give you two DNS server addresses.)

CROSS-REFERENCE: To configure your LAN after installation, see Chapter 15.

---

15. **Choose a firewall configuration.** The use of a firewall has significant impact on the security of your computer. If you are connected to the Internet or to another public network, a firewall can limit the ways an intruder may break into your Linux system. Here are your choices for configuring a firewall during installation:

    - **No firewall** — Select this security level if you are not connected to a public network and do not want to deny requests for services from any computer on your local network. Of course, you can still restrict access to services by starting up only the services you want to offer and by using configuration files to restrict access to individual services.

    - **Enable firewall** — Select this security level if you are connecting your Linux system to the Internet for Web browsing and file downloading (FTP). By default, only services needed to allow Web browsing and basic network setup, DNS replies, and DHCP (to serve addresses) are allowed at this level.

    If you enable the firewall and you know you want to allow access to particular services, you can click the appropriate check boxes and allow incoming requests for the following services: SSH (secure shell to allow remote login), Telnet (an insecure method of remote login), WWW (act as a Web server), Mail (act as a mail server), and/or FTP (act as an FTP server). You can also add a comma-separated list of port numbers to the Other Ports box to open access to those ports, which effectively allows requests to services associated with those port numbers. (The `/etc/services` file lists which services are associated with which port numbers.)

    If you have a LAN that consists of trusted computers, you can click the box representing your interface to that LAN (probably `eth0`). Clicking the box allows access to any services you care to share with the computers on your LAN.

> **TIP:** Adding firewall rules here results in rules being added to the `/etc/sysconfig/iptables` file. The rules are run from the `/etc/init.d/iptables` start-up script when you boot your system. To make permanent changes to your firewall rules, you can use the Configure Firewalling window, as described in Chapter 14.

16. **Choose language support.** Your installation language should be selected automatically as your default language on this screen. You can select to install support for additional languages by clicking the check boxes next to the languages you want. You can click the Select All button to install all supported languages to your system.

17. **Choose a time zone.** Select the time zone from the list of time zones shown. Either click a spot on the map or choose from the scrolling list. To see a more specific view of your location, click World and choose your continent. From the UTC Offset tab, you can choose a time zone according to the number of hours away from Greenwich Mean Time (GMT), known as the UTC offset.

18. **Set root password.** You must choose a password for your root user at this point. The root password provides complete control of your Fedora Linux system. Without it, and before you add other users, you will have no access to your own system. Enter the Root Password, and then type it again in the Confirm box to confirm it. (Remember the root user's password and keep it confidential! Don't lose it!) Click Next to continue.

> **TIP:** Use the `passwd` command to change your password later. See Chapter 14 for suggestions on how to choose a good password. See Chapter 11 for information on setting up user accounts.

> **NOTE:** If you are enabling Security Enhanced Linux (SELinux) on your computer, the security structure of your computer changes. The root user may no longer have complete control of the computer, but instead there may be policies set that prevent any one user from having complete control.

19. **Select Packages.** You are presented with groups of packages at this point. Which packages are selected by default depends on the type of installation you chose earlier. In general, either more workstation-oriented or server-oriented packages are selected. Select the ones you want and click Next.

> **TIP:** You can override your package selections by choosing Mimimal or Everything install groups. Disk space requirements for those install types are described earlier in this chapter.

Because each group represents several packages, you can click the Details button next to each group to select more specifically the packages within that group. Because Workstation and Personal Desktop installations don't add any server packages, this is a good opportunity to add server packages for the services you expect to use.

> **CROSS-REFERENCE:** Appendix B describes the software packages that come with Fedora Linux.

> **TIP:** A listing of all of the software packages is contained in the file `Fedora/base/comps.xml` on the first Fedora installation CD-ROM. It's in XML format, so it is incomprehensible if you can't read XML.

20. **About to Install.** A screen tells you that you are about to begin writing to hard disk. You can still back out now, and the disk will not have changed. Click Next to proceed. (To quit without changes, eject the CD and restart the computer.) Now the file systems are created and the packages are installed. This typically takes from 20 to 60 minutes to complete, although it can take much longer on older computers.

    You are prompted to insert additional installation CDs as they are needed.

21. **Monitor Configuration** — You may be asked to configure your monitor at this point. If it was probed properly, you should be able to just continue.

22. **Finish installing.** When you see the Congratulations screen, you are done. Note the links to Fedora Linux information, eject the CD and click Exit.

Your computer will restart. If you installed GRUB, you will see a graphical boot screen that displays the bootable partitions. Press the up or down arrow keys to choose the partition you want to boot, and press Enter. If Linux is the default partition, you can simply wait a few moments and it will boot automatically.

The first time your system boots after installation, the Fedora Setup Agent runs to do some initial configuration of your system. The next section explains how Fedora Setup Agent works.

Running Fedora Setup Agent

The first time you boot Fedora Linux, after it is installed, the Fedora Setup Agent runs to configure some initial settings for your computer.

> **NOTE:** The Fedora Setup Agent only runs automatically if you have configured Fedora Linux to boot to a graphical login prompt. To start it from a text login, log in as root and switch to init state 5 temporarily (type **init 5**). Log in to the graphical prompt. From a Terminal window as root user, type:
> ```
> # rm /etc/sysconfig/firstboot
> # /usr/sbin/firstboot
> ```

The first screen you see is the Welcome screen. Click the Next button to step through each procedure as follows:

- **License Agreement** — Read and agree to the Fedora License Agreement to be able to continue.

- **Date and Time Configuration** — You can manually enter the date (click the calendar) and time (select hour, minutes, and seconds) or use the network time protocol to have your date and time set automatically from a known time server. Click Enable Network Time Protocol (NTP), then select a time server by clicking the down arrow and selecting a site. Network Time Protocol (NTP) is a service that allows computers to synchronize their date and time clocks with reliable time servers.

> **TIP:** Fedora offers two time servers you can use (click the down arrow in the server box to see them). Or you can type in your own time server. It is better to type an IP address than a name for your time server.

Setting NTP in this way adds your chosen NTP server to the `/etc/ntp.conf` file (see the `server` option). To check that time has been synchronized, type the `ntptrace` command. You should not have to change your firewall for NTP to work, because NTP attempts to punch a hole through your firewall to synchronize your time.

- **Monitor Configuration** — You may be asked to configure your monitor again. Linux should already know your monitor model and allow you to select your screen resolution and color depth.

> **NOTE:** The change from XFree86 to the X.Org X server in Fedora Core 2 results in Fedora asking you to reconfigure your monitor more times than in previous releases.

- **User Account** — For your daily use of Fedora Linux, you should have your own user account. You should typically log in with this user name (of your choosing) and use only the root user to perform administrative tasks. In the first of the four text boxes on the screen, type a user name (something like `jparker` or `alanb`). Next, type your full name (like John W. Parker or Alan Bourne). Then type your password in the Password text box and again in the Confirm Password text box. Click Forward.

  If some form of network authentication is used, such as LDAP, Kerberos, or SMB authentication, you can click the Use Network Login button. See the "Enabling Authentication" sidebar for information on choosing different authentication types.

Enabling Authentication

In most situations, you will enable shadow passwords and MD5 passwords (as selected by default) to authenticate users who log in to your computer from local `passwd` and `shadow` password files. To change that behavior, you can select the Use Network Login button during the User Account setup during Fedora Setup Agent (`firstboot`).

The shadow password file prevents access to encrypted passwords. MD5 is an algorithm used to encrypt passwords in Linux and other UNIX systems. It replaces an algorithm called crypt, which was used with early UNIX systems. When you enable MD5 passwords, your users can have longer passwords that are harder to break than those encrypted with crypt.

If you are on a network that supports one of several different forms of network-wide authentication, you may choose one of the following features:

- **Configure NIS.** Select this button and type the NIS Domain name and NIS server location if your network is configured to use the Network Information System (NIS). Instead of selecting an NIS Server, you can click the check box to broadcast to find the server on your network. For more information on NIS, see Chapter 23.

- **Configure LDAP.** If your organization gathers information about users, you can click this button to search for authentication information in an LDAP server. You can enter the LDAP Server name and optionally an LDAP distinguished name to look up the user information your system needs.

- **Configure Hesiod.** If your organization uses Hesiod for holding user and group information in DNS, you can add the LHS (domain prefix) and RHS (Hesiod default domain) to use for doing Hesiod queries.

- **Configure Kerberos Support.** Click this button to enable network authentication services available through Kerberos. After enabling Kerberos, you can add information about a Kerberos Realm (a group of Kerberos servers and clients), KDC (a computer that issues Kerberos tickets), and Admin server (a server running the Kerberos kadmind daemon).

- **Configure SMB.** Click this tab to configure your computer to use Samba for file and print sharing with Windows systems. If you enable SMB authentication, you can enter the name of the SMB server for your LAN and indicate the Workgroup you want your computer to belong to.

- **Install Additional Software** — If you have Fedora Linux CDs other than those that come with this book, you can install them now by inserting the CD you want to install and clicking the appropriate button.

The Fedora Setup Agent is complete. See Chapter 3 for a description of how to log in to Fedora Linux and start learning how to use Linux.

When Fedora starts up the next time, it will boot up normally to a login prompt. For this release of Fedora, a new graphical boot screen is displayed (instead of a scrolling list of services starting up). If you miss the old scrolling list, you can view it by clicking the Details button or by pressing Ctrl+Alt+F1. Then go back again by pressing Ctrl+Alt+F8.

Installing More Fedora Packages

Unless you did an Everything install, as you go through this book you will probably find that you want to add some Fedora software packages later. To do that, you can use `rpm` (described in Chapter 5), a general-purpose command for installing any software packages in RPM format. Or you can use the Package Management window (`system-config-`

`packages`), which provides the same interface for installing packages that was used in the original installation procedure.

To open the Package Management window, select System Settings → Add/Remove Applications from the main menu on the desktop (or type **system-config-packages** from a Terminal window). The window appears, as shown in Figure 2-1.

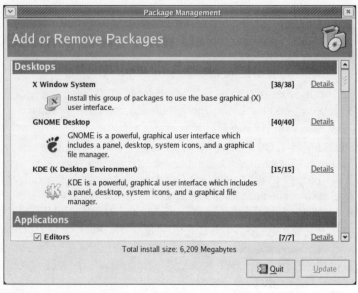

Figure 2-1: Change software packages after Fedora installation using the Package Management window.

Scroll through the major package groups using the scroll bar. After the name and description of each group there is a set of numbers in brackets that shows how many packages are in the group and how many of those are actually installed. Click Details to see the listing of all packages in the group.

The details of each group shows the standard packages in each group (ones that are required if the group is installed at all) and ones that are extra. To add or remove packages from your system, click the check box next to the package so that it is on or off, respectively. Repeat this for each package group, and close the details window.

When you have made all your add or delete selections, click Update on the main Add and Remove Software window. Insert each CD as it is requested. Packages will be added or removed, as you requested.

Special Installation Procedures

If you don't want to, or can't, use the procedure to install Fedora Linux from CD, the procedures in the following sections give you alternatives. The first subsection describes alternate ways of booting the installation, such as PXE (if your computer doesn't have a bootable CD drive). After the install procedure boots, use the "Installing from other media" section that follows to learn how to install Fedora from media other than CD-ROM (using FTP, HTTP, NFS, or hard disk installs). The next subsection describes how to do kickstart installations.

Alternatives for starting installation

You computer may not have a CD drive or may have one that is unbootable, so, you need to find an alternative way to boot the install process. Although booting installation from 1.44 floppy disks is no longer supported (the 2.6 kernel won't fit on one), you have a few other alternatives:

- Boot installation from hard disk
- Do a PXE install

Procedures for starting installation in those two ways are described in the following sections.

Booting installation from hard disk

Booting the install process is similar to booting a regular Linux system. To start an install from your hard disk all you really need to do is:

- Put the files needed to boot installation on your hard disk.
- Configure your boot loader to tell your computer's master boot record about those installation files.

This procedure presumes that there is already a Fedora or Red Hat Linux system running on the system (so you are doing an upgrade or a fresh install of Fedora). It also presumes that you can find a way to get those files on to the hard disk (I'll describe how to do that from a CD that can be mounted even if it can't be booted).

> **NOTE:** See the section earlier in this chapter on setting up install servers, since presumably you need the contents of the Fedora installation CDs accessible from somewhere other than the CDs themselves.

1. Insert Fedora Core 2 CD #1 into the CD drive while Fedora or Red Hat Linux is running.

2. If the CD isn't automatically mounted, as root user type the following to mount it:

   ```
   # mount /mnt/cdrom
   ```

3. Copy the vmlinuz and initrd files from the installation CD to your boot directory:

   ```
   # cd /mnt/cdrom/isolinux
   # cp initrd.img /boot/initrd-boot.img
   # cp vmlinuz /boot/vmlinuz-boot
   ```

> **NOTE:** If you are not able to mount a CD on the machine, you could copy the files from another machine on the network using scp. Or you could download those files to your /boot directory from a Fedora FTP site that contains the Fedora distribution.

4. Change your local /boot/grub/grub.conf file to include an entry for the vmlinux and initrd files you just added to your boot directory. For example:

```
title Fedora Core 2 installation
        root (hd0,0)
        kernel /vmlinuz-boot
        initrd /initrd-boot.img
```

This example assumes that your /boot partition exists on the first partition of your first IDE hard drive (hd0,0 which is /dev/hda1). You could type **df** to see where your /boot partition is located.

5. Reboot your computer.

6. When the GRUB boot screen appears, press the down arrow key to move to the entry that we titled "Fedora Core 2 installation" and press Enter. From here you should be able to start installation normally.

Booting installation using PXE

Another method to begin Fedora installation is to use Pre-eXecution Environment (PXE). With PXE, the installation process begins by setting the BIOS of your computer to look on the network for a PXE server to boot from. For information on how to do a PXE install, refer to /usr/share/doc/syslinux-*/pxelinux.doc. For the PXE install server, you can use the kernel and initrd images from the images/pxeboot directory on the first Fedora CD. You need to be able to set up a DHCP server and Tftp server to complete this procedure.

Installing from other media

Once the installation process has booted (from CD or as described in the previous section), Fedora will let you get the actual packages that are to be installed from a Web server (HTTP), an FTP server, a shared NFS directory, or local hard disk.

> **NOTE:** To use HTTP, FTP, or NFS installations, your computer must be connected to a LAN that can reach the computer containing the Fedora Linux distribution. You cannot use a direct dial-up connection. For a local hard disk install, the distribution must have been copied to a local disk that is not being used for installation. See the section "Setting up an HTTP, FTP, or NFS install server" for details on copying the distribution and making it available.

Beginning installation

You can use CD #1 that comes with this book (or an alternative method described in the previous section) to start a network or hard disk install.

> **NOTE:** For earlier Red Hat and Fedora Core distributions, you could use a floppy disk to boot the install process. Because the 2.6 kernel it too large to fit on a floppy disk, however, this method of starting installation is not supported for Fedora Core 2.

1. **Insert CD #1.**

2. **Reboot the computer.** You should see the Fedora boot screen.

3. **Start askmethod.** Type the following at the boot prompt:

   ```
   boot: linux askmethod
   ```

   You are prompted to select a language.

4. **Select the language.** You are prompted to choose a keyboard type.

5. **Select your keyboard type.** You are prompted to select an installation method.

6. **Choose the installation method.** Select any of the following installation methods: Local CDROM, NFS image, FTP, HTTP, or Hard drive.

7. **Configure the network card.** For any of the network installs, you are asked to select your Ethernet card from the list shown. (This may be detected automatically.) If your card is not on the list, you need to obtain a driver disk that contains the driver needed by your network card.

> **NOTE:** The Fedora project does not currently offer a driver disk, so you need to obtain the appropriate driver on your own.

8. **Configure TCP/IP.** For any of the network install types (NFS, FTP, and HTTP), you are prompted to configure TCP/IP for your computer. (See the section on configuring networking earlier in this chapter for information on how to add to these fields.)

9. **Identify the location of the Fedora Linux distribution.** You must identify the NFS server name, FTP site name, or Web site name that contains the Fedora directory that holds the distribution. Or, if you are installing from hard disk, you must identify the partition containing the distribution and the directory that actually contains the Fedora directory.

> **NOTE:** For an FTP install, if you are not downloading from an anonymous FTP site, you must select the "Use non-anonymous FTP" check box when you identify the server and directory. You will need a user name and password that has access to the shared directory.

10. **Do a checksum.** You are asked if you want to do a checksum on the first disk image (.iso file of the first installation CD) found in that directory. Select Test if you do. This will verify that the image is not corrupted before you begin. Repeat this for each disk image.

11. **Continue with installation.** If the distribution is found in the location you indicated, continue the installation as described in the previous section. The install is text-based.

The next section describes how to set up your own server for installing Fedora.

Setting up an HTTP, FTP, or NFS install server

If you have a LAN connection from your computer to a computer that has about 2.5GB of disk space and offers NFS, FTP, or Web services, you can install Fedora Linux from that server. Likewise, you can install from a spare disk partition by using a hard disk install. The following procedures let you set up a Linux install server by either copying all files from the four CDs or by copying images of the four CDs.

Configuring an install server using files

To do an FTP or HTTP install, you must copy the files from the installation CDs to a directory that you make available to the network. Because there are four installation CDs in the current Fedora distribution, you can't just identify the location of a mounted CD. You must install the contents of all the CDs in the same directory structure on the server's hard disk. For example, you could do the following:

```
# mkdir /tmp/rh
# mount /mnt/cdrom              With first CD inserted
# cp -r /mnt/cdrom/* /tmp/rh/
# umount /mnt/cdrom ; eject /mnt/cdrom
# mount /mnt/cdrom              With second CD inserted
# cp -r /mnt/cdrom/* /tmp/rh/
# umount /mnt/cdrom ; eject /mnt/cdrom
# mount /mnt/cdrom              With third CD inserted
# cp -r /mnt/cdrom/* /tmp/rh/
# umount /mnt/cdrom ; eject /mnt/cdrom
# mount /mnt/cdrom              With fourth CD inserted
# cp -r /mnt/cdrom/* /tmp/rh/
```

Just type **y** when it asks to overwrite some files. The distribution directory must contain at least the RPMS and base directories, which must include all necessary software packages. In this example, all files were copied. Setting up an NFS install server or hard disk install requires copying CD images to the shared NFS directory.

Configuring an install server using disk images

Instead of copying all files from the three installation CDs, you can copy the entire images of each of the three disks to your hard disk for NFS or hard disk installs. To do this, insert the first installation CD and type the following:

```
# mkdir /tmp/rh
# dd if=/dev/cdrom of=/tmp/rh/disk1.iso      With first CD inserted
# umount /mnt/cdrom ; eject /mnt/cdrom
# dd if=/dev/cdrom of=/tmp/rh/disk2.iso      With second CD inserted
# umount /mnt/cdrom ; eject /mnt/cdrom
# dd if=/dev/cdrom of=/tmp/rh/disk3.iso      With third CD inserted
# umount /mnt/cdrom ; eject /mnt/cdrom
```

```
# dd if=/dev/cdrom of=/tmp/rh/disk3.iso    With fourth CD inserted
# umount /mnt/cdrom ; eject /mnt/cdrom
```

NFS server

Add an entry to the /etc/exports file to share the distribution directory you created. Remember, that for NFS installs, this directory must contain CD ISO images. The following entry would make the directory available in read-only form to any computer:

```
/tmp/rh    (ro)
```

Next, restart NFS by typing the following as root user:

```
# /etc/init.d/nfs restart
```

To set the NFS service to be on permanently (it is off by default), type the following as root:

```
# chkconfig nfs on
```

Web server

If your computer is configured as a Web server, you need to simply make the distribution directory available. For example, after creating the distribution directory as described above, type the following:

```
# ln -s /tmp/rh /var/www/html/rh
```

If your computer were named pine.handsonhistory.com, you would identify the install server as pine.handsonhistory.com and the directory as rh.

FTP server

If your computer is configured as an FTP server, you need to make the distribution directory available in much the same way you did with the Web server. For example, after creating the distribution directory as described above, type the following:

```
# ln -s /tmp/rh /var/ftp/pub/rh
```

If your computer were named pine.handsonhistory.com, you would identify the install server as pine.handsonhistory.com and the directory as pub/rh.

Hard disk install

With the ISO images of each CD copied to a disk partition that is not being used for your Fedora Linux install, you can use the hard disk install. If the ISO images exist in the /tmp/rh directory of the first partition of your IDE hard disk, you could identify the device as /dev/hda1 and the directory holding the images as /tmp/rh.

Performing a kickstart installation

If you are installing Fedora on multiple computers, you can save yourself some trouble by preconfiguring the answers to questions asked during installation. The method of automating the installation process is referred to as a *kickstart* installation.

> **CAUTION:** Based on the information you provide in your `ks.cfg` file, kickstart will silently go through and install Fedora without intervention. If this file is not correct, you could easily remove your master boot record and erase everything on your hard disk. Check the `ks.cfg` file carefully and test it on a noncritical computer before trying it on a computer holding critical data.

The general steps of performing a kickstart installation are as follows:

1. **Create a kickstart file.** The kickstart file, named `ks.cfg`, contains the responses to questions that are fed to the installation process.

2. **Install kickstart file.** You have to place the `ks.cfg` on a floppy disk, CD, on a local hard disk, or in an accessible location on the network.

3. **Start kickstart installation.** When you boot the installation procedure, you need to identify the location of the `ks.cfg` file.

Creating the kickstart file

A good way to begin creating your kickstart file is from a sample `ks.cfg` file. When you install Fedora Linux, the installation process places a file called `anaconda-ks.cfg` into the `/root` directory. You can use this file as the basis for the `ks.cfg` file that you will use for your kickstart installs.

The particular `/root/anaconda-ks.cfg` file you get is based on the information you entered during a regular installation (CD, NFS, and so on). Presumably, if you are installing Fedora on other computers for the same organization, multiple computers may have a lot of the same hardware and configuration information. That makes this a great file for you to start creating your `ks.cfg` file from.

> **NOTE:** For further details about how to use kickstart, refer to the Red Hat Linux Configuration Guide. You can get this guide from any Red Hat mirror site. To use a more graphical tool for configuring kickstart, run the `system-config-kickstart` command.

To start, log in as the root user. Then make a copy of the `anaconda-ks.cfg` file to work on.

```
# cp anaconda-ks.cfg ks.cfg
```

Use any text editor to edit the `ks.cfg` file. Remember that required items should be in order and that any time you omit an item, the user will be prompted for an answer. Entries from a `ks.cfg` file that was created from a regular CD installation of Fedora are used as a model for the descriptions below. You should start with your own `anaconda-ks.cfg` file, and as a result, your file will start out somewhat differently. Commented lines begin with a pound sign (#).

The first line in the `ks.cfg` file should indicate whether the installation is an upgrade or an install. The `install` option runs a new installation. You can use the `upgrade` keyword instead to upgrade an existing system. (For an upgrade, the only requirements are a language, an install method, an install device, a keyboard, and a boot loader.)

```
install
```

The method of installation is indicated on the next line. Possible locations for the installation media include: NFS (nfs --server=*servername* --dir=*installdir*), FTP (url --url ftp://*user:passwd@server/dir*), HTTP (url --url http://*server/dir*), or hard drive (harddrive --dir=/*dir* --partition=/dev/*partition*). For the default CD install, you will see:

```
cdrom
```

The required lang command sets the language (and to be more specific, the country as well) in which Fedora is installed. The value is U.S. English (en_US.UTF-8) by default.

```
lang en_US.UTF-8
```

You can install multiple languages to be supported in Fedora Linux. Here is an example of the default being set to U. S. English:

```
langsupport -default en_US.UTF-8 en_US.UTF-8
```

The required keyboard command identifies a United States (us) keyboard by default. More than 70 other keyboard types are supported.

```
keyboard us
```

The required mouse command identifies the mouse type. The following example shows a generic three-button PS/2 type mouse (generic3ps/2). You could replace it with a two-button serial mouse (generic), a two-button PS/2 mouse (genericps/2), or a Microsoft IntelliMouse (msintellips/2). For a serial mouse, identify the device (for example, --device ttyS0 for the COM1 port). To configure other types of mice, you must run mouseconfig. To see other mouse types, run the mouseconfig --help command.

```
mouse generic3ps/2 -device psaux
```

The optional xconfig command can be used to configure your monitor and video card. If you use the skipx command instead (as shown in the following code sample), no X configuration is done. (After the system is installed, run system-config-desktop to set up your X configuration.) When you use the xconfig command, you can identify the type of X server to use based on your video card (--card) and monitor specs (--hysnyc and --vsync). A handful of other options enable you to set the color depth in bits (--depth), the screen resolution (--resolution), whether the default desktop is GNOME or KDE (--defaultdesktop), whether the login screen is graphical (--startxonboot), and the amount of RAM on your video card (--videoram). (All the information after xconfig should actually appear on one line.)

```
skipx
```

```
        or
xconfig --card="ATI Mach64 3D Rage IIC" --videoram=2048 --hsync=30-95
    --vsync=50-180 --resolution=800x600 --depth=16 --startxonboot
    defaultdesktop=GNOME
```

The optional `network` command lets you configure your Fedora system's interface to your
network. The example tells your computer to get its IP address and related network
information from a DHCP server (`--bootproto=dhcp`). If you want to assign a particular IP
address, use the `--bootproto=static` option. Then change the IP address (`--ip`),
netmask (`--netmask`), IP address of the gateway (`--gateway`), and IP address of the DNS
server (`--nameserver`) to suit your system. You can also add a hostname (`--hostname`).

> **NOTE:** Although the `network` values appear to be on three lines, all values must be on the same line.

```
network --bootproto dhcp
        or
network --device=eth0 --bootproto=static --ip=192.168.0.1
    --netmask=255.255.255.0 --gateway=192.168.0.1
    --nameserver=192.168.0.254 --hostname=duck.ab.com
```

The `rootpw` command sets the password to whatever word follows (in the following example,
`paSSword`). It is a security risk to leave this password hanging around, so you should change
this password (with the `passwd` command) after Linux is installed. You also have the option
of adding an encrypted password instead (`--iscrypted g.UJ.RQeOV3Bg -enablemd5`).

```
rootpw paSSword
     or
rootpw --iscrypted g.UJ.RQeOV3Bg --enablemd5
```

The `firewall` command lets you set the default firewall used by your Fedora
system. The default value is `enabled` (if the firewall is turned on). You can also set
`firewall` to `disabled` (no firewall). (These values are described in the installation
procedure earlier in this chapter.) As you can see in the example, you can optionally indicate
that there be no restrictions from host computers on a particular interface
(`--trust eth0`). You can also allow an individual service (`--ssh`) or a particular
port:protocol pair (`--port 1234:upd`).

```
firewall --enabled --trust=eth0 --ssh --port=1234:udp
```

The required `auth` command sets the type of authentication used to protect your
user passwords. The `--useshadow` option enables the `/etc/shadow` file to store your
passwords. The `--enablemd5` option enables up to 256 character passwords. (You would
typically use both.)

```
auth --useshadow --enablemd5
```

The `timezone` command sets the time zone for your Linux system. The default, shown here,
is United States, New York (`America/New_York`). The `-utc` option indicates that the

computer's hardware clock is set to UTC time. If you don't set a time zone, `US/Eastern` is used. Run the `timeconfig` command to see other valid time zones.

```
timezone --utc America/New_York
```

The `bootloader` command sets the location of the boot loader (GRUB, by default). For example, `--location=mbr` adds GRUB to the master boot record. (Use `--location=none` to not add GRUB.) You can also add kernel options to be read at boot time using the append option (`--append hdd=ide-scsi`) or an optional password for GRUB (`--password=GRUBpassword`).

```
bootloader --location=mbr
password=GRUBpassword
```

Partitioning is required for a new install, optional for an upgrade. The code that follows is from the sample `ks.cfg` file. The `clearpart --linux` value removes existing Linux partitions (or use `--all` to clear all partitions) on the first hard drive (`--drives=hda`). The `part /boot`, `/` and `swap`, sets the file system type (`--fstype`) and partition name (`onpart`) for each partition assignment. You can also set sizes of the partitions (`--size`) to however many MB you want.

```
# The following is the partition information you requested
# Note that any partitions you deleted are not expressed
# here so unless you clear all partitions first, this is
# not guaranteed to work
#clearpart --linux --drives=hda
#part /boot --fstype ext3 --size=100 --ondisk=hda
#part / --fstype ext3 --size=700 --grow --ondisk=hda
#part swap --size=128 --grow --maxsize=256 --ondisk=hda
```

To indicate which packages to install, begin a section with the `%packages` command. (A few examples follow.) Designate whole installation groups, individual groups, or individual packages. On the `%packages` line, you can indicate whether or not to resolve dependencies by installing those packages needed by the ones you selected (`--resolvedeps`). After `%packages`, start an entry with an `@` sign for a group of packages, and add each individual package by placing its name on a line by itself. Here is an example:

> **TIP:** You can find a listing of package groups and individual packages on Fedora installation CD #1. Find the `comps` file in the `Fedora/base` directory. However, if you start with the `anaconda-ks.cfg` file that resulted from installing Fedora Linux, you might already have a set of packages that you want to install.

```
%packages --resolvdeps
@ Administration Tools
@ Authoring and Publishing
@ Core
@ DNS Name Server
@ Development Libraries
```

```
@ Development Tools
        .
        .
        .
@ Web Server
@ Windows File Server
@ X Window System
```

> **NOTE:** The %packages command is not supported for upgrades. To do an Everything install, you can remove the package names shown. Then, after the %packages line, you can add an @ everything line.

The %post command starts the post-installation section. After it, you can add any shell commands you want to run after installation is completed. By default, you should have useradd commands for users you added during installation. You can also use the usermod command to add the user's password.

```
%post
/usr/sbin/useradd jake
chfn -f 'John W. Jones' jake
/usr/sbin/usermod -p '$1$ðrãæàÕÖà$kQUMYbFhOh79wECxnTuaH.' jake
```

At this point you should have a working ks.cfg file.

Installing the kickstart file

Once the ks.cfg file is created, you need to put it somewhere accessible to the computer doing the installation. Typically, you will place the file on a floppy disk. However, you can also put the file on a computer that is reachable on the network or on a hard disk.

To copy the file to a floppy disk, create a DOS floppy and copy the file as follows:

```
# mcopy ks.cfg a:
```

When you do the Fedora kickstart installation, have this floppy disk with you. As an alternative, you can copy the ks.cfg file to a CD.

Being able to place the ks.cfg file on a computer on the network requires a bit more configuration. The network must have a DHCP or a BOOTP server configured that is set up to provide network information to the new install computer. The NFS server containing the ks.cfg file must export the file so that it is accessible to the computer installing Linux. To use a ks.cfg file from the local hard disk, you can place the file on any partition that is a Windows (VFAT) or Linux (ext3) partition.

Booting a kickstart installation

If the kickstart file (`ks.cfg`) has been created and installed in an accessible location, you can start the kickstart installation. Here is an example of how you can do a kickstart installation using the Fedora Linux CD and a floppy containing a `ks.cfg` file:

1. Insert the first Fedora CD and restart the computer.

2. When you see the boot prompt, insert the floppy containing the `ks.cfg` file and type the following (quickly, before the installation boots on its own):

   ```
   boot: linux ks=file:fd0/ks.cfg
   ```

   You should see messages about formatting the file system and reading the package list. The packages should install, with the only intervention required being to change CDs. Next you should see a post-install message. Finally, you should see the "Complete" message.

3. Remove the floppy; then press the Spacebar to restart your computer (the CD should eject automatically).

TIP: To avoid having to change CDs with kickstart, do a hard disk or network install. You can install using kickstart over NFS (`ks:nfs:server:path`), from Web server (`ks=http://server/path`), or from your hard drive (`ks=hd:device`).

Special Installation Topics

Some things that you run into during installation merit whole discussions by themselves. Rather than bog down the procedures with details that not everyone needs, I have added the following topics to this section. Descriptions cover things such as reclaiming disk space and partitioning.

Partitioning your disks

The hard disk (or disks) on your computer provides the permanent storage area for your data files, applications programs, and the operating system (such as Fedora). Partitioning is the act of dividing a disk into logical areas that can be worked with separately. There are several reasons you may want to do partitioning:

- **Multiple operating systems** — If you install Fedora on a PC that already has a Windows operating system, you may want to keep both operating systems on the computer. To run efficiently, they must exist on completely separate partitions. When your computer boots, you can choose which system to run.

- **Multiple partitions within an operating system** — To protect from having your entire operating system run out of disk space, people often assign separate partitions to different areas of the Linux file system. For example, if `/home` and `/var` were assigned to separate partitions, then a gluttonous user who fills up the /home partition wouldn't prevent logging daemons from continuing to write to log files in the /var/log directory.

Multiple partitions also make it easier to do certain kinds of backups (such as an image backup). For example, an image backup of /home would be much faster (and probably more useful) than an image backup of the root file system (/).

- **Different file system types** — Different kinds of file systems that have different structures. File systems of different types must be on their own partitions. In Fedora Linux, you need at least one file system type for / (typically ext3) and one for your swap area. File systems on CD-ROM use the iso9660 file system type.

> **TIP:** When you create partitions for Fedora, you will usually assign the file system type as Linux native (using the ext3 type). Reasons to use other types include needing a file system that allows particularly long filenames or many inodes (each file consumes an inode).
>
> For example, if you set up a news server, it can use many inodes to store news articles. Another reason for using a different file system type is to copy an image backup tape from another operating system to your local disk (such as one from an OS/2 or Minix operating system).

If you have only used Windows operating systems before, you probably had your whole hard disk assigned to C: and never thought about partitions. With Fedora Linux, you can do a Server class of install (and have Linux erase the whole disk, take it over, and partition it) or a Personal Desktop or Workstation class (and have Linux keep separate partitions for Windows 9*x*/2000/NT and Linux). With the latest version of Fedora Linux, you also have the opportunity to view and change the default partitioning for the different installation types.

During installation, Fedora enables you to partition your hard disk using the Disk Druid utility (a graphical partitioning tool). The following sections describe how to use Disk Druid (during installation) or fdisk (when Fedora is up and running). See the section "Tips for creating partitions" for some ideas for creating disk partitions.

Partitioning with Disk Druid during installation

During installation, you are given the opportunity to change how your hard disk is partitioned. Fedora recommends using the Disk Druid. The Disk Druid screen is divided into two sections. The top shows general information about each hard disk. The bottom shows details of each partition. Figure 2-2 shows an example of the Disk Druid window.

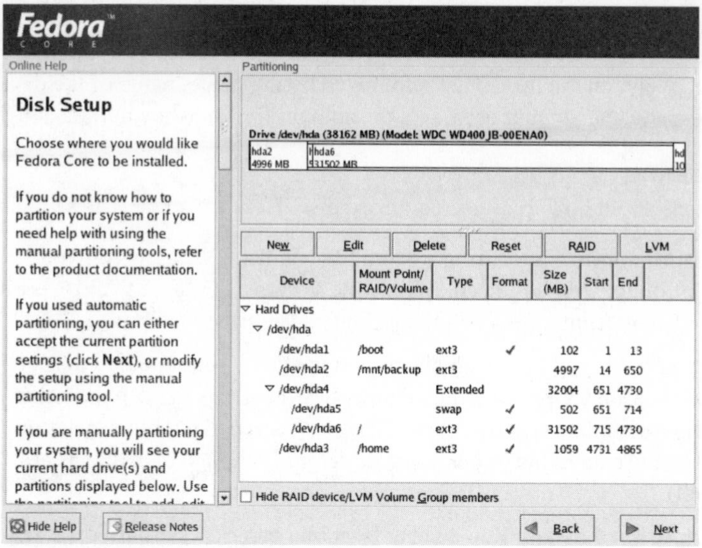

Figure 2-2: Partition your disk during installation from the Disk Setup window.

For each of the hard disk partitions, you can see:

- **Device** — The device name is the name representing the hard disk partition in the /dev directory. Each disk partition device begins with two letters: hd for IDE disks, sd for SCSI disks, ed for ESDI disks, or xd for XT disks. After that is a single letter representing the number of the disk (disk 1 is a, disk 2 is b, disk 3 is c, and so on). The partition number for that disk (1, 2, 3, and so on) follows that.

- **Mount Point/Raid/Volume** — The directory where the partition is connected into the Linux file system (if it is). You must assign the root partition (/) to a native Linux partition before you can proceed. If you are using RAID or LVM, the name of the RAID device or LVM volume appears here.

- **Type** — The type of file system that is installed on the disk partition. In most cases, the file system will be Linux (ext3), Win VFAT (vfat), or Linux swap. However, you can also use the previous Linux file system (ext2), physical volume (LVM), or software RAID.

- **Format** — Indicates whether (check mark) or not (no check mark) the installation process should format the hard disk partition. Partitions marked with a check are erased! So, on a multiboot system, be sure your Windows partitions, as well as other partitions containing data are not checked!

- **Size (MB)** — The amount of disk space allocated for the partition. If you selected to let the partition grow to fill the existing space, this number may be much larger than the requested amount.

- **Start/End** — Represents the partition's starting and ending cylinders on the hard disk.

In the top section, you can see each of the hard disks that are connected to your computer. The drive name is shown first. The Geometry section (Geom) shows the numbers of cylinders, heads, and sectors, respectively, on the disk. That's followed by the model name of the disk. The total amount of disk space, the amount used, and the amount free are shown in megabytes.

Reasons for partitioning

There are different opinions about how to divide up a hard disk. Here are some issues:

- **Do you want to install another operating system?** If you want Windows on your computer along with Linux, you will need at least one Windows (Win95 FAT16, VFAT, or NTFS type), one Linux (Linux ext3), and one Linux swap partition.

- **Is it a multiuser system?** If you are using the system yourself, you probably don't need many partitions. One reason for partitioning an operating system is to keep the entire system from running out of disk space at once. That also serves to put boundaries on what an individual can use up in his or her home directory (although disk quotas are good for that as well).

- **Do you have multiple hard disks?** You need at least one partition per hard disk. If your system has two hard disks, you may assign one to / and one to /home (if you have lots of users) or /var (if the computer is a server sharing lots of data).

Deleting, adding, and editing partitions

Before you can add a partition, there needs to be some free space available on your hard disk. If all space on your hard disk is currently assigned to one partition (as it often is in DOS or Windows), you must delete or resize that partition before you can claim space on another partition. The section on reclaiming disk space discusses how to add a partition without losing information in your existing single-partition system.

> **CAUTION:** Make sure that any data that you want to keep is backed up before you delete the partition. When you delete a partition, all its data is gone.

Disk Druid is less flexible, but more intuitive, than the fdisk utility. Disk Druid lets you delete, add, and edit partitions.

> **TIP:** If you create multiple partitions, make sure that there is enough room in the right places to complete the installation. For example, most of the Linux software is installed in the /usr directory (and subdirectories), whereas most user data are eventually added to the /home or /var directories.

To delete a partition in Disk Druid, do the following:

1. Select a partition from the list of Current Disk Partitions on the main Disk Druid window (click it or use the arrow keys).

2. To delete the partition, click Delete.

3. When asked to confirm the deletion, click Delete.

4. If you made a mistake, click Reset to return to the partitioning as it was when you started Disk Druid.

To add a partition in Disk Druid, follow these steps from the main Disk Druid window:

1. Select New. A window appears, enabling you to create a new partition.

2. Type the name of the Mount Point (the directory where this partition will connect to the Linux file system). You need at least a root (/) partition and a swap partition.

3. Select the type of file system to be used on the partition. You can select from Linux native (ext2 or preferably ext3), software RAID, Linux swap (swap), physical volume (LVM), or Windows FAT (vfat).

TIP: To create a different file system type than those shown, leave the space you want to use free for now. After installation is complete, use `fdisk` to create a partition of the type you want.

---

4. Type the number of megabytes to be used for the partition (in the Size field). If you want this partition to grow to fill the rest of the hard disk, you can put any number in this field (1 will do fine).

5. If you have more than one hard disk, select the disk on which you want to put the partition from the Allowable Drives box.

6. Type the size of the partition (in megabytes) into the Size (MB) box.

7. Select one of the following Additional Size Options:

   - **Fixed size** — Click here to use only the number of megabytes you entered into the Size text box when you create the partition.

   - **Fill all space up to (MB)** — If you want to use all remaining space up to a certain number of megabytes, click here and fill in the number. (You may want to do this if you are creating a VFAT partition up to the 2048MB limit that Disk Druid can create.)

   - **Fill to maximum allowable size** — If you want this partition to grow to fill the rest of the disk, click here.

8. Optionally select Force to Be a Primary Partition if you want to be sure to be able to boot the partition or Check for Bad Blocks if you want to have the partition checked for errors.

9. Select OK if everything is correct. (The changes don't take effect until several steps later when you are asked to begin installing the packages.)

To edit a partition in Disk Druid from the main Disk Druid window, follow these steps:

1. Click the partition you want to edit.

2. Click the Edit button. A window appears, ready to let you edit the partition definition.

3. Change any of the attributes (as described in the add partition procedure). For a new install, you may need to add the mount point (/) for your primary Linux partition.

4. Select OK. (The changes don't take effect until several steps later, when you are asked to begin installing the packages.)

> **NOTE:** If you want to create a RAID device, you need to first create at least two RAID partitions. Then click the RAID button to make the two partitions into a RAID device. For more information on RAID, refer to Chapter 10 or the Red Hat Linux Customization guide. The latter is available from any Red Hat mirror site (such as `ftp.redhat.com`) here: `pub/redhat/linux/current/en/doc/RH-DOCS/rhl-cg-en-9/*`. To create an LVM volume group, you must create at least one partition of type "physical volume (LVM)."

Partitioning with fdisk

The `fdisk` utility does the same job as Disk Druid, but it's no longer offered as an option during Fedora installation. (If you are old school, however, you could press Ctrl+Alt+F2 during the installation process and run `fdisk` from the shell to partition your disk.)

The following procedures are performed from the command line as root user.

> **CAUTION:** Remember that any partition commands can easily erase your disk or make it inaccessible. Back up critical data before using any tool to change partitions! Then be very careful about the changes you do make. Keeping an emergency boot disk handy is a good idea, too.

The `fdisk` command is one that is available on many different operating systems (although it looks and behaves differently on each). In Linux, `fdisk` is a menu-based command. To use `fdisk` to list all your partitions, type the following (as root user):

```
# fdisk -l

Disk /dev/hda: 40.0 GB, 40020664320 bytes
255 heads, 63 sectors/track, 4865 cylinders
Units = cylinders of 16065 * 512 = 8225280 bytes

   Device Boot     Start       End    Blocks   Id  System
/dev/hda1    *         1        13    104391   83  Linux
/dev/hda2             14      4833  38716650   83  Linux
/dev/hda3           4834      4865    257040   82  Linux swap
```

To see how each partition is being used on your current system, type the following:

```
# df -h
Filesystem           Size  Used Avail Use% Mounted on
/dev/hda2            37G   5.4G   30G  16% /
/dev/hda1            99M   8.6M   86M  10% /boot
none                 61M      0   61M   0% /dev/shm
```

From the output of df, you can see that the root of your Linux system (/) is on the /dev/hda2 partition and that the /dev/hda1 partition is used for /boot.

NOTE: If this had been a dual-boot system (with Windows 98), you might have seen a Windows partition from fdisk that looked like the following:

/dev/hda1   *   1   83   666666+   b   Win95 FAT32

You could mount that partition in Linux (to get to your Windows files when Linux is booted) by typing:

 # mkdir /mnt/win

 # mount -t vfat /dev/hda1 /mnt/win

CAUTION: Before using fdisk to change your partitions, I strongly recommend running the df -h command to see how your partitions are currently being defined. This will help reduce the risk of changing or deleting the wrong partition.

To use fdisk to change your partitions, begin (as root user) by typing:

```
# fdisk device
```

where *device* is replaced by the name of the device you want to work with. For example, here are some of your choices:

/dev/hda   For the first IDE hard disk; hdb, hdc, and so on for other IDE disks.

/dev/sda   For the first SCSI hard disk; sdb, sdc, and so on for other SCSI disks.

/dev/rd/c0d0   For a RAID device.

/dev/ida/c0d0   Also for a RAID device.

After you have started fdisk, type **m** to see the options. Here is what you can do with fdisk:

- **Delete a partition** — Type **d** and you are asked to enter a partition number on the current hard disk. Type the partition number and press Enter. For example, /dev/sda2 would be partition number 2. (The deletion won't take effect until you write the change. Until then, it's not too late to back out.)

- **Create a partition** — If you have free space, you can add a new partition. Type **n** and you are asked to enter l for a logical partition (5 or over) or p for a primary partition (1–4). Enter a partition number from the available range. Then choose the first cylinder number from those available. (The output from fdisk -l shown earlier will show you cylinders being used under the Start and End columns.)

Next, enter the cylinder number the partition will end with (or type the specific number of megabytes or kilobytes you want: for example, +50M or +1024K). You just created an ext3 Linux partition. Again, this change isn't permanent until you write the changes.

- **Change the partition type** — Press t to choose the type of file system. Enter the partition number of the partition number you want to change. Type the number representing the file system type you want to use in hexadecimal code. (Type **L** at this point to see a list of file system types and codes.) For a Linux file system, use the number 83; use 82 for a Linux swap partition. For a windows FAT32 file system, you can use the letter b.

- **Display the partition table** — Throughout this process, feel free to type **p** to display (print on the screen) the partition table as it now stands.

- **Saving and quitting** — If you don't like a change you make to your partitions, press **q** to exit without saving. Nothing will have changed on your partition table.

Before you write your changes, display the partition table again and make sure that it is what you want it to be. To write your changes to the partition table, press **w**. You are warned about how dangerous it is to change partitions and asked to confirm the change.

An alternative to the fdisk command is sfdisk. The sfdisk command is command-line–oriented. Type the full command line to list or change partitions. (See the sfdisk man page for details.)

Tips for creating partitions

Changing your disk partitions to handle multiple operating systems can be very tricky. Part of the reason is that each different operating system has its own ideas about how partitioning information should be handled, as well as different tools for doing it. Here are some tips to help you get it right.

- If you are creating a dual-boot system, particularly for Windows ME or Windows XP, try to install the Windows operating system first. Otherwise, the Windows installation may make the Linux partitions inaccessible.

- The fdisk man page recommends that you use partitioning tools that come with an operating system to create partitions for that operating system. For example, the DOS fdisk knows how to create partitions that DOS will like, and the Fedora fdisk will happily make your Linux partitions. Once your hard disk is set up for dual boot, however, you should probably not go back to Windows-only partitioning tools. Use Linux fdisk or a product made for multiboot systems (such as Partition Magic).

- You can have up to 63 partitions on an IDE hard disk. A SCSI hard disk can have up to 15 partitions. You won't need nearly that many partitions.

If you are using Fedora as a desktop system, you probably don't need a lot of different partitions within your Linux system. There are, however, some very good reasons for having multiple partitions for Linux systems that are shared by a lot of users or are public Web servers or file servers. Multiple partitions within Fedora Linux offer the following advantages:

- **Protection from attacks** — Denial-of-service attacks sometimes take action that tries to fill up your hard disk. If public areas, such as /var, are on separate partitions, a successful attack can fill up a partition without shutting down the whole computer. Because /var is the default location for Web and FTP servers, and therefore might hold a lot of data, often entire hard disks are assigned to the /var file system alone.

- **Protection from corrupted file systems** — If you have only one file system (/), corruption of that file system can cause the whole Fedora Linux system to be damaged. Corruption of a smaller partition can be easier to correct and can often allow the computer to stay in service while the corruption is fixed.

Here are some directories that you may want to consider making into separate file system partitions.

- **/boot** — Sometimes the BIOS in older PCs can access only the first 1024 cylinders of your hard disk. To make sure that the information in your /boot directory is accessible to the BIOS, create a separate disk partition (of only about 100MB) for /boot and make sure that it exists below cylinder 1024. Then, the rest of your Linux system can exist outside of that 1024-cylinder boundary if you like. Even with several boot images, there is rarely a reason for /boot to be larger than 100MB. For newer hard disks, you can sometimes avoid this problem by selecting the Linear Mode check boxduring installation. Then the boot partition can be anywhere on the disk.

- **/usr** — This directory structure contains most of the applications and utilities available to Fedora Linux users. Having /usr on a separate partition lets you mount that file system as read-only after the operating system has been installed. This prevents attackers from replacing or removing important system applications with their own versions that may cause security problems. A separate /usr partition is also useful if you have diskless workstations on your local network. Using NFS, you can share /usr over the network with those workstations.

- **/var** — Your FTP (/var/ftp) and Web-server (/var/www) directories are, by default, stored under /var. Having a separate /var partition can prevent an attack on those facilities from corrupting or filling up your entire hard disk.

- **/home** — Because your user account directories are located in this directory, having a separate /home account can prevent an indiscriminate user from filling up the entire hard disk. (Disk quotas, see Chapter 10, represent another way of controlling disk use.)

- **/tmp** — Protecting /tmp from the rest of the hard disk by placing it on a separate partition can ensure that applications that need to write to temporary files in /tmp are able to complete their processing, even if the rest of the disk fills up.

Although people who use Fedora casually rarely see a need for lots of partitions, those who maintain and occasionally have to recover large systems are thankful when the system they need to fix has several partitions. Multiple partitions can localize deliberate damage (such as denial-of-service attacks), problems from errant users, and accidental file system corruption.

Reclaiming disk space from existing partitions

Chances are that your PC came with a Windows operating system already installed on the entire disk. Installing Fedora while keeping Windows on your hard disk presents a problem. Fedora Linux and Windows operating systems are put on separate disk partitions, and right now there is only one partition (and it isn't for Fedora Linux).

If you are in this predicament, but you have a lot of unused space in your Windows partition (at least 2GB or more), follow this procedure to reclaim the disk space.

> **CROSS-REFERENCE:** If, instead of adding Linux to an existing Windows computer, you want to add Windows to your Linux computer, refer to the Linux+Windows+Grub HOWTO. For information on installing Windows NT and Linux on the same computer, refer to the Linux+Windows NT mini-HOWTO.These and other Linux HOWTOs are available from the Linux Documentation Project (www.tldp.org).

Before you begin

Read this section before you begin resizing your Windows partitions!

FIPS is a well-tested utility for resizing DOS FAT and VFAT file systems so that space can be made available to install Linux. To find out what kind of file system is being used on your Windows computer, do the following while Windows is running:

1. Double-click the My Computer icon.

2. Right-click the hard-disk (C:) icon and select Properties.

3. Look at the File system line. If it shows the file system type as FAT or FAT32 the disk partition can be resized with FIPS.

If you are using a Windows 95, Windows 98, or Windows ME computer, providing that you have enough free disk space on the partition, you can probably use FIPS to resize it. If, however, you have a Windows 2000, Windows NT, or Windows XP computer with an NTFS file system, you will have to use some other tools to resize it. Here are some of your choices:

> **CAUTION:** I have not extensively tested the utilities in the following list. I recommend that before deciding to commit to using any of these tools you research them carefully.

- **parted command** — A Fedora Linux utility called parted can be used to resize NTFS file systems. Because it runs in Linux, you need to be able to run it from a boot disk if you currently have a Windows-only system. You can download a boot disk image from the following location and create a boot disk with that image using the boot-disk–creation descriptions in this chapter:

```
ftp://ftp.gnu.org/gnu/parted/bootdisk/
```

The README file in this directory describes which boot image to use and how to use it.

- **Partition Magic** — I've heard good reports from people using Partition Magic (`www.powerquest.com/partitionmagic`) to resize NTFS partitions. Partition Magic also helps you create new partitions and manage them. It supports Windows XP Professional/Home, Windows 95b-98SE, Windows Me, Windows 2000 Professional, and NT 4.0 workstation (SP6a). The cost is currently $70.

- **Acronis OS Selector** — This is another well-regarded product for managing, creating, and resizing partitions. It supports a variety of file system types, including FAT12, FAT16, FAT32, NTFS, and Linux partition types (ext2, ext3 and Linux ReiserFS). It also supports the same Windows platforms that Partition Magic does. The cost is currently $49.99 from `www.acronis.com`.

As I mentioned earlier, if your Windows partition is FAT or VFAT you can continue with the procedure in the next session to resize your hard disk.

Backing up and repartitioning

One way to divide a disk that is currently totally used for DOS (DOS, Windows 9*x*/2000, and so on) is not very complicated, but it can take some time. The method is to do a full system backup of your data, erase the whole disk, repartition the disk, restore your Windows 9*x*/2000 operating system to the hard disk (on a smaller partition), and add Fedora to the hard disk (using new partitions). Whew!

The problem with the backup/repartition approach is that it can be a pain. If your backup device is a 1.44MB floppy disk and your hard disk holds a few gigabytes of data, a full backup is not a pleasant prospect. Alternatively, there is a DOS utility called FIPS.

Using the FIPS utility

The FIPS utility came about to solve the problem of a would-be Linux user with a monolithic DOS/Windows hard disk. With FIPS, you can change the size of your DOS partition without erasing it. Though this process is risky, and nobody recommends it without major "buyer beware" warnings, many use it safely and save a lot of time and effort.

FIPS works by changing the values in the partition table and boot sector. Space is gained by changing the partition table that is used to create a new primary DOS partition. After that, the new DOS partition can be converted to Linux partitions.

CAUTION: Warnings that come with FIPS documentation have mostly to do with older, nonstandard hard disks. I recommend reading the warnings that come with this documentation. You can find them on the Fedora Linux installation CD #1 in the `dosutils/fipsdocs` directory. Especially read `fips.doc`.

Split your DOS (Windows) disk into separate DOS and Linux partitions as follows:

1. **Check your Windows/DOS partition.**

   In a DOS window, run `chkdsk` to check for disk errors. The output shows how your disk space is used, as well as errors found and corrected. Next, run `scandisk` in Windows 9*x*/2000. Scandisk deals with lost file fragments, invalid filenames, and cross-linked files. It also scans for disk surface errors. The point is to correct hard disk errors encountered.

2. **Create a bootable FIPS floppy.**

   You need to create a bootable floppy disk. Insert a blank, 3.5-inch floppy disk in drive A. Then, from DOS (or a DOS window), type the following to create a boot floppy:

   ```
   format a:/s
   ```

   After creating the boot floppy, copy the following files from the first Fedora Linux installation CD (CD #1) to this bootable floppy: `restorrb.exe`, `fips.exe`, and `errors.txt`. (These files are located in the `dosutils/fips20` directory.) To make sure that the bootable floppy is working properly, insert the floppy disk into a PC that has a DOS (Windows 9*x*/2000) partition and reboot the computer. Now make sure that you can access the partition by typing **dir C:** at the prompt.

3. **Defragment your hard disk.**

   Reboot your PC so that Windows 9*x*/2000 starts up. To defragment your disk, so that all of your used space is put in order on the disk, open My Computer, right-click your hard disk icon (C:), select Properties, click Tools, and select Defragment Now.

   Defragmenting your disk can be a fairly long process. The result of defragmentation is that all the data on your disk are contiguous, creating a lot of contiguous free space at the end of the partition. There are cases where you will have to do the following special tasks to make this true:

   - If the Windows swap file is not moved during defragmentation, you must remove it. Then, after you defragment your disk again and run FIPS, you will need to restore the swap file. To remove the swap file, open the Control Panel, open the System icon, and then click the Performance tab and select Virtual Memory. To disable the swap file, click Disable Virtual Memory.

   - If your DOS partition has hidden files that are on the space you are trying to free up, you need to find them. In some cases, you won't be able to delete them. In other cases, such as swap files created by a program, you can safely delete those files. This is a bit tricky because some files should not be deleted, such as DOS system files. You can use the `attrib -s -h` command from the root directory to deal with hidden files.

4. **Reboot (FIPS boot disk).**

   Before you reboot to the FIPS disk, you want to make sure that nothing is written to the hard disk when DOS/Windows shuts down. Look for programs in `config.sys` and `autoexec.bat` that write to disk. When you are satisfied, insert the boot floppy and reboot.

5. **Run FIPS.**

   With your computer now booted in DOS (with C: drive accessible), run the FIPS program by typing:

   ```
   # fips
   ```

   You can quit FIPS at any time by pressing Ctrl+C. If you have more than one hard disk, FIPS will ask which one you want to use. FIPS then displays the partition table and asks you the number of the partition you want to split:

   - Type the number of the partition you want to split. FIPS checks the partition for free space and asks if you want to make a copy of your root and boot sector before you go on (this is recommended).

   - Type **Y** to back up your root and boot sector. FIPS asks if you have your FIPS bootable floppy in the drive.

   - Make sure the floppy is in the drive and type **Y**. FIPS copies a file called `rootboot.000` to your `A:` drive. Then FIPS determines how much free space is available on the partition. If FIPS can't find at least one cylinder free, it probably means that you need to remove a mirror or image file (after you do that, you will have to defragment the drive again before you can rerun FIPS). If all goes well, you will see output that looks similar to the following:

   ```
   Old partition        Cylinder       New Partition
       2753.3 MB             351            35393.2 MB
   ```

   > **NOTE:** If the New Partition doesn't show enough disk space, you may need to go back and remove some files until there is enough free space.

   - Use the right and left arrow keys to choose what cylinder the new partition should start on. When you press those keys, you can see the sizes of the old and new partitions change. When the partitions are the sizes you want, press Enter.

   - When the new partition table appears, you can accept it or re-edit the table.

   - Press **C** to continue if everything is okay. You are asked if you are ready to write the new partition table to disk.

   - Press **Y** to proceed. When FIPS is done, it will say `Bye!` and exit.

6. **Reboot (FIPS boot disk) and test.**

   Reboot from the DOS/FIPS disk again. Then run the `fips` command again, but this time in test mode as follows:

   ```
   # fips -t
   ```

If the partition table looks okay, exit FIPS by pressing Ctrl+C. You can also use a program such as `chkdsk` to be sure the old partition is still working.

> **CAUTION:** If the partitions are not correct, you can restore your original partitioning by running the `restorrb` command from the FIPS floppy disk.

7. **Restart your computer.**

   At this point, you can restart your computer as you would normally (remove the FIPS boot disk). Try using the Windows 9*x*/2000 system to make sure that everything is working okay.

With partitioning done, you can install Fedora Linux using the reclaimed space. (Don't assign the free disk space to anything yet. Just go ahead and install Fedora Linux and assign the Linux partitions you need during installation.)

If you have a problem with FIPS, its creator asks that you make a transcript of the FIPS session (using the `-d` option) and send it to `schaefer@rbg.informatik.th-darmstadt.de`. The transcript will appear in the `fipsinfo.dbg` file.

Using GRUB or LILO boot loaders

A boot loader lets you choose when and how to boot the bootable operating systems installed on your computer's hard disks. GRUB is the only boot loader offered for you to configure during Fedora Core 2 installation. However, Fedora also includes the LILO boot loader, if you want to configure that after Fedora is installed. The following sections describe both GRUB and LILO boot loaders.

Booting your computer with GRUB

With multiple operating systems installed and several partitions set up, how does your computer know which operating system to start? To select and manage which partition is booted and how it is booted, you need a boot loader. The boot loader that is installed by default with Fedora is called the GRand Unified Boot loader (GRUB).

GRUB is a GNU software package (`www.gnu.org/software/grub`) that replaced the LILO as the default boot loader in Fedora. GRUB offers the following features:

- Support for multiple executable formats.
- Support for multiboot operating systems (such as Fedora, FreeBSD, NetBSD, OpenBSD, and other Linux systems).
- Support for non-multiboot operating systems (such as Windows 95, Windows 98, Windows NT, Windows ME, Windows XP, and OS/2) via a chain-loading function. Chain-loading is the act of loading another boot loader (presumably one that is specific to the proprietary operating system) from GRUB to start the selected operating system.

- Support for multiple file system types.

- Support for automatic decompression of boot images.

- Support for downloading boot images from a network.

For more information on how GRUB works, type `man grub` or `info grub`. The `info` command contains more details about GRUB.

Booting with GRUB

When you install Fedora, information needed to boot your computer (with one or more operating systems) is automatically set up and ready to go. Simply restart your computer. When you see the GRUB boot screen (it says GRUB at the top and lists bootable partitions below it), do one of the following:

- **Default** —If you do nothing, the default operating system will boot automatically after a few seconds.

- **Select an operating system** — Use the up and down arrow keys to select any of the operating systems shown on the screen. Then press Enter to boot that operating system.

- **Edit the boot process** — If you want to change any of the options used during the boot process, use the arrow keys to select the operating system you want and type **e** to select it. Follow the next procedure to change your boot options temporarily.

If you want to change your boot options so that they take effect every time you boot your computer, see the section on permanently changing boot options. Changing those options involves editing the `/boot/grub/grub.conf` file.

Temporarily changing boot options

From the GRUB boot screen, you can select to change or add boot options for the current boot session. First, select the operating system you want (using the arrow keys) and type **e** (as described earlier). You will see a graphical screen that contains information like the following:

```
GRUB version 0.94 (639K lower / 128768K upper memory)

root (hd0,0)
kernel /boot/vmlinuz-2.6.5-1.350 ro root=LABEL=/
initrd /boot/initrd-2.6.5-1.350.img

Use the ↑ and ↓ keys to select which entry is highlighted.
Press 'b' to boot, 'e' to edit the selected command in the
boot sequence, 'c' for a command-line, 'o' to open a new line
after ('O' for before) the selected line, 'd' to remove the
selected line, or escape to go back to the main menu.
```

There are three lines in the example of the GRUB editing screen that identify the boot process for the operating system you chose. The first line (beginning with `root`) shows that the entry for the GRUB boot loader is on the first partition of the first hard disk (`hd0,0`). GRUB represents the hard disk as `hd`, regardless of whether it is a SCSI, IDE, or other type of disk. You just count the drive number and partition number, starting from zero.

The second line of the example (beginning with `kernel`) identifies the boot image (`/boot/vmlinuz-2.6.5-1.350`) and several options. The options identify the partition as initially being loaded `ro` (read-only) and the location of the root file system on a partition with the label `LABEL=/`. The third line (starting with `initrd`) identifies the location of the initial RAM disk, which contains the minimum files and directories needed during the boot process.

If you are going to change any of the lines related to the boot process, you would probably change only the second line to add or remove boot options. Here is how you do that:

1. Position the cursor on the `kernel` line and type **e**.

2. Either add or remove options after the name of the boot image. You can use a minimal set of bash shell command-line editing features to edit the line. You can even use command completion (type part of a filename and press Tab to complete it). Here are a few options you may want to add or delete:

    - **Boot to a shell:** If you forgot your root password or if your boot process hangs, you can boot directly to a shell by adding `init=/bin/sh` to the boot line. (The file system is mounted read-only, so you can copy files out. You need to remount the file system with read/write permission to be able to change files.)

    - **Select a run level:** If you want to boot to a particular run level, you can add the word *linux,* followed by the number of the run level you want. For example, to have Fedora Linux boot to run level 3 (multiuser plus networking mode), add `linux 3` to the end of the boot line. You can also boot to single-user mode (1), multi-user mode (2), or X GUI mode (5). Level 3 is a good choice if your GUI is temporarily broken.

3. Press Enter to return to the editing screen.

4. Type **b** to boot the computer with the new options. The next time you boot your computer, the new options will not be saved. To add options so they are saved permanently, see the next section.

Permanently changing boot options

You can change the options that take effect each time you boot your computer by changing the GRUB configuration file. In Fedora, GRUB configuration centers around the `/boot/grub/grub.conf` file.

The `/boot/grub/grub.conf` file is created when you install Fedora. Here is an example of a `grub.conf` file.

```
# grub.conf generated by anaconda
#
# Note that you do not have to rerun grub after making
# changes to this file
# NOTICE: You have a /boot partition.  This means that
#         all kernel and initrd paths are relative to /boot/, eg.
#         root (hd0,0)
#         kernel /vmlinuz-version ro root=/dev/hda6
#         initrd /initrd-version.img
#boot=/dev/hda
default=0
timeout=10
splashimage=(hd0,4)/grub/splash.xpm.gz
title Fedora Linux (2.6.5-1.350)
     root (hd0,4)
     kernel /vmlinuz-2.6.5-1.350 ro root=LABEL=/
     initrd /initrd-2.6.5-1.350.img
title Windows XP
     rootnoverify (hd0,0)
     chainloader +1
```

The `default=0` line indicates that the first partition in this list (in this case Fedora Linux) will be the one that is booted by default. The line `timeout=10` causes GRUB to pause for ten seconds before booting the default partition. (That's how much time you have to press e if you want to edit the boot line, or to press arrow keys to select a different operating system to boot.)

The `splashimage` line looks in the fifth partition on the first disk (`hd0,4`) for the boot partition (in this case `/dev/hda5`, which is the `/boot` partition). GRUB loads `splash.xpm.gz` as the image on the splash screen (`/boot/grub/splash.xpm.gz`). The splash screen appears as the background of the boot screen.

NOTE: GRUB indicates disk partitions using the following notation: (`hd0`, 0). The first number represents the disk, and the second is the partition on that disk. So, (`hd0`, 1) is the second partition (1) on the first disk (0).

The two bootable partitions in this example are `Fedora` and `Windows XP`. The title lines for each of those partitions are followed by the name that appears on the boot screen to represent each partition.

For the Fedora Linux system, the `root` line indicates the location of the boot partition as the second partition on the first disk. So, to find the bootable `kernel` (`vmlinuz-2.6.5-1.350`) and the `initrd` initial RAM disk boot image that is loaded (`initrd-2.6.5-1.350.img`), GRUB looks in the root of `hd0,4` (which is represented by `/dev/hda5` and is eventually mounted as `/boot`). Other options on the `kernel` line set the partition as read-only initially (`ro`) and set the root file system to `/dev/hda6`.

For the Windows XP partition, the `rootnoverify` line indicates that GRUB should not try to mount the partition. In this case, Windows ME is on the first partition of the first hard disk (`hd0,0`) or `/dev/hda1`. Instead of mounting the partition and passing options to the new operating system, the `chainloader +1` indicates to hand control the booting of the operating system to another boot loader. The `+1` indicates that the first sector of the partition is used as the boot loader.

> **NOTE:** Microsoft operating systems require that you use the `chainloader` to boot them from GRUB.

If you make any changes to the `/boot/grub/grub.conf` file, you *do not* need to load those changes. Those changes are automatically picked up by GRUB when you reboot your computer. If you are accustomed to using the LILO boot loader, this may confuse you at first, as LILO requires you to rerun the `lilo` command for the changes to take effect.

Adding a new GRUB boot image

You may have different boot images for kernels that include different features. Here is the procedure for modifying the `grub.conf` file:

1. Copy the new image from the directory in which it was created (such as `/usr/src/linux-2.4/arch/i386/boot`) to the `/boot` directory. Name the file something that reflects its contents, such as `bz-2.4.21`. For example:

   ```
   # cp /usr/src/linux-2.6.5/arch/i386/boot/bzImage /boot/bz-2.6.5
   ```

2. Add several lines to the `/boot/grub/grub.conf` file so that the image can be started at boot time if it is selected. For example:

   ```
   title Fedora Linux (IPV6 build)
       root (hd0,4)
       kernel /bz-2.6.5 ro root=/dev/hda6
       initrd /initrd-2.6.5.img
   ```

3. Reboot your computer.

4. When the GRUB boot screen appears, move your cursor to the title representing the new kernel and press Enter.

The advantage to this approach, as opposed to copying the new boot image over the old one, is that if the kernel fails to boot, you can always go back and restart the old kernel. When you feel confident that the new kernel is working properly, you can use it to replace the old kernel or perhaps just make the new kernel the default boot definition.

Booting your computer with LILO

LILO stands for LInux LOader. Like other boot loaders, LILO is a program that can stand outside the operating systems installed on the computer so you can choose which system to boot. It also lets you give special options that modify how the operating system is booted.

> **NOTE:** LILO was added back for Fedora Core 2. It is not installed by default, but it is available on CD #3 that comes with this book. Unless you have explicitly installed LILO and configured your system to use it, you should read the GRUB section for boot loader information.

If LILO is being used on your computer, it is installed in either the master boot record or the first sector of the root partition. The master boot record is read directly by the computer's BIOS. In general, if LILO is the only loader on your computer, install it in the master boot record. If there is another boot loader already in the master boot record, put LILO in the root partition.

Using LILO

When your computer boots with the Fedora version of LILO installed in the master boot record, a graphical Fedora screen appears, displaying the bootable partitions on the computer. Use the up and down arrow keys on your keyboard to select the one you want and press Enter. Otherwise, the default partition that you set at installation will boot after a few seconds.

If you want to add any special options when you boot, press Ctrl+X. You will see a text-based boot prompt that appears as follows:

```
boot:
```

LILO pauses for a few seconds and then automatically boots the first image from the default bootable partition. To see the bootable partitions again, quickly press Tab. You may see something similar to the following:

```
LILO boot:
linux linux-up dos
boot:
```

This example shows that three bootable partitions are on your computer, called `linux`, `linux-up`, and `dos`. The first two refer to two different boot images that can boot the Linux partition. The third refers to a bootable DOS partition (presumably containing a Windows operating system). The first bootable partition is loaded if you don't type anything after a few seconds. Or you could type the name of the other partition to have that boot instead.

If you have multiple boot images, press Shift, and LILO will ask you which image you want to boot. Available boot images and other options are defined in the `/etc/lilo.conf` file.

Setting up the /etc/lilo.conf file

The `/etc/lilo.conf` file is where LILO gets the information it needs to find and start bootable partitions and images. By adding options to the `/etc/lilo.conf` file, you can change the behavior of the boot process. The following is an example of some of the contents of the /etc/lilo.conf file:

> **NOTE:** Because LILO is not used by default, there is no /etc/lilo.conf file. However, the Fedora Linux installation program creates an /etc/lilo.conf.anaconda file to suit your installation. If you change from GRUB to LILO, you can copy that file to /etc/lilo.conf.

```
prompt
timeout=50
default=linux
boot=/dev/hda
map=/boot/map
install=/boot/boot.b
message=/boot/message
linear

image=/boot/vmlinuz-2.6.5-1.327
        label=linux
        initrd=/boot/initrd-2.6.5-1.327.img
        read-only
        root=/dev/hda6
        append="root=LABEL=/"

other=/dev/hda1
        optional
        label=dos
```

With prompt on, the boot prompt appears when the system is booted without requiring that any keys are pressed. The timeout value, in this case 50 tenths of a second (5 seconds), defines how long to wait for keyboard input before booting the default boot image. The boot line indicates that the bootable partition is on the hard disk represented by /dev/hda (the first IDE hard disk).

The map line indicates the location of the map file (/boot/map, by default). The map file contains the name and locations of bootable kernel images. The install line indicates that the /boot/boot.b file is used as the new boot sector. The message line tells LILO to display the contents of the /boot/message file when booting (that contains the graphical Fedora boot screen that appears). The linear line causes linear sector addresses to be generated (instead of sector/head/cylinder addresses).

In the sample file, there are two bootable partitions. The first (image=/boot/vmlinuz-2.6.5-1.327) shows an image labeled linux. The root file system (/) for that image is on partition /dev/hda6. Read-only indicates that the file system is first mounted read-only, though it is probably mounted as read/write after a file system check. The inidrd line indicates the location of the initial RAM disk image used to start the system.

The second bootable partition, which is indicated by the word *other* in this example, is on the /dev/hda1 partition. Because it is a Windows XP system, it is labeled a DOS file system. The table line indicates the device that contains the partition.

Other bootable images are listed in this file, and you can add another boot image yourself (like one you create from reconfiguring your kernel as discussed in the next section) by installing the new image and changing lilo.conf.

After you change lilo.conf, you then must run the lilo command for the changes to take effect. You may have different boot images for kernels that include different features. Here is the procedure for modifying the lilo.conf file:

1. Copy the new image from the directory in which it was created (such as /usr/src/linux-2.6/arch/i386/boot) to the /boot directory. Name the file something that reflects its contents, such as zImage-2.6.5-1.

2. Add several lines to the /etc/lilo.conf file so that the image can be started at boot time if it is selected. For example:

```
image=/boot/zImage-2.6.5-1
label=new
```

3. Type the lilo -t command (as root user) to test that the changes were okay.

4. Type the lilo command (with no options) for the changes to be installed.

To boot from this new image, either select new from the graphical boot screen or type new and press Enter at the LILO boot prompt. If five seconds is too quick, increase the timeout value (such as 100 for 10 seconds).

Options that you can use in the /etc/lilo.conf file are divided into global options, per-image options, and kernel options. There is a lot of documentation available for LILO. For more details on any of the options described here or for other options, you can see the lilo.conf manual page (type man lilo.conf) or any of the documents in /usr/share/doc/lilo*/doc.

A few examples follow of global options that you can add to /etc/lilo.conf. Global options apply to LILO as a whole, instead of just to a particular boot image.

You can use the default=label option, where label is replaced by an image's label name, to indicate that a particular image be used as the default boot image. If that option is excluded, the first image listed in the /etc/lilo.conf file is used as the default. For example, to start the image labeled new by default, add the following line to lilo.conf:

```
default=new
```

Change the delay from 5 seconds to something greater if you want LILO to wait longer before starting the default image. This gives you more time to boot a different image. To change the value from 5 seconds (50) to 15 seconds (150), add the following line:

```
delay=150
```

You can change the message that appears before the LILO prompt by adding that message to a file and changing the message line. For example, you could create a /boot/boot.message file and add the following words to that file: Choose linux, new, or dos. To have that message appear before the boot prompt, add the following line to /etc/lilo.conf:

```
message=/boot/boot.message
```

All per-image options begin with either an image= line (indicating a Linux kernel) or other= (indicating some other kind of operating system, such as Windows XP). The per-image options apply to particular boot images rather than to all images (as global options do). Along with the image or other line is a label= line, which gives a name to that image. The name is what you would select at boot time to boot that image. Here are some of the options that you can add to each of those image definitions:

- **lock** — This enables automatic recording of boot command lines as the defaults for different boot options.
- **alias=name** — You can replace *name* with any name. That name becomes an alias for the image name defined in the label option.
- **password=*password*** — You can password-protect the image by adding a password option line and replacing *password* with your own password. The password would have to be entered to boot the image.
- **restricted** — This option is used with the password option. It indicates that a password should be used only if command-line options are given when trying to boot the image.

For Linux kernel images, there are specific options that you can use. These options let you deal with hardware issues that can't be autodetected, or provide information such as how the root file system is mounted. Here are some of kernel image–specific options:

- **append** — Add a string of letters and numbers to this option that need to be passed to the kernel. In particular, these can be parameters that need to be passed to better define the hard disk when some aspect of that disk can't be autodetected.
- **ramdisk** — Add the size of the RAM disk that you want to use so as to override the size of the RAM disk built into the kernel.
- **read-only** — Indicates to mount the root file system read-only. It is typically remounted read-write after the disk is checked.
- **read-write** — Indicates to mount the root file system read/write.

Changing your boot loader

If you don't want to use the GRUB boot loader, or if you tried out LILO and want to switch back to GRUB, it's not hard to change to a different boot loader. To switch your boot loader from GRUB to LILO, do the following:

1. Configure the `/etc/lilo.conf` file as described in the "Booting your computer with LILO" section. (Use the contents of `/etc/lilo.conf.anaconda` to start.)

2. As root user from a Terminal window, type the following:

```
# lilo
```

3. The new Master Boot Record is written, including the entries in `/etc/lilo.conf`.

4. Reboot your computer. You should see the LILO boot screen.

To change your boot loader from LILO to GRUB, do the following:

1. Configure the `/boot/grub/grub.conf` file as described in the "Booting your computer with GRUB" section.

2. You need to know the device on which you want to install GRUB. For example, to install GRUB on the master boot record of the first disk, type the following as root user from a Terminal window:

```
# grub-install /dev/hda
```

The new Master Boot Record is written to boot with the GRUB boot loader.

3. Reboot your computer. You should see the GRUB boot screen.

Troubleshooting Your Installation

After you have finished installing Fedora, you can check how the installation went by checking your log files. There are three places to look once the system comes up:

- **/tmp/upgrade.log** — When upgrading packages, output from each installed package is sent to this file. You can see what packages were installed and if any failed.

- **/var/log/dmesg** — This file contains the messages that are sent to the console terminal as the system boots up, including messages relating to the kernel being started and hardware being recognized. If a piece of hardware isn't working, you can check here to make sure that the kernel found the hardware and configured it properly.

- **/var/log/boot.log** — This file contains information about each service that is started up at boot time. You can see if each service started successfully. If a service fails to start properly, there may be clues in this file that will help you learn what went wrong.

If something was set wrong (such as your mouse) or just isn't working quite right (such as your video display), you can always go back after Fedora is running and correct the problem. Here is a list of utilities you can use to reconfigure different features that were set during installation:

- **Changing or adding a mouse** — `system-config-mouse`
- **Changing a keyboard language** — `system-config-keyboard`
- **Adding or deleting software packages** — `system-config-packages` or `rpm`
- **Partitioning** — `fdisk` or `sfdisk`
- **Boot loader** — `/boot/grub/grub.conf` (for GRUB); `lilo` and `/etc/lilo.conf` (for LILO)
- **Networking (Ethernet & TCP/IP)** — `system-config-network`
- **Time zone** — `timeconfig` or `firstboot`
- **User accounts** — `useradd` or `system-config-users`
- **Sound** — `system-config-soundcard`
- **X Window System** — `system-config-display`

Here are a few other random tips that can help you during installation:

- If installation fails because the installation procedure is unable to detect your video card, try restarting installation in text mode. After Fedora Linux is installed and running, use the `system-config-display` command to configure your video card and monitor. (For some cards, such as those from NVIDIA, you need to get and install special drivers from the manufacturer's Web site.)
- If installation completes successfully, but your screen is garbled when you reboot, you should try to get Fedora Linux to boot to a text-login prompt. To do this, add the words `linux 3` to the end of the kernel boot line in GRUB or LILO. Linux will start with the GUI temporarily disabled. Run `system-config-display` to try to fix the problem. (See Chapter 3 for other advice related to fixing your GUI.)
- If your mouse is not detected during installation, you can use arrow keys and the Tab key to make selections.
- If installation improperly probes your hardware or turns on a feature that causes problems with your hardware, you might be able to solve the problem by disabling the offending feature at the install boot prompt. Try adding one or more of the following after the word `linux` at the installation boot prompt: `ide=nodma` (if your system hangs while downloading the image), `apm=off` or `acpi=off` (if you experience random failures during install), or `nousb`, `nopcmcia`, or `nofirewire` (if you suspect that install is hanging on devices of those types).

- Probably the best resource for troubleshooting your installation problems is the Red Hat Support site (www.redhat.com/apps/support). Links from that page can take you to documentation, updates and errata, and information about support programs. If you are having problems with a particular piece of hardware, try searching the Solutions Database, using the name of the hardware in the search box. If you are having problems with particular hardware, chances are someone else did, too.

Summary

Installing Linux is not nearly the adventure it once was. Precompiled binary software and preselected packaging and partitions make most Fedora installations a simple proposition. Improved installation and GUI configuration windows have made it easier for computer users who are not programmers to enter the Linux arena.

Besides providing some step-by-step installation procedures, this chapter discussed some of the trickier aspects of Fedora installation. In particular, specialty installation procedures, ways of partitioning your hard disk, and how to change the boot procedure were described.

Chapter 3

Getting Started with the Desktop

In This Chapter

- Logging in to Linux
- Getting started with the desktop
- Choosing KDE or GNOME desktops
- Using the GNOME desktop environment
- Using the KDE desktop environment
- Getting your desktop to work

The desktop is the most personal feature of your computer. The way that icons, menus, panels, and backgrounds are arranged and displayed should make it both easy and pleasant to do your work. With Fedora Linux, you have an incredible amount of control over how your desktop behaves and how your desktop is arranged.

In the past few versions of Fedora and Red Hat Linux, the desktop has changed dramatically. While going for a "Red Hat" look-and-feel, Red Hat, Inc. set out to standardize how you use Red Hat Linux, regardless of whether you choose KDE or GNOME as your desktop environment. Despite differences in logos and colors, the default Fedora Desktop is very similar to the desktop on Red Hat Enterprise Linux. With the default BlueCurve theme configured on the desktop, you can hardly tell the difference between GNOME and KDE in any of the Red Hat distributions.

Not to be outdone, KDE and GNOME themselves, with recent updates to release 3.2.2 and 2.6, respectively, have stretched beyond the bounds of a simple look-and-feel. With each desktop environment, you can get a full set of desktop applications, features for launching applications, and tools for configuring preferences.

In Fedora Core 2, the XFree86 X server has been replaced by the X.Org X server. The X server provides the framework on which GNOME, KDE, and other desktop applications and window managers rely.

This chapter takes you on a tour of your desktop — going through the process of logging in, trying out some features, and customizing how your desktop looks and behaves. Sections on KDE and GNOME desktops contain reference information on how to set preferences, run applications, configure panels, and work with the file manager. The last section describes how to use the Display Settings window to configure your video card and monitor if they were not properly detected.

Logging in to Red Hat Linux

Because Linux was created as a multiuser computer system, you start by logging in (even if you are the only person using the computer). Logging in accomplishes three functions:

- It identifies you as a particular user.
- It starts up your own shell and desktop (icons, panels, backgrounds, and so on) configurations.
- It gives you appropriate permissions to change files and run programs.

After the computer has been turned on and the operating system has started, you see either a graphical login screen (default) or a text-based login prompt. The text-based prompt should look like this:

```
Fedora Core release 2
Kernel 2.6.5-1 on an i686

localhost login:
```

The graphical login is typically your entry into the graphical user interface (GUI). Figure 3-1 is an example of the login screen you see when you boot the Fedora operating system that comes with this book.

Figure 3-1: A graphical login screen greets Fedora desktop users.

> **NOTE:** If you see a text-based login prompt instead of the graphical login screen, and you want to use the GUI, type your user name and password. Then when you see a command prompt, type **startx** to start up your desktop.

Notice the several menu buttons on the login screen. You can ignore them and simply type your user name and password as prompted. Or you can use these buttons as follows:

- **Language** — Click Option to select a language other than the last language you selected when Fedora was installed. (You may need additional software packages to use different languages.)

- **Session** — When you log in, your graphical desktop usually starts up (either GNOME or KDE). Click Session to choose a different desktop (if available) or to select Failsafe. If you can't remember which desktop to use, you can choose Last (to use the desktop you used most recently) or Default (to use the desktop set as your default). You use Failsafe if you want only a shell interface (the shell is described in Chapter 4).

> **NOTE:** The Failsafe session is used primarily to correct problems when, for some reason, your desktop session won't start properly. For example, graphics settings may be wrong, resulting in a garbled screen. The Failsafe session simply opens a shell window so you can type commands to correct the problem before you log in again. When you are done with a Failsafe session, type **exit** to be allowed to log in again.

- **Reboot** — Click to reboot the computer.
- **Shutdown** — Click to shut down the computer.

To log in, type your user name and, when prompted, your password. You can log in as either a regular user or as the root user:

- **A regular user** — As someone just using the Linux system, you probably have your own unique user name and password. Often, that name is associated with your real name (such as johnb, susanp, or djones). If you are still not sure why you need a user login, see the sidebar "Why Do I Need a User Login?"

- **The root user** — Every Linux system has a *root* user assigned when Linux is installed. The root user (literally type the user name **root**) can run programs, use files, and change the computer setup in any way. Because the root user has special powers, and can therefore do special damage, you usually log in as a regular user (which allows access only to that user's files and those that are open to everyone).

> **CROSS-REFERENCE:** See Chapter 10 for a description of the root user and Chapter 11 for information on how to set up and use other user accounts. Refer to Chapter 14 for suggestions on how to choose a good password.

If your desktop did not start, refer to the "Troubleshooting Your Desktop" section at the end of this chapter. Otherwise, continue on to the next section.

Getting Familiar with the Desktop

Desktop refers to the presentation of windows, menus, panels, icons, and other graphical elements on your computer screen. Originally, computer systems such as Linux operated purely in text mode — no mouse, no colors, just commands typed on the screen. Desktops provide a more intuitive way of using your computer.

Why Do I Need a User Login?

If you are working on a PC, and you are the only one using your Linux computer, you may wonder why you need a user account and password. Unlike Windows, Linux (as its predecessor UNIX) was designed from the ground up to be a multi-user system. Here are several good reasons why you should use separate user accounts:

- Even as the only person using Linux, you want a user name besides root for running applications and working with files so you don't change critical system files by mistake during everyday computer use.

- If several people are using a Linux system, separate user accounts let you protect your files from being accessed or changed by others.

- Networking is probably the best reason for using a Linux system. If you are on a network, a unique user name is useful in many ways. Your user name can be associated with resources on other computers: file systems, application programs, and mailboxes to name a few. Sometimes a root user is not allowed to share resources on remote Linux systems.

- Over time, you will probably change personal configuration information associated with your account. For example, you may add aliases, create your own utility programs, or set properties for the applications you use. By gathering this information in one place, it's easy to move your account or add a new account to another computer in the future.

Like most things in Linux, the desktop is built from a set of interchangeable building blocks. The building blocks of your desktop, to use a car analogy, are:

- The X Window System (which is like the frame of the car),
- The KDE or GNOME desktop environment (which is like a blueprint of how the working parts fit together)
- The Metacity window manager (which provides the steering wheel, seat upholstery, and fuzzy dice on the mirror).
- The Bluecurve desktop theme (the paint job and the pin stripe).

Once Linux is installed (see Chapter 2) and you have logged in (see the previous section), you should see either the GNOME or KDE desktop with the Fedora look-and-feel. At this point,

I'll take you on a tour of the desktop and step you through some initial setup to get your desktop going.

Figure 3-2 shows an example of the Fedora Linux default desktop (GNOME).

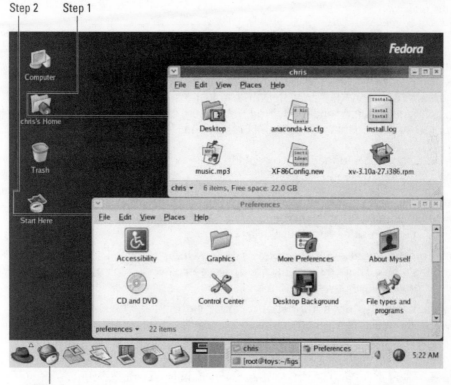

Figure 3-2: After login, Fedora starts you off with a GNOME desktop by default. Steps 1, 2, and 3 are explained in the following section.

Because GNOME is the default desktop for Fedora and other Red Hat personal desktop and workstation installs, I'll start by walking you around the GNOME desktop. As indicated in Figure 3-2, the tour steps you through trying out your home folder, changing some preferences, and configuring your panel.

To understand how Red Hat has created a common look-and-feel for the GNOME and KDE environments, refer to the sidebar, "The Red Hat Look-and-Feel."

Touring your desktop

If you are unfamiliar with the GNOME or KDE desktops that come with Fedora, I suggest you take this quick tour to familiarize yourself with its features.

Step 1: Checking out your home folder

Double-click the *user*'s Home icon on the desktop (it should say something like "bill's Home" or "julie's Home," depending on your user name). The window that appears shows your file manager window (Nautilus in GNOME or Konqueror in KDE) as it displays the contents of your home folder.

The Red Hat Look-and-Feel

Red Hat has done a lot in the past few versions of Red Hat Linux and now Fedora to make KDE and GNOME appear to be the same in many ways. Despite the fact that the differences between KDE and GNOME below the surface are quite dramatic, the way icons, menus, panels, and many Red Hat system tools are presented are the same for the two environments across all Fedora and Red Hat Linux distributions.

To provide a common interface in two desktop environments, you will find the following similarities between the KDE and GNOME desktops in Fedora Core 2:

- **Main menu** — An icon of a red hat on the far left of the panel (in both KDE and GNOME) represents the main menu used in both desktop environments. The menus in both desktops contain similar content.

- **Panel arrangement** — On their panels, both KDE and GNOME start with the same main menu button (just described), the same six desktop applications, a viewer for virtual windows, an area for listed tasks, and a clock.

- **System tools, system settings, and server settings** — These three menus listed on the main menu contain most of the same applications for both desktop environments. This is where Red Hat has added many tools from its growing list of administrative GUI utilities.

- **Icons** — Both KDE and GNOME now start with at least Home, StartHere, Computer, and Trash icons on the desktop. These desktop icons, as well as icons shown on the panel and menus, are specific to Fedora. These icons add a lot to the similar look of both KDE and GNOME in Red Hat Linux.

Although the two desktops now look very much alike in Fedora and offer many of the same Red Hat administrative tools, the two desktop environments are very different in other ways. KDE comes with many more integrated applications and offers more tools for configuring desktop preferences. GNOME tends to be more streamlined, offering a fairly simple, efficient desktop experience.

To choose between KDE and GNOME, I recommend you read the sections on the two desktop environments and compare features in their panels, file managers (Konqueror and Nautilus), and configurable preferences. In general, Red Hat has thrown more weight behind GNOME support.

The location of the home folder (also referred to as a *home directory*) on your computer is usually /home/*user*, where *user* is replaced by your user name. Here are some things to try out with your home folder (assuming the GNOME Nautilus window is your file manager):

1. **Folders** — Create folders and subfolders to store your work (click File → Create Folder, and then type the name of the new folder; something like Images, Music, or Packages).

2. **Open Location** — To open another folder on your computer, click File → Open Location and type a directory name. For our tour, open a folder that has several different file types in it (for example, /usr/share/doc/bash-2.05b).

> **NOTE:** To move down to a subfolder of the current folder, simply double-click that folder. To move up to a parent folder, click the current folder name in the bottom left corner of the window frame. From the menu that opens, you can select to go to any higher level folder from there.

3. **Open With** — Click any object in a folder with the right mouse button, then select Open With. You should be able to see several programs you can use to open the object. For example, you can choose to open a Web page (.html file) with htmlview, Lynx, or Mozilla (provided each of those tools is installed).

4. **Side Pane** — Right-click any folder in the Nautilus file manager window, then select Browse Folder to see the Side Pane. From the box at the top of this pane, choose Information to show information about the selected folder or file. Next choose History to see files and folders previously viewed. Choose Tree to see a hierarchical representation of your file system.

5. **Backgrounds** — Click Edit → Backgrounds and Emblems. Drag-and-drop patterns or colors you like into the pane on your folder window. (I personally like camouflage.) Click Emblems, then drag-and-drop an emblem on a file or folder. Use the emblem to remind yourself of something about the object (such as the fact that it's a personal document or of an urgent nature).

6. **Organize your work** — As you create documents, add music, or download images from your camera, organize them into your home folder or any subfolders. Your home folder is not accessible to any other user on the computer except the root user, so you can safely store your work there. With the files you create, you can:

    - **Move** — Drag-and-drop to move a file to another folder icon or folder window.
    - **Delete** — Drag-and-drop a file to the Trash icon to delete it.
    - **Rename** — Right-click the file, select Rename, and then type the new name.

As with any window, with the Folder window you can:

- **Minimize/Unminimize** — Click the Minimize button (first button, upper-right corner of the title bar) to minimize the window to the window pane. Click the minimized window in the desktop panel to return it to your desktop.

- **Maximize** — Click the Maximize button (second button, upper-right corner of the title bar) to have the window go full screen. (Maximize is now the default action for double-clicking in the title bar. If you prefer the old window shade default, see the Tip below.)

> **TIP:** The window shade feature, where a double-click in the title bar rolls up the window instead of maximizing or restoring it, is not on by default. To turn on that feature from the red hat menu, click Preferences → Windows. From the pop-up window that appears, change Maximize to Roll Up (under Double-click Title Bar to Perform This Action).

- **Delete** — Click the X button (upper-right corner of the title bar) to delete the window.

Step 2: Change some preferences

More than 20 different preference categories are available from the GNOME desktop. Double-click the Start Here icon, and then double-click the Preferences icon. Here are a few preferences you might want to modify when you start out (see the GNOME and KDE preferences sections later in this chapter for further details):

- **Change background** — Double-click the Desktop Background icon. The Desktop Background Preferences window appears, as shown in Figure 3-3. To change the background image, select one of the Desktop Wallpaper images shown. To add your own image, click the Add Wallpaper box (to choose a file from your disk) or drag-and-drop an image onto the Desktop Wallpaper box. For example, from a folder window, type **/usr/share/backgrounds/images** in the Location box. Then drag-and-drop images to the Desktop Wallpaper box to change the background. Select a Style, such as Centered, Fill Screen, Tiled, or Scaled. To just use a color, select No Wallpaper and choose a color under the Desktop Colors selector.

Figure 3-3: Select a color or picture for your desktop background.

- **Choose browsers and editors** — Double-click the Preferred Applications icon. When you open a Web page, text file, mail composer, or shell from the desktop, this preferences window lets you choose which Web browser, text editor, mail reader, or Terminal window to open. Mozilla is the default Web browser, but you can choose Epiphany or Konqueror (the KDE browser) to run on your GUI. If you want a text-based Web browser, select W3M, Lynx, or Links. To use a different Web browser, select Custom and type the name of that browser. Available Mail Readers include Evolution (the default), Balsa, KMail, Mozilla Mail, Sylpheed, and Mutt. For your default text editor, choose the application to open plain-text files from your desktop (by default, gedit is used). The GNOME Terminal is used when you need a shell prompt (you can change that to use KDE Konsole or a standard xterm Terminal). To add a different default terminal, select Custom Terminal and enter the command that starts the Terminal you want.

> **TIP:** The `konsole` command starts the Konsole (KDE) terminal window. Programmers who use many terminal windows at once often prefer Konsole over gnome-terminal (finding it to be more efficient and feature-rich).

- **Add a screensaver** — Double-click the Screensaver icon. Try out a few screen savers (all are used randomly, by default). Click the Only One Screen Saver check box in the Mode box.

  Click different screen savers to see them and click Preview to try them out. Try T3D for a bizarro clock or Rubick to watch how to solve a Rubick's cube.

> **TIP:** Click the Lock Screen After check box and set the number of minutes after which the screen will be locked. This is a good option for an office environment, where you want your screen locked if you wander away for a few minutes. (Be sure to log off of any virtual terminals you may have open.)

- **Change the theme** — Double-click the Theme icon. You can change the entire theme (colors, icons, borders, and so on) for your desktop. The Bluecurve theme is the default theme used by Red Hat Linux. Try any of the others to find one that suits you. Click Theme Details to mix-and-match attributes from different themes. Figure 3-4 shows the window for selecting a theme.

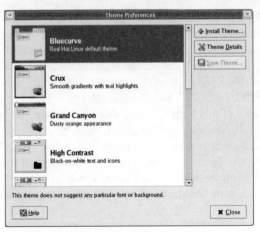

Figure 3-4: Change the default Bluecurve theme.

Step 3: Configure your panel

Most people manage their desktops from the panel that appears at the bottom of the screen. This panel provides an intuitive way to:

- Launch applications
- Change workspaces
- Add useful information (clocks, news tickers, CD players, and so on)

Step through the following procedure to learn about the desktop (GNOME) panel:

1. **Red Hat Menu** — Click the red hat in the panel. Most useful GUI applications and system tools that come with Fedora are available from the menus and submenus of this main red hat menu. Here are a few cool things to do from this menu:

   - **Start an application** — Click Accessories, Games, Graphics, Internet, Office, or Sound & Video menu items, then select any application to run.

   - **Change your settings** — Click the Preferences menu item to change preferences or the System Settings or System Tools menu items to change system-wide settings.

   - **Log out or shutdown** — Click the Logout menu item to log out from your current desktop session, shut down, or reboot your computer.

   - **Launch applications** — Red Hat places icons for popular desktop applications right on the panel. Click any of the icons shown in Figure 3-5 to launch a Web browser (Mozilla), e-mail reader (Evolution), word processor (OpenOffice Writer), presentation creator (OpenOffice Impress), spreadsheet (OpenOffice Calc), or print manager, respectively.

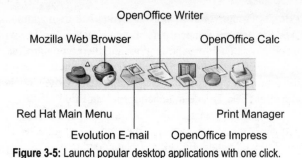

OpenOffice Writer

Mozilla Web Browser   OpenOffice Calc

Red Hat Main Menu   Print Manager

Evolution E-mail   OpenOffice Impress

Figure 3-5: Launch popular desktop applications with one click.

Use workspaces — Click different panels in the Workspace Switcher. Open an application, then click another workspace panel. Workspaces are a great way to have multiple windows and still keep your desktop uncluttered. Notice that there are tiny representations of each window you open on the workspace panel it is in. Drag-and-drop the tiny windows to move them to different workspaces, without leaving your workspace.

Add cool stuff to your panel — Click an empty place in the panel so that a panel menu appears. It should say "Add to Panel" at the top. Because real estate is limited on your panel, I recommend adding a drawer, to which you can add some little applications that run in the panel and icons that launch other applications. To begin, click Add to Panel → Drawer. A Drawer icon appears on your panel (you can drag it where you want it to go. Click to open the drawer, then right-click the open drawer and click Add to Panel. Here are a few things I suggest adding to your panel:

- **Terminal** — From the drawer menu, click Add to Panel → Launcher from menu → System Tools → Terminal. Now, when I ask you to type something into a Terminal window, you can launch one from this drawer.

> **NOTE:** Throughout this book, I give examples that require you to use a Terminal window. Neither the new KDE nor GNOME desktops have a Terminal window launcher on the panel or desktop. I strongly suggest that you add a Terminal window to your desktop or panel in order to launch it easily. The alternative is to right-click the desktop and select Open Terminal.

- **Weather report** — From the drawer menu, click Add to Panel → Accessories → Weather Report. Right-click the temperature icon that appears and choose Preferences. Click the Location tab and select your country, state, and city from the list. Now, whenever you double-click the temperature icon in your drawer, you can see weather conditions and a forecast for your city.

- **Volume control** — From the drawer menu, click Add to Panel → Multimedia → Volume Control. The volume control that appears lets you control audio levels to your sound card (when you play a CD, for example).

- **Popular folder or Web site** — Folders or Web sites that you visit often should be easily accessible. Click Add to Panel → Launcher. From the Create Launcher window, select Link (as the Type) and type a URL or Application, and then type **nautilus** *folder* (where `folder` is replaced by the name of the folder you want to open). Click Icon and choose an icon to represent the item. For example, when I write a book, I have a folder containing chapter files. To add a launcher for that file, I select Application from Launcher Properties (`nautilus /home/chris/rhlbible`). Then I assign an icon (an image of the book cover) to the launcher. Figure 3-6 shows an example of a drawer, with the launchers I just described added to it.

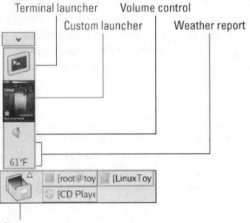

Figure 3-6: A drawer is a great way to contain personal utilities and launchers.

You can do much more with the desktop and the panel. To learn more about configuring your desktop, you can check out the specific descriptions of the GNOME and KDE desktops later in this chapter.

Tips for configuring your desktop

Now that you have experimented with a few items on the desktop, you should configure certain features to get Fedora really working well for you. Most of the tips I describe here will help you get Fedora working well on the network.

> **NOTE:** Some of the tips described here should be carried out by the system administrator. They apply to you if you are the system administrator for your organization, or if you are configuring your own home or office network.

- **Getting Updates** — If you see a blinking red exclamation point icon, it means that updates are available to your Fedora system. These updates can patch dangerous security holes in a timely fashion. The Fedora Project maintains updates on an on-going basis for

each Fedora release. If you are connected to the Internet, double-click that icon and
follow the instructions to download free updates to Fedora software packages.

> **CROSS-REFERENCE:** Refer to Chapters 2 and 10 for more information on using the up2date facility
> and yum repositories to get updates.

- **Set up your network** — You may have already configured your network interfaces
  (dial-up or LAN) during installation. If not, refer to Chapter 15 for setting up a LAN and
  Chapter 16 for setting up an Internet connection.

- **Configure e-mail** — You must identify information about your e-mail account in order
  to use e-mail. Click the Evolution E-mail icon in the panel to start the process of
  configuring e-mail. Refer to Chapter 9 for information on setting up and using e-mail.

- **Configure the Web browser** — Open the Mozilla Web Browser from the panel.
  Although it should work fine at browsing the Internet once you have a network
  connection set up, there are a few things you should do to tune your browser. For
  example, you should choose a home page (click Edit → Preferences, then type a home
  page location); set the browser window's appearance (from the Preferences window,
  click Appearance and select a topic); and import bookmarks (click Bookmarks →
  Manage Bookmarks, then select Tools → Import from the Bookmark Manager window).

> **NOTE:** If you are coming from a Windows environment, you may find that some Web content doesn't
> work well in Mozilla. Refer to Chapter 9 for suggestions on ways to enhance Mozilla to change the
> appearance of some Web pages and improve the ability to play certain multimedia content.

The sections that follow provide more details on using the GNOME and KDE desktops.

Using the GNOME Desktop

GNOME (pronounced *guh-nome*) provides the desktop environment that you get by default
when you install Fedora. This desktop environment provides the software that is between your
X Window System framework and the look-and-feel provided by the window manager.
GNOME is a stable and reliable desktop environment, with a few cool features in it.

The new GNOME 2.6 desktop comes with the most recent version of Fedora. For GNOME
2.6, enhancements include a new spatial user interface that remembers the locations and sizes
of folder windows you open, and returns them to that state when you open them again. Folder
windows also have a new look, making them less cluttered and easier to manage. I describe
these features as I step through the GNOME desktop.

To use your GNOME desktop, you should become familiar with the following components:

- **Metacity (window manager)** — The default window manager for GNOME in Fedora is
  Metacity. The window manager provides such things as themes, window borders, and
  window controls.

- **Nautilus (file manager/graphical shell)** — When you open a folder (for example, by double-clicking the Home icon on your desktop), the Nautilus window opens and displays the contents of the selected folder. Nautilus can also display other types of content, such as shared folders from Windows computers on the network (using SMB).

- **GNOME panel (application/task launcher)** — This panel, which lines the bottom of your screen, is designed to make it convenient for you to launch the applications you use, manage running applications, and work with multiple virtual desktops. By default, the panel contains the main menu (represented by a red hat), desktop application launchers (Mozilla browser, Evolution e-mail, and a set of OpenOffice applications), a workspace switcher (for managing four virtual desktops), window list, and a clock. It also has an icon to alert you when you need software updates.

- **Desktop area**— The windows and icons you use are arranged on the desktop area. The desktop area supports such things a drag-and-drop between applications, a desktop menu (right click to see it), and icons for launching applications. One new icon for GNOME 2.6 is the Computer icon, which consolidates CD drives, floppy drives, the file system and shared network resources in one place.

Besides the components just described, GNOME includes a set of Preferences windows that let you configure different aspects of your desktop. You can change backgrounds, colors, fonts, keyboard shortcuts, and other features relating to the look and behavior of the desktop. Figure 3-7 shows how the GNOME desktop environment appears the first time you log in, with a few windows added to the screen.

The following sections provide details on using the GNOME desktop.

Using the Metacity window manager

The Metacity window manager seems to have been chosen as the default window manager for GNOME in Red Hat Linux because of its simplicity. The creator of Metacity refers to it as a "boring window manager for the adult in you" — then goes on to compare other window managers to colorful, sugary cereal while Metacity is characterized as Cheerios.

There really isn't much you can do with Metacity (except get your work done efficiently). Assigning new themes to Metacity and changing colors and window decorations is done through the GNOME preferences (and is described later). A few Metacity themes exist, but expect the number to grow.

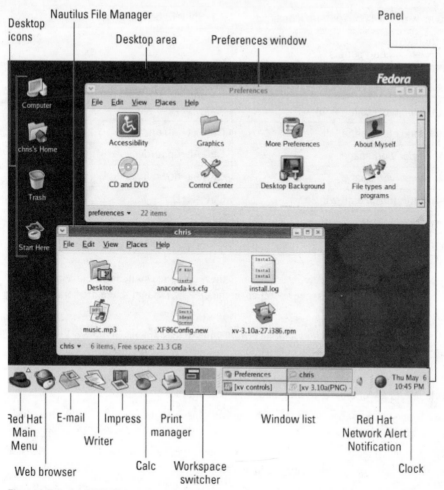

Figure 3-7: In the GNOME desktop environment, you can manage applications from the panel.

Basic Metacity functions that might interest you are keyboard shortcuts and the workspace switcher. Table 3-1 shows keyboard shortcuts to get around the Metacity window manager.

Table 3-1: Metacity Keyboard Shortcuts

Actions	Keystrokes
Window focus cycle forward, with pop-up icons	Alt+Tab
cycle backwards, with pop-up icons	Alt+Shift+Tab
cycle forward, without pop-up icons	Alt+Esc

cycle backwards, without pop-up icons	Alt+Shift+Esc
Panel focus cycle forward among panels	Alt+Ctrl+Tab
cycle backwards among panels	Alt+Ctrl+Shift+Tab
Workspace focus move to workspace to the right	Ctrl+Alt+right arrow
move to workspace to the left	Ctrl+Alt+left arrow
move to upper workspace	Ctrl+Alt+up arrow
move to lower workspace	Ctrl+Alt+down arrow
Minimize/unminimize all windows	Ctrl+Alt+D
Show window menu	Alt-Spacebar
Close menu	Esc

Another Metacity feature that may interest you is the workspace switcher. Four virtual workspaces appear in the workspace switcher on the GNOME panel. Here are some things to do with the workspace switcher:

- **Choose current workspace** — Four virtual workspaces appear in the workspace switcher. Click any of the four virtual workspaces to make it your current workspace.

- **Move windows to other workspaces** — Click any window, each represented by a tiny rectangle in a workspace, to drag-and-drop it to another workspace.

- **Add more workspaces** — Right-click the workspace switcher, and select Preferences. You can add workspaces (up to 32).

- **Name workspaces** — Right-click the workspace switcher and select Preferences. Click in the Workspaces pane to change names of workspaces to any names you choose.

You can view and change information about Metacity controls and settings using the gconf-editor window (type **gconf-editor** from a Terminal window). As the window says, it is not the recommended way of changing preferences. So, when possible, you should change the desktop through GNOME preferences. However, gconf-editor is a good way to see descriptions of each Metacity feature.

From the gconf-editor window, select apps → metacity. Then choose from general, global_keybindings, keybindings_commands, window_keybindings and workspace_names. Click each key to see its value, along with short and long descriptions of the key.

Using the GNOME panel

The GNOME panel is intended to be the place from which you manage your desktop. From this panel you can start applications (from buttons or menus), see what programs are active, and monitor how your system is running. There are also many ways to change the panel — by adding applications or monitors, or by changing the placement or behavior of the panel, for example.

Click any open space on the panel to see the Panel menu. The Panel menu appears as shown in Figure 3-8.

Figure 3-8: Left-click any open spot on the GNOME Panel to see the Panel menu.

From the GNOME Panel menu, you can perform a variety of functions, including:

- **Use the Red Hat menu** — Displayed on the red hat menu are most of the applications and system tools you will use from the desktop.
- **Add to panel** — You can add an applet, menu, launcher, drawer, or button.
- **Delete This panel** — You can delete the current panel.
- **Properties** — Change position, size, and background of the panel.
- **New panel** — You can add panels to your desktop in different styles and locations.

You can also work with items on a panel; for example you can:

- **Move items** — To move items on a panel, simply drag-and-drop them to a new postion.
- **Resize items** — Some elements, such as the Window List, can be resized by clicking an edge and dragging it to the new size.
- **Use the Window List** — Tasks running on the desktop appear in the Window List area. Click a task to have that task minimized or maximized.

The following sections describe some things you can do with the GNOME panel.

Use the Red Hat menu

Click the red hat icon on the panel and you see categories of applications and system tools that you can select. Click the application you want to launch. To add an item to launch from the panel — and to view its properties — right-click it. There is currently no way to add or remove applications to or from this menu from the GUI in GNOME. However, you can manually add items to your GNOME menus.

To add to the red hat menu, create a .desktop file in the /usr/share/applications directory. The easiest way to do that is copy an existing .desktop file that is on the menu you want and modify it. For example, to add a video player to the Sound & Video menu, you could do the following (as root user):

```
# cd /usr/share/applications
# cp gnome-cd.desktop vidplay.desktop
```

Next use any text editor to change the contents of the vidplay.desktop file you created by adding a comment, file to execute, icon to display, and application name. After you save the changes, the new item will immediately appear on the menu (no need to restart anything).

> **CROSS-REFERENCE:** There is a graphical way of modifying your main menu if you are using the KDE desktop. See the Menus bullet in the "Changing panel attributes" section later in this chapter for details.

Adding an applet

1. There are several small GNOME applications, called *applets*, that you can run directly on the GNOME panel. These applets can show information you may want to see on an ongoing basis or may just provide some amusement. To see what applets are available and to add applets that you want to your panel, perform the following steps:Right-click an open space in the panel so that the panel menu appears.

2. Select Add to Panel.

3. Select an applet from one of the following categories:

   - **Accessories** — Has clock, dictionary lookup, stock ticker, and weather report applets.

   - **Actions** — Contains action applets to lock the screen, log out, run an application, take a screen shot, and search the Web.

   - **Amusements** — Includes a fortune-telling fish and eyes that follow your mouse (geyes).

   - **Internet** — Contains an e-mail Inbox monitor and modem lights monitor.

   - **Multimedia** — Includes an applet for playing CDs and a volume control.

   - **Utility** — Includes applets for monitoring battery levels, inserting special characters, running a command line, mounting floppy drives, monitoring systems load, and performing other useful tasks.

4. Select the applet to add from the category you selected. The applet appears on the panel, ready for you to use. Figure 3-9 shows, from left to right, geyes, system monitor, CD player, stock ticker, e-mail Inbox monitor, and dictionary lookup applets.

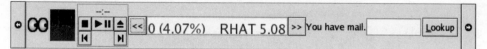

Figure 3-9: Applets let you monitor activities, play CDs, watch your mail, or look up dictionary words.

After an applet is installed, right-click it to see what options are available. For example, select Preferences for the stock ticker, and you can add or delete stocks whose prices you want to monitor. If you don't like the applet's location, right-click it, click Move, slide the mouse until the applet is where you want it (even to another panel), and click to set its location.

If you no longer want an applet to appear on the panel, right-click it, and then click Remove From Panel. The icon representing the applet will disappear. If you find that you have run out of room on your panel, you can add a new panel to another part of the screen, as described in the next section.

Adding another panel

You can have several panels on your GNOME desktop. You can add panels that run along the entire bottom, top, or side of the screen. To add a panel, do the following:

1. Right-click an open space in the panel so that the Panel menu appears.
2. Select New Panel. A new panel appears at the top of the screen.
3. Right-click an open space in the new panel and select Properties.
4. From the Panel Properties, select where you want the panel from the Orientation box (Top, Bottom, Left or Right).

After you've added a panel, you can add applets or application launchers to it as you did to the default panel. To remove a panel, right-click it and select Delete This Panel.

Adding an application launcher

Icons on your panel represent a Web browser and several office productivity applications. You can add your own icons to launch applications from the panel as well. To add a new application launcher to the panel, do the following:

1. Right-click in an open space on the panel.
2. Select Add to Panel → Launcher from the menu. All application categories from your main desktop menu (the one under the red hat) appear.
3. Select the category of application you want; then select the application. An icon representing the application appears.

To launch the application you just added, single-click it.

If the application you want to launch is not on your red hat menu, you can build one yourself as follows:

1. Right-click in an open space on the panel.

2. Select Add to Panel → Launcher. The Create Launcher window appears.

3. Provide the following information for the application that you want to add:

   - **Name** — A name to identify the application (this appears in the tool tip when your mouse is over the icon).

   - **Generic Name** — A name to identify the type of application.

   - **Comment** — A comment describing the application. Like with Name, this information appears when you later move your mouse over the launcher.

   - **Command** — The command line that is run when the application is launched. You should use the full path name, plus any required options.

   - **Type** — Select Application (to launch an application). (Other selections include Link, to open a Web address in a browser or FSDevice to open a file system.)

   - **Run in Terminal** — If it is a character-based or ncurses application. (Applications written using the curses library run in a Terminal window but offer screen-oriented mouse and keyboard controls.)

4. Click the Icon box (it might say No Icon). Select one of the icons shown and click OK. Alternatively, you can browse the Red Hat Linux file system to choose an icon.

> **NOTE:** Icons available to represent your application are contained in the `/usr/share/pixmaps` directory. These icons are either in png or xpm formats. If there isn't an icon in the directory you want to use, create your own and assign it to the application.

5. Click OK.

The application should now appear in the panel. Click it to start the application.

Adding a drawer

By adding a drawer to your GNOME panel, you can add several applets and launchers and have them take up only one slot on your panel. You can use the drawer to show the applets and launchers as though they were being pulled out of a drawer icon on the panel.

To add a drawer to your panel, right-click the panel and then select Add to Panel → Drawer. The drawer should appear on the panel. The drawer behaves just like a panel. Right-click the drawer area, and add applets or launchers to it as you would to a panel. Click the drawer icon to retract the drawer.

Figure 3-10 shows a portion of the panel that includes an open drawer. This example includes icons for launching a Terminal window, the GIMP, and the Ethereal window.

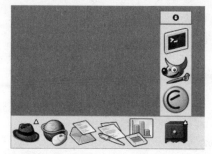

Figure 3-10: Add launchers or applets to a drawer on your GNOME panel.

Changing panel properties

Properties you can change that relate to a panel are limited to the orientation, size, hiding policy, and background. To open the Panel properties window that applies to a specific panel, right-click on an open space on the panel, then choose Properties. The Panel Properties window that appears includes following values:

- **Name** — Contains a name by which you identify this panel.

- **Orientation** — You can move the panel to different locations on the screen by clicking on a new position.

- **Size** — You can select the size of your panel by choosing its height in pixels (48 pixels by default).

- **Expand** — Click this check box to have the panel expand to fill the entire side or unselect the check box to make the panel only as wide as the applets it contains.

- **Autohide** — You can select whether or not a panel is automatically hidden (appearing only when the mouse pointer is in the area).

- **Show hide buttons** — You can choose whether or not the Hide/Unhide buttons (with pixmap arrows on them) appear on the edges of the panel.

- **Arrows on hide buttons** — If you select "Show hide buttons" you can select to either have arrows on those buttons or not.

- **Background** — From the Background tab, you can assign a color to the background of the panel, assign a pixmap image, or just leave the Default (which is based on the current system theme). Click the Background Image check box if you want to select an Image for the background, then select an image, such as a tile from `/usr/share/backgrounds/tiles` or other directory.

> **TIP:** I usually turn on the AutoHide feature and turn off the Hide buttons. Using AutoHide gives you more space to work with on your desktop. When you move your mouse to the edge where the panel is, it pops up — so you don't need Hide buttons.

Using the Nautilus file manager

At one time, file managers did little more than let you run applications, create data files, and open folders. These days, as the information a user needs expands beyond the local system, file managers are expected to also display Web pages, access FTP sites, and play multimedia content. The Nautilus file manager, which is the default GNOME file manager, is an example of just such a file manager.

When you open the Nautilus file manager window (from the GNOME main menu or by opening the Home icon or other folder on your desktop), you see the name of the location you are viewing (such as the folder name) and what that location contains (files, folders, and applications). Figure 3-11 is an example of the file manager window displaying the home directory of a user named chris (/home/chris).

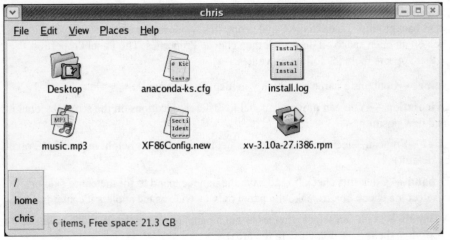

Figure 3-11: Move around the file system, open directories, launch applications, and open Samba folders.

In GNOME 2.6, the default Nautilus window has been greatly simplified to show fewer controls and provide more space for file and directory icons. Double-click a folder to open that folder in a new window. Select your folder name in the lower left corner of the window to see the file system hierarchy above the current folder (as shown in Figure 3-11). Whatever size, location, and other setting you had for the folder the last time you opened it, GNOME will remember and return it to that state the next time you open it.

To see more controls, as Nautilus had in previous version, right-click a folder and select Browse Folder to open it. Icons on the toolbar of the Nautilus window let you move forward and back among the directories and Web sites you visit. To move up the directory structure, click the up arrow. To refresh the view of the folder or Web page, click the Reload button. The Home button takes you to your home page and the Computer button lets you see the same type of information you would see from a My Computer icon on a Windows system (CD drive, floppy drive, hard disk file systems, and network folders).

NOTE: One note about viewing HTML content (in other words, Web pages). The version of Nautilus that originally came with GNOME 2.6 did not properly display HTML content. Depending on how the fix for this problem falls out, HTML content may not be displayed in the Nautilus window. Instead, you might have the option of launching an external window (such as Mozilla or Epiphany) to display that content.

Icons in Nautilus often indicate the type of data that a particular file contains. The contents or file extension of each file can determine which application is used to work with the file. Or, you can right-click an icon to open the file it represents with a particular application or viewer.

Some of the more interesting features of Nautilus are described below:

- **Sidebar** — From the Browse Folder view described previously, click on View → Side Pane to have a sidebar appear in the left column of the screen. From the sidebar, you can click on tabs that represent different types of information you can select. The Tree tab shows a tree view of the directory structure, so you can easily traverse your directories.

  The Notes tab lets you add notes that become associated with the current Directory or Web page. The History tab displays a history of directories and Web sites you have visited, allowing you to click those items to return to the sites they represent. Right-click in the sidebar to choose which of the sidebar tabs are displayed.

- **Windows File and Printer Sharing** — If your computer is connected to a LAN on which Windows computers are sharing files and printers, you can view those resources from Nautilus. Type **smb:** in the Open Location box (click File → Open Location to get there) to see available workgroups. Click a workgroup to see computers from that workgroup that are sharing files and printers. Figure 3-12 shows an example of Nautilus displaying icons representing Windows computers in a workgroup called estreet (`smb://estreet`).

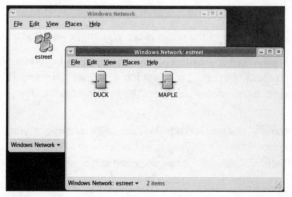

Figure 3-12: Display shared Windows file and printer servers (SMB) in Nautilus.

- **MIME types and file types** — To handle different types of content that may be encountered in the Nautilus window, you can set applications to respond based on MIME type and file type. With a folder being displayed, right-click a file for which you want to assign an application. Click either Open With an Application or Open With a

Viewer. If no application or viewer has been assigned for the file type, click Associate Application to be able to select an application. From the Add File Types window, you can add an application based on the file extension and MIME type representing the file.

CROSS-REFERENCE: For more information in MIME types, see the description of MIME types in the "Changing GNOME preferences" section later in this chapter.

- **Drag-and-Drop** — You can use drag-and-drop within the Nautilus window, between the Nautilus and the desktop, or between multiple Nautilus windows. As other GNOME-compliant applications become available, they are expected to also support the GNOME drag-and-drop feature.

If you need more information on the Nautilus file manager, visit the GNOME Web site (www.gnome.org/nautilus).

Changing GNOME preferences

There are many ways to change the behavior, look, and feel of your GNOME desktop. Most GNOME preferences can be modified from windows you can launch from the main red hat menu or from the Preferences folder. You can open that folder from the red hat menu by clicking Preferences → Control Center (or typing **preferences:** in the Nautilus Open Location box).

Unlike earlier versions of GNOME for Fedora and Red Hat Linux, boundaries between preferences relating to the window manager (Metacity), file manager (Nautilus), and the GNOME desktop itself have been blurred. Preferences for all of these features are in the Preferences window. Figure 3-13 shows the Preferences window, with icons that represent features you can change.

The following items highlight some of the preferences you might want to change:

- **Accessibility** — If you have difficulty operating a mouse or keyboard, the Keyboard Accessibility Preferences (AccessX) window lets you adapt mouse and keyboard settings to make those devices more accessible. From the Preferences window, open Accessibility.

- **Desktop Background** — From Desktop Background Preferences, you can choose a solid color or an image to use as wallpaper. If you choose to use a solid color (by selecting No Wallpaper), click the Color box, choose a color from the palette, and select OK.

  To use wallpaper for your background, open a folder containing the image you want to use. Then drag the image into the Desktop Wallpaper pane on the Desktop Preferences window. You can choose from a variety of images in the /usr/share/nautilus/patterns and /usr/share/backgrounds/tiles directories. Then, choose to have the image as wallpaper that is tiled (repeated pattern), centered, scaled (in proportion), or stretched (using any proportion to fill the screen).

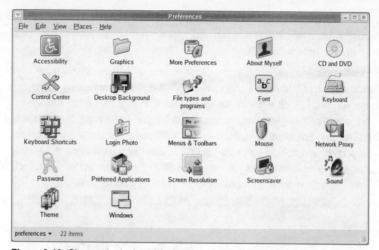

Figure 3-13: Change the look-and-feel of your desktop from the Preferences window.

- **CD and DVD Properties** — Even if you don't change CD properties, it is important to know what happens when you insert a Data CD, Audio CD, Blank CDs, or DVD (video) disk. These properties are associated with a feature called *magicdev*, which is a bit controversial.

    For Data CDs , the CD is mounted when it is inserted, any auto-run program on the CD is run, and a file manager window opens for the CD you inserted. If you would rather mount and open the CD as you choose, you can turn off any or all of these preferences.

    For Audio CDs, the gnome-cd player is launched and the CD begins playing. You can type in a different CD player, if you like, or clear the Run command when CD is inserted check box so that you can choose which player to use later.

    For Blank CDs, a CD-burning utility is launched through the Nautilus window. After that, you can burn audio files or data to the blank CD.

    For DVD (Video), the DVD is not set to play automatically. If you have a player installed that can play the content of DVDs that you have, turn on this feature and add the command to run the player into the Command box.

- **File Types and Programs** — The File Types and Programs preferences can help you understand the different types of data files that GNOME knows about. Double-click this icon to see data types (audio, documents, images, information, and so on) that have definitions in GNOME. Then choose a particular data type (such as Audio, ogg audio).

    From the Edit file type window that appears, you can see the information assigned to the file type. So, for example, when data that ends with a .ogg extension appears in a Nautilus window, you can see the icon that will represent the file, the mime type assigned to the file, and the action (if any) is taken when you open the file.

You can modify any file type that appears in these preferences windows. You can choose what applications are run and and what icons represent data of this type. You can even create your own data types.

- **Screensaver** — You can choose from dozens of screensavers from the Screensaver window. Select Random Screensaver to have your screen saver chosen randomly from those you mark with a check, or select one that you like from the list to use all the time. Next, choose how long your screen must be idle before the screensaver starts (default is 10 minutes). For random screen savers, you can select how long before cycling to the next screen saver. You can also choose to require a password or to enable power management to shut down your monitor after a set number of minutes (Advanced Tab). Figure 3-14 shows the Screensaver Preferences dialog box.

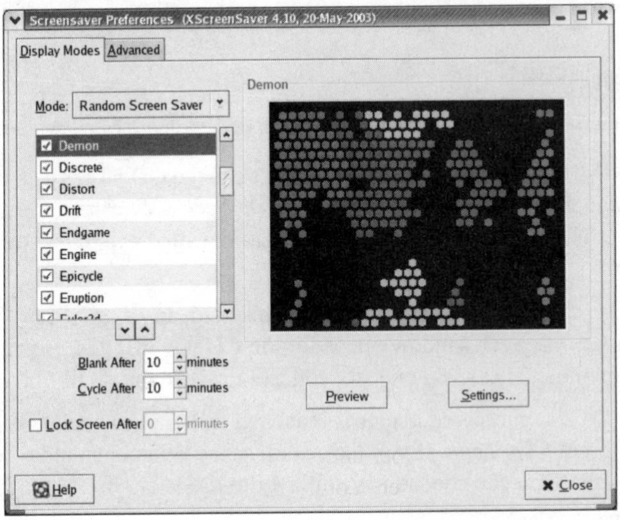

Figure 3-14: Select specific or random screen savers from the Screensaver Preferences dialog box.

- **Theme Selector** — You can choose to have an entire theme of elements be used on your desktop. A desktop theme affects not only the background, but also the way that many buttons and menu selections appear. There are only a few themes available for the window manager (Metacity) in the Fedora distribution. You can get a bunch of other Metacity themes from `themes.freshmeat.net` (click on Metacity).

Click Install theme; then click the Window Border tab to select from different themes that change the title bar and other borders of your windows. Click the Icons tab to choose different icons to represent items on your desktop. Themes change immediately as you click or when you drag a theme name on the desktop.

Exiting GNOME

When you are done with your work, you can either log out from your current session or shut down your computer completely. To exit from GNOME, do the following:

1. Click the red hat menu button.

2. Select Log Out from the menu. A pop-up window appears, asking if you want to Log out, Shut down, or Restart the computer.

> **TIP:** At this point, you can also select to save your session by clicking Save current setup. This is a great way to have the applications that you use all the time restart the next time you log in. Make sure you save your data before you exit, however. Most applications do not yet support the data-saving feature.

3. Select Log out from the pop-up menu. This will log you out and return you to either the graphical login screen or to your shell login prompt. If, instead, you select Shut Down, the system is shut down; if you select Reboot, the system is restarted.

4. Select OK to finish exiting from GNOME.

If you are unable to get to the Log out button (if, for example, your Panel crashed), there are two other exit methods. Try one of these two ways, depending on how you started the desktop:

- If you started the desktop by typing **startx** from your login shell, press Ctrl+Alt+F1 to return to your login shell. Then type Ctrl+C to kill the desktop.

- If you started the desktop from a graphical login screen, first open a Terminal window (right-click the desktop and then select New Terminal). In the Terminal window, type **ps x | more** to see a list of running processes. Look for a command named gnome-session and determine its number under the PID column. Then type **kill -9 *PID*** , where *PID* is replaced by the PID number. You should see the graphical login screen.

Although these are not the most graceful ways to exit the desktop, they work. You should be able to log in again and restart the desktop.

Using the KDE Desktop

The KDE desktop was developed to provide an interface to Linux and other UNIX systems that could compete with MacOS or Microsoft Windows operating systems for ease of use. Integrated within KDE are tools for managing files, windows, multiple desktops, and applications. If you can work a mouse, you can learn to navigate the KDE desktop. Fedora includes version 3.2.2 of KDE.

> **NOTE:** KDE is not installed by default for Fedora personal desktop and workstation installations. Therefore, to use the procedures in this section, you might have to install KDE. During installation, you could use a Custom install type to install KDE. Otherwise, see Chapter 2 for information on how to use the Package Management window so you can add KDE.

The lack of an integrated, standardized desktop environment in the past has held back Linux and other UNIX systems from acceptance on the desktop. While individual applications could run well, you rarely could drag-and-drop files or other items between applications. Likewise, you couldn't open a file and expect the machine to launch the correct application to deal with it or save your windows from one login session to the next. KDE provides a platform for developers to create programs that easily share information and detect how to deal with different data types.

The following section describes how to get started with KDE. This includes using the KDE Setup wizard, maneuvering around the desktop, managing files, windows, virtual desktops, and adding application launchers.

Starting with KDE

You can select the KDE desktop from the login screen (provided that KDE is installed). Choose Session → KDE. Then type your login name and password, as prompted. The KDE desktop should appear, as shown in Figure 3-15.

KDE desktop described

You may notice that, in Fedora, KDE looks very similar to GNOME. That's because both begin with the same icons and background. Beneath the surface, however, you will notice that there are a lot more tools with KDE for configuring and using your desktop.

Here are some descriptions of what you will find on the KDE desktop for Fedora:

- **Desktop icons** — The desktop starts with several icons on it to provide quick access to selected features. By default, you will probably have an icon that gives you access to your home directory. You will also see icons representing your removable drives (CDs, DVDs, and floppies), the Start Here icon (to open applications), and the Trash icon.

- **Panel** — The panel provides some quick tools for launching applications and managing the desktop. You can adapt the panel to your needs by resizing it, adding tools, and changing the look-and-feel. By default, you start with the same icons you had in GNOME: one for your Web browser and several for office-productivity applications.

- **Red hat menu** — This panel button is represented by a red fedora icon. Click this button to see a menu of applications, utilities, and configuration tools that are available to run on your KDE desktop.

- **Web Browser** — This panel button looks like a globe with a mouse on it. Click it to open the Mozilla Web Browser.

- **Evolution Email** — This panel button is the image of an envelope with a letter on it. Click it to open the Evolution window for sending, receiving, and managing e-mail.

Konqueror File Manager   KDE Info Center

Figure 3-15: Manage files and applications graphically with the KDE desktop.

- **Writer** — This button, which includes a pen and paper, launches the OpenOffice Writer word-processing window.

- **Impress** —This button includes a bar chart image and launches the OpenOffice Impress presentation window. Impress lets you create presentations similar to those produced by Microsoft PowerPoint.

- **Calc** — This button includes an image of a pie chart and launches the OpenOffice Calc spreadsheet application.

- **Print Manager** — This button opens a Print Manager window to manage printers and view queued print jobs.

- **Desktop Pager** — This box on the panel consists of your virtual desktops, which contain small views of each desktop. There are four virtual desktops available to you, by default. These are labeled 1, 2, 3, and 4. You begin your KDE session on virtual desktop 1. You can change to any of the four desktops by clicking it.

- **Taskbar** — This button shows the tasks that are currently running on the desktop. The window that is currently active appears pressed in. Click a task to toggle between opening and minimizing the window.

- **Klipper** — This button looks like a clipboard. Click it if you want to clear your desktop's clipboard.

- **Red Hat Network Alert Notification Tool** — When software updates are available to Fedora, this changes from a checkmark to a blinking, red exclamation mark. Click it to use the up2date facility to get software updates.

- **Clock** — The current time and date are shown on the far right-hand side of the panel. Click them to see a calendar for the current month. Click the arrow keys on the calendar to move forward and back to other months.

- **Konqueror** — The default file manager for KDE.

- **KDE Info Center** — The window for viewing desktop preferences and system status information.

Getting around the desktop

Navigating the desktop is done with your mouse and keyboard. You can use a two-button or three-button mouse. Using the keyboard to navigate requires some Alt and Ctrl key sequences.

Using the mouse

The responses from the desktop to your mouse depend on which button you press and where the mouse pointer is located. Table 3-2 shows the results of clicking each mouse button with the mouse pointer placed in different locations.

The mouse actions in the table are all single-click actions. Use single-click with the left mouse button to open an icon on the desktop. On a window title bar, double-clicking results in a window-shade action, where the window scrolls up and down into the title bar.

Table 3-2: Mouse Actions

Pointer Position	Mouse Button	Results
Window title bar or frame (current window active)	Left	Raise current window.
Window title bar or frame (current window active)	Middle	Lower current window.
Window title bar or frame (current window active)	Right	Open operations menu.

Pointer Position	Mouse Button	Results
Window title bar or frame (current window not active)	Left	Activate current window and raise it to the top.
Window title bar or frame (current window not active)	Middle	Activate current window and lower it.
Window title bar or frame (current window not active)	Right	Open operations menu without changing position.
Inner window (current window not active)	Left	Activate current window, raise it to the top, and pass the click to the window.
Inner window (current window not active)	Middle	Activate current window and pass the click to the window.
Inner window (current window not active)	Right	Activate current window and pass the click to the window.
Any part of a window	Middle (plus hold Alt key)	Toggle between raising and lowering the window.
Any part of a window	Right (plus hold Alt key)	Resize the window.
On the desktop area	Left (hold and drag)	Select a group of icons.
On the desktop area	Right	Open system pop-up menu.

Using keystrokes

If you don't happen to have a mouse or you just like to keep your hands on the keyboard, there are several keystroke sequences you can use to navigate the desktop. Here are some examples:

- **Step through desktops** (Ctrl+Tab) — To go from one virtual desktop to the next, hold down the Ctrl key and press the Tab key until you see the desktop that you want to make current. Then release the Ctrl key to select that desktop.

- **Step through windows** (Alt+Tab) — To step through each of the windows that are running on the current desktop, hold down the Alt key and press the Tab key until you see the one you want. Then release the Alt key to select it.

- **Open Run Command box** (Alt+F2) — To open a box on the desktop that lets you type in a command and run it, hold the Alt key and press F2. Next, type the command in the box and press Enter to run it. You can also type a URL into this box to view a Web page.

- **Close the current window** (Alt+F4) — To close the current window, press Alt+F4.

- **Close another window** (Ctrl+Alt+Esc) — To close an open window on the desktop, press Ctrl+Alt+Esc. When a skull and cross bones appears as the pointer, move the pointer over the window you want to close and click the left mouse button. (This is a good technique for killing a window that has no borders or menu.)

- **Switch virtual desktops** (Ctrl+F1, F2, F3 or F4 key) — To step through virtual desktops, press and hold the Ctrl key and press F1, F2, F3, or F4 to go directly to desktop one, two, three, or four, respectively. You could do this for up to eight desktops, if you have that many configured.

- **Open window operation menu** (Alt+F3) — To open the operations menu for the active window, press Alt+F3. When the menu appears, move the arrow keys to select an action (Move, Size, Minimize, Maximize, and so on), then press Enter to select it.

Managing files with the Konqueror File Manager

The Konqueror File Manager helps elevate the KDE environment from just another X window manager to an integrated desktop that can compete with GUIs from Apple Computing or Microsoft. The features in Konqueror rival those that are offered by those user-friendly desktop systems. Figure 3-16 shows an example of the Konqueror File Manager window.

Some of Konqueror's greatest strengths over earlier file managers are the following:

- **Network desktop** — If your computer is connected to the Internet or a LAN, features built into Konqueror let you create links to files (using FTP) and Web pages (using HTTP) on the network and open them within the Konqueror window. Those links can appear as file icons in a Konqueror window or on the desktop. When a link is opened (single-click), the contents of the FTP site or Web page appears right in the Konqueror window.

- **Web browser interface** — The Konqueror interface works like Mozilla, Internet Explorer, or another Web browser in the way you select files, directories, and Web content. A single-click opens a file, link to a network resource, or application program. You can also open content by typing Web-style addresses in a Location box.

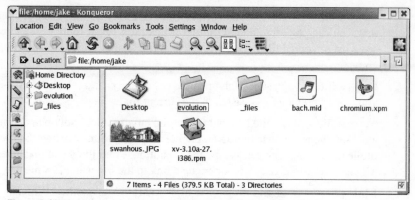

Figure 3-16: Konqueror provides a network-ready tool for managing files.

> **TIP:** Web pages that contain Java content will run by default in Konqueror starting with this release. To check that Java support is turned on, choose Settings → Configure Konqueror. From the Settings window, click Java & JavaScript and select the Java tab. To enable Java, click the Enable Java Globally box and click Apply.

- **File types and MIME types** — If you want a particular type of file to always be launched by a particular application, you can configure that file yourself. KDE already has dozens of MIME types defined that can automatically detect particular file and data types and start the right application. There are MIME types defined for audio, image, text, video, and a variety of other content types.

Of course, you can also perform many standard file manager functions with Konqueror. For manipulating files, you can use features like Select, Move, Cut, Paste, and Delete. You can search directories for files, create new items (files, folders, and links, to name a few), view histories of the files and Web sites you have opened, and create bookmarks.

Working with files

Because most of the ways of working with files in Konqueror are quite intuitive (by intention), I'll just give a quick rundown of how to do basic file manipulation:

- **Open a file** — Double-click a file. The file will open right in the Konqueror window, if possible, or in the default application set for the file type. You can also open a directory (to make it the current directory), application (to start the application), or link (to open the target of a link) in this way.

- **Choose an application** — Single-click to highlight it or right mouse button to open a menu. When you right-click a data file, select the Open With menu. The menu that appears shows which applications are set up to open the file.

- **Delete a file** — Right-click and select Delete. You are asked if you really want to delete the file. Click Yes to permanently delete it.

- **Copy a file** — Right-click and select Copy. This copies the file to your clipboard. After that, you can paste it to another folder. Click the Klipper (clipboard) icon in the panel to see a list of copied files. (See the "Move a file" bullet for a drag-and-drop method of copying.)

- **Paste a file** — Right-click (an open area of a folder) and select Paste. A copy of the file you copied previously is pasted in the current folder.

- **Move a file** — With the original folder and target folder both open on the desktop, press and hold the left mouse button on the file you want to move, drag the file to an open area of the new folder, and release the mouse button. From the menu that appears, click Move. (You could also copy or create a link to the file using this menu.)

- **Link a file** — Drag-and-drop a file from one folder to another. When the menu appears, click Link Here. (A linked file lets you access a file from a new location without having to make a copy of the original file. When you open the link, a pointer to the original file causes it to open.)

There are also several features for viewing information about the files and folders in your Konqueror windows:

- **View quick file information** — Position the mouse pointer over the file. When a mouse pointer is over a file in a Konqueror window, information appears in the window footer. This includes the filename, file size, and file type.

- **View hidden files** — Select View → Show Hidden Files. This allows you to see files that begin with a dot (.). Dot files tend to be used for configuration and don't generally need to be viewed in your daily work.

- **View file system tree** — Select View → View Mode → Tree View. This presents a tree view of your folder, displaying folders above the current folder in the file system. You can click a folder in the tree view to jump directly to that folder. There are also Multicolumn, Detailed List, and Text views available.

- **Change icon view** — Select View → Icon Size, and then choose Large, Medium, or Small to select the size of the icons that are displayed in the window. You can also choose Default Size, to return to the default icon size.

To act on a group of files at the same time, there are a couple of actions you can take. Choose Edit → Selection → Select. A pop-up window lets you match all (*) or any group of documents indicated by typing letters, numbers, and wildcard characters. Or, to select a group of files, click in an open area of the folder and drag the pointer across the files you want to select. All files within the box will be highlighted. When files are highlighted, you can move, copy, or delete the files as described earlier.

Searching for files

If you are looking for a particular file or folder, you can use the Konqueror Find feature. To open a Find window to search for a file, choose Tools → Find File and the Find box will appear in your Konqueror window. You could also start the kfind window by typing **kfind** from a Terminal window. Figure 3-17 shows the kfind window.

Simply type the name of the file you want to search for (in the Named text box) and the folder, including all subfolders, you want to search in (in the Look in text box). Then click the Find button. Use metacharacters, if you like, with your search. For example, search for * . rpm to find all files that end in . rpm or z* . doc to find all files that begin with z and end with . doc. You can also select to have the search be case-sensitive or click the Help button to get more information on searching.

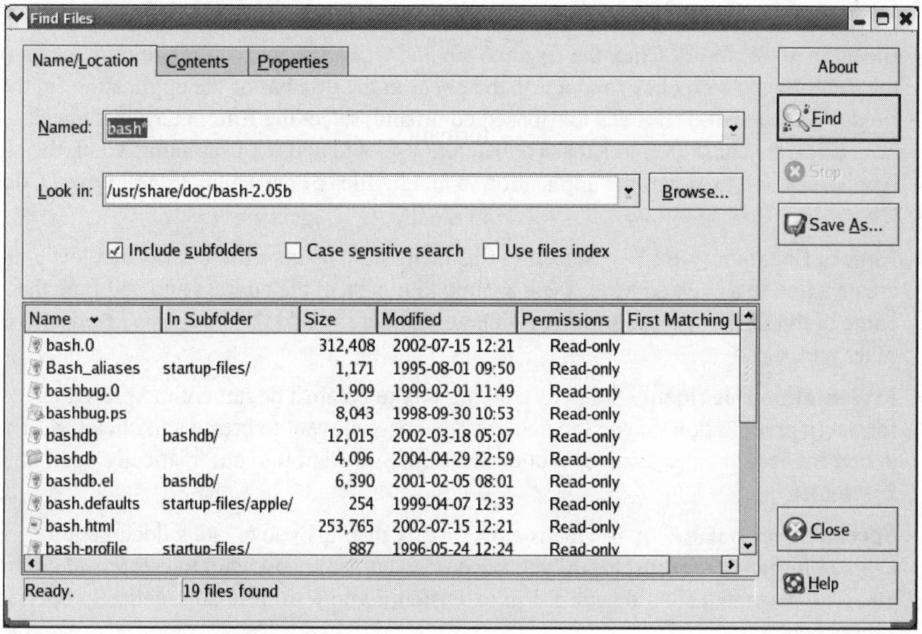

Figure 3-17: Search for files and folders from the kfind window.

To further limit your search, you can click the Date Range tab, then enter a date range (between), a number of months before today (during the previous x months), or the number of days before today (during the previous x days). Select the Advanced tab to choose to limit the search to files of a particular type (of Type), files that include text that you enter (Containing Text), or that are of a certain size (Size is) in kilobytes.

Creating new files and folders

You can create a variety of file types when using the Konqueror window. Choose Edit →
Create New, and select Folder (to create a new folder) or one of the following types under the
File submenu:

- **Illustration Document** — Opens a dialog box that lets you create a document in
  kontour format (an illustration). Type the document name you want to create and click
  OK. The document should have a `.kil` extension if you want it to automatically open in
  kontour.

- **HTML File** — Opens a dialog box that lets you type the name of an HTML file to
  create.

- **Link to Application** — Opens a window that lets you type the name of an application.
  Click the Permissions tab to set file permissions (Exec must be on if you want to run the
  file as an application). Click the Execute tab and type the name of the program to run (in
  the field: Execute on click) and a title to appear in the title bar of the application (in the
  field: Window Title). If it is a text-based command, select the Run in terminal check
  box. Click the check box to Run as a different user and add the user name. Click the
  Application tab to assign the application to handle files of particular MIME types. Click
  OK.

- **Link to Location (URL)** — Selecting this menu item opens a dialog box that lets you
  create a link to a Web address. Type a name to represent the address and and type the
  name of the URL (Web address) for the site. (Be sure to add the `http://`, `ftp://`, or
  other prefix.)

- **Presentation Document** — Opens a dialog box to create a document in kpresenter
  format (a presentation). Type the document name you want to create and click OK. The
  document should have a .kpr or .kpt extension if you want it to automatically open in
  kpresenter.

- **Spread Sheet Document** — Opens a dialog box that lets you create a document in
  kspread format (a spreadsheet). Type the document name you want to create and click
  OK. The document should have a .ksp extension if you want it to automatically open in
  kspread.

- **Text Document** — Opens a dialog box that enables you to create a text document in
  KWord. Type a filename for the text file and click OK. The document should have a .txt,
  .kwd, or .kwt extension if you want it to open automatically in Kword.

- **Text File** — Opens a dialog box that lets you create a document in text format and place
  it in the Konqueror window. Type the name of the text document to create and click OK.

Under the Device submenu, you can make the following selections:

- **CD-ROM Device** — Opens a dialog box that lets you type a new CD-ROM device
  name. Click the Device tab and type the device name (`/dev/cdrom`), the mount point

(such as /mnt/cdrom), and the file system type (you can use iso9660 for the standard CD-ROM file system, ext2 for Linux, or msdos for DOS). When the icon appears, you can open it to mount the CD-ROM and display its contents.

- **CDWRITER Device** — From the window that opens, enter the device name of your CD writer.

- **CD/DVD-ROM Device** — Opens a dialog box that lets you type a new CD-ROM or DVD-ROM device name. Click the Device tab and type the device name (/dev/cdrom), the mount point (such as /mnt/cdrom), and the file system type (you can use iso9660 for the standard CD-ROM file system, ext2 for Linux, or msdos for DOS). When the icon appears, you can open it to mount the CD-ROM or DVD-ROM and display its contents.

- **Camera Device** — In the dialog box that opens, identify the device name for the camera devices that provides access to your digital camera.

- **Floppy Device** — Opens a dialog box to type a new floppy name. Click the Device tab and type the device name (/dev/fd0), the mount point (such as /mnt/floppy), and the file system type (you can use auto to autodetect the contents, ext2 for Linux, or msdos for DOS). When the icon appears, open it to mount the floppy and display its contents.

- **Hard Disc Device** — Opens a dialog box that lets you type the name of a new hard disk or hard-disk partition. Click the Device tab and type the device (/dev/hda1), the mount point (such as /mnt/win), and the file system type (you can use auto to autodetect the contents, ext2 or ext3 for Linux, or vfat for a Windows file system). When the icon appears, you can open it to mount the file system and display its contents.

Creating MIME types and applications are described later in this chapter.

Using other browser features

Because Konqueror performs like a Web browser as well as a file manager, it includes several other browser features. For example, you can keep a bookmark list of Web sites you have visited, using the bookmarks feature. Any bookmarks that you add to your bookmarks list show up in the drop-down menu that appears when you click Bookmarks. Select from that list to return to a site. There are several ways to add and change your bookmarks list:

- **Add Bookmark** — To add the address of the page that is currently being displayed to your bookmark list, choose Bookmarks → Add Bookmark. The bookmark is silently added. The next time you click Bookmarks, you will see the bookmark you just added on the Bookmarks menu. In addition to Web addresses, you can also bookmark any file or folder.

- **Edit Bookmarks** —Select Bookmarks → Edit Bookmarks to open a tree view of your bookmarks. From the Bookmark Editor window that appears, you can change the URLs, the icon, or other features of the bookmark. There is also a nice feature that lets you check the status of the bookmark (that is, the address available).

- **New Bookmark Folder** — You can add a new folder of bookmarks to your Konqueror bookmarks list. To create a bookmarks folder, choose Bookmarks → New Folder. Then type a name for the new Bookmarks folder and click OK. The new bookmark folder appears on your bookmarks menu. You can add the current location to that folder by clicking on the folder name and selecting Add Bookmark.

Configuring Konqueror options

You can change many of the visual attributes of the Konqueror window. You can select which menu bars and toolbars appear. You can have any of the following bars appear on the Konqueror window: Menu bar, Toolbar, Extra Toolbar, Location Toolbar, Bookmark Toolbar. Select Settings and then click the menu item for the bar you want to have appear (or not appear). The bar appears when the checkmark is shown next to it.

You can modify a variety of options for Konqueror by choosing Settings → Configure Konqueror. The Konqueror Settings window appears, offering the following options:

- **Behavior (File)** — Changes file manager behavior.
- **Appearance** — Changes file manager fonts and colors.
- **Previews & Meta-Data** — An icon in a Konqueror folder can be made to ressemble the contents of the file it represents. For example, if the file is a JPEG image, the icon representing the file could be a small version of that image. Using the Previews features, you can limit the size of the file used (1MB is the default) since many massive files could take too long to refresh on the screen. You can also select to have any thumbnail embedded in a file to be used as the icon or have the size of the icon reflect the shape of the image used.
- **File Associations** — Describes which programs to launch for each file type.
- **Web Behavior**— Click the Behavior (Browser) button to open a window to configure the Web browser features of Konqueror. By enabling Form Completion, Konqueror can save form data you type and, at a later time, fill that information into other forms. If your computer has limited resources, you can speed up page display by clearing the Automatically load images check box or by disabling animations.
- **Java and JavaScript** — Use this selection to enable or disable Java and JavaScript content contained in Web pages in your Konqueror window.
- **Fonts** — Choose which fonts to use, by default, for various fonts needed on Web pages (standard font, fixed font, serif font, sans serif font, cursive font, and fantasy font). The serif fonts are typically used in body text, while sans serif fonts are often used in headlines. You can also set the Minimum and Medium font sizes.

- **Web Shortcuts** — Click the Web Shortcuts button to see a list of keyword shortcuts you can use to go to different Internet sites. For example, follow the word "ask" with a search string to search the Ask Jeeves (www.ask.com) Web site. (This feature doesn't appear to be working at the moment.)

- **History Sidebar** — Click here to modify the behavior of the list of sites you have visited (the history). By default, the most recent 500 URLs are stored, and after 90 days, a URL is dropped from the list. You will also find a button to clear your history. (To view your history list in Konqueror, open the left side panel, then click the tiny scroll icon.)

- **Cookies** — Click the Cookies button to select whether or not cookies are enabled in Konqueror. By default, you are asked to confirm that it is okay each time a Web site tries to create or modify a cookie. You can change that to either accept or reject all cookies. You can also set policies for acceptance or rejection of cookies based on host and domain names.

- **Cache** — Click the Cache button to indicate how much space on your hard disk can be used to store the sites you have visited (based on the value in the Disk Cache Size field).

- **Proxy** — Click the Proxy button if you are accessing the Internet through a proxy server. You need to enter the address and port number of the computer providing HTTP and/or FTP proxy services.

- **Stylesheets** — Click the Stylesheets button to select whether to use the default stylesheet, a user-defined stylesheet, or a custom stylesheet. The stylesheet sets the font family, font sizes, and colors that are applied to Web pages. (This won't change particular font requests made by the Web page.) If you select a custom stylesheet, click the Customize tab to customize your own fonts and colors.

- **Crypto** — Click the Crypto button to display a list of secure certificates that can be accepted by the Konqueror browser. By default, Secure Socket Layer (SSL) version 2 and 3 certificates are accepted, as is TLS support (if supported by the server). You can also select to be notified when you are entering or leaving a secure Web site.

- **Browser Identification** — Click the Browser Identification button to set how Konqueror identifies itself when it accesses a Web site. By default, Konqueror tells the Web site that it is the Mozilla Web browser. You can select Konqueror to appear as different Web browsers to specific sites. You must sometimes do this when a site denies you access because you do not have a specific type of browser (even though Konqueror may be fully capable of displaying the content).

- **Plugins** — Click the Plugins button to see a list of directories that Konqueror will search to find plug-ins. Konqueror can also scan your computer to find plug-ins that are installed for other browsers in other locations.

- **Performance** — Select the Performance button to see configuration settings that can be used to improve Konqueror performance. You can preload an instance after KDE startup or minimize memory usage.

Creating an Image Gallery with Konqueror

There's a neat feature in Konqueror that lets you create a quick image gallery. The feature takes a directory of images, creates thumbnails for each one, and generates an HTML (Web) page. The HTML page includes a title you choose, all image thumbnails arranged on a page, and links to the larger images. Here's how you do it:

1. Add images you want in your gallery to any folder (for example, /home/jake/images). Make sure they are sized, rotated, and cropped the way you like before beginning. (Try The Gimp for manipulating your images by typing **gimp&** from a Terminal.)

2. Open the folder in Konqueror (for example, type **/home/jake/images** in the Location box).

3. Click Tools → Create Image Gallery. The Create Image Gallery window appears.

4. Type a title for the image gallery into the Page Title box. You can also select other attributes of the gallery, such as the number of rows, information about the image to appear on the page (name, size, and dimension), the fonts, and the colors to use.

5. Click OK.

Konqueror generates the thumbnails and adds them to the thumbs directory. The image gallery page itself opens and is saved to the images.html file. (Select the Folders button to save the gallery under a different name. You can also have Konqueror create galleries in recursive subfolders to a depth you choose.) You can now copy the entire contents of this directory to a Web server and publish your pictures on the Internet. Figure 3-18 shows an example of a Konqueror image gallery.

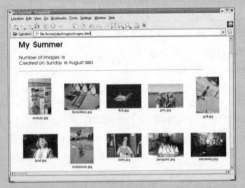

Figure 3-18: Create an image gallery in Konqueror.

Managing windows

If you have a lot of windows open at the same time, tricks for organizing and managing the windows on your desktop are very helpful. KDE helps you out by maintaining window lists you can work with and shortcuts for keeping the windows in order.

Using the taskbar

When you open a window, a button representing the window appears in the taskbar at the bottom of the screen. Here is how you can manage windows from the taskbar:

- **Toggle windows** — You can left-click any running task in the taskbar to toggle between opening the window and minimizing it.

- **Move windows** — You can move a window from the current desktop to any other virtual desktop. Right-click any task in the taskbar, select To Desktop, then select any desktop number. The window moves to that desktop.

All the windows that are running, regardless of which virtual desktop you are on, appear in the taskbar. If there are multiple windows of the same type shown as a single task, you can right-click that task; then select "All to Desktop" to move all related windows to the desktop you pick.

Uncluttering the desktop

If your windows are scattered willy-nilly all over the desktop, here are a couple of ways you can make your desktop's appearance a little neater:

- **Unclutter windows** — Right-click the desktop, and then click Windows → Unclutter Windows on the menu. All windows that are currently displayed on the desktop are lined up along the left side of the screen (or aligned with other windows), from the top down.

- **Cascade windows** — Right-click the desktop, and then click Windows → Cascade windows on the menu. The windows are aligned as they are with the Uncluttered selection, except that the windows are each indented starting from the upper-left corner.

Moving windows

The easiest way to move a window from one location to another is to place the pointer on the window's title bar; while holding down the mouse button, move the mouse so the window goes to a new location, and release the mouse button to drop the window. Another way to do it is to click the window menu button (top left corner of the title bar), click Move, move the mouse to relocate the window, and then click again to place it.

If somehow the window gets stuck in a location where the title bar is off the screen, there is a way you can move it back to where you want it. Hold down the Alt key and press the left mouse button in the inner window. Then move the window where you want it and release.

Resizing windows

To resize a window, place the pointer over a corner or side of the window border, and, while holding down the mouse button, move it until it is the size you want. Grabbing a corner lets you resize vertically and horizontally at the same time. Grabbing the side lets you resize in only one direction.

You can also resize a window from the window menu button. Click the window menu button (top left corner of the title bar) and select Size. Move the mouse until the window is resized and click to leave it there.

Pinning windows on top or bottom

You can set a window to always stay on top of all other windows or always stay under them. Keeping a window on top can be useful for a small window that you want to always refer to (such as a clock or a small TV viewing window). To pin a window on top of the desktop, click in the window title bar. From the menu that appears, select Advanced → Keep Above Others. Likewise, to keep the window on the bottom, select Advanced → Keep Below Others.

Using virtual desktops

To give you more space to run applications than will fit on your physical screen, KDE gives you access to several virtual desktops at the same time. Using the 1, 2, 3, and 4 buttons on the Panel, you can easily move between the different desktops. Just click the one you want.

If you want to move an application from one desktop to another, you can do so from the window menu. Click the window menu button for the window you want to move, click To Desktop, then select Desktop 1, 2, 3, or 4. The window will disappear from the current desktop and move to the one you selected.

Configuring the desktop

If you want to change the look, feel, or behavior of your KDE desktop, the best place to start is the KDE Control Center. The KDE Control Center window lets you configure dozens of attributes associated with colors, fonts, backgrounds, and screen savers used by KDE. You can also change attributes relating to how you work with windows and files.

To open the KDE Control Center from the desktop, open a Terminal window and type kcontrol. The KDE Control Center window appears, as shown in Figure 3-19.

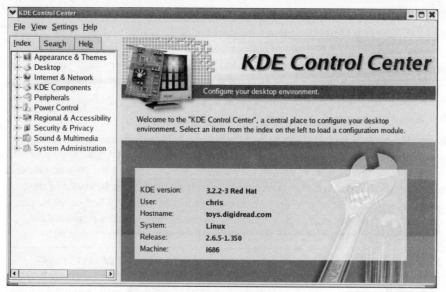

Figure 3-19: Configure your desktop from the KDE Control Center.

Click the plus (+) sign next to topics you want to configure. Then select the particular item you want to configure. The following sections describe some of the features you can configure from the KDE Control Center.

Changing the display

There are several ways you can change the look-and-feel of your desktop display. Under the Appearance & Themes topic (click the plus sign), you can change Background, Colors, Fonts, Icons, Launch Feedback, Panel, Screen Saver, Style, Theme Manager, and Window Decoration.

Here are a few of the desktop features you may want to change:

- **Change the background** — Under the Appearance & Themes heading in the KDE Control Center, select Background. You can remove the checkmark next to Common Background to choose to have a common background for all four of your virtual desktops or assign backgrounds to individual desktops.

  First select the Mode: Flat (single color); Pattern (two colors and click Setup to select a pattern); Background Program (click Setup to choose a program to run on the background); Horizontal Gradient (two colors that fade from left to right); Vertical Gradient (two colors that fade from top to bottom); Pyramid Gradient (two colors that fade from outside in); Pipecross Gradient (two colors that fade from the outside to a cross in the middle); and Elliptic Gradient (two colors that fade from outside to an ellipse in the middle).

If you prefer to use a wallpaper on the background, click the Wallpaper tab and select a desktop. Choose a Mode (to indicate the position of the wallpaper) and click the Wallpaper list box to scroll down to choose the wallpaper. If you have a JPEG image you would like to use instead, click the Browse button to select the image you want from your file system. Click the Multiple check box if you want to assign several wallpapers that change at set intervals.

Click Apply to apply your selections.

- **Change the screensaver** — Under the Appearance & Themes heading, select Screen Saver. From the window that appears, select from about 160 different screen savers. My favorite is Slide Show, where you can have a slide show of images for your screen saver. Click Setup to identify an image directory or otherwise modify the behavior of the screen saver. Under settings, select how many minutes of inactivity before the screen saver turns on. You can also click Require Password to require that a password be entered before you can access your display after the screen saver has come on.

> **TIP:** If you are working in a place where you want your desktop to be secure, be sure to turn on the Require Password feature. This prevents others from gaining access to your computer when you forget to lock it or shut it off. If you have any virtual terminals open, switch to them and type **vlock** to lock each of them as well. (You need to install the vlock package if the `vlock` command isn't available.)

- **Change fonts** — You can assign different fonts to different places in which fonts appear on the desktop. Under the Appearance and Themes heading, select Fonts. Select one of the categories of fonts (General, Fixed width, Toolbar, Menu, Window title, Taskbar and Desktop fonts). Then click the Choose check box to select a font from the Select Font list box that you want to assign to that category. If the font is available, you will see an example of the text in the Sample text box.

> **TIP:** To use 100 dpi fonts, you need to add an entry for 100 dpi fonts to `/etc/X11/xorg.conf` file. After you make that change, you need to restart the X server for it to take effect.

Other attributes you can change for the selected fonts are size (in points) and character set (to select an ISO standard character set). Select Apply to apply the changes.

- **Change the colors** — Under the Appearance & Themes heading in the KDE Control Center, select Colors. The window that appears lets you change the color of selected items on the desktop. Select a whole color scheme from the Color Scheme list box. Or select an item from the Widget color box to change a particular item. Items you can change include text, backgrounds, links, buttons, and title bars.

Changing panel attributes

For most people, the Panel is the place where they select which desktop is active and which applications are run. You can change some of the behavior of the panel from the KDE Control

Center. (Select Panels under the Appearance & Themes heading.) However, you can do more to modify the panel from the panel itself.

Right-click any empty space on your panel, and then select Configure Panel. You can change these features from the Settings window that appears:

- **Arrangement** — Change the location of the panel by clicking on Top, Left, Bottom, or Right in the Panel Location list box. The Panel Style selection lets you change the size of the Panel from Medium to Tiny, Small, or Large.

- **Hiding** — Certain selections allow you to autohide the panel or use hide buttons. Under the Hide Mode heading, choose whether to hide only when a panel hiding button is clicked or to hide automatically after a set number of seconds when the cursor is not in the panel area. You can also show or not show hiding buttons. Sliders let you select the delay and speed at which panels and buttons are hidden.

- **Menus** — Unlike with the GNOME main menu, you have the ability to manipulate the main menu from the GUI in KDE. Click the Edit K Menu button. The KDE Menu editor that appears lets you cut, copy, paste, remove, and modify submenus and applications from your main menu.

Adding application launchers and MIME types

You want to be able to quickly access the applications that you use most often. One of the best ways to make that possible is to add icons to the panel or the desktop that can launch the applications you need with a single click. Procedures for adding applications to the panel and desktop are described in the following sections.

Adding applications to the panel

You can add any KDE application to the KDE panel quite easily. Here's how:

1. Right-click an open space on the panel.
2. Choose Add → Application Button.
3. Select one of the categories of applications.
4. Click any application from the category you selected (or select Add this menu to add the whole menu of applications).

An icon representing the application should immediately appear on the panel. (If the panel seems a bit crowded, you might want to remove some applications you don't use.) At this point, you can change any properties associated with the application by right-clicking the application icon in the panel and then selecting Preferences. Here are the properties you can change:

- **General** — Lets you change the filename associated with the icon. (This is not recommended, since the filename is not exposed from the panel.) You can also click the icon on this tab to select a different icon to represent it.

- **Permissions** — Lets you change read, write, and execute permissions associated with the application. Because this is a special KDE link file (.kdelnk or .desktop), it only needs to be readable by all and not executable.

- **Execute** — Lets you change the complete command line that is run when the command is executed, as well as the icon representing the application. Click Run in terminal if the application is a text-based, and not a GUI-based, application.

- **Application** — Lets you add a Comment to the application. This comment is displayed as a tool tip when the pointer is positioned over the icon. The Name you enter is what appears in the title bar for the application. If you want the application to be launched if a particular type of data (MIME Type) is encountered, you can click a File Type in the right text box, then click the left arrow button to move the MIME Type to the left box.

If you decide later that you no longer want this application to be available on the panel, right-click it and click Remove. To move it to a different location on the panel, right-click it, click Move, move it to where you want it on the panel, and click again.

Adding applications to the desktop

To add an application to the desktop, you can use the desktop menu. Here's how:

1. Right-click an open area of the desktop.

2. Select Create New → Link to Application from the menu.

3. In the Properties window that appears, replace the Program name. (This name will appear under the icon on the desktop.)

4. Add Permissions, Execute, and Application information for the application as described in the previous section about adding applications to the panel. In this case, much of the information will have to be entered manually. You will at least want to enter the command to run, along with any options, on the Execute tab. You will probably also want to enter the Comment and Name on the Application tab. Click OK to save the application icon to the desktop.

If you decide later that you no longer want this application to be available on the desktop, right-click it and click Delete or Move to Trash.

Troubleshooting Your Desktop

If your desktop is not functioning properly (or at all) it may be that your video card was not configured properly. This section helps you get your video card configured properly and your desktop up and running smoothly.

GUI doesn't work at start-up

If Fedora has been successfully installed (along with the desired desktop environment) but the GUI wasn't set to start at boot time, you may only see a simple text-based login prompt when you start Fedora. This login prompt may look something like this:

```
Fedora Core release 2
Kernel 2.6.5 on an i686
YourComputer login:
```

Log in as the root user. As noted earlier, you can check if you have a GUI that is at least working well enough for you to correct it. Type the following command:

```
# startx
```

If the desktop works fine when you type **startx**, you might want to change to a graphical login, so the GUI starts automatically every time. See the "What Happens During Desktop Startup" sidebar for information on booting to a GUI.

If your GUI is so distorted you can't even see to correct it, switch to a virtual terminal to correct the problem. For example, hold the Ctrl and Alt keys, and press F2. You will see a plain text login prompt. Log in as root user and type **init 3** to make the garbled GUI login screen go away. Then you can try tuning your video card as described in the following section.

What Happens During Desktop Startup?

The X server and graphical login screen is started by the `prefdm` script. By default, the login screen is displayed by the GNOME display manager (`gdm` command), which handles both logging in and starting the desktop environment for your console monitor, as well as graphical logins from other computers and X terminals. (If you don't like the way the login screen appears, run `gdmsetup` as root user. It will let you change the login greeter screen or even allow no-password logins.)

The `prefdm` script is launched only if the run level in the `/etc/inittab` file is set to 5, as follows:

```
id:5:initdefault:
```

If the `initdefault` state is 3, the system boots to a text-based login prompt. See Chapter 12 for information on Linux run states and start-up processes.

If you are unable to get the video card and monitor configured properly, or if you don't need a GUI, you can configure the computer to start up in text mode. To do this using any shell text editor (such as the `vi` command described in Chapter 3), change the `initdefault` line in the `/etc/inittab` file from `id:5:initdefault:` to `id:3:initdefault`.

If you prefer to have Fedora boot to a GUI, change the 3 to a 5.

> **TIP:** Switching virtual terminals is a great way to get out of a GUI that is broken or stuck and run the commands you need to fix a problem. You can use any function key from F1 through F8 with Ctrl+Alt to switch terminals. The GUI itself is probably on the F7 virtual terminal. Linux experts use virtual terminals during Fedora installation to debug a problem or during startup to view text startup messages.

Tuning your video card and monitor

If your GUI is starting up but needs some tuning (to get better resolution, more colors, or to fix flickering), you can use the Display Settings window to fix your desktop. For the current Fedora version, the Display Settings window was enhanced so that you can use it from a command with no GUI running. The next sections describe how to run the Display Settings window, then how to review the resulting `xorg.conf` file to understand your settings.

Running the Display Settings window

Red Hat recently replaced the `Xconfigurator` tool with a new Display Settings window (`system-config-display` command). This window lets you set the most basic functions relating to your display, monitor, and video card. The Display Settings window is easy-to-use and no longer requires a running X desktop to use it.

To open the Display Settings window from the Red Hat menu, click System Settings → Display. To open that window from a text prompt (even with no GUI running), type **system-config-display** (as root). The Display Settings window appears, as shown in Figure 3-20.

From the Settings tab, you can try different resolutions (screen width and height in pixels) and color depth (from 256 colors to millions of color). Click the Hardware tab to try to configure your monitor and video card. Click the Dual head tab if you have a video card that supports two monitors that you can use side-by-side with Fedora. Click OK to save your changes.

Here are a few tips for using the Display Settings window:

- If you know your monitor type, but it is not being detected, click the Hardware tab and then click Configure. You can select the monitor from a list of monitors (by manufacturer) or, if it's not on the list, enter information about the monitor's horizontal and vertical sync rates from the manufacturer's instructions.

- If you don't know the vertical and horizontal sync rates, you can choose a generic monitor from the list. You could simply choose a generic CRT or Generic LCD at a resolution you would expect the monitor to support.

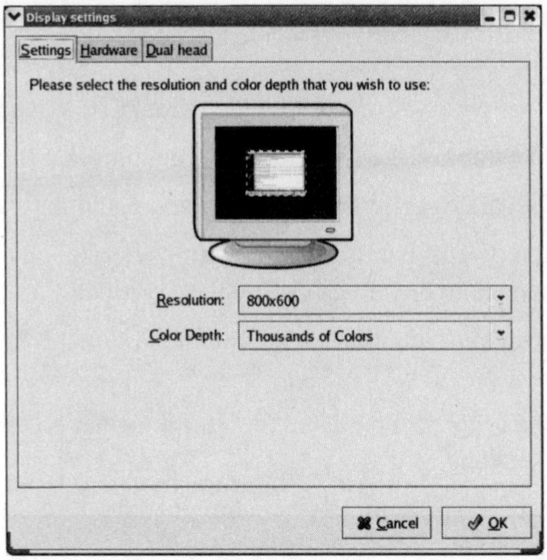

Figure 3-20: Use the Display Settings window to configure basic desktop, video card, and monitor settings.

Changes made in the Display Settings window result in the creation of a new /etc/X11/xorg.conf file. The next section describes what the xorg.conf file contains.

TIP: If the Display Settings window fails to create a working xorg.conf file, you can try another approach. With no GUI on as root user, type the following commands from a shell:

```
# Xorg -configure
# X -xf86config /root/xorg.conf.new
```

The first line creates xorg.conf.new in the /root directory. The second tries to start your GUI with that new config file. If the GUI works, copy /root/xorg.conf.new to /etc/X11/xorg.conf. You may need to run system-config-mouse to get the mouse working properly after this.

Understanding the xorg.conf file

For Fedora Core 2, the XFree86 X server was replaced by the X server from X.Org. Although that change should be invisible to most users, if you like to change X settings directly, you need to know that the main X configuration file is now /etc/X11/xorg.conf and not /etc/X11/XF86Config.

The xorg.conf file (located in the /etc/X11 directory) contains definitions used by the X server to use your video card, keyboard, mouse, and monitor. In general, novice users should not edit this file directly. For some video cards, however, manual configuration may be required to get the card working properly.

The following is a description of the basic information contained in the xorg.conf file:

- **ServerLayout section** — Binds input and output devices for your X session. Lets you set server definitions for different X servers (if necessary).

- **Module section** — Describes which X server modules should be loaded.

- **Files section** — Sets the locations of the RGB (color) , modules and fonts databases.

- **InputDevice sections** — Separate sections identify keyboard and mouse input devices.

- **Monitor section** — Sets the type of monitor, along with its horizontal sync rate, vertical refresh rate, and settings needed to operate at different resolutions.

- **Device section** — Identifies your video card and, optionally, video RAM and clock information for the chipset.

- **Screen section** — Binds the graphics board and monitor information to be referenced later by the ServerLayout section.

- **Keyboard section** — Sets keyboard settings, including the layout of the keyboard and the way certain key sequences are mapped to the keyboard.

- **Pointer section** — Selects the pointer you are using (typically a mouse linked to /dev/mouse). Also sets speed and button emulation, when appropriate.

- **DRI** — Provides information for Direct Rendering Infrastructure (used for accelerated 3D graphics).

Configuring video cards for gaming

Some games and video players require special features to work properly (or at all, in some cases). For games that require 3D hardware acceleration, including some that run under TransGaming's WineX, TransGaming recommends using NVIDIA GeForce Graphics cards.

Because only basic NVIDIA video card drivers are included in Fedora (NVIDIA's own drivers are not open source), you need to get NVIDIA drivers yourself to use those cards for gaming. You can download NVIDIA drivers for Linux from:

```
www.nvidia.com/object/linux_display_archive.html
```

Select the latest drivers from the list (look for version 1.0-5336 or later). Download and install the drivers as described.

Games that don't require 3D hardware acceleration should work fine with most video cards that are supported by the X.Org X server drivers.

> **TIP:** To use hardware DRI acceleration on Voodoo 3 cards, you must have your display set to use 16bpp resolution. On Voodoo 5 cards, only 16bpp and 24bpp resolutions are supported.

Getting more information

If you tried configuring X and you still have a server that crashes or has a garbled display, your video card may either be unsupported or may require special configuration. Here are several locations you can check for further information:

- **X.Org** (www.x.org) — The latest information about the X servers that come with Fedora is available from the X.Org Web site. X.Org is the freeware version of X recently used by many major Linux distributions to replace the XFree86 X server.

- **Red Hat Support** (www.redhat.com/support) — Search the Red Hat support database for the model of your card. There may already be reports of problems (and hopefully fixes) related to your card.

- **X documentation** — README files that are specific to different types of video cards are delivered with the X.Org X server. Visit the X doc directory (/usr/X11R6/lib/X11/doc) for a README file specific to the type of video card (or more specifically, the video chipset) you are using. A lot of good information can also be found on the xorg.conf man page (type **man** xorg.conf).

Summary

The X Window System provides the basis for most graphical user interfaces available for Fedora and other Linux systems today. Although X provides the framework for running and sharing applications, the GNOME and KDE desktop environments, along with a window manager and theme, provide the look-and-feel of your desktop.

Using various configuration files and commands, you can change nearly every aspect of your graphical environment. Backgrounds can be assigned a single color or can be filled with single or tiled graphic images. Menus can be changed or enhanced. Multiple virtual workspaces can be used and managed.

After reading this chapter, you should feel comfortable working with the GNOME and KDE desktops. The next chapter should help you work from the traditional command line interface, referred to as the shell.

Chapter 4

Using Linux Commands

This chapter presents a view of Linux from the shell. The *shell* is a command-line interpreter that lets you access some of the most critical Linux tools. The shell is powerful, complex, and almost completely unintuitive.

Although, at first, it isn't obvious how to use the shell, with the right help you can quickly learn many of the most important shell features. This chapter is your guide to working with the Linux system commands, processes, and file system from the shell. It describes the shell environment and helps you tailor it to your needs. It also describes how to use and move around the file system.

The Shell Interface

There are several ways to get to a shell interface in Linux. Common ways are:

- **No GUI** — If your Linux system has no GUI (or one that isn't working at the moment), you must enter commands from the shell.

- **A Terminal window** — With the desktop GUI running, you can open a Terminal window (right-click on the desktop, then click Open Terminal) to start a shell. You can begin typing commands into the Terminal window.

If you are using a shell interface, the first thing you see is the shell prompt. The default prompt for a user is simply a dollar sign:

```
$
```

The default prompt for the root user is a pound sign (also called a hash mark):

```
#
```

For most Linux systems, the $ or # prompts are preceded by your user name, system name, and current directory name. So, for example, a login prompt for the user named jake on a computer named pine with /tmp as the current directory would appear as:

```
[jake@pine tmp]$
```

You can change the prompt to display any characters you like. You could use as your prompt the current directory, the date, the local computer name, or any string of characters. (To configure your prompt, see the "Setting your prompt" section later in this chapter.)

Although there are a tremendous number of features available with the shell, it's easy to begin by just typing a few commands. Try some of the commands shown in the remainder of this section to become familiar with your current shell environment.

> **TIP:** If, instead of a shell prompt, you see a GUI when you log in, you can still try out the shell commands shown in the next section. To access a shell from the GUI, you can open a Terminal window by right-clicking on your desktop and selecting Open Terminal.

In the examples that follow, the $ or # symbols indicate a prompt. The prompt is followed by the command that you type and then by Enter or Return (depending on your keyboard). The lines that follow show the output that results from the command.

Checking your login session

When you log in to a Linux system, Linux views you as having a particular identity. That identity includes your user name, group name, user ID, and group ID. Linux also keeps track of your login session: it knows when you logged in, how long you have been idle, and where you logged in from.

To find out information about your identity, use the id command as follows:

```
$ id
  uid=501(chris) gid=105(sales) groups=105(sales),4(adm),7(lp)
```

This shows that the user name is chris, which is represented by the numeric user ID (uid) 501. Here, the primary group for chris is called sales, which has a group ID (gid) of 105. Chris also belongs to other groups called adm (gid 4) and lp (gid 7). These names and numbers represent the permissions that chris has to access computer resources. (Permissions are described later in this chapter in the section on working with files.)

You can see information about your current login session by using the who command. In the following example, the -m option tells the who command to print information about the current user, -u says to add information about idle time and the process ID, and -H asks that a header be printed:

```
$ who -umH
NAME         LINE         TIME                 IDLE      PID    COMMENT
chris        tty1         Jan 13 20:57           .       2013
```

The output from this who command shows that the user name is chris. Here, chris is logged in on tty1 (which is the monitor connected to the computer), and his login session began at 20:57 on January 13. The IDLE time shows how long the shell has been open without any command being typed (the dot indicates that it is currently active). COMMENT would show the name of the remote computer the user had logged in from, if that user had logged in from another computer on the network, or the name of the local X display if you were using a Terminal window (such as :0.0).

Checking directories and permissions

Associated with each shell is a location in the Linux file system known as the *current* or *working directory.* As previously mentioned, each user has a directory that is identified as the user's home directory. When you first log in to Linux, you begin with your home directory as the current directory.

When you request to open or save a file, your shell uses the current directory as the point of reference. Simply give a filename when you save a file, and it will be placed in the current directory. Alternatively, you can identify a file by its relation to the current directory (relative path). Or you can ignore the current directory and identify a file by the full directory hierarchy that locates it (absolute path). The structure and use of the file system is described in detail later in this chapter.

To find out what your current directory is, type the pwd command:

```
$ pwd
/usr/bin
```

In this example, the current/working directory is /usr/bin. To find out the name of your home directory, type the echo command, followed by the $HOME variable:

```
$ echo $HOME
/home/chris
```

In the preceding example, the home directory is /home/chris. To get back to your home directory, you can simply type the change directory (cd) command. Although cd, followed by a directory name, changes the current directory to the directory that you choose, simply typing cd (with no directory name) takes you to your home directory:

```
$ cd
```

At this point, list the contents of your home directory, using the ls command. Either you can type the full path to your home directory to list its contents, or you can use the ls command without a directory name to list the contents of the current directory. Using the -a option to ls enables you to view the hidden files (dot files) as well as all other files. With the -l option, you can see a long, detailed list of information on each file. (You can put multiple single-letter options together after a single dash, for example, -la.)

```
$ ls -la /home/chris
total 158
drwxrwxrwx    2   chris   sales    1024   May 12 13:55 .
drwxr-xr-x    3   root    root     1024   May 10 01:49 ..
-rw-------    1   chris   sales    2204   May 18 21:30 .bash_history
-rw-r--r--    1   chris   sales      24   May 10 01:50 .bash_logout
-rw-r--r--    1   chris   sales     230   May 10 01:50 .bash_profile
-rw-r--r--    1   chris   sales     124   May 10 01:50 .bashrc
drw-r--r--    1   chris   sales    4096   May 10 01:50 .kde
-rw-rw-r--    1   chris   sales  149872   May 11 22:49 letter
```

Displaying a long list (-l option) of the contents of your home directory shows you more about file sizes and directories. Directories such as the current directory (.) and the directory above the current directory (..) are noted as directories by the letter d at the beginning of each entry. In this case, dot (.) represents /home/chris and two dots (..), which is also referred to as the parent directory, represents /home. The /home directory is owned by root. All other files are owned by the user chris (who belongs to the sales group).

The file or directory names shown on the right are mostly dot (.) files that are used to store GUI properties (.kde directory) or shell properties (.bash files). The only non-dot file shown in this example is the one named letter. At the beginning of each line are the permissions set for each file. (Permissions and configuring shell property files are described later in this chapter.) Other information in the listing includes the size of each file in bytes (column 4) and the date and time each file was most recently modified (column 5).

Checking system activity

In addition to being a multiuser operating system, Linux is also a multitasking system. *Multitasking* means that many programs can be running at the same time. An instance of a running program is referred to as a *process*. Linux provides tools for listing running processes, monitoring system usage, and stopping (or killing) processes when necessary.

The most common utility for checking running processes is the ps command. With ps, you can see which programs are running, the resources they are using, and who is running them. The following is an example of the ps command:

```
$ ps -au
USER    PID %CPU %MEM  VSZ    RSS   TTY    STAT START   TIME COMMAND
root    2146 0.0  0.8 1908   1100  ttyp0   S    14:50   0:00 login -- jake
jake    2147 0.0  0.7 1836   1020  ttyp0   S    14:50   0:00 -bash
jake    2310 0.0  0.7 2592    912  ttyp0   R    18:22   0:00 ps -au
```

In this example, the -a option asks to show processes of all users who are associated with your current terminal, and the -u option asks that user names be shown, as well as other information such as the time the process started and memory and CPU usage. The concept of terminal comes from the old days, when people worked exclusively from character terminals, so a terminal typically represented a single person at a single screen. Now you can have many "terminals" on one screen by opening multiple Terminal windows.

On this shell session, there isn't much happening. The first process shows that the user named jake logged in to the login process (which is controlled by the root user). The next process shows that jake is using a bash shell and has just run the ps -au command. The terminal device ttyp0 is being used for the login session. The STAT column represents the state of the process, with R indicating a currently running process and S representing a sleeping process.

The USER column shows the name of the user who started the process. Each process is represented by a unique ID number referred to as a process ID (PID). (You can use the PID if you ever need to kill a runaway process.) The %CPU and %MEM columns show the percentage of the processor and random access memory, respectively, that the process is consuming. VSZ (virtual set size) shows size of the image process (in kilobytes), and RSS (resident set size) shows the size of the program in memory. START shows the time the process began running, and TIME shows the cumulative system time used.

Many processes running on a computer are not associated with a terminal. A normal Linux system has many processes running in the background. Background system processes perform such tasks as logging system activity or listening for data coming in from the network. They are often started when Fedora boots up and runs continuously until it shuts down. To see and thereby monitor all the processes running on your Fedora system, type:

```
$ ps -aux | less
```

I added the pipe (|) and the less command to ps -aux to allow you to page through the many processes that will appear on your screen. Use the spacebar to page through and type **q** to end the list. You can also use the arrow keys to move one line at a time through the output. A pipe lets you direct the output of one command to be the input of the next command.

Exiting the shell

To exit the shell when you are done, either type **exit** or press Ctrl+D. If you are exiting from your login shell (the shell that started when you first logged in), type **logout** to exit the shell.

I just showed a few commands designed to familiarize you quickly with your Linux system. There are hundreds of other commands that you can try that are contained in directories such as /bin and /usr/bin. There are also administrative commands in /sbin or /usr/sbin directories. Many of these commands are described in the remainder of this chapter.

Understanding the Linux Shell

Before icons and windows took over computer screens, you typed commands to run most computers. On UNIX systems, from which Linux was derived, the program used to interpret and manage commands was referred to as the shell.

The shell provides a way to run programs, work with the file system, compile computer code, and manage the computer. Although the shell is less intuitive than common GUIs, most Linux experts consider the shell to be much more powerful than GUIs. Because shells have been around for so long, many advanced features have been built into them. Many old-school Linux administrators and programmers primarily use a GUI as a way to open lots of shells.

The Linux shell illustrated in this chapter is called the *bash* shell, which stands for Bourne Again SHell. The name is derived from the fact that bash is compatible with the first UNIX shell: the Bourne shell (represented by the sh command). Other popular shells include the C Shell (*csh*), which is popular among BSD UNIX users, and the Korn Shell (*ksh*), which is popular among UNIX System V users. Linux also has a *tcsh* shell (a C shell look-alike) and an *ash* shell (another Bourne shell look-alike).

> **NOTE**: While you can invoke the Bourne shell with /bin/sh, the command actually runs the bash shell in sh compatibility mode. Running /bin/sh produces a shell that behaves more like sh than bash, but you will probably be able to use bash scripting concepts that the real Bourne shell wouldn't recognize.

Although most Linux users have a preference for one shell or another, when you know how to use one shell, you can quickly learn any of the others by occasionally referring to the shell's man page (for example, type **man bash**). In Linux, the bash shell is roughly compatible with the sh shell.

Using the Shell in Linux

When you type a command in a shell, you can also include other characters that change or add to how the command works. In addition to the command itself, these are some of the other items that you can type on a shell command line:

- **Options** — Most commands have one or more options you can add to change their behavior. Options typically consist of a single letter, preceded by a dash. You can also often combine several options after a single dash. For example, the command ls -la lists the contents of the current directory. The -l asks for a detailed (long) list of information, and the -a asks that files beginning with a dot (.) also be listed. When a single option consists of a word, it is usually preceded by a double dash (--). For example, to use the help option on many commands, you would enter --help on the command line.

- **Arguments** — Many commands also accept arguments after any options are entered. An argument is an extra piece of information, such as a filename, that can be used by the command. For example, cat /etc/passwd displays the contents of the /etc/passwd file on your screen. In this case, /etc/passwd is the argument.

- **Environment variables** — The shell itself stores information that may be useful to the user's shell session in what are called *environment variables*. Examples of environment variables include $SHELL (which identifies the shell you are using), $PS1 (which defines your shell prompt), and $MAIL (which identifies the location of your mailbox).

> **TIP:** You can check your environment variables at any time. Type `declare` to list the current environment variables. Or you can type `echo $VALUE`, where `VALUE` is replaced by the name of a particular environment variable you want to list.

- **Metacharacters** — These are characters that have special meaning to the shell. Metacharacters can be used to direct the output of a command to a file (`>`), pipe the output to another command (`|`), or run a command in the background (`&`), to name a few. Metacharacters are discussed later in this chapter.

To save you some typing, there are shell features that store commands you want to reuse, recall previous commands, and edit commands. You can create aliases that allow you to type a short command to run a longer one. The shell stores previously entered commands in a history list, which you can display and from which you can recall commands. This is discussed further in the remainder of this section.

Unless you specifically change to another shell, the bash shell is the one you use with Fedora. The bash shell contains most of the powerful features available in other shells. Although the description in this chapter steps you through many bash shell features, you can learn more about the bash shell by typing `man bash`. For other ways to learn about using the shell, refer to the sidebar "Getting Help with Using the Shell."

Locating commands

If you know the directory that contains the command you want to run, one way to run it is to type the full path to that command. For example, you run the `date` command from the `/bin` directory by typing:

```
$ /bin/date
```

Of course, this can be inconvenient, especially if the command resides in a directory with a long name. The better way is to have commands stored in well-known directories, and then add those directories to your shell's PATH environment variable. The path consists of a list of directories that are checked sequentially for the commands you enter. To see your current path, type the following:

```
$ echo $PATH
/bin:/usr/bin:/usr/local/bin:/usr/bin/X11:/usr/X11R6/bin:/home/chris/bin
```

The results show the default path for a regular Linux user. Directories in the path list are separated by colons. Most user commands that come with Linux are stored in the `/bin`, `/usr/bin`, or `/usr/local/bin` directories. Although most graphical commands (that are used with GUIs) are contained in /usr/bin, there are some special X commands that are in `/usr/bin/X11` and `/usr/X11R6/bin` directories. The last directory shown is the bin directory in the user's home directory.

> **TIP:** If you want to add your own commands or shell scripts, place them in the `bin` directory in your home directory (such as `/home/chris/bin` for the user named chris). This directory is automatically added to your path. So as long as you add the command to your bin with execute permission (described in the "Understanding file permissions" section), you can immediately begin using the command by simply typing the command name at your shell prompt.

Getting Help with Using the Shell

When you first start using the shell, it can be intimidating. All you see is a prompt. How do you know which commands are available, which options they use, or how to use more advanced features? Fortunately, lots of help is available. Here are some places you can look to supplement what you learn in this chapter:

- Check the PATH — Type `echo $PATH`. You see a list of the directories containing commands that are immediately accessible to you. Listing the contents of those directories displays most standard Linux commands.

- Use the `help` command — Some commands are built into the shell, so they do not appear in a directory. The `help` command lists those commands and shows options available with each of them. (Type `help | less` to page through the list.) For help with a particular built-in command, type `help command`, replacing `command` with the name that interests you. The `help` command only works with the bash shell.

- Use `--help` with the command — Many commands include a `--help` option that you can use to get information about how the command is used. For example, type `date --help | less`. The output shows not only options, but also time formats you can use with the date command.

- Use the `man` command — To learn more about a particular command, type `man command`. (Replace `command` with the command name you want.) A description of the command and its options appears on the screen.

If you are the root user, directories containing administrative commands are in your path. These directories include `/sbin` and `/usr/sbin`.

The path directory order is important. Directories are checked from left to right. So, in this example, if there is a command called `foo` located in both the `/bin` and `/usr/bin` directories, the one in `/bin` is executed. To have the other `foo` command run, you either type the full path to the command or change your PATH variable. (Changing your PATH and adding directories to it are described later in this chapter.)

Not all the commands that you run are located in directories in your PATH. Some commands are built into the shell. Other commands can be overridden by creating aliases that define any commands and options that you want the command to run. There are also ways of defining a function that consists of a stored series of commands. Here is the order in which the shell checks for the commands you type:

1. **Aliases** — Names set by the `alias` command that represent a particular command and a set of options. (Type **alias** to see what aliases are set.) Often, aliases allow you to define a short name for a long, complicated command.

2. **Shell reserved word** — Words that are reserved by the shell for special use. Many of these are words that you would use in programming-type functions, such as `do`, `while`, `case`, and `else`.

3. **Function** — A set of commands that are executed together within the current shell.

4. **Built-in command** — A command that is built into the shell.

5. **File system command** — This is a command that is stored in and executed from the computer's file system. (These are the commands that are indicated by the value of the PATH variable.)

To find out where a particular command is taken from, you can use the `type` command. (If you are using a shell other than `bash`, use the `which` command instead.) For example, to find out where the bash shell command is located, type the following:

```
$ type bash
bash is /bin/bash
```

Try these few words with the `type` command to see other locations of commands: `which`, `case`, and `return`. If a command resides in several locations, you can add the `-a` option to have all the known locations of the command printed.

> **TIP:** Sometimes you run a command and receive an error message that the command was not found or that permission to run the command was denied. In the first case, check that you spelled the command correctly and that it is located in your PATH. In the second case, the command may be in the PATH, but may not be executable. Adding execute permissions to a command is described later in this chapter.

Rerunning commands

It's annoying, after typing a long or complex command line, to learn that you mistyped something. Fortunately, some shell features let you recall previous command lines, edit those lines, or complete a partially typed command line.

The *shell history* is a list of the commands that you have entered before. Using the `history` command, you can view your previous commands. Then, using various shell features, you can recall individual command lines from that list and change them however you please.

The rest of this section describes how to do command-line editing, how to complete parts of command lines, and how to recall and work with the history list.

Command-line editing

If you type something wrong on a command line, the bash shell ensures that you don't have to delete the entire line and start over. Likewise, you can recall a previous command line and change the elements to make a new command.

By default, the bash shell uses command-line editing that is based on the `emacs` text editor. So, if you are familiar with `emacs`, you probably already know most of the keystrokes described here.

> **TIP:** If you prefer the `vi` command for editing shell command lines, you can easily make that happen. Add the line
>
> ```
> set -o vi
> ```
>
> to the `.bashrc` file in your home directory. The next time you open a shell, you can use `vi` commands (as described in the tutorial later in this chapter) to edit your command lines.

To do the editing, you can use a combination of control keys, meta keys, and arrow keys. For example, Ctrl+f means to hold the control key and type f. Alt+f means to hold the Alt key and type f. (Instead of the Alt key, your keyboard may use a Meta key or the Esc key instead. On a Windows keyboard, you can sometimes use the Windows key.)

To try out a bit of command-line editing, type the following command:

```
$ ls /usr/bin | sort -f | more
```

This command lists the contents of the `/usr/bin` directory, sorts the contents in alphabetical order (regardless of upper- and lowercase), and pipes the output to `more` (so you can page through the results). Now, suppose you want to change `/usr/bin` to `/bin`. You can use the following steps to change the command:

1. Press Ctrl+a. This moves the cursor to the beginning of the command line.
2. Press Ctrl+f or the right arrow (→) key. Repeat this command a few times to position the cursor under the first slash (/).
3. Press Ctrl+d. Type this command four times to delete `/usr`.
4. Press Enter. This executes the command line.

As you edit a command line, at any point you can type regular characters to add those characters to the command line. The characters appear at the location of your cursor. You can use right (→) and left (←) arrows to move the cursor from one end to the other on the command line. You can also press the up (↑) and down (↓) arrow keys to step through previous commands in the history list to select a command line for editing. (See the discussion on command recall for details on how to recall commands from the history list.)

There are many keystrokes you can use to edit your command lines. Table 4-1 lists the keystrokes that you can use to move around the command line.

Table 4-1: Keystrokes for Navigating Command Lines

Keystroke	Full Name	Meaning
Ctrl+f	Character forward	Go forward one character.
Ctrl+b	Character backward	Go backward one character.
Alt+f	Word forward	Go forward one word.
Alt+b	Word backward	Go backward one word.
Ctrl+a	Beginning of line	Go to the beginning of the current line.
Ctrl+e	End of line	Go to the end of the line.
Ctrl+l	Clear screen	Clear screen and leave line at the top of the screen.

Table 4-2 lists the keystrokes for editing command lines.

Table 4-2: Keystrokes for Editing Command Lines

Keystroke	Full Name	Meaning
Ctrl+d	Delete current	Delete the current character.
Backspace or Rubout	Delete previous	Delete the previous character.
Ctrl+t	Transpose character	Switch positions of current and previous characters.
Alt+t	Transpose words	Switch positions of current and previous characters.
Alt+u	Uppercase word	Change the current word to uppercase.
Alt+l	Lowercase word	Change the current word to lowercase.
Alt+c	Capitalize word	Change the current word to an initial capital.
Ctrl+v	Insert special character	Add a special character. For example, to add a Tab character, press Ctrl+v+Tab.

Table 4-3 lists the keystrokes for cutting and pasting text on a command line.

Table 4-3: Keystrokes for Cutting and Pasting Text in Command Lines

Keystroke	Full Name	Meaning
Ctrl+k	Cut end of line	Cut text to the end of the line.
Ctrl+u	Cut beginning of line	Cut text to the beginning of the line.
Ctrl+w	Cut previous word	Cut the word located behind the cursor.
Alt+d	Cut next word	Cut the word following the cursor.
Ctrl+y	Paste recent text	Paste most recently cut text.
Alt+y	Paste earlier text	Rotate back to previously cut text and paste it.
Ctrl+c	Delete whole line	Delete the entire line.

Command line completion

To save you a few keystrokes, the bash shell offers several different ways of completing partially typed values. To attempt to complete a value, type the first few characters, and then press Tab. Here are some of the values you can type partially:

- **Environment variable** — If the text begins with a dollar sign ($), the shell completes the text with an environment variable from the current shell.
- **User name** — If the text begins with a tilde (~), the shell completes the text with a user name.
- **Command, alias, or function** — If the text begins with regular characters, the shell tries to complete the text with a command, alias, or function name.
- **Host name** — If the text begins with an at (@) sign, the shell completes the text with a host name taken from the /etc/hosts file.

> **TIP:** To add host names from an additional file, you can set the HOSTFILE variable to the name of that file. The file must be in the same format as /etc/hosts.

Here are a few examples of command completion. (When you see <Tab>, it means to press the Tab key on your keyboard.) Type the following:

```
$ echo $OS<Tab>
$ cd ~ro<Tab>
$ fing<Tab>
$ mail root@loc<Tab>
```

The first example causes $OS to expand to the $OSTYPE variable. In the next example, ~ro expands to the root user's home directory (~root/). Next, fing expands to the finger command. Finally, the address of root@loc expands to computer name localhost.

Of course, there will be times when there are several possible completions for the string of characters you have entered. In that case, you can check the possible ways text can be expanded by pressing Esc+? (or by pressing Tab twice) at the point where you want to do completion. This shows the result you would get if you checked for possible completions on $P.

```
$ echo $P<Esc+?>
$PATH $PPID $PS1 $PS2 $PS4 $PWD
$ echo $P
```

In this case, there are six possible variables that begin with $P. After possibilities are displayed, the original command line returns, ready for you to complete it as you choose.

If text you are trying to complete is not preceded by a $, ~, or @, you can still try to complete the text with a variable, user name, or host name. Press the following to complete your text:

- **Alt+~** — Complete the text before this point as a user name.
- **Alt+$** — Complete the text before this point as a variable.
- **Alt+@** — Complete the text before this point as a host name.
- **Alt+!** — Complete the text before this point as a command name (alias, reserved word, shell function, shell built-in command, and filenames are checked in that order). In other words, complete this key sequence with a command that you previously ran.
- **Ctrl+x+/** — List possible user name text completions.
- **Ctrl+x+$** — List possible environment variable completions.
- **Ctrl+x+@** — List possible host name completions.
- **Ctrl+x+!** — List possible command name completions.

Command line recall

After you type a command line, that entire command line is saved in your shell's history list. The list is stored in a history file, from which any command can be recalled to run again. After it is recalled, you can modify the command line, as described earlier.

To view your history list, use the history command. Type the command without options or followed by a number to list that many of the most recent commands. For example:

```
$ history 8
 382 date
 383 ls /usr/bin | sort -a | more
 384 man sort
 385 cd /usr/local/bin
```

```
386 man more
387 useradd -m /home/chris -u 101 chris
388 passwd chris
389 history 8
```

A number precedes each command line in the list. There are several ways to run a command immediately from this list, including:

- **Run Command Number (!n)** — Replace the *n* with the number of the command line, and the command line indicated is run. For example, to repeat the date command shown as command number 382 from the previous history listing, you could type the following:

```
$ !382
date
Thu May 13 21:30:06 PDT 2004
```

- **Run Previous Command (!!)** — Runs the previous command line. So, to immediately run that same date command again, type the following:

```
$ !!
date
Thu May 13 21:30:39 PDT 2004
```

- **Run Command Containing String (!?*string*?)** — Runs the most recent command that contains a particular *string* of characters. So, for example, you could run the date comand again by just searching for part of that command line as follows:

```
$ !?dat?
date
Thu May 13 21:32:41 PDT 2004
```

Instead of just running a history command line immediately, you can recall a particular line and edit it. You can use these keys to do that:

- **Step (Arrow Keys)** — Press the up (↑) and down (↓) arrow keys to step through each command line in your history list to arrive at the one you want. (Ctrl+p and Ctrl+n do the same functions, respectively.)

- **Reverse Incremental Search (Ctrl+r)** — After you press these keys, you are asked to enter a search string to do a reverse search. As you type the string, a matching command line appears that you can run or edit.

- **Forward Incremental Search (Ctrl+s)** — After you press these keys, you are asked to enter a search string to do a forward search. As you type the string, a matching command line appears that you can run or edit.

- **Reverse Search (Alt+p)** — After you press these keys, you are asked to enter a string to do a reverse search. Type a string and press Enter to see the most recent command line that includes that string.

- **Forward Search (Alt+n)** — After you press these keys, you are asked to enter a string to do a forward search. Type a string, and press Enter to see the most recent command line that includes that string.

- **Beginning of History List (Alt+<)** — Brings you to the first entry of the history list.

- **End of History List (Alt+>)** — Brings you to the last entry of the history list.

Another way to work with your history list is to use the `fc` command. Type **fc** followed by a history line number, and that command line is opened in a text editor. Make the changes that you want. When you exit the editor, the command runs. You could also give a range of line numbers (for example, `fc 100 105`). All the commands open in your text editor, and then run one after the other when you exit the editor.

The history list is stored in the `.bash_history` file in your home directory. Up to 1000 history commands are stored for you by default.

Connecting and expanding commands

A truly powerful feature of the shell is the capability to redirect the input and output of commands to and from other commands and files. To allow commands to be strung together, the shell uses metacharacters. As noted earlier, a metacharacter is a typed character that has special meaning to the shell for connecting commands or requesting expansion.

Piping commands

The pipe (|) metacharacter connects the output from one command to the input of another command. This lets you have one command work on some data, then have the next command deal with the results. Here is an example of a command line that includes pipes:

```
$ cat /etc/password | sort | more
```

This command lists the contents of the `/etc/password` file and pipes the output to the `sort` command. The `sort` command takes the user names that begin each line of the `/etc/password` file, sorts them alphabetically, and pipes the output to the `more` command. The `more` command displays the output one page at a time, so that you can go through the output a line or a page at a time.

Pipes are an excellent illustration of how UNIX, the predecessor of Linux, was created as an operating system made up of building blocks. A standard practice in UNIX was to connect utilities in different ways to get different jobs done. For example, before the days of graphical word processors, users created plain-text files that included macros to indicate formatting. To see how the document really appeared, they would use a command such as the following:

```
$ gunzip < /usr/share/man/man1/grep.1.gz | nroff -c -man | less
```

In this example, the contents of the `grep` man page (`grep.1.gz`) are directed to the `gunzip` command to be unzipped. The output from `gunzip` is piped to the `nroff` command to format the man page using the manual macro (-man). The output is piped to the less command to display the output. Because the file being displayed is in plain text, you could have substituted any number of options to work with the text before displaying it. You could sort the contents, change or delete some of the content, or bring in text from other documents. The key is that, instead of all those features being in one program, you get results from piping and redirecting input and output between multiple commands.

Sequential commands

Sometimes you may want a sequence of commands to run, with one command completing before the next command begins. You can do this by typing several commands on the same command line and separating them with semicolons (;):

```
$ date ; troff -me verylargedocument | lpr ; date
```

In this example, I was formatting a huge document and wanted to know how long it would take. The first command (date) showed the date and time before the formatting started. The troff command formatted the document and then piped the output to the printer. When the formatting was done, the date and time was printed again (so I knew how long the troff command took to complete).

Background commands

Some commands can take a while to complete. Sometimes you may not want to tie up your shell waiting for a command to finish. In those cases, you can have the commands run in the background by using the ampersand (&).

Text formatting commands (such as nroff and troff, described earlier) are examples of commands that are often run in the background to format a large document. You also might want to create your own shell scripts that run in the background to check continuously for certain events to occur, such as the hard disk filling up or particular users logging in.

Here is an example of a command being run in the background:

```
$ troff -me verylargedocument | lpr &
```

There are other ways of managing background and foreground processes (described in the "Managing background and foreground processes" section).

Expanding commands

With command substitution, you can have the output of a command interpreted by the shell instead of by the command itself. In this way, you can have the standard output of a command become an argument for another command. The two forms of command substitution are $(command) or 'command'.

The command in this case can include options, metacharacters, and arguments. Here is an example of using command substitution:

```
$ vi $(find /home | grep xyzzy)
```

In this command line, the command substitution is done before the vi command is run. First, the find command starts at the /home directory and prints out all files and directories below that point in the file system. This output is piped to the grep command, which filters out all files except for those that include the string xyzzy. Finally, the vi command opens all filenames for editing (one at a time) that include xyzzy.

This particular example might be useful if you knew that you wanted to edit a file for which you knew the name but not the location. As long as the string was uncommon, you could find and open every instance of a filename existing beneath a point you choose in the file system.

Expanding arithmetic expressions

There may be times when you want to pass arithmetic results to a command. There are two forms you can use to expand an arithmetic expression and pass it to the shell: $[*expression*] or $((*expression*)). Here is an example:

```
$ echo "I am $[2004 - 1957] years old."
I am 47 years old.
```

In this example, the shell interprets the arithmetic expression first (2004 - 1957), and then passes that information to the echo command. The echo command displays the text, with the results of the arithmetic (47) inserted.

Expanding variables

Environment variables that store information within the shell can be expanded using the dollar sign ($) metacharacter. When you expand an environment variable on a command line, the value of the variable is printed instead of the variable name itself, as follows:

```
$ ls -l $BASH
-rwxr-xr-x 1 root   root   625516 Dec 5 11:13 /bin/bash
```

Using $BASH as an argument to ls -l causes a long listing of the bash command to be printed. For more information on shell environment variables, see the following section.

Using shell environment variables

Every active shell stores pieces of information that it needs to use in what are called *environment variables*. An environment variable can store things such as locations of configuration files, mailboxes, and path directories. They can also store values for your shell prompts, the size of your history list, and type of operating system.

To see the environment variables currently assigned to your shell, type the `declare` command. (It will probably fill more than one screen, so type `declare | more`.) You can refer to the value of any of those variables by preceding it with a dollar sign (`$`) and placing it anywhere on a command line. For example:

```
$ echo $USER
chris
```

This command prints the value of the USER variable, which holds your user name (`chris`). Substitute any other value for USER to print its value instead.

Common shell environment variables

When you start a shell (by logging in or opening a Terminal window), a lot of environment variables are already set. Here are some variables that are either set when you use a bash shell or that can be set by you to use with different features.

- BASH — Contains the full path name of the `bash` command. This is usually `/bin/bash`.

- BASH_VERSION — A number of the current version of the `bash` command.

- EUID — This is the effective user ID number of the current user. It is assigned when the shell starts, based on the user's entry in the `/etc/passwd` file.

- FCEDIT — If set, this variable indicates the text editor used by the `fc` command to edit `history` commands. If this variable isn't set, the `vi` command is used.

- HISTFILE — The location of your history file. It is typically located at `$HOME/.bash_history`.

- HISTFILESIZE — The number of history entries that can be stored. After this number is reached, the oldest commands are discarded. The default value is 1000.

- HISTCMD — This returns the number of the current command in the history list.

- HOME — This is your home directory. It is your current working directory each time you log in or type the `cd` command with any options.

- HOSTTYPE — A value that describes the computer architecture on which the Linux system is running. For Intel-compatible PCs, the value is i386, i486, i586, i686, or something like i386-linux. For AMD 64-bit machines, the value is x86_64.

- MAIL — This is the location of your mailbox file. The file is typically your user name in the `/var/spool/mail` directory.

- OLDPWD — The directory that was the working directory before you changed to the current working directory.

- OSTYPE — A name identifying the current operating system. For Fedora, the OSTYPE value is either linux or linux-gnu, depending on the type of shell you are using (Bash can run on other operating systems as well.)

- PATH — The colon-separated list of directories used to find commands that you type. The default value for regular users is:

```
/bin:/usr/bin:/usr/local/bin:/usr/bin/X11:/usr/X11R6/bin:~/bin
```

  For the root user, the value also includes /sbin, /usr/sbin, and /usr/local/sbin.

- PPID — The process ID of the command that started the current shell (for example, its parent process).

- PROMPT_COMMAND — Can be set to a command name that is run each time before your shell prompt is displayed. Setting PROMPT_COMMAND=date lists the current date/time before the prompt appears.

- PS1 — Sets the value of your shell prompt. There are many items that you can read into your prompt (date, time, user name, host name, and so on). Sometimes a command requires additional prompts, which you can set with the variables PS2, PS3, and so on. (Setting your prompt is described later in this chapter.)

- PWD — This is the directory that is assigned as your current directory. This value changes each time you change directories using the cd command.

- RANDOM — Accessing this variable causes a random number to be generated. The number is between 0 and 99999.

- SECONDS — The number of seconds since the time the shell was started.

- SHLVL — The number of shell levels associated with the current shell session. When you log in to the shell, the SHLVL is 1. Each time you start a new bash command (by, for example, using su to become a new user, or by simply typing bash), this number is incremented.

- TMOUT — Can be set to a number representing the number of seconds the shell can be idle without receiving input. After the number of seconds is reached, the shell exits. This is a security feature that makes it less likely for unattended shells to be accessed by unauthorized people. (This must be set in the login shell for it to actually cause the shell to log out the user.)

- UID — The user ID number assigned to your user name. The user ID number is stored in the /etc/password file.

Set your own environment variables

Environment variables can provide a handy way of storing bits of information that you use often from the shell. You can create any variables that you want (avoiding those that are already in use) so that you can read in the values of those variables as you use the shell. (The bash man page lists variables already in use.)

To set an environment variable temporarily, you can simply type a variable name and assign it to a value. Here is an example:

```
$ AB=/usr/dog/contagious/ringbearer/grind ; export AB
```

This example causes a long directory path to be assigned to the AB variable. The export AB command says to export the value to the shell so that it can be propagated to other shells you may open. With AB set, you can go to the directory by typing the following:

```
$ cd $AB
```

> **TIP:** You may have noticed that environment variables shown here are in all caps. Though case does matter with these variables, setting them as uppercase is a convention, not a necessity. You could just as easily set a variable to xyz as to XYZ (they are not the same, but either will work).

The problem with setting environment variables in this way is that as soon as you exit the shell in which you set the variable, the setting is lost. To set variables more permanently, you should add variable settings to a bash configuration file, as described later in this section.

If you want to have other text right up against the output from an environment variable, you can surround the variable in braces. This protects the variable name from being misunderstood. For example, if you wanted to add a command name to the AB variable shown earlier, you could type the following:

```
$ echo ${AB}/adventure
/usr/dog/contagious/ringbearer/grind/adventure
```

Remember that you must export the variable so that it can be picked up by other shell commands. You must add the export line to a shell configuration file for it to take effect the next time you log in. The export command is fairly flexible. Instead of running the export command after you set the variable, you could do it all in one step, as follows:

```
$ export XYZ=/home/xyz/bin
```

You can override the value of any environment variable. This can be temporary by simply typing the new value. Or you can add the new export line to your $HOME/.bashrc file. One useful variable to update is PATH. Here is an example:

```
$ export PATH=$PATH:/home/xyz/bin
```

In this example, I added the /home/xyz/bin directory to the PATH, a useful technique if you want to run a bunch of commands from a directory that is not normally in your PATH, without typing the full or relative path each time.

If you decide that you no longer want a variable to be set, you can use the unset command to erase its value. For example, you could type unset XYZ, which would cause XYZ to have no value set. (Remember to remove the export from the $HOME/.bashrc file — if you added it there — or it will return the next time you open a shell.)

Managing background and foreground processes

If you are using Linux over a network or from a *dumb* terminal (a monitor that allows only text input with no GUI support), your shell may be all that you have. You may be used to a windowing environment where you have a lot of programs active at the same time so that you can switch among them as needed. This shell thing can seem pretty limited.

Although the bash shell doesn't include a GUI for running many programs, it does let you move active programs between the background and foreground. In this way, you can have a lot of stuff running, while selectively choosing the one you want to deal with at the moment.

There are several ways to place an active program in the background. One mentioned earlier is to add an ampersand (&) to the end of a command line. Another way is to use the at command to run commands in a way in which they are not connected to the shell. (See Chapter 12 for more information about the at command.)

To stop a running command and put it in the background, press Ctrl+z. After the command is stopped, you can either bring it to the foreground to run (the fg command) or start it running in the background (the bg command).

Starting background processes

If you have programs that you want to run while you continue to work in the shell, you can place the programs in the background. To place a program in the background at the time you run the program, type an ampersand (&) at the end of the command line. For example:

```
$ find /usr > /tmp/allusrfiles &
```

This command finds all files on your Linux system (starting from /usr), prints those filenames, and puts those names in the file /tmp/allusrfiles. The ampersand (&) runs that command line in the background. To check which commands you have running in the background, use the jobs command, as follows:

```
$ jobs
[1]   Stopped (tty output)  vi /tmp/myfile
[2]   Running         find /usr -print > /tmp/allusrfiles &
[3]   Running         nroff -man /usr/man2/* >/tmp/man2 &
[4]-  Running         nroff -man /usr/man3/* >/tmp/man3 &
[5]+  Stopped         nroff -man /usr/man4/* >/tmp/man4
```

The first job shows a text-editing command (vi) that I placed in the background and stopped by pressing Ctrl+z while I was editing. Job two shows the find command I just ran. Jobs three and four show nroff commands currently running in the background. Job five had been running in the shell (foreground) until I decided too many processes were running and pressed Ctrl+z to stop job five until a few processes had completed.

The plus sign (+) next to number 5 shows that it was most recently placed in the background. The minus sign (-) next to number 4 shows that it was placed in the background just before the most recent background job. Because job 1 requires terminal input, it cannot run in the background. As a result, it is Stopped until it is brought to the foreground again.

> **TIP:** To see the process ID for the background job, add an -1 option to the jobs command. If you type ps, you can use the process ID to figure out which command is for a particular background job.

Using foreground and background commands

Continuing with the example, you can bring any of the commands on the jobs list to the foreground. For example, to edit myfile again, type:

```
$ fg %1
```

As a result, the vi command opens again, with all text as it was when you stopped the vi job.

> **CAUTION:** Before you put a text processor, word processor, or similar program in the background, make sure you save your file. It's easy to forget you have a program in the background and you will lose your data if you log out or the computer reboots later on.

To refer to a background job (to cancel or bring it to the foreground), use a percent sign (%) followed by the job number. You can also use the following to refer to a background job:

- % — A percent sign alone refers to the most recent command put into the background (indicated by the plus sign). This action brings the command to the foreground.
- %string — Refers to a job where the command begins with a particular *string* of characters. The *string* must be unambiguous. (In other words, typing %vi when there are two vi commands in the background results in an error message.)
- %?string — Refers to a job where the command line contains a string at any point. The string must be unambiguous or the match will fail.
- %-- — Refers to the previous job stopped before the one most recently stopped.

If a command is stopped, you can start it running again in the background using the bg command. For example, take job number 5 from the jobs list in the previous example:

```
[5]+ Stopped              nroff -man man4/* >/tmp/man4
```

Type the following:

```
$ bg %5
```

After that, the job runs in the background. Its jobs entry appears as follows:

```
[5]  Running              nroff -man man4/* >/tmp/man4 &
```

Configuring your shell

You can tune your shell to help you work more efficiently. Your prompt can provide pertinent information each time you press Enter. You can set aliases to save your keystrokes and permanently set environment variables to suit your needs. To make each change occur when you start a shell, you can add this information to your shell configuration files.

Several configuration files support how your shell behaves. Some of the files are executed for every user and every shell. Others are specific to the user who creates the configuration file. Here are the files that are of interest to anyone using the bash shell in Linux:

- /etc/profile — This file sets up user environment information for every user. It is executed when you first log in. This file provides values for your path, as well as setting environment variables for such things as the location of your mailbox and the size of your history files. Finally, /etc/profile gathers shell settings from configuration files in the /etc/profile.d directory.

- /etc/bashrc — This file is executed for every user who runs the bash shell, each time a bash shell is opened. It sets the default prompt and may add one or more aliases. Values in this file can be overridden by information in each user's ~/.bashrc file.

- ~/.bash_profile — This file is used by each user to enter information that is specific to their own use of the shell. It is executed only once, when the user logs in. By default it sets a few environment variables and executes the user's .bashrc file.

- ~/.bashrc — This file contains the information that is specific to your bash shells. It is read when you log in and also each time you open a new bash shell. This is the best location to add environment variables and aliases so that your shell picks them up.

- ~/.bash_logout — This file executes each time you log out (exit the last bash shell). By default, it simply clears your screen.

To change the /etc/profile or /etc/bashrc files, you must be the root user. Users can change the information in the $HOME/.bash_profile, $HOME/.bashrc, and $HOME/.bash_logout files in their own home directories.

The following sections provide ideas about items to add to your shell configuration files. In most cases, you add these values to the .bashrc file in your home directory. However, if you administer a system, you may want to set some of these values as defaults for all of your Linux system's users.

Setting your prompt

Your prompt consists of a set of characters that appear each time the shell is ready to accept a command. The PS1 environment variable sets what the prompt contains. If your shell requires additional input, it uses the values of PS2, PS3, and PS4.

When your Fedora system is installed, your prompt is set to include the following information: your user name, your host name, and the base name of your current working directory. That information is surrounded by brackets and followed by a dollar sign (for regular users) or a pound sign (for the root user). Here is an example of that prompt:

```
[chris@myhost bin]$
```

If you change directories, the bin name would change to the name of the new directory. Likewise, if you were to log in as a different user or to a different host, that information would change.

You can use several special characters (indicated by adding a backslash to a variety of letters) to include different information in your prompt. These can include your terminal number, the date, and the time, as well as other pieces of information. Here are some examples:

- \! — Shows the current command history number. This includes all previous commands stored for your user name.
- \# — Shows the command number of the current command. This includes only the commands for the active shell.
- \$ — Shows the user prompt ($) or root prompt (#), depending on which user you are.
- \W — Shows only the current working directory base name. For example, if the current working directory was /var/spool/mail, this value would simply appear as mail.
- \[— Precedes a sequence of nonprinting characters. This could be used to add a terminal control sequence into the prompt for such things as changing colors, adding blink effects, or making characters bold. (Your terminal determines the exact sequences available.)
- \] — Follows a sequence of nonprinting characters.
- \\ — Shows a backslash.
- \d — Displays the day, month, and number of the date. For example: Sat Jan 23.
- \h — Shows the host name of the computer running the shell.
- \n — Causes a newline to occur.
- \nnn — Shows the character that relates to the octal number replacing *nnn*.
- \s — Displays the current shell name. For the bash shell, the value would be bash.
- \t — Prints the current time in hours, minutes, and seconds (for example, 10:14:39).
- \u — Prints your current user name.
- \w — Displays the full path to the current working directory.

TIP: If you are setting your prompt temporarily by typing at the shell, you should put the value of PS1 in quotes. For example, you could type export PS1=" [\t \w]\$ " to see a prompt that looks like this: [20:26:32 /var/spool]$.

To make a change to your prompt permanent, add the value of PS1 to your .bashrc file in your home directory (assuming that you are using the bash shell). There may already be a PS1 value in that file that you can modify.

Adding environment variables

You may consider adding a few environment variables to your .bashrc file. These can help make working with the shell more efficient and effective:

- TMOUT — This sets how long the shell can be inactive before bash automatically exits. The value is the number of seconds for which the shell has not received input. This can be a nice security feature, in case you leave your desk while you are still logged in to Linux. So as not to be logged you off while you are working, you may want to set the value to something like TMOUT=1800 (to allow 30 minutes of idle time).

- PATH — As described earlier, the PATH variable sets the directories that are searched for commands you use. If you often use directories of commands that are not in your PATH, you can permanently add them. To do this, add a PATH variable to your .bashrc file. For example, to add a directory called /getstuff/bin, add the following:

```
PATH=$PATH:/getstuff/bin ; export PATH
```

This example first reads all the current path directories into the new PATH ($PATH), adds the /getstuff/bin directory, and then exports the new PATH.

> **CAUTION:** Some people add the current directory to their PATH by adding a directory identified simply as a dot (.), as follows:
>
> ```
> PATH=.:$PATH ; export PATH
> ```
>
> This lets you always run commands in your current directory (which people may be used to if they have used DOS). However, the security risk with this procedure is that you could be in a directory that contains a command that you don't intend to run from that directory. For example, a hacker could put an ls command in a directory that, instead of listing the content of your directory, does something devious.

- WHATEVER — You can create your own environment variables to provide shortcuts in your work. Choose any name that is not being used and assign a useful value to it. For example, if you do a lot of work with files in the /work/time/files/info/memos directory, you could set the following variable:

```
M=/work/time/files/info/memos ; export M
```

You could make that your current directory by typing cd $M. You could run a program from that directory called hotdog by typing $M/hotdog. You could edit a file from there called bun by typing vi $M/bun.

Adding aliases

Setting aliases can save you even more typing than setting environment variables. With aliases, you can have a string of characters execute an entire command line. You can add and list aliases with the `alias` command. Here are some examples:

```
alias p='pwd ; ls -CF'
alias rm='rm -i'
```

In the first example, the letter p is assigned to run the command `pwd`, and then to run `ls -CF` to print the current working directory and list its contents in column form. The second runs the `rm` command with the `-i` option each time you simply type **rm**. (This is an alias that is often set automatically for the root user, so that instead of just removing files, you are prompted for each individual file removal. This prevents you from removing all the files in a directory by mistakenly typing something such as `rm *`.)

While you are in the shell, you can check which aliases are set by typing the `alias` command. If you want to remove an alias, you can type **unalias**. (Remember that if the `alias` is set in a configuration file, it will be set again when you open another shell.)

Working with the Linux File System

The Linux file system is the structure in which all the information on your computer is stored. Files are organized within a hierarchy of directories. Each directory can contain files, as well as other directories.

If you were to map out the files and directories in Fedora, it would look like an upside-down tree. At the top is the root directory, which is represented by a single slash (/). Below that is a set of common directories in the Linux system, such as `bin`, `dev`, `home`, `lib`, and `tmp`, to name a few. Each of those directories, as well as directories added to the root, can contain subdirectories.

Figure 4-1 illustrates how the Linux file system is organized as a hierarchy. To illustrate how directories are connected, Figure 4-1 shows a `/home` directory that contains subdirectories for three users: `chris`, `mary`, and `tom`. Within the `chris` directory are subdirectories: `briefs`, `memos`, and `personal`. To refer to a file called `inventory` in the `chris/memos` directory, you could type the full path of `/home/chris/memos/inventory`. If your current directory were `/home/chris/memos`, you could refer to the file as simply `inventory`.

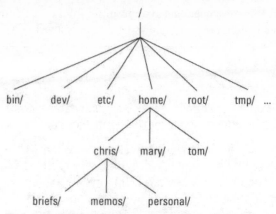

Figure 4-1: The Linux file system is organized as a hierarchy of directories.

Some of the Linux directories that may interest you include the following:

- /bin — Contains common Linux user commands, such as ls, sort, date, and chmod.
- /boot — Has the bootable Linux kernel and boot loader configuration files (GRUB).
- /dev — Contains files representing access points to devices on your systems. These include terminal devices (tty*), floppy disks (fd*), hard disks (hd*), RAM (ram*), and CD-ROM (cd*). (Users normally access these devices directly through the device files.)
- /etc — Contains administrative configuration files.
- /home — Contains directories assigned to each user with a login account.
- /mnt — Provides a location for mounting devices, such as remote file systems and removable media (with directory names of cdrom, floppy, and so on).
- /proc — Provides a mechanism for the kernel to send information to processes.
- /root — Represents the root user's home directory.
- /sbin — Contains administrative commands and daemon processes.
- /sys — A /proc-like file system, new in Fedora Core 2 and intended to contain files for getting hardware status and reflecting the system's device tree as it is seen by the kernel. It pulls many of its functions from /proc.
- /tmp — Contains temporary files used by applications.
- /usr — Contains user documentation, games, graphical files (X11), libraries (lib), and a variety of other user and administrative commands and files.
- /var — Contains directories of data used by various applications. In particular, this is where you would place files that you share as an FTP server (/var/ftp) or a Web server (/var/www). It also contains all system log files (/var/log).

The file systems in the DOS or Microsoft Windows operating systems differ from Linux's file structure. See the sidebar on the Linux file system versus Windows-based file systems.

Linux File Systems versus Windows-based File Systems

Although similar in many ways, the Linux file system has some striking differences from file systems used in MS-DOS and Windows operating systems. Here are a few:

- In MS-DOS and Windows file systems, drive letters represent different storage devices (for example, A: is a floppy drive and C: is a hard disk). In Linux, all storage devices are fit into the file system hierarchy. So, the fact that all of /usr may be on a separate hard disk or that /mnt/rem1 is a file system from another computer is invisible to the user.

- Slashes, rather than backslashes, are used to separate directory names in Linux. So, C:\home\chris in an MS system is /home/chris in a Linux system.

- Filenames almost always have suffixes in DOS (such as .txt for text files or .doc for word-processing files). Although at times you can use that convention in Linux, three-character suffixes have no required meaning in Linux. They can be useful for identifying a file type.

- Every file and directory in a Linux system has permissions and ownership associated with it. Security varies among Microsoft systems. Because DOS and MS Windows began as single-user systems, file ownership was not built into those systems when they were designed. Later releases added features such as file and folder attributes to address this problem.

Creating files and directories

As a Fedora user, most of the files you save and work with will probably be in your home directory. Here are commands you use to create and use files and directories:

- cd — Change to another current working directory
- pwd — Print the name of the current working directory
- mkdir — Create a directory
- chmod — Change the permission on a file or directory
- ls — List the contents of a directory

The following procedure steps you through creating directories within your home directory, moving among your directories, and setting appropriate file permissions:

1. First, go to your home directory. To do this, simply type **cd**. (For other ways of referring to your home directory, see the sidebar on identifying directories.)

2. To make sure that you got to your home directory, type **pwd**. When I do this, I get the following response (yours will reflect your home directory):

   ```
   $ pwd
   /home/chris
   ```

3. Create a new directory called test in your home directory, as follows:

   ```
   $ mkdir test
   ```

4. Check the permissions of the directory by typing:

   ```
   $ ls -ld test
   drwxr-xr-x  2 chris   sales    1024  Jan 24 12:17 test
   ```

   Notice that this listing says that test is a directory (d), the owner is chris, the group is sales, and the file was most recently modified on Jan 24 at 12:17 p.m. Suppose that you want to prevent everyone else who uses this computer from using or viewing the files in this directory. The permissions for the directory are rwxr-xr-x. I explain what these permissions mean later in this section.

   > **NOTE:** When you add a new user in Fedora, by default, the user is assigned to a group of the same name. For example, in the preceding text, the user chris would be assigned to the group chris. This approach to assigning groups is referred to as the user private group scheme. For more information on user private groups, refer to Chapter 11.

5. For now, type the following:

   ```
   $ chmod 700 test
   ```

   This step changes the permissions of the directory to give you complete access and everyone else no access at all. (The new permissions should read like rwx------.)

6. Next, make the test directory your current directory as follows:

   ```
   $ cd test
   ```

Identifying Directories

When you need to identify your home directory on a shell command line, you can use the following:

- $HOME — This environment variable stores your home directory name.
- ~ — The tilde (~) represents your home directory on the command line.

You can also use the tilde to identify someone else's home directory. For example, ~chris would be expanded to the chris home directory (probably /home/chris).

Other special ways of identifying directories in the shell include the following:

- . — A single dot (.) refers to the current directory.
- . . — Two dots (. .) refers to a directory directly above the current directory.
- $PWD — This environment variable refers to the current working directory.
- $OLDPWD — This environment variable refers to the previous working directory before you changed to the current one.

Using metacharacters and operators

To make more efficient use of your shell, the bash shell lets you use certain special characters, referred to as metacharacters and operators. Metacharacters can help you match one or more files without typing each file completely. Operators let you direct information from one command or file to another command or file.

Using file-matching metacharacters

To save you some keystrokes and to be able to refer easily to a group of files, the bash shell lets you use metacharacters. Anytime you need to refer to a file or directory, such as to list it, open it, or remove it, you can use metacharacters to match the files you want. Here are some useful metacharacters for matching filenames:

- * — This matches any number of characters.
- ? — This matches any one character.
- [. . .] — This matches any one of the characters between the brackets, which can include a dash-separated range of letters or numbers.

To try out some of these file-matching metacharacters, go to an empty directory (such as the test directory described in the previous section) and create some files. Here's an example of how to create some empty files:

```
$ touch apple banana grape grapefruit watermelon
```

The next few commands show you how to use shell metacharacters to match filenames so they can be used as arguments to the `ls` command. Using the metacharacters shown below, you can match the filenames you just created with the `touch` command. Type the following commands and see if you get the same responses:

```
$ ls a*
apple
$ ls g*
grape
grapefruit
$ ls g*t
grapefruit
$ ls *e*
apple grape grapefruit watermelon
$ ls *n*
banana watermelon
```

The first example matches any file that begins with an a (`apple`). The next example matches any files that begin with g (`grape`, `grapefruit`). Next, files beginning with g and ending in t are matched (`grapefruit`). Next, any file that contains an e in the name is matched (`apple`, `grape`, `grapefruit`, `watermelon`). Finally, any file that contains an n is matched (`banana`, `watermelon`).

Here are a few examples of pattern matching with the question mark (`?`):

```
$ ls ????e
apple grape
$ ls g???e*
grape grapefruit
```

The first example matches any five-character file that ends in e (`apple`, `grape`). The second matches any file that begins with g and has e as its fifth character (`grape`, `grapefruit`).

Here are a few examples of using braces to do pattern matching:

```
$ ls [abw]*
apple banana watermelon
$ ls [agw]*[ne]
apple grape watermelon
```

In the first example, any file beginning with a, b, or w is matched. In the second, any file that begins with a, g, or w and also ends with either n or e is matched. You can also include ranges within brackets. For example:

```
$ ls [a-g]*
apple banana grape grapefruit
```

Here, any file names beginning with a letter from a through g is matched.

Using file-redirection metacharacters

Commands receive data from standard input and send it to standard output. Using pipes (described earlier), you can direct standard output from one command to the standard input of another. With files, you can use less than (<) and greater than (>) signs to direct data to and from files. Here are the file redirection characters:

- < — Direct the contents of a file to the command.
- > — Direct the output of a command to a file, deleting the existing file.
- >> — Direct the output of a command to a file, adding the output to the end of the existing file.

Here are some examples of command lines where information is directed to and from files:

```
$ mail root < ~/.bashrc
$ man chmod | col -b > /tmp/chmod
$ echo "I finished the project on $(date)" >> ~/projects
```

In the first example, the contents of the .bashrc file in the home directory are sent in a mail message to the computer's root user. The second command line formats the chmod man page (using the man command), removes extra back spaces (col -b) and sends the output to the file /tmp/chmod (erasing the previous /tmp/chmod file, if it exists). The final command results in the following text being added to the user's project file:

```
I finished the project on Sat Oct 25 13:46:49 PST 2003
```

Understanding file permissions

After you've worked with Linux for a while, you are almost sure to get a "Permission denied" message. Permissions associated with files and directories in Linux were designed to keep users from accessing other users' private files and to protect important system files.

The nine bits assigned to each file for permissions define the access that you and others have to your file. Permission bits appear as rwxrwxrwx. The first three bits apply to the owner's permission, the next three apply to the group assigned to the file, and the last three apply to all others. The r stands for read, the w stands for write, and the x stands for execute permissions. If a dash appears instead of the letter, it means that permission is turned off for that associated read, write, or execute.

You can see the permission for any file or directory by typing the ls -ld command. The named file or directory appears as those shown in the following example:

```
$ ls -ld ch3 test
-rw-rw-r--  1 chris  sales    4983  Jan 18 22:13 ch3
drwxr-xr-x 2 chris  sales    1024  Jan 24 13:47 test
```

The first line shows a file (ch3) that has read and write permission for the owner and the group. All other users have read permission, which means they can view the file but cannot change its contents or remove it. The second line shows a directory (indicated by the letter d before the permission bits). The owner has read, write, and execute permission, while the group and other users have only read and execute permissions. As a result, only the owner can add, change, or delete files in that directory. Any other user, however, can only read the contents, change to that directory, and list the contents of the directory.

If you own a file, you can change the permission on it as you please. You can do this with the chmod command. For each of the three sets of permission on a file (read, write, and execute), r is assigned to the number 4, w to 2, and x to 1. So to make permissions wide open for yourself as owner, you would set the first number to 7 (4 plus 2 plus 1). The same would be true for group and other permission. Any combination of permissions can result from 0 (no permission) through 7 (full permission).

Here are some examples of how to change permission on a file and what the resulting permission would be:

```
chmod 777 files   →   rwxrwxrwx
chmod 755 files   →   rwxr-xr-x
chmod 644 files   →   rw-r--r-
chmod 000 files   →   ---------
```

You can also turn file permissions on and off using plus (+) and minus (-) signs, respectively. This can be done for the owner user (u), owner group (g), others (o), and all users (a). For example, each time starting with a file that has all permissions open (rwxrwxrwx), here are some chmod examples with resulting permissions after using a minus sign:

```
chmod a-w files   →   r-xr-xr-x
chmod o-x files   →   rwsrwsrw-
chmod go-rwx files   →   rwx------
```

Likewise, here are some examples, starting with all permissions closed (---------) where the plus sign is used with chmod to turn permissions on:

```
chmod u+rw files   →   rw-------
chmod a+x files   →   --x--x--x
chmod ug+rx files   →   r-xr-x---
```

When you try to create a file, by default it is given the permission rw-r--r--. A directory is given the permission rwxr-xr-x. These default values are determined by the value of umask. Type **umask** to see what your umask value is. For example:

```
$ umask
022
```

The umask value masks the permissions value of 666 for a file and 777 for a directory. The umask value of 022 results in permission for a directory of 755 (rwxr-xr-x). That same umask results in a file permission of 644 (rw-r--r--). (Execute permissions are off by default for regular files.)

TIP: Here's a great tip for changing the permission for lots of files at once. Using the -R options of chmod, you could change the permission for all of the files and directories within a directory structure at once. For example, if you wanted to open permissions completely to all files and directories in the /tmp/test directory, you could type the following:

```
$ chmod -R 777 /tmp/test
```

This command line runs chmod recursively (-R) for the /tmp/test directory, as well as any files or directories that exist below that point in the file system (for example, /tmp/test/hat, /tmp/test/hat/caps, and so on). All would be set to 777 (full read/write/execute permissions).

CAUTION: The -R option of chmod works best if you are opening permissions completely or adding execute permission (as well as the appropriate read/write permission). The reason is that if you turn off execute permission recursively, you close off your ability to change to any directory in that structure. For example, chmod -R 644 /tmp/test turns off execute permission for the /tmp/test directory, then fails to change any files or directories below that point.

CROSS-REFERENCE: If you are using Security Enhanced Linux, working with file permissions will be quite different than the method described here (with security enhancement turned off). See Chapter 28 for more information.

Moving, copying, and deleting files

Commands for moving, copying, and deleting files are fairly straightforward. To change the location of a file, use the mv command. To copy a file from one location to another, use the cp command. To remove a file, use the rm command. Here are some examples:

```
$ mv abc def
$ mv abc ~
$ cp abc def
$ cp abc ~
$ rm abc
$ rm *
```

Of the two move (mv) commands, the first moves the file abc to the file def in the same directory (essentially renaming it), whereas the second moves the file abc to your home directory (~). The first copy command (cp) copies abc to the file def, whereas the second copies abc to your home directory (~). The first remove command (rm) deletes the abc file; the second removes all the files in the current directory (except those that start with a dot).

NOTE: For the root user, the mv, cp, and rm commands are aliased to each be run with the -i option. This causes a prompt to appear asking you to confirm each move, copy, and removal, one file at a time. This is done to prevent the root user from messing up a large group of files by mistake.

Using the vi Text Editor

It's almost impossible to use Linux for any period of time and not need to use a text editor. If you are using a GUI, you can run `gedit`, which is fairly intuitive for editing text. Most Linux shell users will use either the `vi` or `emacs` commands to edit text files. The advantage of `vi` or `emacs` over a graphical editor is that you can use it from any shell, a character terminal, or a character-based connection over a network (using `telnet` or `ssh`, for example). No GUI is required.

This section provides a brief tutorial of the `vi` text editor. Any time in this book that I suggest you manually edit a configuration file, you can use `vi` to do that editing (from any shell). (If `vi` doesn't suit you, see the "Exploring Other Text Editors" sidebar for other options.)

The `vi` editor is difficult to learn at first. But when you know it, you will be able to edit and move around quickly and efficiently within files. Your fingers never have to leave the keyboard to pick up a mouse or press a function key.

Exploring Other Text Editors

There are dozens of text editors available to use with Linux. Here are a few contained in Fedora that you can try out if you find `vi` to be too taxing:

- **gedit** — The GNOME text editor that runs in the GUI.

- **jed** — This screen-oriented editor was made for programmers. Using colors, `jed` can highlight code you create so you can easily read the code and spot syntax errors. Use the Alt key to select menus to manipulate your text.

- **joe** — The `joe` editor is similar to many PC text editors. Use control and arrow keys to move around. Type Ctrl+C to exit with no save or Ctrl+X to save and exit.

- **kate** — A nice-looking editor that comes in the kdebase package. It has lots of bells-and-whistles, such as highlighting for different types of programming languages and controls for managing word wrap.

- **kedit** — A GUI-based text editor that comes with the KDE desktop.

- **mcedit** — With `mcedit`, function keys help you get around, save, copy, move, and delete text. Like `jed` and `joe`, `mcedit` is screen-oriented.

- **nedit** – An excellent programmer's editor. You need to install the optional nedit package to get this editor.

- If you use ssh to log in to other Linux computers on your network, you can use any editor to edit files. A GUI-based editor will pop up on your screen. When no GUI is available, you will need a text editor that

> runs in the shell, such as `vi`, `jed` or `joe`.

Starting with vi

Most often, you start `vi` to open a particular file. For example, to open a file called `/tmp/test`, type the following command:

```
$ vi /tmp/test
```

If this is a new file, you should see something similar to the following:

```
~
~
~
~
~
"/tmp/test" [New File]
```

The box at the top represents where your cursor is. The bottom line keeps you informed about what is going on with your editing (here you just opened a new file). In between, there are tildes (~) as filler because there is no text in the file yet. Now here's the intimidating part: there are no hints, menus, or icons to tell you what to do. On top of that, you can't just start typing. If you do, the computer is likely to beep at you. And some people complain that Linux isn't friendly.

The first things you need to know are the different operating modes. The `vi` editor operates in either command mode or input mode. When you start `vi`, you are in command mode. Before you can add or change text in the file, you have to type a command to tell `vi` what you want to do. A command consists of one or two letters and an optional number. To get into input mode, you need to type an input command. To start out, type either of the following input commands:

- `a` — Add. After you type a, you can input text that starts to the right of the cursor.

- `i` — Insert. After you type i, you can input text that starts to the left of the cursor.

Type a few words and press Enter. Repeat that a few times until you have a few lines of text. When you are done typing, press Esc. You are now back in command mode. Now that you have a file with some text in it, try moving around in your text with the following keys or letters:

> **TIP:** Remember the Esc key! It always places you back into command mode.

- **Arrow keys** — Use the arrow keys to move up, down, left, or right in the file one character at a time. To move left and right you can also use Backspace and the Spacebar, respectively. If you prefer to keep your fingers on the keyboard, use h (left), l (right), j (down), or k (up) to move the cursor.

- **w** — Moves the cursor to the beginning of the next word.

- **b** — Moves the cursor to the beginning of the previous word.
- **0 (*zero*)** — Moves the cursor to the beginning of the current line.
- **$** — Moves the cursor to the end of the current line.
- **H** — Moves the cursor to the upper-left corner of the screen (first line on the screen).
- **M** — Moves the cursor to the first character of the middle line on the screen.
- **L** — Moves the cursor to the lower-left corner of the screen (last line on the screen).

Now that you know how to input text and move around, the only other editing you need to know is how to delete text. Here are a few vi commands for deleting text:

- **x** — Deletes the character under the cursor.
- **X** — Deletes the character directly before the cursor.
- **dw** — Deletes from the current character to the end of the current word.
- **d$** — Deletes from the current character to the end of the current line.
- **d0** — Deletes from the previous character to the beginning of the current line.

If you feel pretty good about creating text and moving around the file, you may want to wrap things up. Use the following keystrokes for saving and quitting the file:

- **ZZ** — Save the current changes to the file and exit from vi.
- **:w** — Save the current file but continue editing.
- **:wq** — Same as ZZ.
- **:q** — Quit the current file. This works only if you don't have any unsaved changes.
- **:q!** — Quit the current file and *don't* save the changes you just made to the file.

> **TIP:** If you've really trashed the file by mistake, the :q! command is the best way to exit and abandon your changes. The file reverts to the most recently changed version. So, if you just did a :w, you are stuck with the changes up to that point. If you just want to undo a few bad edits, press u to back out of changes.

You have learned a few vi editing commands. I describe more commands in the following sections. However, before I do, here are a few tips to smooth out your first trials with vi:

- **Esc** — Remember that Esc gets you back to command mode. (I've watched people press every key on the keyboard trying to get out of a file.) Esc followed by ZZ gets you out of command mode, saves the file, and exits.
- **u** — Press u to undo the previous change you made. Continue to press u to undo the change before that, and the one before that.
- **Ctrl+r** — If you decide you didn't want to undo the previous command, use Ctrl+r for Redo. Essentially, this command undoes your undo.

- **Caps Lock** — Beware of hitting Caps Lock by mistake. Everything you type in vi has a different meaning when the letters are capitalized. You don't get a warning that you are typing capitals — things just start acting weird.

- **:!** *command* — You can run a command while you are in vi using : ! followed by a command name. For example, type **:!date** to see the current date and time, type **:!pwd** to see what your current directory is, or type **:!jobs** to see if you have any jobs running in the background. When the command completes, press Enter and you are back to editing the file. You could even do that with a shell (:!bash) to run a few commands from the shell, then type **exit** to return to vi. (I recommend doing a save before escaping to the shell, just in case you forget to go back to vi.)

- **-- INSERT --** — When you are in insert mode, the word INSERT appears at the bottom of the screen. Other messages also appear at the line at the bottom of the screen.

- **Ctrl+g** — If you forget what you are editing, pressing these keys displays the name of the file that you are editing and the current line that you are on. It also displays the total number of lines in the file, the percentage of how far you are through the file, and the column number the cursor is on. This just helps you get your bearings after you've stopped for a cup of coffee at 3a.m.

Moving around the file

Besides the few movement commands described earlier, there are other ways of moving around a vi file. To try these out, open a large file that you can't do much damage to. (Try copying /var/log/messages to /tmp and opening it in vi.) Here are some movement commands you can use:

- **Ctrl+f** — Page ahead, one page at a time.
- **Ctrl+b** — Page back, one page at a time.
- **Ctrl+d** — Page ahead 1/2 page at a time.
- **Ctrl+u** — Page back 1/2 page at a time.
- **G** — Go to the last line of the file.
- **1G** — Go to the first line of the file. (Use any number to go to that line in the file.)

Searching for text

To search for the next occurrence of text in the file, use either the slash (/) or the question mark (?) character. Within the search, you can also use metacharacters. Here are some examples:

- /hello — Searches forward for the word hello.
- ?goodbye — Searches backward for the word goodbye.

- /The.*foot — Searches forward for a line that has the word The in it and also, after that at some point, the word foot.

- ?[pP]rint — Searches backward for either print or Print. Remember that case matters in Linux, so using brackets can search for words that could have different capitalization.

The vi editor was originally based on the ex editor. That editor did not let you work in full-screen mode. However, it did enable you to run commands that let you find and change text on one or more lines at a time. When you type a colon and the cursor goes to the bottom of the screen, you are essentially in ex mode. Here is an example of some of those ex commands for searching for and changing text. (I chose the words Local and Remote to search for, but you can use any appropriate words.)

- :g/Local — Searches for the word Local and prints every occurrence of that line from the file. (If there is more than a screenful, the output is piped to the more command.)

- :s/Local/Remote — Substitutes Remote for the word Local on the current line.

- :g/Local/s//Remote — Substitutes the first occurrence of the word Local on every line of the file with the word Remote.

- :g/Local/s//Remote/g— Substitutes every occurrence of the word Local with the word Remote in the entire file.

- :g/Local/s//Remote/gp — Substitutes every occurrence of the word Local with the word Remote in the entire file, then prints each line so that you can see the changes (piping it through more if output fills more than one page).

Using numbers with commands

You can precede most vi commands with numbers to have the command repeated that number of times. This is a handy way to deal with several lines, words, or characters at a time. Here are some examples:

- 3dw — Deletes the next three words.

- 5cl — Changes the next five letters (that is, removes the letters and enters input mode).

- 12j — Moves down 12 lines.

Putting a number in front of most commands just repeats those commands. At this point, you should be fairly proficient at using the vi command.

> **NOTE**: When you invoke vi on Fedora Core, you're actually invoking the vim text editor, which runs in vi compatibility mode. Those who do a lot of programming might prefer vim, because it shows different levels of code in different colors. vim has other useful features, such as the ability to open a document with the cursor at the same place where it was when you last exited that file.

Summary

Working from a shell command-line interpreter within Linux may not be as simple as using a GUI, but it offers many powerful and flexible features. This chapter describes how to log in to Fedora and use shell commands. Features for running commands include recalling commands from a history list, completing commands, and joining commands.

This chapter describes how shell environment variables can be used to store and recall important pieces of information. It also teaches you to modify shell configuration files to tailor the shell to suit your needs. Finally, this chapter describes how to use the Linux file system to create files and directories, use permissions, and work with files (moving, copying, and removing them), and how to edit text files from the shell using the vi command.

Part II

Using Fedora

Chapter 5: Accessing and Running Applications

Chapter 6: Publishing with Fedora

Chapter 7: Playing Games with Fedora

Chapter 8: Multimedia in Fedora

Chapter 9: Tools for Using the Internet and the Web

Chapter 5

Accessing and Running Applications

In This Chapter

- Using Fedora as an application platform
- Obtaining Fedora applications
- Installing Fedora applications
- Running X Window applications
- Using emulators to run applications from other operating systems
- Running DOS applications
- Running Windows applications with WINE

To get your work done on a computer, you use application programs. Applications let you create documents, crunch data, and communicate with others. As an engine for running applications, Fedora is becoming more viable every day. Not too long ago, there were only a handful of user-friendly applications available. Now there are hundreds — and they're getting more powerful and friendlier all the time.

This chapter describes how to get applications for Fedora and run them. In particular, it teaches you how to download applications from the Internet and install them. For running native Linux applications, this chapter focuses on graphical-based applications (run on an X desktop, including applications distributed over the network).

Besides programs that were specifically created for (or ported to) Linux, it is possible to run applications that were intended for other operating systems. This chapter describes emulators and compatibility software that are available to use with Fedora for running applications created for Windows, DOS, and Macintosh operating systems.

Using Fedora as an Application Platform

Although operating systems are nice (and necessary), people use desktop computers to run application programs. A strong case can be made for using Fedora as a server, but as a desktop system, Fedora is still some distance away from challenging the dominance of the Microsoft Windows operating systems for several reasons:

- Although you can get word processing programs, spreadsheet programs, graphics programs, and almost any other type of application that you want for Linux, many of the most popular applications in each category don't run well in Linux or don't run at all. For example, the latest Microsoft Office product will not run in Linux (though Codeweavers.com and others were successful in running earlier versions of Microsoft Office in Linux). If your company uses Microsoft Word for word processing or Microsoft Excel for spreadsheets, you could try using those files with OpenOffice in Fedora Core. However, those files won't always convert cleanly. Also, many proprietary features that Microsoft Office locks you into (such as macros, scripts, and forms/fields) are not supported fully (or in some cases, at all) in OpenOffice.

- There are many more commercial, battle-tested desktop applications for the Microsoft Windows operating systems than there are for Linux. Because the market is so huge for desktop Windows systems, many software companies develop their products solely for that market.

- Linux applications, as a rule, have historically been more difficult to configure and use than many commercial Windows applications.

That's the bad news. The good news is that Linux is significantly gaining ground. You can now use Linux on your desktop to do almost everything you would want to do on a desktop computer with Microsoft Windows. The time is coming when you will be able to replace the operating systems on the desktop computers in your home or office with Fedora. I believe that, in the long term, Linux could become a preferred operating system for running applications. Here are some reasons:

- Many people believe that networked applications will drive the future of computing. Unlike the first Microsoft Windows systems, which had their roots in the single-user, one-task-at-a-time DOS system, Linux is based on UNIX systems. UNIX was designed from the ground up to deal with many users and many tasks in a networked environment. Fedora offers a strong foundation for networked applications.

- A huge development community is working on open source applications to meet the needs of the Linux community. Recently, some strong commercial offerings have been added.

- In the spirit of Linux and the GNU (which stands for "*GNU is Not UNIX*"), most application programs are free or inexpensive. As a result, you can try out most applications for little or no money. Getting started running Linux applications can be done at a small cost. For example, OpenOffice (the open source version of StarOffice) comes with Fedora Core and the boxed set of StarOffice is only $79.95 (from www.sun.com/staroffice), whereas Microsoft Office will cost you hundreds of dollars. Although you can buy components such as Microsoft Word separately, even they can cost several hundred dollars apiece.

- The transition for desktop users from Windows to Linux is becoming easier, with great strides being made by projects such as the WINE project. WINE (described later in this chapter) lets you run many Windows programs directly in Linux. WINE also provides a path for application developers to more simply port their Windows code to run in Linux. So far, the greatest strides have come in getting Windows games and office productivity applications running in Linux.

The bottom line is that it will take some effort for most people to discard their Microsoft Windows operating systems completely. However, if you are committed to making Fedora Core your sole application platform, there are several ways to ease that transition. Emulation programs let you run many programs that were created for other operating systems. Conversion programs can help you convert graphics and word processing data files from other formats to those supported by Linux applications.

> **CROSS-REFERENCE:** See Chapter 6 for information on importing and exporting word processing and graphics files.

If you are running Linux on a PC, chances are that you already paid for a Microsoft Windows 95, 98, ME, XP, NT, or 2000 operating system. You can either run the different operating systems on different PCs or have Windows and Linux on separate partitions of your hard disk. The latter requires that you reboot each time you want to switch operating systems.

The following section describes applications that run in Fedora that you can use to replace the Windows applications you are used to.

Finding Common Desktop Applications in Linux

If you are going to use Linux as a desktop computer system, you have to be able to write documents, work with graphics, and crunch numbers. You probably also have other favorite applications, like a music player, Web browser, and e-mail reader.

> **NOTE:** Using WINE technology, the people at Codeweavers, Inc. offer a CrossOver Office product that lets you install and run Microsoft Office in Linux. See the "Running Windows Applications with WINE" section later in this chapter.

To give you a snapshot of what desktop applications are available, Table 5-1 contains a list of popular Windows applications, equivalent Linux applications, and where you can find the Linux applications. Although many of these applications have not reached the level of sophistication of their Windows counterparts, they can be cost-effective alternatives.

Table 5-1: Windows-Equivalent Linux Applications

Windows Applications	Linux Applications	Where to Get Linux Applications	Cost
Microsoft Office (office productivity suite)	OpenOffice (`openoffice.org`)	Included on Fedora Core CDs	Free
	Koffice	Included on Fedora Core CDs	Free
	StarOffice	`www.sun.com/staroffice`	$75.95
Microsoft Word (word processor)	OpenOffice Writer	Included on Fedora Core CDs	Free
	AbiWord	Included on Fedora Core CDs	Free
	kword	Included on Fedora Core CDs	Free
Microsoft Excel (spreadsheet)	OpenOffice Calc	Included on Fedora Core CDs	Free
	gnumeric	Included on Fedora Core CDs	Free
	kspread	Included on Fedora Core CDs	Free
Microsoft Powerpoint (presentation)	OpenOffice Impress	Included on Fedora Core CDs	Free
	kpresenter	Included on Fedora Core CDs	Free
Microsoft Internet Explorer (Web browser)	mozilla	Included on Fedora Core CDs	Free
	epiphany	Included on Fedora Core CDs	Free
	konqueror	Included on Fedora Core CDs	Free
	opera	`www.opera.com`	Free download
Microsoft Outlook (e-mail reader)	evolution	Included on Fedora Core CDs	Free
	kmail	Included on Fedora Core CDs	Free
	Mozilla Mail	Included on Fedora Core CDs	Free
Adobe Photoshop (image editor)	The Gimp (gimp)	Included on Fedora Core CDs	Free
Microsoft Front Page (HTML editor)	quanta	Included on Fedora Core CDs	Free
Quicken or Microsoft Money (personal finance)	gnucash	Included on Fedora Core CDs	Free

Windows Applications	Linux Applications	Where to Get Linux Applications	Cost
AutoCAD (computer-aided design)	LinuxCad	`www.linuxcad.com`	$89

The following sections describe how to find and work with application programs that are included or available specifically for Linux.

Obtaining Fedora Applications

Unfortunately, you won't be able to walk into the average computer store and find a lot of Linux application programs. The best way to get Linux applications (other than those included with your Fedora system) is to download them from the Internet. They can also be ordered on CD-ROM from several Linux Web sites.

Software packages that are specifically compiled and packaged for Fedora and other Red Hat Linux distributions are almost always available in RPM format. So when you begin scouring the Internet for Red Hat software (as described later in this chapter), look for software repositories of RPM packages built specifically for the version of Fedora Core that you are using.

Investigating your desktop

More and more high-quality desktop applications are being packaged with Fedora Core, mostly as part of the GNOME or KDE desktop environments. In other words, to start finding some excellent office applications, games, multimedia players, and communications tools, you don't have to look any further than the red hat menu button on your desktop.

So before you start hunting around the Internet for the software you need, see if you can use something already installed with Fedora. The chapters that follow this one describe how to use publishing tools, play games, work with multimedia, and communicate over the Internet — all with programs that are either on the CDs that come with this book or are easily attainable. Appendix B contains a list of the software packages that are included with the complete version of Fedora Core that is packaged with this book.

> **TIP:** To keep up with fixes to software packages that are part of the Fedora Core distribution, Red Hat offers a service for automatically downloading and installing packages. Chapter 10 shows you how to use `up2date` and the yum commands to update your Fedora Core software.

Finding applications on the Internet

If you don't already know the names of applications you want to use, there are a lot of places to look for Linux applications on the Internet. If you do know what you want, your best bet might be to head for a software repository that has packages built specifically for Fedora.

Your best bet for getting high-quality, popular applications that are outside of the Linux distribution you are using is to go to a software repository that has created RPMs of the software that are particular to your distribution. Refer to the "Downloading and installing applications with yum" section later in this chapter for instructions on how to find and access yum repositories built for Fedora distributions.

Here are a few Web sites that you can browse to find detailed information about software that runs in Linux:

- **Freshmeat** (www.freshmeat.net) — This site maintains a massive index of Linux software. You can do keyword searches for software projects or browse for software by category.

- **SourceForge** (www.sourceforge.net) — This site hosts thousands of open source software projects. You can download software and documentation from those projects through the SourceForge site.

- **Tucows Linux site** (linux.tucows.com) — Both free and commercial software for Linux is available from the Tucows Linux Web site. This site also features news articles on Linux and a listing of software downloads from the site by category.

When you purchase a commercial boxed application, you usually get the application on CD. Installation is often simplified, and hard copy documentation is provided. Of course, when you download software, you get immediate gratification — you don't even have to get up from your desk.

TIP: Sometimes software packages will be available in both libc5 and libc6 formats. This designation refers to the version of C programming-language libraries used by the application. If you have a choice, choose the libc6 packages. These are compatible with Red Hat Linux 7 and later (or any Linux kernel version 2.2 and higher). In fact, all major Linux distributions now use libc6. Better yet, look for packages designated for the specific distribution you are using (such as Fedora Core 2, Red Hat Linux 9, and so on.).

You can visit FTP sites containing RPM packages if you already have some idea of what you are looking for. You can start by reading the README and INDEX files for a particular software product to get your bearings. Here are a few sites that are particularly good for finding RPM packages:

- **Fedora.us** (www.fedora.us) — The Fedora project expects to make the Fedora.us site the recommended site for getting extra software packages to run on your Fedora system. Look for that site to become the official Fedora Extras site for getting quality software that is outside of the main Fedora distribution.

- **Rpmfind** (www.rpmfind.net) — Open source software that is already packaged in the RPM Package Management (RPM) format is available from this site. Do a keyword search from this Web site, then download the appropriate RPM from the search results.

- **FreshRPMs** (www.freshrpms.net) — Another site with a good selection of high-quality RPMs.

- **Fedora Download Mirrors** (http://fedora.redhat.com/download/mirrors.html) — Go to this page for a listing of download sites containing Fedora Core software that you can download. Most of these sites also have a variety of freeware and shareware applications that are usable with Linux.

Often, you can't just download a single software package to get the software in that package to work. Many packages depend on other packages. For example, software packages for playing audio and video typically rely on other software packages for decoding different kinds of content. To deal with this issue, Fedora Core has included the yum package.

Downloading and installing applications with yum

The Yellow Dog Updater, Modified (yum) software package lets you install and update selected software packages in RPM format from software repositories on the Web. Once you know the software package that you want, yum is probably the best way to download and install that package.

The yum package is included on the Fedora Core CDs that come with this book. To use yum to install RPM software packages, follow these basic steps:

1. **Determine the software package you want.** Many popular add-on packages for Fedora are already built for specific versions of Fedora Core and Red Hat Linux (Red Hat 8, 9, Fedora Core 1, 2 and so on) and stored in software repositories on the Internet. A small list of repositories are available from the yum Web site at http://linux.duke.edu/projects/yum/repos. You can click any of the repository names to display the exact information to copy and paste into your yum.conf file.

2. **Configure yum.** You need to configure the /etc/yum.conf file to point to the repository that contains the software you want. Then you can install any package that repository contains.

3. **Run yum.** The yum command can be used to download and install any package from the yum repository, including any packages the one you want depends on.

> **CAUTION:** In Red Hat Linux, and so far also in Fedora Core, Red Hat, Inc. has gone to great lengths to ensure that software it provides is of good quality and unimpaired by legitimate patent claims. When you download packages outside of a Red Hat distribution of Linux, you are on your own to check the quality and legality of that software.

Besides downloading and installing new software packages, yum can also be used to check for available updates and list various kinds of information about available packages.

Configuring yum (/etc/yum.conf)

The /etc/yum.conf file already comes preconfigured to be able to install Fedora Core base system packages as well as updates. So, to update your system with packages that are part of the current Fedora Core release, you probably don't need to update yum.conf at all.

To be able to download from a repository that contains software that is not in a Fedora Core distribution, you need to add that repository to the /etc/yum.conf file. Here is an example of an entry in yum.conf that points to such a repository:

```
[freshrpms-fc-1]
name=Freshrpms packages for Fedora Core 2
baseurl=http://ayo.freshrpms.net/fedora/linux/2/i386/freshrpms
```

In this example, for freshrpms-fc-1, the repository is named Freshrpms packages for Fedora Core 2. When you request a software package with yum, it looks in subdirectories of http://ayo.freshrpms.net/fedora/linux/2/i386/freshrpms.

> **NOTE:** As of this writing, the Fedora Core 2 repositories were not available from the location noted. Until they are, try http://ayo.freshrpms.net/fedora/linux/1/i386/freshrpms instead.

Running yum to download and install RPMs

With the repository identified in your yum.conf file, downloading and installing an RPM you want is as simple as running yum with the install option to request the RPM. With an active connection to the Internet, open a Terminal window as root user.

The first thing yum does is download headers for all packages you might want from the repository. Then, after presenting you with the list of dependencies it thinks you need, it asks if you want to install the necessary packages. Here is an example of using the yum command to download the mplayer media player:

```
# yum install mplayer
Gathering header information file(s) from server(s)
Server: Fedora Core 2
Server: Freshrpms packages for Fedora Core 2
Finding updated packages
Downloading needed headers
Resolving dependencies
..Dependencies resolved
I will do the following:
[install: mplayer 1.0-0.9.20040415.1.fc2.fr.i386]
I will install/upgrade these to satisfy the dependencies:

    .
    .
    .

Is this ok [y/N]: y
```

```
        .
        .
        .
Getting mplayer-fonts-1.1-1.fr.noarch.rpm
Getting mplayer-1.0-0.1.20031002.fr.i386.rpm
Calculating available disk space - this could take a bit
mplayer-fonts 100 % done 2/14
mplayer 100 % done 14/14
Installed:  mplayer 1.0-0.1.20031002.fr.i386
Dep Installed: mplayer-fonts 1.1-1.fr.noarch
Transaction(s) Complete
```

As you can see from this example, yum checked three different software repositories: Fedora Core 2(Base and Updates) and Freshrpms packages for Fedora Core 2. After listing the dependencies, yum asks if it is OK to install them. Type **y** and the package and all its dependencies are installed.

Using yum for listing and updating packages

Besides downloading and installing new RPM packages, yum can also be used to list available packages and update packages that are already installed. The following examples illustrate some uses of yum.

```
# yum check-update
```

The check-update option causes yum to check the software repositories for available updated versions of RPM packages you have installed. If you see a package you want to update, you can use the update option. For example, to update the nmap-frontend package, you could type the following:

```
# yum update nmap-frontend
```

If you want to see a list of all packages that are available for download from the repositories you have entered, type the following:

```
# yum list | less
```

Adding the less command to the end lets you scroll through the list of software (it could be long, depending on which repositories you point to). If you try to install a package and it fails with a message like "package xyzpackage needs xyzfile (not provided)" you can check for packages that include the missing file using the provides option as follows:

```
# yum provides missingfile
```

With the provides option, yum will search your repositories for whatever file you enter (instead of missingfile) and return the name of any packages it finds that include that file.

Downloading Linux software

Instead of using yum to download and install software RPMS, you can simply browse for Linux software on the Internet and download it using a Web browser (such as Mozilla) or an FTP program (such as the ncftp command). The browser often enables you to view the contents of an FTP site through a Web interface (look for an index.html file in an FTP directory). An ftp command (such as ncftp) has more options, but is less intuitive. There are also GUI-based FTP applications, such as gFTP, to make FTP services easier to use. (The gFTP command is described in Chapter 9.)

> **NOTE:** The following procedures assume that you have a connection to the Internet.

Downloading with Mozilla

To download a Linux software package from the Internet using Mozilla, follow this procedure:

1. From the desktop panel, start Mozilla.

2. Type the name of an FTP site that has Linux software in the location box and press Enter.

3. To move around the FTP site, click Up to Higher Level Directory to move up, or click on a directory to move down.

4. When you find a package that you want to install, position the cursor over it, click the right mouse button, and then select Save Link Target As.

5. In the Save As window, click the Go Up a Level button to move up, or click a directory to go down until you find where you would like to save the package.

6. Click Save.

As the package is downloaded to your computer, a dialog box displays the progress. Mozilla now has a nice, fairly new download manager that makes it easier to watch the progress of multiple downloads. When the download is complete, the application is ready to be uncompressed and installed (or simply installed if you have an RPM file).

Downloading with ncFTP

If you want to use a text-based means of downloading files (instead of Mozilla), you can use any of several FTP commands that come with Red Hat Linux. One FTP client that I like to use is the ncftp command. (Other options are the ftp and lftp commands.) Here's an example of an ncftp procedure:

> **TIP:** The sftp command is a more secure way to connect to FTP servers. However, the FTP server needs to support ssh requests for sftp to work (which they don't all do). To try an sftp command to connect to an FTP server, use a comand like the following: sftp user@ftp.example.com. Once you are connected, use the commands in the following procedure to get around.

1. From a shell or a Terminal window, type **ncftp** *location*, where *location* is the name of an FTP site. For example:

```
$ ncftp metalab.unc.edu
```

or

```
$ ncftp -u jake ftp://ftp.myveryownsrver.com
```

With no user name, as in the first example, ncftp logs you in as the anonymous user. (As an alternative, you could append the user name to the address. For example, jake@ftp://ftp.myveryownsrver.com.)

With a user name (for example, -u jake), you are prompted to enter the password for that user at the FTP site.

2. When your login is accepted, you can use these commands to find the software package or document that you are looking for:

- **ls** — To list the contents of the current directory.

- **cd** *dir* — To change the current directory to the subdirectory *dir*. If you prefer, you can use two dots (cd ..) to go up a directory level. For example, try cd /pub/Linux/apps/doctools.

3. Type **binary** (to make sure the file is downloaded as a binary file).

4. To download a file from the current working directory, type **get** *file* where *file* is the application name. For example, to download the whichman application while /pub/Linux/apps/doctools is the current directory, type:

```
> get whichman-2.1.tar.gz
```

5. When the download is complete, type **exit**.

> **TIP:** Before you start the ncftp command, make sure that your current directory is the one in which you want to download the file. Alternatively, you could change to the directory you want by using the lcd command within ncftp. For example, to change to /tmp/abcapp, type **lcd /tmp/abcapp**.

Understanding package names and formats

Whenever possible, you want to install the applications you use with Fedora Core from software packages in RPM format (files with a .rpm extension). However, if an RPM isn't available, the software that you want may come in other package formats.

Say you just downloaded a file from the Internet that contains lots of names, numbers, dots, gzs, and tars. What does all that stuff mean? Well, when you break it down, it's really not that complicated.

Most of the names of archive files containing Linux applications follow the GNU-style package-naming conventions. The following example illustrates the package-naming format:

```
mycoolapp-4.2.3-1.i386.rpm
mycoolapp-4.2.3.tar.gz
mycoolapp-4.2.3.src.tar.gz
mycoolapp-4.2.3.bin.SPARC.tar.gz
mycoolapp-4.2.3.bin.ELF.static.tar.gz
```

These examples represent several different packages of the same software application. The name of this package is `mycoolapp`. Following the package name is a set of numbers that represent the version of the package. In this case, it is version 4.2.3 (the major version number is 4, followed by minor version number and patch level 2.3). After the version number is a dot, followed by some optional parts, which are followed by indications of how the file is archived and compressed.

The first line shows a package that is in the RPM Package Manager (`.rpm`) format. The `.i386` before the `.rpm` indicates that the package contains binaries that are built to run Intel i386 architecture computers (in other words, PCs). The -1 indicates the build level (the same package may have been rebuilt multiple times to make minor changes). See the sidebar "Using RPMs versus Building from Source" for the pros and cons of using prebuilt RPM binary packages as opposed to compiling the program yourself.

In the next two lines of the previous example, each file contains the source code for the package. The files that make up the package were archived using the `tar` command (`.tar`) and compressed using the `gzip` command (`.gz`). You use these two commands (or just the `tar` command with the `-z` option) to expand and uncompress the packages when you are ready to install the applications.

Between the version number and the `.tar.gz` extension there can be optional tags, separated by dots, which provide specific information about the contents of the package. In particular, if the package is a binary version, this information provides details about where the binaries will run. In the third line, the optional `.src` tag was added because the developer wanted to differentiate between the source and binary versions of this package. In the fourth line, the `.bin.SPARC` detail indicates that it is a binary package, ready to run on a SPARC workstation. The final line indicates that it is a binary package, consisting of statically linked ELF format executables.

Using Binary RPMs versus Building from Source

Binaries created in RPM format are easily installed, managed, and uninstalled using Red Hat tools. This is the recommended installation method for Fedora Core novices. Sometimes, however, building an application from source code may be preferable. Here are some arguments on both sides:

- RPM — Installing applications from an RPM archive is easy. After the application is installed, there are both shell commands and GUIs for managing, verifying, updating, and removing the RPM package. You don't need to know anything about Makefiles or compilers. When you install an RPM package, RPM tools even check to make sure that other packages that the package depends on are installed. Because Red Hat has released RPM under the GPL, other Linux distributions also use it to distribute their software. Thus, most Linux applications are, or will be, available in RPM format.

- Source code — Not all source-code packages are made into RPM binaries. If you use RPM, you may find yourself with software that is several versions old, when you could simply download the latest source code and run a few tar and make commands. Also, by modifying source code, you can tailor the package to better suit your needs.

For more information on RPMs, refer to the *Red Hat RPM Guide* by Eric Foster-Johnson (Red Hat Press/Wiley, 2003).

Here is a breakdown of the parts of a package name:

- **name** — This is generally an all-lowercase string of characters that identifies the application.
- **dash (-)**
- **version** — This is shown as major to minor version number from left to right.
- **dot (.)**
- **src or bin** — This is optional, with src usually implied if no indication is given.
- **dot (.)**
- **type of binary** — This is optional and can include several different tags to describe the content of the binary archive. For example, i386 indicates binaries intended for Intel architectures (Pentium CPU) and SPARC indicates binaries for a Sparc CPU.
- **dot (.)**
- **archive type** — Often tar is used (.tar)
- **compression type** — Often gzip is used (.gzip)

Using different archive and document formats

Many of the software packages that are not associated with a specific distribution (such as Fedora Core or Debian) use the tar/gzip method for archiving and compressing files. However, you may notice files with different suffixes at software project sites.

NOTE: Because we are using Fedora Core, most of the software applications we install are in RPM Package Management format (`.rpm`). Unless you want to build the software yourself — in which case you'll need the source code — RPM is the format to look for. When it is available, an RPM package from a Fedora Core download site will provide your best chance for getting a software package that will run without modification on a Fedora Core system. The next best is probably `fedora.us`.

Table 5-2 describes the different file formats that you will encounter as you look for software at a Linux FTP site. Table 5-3 lists some of the common document formats that are used in distributing information in Linux.

Table 5-2: Linux Archive File Formats

Format	*Extension*	*Description*
Gzip file	`.gz` or `.z`	File was compressed using the GNU `gzip` utility. It can be uncompressed using the `gzip` or `gunzip` utilities (they are both the same).
Tar file	`.tar`	File was archived using the `tar` command. `tar` is used to gather multiple files into a single archive file. You can expand the archive into separate files using `tar` with different options.
Tar and Gzip file	`.tgz`	A common practice for naming files that are `tar` archives that were compressed with `gzip` is to use the `.tgz` extension.
Bzip2	`.bz2`	File was compressed with the `bzip2` program.
Tar/compressed	`.taz` or `.tz`	File was archived with `tar` and compressed with the UNIX `compress` command.
Linux Software Map	`.lsm`	File contains text that describes the content of an archive.
Debian Binary Package	`.deb`	File is a binary package used with the Debian Linux distribution. (See descriptions of how to convert Debian to Red Hat formats later in this chapter.)
RPM Package Management	`.rpm`	File is a binary package used with Fedora Core. Format also available to other Linux distributions.

Table 5-3: Linux Document Formats

Format	Extension	Description
Hypertext Markup Language	`.html` or `.htm`	File is in hypertext format for reading by a Web browser program (such as Mozilla).
PostScript	`.ps`	File is in PostScript format for outputting on a PostScript printer.
SGML	`.sgml`	File is in SGML, a standard document format. SGML is often used to produce documents that can later be output to a variety of formats.
DVI	`.dvi`	File is in DVI, the output format of the LaTeX text-processing tools. Convert these files to PostScript or Hewlett-Packard's PCL using the `dvips` and `dvilj` commands.
Plain text		Files in Fedora without a suffix are sometimes plain-text files (in ASCII format). (One note of caution: A lot of the commands in Linux, such as those in `/usr/bin` and `/usr/sbin`, have no extension either. If you have a file with no extension, it's best to use the `file` command on it before proceeding with any operation. In fact, using `file` on a previously untested file can prevent problems. A `.txt` file full of binary code could be used to exploit a text editor and do malicious things to the system.)

If you are not sure what format a file is in, use the `file` command as follows:

```
$ file filename
```

This command tells you if it is a GNU `tar` file, RPM, `gzip`, or other file format. (This is a good technique if a file was renamed and lost its extension.)

Installing Fedora Applications

The first part of this section describes how to install and manage applications using tools created for RPM archive files. Later in this section, you will learn how to build and install applications that come as source code packages.

NOTE: The `rpm` command can be used to install any packages that are in RPM format. If you need to install RPM packages that are part of your Fedora Core distribution, you can use the Package Management window to add and remove packages instead of the `rpm` command. The Package Management window is described in Chapter 2. To upgrade existing packages, you can use the `up2date` command (described in Chapter 10) or `yum` command (described earlier in this chapter).

Installing and managing RPM files

When you get an application that is packaged in RPM format, you typically get a single file. The command used to work with RPM package files is rpm. To manage RPM packages, the rpm command has options that let you list all the packages that are installed, upgrade existing packages to newer versions, and query packages for information (such as the files or documentation included with the package). There is also a verify option to check that all files that make up the package are present and unchanged.

The rpm command has the following modes of operation:

- install (-i)
- upgrade (-U)
- freshen (-F)
- query (-q)
- verify (-V)
- signature check (--checksig)
- uninstall (-e)
- rebuild database (--rebuilddb)
- fix permissions (--setperms)
- set owners/groups (--setugids)
- show RC (--showrc)

With these options, you can install RPM packages and verify that their contents are properly installed, correcting any problems that occur. You can also do special things, such as rebuild the RPM database and modify ownership. You must be logged in as the root user to add or remove packages. You may, however, list installed packages, query packages for information, or verify a package's contents without root permission.

The following sections describe how to use rpm to install and work with your RPM applications.

Installing with rpm

To install an RPM archive file with the rpm command that is not yet installed on your system, most people generally use the same options they would if they were upgrading (the -U option). Here's an example of a command line you could use to install a new RPM package.

```
# rpm -U [options] package
```

Package is the name of the RPM archive file. This package may be in the current directory, on a mounted CD (for example, /mnt/cdrom/Fedora/RPMS/*whatever*.rpm), or on an accessible FTP site (for example,

```
ftp://sunsite.unc.edu/pub/Linux/games/strategy/galaxis-1.7-
1.i386.rpm).
```

> **CAUTION:** Interrupting rpm during a package installation can leave stale lock files and possibly corrupt the database. As a result, subsequent rpm commands may hang. If this happens, you can probably correct the problem by removing old database locks. If that doesn't work, you can also try checking whether the database is corrupt and, if so, rebuilding the RPM database. Rebuilding the database can tak a long time, so only do it if the other options don't clear up the problem. Here's how to remove lock files, check the database, and rebuild the database (as root user):
>
> # **rm -f /var/lib/rpm/__db***
>
> # **db_verify /var/lib/rpm/Packages**
>
> Along with the -U option, you can use the following options to get feedback during a new installation:

- **-v** — Prints debugging information during installation. This is a good way to see everything that happens during the install process. (This output can be long, so you may want to pipe it to the less command.) You can get more information by adding multiple -v options (for example, -vv).

- **-h** — Prints 50 hash marks (#) as the package unpacks. The intent is to see the progress of the unpacking process (so you can tell if the program is still working or stalled).

- **-percent** — Prints the percentage of the total package that has been installed throughout the install process.

Before installing a package, rpm checks to make sure that it is not overwriting newer files or installing a package that has dependencies on other packages that are not installed. The following install options can be used to override conditions that may otherwise cause the installation to fail:

- **--force** — Forces the contents of the current package to be installed, even if the current package is older than the one already installed, contains files placed there by other packages, or is already installed. (This is the same as using the oldpackage, replacefiles, and replacepkgs options.) Although it is dangerous to do so, people often use this option to override any issue that might cause the package install to fail (such as an older RPM).

- **--oldpackage** — Forces the package to be installed, even if the current package is older than the one already installed.

- **--replacefiles** — Forces files in this package to be installed, even if the files were placed there by other packages.

- **--replacepkgs** — Forces packages in this archive to be installed, even if they are already installed on the system.

- **--nodeps** — Skips package dependency checks and installs the package, even if packages it depends on are not installed. This option should be used with extreme caution! By not resolving dependencies properly, you can end up with broken software.
- **--ignorearch** — Forces package to be installed, even if the binaries in the package don't match the architecture of your host computer.
- **--excludedocs** — Excludes any man pages, texinfo documents, or other files marked as documentation.
- **--ignoreos** — Forces package to be installed, even if the binaries in the package don't match the architecture of your operating system.

The following is a simple `rpm` command line used to install an RPM archive:

```
# rpm -U RealPlayer-8.0-1.i386.rpm
```

I like to see some feedback when I install something (by default, `rpm` is suspiciously quiet when it succeeds). Here is what the command looks like when I add the `-vv` option to get more verbose feedback, along with some of the output:

```
# rpm -Uvv RealPlayer-8.0-1.i386.rpm
D: =============== RealPlayer-8.0-1.i386.rpm
D: Expected size:      4978643 = lead(96)+sigs(100)+pad(4)+data(4978443)
D:   Actual size:      4978611
D: RealPlayer-8.0-1.i386.rpm: MD5 digest: OK
(f8080e7c3c32eacc6912a5afb364479a)
D:  added binary package [0]
D: found 0 source and 1 binary packages
D: opening  db environment /var/lib/rpm/Packages joinenv
   .
   .
   .
D: installing binary packages
D: opening  db environment /var/lib/rpm/Packages joinenv
D: opening  db index       /var/lib/rpm/Packages create mode=0x42
   .
   .
   .
D: closed   db index       /var/lib/rpm/Basenames
D: closed   db index       /var/lib/rpm/Name
D: closed   db index       /var/lib/rpm/Packages
D: closed   db environment /var/lib/rpm/Packages
```

From this output, you can see that `rpm` finds one binary package in this archive, verifies the checksum, opens the RPM database, installs the packages, and closes the database when done. Another way to verify that the install is actually working is to add the `-h` option, as follows:

```
# rpm -Uvh RealPlayer-8.0-1.i386.rpm
RealPlayer   #################################################
```

With the -h option, rpm chugs out 50 hash marks (#) until the package is done installing. As you can see, when everything goes well, installing with rpm is quite simple. Some problems can occur, however. Here are a couple of them:

- **Package dependencies errors** — If the package you are installing requires an additional package for it to work properly, you will see an error noting the missing package. You should get and install that package before trying your package again. (You can override the failure with install options described above, but I don't recommend that because your package may not work without the dependent package.)

- **Nonroot user errors** — If rpm -U is run by someone who is not the root user, the command will fail. The output will indicate that the /var/lib/rpm database could not be opened. Log in as root user and try again.

Upgrading packages with rpm

The upgrade option (-U) with rpm can, as you might expect, also be used to upgrade existing packages. The format is the same as described above:

```
# rpm -U [options] package
```

> **TIP:** Although there is a separate install option (-i), I recommend using the -U option whether you are doing a new install or an upgrade. With -U, the package installs in either case. So rpm -U always works (with one exception), while rpm -i fails if the package is already installed.
>
> The exception is when you are installing kernel packages. Use -i when installing a new kernel or your old (and presumably, working) kernel will be removed and you could be stuck with an unbootable system!

One issue when upgrading is installing an older version of a package. For example, if you install a new version of some software and it doesn't work as well, you will want to go back to the old version. To do this, you can use the --oldpackage option as follows:

```
# rpm -U --oldpackage AnotherLevel-0.7.4-1.noarch.rpm
```

If a later package of this name already exists, it is removed and the older version is installed.

Freshening packages with rpm

An option that is similar to the upgrade (-U) option is the freshen (-F) option. The main difference between the two is what happens if the RPM you are updating or freshening is not already installed on your Fedora system. The -U can do either a fresh install or an upgrade. The -F will only do an upgrade (so if the package is not already installed, rpm -F will do nothing).

A great use for freshen is when you have a directory full of updated RPM files that you want to install on your system. But, you only want to update those packages that are already installed. In other words, there may be a lot of RPMs in the directory you don't want. Freshen lets you just update the package you already have.

Let's say that you downloaded a directory of RPMs and you want to selectively freshen the ones you have installed. With the directory of RPMs as your current directory, you could type:

```
# rpm -Fhv *.rpm
```

Packages already installed are updated with the new RPMs. All other RPMs are skipped.

> **CAUTION:** Again, note that you should not do freshens or upgrade on kernel packages, since it might cause your only working kernel to be removed when you add the new one.

Removing packages with rpm

If you no longer want to use a package (or you just want to recover some disk space), use the -e option to remove a package. In its simplest form, you use rpm with the -e option as follows:

```
# rpm -e package
```

If there are no dependencies on this package, it is silently removed. Before you remove a package, however, you may want to do a quick check for dependencies. The -q option is used for a variety of query options. (Checking for dependencies isn't necessary because rpm checks for dependencies before it removes a package. You may want to do this for your own information, however.) To check for dependencies, do the following:

```
# rpm -q --whatrequires package
```

If you decide to remove the package, I recommend using the -vv option with rpm -e. This lets you see the actual files that are being removed. I also suggest that you either direct the output to a file or pipe it to the less command because the output often runs off the screen. For example:

```
# rpm -evv jpilot | less
```

This example removes the jpilot package and shows you the files that are being removed one page at a time. (Press the Spacebar to page through the output.)

Other options that you can run with rpm -e can be used to override conditions that would prevent the package from being removed or to prevent some processing (such as not running preuninstall and postuninstall scripts). Three of those options are as follows:

- **--nodeps** — Uninstall the package without checking for dependencies.
- **--noscripts** — Uninstall the package without running any preuninstall or postuninstall scripts.
- **--notriggers** — Uninstall the package without executing scripts that are triggered by removing the package.

If you feel nervous about boldly removing a package, you can always run the uninstall in test mode (--test) before you do the real uninstall. Test mode shows you everything that would happen in the uninstall without actually uninstalling. (Add the `--vv` option to see the details.) Here's an example:

```
# rpm -evv --test jpilot | less
D: opening  db environment /var/lib/rpm/Packages joinenv
D: opening  db index       /var/lib/rpm/Packages rdonly mode=0x0
D: locked   db index       /var/lib/rpm/Packages
D: opening  db index       /var/lib/rpm/Name rdonly mode=0x0
D: opening  db index       /var/lib/rpm/Pubkeys rdonly mode=0x0
    .
    .
    .

D: closed   db index       /var/lib/rpm/Name
D: closed   db index       /var/lib/rpm/Packages
D: closed   db environment /var/lib/rpm/Packages
```

If the results look fine, you can run the command again, without the `--test` option, to have the package removed.

Querying packages with rpm

You can use the query options (`-q`) of `rpm` to get information about RPM packages. This can be simply listing the packages that are installed or printing detailed information about a package. Here is the basic format of an `rpm` query command (at least one option is required):

```
# rpm -q [options]
```

The following list shows some useful options you can use with an `rpm` query:

- **-qa** — Lists all installed packages.
- **-qf** *file* — Lists the package that owns *file*. (The file must include the full path name or `rpm` assumes the current directory.)
- **-qi** *package* — Lists lots of information about a package.
- **-qR** *package* — Lists components (such as libraries and commands) that *package* depends on.
- **-ql** *package* — Lists all the files contained in *package*.
- **-qd** *package* — Lists all documentation files that come in *package*.
- **-qc** *package* — Lists all configuration files that come in *package*.
- **-qp** *[option] package* — Query packages that are not yet installed. Using this option, along with other query options, allows you to query packages you have that are not yet installed.

To list all the packages installed on your computer, use the `-a` query option. Because this is a long list, you should either pipe the output to `less` or, possibly, use `grep` to find the package you want. The following command line displays a list of all installed RPM packages, and then shows only those names that include the string of characters xfree. (The -i option to grep says to ignore case.)

```
# rpm -qa |grep -i xorg
```

If you are interested in details about a particular package, you can use the rpm -i query option. In the following example, information about the dosfstools package (for working with DOS file systems in Linux) is displayed:

```
# rpm -qi dosfstools
Name         : dosfstools           Relocations: (not relocateable)
Version      : 2.8                            Vendor: Red Hat, Inc.
Release      : 5            Build Date: Mon 16 Feb 2004 02:59:38 PM PST
Install Date: Thu 29 Apr 2004 02:15:35 PM PST
Build Host   : tweety.devel.redhat.com
Group        : Applications/System Source RPM:dosfstools-2.8-12.src.rpm
Size         : 70346                          License: GPL
Signature    : DSA/SHA1, Wed 17 Mar 2004 11:48:55 AM PST, Key ID
               da84cbd430c9ecf8
Packager     : Red Hat, Inc. <http://bugzilla.redhat.com/bugzilla>
Summary      : Utilities for making and checking MS-DOS FAT
               filesystems on Linux.
Description :
The dosfstools package includes the mkdosfs and dosfsck utilities,
which respectively make and check MS-DOS FAT filesystems on hard
drives or on floppies.
```

To find out about a package's contents, you can use the -l (list) option with your query. The following example shows the complete path names of files contained in the xpilot package:

```
# rpm -ql dosfstools | less
/sbin/dosfsck
/sbin/fsck.msdos
/sbin/fsck.vfat
/sbin/mkdosfs
/sbin/mkfs.msdos
/sbin/mkfs.vfat
/usr/share/man/man8/dosfsck.8.gz
    .
    .
    .
```

Would you like to know how to use the components in a package? Using the -d option with a query will display the documentation (man pages, README files, HOWTOs, and so on) that is included with the package. If you are having trouble getting your X Window System running properly, you can use the following command line to find documents that may help:

```
# rpm -qd xorg-x11 | less
/usr/X11R6/man/man1/Xmark.1x.gz
/usr/X11R6/man/man1/Xorg.1x.gz
```

```
/usr/X11R6/man/man1/Xserver.1x.gz
/usr/X11R6/man/man1/appres.1x.gz
/usr/X11R6/man/man1/atobm.1x.gz
/usr/X11R6/man/man1/bitmap.1x.gz
/usr/X11R6/man/man1/bmtoa.1x.gz
        .
        .
        .
```

Many packages have configuration files associated with them. To see what configuration files are associated with a particular package, use the `-c` option with a query. For example, this is what you would type to find configuration files that are used with the ppp package:

```
# rpm -qc ppp
/etc/pam.d/ppp
/etc/ppp/chap-secrets
/etc/ppp/options
/etc/ppp/pap-secrets
```

If you ever want to know which package a particular command or configuration file came from, you can use the `-qf` option. In the following example, the `-qf` option displays the fact that the chgrp command comes from the fileutils package:

```
# rpm -qf /bin/chgrp
fileutils-4.1-4
```

Before you install a package, you can do the same queries on it that you would do on an installed package. This can be a great tool for finding information from a package while it is in your current directory, or even in a software repository. Here is an example of using the `-qp` option with `-i` to see the description of a package in a software repository:

```
# rpm -qp -i \
http://ayo.freshrpms.net/fedora/linux/1/i386/freshrpms/RPMS/blackbox-0.65.0-\
8.1.fc1.fr.i386.rpm
Name        : blackbox        Relocations: (not relocatable)
Version     : 0.65.0          Vendor: Freshrpms.net
Release     : 8.1.fc1.fr      Build Date: Thu 25 Mar 2004 12:45:45 PM PST
Install Date: (not installed) Build Host: python2.freshrpms.net
   .
   .
   .
Blackbox is a window manager for the X Window environment, which is...
```

In the previous example, the long command line shown on three lines should actually be typed on one line. If you are concerned about the content or legality of downloading a package, this example is a way to read the description of a package before you even download it.

In the following example, the command lists the files contained in a package that is in the current directory:

```
# rpm -qp -l RealPlayer-8.0-1.i386.rpm
```

Again, this is an excellent way to find out what is in a package before you install it.

Verifying packages with rpm

If something in a software package isn't working properly, or if you suspect that your system has been tampered with, the verify (-V) option of rpm can help you verify installed software against its original software package. Information about each installed package is stored on your computer in the RPM database. By using the verify option, you can check whether any changes were made to the components in the package.

> **NOTE:** The verify option uses the uppercase letter (-V), while the verbose option uses the lowercase (-v).

Various file size and permissions tests are done during a verify operation. If everything is fine, there is no output. Any components that have changed from when they were installed will be printed along with information indicating how they were changed. Here's an example:

```
# rpm -V ppp
S.5....T c /etc/ppp/chap-secrets
S.5....T c /etc/ppp/options
S.5....T c /etc/ppp/pap-secrets
```

This output shows that the ppp package (used to dial up a TCP/IP network such as the Internet) has had three files changed since it was installed. The notation at the beginning shows that the file size (S), the MD5 sum (5), and the modification time (T) have all changed. The letter c shows that these are all configuration files. By reviewing these files to see that the changes were only those that I made to get PPP working, I can verify that the software is okay.

The indicators that you may see when you verify the contents of a configuration file are:

- **5 — MD5 Sum** — An MD5 checksum indicates a change to the file contents.
- **S — File size** — The number of characters in the file has changed.
- **L — Symlink** — The file has become a symbolic link to another file.
- **T — Mtime** — The modification time of the file has changed.
- **D — Device** — The file has become a device special file.
- **U — User** — The user name that owns the file has changed.
- **G — Group** — The group assigned to the file has changed.
- **M — Mode** — If the ownership or permission of the file changed.

> **TIP:** A utility is available to browse the contents of RPM files from Microsoft Windows. With the rpmbrowser.exe utility, you can list and extract files from an RPM distribution. This utility is available from winsite.com (search for rpmbrowser from www.winsite.com/search).

Building and installing from source code

If no binary version of the package that you want is available, or if you just want to tailor a package to your needs, you can always install the package from source code. Source-code CDs for Fedora Core contain the source code equivalent (SRPMs) of the binary packages you installed. You can modify the source code and rebuild it to suit your needs.

> **NOTE:** To get CDs of the Fedora source code, see the mail-in coupon at the back of the book. Kernel source code is included on CD #3 with this book.

Software packages that are not available in RPM format are typically available in the form of a tarball (a bunch of files grouped together into a single file formatted by the `tar` utility) that has been compressed (typically by the `gzip` utility). Although the exact instructions for installing an application from a source code archive vary, many packages that are in the .tgz, .gz and .tar formats follow the same basic procedure.

> **TIP:** Before you install from source code, you will need to install a variety of software development packages. If you have the disk space, I recommend that you install all software development packages that are recommended during Red Hat installation.

The following is a minimal list of C-programming software development tools:

- **gcc** — Contains the `gcc` (GNU C compiler) compiler.
- **make** — Contains the `make` command for making the binaries from Makefiles.
- **glibc** — Contains important shared libraries, the C library, and the standard math library.
- **glibc-devel** — Contains standard header files needed to create executables.
- **binutils** — Contains utilities needed to compile programs (such as the assembler and linker).
- **kernel-source** — Contains the Linux kernel source code and is needed to rebuild the kernel.
- **libc** — Contains libraries needed for programs that were based on `libc` 5, so older applications can run on `glibc` (`libc` 6) systems.

Installing software in SRPM format

To install a source package from the Fedora Core source CDs, do the following:

1. Insert a Fedora Core source CD into the CD-ROM drive. It should mount automatically. (If it doesn't, type **mount /mnt/cdrom** in a Terminal window as root.)

2. Change to the source directory on the CD. For example:

```
# cd /mnt/cdrom/SRPMS
```

3. Choose the package you want to install (type **ls** to see the packages) and install it using the following command:

```
# rpm -iv packagename*.src.rpm
```

(Replace *packagename* with the name of the package you are installing.) The source is installed in the Fedora Core source tree (/usr/src/redhat). Spec files are copied to /usr/src/redhat/SPECS.

4. Change to the SPECS directory as follows:

```
# cd /usr/src/redhat/SPECS
```

5. Unpack the source code as follows:

```
# rpmbuild -bp packagename*.spec
```

6. The package's source code is installed to the /usr/src/redhat/BUILD/*package* directory, where *package* is the name of the software package.

7. You can now make changes to the files in the package's BUILD directory. Read the README, Makefile, and other documentation files for details on how to build the individual package.

Installing software in tar.gz or tar.bz2 formats

Here are some generic instructions that you can use to install many Linux software packages that are in the gzip or tar format:

1. Get the source code package from the Internet or from a CD distribution and copy it into an empty directory (preferably using a name that identifies the package).

2. Assuming the file is compressed using gzip, uncompress the file using the following command:

```
# gunzip package.tar.gz
```

The result is that the package is uncompressed and the .gz is removed from the package name (for example, *package.tar*).

3. From the resulting tar archive, run the tar command as follows:

```
# tar xvf package.tar
```

This command extracts the files from the archive and copies them to a subdirectory of the current directory. (using tar xvfz   package.tar.gz you can do steps 2 and 3 in one step.)

4. Change directories to the new subdirectory created in Step 3, as follows:

```
# cd package
```

5. Look for a file called INSTALL or README. One of these files should give you instructions on how to proceed with the installation. In general, the make command is used to install the package. Here are a few things to look for in the current directory:

If there is a Make.in file, try running:

```
# ./configure –prefix=/usr/local
# make all
```

If there is an Imake file, try running:

```
# xmkmf –a
# make all
```

If there is a Make file, try running:

```
# make all
```

After the program is built and installed, you might have to do additional configuration. You should consult the man pages and/or the HOWTOs that come with the software for information on how to proceed.

> **TIP:** Even if you are not a programmer, reading the source code used to make a program can often give you insight into how that program works. Sometimes notes may be in the source code, but never make it into the documentation.

To try out this procedure, I downloaded the whichman package, which includes utilities that let you find manual pages by entering keywords. The file I downloaded, whichman-2.2.tar.gz, was placed in a directory that I created called /usr/src/which. I then ran the gunzip and tar commands, using whichman-2.2.tar.gz and whichman-2.2.tar as arguments, respectively.

I changed to the new directory, cd /usr/sw/which/whichman-2.2. I then listed its contents. The README file contained information about the contents of the package and how to install it. As the README file suggested, I typed **make**, and then **make install**. The commands whichman, ftwhich, and ftff were installed in /usr/bin. (At this point, you can check the man page for each component to see what it does.)

The last thing I found in the README file was that a bit of configuration needed to be done. I added a MANPATH variable to my $HOME/.bashrc to identify the location of man pages on my computer to be searched by the whichman utility. The line I added looked like this:

```
export
MANPATH=/usr/share/man:/usr/man/man1:/usr/X11R6/man:/usr/share/doc/samba-
2.2.3a/docs
```

In case you are wondering, whichman, ftwhich, and ftff are commands that you can use to search for man pages. They can be used to find several locations of a man page, man pages that are close to the name you enter, or man pages that are located beneath a point in the directory structure, respectively.

Running X Window Applications

Setting up and configuring the X Window System to your liking is the hard part. By comparison, using X to run applications is relatively easy. If you have used Microsoft Windows operating systems, you already know the most basic ways of running an application from a graphical desktop. X, however, provides a much more flexible environment for running native Linux applications.

> **CROSS-REFERENCE:** See Chapter 3 for information on setting up an X desktop.

Starting applications from a menu

To run applications on your own desktop, most X window managers provide a menu, similar to the Microsoft Start menu, to display and select X applications. Applications are usually organized in categories. From the GNOME or KDE desktops in Fedora Core, open the red hat menu, select the category, and then select the application to run. Figure 5-1 shows an example of the Fedora Core Main Menu and the Sound & Video subsubmenu.

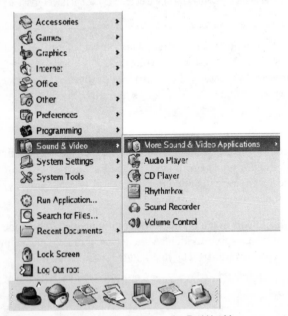

Figure 5-1: Starting X applications from the Red Hat Menu.

Starting applications from a Run Application window

Not all installed applications appear on the menus provided with your window manager. For running other applications, some window managers provide a window, similar to the Run Application window, that lets you type in the name of the program you want to run.

To access the Run Application window:

1. Open the red hat menu.

2. Click Run Application. The Run Application window appears.

3. Click Show List of Known Applications, click the program you want, and then click Run.

    If the application you want isn't on the list, you can either type the command you want to run (along with any options) and click Run, or you can click Append File to browse through directories to select a program to run. If you are running a program that needs to run in a Terminal window, such as the `vi` command, click the Run in Terminal button before running the command. Figure 5-2 is an example of the Run Application window.

Figure 5-2: Select a program to run from the list in the Run Application window.

Starting applications from a Terminal window

I often prefer to run an X application, at least for the first time, from a Terminal window. There are several reasons why I prefer a Terminal window to selecting an application from a menu or Run Application window:

*   If there is a problem with the application, you see the error messages. Applications started from a menu or Run Application usually just fail silently.

- Applications from menus run with set options. If you want to change those options, you have to change the configuration file that set up the menu and make the changes there.

- If you want to try out a few different options with an application, a Terminal window is an easy way to start it, stop it, and change its options.

When you have found an application and figured out the options that you like, you can add it to a menu or a panel (if your window manager supports those features). In that way, you can run a program exactly as you want, instead of the way it is given to you on a menu.

Here is a procedure to run X applications from a Terminal window:

1. Open a Terminal window from your desktop (look for a Terminal icon on your Panel or a Terminal selection on a menu.)

2. Type

   ```
   $ echo $DISPLAY
   ```

   The result should be something similar to the following:

   ```
   :0.0
   ```

   This indicates that the Terminal window will, by default, direct any X application you run from this window to display 0.0 on your local system. (If you don't see a value when you type that command, type **export DISPLAY=:0.0** to set the display value.)

3. Type the following command:

   ```
   $ xmms &
   ```

   The xmms program should appear on your desktop, ready to work with. You should note the following:

   - The xmms command runs in the background of the Terminal window (&). This means that you can continue to use the Terminal window while xmms is running.

   - I encountered no errors running xmms on this occasion. With other applications, however, text sometimes appeared in the Terminal window after the command was run. The text may say that the command can't find certain information or that certain fonts or colors cannot be displayed. That information would have been lost if the command were run from a menu.

4. If you want to know what options are available, type:

   ```
   $ xmms --help
   ```

5. Try it with a few options. For example, if you want to begin by playing a file and you have a WAV audio file named file.wav, you could type:

   ```
   $ xmms file.wav
   ```

6. When you are ready to close the xmms window, you can either do so from the xmms window (right-click on the xmms window and select Exit) or you can kill the process in the Terminal window. Type **jobs** to see the job number of the process. If it was job number 2, for example, you would type **kill %2** to kill the xmms program.

You should try running a few other X commands. A few old X commands you might try are xeyes or xcalc.

Running remote X applications

X lets you start an application from anywhere on the network and have it show up on your X display. Instead of being limited by the size of your hard disk and the power of your CPU and RAM, you can draw on resources from any computer that gives you access to those resources.

Think about the possibilities. You can work with applications launched from any other computer that can run an X application — from a small PC to a supercomputer. Given the proper permission, you can work with files, printers, backup devices, removable drives, other users, and any other resources on the remote computer as though you were on that computer.

With this power, however, comes responsibility. You need to protect the access to your display, especially in networks where the other machines and users are not known or trusted. For example, you wouldn't want to allow anyone to display a login screen on your display, encouraging you to inadvertently give some cracker your login and password.

Traditionally, to run remote X applications, you basically only need to know how to identify remote X displays and how to use whatever security measures are put in place to protect your network resources. Using ssh to launch X applications is even simpler and more secure than the traditional method. Those issues are described in the following sections.

Traditional method to run remote X applications

If there is an X application installed on another computer on your network and you want to use it from your desktop, follow these steps:

*   Open permissions to your X server so that the remote application can use your display.

*   Identify your X server display to the application when it starts up.

When you run an X client on your local system, your local display is often identified as : 0, which represents the first display on the local system. To identify that display to a remote system, however, you must add your computer's host name. For example, if your computer were named *whatever*, your display name would be:

```
whatever:0
```

> **TIP:** In most cases, the host name is the TCP/IP name. For the computers on your local network, the name may be in your `/etc/hosts` file, or it may be determined using the Domain Name System (DNS) service. You could also use a full domain name, such as `hatbox.handsonhistory.com`. X does support other types of transport, although transports other than TCP/IP aren't used much anymore.

You will probably use the display name in this form most of the time you run a remote X application. In certain cases, however, the information may be different. If your computer had multiple X displays (keyboard, mouse, and monitor), you may have numbers other than `:0` (`:1`, `:2`, and so on). It is also possible for one keyboard and mouse to be controlling more than one monitor, in which case you could add a screen number to the address, like this:

```
whatever:0.1
```

This address identifies the second screen (`.1`) on the first display (`:0`). The first screen is identified as `.0` (which is the default because most displays only have one screen). Unless you have multiple physical screens, however, you can skip the screen identifier.

There are two ways to identify your display name to a remote X application:

- `DISPLAY` **shell variable** — The `DISPLAY` shell variable can be set to the system name and number identifying your display. After this is done, the output from any X application run from that shell will appear on the display indicated. For example, to set the `DISPLAY` variable to the first display on `whatever`, type one of the following:

  ```
  export DISPLAY=whatever:0
  ```

  or

  ```
  setenv DISPLAY whatever:0
  ```

  The first example shows how you would set the DISPLAY variable on a `bash` or `ksh` shell. The second example works for a `csh` shell.

- `-display` **option** — Another way to identify a remote display is to add the `-display` option to the command line when you run the X application. This overrides the `DISPLAY` variable. For example, to open an `xterm` window on a remote system so that it appears on the first display on `whatever`, type the following:

  ```
  xterm -display whatever:0
  ```

With this information, you should be able to run an X application from any computer that you can access from your local computer. The following sections describe how you may use this information to start a remote X application.

Launching a remote X application

Suppose you want to run an application from a computer named `remote1` on your local area network (in your same domain). Your local computer is `local1`, and the remote computer is remote1. The following steps show how to run an X application from remote1 from your X display on local1.

> **CAUTION:** This procedure assumes that no special security procedures are implemented. It is the default situation and is designed for sharing applications among trusted computers (usually single-user workstations) on a local network. This method is inherently insecure and requires that you trust all users on computers to which you allow access. If you require a more secure method, refer to the section "Using SSH to run remote X applications" later in this chapter.

1. Open a Terminal window on the local computer.

2. Allow access for the remote computer (for example, remote1) to the local X display by typing the following from the Terminal window:

```
$ xhost +remote1
remote1 being added to access control list
```

3. Log in to the remote computer using any remote login command. For example:

```
$ telnet -l user remote1
Password:
```

   Replace *user* with the name of the user login that you have on the remote computer. You will be prompted for a password.

> **NOTE:** By default, the telnet service is not enabled in Fedora Core. The server (in this example, remote1) must consider the security consequences of enabling remote login services.

4. Type the password for the remote user login. (You are now logged in as the remote user in the Terminal window.)

5. Set the DISPLAY variable on the remote computer to your local computer. For example, if your computer were named pine in the local domain, the command could appear as:

```
$ export DISPLAY=pine:0
```

   (If you are using a csh shell on the remote system, you may need to type **setenv DISPLAY pine:0**.)

6. At this point, any X application you run from the remote system from this shell will appear on the local display. For example, to run a remote Terminal window so that it appears locally, type:

```
$ xterm -title "Terminal from Remote1"
```

   The Terminal window appears on the local display with *Remote1* in the title bar.

> **TIP:** As a rule, I use the -title option when I run remote X applications. In the title, I try to indicate the remote computer name. That way, I am reminded that the application is not running locally.

You need to remember some things about the remote application that appears on your display:

- If you only use the login to run remote applications, you can add the line exporting the DISPLAY variable to a user configuration file on the remote system (such as .bashrc, if you use the bash shell). After that, any application that you run will be directed to your local display.

- Even though the application looks as though it is running locally, all the work is being done on the remote system. For example, if you ran a word processing program remotely, it would use the remote CPU and when you save a file, it is saved to the remote file system.

> **CAUTION:** Don't forget when a remote shell or file editor is open on your desktop. Sometimes people forget that a window is remote and will edit some important configuration file on the remote system by mistake (such as the /etc/fstab file). You could damage the remote system with this type of mistake.

Securing remote X applications

There are several different traditional methods available to prevent just any X application from appearing on your display. Each method offers a different level of security, as well as different amounts of setup. The major security methods that are supported include:

- **Host Access** — This method, described earlier as a default method, lets you decide which host computers can have access to your computer's X display. Use the xhost command to indicate those computers that are allowed access (xhost +*hostname*) and those that are not (xhost -*hostname*). If you allow a host access, any user from that computer is allowed access. This security method works best with small networks and single-user computers owned by people you trust.

- **Magic Cookie** — This method, referred to as the MIT-MAGIC-COOKIE-1 method, lets you grant an individual user remote access to your display. The remote client must present a valid cookie before it can access your display.

  The steps go something like this: You generate a magic cookie (using the mcookie command); you refer to the cookie when you start your X server (usually from a copy of the cookie in your $HOME/.Xauthority file); you distribute this cookie to remote computers that want to show X clients on your display; and the remote client refers to this cookie when it starts.

There are other X security methods that are also based on storing one or more randomly generated keys in the .Xauthority file. XDM-AUTHORIZATION-1 uses a two-part key — a DES encryption key (56-bit) and some random data (64-bit) — to enable access. When a system supports secure RPC, the SUN-DES-1 method can be used to enable access by setting up public and private key pairs that can be validated on a per user basis. Finally, the MIT-KERBEROS-5 method enables both the X client and X server to validate each other (using a Kerberos trusted third party).

> **CROSS-REFERENCE:** For more information about Kerberos, visit the Kerberos home page at
> `web.mit.edu/kerberos/www/`.

Using SSH to run remote X applications

Not only does the `ssh` command provide a secure mechanism for logging in to a remote
system, it also provides a way of securely running remote X applications. After you log in to
the remote computer using `ssh`, you can use that secure channel to forward X applications
back to your local display. Here is an example:

1. Type the following `ssh` command to log in to a remote computer:

   ```
   $ ssh jake@remote1
   jake@remote1's password: *******
   ```

2. After you are logged in, type any X command and the window associated with that
   command appears on your local display. For example, to start the `gedit` command, type:

   ```
   $ gedit &
   ```

For this to work, you don't need to open your local display (using `xhost`). The reason this
works is because the SSH daemon (`sshd`) on the remote system sets up a secure channel to
your computer for X applications. So as not to interfere with any real display numbers, the
SSH daemon (by default) uses the display name of `localhost:10.0`.

This X forwarding feature is on by default with Red Hat Linux systems. The `ForwardX11`
`yes` option set in the `/etc/ssh/ssh_config` file (remotely) is what allows this to work.

Running Microsoft Windows, DOS, and Macintosh Applications

Linux is ready to run most applications that were created specifically for Linux, the X Window
System, and many UNIX systems. Many other applications that were originally created for
other operating systems have also been ported to Linux. There are still, however, lots of
applications created for other operating systems for which there are no Linux versions.

Linux can run some applications that are intended for other operating systems using *emulator*
programs. An emulator, as the name implies, tries to act like something it is not. In the case of
an operating system, an emulator tries to present an environment that looks to the application
like the intended operating system.

> **NOTE:** The most popular of these emulators, called WINE, is not really an emulator at all. WINE is a
> mechanism that implements Windows application-programming interfaces; rather than emulating Microsoft
> Windows, it provides the interfaces that a Windows application would expect. In fact, some people claim
> that WINE stands for "WINE Is Not an Emulator."

In the following sections, I discuss emulators that enable you to run applications that are intended for the following operating systems:

- DOS
- Microsoft Windows 3.1
- Microsoft Windows 95
- Microsoft Windows 98
- Microsoft Windows 2000
- Microsoft Windows NT
- Microsoft Windows XP
- Macintosh (Mac OS)

> **NOTE:** In theory, any application that is Win32-compatible should be able to run using software such as WINE (described later). Whether or not a Microsoft Windows application will run in an emulator in Linux must really be checked on a case-by-case basis.

Available emulation programs include:

- DOSEMU, for running DOS programs. (DOSEMU is available from `http://dosemu.sourceforge.net`).
- WINE, which lets you run Windows 3.1, Windows 95, Windows 98, Windows 2000, Windows NT, and Windows XP binaries. (Windows NT and XP programs are not well supported.)
- ARDI Executor, which enables you to run applications that are intended for the Macintosh operating system (MAC OS).

In general, the older and less complex the program, the better chance it has to run in an emulator. Character-based applications generally run better than graphics-based applications. Also, programs tend to run slower in emulation, due sometimes to additional debugging code put into the emulators.

Running DOS applications

Because Linux was originally developed on PCs, a variety of tools were developed to help developers and users bridge the gap between Linux and DOS systems. A set of Linux utilities called *mtools* enables you to work with DOS files and directories within Linux. A DOS emulator called `dosemu` lets you run DOS applications within a DOS environment that is actually running in Linux (much the way a DOS window runs within a Microsoft Windows operating system).

Using mtools

mtools are mostly DOS commands that have the letter *m* in front of them and that run in Linux (though there are a few exceptions that are named differently). Using these commands, you can easily work with DOS files and file systems. Table 5-4 lists mtools that are available with Linux (if you have the mtools package installed).

Table 5-4: mtools Available with Linux

Command	*Function*
mattrib	The DOS attrib command, which is used to change an MS-DOS file attribute flag.
mbadblocks	The DOS badblocks command, which tests a floppy disk and marks any bad blocks contained on the floppy in its FAT.
mcd	The DOS cd command, which is used to change the working directory to another DOS directory. (The default directory is A:\) that is used by other mtools.
mcheck	The DOS check command, which is used to verify a file.
mcopy	The DOS copy command, which is used to copy files from one location to another.
mdel	The DOS del command, which is used to delete files.
mdeltree	The DOS deltree command, which deletes an MS-DOS directory along with the files and subdirectories it contains.
mdir	The DOS dir command, which lists a directory's contents.
mdu	The Linux du command, which is used to show the amount of disk space used by a DOS directory.
mformat	The DOS format command, which is used to format a DOS floppy disk.
minfo	This command is used to print information about a DOS device, such as a floppy disk.
mkmanifest	This command is used to create a shell script that restores Linux filenames that were truncated by DOS commands.
mlabel	The DOS label command, which is used to make a DOS volume label.
mmd	The DOS md command, which is used to create a DOS directory.
mmount	This command is used to mount a DOS disk in Linux.
mmove	The DOS move command, which is used to move a file to another directory and/or rename it.

Command	Function
mrd	The DOS `rd` command, which is used to remove a DOS directory.
mren	The DOS `ren` command, which is used to rename a DOS file.
mshowfat	This command is used to show the FAT entry for a file in a DOS file system.
mtoolstest	This command is used to test the `mtools` configuration files.
mtype	The DOS `type` command, which is used to display the contents of a DOS text file.
mzip	This command is used to perform operations with Zip disks, including eject, write protect, and query.

I usually use the `mtools` to copy files between my Linux system and a Windows system that is not on my network. I most often use mcopy, which lets me copy files using drive letters instead of device names. In other words, to copy the file vi.exe from floppy drive A: to the current directory in Linux, I would type:

```
# mcopy a:\vi.exe .
```

> **CAUTION:** By default, the floppy-disk drive can be read from or written to only by the root user and the floppy group. To make the floppy drive accessible to everyone (assuming it is floppy drive A:), type the following as root user: **chmod 666 /dev/fd0**.

Using dosemu

The DOS emulator package dosemu does not come with Fedora Core distributions. To use dosemu, download the dosemu RPM file from dosemu.sourceforge.net.

With the utilities that come with the dosemu package, you can run DOS applications, as well as use your computer as if it were running DOS. This includes accessing hardware, working with DOS configuration files, and using the DOS file system.

The following commands can be used to start dosemu within Linux:

- **dosemu** — Starts the DOS emulator in any shell.
- **xdosemu** — Starts the DOS emulator in its own X window.
- **xtermdos** — Starts the DOS emulator in an xterm window.
- **dosdebug** — Starts a debug program to view information and error messages about a running DOS program.

Basic information about your DOS environment is set in the `/etc/dosemu/dosemu.conf` file. The following list describes how the DOS environment is set up and how to change it:

- **CPU** — The CPU is set to emulate an 80386 (Intel 386-compatible). You can change the `$_cpu` value to 80486 or 80586 (for Pentium).

- **Keyboard** — The keyboard is set to `auto`, which tries to set the keyboard based on the current Linux console settings. You can specifically change the keyboard type by setting the `$_layout` value to a variety of other country/language combinations listed in the `dosemu.conf` file (such as `us` for US/English, `de` for German, or `it` for Italian).

- **X Settings** — There are several X settings (beginning with `$_X`) that let you change things such as the title in the DOS window, the font used, and the cursor blink rate.

- **Floppy Disks** — Floppy disk A (`/dev/fd0`) is set to a 3.5-inch floppy (`threeinch`) and floppy disk B (`/dev/fd1`) is not assigned. Either disk can be assigned to be 3.5-inch (`threeinch`), 5.25-inch (`fiveinch`), `atapi`, or `empty`.

- **Hard Disk Images** — The file system that appears when you start DOS is actually a disk image file stored in `/var/lib/dosemu`. By default, `dosemu` uses `hdimage.first` (which is linked to `hdimage.freedos`). You can change that to another DOS image or to a DOS file system (such as `/dev/hda1`, if that partition were a DOS partition).

- **Serial Ports** — No serial ports are assigned by default. You can assign any of the serial ports (`$_com1` to `$_com4`) to a device such as a modem (`/dev/modem`), a mouse (`/dev/mouse`), or a terminal line (`/dev/tty0`).

The `dosemu` package is set up for the root user. It is not very secure to allow multiple users to have access to DOS because DOS does not have the same security protections for files and devices that Linux does. If you want other users on your Linux system to use DOS, however, edit the `/etc/dosemu.users` file so that it includes the following lines:

```
root c_all
all c_all
```

For more information on `dosemu`, visit the `dosemu` home page at `www.dosemu.org`.

Running Microsoft Windows applications with WINE

The WINE project (`www.winehq.com`) has been making great strides in getting applications that were created for Microsoft Windows to run in Linux and other operating systems. WINE is not really an emulator, because it doesn't emulate the entire Windows operating system. Instead, because it implements Win32 application programming interfaces (APIs) and Windows 3.*x* interfaces, the WINE project is more of a "Windows compatibility layer."

To get WINE for your Fedora system, you can go to the following places:

- **Download sites** — You can download WINE free of charge from several different Web sites. Check `winehq.com` for a list of download sites. I downloaded the latest RPMs built for Fedora Core 1 from this site: `http://sourceforge.net/projects/wine/`. (If a Fedora Core 2 version becomes available you should probably use that instead.)

  WINE daily builds are available from `http://wine.dataparty.no` (in RPM format). If you get the daily build, follow the instructions from `http://wine.dataparty.no/install.html`.

- **WineX** — A commercial version of WINE, called WineX, is available from TransGaming, Inc. (`www.transgaming.com`). TransGaming focuses on running Windows games in Linux, using WINE as its base. See Chapter 7 for descriptions of WineX.

- **CodeWeavers** — If you need Microsoft Office or Web browser plug-ins, CodeWeavers (`www.codeweavers.com`) offers CrossOver Office and CrossOver Plug-in, respectively. Although these products cost some money, they offer friendly interfaces for installing and managing the Windows software and browser plug-ins that it supports.

While it's true that you can run many Windows applications using WINE, some fiddling is still required to get many Windows applications to work. If you are considering moving your desktop systems from Windows to Linux, the current state of WINE provides an opportunity to see if some Windows applications you need might run in Linux.

> **CAUTION:** I suggest that you test any application you want to use in WINE before you put it on any computer that is a critical part of your work. Although I haven't done serious damage to my computer, WINE still freezes up the desktop under certain conditions. Please check with the organizations listed in the bullet lists for specific issues related to running Windows applications in Fedora.

Besides developing software, the WINE project maintains a database of applications that run under WINE. More than 1000 applications are listed, although many of them are only partially operational. The point is, however, that the list of applications is growing, and special attention is being paid to getting important Windows 98 and 2000 applications running.

Although not open-source products, VMware and Win4Lin are other good ways to run Windows applications along with a Linux system on the same running computer. With VMware you can simultaneously run Microsoft Windows 98/NT/2000/XP and Linux operating systems on the same PC. You can get more information about VMware from `www.vmware.com`. Win4Lin (`www.netraverse.com`) lets you run Windows applications in a running Linux system.

The next section describes how to set up Linux to run Microsoft Windows applications using WINE.

Understanding WINE

For WINE to let you run Microsoft Windows applications, it needs to have an environment set up that looks like a Microsoft Windows system. The following section takes you through the steps of installing and configuring the latest released wine RPM for Fedora Core (under Red Hat Packages) from `sourceforge.net/projects/wine`.

When you install the wine package in Fedora Core, the package creates `/etc/wine/wine.conf` and `/etc/wine/system.reg` files that, like the Windows registry, identify the locations of components an application would need in a Microsoft Windows operating system.

The location of the basic Microsoft Windows operating-system directories for WINE is the `$HOME/.wine/c` directory for each user, which looks like the C: drive to wine. The `/usr/share/wine-c` directory contains the system-wide version of this directory that each user can point to. Table 5-5 shows how C: and other Windows drive letters are mapped to Linux directories and devices.

Table 5-5: Microsoft Windows Drive Letters in WINE

Description	Drive Letter or Name	Linux Directory or Output Location	Linux Device Name (If Applicable)
Floppy drive	A:	`/mnt/floppy`	/dev/fd0
Hard disk #1	C:	`$HOME/.wine/c` `/usr/share/wine-c`	
CD-ROM	D:	`/mnt/cdrom`	/dev/cdrom
Temp directory	E:	`/tmp`	
User's home directory	F:	`$HOME` (user's home directory)	
Root directory	Z:	`/`	
Serial ports	COM1		/dev/ttyS0
	COM2		/dev/ttyS1
	COM3		/dev/ttyS2
	COM4		/dev/modem
Parall ports	Lpt1		/dev/lp0
Print spooler	LPT1	Pipes printer jobs to the `lpr` command (`| lpr`)	

Description	Drive Letter or Name	Linux Directory or Output Location	Linux Device Name (If Applicable)
WineLook	Win95 (how the system appears to apps: Win31, Win98, or the default Win95)		

Within the `/usr/share/wine-c` directory (that is, your C: drive), you should see some things that are familiar to you if you are coming from an older Windows environment: `autoexec.bat` and `config.sys` files (empty to start with), and `My Documents`, `Program Files`, and `windows` directories.

Assuming that the basic directory structure is okay with you, you may still want to consider changing a few items. For example, you may want to change the command to print documents (set in the `/etc/wine/wine.conf` file) to something other than the "`| lpr`" command to use a particular printer or add some Linux printing options.

> **NOTE:** For details on configuring the `wine.conf` file, see the Wine User Guide. That guide (`wine-user.pdf`) is stored in the `/usr/share/doc/wine*` directory when you install the wine RPM for Fedora Core.

Setting up Microsoft Windows applications

The best way to understand how to set up and run a Microsoft Windows application is to step through the process of getting a simple Microsoft Windows accessory to run in WINE. To do this procedure, you will need the following:

- The wine package installed in your Fedora Core system.
- Access to Microsoft Windows components, including the executable program you want to run and the DLL files the executable needs to run.

If you have a dual-boot system (Fedora Core and Microsoft Windows), the best way to do this procedure is to have Linux running with the Windows partition mounted somewhere so that you can copy the files you need. Otherwise, you should skip the first step and copy the files you need from a floppy or CD, or over the network.

In this example, I want to be able to run the Microsoft Paint program (`mspaint.exe`) from Windows in Linux using WINE. Here is an example of how to go about it.

1. If you have a dual-boot system start by mounting the Windows partition. Here's how:
   - As the root user, from a Terminal window, type:

```
# fdisk -l
```

This lists your hard-disk partitions. Look for a partition that is listed as something like WIN95 FAT32.

- Make a directory on which to mount your Windows partition. For example, to use the /mnt/win directory, type:

```
# mkdir /mnt/win
```

- Assuming that the Windows partition is on the first partition of the first IDE hard disk (/dev/hda1), type the following to mount the Windows partition:

```
# mount -t vfat /dev/hda1 /mnt/win
```

At this point you should have a mounted Windows partition available from /mnt/win.

- To make that partition permanently available to you from Linux, add the following line to your /etc/fstab file:

```
/dev/hda1              /mnt/win          vfat       defaults    0   0
```

The preceding entry causes the Microsoft Windows partition to mount automatically on /mnt/win each time your Fedora Core system boots up.

> **NOTE:** For the purposes of the rest of this procedure, I assume that you have a Microsoft Windows system accessible from /mnt/win. If this is not the case, you need to find a way to copy files from your Microsoft Windows system on another computer to the locations described in this procedure.

2. Copy the mspaint.exe program to a location accessible from your Linux computer. For example, with a mounted Microsoft Windows partition as previously described, you could type:

```
# cp /mnt/win/Program\ Files/Accessories/mspaint.exe /bin/
```

3. Run the wine command with mspaint.exe as an argument to see if it can run or if it needs some added DLL files.

```
# wine /bin/mspaint.exe
err: module:PE_fixup_imports Module (file) MFC42.DLL (which is
         needed by Z:\a\mspaint.exe) not found
```

This says that you need the mfc42.dll file to be able to run mspaint.exe.

4. Next, copy the necessary DLL file from the Microsoft Windows partition. For example:

```
# cp /mnt/win/windows/system/mfc42.dll /usr/share/wine-
c/windows/system/
```

5. With the proper DLL files installed, type **wine /bin/mspaint.exe** again and the Microsoft Paint window opens. An example of the Paint window running in Fedora Core is shown in Figure 5-3.

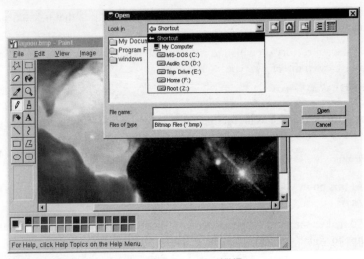

Figure 5-3: Running Paint in Red Hat Linux using WINE.

In Figure 5-3, Paint is displaying a bitmap image that I opened from the Fedora Core file system. Choose File → Open. In the Open dialog box, you can see how the application views the locations available to it. The C:, D:, E:, F:, and Z: drives all represent the locations shown in Table 5-5. (The computer in the example didn't have a floppy, or you would also see the A: drive.)

Finding Microsoft Windows applications for WINE

Applications that have been tested to run under WINE are maintained at the Wine Application Database (http://appdb.codeweavers.com/). The database is divided into the following categories:

- Educational Software and Computer-Based Training
- Games
- Multimedia
- Networking & Communications
- Productivity
- Programming / Software Engineering
- Reference, Documentation, and Information
- Scientific, Technical, and Mathmatical
- Special Purpose
- Utilities

Hundreds of applications have been submitted for the database. Most of the packages that have been tested are games. In most cases, the person listing the application describes the platform he or she tested on and any experiences he or she had getting it to run. The host of the list, codeweavers.com, asks that you create a login to access the database.

Running Macintosh applications with ARDI Executor

Besides enabling you to run many popular older Macintosh applications on the PC, ARDI Executor (www.ardi.com) from ARDI, Inc. lets you work with Mac-formatted floppies and a variety of Mac drives. Find more about ARDI Executor from www.ardi.com/executor.php.

ARDI also maintains a listing of compatible Mac software in its Compatibility Database. There are literally hundreds of Mac applications listed. Each application is color coded (green, yellow, orange, red, or black) to indicate how well the software runs under ARDI. Green and yellow are fully usable and largely usable, respectively. Orange is mostly unusable. Red means the application won't run at all, and black means it won't run because it requires features that aren't implemented in ARDI. At a glance, about two-thirds of the applications listed were either green or yellow.

> **CROSS REFERENCE:** With Mac OS X being based on a Linux-like operating system, more and more cross-platform applications will be available for Linux and the Mac. Interoperating Mac OS X with Linux systems is discussed in more detail in Chapter 26.

Summary

Between applications written directly for Linux and other UNIX systems, those that have been ported to Linux, and those that can run in emulation, hundreds of applications are available to be used with Fedora Core systems. There are dozens of locations on the Internet for downloading Linux applications, and many more that can be purchased on CD.

To simplify the process of installing and managing your Linux applications, Red Hat developed the RPM Package Manager (RPM). Using tools developed for RPM, such as the rpm command, you can easily install, remove, and perform queries on Linux RPM packages.

Of the types of applications that can run in Linux, those created for the X Window System provide the greatest level of compatibility and flexibility when used in Linux. However, using emulation software, it is possible to run applications intended for DOS, Microsoft Windows 95/98/2000/NT/XP, and Macintosh operating systems.

Chapter 6

Publishing with Fedora

In This Chapter

- Using OpenOffice.org
- Using commercial word processors
- Creating documents with Groff and LaTeX
- Creating DocBook documents
- Printing documents with Linux
- Displaying documents with ghostscript and Acrobat
- Working with graphics
- Using scanners driven by SANE

To survive as a desktop system, an operating system must be able to perform at least one task well: produce documents. It's no accident that, after Windows, Microsoft Word (often bundled into Microsoft Office) is the foundation of Microsoft's success on the desktop. Fedora includes tools for producing documents, manipulating images, scanning, and printing. Almost everything you would expect a publishing system to do, you can do with Fedora.

OpenOffice.org is a powerful open-source office suite available as part of the Fedora distribution. Based on the Sun Microsystem Star Office productivity suite, OpenOffice.org includes a word processor, spreadsheet, presentation manager, and other personal productivity tools. In many cases, OpenOffice.org can act as a drop-in replacement for Microsoft Office.

The first document and graphics tools for Linux were mostly built on older, text-based tools. Recently, more sophisticated tools for writing, formatting pages, and integrating graphics have been added. Despite their age, many of the older publishing tools (such as Groff and LaTeX) are still used by people in the technical community.

In this chapter, I describe both text-based and GUI-based document preparation software for Fedora. I also describe tools for printing and displaying documents, as well as software for working with images.

Using OpenOffice.org

Some have called OpenOffice.org a significant threat to Microsoft's dominance of the desktop market. If a need to work with documents in Microsoft Word format has kept you from using Linux as your desktop computer, OpenOffice.org is a big step toward removing that obstacle.

> **NOTE:** If you are willing to pay a few dollars, CrossOver Office from Codeweavers.com lets you install and run older versions of Microsoft Office (97, 2000, XP, and so on) from your Linux desktop. See Chapter 5 for further information or check out `www.codeweavers.com/products/office`.

Fedora includes the entire OpenOffice.org suite of desktop applications. Based on the StarOffice source code, OpenOffice.org consists of the following office-productivity applications:

- OpenOffice.org **Writer** — A word-processing application that can work with documents in file formats from Microsoft Word, StarOffice, and several others. Writer also has a full set of features for using templates, working with fonts, navigating your documents, including images and effects, and generating tables of contents.

- OpenOffice.org **Calc** — A spreadsheet application that lets you incorporate data from Microsoft Excel, StarOffice, Dbase, and several other spreadsheet formats. Some nice features in Calc enable you to create charts, set up database ranges (to easily sort data in an area of a spreadsheet), and use the data pilot tool to arrange data in different points of view.

- OpenOffice.org **Draw** — A drawing application that enables you to create, edit, and align objects; incorporate textures; include textures and colors; and work with layers of objects. It lets you incorporate images, vector graphics, AutoCAD, and a variety of other file formats into your drawings. Then, you can save your drawing in the OpenOffice.org Drawing or StarDraw formats.

- OpenOffice.org **Math** — A calculation program that letsyou create mathematical formulas.

- OpenOffice.org **Impress** — A presentation application that includes a variety of slide effects. Using Impress, you can create and save presentations in the Microsoft PowerPoint, StarDraw, and StarImpress formats.

Unlike other applications that were created to work with Microsoft document and data formats, OpenOffice.org (although not perfect) does a very good job of opening and saving those files with fewer problems. Very basic styles and formatting that open in OpenOffice.org often don't look noticeably different from the way they appear in Microsoft Office. In other cases, such things as bullets, alignment and indentation can appear quite different in Writer than they do in Word. Also, some features such as macros and scripting features in Word may not work at all in Writer.

Icons for launching Writer, Impress, and Calc are placed on the Fedora desktop panel. Alternatively, to open those and other OpenOffice.org applications, click Office from the main menu. Then select the OpenOffice.org application you want to open. Figure 6-1 shows an example of OpenOffice.org Writer displaying and working with a document file that was originally created in Microsoft Word.

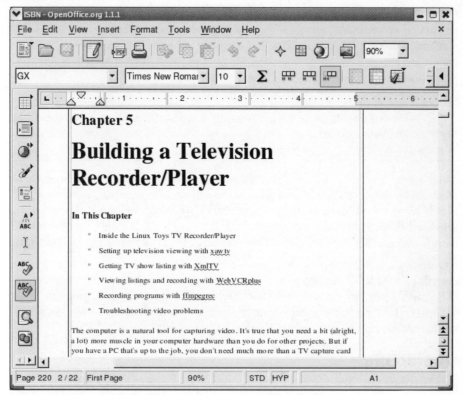

Figure 6-1: Work with Microsoft Word documents in OpenOffice.org Writer.

The controls in OpenOffice.org are similar to the ones you would find in Word. Toolbars include boxes for identifying filenames, changing styles, font types, and font sizes. Buttons let you save and print the file, change the text alignment, and cut, copy, and paste text. In other words, Writer includes almost everything you expect in an advanced word processor. In addition, Writer includes a handy PDF button to output a file directly to the PDF format. This is very useful for exchanging documents or placing data on the Internet.

> **NOTE**: Find out more about OpenOffice.org at `www.OpenOffice.org`. Also note that technically, the name of the suite is OpenOffice.*org*, for copyright reasons associated with simply calling it OpenOffice.

Other Word Processors

Other free word processors that come with Fedora include AbiWord and KOffice (which is part of the KDE desktop). As for commercial offerings, there is StarOffice from Sun Microsystems.

- **StarOffice** — The StarOffice productivity suite contains applications for word processing, spreadsheets, presentation graphics, e-mail, news, charting, and graphics. It was created to run on Linux systems, but it runs in other environments as well. It can import and export a variety of Microsoft file formats. StarOffice is owned by Sun Microsystems, which sells it as a commercial product.

> **NOTE:** One reason for paying for StarOffice when you can get OpenOffice.org software for free is that you get a bunch of extras with StarOffice. The extras that come with StarOffice include a spellchecker, clip art, many more file converters (although the best ones are for converting Microsoft formats), a database module, and technical support.

- **AbiWord** — The AbiWord word processor (`abiword` command) is the first application produced by the AbiSource project (`www.abisource.com`). Besides working with files in its own AbiWord format (.abw and .zabw), AbiWord can import files in Microsoft Word and several other formats. If AbiWord is not installed, you can install the abiword package from the second installation CD (CD #2) that comes with this book.

- **KOffice** — The KOffice package contains a set of office productivity applications designed for the KDE desktop. It includes a word processor (KWord), spreadsheet (KSpread), a presentation creator (KPresenter), and a diagram drawing program (KChart). These applications can be run separately or within a KOffice Workspace. (The koffice package is on CD #2 of the disks that come with this book.)

Using StarOffice

The StarOffice suite from Sun Microsystems Inc. (`www.sun.com/staroffice`) is a product that runs on Linux, UNIX, and Windows operating systems. Like OpenOffice.org, StarOffice contains many features that make it compatible with Microsoft Office applications. In particular, it includes the capability to import Microsoft Word and Excel files.

StarOffice is probably the most complete integrated office suite for Linux. It includes:

- **StarOffice Writer** — This is the StarOffice word processing application. It can import documents from a variety of formats, with special emphasis on Word documents.

- **StarOffice Calc** — This is the spreadsheet program that comes with StarOffice. You can import spreadsheets from Microsoft Excel and other popular programs.

- **StarOffice Impress** — This module enables you to create presentations.

- **StarOffice Draw** — This is a vector-oriented drawing program. It includes the capability to create 3D objects and to use texturing.

- **StarOffice Base** — You can manage your data with StarBase, a friendly front end for databases. It can access a variety of database interfaces.

There are also other tools in StarOffice that enable you to create business graphics, edit raster images, and edit mathematical formulas (StarOffice Math).

You can download StarOffice 7 for Linux or purchase a boxed set from the StarOffice Web site at www.sun.com/staroffice. Although StarOffice was once available free for download, the current price to download the software for home users is $75.95.

> **NOTE**: OpenOffice.org is an open-source project sponsored by Sun Microsystems. Sun takes the OpenOffice.org source code and uses it (along with other modules) to create StarOffice. This is very similar to Mozilla, an open-source Web browser, and Netscape, a commercial product built from the Mozilla sources.

AbiWord

The AbiWord word processor is a very nice, free word processor from the AbiSource project (www.abisource.com). If you are creating documents from scratch, AbiWord includes many of the basic functions you need to create good-quality documents.

With AbiWord, you can select what type of document the file contains. You can select to read the file in the following formats:

- AbiWord (.abw)
- GZipped AbiWord (.zabw)
- Rich Text Format (.rtf)
- Microsoft Word (.doc)
- UTF8 (.utf8)
- Text (.txt)

AbiWord doesn't yet import all of these file types cleanly. Although the recent version of AbiWord supports Word styles, sometimes tables, graphics, and other features don't translate perfectly. If you want to work with a Word document in AbiWord, open it as AbiWord, correct any font problems, and save the document in AbiWord format. AbiWord has vastly improved in the past few releases, but you can still have problems if you need to exchange files with others who are using Word. (To keep files in the Word format, OpenOffice.org and StarOffice work much better, but not perfectly.)

AbiWord is a great first try as a usable word processor. Recently added features, such as styles and bullets, continue to make AbiWord a more useful word processing tool. It's not competitive with comparable commercial products, but its developers continue to improve it.

Using KOffice

There is now a KDE office suite of applications that go with the KDE desktop. The KOffice package has the basic applications you would expect in an integrated office suite: a word processor (KWord), spreadsheet (KSpread), a presentation creator (KPresenter), and a diagram drawing program (KChart).

You can start by opening the KOffice Workspace (from the red hat menu, Office → More Office Applications → KOffice Workspace). From the workspace window that opens, you can select from the different office applications from the left column. Open multiple documents in any of the applications. Then click on Documents in the left column to choose which one to display at the moment.

Figure 6-2 shows the KOffice workspace, displaying a KWord document.

You can work with a variety of document, spreadsheet, and image types; not many commercial document types are supported yet. So you may need to import documents using other tools before you can read them into KWord. The KSpread can open several different spreadsheet styles, however, such as Microsoft Excel and GNUmeric spreadsheets.

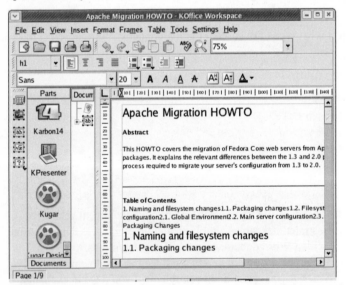

Figure 6-2: The KOffice Workspace lets you work with multiple KDE office applications at once.

Using Traditional Linux Publishing Tools

With old-school text processors (such as Groff and TeX), you can ignore document appearance while writing. Plain-text macros instruct post-processors how to lay out a document for printing after writing is done. With word processors (such as OpenOffice.org

Word and StarOffice Writer), you mark up text and see the basic layout of the document as you write.

Some attributes of the traditional Linux publishing tools make them particularly well suited for certain types of document publishing. Groff and LaTeX (which is based on TeX) come with Fedora and have been popular among technical people. Reasons for that include:

- You can manipulate files in plain text. Using tools such as `sed` and `grep`, you can scan and change one document or hundreds with a single command or script.

- Scientific notation is supported. With `geqn`, you can create complex equations. LaTeX and TeX are suited for technical notation. Some math publications require LaTeX.

- Editing can be faster because traditional Linux documents are created with a text editor. You usually get better performance out of a text editor than a word processor.

Simple page layouts work well with Linux documentation tools. For example, a technical book with a few flow charts and images can be easily produced and maintained using Groff or TeX documentation tools. Letters and memos are also easy to do with these tools. And, of course, Linux man pages are created with text-based tools.

Also, Linux likes PostScript. Although people think of PostScript as a printing language, it is really more of a programming language (you could write PostScript code directly). Most Linux document-processing software includes print drivers for PostScript. Also, some documents on the Web are distributed in PostScript (`.ps`).

The drawback to the traditional Linux document tools is that they are not intuitive. Although there are some easier front-ends to LaTeX (see the description of LyX later on), if you are creating documents in a text editor, you need to learn what macros to type into your documents and which formatting and print commands to use.

> **NOTE:** For many years, the UNIX system documentation distributed by AT&T was created in troff/nroff formats, which predate Groff. The documents used separate macro packages for man pages and guide material. Using a source code control system (SCCS), thousands of pages of documentation could be ported to different UNIX systems. Today, Fedora still includes the same tools to work with man pages.

Creating Documents in Groff or LaTeX

You can create documents for either of Linux's Groff (troff/nroff) or LaTeX (TeX) styles of publishing using any text editor. Fedora comes with several text editors, or you can download others from the Internet. See the "Choosing a Text Editor" sidebar for more information.

The process of creating documents in Groff or LaTeX consists of the following general steps:

1. Create a document with any text editor. The document will contain text and markup.

2. Format the document using a formatting command that matches the style of the document that you created (for example, with `groff` or `latex`). During this step, you may need to indicate that the document contains special content, such as equations (`eqn` command), tables (`tbl` command), or line drawings (`pic` command).

3. Send the document to an output device. The device may be a printer or display program.

If you are used to a word processor with a GUI, you may find these publishing tools difficult. In general, Groff is useful to create man pages for Linux. LaTeX is useful if you need to produce mathematical documents, perhaps for publication in a technical journal.

Text processing with Groff

The `nroff` and `troff` text formatting commands were the first interfaces available for producing typeset quality documents with the UNIX system. They aren't editors; rather, they are commands that you send your text through, with the result being formatted pages:

- **nroff** — Produces formatted plain text and includes the ability to do pagination, indents, and text justification, as well as other features.

- **troff** — Produces typeset text, including everything `nroff` can do, plus the ability to produce different fonts and spacing. The `troff` command also supports kerning.

Choosing a Text Editor

Hardcore UNIX or Linux users tend to edit files with either the vi or emacs text editor. These editors have been around a long time and are hard to learn, but efficient to use. (Your fingers never leave the keyboard.) The emacs editor has some GUI support, though it will run fine in a Terminal window. There are also GUI versions of vi and emacs that add menu and mouse features to the editors. These are GVim (`gvim` command in the vim-X11 package) and Xemacs (`xemacs` command) editors.

Some of the other, simpler text editors that can run on your graphical desktop are:

- **gedit** (`gedit` command) — This text editor, which comes with Fedora, is the lightweight text editor for GNOME. It has simple edit functions (cut, copy, paste, and select all) and settings let you set indentations and word wrap. Special functions, such as a spell checker and a diff feature are included. You can start gedit by typing **gedit** from a Terminal window. Go to `http://gedit.sourceforge.net` for more information.

- **Advanced Editor** (`kwrite` command) — This text editor includes a menu bar to create, open, or save files. It also has simple edit functions (cut, copy, paste, undo, and help). Other edit features let you set indents, find and replace text, and select all text. This tool comes with the KDE desktop, so you can access it by selecting Accessories → More Accessories → Kwrite.

- **Text Editor** (`kedit` command) — Another simple text editor. Features let you open files from your file system or from a URL. It also includes a convenient toolbar and a spell checker. It comes with the KDE desktop, so you can access it by selecting Accessories → More Accessories → Text Editor.

- **nedit** (`nedit` command) – nedit is a rather plain-looking, but very advanced, X-based text editor. It provides all the usual editing functions as well as syntax-highlighting modes for a plethora of programming languages, as well as an advanced macro system. Despite its advanced features, it is also simple for beginners to figure out and use.

- **joe** (`joe` command) – joe is a text-mode editor which is much simpler than either vi or emacs. joe also has the ability to mimic other text editors, such as vi, emacs, pico, and even the late, lamented WordStar. In addition to standard features like search and replace, arrow key movements for the cursor, and so on, joe also offers macros, code editing features, and the ability to move or format large chunks of text easily.

The `groff` command is the front-end for producing `nroff/troff` documentation. Because Linux man pages are formatted and output in Groff, most of the examples here help you create and print man pages with Groff.

People rarely use primitive `nroff/troff` markup. Instead, there are common macro packages that simplify creating `nroff/troff` formatted documents, which include:

- **man** — The man macros are used to create Linux man pages. You can format a man page using the `-man` option to the `groff` command.

- **mm** — The mm macros (memorandum macros) were created to produce memos, letters, and technical white papers. This macro package includes macros for creating a table of contents, lists of figures, references, and other features that are helpful for producing technical documents. You can format an mm document using the `-mm groff` option.

- **me** — The me macros were popular for producing memos and technical papers on Berkeley UNIX systems. Format an me document using the `-me groff` option.

Groff macro packages are stored in `/usr/share/groff/*/tmac`. The man macros are called from the `an.tmac` file, mm macros are from `m.tmac`, and me macros are from `e.tmac`. The naming convention for each macro package is *xxx*.`tmac`, where *xxx* is replaced by one or more letters representing the macro package. In each case, you can understand the name of the macro package by adding an m to the beginning of the file suffix.

TIP: Instead of noting a specific macro package, you can use `-mandoc` to choose a macro package.

When you run the `groff` formatting command, you can indicate on the command line which macro packages you are using. You can also indicate that the document should be run through any of the following commands that preprocess text for special formats:

- **eqn** — This preprocessor formats macros that produce equations in groff.
- **pic** — This preprocessor formats macros that create simple line drawings in groff.
- **tbl** — This preprocessor formats macros that produce tables within groff.

The formatted Groff document is output for a particular device type. The device can be a printer, a window, or (for plain text) your shell. Here are output forms supported by Groff:

- **ps** — Produces PostScript output for PostScript printer or a PostScript previewer.
- **lj4** — Produces output for an HP LaserJet4 printer or other PCL5-compatible printer.
- **ascii** — Produces plain-text output that can be viewed from a Terminal window.
- **dvi** — Produces output in TeX dvi, to output to a variety of devices described later.
- **X75** — Produces output for an X11 75 dots/inch previewer.
- **X100** — Produces output for an X11 100 dots/inch previewer.
- **latin1** — Produces typewriter-like output using the ISO Latin-1 character set.

Formatting and printing documents with Groff

You can try formatting and printing an existing Groff document using any man pages on your Fedora system (such as those in /usr/share/man/*). (Those man pages are compressed, so you can copy them to a temporary directory and unzip them to try out Groff.)

These commands copy the chown man page to the /tmp directory and unzips it. Then, groff formats the chown man page in plain text so you can page through it on your screen.

```
$ cp /usr/share/man/man1/chown.1.gz /tmp
$ gunzip /tmp/chown.1.gz
$ groff -Tascii -man /tmp/chown.1 | less
```

In the previous example, the chown man page (chown.1.gz) is copied to the /tmp directory, is unzipped (using gunzip), and is output in plain text (-Tascii) using the man macros (-man). The output is piped to less, to page through it on your screen. Instead of piping to less (| less), you could direct the output to a file (> /tmp/chown.txt).

To format a man page for typesetting, you could specify PostScript or HP LaserJet output. You should either direct the output to a file or to a printer. Here are a couple of examples:

```
$ groff -Tps -man /tmp/chown.1 > /tmp/chown.ps
$ groff -Tlj4 -man -l /tmp/chown.1
```

The first example creates PostScript output (-Tps) and directs it to a file called /tmp/chown.ps. That file can be read by a PostScript previewer (such as ghostscript) or sent to a printer (lpr /tmp/chown.ps). The next example creates HP LaserJet output (-Tlj4) and directs it to the default printer (-l option).

Creating a man page with Groff

Before HOW-TOs and info files, man pages were the foundation for information about UNIX (and UNIX-like) systems. Each command, file format, device, or other component either had its own man page or was grouped on a man page with similar components. To create your own man page requires that you learn a few macros (in particular, man macros). Figure 6-3 shows the source for a fictitious man page for a command called waycool.

> **TIP:** Most man pages are stored in subdirectories of /usr/share/man. Before you create a man page, refer to similar man pages to see the markup and the headings they include. In man1 are commands; man2 has system calls; man3 has library functions; man4 has special device files (/dev/*); man5 has file formats; man6 has games; man7 has miscellaneous components; and man8 has administrative commands.

A few other kinds of macros are used in the man page. The .IP macros format indented paragraphs for things such as options. The man page also contains some lower-level font requests; for example, \fB says to change the current font to bold, \fI changes the font to italic, and \fR changes it back to regular font. (This markup is better than asking for a particular font type because it just changes to bold, italic, or regular for the current font.) Figure 6-4 shows what the waycool man page looks like after it is formatted with groff:

```
$ groff -man -Tps -l waycool.1
```

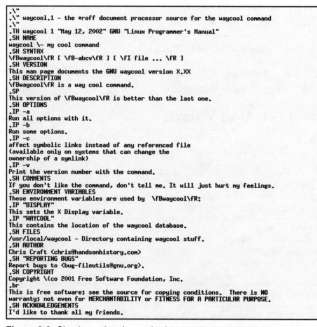

```
.\"
.\" waycool.1 - the *roff document processor source for the waycool command
.\"
.TH waycool 1 "May 12, 2002" GNU "Linux Programmer's Manual"
.SH NAME
waycool \- my cool command
.SH SYNTAX
\fBwaycool\fR [ \fB-abcv\fR ] [ \fI file ... \fR ]
.SH VERSION
This man page documents the GNU waycool version X.XX
.SH DESCRIPTION
\fBwaycool\fR is a way cool command.
.SP
This version of \fBwaycool\fR is better than the last one.
.SH OPTIONS
.IP -a
Run all options with it.
.IP -b
Run some options.
.IP -c
affect symbolic links instead of any referenced file
(available only on systems that can change the
ownership of a symlink)
.IP -v
Print the version number with the command.
.SH COMMENTS
If you don't like the command, don't tell me. It will just hurt my feelings.
.SH ENVIRONMENT VARIABLES
These environment variables are used by  \fBwaycool\fR:
.IP "DISPLAY"
This sets the X Display variable.
.IP "WAYCOOL"
This contains the location of the waycool database.
.SH FILES
/usr/local/waycool - Directory containing waycool stuff.
.SH AUTHOR
Chris Craft <chris@handsonhistory.com>
.SH "REPORTING BUGS"
Report bugs to <bug-fileutils@gnu.org>.
.SH COPYRIGHT
Copyright \(co 2001 Free Software Foundation, Inc.
.br
This is free software; see the source for copying conditions.  There is NO
warranty; not even for MERCHANTABILITY or FITNESS FOR A PARTICULAR PURPOSE.
.SH ACKNOWLEDGEMENTS
I'd like to thank all my friends.
```

Figure 6-3: Simple markup is required to create man pages.

```
waycool(1)                    Linux Programmer's Manual                    waycool(1)


NAME
        waycool – my cool command
SYNTAX
        waycool [ -a bcv ] [ file ... ]
VERSION
        This man page documents the GNU waycool version X.XX
DESCRIPTION
        waycool is a way cool command.  This version of waycool is better than the last one.
OPTIONS
        -a      Run all options with it.
        -b      Run some options.
        -c      affect symbolic links instead of any referenced file (available only on systems that can change the
                ownership of a symlink)
        -v      Print the version number with the command.
COMMENTS
        If you don't like the command, don't tell me. It will just hurt my feelings.
ENVIRONMENT VARIABLES
        These environment variables are used by waycool:
        DISPLAY
                This sets the X Display variable.
        WAYCOOL
                This contains the location of the waycool database.
FILES
        /usr/local/waycool - Directory containing waycool stuff.
AUTHOR
        Chris Craft <chris@handsonhistory.com>
REPORTING BUGS
        Report bugs to <bug-fileutils@gnu.org>.
COPYRIGHT
        Copyright © 2001 Free Software Foundation, Inc.
        This is free software; see the source for copying conditions.  There is NO warranty; not even for MER-
        CHANTABILITY or FITNESS FOR A PARTICULAR PURPOSE.
ACKNOWLEDGEMENTS
        I'd like to thank all my friends.
```

Figure 6-4: Man page formatting adds headers and lays out the page of text.

Table 6-1 lists the macros that you can use on your man pages. These macros are described on the man(7) manual page (type **man 7 man** to view that page).

Table 6-1: Man Macros

Macro	Description
.B	Bold
.BI	Bold, then italics (alternating)
.BR	Bold, then roman (alternating)
.DT	Set default tabs
.HP	Begin a hanging indent
.I	Italics
.IB	Italics, then bold (alternating)
.IP	Begin hanging tag. For options. Long tags use .TP.
.IR	Italics, then roman (alternating)
.LP	Begin paragraph
.PD	Set distance between paragraphs

Macro	Description
.PP	Begin paragraph
.RB	Roman, then bold (alternating)
.RE	End relative indent (after .RS)
.RI	Roman, then italics (alternating)
.RS	Begin relative indent (use .RE to end indent)
.SB	Small text, then bold (alternating)
.SM	Small text. Used to show words in all caps.
.SH	Section head
.SS	Subheading within a .SH heading.
.TH	Title heading. Used once at the beginning of the man page.
.TP	Begin a hanging tag. Begins text on next line, not same line as tag.

Creating a letter, memo, or white paper with Groff

Memorandum macros (which are used with the -mm option of Groff) were once popular among UNIX users for producing technical documents, letters, and memos. Although more modern word processors with a variety of WYSIWYG templates have made mm outdated, in a pinch mm can still be a quick way to create a typeset-style document in a text environment.

To format and print (to a PostScript printer) a document with mm macros, use the following:

```
$ groff -mm -Tps -l letter.mm
```

The following is a simple example of how to use mm macros to produce a letter:

```
.WA "Christopher T. Craft"
999 Anyway Way
Anytown, UT 84111 USA
.WE
.IA
John W. Doe
111 Notown Blvd.
Notown, UT 84111
.IE
.LO RN "Our telephone conversation"
.LO SA "Dear Mr. Doe:"
.LT
In reference to our telephone conversation on the 4th, I am calling to
confirm our upcoming appointment on the 18th. I look forward to
discussing the merger. I believe we have a win-win situation here.
```

```
.FC "Yours Truly,"
.SG
```

The output of the letter, if you use the `groff` command line mentioned in the paragraph preceding the code example, is shown in Figure 6-5.

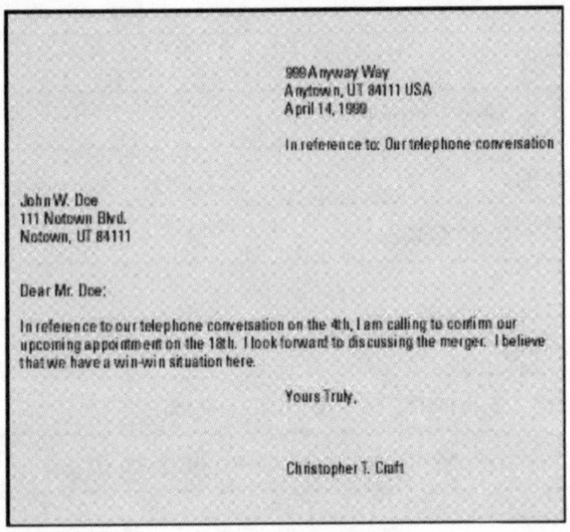

Figure 6-5: Create a simple letter using mm macros.

The mm macros were often used to produce technical memos. The following is an example of a sign-off sheet that might go at the front of a larger technical memo.

```
.TL
Merger Technical Specifications
.AF "ABC Corporation"
.AU "Christopher Craft"
.AT "President"
.AS
This memo details the specifications for the planned merger.
.AE
.MT "Merger Description and Marching Orders"
As a result of our talks with XYZ corporation, we plan to go
forward with the merger. This document contains the following:
.BL
.LI
Schedule and time tables.
.LI
Financial statements.
.LI
Asset allocations.
.LE
.SP
Please add any corrections you have, then sign the approval line
indicated at the bottom of this sheet.
.FC
.SG
```

```
.AV "John W. Doe, XYZ Corporation President"
.AV "Sylvia Q. Public, XYZ Corporation CFO"
.NS
Everyone in the corporation.
.NE
```

Figure 6-6 shows the output of this memo.

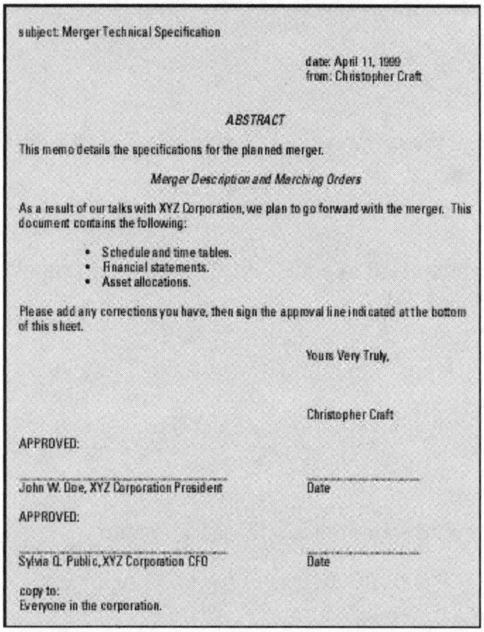

Figure 6-6: Add headings and approval lines automatically to memos.

> **NOTE:** For a complete listing of mm macros, see the `groff_mm` man page. More than 100 mm macros exist. Also, dozens of defined strings let you set and recall information (such as figure names, tables, table of contents information, and text) that is automatically printed with different headings.

Adding equations, tables, and pictures

To interpret special macros for equations, tables, and line drawings, you can run separate commands (`eqn`, `tbl`, and `pic` commands) on the file before you run the `groff` command. Alternatively, you can add options to the `groff` command line to have the file preprocessed automatically by any of the commands (`-e` for `eqn`, `-t` for `tbl`, and `-p` for `pic`).

Here are some examples of EQN, TBL, and PIC markup included in a Groff document. The first example shows an equation that can be processed by `eqn` for a Groff document:

```
.EQ
a ~ mark = ~ 30
.EN
.sp
.EQ
a sup 2 ~ + ~ b sup 2~lineup = ~ 1000
.EN
.sp
.EQ
x sup 3 ~ + ~ y sup 3 ~ + ~ z sup 3~lineup = ~ 1400
.EN
```

If this appeared in a memo called memoeqn.mm, the memo would be preprocessed by eqn and then sent to the printer using the following command:

```
$ groff -Tps -l -mm -e memoeqn.mm
```

All data between the .EQ and .EN macros are interpreted as equations. The resulting output from the equation would appear as shown in Figure 6-7.

$$a = 30$$
$$a^2 + b^2 = 1000$$
$$x^3 + y^3 + z^3 = 1400$$

Figure 6-7: Produce equations in documents with the use of the eqn command's .EQ and .EN macros.

To create a table in a Groff document, use the .TS and .TE macros of the tbl preprocessor. The following is an example of the markup used to produce a simple table.

```
.TS
center, box, tab(:);
c s s
c | c | c
l | l | l.
Mergers and Acquisitions Team
=
Employee:Title:Location
=_
Jones, James:Marketing Manager:New York Office
Smith, Charles:Sales Manager:Los Angeles Office
Taylor, Sarah:R&D Manager:New York Office
Walters, Mark:Information Systems Manager:Salt Lake City Office
Zur, Mike:Distribution Manager:Portland Office
.TE
```

After the .TS macro starts the table, the next line indicates that the table should be centered on the page (center) and surrounded by a line box and that a colon will be used to separate the data into cells (tab(:)). The next line shows that the heading should be centered in the box (c) and should span across the next two cells (s s). The line after that indicates that the heading of each cell should be centered (c | c | c) and that the data cells that follow should be left justified (1 | 1 | 1).

> **CAUTION:** There must be a period at the end of the table definition line. In this case, it is after the 1 | 1 | 1. line. If the period is not there, tbl will try to interpret the text as part of the table definition. In this case, tbl will fail and stop processing the table, so the table will not print.

The rest of the information in the table is the data. Note that the tab separators are colon characters (:). When the table is done, you end it with a .TE macro. If the table were in a memo called memotbl.mm, tbl could preprocess the memo and then send it to the printer using the following command:

```
$ groff -Tps -l -mm -t memotbl.mm
```

Data between .TS and .TE macros are interpreted as tables. Figure 6-8 displays this example.

Employee	Title	Location
Jones, James	Marketing Manager	Jones, James
Smith, Charles	Sales Manager	Smith, Charles
Taylor, Sarah	R&D Manager	Taylor, Sarah
Walters, Mark	Information Systems Manager	Walters, Mark
Zur, Mike	Distribution Manager	Zur, Mike

Figure 6-8: Set how text is justified and put in columns with the use of the tbl command's .TS and .TE macros.

The PIC macros (.PS and .PE) let you to create simple diagrams and flow charts to use in Groff. PIC is really only qualified to create simple boxes, circles, ellipses, lines, arcs, splines, and some text. The following is some PIC code that could be in a Groff document:

```
.PS
box invis "Start" "Here"; arrow
box "Step 1"; arrow
circle "Step 2"; arrow
ellipse "Step 3"; arrow
box "Step 4"; arrow
box invis "End"
.PE
```

After the .PS, the first line indicates an invisible box (invis) that contains the words Start Here, followed by an arrow. That arrow connects to the next box containing the words Step 1. The next elements (connected by arrows) are a circle (Step 2), an ellipse (Step 3), another box (Step 4), and another invisible box (End). The .PE indicates the end of the pic drawing.

If these lines appeared in a document called memopic.mm, you could preprocess the PIC code and print the file using the following command:

```
$ groff -Tps -l -mm -p memopic.mm
```

Figure 6-9 shows an example of this drawing.

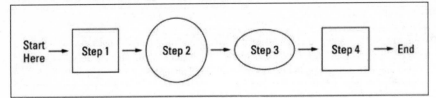

Figure 6-9: Create simple flow diagrams with the pic command's .PS and .PE macros.

Text processing with TeX/LaTeX

TeX (pronounced *tech*) is a collection of commands used primarily to produce scientific and mathematical typeset documents. The most common way to use TeX is by calling a macro package. The most popular macro package for Tex is LaTeX, which takes a higher-level approach to formatting TeX documents. TeX and LaTeX tools are contained in the tetex-latex package.

> **NOTE:** The tetex-* packages needed to use the TeX examples shown in this book are found on CD #2 that accompanies this book. The tetex-doc package is on CD # 4.

TeX interprets the LaTeX macros from the latex format file (`latex.fmt`). By default, the `latex.fmt` and `plain.fmt` format files are the only ones that are automatically built when the TeX package is installed. Other macro files that you can use with TeX include:

- **amstex** — Mathematical publications, including the American Mathematical Society uses this as their official typesetting system.
- **eplain** — Includes macros for indexing and table of contents.
- **texinfo** — Macros used by the Free Software Foundation to produce software manuals. Text output from these macros can be used with the Linux `info` command.

You can create a TeX/LaTeX file using any text editor. After the text and macros are created, you can run the `tex` command (or one of several other related utilities) to format the file. The input file is in the form `filename.tex`. The output is generally three different files:

- **`filename.dvi`** — This is the device-independent output file that can be translated for use by several different types of output devices (such as PostScript).
- **`filename.log`** — This is a log file that contains diagnostic messages.
- **`filename.aux`** — This is an auxiliary file used by LaTeX.

The .dvi file produced can be formatted for a particular device. For example, you could use the `dvips` command to output the resulting .dvi file to your PostScript printer (`dvips filename.dvi`). Or you could use the `xdvi` command to preview the dvi file in X.

Creating and formatting a LaTeX document

Because LaTeX is the most common way of using TeX, this section describes how to create and format a LaTeX document. A LaTeX macro (often referred to as a command) appears in a document in one of the two following forms:

- *\string{option}*[*required*] — First there is a backslash (\), which is followed by a string of characters. (Replace `string` with the name of the command.) Optional arguments are contained in braces ({ }), and required arguments are in brackets ([]).

- *\?{option}*[*required*] — First there is a backslash (\), which is followed by a single character that is not a letter. (Replace `?` with the command character.) Optional arguments are contained in braces ({ }), and required arguments are in brackets ([]).

Each command defines some action to be taken. The action can control page layout, the font used, spacing, paragraph layout, or a variety of other actions on the document. The minimum amount of formatting that a LaTeX document can contain is the following:

```
\documentclass{name}
\begin{document}
   TEXT GOES HERE!
\end{document}
```

You should replace `{name}` with the name of the class of document you are creating. Valid document classes include article, book, letter, report, and slides. The text for the file, along with your formatting commands, goes between the `begin` and `end` document commands.

The best way to get started with LaTeX is to use the LyX editor. LyX provides a GUI for creating LaTeX documents. It also contains a variety of templates you can use instead of just creating a document from scratch. Figure 6-10 shows an example of the LyX editor.

> **NOTE:** The LyX editor doesn't come with Fedora. Find an RPM package for LyX from the LyX site at `ftp://ftp.lyx.org/pub/lyx/bin`. Look for a Fedora or Red Hat RPM.

If you want to edit LaTeX in a regular text editor, you need to be familiar with the LaTeX commands. For a complete listing of the LaTeX commands, type `info latex` and then go to the section "Commands within a LaTeX document."

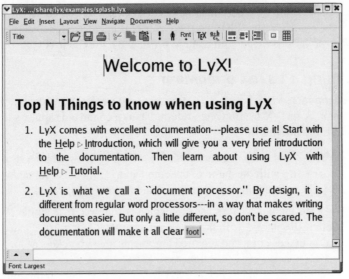

Figure 6-10: Create LaTeX documents graphically with the LyX editor.

Using the LyX LaTeX Editor

Start the LyX LaTeX editor with the lyx command. LyX comes with a lot of supporting documentation. Click Help to select a Tutorial, User's Guide, or other information.

To start your first document, I recommend that you select one of the templates provided with LyX. Templates are located in /usr/share/lyx/templates. To open a template, click File → New from Template. A list of available templates appears. You can use them to create letters, slides, and articles, for example.

Besides offering standard editing functions, such as cut, copy, and paste, you can perform a variety of markup functions from the Layout menu. As for mathematical functions, the Math menu enables you to insert fractions, square root, exponent, sum, and integral functions into your document. When you are done, you can:

- Print the file to a PostScript printer or output a PostScript (.ps) file. (Click File → Print, select the printing method, and then click OK.)

- Export the file to LaTeX, DVI, PostScript, or ASCII Text. (Click File → Export and choose from the list of file formats.)

LyX calls itself a WYSIWYM editor — What You Say Is What You Mean. As a result, what you see on the screen as you edit is not exactly what the printed document will look like. For example, no extra white space will appear between lines by pressing Enter multiple times.

Because LyX supports style files, it enables you to create documents that meet several different standards. For example, LyX supports typesetting for the American Mathematics Society (AMS) journals using the article text class. Other text classes supported include:

- **article** — One-sided paper with no chapters.
- **report** — Two-sided report, tending to be longer than an article.
- **book** — Same as report, with additional front and back matter.
- **slides** — For producing transparencies.
- **letter** — Includes special environments for addresses, signatures, and other elements.

Printing LaTeX files

Whether you create your own LaTeX file, export one from the LyX LaTeX editor, or download one from the Internet, several utilities are available to format, print, or display the output. Here are some of your choices:

- To format a LaTeX file (`filename.tex`), run the following command:

```
$ latex filename.tex
```

- To print a DVI file (`filename.dvi`), send it to your default PostScript printer, and type the following:

```
$ dvips filename.dvi
```

- To display a DVI file in an X window, type the following:

```
$ xdvi filename.dvi
```

- To print a DVI file to a PCL printer, such as an HP LaserJet, type the following:

```
$ dvicopy filename.dvi
$ dvilj filename.dvi
```

- The `dvilj` command doesn't support virtual fonts directly. The `dvicopy` command converts the fonts so that the PCL printer can handle them.

Converting documents

Documents can come to you in many different formats. Search just some of the Linux FTP sites on the Internet and you will find files in PostScript, DVI, man, PDF, HTML, and TeX. There are also a variety of graphics formats. Fedora comes with lots of utilities to convert documents and graphics from one format to another. The following is a list of document and graphics conversion utilities:

- **dos2unix** — Converts a DOS text file to a UNIX (Linux) text file.

- **fax2ps** — Converts TIFF facsimile image files to a compressed PostScript format. The PostScript output is optimized to send to a printer on a low-speed line. This format is less efficient for images with a lot of black or continuous tones. (In those cases, tiff2ps might be more effective.)

- **fax2tiff** — Converts fax data (Group 3 or Group 4) to a TIFF format. The output is either low-resolution or medium-resolution TIFF format.

- **g32pbm** — Converts a Group 3 fax file (either digifax or raw) to a portable bitmap.

- **gif2tiff** — Converts a GIF (87) file to a TIFF format.

- **man2html** — Converts a man page to an HTML format.

- **pal2rgb** — Converts a TIFF image (palette color) to a full-color RGB image.

- **pbm2g3** — Converts a portable bitmap image to a fax file (Group 3).

- **pdf2dsc** — Converts a PDF file to a PostScript document dsc file. The PostScript file conforms to Adobe Document Structuring Conventions (DSC). The output enables PostScript readers (such as Ghostview) to read the PDF file a page at a time.

- **pdf2ps** — Converts a PDF file to a PostScript file (level 2).

- **pfb2pfa** — Converts Type 1 PostScript font (binary MS-DOS) to ASCII-readable.

- **pk2bm** — Converts a TeX pkfont font file to a bitmap (ASCII file).

- **ppm2tiff** — Converts a PPM image file to a TIFF format.

- **ps2ascii** — Converts PostScript or PDF files to ASCII text.

- **ps2epsi** — Converts a PostScript file to Encapsulated PostScript (EPSI). Some word processing and graphic programs can read EPSI. Output is often low quality.

- **ps2pdf** — Converts PostScript file to Portable Document Format (PDF).

- **ps2pk** — Converts a Type 1 PostScript font to a TeX pkfont.

- **pstotext** — Converts a PostScript file to ASCII text. pstotext is similar to ps2ascii, but handles font encoding and kerning better than ps2ascii. pstotext doesn't convert PDFs.

- **ras2tiff** — Converts a Sun raster file to a TIFF format.

- **texi2html** — Converts a Texinfo file to HTML.

- **tiff2bw** — Converts an RGB or Palette color TIFF image to a grayscale TIFF image.

- **tiff2ps** — Converts a TIFF image to PostScript.

- **unix2dos** — Converts a UNIX (Linux) text file to a DOS text file.

Besides these tools many graphical applications, such as The GIMP, let you save images into several different formats (BMP, JPEG, PNG, TIFF, and so on), using the Save As feature.

Creating DocBook documents

Documentation projects often need to produce documents that are output in a variety of formats. For example, the same text that describes how to use a software program may need to be output as a printed manual, an HTML page, and a PostScript file. The standards that have been embraced most recently by the Linux community for creating what are referred to as *structured documents* are SGML, XML, and DocBook.

Understanding SGML and XML

Standard Generalized Markup Language (SGML) was created to provide a standard way of marking text so that it could be output later in a variety of formats. Because SGML markup is done with text tags, you can create SGML documents using any plain-text editor. Documents consist of the text of your document and tags that identify each type of information in the text.

Unlike markup languages such as Groff and HTML, SGML markup is not intended to enforce a particular look when you are creating the document. So, for example, instead of marking a piece of text as being bold or italic, you would identify it as an address, paragraph, or a name. Later, a style sheet would be applied to the document to take the tagged text and assign a look and presentation.

Because SGML consists of many tags, to simplify producing documents based on SGML other projects have cropped up to better focus the ways in which SGML is used. In particular, the Extensible Markup Language (XML) was created to offer a manageable subset of SGML that would be specifically tailored to work well with Web-based publishing.

So far in describing SGML and XML, I have only referred to the frameworks that are used to produce structured documents. Specific documentation projects need to create and, to some extent, enforce specific markup definitions for the type of documents they need to produce. These definitions are referred to as Data Type Definitions (DTDs). For documentation of Linux itself and other open source projects, DocBook has become the DTD of choice.

Understanding DocBook

DocBook is a DTD that is well suited for producing computer software documents in a variety of formats. It was originally created by the OASIS Consortium (www.oasis-open.org) and is now supported by many different commercial and open-source tools.

DocBook's focus is on marking content, instead of indicating a particular look (that is, font type, size, position, and so on.). It includes markup that lets you automate the process of creating indices, figure lists and tables of contents, to name a few. Tools in Fedora let you output DocBook documents into HTML, PDF, DVI, PostScript, RTF, and other formats.

DocBook is important to the Linux community because many open-source projects are using DocBook to produce documentation. For example, the following is a list of organizations, and related Web sites, that use DocBook to create the documents that describe their software:

- Linux Documentation Project (`www.tldp.org/LDP/LDP-Author-Guide`)
- GNOME Documentation
  (`developer.gnome.org/projects/gdp/handbook/gdp-handbook`)
- KDE Documentation Project (`www.kde.org/documentation`)
- FreeBSD Documentation Project (`www.freebsd.org/docproj`)

If you want to contribute to any of the above documentation projects, refer to the Web sites for each organization. In all cases, they publish writers' guides or style guides that describe the DocBook tags that they support for their writing efforts.

Creating DocBook documents

You can create the documents in any text editor, using tags that are similar in appearance to HTML tags (with beginning and end tags appearing between less-than and greater-than signs). There are also word processing programs that allow you to create DocBook markup.

The following procedure contains an example of a simple DocBook document produced with a plain-text editor and output into HTML using tools that come with Fedora.

1. Create a directory in your home directory to work in and go to that directory. For example, you could type the following from a Terminal window:

```
$ mkdir $HOME/doctest
$ cd $HOME/doctest
```

2. Open a text editor to hold your DocBook document. For example, you could type:

```
$ gedit cardoc.sgml
```

(A text editor such as `jedit`, which you can get at `www.jedit.org`, can also be useful for dealing with the long tag names used in docbook.)

3. Enter the tags and text that you want to appear in your document. Most DocBook documents are either `<book>` type (large, multi-chapter documents) or `<article>` type (single chapter documents). To try out a DocBook document, type the following:

```
<xml version="1.0">
<article>
  <title>Choosing a new car</title>
  <artheader>
    <abstract>
      In this article, you will learn how to price,
      negotiate for, and purchase an automobile.
    </abstract>
  </artheader>
  <section>
    <title>Getting Started</title>
    <para>
```

```
      The first thing you will learn is how to figure out
      what you can afford.
    </para>
  </section>
  <section>
    <title>The Next Step</title>
    <para>
    After you know what you can afford, you can begin your
    search.
    </para>
  </section>
</article>
```

There are a few things you should notice about this document. The entire document is wrapped in article tags (`<article> </article>`). The article title is in title tags (`<title> </title>`). The section tags (`<section> </section>`) indicate sections of text that have a title and paragraph each. These sections can later be treated separately in the TOC.

4. Save the file and exit from the text editor.

5. Next, you can try translating the document you just created into several different formats. For example, to create HTML output you could type the following:

```
$ db2html cardoc.sgml
```

The result is a new directory called `cardoc`. The result from db2html in the `cardoc` directory was: stylesheet-images directory, `t2.html` file, and `x12.html` file.

6. To view the HTML file just created, I typed the following:

```
$ epiphany $HOME/doctest/cardoc/t2.html
```

Figure 6-11 shows an example of the output created from the db2html command. The screen on the left shows the first page. Click the Next link at the top of the page. The second page that you see is shown on the right. During conversion to HTML, the db2html command adds Next/Previous buttons to each page. It also puts the title of each section in a Table of Contents on page one and in the browser's title bar.

From this point, you can continue to add content and different types of tags. If you are writing documents for a particular project (such as the Linux projects mentioned earlier), you should get information on the particular tags and other style issues they require.

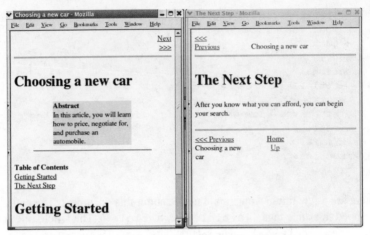

Figure 6-11: The DocBook file is output in HTML with the db2html command.

Converting DocBook documents

The previous example shows how to create a simple DocBook document and convert it to HTML output. The following Fedora utilities convert DocBook to other formats:

- **docbook2dvi** — Converts a DocBook file to Device Independent file format.
- **docbook2html** — Converts a DocBook file to HTML format.
- **docbook2man** — Converts a DocBook file to man page format.
- **docbook2pdf** — Converts a DocBook file to Portable Document Format (PDF).
- **docbook2ps** — Converts a DocBook file to PostScript format.
- **docbook2rtf** — Converts a DocBook file to Rich Text Format (RTF).
- **docbook2tex** — Converts a DocBook file to TeX format.
- **docbook2texi** — Converts a DocBook file to GNU TeXinfo format.
- **docbook2txt** — Converts a DocBook file to a bare text format.

Printing Documents with Fedora

Printing in Red Hat Linux is provided by the Common UNIX Printing System (CUPS) service. The LPRng service, which is no longer included with Fedora, still can be obtained from Red Hat FTP sites and some Fedora software repositories. Both services, however, let you print using the same basic set of printing commands described in this section.

> **CROSS-REFERENCE:** See Chapter 10 for a description of how to use the Alternatives system to choose between LPRng and CUPS as the default print service. For information on configuring local and remote printers for Fedora, see Chapter 17.

As a non-administrative user, you don't have a lot of control over how the printers are configured. You can, however, check which printers are available to print to, check the status of print queues (documents waiting to print), and remove any of your own queued print jobs.

Printing to the default printer

When your system administrator (or you) configured printers for your computer, one of those printers was defined as the default printer. If you are not sure which printer is your default, type `system-config-printer` and look for the printer with the check by it.

Most graphical word processors, such as StarOffice and OpenOffice.org, let you choose a printer from those available. Some of the less sophisticated Linux utilities that run from the command line, however, use only the default printer. For example, `dvips` (to print a PostScript file) and `groff -l` (to print a troff/nroff file) automatically send the output to the default printer.

As a regular user, you can override the default printer using the `PRINTER` environment variable. For example, if the default printer on your computer is `lp0` and you want to print regularly to `lp1`, change your default printer by setting the `PRINTER` variable as follows:

```
$ export PRINTER=lp1
```

To have this take effect all the time, you could add this line to one of your shell configuration files (such as `$HOME/.bashrc`, if you use the bash shell).

Printing from the shell

The `lpr` command is used to print files from the shell. You can use `lpr` to print whether the LPRng or CUPS print service is being used. If you have a file already formatted, use `lpr` to print it. For example, if you have a PostScript output file (`file.ps`) and you want to print it to your PostScript printer, use the following command line:

```
$ lpr file.ps
```

If you want to specify a particular printer (other than the default), add the `-Pprinter` option. For example, to print to the lp0 printer, you could type the following:

```
$ lpr -Plp0 file.ps
```

If you want to print more than one copy of a document, use the `-#num` option, where *num* is replaced by the number of copies you want. For example, to print five copies of a file, use:

```
$ lpr -#5 file.ps
```

The `lpr` command can also accept standard output for printing. For example, you could print the output of a `groff` command by piping that output to `lpr` as follows:

```
$ groff -Tps -man /tmp/chown.1 | lpr -Plp0
```

> **TIP:** The enscript command (in the enscript package) is another useful tool for printing plain-text files. It converts the files to PostScript and sends them to a printer or to a specified file.

Checking the print queues

To check the status of print jobs that have been queued, you can use the lpq command. By itself, lpq prints a listing of jobs that are in the queue for the default printer. For example:

```
$ lpq
hp is ready and printing
Rank        Owner      Job   Files              Total Size
active      root        3     hosts              1024 bytes
1st         root        7     (stdin)            625 bytes
2nd         root        8     memo1.ps           12273 bytes
3rd         chuck       9     bikes.ps           10880 bytes
```

The output from lpq shows the printer status and the files waiting to be printed. Rank lists the order in which they are in the queue. Owner is the user who queued the job. Job shows the job number. The Files column shows the name of the file or standard output (if the file was piped or directed to lpr). Total Size shows how large each file is in bytes.

You can add options to lpq to print different kinds of information. By adding -Pprinter, you can see the queue for any available printer. You can also add the job number (to see the status of a particular print job) or a user name (to see all queued jobs for a user).

Removing print jobs

If you have ever printed a large document by mistake, you understand the value of being able to remove a print job from the queue. Likewise, if a printer is going to be down for a while and everyone has already printed their jobs to another printer, it's sometimes nice to be able to clear all the print jobs when the printer comes back online.

Remove print jobs in Fedora using lprm. For example, to remove all jobs for the user named bill (assuming you are either bill or the root user), type the following:

```
$ lprm bill
```

The root user can remove all print jobs from the queue. To do this you add a dash (-) to the lprm command line as follows:

```
$ lprm -
```

You can also remove queued print jobs for a particular printer (-Pprinter) or for a particular job number by just adding the job number to the lprm command line.

Checking printer status

Sometimes nothing comes out of a printer and you have no idea why. The `lpc` command is a printer status command that might give you a clue as to what is going on with your printer. The `lpc` command is intended for administrators, so it may not be in your default PATH. To start the `lpc` command, type the following:

```
# /usr/sbin/lpc
lpc> status
hp:
            printer is on device 'lpd' speed -1
            queing is enabled
            printing is enabled
            no entries
            daemon present
lpc>
```

When the command returns the `lpc>` prompt, type the word **status**. This example shows the status of printer `hp`. Here, queuing and printing are enabled. The printer shows no problems, no print jobs are waiting. To quit the `lpc` command, type `exit` at the `lpc>` prompt.

Displaying Documents with Ghostscript and Acrobat

Fedora publishing can be very paper-intensive if you send a Groff or LaTeX document to the printer each time you want to make a change to the document's content or formatting. To save paper and time spent running around, you can use some print preview programs to display a document on the screen as it will appear on the printed page. The following sections describe the `ghostscript` command for displaying PostScript files and the Adobe Acrobat reader for displaying Portable Document Format (PDF) files.

Using the ghostscript and gv commands

To display PostScript or PDF documents in Fedora, you can use the `ghostscript` command. The `ghostscript` command is a fairly crude interface, intended to let you step through documents and interpret them one line at a time. (If the `ghostscript` command is not installed on your system, you can get it by installing the ghostscript package from CD #1 that comes with this book.)

You can display any PS or .PDF file you happen to have on your computer. For example, if the samba package is installed, you could type the following to display a PDF file (otherwise, you could find your own PDF file to try it):

```
$ ghostscript /usr/share/doc/samba-*/docs/Samba-HOWTO-Collection.pdf
>>showpage, press <return> to continue<<
```

At the prompt, press Enter (or Return) to go through the file one page at a time. When you have reached the end of the document, you can type the name of another PostScript or PDF file and page through that file. When you are done, type **quit**.

The ggv command (GNOME ghostview) is another, more friendly way of viewing PostScript files. (If the ggv command is not installed on your system, you can get it by installing the ggv package from CD #3 that comes with this book.)

To use ggv to open a file called rbash.ps, you would type the following:

```
$ ggv /usr/share/doc/bash-doc-*/bashref.ps
```

When the ghostview window opens, you can see the document. Left-click on the page and move it up and down to scroll the document. Use the Page Up and Page Down keys to page through the document. You can click on a page number in the left column to jump to a particular page or click the Print All button to print the entire document.

Using Adobe Acrobat Reader

The Portable Document Format (PDF) provides a way of storing documents as they would appear in print. With Adobe Acrobat Reader, you can view PDF files in a very friendly way. Adobe Acrobat makes it easy to move around within a PDF file. A PDF file may include hyperlinks, a table of contents, graphics, and a variety of type fonts.

A recent version of the Adobe Acrobat Reader (version 5.08) is available in RPM format from Guru Labs (www.gurulabs.com/downloads.html). This version can use many PDF features that aren't available in other PDF readers, including some new compression features in version 1.4. (While you are at it, you can install the Acrobat Plug-in RPM, to use the same reader to play PDF content when you browse the Web).

After you install Adobe Acrobat Reader, type the following command to start the program:

```
$ acroread
```

Click File → Open, and then select the name of a PDF file you want to display. Figure 6-12 shows an example of a PDF file viewed in Adobe Acrobat Reader.

Acrobat Reader has a lot of nice features. For example, you can display a list of bookmarks alongside the document and click on a bookmark to take you to a particular page. You can also display thumbnails of the pages to quickly scroll through and select a page.

Figure 6-12: Display PDF files in the Adobe Acrobat Reader.

Using the menu bar or buttons, you can page through the PDF document, zoom in and out, go to the beginning or end of the document, and display different views of the document (as well as display bookmarks and page thumbnails). To print a copy, click File → Print.

Working with Graphics

Tools for creating and manipulating graphics are becoming both more plentiful and more powerful in Fedora. Leading the list is the GNU Image Manipulation Program (GIMP). GIMP lets you compose and author images as well as retouch photographs. Other tools that come with Fedora for creating graphics include `ksnapshot` (a program for taking screen captures) and `kpaint` (for working with bitmap images).

> **CROSS-REFERENCE:** See Chapter 8 for descriptions of other multimedia applications, such as the gphoto window for working with images from digital cameras.

Manipulating images with GIMP

The GIMP is a free software program that comes with Fedora for manipulating photographs and graphical images. To create images with GIMP, you can either import a drawing, photograph, or 3D image, or you can create one from scratch. You can start GIMP from the system menu by clicking Graphics → The GIMP or by typing `gimp&` from a Terminal window.

Figure 6-13 shows an example of GIMP.

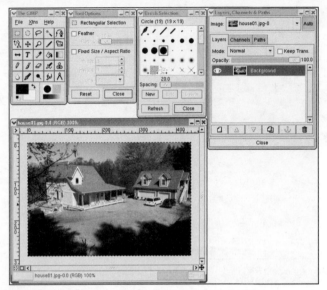

Figure 6-13: GIMP is a powerful tool for graphic manipulation.

> **NOTE:** If GIMP is not on your system or is not installed properly, you can install it from CD # 1 that comes with this book. There are also gimp plugin and extra utilities on CD #2. Alternatively, you can obtain the latest copy of GIMP from `www.gimp.org`.

In many ways, GIMP is similar to Adobe Photoshop. Some people feel that GIMP's scripting features are comparable to, or even better than, Actions in Adobe Photoshop. One capability that GIMP lacks, however, is support for CMYK separations. If CMYK is not critical for your graphics needs, you will probably find GIMP to be just as powerful and flexible as Photoshop in many ways.

One of the easiest ways to become familiar with GIMP is to crop, or trim, an image file already on your computer. To crop a file, follow these steps:

1. Start GIMP and open an image file.

2. Right-click on the image. From the contextual menu that appears, select Tools → Transform Tools → Crop and Resize. The crop cursor appears (two overlapping L shapes), as does the Crop and Resize Information window.

3. Position the crop cursor at the upper left-hand corner of the area of the image that you want to crop. Click and drag the cursor to the lower right-hand corner of the area to be cropped. A selection rectangle will appear around the selected area as you do so.

4. Release the mouse button. Four "selection handles" will appear in the corners of the border around the selected area. Click and drag the handles to resize the border.

5. When the border is in the right place, click the Crop button in the Information window. The image will be cropped to the border.

> **TIP**: If you make a mistake, select Edit → Undo from the GIMP menu or press the Ctrl+Z key combination.

Taking screen captures

If you want to show examples of the work you do on Fedora, you can use the Screen Capture program to capture screen images. (The ksnapshot command is part of the kdegraphics package contained on CD #2.)

To open Screen Capture, from the red hat menu click Graphics → Ksnapshot (or type ksnapshot). Figure 6-14 shows an example of the Screen Capture program.

When Screen Capture first opens, it takes a snapshot of the full desktop. Buttons on the window let you:

-   **New Snapshot** — Select the capture mode (Full Screen, Window under cursor, or Region). Click here to take a new snapshot of the selected content.
-   **Save As** — Save the snapshot to a file in X bitmap, windows icon, PNG, portable pixmap, JPEG, X pixmap, Encapsulated PostScript, or WIndows BMP formats.
-   **Print** — Have the snapshot sent to your printer.

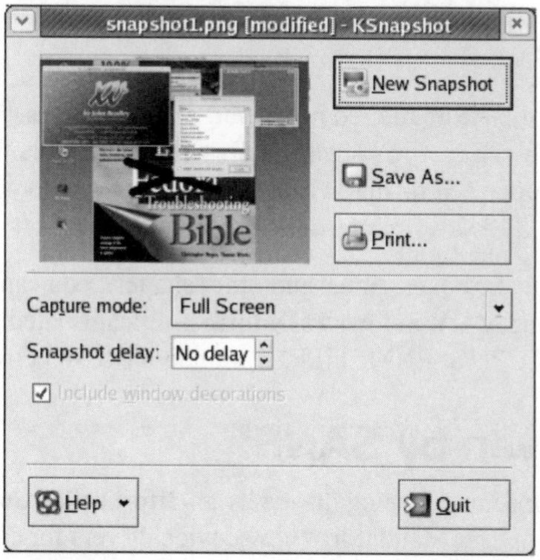

Figure 6-14: Grab a picture of your desktop or selected window with Screen Capture.

Modifying images with KPaint

Using the KPaint window, a utility that comes with KDE (in the kdegraphics package on CD #2), you can work with and convert images in several formats. Figure 6-15 shows an example of KPaint.

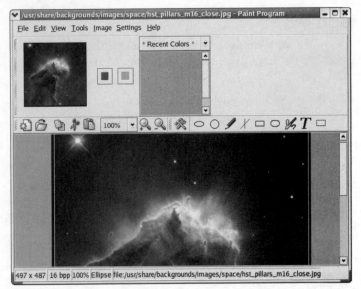

Figure 6-15: Edit bitmap images with KPaint.

Start KPaint from either the desktop (from the red hat menu, click Graphics → Paint Program) or from a Terminal window (`/usr/bin/kpaint&`). Start with either a blank canvas or by opening an image in one of the supported formats (File → Open, browse for a file, and then click OK). Look in the `/usr/share/backgrounds` directory for graphics to try.

The painting tools let you draw ovals, boxes, lines, and other shapes. You can save the file to several different formats, including MS Windows PCX format, Encapsulated PostScript image, MS Windows icons, JPEG, PNG, PNM, TIFF, X bitmap, or X Window pixmap.

Using Scanners Driven by SANE

Software for using a scanner with Linux is being driven by an effort called Scanner Access Now Easy (SANE). This effort hopes to standardize how device drivers for equipment such as scanners, digital still cameras, and digital video cameras are created, as well as help simplify the interfaces for applications that use those devices.

SANE is now included with the Fedora distribution. The sane-backend and sane-frontend packages are on CD #1, while the xsane and xsane-gimp packages are on CD #2. You can get the latest SANE driver packages from www.sane-project.org.

Someone wanting to use Linux as a publishing platform is generally interested in two issues about scanners: which scanners are supported and which applications are available to use the scanners. In general, more SCSI scanners are supported than parallel scanners.

Because of the ongoing development effort, new scanners are being supported all the time. You can find a current list of supported scanners at `www.sane-project.org/sane-supported-devices.html`, with USB scanners listed at `www.buzzard.me.uk/jonathan/scanners-usb.html`. As for applications, these are currently available with Fedora:

- **xsane** — This is an X-based graphical front end for SANE scanners; `xsane` can work as a GIMP plug-in or as a separate application (from the red hat menu, select Graphics → Scanning). It supports 8-bit output in JPG, TIFF, PNG, PostScript, and PNM formats. There is experimental 16-bit support for PNM (ASCII), PNG, and raw formats.

- **scanimage** — This is a command-line interface for obtaining scanned images. It supports the same formats as `xscanimage`. The command acquires the scanned image, and then directs the data to standard output (so you can send it to a file or pipe it to another program).

In addition to these applications, the OpenOffice.org suite supports SANE.

Because of the architecture of SANE scanner drivers, it is possible to separate scanner drivers from scanner applications. This makes it possible to share scanners across a network.

Summary

In recent times, modern GUI-based publishing tools have augmented the text-based publishing tools that have always been available with Fedora (and other Red Hat Linux systems). Powerful open-source publishing tools such as OpenOffice.org are becoming competitive with commercial office suites. Traditional publishing tools such as Groff (which implements traditional troff/nroff text processing) and LaTeX (a TeX macro interface that is particularly suited for scientific and mathematical publishing) are still available with Fedora.

Chapter 7

Playing Games with Fedora

In This Chapter

- Basic Linux gaming information
- X Window games
- Commercial Linux games
- Transgaming and WineX gaming

The advancement of computer games has mirrored the improvements in computers themselves. In the 1970s, the first games for UNIX systems were visually simple and could run on slow, character-based terminal connections. Today, games that combine graphics, animation, and sound have helped drive improvements in computer technology in general.

Availability of gaming software that you can use with Linux is similar to that of Linux publishing software. A lot of the old software is still around (and is free), while newer software is available in demo form but costs some money to get a full version. Some experts predict that gaming will be the software category that brings Linux into homes. Although the number of popular game applications is limited at the moment, like everything else in Linux, more are becoming available each day.

This chapter addresses the current state of gaming in Linux, including the basics on getting your gaming environment going, and hardware considerations for gaming. It describes the free games (mostly fairly simple X Window games) that come with Fedora or that can be easily downloaded. For running games that were created for other platforms, this chapter describes game emulators such as WineX.

This chapter also discusses some popular commercial games that have demo versions available for Linux. If you like the demos, you can purchase these games, which run natively in Linux.

Basic Linux Gaming Information

There isn't much you need to know to run most of the X Window-based games that come with Fedora. The following sections describe basic information about Linux gaming.

Where to get information on Linux gaming

To find news on the latest games available for Linux, as well as links to download sites, go to some of the several Web sites available. Here are a few to get you started:

- **TransGaming Technologies** (www.transgaming.com) — This company's mission is to bring games from other platforms to Linux.

- **The Linux Game Tome** (http://happypenguin.org) — This site features a database of descriptions and reviews of tons of games that run in Linux. You can do keyword searches for games listed at this site. The site also includes links to where you can get the different games, as well as links to other gaming sites.

- **Linuxgames.com** (http://linuxgames.com) — This site can give you some very good insight into the state of Linux gaming. There are links to HOW-TOs and Frequently Asked Questions (FAQs), as well as forums for discussing Linux games. There are also links to Web sites that have information on a particular game you are interested in.

- **id Software** (www.idsoftware.com) — Go to the id Software site for information on Linux demo versions for Quake and Return to Castle Wolfenstein.

- **Linuxgamepublishing.com** (www.linuxgamepublishing.com) — A new entrant into the Linux gaming world, linuxgamepublishing.com aims to be a one-stop shopping portal for native Linux games, as well as for ports of games from other platforms. At the time of writing, they offered 15 games. Note that to purchase games from this site, you must create a user account.

- **Loki Entertainment Software** (www.lokigames.com) — Loki provided ports of best-selling games to Linux, but went out of business in 2001. Its products included Linux versions of Civilization: Call to Power, Myth II: Soulblighter, SimCity 3000, Railroad Tycoon II, and Quake III Arena. The Loki Demo Launcher is still available to see demo versions of these games, and some boxed sets are available for very little money.

- **Tux Games** (www.tuxgames.com) — If you are ready to purchase a game, the Tux Games Web site is dedicated to the sale of Linux games. Besides offering Linux gaming news and products, the site lists its top-selling games and includes notices of games that are soon to be released.

- **Linux Gamers' FAQ** (http://icculus.org/lgfaq) — This FAQ contains a wealth of information about free and commercial Linux games. It lists gaming companies that have ported their games to Linux, tells where to get Linux games, and answers queries related to common Linux gaming problems. For a list of Linux games without additional information, see http://icculus.org/lgfaq/gamelist.php.

If the idea of developing your own games interests you, try the Linux Game Development Center (http://lgdc.sunsite.dk).

Getting started with Linux gaming

How you get started with Linux gaming depends on how serious you are about it. If all you want to do is play a few games to pass the time, you can find plenty of diverting X Window games that come with Linux. If you want to play more powerful commercial games, you can choose from:

- **Games for Microsoft Windows (WineX)** — Many of the most popular commercial games created to run on Microsoft operating systems will run in Linux using WineX. To get RPM versions of WineX, you must sign up for a WineX subscription at `Transgaming.com`.

- **Games for Linux (id Software and others)** — Certain popular games have Linux versions available. Most notably, id Software offers its DOOM and Return to Castle Wolfenstein in Linux versions.

Games are still available from the now defunct company Loki Software, Inc. I just purchased Myth II: Soulblighter and Heretic II for Linux over the Internet for a few dollars.

Choosing a video card for gaming

Because high-end games place extraordinary demands on your video hardware, choosing a good video card and configuring it properly is one of the keys to ensuring a good gaming experience. Although basic video card configuration is covered in Chapter 3, for advanced gaming you may need to go beyond what a low-end card can do for you.

One feature that many games may require of your video card is Direct Rendering Infrastructure (DRI). Whether you are running the games using WineX or natively in Linux, to play demanding games in Linux you need a card that supports DRI to do hardware acceleration. Here is a list of video cards that support DRI from the DRI project site (`http://dri.sourceforge.net/`):

- **3dfx** — Although 3dfx Interactive, Inc. is no longer in business, you can still find 3dfx cards that support DRI. In particular, the Voodoo (3, 4, and 5) and Banshee chip sets have drivers that support DRI. Voodoo 5 cards support 16 and 24 bpp. Scan Line Interleaving (SLI), where two or more 3D processors work in parallel (to result in higher frame rates), is not supported for 3dfx cards.

- **3Dlabs** — Graphics cards containing the MX/Gamma chipset from 3Dlabs have drivers available that support DRI in Linux.

- **ATI Technologies** — Chipsets from ATI Technologies that support DRI include the Mach64 (Rage Pro), Radeon 7X00 (R100), Radeon 2 / 8500 (R200), and Rage 128 (Standard, Pro, Mobility). Cards based on these chip sets include All-in-Wonder 128, Rage Fury, Rage Magnum, Xpert 99, Xpert 128, and Xpert 2000. Note that there is no support under Fedora Core for ATI 9X00 cards; use a 7500-series card or older instead.

- **Intel** — Supported video chipsets from Intel include the i810 (e, e2, and -dc100), i815 and i815e.

- **Matrox** — The Matrox chipsets that have drivers that support DRI include the G200, G400, and G450. Cards that use these chips include the Millennium G450, Millennium G400, Millennium G200, and Mystique G200.

- **NVIDIA** — Cards from NVIDIA are not supported by DRI because NVIDIA has not released hardware specifications to DRI developers. However, NVIDIA cards work for most Linux games. To get NVIDIA drivers, which are produced by NVIDIA but are not open source drivers, you must download them from the NVIDIA Web site (www.nvidia.com). On the NVIDIA home page, click the download button and follow the instructions for downloading and installing the correct drivers for your card on Fedora systems. RPM packages are available.

To find out whether DRI is working on your current video card, type the following:

```
$ glxinfo | grep rendering
direct rendering: Yes
```

This example shows that direct rendering is supported. If it were not supported, the output would say No instead of Yes.

X Window Games

The X Window System created a great opportunity for games in Fedora and other UNIX systems to become graphical based rather than character based. So, instead of having little character symbols representing robots and arrows, the games could actually show pictures of little robots and arrows.

A lot of diverting games come with Fedora and run in X. Unless otherwise noted, all of the X games described in this section are free. Also, the GNOME and KDE environments that come on the CDs (described in Chapter 3) each have a set of games associated with it.

GNOME games

The GNOME games consist of some old card games and a bunch of games that look suspiciously like games you would find on Windows systems. If you are afraid of losing your favorite desktop diversion (such as Solitaire, FreeCell, and Minesweeper) when you leave Windows, have no fear. You can find many of them under GNOME games.

Table 7-1 lists the games available by selecting Games from the Red Hat menu. In this release, many KDE games (shown in Table 7-2) are also on this menu.

Table 7-1: GNOME Games

Game	Description
AisleRiot (solitaire)	Lets you select from among 28 different solitaire card games.
Chess	Gnuchess game in X. (Runs the `xboard` and `gnuchess` commands.)
Chromium Configuration	Set options such as skill level, screen size, and sound for Chromium.
Chromium	Deliver supplies to troops in battle in this action game.
FreeCell	A popular solitaire card game.
Freeciv (Isometric tileset)	In this strategy game, you try to lead your civilization to extinguish all others. (Uses Isometric tile set to represent cities, oceans, and other terrain.)
Freeciv Server (new game)	Server program needed to play Freeciv.
Ataxx	Board game where you flip over circles to consume enemy pieces.
Lines	Match five colored balls in a row to score points.
Four-In-A-Row	Drop balls to beat the game at making four in a row.
Nibbles	Steer a worm around the screen while avoiding walls.
Robots	Later version of Gnobots, which includes movable junk heaps.
Mines	Minesweeper clone. Click on safe spaces and avoid the bombs.
Stones	Move around a cave, collect diamonds, and avoid rocks.
Tetravex	A clone of Tetravex from the GNOME project. Move blocks so that numbers on each side align.
Klotski	Move pieces around to allow one piece to escape.
Tali	Yahtzee clone. Roll dice to fill in categories.
Iagno	Flip black and white chips to maneuver past the opponent.
Maelstrom	Navigate a spaceship through an asteroid field.
Mahjongg	Classic Asian tile game.
Same GNOME	Eliminate clusters of balls for high score.
Tux Racer	Steer a penguin as he races down a hill on his belly.

KDE games

If you install KDE, there are a bunch of games in the kdegames package. If you did not install the KDE desktop, you can install the kdegames package separately from CD #2. To see the KDE games (along with some GNOME games) on the Red Hat menu, select Games, then choose the game you want. The games available in KDE are listed by category in Table 7-2.

Table 7-2: Games for the KDE Desktop

Game	Description
Arcade Games	
KAsteroids	Destroy asteroids in the classic arcade game.
KBounce	Add walls to block in bouncing balls.
KFoul Eggs	Squish eggs in this Tetris-like game.
Klickety	Click color groups to erase blocks in this adaptation of Clickomania.
Kolf	Play a round of virtual golf.
KSirtet	Tetris clone. Try to fill in lines of blocks as they drop down.
KSmileTris	Tetris with smiley faces.
KSnakeRace	Race your snake around a maze.
KSpaceDuel	Fire at another spaceship as you spin around a planet.
KTron	Snake-style race game.
Boardgames	
Atlantik	Play this Monopoly-like game against other players on the network.
KBackgammon	Online version of backgammon.
KBattleship	Sink the opponent's battleship in this online version of the board game.
KBlackBox	Find hidden balls by shooting rays.
Kenolaba	Move game pieces to push opponents' pieces off the board.
KMahjongg	Classic oriental tile game.
KReversi	Flip game pieces to outmaneuver the opponent.
Shisen-Sho	Tile game similar to Mahjongg. Very addicting.
Kwin4	Drop colored pieces to get four pieces in a row.

Game	Description
Cardgames	
Patience	Choose from nine different solitaire card games.
KPoker	Video poker clone. Play five-card draw, choosing which cards to hold and which to throw.
Lieutenant Skat	Play the card game Skat.
Megami	Play four blackjack hands against a dealer.
Tactics and Strategy	
KJumping Cube	Click squares to increase numbers and take over adjacent squares.
KAtomic	Move pieces to create different chemical compounds.
Konquest	Expand your interstellar empire in this multiplayer game.
Kolor Lines	Move marbles to form five-in-a-row and score points.
KMines	Minesweeper clone. Click safe spaces and avoid the bombs.
KSokoban	The Japanese warehouse keeper game.
SameGame	Erase game pieces to score points.

The games on the KDE menu range from diverting to quite challenging. If you are used to playing games in Windows, KMines and Patience will seem like old favorites. KAsteroids and KPoker are good for the mindless game category. For a mental challenge (it's harder than it looks), try KSokoban. For a challenging multiuser game on the GNOME menu, try Freeciv. For chess enthusiasts, there is Chess (xboard version of gnuchess).

The following sections describe a couple of the more interesting games that come with Fedora. First is the xboard game and some related chess programs. Next is a description of Freeciv.

Chess games

Chess was one of the first games played on computer systems. While the game hasn't changed over the years, the way it's played on computers has. The set of chess programs that come with Fedora lets you play against the computer (in text or graphical modes), have the computer play against itself, or replay stored chess games. You can even play chess against other users on the Internet using Internet Chess Servers (ICS).

The xboard program is an X-based chess game that provides a graphical interface for gnuchess. GNU Chess (represented by the gnuchess package) describes itself as a communal chess program. It has had many contributors, and it seeks to advance a "more open and friendly environment of sharing" among the chess community. With xboard, you can move graphical pieces with your mouse. To play against the computer, click Games → Chess from the Red Hat menu, then start by just moving a piece with your mouse. While in the xboard window, select Mode → Two Machines to have the computer play itself. Select File → Load Game to load a game in Portable Game Notation (PGN). Figure 7-1 shows the xboard window with a "Two Machines" game in progress.

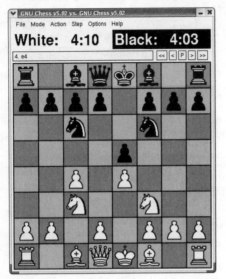

Figure 7-1: In the xboard window, you can set xgame to either play against the computer or to replay saved games.

You can use xboard to play online against others by connecting an xboard session to an Internet Chess Server (ICS). To start xboard as an interface to an ICS, type the following command line:

```
$ xboard -ics -icshost name
```

In this example, *name* should be replaced by the name of the ICS host (see the list of hosts below). In ICS mode, you can just watch games, play against other users, or replay games that have finished. The ICS host acts as a gathering place for enthusiasts who want to play chess against others on the Internet, watch games, participate in tournaments, or just meet chess people. Here are ICS host computers you can connect to by substituting *name* above with the address shown below:

- **Internet Chess Club: ICC** (chessclub.com)
- **Chess.net** (chess.net)
- **Free Internet Chess Server** (freechess.org)

Freeciv

With Freeciv, you create a civilization that challenges competing civilizations for world dominance. The version of Freeciv that comes with Fedora contains both client software (to play the game) and server software (to connect players together). You can connect to your server and try the game yourself or (with a network connection) play against up to 14 other players on the Internet.

You can start Freeciv from the Red Hat menu (as a non-root user) by clicking Games → FreeCiv (Isometric tile set). If Freeciv doesn't start, try starting it from a Terminal window by typing:

```
$ civ &
```

Figure 7-2 shows the two windows that appear when you start Freeciv. The Connect to Freeciv Server window contains your user name, host name, and port number. The Freeciv window is where you play the game.

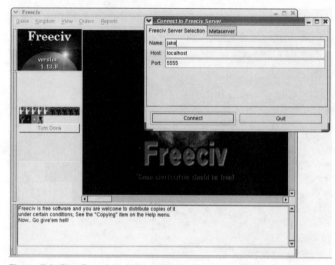

Figure 7-2: Play Freeciv to build civilizations and compete against others.

> **NOTE:** If Freeciv won't start, one reason may be because you are logged in as root. You must be logged in as a regular user to run the `civ` command.

Starting Freeciv

You can play a few games by yourself, if you like, to get to know the game before you play against others on the network. The following procedure describes how to start your first practice Freeciv game.

1. Start Freeciv from the Red Hat menu (Games → FreeCiv, or type **civ&**).The Freeciv windows appear, as shown in Figure 7-2.

2. From a Terminal window, start the Freeciv server by typing:

```
$ civserver
This is the server for Freeciv version 1.13.0
You can learn a lot about Freeciv at http://www.freeciv.org/
2: Now accepting new client connections.

For introductory help, type 'help'.
>
```

3. Click Connect in the Connect to Freeciv Server window.

4. At the server prompt, type the following:

```
> start
Starting game.
2: Loading rulesets
>
```

A What Nation Will You Be? window appears on the client, as shown in Figure 7-3.

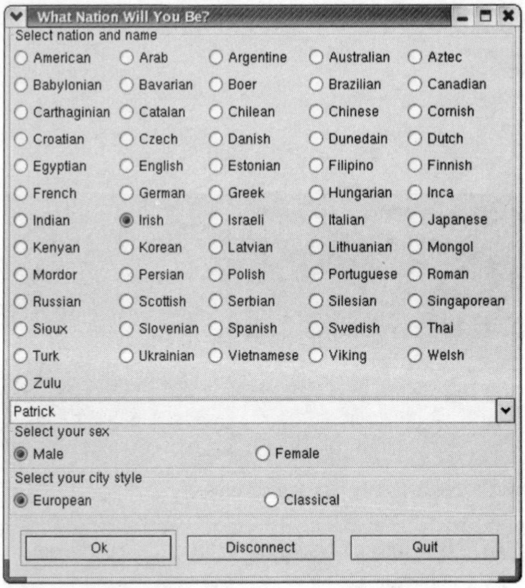

Figure 7-3: Choose a nation to begin Freeciv.

5. After you start Freeciv from the server prompt, choose a nation, the name of a leader, your gender, and the style of the city, and then click OK. At this point, you are ready to return to the Freeciv window.

Beginning with Freeciv

Check out the Freeciv window. Here are things you should know before you start the game. (You can find more help at the Freeciv site: www.freeciv.org.)

- Click the Help button for topical information on many different subjects that will be useful to you as you play.

- The world (by default) is 80 x 50 squares, with 11 x 8 squares visible at a time.

- The active square contains an icon of the active unit (flashing alternatively with the square's terrain).

- Some squares contain special resources. Press and hold the middle mouse button for information on what special resources a square contains. (With a two-button mouse, hold the Ctrl key and click the right mouse button.) Try this a few times to get a feel for the land around you. This action also identifies any units on the terrain, as well as statistics for the unit.

- To see the world outside of your 11 x 8 viewing area, click the scroll bars outside of the map. At first the world outside will be black. As units are added, areas closer to those units will be visible. (Press the letter **c** to return to the active part of your map.)

- An overview map is in the upper-left corner of the Freeciv window. As the world becomes more civilized, this provides a good way to get an overview of what is going on. Right-click a spot on the overview map to have your viewport centered there.

- The menu bar contains buttons you can use to play the game. The Game menu lets you change settings and options, view player data, view messages, and clear your log. The Kingdom menu lets you change tax rates, find cities, and start revolutions. The View menu lets you place a grid on the map or center the view. The Orders menu is where you choose the items you build and the actions you take. The Reports menu lets you display reports related to cities, military, trade, and science, as well as other special reports.

- A summary of the economy of your civilization appears under the overview map. Information includes number of people, current year, money in the treasury, and percent of money distributed to tax, luxury, and science.

- Ten icons below the overview information represent how money is divided between luxuries (an entertainer), research (a researcher), and taxes (a tax collector). Essentially, these icons represent how much of your resources are placed into improving each of those attributes of your community.

- When you have made all your moves for a turn, click Turn Done. Next to that, a lightbulb indicates the progress of your research (increasing at each turn). A sun icon starts clear, but becomes brighter from pollution to warn of possible global warming. A government symbol indicates that you begin with a despotic government. The last icon tells you how much time is left in a turn.

The Unit box shows information about your current unit. You begin with two Settlers units and one Explorer unit.

Building your civilization

Start building your civilization. Here are things to try, as suggested by the Freeciv manual:

- To change the distribution of money, choose Kingdom → Tax Rates. Move the slider bars to redistribute the percentage of assets assigned to luxury, research, and taxes. Try increasing research and reducing taxes to start off.

- Change the current unit to be a settler as follows: click the stack of units on the map and click one of the Settlers from the menu that appears.

- Begin building a city by clicking on Orders → Build City. When prompted, type a name for the city and click OK. The window that appears shows information about the city. It starts with one happy citizen, represented by a single icon (more citizens will appear as the game progresses).

- The Food, Prod, and Trade lines reflect the raw productivity statistics for the city. The first number shows how much is being produced, the second (in parens) shows the surplus above what is needed to support the units. The Gold, Luxury, and Science lines indicate the city's trade output. Granary numbers show how much food is stored and the size of the food store. The pollution level begins at zero.

- The Units at this point are not yet supported by a city (so nothing appears under Supported Units). When Units require support, they will be assigned to cities, and they will draw on city resources. Units present appear under that heading.

- The map area shown consists of 21 squares that make up the city. The number 1 indicates the size of the city. The number 211 reflects the production of food, manufacturing production, and trade, respectively. The number 210 shows where the city's citizen is working and the results of the work.

- The Phalanx line shows that the city can build a Phalanx and that it will take 20 production points to produce. Click Change to view other units the city could produce, select one you want to build, and click Change. Below that is a list of your current buildings (of which you have only a Palace to start out).

- Close the city window by clicking Close.

Exploring your world

To begin exploring, move the Settler.

1. Using the numeric keypad, press the 9 key three times to begin exploring. You can move the explorer up to three times per turn. You begin to see more of the world.

2. When the next unit (the Settler) begins blinking, move it one square in another direction. Click Turn Done. Information for the city will be updated.

3. Click the City to see the city window. Notice that information about the city has been updated. In particular, you should see food storage increase. Close the city window.

4. Continue exploring and build a road. With the explorer flashing, use the numeric keypad to move it another three sections. When the Settler begins blinking, press **r** to build a road. A small R appears on the square to remind you that the Settler is busy building a road. Click Turn Done.

Using more controls and actions

Now that you have some understanding of the controls and actions, the game can begin taking a lot of different directions. Here are a few things that might happen next and things you can do:

- After you take a turn, the computer gets a chance to play as well. As it plays, its actions are reported to you. You can make decisions on what to do about those actions. Choose Game → Message Options. The Message options window appears, containing a listing of different kinds of messages that can come from the server and how they will be presented to you.

- As you explore, you will run into other explorers and eventually other civilizations. Continue exploring by selecting different directions on your numeric keypad.

- Continue to move the Settler one square at a time, after it has finished creating the road. (The Settler will blink again when it is available.) Click Turn Done.

- At this point, you should see a message that your city has finished building Warriors. When buildings and units are complete, you should usually check out what has happened. Click the message associated with the city, then click Popup City. The city window appears, showing you that it has additional population. The food storage may appear empty, but the new citizens are working to increase the food and trade. You may see an additional warrior unit.

- A science advisory may also appear at this point to let you choose your city's research goals. Click Change and select Writing as your new research goal. You can then select a different long-term goal as well. Click Close when you are done.

- If your new Warrior is now blinking, press the s key to assign sentry mode to the Warrior.

You should be familiar with some of the actions of Freeciv at this point. To learn some basic strategies for playing the game, choose Help → Help Playing.

Commercial Linux Games

When Loki Software, Inc. closed its doors a few years ago, the landscape of commercial gaming in Linux changed. Loki produced Linux ports of popular games, including Myth II and

Civilization: Call to Power, to name a few. Today, commercial games that run natively are led by several popular games from id Software (described in the next section).

Although Loki Software, Inc. is gone, certain Loki Games are still available for purchase on the Web. Although they sell for a fraction of their original price, you are on your own if they don't work since Loki Software is no longer there to support them. The Loki Games Demo is still around, if you want to get a feel for a particular Loki game before it disappears completely (I describe how to find demo and packaged Loki Games later in this chapter).

In the wake of Loki's demise, TransGaming Technologies has been working on an approach to bringing popular games to Linux that relies on a version of WINE called WineX. In most cases, instead of having different ports of popular games (as Loki did), Transgaming lets users run existing Windows games in Linux by adapting WineX to each game that needs a tweak here and there.

While the state of Linux gaming has improved somewhat since the last edition of this book, Linux is still not the gaming platform that many enthusiasts wish it would be. Most serious gamers still maintain a Windows partition to support their gaming habits. According to top game developers, there are significant hurdles — both technological and economic — that hinder development of games for Linux. Issues with video and audio hardware, as well as problems with GNU/Linux development itself (in particular, `glibc`), have made new games difficult to produce. In addition, the relatively small size of the Linux gaming market means that incentives to overcome these issues are not particularly strong. However, as you will see in the remainder of this chapter, there are plenty of titles to amuse the Linux user, whether a casual gamer or one more hardcore.

id Software Games

Among the most popular games running natively in Linux are Quake III Arena, and Return to Castle Wolfenstein from id Software, Inc. You can purchase Linux versions of these games or download demos of each game before you buy.

> **NOTE:** If you have trouble getting any id Software games running in Linux, refer to the Linux FAQs available from id Software at: `http://zerowing.idsoftware.com/linux`.

Quake III Arena

Quake III Arena is a first-person shooter-type game where you can choose from lots of weapons (lightning guns, shotguns, grenade launchers, and so on) and pass through scenes with highly detailed 3D surfaces. You can play alone or against your friends. There are multiplayer death-match and capture-the-flag competitions.

A demo version of Quake III Arena for Linux is available from the id Software Web site (look for the demo link at `www.idsoftware.com/games/quake/quake3-gold/` and look for the Linux demo). Figure 7-4 shows a screenshot from Quake III Arena.

Figure 7-4: Quake III Arena is a popular first-person shooter game that runs in Linux.

Return to Castle Wolfenstein

Mixing World War II action with creatures conjured up by Nazi scientists, you battle with the Allies to destroy the Third Reich. Return to Castle Wolfenstein is based on the Quake III Arena engine. The game offers single-player mode as well as team-based multiplayer mode.

If you purchase Return to Castle Wolfenstein for Linux, you actually get the Windows version with an extra Linux installer. If you already have the Windows version, you can download the Linux installer and follow some instructions to get it going. I downloaded the installer called `wolf-linux-1.31.x86.run` from `www.idsoftware.com/games/wolfenstein/rtcw/index.php?game_section=updates`. The INSTALL file (in `/usr/local/games/wolfenstein`) describes what files you need to copy from the Windows CD.

To get a demo of Return to Castle Wolfenstein, go to `www.idsoftware.com/games/wolfenstein/rtcw/index.php?game_section=overview`. Both a single-player and a multiplayer demo are available.

> **WARNING:** You need an NVIDIA card to run Return to Castle Wolfenstein.

Figure 7-5 is a screenshot from Return to Castle Wolfenstein running in Linux.

Figure 7-5: Return to Castle Wolfenstein combines strange creatures and WWII battles.

TransGaming and WineX gaming

TransGaming Technologies brings to Linux some of the most popular games that currently run on the Windows platforms. Working with WINE developers, TransGaming is developing WineX, which enables you to run many different games on Linux that were originally developed for Windows. Although TransGaming is producing a few games that are packaged separately and tuned for Linux, in most cases it sells you a subscription service to WineX instead of the games. That subscription service lets you stay up-to-date on the continuing development of WineX so you can run more and more Windows games.

> **NOTE:** Unfortunately, the kernel that ships with Fedora does not work with WineX. To use WineX in Fedora, TransGaming recommends that you download a vanilla kernel from `kernel.org` and boot that on your Fedora system before running games with WineX.

To get Windows games to run in Linux, WineX particularly needs to develop Microsoft DirectX features that are required by many of today's games. There are also issues relating to CD keys and hooks into the Windows operating system that must be overcome (such as requiring Microsoft Active Desktop). In fact, a WineX subscription has value, in part, because it lets you vote on which games you'd like to see TransGaming work on next.

A full list of games supported by TransGaming, as well as indications of how popular they are and how well they work, is available from the TransGaming site (search for the games that interest you by going to `www.transgaming.com` and clicking on Games). More than 100 games are currently listed with a rating of 4 out of 5 (meaning that the game will run well, if not flawlessly). Eight games are rated a 5 (meaning that they run flawlessly).

NOTE: The Windows version of The Sims doesn't run under WineX. You need to purchase The Sims for Linux. Although TransGaming believes that Sims for Linux will run on any recent Linux distribution, such as Fedora or Red Hat Linux, that supports installation of RPMs, the product was optimized to run under Mandrake Linux.

Support or major enhancements for the following games were recently added to WineX 3.3.1:

- Morrowind
- Grand Theft Auto: Vice City
- Battlefield 1942
- Medal of Honor: Allied Assault
- Steam
- Dark Age of Camelot
- Max Payne 2

Here is a list of some of the most popular games that are being used by the TransGaming community (though they may or may not have been tested by TransGaming) and that are said to run well in WineX (rated a 4 or 5). I suggest you check the TransGaming list yourself for additions and changes:

- Half-Life and Counter-Strike
- Diablo II
- StarCraft
- Baldur's Gate 2
- Jedi Knight 2: Jedi Outcast
- Max Payne
- Return to Castle Wolfenstein
- American McGee's Alice
- Command & Conquer Red Alert 2
- Baldur's Gate
- Total Annihilation
- DeusEx
- The Sims (Mandrake Gaming Edition)
- Fallout 2
- Warcraft II

With WineX 3.1, Transgaming added a new Point2Play feature. Point2Play provides a graphical window for installing, configuring, and testing WineX on your computer. It also lets you install and organize your games so you can launch them graphically. Figure 7-6 shows an example of the Transgaming Point2Play window:

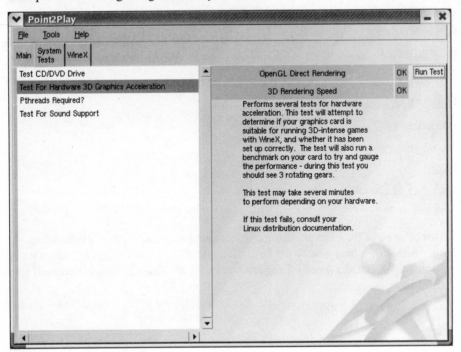

Figure 7-6: Use the Point2Play window to check computer hardware for WineX gaming.

Other features in the new Point2Play window include the ability to select among different installed versions of WineX for running applications and tools for individually configuring how each game runs under WineX. (If a game won't run from the GUI, try launching it from a Terminal window.

To get binary copies (ones that are already compiled to run) of WineX and Point2Play, you need to subscribe to TransGaming. For details on how to become a "TransGamer," click on the Subscribe Here link on the TransGaming home page (www.transgaming.com). Benefits currently include:

- Downloads of the latest version of WineX.
- Access to WineX support forums.
- Ability to vote on which games you want TransGaming to support next.
- Subscription to the WineX newsletter.

Source code for WineX should be available in the near future if you want to build your own WineX package. To check availability, try the SourceForge.net project site for WineX (sourceforge.net/projects/winex).

Loki Software game demos

To encourage people to get to know their games, Loki offered a demo program that let you choose from among more than a dozen of its games to download and try. Although Loki Software, Inc. is no longer in business, you can still find some of its games for sale. For example, a recent search for Loki at Amazon.com turned up 16 different Loki games (including the ones described here), with many selling for $9.99.

> **WARNING:** If you try to download any of the demos described in the next sections, make sure you have plenty of disk space available. It is common for one of these demos to require several hundred megabytes of disk space.

The Loki Demo Launcher for downloading demos is still available from the Demo Launcher page (`www.lokigames.com/products/demos.php3`). From that page, there are links to FTP sites from which you can download the Demo Launcher. The file that you want to save is `loki_demos-full-1.0e-x86.run`. Save it to a directory (such as `/tmp/loki`) and do the following:

1. Change to the directory where you downloaded the demo. For example:

   ```
   # cd /tmp/loki
   ```

> **NOTE:** You may not need to be root user to install these games. However, the default paths where the Demo Launcher tries to write by default are only accessible to the root user.

2. As root user, run the following command (the program may have a different name if it has been updated):

   ```
   # sh loki_demos-full-1.0e.x86.run
   ```

   If you have not used the Demo Launcher before, a screen appears asking you to identify the paths used to place the Install Tool.

3. If the default locations shown are okay with you, click Begin Install.

   Assuming that there was no problem writing to the install directories, you should see an Install Complete message.

4. Click Exit. Next, you should see the Uninstall Tool window.

5. If the paths for holding the Uninstall Tool are okay, click Begin Install. The Install Complete message appears.

6. Click Exit. The window that appears allows you to set the locations for installing the Demo Pack.

7. If the paths are okay, click Begin Install.

   Next, you should see a box that shows the different demo games that are available. As you move the cursor over each game, the disk space is displayed for that game. Click the games you want to install and then click Continue. A window appears, displaying the progress of each download.

8. You may need to click an Update button to complete the update and Finish to finish it.

   The demo should now be ready to start.

9. Either click Play or type `loki_demos` from a Terminal window to start the program.

10. Select to start the game, and you're ready to go.

The following sections describe a few games that may still be available. Again, these games may not be available for long.

Civilization: Call to Power

You can build online civilizations with Civilization: Call to Power (CCP). Like earlier versions and public spin-offs (such as the Freeciv described earlier in this chapter), Civilization: Call to Power for Linux lets you explore the world, build cities, and manage your empire. This latest version offers multiplayer network competition and extensions that let you extend cities into outer space and under the sea.

If you like the Freeciv game that comes with Fedora, you will love CCP. Engaging game play is improved with enhanced graphics, sound, and animation. English, French, German, Italian, and Spanish versions are available.

The CCP demo comes with an excellent tutorial to start you out. If you have never played a civilization game before, the tutorial is a great way to start. Figure 7-7 shows an example of a scene from the Civilization: Call to Power for Linux demo.

Figure 7-7: Civilization: Call to Power features excellent graphics and network play.

Myth II: Soulblighter

If you like knights and dwarves and storming castles, Myth II: Soulblighter for Linux might be for you. In Myth II, you are given a mission and some troops with various skills. From there, you need strategy and the desire to shed lots of virtual blood to meet your goal.

Myth II was created by Bungie Software (www.bungie.com) and ported to Linux by Loki Entertainment Software (www.lokigames.com). This version of the popular Myth game includes improved graphics and new scenarios.

A demo version is available that runs well in Fedora. You can get it via the Demo Launcher described earlier. As usual, you will need a fairly powerful computer (at least a Pentium 133 MHz, 32MB RAM, 80MB swap space, and 100MB of free disk space). You need network hardware for multiuser network play (network card or dialup) and a sound card if you want audio. A screenshot of Myth II is shown in Figure 7-8.

Figure 7-8: Use warriors, archers, and dwarves to battle in Myth II.

Heretic II

Based on the Quake Engine, Heretic II sets you on a path to rid the world of a deadly, magical plague. As the main character, Corvus, you explore dungeons, swamps, and cities to uncover and stop the plague. The graphics are rich and the game play is quite engaging.

You will experience some crashing problems with Heretic II out-of-the-box. Be sure to check for the update to Heretic II at `updates.lokigames.com`, which should fix most of the problems.

Neverwinter Nights

BioWare (`www.bioware.com`) has recently dipped its foot into Linux gaming waters with a Linux client for its wildly popular Neverwinter Nights game. Neverwinter Nights is a classic role-playing game in the swords-and-sorcery mold. You can develop your character and go adventuring, or play online with others via a LAN or over the Internet. You can even build your own worlds and host adventures as the Dungeon Master. Neverwinter Nights is licensed by Wizards of the Coast to use Dungeons & Dragons rules and material.

In order to use the Neverwinter Nights Linux client, you must purchase the game itself from BioWare. You must also have access to certain files from a Windows installation of the game. If you or a friend have the Windows version already, you can grab the files from that version. Otherwise, you'll find them online in a number of locations. See the installation instructions at `http://nwn.bioware.com` for links.

Summary

While Linux has not yet become a dominant gaming platform, you can still spend your time on plenty of games running on Fedora. Old UNIX games that have made their way to Linux include a variety of X Window-based games. There are card games, strategy games, and some action games.

On the commercial front, Civilization: Call to Power for Linux and Myth II are available to use on your Fedora system, but will soon disappear because Loki Software (which ported those applications to Linux) went out of business. The future of high-end Linux gaming might be in the hands of TransGaming Technologies, which has created WineX from current WINE technology to allow Windows games to run in Linux.

Commercial games that run natively in Linux are also available. These include games from id Software, such as Quake III Arena and Return to Castle Wolfenstein.

Chapter 8

Multimedia in Fedora

In This Chapter

- Listening to audio in Fedora
- Using Webcams and TV cards
- Playing video in Fedora
- Using a digital camera
- Creating music CDs

In this chapter, you learn to add sound, video, digital images, and other multimedia support to your Fedora system. The chapter describes how to configure a sound card to work with Fedora. Then it tells you how to get and use software to play music CDs and a variety of sound formats from your Fedora system.

Video clips that are readily available on the Internet in formats such as AVI, OGG, and QuickTime can be viewed using several different players in or available for Fedora Core 2. Also, you can view live television and video using TV cards and Webcams.

Because CD-ROM is the medium of choice for recorded music, this chapter describes how to set up and use CD burners to create your own music CDs. After your CD burner is set up to record music, you can use the same CD burner to back up your data or to create software CDs.

Listening to Audio

If you want the sound on your computer to be more than the speaker on your PC going "bing" occasionally, you must have a separate sound card or one built into your computer's motherboard. Games are a reason to add a sound card, if the games rely on sound effects or other audio cues. Also, sound cards let you play music and communicate on the Internet using a variety of communications tools.

Most modern PCs include a sound card, often integrated into the motherboard. In the rare case that one isn't included (or the slightly more common case where it isn't supported in Linux), you can add a supported sound card starting for only a few dollars.

To give you an idea of the features that a sound card can provide, the following list summarizes features that are included in the popular Sound Blaster 16 sound card:

- **Sound recording and playback** — The card can convert analog sound into 8-bit or 16-bit digital numbers. To convert the sound, the board samples the sound in waves from 5 kHz to 48 kHz, or 5,000 to 48,100 times per second. (Of course, the higher the sampling, the better the sound and larger the output.)

- **Full-duplex support** — This allows for recording and playback to occur at the same time. This is particularly useful for bidirectional Internet communication or simultaneous recording and playback.

- **Input/output ports** — Several different ports on the board enable you to connect other input/output devices. These ports include:

  - **Line-In** — Connects an external CD player, cassette deck, synthesizer, MiniDisc, or other device for recording or playback. If you have a television card, you might also patch that card's line out to your sound card's line in.

  - **Microphone** — Connects a microphone for audio recording or communications.

  - **Line-Out (Speaker Out)** — Connects non-powered speakers, headphones, or a stereo amplifier.

  - **Joystick/MIDI** — Connects a joystick for gaming or MIDI device.

  - **Internal CD Audio** — This internal port connects the sound card to your computer's internal CD-ROM board (this port isn't exposed when the board is installed).

Sound drivers provided in Linux come from many sources, including a project that no longer exists: Open Sound System/Free (OSS/Free). However, the Advanced Linux Sound Architecture (ALSA) is the sound system that is integrated into the 2.6 kernel that comes with Fedora Core 2. The older OSS drivers are useful if ALSA does not support your sound card.

> **CAUTION:** Before you install a separate sound driver distribution, check to see if your current Red Hat distribution already has the most recent sound driver. When possible, use the driver that's distributed with the kernel. If you have tried the procedures in this book and you still don't have a working sound card, visit the Advanced Linux Sound Architecture at `www.alsa-project.org` site, home of the ALSA sound architecture. If that fails, then read the following file: `/usr/src/linux*/Documentation/sound/oss/README.OSS`. Also, you can visit `www.linux.org.uk/OSS` for a list of supported cards.

The devices that the audio programs use to access audio hardware in Fedora include:

- **/dev/audio, /dev/audio1** — Devices that are compatible with Sun workstation audio implementations (audio files with the .au extension).

- **/dev/cdrom** — Device representing your first CD-ROM drive. (Additional CD-ROM drives are located at `/dev/cdrom1`, `/dev/cdrom2`, and so on.)

- **/dev/dsp, /dev/dsp1** — Digital sampling devices, which many audio applications identify to access your sound card.

- **/dev/mixer, /dev/mixer1** — Sound-mixing devices.

- **/dev/sequencer** — Device that provides a low-level interface to MIDI, FM, and GUS.

- **/dev/midi00** — Device that provides raw access to midi ports.

- **/dev/sndstat** — Device that displays the status of sound drivers.

TIP: Nodes in the `/dev` directory, such as `/dev/audio`, aren't just regular files. They represent access points to the physical devices (hard disks, COM ports, and so on) that are connected to your system, or to pseudo-devices (such as Terminal windows). For example, to find out the device of your current Terminal window, type `tty`. Then send some data to that device. For example, if your device name is `/dev/pts/0`, type:

```
$ echo "Hello There" > /dev/pts/0
```

The words "Hello There" appear in that Terminal window. You can try sending messages among several Terminal windows. If a user who is logged on to the computer has terminal permissions open, you can send messages to him or her in this way, too. (I knew people who would send a dictionary file to an unsuspecting user's terminal. Although it wasn't destructive, it was annoying if you were trying to get work done.)

For general information about sound in Linux, see the Sound-HOWTO (for tips about sound cards and general sound issues) and the Sound-Playing-HOWTO (for tips on software for playing different types of audio files).

NOTE: You can find Linux HOWTOs at `www.tldp.org`.

Configuring your sound card

During the first start-up after you install Fedora, the Firstboot setup agent tries to detect and configure your sound card. If that process was successful, you can skip this procedure. If your sound card wasn't detected or if you add a card later, here are a few things you can try:

- Insert a music CD into the drive and see if it plays.

TIP: Audio volume is set fairly low by default. If you can barely hear your audio, click Sound & Video → Volume Control (from the red hat menu) to increase the volume level. Move the sliders to adjust the volume to your taste. Alternatively, from the command line type **aumix -v 100** in a Terminal window to turn the volume all the way up, so you can adjust sound from your volume knobs.

- From the red hat menu, click System Settings → Soundcard Detection (this runs the `system-config-soundcard` command). If your sound card was detected, an Audio Devices window should appear, as shown in Figure 8-1. Click the Play Test Sound button and you should hear a test sound. Click OK to finish up.

Figure 8-1: The Audio Devices (system-config-soundcard) window detects your sound card.

At this point, you can try playing an audio file. Insert a CD and open one of the CD players described in the following section.

> **TIP:** If there is a data CD in your CD drive, you may not be able to simply eject it to play your music CD. To eject a data CD, close any windows that may have an open file from the CD, then unmount the CD in your drive (if one is mounted) by typing **umount /mnt/cdrom** as root user from a Terminal window. Then you can eject the old CD and place an audio CD in the drive. If the CD appears as an icon on the desktop, you can right-click the CD icon and select Eject to eject the disc.

Choosing an audio CD player

The player that pops up automatically when you insert a CD (on the GNOME desktop) is the gnome-cd player. However, several CD players that come with Fedora Core can be used to play CDs. Here are your choices for playing CDs with Fedora Core:

- **CD Player (gnome-cd)** — This is the default CD player for the GNOME desktop. Besides having standard play buttons, this player lets you get track information automatically from a CD database (such as `freedb.org`). Or, if your CD isn't listed in the database, you can enter your own track information manually.

- **Rhythmbox (rhythmbox)** — Import and manage your CD collection with Rhythmbox music management and playback software for GNOME. Rhythmbox uses Gstreamer on the audio backend and compresses music using Ogg Vorbis audio format. Besides allowing you to create playlists of your music library, Rhythmbox also has features for playing Internet radio stations.

- **KsCD Player (kscd)** — The KsCD player comes with the KDE desktop. To use KsCD, the kdemultimedia package must be installed. From the red hat menu (KDE desktop), select Sound & Video → KsCD (or type **kscd** from a Terminal window). Like gnome-cd, this player lets you get title, track, and artist information from the CD database. KsCD, however, also lets you submit information you type in yourself to a CD database (if your CD isn't found there).

- **Grip (grip)** — While the Grip window is primarily used as a CD ripper, it can also play CDs. Select Sound & Video → More Sound & Video Applications → Grip. It includes tools for gathering data from and submitting data to CD databases. It also includes tools for copying (ripping) CD tracks and converting them to different formats (encoding). (The grip package must be installed to use this command.)

- **CDPlay (cdp)** — If you don't have access to the desktop, you can use the text-based cdp command. This player lets you use keyboard keys to play your CD, select tracks, go forward or back, or eject. (The cdp package must be installed to use this command.)

- **X Multimedia System (xmms)** — The xmms player plays a variety of audio formats, but can also play directly from a CD.

If you prefer to use one of these players, you can disable automatic startup of gnome-cd by disabling automatic play in your CD Properties window (as described in the next section). The gnome-cd and cdp CD players are then described.

> **NOTE:** If you try some of these CD players and your CD-ROM drive is not working, see the sidebar "Troubleshooting Your CD-ROM" for further information.

Automatically playing CDs

When you put an audio CD into your CD-ROM drive, a CD player automatically pops up on your desktop. If you are using the GNOME desktop, you can thank magicdev. The magicdev process monitors your CD-ROM drives and opens a CD player when it sees an audio CD.

The fact that inserting a CD starts a player automatically is nice to some people and annoying to others. If you just want the CD to play, this behavior is a good thing. However, if you want to choose your own CD player or not play the CD until you choose, you may find auto-playing a bother. If you insert a data CD or a blank CD, magicdev exhibits different behavior. Here is what magicdev does by default:

- **Audio CD** — When the music CD is inserted, magicdev starts the gnome-cd CD player and starts to play the first track of the CD.

- **Data CD** — When a data CD is inserted, the CD is mounted on your file system, any auto-run program that may be on the CD is launched, and a CD icon appears on the desktop. The first CD drive's mount point (/dev/cdrom) is /mnt/cdrom. If you have two drives, the second (/dev/cdrom1) is mounted on /mnt/cdrom1 (and so on).

- **Blank CD** — When a blank CD is inserted, a nautilus window opens with burn:/// as the location.

You can change the behavior of magicdev for the GNOME desktop on the CD and DVD preferences window. As you might guess from its name, you can change the behavior for both CDs and DVDs as follows:

1. From the red hat menu, click Preferences → CD and DVD. The CD and DVD preferences window appears.

2. For Data CDs, select from the following options:

   • **Mount discs when inserted** — If this is selected, when a data CD is inserted it is automatically mounted in a subdirectory of /mnt. This option is on by default.

   • **Start auto-run program on newly mounted discs** — If this is selected, after a data CD is mounted, the user is asked to choose whether to run an auto-run program from the CD. This option is on by default if the first option is checked.

3. For Audio CDs, you can select the "Run command when audio CD is inserted" check box to have the CD start playing automatically after it's inserted. The command shown in the box labeled Command is used to play the CD. By default, the option is on, and the gnome-cd player is chosen for you.

4. For blank CDs, the nautilus window opens with burn:/// as the location. With this feature enabled, you can drag-and-drop files on the nautilus window to gather the files you want to write to CD. Click Write to CD to burn the selected files to the CD.

5. For DVDs, click the check box next to "Run command when DVD (video) is inserted" to have the DVD play automatically (using the vlc command) when you insert a DVD.

6. Click Close.

Troubleshooting Your CD-ROM

If you are unable to play CDs on your CD-ROM drive, here are a few things you can check to correct the problem:

- Verify that your sound card is installed and working properly (see "Configuring your sound card" earlier in this chapter).

- Verify that the CD-ROM drive was detected when you booted Linux. If your CD-ROM drive is an IDE drive, type **dmesg | grep ^hd**. You should see messages about your CD-ROM that look like this: "hdc: CD-ROM CDU701, ATAPI CDROM drive" or this: "hdc: ATAPI 14X CD-ROM drive, 128kB Cache".

- If you see no indication of a CD-ROM drive, verify that the power supply and cables to the CD-ROM are connected. To make sure that the hardware is working, you can also boot to DOS and try to access the CD.

- Try inserting a software CD-ROM. If you are running the GNOME or KDE desktop, a desktop icon should appear indicating that the CD mounted by itself. If no such icon appears, go to a Terminal window and type **mount /mnt/cdrom**. Then change to the /mnt/cdrom directory and list the contents using the command cd /mnt/cdrom; ls. This tells you if the CD-ROM is accessible.

- If you get the CD-ROM working, but it fails with the message "CDROM device:

Permission denied" when you try to play music as a nonroot user, the problem may be that /dev/cdrom (which is typically a link to the actual hardware device) is not readable by anyone but root. Type **ls -l /dev/cdrom** to see what the device is linked to. Then (as the root user), if, for example, the CD device were /dev/hdc, type **chmod 644 /dev/hdc** to enable all users to read your CD-ROM and to enable the root user to write to it. One warning: if others use your computer, they will be able to read any CD you place in this drive.

Playing CDs with gnome-cd

Like most graphical CD players, the gnome-cd player has controls that look similar to what you would see on a physical CD player. If you are using the GNOME desktop, from the System Menu select Sound & Video → CD Player, or from a Terminal window, type:

```
$ gnome-cd &
```

If your computer is connected to the Internet, then for most CDs, you'll see the title and artist information. Even obscure artists are represented in the free online databases. If the information isn't available, you can enter it yourself.

The interface for adding information about the CD and its tracks is very nice. Click the Open Track Editor button. You can add Artist and Title information about the CD. Then you can select each track to type in the track name. To add the name of the artist and the disc title, click in the appropriate text box and type in that information. Figure 8-2 shows the CD Player and the CDDB Track Editor.

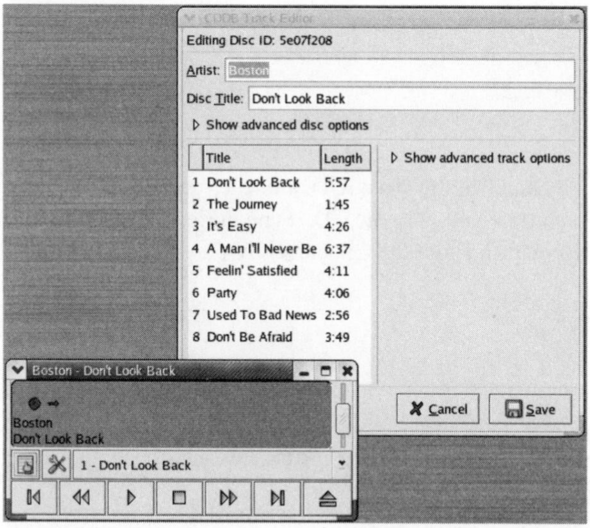

Figure 8-2: Play CDs and store artist, title, and track information with gnome-cd.

Playing CDs with cdp

If you are working from a dumb terminal or just don't have your X desktop running, you can run the cdp utility (which comes with Fedora) to play CDs. I don't suggest running this utility from a Terminal window; it doesn't display properly. First, insert the music CD you want to play. Then, to start cdp, at a shell prompt type:

```
$ cdp
```

You should see a blue screen containing the cdp display. If instead of starting on the first track you want to start on another track (for example, track 5), type:

```
$ cdp play 5
```

When cdp starts, you can see all the tracks, how long each track plays, and total play time. To control the play of the CD, use the following controls (turn on Num Lock to use these numbers from the numeric keypad):

- **9** — Play
- **8** — Pause/Resume
- **7** — Stop
- **6** — Next Track
- **5** — Replay Current Track
- **4** — Previous Track
- **3** — Forward 15 Seconds
- **2** — Quit (Stop Music, Exit, and Eject)
- **1** — Back 15 Seconds
- **0** — Exit (Continue Music and Exit)
- **.** — Help (Press the period key)

The cdp display also lets you enter the names of the artist, CD, and each song. Because this information is saved, you can see it each time you play the CD. Type these commands while the cdp display is showing to edit information about the CD currently playing:

- **a** — Edit the Artist Name and press Enter.
- **c** — Edit the CD Name and press Enter.
- **Enter** — Edit the title of the current song and press Enter again.

CAUTION: If you try to edit a song name and cdp crashes, type **eject** to stop the CD from playing. Editing the song name seems to work better if you pause the song first.

The arrow keys are also pretty handy for controlling CDs in `cdp`. The up arrow is for pause/play, and the left arrow is to go back a track. The right arrow is to go forward a track, and the down arrow is to eject.

Playing music with Rhythmbox Audio Player

Rhythmbox provides the GNOME music player that lets you do everything, at least according to the Rhythmbox documentation. You can play music files, import music from CDs, and play Internet radio stations, all from one interface.

The first time you run Rhythmbox, the program displays a setup wizard. You can tell Rhythmbox where you store your music files, and Rhythmbox will index, sort, and help you maintain a music library, with the wizard dialog shown in Figure 8-3.

Figure 8-3: Defining where you store your music.

After you've gone through the setup wizard, you'll see the main music library interface (see Figure 8-4). Rhythmbox makes it easy to organize even large collections of music files.

Figure 8-4: Viewing a music library with Rhythmbox.

NOTE: The Red Hat and Fedora versions of Linux do not include support for playing MP3 files, due to patent issues. You can download updates for Rhythmbox at `gstreamer.net`. You want the package `gstreamer-plugins-mp3`.

In addition to playing music files, Rhythmbox can launch Sound Juicer to rip CDs (see the section on Ripping CDs with Grip for more on ripping CD audio). Rhythmbox can also play Internet radio stations. The easiest way to do this is to find a streaming radio station (you want to look for Shoutcast PLS files, usually with a .pls extension). Save the PLS file, and then double-click on the file in the Nautilus file browser. Nautilus comes configured to launch Rhythmbox for playing audio. Figure 8-5 shows Rhythmbox with three Internet radio stations.

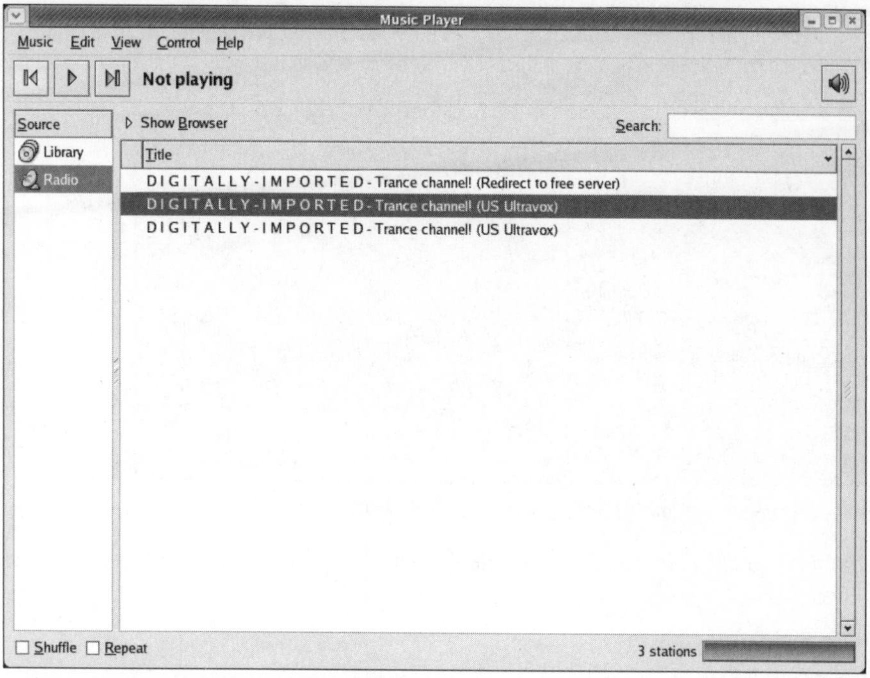

Figure 8-5: Rhythmbox playing Internet radio.

> **TIP**: The site www.di.fm lists a number of free Internet radio channels.

Playing music with XMMS Audio Player

The XMMS (X Multimedia System) Audio Player provides a graphical interface for playing music files in MP3, Ogg Vorbis, WAV, and other audio formats. XMMS has some nice extras too, which include an equalizer, a playlist editor, and the ability to add more audio plugins. If the player looks familiar to you, that's because it is styled after the Windows winamp program.

> **NOTE:** Red Hat removed all software that does MP3 encoding or decoding due to patent concerns related to MP3 format. Although the XMMS player was designed to play MP3 files, the XMMS plug-in required to actually decode MP3 is not included with Fedora Core. To add MP3 support back into Fedora Core, you can get and install an MP3 plugin. One place to get RPM packages that support MP3 decoding is http://rpm.livna.org. They are also available from other sources, including www.xmms.org and www.gurulabs.com/downloads.html.

You can start the XMMS Audio Player by selecting Sound & Video → Audio Player or by typing the xmms command from a Terminal window. Figure 8-6 consists of the XMMS Audio Player with the associated equalizer (below) and the Playlist Editor (to the right).

NOTE: Although the default theme is one that matches the Fedora Blue Curve theme, you can change the look of xmms by right-clicking on xmms and selecting Options → Skin Browser. The theme shown in Figure 8-6 is called BrushedMetal_Xmms.

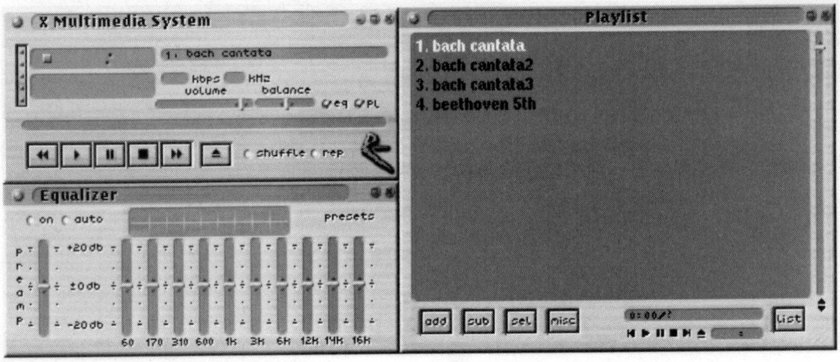

Figure 8-6: Play Ogg Vorbis and other audio files from the XMMS playlist.

As noted earlier, you can play several audio file formats. Supported audio file formats include the following:

- MP3 (with added plugin)
- Ogg Vorbis
- WAV
- AU
- CD Audio
- CIN Movies

You can get many more audio plugins from xmms.org. The XMMS Audio Player can be used in the following way:

1. Obtain music files by either:
   - Ripping songs from a CD or copying them from the Web so that they are in an accessible directory.
   - Inserting a music CD in your CD-ROM drive. (Xmms expects the CD to be accessible from /dev/cdrom.)

2. From the red hat menu, select Sound & Video → Audio Player. The X Multimedia System player appears.

3. Click the Eject button. The Load files window appears.

4. If you have inserted a CD, the contents of /mnt/cdrom appear in the Files pane. Select the files you want to add to your Playlist and click the Add Selected Files or the Add all

Files in Directory button to add all songs from the current directory. To add audio files from your file system, browse your files and directories and click the same buttons to add the audio files you want. Select Close.

5. Click the Play List button (the tiny button marked PL) on the console. A Playlist Editor window appears.

6. Double-click the music file, and it starts to play.

7. With a file selected and playing, here are a few actions you can take:

   - **Control play** — Buttons for controlling play are what you may expect to see on a physical CD player. From left to right, the buttons let you go to a previous track, play, pause, stop, go to the next track, or eject the CD. The eject button opens a window, allowing you to load the next file.

   - **Adjust sound** — Use the left slider bar to adjust the volume. Use the right slider bar to change the right-to-left balance.

   - **Display time** — Click in the elapsed time area to toggle between elapsed time and time remaining.

   - **View file information** — Click the button in the upper-left corner of the screen to see the XMMS menu. Then select View File Info. You can often find out a lot of information about the file: title, artist, album, comments, and genre. For an Ogg file, you can see specific information about the file itself, such as the format, bit rate, sample rate, frames, file size, and more. You can change or add to the tag information and click Save to keep it.

8. When you are done playing music, click the Stop button to stop the current song. Then click the X in the upper-right corner of the display to close the window.

Special features of the XMMS Audio Player let you adjust high and low frequencies using a graphic equalizer and gather and play songs using a Playlist Editor. Click the button marked EQ next to the balance bar on the player to open the Equalizer. Click the button marked PL next to that to open the Playlist Editor.

Using the Equalizer

The Equalizer lets you use slider bars to set different levels to different frequencies played. Bars on the left adjust lower frequencies, and those on the right adjust higher frequencies. Click the EQ button to open the Equalizer. Here are tasks you can perform with the Equalizer:

- If you like the settings you have for a particular song, you can save them as a Preset. Set each frequency as you like it and click the Preset button. Then choose Save → Preset. Type a name for the preset and click OK.

- To reload a preset you created earlier, click the Preset button and select Load → Preset. Select the preset you want and click OK to change the settings.

The small window in the center/top of the Equalizer shows the sound wave formed by your settings. You can adjust the Preamp bar on the left to boost different levels in the set range.

Using the Playlist Editor

The Playlist Editor lets you put together a list of audio files that you want to play. You can add and delete files from this list, save them to a file, and use them again later. Click the PL button in the XMMS window to open the Playlist Editor.

The Playlist Editor allows you to:

- **Add files to the playlist** — Click the Add button. The Load Files window appears. Select the directory containing your audio files (it's useful to keep them all in one place) from the left column. Then either select a file from the right column and click Add selected files or click Add all files in the directory. Click OK. The selected file or files appear in the playlist. You can also drag music files from the nautilus file manager onto the playlist window to add the files to the playlist.

- **Select files to play** — To select from the files in the playlist, use the previous track and next track buttons in the main XMMS window. The selected file is highlighted. Click the Play button to play that file. Alternatively, you can double-click on any file in the playlist to start it playing.

- **Delete files from the playlist** — To remove files from the playlist, select the file or files you want to remove (next/previous track buttons), right-click the playlist window, and click Remove → Selected . The selected files are removed.

- **Sort files on the playlist** — To sort the playlist in different ways, click and hold the Misc button and move the mouse to select Sort List. Then you can select Sort List to sort by Title, Filename, Path and Filename, or Date. You can also randomize or reverse the list.

- **Save the playlist** — To save the current playlist, hold the mouse button down on the List button and then select Save. Browse to the directory you want, and then type the name you want to assign to the playlist and click OK.

- **Load the playlist** — To reload a saved playlist, click the List button. Select a previously saved playlist from the directory in which you saved it and click OK.

There is also a tiny set of buttons on the bottom of the Playlist Editor screen. These are the same buttons as those on the main screen used for selecting different tracks or playing, pausing, stopping, or ejecting the current track.

Using MIDI audio players

MIDI stands for Musical Instrument Digital Interface. MIDI files are created from synthesizers and other electronic music devices. MIDI files tend to be smaller than other kinds of audio files because, instead of storing the complete sounds, they contain the notes played. The MIDI player reproduces the notes to sound like a huge variety of MIDI instruments.

There are lots of sites on the Internet for downloading MIDI files. Try the Ifni MIDI Music site (www.ifni.com), which contains songs by the Beatles, Led Zeppelin, Nirvana, and others organized by album. Most of the MIDI music is pretty simple, but you can have some fun playing with it.

Fedora comes with the kmid MIDI player. Kmid is not installed by default (find it in the kdemultimedia package on CD #2). Kmid provides a GUI interface for midi music, including the ability to display karaoke lyrics in real time. There is also the timidity MIDI player (from the timidity++ package on CD #4), which lets you run MIDI audio from a Terminal window.

> **NOTE:** Use the timidity or kmid MIDI player if your sound card doesn't include MIDI support. Both can convert MIDI input into WAV files that can play on any sound card. To start timidity, type **timidity file.mid &** at the command-line prompt.

To start kmid, select Sound & Video → KMid (or type **kmid &** from a Terminal window).

Performing audio file conversion and compression

There are many different formats for storing and compressing speech and music files. Because music files can be large, they are typically stored in a compressed format. While MP3 has been the compression format of choice, Ogg Vorbis is quickly becoming a favorite format for compressing music in the open-source community. Ogg Vorbis has the added benefit over MP3 of not being encumbered by patents.

Tools that come with Fedora for converting and compressing audio files include:

- **sox** — A general-purpose tool for converting audio files among a variety of formats.
- **oggenc** — A tool for specifically converting music files to Ogg Vorbis format.

Converting audio files with Sox

If you have a sound file in one format, but you want it to be in another format, Linux offers some conversion tools you can use to convert the file. The Sox utility can translate to and from any of the audio formats listed in Table 8-1.

> **TIP:** Type **sox -h** to see the supported audio types. This also shows supported options and effects.

Table 8-1: Sound Formats Supported by Sox Utility

File Extension or Pseudonym	Description	File Extension or Pseudonym	Description
.8svx	8SVX Amiga musical instrument description format.	.aiff	Apple IIc/IIgs and SGI AIFF files. May require a separate archiver to work with these files.

File Extension or Pseudonym	Description	File Extension or Pseudonym	Description
.au, .snd	Sun Microsystems AU audio files. This is a popular format.	.avr	Audio Visual Research format, used on the Mac.
.cdr	CD-R files used to master compact disks.	.cvs	Continuously variable slope delta modulation, which is used for voice mail and other speech compression.
.dat	Text data files, which contain a text representation of sound data.	.gsm	Lossy Speech Compression (GSM 06.10), used to shrink audio data in voice mail and similar applications.
.hcom	Macintosh HCOM files.	.maud	Amiga format used to produce sound that is 8-bit linear, 16-bit linear, A-law, and u-law in mono or stereo.
.ogg	Ogg Vorbis compressed audio, which is best used for compressing music and streaming audio.	.ossdsp	Pseudo file, used to open the OSS /dev/dsp file and configure it to use the data type passed to Sox. Used to either play or record.
.prc	Psion record.app format, newer than the WVE format.	.sf	IRCAM sound files, used by CSound package and MixView sample editor.
.sph	Speech audio SPHERE (Speech Header Resources) format from NIST (National Institute of Standards and Technology).	.smp	SampleVision files from Turtle Beach, used to communicate with different MIDI samplers.
.sunau	Pseudo file, used to open a /dev/audio file and set it to use the data type being passed to Sox.	.txw	Yamaha TX-16W from a Yamaha sampling keyboard.

File Extension or Pseudonym	Description	File Extension or Pseudonym	Description
`.vms`	Used to compress speech audio for voice mail and similar applications.	`.voc`	Sound Blaster VOC file.
`.wav`	Microsoft WAV RIFF files. This is the native Microsoft Windows sound format.	`.wve`	8-bit, a-law, 8 kHz sound files used with Psion Palmtop computers.
`.raw`	Raw files (contain no header information, so sample rate, size, and style must be given).	`.ub, .sb, .uw, .sw, .ul, .al, .lu, .la, .sl`	Raw files with set characteristics. ub is unsigned byte; sb is signed byte; uw is unsigned word; sw is signed word; and ul is ulaw.

If you are not sure about the format of an audio file, you can add the .auto extension to the filename. This triggers Sox to guess what kind of audio format is contained in the file. The .auto extension can only be used for the input file. If Sox can figure out the content of the input file, it translates the contents to the sound type for the output file you request.

In its most basic form, you can convert one file format (such as a WAV file) to another format (such as an AU file) as follows:

```
$ sox file1.wav file1.au
```

To see what Sox is doing, use the -V option. For example:

```
$ sox -V file1.wav file1.voc

sox: Reading Wave file: Microsoft PCM format, 2 channel, 44100 samp/sec
sox: 176400 byte/sec, 4 block align, 16 bits/samp, 50266944 data bytes
sox: Input file: using sample rate 11025
        size bytes, style unsigned, 1 channel
sox: Input file1.wav: comment "file1.wav"

sox: Output file1.voc: using sample rate 44100
        size shorts, encoding signed (2's complement), 2 channels
sox: Output file: comment "file1.wav"
```

You can apply sound effects during the Sox conversion process. The following example shows how to change the sample rate (using the -r option) from 10,000 kHz to 5,000 kHz:

```
$ sox -r 10000 file1.wav -r 5000 file1.voc
```

To reduce the noise, you can send the file through a low-pass filter. Here's an example:

```
$ sox file1.voc file2.voc lowp 2200
```

For more information on Sox and to get the latest download, go to the SoX — Sound eXchange — home page (`sourceforge.net/projects/sox/`).

Compressing music files with oggenc

The `oggenc` command takes music or other audio data and converts it from uncompressed formats (such as WAV, raw, or AIFF) to the compressed OGG Vorbis format. Using OGG Vorbis, audio files can be significantly reduced in size without a noticeable loss of sound quality. (Using the default settings in `oggenc`, I reduced a 48MB WAV music file to 4MB.)

In its most basic form, you can use `oggenc` with one or more WAV or AIFF files following it. For example:

```
$ oggenc *.wav
```

This command would result in all files ending with `.wav` in the current directory to be converted to OGG Vorbis format. An OGG file is produced for each WAV file, with `oggenc` substituting `.ogg` for `.wav` as the file suffix for the compressed file. OGG Vorbis files can be played in many different audio players in Linux, including the XMMS player (described earlier).

> **TIP:** If you want to rip music files from a CD and compress them, you can use the `grip` window (described later in this chapter). Grip allows you to select `oggenc` as the tool to do the file compression.

> **CROSS-REFERENCE:** If you are interested in making a CD jukebox that rips, records, and compresses music CDs using `oggenc` and other open source software, check out the book *Linux Toys* by Christopher Negus and Chuck Wolber from Wiley Publishing.

Viewing TV and Webcams

Getting TV cards, Webcams, and other video devices to play in Linux is still a bit of an adventure. Most manufacturers of TV cards and Webcams are not losing sleep to produce Linux drivers. As a result, most of the drivers that bring video to your Linux desktop have been reverse-engineered (that is, they were created by software engineers who watched what the video device sent and received, rather than seeing the actual code that runs the device).

The first, and probably biggest, trick is to get that TV card or Webcam that is supported in Linux. Once you are getting video output from that device (typically available from `/dev/video0`), you can try out a couple of applications to begin using it. This section describes the Tvtime program for watching television and the GnomeMeeting program for video conferencing.

Watching TV with Tvtime

The Tvtime program (tvtime command) lets you display video output, in particular television channels, on your desktop. You can change the channels, adjust volume, and fine-tune your picture. In addition, tvtime sports a slick on-screen display and support for a widescreen display.

Tvtime will display, by default, any device producing video on the /dev/video0 device. Therefore, you can use tvtime to view Webcams as well as receive television channels. The following sections describe how to choose a TV capture card and use tvtime to watch television on your desktop.

> **NOTE:** Tvtime will not display output from some low-quality Webcams. To use your Webcam, consider obtaining the xawtv package, which is available from most Fedora software repositories.

Getting a supported TV card

Video4Linux is the video interface included with Fedora. It supports a variety of TV capture cards and cameras.

To see a list of supported TV cards that you can use with tvtime, refer to the CARDLIST and Cards files. To view these files, you need to have the kernel-source package installed. You'll find the Cards file in the following location on your Linux system:

```
/usr/src/linux*/Documentation/video4linux/bttv/Cards
```

The Cards file applies to the Video4Linux bttv driver. In addition, look at all files starting with CARDLIST in the following location on your location:

```
/usr/src/linux*/Documentation/video4linux/CARDLIST*
```

Video4Linux is designed to autodetect your TV capture card and load the proper modules to activate it. So install the TV-card hardware (with the appropriate connection to your TV reception), boot Fedora, and run the tvtime command as described in the next section. You should be able to see video displayed on your tvtime window.

If your card appears not to be working, here are a few things you can try:

1. To see if your TV card was properly seated in its slot and detected by Linux, type the following:

   ```
   $ /sbin/lspci
   ```

   This will show you a list of all valid PCI cards on your computer. If nothing shows up for the card, you probably have a hardware problem.

2. It is possible that the card is there, but the right card type is not being detected. Improper detection is most likely if you have a card for which there are several revisions, with each requiring a different driver. If you think your card is not being properly detected, find

your card in the CARDLIST files. Then add the appropriate line to the /etc/modprobe.conf file. For example, to add a Prolink PV-BT878P, revision 9B card, add the following line to /etc/modprobe.conf:

```
options    bttv   card=72
```

You can also add other options listed in the Insmod-options file for the bttv driver. If you are still having problems getting your card to work, a mailing list is available on which you can ask questions about Video4Linux issues. The location is:

```
http://listman.redhat.com/mailman/listinfo/video4linux-list
```

One possible reason that you don't see any video when you try to run tvtime or other video applications is that some other person or video application already has the video driver open. Only one application can use the video driver at a time in Fedora. Another quirk of video4linux is that the first person to open the device on your system becomes the owner. So you might need to open the permissions of the driver to allow people other than the first person to use it to access the video4linux driver.

Running tvtime

To start up the tvtime viewer, simply select the TVtime Televison Viewer choice from the Sound & Video menu. Or, type the following from a Terminal window on your desktop:

```
$ tvtime &
```

A video screen should appear in a window on the desktop. Click the left mouse button on the window to see a list of stations. Click the right mouse button to see the on-screen Setup menu.

Here are a few things you can now do with your tvtime on-screen display:

- **Configure input** — This choice allows you to change the video source, choose the television standard (which defaults to NTSC for the USA), and change the resolution of the input.
- **Set up the picture** — Adjust the brightness, contrast, color and hue.
- **Adjust the video processing** — You can control the attempted frame rate, configure the deinterlacer, or add an input filter.
- **Adjust output** — Control the aspect ratio (for 16:9 output, for example), apply a matte, or set the overscan mode.

Video conferencing with GnomeMeeting

The GnomeMeeting window lets you communicate with other people over a network through video, audio, and typed messages. Because GnomeMeeting supports the H323 protocol, you can use it to communicate with people using other popular video-conferencing clients, such as Microsoft NetMeeting, Cu-SeeMe, and Intel VideoPhone.

> **NOTE**: GnomeMeeting does not support the NetMeeting shared whiteboard functions, just video conferencing.

To be able to send video, you need a Webcam that is supported in Linux. Although not all Webcams are supported in Linux, you still have a few dozen models to choose from. The following sections show you how to set up your Webcam and use GnomeMeeting for video conferencing.

Getting a supported Webcam

As with support for TV capture cards, Webcam support is provided through the video4linux interface. Some of the supported cameras have a parallel-port interface, although most Webcams currently supported in Linux require a USB port.

> **NOTE:** At the time of this writing, Fedora Core 2 was not properly detecting and configuring any Webcam that I tested. The following procedure describes how a Webcam was configured in Fedora Core 1. Look for software updates to Fedora Core 2 to see if the problem gets fixed.

To see if your Webcam is supported, check the `/usr/src/linux*/Documentation` directory. A few parallel-port video cameras are described in the `video4linux` subdirectory; however, the bulk of the supported cameras are listed in the `usb` directory.

> **TIP:** After doing some research myself, I purchased a Logitech QuickCam Pro 3000. The driver for this Webcam was made for a Philips USB Webcam, but it also works for Webcams from Logitech, Samsung, Creative Labs, and Askey. Before making the purchase, I checked out the description of the driver at `www.smcc.demon.nl/webcam`.

Supported USB cameras should be autodetected, so that when you plug them in the necessary modules are loaded automatically. Just start up GNOME Meeting (`gnomemeeting` command) , and if everything is working you should see video from your Webcam on your Linux desktop. Here are a few things I typed to check that my Webcam was working properly:

```
# lsmod
pwc                    43392   1
videodev                5120   2  [pwc]
usbcore                59072   1  [audio pwc usb-uhci]
```

The output from `lsmod` shows that the `pwc` driver was loaded and associated with the `videodev` module and `usbcore` module. To see information about the pwc module (which is specific to this Webcam), I typed the following `modinfo` command:

```
# modinfo -p pwc
filename:     /lib/modules/2.4.20-2.48/kernel/drivers/usb/pwc.o
description:  "Philips USB webcam driver"
author:       "Nemosoft Unv. <nemosoft@smcc.demon.nl>"
license:      "GPL"
```

```
parm:          size string, description "Initial image size. One of
               sqcif, qsif, qcif, sif, cif, vga"
parm:          fps int, description "Initial frames per second. Varies
               with model, useful range 5-30"
parm:          fbufs int, description "Number of internal frame buffers
               to reserve"
parm:          mbufs int, description "Number of external (mmap()ed)
               image buffers"
parm:          trace int, description "For debugging purposes"
parm:          power_save int, description "Turn power save feature in
               camera on or off"
parm:          compression int, description "Preferred compression
               quality. Range 0 (uncompressed) to 3 (high compression)"
parm:          leds int array (min = 2, max = 2), description "LED on,off
               time in milliseconds"
parm:          dev_hint string array (min = 0, max = 10), description
               "Device node hints"
```
The output shows that pwc is a Philips USB Webcam driver. It also shows options that you can set with the pwc module in order to change the image size, frames per second, and debugging level, among other things. The information about options for your Webcam driver can be useful later if you want to tune the behavior of your Webcam or track down a problem.

Running GnomeMeeting

To start GnomeMeeting from a Terminal window, type **gnomemeeting &.** If it is not installed, you can install the gnomemeeting package from the second Fedora Core installation CD (CD #2). The first time you run GnomeMeeting, the GnomeMeeting Configuration Assistant starts. The assistant lets you enter the following information:

- **Personal Data** — Your first name, last name, e-mail address, comment, and location. You can also select whether or not you want to be listed in the GnomeMeeting ILS directory.

- **Connection Type** — Indicate the speed of your Internet connection (56K modem, ISDN, DSL/Cable, T1/LAN or Custom).

Figure 8-7 shows the GnomeMeeting window with the history log to the right and the address book behind.

In the GnomeMeeting window that opens you can click on the book icon to open a search window (shown to the upper right in Figure 8-7). The search window enables you to connect to an ILS directory. By typing a name into the search filter, you can search for people who might be connected to that server by first name, last name, e-mail address, or location. Select a person from the list that appears and, if he or she accepts your call, you can begin video-conferencing.

Tabs beneath the video window let you adjust your audio levels and video appearance. The History tab shows a log of your activities.

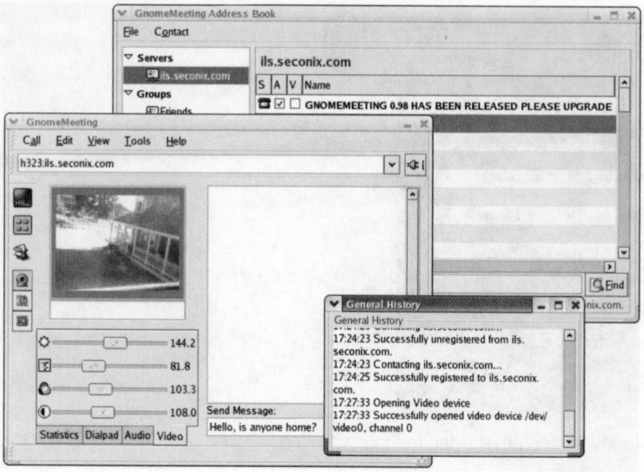

Figure 8-7: Connect to ILS servers to video-conference with GnomeMeeting.

Playing Video

Although several fairly high-quality video players are available for Linux, none are included in the Fedora Core distribution. Legal issues surrounding the playing of encoded DVD movies in Linux might be responsible for keeping players such as the Mplayer (`freshmeat.net/mplayer`), Ogle (`http://www.dtek.chalmers.se/groups/dvd`), and Xine (`xine.sourceforge.net`) video players out of this distribution.

By most accounts, however, if you don't download and use the DeCCS (software for decrypting DVD movies), you can get and use these video players to play a variety of video content for personal use. The following sections provide descriptions of video applications to use with Fedora.

> **CROSS-REFERENCE:** The `mplayer` video player, along with various tools for creating your own videos and TV recordings in Fedora, are available with the book *Linux Toys* by Christopher Negus and Chuck Wolber from Wiley Publishing. Those tools are described for making simple home video archive, television recorder, and streaming media projects.

Watching Video with Xine

The xine player is an excellent application for playing a variety of video and audio formats. You can get xine from `xine.sourceforge.net` or by downloading RPMs from `freshrpms.net`.

You can start the xine player by typing **xine&** from a Terminal window. Figure 8-8 shows an example of the xine video player window and controls.

Figure 8-8: Play video CDs, MP3s, Quicktime, and other video formats with xine.

NOTE: When you try to install xine, it will tell you if you need any additional packages. If your xine player fails to start, see the "Xine tips" section later in this chapter.

Xine supports a bunch of video and audio formats, including:

- MPEG (1, 2, and 4)
- Quicktime (see "Xine tips" if your Quicktime content won't play)
- WMV
- DVDs, CDs, and VCDs
- Motion JPEG
- MPEG audio (MP3)
- AC3 and Dolby Digital audio
- DTS audio
- Ogg Vorbis audio

Xine can understand different file formats that represent a combination of audio and video. These include .mpg (MPEG program streams), .ts (MPEG transport streams), .mpv (raw MPEG audio/video streams), .avi (MS AVI format), and .asf (Advanced Streaming format). While xine can play Video CDs and DVDs, it can't play encrypted DVDs or Video-on-CD hybrid format as xine is delivered (because of the legal issues mentioned earlier related to decrypting DVDs).

Using xine

With xine started, right-click in the xine window to see the controls. The quickest way to play video is to click one of the following buttons, then press the Play button (right arrow or play, depending on the skin you are using):

- VCD (looks for a video CD)
- DVD (looks for a DVD in `/dev/dvd`)
- CDA (looks a music CD in `/dev/cdaudio`)

Next, you can use the Pause/resume, Stop, Play, Fast motion, Slow motion, or Eject buttons to work with video. You can also use the Previous and Next buttons to step to different tracks. The controls are very similar to what you would expect on a physical CD or DVD player.

To select individual files, or to put together your own list of content to play, you can use the Playlist feature.

Creating playlists with xine

Click the Playlist button on the left side of the xine control window. A Playlist Editor appears, showing the files on your current playlist. You can add and delete content from this list, then save the list to call on later. Here's how you use the xine Playlist Editor:

- **CDA, DVD, or VCD** — Click any of the buttons that represent a particular CD or DVD. All content from that CD or DVD is added to the playlist.
- **Add** — Click the Add button to see the MRL Browser window. From that window, click File to choose a file from your Linux file system to add to the list. Click Select to add that file to the Playlist Editor.
- **Move up/Move down** — Use the Move up selected MRL and Move down selected MRL buttons to move up and down the playlist.
- **Delete** — Click the Delete Selected MRL button to remove the current selection.
- **Delete all** — Click the Delete All Entries button to clear the whole playlist.
- **Save** — Click the Save button to save the playlist to your home directory (`$HOME/.xine/playlist`).
- **Load** — To read in the playlist you saved, click the Load button.

The xine content is identified as media resource locators (MRLs). Each MRL is identified as a file, DVD, or VCD. Files are in the regular file path (`/path/file`) or preceded by `file:/`, `fifo:/`, or `stdin:/`. DVDs and VCD are preceded by `dvd` and `vcd`, respectively (for example, `vcd://01`).

To play your playlist, click the Play button (arrow key) on the Playlist Editor.

Xine tips

Getting video and audio to work properly can sometimes be a tricky business. Here are a few quick tips if you are having trouble getting xine to work properly (or at all):

- **Xine won't start** — To work best, xine needs an X driver that supports xvid. If there is no xvid support for your video card in X, xine will shut down immediately when it tries to open the default Xv driver. If this happens to you, try starting xine with the X11 video driver (which is slower, but should work) as follows:

```
$ xine -VXSHM
```

- **Xine playback is choppy** — If playback of files from you hard disk is choppy, there are a couple of settings you can check: 32-bit IO and DMA. (If these two features are supported by your hard disk, they will generally improve hard disk performance.)

> **CAUTION:** Improper disk settings can result in destroyed data on your hard disk. Do this procedure at your own risk. This procedure is only for IDE hard drives (NO SCSI)! Also, be sure to have a current backup and no activity on your hard disk if you change DMA or IO settings as described below.

First, test the speed of hard disk reads. To test the first IDE drive (/dev/hda), type:

```
# hdparm -t /dev/hda
Timing buffered disk reads: 64 MB in 19.31 seconds = 3.31 MB/sec
```

To see your current DMA and IO settings, as root user type:

```
# hdparm -c -d /dev/hda
/dev/hda:
 I/O support = 0 (default 16-bit)
 using_dma   = 0 (off)
```

This shows that both 32-bit IO and DMA are off. To turn them on, type:

```
# hdparm -c 1 -d 1 /dev/hda
/dev/hda:
 I/O support = 1 (32-bit)
 using_dma   = 1 (on)
```

With both settings on, test the disk again:

```
# hdparm -t /dev/hda
Timing buffered disk reads: 64 MB in 2.2 seconds = 28.83 MB/sec
```

As you can see from this example, buffered disk reads of 64 MB went from 19.31 seconds to 2.2 seconds after changing the parameters described. Playback should be much better now.

- **Xine won't play particular media** — Messages such as `no input plug-in` mean that either the file format you are trying to play is not supported or it requires an additional plug-in (as is the case with playing DVDs). If the message is `maybe xyx is a broken file`, the file may be a proprietary version of an otherwise supported format. For example, I had a Quicktime video fail that required an SVQ3 codec (which is currently not supported under Linux), though other Quicktime files will play fine.

> **NOTE:** The CrossOver Plugin (described in Chapter 9) can be used to play a variety of content, including the version of Quicktime just mentioned.

Using RealPlayer

A tremendous amount of content is available on the Internet in the RealMedia and RealAudio formats. You can see and hear video clips of popular musicians and comics. You can view live events, such as conferences, news stories, and concerts. You can also listen to your favorite radio stations when you are out of town.

To play RealMedia and RealAudio content you need, as you may have guessed, RealPlayer. Real Networks (www.real.com) is a leader in streaming media on the Internet. More than 50 million unique users have registered with Real Networks and their Web site, downloading more than 175,000 files per day. And that's not even the good news. The good news is that RealPlayer is available to run in Fedora.

RealPlayer for Linux is available via the Linux area of download.com or tucows.com. Or, try this site: http://proforma.real.com/real/player/unix/unix.html. This player is not supported by Real Networks directly. In addition, Real has opened up the source code to the RealPlayer under the name Helix DNA Client. (Currently, RealPlayer is built on top of the Helix DNA Client.) You can download the Helix source code from helixcommunity.org.

The instructions for configuring RealPlayer are delivered in HTML format, so you can read it in Mozilla or some other Web browser. If any patches or workarounds are required, you can find them in the Real Networks Knowledge Base. To get there, click Support (from most Real Networks pages), then click Knowledge Base. When there, query for the word Linux to find any problem reports and fixes.

When you install RealPlayer, you are asked if you want to configure it to be used as a Netscape plug-in (which I recommend you do so you can play real content in Mozilla). After that, when you open any Real content in your browser, RealPlayer opens to handle it. Alternatively, you can start RealPlayer from a Terminal window on your desktop by typing the following:

```
$ realplay &
```

Real Networks has gone to a subscription model for its content. You sign up and pay a monthly fee to get RealPlayer content. To see what is available, and to decide if it is worth signing up, I suggest starting at the RealGuide site (realguide.real.com). Besides describing the Real Networks content that is available, there are a few clips at this site you can try out.

Using a Digital Camera with gtkam and gphoto2

With the gtkam window, you can download and work with images from digital cameras. The gtkam window is a front end to gPhoto2, which provides support for dozens of digital cameras in Linux. The gtkam window works by attaching a supported digital camera to a serial or USB port on your computer. You can view thumbnails of the digital images from the camera, view full-size images, and download the ones you select from the camera to your hard disk.

> **NOTE:** If you have a camera that saves images to a floppy disk, just insert that disk into your disk drive and the contents of the disk should open automatically on your desktop. In addition, if your camera saves images to SD or CF cards, you can purchase a USB card reader and view these files from Linux.

Check the gPhoto2 Web site (`http://www.gphoto.org/proj/libgphoto2/support.php`) for information on supported cameras as well as other topics related to gPhoto. Here is a list of currently supported digital cameras.

- **AEG** — Supported model: Snap 300
- **Agfa ePhoto** — Supported models: 307, 780, 780C, 1280, 1680, and CL18
- **Aiptek** – Supported models: PalmCam Trio, and PenCam Trio
- **Apple QuickTake** — Supported model: 200
- **Argus** — Supported models: DC-100, DC-1500, DC-1510, DC-2000, and DC-2200
- **Barbie**
- **Canon** — Supported models: IXY Digital, IXY Digital 300, MV630i, MVX2i, Optura 10, Optura 20, Optura 200 MC, and ZR70MC
- **Canon Digital**— Suported models: IXUS, IXUS 2, IXUS 300, IXUS 330, IXUS 400, IXUS i, IXUS II, IXUS v, IXUS v2, and IXUS v3
- **Canon EOS** - Supported models: 10D, 300D, D30, Digital Rebel, Kiss Digital
- **Canon PowerShot** — Supported models: A5, A5 Zoom, A10, A20, A50, A60, A70, A80, A100, A200, A300, G1, G2, G3, G5, Pro70, Pro90 IS, S10, S20, S30, S40, S45, S50, S100, S110, S200, S210, S300, S400, and SD100
- **Casio QV** — Supported models: 10, 10A, 11, 30, 70, 100, 200, 700, and 5000SX
- **Chinon** — Supported model: ES-1000
- **CoolCam** — Supported model: CP086
- **Digitaldream** — Supported models: 200, l'elegante, l'elite, l'espion, l'esprit, and la ronde
- **Dynatron** — Supported model: Dynacam 800
- **Epson PhotoPC** — Supported models: 300z, 500, 550, 600, 700, 800, and 850z

- **Fuji** — Supported models: ix-100, DS-7, DX-5, DX-10, IX-1, MX-500, MX-600, MX-700, MX-1200, MX-1700, MX-2700, and MX-2900

- **Generic Soundvision** — Supported model: Clarity2

- **Hawking** — Supported model: DC120

- **Hot Wheels**

- **Hewlett-Packard PhotoSmart** — Supported models: 618, 912, C20, C30, C200, C500, 120, 318, 320, 43x, 612, 620, 715, 720, 812, 850, and 935

- **IOMagic** — Supported models: 400, 420

- **Jentoptik** — Supported models: JD11, JD12 800ff

- **KBGear** — Supported model: JamCam

- **Kodak DC** — Supported models: CX4200, CX4210, CX4230, CX4300, CX6200, CX6230, CX6330, DC120, DC220, DC240, DC260, DC265, DC280, DC290, DC3200, DC3400, DC4800, DC5000, DX3215, DX3500, DX3600, DX3700, DX3900, DX4330, DX4530, DX4900, DX6340, DX6440, DX6490, LS420, LS443, LS663, and MC3

- **Konica** — Supported models: e-mini, Q-EZ, Q-M100, Q-M100V, Q-M200

- **Leica** — Supported model: Digilux Zoom.

- **Media-Tech** — Supported model: mt-406

- **Minolta** — Supported model: Dimage V

- **Mustek** — Supported model: VDC-3500

- **Nicon CoolPix** — Supported models: 100, 300, 600, 700, 800, 880, 900, 900S, 910, 950, 950S, 990, 995, 2000, 2100, 2500, 3100, 3500, 4300, 4500, 5000, 5400, 5700, and SQ

- **Olympus** — Supported models: D-100Z, D-200L, D-220L, D-300L, D-320L, D-330R, D-340L, D-340R, D-360L, D-400L Zoom, D-450Z, D-460Z, D-500L, D-560Z, D-600L, D-600XL, D-620L, C-350Z, C-400, C-400L, C-410, C-410L, C-420, C-420L, C-800, C-800L, C-820, C-820L, C-830L, C-840L, C-860L, C-900 Zoom, C-900L Zoom, C-1000L, C-1400L, C-1400XL, C-2000Z, C-2020Z, C-2040Z, C-21000UZ, C-2500L, C-3000Z, C-3020Z, C-3030Z, C-3040Z, and X-250

- **Oregon Scientific** — Supported models: DShot II and DShot III

- **Panasonic** — Supported models: Coolshot KXL-600A and KXL-601A, and NV-DCF5E, DC1000, DC1580, PV-L691, and PV-L859

- **Pencam** — Supported model: Tevion MD 9456

- **Philips** — Supported models: ESP2, ESP50, ESP60, ESP70, ESP80 and ESP80SXG

- **Polaroid** — Supported models: PDC 640, PDC 2300Z, and DC700

- **Ricoh RDC** — Supported models: 300, 300Z, 4200, 4300, and 5000

- **Samsung** — Supported models: Kenox SSC-350N and Digimax 800K

- **Sanyo** — Supported models: DSC-X300, DSC-X350, VPC-G200, VPC-G210, VPC-G200EX, and VPC-G250

- **Sony** — Supported models: DSC-F1, DSC-F55, DSC-F707V, DSC-P30, DSC-P31, DSC-P32, DSC-P5, DSC-P50, DSC-P52, DSC-P72, DSC-P92, DSC-S75, DSC-S85, DSC-U20, DSC-V1, Memory Stick Adapter, MSAC-SR1, and DCR-PC100

- **Toshiba** — Supported model: PDR-M1

More cameras in experimental or testing status are listed on the gPhoto2 Web site. In addition, new cameras are added frequently.

Downloading digital photos with gtkam

The following procedure describes how to download images from your digital camera.

1. Using a cable provided with your digital camera, connect your camera to the USB or COM port on your computer. (I had better luck with the USB port.)

2. Set your camera to be in Send and Receive mode.

3. From the main red hat menu, choose Graphics → Digital Camera Tool. The gtkam window appears.

4. Click Camera → Add Camera. The Select Camera window appears.

5. Click the down arrow next to the Model box, select your camera, and click Detect.

6. Click Apply, then OK. Your camera model should be listed in the gtkam window.

7. To begin downloading images from your digital camera, click the camera name that appears in the left column, and then select the folder containing the images from that camera. After the images download (which can take a while), thumbnails appear in the main gtkam window, as shown in Figure 8-9.

8. Select the images you are interested in, and click the Save Selected Photos button to save the selected images. The Save Photos window that appears lets you choose a directory to save them to. You can rename the images or just use the names assigned by the camera.

9. Choose images you want to delete, and click the Delete button to delete them.

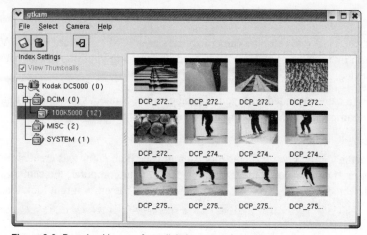

Figure 8-9: Download images from digital cameras from the gtkam window.

Using your camera as a storage device

Instead of using gtkam or gphoto to download pictures to Linux, some digital cameras let you treat them like a storage device to manage pictures. By mounting a digital camera as a USB mass storage device, you can view, copy, delete, and move the pictures on your camera as you would files on a hard disk or CD (just at a lower speed).

The following list is a partial summary of digital cameras that can be used as a USB storage device:

- **Casio** — Supported models: QV-2400UX, QV-2x00, QV-3x00, QV-4000 and QV-8000
- **Fuji** — FinePix 1300, 1400Zoom, 2300Zoom, 2400Zoom, 2800Zoom, 4200Z, 4500, 4700 Zoom, 4900 Zoom, 6800 Zoom, A101, A201, and S1 Pro
- **HP** — PhotoSmart 315, 318xi, 618, and C912
- **Konica** — KD200Z, KD400Z, and Revio KD300Z
- **Kyocera** — Finecam s3
- **Leica** — Digilux 4.3
- **Minolta** — Dimage 5, Dimage 7, and Dimage X
- **Nikon** — CoolPix 2500, 885, 5000, 775, and 995
- **Olympus** — Brio Zoom D-15, C-100, C-200Z, C-2040, C-220Z, C-2Z, C-3020Z, C-3040Z, C-4040Zoom, C-700, C-700UZ, C-860L, D-510, D-520Z, E-10, and E-20
- **Pentax** — EI2000, Optio 330, and Optio 430
- **Sony** — DSC-F505, DSC-F505V, DSC-F707, DSC-P1, DSC-P20, DSC-P5, DSC-P71, DSC-S30, DSC-S70, DSC-S75, DSC-S85, MVC-CD300, and MVC-FD92
- **Vivitar** — Vivicam 3550

- **Yashica** — Finecam s3

To Linux, the USB mass storage camera appears as a SCSI drive containing a VFAT file system with image files on it. Here's a procedure for using your digital camera as a USB storage device:

1. Using a cable provided with your digital camera, connect your camera to a USB port on your computer and turn it on so it is ready to send and receive data.

2. Boot your computer to Fedora.

3. Open the /etc/fstab file as root user and see if an entry was created for your digital camera. If you have no other SCSI devices on your computer, the camera will probably be detected as /dev/sda1 device. Here is what the entry might look like:

```
/dev/sda1      /mnt/camera      auto      defaults, user,noauto      0 0
```

   If no such entry appears, create the entry, possibly using vfat instead of auto. Create the mount point directory (as root user, type **mkdir /mnt/camera**).

4. As root user, type the mount command to mount the camera: **mount /mnt/camera**.

5. Open the /mnt/camera directory as you would any other directory from the shell or from a file manager. Copy, delete, move, and rename files as you would any files on your hard disk.

6. When you are done, be sure to unmount the camera as follows (as root user from a Terminal window).

```
# umount /mnt/camera
```

> **CAUTION:** If you unplug your camera without unmounting the file system, it could damage the files on your camera.

You can follow the previous procedure to use other USB mass storage devices (CD drives, keychains, and so on) in Linux. Use different mount directories (such as /mnt/keychain) and check which SCSI device is being assigned to the USB storage device.

To see if your USB storage device can be seen by Linux, you can check the /var/log/dmesg file or run the usbview command. Either of those places will tell you if the device is being detected properly by Linux.

Recording Music CDs

Writable CD-ROM drives are fast becoming a standard device on computers. Where once you had to settle for a floppy disk (1.44MB) or a Zip disk (100MB) to store personal data, a CD-ROM burner lets you store more than 600MB of data in a format that can be exchanged with most computers. On top of that, you can create CD music disks!

Both graphical and command-line tools exist for creating CDs in Red Hat Linux. The cdrecord command lets you create audio and data CDs from the command line. Using cdrecord you can write to CD-Recordable (CD-R) and CD-Rewritable (CD-RW) drives. The cdrecord command is described in the next section of this chapter.

Creating an audio CD with cdrecord

You can use the cdrecord command to create either data or music CDs. You can create a data CD by setting up a separate file system and copying the whole image of that file system to CD. Creating an audio CD consists of selecting the audio tracks you want to copy and copying them all at once to the CD.

This section focuses on using cdrecord to create audio CDs. The cdrecord command can use audio files in .au, .wav, or .cdr format, automatically translating them when necessary. If you have audio files in other formats, you can convert them to one of the supported formats by using the sox command (described previously in this chapter).

> **CROSS-REFERENCE:** See Chapter 13 for how to use cdrecord to create data CDs.

One way to create an audio CD is to copy the music tracks you want to a directory; then copy them to the writable CD. To extract the tracks, you can use the cdda2wav command. Then you write them to CD by using the cdrecord command. Here's an example:

1. Create a directory to hold the audio files, and change to that directory. Make sure the directory can hold up to 660MB of data (or less if you are burning fewer songs). For example:

```
# mkdir /tmp/cd
# cd /tmp/cd
```

2. Insert the music CD into your CD-ROM drive. (If a CD player opens on the desktop, close it.)

3. Extract the music tracks you want by using the cdda2wav command. For example:

```
# cdda2wav -D /dev/cdrom -B
```

This example reads all of the music tracks from the CD-ROM drive. The -B option says to output each track to a separate file. By default, the cdda2wav command outputs the files to the WAV audio format.

Instead of extracting all songs, you can choose a single track or a range of tracks to extract. For example, to extract tracks 3 through 5, add the -t3+5 option. To extract just track 9, add -t9+9. To extract track 7 through the end of the CD, add -t7.

> **NOTE:** If you have a low-quality CD drive or an imperfect CD, cdda2wav might not be the best ripping tool. Instead of cdda2wav, you could use cdparanoia -B to extract songs from the CD to hard disk.

4. When cdda2wav is done, insert a blank CD into your writable CD drive.

5. Use the cdrecord command to write the music tracks to the CD. For example:

```
# cdrecord -v dev=/dev/cdrom -audio *.wav
```

The options to cdrecord tell the command to create an audio CD (-audio) on the writable CD device located at /dev/cdrom. The cdrecord command writes all files from the current directory that end in .wav. The -v option causes verbose output.

If you want to change the order of the tracks, you can type their names in the order you want them written (instead of using *.wav). If your CD writer supports higher speeds, you can use the speed option to double (speed=2) or to quadruple (speed=4) the writing speed.

After you have created the music CD, indicate the contents of the CD on the label side of the CD. The CD should now be ready to play on any standard music CD player.

Ripping CDs with Grip

The Grip window provides a more graphical method of copying music from CDs to hard disk. You can then play the songs directly from your hard disk or burn them back on to a blank CD. Besides just ripping music, you can also compress each song as you extract it from the CD.

You can open Grip from the red hat menu by selecting Sound & Video → Grip (or by typing grip from a Terminal window). Figure 8-10 shows an example of the Grip window.

Figure 8-10: Rip and play songs from the Grip window.

To rip audio tracks from a CD with grip, do the following:

1. With the Grip window open, insert a music CD into your CD drive. If you have an active connection to the Internet and the CD is known to the CD database, then title, artist, and track information appear for the CD.

2. Left-click on each track that you want to rip (that is, copy to your hard disk). A check mark appears under the Rip column for the song.

3. Click the Config tab at the top of the page, then select Encode.

4. You can select the type of encoder used to compress the music by clicking the Encoder box and selecting an encoder (by default, `oggenc` compresses files in Ogg Vorbis).

5. Click the Rip tab at the top of the page. The Rip tab appears.

6. Click one of the following:

    -   **Rip+Encode** — This rips the selected songs and (if you left in the default oggenc compression as described previously) compresses them in Ogg Vorbis format. You need an Ogg Vorbis player to play the songs after they have been ripped in this format (there are many Ogg Vorbis players for Linux).

    -   **Rip only** — This rips the selected songs in WAV format. You can use a standard CD player to play these songs. (When I tried this, the same song ripped in WAV was twelve times larger than the Ogg Vorbis file.)

        Songs are copied to the hard disk in the format you selected. By default, the files are copied into a subdirectory of `$HOME/ogg` (such as `/home/jake/ogg`). The subdirectory is named for the artist and CD. For example, if the user jake were ripping the song called High Life by the artist Mumbo, the directory containing ripped songs would be `/home/jake/ogg/mumbo/high_life`. Each song file would be named for the song (for example, `fly_fly_fly.wav`).

At this point you can play any of the files using a player that can play WAV or Ogg files, such as XMMS. Or you can copy the files back to the CD using `cdrecord`. Because the filenames are the song names, they don't appear in the same order as they appear on the CD. So if you want to copy them back to a writable CD in the same order where they originally appeared, you may have to type each filename on the `cdrecord` command line. For example:

```
# cdrecord -v dev=/dev/cdrom -audio fly_fly.wav big_news.wav
about_time.wav
```

The Grip window can also be used to play CDs. Use the buttons on the bottom of the display to play or pause, skip ahead or back, stop, and eject the CD. The Toggle track display button lets you shrink the size of the display so it doesn't take up much space on the desktop. Click Toggle disc editor to see and change title, artist, and track information.

In addition to grip, Fedora includes the Sound Juicer CD Ripper, which you can launch by selecting Sound & Video → Sound Juicer CD Ripper from the red hat menu. Sound Juicer can also extract, or rip, files from an audio CD. I found Sound Juicer had slightly better quality when ripping a CD.

Creating CD labels with cdlabelgen

The `cdlabelgen` command can be used to create tray cards and front cards to fit in CD jewel cases. You gather information about the CD and `cdlabelgen` produces a PostScript output file that you can send to the printer. The cdlabelgen package also comes with graphics (in `/usr/share/cdlabelgen`) that you can incorporate into your labels.

Here is an example of a `cdlabelgen` command line that you can use to generate a CD label file in PostScript format. (Type it all on one line or use backslashes, as shown here, to put it on multiple lines.)

```
cdlabelgen -c "Grunge is Gone" -s "Yep HipHop" \
-i "If You Feed Me%Sockin Years%City Road%Platinum and Copper%Fly Fly \
Fly%Best Man Spins%What A Headache%Stayin Put Feelin%Dreams Do Go \
Blue%Us%Mildest Schemes" -o yep.ps
```

In this example, the title of the CD is indicated by `-c "Grunge is Gone"` and the artist by the `-s "Yep HipHop"` option. The tracks are entered after the `-i` option, with each line separated by a `%` sign. The output file is sent to the file `yep.ps` with the `-o` option. To view and print the results, you can use the `ggv` command as follows:

```
$ ggv yep.ps
```

The results of this example are shown in Figure 8-11.

Figure 8-11: Generate CD jewel case labels with cdlabelgen and print them with ggv.

You will probably want to edit the command and re-run ggv a few times to get the CD label correct. When you are ready to print the label (assuming you have a printer configured for your computer), click Print All to print the label.

Summary

Getting your Fedora system set up for sound and video can take some doing, but once it's done you can play most audio and video content that is available today. This chapter takes you through the steps of setting up and troubleshooting your sound card, and explains how to find software to play music through that card.

Live video from TV cards and Webcams in the sections on Tvtime and GnomeMeeting, respectively. Finally, I cover the xine player for playing a variety of video formats and the gtkam window for downloading images from a digital camera. If your computer has a CD burner, use the descriptions in this chapter to create your own music CDs and CD labels.

## Chapter 9

Tools for Using the Internet and the Web

In This Chapter

- Understanding Internet tools
- Browsing the Web
- Communicating via e-mail
- Participating in newsgroups
- Using Gaim Instant Messaging
- Using remote login, copy, and execution commands

With your Fedora Core system connected to the Internet, you can take advantage of dozens of tools for browsing the Web, downloading files, getting e-mail, and participating in newsgroups. In most cases, you have several choices of GUI and command-line applications for using Internet services from your Linux desktop or shell.

This chapter describes some of the most popular tools available with Fedora Core for working with the Internet. These descriptions include Web browsers, e-mail readers, newsreaders, instant messaging clients, and commands for login and remote execution.

Overview of Internet Tools

The most important client Internet program these days is the Web browser. Fedora Core includes the Mozilla software suite, which includes a Web browser along with other Web client software for downloading files, reading e-mail, participating in newsgroups, and creating Web pages (to name a few). Other Web browsers, some of which incorporate Mozilla features, also come with Fedora Core. These include:

- **Epiphany** — This Web browser is integrated with the GNOME desktop, allowing you to take advantage of GNOME themes, drag-and-drop, and translation features. On the inside, Epiphany relies on Mozilla's rendering engine. Like recent versions of Mozilla,

Epiphany supports multiple tabs, each containing a different Web page, as well as multiple windows.

- **Konqueror** — Although Konqueror is the file manager for the KDE desktop, it can also display Web content. Using Konqueror, you can easily go back and forth between Web sites and local files and folders.

Running a close second to Web browsers is the e-mail reader (referred to in network standards terms as a Mail User Agent, or MUA). Ximian Evolution is the recommended e-mail client for Fedora Core. Other options include the Mozilla integrated e-mail client, the Sylpheed mail client, or the KDE KMail program. There's also a groupwise application that comes with KDE called Kontact that includes an e-mail client. Mail programs that have been around in Linux and other UNIX systems since the time when most mail was plain text include mutt, pine, and mail.

You can choose from thousands of newsgroups to participate in discussions on the Internet. Fedora Core has several newsreaders available. Again, Mozilla includes an application for participating in newsgroups. Also, the Pan and slrn newsreaders are available.

Besides browsing, e-mail, and news, there are many ways of communicating with other computers and users on the Internet. Older UNIX commands such as `rlogin`, `rsh`, and `rcp` are supported in Linux to do remote login, run remote commands, and copy files remotely. In recent years, OpenSSH commands (`ssh`, `scp`, and `sftp`) have become preferable to the "r" commands because they offer greater security.

Browsing the Web

Although the Internet has been around since the 1960s, the Web is a relatively new technology (it was created in 1985). The Web places an additional framework over Internet addresses that were once limited to host names and domain names. Before the Web, finding resources on the Internet was difficult. However, the Web now provides several features that make it much easier to access these resources:

- **Uniform Resource Locators (URLs)** — URLs identify the location of resources on the Web. Besides identifying the domain and host on which a resource resides, they can also identify the type of content and the specific location of the content.

- **Hypertext Markup Language (HTML) Web pages** — When people talk about a Web page, they are generally referring to information that is presented in HTML format. HTML changed the Internet from a purely plain-text–based resource to one that could present graphics and font changes. An HTML page can also contain hypertext links. Links are the threads that join together the Web, enabling someone viewing a Web page to be immediately transported to another Web page (or other content) by simply selecting a linked text string or image on the page.

The primary tool for displaying HTML Web pages is the Web browser. Mozilla is the most popular Web browser for Fedora Core. It displays HTML (Web pages) as well as other types of Web content. Now, even file managers, made for displaying local files and folders, have been extended to be able to display Web content (see the description of Konqueror file manager in Chapter 3).

This section contains general information about the Web and some specific hints for using Mozilla to browse the Web from your Fedora Core system.

Uniform Resource Locators

To visit a site on the Internet, you either type a URL into the location box on your browser or click on a link (either on a Web page or from a menu or button on the browser). Although URLs are commonplace these days — you can find them on everything from business cards to cereal boxes — you may not know how URLs are constructed. The URL form is as follows:

```
protocol://host-domain/path
```

The protocol identifies the kind of content that you are requesting. By far, the most common protocol you come across is Hypertext Transfer Protocol (HTTP). HTTP is the protocol used to request Web pages. In addition to HTTP, however, there are other protocols that might appear at the beginning of a Web address. Instead of showing you a Web page, these other types of protocols may display different kinds of information in your browser, or open a completely different application for working with the content.

Table 9-1 lists some of the protocols that can appear in a Web URL.

Table 9-1: Protocols in Web URLs

Protocol Name	Description
http	Hypertext Transfer Protocol. Used to identify HTML Web pages and related content.
file	Identifies a file on a specific host. Most often used to display a file from your local computer.
ftp	File Transfer Protocol. Identifies a location where there are file archives from which you might want to download files.
gopher	Gopher Protocol. Provides databases of text-based documents that are distributed across the Internet. (Gopher is nearly obsolete.)
mailto	Electronic Mail Address. Identifies an e-mail address, such as `mailto:joe@example.com`. (Usually opens a mail composer.)
news	USENET newsgroup. Identifies a newsgroup, such as `news://news.myisp.com/comp.os.linux.networking`. If you type this address into Mozilla, a window appears with the newsgroup displayed from the news server you identified.
nntp	USENET news using `nntp` protocol.

| telnet | Log in to a remote computer and begin an interactive session. An example of a telnet address is `telnet://localhost`. (Replace `localhost` with any host or IP address that allows you to log in.) |
| wais | Wide Area Information Server protocol. A WAIS address might look like the following: `wais://handsonhistory.com/waisdb`. (Like gopher, WAIS databases are nearly obsolete.) |

The first part of a URL is the protocol. You don't always have to type the protocol. Most browsers are good at guessing the content you are looking for (mostly it guesses HTTP). If the address you type starts with www, it assumes HTTP; if it starts with `ftp`, it assumes FTP.

The second part of a URL takes you to the computer that is hosting the Web content. By convention, Web servers begin with www (or sometimes home). However, if you type the correct protocol (usually `http`), you will be directed to the right service at the host computer. The next piece of this name is just the host.domain style of Internet address that is always used with the Internet (such as `redhat.com`, `linuxtoys.net`, or `whitehouse.gov`). An optional port number can be tacked on to the host.domain name. For example, to request the port used for HTTP services (port 80) from the host called `www.linuxtoys.net`, you can type `http://www.linuxtoys.net:80`.

> **TIP:** You can identify a specific port number to request the service attached to the port on the computer you request. A port number is a lot like a telephone extension in a big company. A main telephone number (like the host.domain name) gets you to a company switchboard. The telephone extension (like the port number) connects you to the right person (like the service associated with a port).

The third part of a URL identifies the location of the content on the host computer. Sections in a Web page can be identified with a pound sign (#) and an identifier following the Web page location. For example, the craft section of the `bsched.htm` page at `handsonhistory.com` would appear as:

`http://www.handsonhistory.com/bsched.htm#craft`

The filename extension (such as `.htm` or `.html`) further identifies the content type.

Web pages

If you look at the HTML source code that produces Web pages, you see that it consists of a combination of information and markup tags, all of which are in plain-text format. The idea was to have Web pages be very portable and flexible. You can create a Web page with vi, emacs, gedit, Notepad, or any text editor on any computing platform. Or simplified front-end programs can be used to provide WYSIWYG (What You See Is What You Get) interfaces that let you see what you are creating as you go.

HTML tags are set apart by right and left angle brackets. Tags come in pairs, with a beginning tag, the information, and then an ending tag. The beginning tag contains the tag name, while an ending tag contains a forward slash (/) and the tag name. Here is a minimal HTML page:

```
<HTML>
<HEAD>
<TITLE>Greetings from Washington</TITLE>
</HEAD>
<BODY>
Here we are in beautiful Tacoma.
</BODY>
</HTML>
```

You can see that the document begins and ends with HTML tags (`<HTML>` and `</HTML>`). The beginning part of the Web page is contained within the HEAD tags. The body of the page is contained within the BODY tags. The title of the page is set apart by TITLE tags.

Between the beginning and ending BODY tags, you can add all kinds of stuff. You can have different types of bulleted or numbered lists. You can have headings, images, and text. More complex pages can include forms, dynamic HTML (which changes the content as you move or select items), or special data. Figure 9-1 is an example of a Web page as it appears in Mozilla.

Some of the HTML code that was used to create the Web page shown in Figure 9-1 is shown here. The title of the Web page appears between two TITLE tags.

```
<TITLE>Swan Bay Folk Art Center - American Crafts
in Port Republic, NJ</TITLE>
```

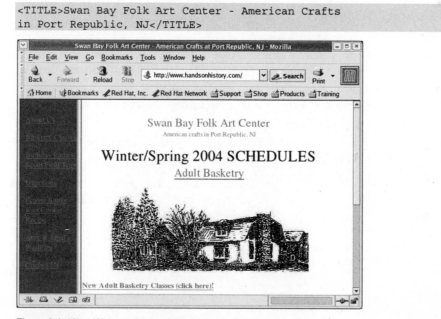

Figure 9-1: Many Web pages contain text, images, headings, and links.

The following code is used to create a link that opens a new mail message window:

```
A HREF="mailto:webmaster@handsonhistory.com">Contact Us</A>;
```

The text `Contact Us` is a link to an e-mail address. When someone clicks that link, a new message window appears, allowing that person to send e-mail to that address.

```
<FONT FACE="Copperplate Gothic Bold"><A HREF="bsched.htm">
Adult Basketry </A></FONT>
```

A special font face was used for the words `Adult Basketry`, with the words pointing to a link to another HTML page. If someone were to click on those words, the `bsched.htm` page would appear.

Web browsing with Mozilla

During the early 1990s, Netscape Navigator was the most popular Web browser. When it became apparent that Netscape was losing its lead to Microsoft Internet Explorer, the source code for Netscape was released to the world as open-source code.

Mozilla.org was formed to coordinate the development of the new browser from that code. The result was the Mozilla browser that is now available with Fedora Core, as well as with many other computing platforms. The availability on multiple platforms is great, especially if you must switch between Linux and Windows, for example, using Windows at work and Linux at home. Mozilla looks and acts the same on many platforms.

At the center of Mozilla, of course, is the Navigator Web browser. Mozilla also includes the following features:

- **Mail and Newsgroups** — A full-featured program for sending, receiving, and managing e-mail, as well as for using newsgroups. (The mozilla-mail RPM must be installed.)
- **IRC Chat** — An Internet Relay Chat (IRC) window, called ChatZilla, for participating in online, typed conversations. (The mozilla-chat package must be installed.)
- **Composer** — A Web page (HTML) composer application.
- **Address Book** — An application to manage names, addresses, and telephone numbers. (This feature is also part of the mozilla-mail RPM package.)

You can click the Mozilla Web Browser icon directly on the desktop panel to start Mozilla. Or you can open Mozilla from the desktop menu (beginning from the red hat) by selecting Internet → Mozilla Web Browser. Figure 9-2 shows the Mozilla home page (www.mozilla.org) as displayed by the Mozilla browser.

Figure 9-2: Mozilla is the open-source Web browser based on Netscape source code.

Mozilla has all the basic features you need in a Web browser and a few special features. The following sections describe how to get the most out of your Mozilla Navigator Web browser.

Setting up Mozilla Navigator

There are many things you can do to configure Mozilla to run like a champ. The following sections describe some ways to customize your browsing experience in Mozilla Navigator.

Setting Navigator preferences

You can set your Mozilla Navigator preferences in the Preferences window. To open Mozilla preferences, click Edit → Preferences. The Preferences window appears, as shown in Figure 9-3.

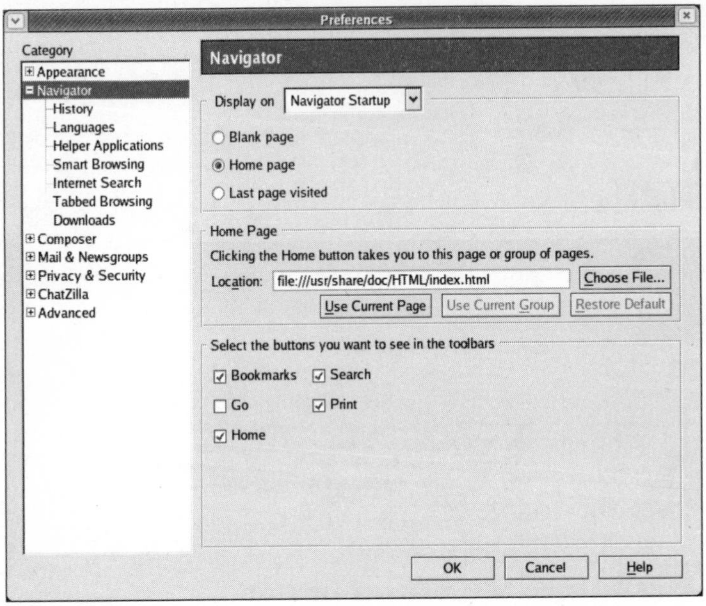

Figure 9-3: Change settings for navigating the Web from Mozilla's Preferences window

The following list shows some Navigator preferences that you might want to change:

- **Navigator** — Besides selecting the location to use as your home page, you can choose which buttons you see on the toolbar.

- **History** — Choose how long to store addresses of pages you visit. You can also select to clear your history and/or the sites you have typed in your location bar.

- **Languages** — Set a list of preferences for the particular language a Web page should be displayed in, if the page is available in several languages.

- **Helper Applications** — Set up applications to use to handle different types of data that may be encountered while browsing the Web.

- **Smart Browsing** — Choose to do keyword searches when you type partial addresses in the Location box. Smart browsing is off by default, so typing `netscape` would cause Mozilla to look for `www.netscape.com` instead of searching for `netscape` links.

- **Internet Search** — Select which search engine to use for Internet searches. You can also change how the Search tab is used with searches.

- **Tabbed Browsing** — Use these selections to have search results appear in tabs on the Mozilla Navigator window, as opposed to appearing in the full screen.

- **Download** — Choose what you see during downloads from the Internet (a download manager, a progress dialog, or nothing).

The Advanced Preferences can be used to fine-tune your Web browsing experience, as well as specify what content you open can and can't do on your computer. Here are some Advanced Preferences that might interest you:

- **Scripts & Plugins** — The Web content you choose can try to open, move, resize, raise and lower windows. It can request to change your images, status bar text, or bits of information stored in what are called *cookies*. These preferences let you restrict what the content you request can do.

- **Cache** — By default, the most recent 4MB of Web pages you visit are stored in RAM and the most recent 50MB of pages you visit are stored on your hard disk. If a page is not out-of-date, caching makes it possible to return to a page quickly, without needing to reload from the original Web server. Cache preferences let you change how much information is cached, where hard disk cache is located. Other cache preferences let you clear all memory and disk cache immediately.

- **Proxies** — If you have direct access to the Internet, you don't need to change any proxy settings. However, if you need to access the Internet via a proxy server, you can identify the location of that server (or servers) here. To access the Web via proxy servers, you must explicitly identify the proxy server to use for each type of content you request (HTTP, SSL, FTP, Gopher, and SOCKS).

- **HTTP Networking** — If you are using a proxy server, that proxy server may require that you make HTTP requests using either HTTP/1.0 or HTTP/1.1 standards (1.1 is the default).

- **Software Installation** — When a request for Web content results in that content trying to install software on your computer, you can either allow that to happen (with prompting) or not allow any software updates, based on how this preference is set.

- **Mouse Wheel** — If your mouse has a wheel, you can change how Mozilla behaves when you use that wheel. By default, the mouse wheel scrolls a line at a time.

- **DOM Inspector** — Turn this on to check the structure of a Web page (for debugging). This is very useful if you need to create Web pages, especially dynamic Web pages.

Adding helper apps

Although the main type of content provided by Web pages is HTML, many other content types can be displayed, played, or presented by a Web browser. Most additional data encountered by Mozilla is handled in one of two ways: plug-ins or helper apps.

Plug-ins are self-contained programs that allow data to play within the Mozilla window. A helper app can be any program that is available on your Red Hat Linux system. It is up to you to identify the plug-in or helper app to launch when a certain type of data is encountered.

Mozilla determines what helper app or plug-in to launch based on the following criteria:

- **Suffixes** — If the browser is reading a file that has a particular suffix attached to the filename (such as exe for an application or gz for a compressed zip file), it can use that suffix to determine the file's contents. When a file's suffix matches a suffix configured for a particular helper app or plug-in, the helper app or plug-in is used to play or display the data.

- **MIME type** — Because data may come to the browser in a stream or have no suffix, Mozilla can use the MIME type attached to the data to determine which plug-in or helper app to use. (MIME stands for Multipurpose Internet Mail Extensions.)

You can add your own helper app to automatically handle a particular type of data in your browser. Here's how:

1. Choose Edit → Preferences. The Mozilla Preferences window appears.

2. Click the plus next to the Navigator category, and select Helper Applications.

3. Click New Type. A dialog box appears that enables you to add information about the helper app and the data that it can handle.

4. Type in a description of the data, the MIME type, and the file suffixes (if any) on files that contain that type of data.

NOTE: When you add the suffix, don't include the dot.

---

5. Choose an application to handle the data type. If the application needs a Terminal window to run, type **xterm -e**, followed by the command line you need to enter. This executes the command in an xterm window, reading in data as needed.

6. Click OK when you are done.

The next time you open data in Mozilla of the type you just added, a pop-up window will ask you if you want to use the application you just entered to open the data.

Adding plug-ins

There are not many plug-ins available for use in the version of Mozilla that comes with Fedora Core. To see a list of plug-ins associated with your Mozilla browser, choose Help → About Plug-ins. You will probably see one plug-in: Plugger. If Plugger isn't installed, you can install it from CD #3. Plugger (http://fredrik.hubbe.net/plugger.html) is a multimedia plug-in that handles QuickTime, MPEG, MP2, AVI, SGI-movie, TIFF, DL, IFF-anim, MIDI, Soundtracker, AU, WAV, and Commodore 64 audio files by relying on external programs to play the data. Recently, Plugger has also added support for displaying a variety of Microsoft file types.

Here is a list of some free plug-ins available for Mozilla that work with Fedora Core.

- **Adobe Acrobat Plug-in** (www.adobe.com/support/downloads) — Displays files in Adobe Systems' PDF (Portable Document Format) format.

- **Cult3D Plug-in** (www.cult3d.com) — Displays high-quality, interactive real-time 3D images on the Web. This plug-in is from Cycore Computers. (Click Download to find the plug-in. There is a cult3d RPM available that requires tailoring to work in Mozilla.)

- **DjVu Plug-in** (djvu.sourceforge.net) — Displays images in DjVu image compression technology. This plug-in is from AT&T.

- **Real Audio** (www.real.com) — Plays Real Audio and Video content. (To use the Real Play plug-in in Mozilla, you need the RealPlayer and realplay-nplugin RPMs, available by searching rpmfind.net).

- **Macromedia Flash Player** (www.macromedia.com) — Displays multimedia vector graphics and animation. This plug-in is from Macromedia, Inc. Flash Player is available for Fedora Core, but Macromedia's Shockwave plug-in is not yet available for Linux.

More plug-ins may be added in the future for use with Fedora Core. Mozilla now offers a great new Web site for getting plug-ins for Linux that run in Mozilla: http://plugindoc.mozdev.org/linux.html. The site contains links to download plug-ins and instructions for installing them.

When you download a plug-in, follow the instructions that come with the plug-in for installing it. If the plug-in comes in an RPM file, install it as you would any other software package in Red Hat Linux (rpm -Uvh *package* command). Otherwise, probably just copy the plug-in file (a .so file) to the system plug-in directory (probably /usr/lib/mozilla/plugins) or your personal plug-ins directory (probably $HOME/.mozilla/plugins). When you restart Mozilla, the plug-ins will automatically be picked up from those locations.

> **NOTE:** The CrossOver Plugin is a commercial product that lets you use many Windows plug-ins in Mozilla. See the section "Adding a CrossOver Plugin" later in this chapter for details.

Using Mozilla Navigator controls

If you have used a Web browser before, the controls are probably as you might expect: location box, forward and back buttons, file and edit menus, and so on. There are a few controls with Mozilla, however, that you might not be used to seeing. Here are some examples:

- **Using the sidebar** — Press the F9 function key to toggle the sidebar on and off. Click a What's Related, Search, Bookmarks, or History tab (or add your own tab as described earlier). Add your own bookmarks, return to pages from your history list, or search for Web content.

- **Sending Web Content** — You can send an e-mail containing either the current Web page (File → Send Page) or the URL of the current Web page (File → Send Link) to selected recipients.

- **Searching the Internet** — You can search the Internet for a keyword phrase in many different ways. Choose Tools → Search the Web to open a Netscape Web site that lets you search the Internet. Or type one or more keywords in the Location box, and click Search. Then, of course, you can use the sidebar for searches as described earlier.

- **Viewing Information about a Page** — You can view information about the location of a Web page, the location of each of its components, the dates the page was modified, and other information by choosing View → Page Info. Figure 9-4 shows the Page Info window for a Web page. Click the Links tab to see links on that page to other content on the Web. Click the Security tab to see information about verification and encryption used on the page.

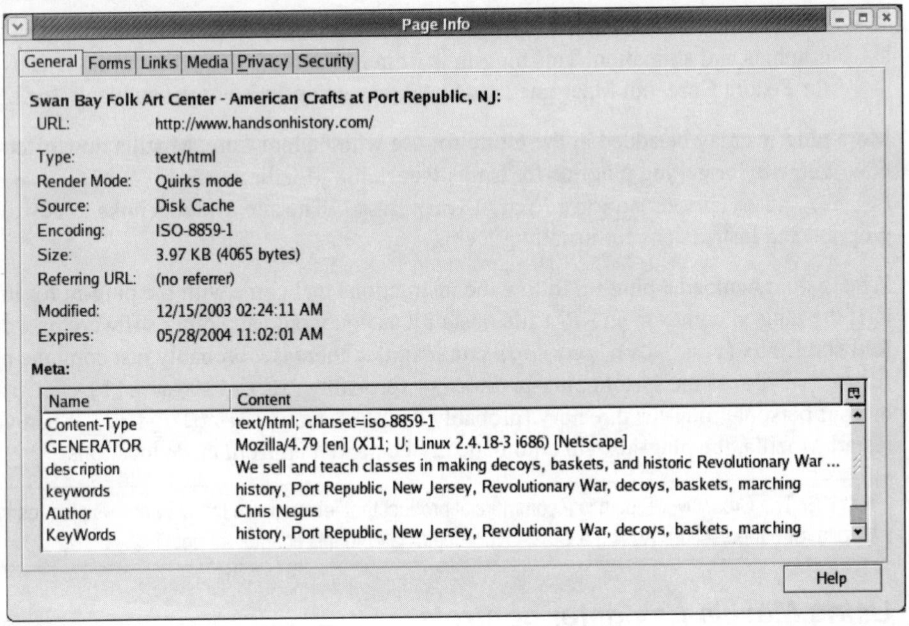

Figure 9-4: Display information about a Web page by selecting Page Info.

Improving Mozilla browsing

Every Web site you visit with Mozilla is not going to play well. Some sites don't follow standards, use unreadable fonts, choose colors that make it hard to see, or demand that you use a particular type of browser to view their content. To improve your browsing experience, there are several things you can add to Mozilla.

Adding a CrossOver Plugin

QuickTime 5 movies, Shockwave Director multimedia content, and various Microsoft movie, file, and data formats simply will not play natively in Mozilla Navigator. Using software built on WINE for Linux on x86-based processors, CodeWeavers (www.codeweavers.com) created the CrossOver Plugin. Although it costs a few dollars ($24.95 U.S. for a one-user-at-a-time type license), the CrossOver Plugin lets you play some content that you simply could not otherwise use in Linux.

After you install the CrossOver Plugin, you see a nice Plugin Setup window that lets you selectively install plug-ins for QuickTime 6, Windows Media Player 6.4, Shockwave 8.5, Flash 6, and Microsoft Word, Excel, and PowerPoint viewers. (Support for later versions of these content formats may be available by the time you read this.) You can also install other multimedia plug-ins, as well as a variety of fonts to use with those plug-ins.

> **TIP:** Although I have had CrossOver Plugin running well in earlier versions of Red Hat Linux, at the time of writing it was not yet working in the current version of Fedora Core. Check with CodeWeavers to see if they have corrected CrossOver Plugin to run in the latest version of Fedora Core.

Adding a Preferences toolbar

Did you ever run into a Web page that required you to use a particular type or version of a browser or had fonts or colors that made a page unreadable? The Mozilla preferences toolbar called PrefBar2 lets you try to spoof Web sites into thinking you are running a different browser. It also lets you choose settings that might improve colors, fonts, and other attributes on difficult-to-read pages.

You can install the neat little toolbar from the Mozdev.org site (`prefbar.mozdev.org`). Click the Install link; then, after it is installed, restart Mozilla.

> **TIP**: You must have write permissions to `/usr/lib/mozilla-1.6` for the Install link to work. This may require you to log in as root, start Mozilla, install the Preferences Toolbar, and then log out as root.

Figure 9-5 shows an example of PrefBar2 that has been installed in Mozilla.

Figure 9-5: Change colors, fonts, and browser types on the fly with Mozdev.org Preferences Toolbar.

The default set of buttons let you do the following:

- **Colors** — Change between default colors and those set on the Web page.
- **Images** — Toggle between having images loaded or not loaded on pages you display.
- **JavaScript** — Allow or disallow JavaScript content to play in Mozilla Navigator.
- **Clear Cache** — Deletes all cached content from memory and disk.
- **Kill Flash** — Kills all embedded Flash content on the current page.

- **Real UA** — Choose to have your browser identified as itself (current version of Mozilla) or any of the following: Mozilla 1.0 (in Windows 98), Netscape Navigator 4.7 (in Macintosh), Netscape 6.2 (in Linux), Internet Explorer 5.0 (in Macintosh), or Internet Explorer 6.0 (in Windows XP).

The user agent (UA) setting is very useful when dealing with Web sites that require Internet Explorer (IE) (and usually IE on Windows, not MacOS). The IE 6.0 WinXP setting is good enough to allow Mozilla to log on to the Microsoft Exchange webmail service, which is usually set up to require IE. If you want to run Linux in a mostly Windows organization, install the Preferences toolbar.

Click the Customize button to add other buttons to the Preferences toolbar. You can add buttons to clear your History or Location bar entries. You can even add a Popups button to prevent a page from opening a pop-up window from Mozilla.

Many of the preferences take effect immediately. Others may require you to restart Mozilla.

Adding Java support

If you want to display some Java content, but you only see a broken puzzle piece and a failure message that says you need a plug-in to view application/x-java-whatever content, you can install the software you need from the Sun Microsystems Web site (www.sun.com). Here's how:

1. Download the Java 2 Runtime Environment package from java.sun.com/download. (Look for a Java 2 Platform, Standard Edition that runs on Linux, then download the Java 2 Runtime Environment package. I used j2re-1_4_2-linux-i586-rpm.bin.)

2. Make the package executable and execute it to extract the RPM, as follows:

```
# chmod 755 j2re*-rpm.bin
# ./j2re*-rpm.bin
```

3. Install the j2re* package (as root user), just as you would any software RPM package.

```
# rpm -Uvh j2re*rpm
```

4. Change to the Java plug-in directory and create a link from the Java plug-in to the Mozilla plug-ins directory. (Instead of *, you could type the whole j2re directory name.)

```
$ cd /usr/java/j2re*/plugin/i386/ns610/
$ ln -s libjavaplugin_oji.so /usr/lib/mozilla/plugins/
```

5. Close any open Mozilla windows, then open a new Mozilla window.

6. Click Help → About Plug-ins. You should see a listing for the Java plug-in and lots of supported Java MIME types.

7. To see if the Java plug-in is working, you could try out some games from the Java Software Showcase (http://java.sun.com/getjava/showcase.html).

Doing cool things with Mozilla

There are some neat bells and whistles built into Mozilla that can make your browsing more pleasant. Here are a few of those features that you can try out:

Using tabbed browsing

If you go back and forth among several Web pages, you can use the tabbed browsing feature to hold multiple pages in your browser window at once. You can open a new tab for browsing by simply selecting File → New → Navigator Tab or by pressing Ctrl+t. You can also tailor how tabbed browsing works from a Web page or from the Location box. Here's how:

1. Click Edit → Preferences. The Preferences window appears.

2. Click Tabbed Browsing under the Navigator category.

3. Click one or both of these boxes, depending on how you want to use tabbed browsing:

   - **Middle-click, Control+click or Control+Enter on links in a Web page** — Selecting this box lets you open a link to another Web page in a new tab. For this to work, click the middle mouse button on a link, hold the Ctrl key while you click the left mouse button on a link, or (with the link highlighted) hold the Ctrl key and press Enter.

   - **Control+Enter in the Location bar** — After you type a Web address (URL) into the Location box, hold the Ctrl key and press Enter to open the new page in a tab.

4. Click OK. You can begin using the tabbed browser feature from your Mozilla Navigator.

A tab for each tabbed page appears at the top of the Navigator pane. To close a tab, create a new tab, bookmark a group of tabs, or reload tabs, right-click one of the tabs at the top of the pane. A drop-down menu lets you choose the function you want.

One of the easiest ways to open a link in a tab is to right-click over a link on an HTML page. Select the Open Link in New Tab choice.

Using the DOM Inspector

If you are debugging a Web page that you are creating, the Document Object Model (DOM) Inspector can be useful for checking out the structure of your page. To open the DOM inspector, from the Mozilla window click Tools → Web Development → DOM Inspector.

From the DOM Inspector window, type the URL to the Web page you want to check out. The nodes, representing the head, body, tables, fonts, and so on, appear in the left column. Values for each node appear in the right column. Click a node name and the selected area is highlighted on the page below, with the node value appearing to the right.

Resizing the Web page

There is a nice keyboard shortcut that lets you quickly resize the text on most Web pages in Mozilla. Hold the Ctrl key and press the plus (+) or minus (-) keys. The text on the Web page will (in most cases) get larger or smaller, respectively. That page with the insanely small type font is suddenly readable.

Using text-based Web browsers

If you become a Linux administrator or power user, over time you will inevitably find yourself working on a computer from a remote login or where there is no desktop GUI available. At some point while you are in that state, you will probably want to check an HTML file or a Web page. To solve the problem, Fedora Core includes several text-based Web browsers.

With text-based Web browsers, any HTML file available from the Web, your local file system, or a computer where you're remotely logged in can be accessed from your shell. There's no need to fire up your GUI or read pages of HTML markup if you just want to take a peek at the contents of a Web page. Besides letting you call up Web pages, move around with those pages, and follow links to other pages, some of these text-based browsers even display graphics right in a Terminal window!

Which text-based browser you use is a matter of which you are more comfortable with. Browsers that are available include:

- **links** — With `links`, you can open a file or a URL, and then traverse links from the pages you open. Use search forward (`/string`) and back (`?string`) features to find text strings in pages. Use up and down arrows to go forward and back among links. Then press Enter to go to the current link. Use the right and left arrow keys to go forward and back among pages you have visited. Press Esc to see a menu bar of features to select from.

- **lynx** — The `lynx` browser has a good set of help files that come with it (press the ? key). Step through pages using the Spacebar. Though `lynx` can display pages containing frames, it cannot display them in the intended positioning. Use the arrow keys to display the selected link (right arrow), go back to the previous document (left arrow), select the previous link (up arrow), and select the next link (down arrow).

- **w3m** — The `w3m` text-based Web browser can display HTML pages containing text, links, frames, and tables. It even tries to display images (though it is a bit shaky). There are both English and Japanese help files available (press H with `w3m` running). You can also use `w3m` to page through an HTML document in plain text (for example, `cat index.html | w3m -T text/html`). Use the Page Up and Page Down keys to page through a document. Press Enter on a link to go to that link. Press the B key to go back to the previous link. Search forward and back for text using / and ? keys, respectively.

> **NOTE**: You must install the elinks package to get links, the lynx package to get lynx, and the w3m package to get w3m.

The `w3m` command seems the most sophisticated of these browsers. It features a nice default font selection, seems to handle frames neatly, and its use of colors also makes it easy to use. The `links` browser lets you use the mouse to cut and paste text.

You can start any of these text-based Web browsers by giving it a filename, or if you have an active connection to the network, a Web address. For example, to read the w3m documentation (which is in HTML format) with a w3m browser, you can type the following from a Terminal window or other shell interface:

```
$ w3m /usr/share/doc/w3m-0*/doc/MANUAL.html
```

An HTML version of the W3M Manual is displayed. You can also have started w3m without giving it a filename (in which case, you will have to open one later from the menu). Or you can give w3m a URL to a Web page, such as the following:

```
$ w3m www.handsonhistory.com
```

After a page is open, you can begin viewing the page and moving around to links included in the page. Start by using the arrow keys to move around and select links. Use the Page Up and Page Down keys to page through text.

Communicating with E-mail

To manage your e-mail, Fedora Core features the Ximian Evolution mail program. Mozilla also includes a graphical application for reading, managing, and sending e-mail. The Mozilla mail client is useful if you also have to work on Windows or other non-Linux systems. If not, I recommend Evolution.

If you don't mind text-based interfaces, or if you are a UNIX person who likes to sort, grep, troff, col, and cat your e-mail, there are still plenty of UNIX-like mail tools around. The mail command itself provides an easy-to-use interface for plain-text messages sent to other users on your UNIX system or on your LAN. There are also text-based mail applications, such as the mutt command, that let you handle mail attachments.

After covering some e-mail basics, this section will lead you through the steps that allow you to use e-mail with Evolution and Mozilla Mail. If you are interested in text-based, command-driven mail tools, some of which have been around UNIX systems for many years, you will also find descriptions of many of those commands in this section.

E-mail basics

E-mail is one of the oldest uses of computer networks — predating the Web by more than 20 years. In fact, e-mail was one of the first applications used to transport information on the Internet, when the Internet consisted of only a few computers.

Today, there are millions of users around the world who have e-mail addresses. Although there are several different styles of e-mail addressing, by far the most popular e-mail address format is the domain style address (used with the Internet and other TCP/IP networks). The e-mail address consists of a user name and domain name, separated by an @ sign. For example:

```
webmaster@handsonhistory.com
```

As someone using e-mail, you need a program (such as Ximian Evolution) that enables you to get your e-mail, manage your e-mail messages, and send messages. Although mail messages were originally only plain text, and still are in most cases today, there are some newer features that let you enhance the kinds of content that you can send and receive. Here are two ways to enhance your mail messages:

- **Attachments** — You can attach files to your mail messages. Attachments can contain data that you couldn't ordinarily keep in a mail message, such as a binary program, a word processing file, or an image. The recipient of the mail attachment can either save the file to a local hard disk or open it in a program designed to read the attachment.

- **HTML** — The same stuff used to create Web pages can be included in mail messages you create with certain mail clients (including Evolution and Mozilla Mail). This lets you change fonts and colors, add backgrounds, insert images, or add HTML features.

> **CAUTION:** To people who use text-based mail clients, HTML content can't be interpreted (it shows up as a bunch of markers that overwhelm the text). In general, don't use HTML in messages that are being distributed to a large group of people (such as in a newsgroup). Also, e-mail was never intended to transport large attachments. For larger files, try copying to an FTP site instead of sending e-mail attachments.

Depending on the mail program you are using (which is also referred to as a Mail User Agent or MUA), e-mail management features let you direct incoming e-mail into different folders and sort messages by date, sender, or other attributes. E-mail sending features let you reply to messages, forward messages, and draw names from an address book or directory server.

> **CROSS-REFERENCE:** If you don't have an e-mail account, you can set up your own e-mail server using Fedora Core. For information on setting up a mail server, see Chapter 19.

Using Evolution e-mail

Evolution is the preferred application for sending and managing e-mail in Fedora Core. Fedora Core developers gave it a prime spot on the desktop, just to the right of the red hat main menu and Web browser icons. After you launch Evolution for the first time and run the Startup Assistant, the Evolution window appears, showing the different types of operations you can perform.

Figure 9-6 shows an example of the Evolution window. Evolution is a groupware application, combining several types of applications that help groups of people communicate and work together. The features of Evolution include:

- **E-mail** — Includes a complete set of features for getting, reading, managing, composing, and sending e-mail on one or more e-mail accounts.

- **Calendar** — Create and manage appointments on your personal calendar. You can e-mail appointment information to others and do keyword searches of your calendar.

- **Tasks** — Organize ongoing tasks into folders.

- **Contacts** — Create contact information for friends and associates, such as names, addresses, and telephone numbers. A Categories feature helps you remember who gets birthday and anniversary gifts.

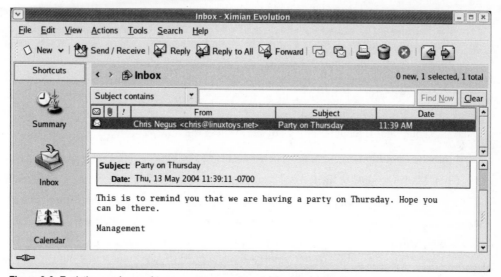

Figure 9-6: Evolution can be used to manage your mail, appointments, and tasks.

In the next section, I focus on the Summary and E-mail features of Evolution.

Setting Evolution preferences

To really make Evolution your own, you can set preferences that are particular to you. Certain settings let you choose the information that appears on the Summary page when you start Evolution. Other settings let you choose how your e-mail is gathered and sorted.

Changing Summary settings

You can change Summary settings by performing the following steps:

1. From the Evolution main window, select Tools → Settings.

2. Select Summary Preferences (left column). You can change the following Summary settings:

   - **Mail** — Select which folders should appear on the Summary window. By default, only the Mail Summary link appears, but no specific folders are shown.

   - **News Feeds** — Select from a variety of news feeds, to have headlines and links to news stories added to your Summary page. Click the News Feeds tab, choose the news headlines that interest you, and click Add to have them appear on the list. By default, news headlines will refresh every 10 minutes (600 seconds), and up to 10 headlines will appear for each feed (both values are configurable).

- **Weather** — Choose to have weather for a particular city appear on your Summary page. Click the Weather tab, select the country, state, and city for which you want to see weather, and then click Add to make the change.

- **Schedule** — Choose how many days of scheduled appointments to appear on your Summary page. Click the Schedule tab and select one day, five days, one week, or one month of appointments. Also, select to show all or just today's tasks.

3. Click Apply to apply the changes.

Changing Mail Accounts settings

You can change Mail Accounts settings by performing the following steps:

1. From the Evolution main window, select Tools → Settings.

2. Click Mail Accounts in the left column.

3. Select the mail account to change and click Edit. The Evolution Account Editor appears.

4. Here are a few items you may want to change for your e-mail account:

- **Signature** — Have a signature appear on every e-mail message you send. Either click the Default signature box and select Autogenerated (to use name and e-mail address as a signature) or click Add New Signature to create a signature.

- **Receiving** — By default, Evolution checks your mail server for your mail every 10 minutes. Once downloaded, each message is erased from the server. To change automatic e-mail checking and options to leave messages on the server, select the Receiving Options tab and make the changes you want.

- **Automatic copy** — You can have every message you send copied to one or more other users. This is a nice feature if you write important e-mail that you want to archive to a different e-mail account. Select the Defaults tab, then click the check box next to Always Cc or Always Bcc. Next, type the correct e-mail address.

- **Security** — To help validate that you are who you say you are and keep your e-mail private, Evolution lets you use PGP (Pretty Good Privacy) encryption keys. Click the Security tab, then enter your PGP/GPG Key ID. Choose settings for signing and encryption as appropriate.

5. Click Apply to apply the changes.

Receiving, composing, and sending e-mail

Evolution offers a full set of features for sending, receiving and managing your e-mail. I personally prefer the Folder to the Shortcut view for working with Evolution (click View → Folder Bar to turn it on; click View → Shortcut Bar to turn it off).

Here are some tips for sending, reading, and receiving mail:

- **Read e-mail** — Click Inbox in the Folder column. Your messages appear to the right.

- **Delete e-mail** —After you have read a message, select it and press the Delete key. Click View → Hide Deleted Messages to toggle whether or not you see deleted messages. Click Actions → Expunge to permanently remove all messages marked for deletion in the current folder.

- **Send and receive** — Click the Send/Receive button to send any e-mail queued to be sent and receive any e-mail waiting for you at your mail server.

- **Compose e-mail** — Click New → Mail Message. A Compose a Message window appears. Type the e-mail address, a message for the subject line, and the body of the message. Click Send when you are finished. Buttons on the Compose window let you add attachments, cut and paste text, choose a format (HTML or plain text), and sign the message (if you have set up appropriate keys).

- **Create folders** — If you like to keep old messages, you may want to save them outside your Inbox (so it won't get too junked up). Right-click on the Inbox, then select New Folder. Type a folder name and click OK (to store it as a subfolder to your Inbox).

- **Sort messages** — With new folders created, you can easily sort messages from your Inbox to another folder. The easiest way is to simply drag-and-drop each message (or a set of selected messages) from the message pane to the new folder.

- **Search messages** — Type a keyword in the search box over your e-mail message pane and select whether to search your message subject lines, sender, recipient, or message body. Click Find Now to search for the keyword. After viewing the messages, click Clear to have the other messages reappear.

- **Filter messages** — You can take action on an e-mail message before it even lands in your Inbox. Click Tools → Filters. A Filters window appears that lets you add filters to deal with incoming or outgoing messages. Click Add to create criteria and set actions.

  For example, you could have all messages from a particular sender, subject, date, status, or size sorted to a selected folder. Or you could have messages matching your criteria deleted, assigned a color, or respond by playing a sound clip.

> **CROSS-REFERENCE:** Refer to Chapter 19 for information on using Spamassassin, along with Evolution filters, to sort out SPAM from your real e-mail messages.

Besides the features mentioned in the previous list, Evolution supports many common features, such as printing, saving, and viewing e-mail messages in various ways. The help system that comes with Evolution (click the Help button) includes a good manual, FAQ, and service for reporting bugs.

Mozilla Mail client

The Mozilla Mail client program provides a simple interface for using e-mail in Fedora Core. You can access the Mozilla Mail window from your Mozilla browser window by choosing Tasks → Mail & Newsgroups. Figure 9-7 shows an example of the Mozilla Mail window that is ready to use mail and news.

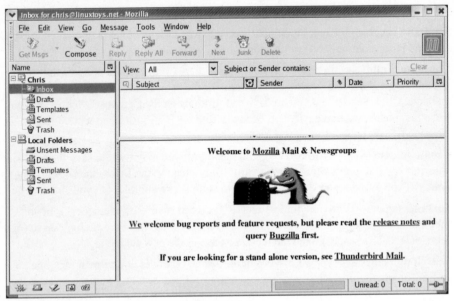

Figure 9-7: Manage your e-mail from the Mozilla Mail window.

As with Evolution e-mail, you need to provide some information about your mail account before you can connect to your mail server and use Mozilla Mail.

> **TIP:** A new Junk Mail feature was recently added to Mozilla Mail. With Junk Mail, Mozilla Mail automatically tags any message it believes to be junk mail with a blue recycle-bin icon. Using the Junk Toolbar, you train the Junk Mail feature by telling it when a message is or isn't junk mail. After you have identified which messages are junk mail, you can automatically move incoming junk mail to the Junk folder.

Connecting to the mail server

You must identify information about yourself and your mail server before you can download or send mail messages. The first time you open Mozilla Mail, an Account Wizard appears. Select to set up an e-mail account; then enter the following information as you are prompted for it:

- **Your Name** — The name to appear on messages you send (for example, John Smith).
- **Your E-mail Address** — The *name@domain* address that is assigned to you.

- **Incoming Mail Server** — The name or IP address of the mail server from which you get your messages. You also need to know what type of server it is (POP or IMAP). POP and IMAP servers require a login and password. POP stands for Post Office Protocol. IMAP stands for Internet Message Protocol.

- **Outgoing Mail Server** — If there is a different outgoing mail server, you need the name or IP address of that server. Likewise, you will probably need login and password information to send mail through that server. You can choose to use Secure Socket Layer (SSL) to protect your outgoing messages (if it is supported by the server).

After the wizard has created the account, you are prompted for the password for your account on the mail server. Using that password, Mozilla Mail will download all your messages from the mail server. It will try to download messages again every 10 minutes. Or, you can click the Get Msgs button to download messages immediately.

If you want to change how often mail is downloaded, or other features of your account, click Edit → Mail & Newsgroup Account Settings. Under the e-mail account you added are categories to change the set-up and behavior of the account. (Click Server Settings to change how often, if at all, new messages are automatically downloaded from the mail server.)

Managing incoming mail

There are various ways to store and manage the e-mail messages in Mozilla Mail. The following is a quick rundown of how to use Mozilla Mail for managing incoming mail:

- Your e-mail messages are typically stored on a mail server that is contacted over the network. To download your mail messages immediately from the mail server, click File → Get New Messages (or click Get Msgs on the toolbar).

- Mail messages are stored in folders under the Mail Folders heading in the left column. There should be a separate heading for each mail account you have. For each mail account, incoming messages are stored (by default) in your Inbox folder. You can create additional folders to better keep track of your mail (right-click on Inbox, then select New Folder to add a folder). Other folders contain drafts of messages set aside for a time (Drafts), templates for creating messages (Templates), messages you have sent (Sent), and messages that you have discarded (Trash).

- Messages are sorted by date for the folder you select, in the upper-right corner of the display. Click on the heading over the messages to sort by subject, sender, or priority.

- When you select a message, it appears in the lower-right corner of the display.

Composing and sending mail

To compose e-mail messages, you can either start from scratch or respond to an existing e-mail message. The following are some quick descriptions of how to create outgoing mail:

- To create a new message, choose File → New → Message (or Compose on the toolbar).

- To reply to a mail message, click on the message on the right side of your screen, and then choose Message → Reply (to reply only to the author of the message) or Message → Reply to All (to reply to everyone listed as copied on the message).

- To forward a mail message, choose Message → Forward. You can also forward a message and have it appear in the text (Message → Forward As → Inline) or as an attachment (Message → Forward As → Attachment).

In each case of outgoing mail, a mail Compose window appears, in which you compose your e-mail message. As you compose your message in the Compose window, you can:

- Add e-mail addresses from your personal address book (or from one of several different directory servers) by choosing Options → Select Addresses. A list of your stored addresses appears for you to choose from. Click Collected Addresses to see a list of addresses that have been collected from e-mail messages you have received.

- Add attachments to the message (such as a word processing file, image, or executable program) by choosing File → Attach File. After that, you can select a file from your file system to attach. (You can also choose File → Attach Web Page to choose the URL of a Web page that you want to attach.)

- Add certificates or view security information about your mail message by selecting View → Message Security Info. In the window that appears, you can view general security information about the message.

When you are finished composing the message, click Send to send the message. If you prefer, queue the message to be sent later by choosing File → Send Later. (Send Later is useful if you have a dial-up connection to the network and you are not currently online.)

> **TIP:** If you want to quit and finish the e-mail message later, you can choose File → Save As → Draft. Then click the X in the upper-right corner to close the window. When you are ready to resume work on the message, click the Draft folder in the Mozilla Mail window and double-click the message.

Text-based mail programs

There are many text-based mail programs for reading, sending, and working with your mail. Many of these programs have been around for a long time, so they are full of features and have been well debugged. As a group, however, they are not very intuitive. The following sections describe some text-based commands.

> **TIP:** Most of these programs use the value of your $MAIL environment variable as your local mailbox. Usually, that location is /var/spool/mail/*user*, where *user* is your user name. To set your $MAIL so that it points to your Mozilla mailbox (so you can use either Mozilla Mail or a text-based mail program), add the following line to one of your startup files:
>
> ```
> export MAIL=$HOME/.mozilla/default/*/Mail/hostname/Inbox
> ```
>
> If you usually use Mozilla for mail, set this variable temporarily to try out some of these mail programs.

Mail readers and managers

Mail readers described below are text-based and use the entire screen. Although some features are different, menu bars show available options right on the screen.

Mutt mail reader

> **NOTE:** To use the mutt mail reader you must have the mutt software package installed from CD #1.

The mutt command is a text-based, full-screen mail user agent for reading and sending e-mail. The interface is quick and efficient. Type **mutt** to start the mail program. Move arrow keys up and down to select from your listed messages. Press Enter to see a mail message and type **i** to return to the Main menu.

The menu bar indicates how to mark messages for deletion or undelete them, save messages to a directory, or reply to a message. Type **m** to compose a new message and it opens your default editor (for me, vi) to create the message. Type **y** to send the message. If you want to read mail without having your fingers leave your keyboard, mutt is a nice choice. (It even handles attachments!)

Pine mail reader

> **NOTE:** To use the pine mail reader, you must have the pine software package installed. The pine package is not distributed with Fedora Core. You can go to ftp://people.redhat.com/mharris/pine to get a pine package.

The pine mail reader is another full-screen mail reader, but it offers many more features than does mutt. With pine, you can manage multiple mail folders. You can also manage newsgroup messages, as well as mail messages. As text-based applications go, pine is quite easy to use. It was developed by a group at the University of Washington for use by students on campus, but has become widely used in UNIX and Linux environments.

Start this mail program by typing **pine**. The following menu is displayed, from which you can select items by typing the associated letter or using up and down arrows and pressing Enter:

```
?   HELP                - Get help using Pine
C   COMPOSE MESSAGE     - Compose and send a message
I   MESSAGE INDEX       - View messages in current folder
```

```
L   FOLDER LIST      - Select a folder to view
A   ADDRESS BOOK     - Update address book
S   SETUP            - Configure Pine Options
Q   QUIT             - Leave the Pine program
```

To read your e-mail, select either I or L. Commands are listed along the bottom of the screen and change to suit the content you are viewing. Left (←) and right (→) arrow keys let you step backward and forward among the pine screens.

Mail reader

The mail command was the first mail reader for UNIX. It is text-based, but not screen-oriented. Type **mail** and you will see the messages in your mailbox. Because mail is not screen-oriented, you just get a prompt after message headings are displayed — you are expected to know what to do next. (You can use the Enter key to step through messages.) Type **?** to see which commands are available.

While in mail, type **h** to see mail headings again. Simply type a message number to see the message. Type **d#** (replacing # with a message number) to delete a message. To create a new message, type **m**. To respond to a message, type **r#** (replacing # with the message number).

Participating in Newsgroups

Usenet news is another feature that has been around almost as long as the Internet. Using a newsreader, and even many regular mail readers, you can select from literally thousands of topics and participate in discussions on those topics. To participate, you simply read the messages people have posted to the group, respond to those that you have something to say about, and send your own messages to start a discussion yourself.

To get started, you basically need a newsreader and access to a news server computer. As with e-mail, Mozilla uses Mozilla Mail to let you participate in newsgroups. Another popular newsreader that comes with Fedora Core is called Pan.

> **TIP:** If you have never used a newsgroup before, check out the news.announce.newusers newsgroup. This newsgroup exists to answer questions from new users.

Mozilla for newsgroups

The same Mozilla Mail window you use for e-mail can be used to participate in newsgroups. Before you can begin using newsgroups, you need to identify the news server you are using, identify yourself, and choose the newsgroups you want to access.

Connecting to the news server

To begin using newsgroups, open the Preferences window from Mozilla and add the news server's name and port number as follows:

1. From the Mozilla Navigator window, click Window → Mail & Newsgroups.

2. From the Mail window, choose Edit → Mail & Newsgroups Account Settings to bring up the window to create the news server account.

3. In the Mail & Newsgroups Account Settings window, click Add Account. The Account Wizard window appears.

4. Click Newsgroup Account and click Next. You are asked to identify yourself.

5. Type your name (as you would have it appear to people in newsgroups) and your e-mail address (where you would like newsgroup participants to send you mail), and click Next.

6. Type the address of your news server (such as `news.handsonhistory.net`) and, if necessary, the port number for news on that server; then click Next. (The default news port is 119. You can obtain the name of the news server from your ISP or your system administrator at work. By convention, the name often has "news" or "nw" at the beginning.)

7. Type a name to represent the news account (it can be the server address), and click Next.

8. If the information you have entered looks correct, click Finish. The news server you have just added should now appear in your Mail & Newsgroups Account Settings window.

9. With the basic newsgroup settings in place, you can now set a variety of options to define how your newsgroup interface behaves. For example, you can change the following:

   - **Account Settings** — Besides the Account Name, Your Name, and E-mail Address (which should already be there), you can identify a different Reply-to e-mail address, identify your organizaiton, and attach a signature. You can also have messages you send to newsgroups be in HTML format (usually you should not use HTML in newsgroups).

   - **Copies & Folders** — You can choose to have messages you send to newsgroups copied to your Sent folder (default). You can also choose to have blind copies of the messages sent to yourself or another e-mail address.

   - **Addressing** — If you have preferences set in an LDAP server, you can choose to have those preferences used with this news account.

   - **Offline & Disk Space** — You can limit the amount and size of news messages that are downloaded to your computer. You can also select how many messages are kept when you clean up your news messages.

   - **Server Settings** — For the news server, you can change the port number you connect to (usually 119 for news servers), whether or not to use a secure connection, how often you should check the server for messages, and whether or not you want to be prompted before downloading more than a set number of messages (500 by default).

10. Click OK.

If your news server was properly identified and your connection to that server is working, you can click on the news server's name in the Mozilla Mail window to begin participation in newsgroups. Connection to the news server occurs when you select news in that window. You must have a Mozilla mail account configured to post messages to a newsgroup.

Using newsgroups

To participate in newsgroups, you need to choose the ones that interest you from a list of available newsgroups. Before you start using newsgroups, create a valid mail account through Mozilla Mail (so you can fully participate once you begin). You can then subscribe to your favorite newsgroups so that they are available every time you use Mozilla.

Subscribing to newsgroups

The following procedure describes how to subscribe to a newsgroup in Mozilla.

1. Open Mozilla Mail & Newsgroups (Window → Mail & Newsgroups from Mozilla).

2. Right-click the news server name in the left column; then click Subscribe. A Subscribe window appears, as shown in Figure 9-8.

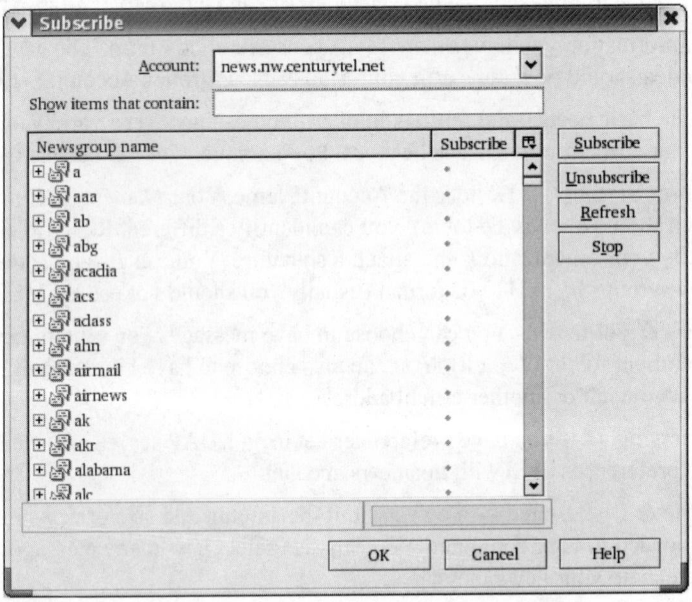

Figure 9-8: Choose from thousands of newsgroups in the newsgroup subscription window in Mozilla.

What appears (after a few minutes) are top-level newsgroup names. Newsgroups are organized in a hierarchy, similar to Internet domain names — levels are separated by dots (although newsgroup names start at the left and go down to the right).

3. Click the arrow sign next to a category to see which groups in that category interest you.

4. When you see a newsgroup that interests you, click it and select Subscribe.

5. Click OK. The subscribed newsgroup appears in your Mail & Newsgroups window under the name of the news server.

6. Click the newsgroup in the Mail & Newsgroups window. Recent messages from that newsgroup are downloaded to your Messenger window.

Reading newsgroup messages

Reading newsgroup messages is similar to reading mail messages. You simply select a message that interests you or move to it using the up and down arrow keys. The message will appear in the message pane in the lower-right corner of the Mail & Newsgroups window.

The concept of threads should be mentioned here: When someone posts a message to a newsgroup, usually one or more people respond to it. Because it is useful to read messages and responses together, these messages are grouped together in *threads*. A plus (+) next to a message indicates there are responses to that message. Click the plus to see available threads. Threads make it easy to see messages on a topic that interests you or skip a topic that doesn't.

The Pan newsreader

> **NOTE:** To use pan, you need to install the pan RPM package from CD # 2 that comes with this book. For further information about pan, refer to: `http://pan.rebelbase.com`.

The Pan newsreader is a graphical application for reading, managing, and interacting with newsgroups. It is particularly adept at displaying attached pictures and downloading binaries. The interface is very intuitive and easy to use.

Pan is designed for the GNOME desktop. If you are running another desktop environment, however, you can still use Pan as long as you have the gnome-libs software package installed. After that, Pan works on KDE, Window Maker, or other desktop environments.

To open the Pan newsreader from the main red hat menu, choose Internet → More Internet Applications → Pan. The first time you start Pan, the Pan wizard runs to let you set up the newsreader. Have your e-mail address and your news server's name ready. When the wizard is done, you can download the list of newsgroups available from your news server.

Instant Messaging with Gaim

Gaim is an Instant Messaging client program that runs in Linux. Because it is based on the America Online (AOL) Open IM architecture (`www.aim.com`), it has the same messaging features you get from AOL's own messaging application.

To start Gaim from a red hat desktop menu, choose Internet → Messaging Client. Figure 9-9 contains an example of the Gaim window.

Figure 9-9: Access your AOL Instant Messaging using Gaim.

From the main Gaim window, you have the following options:

- **Accounts** — Add screen names, passwords, and options associated with your AOL Instant Messaging accounts.

- **Signon** — Sign on to AOL Instant Messaging by using your selected screen name.

- **Preferences** — Set preferences associated with AOL Instant Messaging and Chat windows. You can also load plug-ins that can perform special functions, such as spell checking and auto-reconnection.

Besides AOL IM protocols, Gaim supports other messaging protocols, including instant messaging protocols from Yahoo!, MSN, ICQ, Jabber, and IRC.

Using Remote Login, Copy, and Execution

This section describes some features for allowing users to use resources across a network. They are the `telnet`, `ssh`, `ftp`, `wget`, `rsync`, `rlogin`, `rcp`, and `rsh` commands.

> **CROSS-REFERENCE:** Only the ssh service is turned on by default in Fedora Core. That is because the other remote login, execution, and copy commands described here do not provide encrypted communications by default, and so they can represent significant security risks. For information on how to turn on the services described in this chapter on a Fedora Core server, refer to Chapter 14 and Appendix C.

Two of the commands described in this section that are generally available are remote login and file transfer programs: `telnet` and `ftp`, respectively. Other commands for accessing FTP servers are `ncftp` and `gFTP`.

Two newer commands for copying files over the network are `wget` and `rsync`. Both of these tools can be used for efficiently downloading files that you can identify on the network.

Other commands described in this section are more specific to Fedora Core and other UNIX systems, but they provide simplified ways of copying files, logging in, and executing commands among trusted systems: `rcp`, `rlogin`, and `rsh`, respectively. Also, a more secure tool for remote login, called `ssh`, is included with Fedora Core. The `ssh` command can be used for remote execution as well.

Using telnet for remote login

Telnet is a service provided by many different types of computer systems to enable remote users to log in to their machines over TCP/IP networks. The `telnet` command is the client program that you use to do the remote login. The most common way to use telnet is with a host name. The following is a typical telnet session:

```
$ telnet maple
Trying 10.0.0.11 ...
Connected to maple.linuxtoys.net (10.0.0.11).
Escape character is '^]'.
Fedora Core release 2
Kernel 2.6.5-1 on an i686
login: mike
Password: ********
Last login: Mon May 31 13:15:57 from pine
[mike@maple mike]$
```

This example shows what happens when the `telnet` command is used to log in from a computer named `pine` to a computer named `maple` by typing `telnet maple`. My computer tries to connect to the telnet port on `maple` (IP address `10.0.0.11`). Because `maple` is also a Fedora system, once the connection is established, I see the standard `login:` prompt. I type the user name (`mike`) and the password when prompted. When the login and password are accepted, I see the shell prompt for the user named `mike`.

The telnet service is disabled by default on Fedora Core systems (as are most network services). So, to be able to log in to your computer using telnet, refer to Appendix C for information on how to turn on the telnet service.

Here are a few useful options you can use with telnet:

- **-a** — Automatic login. With this option, your computer attempts to log in to the remote computer using your local user name. So, if you are logged in to your computer as `mike`, when you use `telnet` to log in to a remote computer, the remote computer assumes that you want to log in as `mike`. It simply prompts you for `mike`'s password.

- **-l** *user* — User name. This option is similar to the `-a` option, except that instead of using your current user name, you can ask to log in using any user name you choose.

- **-r** — Rlogin-style interface. This option lets you use tilde (~) options. For example, to disconnect while in rlogin mode, type **~.** (tilde+dot), or to suspend the telnet session, type **~^z** (tilde+Ctrl+z). Only use ~. if your remote shell is hung (exit is a better way to quit normally). If you use ~^z to suspend your telnet session temporarily, you are returned to your local system shell. To get back to the suspended session, type **fg** to put telnet back in the foreground. See the description of `rlogin` later in this chapter for more features you can use in rlogin mode.

Another way to use `telnet` is in command mode. Instead of using a host name, simply type the word **telnet**. You will see a `telnet` prompt as follows:

```
$ telnet
telnet>
```

At this point, there are several commands available to you. You are not yet connected to a remote host. To open a login session to a remote computer from the telnet prompt (for example, to a computer named `maple`), type:

```
telnet> open maple
```

After you do connect to a remote computer, you can return to the telnet session at any time by typing `Ctrl+]`. Here are other options you can use during your telnet session:

- **?** — Print help information.
- **!** — Escape to the shell.
- **close** — If you have an open connection, type **close** to close it.
- **display** — Shows the operating parameters that are in effect.
- **logout** — Logs you off any remote connection in this session and closes it.
- **mode** — Tries to enter line mode or character mode. (Type **mode ?** to see other options that go with the mode option.)
- **quit** — Close telnet and exit.
- **z** — Suspend the current telnet session.

If you suspend a telnet session or escape to the shell, return to telnet by typing `fg`.

Copying files with FTP

Like telnet, FTP is a protocol that is available on many different operating systems. Archives of files on the Internet are stored on what are called FTP servers. To connect to those servers from Fedora Core, you can either type the URL of that server into a Web browser or you can use the `ftp` command or graphical FTP windows such as gFTP. Of the other FTP client programs available with Fedora Core, my favorite is the `ncftp` command.

> **TIP**: The ftp program runs on Windows as well. All of the commands listed here run on UNIX, Linux, and Windows versions of the ftp program.

Using the ftp command

The `ftp` command is available on Fedora Core, as well as every other Linux and UNIX system, for copying files to and from FTP servers. Like telnet, FTP has a command mode or you (more typically) can use it to connect directly to a remote computer. For example:

```
$ ftp maple
Connected to maple.
220 (vsFTPd 1.1.3)
Name (maple:mike): jake
331 Please specify the password.
Password: *********
230 Login successful. Have fun.
Remote system type is UNIX.
Using binary mode to transfer files.
ftp>
```

In this example, `ftp` connects to a computer called `maple` (`ftp maple`). When I was prompted for a name, it assumed that I was going to use my current login name on `maple` (`maple:mike`). I could have pressed Enter to use the name `mike`, but instead I logged in as `jake` and typed the password when prompted. The password was accepted and, after some information was printed, I was given an `ftp>` prompt.

Because FTP is used for public servers, you can often log in using the word `anonymous` as your user name. By entering a valid e-mail address as your password, you can enter the anonymous FTP site and download files that the server makes available to the public.

Unlike telnet, instead of being in a regular UNIX shell after I logged in with FTP, I was placed in FTP command mode. Command mode with FTP includes a whole lot of commands for moving around the remote file system and for copying files (which is its main job).

FTP directory commands

To get your bearings and move around the remote file system, you could use some of the following commands from the `ftp>` prompt. The commands are used to work with both the remote and local directories associated with the FTP connection.

- **pwd** — Shows the name of the current directory on the remote system.
- **ls** — Lists the contents of the current remote directory using the UNIX `ls` command. You can use any valid `ls` options with this command, provided that they are supported by the particular FTP server you are connected to.
- **dir** — Same as `ls`.
- **cd** — Use the `cd` command to move to the named directory on the remote system.

- **cdup** — Moves up one directory in the file system.

- **lcd** — Use the `lcd` command to move to the named directory on the local system.

If you want to make changes to any of the remote files or directories, use the following commands:

- **mkdir** — Creates a directory on the remote system.

- **rename** — Renames a file or directory on the remote system.

- **rmdir** — Removes a remote directory.

- **delete** — Removes a remote file.

- **mdelete** — Removes multiple remote files.

Depending on how the FTP server is configured, you may or may not be able to execute some of the file and directory commands shown above. In general, if you log in as the anonymous user, you will not be able to modify any files or directories. You will only be able to download files. If you have a real login account, you will typically have the same read and write permission you have when you enter the computer using a standard login prompt.

FTP file copying commands

Before you copy files between the remote and local systems, consider the type of transfer you want to do. The two types of transfer modes are:

- **binary** — For transferring binary files (such as data files and executable commands). This is also referred to as an image transfer.

- **ascii** — For transferring plain-text files.

The Linux `ftp` command seems to set the default to binary when you start FTP. Binary seems to work well for either binary or text files. However, binary transfers may not work transferring ASCII files from non-UNIX systems. If you transfer an executable file in ASCII mode, the file may not work when you try to run it on your local system.

Most file copying is done with the `get` and `put` commands. Likewise, you can use the `mget` and `mput` commands to transfer multiple files at once. Some FTP servers will even allow you to use matching characters (for example, `mget abc*` to get all files beginning with the letters abc). Here are descriptions of those commands:

- **get file** — Copies a file from the current directory on the remote file system and copies it to the current directory on the local file system. You can use a full path along with the filename. Here are some examples:

```
ftp> get route
ftp> get /tmp/sting
```

The first example takes the file route from the current remote directory and copies it to the current local directory. The second example copies the file /tmp/sting from the remote system to the file tmp/sting relative to the current directory on the local system. So if your current directory were /home/jake, ftp would try to copy the file to /home/jake/sting.

- **put** *file* — Copies a file from the current local directory to the current remote directory. The usage of this command is essentially the same as the get command, except that files are copied from the local to the remote system.

> **NOTE:** Anonymous FTP sites (described later) usually let you copy files *from* them, but not *to* them. If they do allow you to put files on their servers, it will usually be in a restricted area.

- **mget** *file* ... — This command lets you download multiple files at once. You can specify multiple files either individually or by using metacharacters (such as the asterisk). FTP prompts you for each file to make sure you want to copy it.

- **mput** *file* ... — This command lets you put multiple files on the remote computer. Like mget, mput prompts you before transferring each file.

FTP exiting commands

While a connection is open to a remote computer from an FTP client in Fedora, you can use several commands to either temporarily or permanently exit from that connection. Here are some useful commands:

- **!** — This command temporarily exits you to the local shell. After you have done what you need to do, type **exit** to return to your FTP session. You can also use this command to run other local commands. For example, you can type **!pwd** to see what the current directory is on the local system, **!uname -a** to remind yourself of your local system name, or **!ls -l** to see the contents of your current directory.

- **close** — Closes the current connection.

- **bye** — Closes the connection and exits the ftp command.

Using the ncftp command

By virtue of being an FTP client program, the ncftp command supports all the standard commands you would expect to find in an FTP client (get, put, ls, cd, and so on). However, ncftp has added features that make it more efficient and friendlier than most FTP clients.

With ncftp, you can connect to an FTP server in the same way you did with ftp. One convenient difference is that if you enter no user name, ncftp assumes you want to use the anonymous user name and just logs you in. Here is an example:

```
$ ncftp ns1
NcFTP 3.1.5 (Oct 13, 2002) by Mike Gleason (ncftp@ncftp.com).
Connecting to 63.240.14.64...
(vsFTPd 1.1.3).
Logging in...
Login successful. Have fun.
Sorry, I don't do help.
Logged in to ns1.
ncftp / >
```

To log in as a user name other than anonymous, add a -u *user* option, where *user* is replaced by the name you want to log in as. Enter the password as prompted to continue.

Using ncftp

After you are logged in, there are a few nice features you can use that aren't available with other FTP clients. Here are some examples:

- **bookmark** — If you are visiting a site that you want to return to, type the bookmark command and type a name to identify that site. The next time you start an ncftp session, type the bookmark name as an option. Not only are you logged into the FTP site you bookmarked; you are taken to the directory where you set the bookmark.

- **lls, lcd, lmkdir, lpwd** — There is a set of commands that enables you to move around the local file system. Just place a letter "l" in front of standard shell commands like ls, cd, mkdir, pwd, rm and rmdir and you can move around and work with your local file system while you are in ncftp.

- **rhelp, site** — Use rhelp to see commands that are recognized by the remote FTP server. To see commands that are specific to the FTP server, type **help**.

- **Auto-resume** — If you were disconnected in the middle of a large download, you will appreciate this new feature. After a connection is broken during a download, reconnect to the FTP site and begin downloading the file again in the same local directory. The ncftp command resumes downloading where it left off.

Using ncftp for background transfers

If you are moving around to different parts of the FTP site, or jumping between different sites, you might not want to wait around for a file transfer to complete before you can go somewhere else. The ncftp command has an excellent feature for placing transfer commands in a spool file and then running them in the background immediately or later.

To select a file for background transfer, use the bgget command. Here is an example:

```
ncftp /pub > bgget wireless.doc
•Spooled: get wireless.doc
ncftp /pub > jobs
---Scheduled-For-----Host-----------Command-------------------
2003-09-01  18:38 maple            GET wireless.doc
ncftp /pub > bgstart
Background process started.
Watch the "/home/br/.ncftp/spool/log" file to see how it is progressing
```

In this example, the bgget command spools the wireless.doc file from the remote current directory (/pub) and sets it to be copied to the local current directory. Typing the jobs command shows that the job (GET wireless.doc), from the host named maple, is scheduled to run immediately (6:38 p.m., September 1, 2003). By running the bgstart command this process, and any other spooled jobs, are run immediately.

Instead of starting the background transfers immediately you can do them later. For background jobs spooled for transfer, the transfer begins when you quit ncftp, leave your current FTP site or go to another FTP site. In this way, the program that does the transfer (ncftpbatch) can take over your current login session to do the transfer.

If you wanted to wait even longer to do the transfers, you can pass an option to the bgget command to have it start the transfer at a particular time. Here is an example:

```
ncftp /pub > bgget -@ 2003090410000 wireless.doc
```

With this command, the transfer is set to run at 1 a.m. on September 4, 2003 to transfer the file called wireless.doc. Again, you can check the .ncftp/spool/log file in your home directory to see if the transfer has completed.

Using the gFTP window

If you prefer a more graphical interface for accessing FTP servers, you can use the gFTP window. You can open a gFTP window by typing gftp or by choosing Internet → gFTP from the Red Hat menu on the desktop. Figure 9-10 shows an example of the gFTP window.

Unlike the ftp command, the gFTP window lets you simultaneously see the contents of the current remote and local directories. To transfer a file from one side to the other, simply double-click it or drag-and-drop it to the other pane. (Normally, you will just be copying files from FTP sites, unless a site provides you with permission to write to it.)

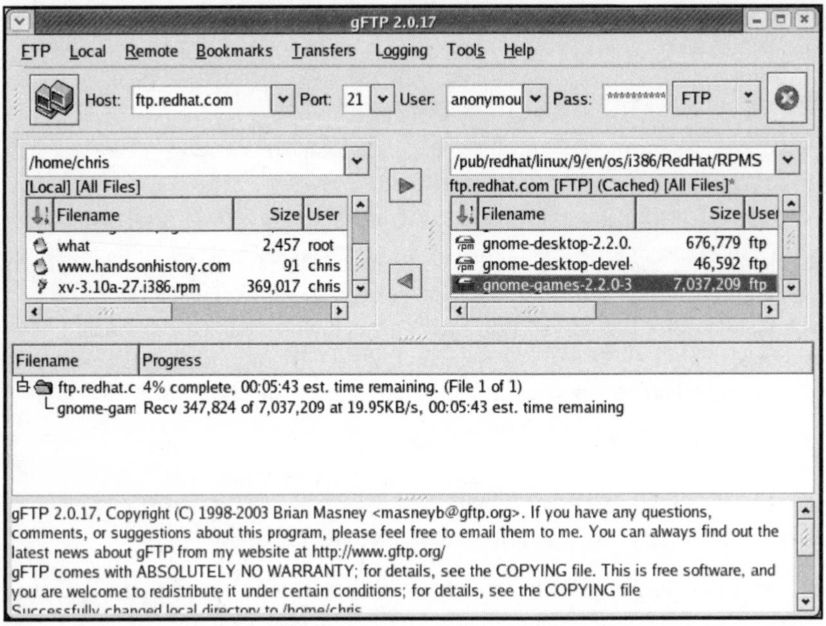

Figure 9-10: View local and remote files simultaneously from the gFTP window.

Follow this procedure to connect to an FTP site:

1. Type the name of the FTP server to which you want to connect (for example, `ftp.redhat.com`) into the Host box.

2. Type the port number on the FTP server (you can leave this blank to use the default port number 21).

3. Type the user name used to log in to the FTP server. Use the default `anonymous` if you don't have a specific user name and the server is pubically accessible.

4. Type the password for the user name you entered. The convention with FTP servers is to use your e-mail address as the password.

5. Click the icon displaying two little monitors to connect to the FTP site.

6. If you entered the information correctly, the bottom pane on the window should show that the transfer was complete and the right pane should show the contents of the current directory of the FTP site. Here are some actions you can take once you are connected:

   - **Move around.** Double-click a directory to move to that directory or two dots (. .) to move up a level. You can do this on both the remote and local directories.

   - **Drag-and-drop files.** You can drag-and-drop files from the FTP site on to the left pane (representing your current local directory).

- **Save this site.** If you want to return to this site later, choose Bookmarks → Add Bookmark. A pop-up window lets you name this site for the bookmarks list. After you do, you can select that entry from the list at a later date to connect to that site. The gFTP window will have stored not only the host name, but also the port, user name, and password. So you are just one click away from connecting. This is one of the best features of graphical FTP programs such as gFTP.

A nice feature of gFTP is that it stores log information. Choose Logging → View Log. A window appears showing you the conversations that have taken place between your computer and each FTP site. You can look at these messages to see what is wrong if you are unable to connect to a site or to remember where you have been and what you have done on an FTP site.

Getting files with wget

If you already know where a file is on the network, there are more efficient ways of downloading that file than opening an FTP session, moving around the FTP server, and running the get command. The wget command is a simple, efficient tool for doing non-interactive downloads of files over the Internet.

If there is a file you want to download from an FTP site or Web server (HTTP), and you know exactly where the file is, wget is a good way to download. The wget command is very useful if you want to copy a whole site, recursively, from one computer to another (for example, containing user home directories). When downloading from FTP sites, wget can let you just download as the anonymous user or add your own user name and password to the command line.

Here is an example of using wget to get a file from an FTP site:

```
$ wget ftp://ftp.redhat.com/pub/contrib/libc6/i386/zsh-4.1.1-1.i386.rpm
--01:53:33-  ftp://ftp.redhat.com/pub/contrib/libc6/i386
=  `zsh-4.1.1-1.i386.rpm`
Resolving ftp.redhat.com ... done.
Conecting to ftp.redhat.com[216.148.218.201]:21... connected.
Loggin in as anonymous ... Logged in!
==> SYST ... done.    ==> PWD ... done.
==> TYPE I ... done.  ==> CWD /pub/contrib/libc6/i386 ... done.
==> PASV ... done.    ==> RETR zsh-4.1.1-1.i386.rpm... done.
Length: 2,541,655 (unauthoritative)

100%[================================>] 2,541,655 50.31K/s  ETA 00:00
05:16:39 (50.31 KB/s) - `zsh-4.1.1-1.i386.rpm` saved [2541655]
```

By the first part of the URL (ftp://), wget knows you are copying a file from using FTP to the current directory (.) on the local host. After resolving the address (ftp.redhat.com), wget connects to the site, logs in as the anonymous user, changes the working directory (to /pub/contrib/libc6/i386), and transfers the file. As the file downloads, wget shows the progress of the download, then exits.

If you need to log in as a user other than anonymous, you can add that information to the command line or to a .netrc file in your home directory (type **man netrc** to see the format of that file). Here is an example of adding the password to the command line:

```
$ wget ftp://joe:my67chevy@ftp.handsonhistory.com/memo1.doc .
```

> **CAUTION:** Adding a password to a command line leaves the password exposed to onlookers. This practice is generally discouraged, except in cases where no one can see your monitor or your history files.

In the previous example, the user logs in as joe with the password my67chevy. The wget then copies the file memo1.doc from the current directory on the host computer named ftp.handsonhistory.com. That current directory is most likely /home/joe.

Using wget, you can download files from Web servers as well. The wget command downloads files using the http protocol, if file addresses begin with http://. Downloading a single file, you would use the same form as you would for an FTP file (for example: wget http://host/file.). The best wget option for HTTP downloads is -r (recursive).

A recursive download lets you choose a point at a Web site and download all content below that point. Here is an example of a recursive download used to download the contents of the www.handsonhistory Web site.

```
$ wget -r www.handsonhistory.com .
```

In this example, the directory structure making up the www.handsonhistory.com Web site is copied below the current directory in the directory www.handsonhistory.com. This is useful if you want to move the contents of a Web site from one computer to another.

> **CAUTION:** Downloading an entire Web site can result in a massive amount of data being downloaded. If you only want part of a Web site, start from a point lower in the site's structure. Because content is taken by following links, if there is content in a directory at the Web site that isn't in a link, it won't be downloaded.

> **NOTE:** Another command that you might be interested in, similar to wget, is the curl command. Like wget, curl can download files using the ftp or http protocols. However, it also includes support for secure http (https), telnet and gopher protocols. Curl can also do multiple file transfers on the same connection.

Using ssh for remote login/remote execution

Although the telnet and rlogin login commands and rsh remote execution command have been around much longer, the ssh command is the preferred tool for remote logins and executions. The reason is that ssh provides encrypted communication so you can use it securely over insecure, public networks between hosts that don't know each other.

In the following example, ssh is being used to log in to a computer named maple. Because no user is specified, ssh tries to log in as the current user (which is the root user in this case).

```
# ssh maple
root@maple's password:
```

If you wanted to log in as a different user, you could use the -1 option. For example, to log in to the computer named maple as the user named jake, you could type the following:

```
# ssh jake@maple
jake@maple's password:
```

The ssh command can also be used to execute a command on the remote computer. For example, if you wanted to monitor the messages file on a remote computer for a minute, you could type the following command:

```
# ssh root@maple "tail -f /var/log/messages"
root@maple's password:
```

After you typed the password in the above case, the last several lines of the /var/log/messages file on the remote computer would be displayed. As messages were received, they would continue to be displayed until you decided to exit (press Ctrl+D).

> **NOTE:** Find out more about the ssh command from the SSH Web site (www.openssh.org).

Using scp for remote file copy

The scp command is a simple yet secure way of copying files among Linux systems. It uses the underlying ssh facility, so if ssh is enabled, so is scp. Here is an example of using scp to copy a file from one computer to another:

```
# scp myfile toys.linuxtoys.net:/home/chris
root@toys.linuxtoys.net's password: ******
```

In this example, the file myfile is copied to the computer named toys.linuxtoys.net in the /home/chris directory. If you don't provide a user name (as is the case here), scp assumes you are using the current user name. Unlike some tools that provide remote login, scp and ssh do allow you to login as root user over the network, by default. (Many people turn off this feature for security reasons.)

To use scp with a different user name, you can append the user name with an @ character. For example, chris@toys.linuxtoys.net:/home/chris would attempt to log in as the user named chris to do the file copy.

The first time you connect to a remote computer using scp or ssh, those commands try to establish the authenticity of the remote host. If it cannot establish the host's authenticity, it will display the RSA key fingerprint and ask you if you want to continue. If you type yes, scp will not question the authenticity of that computer again for subsequent scp commands.

However, if the RSA key fingerprint should change in the future for the remote computer (which will happen if, for example, the operating system is reinstalled on that computer), scp will refuse to let you connect to that remote computer. To override that refusal, you need to edit your $HOME/.ssh/known_hosts file and delete the entry for the remote computer. You can then verify the authenticity of the remote computer and continue to use scp.

Using the "r" commands: rlogin, rcp, and rsh

The `rlogin`, `rcp`, and `rsh` commands all use the same underlying security mechanism to enable remote login, remote file copy, and remote execution, respectively, among computers. These commands are included with Fedora Core to be compatible with legacy UNIX systems. Because "r" commands are inherently insecure, however, most people use `ssh` and `scp` commands to provide the same functionality in a more secure way.

> **CROSS REFERENCE:** For a description of these "r" commands, refer to the *Red Hat Linux Bible* Web site at Wiley Publishing: `www.wiley.com/compbooks/negus`.

Summary

Most use of the World Wide Web centers on the Web browser. Mozilla is popular with Fedora Core, and is accessible from a button on your desktop. The e-mail program that comes with Mozilla, called Mozilla Mail, provides almost everything you need for reading, sending, and managing your mail. Ximian Evolution, which can also be used for managing your e-mail, is now the preferred mail reader for Fedora Core. To read newsgroups, you can also use Mozilla or the Pan newsreader.

Commands such as `telnet` (for remote login) and `ftp` (for remote file copying) are available for communicating with remote computers from the command line in Fedora Core. There are also improved programs for remote login and file copy, such as `ssh`, `scp`, and `ncftp`.

Part III
Administering Fedora

Chapter 10

Understanding System Administration

In This Chapter

- Using the root login
- Administrative commands, configuration files, and log files
- Graphical administration tools
- Working with the file system
- Working with hardware devices
- Monitoring system performance
- Managing battery power on laptops
- Getting Red Hat software updates

Fedora Linux, like other UNIX systems, was intended for use by more than one person at a time. Multiuser features allow many people to have accounts in Fedora, with their data kept secure from others. Multitasking allows many people to use the computer at the same time. Sophisticated networking protocols and applications make it possible for a Linux system to extend its capabilities to network users and computers around the world. The person assigned to manage all of this stuff is referred to as the *system administrator*.

Even if you are the only person using a Linux system, system administration is still set up to be separate from other computer use. To do most tasks, you need to be logged in as the root user (also referred to as the super user). Other users cannot change, or in some cases, even see some of the configuration information for a Linux system. In particular, security features such as passwords are protected from general view.

This chapter describes the general principles of Fedora system administration. In particular, this chapter covers some of the basic tools you need to administer your Fedora system. It also helps teach you how to work with file systems and monitor the setup and performance of your Linux system.

> **NOTE:** Security Enhanced Linux drastically changes the rules of how system administration is done in Linux systems. By default, SE Linux is turned off. However, for those systems where SE Linux is turned on, refer to Chapter 28 for information on how SE Linux handles issues of ownership, access rights, and many other issues.

Using the root Login

The root user has complete control of the operation of your Fedora system. That user can open any file or run any program. The root user also installs software packages and adds accounts for other people who use the system.

When you first install Fedora, you should add a password for the root user. You need to remember and protect this password. You will need it to log in as root or to obtain root permission while you are logged in as some other user.

The home directory for the root user is /root. The home directory and other information associated with the root user account is located in the /etc/passwd file. Here is what the root entry looks like in the /etc/passwd file:

```
root:x:0:0:root:/root:/bin/bash
```

This shows that for the user named root, the user ID is set to 0 (root user), the group ID is set to 0 (root group), the home directory is /root, and the shell for that user is /bin/bash. You can change the home directory or the shell used by editing the values in this file.

> **CROSS-REFERENCE:** See the section on setting up users in Chapter 11 for more information about the /etc/passwd file.

Among the defaults that are set for the root user are aliases for certain commands that could have dangerous consequences. Aliases for the rm, cp, and mv commands allow those commands to be run with the -i option. This prevents massive numbers of files from being removed, copied, or moved by mistake. The -i option causes each deletion, copy, or move to prompt you before the actual change is made.

Becoming Super User (The su Command)

Though the normal way to become the super user is to log in as root, sometimes that is not convenient. For example, you may be logged into a regular user account and just want to make a quick administrative change to your system without having to log out and log back in. Or, you may need to log in over the network to make a change to a Linux system but find that the system doesn't allow root users in from over the network (a common practice).

The answer is that you can use the su command. From any Terminal window or shell, you can simply type:

```
$ su
Password: ******
#
```

When you are prompted, type in the root user's password. The prompt for the regular user ($) will be changed to the super user prompt (#). At this point, you have full permission to run any command and use any file on the system. However, one thing that the su command doesn't do when used this way is read in the root user's environment. As a result, you may type a command that you know is available and get the message "command not found." To fix this problem, you can use the su command with the dash (-) option instead, as follows:

```
$ su -
Password: ******
#
```

You still need to type the password, but after you do that, everything that normally happens at login for the root user will happen after the su command is completed. Your current directory will be root's home directory (probably /root), and things like the root user's PATH variable will be used. If you became the root user by just typing su, rather than su -, you would not have changed directories or the environment of the current login session.

> **TIP:** When you become super user during someone else's session, a common mistake is to leave files or directories behind in the user's directories that are owned by root. If you do this, be sure to use the chown or chmod command to make the files and directories you modify open to the user that you want to own them. Otherwise, you will probably get a phone call in a short time, asking you to come back and fix it.

You can also use the su command to become another user than root. For example, to have the permissions of a user named chum, you could type the following:

```
$ su - chum
```

Even if you were root user before you typed this command, you would only have the permission to open files and run programs that are available to chum. As root user, however, after you type the su command to become another user, you don't need a password to continue. If you type that command as a regular user, you must type the new user's password.

When you are finished using super user permissions, return to the previous shell by exiting the current shell. Do this by pressing Ctrl+D or by typing **exit**. If you are the administrator for a computer that is accessible to multiple users, don't leave a root shell open on someone else's screen (unless you want to let that person do anything they like to the computer)!

When you run GUI tools as a regular user, you are usually prompted for the root password (as described the section "Using graphical administration tools" later in this chapter). If a GUI tool fails and doesn't prompt you for a password, refer to the "Becoming Super User in X" sidebar.

Learning about Administrative GUI Tools, Commands, Configuration Files, and Log Files

Fedora and Red Hat Linux systems have advanced enough in recent releases that you can now do most system administration from your desktop GUI, bypassing the shell altogether. Whether you administer Fedora from the GUI or from a shell, however, underlying your activities are many administrative commands, configuration files, and log files.

Becoming Super User in X

There may be times when an X GUI is running on Linux as a non-root user and you want to run a graphical administration program. In most cases, the GUI administration program will simply prompt you for the root password to continue. However, if the program fails, saying that you don't have permission to run the command, here is what you can do:

First, open a Terminal window on the X desktop.

Then, open permission to the X window display to everyone on the local computer (this is just a temporary measure) by typing:

```
$ xhost +localhost
```

Type the following and enter the root password when prompted, to become super user:

```
$ su -
Password: ******
#
```

Next, type the following to see the current display value:

```
# echo $DISPLAY
```

If the value is something like :0 or :0.0, any X command you run from that shell will appear on the console terminal for the computer. If you are at the console and that's what you see, then you can skip the next step. If you see no value (which is quite possible) or the wrong value, you must set the DISPLAY variable.

Type the following (assuming you are using a bash or sh shell):

```
# export DISPLAY=:0
```

At this point, you can run any administrative X command (such as neat or system-config-packages) and have it appear on your X desktop. If you are running an administrative command from a remote computer and you want it to appear on your local desktop, you can set the DISPLAY to host:0, where host is replaced by the name of your computer.

When you are done, be sure to exit the application you are running. Then restore the
security of your X desktop by typing the following:

```
$ xhost -
```

Understanding where GUI tools, commands, and files are located and how they are used will
help you effectively maintain your Fedora system. Although most administrative features are
intended for the root user, other administrative users (described later in this section) have
limited administrative capabilities.

Using graphical administration tools

The trend over the past few versions of Fedora and other Red Hat Linux distributions has been
to steer clear of the massive administrative interfaces (such as `linuxconf` and `Webmin`) and
instead to offer graphical windows that perform individual administrative tasks. Instead of
sharing one monolithic interface, they share common menus. Individual graphical windows for
configuring a network, adding users, or setting up printers can be launched from that menu.

NOTE: In Fedora Core 1 and previous versions of Red Hat Linux, the GUI administrations tools all began
with `redhat-`, such as `redhat-config-network` and `redhat-logviewer`. Starting with
Fedora Core 2, those names have all changed to `system-`, resulting in names like `system-config-network` and `system-logviewer`.

To administer your Fedora system through the GNOME or KDE desktops, Red Hat Inc. has
provided a common menu (Red Hat calls it the Main Menu; I refer to it as the red hat menu).
In GNOME click the red hat; in KDE, click the K icon in the lower-left corner of the desktop.

Because these administrative tasks require root permission, if you are logged in as a regular
user you must enter the root password before the GUI application's window opens. For
example, if you launch the System Logs window (System Tools → System Logs) from the
GNOME menu as a regular user, you see the pop-up window shown in Figure 10-1.

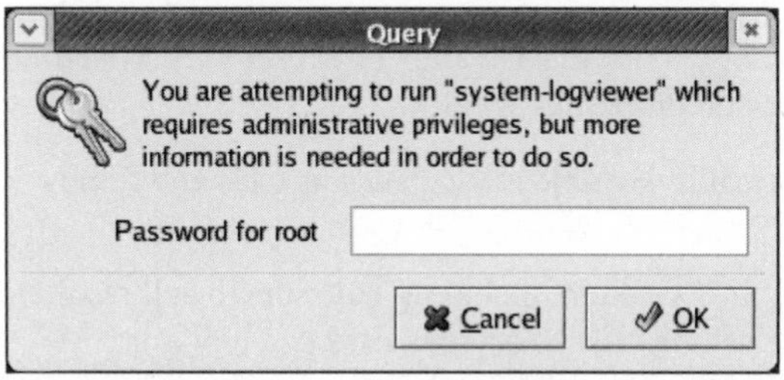

Figure 10-1: Enter the root password to open system administration windows from a regular user's GUI.

After you have entered the root password, most of the system configuration tools will open without requiring you to retype the password during this login session. Look for a "keys" icon in the lower right corner of the panel, indicating that you have root authorization. Click the keys to open a pop-up window that lets you remove authorization. Otherwise, authorization goes away when you close the GUI window.

> **NOTE:** As you configure different features on your Fedora or Red Hat Linux system, you are asked to launch different individual graphical windows. In general, if you have a choice of tools for configuring a server or adding a feature, I recommend that you use the tool provided with your distribution. That's because the Red Hat GUI tools more often integrate closely with the way Fedora and Red Hat systems store and manage their configuration information.

The following list describes many of the GUI-based windows you can use to administer your Fedora or Red Hat Linux system. Start these windows from the System Settings or System Tools submenus on your red hat menu:

- **Server Settings** — This submenu accesses the following server configuration windows:

  - **Domain Name System** — Create and configure zones if your computer is acting as a DNS server.

  - **HTTP**— Configure your computer as an Apache Web server.

  - **NFS**— Set up directories from your system to be shared with other computers on your network using the NFS service.

  - **Samba**— Configure Windows (SMB) file sharing. (To configure other Samba features, you can use the SWAT window. SWAT is described in Chapter 18.)

  - **Services** —Display and change which services are running on your Fedora system at different run levels.

- **Add/Remove Applications** — Manage software packages in the Fedora distribution.

- **Authentication** —Change how users are authenticated on your system. Usually, Shadow Passwords and MD5 Passwords are selected. However, if your network supports LDAP, Kerberos, SMB, NIS, or Hesiod authentication, you can select to use any of those authentication types.

- **Date & Time** —Set the date and time or choose to have an NTP server keep system time in sync. Figure 10-2 shows the Date/Time Properties window.

- **Disk Management** — Mount and format removable media, such as CDs and floppy disks.

- **Display** — Change the settings for your X desktop, including color depth and resolution for your display. You can also choose settings for your video card and monitor.

- **Hardware Browser** — View information about your computer's hardware.

- **Internet Configuration Wizard** — Create initial configurations for connecting to the Internet via Ethernet, ISDN, modem, and other types of network equipment.

- **Keyboard** — Choose the type of keyboard you are using, based on language.

- **Kickstart** —Create a Kickstart configuration file that can be used to install multiple Fedora systems without user intervention.

- **Language** — Select the default language used for the system.

- **Login Screen** — Control how your login screen appears and behaves.

- **Mouse** — Configure your mouse.

- **Network** —Manage your current network interfaces, as well as add interfaces.

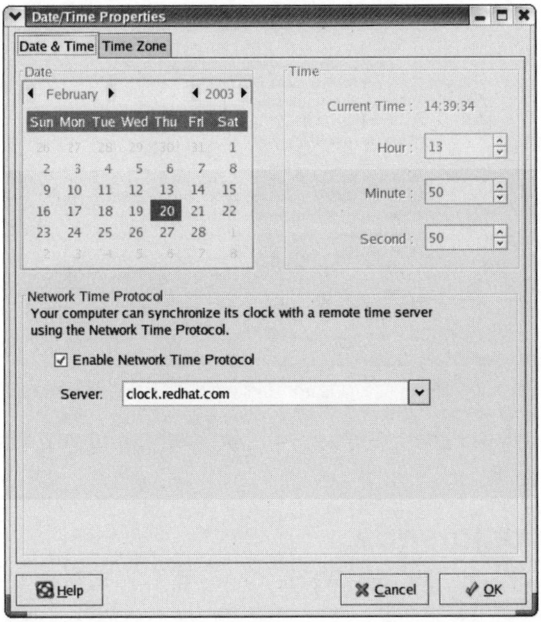

Figure 10-2: Choose an NTP server or set date and time in the Date/Time Properties window.

- **Network Device Control** — Display the active profile for network devices.

- **Printing Manager** —Configure local and network printers.

- **Red Hat Network** —Register your computer with the Red Hat Network to get free software updates.

- **Root Password** — Change the root password.

- **Security Level** — Configure your firewall to allow or deny services to computers from the network.

- **Soundcard Detection** — Tries to detect and configure your sound card.

- **System Logs** — Displays system log files and lets you search them for keywords. Figure 10-3 shows the Boot Log being displayed in the System Logs window.

- **System Monitor** — Shows information about running processes and resource usage.

- **Task Scheduler** — Schedules tasks to be run at set times.

- **Users & Groups** — Lets you add, display, and change user and group accounts for your Fedora system.

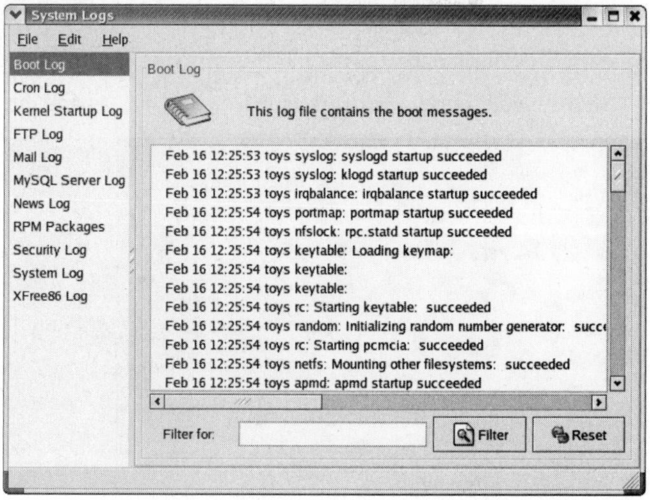

Figure 10-3: Show log files of activities from system boot, FTP, mail, news, and other services.

Procedures for using the various system graphical administrative tools are discussed throughout the book.

Administrative commands

Many commands are intended only for root. When you log in as root, your $PATH variable is set to include some directories that contain commands for the root user. These include the following directories:

- **/sbin** — This contains commands for modifying your disk partitions (such as fdisk), changing boot procedures (grub), and changing system states (init).

- **/usr/sbin** — This contains commands for managing user accounts (such as useradd) and configuring your mouse (mouseconfig). Commands that run as daemon processes are also contained in this directory. (Look for commands that end in "d" such as sshd, pppd, and crond.)

Some administrative commands are contained in regular user directories (such as /bin and /usr/bin). This is especially true of commands that have some options available to everyone. An example is the `/bin/mount` command, which anyone can use to list mounted file systems, but only root can use to mount file systems.

To find commands that are intended primarily for the system administrator, check out the section 8 manual pages (usually in `/usr/share/man/man8`). They contain descriptions and options for most Linux administrative commands.

Some third-party applications will add administrative commands to directories that are not in your PATH. For example, an application may put commands in `/usr/local/bin`, `/opt/bin`, or `/usr/local/sbin`. In those cases, you may want to add those directories to your PATH.

Administrative configuration files

Configuration files are another mainstay of Linux administration. Almost everything you set up for your particular computer — user accounts, network addresses, or GUI preferences — is stored in plain-text files. This has some advantages and some disadvantages.

The advantage of plain-text files is that it is easy to read and change them. Any text editor will do. On the downside, however, is that as you edit configuration files, no error checking is going on. You have to run the program that reads these files (such as a network daemon or the X desktop) to find out if you set up the files correctly. A comma or a quote in the wrong place can sometimes cause a whole interface to fail.

Throughout this book, I describe the configuration files you need to set up the different features that make up Fedora systems. In terms of a general perspective on configuration files, however, there are several locations in a Fedora file system where configuration files are stored. Here are some of the major locations:

- **$HOME** — All users store information in their home directories that directs how their login accounts behave. Most configuration files in $HOME begin with a dot (.), so they don't appear as a user's directory when you use a standard `ls` command (you need to type `ls -a` to see them). There are dot files that define how each user's shell behaves, the desktop look and feel , and options used with your text editor. There are even files (such as `.ssh/*` and `.rhosts`) that configure network permissions for each user.

- **/etc** — This directory contains most of the basic Linux system-configuration files. The following `/etc` configuration files are of interest:

  - **adjtime** — Holds to data to adjust the hardware clock (see the `hwclock` man page).

  - **aliases** — Can contain distribution lists used by the Linux mail service.

  - **bashrc** — Sets system-wide defaults for bash shell users. (By default, it sets the shell prompt to include current user name, host name, current directory, and other values.)

  - **cdrecord.conf** — Contains defaults used for recording CDs.

  - **crontab** — Sets cron environment and times for running automated tasks.

- **csh.cshrc** (or **cshrc**) — Sets system-wide defaults for csh (C shell) users.

- **exports** — Contains a list of local directories that are available to be shared by remote computers using the Network File System (NFS).

- **fdprm** — Sets parameters for common floppy disk formats.

- **fedora-release** — Contains a string identifying the current Fedora Core release.

- **fstab** — Identifies the devices for common storage media (hard disk, floppy, CD-ROM, and so on) and locations where they are mounted in the Linux system. This is used by the `mount` command to choose which file systems to mount.

- **group** — Identifies group names and group IDs (GIDs) that are defined on the systems. Group permissions in Fedora are defined by the second of three sets of rwx (read, write, execute) bits associated with each file and directory.

- **gshadow** — Contains shadow passwords for groups.

- **host.conf** — Sets the locations in which domain names (for example, redhat.com) are searched for on TCP/IP networks (such as the Internet). By default, the local hosts file is searched, then any nameserver entries in `resolv.conf`.

- **hosts** — Contains IP addresses and host names that you can reach from your computer. (Usually this file is used just to store names of computers on your LAN or small private network.)

- **hosts.allow** — Lists host computers that are allowed to use certain TCP/IP services from the local computer.

- **hosts.deny** — Lists host computers that are *not* allowed to use certain TCP/IP services from the local computer (doesn't exist by default).

- **inittab** — Contains information that defines which programs start and stop when Fedora boots, shuts down, or goes into different states in between. This is the most basic configuration file for starting Linux.

- **issue** — Contains the lines that are displayed when a terminal is ready to let you log in to Fedora from a local terminal, or the console in text mode.

- **issue.net** — Contains login lines that are displayed to users who try to log in to the Linux system from a computer on the network using the telnet service.

- **lilo.conf** — Sets Linux boot loader (lilo) parameters to boot the computer. In particular, it lists information about bootable partitions on your computer. (If you are using grub, which replaced lilo as the default boot manager, the `lilo.conf.anaconda` file is available. You can copy that file to `lilo.conf` to switch to LILO.)

- **mail.rc** — Sets system-wide parameters associated with using mail.

- **man.config** — Used by the `man` command to determine the default path to the location of `man` pages.

- **modules.conf** — Contains aliases and options related to loadable kernel modules used by your computer.

- **mtab** — Contains a list of file systems that are currently mounted.

- **mtools.conf** — Contains settings used by DOS tools in Linux.

- **named.conf** — Contains DNS settings if you are running your own DNS server.

- **ntp.conf** — Includes information needed to run the Network Time Protocol (NTP).

- **passwd** — Stores account information for all valid users for the system. Also includes other information, such as the home directory and default shell.

- **printcap** — Contains definitions for the printers configured for your computer.

- **profile** — Sets system-wide environment and start-up programs for all users. This file is read when the user logs in.

- **protocols** — Sets protocol numbers and names for a variety of Internet services.

- **redhat-release** — Contains a string identifying the current Red Hat release. (This file exists on Red Hat Linux and Red Hat Enterprise Linux systems. On Fedora systems, this file exists as a link to the `fedora-release` file, so that applications that look for release information in the `redhat-release` file won't fail.)

- **resolv.conf** — Identifies the locations of DNS name server computers that are used by TCP/IP to translate Internet host.domain names into IP addresses.

- **rpc** — Defines remote procedure call names and numbers.

- **services** — Defines TCP/IP services and their port assignments.

- **shadow** — Contains encrypted passwords for users who are defined in the `passwd` file. (This is viewed as a more secure way to store passwords than the original encrypted password in the `passwd` file. The `passwd` file needs to be publicly readable, whereas the `shadow` file can be unreadable by all but the root user.)

- **shells** — Lists the shell command-line interpreters (`bash`, `sh`, `csh`, and so on) that are available on the system, as well as their locations.

- **sudoers** — Sets commands that can be run by users, who may not otherwise have permission to run the command, using the `sudo` command. In particular, this file is used to provide selected users with root permission.

- **syslog.conf** — Defines what logging messages are gathered by the `syslogd` daemon and what files they are stored in. (Typically, log messages are stored in files contained in the `/var/log` directory.)

- **termcap** — Lists definitions for character terminals, so that character-based applications know what features are supported by a given terminal. Graphical terminals and applications have made this file obsolete to most people. (Termcap was the BSD UNIX way of storing terminal information; UNIX System V used definitions in `/usr/share/terminfo` files.)

- **xinetd.conf** — Contains simple configuration information used by the `xinetd` daemon process. This file mostly points to the `/etc/xinetd.d` directory for information about individual services (described later in this chapter).

- **/etc/X11** — Contains subdirectories that each contain system-wide configuration files used by X and different X window managers available for Linux. The `xorg.conf` file (which makes your computer and monitor usable with X) and configuration directories containing files used by `xdm` and `xinit` to start X are in here.

  Directories relating to window managers contain files that include the default values that a user will get if that user starts one of these window managers on your system. Window managers that may have system-wide configuration files in these directories include GNOME (`gdm`) and Twm (`twm`).

> **NOTE:** Some files and directories in `/etc/X11` are linked to locations in the `/usr/X11R6` directory.

- **/etc/alternatives** — Contains links that the alternatives facility uses to enable a system administrator to exchange one service with another in a way that is invisible to users. (Currently, only mail and printing use the alternatives service.)

- **/etc/amanda** — Contains files and directories that allow the amanda facility to do network backups of other Linux and UNIX systems.

- **/etc/cipe** — Holds if-up and if-down scripts to start a CIPE virtual private network.

- **/etc/cron*** — Directories in this set contain files that define how the `crond` utility runs applications on a daily (`cron.daily`), hourly (`cron.hourly`), monthly (`cron.monthly`), or weekly (`cron.weekly`) schedule.

- **/etc/cups** — Contains files that are used to configure the CUPS printing service.

- **/etc/default** — Contains files that set default values for various utilities. For example, the file for the `useradd` command defines the default group number, home directory, password expiration date, shell, and skeleton directory (`/etc/skel`) that are used when creating a new user account.

- **/etc/httpd** — Contains a variety of files used to configure the behavior of your Apache Web server (specifically, the `httpd` daemon process).

- **/etc/init.d** — Contains the permanent copies of run-level scripts. These scripts are linked to files in the `/etc/rc?.d` directories to have each service associated with a script started or stopped for the particular run level. The *?* is replaced by the run-level number (0 through 6).

- **/etc/mail** — Contains files used to configure your sendmail mail service.

- **/etc/pcmcia** — Contains configuration files that allow you to have a variety of PCMCIA cards configured for your computer. (PCMCIA slots are those openings on your laptop that allow you to have credit card–sized cards attached to your computer. You can attach such devices as modems and external CD-ROMs.)

- **/etc/postfix** — Contains configuration files for the postfix mail transport agent.

- **/etc/ppp** — Contains several configuration files used to set up Point-to-Point protocol (so that you can have your computer dial out to the Internet).

- **/etc/rc?.d** — There is a separate `rc?.d` directory for each valid system state: `rc0.d` (shutdown state), `rc1.d` (single-user state), `rc2.d` (multiuser state), `rc3.d` (multiuser plus networking state), `rc4.d` (user-defined state), `rc5.d` (multiuser, networking, plus GUI login state), and `rc6.d` (reboot state).

- **/etc/security** — Contains files that set a variety of default security conditions for your computer. These files are part of the pam (pluggable authentication modules) package.

- **/etc/skel** — Any files contained in this directory are automatically copied to a user's home directory when that user is added to the system. By default, most of these files are dot (.) files, such as `.kde` (a directory for setting KDE desktop defaults) and `.bashrc` (for setting default values used with the bash shell).

- **/etc/squid** — Contains configuration files for the Squid proxy caching server.

- **/etc/sysconfig** — Contains important system configuration files that are created and maintained by various Fedora services (including `iptables`, `samba`, and most networking services).

- **/etc/uucp** — Contains configuration files used with Taylor UUCP (a nonstandard version of the uucp facility that is used to create modem, direct line, and other serial connections with other computers).

- **/etc/vsftpd** — Contains configuration files used to set up the vsftpd FTP server.

- **/etc/xinetd.d** — Contains a set of files, each of which defines a network service that the `xinetd` daemon listens for on a particular port. When the `xinetd` daemon process receives a request for a service, it uses the information in these files to determine which daemon processes to start to handle the request.

Administrative log files

One of the things that Linux does well is keep track of itself. This is a good thing, when you consider how much can go wrong with a complex operating system. Sometimes you are trying to get a new facility to work and it fails without giving you the foggiest reason why. Other times you want to monitor your system to see if people are trying to access your computer illegally. In any of those cases, you can use log files to help track down the problem.

The main utilities for logging error and debugging messages for Linux are the `syslogd` and `klogd` daemons. General system logging is done by `syslogd`. Logging that is specific to kernel activity is done by `klogd`. Logging is done according to information in the `/etc/syslog.conf` file. Messages are typically directed to log files that are usually in the `/var/log` directory.

Fedora includes a System Logs window (System Tools → System Logs) you can use to view and search system log files from the desktop. See Chapter 14 for a description of that window and of the log files you can view with it.

Using other administrative logins

You don't hear much about other administrative logins (besides root) being used with Fedora. It was a fairly common practice in UNIX systems to have several different administrative logins that allowed administrative tasks to be split among several users. For example, a person sitting near a printer could have lp permissions to move print jobs to another printer if they knew a printer wasn't working.

In any case, these administrative logins are available with Linux, so you may want to look into using them. At the very least, because individual software packages such as bind, squid, and amanda set up permissions for their log files and configuration files based on their administrative logins, maintaining those permissions can prevent someone who hacks into one of those services from gaining control of the whole computer.

> **TIP:** Because most Fedora administrative features are expected to be administered by the root user, e-mail for other administrative accounts is routed to the root user. If you want other administrative users to receive their own e-mail, delete the aliases for those users from the /etc/aliases file.

Understanding administrative logins

Here are some of the administrative logins that are configured automatically for Linux systems. By tradition, these logins are assigned UID numbers under 100. Here are examples:

> **TIP:** Most administrative logins have no passwords by default. They also typically have /sbin/nologin assigned as their shell, so if you try to log in as one of these users, you see a "This account is currently not available" message. That's why you can't use an administrative login separately until you assign it a password and shell (such as /bin/bash).

- **lp** — This user can control some printing features. Having a separate lp administrator allows someone other than the super user to do such things as move or remove lp logs and print spool files. The home directory for lp is /var/spool/lpd.

- **mail** — This user can work with administrative e-mail features. The mail group has group permissions to use mail files in /var/spool/mail (which is also the mail user's home directory).

- **uucp** — This user owns various uucp commands (once used as the primary method for dial-up serial communications). It is the owner of log files in /var/log/uucp, spool files in /var/spool, administrative commands (such as uuchk, uucico, uuconv, and uuxqt) in /usr/sbin, and user commands (uucp, cu, uuname, uustat, and uux) in /usr/bin. The home directory for uucp is /var/spool/uucp.

- **bin** — This user owns many commands in /bin in traditional UNIX systems. This is not the case in Fedora, because root tends to own most executable files. The home directory of bin is /bin.

- **news** — This user could do administration of Internet news services, depending on how you set permission for /var/spool/news and other news-related resources. The home directory for news is /etc/news.

Using sudo for assigning administrative privilege

One way to give full or limited root privileges to any non-root user is to set up the sudo facility. That simply entails adding the user to /etc/sudoers and defining what privilege you want that user to have. Then the user can run any command he or she is privileged to use by preceding that command with the sudo command.

The following is an example of how to use the sudo facility to cause any users that are added to the wheel group to have full root privileges:

1. As the root user, edit the /etc/sudoers file by running the visudo command:

   ```
   # /usr/sbin/visudo
   ```

   By default, the file is opened in vi, unless your EDITOR variable happens to be set to some other editor acceptable to visudo (for example, export EDITOR=gedit) The reason for using visudo is that the command will lock the /etc/sudoers file and do some basic sanity-checking of the file to ensure it was edited correctly.

   NOTE: If you are stuck here, refer to the vi tutorial in Chapter 4 for information on using the vi editor.

2. Uncomment the following line to allow users in the group named wheel to have full root privileges on the computer:

   ```
   %wheel        ALL=(ALL)        ALL
   ```

   The previous line causes the user to be prompted for a password to be allowed to use administrative commands. To allow users in the wheel group to have that privilege without using a password, uncomment the following line instead:

   ```
   %wheel        ALL=(ALL)        NOPASSWD: ALL
   ```

3. Save the changes to the /etc/sudoers file (in vi, type **ZZ**).

4. Still as root user, open the /etc/group file in any text editor and add the users you want to have root privilege to the wheel line. For example, if you were to add the users mary and jake to the wheel group, the line would appear as follows:

   ```
   wheel:x:10:root,mary,jake
   ```

At this point, the users `mary` and `jake` can run the `sudo` command to run commands, or parts of commands, that are normally restricted to the root user. The following is an example of a session by the user `jake` after he has been assigned `sudo` privileges:

```
[jake]$ sudo umount /mnt/win

We trust you have received the usual lecture from the local System
Administrator. It usually boils down to these two things:

        #1) Respect the privacy of others.
        #2) Think before you type.

Password: ********
[jake]$ mount /mnt/win
mount: only root can mount /dev/hda1 on /mnt/win
[jake]$ sudo mount /mnt/win
[jake]$
```

In the above session, the user `jake` runs the `sudo` command so he can unmount the `/mnt/win` file system (using the `umount` command). He is given a warning and asked to provide his password (this is `jake`'s password, *not* the root password).

Notice that even after `jake` has given the password, he must still use the `sudo` command to run the command as root (the first mount fails, but the second succeeds). Notice that he was not prompted for a password for the second `sudo`. That's because after entering his password successfully he can enter as many `sudo` commands as he wants for the next five minutes without having to enter it again. (You can change the timeout value from five minutes to however long you want by setting the `passwd_timeout` value in the `/etc/sudoers` file.)

The preceding example grants a simple all-or-nothing administrative privilege to everyone you put in the `wheel` group. However, the `/etc/sudoers` file gives you an incredible amount of flexibility in permitting individual users and groups to use individual applications or groups of applications. I recommend you refer to the `sudoers` and `sudo` man pages for information about how to tune your `sudo` facility.

Administering Your Fedora System

Your Linux system administrator duties don't end after you have installed Fedora. Your ongoing job as a Linux system administrator includes the following tasks:

- **Configuring hardware** — Often when you add hardware to your Fedora computer, that hardware will be automatically detected and configured by tools such as kudzu. In those cases where the hardware was not properly set up, you can use commands such as `lsmod`, `modprobe`, `insmod`, and `rmmod` to configure the right modules to get the hardware working.

- **Managing file systems and disk space** — You must keep track of the disk space being consumed, especially if your Fedora system is shared by multiple users. At some point, you may need to add a hard disk or track down what is eating up your disk space (you can use commands like `find` to do this).

- **Monitoring system performance** — You may have a run-away process on your system or you may just be experiencing slow performance. Tools that come with Fedora can help you determine how much of your CPU and memory are being consumed.

- **Keeping software up2date** — Corrections to Fedora software, especially those related to security issues, should be incorporated into your system as time goes on. The Red Hat Network offers the up2date service for Red Hat Enterprise Linux systems and yum and apt repositories for Fedora systems to ensure that you get critical fixes.

The aforementioned administrative tasks are described in the rest of this chapter. Later chapters cover other administrative topics, such as managing user accounts (Chapter 11), automating system tasks (Chapter 12), system backups and restores (Chapter 13), and securing your system (Chapter 14). Tasks related to network administration are covered in Chapters 15 through 26.

Configuring Hardware

The following section describes how to add and reconfigure hardware using kudzu. The section after that describes how to manage loadable modules when hardware isn't being detected and configured properly.

Reconfiguring hardware with kudzu

When you add or remove hardware from your computer and reboot Fedora, a window appears during the reboot process advising that hardware has either been added or removed and asking if you want to reconfigure it. The program that detects and reconfigures your hardware is called kudzu.

The kudzu program is a hardware autodetection and configuration tool that runs automatically at boot time. If you like, you can also start kudzu while Fedora is running. In either case, here is what kudzu does:

1. It checks the hardware connected to your computer.

2. It compares the hardware it finds to the database of hardware information stored in the `/etc/sysconfig/hwconf` file.

3. It prompts you to change your system configuration, based on new or removed hardware that was detected.

The following is a list of hardware that kudzu can detect (according to the kudzu README file), followed by a description of what kudzu does to configure the device. Other devices may be detected as well (such as USB devices).

- **Network devices** — Adds an Ethernet interface alias (eth0, eth1, and so on) if necessary and either migrates the old device configuration or creates a new one.
- **SCSI** — Adds an alias for scsi_hostadapter.
- **Sound card** — Runs the sndconfig command to configure and test the sound card.
- **Mouse** — Links the new mouse device to /dev/mouse and runs the mouseconfig command to configure and test the mouse.
- **Modem** — Links the new modem device to /dev/modem.
- **CD-ROM** — Links the CD-ROM device to /dev/cdrom.
- **Scanner** — Links the new scanner device to /dev/scanner.
- **Keyboard** — Runs the kbdconfig command to reconfigure the keyboard. Also, if you are using a serial console, it makes sure /etc/inittab and /etc/securetty are configured to be used by a serial console.

The following is a list of actions kudzu takes when a device is removed:

- **Network** — Removes the alias for the Ethernet interface (eth0, eth1, and so on).
- **SCSI** — Removes the alias for the SCSI host adapter (scsi_hostadapter).
- **Mouse** — Removes the link to /dev/mouse.
- **Modem** — Removes the link to /dev/modem.
- **CD-ROM** — Removes the link to /dev/cdrom.
- **Scanner** — Removes the link to /dev/scanner.

To run kudzu, either reboot (during the reboot, kudzu is run automatically) or switch to a virtual terminal (Ctrl+Alt+F2), log in as root, and run the kudzu command. For any hardware that has been added or removed since the last time kudzu was run, you are asked if you want to configure it, not configure it, or do nothing.

Configuring modules

In a perfect world, after installing and booting Linux, all of your hardware should be detected and available for access. While Fedora and other Red Hat Linux systems are rapidly moving closer to that world, there are times when you must take special steps to get your computer hardware working.

Fedora systems come with tools for configuring the drivers that stand between the programs you run (such as CD players and Web browsers) and the hardware they use (such as CD-ROM drives and network cards). The intention is to have the drivers your system needs most often built into the kernel; these are called *resident drivers*. Other drivers that are added dynamically as needed are referred to as *loadable modules*.

Finding available modules

If you have installed the Linux kernel source code (kernel-source package), source code files for available drivers are stored in subdirectories of the `/usr/src/linux-2.6*/drivers` directory. There are several ways of finding information about these drivers:

- **make xconfig** — With `/usr/src/linux-2.6*` as your current directory, type **make xconfig** from a Terminal window on the desktop. Select the category of module you are interested in and click Help next to the driver that interests you. The help information that appears tells you the module name and a description of the driver.

- **Documentation** — The `/usr/src/linux-2.6*/Documentation` directory contains lots of plain-text files describing different aspects of the kernel and related drivers.

- **kernel-doc** — The kernel-doc software package (available on CD #3 of the Fedora Core distribution) contains a large set of documents describing the kernel and drivers. These documents are stored in the `/usr/share/doc/kernel-doc*` directory.

After modules have been built, they are installed in the `/lib/modules/2.6*` directory. The name of the directory is based on the current release number of the kernel. Modules that are in that directory can then be loaded and unloaded as they are needed.

> **NOTE:** In previous releases, Fedora and other Red Hat Linux systems stored modules in the `/lib/modules` directory, rather than the `/lib/modules/2.6*` directory. This new structure allows you to store modules on your system that relate to different kernel versions you may be running.

Listing loaded modules

To see which modules are currently loaded into the running kernel on your computer, you can use the `lsmod` command. Here's an example:

```
# lsmod
Module                  Size  Used by
snd_seq_oss            38912  0
snd_seq_midi_event      9344  1 snd_seq_oss
snd_seq                67728  4 snd_seq_oss,snd_seq_midi_event
snd_seq_device          8328  2 snd_seq_oss,snd_seq
.
.
.
autofs                 16512  0
ne2k_pci                9056  0
8390                   13568  1 ne2k_pci
ohci1394               41860  0
```

```
ieee1394              284464   1 ohci1394
floppy                 65712   0
sg                     36120   0
scsi_mod              124600   1 sg
parport_pc             39724   0
parport                47336   1 parport_pc
ext3                  128424   2
jbd                    86040   1 ext3
```

This output shows a variety of modules that have been loaded on a Linux system. The modules loaded on this system include several to support the ALSA sound system, including some that provide OSS compatibility (snd_seq_oss).

To find information about any of the loaded modules, you can use the `modinfo` command. For example, you could type the following:

```
# modinfo -d snd-seq-oss
"OSS-compatible sequencer module"
```

Not all modules have descriptions available. In this case, however, the snd-seq-oss module is described as an OSS-compatible sequencer module. You can also use the `-a` option to see the author of the module or `-n` to see the object file representing the module. The author information often has the e-mail address of the driver's creator, so you can contact the author if you have problems or questions about it.

Loading modules

You can load any module that has been compiled and installed (to the `/lib/modules` directory) into your running kernel using the `modprobe` command. The most common reasons for loading a module are that you want to use a feature temporarily (such as loading a module to support a special file system on a floppy you want to access) or to identify a module that will be used by a particular piece of hardware that could not be autodetected.

Here is an example of the `modprobe` command being used to load the parport module. The parport module provides the core functions to share parallel ports with multiple devices.

```
# modprobe parport
```

After parport is loaded you can load the parport_pc module to define the PC-style ports available through the interface. The parport_pc module lets you optionally define the addresses and IRQ numbers associated with each device sharing the parallel port. For example:

```
# modprobe parport_pc io=0x3bc irq=auto
```

In the previous example, a device is identified as having an address of 0x3bc. The IRQ for the device is autodetected.

The `modprobe` command loads modules temporarily. At the next system reboot, the modules you enter disappear. To permanently add the module to your system, add the `modprobe` command line to one of the start-up scripts that are run a boot time.

> **NOTE:** An alternative to using `modprobe` is the `insmod` command. The advantage of using `modprobe`, however, is that `insmod` will only load the module you request, while `modprobe` will try to load other modules that the one you requested is dependent on.

Removing modules

You can remove a module from a running kernel using the `rmmod` command. For example, to remove the module parport_pc from the current kernel, type the following:

```
# rmmod parport_pc
```

If the module is not currently busy, the parport_pc module is removed from the running kernel.

Managing File Systems and Disk Space

File systems in Linux are organized in a hierarchy, beginning from root (/) and continuing downward in a structure of directories and subdirectories. As an administrator of a Fedora system, it is your duty to make sure that all the disk drives that represent your file system are available to the users of the computer. It is also your job to make sure there is enough disk space in the right places in the file system for users to store what they need.

File systems are organized differently in Linux than they are in Microsoft Windows operating systems. Instead of drive letters (for example, A:, B:, C:) for each local disk, network file system, CD-ROM, or other type of storage medium, everything fits neatly into the directory structure. It is up to an administrator to create a mount point in the file system and then connect the disk to that point in the file system.

> **CROSS-REFERENCE:** Chapter 2 provides instructions for using Disk Druid to configure disk partitions. Chapter 4 describes how the Linux file system is organized.

The organization of your file system begins when you install Linux. Part of the installation process is to divide your hard disk (or disks) into partitions. Those partitions can then be assigned to:

- A part of the Linux file system,
- Swap space for Linux, or
- Other file system types (perhaps containing other bootable operating systems)

For our purposes, I want to focus on partitions that are used for the Linux file system. To see what partitions are currently set up on your hard disk, use the `fdisk` command as follows:

```
# fdisk -1

Disk /dev/hda:  40.0 GB, 40020664320
255 heads, 63 sectors/track, 4825 cylinders
Units = cylinders of 16065 * 512 bytes = 8225280 bytes

   Device Boot    Start       End     Blocks   Id  System
/dev/hda1    *        1        13        104    b  Win95 FAT32
/dev/hda2            84        89      48195   83  Linux
/dev/hda3            90       522    3478072+  83  Linux
/dev/hda4           523       554     257040    5  Extended
/dev/hda5           523       554     257008+  82  Linux swap
```

This output shows the disk partitioning for a computer able to run both Linux and Microsoft Windows. You can see that the Linux partition on /dev/hda3 has most of the space available for data. There is a Windows partition (/dev/hda1) and a Linux swap partition (/dev/hda5). There is also a small /boot partition (46MB) on /dev/hda2. In this case, the root partition for Linux has 3.3GB of disk space and resides on /dev/hda3.

Next, to see what partitions are actually being used for your Linux system, you can use the mount command (with no options). The mount command can show you which of the available disk partitions are actually mounted and where they are mounted.

```
# mount
/dev/hda3 on / type ext3 (rw)
/dev/hda2 on /boot type ext3 (rw)
/dev/hda1 on /mnt/win type vfat (rw)
none on /proc type proc (rw)
none on /sys type sysfs (rw)
none on /dev/pts type devpts (rw,gid=5,mode=620)
none on /dev/shm type tmpfs (rw)
none on /proc/sys/fs/binfmt_misc type binfmt_misc (rw)
/dev/cdrom on /mnt/cdrom type iso9660 (ro,nosuid,nodev)
```

> **NOTE:** You may notice that /proc, /sys, /dev/pts, /proc/sys/fs/binfmt_misc, /dev/shm, and other entries not relating to a partition are shown as file systems. This is because they represent different file system types (proc and devpts, and so on). The word none, however, indicates that they are not associated with a separate physical partition.

The mounted Linux partitions in this case are /dev/hda2, which provides space for the /boot directory (which contains data for booting Linux), and /dev/hda3, which provides space for the rest of the Linux file system beginning from the root directory (/). This particular system also contains a Windows partition that was mounted in the /mnt/win directory and a CD that was mounted in its standard place: /mnt/cdrom. (With most GUI interfaces, the CD is typically mounted automatically when you insert it.)

After the word `type`, you can see the type of file system contained on the device. (See the description of different file system types later in this chapter.) Particularly on larger Linux systems, you may have multiple partitions for several reasons:

- **Multiple hard disks** — You may have several hard disks available to your users. In that case you would have to mount each disk (and possibly several partitions from each disk) in different locations in your file system.

- **Protecting different parts of the file system** — If you have many users on a system, and the users consume all of the file system space, the entire system can fail. For example, there may be no place for temporary files to be copied (so the programs writing to temporary files may fail), and incoming mail may fail to be written to mail boxes. With multiple mounted partitions, if one partition runs out, others can continue to work.

- **Backups** — There are some fast ways to back up data from your computer that involve copying the entire image of a disk or partition. If you want to restore that partition later, you can simply copy it back (bit-by-bit) to a hard disk. With smaller partitions, this approach can be done fairly efficiently.

- **Protecting from disk failure** — If one disk (or part of one disk) fails, by having multiple partitions mounted on your file system, you may be able to continue working and just fix the one disk that fails.

When a disk partition is mounted on the file system, all directories and subdirectories below that mount point are then stored on that partition. So, for example, if you were to mount one partition on / and one on `/usr`, everything below the `/usr` mount point would be stored on the second partition while everything else would be stored on the first partition. If you then mounted another partition on `/usr/local`, everything below that mount point would be on the third partition, while everything else below `/usr` would be on the second partition.

> **TIP:** What if a remote file system is unmounted from your computer, and you go to save a file in that mount point directory? What happens is that you will write the file to that directory and it will be stored on your local hard disk. When the remote file system is remounted, however, the file you saved will seem to disappear. To get the file back, you will have to unmount the remote file system (causing the file to reappear), move the file to another location, remount the file system, and copy the file back there.

Mount points that are often mentioned as being candidates for separate partitions include /, `/boot`, `/home`, `/usr`, and `/var`. The root file system (/) is the catchall for directories that aren't in other mount points. The root file system's mount point (/) is the only one that is required. The `/boot` directory holds the images needed to boot the operating system. The `/home` file systems is where all the user accounts are typically stored. Applications and documentation are stored in `/usr`. Below the `/var` mount point is where log files, temporary files, server files (Web, FTP, and so on), and lock files are stored (that is, items that need disk space for your computer's applications to keep running).

> **CROSS-REFERENCE:** See Chapter 2 for further information on partitioning techniques.

The fact that multiple partitions are mounted on your file system is invisible to people using your Linux system. The only times they will care will be if a partition runs out of space or if they need to save or use information from a particular device (such as a floppy disk or remote file system). Of course, any user can check this by typing the mount command.

Mounting file systems

Most of your hard disks are mounted automatically for you. When you installed Fedora, you were asked to create partitions and indicate the mount points for those partitions. When you boot Fedora, all Linux partitions residing on hard disk should typically be mounted. For that reason, this section focuses mostly on how to mount other types of devices so that they become part of your Linux file system.

Besides being able to mount other types of devices, you can also use mount to mount other kinds of file systems on your Linux system. This means that you can store files from other operating systems or use file systems that are appropriate for certain kinds of activities (such as writing large block sizes). The most common use of this feature for the average Linux user, however, is to allow that user to obtain and work with files from floppy disks or CD-ROMs.

Supported file systems

To see file system types that are currently available to be used on your system, type **cat /proc/filesystems**. The following file system types are supported in Linux, although they may not be in use at the moment or they may not be built into your current kernel (so they may need to be loaded as modules):

- **adfs** — This is the acorn disc file system, which is the standard file system used on RiscOS operating systems.

- **befs** — This is the file system used by the BeOS operating system.

- **cifs** — The Common Internet File System (CIFS) is the virtual file system used to access servers that comply with the SNIA CIFS specification. CIFS is an attempt to refine and standardize the SMB protocol used by Samba and Windows file sharing.

- **ext3** — The ext file systems are the most common file systems used with Linux. The ext3 file system was new for Red Hat Linux 7.2 and is currently the default file system type in most Linux systems (including Fedora). The root file system (/) must be ext3, ext2, or minux. The ext3 file system is also referred to as the Third Extended file system. The ext3 file system includes journaling features that improve a file system's ability to recover from crashes, as compared to ext2 file systems.

- **ext2** — The default file system type for versions of Red Hat Linux previous to 7.2. Features are the same as ext3, except that ext2 doesn't include journaling features.

- **ext** — This is the first version of ext3. It is not used very often anymore.

- **iso9660** — This file system evolved from the High Sierra file system (which was the original standard used on CD-ROM). Extensions to the High Sierra standard (called

Rock Ridge extensions), allow iso9660 file systems to support long filenames and UNIX-style information (such as file permissions, ownership, and links). This file system type is used when you mount a CD-ROM.

- **kafs** — This is the AFS client file system. It is used in distributed computing environments to share files with Linux, Windows, and Macintosh clients.

- **minix** — This is the Minix file system type, used originally with the Minix version of UNIX. It only supports filenames of up to 30 characters.

- **msdos**— This is an MS-DOS file system. You can use this type to mount floppy disks that come from Microsoft operating systems.

- **vfat** — This is the Microsoft extended FAT (VFAT) file system.

- **umsdos** — This is an MS-DOS file system with extensions to allow features that are similar to UNIX (including long filenames).

- **proc** — This is not a real file system, but rather a file-system interface to the Linux kernel. You probably won't do anything special to set up a proc file system. However, the /proc mount point should be a proc file system. Many utilities rely on /proc to gain access to Linux kernel information.

- **reiserfs** — This is the ReiserFS journaled file system.

- **swap** — This is used for swap partitions. Swap areas are used to hold data temporarily when RAM is currently used up. Data is swapped to the swap area, then returned to RAM when it is needed again.

- **nfs** — This is the Network File System (NFS) type of file system. File systems mounted from another computer on your network use this type of file system.

CROSS-REFERENCE: Information on using NFS to export and share file systems over a network is contained in Chapter 18.

- **hpfs** — This file system is used to do read-only mounts of an OS/2 HPFS file system.

- **ncpfs** — This relates to Novell NetWare file systems. NetWare file systems can be mounted over a network.

CROSS-REFERENCE: For information on using NetWare file systems over a network, see the section on setting up a file server in Chapter 18.

- **ntfs** — This is the Windows NT file system. It is supported as a read-only file system (so that you can mount and copy files from it). Read-write support is available, but considered unreliable (some say, dangerous).

- **affs** — This file system is used with Amiga computers.

- **ufs** — This file system is popular on Sun Microsystems operating systems (that is, Solaris and SunOS).

- **xenix** — This was added to be compatible with Xenix file systems (one of the first PC versions of UNIX). The system is obsolete and will probably be removed eventually.

- **xiafs** — This file system supports long filenames and larger inodes than file systems such as minux.

- **coherent** — This is the file system type used with Coherent or System V files. Like the xenix file system type, it will be removed at some time in the future.

Using the fstab file to define mountable file systems

The hard disks on your local computer and the remote file systems you use every day are probably set up to automatically mount when you boot Linux. The definitions for which of these file systems are mounted are contained in the /etc/fstab file. Here's an example of an /etc/fstab file:

```
LABEL=/          /              ext3      defaults             1 1
LABEL=/boot      /boot          ext3      defaults             1 2
none             /dev/pts       devpts    gid=5,mode=620       0 0
none             /dev/shm       tmpfs     defaults             0 0
none             /proc          proc      defaults             0 0
/dev/hda5        swap           swap      defaults             0 0
/dev/cdrom       /mnt/cdrom     udf,iso9660  noauto,owner,kudzu,ro 0 0
/dev/hda1        /mnt/win       vfat      noauto               0 0
/dev/fd0         /mnt/floppy    auto      noauto,owner         0 0
```

All file systems listed in this file are mounted at boot time, except for those set to noauto in the fourth field. In this example, the root (/) and boot (/boot) hard disk partitions are mounted at boot time, along with the /proc, /dev/shm and /dev/pts file systems (which are not associated with particular devices). The floppy disk (/dev/fd0) and CD-ROM drives (/dev/cdrom) are not mounted at boot time. Definitions are put in the fstab file for floppy and CD-ROM drives so that they can be mounted in the future (as described later).

I also added one additional line for /dev/hda1, which allows me to mount the Windows (vfat) partition on my computer so I don't have to always boot Windows to get at the files on my Windows partition.

> **NOTE:** To access the Windows partition described above, I must first create the mount point (by typing `mkdir /mnt/win`). I can then mount it when I choose by typing (as root) `mount /mnt/win`

You find the following in each field of the fstab file:

- **Field 1** — The name of the device representing the file system. The word none is often placed in this field for file systems (such as /proc and /dev/pts) that are not associated with special devices. Notice that this field can now include the LABEL option. Using LABEL, you can indicate a universally unique identifier (UUID) or volume label instead of a device name. The advantage to this approach is that, since the partition is identified by volume name, you can move a volume to a different device name and not have to change the `fstab` file.

- **Field 2** — The mount point in the file system. The file system contains all data from the mount point down the directory tree structure, unless another file system is mounted at some point beneath it.

- **Field 3** — The file system type. Valid file system types are described in the "Supported file systems" section earlier in this chapter.

- **Field 4** — Options to the `mount` command. In the preceding example, the `noauto` option prevents the indicated file system from being mounted at boot time. Also, `ro` says to mount the file system read-only (which is reasonable for a CD-ROM drive). Commas must separate options. See the `mount` command manual page (under the `-o` option) for information on other supported options.

> **TIP:** Normally, only the root user is allowed to mount a file system using the `mount` command. However, to allow any user to mount a file system (such as a file system on a floppy disk), you could add the `user` option to Field 4 of `/etc/fstab`.

- **Field 5** — The number in this field indicates whether or not the indicated file system needs to be dumped. A number 1 assumes that the file system needs to be dumped. A number 2 assumes that the file system doesn't need to be dumped.

- **Field 6** — The number in this field indicates whether or not the indicated file system needs to be checked with `fsck`. A number 1 assumes that the file system needs to be checked. A number 2 assumes that the file system doesn't need to be checked.

If you want to add an additional local disk or an additional partition, you can create an entry for the disk or partition in the `/etc/fstab` file. To get instructions on how to add entries for an NFS file system, see Chapter 18.

Using the mount command to mount file systems

Your Fedora or Red Hat Linux system automatically runs `mount -a` (mount all file systems) each time you boot. For that reason, you would typically only use the `mount` command for special situations. In particular, the average user or administrator uses `mount` in two ways:

- To display the disks, partitions, and remote file systems that are currently mounted.

- To temporarily mount a file system.

Any user can type the `mount` command (with no options) to see what file systems are currently mounted on the local Linux system. The following is an example of the `mount` command. It shows a single hard disk partition (`/dev/hda1`) containing the root (`/`) file system, and proc and devpts file system types mounted on `/proc` and `/dev`, respectively. The last entry shows a floppy disk, formatted with a standard Linux file system (ext3) mounted on the `/mnt/floppy` directory.

```
$ mount
/dev/hda3 on / type ext3 (rw)
none on /proc type proc (rw)
none on /sys type sysfs (rw)
none on /dev/shm type tmpfs (rw)
/dev/hda2 on /boot type ext3 (rw)
none on /dev/pts type devpts (rw,gid=5,mode=0620)
/dev/fd0 on /mnt/floppy type ext3 (rw)
```

The most common devices to mount by hand are your floppy disk and your CD-ROM. However, depending on the type of desktop you are using, CD-ROMs and floppy disks may be mounted for you automatically when you insert them. (In some cases, the autorun program may also run automatically. For example, autorun may start a CD music player or software package installer to handle the data on the medium.)

If you want to mount a file system manually, however, the /etc/fstab file helps make it simple to mount a floppy disk or a CD-ROM. In some cases, you can use the mount command with a single option to indicate what you want to mount, and information is taken from the /etc/fstab file to fill in the other options. Entries probably already in your /etc/fstab file let you do these quick mounts in the following two cases:

- **CD-ROM** — If you are mounting a CD-ROM that is in the standard ISO 9960 format (as most software CD-ROMs are), you can mount that CD-ROM by placing it in your CD-ROM drive and typing the following:

```
# mount /mnt/cdrom
```

By default, your CD-ROM is mounted on the /mnt/cdrom directory. (The file system type, device name, and other options are filled in automatically.) To see the contents, type **cd /mnt/cdrom**, then type **ls**. Files from the CD-ROM's root directory will be displayed.

- **Floppy Disk** — If you are mounting a floppy disk that is in the standard Linux file system format (ext3), you can mount that floppy disk by inserting it in your floppy drive and typing the following:

```
# mount /mnt/floppy
```

The file system type (ext3), device (/dev/fd0), and mount options are filled in from the /etc/fstab file. You should be able to change to the floppy disk directory (cd /mnt/floppy) and list the contents of the floppy's top directory (ls).

> **NOTE:** In both of the two previous cases, you could give the device name (/dev/cdrom or /dev/fd0, respectively) instead of the mount point directory to get the same results.

Of course, it is possible that you may get floppy disks you want to use that are in all formats. Someone may give you a floppy containing files from a Microsoft operating system (in MS-

DOS format). Or you may get a file from another UNIX system. In those cases, you can fill in your own options, instead of relying on options from the /etc/fstab file. In some cases, Linux autodetects that the floppy disk contains an MS-DOS (or Windows vfat) file system and mount it properly without additional arguments. However, if it doesn't, here is an example of how to mount a floppy containing MS-DOS files:

```
# mount -t msdos /dev/fd0 /mnt/floppy
```

This shows the basic format of the mount command you would use to mount a floppy disk. You could change msdos to any other supported file system type (described earlier in this chapter) to mount a floppy of that type. Instead of using floppy drive A: (/dev/fd0), you could use drive B: (/dev/fd1) or any other accessible drive. Instead of mounting on /mnt/floppy, you could create any other directory and mount the floppy there.

Here are some other useful options you could add along with the mount command:

- **-t auto** — If you aren't sure exactly what type of file system is contained on the floppy disk (or other medium you are mounting), use the -t auto option to indicate the file system type. The mount command will query the disk to try to guess what type of data it contains.

- **-r** — If you don't want to make changes to the mounted file system (or can't because it is a read-only medium), use this option when you mount it. This will mount it read-only.

- **-w** — This mounts the file system with read/write permission.

Another valuable way to use the mount command has to do with disk images. If you download a CD or floppy disk image from the Internet and you want to see what it contains, you can do so without burning it to CD or floppy. With the image on your hard disk, create a mount point and use the -o loop option to mount it locally. Here's an example:

```
# mkdir /mnt/mycdimage
# mount -o loop whatever-i386-disc1.iso /mnt/mycdimage
```

In this example, the disk image file (whatever-i386-disc1.iso) residing in the current directory is mounted on the /mnt/mycdimage directory I just created. I can now cd to that directory, view the contents of it and copy or use any of its contents. This is useful for downloaded CD images that you want to install software from without having to burn the image to CD. When you are done, just type umount /mnt/cdimage to unmount it.

Other options to mount are available only for a specific file system type. See the mount manual page for those and other useful options.

Using the umount command to unmount a file system

When you are done using a temporary file system, or you want to unmount a permanent file system temporarily, you can use the umount command. This command detaches the file system from its mount point in your Linux file system. To use `umount`, you can give it either a directory name or a device name. For example:

```
# umount /mnt/floppy
```

This unmounts the device (probably /dev/fd0) from the mount point /mnt/floppy. You could also have done this using the form:

```
# umount /dev/fd0
```

In general, it's better to use the directory name, because the `umount` command will fail if the device is mounted in more than one location.

If you get a message that the "device is busy," the `umount` request has failed. The reason is that either a process has a file open on the device or that a you have a shell open with a directory on the device as a current directory. Stop the processes or change to a directory outside of the device you are trying to unmount for the `umount` request to succeed.

An alternative for unmounting a busy device is the `-l` option. With `umount -l` (a lazy unmount), the unmount happens as soon as the device is no longer busy. To unmount a remote NFS file system that is no longer available (for example, the server went down), you can use the `umount -f` option to forcibly unmount the NFS file system.

Using the mkfs command to create a file system

It is possible to create a file system, for any supported file system type, on a disk or partition that you choose. This is done with the `mkfs` command. While this is most useful for creating file systems on hard disk partitions, you can create file systems on floppy disks or re-writable CDs as well.

Here is an example of using `mkfs` to create a file system on a floppy disk:

```
# mkfs -t ext3 /dev/fd0
mke2fs 1.34, (25-Jul-2003)
Filesystem label=
OS type: Linux
Block size=1024 (log=0)
Fragment size=1024 (log=0)
184 inodes, 1440 blocks
72 blocks (5.00%) reserved for the super user
First data block=1
1 block group
8192 blocks per group, 8192 fragments per group
184 inodes per group

Writing inode tables: done

Filesystem too small for a jounal
Writing superblocks and filesystem accounting information: done
```

```
The filesystem will be automatically checked every 32 mounts or
180 days, whichever comes first. Use tune2fs -c or -i to override.
```

You can see the statistics that are output with the formatting done by the mkfs command. The number of inodes and blocks created are output. Likewise, the number of blocks per group and fragments per group are also output. You could now mount this file system (mount /mnt/floppy), change to it as your current directory (cd /mnt/floppy), and create files on it as you please.

Adding a hard disk

Adding a new hard disk to your computer so that it can be used by Linux requires a combination of steps described in previous sections. The general steps are as follows:

1. Install the hard disk hardware.
2. Identify the partitions on the new hard disk.
3. Create the file systems on the new hard disk.
4. Mount the file systems.

The easiest way to add a hard disk to Linux is to have the entire hard disk devoted to a single Linux partition. You can have multiple partitions, however, and assign them each to different types of file systems and different mount points, if you like. The following procedure describes how to add a hard disk containing a single Linux partition. Along the way, however, it also notes which steps you need to repeat to have multiple file systems with multiple mount points.

> **NOTE:** This procedure assumes that Fedora is already installed and working on the computer. If this is not the case, follow the instructions for adding a hard disk on your current operating system. Later, when you install Fedora, you can identify this disk when you are asked to partition your hard disk(s).

1. Install the hard disk into your computer. Follow the manufacturer's instructions for physically installing and connecting the new hard disk. If, presumably, this is a second hard disk, you may need to change jumpers on the hard disk unit itself to have it operate as a slave hard disk. You may also need to change the BIOS settings.
2. Boot your computer to Linux.
3. Determine the device name for the hard disk. As root user from a shell, type:

```
# dmesg | less
```

From the output, look for an indication that the new hard disk was found. For example, if it is a second IDE hard disk, you should see hdb: in the output. For a second SCSI drive, you should see sdb: instead. Be sure you identify the right disk or you will erase all the data from disks you probably want to keep!

4. Use the `fdisk` command to create partitions on the new disk. For example, if you are formatting the second IDE disk (hdb), you could type the following:

```
# fdisk /dev/hdb1
```

5. If the disk had existing partitions on it, you can change or delete those partitions now. Or, you can simply reformat the whole disk to blow everything away. Use p to view all partitions and d to delete a partition.

6. To create a new partition, type the following:

```
n
```

You are asked to choose an extended or primary partition.

7. To choose a primary partition, type the following:

```
p
```

You are asked the partition number.

8. If you are creating the first partition (or for only one partition), type the number one:

```
1
```

You are asked to enter the first cylinder number (with one being the default).

9. To begin at the second cylinder, type the number two as follows:

```
2
```

You are asked to enter the last cylinder.

10. If you are using the entire hard disk, use the last cylinder number shown. Otherwise, choose the ending cylinder number or indicate how many megabytes the partition should have.

11. To create more partitions on the hard disk, repeat steps 6 through 10 for each partition.

12. Type **w** to write changes to the hard disk. At this point, you should be back at the shell.

13. To make a file system on the new disk partition, use the `mkfs` command. By default, this command creates an ext2 file system, which is useable by Linux. To create an ext2 file system on the first partition of the second hard disk, type the following:

```
# mkfs -t ext3 /dev/hdb1
```

If you created multiple partitions, repeat this step for each partition (such as /dev/hdb2, /dev/hdb3, and so on).

> **TIP:** If you don't use `-t ext3` as shown above, an ext2 file system is created by default. Use other commands, or options to this command, to create other file system types. For example, use `mkfs.vfat` to create a VFAT file system, `mkfs.msdos` for DOS, or `mkfs.reiserfs` for Reiser file system type. The `tune2fs` command, described later in this section, can be used to change an ext2 file system to an ext3 file system.

14. Once the file system is created, you can have the partition permanently mounted by editing the `/etc/fstab` and adding the new partition. Here is an example of a line you might add to that file:

```
/dev/hdb1              /abc           ext3         defaults       1 1
```

In this example, the partition (`/dev/hdb1`) is mounted on the `/abc` directory as an ext3 file system. The `defaults` keyword causes the partition to be mounted at boot time. The numbers `1 1` cause the disk to be checked for errors. Add one line like the one shown above for each partition you created.

15. Create the mount point. For example, to mount the partition on `/abc` (as shown in the previous step), type the following:

```
# mkdir /abc
```

Create your other mount points if you created multiple partitions. The next time you boot Fedora, the partition will be automatically mounted on the `/abc` directory, as will any other partitions you added.

After you have created the file systems on your partitions, a nice tool for adjusting those file systems is the `tune2fs` command. Using `tune2fs`, you can change volume labels, how often the file system is checked, and error behavior. You can also use `tune2fs` to change an ext2 file system to an ext3 file system so the file system can use journaling. For example:

```
# tune2fs -j /dev/hdb1
tune2fs 1.35-WIP, (07-Dec-2003)
Creating journal inode: done
This filesystem will be automatically checked every 38 mounts or
180 days, whichever comes first. Use tune2fs -c or -i to override.
```

By adding the `-j` option to `tune2fs`, you can change either the journal size or attach the file system to an external journal block device. After you have used `tune2fs` to change your file system type, you probably need to correct your `/etc/fstab` file to include changing the file system type from ext2 to ext3.

Using RAID disks

RAID (Redundant Arrays of Independent Disks) is used to spread the data used on a computer across multiple disks, while appearing to the operating system as if it is dealing with a single disk partition. Using the different RAID specifications, you can achieve the following advantages:

- **Improved disk performance** — RAID0 uses a feature called *striping*, where data is striped across multiple RAID partitions. Striping can improve disk performance by spreading the hits on a computer's file system across multiple partitions, which are presumably on multiple hard disks.

- **Mirroring** — RAID1 uses partitions from multiple hard disks as mirrors. That way, if one of the partitions becomes corrupted or the hard disk goes down, the data exists on a partition from another disk because it has continuously maintained an exact mirror image of the original partition.

- **Parity** — Although striping can improve performance, it can increase the chance of data loss, since any hard-disk crash in the array can potentially cause the entire RAID device to fail. Using a feature called *parity*, information about the layout of the striped data is kept so that data can be reconstructed if one of the disks in the array crashes. RAID3, 4, and 5 implement different levels of parity.

During installation of Fedora, you can use the Disk Druid window to create RAID0, RAID1, and RAID5 disk arrays. The following procedures describe how to set up RAID disks during installation.

Before you begin creating RAID partitions when you install Fedora, you will probably want to start with a computer that has two or more hard disks. The reason is that, if you don't have multiple hard disks, you won't get the performance gains that come from spreading the hits on your computer among multiple disks. Likewise, mirroring will be ineffective if all RAID partitions are on the same disk, because the failure of a single hard disk would still potentially cause the mirrored partitions to fail as well.

For example, you might begin with 30GB of free disk space on your first hard disk (/dev/hda) and 30GB of free disk space on your second hard disk (/dev/hdb). During the Fedora installation procedure, select to partition your disk with Disk Druid. Then follow this procedure:

1. From the Disk Setup (Disk Druid) window, click the RAID button. A RAID Options window appears.

2. Select Create a Software RAID Partition, and click OK. The Add Partition window appears.

3. With Software RAID selected as the File System Type, choose the drive you want to create the partition on and choose the size (in megabytes). Then click OK.

4. Repeat steps 2 and 3 (presumably creating software RAID partitions on different hard disks until you have created all the RAID partitions you want to use).

5. Click the RAID button again. Select Create a RAID Device [default=/dev/md0] and click OK. The Make RAID Device window appears, as shown in Figure 10-4.

6. You need to select the following information about your RAID device and click OK:

- **Mount Point** — The point in the file system associated with the RAID device. You might be creating the RAID device for a part of the file system for which you expect there to be a lot of hits on the hard disk (such as the /var partition).

- **File System Type** — For a regular Linux partition, choose ext3. You can also select LVM, swap, or VFAT as the file system type.

- **RAID Device** — The first RAID device is typically md0 (for /dev/md0).

- **RAID Level** — Allowable RAID levels are RAID0, RAID1, and RAID5. RAID0 is for striping (essentially dividing the RAID device into stripes across RAID partitions you have selected). RAID1 is for mirroring so that the data is duplicated across all RAID partitions. RAID5 is for parity, so there is always one backup disk if a disk goes bad. You need at least three RAID partitions to use RAID5.

- **RAID Members** — From the RAID partitions you created, select which ones are going to be members of the RAID device you are creating.

- **Number of spares** — Select how many spares are available to the RAID device.

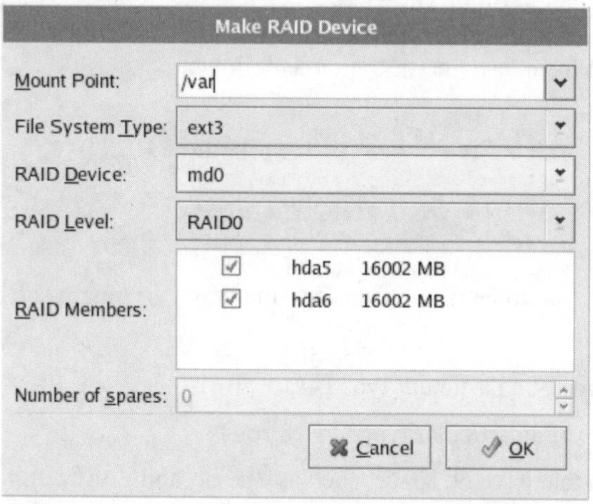

Figure 10-4: Join multiple RAID partitions to form a single RAID device.

The new RAID Device should appear on the Disk Setup (Disk Druid) window. Click Next to continue with installation.

Once installation is complete, you can check your RAID devices by using a variety of tools that come with Fedora. Commands for working with RAID partitions come in the raidtools package. Using raidtools commands, you can list and reconfigure your RAID partitions.

Checking system space

Running out of disk space on your computer is not a happy situation. Using tools that come with Fedora, you can keep track of how much disk space has been used on your computer, and you can keep an eye on users who consume a lot of disk space.

Displaying system space with df

You can display the space available in your file systems using the df command. To see the amount of space available on all of the mounted file systems on your Linux computer, type **df** with no options:

```
$ df
Filesystem    1k-blocks      Used   Available   Use%   Mounted on
/dev/hda3     30645460    2958356    26130408    11%   /
/dev/hda2        46668       8340       35919    19%   /boot
/dev/fd0          1412         13        1327     1%   /mnt/floppy
```

The output here shows the space available on the hard disk partition mounted on the root partition (/dev/hda1), /boot partition (/dev/hda2), and the floppy disk mounted on the /mnt/floppy directory (/dev/fd0). Disk space is shown in 1K blocks. To produce output in a more human-readable form, use the -h option as follows:

```
$ df -h
Filesystem       Size  Used  Avail  Use%  Mounted on
/dev/hda3         29G  2.9G    24G   11%  /
/dev/hda2         46M  8.2M    25M   19%  /boot
/dev/fd0         1.4M   13k   1.2M    1%  /mnt/floppy
```

With the df -h option, output appears in a friendlier megabyte or gigabyte listing. Other options with df let you:

- Print only file systems of a particular type (-t type)
- Exclude file systems of a particular type (-x type)
- Include file systems that have no space, such as /proc and /dev/pts (-a)
- List only available and used inodes (-i)
- Display disk space in certain block sizes (--block-size=#)

Checking disk usage with du

To find out how much space is being consumed by a particular directory (and its subdirectories), you can use the du command. With no options, du lists all directories below the current directory, along with the space consumed by each directory. At the end, du produces total disk space used within that directory structure.

The du command is a good way to check how much space is being used by a particular user (du /home/user1) or in a particular file system partition (du /var). By default, disk space is displayed in 1K block sizes. To make the output more friendly (in kilobytes, megabytes, and gigabytes), use the -h option as follows:

```
$ du -h /home/jake
114k    /home/jake/httpd/stuff
234k    /home/jake/httpd
137k    /home/jake/uucp/data
701k    /home/jake/uucp
1.0M    /home/jake
```

The output shows the disk space used in each directory under the home directory of the user named jake (/home/jake). Disk space consumed is shown in kilobytes (k) and megabytes (M). The total space consumed by /home/jake is shown on the last line.

Finding disk consumption with find

The find command is a great way to find file consumption of your hard disk using a variety of criteria. You can get a good idea of where disk space can be recovered by finding files that are over a certain size or were created by a particular person.

> **NOTE:** You must be root user to run this command effectively, unless you are just checking your personal files.

In the following example, the find command searches the root file system (/) for any files owned by the user named jake (-user jake) and prints the filenames. The output of the find command is then listed with a long listing in size order (ls -ldS). Finally that output is sent to the file /tmp/jake. When you read the file /tmp/jake, you will find all of the files that are owned by the user jake, listed in size order. Here is the command line:

```
# find / -user jake -print -xdev | xargs ls -ldS > /tmp/jake
```

> **TIP:** The -xdev option prevents file systems other than the selected file system from being searched. This is a good way to cut out a lot of junk that may be output from the /proc file system. It could also keep large remotely mounted file systems from being searched.

The next example is similar to the previous one, except that instead of looking for a user's files, this command line looks for files that are larger than 100 kilobytes (-size 100k):

```
# find / -size 100k -print -xdev | xargs ls -ldS > /tmp/size
```

You can save yourself a lot of disk space by just removing some of the largest files that are no longer needed. Open the /tmp/size file in this example and large files are sorted by size.

Monitoring System Performance

If your Linux system is being used as a multiuser computer, sharing the processing power of that computer can be a major issue. Likewise, any time you can stop a runaway process or reduce the overhead of an unnecessary program running, your Linux server can do a better job serving files, Web pages, or e-mail to the people that rely on it.

Utilities are included with Linux that can help you monitor the performance of your Linux system. The kinds of features you want to monitor in Linux include CPU usage, memory usage (RAM and swap space), and overall load on the system. The following sections describe tools for monitoring Linux.

Watch computer usage with System Monitor

If you like visual representations of your system use, the System Monitor provides a great way to see how much your system is being used. To open the System Monitor from the red hat menu, select System Tools → System Monitor. Figure 10-5 shows the System Monitor window with the Resource Monitor tab selected.

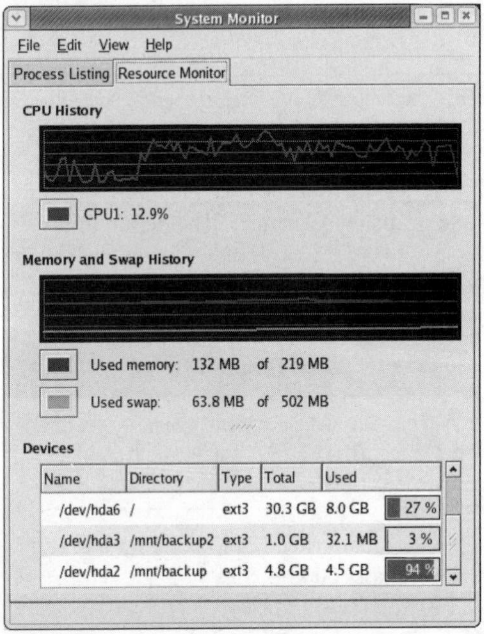

Figure 10-5: System Monitor graphically displays your system's CPU and memory usage.

On the Resource Monitor window, lines scroll from right to left, indicating the percentage of your CPU being used as it rises and falls. You can also see how much of your total memory (RAM) is being used at the moment (and over time), as well as the amount of swap space being used. Scroll the devices at the bottom of the window to see the space being consumed on each of your hard disk partitions.

Click the Process Listing tab to see a listing of processes that are running currently. Click the columns in that tab to sort processes by name, user (who launched the process), memory use, percentage of CPU being consumed by the process, and process ID.

The example in Figure 10-5 shows a computer that is running with only 128MB of RAM. The Memory Used is running near the maximum, indicating the likely occurrence of performance problems as RAM fills up and data has to be moved to swap space. The CPU used is only about 19 percent, which indicates that the CPU is keeping up with the demand.

Monitoring CPU usage with top

Start the top utility in a Terminal window, and it displays the top CPU consuming processes on your computer. Every five seconds, top will determine which processes are consuming the most CPU time and display them in descending order on your screen.

By adding the -S option to top, you can have the display show you the cumulative CPU time that the process, as well as any child processes that may already have exited, has spent. If you want to change how often the screen is updated, you can add the -d secs option, where secs is replaced by the number of seconds between updates.

By default, processes are sorted by CPU usage. You can sort processes numerically by PID (press N), by age (press A), by resident memory usage (press M), by time (press T), or back to CPU usage (press P). Figure 10-6 shows an example of top running in a Terminal window.

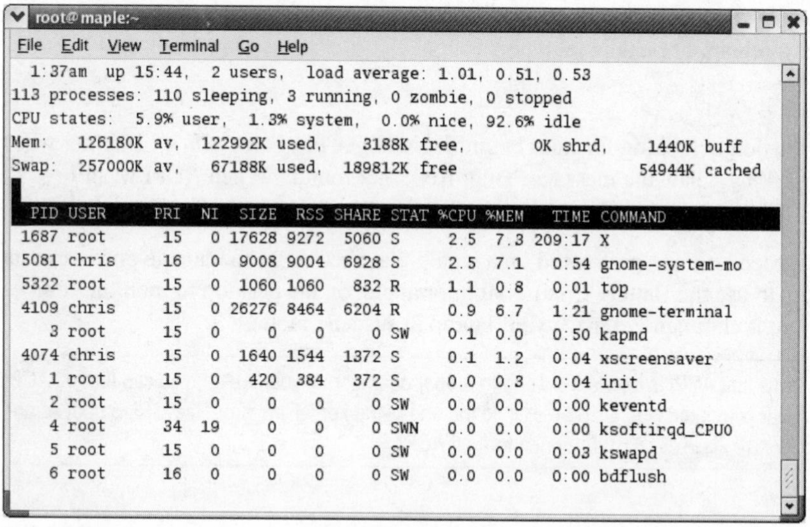

Figure 10-6: Running processes appear in CPU usage order by default in the top window.

Monitoring power usage on laptop computers

To effectively use a laptop computer, you need to be able to monitor and manage the laptop's power usage. Using tools provided in Fedora, you can configure your laptop to:

- Monitor the battery level.
- Notify you when the battery is low.
- Notify you when the battery is fully charged.
- Show when the laptop is plugged in.
- Suspend the current session.

Fedora offers two facilities that do power management: APM and ACPI.

- **Advanced Power** Management (APM) — APM can be used to monitor the battery of your notebook and notify user-level programs to tell you when your battery is low. It can also be used to place your laptop into suspend mode.
- Advanced Configuration and Power Interface (ACPI) — Besides monitoring power features on your laptop, ACPI can also do thermal control, motherboard configuration, and change power states.

Many older laptops do not include support for ACPI in the BIOS, so you must use APM to monitor and manage your batteries. For some newer laptops, ACPI may be required. In general, ACPI offers a more complete feature set for power management, but APM has more user-level support today.

To check whether ACPI or APM are supported on your Fedora system, you can use the dmesg command after a reboot. For example, type:

```
# dmesg | less
```

Page through the output looking for lines beginning with ACPI or amp. On a computer where APM wasn't working, I saw the message "amp: BIOS not found." When ACPI wasn't working, I saw the message "ACPI: System description tables not found."

The following procedure was performed on a laptop that used APM to manage power events. It describes how to use the Battery Charge Monitor applet on the desktop to monitor your battery and the apm command to place your laptop in suspend mode.

> **NOTE:** If it seems that ACPI is interfering with the proper operation of your laptop, you can turn off ACPI when you boot your computer. Add acpi=off to the end of the kernel line (from the GRUB boot screen or the /boot/grub/grub.conf file) to turn off ACPI.

Using the battery status applet

If you are using the GNOME desktop, you can add a Battery Status Monitor to your panel to keep track of the power levels of your battery. The following procedure steps you through adding the monitor to your panel and configuring it to behave as you like:

1. Right-click the GNOME panel; then select Add to Panel → Utility → Battery Charge Monitor. When the Battery Charge Monitor applet appears on the panel, you can stop here if you like. The applet will:

   - Include a battery icon that appears green (with the battery above a 40% charge), yellow (25%-40%), orange (15%-25%) or red (under 15%).

   - Show a power cord if the laptop is plugged in.

   - Notify you with at pop-up window when the battery charge is low.

   - Notify you with a pop-up window when the battery is fully charged.

   - Display the percent charged and whether the battery is currently charging when you move the mouse pointer over the applet icon.

   Continue with the following steps if you want to change that behavior.

2. Right-click the Battery Charge monitor applet, then select Preferences. Figure 10-7 shows the Battery Charge Monitor Preferences window and the applet in the panel.

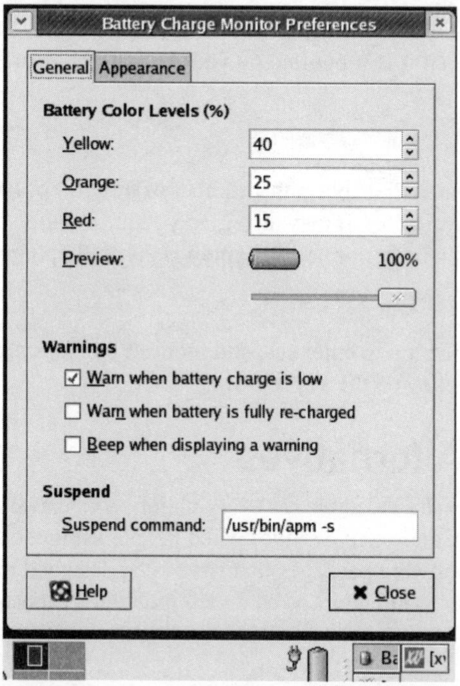

Figure 10-7: View battery status and change preferences with the Battery Charge Monitor.

3. Change any of the following values related to your battery monitor:

    - **Battery color levels** — You can change the levels at which the battery icon changes from green, yellow, orange, and red.

    - **Warnings** — Select whether or not you want to be notified (with a pop-up) when the battery charge is low or fully charged. You can also select to have the laptop beep if either case is true.

    - **Suspend command** — Add a command to put the laptop in suspend mode. (Try the apm -s command as described in the next section.) With a Suspend command set, you can right-click the icon and choose Suspend Computer to suspend your laptop.

    - **Appearance** — Select the Appearance tab. From there, you can choose which icons appear on the applet (battery, power cord, or percent charged). You can also change whether the progress bar on the battery moves up or down as power empties.

> **NOTE:** If, when you try to add the Battery Charge Monitor icon to the panel, a pop-up window tells you that the operation fails, it may be that the apmd daemon isn't running. You can try starting the apmd service (as root user; type **service apmd start**). If, however, APM is shown as not supported in your dmesg file, you can try turning on APM support in your laptop's BIOS.

Using apm to enter suspend mode

The apm command lets you view information about your computer's power management and put the computer in suspend mode (if it is supported on your laptop). Here are some examples of using the apm command:

```
# apm -m
```

Using the -m option, the apm command displays the number of minutes of battery life remaining (if that information is available). It may also give you information about the status of how the battery is charging and whether or not the laptop is currently plugged in.

```
# apm -s
```

The -s option of apm causes the laptop to enter suspend mode. You can start up the laptop again, in most cases, by pressing a key on the keyboard.

Choosing Software Alternatives

Because several software packages are available for every major service available in Linux (such as mail, printing, and so on), there will be times when people using the system will prefer one service over another. Software packages that have been designed to work with the alternatives system can be configured in Fedora to let an administrator choose which of the alternatives to a particular service he or she wants to use by default.

Selecting mail and printing alternatives

Beginning with Red Hat Linux 7.3, which was the first version to offer the alternatives feature, two major services were configured to use alternatives: mail transport and printing services. The alternatives facility lets users choose the following, related to mail transport and printing:

- **Mail Transport Agent (MTA)** — If the sendmail, exim and postfix mail transport agents are installed, as an administrator you can choose which of those services is the default for sending and receiving e-mail.

- **Printing** — If both LPRng and CUPS printing services are installed, you can choose which service is the default for printing documents.

As an administrator, you still need to configure each alternative service to work. Descriptions for configuring sendmail and postfix mail-transport agents are contained in Chapter 19. Information on setting up the CUPS printing service is in Chapter 17. (LPRng is no longer delivered with Fedora , although it is still available from sites such as `rpmfind.net`. Likewise, the feature for switching the printing service described below is not included with Fedora, but can still be found in earlier Red Hat Linux systems.)

In terms of setting up the alternatives side of mail services, much of the work of creating links so that the services can be chosen has already been done. Links relating to the default services are set up in the `/etc/alternatives` directory. Definitions that identify the alternative components of sendmail, exim, and postfix mail servers are contained in the `/var/lib/alternatives` directory.

Because much of the configuration has been done in advance, the first step in switching between the different mail services installed on your computer is only a couple of clicks away. To switch the default mail services on your computer, do the following:

1. To switch mail service, select System Tools → Mail Transport Agent Switcher. The switcher window appears.

2. Click on the service you want to switch to —Sendmail, Exim or Postfix for mail. (If the one you want is already selected, you can just cancel.)

    If the switch is successful, a pop-up window tells you to restart the new service.

3. Close the pop-up window.

The next time your computer boots, your new printing or mail service takes over that service. All the links are in place and the start-up scripts are changed. However, your system is still running the old service. The start-up scripts for those services are in the `/etc/init.d` directory. They are as follows:

- `exim`   For the Exim mail service
- `sendmail`   For the Sendmail mail service
- `postfix`   For the Postfix mail service

To stop the old service so that the new one can take over, type the following (replacing *service* with the name of the service you want to stop):

```
# /etc/init.d/service stop
```

To start the new service, type the following (replacing *service* with the name of the service you want to start):

```
# /etc/init.d/service start
```

Providing that the new service was configured properly, it should now be available to the users of your computer.

Using mail alternatives

The mail-transport services that the alternatives facility allows you to change rely on many of the same command names. For example, both Postfix and Sendmail have a `newalias` command and `mailq` commands for updating aliases and checking the mail queue, respectively.

So, to the user, a change in the local mail service should (in theory) be nearly invisible. Users can send mail as they always did and the fact that a different mail transport is being used should make no difference.

Getting Linux Software "up2date"

The up2date facility is the preferred method from Red Hat, Inc. for updating Fedora and Red Hat Enterprise Linux software. Using up2date, you can determine if any software packages in your Linux distribution have updates available, and you can ask to have them downloaded and installed automatically.

Fixes and improvements continue after a distribution, such as Fedora Core or Red Hat Enterprise Linux, is released. You can incorporate those fixes and features into your system, using a connection to the Internet and up2date.

This section tells you how to determine which updates are available to your Fedora system. Then it describes how you can register to use the up2date tool to gather those updates.

With the advent of Fedora Core, the up2date facility has been modified to allow you to not only download software from Red Hat FTP sites, but also from repositories of software built to work with the `apt` and `yum` facilities.

CROSS REFERENCE: For detailed descriptions of apt and yum, refer to Chapter 5.

Getting updates from Fedora repositories

Fedora includes software that automatically notifies you of available updates and lets you easily download and install them on your Fedora system. The service is called up2date.

The up2date utility provides a mechanism that can:

- Alert you to the latest fixes and enhancements available for Fedora.
- Install the packages that include those changes to your system.

Using the Red Hat Network alert notification tool

To start the process of getting notifications of updates, you don't have to go further than your desktop. A round icon with an exclamation point in the middle appears on the desktop panel, ready to help you check for critical updates to Fedora.

> **NOTE:** If the Red Hat Network Alert icon is not on your desktop, you can put it there by selecting the red hat menu on your desktop panel, then clicking System Tools → Red Hat Network Alert Icon.

Figure 10-8 shows you what the Red Hat Network Alert icon looks like when updates are available. (If no updates are available, a blue checkmark icon appears instead.)

Figure 10-8: The Red Hat Network alert notification tool appears as a round icon on your desktop panel.

Right-click the icon and select Configuration from the context menu. The Red Hat Network Alert Notification Tool window appears. Follow these steps to begin the process of getting updates:

1. From the Red Hat Network Alert Notification Tool window, click Forward. The Terms of Service window appears.

2. Read the Terms of Service. Then either click Forward (to continue) or click Remove From Panel (to remove the icon and not use the service). If you continue, the Proxy Configuration window appears.

3. If you need to go through a proxy server to get to the Internet for HTTP (Web) service, click Enable HTTP Proxy, identify the location of the proxy server, and then add any authentication information you need to connect to that server. Click Forward to continue.

4. On the Configuration Complete window that appears, click Apply. At this point, the red icon turns blue and changes from an exclamation point to a check mark.

5. Because Fedora Core is not an official Red Hat product, you do not need to register with Red Hat Network to get updates. For Red Hat Enterprise Linux, however, you can

register with Red Hat Network to check for software updates, as described in the next section.

Registering with Red Hat Network

To register a Red Hat Enterprise Linux system with Red Hat Network, you can click the RHN icon, use the `rhn_register` command or simply look for the Red Hat Network Configuration window to pop up when you run up2date. Using any of these methods requires a connection to the Internet and root access to your computer — the latter because the registration process needs to access your computer's RPM database. Though only the first computer you register can receive free automatic updates, you can register as many computers as you want with this tool. Here's how it works:

1. From a Terminal window type **rhn_register**. The first time you run this, the Red Hat Network Configuration window appears.

2. Select each of the following tabs to fill out basic configuration information:

   • **General** — Select an RHN server to get your updates. One should already be entered. If you need to go through an http proxy or provide a user name and password to reach the server, enter that information on this tab as well.

   • **Retrieval /Installation** — Set preferences here related to whether or not packages are immediately installed after they are downloaded and whether or not they are kept on your hard disk or deleted after installation. By default, packages are installed after retrieval, verified using GPG, and the RPMs are removed after they are installed. Packages that have had modifications to configuration files are not upgraded.

   • **Package Exceptions** — By default, any kernel packages are not upgraded. You can add other packages, or even selected files, to skip.

3. If you do not have the Red Hat, Inc. public key on your keyring (and you selected to use GPG as is set by default), you are prompted to install the key. Click Yes to install the key. The Welcome to Red Hat Update Agent window appears.

4. Click Forward. The Review the Red Hat Privacy Statement window appears.

5. Read the explanation of the registration procedure and click Next. The Red Hat Privacy Statement appears. This statement tells you, among other things, how your personal information is used and how Red Hat uses cookies to track activities.

6. Read the privacy statement. If it is acceptable, click Forward. The Login window appears.

7. Add information to create a user account and click Forward. The information you provide includes:

   • **User name** — Type a name of your choosing.

   • **Password** — Type a password (then type it again in the next box to verify it).

   • **E-mail address** — Type the address at which you would like Red Hat to contact you.

The Register a User Account window appears.

Add the information and click Forward. The next screen asks for some personal information, including name, address, phone number, fax number, and how you would like to be contacted (e-mail, regular mail, phone, fax, or e-newsletter).

8. A Register a System Profile-Hardware window appears. This window displays information about your Red Hat Linux version, host name, IP address, CPU mode, CPU speed, and memory.

9. Select a profile name (the host name is used by default) or service ID number (which can be the computer's serial number) and click Forward.

The registration process begins building a list of packages installed on your computer. These are gathered so they can become part of your system profile. These packages are then displayed in the Register a System Profile-Packages window.

10. Check that the packages that appear in the window are all okay to include in your system profile (unselecting the ones you don't want to include) and click Next. The Send Profile Information to Red Hat Network window appears.

11. Click Forward to register the system-profile information with the Red Hat Network. (Or choose not to send the information by clicking Cancel.) Your information is sent and the Registration Finished window appears.

12. Click Forward to end the session.

After you have finished registering with Red Hat Network you can go to the RNH site and log in to use the service. You are now also ready to run the up2date command to update your software packages.

Getting Updates

After you have registered your computer with Red Hat Network you can use the up2date command (or right-click the notification icon and click Launch up2date) to find and install updates. As with rhn_register, you need root access to your computer to run up2date. This is because up2date needs permission to change configuration files and install packages.

The up2date configuration file (/etc/sysconfig/rhn/up2date) determines the behavior of up2date. Here are a few of the key settings in the up2date configuration file to help you understand what up2date will do when you launch it:

- Debugging is disabled by default. Change debug=0 to debug=1 to turn on debugging if you are having trouble with up2date.

- Downloaded packages are stored in the /var/spool/up2date directory. After they are installed, the packages are deleted (by default).

- The up2date log file is /var/log/up2date. You can open the file in any text editor to see descriptions of everything up2date did.

- Any packages that begin with the word `kernel` are skipped. Add other package names you want skipped to the `pkgSkipList=kernel*` entry. You can use shell wildcard characters, such as the asterisk shown in the example, to match all kernel packages.

The up2date configuration file contains other settings that you can use to further refine your up2date session. For example, you can identify an HTTP proxy server, change the number of failed network-connection attempts that must occur before an exit, or indicate that you want to retrieve source packages along with the binary packages.

The up2date sources file (`/etc/sysconfig/rhn/sources`) is another configuration file you might consider making enhancements to. In particular, if you want to get updates of packages already installed on your system from yum or apt repositories, you can add the locations of those repositories to this file. The following two lines contain examples of entries you could add to the sources file for `yum` and `apt` repositories, respectively:

```
yum fedora-core-i386-stable http://download.fedora.us/fedora/fedora/2/i386
apt freshrpms-9-i386 http://ayo.freshrpms.net/fedora/linux/1/i386 updates freshrpms
```

The `yum` example shows the service as `yum` and the channel name is `fedora-core-i386-stable`, followed by the location of the yum repository. In the `apt` example, the repository is divided into three parts: the host name, path, and final directory. Notice that in this example, both `updates` and `freshrpms` directories are available repositories. Once you have added a line similar to the ones just shown, they appear as channels in the Channel window when you run up2date.

To use the official locations for packages from Red Hat Inc., you can simply use the default up2date settings. Here's an example of an up2date session:

1. Type **up2date** or click the notification icon and select Launch up2date. If your system does not yet have the Red Hat public key, you will be asked if you want to have up2date install it. (The key is needed to verify that the packages you are receiving are signed by Red Hat.)

2. Click Yes to install the key. The Red Hat Update Agent window appears.

3. Click Forward. The Channels window appears.

4. The Channel indicates the version of Red Hat Linux you are running. Select the Channel appropriate to your Red Hat installation and click Forward. The Update Agent begins checking your available packages.

5. The Available Package Updates window appears, displaying packages available for updates. Click each package you want to update or click Select All Packages to have all applicable packages updated. You can click on a package and then click View Advisory to see which advisories are addressed by updates for the package.

6. Click Forward to continue. The Update Agent begins testing packages to check for dependencies among the packages you are updating. If any dependencies arise from the

packages you selected, the Packages Required to Solve Dependencies window appears, listing the additional packages you need.

7. Click Forward to have the packages shown included in the updates (or click the back button to change your package list). The Retrieving Packages window appears and notes the progress as the packages are downloaded from the Red Hat Network.

8. Click Forward to begin downloading the packages to your computer. (This may take a while, depending on the speed of your Internet connection and the number of packages you are downloading.)

9. When all packages are downloaded, click Forward. The Installing Packages window appears.

10. Click Forward to begin installing the packages you have downloaded.

11. When all the packages are installed, click Next. The All Finished window appears, displaying the package name and version for each package that was installed.

12. Click Finish to end the session.

If you are interested in seeing how the upgrades went, you can do the following:

- Check the log file (/var/log/up2date).

- See if any packages were left behind in the spool directory (/var/spool/up2date).

Though you don't necessarily have to reboot Linux at this point, if new daemon processes are installed with any of the updated packages you might want to restart them. For example, to restart your Web server (httpd daemon), you could type the following as root user:

```
# /etc/init.d/httpd restart
```

Using the Red Hat Network

If you decide to create an account with Red Hat Network you can log in to the RHN site and take advantage of the services it offers. Services that you receive simply by registering with the Red Hat Network Web site include:

- The ability to view complete listings of available errata, including security, bug fixes, and enhancement alerts. Errata are organized by Red Hat Linux version, to take the guesswork out of figuring out compatibility issues.

- E-mail alerts of errata and notification of new packages available to fix the problem.

- An entitlement manager that shows you which systems you are entitled to manage through RHN and lets you add more systems.

- A feature for scheduling actions, such as automatic package update at a specified time.

Go to the Red Hat Network site (rhn.redhat.com) and log in using the user name and account you created during the rhn_register session described earlier. Traverse the RHN site using links on this page. Available sections include:

- **Your RHN** — Contains notifications of the systems that may contain outdated packages. Sections in Your RNN include: Your Account (which contains personal information, such as name, address, e-mail, and so on) and Your Preferences (where you can specify whether or not you want to receive e-mail errata).

- **Systems** — Lets you view a System List, which contains all the systems you have registered with RHN, or use a search tool to search your list of systems.

- **Errata** — From the Errata page you can display all errata, show only those that apply to your system, or do keyword searches of available errata.

- **Channels** — A channel designates a version of Red Hat Enterprise Linux that has package updates associated with it. By selecting the Channel List in this section, you can see what package versions are available for the Red Hat Enterprise Linux version you are using.

- **Schedule** — You can schedule package installations to occur at a later time. From this page you can also see pending, completed, and archived actions.

- **Help** — For more help with Red Hat Network, the Help Desk offers the RHN FAQ, a customer-service support link, support forums, and the RHN Reference Guide.

Summary

Although you may be using Fedora as a single-user system, many of the tasks you must perform to keep your computer running are defined as administrator tasks. A special user account called the root user is needed to do many of the things necessary to keep Fedora working as you would like it to. If you are administering a Fedora system that is used by lots of people, the task of administration becomes even larger. You must be able to add and support users, maintain the file systems, and ensure that system performance serves your users well.

To help the administrator, Fedora comes with a variety of command-line utilities and graphical windows for configuring and maintaining your system. The kudzu program can be used to probe and reconfigure Fedora when you add or remove hardware. Commands such as mkfs and mount let you create and mount file systems, respectively. Tools like System Monitor and top let you monitor system performance.

Another important part of system administration is keeping up with the latest software fixes and enhancements to Fedora and Red Hat Linux. Using the up2date facility, which is part of the Red Hat Network, you can automatically download and install updates to software packages on your system.

## Chapter 11

Setting Up and Supporting Users

In This Chapter

- Creating user accounts
- Setting user defaults
- Creating portable desktops
- Providing support to users
- Deleting user accounts
- Checking disk quotas
- Sending mail to all users

One of the more fundamental tasks of administering a Linux system is setting up and supporting user accounts. Computers, after all, are tools to be used by people. Apocalyptic science fiction plots aside, computers have no purpose without users.

When you install Fedora, you are required to create the root (administrator) user account. The first time you boot Fedora, you are asked to create a regular user account, using any name you choose. Several other administrative user accounts that you will probably never use directly are set up automatically.

> **CROSS-REFERENCE:** For a description of the root user account and how to use it, see Chapter 10.

This chapter discusses the basics of setting up a user account and offers tips on easing the burden of supporting a large number of Linux users.

Creating User Accounts

Every person who uses your Fedora system should have a separate user account. Having a user account provides each person with an area in which to securely store files, as well as a means of tailoring his or her user interface (GUI, path, environment variables, and so on) to suit the way that he or she uses the computer.

> **CROSS-REFERENCE**: If you have multiple users, you'll also need to be concerned about backup and recovery issues. See Chapter 13 for more information.

You can add user accounts to your Fedora system in several ways. This chapter describes how to use the `useradd` command to add user accounts to Fedora from the command line, and how to use the User Manager window to add users from the desktop.

> **NOTE**: If you are using Security Enhanced Linux, `useradd`, `usermod`, and other user-related commands may work differently than the way in which they are shown here. See Chapter 28 for more information on SE Linux.

Adding users with useradd

The most straightforward method for creating a new user from the shell is with the `useradd` command. After opening a Terminal window with root permission, you simply invoke the `useradd` command at the command prompt, with details of the new account as parameters.

The only required parameter to `useradd` is the login name of the user, but you will probably want to include some additional information. Each item of account information is preceded by a single letter option code with a dash in front of it. Table 11-1 lists the options that are available with the `useradd` command.

Table 11-1: useradd Command Options

Option	Description
-c "comment"	Provide a description of the new user account. Usually just the person's full name. Replace comment with the name of the user account. If the comment contains multiple words, use quote marks.
-d home_dir	Set the home directory to use for the account. The default is to name it the same as the login name and to place it in /home. Replace home_dir with the directory name to use.
-D	Rather than create a new account, save the supplied information as the new default settings for any new accounts that are created.
-e expire_date	Assign the expiration date for the account in MM/DD/YYYY format. Replace expire_date with the expiration date to use.
-f inactivity	Set the number of days after a password expires until the account is permanently disabled. Setting this to 0 disables the account immediately after the password has expired. Setting it to -1 disables the option, which is the default behavior. Replace inactivity with the number to use.

Option	Description
-g *group*	Set the primary group (as listed in the /etc/group file) that the new user will be in. Replace *group* with the group name to use.
-G *grouplist*	Add the new user to the supplied comma-separated list of groups.
-k *skel_dir*	Set the skeleton directory containing initial configuration files and login scripts that should be copied to a new user's home directory. This parameter can only be used in conjunction with the -m option. Replace *skel_dir* with the directory name to use.
-m	Automatically create the user's home directory and copy the files in the skeleton directory (/etc/skel) to it.
-M	Do not create the new user's home directory, even if the default behavior is set to create it.
-n	Turn off the default behavior of creating a new group that matches the name and user ID of the new user.
-o	Use with -u *uid* to create a user account that has the same UID as another user name. (This effectively lets you have two different users with authority over the same set of files and directories.)
-p *passwd*	Enter a password for the account you are adding. This must be an encrypted password. Instead of adding an encrypted password here, you can simply use the passwd *user* command later to add a password for *user*.
-r	Allows you to create a new account with a user ID in the range reserved for system accounts.
-s *shell*	Specify the command shell to use for this account. Replace *shell* with the command shell.
-u *user_id*	Specify the user ID number for the account. The default behavior is to automatically assign the next available number. Replace *user_id* with the ID number.

As an example, let's create an account for a new user named Mary Smith with a login name of mary. First, log in as root, then type the following command:

```
# useradd -c "Mary Smith" mary
```

> **TIP:** When you choose a user name, don't begin with a number (for example, 06jsmith). Also, it is best to use all lowercase letters, no control characters or spaces, and a maximum of eight characters. The `useradd` command allows up to 32 characters, but some applications can't deal with user names that long. Tools such as `ps` display UIDs instead of names if names are too long. Having users named Jsmith and jsmith can cause confusion with programs (such as sendmail) that don't distinguish case.

Next, set Mary's initial password using the `passwd` command. It prompts you to type the password twice. (Asterisks are shown here to represent the password you type. Nothing is actually displayed when you type the password.)

```
# passwd mary
Changing password for user mary.
New password: *******
Retype new password: *******
```

> **CROSS-REFERENCE:** Refer to Chapter 14 for tips on picking good passwords.

In creating the account for Mary, the `useradd` command performs several actions:

- Reads the `/etc/login.defs` file to get default values to use when creating accounts.
- Checks command-line parameters to find out which default values to override.
- Creates a new user entry in the `/etc/passwd` and `/etc/shadow` files based on the default values and command-line parameters.
- Creates any new group entries in the `/etc/group` file.
- Creates a home directory based on the user's name and located in the `/home` directory.
- Copies any files located within the `/etc/skel` directory to the new home directory. This usually includes login and application startup scripts.

The preceding example uses only a few of the available `useradd` options. Most account settings are assigned using default values. Here is an example that uses a few more options:

```
# useradd -m -g users -G wheel,sales -s /bin/tcsh -c "Mary Smith" mary
```

In this case, the `useradd` command is told to create a home directory for `mary` (`-m`), make `users` the primary group she belongs to (`-g`), add her to the groups `wheel` and `sales`, and assign `tcsh` as her primary command shell (`-s`). This results in a line similar to the following being added to the `/etc/passwd` file:

```
mary:x:502:100:Mary Smith:/home/mary:/bin/tcsh
```

In the `/etc/passwd` file, each line represents a single user account record. Each field is separated from the next by a colon (`:`) character. The field's position in the sequence determines what it is. As you can see, the login name is first. The password field contains an `x` because we are using a shadow password file to store encrypted password data. The user ID selected by the `useradd` command was 502. The primary group ID is 100, which corresponds to the `users` group in the `/etc/group` file. The comment field was correctly set to Mary Smith, the home directory was automatically assigned as `/home/mary`, and the command shell was assigned as `/bin/tcsh`, exactly as specified with the `useradd` options.

By leaving out many of the options (as I did in the first useradd example), defaults are assigned in most cases. For example, by not using `-g users` or `-G wheel,sales`, a group named mary would have been created and assigned to the new user. Likewise, excluding `-s /bin/tcsh`, causes `/bin/bash` to be assigned as the default shell.

The `/etc/group` file holds information about the different groups on your Fedora system and the users who belong to them. Groups are useful for allowing multiple people to share access to the same files while denying access to others. If you peek at the `/etc/group` file, you should find something similar to this:

```
bin:x:1:root,bin,daemon
daemon:x:2:root,bin,daemon
sys:x:3:root,bin,adm
adm:x:4:root,adm,daemon
tty:x:5:
disk:x:6:root
lp:x:7:daemon,lp
mem:x:8:
kmem:x:9:
wheel:x:10:root,joe,mary
       .
       .
       .
nobody:x:99:
users:x:100:
chris:x:500
sheree:x:501
sales:x:601:bob,jane,joe,mary
```

Each line in the group file contains the name of a group, the group ID number associated with it, and a list of users in that group. By default, each user is added to his or her own group, beginning with GID 500. Note that `mary` was added to the `wheel` and `sales` groups instead of having her own group.

It is actually rather significant that `mary` was added to the `wheel` group. By doing this, you grant her the ability to use the `sudo` command to run commands as the root user (provided that `sudo` was configured as described in Chapter 10).

In this example, we used the `-g` option to assign `mary` to the `users` group. If you leave off the `-g` parameter, the default behavior is for `useradd` to create a new group with the same name and ID number as the user, which is assigned as the new user's primary group. For example, look at the following `useradd` command:

```
# useradd -m -G wheel,sales -s /bin/tcsh -c "Mary Smith" mary
```

It would result in a /etc/passwd line like this:

```
mary:x:502:502:Mary Smith:/home/mary:/bin/tcsh
```

It would also result in a new group line like this:

```
mary:x:502:
```

Note that the user ID and group ID fields now have the same number. If you set up all of your users this way, you will have a unique group for every user on the system, which allows for increased flexibility in the sharing of files among your users.

Adding users with User Manager

If you prefer a graphical window for adding, changing, and deleting user accounts, you can use the User Manager window. To open the window from the GNOME desktop, click System Settings → Users and Groups (or type system-config-users from a Terminal window as root user). Figure 11-1 shows an example of that window.

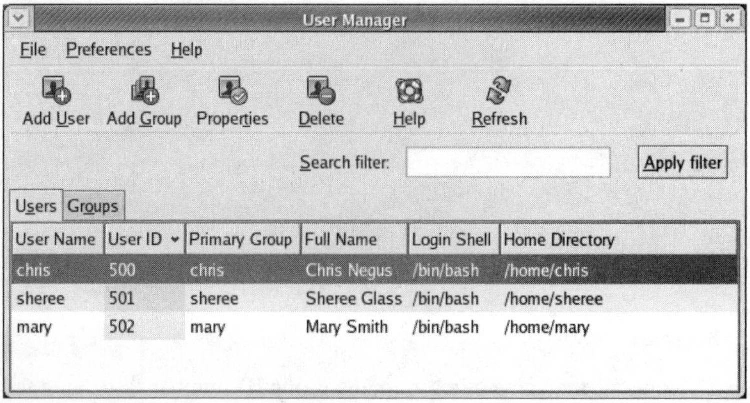

Figure 11-1: Manage users from the User Manager window.

When you open the User Manager window, you see a list of all regular users who are currently added to your computer. Administrative users (UID 1 through 100) are not displayed. For each user, you can see the user name, UID, primary group, full name, login shell, and home directory. Click on any of those headings to sort the users by that information.

To add a new user from the User Manager window, do the following:

1. Click the Add User icon to open the Create New User window (see Figure 11-2).

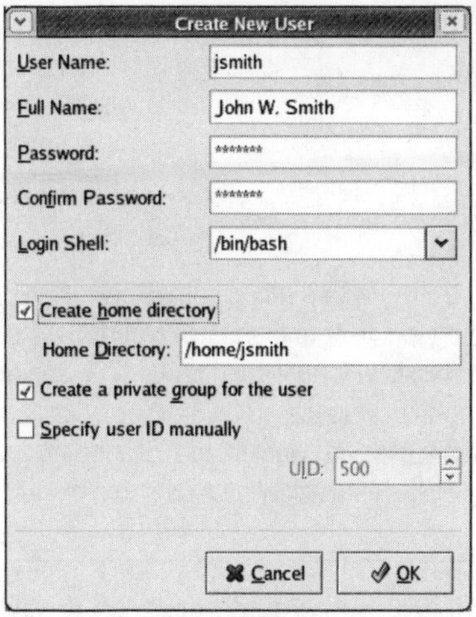

Figure 11-2: The Create New User window

2. Type the requested information in the following fields:

- **User Name** — A single word to describe the user. Typically, the user name is eight characters, all lowercase, containing the user's real first name, last name, or (more often) a combination of the two (such as jwjones).

- **Full Name** — The user's full name (usually first name, middle initial, and last name). This name is typically just used for display, so using upper- and lowercase is fine.

- **Password** — The user's initial password. (Ask the user to change this password the first time he or she logs in to the new account, using the `passwd` command.)

- **Confirm Password** — Type the password again, to make sure you entered it correctly.

- **Login Shell** — The default shell (for entering typed commands) that the user sees when first logging in to Fedora from a character display.

- **Create home directory** — By default, this box is selected and the user's home directory (as indicated by the Home Directory field) is created automatically.

- **Home Directory** — By default, the user is given a home directory of the user's name in the `/home` directory. (For example, the user sheree would be assigned `/home/sheree` as her home directory.) Change this field if you want to assign the user to a different home directory.

- **Create a private group for the user** — Check this box if you want a group by the same name as the user, created for this user. The name is added to the `/etc/group` file. This feature is referred to as user private groups (UPGs).

TIP: Using UPGs can be a benefit for sharing a directory of files among several users. Here's an example:

```
# useradd -m projectx
```

```
# mkdir /usr/local/x
# chown root.projectx /usr/local/x

# chmod 2775 /usr/local/x
# ls -ld /usr/local/x
drwxrwsr-x 2 root projectx 4096 Aug 18 01:54 /usr/local/x
# gpasswd -a nextuser projectx
```

In this example, you create a user named `projectx` (with a group named `projectx`). Create a `/usr/local/x` directory and have it owned by root user and projectx group. Set the setuid bit to be on for the group (2), open full read/write/execute permissions for user and group (77), and open read and execute permissions for everyone else (5). Add each user to the group that you want to be able to write to the projectx directory (replace `nextuser` with the user you want to add). After that, regardless of a user's primary group, any file created in the `/usr/local/x` directory by a user can be read or modified by anyone in the projectx group.

- **Specify user ID manually** — Typically, you would not check this box, so that the UID for the new user would be assigned automatically. New UIDs for regular users start at 500. However, if you want to assign a particular UID for a user (for example, if you want to match the UID with the user's UID from another computer on your network), click this box and type the number you want to use in the UID box.

3. Click OK when you are done. The new user is added to the `/etc/passwd` and `/etc/group` files. The user account is now available for that user to login.

Setting User Defaults

The `useradd` command and User Manager window both determine the default values for new accounts by reading the `/etc/login.defs` file. You can modify those defaults by either editing that file manually with a standard text editor or by running the `useradd` command with the `-D` option. If you choose to edit the file manually, here is what you face:

```
# *REQUIRED*
# Directory where mailboxes reside, _or_ name of file, relative to the
# home directory. If you _do_ define both, MAIL_DIR takes precedence.
# QMAIL_DIR is for Qmail
#
#QMAIL_DIR      Maildir
MAIL_DIR        /var/spool/mail
#MAIL_FILE      .mail

# Password aging controls:
#
# PASS_MAX_DAYS Maximum number of days a password may be used.
# PASS_MIN_DAYS Minimum number of days allowed between password changes.
# PASS_MIN_LEN  Minimum acceptable password length.
# PASS_WARN_AGE Number of days warning given before a password
# expires.
```

```
#
PASS_MAX_DAYS        99999
PASS_MIN_DAYS        0
PASS_MIN_LEN         5
PASS_WARN_AGE        7

#
# Min/max values for automatic uid selection in useradd
#
UID_MIN                     500
UID_MAX                   60000

#
# Min/max values for automatic gid selection in groupadd
#
GID_MIN                     500
GID_MAX                   60000

#
# If defined, this command is run when removing a user.
# It should remove any at/cron/print jobs etc. owned by
# the user to be removed (passed as the first argument).
#
#USERDEL_CMD /usr/sbin/userdel_local

#
# If useradd should create home directories for users by default.
# On RH systems, we do. This option is ORed with the -m flag on
# useradd command line.
#
CREATE_HOME yes
```

Blank lines and comments beginning with a pound sign (#) are ignored. All other lines contain keyword/value pairs. For example, the keyword MAIL_DIR is followed by some white space and the value /var/spool/mail. This tells useradd that the initial user e-mail mailbox is created in that directory. Following that are lines that enable you to customize the valid range of automatically assigned user ID numbers or group ID numbers. A comment section that explains that keyword's purpose precedes each keyword. Altering a default value is as simple as editing the value associated with that keyword and then saving the login.defs file.

If you want to view the defaults, type the useradd command with the -D option as follows:

```
# useradd -D
GROUP=100
HOME=/home
INACTIVE=-1
EXPIRE=
SHELL=/bin/bash
SKEL=/etc/skel
```

You can also use the -D option to change defaults. When run with this flag, useradd refrains from actually creating a new user account; instead, it saves any additionally supplied options as the new default values in /etc/login.defs. Not all useradd options can be used in conjunction with the -D option. You can use only the five options listed in Table 11-2.

Table 11-2: useradd Options for Changing User Defaults

Options	Description
-b *default_home*	Set the default directory in which user home directories will be created. Replace *default_home* with the directory name to use. Usually this is /home.
-e *default_expire_date*	Set the default expiration date on which the user account is disabled. The *default_expire_date* value should be replaced with a date in the form MM/DD/YYYY — for example, 10/15/2001.
-f *default_inactive*	Set the number of days after a password has expired before the account is disabled. Replace *default_inactive* with a number representing the number of days.
-g *default_group*	Set the default group that new users will be placed in. Normally useradd creates a new group with the same name and ID number as the user. Replace *default_group* with the group name to use.
-s *default_shell*	Set the default shell for new users. Normally this is /bin/sh. Replace *default_shell* with the full path to the shell that you want as the default for new users.

To set any of the defaults, give the -D option first; then add any of the defaults you want to set. For example, to set the default home directory location to /home/everyone and the default shell to /bin/tcsh, type the following:

```
# useradd -D -b /home/everyone -s /bin/tcsh
```

Besides setting up user defaults, an administrator can create default files that are copied to each user's home directory for use. These files can include login scripts and shell configuration files (such as .bashrc). The following sections describe some of these files.

Supplying initial login scripts

Many Linux applications, including the command shell itself, read a configuration file at startup. It is traditional practice that these configuration files are stored in the users' home directories. In this way, each user can customize the behavior of the command shell and other applications without affecting that behavior for other users. In this way, global defaults can be assigned from /etc/profile, then those settings can be enhanced or overridden by a user's personal files.

The bash command shell, for example, looks for a file called .bashrc in the current user's home directory whenever it starts up. Similarly, the tcsh command shell looks for a file called .tcshrc in the user's home directory. You may see a repeating theme here. Startup scripts and configuration files for various applications usually begin with a dot (.) character and end in the letters rc. You can supply initial default versions of these and other configuration files by placing them in the /etc/skel directory. When you run the useradd command, these scripts and configuration files are copied to the new user's home directory.

Supplying an initial .bashrc file

By supplying your users with an initial .bashrc file, you give them a starting point from which they can further customize their shell environment. Moreover, you can be sure that the file is created with the appropriate access permissions so as not to compromise system security.

The .bashrc script is run each time the user starts a new bash shell. So, security is a concern. It is also a good place to supply useful command aliases and additions to the command search path. Here's an example:

```
# .bashrc
# User specific aliases and functions
alias rm='rm -i'
alias cp='cp -i'
alias mv='mv -i'

if [ -f /etc/bashrc ]; then
        . /etc/bashrc
fi

PATH=$PATH:/usr/bin:/usr/local/bin
export PATH
```

This sample .bashrc file creates aliases for the rm, cp, and mv commands that result in a -i option always being used (unless overridden with the -f option). This protects against the accidental deletion of files. Next, the file executes the /etc/bashrc (if it exists) to read any further global bash values. This file also sets the search path.

Supplying an initial .tcshrc file

The following example .tcshrc file does basically the same thing as the preceding .bashrc example. However, this file (which is for the root user) has the additional task of setting the appearance of the command prompt:

```
# .tcshrc
```

```
# User specific aliases and functions

alias rm 'rm -i'
alias cp 'cp -i'
alias mv 'mv -i'

setenv PATH "$PATH:/usr/bin:/usr/local/bin"

set prompt='[%n@%m %c]# '
```

Instead of using the export command to set environment variables, the tcsh shell uses the setenv command. In the example, setenv is used to set the PATH variable. The shell prompt is set to include your user name (%n), your computer name (%m), and the name of the current directory (%c). So, if you were to use the tcsh shell as the root user on a computer named maple with /tmp as your current directory, your prompt would appear as follows:

```
[root@maple /tmp]#
```

The .tcshrc file can also be named .cshrc. The tcsh shell is really an extended version of the csh shell (in fact, you can invoke it by the csh name). When a tcsh shell is started, it first looks for a .tcshrc file in the current user's home directory. If it can't find a file by that name, it looks for the other name, .cshrc. Thus, either name is appropriate.

Configuring system-wide shell options

Allowing individually customizable shell startup files for each user is a very flexible and useful practice. But sometimes you need more centralized control than that. You may have an environment variable or other shell setting that you want set for every user, without exception. If you add that setting to each individual shell, the user has the ability to edit that file and remove it. Furthermore, if that setting must be changed in the future, you must change it in every single user's shell startup file.

Fortunately, there is a better way. There are default startup files that apply to all users of the computer that each command shell reads before reading the user-specific files. In the case of the bash command shell, it reads the /etc/bashrc file before doing anything else.

Similarly, the tcsh shell reads the /etc/csh.cshrc file before processing the .cshrc or .tcshrc file found in the user's home directory. The following /etc/csh.cshrc file ships with Fedora:

```
# /etc/cshrc
#
# csh configuration for all shell invocations.

# by default, we want this to get set.
# Even for non-interactive, non-login shells.
 [ `id -gn` = `id -un` -a `id -u` -gt 99 ]
if $status then
```

```
    umask 022
else
    umask 002
endif

if ($?prompt) then
  if ($?tcsh) then
    set prompt='[%n@%m %c]$ '
  else
    set prompt=\[`id -nu`@`hostname -s`\]\$\
  endif
endif
```

The `/etc/cshrc` and `/etc/bashrc` files set a variety of shell environment options. If you want to modify or add to the shell environment supplied to every single user on the system, the `/etc/bashrc` or `/etc/cshrc` files are the place to do it.

Setting system profiles

Some of the most basic information assigned to each user is added from the `/etc/profile` file. So, if you want to change any of the following information, you can start from `/etc/profile`. Here are some values contained in `/etc/profile`:

- **PATH** — Assigns the default PATH for the root user and for all other users. You might change this value to add paths to local directories containing applications all users need.

- **ulimit** — Sets the maximum allowable file size the user can create from the shell to be unlimited. You can use `ulimit` to restrict maximum file size if you find that users are creating enormous files. As defined in the `/etc/profile` file, `ulimit` sets no limit to the size of files a user can create. However, it does prevent core files (normally created when a process crashes) from being created.

- **Environment variables** — Shell environment variables that are needed for standard operation are assigned in this file. These include USER (set by the `id -un` command), LOGNAME (same as USER), MAIL (set to `/var/spool/mail/$USER`), HOSTNAME (set to `/bin/hostname`), and HISTSIZE (which sets shell command history to 1000 items).

- **INPUTRC** — Sets keyboard mappings for particular situations, based on the contents of the `/etc/inputrc` file. In particular, the `inputrc` file makes sure that the Linux console and various Terminal windows (`xterm` and `rxvt`) all behave sanely.

The last thing that the `/etc/profile` file does is look at the contents of the `/etc/profile.d` directory and source in the files that it finds. Each file contains settings that define environment variables or aliases that affect how users can use the shell. For example, the `lang.sh` and `lang.csh` files identify the locations of foreign language files. The `vim` files create aliases that cause `vim` to be used when `vi` is typed. The `which-2.sh` file defines a set of options used by the which command. You can modify the profile.d files or add your own to have environment variables and aliases set for all of your users.

Creating Portable Desktops

Linux is an operating system that was born on the Internet, so it is not surprising that it has strong networking capabilities. This makes Linux an excellent server, but it also allows Linux to be an excellent desktop workstation, especially in a highly networked environment. Fedora lets you easily set up your users with a portable desktop that follows them from computer to computer. With other leading desktop operating systems, it is not nearly as easy.

Normally, a Linux user's home directory is located within the /home directory. As an alternative, within the home directory you can create a directory named after the system's host name. Within that directory, create the users' home directories. Thus, on a Linux system named dexter, the user mary would have a home directory of /home/dexter/mary instead of /home/mary. There is a very good reason for doing this.

If you are logged into the Linux system ratbert and would like to access your home directory on dexter as if it were stored locally, the best approach is to use Network File System (NFS) to mount dexter's /home directory on the /home on ratbert. This results in having the same contents of your home directory available to you no matter which machine you log in to.

> **CROSS-REFERENCE:** You can read more about NFS in Chapter 18.

To mount dexter's /home directory as described, you would add a line similar to the following in ratbert's /etc/fstab file:

```
dexter:/home /home nfs defaults 0 0
```

You would also add an entry such as the following in dexter's /etc/exports directory:

```
/home ratbert
```

Now, when ratbert boots up, it automatically mounts dexter's home partition over the network. This enables you to treat the remote files and directories on dexter's /home as if they are locally stored on ratbert. Unfortunately, this has the side effect of "covering up" ratbert's actual /home directory.

This is where the extra directory level based on the system name comes to the rescue. With all of dexter's home directories located in /home/dexter and all of ratbert's home directories located in /home/ratbert, we can remove the danger of one system covering up the home directories of another. In fact, let's take this example one step further: Imagine a scenario in which the systems dexter, ratbert, and daffy all have portable desktops that are shared with the other systems. The /etc/fstab and /etc/exports files for each system should have the following lines added to them.

The /etc/exports and /etc/fstab files for dexter are as follows:

/etc/exports file

```
/home/dexter ratbert,daffy
```

/etc/fstab file

```
ratbert:/home/ratbert /home/ratbert nfs defaults 0 0
daffy:/home/daffy     /home/daffy   nfs defaults 0 0
```

The /etc/exports and /etc/fstab files for ratbert are:

/etc/exports

```
/home/ratbert dexter,daffy
```

/etc/fstab

```
dexter:/home/dexter /home/dexter nfs defaults 0 0
daffy:/home/daffy   /home/daffy  nfs defaults 0 0
```

The /etc/exports and /etc/fstab files for daffy are:

/etc/exports

```
/home/dexter ratbert,dexter
```

/etc/fstab

```
ratbert:/home/ratbert /home/ratbert  nfs defaults 0 0
dexter:/home/dexter   /home/dexter   nfs defaults 0 0
```

As you can see, each system uses NFS to mount the home directories from the other two systems. A user can travel from server to server and see exactly the same desktop on each system.

Providing Support to Users

Creating new user accounts is just one small administrative task among many. No single chapter can adequately discuss all the tasks that are involved in the ongoing support of users. But I share with you a few hints and procedures to ease that burden.

Creating a technical support mailbox

E-mail is a wonderful communication tool, especially for the overworked system administrator. People usually put more thought and effort into their e-mail messages than into the voice messages that they leave. A text message can be edited for clarity before being sent, and important details can be cut and pasted from other sources. This makes e-mail an excellent method for Linux users to communicate with their system administrator.

In an office with only a few users, you can probably get away with using your personal mailbox to send and receive support e-mails. In a larger office, however, you should create a separate mailbox reserved only for technical support issues. This has several advantages over the use of your personal mailbox:

- Support messages will not be confused with personal, nonsupport-related messages.

- Multiple people can check the mailbox and share administrative responsibility without needing to read each other's personal e-mail.

- Support e-mail is easily redirected to another person's mailbox when you go on vacation. Your personal e-mail continues to go to your personal mailbox.

One easy solution is to simply create a support e-mail alias that redirects messages to an actual mailbox or list of mailboxes. For example, suppose you want to create a support alias that redistributes e-mail to the user accounts for support staff members Joe, Mary, and Bob. You would log in as root, edit the `/etc/aliases` file, and add lines similar to the following:

```
# Technical support mailing list
support: joe, mary, bob
```

After saving the file, you need to run the `newaliases` command to recompile the `/etc/aliases` file into a database format. Now your users can send e-mail to the support e-mail address, and the message is automatically routed to everyone on the list. When a member of the list responds to that message, he or she should use the Reply To All option so that the other support staff members also see the message. Otherwise, multiple people may attempt to solve the same problem, resulting in wasteful duplication of effort.

You may also choose to create a support user account. The technical support staff would log in to this account to check messages and send replies. In this manner, all replies are stamped with the support login name and not the personal e-mail address of a staff member.

Resetting a user's password

One common (if not *the* most common) problem that your users will encounter is the inability to log in because:

- They have the Caps Lock key on.
- They have forgotten the password.
- The password has expired.

If the Caps Lock key is not on, then you probably need to reset the individual's password. You can't look up the password because Linux stores passwords in an encrypted format. Instead, use the `passwd` command to assign a new password to the user's account. Give the user the new password (preferably in person), but then set the password to expire soon so that he or she must choose one (hopefully, a new one that is more easily remembered).

If you must reset a user's password, do so with the `passwd` command. While logged in as root, type `passwd` followed by the login name you are resetting. You are prompted to enter the password twice. For example, to change the password for `mary`, type:

```
# passwd mary
```

After resetting the password, set it to expire so that the user is forced to change it the next time she logs in. You can use the `chage` command to set an expiration period for the password and to trick the system into thinking that the password is long overdue to be changed.

```
# chage -M 30 -d 0 mary
```

The `-M 30` option tells the system to expire Mary's password every 30 days. The `-d 0` option tricks the system into thinking that her password has not been changed since January 1, 1970.

CROSS-REFERENCE: Administrators who support multiple users might want to consider some newer technologies which make life easier, like centralized e-mail address books using LDAP. See Chapter 22 for more information.

Modifying Accounts

Occasionally, a user needs more done to an account than just a resetting of the password. You may need to change the groups that user is in, or the drive that a home directory resides on. The following sections explain how to modify user accounts using one of two methods: `usermod` or the User Manager window.

Modifying user accounts with usermod

The `usermod` command is similar to the `useradd` command and even shares some of the same options. However, instead of adding new accounts, it enables you to change various details of existing accounts. When invoking the `usermod` command, you must provide account details to change followed by the login name of the account. Table 11-3 lists the available options for the `usermod` command.

Table 11-3: usermod Options for Changing Existing Accounts

Options	*Description*
`-c "comment"`	Change the description field of the account. You can also use the `chfn` command for this. Replace `comment` with a name or other description of the user account. Since the comment can contain multiple words, the quotes are necessary.
`-d home_dir`	Change the home directory of the account to the specified new location. If the `-m` option is included, copy the contents of the home directory as well. Replace `home_dir` with the full path to the new directory.

Options	Description
-e *expire_date*	Assign a new expiration date for the account, replacing *expire_date* with a date in MM/DD/YYYY format.
-f *inactivity*	Set the number of days after a password expires until the account is permanently disabled. Setting *inactivity* to 0 disables the account immediately after the password has expired. Setting it to -1 disables the option, which is the default behavior.
-g *group*	Change the primary group (as listed in the /etc/group file) that the user is in. Replace *group* with the name of the new group.
-G *grouplist*	Set the list of groups that user belongs to. Replace *grouplist* with a list of groups.
-l *login_name*	Change the login name of the account to the name supplied after the -l option. Replace *login_name* with the new name. This does not automatically change the name of the home directory; use the -d and -m options for that.
-m	This option is used only in conjunction with the -d option. It causes the contents of the user's home directory to be copied to the new directory.
-o	This option is used only in conjunction with the -u option. It removes the restriction that user IDs must be unique.
-s *shell*	Specify a new command shell to use with this account. Replace *shell* with the full path to the new shell.
-u *user_id*	Change the user ID number for the account. Replace *user_id* with the new user ID number. Unless the -o option is used, the ID number must not be in use by another account.

Assume that a new employee named Jenny Barnes will be taking over Mary's job. We want to convert the mary account to a new name (-l jenny), new comment (-c "Jenny Barnes"), and home directory (-d /home/jenny). We could do that with the following command:

```
# usermod -l jenny -c "Jenny Barnes" -m -d /home/jenny mary
```

Furthermore, if after converting the account we learn that Jenny prefers the tcsh shell, we could make that change with the -s option (-s /bin/tcsh):

```
# usermod -s /bin/tcsh jenny
```

Instead, we could use the chsh command to change the shell. The following is an example:

```
# chsh -s /bin/tcsh jenny
```

The `chsh` command is handy because it enables a user to change his or her own shell setting. Simply leave the user name parameter off when invoking the command, and `chsh` assumes the currently logged-in user as the account to change.

Modifying user accounts with User Manager

To use the desktop to change an existing account, you can use the User Manager. Here's how to add a new user from the User Manager window:

1. From the red hat menu, select System Settings→ Users and Groups (or type `system-config-users` from a Terminal window as root user). The main User Manager window appears.

2. Select the user name of the account you want to modify, then click the Properties button to open the User Properties window (see Figure 11-3).

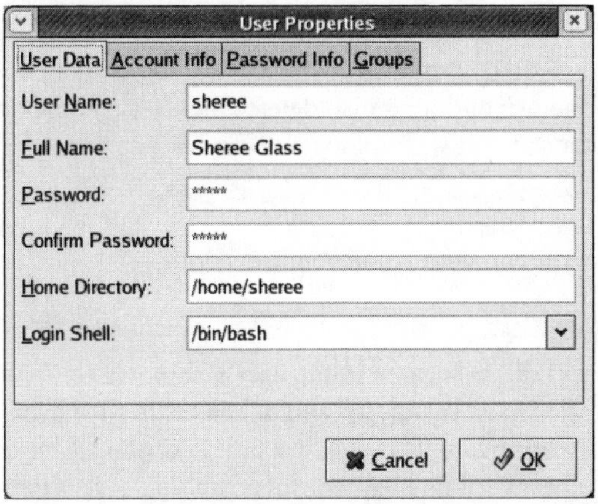

Figure 11-3: Choose Properties to modify an existing user account.

3. There are four tabs of information you can modify for the user you selected:

   - **User Data** — This tab contains the user information you created when you first added the user account.

   - **Account Info** — Select the Enable Account Expiration check box, then type a date if you want the account to become inaccessible after a particular date. Select the Local Password is Locked check box if you want to prevent access to the account but not delete it. (The latter is a good technique when an employee is leaving the company or if you want to lock out a customer whose account is temporarily disabled. The information isn't removed, it just isn't accessible.)

   - **Password Info** — Select Enable Password Expiration if you want to control expiration of the user's password. By default, passwords don't expire. Here are your options: "Days before change allowed" (forces the user to keep the password for at least a set number of days before it can be changed); "Days before change required" (allows the user to keep the same password for at least the set number of days); "Days warning before change" (sets how many days before the password expiration day that the user is warned to change the password); "Days before account inactive" (sets the number of days after which the account is deactivated).

- **Groups** — Select from the list of available groups to add the user to one or more of those groups.

4. Click OK to apply the changes to the user account.

Deleting User Accounts

Occasionally, it is necessary to remove a user account from your Linux system. This can be done with either the `userdel` command or the User Manager window.

Deleting user accounts with userdel

The `userdel` command takes a single argument, which is the login name of the account to delete. If you supply the optional `-r` option, it also deletes the user's home directory and all the files in it. To delete the user account with login name `mary`, you would type this:

```
# userdel mary
```

To wipe out her home directory along with her account, type this:

```
# userdel -r mary
```

Files owned by the deleted user but not located in the user's home directory will not be deleted. The system administrator must search for and delete those files manually. The `find` command comes in very handy for this type of task. I won't describe all the capabilities of the `find` command (that would take a very fat chapter of its own). I do, however, provide a few simple examples of how to use `find` to locate files belonging to a particular user, even when those files are scattered throughout a file system. You can even use the `find` command to delete or change the ownership of files as they are located. Table 11-4 has a few examples of the `find` command in action.

Table 11-4: Using find to Locate and Change User Files

Find Command	Description
`find / -user mary`	Search the entire file hierarchy (start at /) for all files and directories owned by `mary` and print the filenames to the screen.

Find Command	Description
`find /home -user mary -exec rm -i {} \;`	Search for all files and subdirectories under /home owned by mary. Run the rm command interactively to delete each file.
`find / -user mary -exec chown jenny {} \;`	Search for all files and subdirectories under /home that are owned by user mary and run the chown command to change each file so that it is owned by jenny instead.
`find / -uid 500 -exec chown jenny {} \;`	This command is basically the same as the previous example, but it uses the user ID number instead of the user name to identify the matching files. This is useful if you have deleted a user before converting her files.

There are a few common things about each invocation of the find command. The first parameter is always the directory to start the recursive search in. After that come the file attributes to match. You can use the -exec parameter to run a command against each matching file or directory. The { } characters designate where the matching filename should be filled in when find runs the -exec option. The \; at the end simply tells Linux where the command ends. These are only a few of find's capabilities. I encourage you to read the online man page to learn more about find. (Type **man find** to view the page.)

Deleting user accounts with User Manager

To delete a user from the User Manager window, simply click the line representing the user account, then click the Delete button.

- The information about the user is removed from the /etc/passwd file; thus, the user can no longer log in.
- The home directory and all files owned by the user will still exist. However, a listing of files previously owned by that user (ls -l) will show only the former user's UID, but no name, as the owner.

See the description in the previous section for information about how to find and remove files previously owned by the user.

> **TIP:** You may want to transfer the ownership of the files from the old user to the new user (if, for example, a new employee is taking over the work of an employee who is leaving the company). In that case, after you delete the old user, you can create a new user account using the same UID as the old account (with a new password, of course). The new user will immediately have ownership of all files owned by the deleted user.

Checking Disk Quotas

Limited disk space can be another source of user support calls. Fedora offers the quotas software package for limiting and displaying the amount of disk space that a user can consume. You can also use the du command to see how much disk space has been used in a particular directory (and related subdirectories). To automate the process of checking for disk space, you can create your own script. The following sections describe these ways of dealing with potential disk space problems.

Using quota to check disk usage

A careless or greedy user can gobble up all the space on your hard disk and, possibly, bring your computer to a halt. By using disk quotas, you can limit the amount of disk resources a user or group can use up.

The quota package contains a set of tools that lets you limit the amount of disk space (based on disk blocks) and files (based on inodes) that a user can consume. Using quotas, you can limit the amount of usage (on a per-user and -group basis) for each file system on your computer. The general steps for setting disk quotas are:

1. Edit the /etc/fstab file
2. Create quota files
3. Create and start a quota startup script
4. Creat quota rules
5. Check quotas

You set quotas on disk partitions listed in your /etc/fstab file. For computers that are shared by many users, there might be a separate /home or /var partition where users are expected to put all their data. That kind of partition boundary can prevent an entire disk from being consumed by one user. Quotas on the /home or /var partition can make sure that the space within those partitions are shared fairly among your computer's users.

The procedure that spans the next few sections assumes that you have a separate /home partition on your computer for which you want to create quotas. You could use any partition, not just the /home partition shown in the procedure. For example, if you have only one partition mounted at the root of the files system (/), you could set quotas for your entire file system by replacing /home with / in the following example.

Editing the /etc/fstab file

You need to add quota support to the file system. To do that, edit the `/etc/fstab` file and add the `usrquota` option to field number four of the partition for which you want to set quotas. Here is an example of a line from `/etc/fstab`:

```
/dev/hda2      /home      ext3      defaults,usrquota,grpquota        1 2
```

Here, the `/home` file system is used to allow disk quotas for all users' home directories under the `/home` directory.

Before the `usrquota` option can take effect, the file system must be remounted. This happens automatically when you reboot, which you will have to do if you are setting quotas for the root (/) file system. Otherwise, you might be able to use the `umount` and `mount` commands to cause the `usrquota` option to take effect.

Creating quota files

You need to have `aquota.user` and/or `aquota.group` files in the root directory of the partition on which you want to establish disk quotas. To add quotas based on individual users, you need an `aquota.user` file, while `aquota.group` is needed to set quotas based on groups. One way to create these files is with the `quotacheck` command. Here is an example of the `quotacheck` command to create an initial `aquota.user` file:

```
# quotacheck -c /home
```

A `/home/aquota.user` file is created from the previous command. (To create an initial `aquota.group` file, type `touch /home/aquota.group`.) Next, you must create the disk usage table for the partition. Here's an example of how to do that:

```
# quotacheck -vug /home
```

The `quotacheck` command in this example looks at the file system partition mounted on `/home` and builds a table of disk usage. The `-v` option produces verbose output from the command, the `-u` option causes user quotas to be examined, and the `-g` option causes group quotas to be examined. Permissions on the two files are set so only root can access them (`chmod 600 aquota.*`).

Creating a quota startup script

If the quota package doesn't include a startup script (and it doesn't with the current Fedora distribution), you can create your own. You want this script to check quotas (`quotacheck` command), start the quota service (`quotastart` command) and turn off the service (`quotaoff` command).

Open a new file called `/etc/init.d/quota` as root user, using any text editor. Here is an example of the content you can add to that file:

```
#!/bin/bash

# init file for quota
#
# description: Checks disk quotas
#
# processname: quota
# chkconfig: - 90 90
# source function library
. /etc/rc.d/init.d/functions

case "$1" in
  start)
    echo -n "Checking quotas: "
        daemon /sbin/quotacheck -avug
    echo
    echo -n "Starting quotas: "
        daemon /sbin/quotaon -avug
    echo
    ;;
  stop)
    echo -n "Shutting down quotas: "
    daemon /sbin/quotaoff -a
    echo
    ;;
  restart)
        $0 stop
        $0 start
        ;;
  *)
    echo "Usage: quota {start|stop|restart}"
    exit 1
esac

exit 0
```

The quota script, when started, first runs the quotacheck command to check all file systems for which quota checking is on. Then it turns on quota checking with the quotaon command. The line # chkconfig: - 90 90 defines the names assigned to the startup script (S90quota or K90quota) when it is added to the individual runlevel directories. When you run chkconfig --add quota in the next step those scripts are automatically put in the correct runlevel directories.

Turn on the quota startup script

If you created a quota file, as described in the previous step, you need to make it executable and set it to start automatically when you start Fedora. To do those things, type the following as root user:

```
# chmod 755 /etc/init.d/quota
# chkconfig --add quota
```

At this point, links are created so that your quota script starts when Fedora boots.

Creating quota rules

You can use the edquota command to create quota rules for a particular user or group. (Valid users and groups are listed in the /etc/passwd and /etc/group files, respectively). Here is an example of an edquota command to set quotas for a user named jake.

> **NOTE:** The edquota command uses the vi text editor to edit your quota files. To use a different editor, change the value of the EDITOR or VISUAL environment variable before running edquota. For example, to use the emacs editor, type the following before running edquota:
>
> ```
> #   export EDITOR=emacs
> ```

```
# edquota -u jake
Disk quotas for user jake (uid 501)
  Filesystem           blocks    soft    hard   inodes    soft    hard
  /dev/hda2               596       0       0        1       0       0
~
~
~
"/tmp//EdP.aBY1zYC" 3L, 215C
```

This example shows that user quotas can be set for the user jake on the /dev/hda2 partition (which is /home in our example). Currently, jake has used 596 blocks (a block equals 1K on this ext3 file system). One file was created by jake (represented by 1 inode). To change the disk usage limits, you can edit the zeros (unlimited use) under the soft and hard heading for blocks and inodes.

Soft limits set limits that you don't want a user or group to exceed. Hard limits set the boundaries that you will not let a user or group exceed. After a set grace period that a soft limit is exceeded (which is seven days, by default), the soft limit becomes a hard limit. (Type **edquota -t** to check and change the grace periods that you have set.)

Here is an example of how the line in the previous edquota example could be changed:

```
/dev/hda2               596  512000  716800        1     800    1000
```

In this example, the soft limit on the number of blocks that the user jake could consume on the /dev/hda2 device (/home) is 512000 blocks (or 500MB) the hard limit is 716800 blocks (or 700MB). Soft and hard limits on inodes are 800 and 1000, respectively. If either of the soft limits are exceeded by the user jake, he has seven days to get back under the limit, or he will be blocked from using any more disk space or inodes.

Further attempts to write to a partition after the hard limit has been exceeded results in a failure to write to the disk. When this happens, the user who tries to create the file that exceeds his limit will see a message like the following:

```
ide0(3,2): write failed, user block limit reached.
cp: writing 'abc.doc': Disk quota exceeded
```

Instead of assigning quotas to users, you can assign quotas to any group listed in the /etc/group file. Instead of the -u option to edquota, use the -g options followed by a group name.

Updating quota settings

After you have changed quota settings for a user, you should rerun the quotacheck command. You should also run the quotacheck command periodically, to keep the quota records up to date. One way to do that is to run the quotacheck command weekly using a cron entry.

Checking quotas

To report on how much disk space and how many inodes each user on your computer (for which you have set quotas) has consumed, use the repquota command. Here is an example of the repquota command for reading quota data relating to all partitions that are using quotas:

```
# repquota -a
*** Report for user quotas on device /dev/hda2
Block grace time: 7days: Inode grace time: 7days
                       Block limits               File limits
User           used    soft    hard    grace    used   soft   hard   grace
root     --  1973984      0       0              2506      0      0
jake     --     1296    700    1700    6days        3      0      0
```

In this previous example, jake has exceeded his soft limit of 700 blocks. He currently has six days left in his grace period to remove enough files so that the soft limit does not become the hard limit.

Using du to check disk use

You can discover the most voracious consumers of disk space using the du command. Invoke du with the -s option and give it a list of directories; it reports the total disk space used by all the files in each directory. Add an -h option to display disk space used in numbers, followed by kilobytes (k), megabytes (M), or gigabytes (G). The -c option adds a total of all requested directories at the end. The following checks disk usage for several home directories:

```
# du -h -c -s /home/tom /home/bill /home/tina /home/sally
```

This should result in a list of all of your users' home directories preceded by the number of kilobytes that each directory structure uses. It looks something like this:

```
339M    /home/tom
81M     /home/bill
31M     /home/tina
44k     /home/sally
450M    total
```

Removing temp files automatically

Some potential disk-consumption problems are set up to take care of themselves. For example, directories for storing temporary files used by applications (such as /tmp and /var/tmp) can consume lots of disk space over time. To deal with the problem, Fedora includes the tmpwatch facility. The tmpwatch command runs from the cron file /etc/cron.daily/tmpwatch to delete unused temporary files. Here's what that file contains:

```
/usr/sbin/tmpwatch 240 /tmp
/usr/sbin/tmpwatch 720 /var/tmp
for d in /var/{cache/man,catman}/{cat?,X11R6/cat?,local/cat?}; do
    if [ -d "$d" ]; then
    /usr/sbin/tmpwatch -f 720 $d
    fi
done
```

Each day, this tmpwatch script runs to delete temporary files that haven't been used for a while. Files from the /tmp and /var/tmp directories are removed after 240 and 720 hours of not being accessed, respectively. Temporary man page files stored in /var/cache subdirectories are also checked and deleted after 720 hours of disuse.

Sending Mail to All Users

Occasionally, you need to send messages to all users on your system. Warning users of planned downtime for hardware upgrades is a good example. Sending e-mail to each user individually is extremely time consuming and wasteful; this is precisely the kind of task that e-mail aliases and mailing lists were invented for. Keeping a mailing list of all the users on your system can be problematic, however. If you are not diligent about keeping the mailing list current, it becomes increasingly inaccurate as you add and delete users. Also, if your system has many users, the mere size of the alias list can become unwieldy.

The following script, called mailfile, provides a simple method of working around these problems. It grabs the login names from the /etc/passwd file and sends e-mail to all users.

```
#!/bin/csh
```

```
#
# mailfile: This script mails the specified file to all users
#           of the system.  It skips the first 17 accounts so
#           we do not send the email to system accounts like
#           'root'.
#
# USAGE: mailfile "Subject goes here" filename.txt


#
# Check for a subject
#
if ( `echo $1 | awk '{ print $1 }'` == "" ) then
    echo You did not supply a subject for the message.
    echo Be sure to enclose it in quotes.
    exit 1
else
    # Get the subject of the message
    set subject=$1
endif


#
# Check for a filename
#
if ( $2 == "" ) then
    echo You did not supply a file name.
    exit 2
else
    # Get the name of the file to send
    set filename=$2
endif


#
# Check that the file exists
#
if ( -f $filename ) then
   echo Sending file $filename
else
   echo File does not exist.
   exit 3
endif


#
# Loop through every login name, but skip the first 17 accounts
#
foreach user ( `awk -F: '{ print $1 }' /etc/passwd | tail +17` )
    # Mail the file
    echo Mailing to $user
    mail -s "$subject" $user < $filename
```

```
    # sleep for a few seconds so we don't overload the mailer
    # On fast systems or systems with few accounts, you can
    # probably take this delay out.
    sleep 2
end
```

The script accepts two parameters. The first is the subject of the e-mail message, which is enclosed in quotes. The second is the name of the file containing the text message to send. Thus, to send an e-mail message to all users warning them about an upcoming server hardware upgrade, I may do something similar to the following:

```
mailfile "System upgrade at 5:00pm" upgrade.txt
```

The file `upgrade.txt` contains the text of the message to be sent to each user. The really useful thing about this approach is that I can save this text file and easily modify and resend it the next time I upgrade the system.

> **TIP:** If your users log in to your system using text-based logins instead of graphical logins, you can add messages to the `/etc/motd` file to have them reach your users. Any text in that file will be displayed on each user's screen after the user logs in and before the first shell prompt appears.

Summary

It is not uncommon for a Linux system to be used as a single-task server with no actual users. It sits quietly in a server room, serving Web pages or handling domain name service, never crashing, and rarely needing attention. This is not always the case, however. You may have to support users on your Linux system, and that can be the most challenging part of your system administration duties.

Fedora provides a variety of tools that help you with your administrative chores. The `useradd`, `usermod`, and `userdel` commands enable easy command-line manipulation of user account data. Furthermore, creating a support mailbox and building shell scripts to automate repetitive tasks lightens your load even more. Fedora Linux builds on top of the rich history of UNIX and provides an ideal platform to support the diverse needs of your users.

Chapter 12

Automating System Tasks

You'd never get any work done if you typed every command that needs to be run on your Fedora system when it starts. Likewise, you could work more efficiently if you grouped together sets of commands that you run all the time. Shell scripts can handle these tasks.

A *shell script* is a group of commands, functions, variables, or just about anything else you can use from a shell. These items are typed into a plain-text file. That file can then be run as a command. Fedora uses system initialization shell scripts during system startup to run commands needed to get things going. You can create your own shell scripts to automate the tasks you need to do regularly.

This chapter provides a rudimentary overview of the inner workings of shell scripts and how they can be used. You learn how shell scripts are responsible for the messages that scroll by on the system console during booting and how simple scripts can be harnessed to a scheduling facility (such as `cron` or `at`) to simplify administrative tasks.

You also learn to fine-tune your machine to start at the most appropriate run level and to run only services you need. With that understanding, you'll be able to personalize your computer and cut down on the amount of time you spend repetitively typing the same commands.

Understanding Shell Scripts

Have you ever had a task that you needed to do over and over that took a lot of typing on the command line? Do you ever think to yourself, "Wow, I wish there was just one command I could type to do all this of this"? Maybe a shell script is what you're after.

Shell scripts are the equivalent of batch files in MS-DOS, and can contain long lists of commands, complex flow control, arithmetic evaluations, user-defined variables, user-defined functions, and sophisticated condition testing. Shell scripts are capable of handling everything from simple one-line commands to something as complex as starting up your Fedora system.

In fact, as you will read in this chapter, Fedora does just that. It uses shell scripts (/etc/rc.d/rc.sysint and /etc/rc) to check and mount all your filesystems, set up your consoles, configure your network, launch all your system services, and eventually provide you with your login screen. While there are nearly a dozen different shells available in Fedora, the default shell is called bash, the Bourne-Again shell.

Executing and debugging shell scripts

One of the primary advantages of shell scripts is that they can be opened in any text editor to see what they do. A big disadvantage is that shell scripts often execute more slowly than compiled programs. There are two basic ways to execute a shell script:

- The filename is used as an argument to the shell (as in bash myscript). In this method, the file does not need to be executable; it just contains a list of shell commands. The shell specified on the command line is used to interpret the commands in the script file. This is most common for quick, simple tasks.

- The shell script may also have the name of the interpreter placed in the first line of the script preceded by #! (as in #!/bin/bash), and have its execute bit set (using chmod +x). You can then run your script just like any other program in your path simply by typing the name of the script on the command line.

> **CROSS-REFERENCE:** See Chapter 4 for more details on chmod and read/write/execute permissions.

When scripts are executed in either manner, options to the program may be specified on the command line. Anything following the name of the script is referred to as a *command-line argument*.

As with writing any software, there is no substitute to clear and thoughtful design and lots of comments. The pound sign (#) prefaces comments and can take up an entire line or exist on the same line as script code. It's best to implement more complex shell scripts in stages, making sure the logic is sound at each step before continuing. Here are a few good, concise tips to make sure things are working as expected during testing:

- Place an echo statement at the beginning of lines within the body of a loop. That way, rather than executing the code, you can see what will be executed without making any permanent changes.

- To achieve the same goal, you could place dummy echo statements throughout the code. If these lines get printed, you know the correct logic branch is being taken.

- You could use set +x near the beginning of the script to display each command that is executed or launch your scripts using sh -x *myscript*.

Understanding shell variables

Often within a shell script, you want to reuse certain items of information. During the course of processing the shell script, the name or number representing this information may change. To store information used by a shell script in a way that it can be easily reused, you can set variables. Variable names within shell scripts are case-sensitive and can be defined in the following manner:

```
NAME=value
```

The first part of a variable is the variable name, and the second part is the value set for that name. Variables can be assigned from constants, like text or numbers. This is useful for initializing values or saving lots of typing for long constants. Here are examples where variables are set to a string of characters (CITY) and a numeric value (PI):

```
CITY="Springfield"
PI=3.14159265
```

Variables can contain the output of a command or command sequence. You can accomplish this by either enclosing the command in backticks (`) or by enclosing the command in parentheses. This is a great way to get information that can change from computer to computer or from day to day. Here we set the output of the uname -n command to the MACHINE variable. Then we use parentheses to set NUM_FILES to the number of files in the current directory by piping (|) the output of the ls command to the word count command (wc -l).

```
MACHINE=`uname -n`
NUM_FILES=(/bin/ls | wc -l)
```

Variables can also contain the value of other variables. This is useful when you have to preserve a value that will change so you can use it later in the script. Here BALANCE is set to the value of the CurBalance variable.

```
BALANCE="$CurBalance"
```

> **NOTE:** When assigning variables, use only the variable name (for example, BALANCE). When referenced, meaning you want the *value* of the variable, precede it with a dollar sign (as in $CurBalance).

Special Shell Variables

There are special variables that the shell assigns for you . The most commonly used variables are called the *positional parameters* or *command line arguments* and are referenced as $0, $1, $2, $3…$n. $0 is special and is assigned the name used to invoke your script; the remainder are assigned the values of the parameters passed on the command line. For instance, if the shell script named myscript were called as:

```
myscript foo bar
```

the positional parameter $0 would be `myscript`, $1 would be `foo`, and $2 would be `bar`.

Another variable, $#, tells you how many parameters your script was given. In our example, $# would be 2. Another particularly useful special shell variable is $?, which receives the exit status of the last command executed. Typically, a value of zero means everything is okay, and anything other than zero indicates an error of some kind. For a complete list of special shell variables, refer to the `bash` man page .

Parameter expansion in bash

As mentioned earlier, if you want the value of a variable, you precede it with a $ (for example, $CITY). This is really just a shorthand for the notation ${CITY}; curly braces are used when the value of the parameter needs to be placed next to other text without a space. Bash has special rules that allow you to expand the value of a variable in different ways. Going into all the rules is probably a little overboard for a quick introduction to shell scripts, but Table 12-1 presents some common constructs that you're likely to see in bash scripts you find on your Fedora box.

Table 12-1: Examples of bash Parameter Expansion

Construction	Meaning
`${var:-value}`	If variable is unset or empty, expand this to *value*
`${var#pattern}`	Chop the shortest match for *pattern* from the end of *var*'s value
`${var##pattern}`	Chop the longest match for *pattern* from the end of *var*'s value
`${var%pattern}`	Chop the shortest match for *pattern* from the front of *var*'s value
`${var%%pattern}`	Chip the longest match for *pattern* from the front of *var*'s value

Try typing the following commands from a shell to test out how parameter expansion works:

```
# THIS="Example"
# THIS=${THIS:-"Not Set"}
# THAT=${THAT:-"Not Set"}
# echo $THIS
Example
# echo $THAT
Not Set
```

In the previous examples, the THIS variable is set to the word Example. In the next two lines, the THIS and THAT variables are set to their current values or to Not Set, if they are not currently set. Notice that because we just set THIS to the string Example, when we echo the value of THIS it appears as Example. However, since THAT was not set, it appears as Not Set.

> **NOTE:** For the rest of this section, I show how variables and commands may appear in a shell script. To try out any of those examples, however, you can simply type them into a shell as shown in the previous example.

In the following example, set `MYFILENAME` to `/home/digby/myfile.txt`. Next, the `FILE` variable is set to `myfile.txt` and `DIR` is set to `/home/digby`. In the `NAME` variable, the file name is cut down to simply `myfile`, then in the `EXTENSION` variable the file extension is set to `txt`. (To try these out, you can type them at a shell prompt as we did with the previous example, then echo the value of each variable to see how it is set.)

```
MYFILENAME="/home/digby/myfile.txt"
FILE=${MYFILENAME##*/}              #FILE becomes "myfile.txt"
DIR=${MYFILENAME%/*}               #DIR becomes "/home/digby"
NAME=${FILE%.*}                    #NAME becomes "myfile"
EXTENSION=${FILE#*.}               #EXTENSION becomes "txt"
```

Performing arithmetic in shell scripts

Bash used *untyped* variables, meaning it normally treats variables as strings or text, but can change them on the fly if you want it to. Unless you tell it otherwise with `declare`, your variables are just a bunch of letters to bash. But when you start trying to do arithmetic with them, bash will convert them to integers if it can. This makes it possible to do some fairly complex arithmetic in bash.

Integer arithmetic can be performed using the built-in `let` command or through the external `expr` or `bc` commands. After setting the variable `BIGNUM` value to `1024`, the three commands that follow would all store the value `64` in the `RESULT` variable:

```
BIGNUM=1024
let RESULT=$BIGNUM/16
RESULT=`expr $BIGNUM / 16`
RESULT=`echo "$BUGNUM / 16" | bc -l`
```

> **NOTE:** While most elements of shell scripts are relatively freeform (where whitespace, such as spaces or tabs, is insignificant), both `let` and `expr` are particular about spacing. The `let` command insists on no spaces between each operand and the mathematical operator, whereas the syntax of the `expr` command requires whitespace between each operand and its operator. In contrast to those, `bc` isn't picky about spaces, but can be trickier to use because it does floating-point arithmetic.

To see a complete list of the kinds of arithmetic you can perform using the `let` command, type **help let** at the bash prompt.

Using programming constructs in shell scripts

One of the features that make shell scripts so powerful is that their implementation of looping and conditional execution constructs similar to those found in more complex scripting and programming languages. You can use several different types of loops, depending on your needs.

The "if... then" statements

The most commonly used programming construct is conditional execution, or the "if" statement. It is used to perform actions only under certain conditions. There are several variations, depending on whether you're testing one thing, or want to do one thing if a condition is true, but another thing if a condition is false, or if you want to test several things one after the other.

The first if...then example tests if VARIABLE is set to the number 1. If it is, then the echo command is used to say that it is set to 1.

```
if [ $VARIABLE -eq 1 ] ; then
echo "The variable is 1"
fi
```

Instead of using -eq, you can use the equals sign (=), as shown in the following example. Using the else statement, different words can be echoed if the criterion of the if statement isn't met ($STRING = "Friday").

```
if [ $STRING = "Friday" ] ; then
echo "WhooHoo!  Friday!"
else
echo "Will Friday ever get here?"
fi
```

You can also reverse tests with an exclamation mark (!). In the following example, if STRING is not Monday, then "At least it's not Monday" is echoed.

```
if [ $STRING != "Monday" ] ; then
    echo "At least it's not Monday"
fi
```

In the following example, elif is used to test for an additional condition (is filename a file or a directory).

```
if [ -f $filename ] ; then
    echo "$filename is a regular file"
elif [ -d $filename ] ; then
    echo "$filename is a directory"
else
    echo "I have no idea what $filename is"
fi
```

As you can see from the preceding examples, the condition you are testing is placed between square brackets [ ]. When a test expression is evaluated, it will return either a value of 0, meaning that it is true, or a 1, meaning that it is false. Table 12-2 lists the conditions that are testable and is quite a handy reference. (If you're in a hurry, you can type **help test** on the command line to get the same information.)

Table 12-2: Operators for Test Expressions

Operator	What Is Being Tested?
-a *file*	Does the file exist? (same as −e)
-b *file*	Is the file a special block device?
-c *file*	Is the file character special (for example, a character device)? Used to identify serial lines and terminal devices.
-d *file*	Is the file a directory?
-e *file*	Does the file exist? (same as -a)
-f *file*	Does the file exist, and is it a regular file (for example, not a directory, socket, pipe, link, or device file)?
-g *file*	Does the file have the set-group-id bit set?
-h *file*	Is the file a symbolic link? (same as −L)
-k *file*	Does the file have the sticky bit set?
-L *file*	Is the file a symbolic link?
-n *string*	Is the length of the string greater than 0 bytes?
-O *file*	Do you own the file?
-p *file*	Is the file a named pipe?
-r *file*	Is the file readable by you?
-s *file*	Does the file exist, and is it larger than 0 bytes?
-S *file*	Does the file exist, and is it a socket?
-t *fd*	Is the file descriptor connected to a terminal?
-u *file*	Does the file have the set-user-id bit set?
-w *file*	Is the file writable by you?
-x *file*	Is the file executable by you?
-z *string*	Is the length of the string 0 (zero) bytes?
expr1 -a *expr2*	Are both the first expression and the second expression true?
expr1 -o *expr2*	Is either of the two expressions true?
file1 -nt *file2*	Is the first file newer than the second file (using the modification timestamp)?
file1 -ot *file2*	Is the first file older than the second file (using the modification timestamp)?

Operator	What Is Being Tested?
`file1 -ef file2`	Are the two files associated by a link (a hard link or a symbolic link)?
`var1 = var2`	Is the first variable equal to the second variable?
`var1 -eq var2`	Is the first variable equal to the second variable?
`var1 -ge var2`	Is the first variable greater than or equal to the second variable?
`var1 -gt var2`	Is the first variable greater than the second variable?
`var1 -le var2`	Is the first variable less than or equal to the second variable?
`var1 -lt var2`	Is the first variable less than the second variable?
`var1 != var2`	Is the first variable not equal to the second variable?
`var1 -ne var2`	Is the first variable not equal to the second variable?

There is also a special shorthand method of performing tests that can be useful for simple *one-command* actions. In the following example, the two pipes (| |) indicate that if the directory being tested for doesn't exist (`-d dirname`), then make the directory (`mkdir $dirname`).

```
# [ test ] || {action}
# Perform simple single command {action} if test is false
[ -d $dirname ] || mkdir $dirname
```

Instead of pipes, you can use two ampersands to test if something is true. In the following example, a command is being tested to see if it includes at least three command-line arguments.

```
# [ test ] && {action}
# Perform simple single command {action} if test is true
[ $# -ge 3 ] && echo "There are at least 3 command line arguments."
```

The case command

Another frequently used construct is the `case` command. Similar to a `switch` statement in programming languages, this can take the place of several nested `if` statements. A general form of the `case` statement is as follows:

```
case "VAR" in
   Result1)
      { body };;
   Result2)
      { body };;
   *)
      { body } ;;
esac
```

One use for the `case` command might be to help with your backups. The following case statement tests for the first three letters of the current day (case `date +%a` in). Then, depending on the day, a particular backup directory (BACKUP) and tape drive (TAPE) is set.

```
# Our VAR doesn't have to be a variable,
# it can be the output of a command as well
# Perform action based on day of week
case `date +%a` in
   "Mon")
        BACKUP=/home/myproject/data0
        TAPE=/dev/rft0
# Note the use of the double semi-colon to end each option
        ;;
# Note the use of the "|" to mean "or"
   "Tue" | "Thu")
        BACKUP=/home/myproject/data1
        TAPE=/dev/rft1
        ;;
   "Wed" | "Fri")
        BACKUP=/home/myproject/data2
        TAPE=/dev/rft2
        ;;
# Don't do backups on the weekend.
   *)
        BACKUP="none"
        TAPE=/dev/null
        ;;
esac
```

The asterisk (*) is used as a catchall, similar to the `default` keyword in the C programming language. In this example, if none of the other entries are matched on the way down the loop, the asterisk is matched, and the value of BACKUP becomes none. Note the use of esac, or case spelled backwards, to end the case statement.

The "for . . . do" loop

Loops are used to perform actions over and over again until a condition is met or until all data has been processed. One of the most commonly used loops is the `for . . . do` loop. It iterates through a list of values, executing the body of the loop for each element in the list. The syntax and a few examples are presented here:

```
for VAR in LIST
do
    { body }
done
```

The `for` loop assigns the values in `LIST` to `VAR` one at a time. Then for each value, the body in braces between `do` and `done` is executed. `VAR` can be any variable name, and `LIST` can be composed of pretty much any list of values or anything that generates a list.

```
for NUMBER in 0 1 2 3 4 5 6 7 8 9
do
    echo The number is $NUMBER
done
```

```
for FILE in `/bin/ls`
do
    echo $FILE
done
```

```
# You can also write it this way, which is somewhat cleaner.
for NAME in John Paul Ringo George ; do
    echo $NAME is my favorite Beatle
done
```

Each element in the `LIST` is separated from the next by whitespace. This can cause trouble if you're not careful, since some commands, like `ls -l`, output multiple fields per line, each separated by whitespace.

If you're a die-hard C programmer, bash allows you to use C syntax to control your loops.

```
LIMIT=10
# Double parentheses, and no $ on LIMIT even though it's a variable!
for ((a=1; a <= LIMIT ; a++)) ; do
  echo "$a"
done
```

The "while . . . do" and "until . . . do" loops

Two other possible looping constructs are the `while...do` loop and the `until...do` loop. The structure of each is presented here:

```
while condition        until condition
do                     do
    { body }               { body }
done                   done
```

The `while` statement executes while the condition is true. The `until` statement executes until the condition is true, in other words, while the condition is false.

Here is an example of a `while` loop that will output the number `0123456789`:

```
N=0
while [ $N -lt 10 ] ; do
    echo -n $N
    let N=$N+1
```

```
done
```

Another way to output the number 0123456789 is to use an until loop as follows:

```
N=0
until [ $N -eq 10 ] ; do
    echo -n $N
    let N=$N+1
done
```

Some useful external programs

Bash is great and has lots of built-in commands, but it usually needs some help to do anything really useful. Some of the most common useful programs you'll see used are grep, cut, tr, and sed. Like all the best UNIX tools, most of these programs are designed to work with standard input and standard output, so you can easily use them with pipes and shell scripts.

The General Regular Expression Parser (grep)

The name sounds intimidating, but grep is just a way to find patterns in files or text. Think of it as a useful search tool. Getting really good with regular expressions is quite a challenge, but many useful things can be accomplished with just the simplest forms.

For example, you can display a list of all regular user accounts by using grep to search for all lines that contain the text /home in the /etc/passwd file as follows:

```
grep /home /etc/passwd
```

Or you could find all environment variables that begin with HO using the following command:

```
env | grep ^HO
```

To find a list of options to use with the grep command, type **man grep**.

Remove sections of lines of text (cut)

The cut command can extract specific fields from a line of text or from files. It is very useful for parsing system configuration files into easy-to-digest chunks. You can specify the field separator you want to use and the fields you want, or you can break a line up based on bytes.

The following example lists all home directories of users on your system. Using an earlier example of the grep command, this line pipes a list of regular users from the /etc/passwd file, then displays the sixth field (-f6) as delimited by a colon (-d':').

```
grep /home /etc/passwd | cut -f6 -d':'
```

Translate or delete characters (tr)

The `tr` command is a character-based translator that can be used to replace one character or set of characters with another or to remove a character from a line of text.

The following example translates all uppercase letters to lowercase letters and displays the words "mixed upper and lower case" as a result:

```
FOO="Mixed UPpEr aNd LoWeR cAsE"
echo $FOO | tr [A-Z] [a-z]
```

In this example, the `tr` command is used on a list of file names to rename any files in that list so that any spaces contained in a file name are translated into underscores:

```
for file in * ; do
   d=`echo $file | tr [:blank:] [_]`
   [ "$file" -eq "-d" ] || mv "$file" "$d"
done
```

The Stream Editor (sed)

The `sed` command is a simple scriptable editor, and as such can perform only simple edits, such as removing lines that have text matching a certain pattern, replacing one pattern of characters with another, and other simple edits. To get a better idea of how `sed` scripts work, there's no substitute for the online documentation, but here are some examples of common uses.

You can use the `sed` command to essentially do what we did earlier with the `grep` example: search the `/etc/passwd` file for the word `home`. Here the sed command searches the entire `/etc/passwd` file, searches for the word `home`, and prints any line containing the word `home`.

```
sed -n -e '/home/p' /etc/passwd
```

In this example, `sed` searches the file `somefile.txt` and replaces every instance of the string `Mac` with `Linux`. The output is then sent to the `fixed_file.txt` file.

```
sed -e 's/Mac/Linux/' somefile.txt > fixed_file.txt
```

You can get the same result using a pipe:

```
cat somefile.txt | sed -e 's/Mac/Linux/' > fixed_file.txt
```

By searching for a pattern and replacing it with a null pattern, you delete the original pattern. This example searches the contents of the `somefile.txt` file and replaces extra blank spaces at the end of each line (s/ *$) with nothing (//). Results go to the `fixed_file.txt` file.

```
cat somefile.txt | sed -e 's/ *$//' > fixed_file.txt
```

Trying some simple shell scripts

Sometimes the simplest of scripts can be the most useful. If you type the same sequence of commands repetitively, it makes sense to store those commands (once!) in a file. Here are a couple of simple, but useful, shell scripts.

A simple telephone list

This idea has been handed down from generation to generation of old UNIX hacks. It's really quite simple, but it employs several of the concepts just introduced.

```
#!/bin/bash
# (@)/ph
# A very simple telephone list
# Type "ph new name number" to add to the list, or
# just type "ph name" to get a phone number

PHONELIST=~/.phonelist.txt

# If no command line parameters ($#), there
# is a problem, so ask what they're talking about.
if [ $# -lt 1 ] ; then
   echo "Whose phone number did you want?"
   exit 1
fi

# Did you want to add a new phone number?
if [ "$1" = "new" ] ; then
   shift
   echo $* >> $PHONELIST
   echo $* added to database
   exit 0
fi

# Nope. But does the file have anyting in it yet?
# This might be our first time using it, after all.
if [ ! -s $PHONELIST ] ; then
   echo "No names in the phone list yet!"
   exit 1
else
   grep -q "$*" $PHONELIST        # Quietly search the file
   if [ $? -ne 0 ] ; then         # Did we find anything?
      echo "Sorry, that name was not found in the phone list"
      exit 1
   else
      grep "$*" $PHONELIST
   fi
fi
exit 0
```

A Simple Backup Script

Since nothing works forever and mistakes happen, backups are just a fact of life when dealing with computer data. This simple script will back up all the data in the home directories of all the users on your Fedora system.

```
#!/bin/bash
# (@)/my_backup
# A very simple backup script
#

TAPE=/dev/rft0

# Rewind the tape device $TAPE
mt $TAPE rew
# Get a list of home directories
HOMES=`grep /home /etc/passwd | cut -f6 -d': '`
# Backup the data in those directories
tar cvf $TAPE $HOMES
# Rewind and eject the tape.
mt $TAPE rewoffl
```

> **CROSS-REFERENCE:** See Chapter 13 for details on backing up and restoring files.

System Initialization

When you turn on your computer, a lot happens even before Fedora starts up. Here are the basic steps that occur each time you boot up your computer to run Fedora:

1. **Boot hardware** — Based on information in the computer's read-only memory (referred to as the BIOS), your computer checks and starts up the hardware. Some of that information tells the computer which devices (floppy disk, CD, hard disk, and so on) to check to find the bootable operating system.

2. **Start boot loader** — Typically, the BIOS checks the master boot record on the primary hard disk to see what to load next. With Fedora installed, the GRUB boot loader is started, allowing you to choose to boot Fedora or another installed operating system.

3. **Boot the kernel** — Assuming that you selected to boot Fedora, the Linux kernel is loaded. That kernel mounts the basic file systems and transfers control to the init process. The rest of this section describes what happens after the kernel hands off control of system startup to the init process.

Starting init

In the boot process, the transfer from the kernel phase (the loading of the kernel, probing for devices, and loading drivers) to init is indicated by the following lines:

```
INIT: version 2.85 booting
```

```
Welcome to Fedora Core
Press "I" to enter interactive startup.
```

The init program, part of the SysVinit RPM package, is now in control. Known as "the father of all processes," the output from ps always lists `init` as PID (process identifier) 1. Its actions are directed by the `/etc/inittab` file, which is reproduced next.

The inittab file

The following example shows the contents of the `/etc/inittab` file as it is delivered with Fedora:

```
#
# inittab       This file describes how the INIT process should set up
#               the system in a certain run level.

    .
    .
    .

id:3:initdefault:

# System initialization.
si::sysinit:/etc/rc.d/rc.sysinit

l0:0:wait:/etc/rc.d/rc 0
l1:1:wait:/etc/rc.d/rc 1
l2:2:wait:/etc/rc.d/rc 2
l3:3:wait:/etc/rc.d/rc 3
l4:4:wait:/etc/rc.d/rc 4
l5:5:wait:/etc/rc.d/rc 5
l6:6:wait:/etc/rc.d/rc 6

# Trap CTRL-ALT-DELETE
ca::ctrlaltdel:/sbin/shutdown -t3 -r now

# When our UPS tells us power has failed, assume we have a few minutes
# of power left. Schedule a shutdown for 2 minutes from now.
# This does, of course, assume you have powerd installed and your
# UPS connected and working correctly.
pf::powerfail:/sbin/shutdown -f -h +2 "Power Failure; System Shutting Down"

# If power was restored before the shutdown kicked in, cancel it.
pr:12345:powerokwait:/sbin/shutdown -c "Power Restored; Shutdown Cancelled"

# Run gettys in standard runlevels
1:2345:respawn:/sbin/mingetty tty1
2:2345:respawn:/sbin/mingetty tty2
3:2345:respawn:/sbin/mingetty tty3
4:2345:respawn:/sbin/mingetty tty4
5:2345:respawn:/sbin/mingetty tty5
```

```
6:2345:respawn:/sbin/mingetty tty6

# Run xdm in runlevel 5
# xdm is now a separate service
x:5:respawn:/etc/X11/prefdm -nodaemon
```

Format of the inittab file

The plain-text `inittab` file consists of several colon-separated fields in the format:

```
id:runlevels:action:command
```

The `id` field is a unique identifier, one to four alphanumeric characters in length that represents a particular action to take during system startup. The `runlevels` field contains a list of run levels in which the command will be run. Common run levels are 0, 1, 2, 3, 4, 5, and 6 (s and S represent single-user mode, which is equivalent to 1). Run levels 7, 8, and 9 can also be used as the special run levels associated with the on demand action (a, b, and c, which are equivalent to A, B, and C). The next field represents the type of action to be taken by `init` (valid actions and the results of those actions are listed in Table 12-3), and the last field is the actual command that is to be executed.

Table 12-3: Valid init Actions

Action	How the Command Is Run
once	The command is executed once when entering the specified run level.
wait	The same as `once`, but `init` waits for the command to finish before continuing with other `inittab` entries.
respawn	The process is monitored, and a new instance is started if the original process terminates.
powerfail	The command is executed on receiving a `SIGPWR` signal from software associated with a UPS unit.
powerwait	The same as `powerfail`, but `init` waits for the command to finish.
powerwaitok	The command is executed on receiving a `SIGPWR` signal if the `/etc/powerstatus` file contains the word OK. This is generally accomplished by the UPS software, and indicates that a normal power level has been restored.
ondemand	The command is executed when `init` is manually instructed to enter one of the special run levels a, b, or c (equivalent to A, B, and C, respectively). No change in run level actually takes place. The program is restarted if the original process terminates.
sysinit	The command is executed during the system boot phase; the `runlevels` field is ignored.

Action	How the Command Is Run
boot	The command is executed during the system boot phase, after all sysinit entries have been processed; the runlevels field is ignored.
bootwait	The same as boot, but init waits for the command to finish before continuing with other inittab entries; the runlevels field is also ignored.
initdefault	The run level to enter after completing the boot and sysinit actions.
off	Nothing happens (perhaps useful for testing and debugging).
ctrlaltdel	Traps the Ctrl+Alt+Del key sequence, and is typically used to gracefully shut down the system.
kbrequest	Used to trap special key sequences, as interpreted by the keyboard handler.

Breakdown of the inittab file

Because the inittab file is a configuration file, not a sequential shell script, the order of lines is not significant. Lines beginning with a hash (#) character are comments and are not processed.

The first non-commented line in the preceding sample inittab file sets the default run level to 3. A default of 3 means that, following the completion of all commands associated with the sysinit, boot, and bootwait actions, run level 3 will be entered (booting to a text-based login). The other common initdefault level is run level 5 (booting to a GUI login screen). Table 12-4 describes each of the run levels and helps you choose the run level that is best suited as the default in your environment.

Table 12-4: Possible Run Levels

Run Level	What Happens in This Run Level
0	All processes are terminated and the machine comes to an orderly halt. As the inittab comments point out, this is not a good choice for initdefault, because as soon as the kernel, modules, and drivers are loaded, the machine will halt.
1, s, S	This is single-user mode, frequently used for system maintenance and where it may be preferable to have few processes running and no services activated. In single-user mode, the network is nonexistent, the X server is not running, and it is possible that some file systems are not mounted.

Run Level	What Happens in This Run Level
2	Multiuser mode. Multiple user logins are allowed, all configured file systems are mounted, and all processes except X, the `at` daemon, the `xinetd` daemon, and NIS/NFS are started. If your machine doesn't have (or perhaps doesn't need) a permanent network connection, this is a good choice for `initdefault`.
3, 4	Multiuser mode with network services. Run level 3 is the typical value for `initdefault` on a Fedora server, but run level 4 (generally left to be user-defined) is almost identical in a default Fedora configuration.
5	Multiuser mode with network services and X. This run level starts the X server and presents a graphical login window, visually resembling any of the more expensive UNIX-based workstations. This is a common `initdefault` value for a Fedora workstation or desktop system.
6	All processes are terminated and the machine is gracefully rebooted. Again, the comments in the `inittab` file mention that this is not a good choice for `initdefault`, perhaps even worse than run level 0. The effect is a possibly infinite cycle of booting, followed by rebooting.
7, 8, 9	Generally unused and undefined, these run levels have the potential to meet any needs not covered by the default options.
a, b, c, A, B, C	Used in conjunction with the `ondemand` action. These don't really specify a run level but can launch a program or daemon "on demand" if so instructed.

NOTE: If there is no `initdefault` specified in the `inittab` file, the boot sequence will be interrupted and you will be prompted to specify a default run level into which the machine will boot.

The next line in the `inittab` file instructs `init` to execute the `/etc/rc.d/rc.sysinit` script before entering the default run level. This script performs many initialization routines such as choosing a `keymap` file, checking and mounting `root` and `proc` file systems, setting the clock and hostname, configuring swap space, cleaning up `temp` files, and loading modules.

The seven following lines control the commands executed within each major run level. In each, the `/etc/rc.d/rc` script is called, using the desired run level as an argument. It, in turn, descends into the appropriate directory tree (for example, the `/etc/rc3.d` directory is entered for run level 3).

The `ctrlaltdel` action in the `inittab` file tells `init` to perform exactly what PC users would expect if the Ctrl, Alt, and Delete keys were pressed simultaneously. The system reboots itself in an orderly fashion (a switch to run level 6) after a three-second delay.

The next two lines (with their comments) deal with graceful shutdowns if you have an uninterruptible power supply (UPS) and software installed. The first line initiates a halt (a switch to run level 0) two minutes after receiving a signal from the UPS indicating a power failure. The second line cancels the shutdown in the event that power is restored.

The six `getty` lines start up virtual consoles to allow logins. These processes are always running in any of the multiuser run levels. When someone connected to a virtual console logs out, that `getty` process dies, then `respawn` action tells `init` to start a new `getty` process.

The last line indicates that as long as the system is in run level 5, the "preferred display manager" (xdm, gnome, KDE, and so on) will be running. This presents a graphical login prompt rather than the usual text-based login, and eliminates the need to run `startx` to start the GUI.

System Startup and Shutdown

During system startup, a series of scripts are run to start the services that you need. These include scripts to start network interfaces, mount directories, and monitor your system. Most of these scripts are run from subdirectories of `/etc/rc.d`. The program that starts most of these services up when you boot and stops them when you shut down is the `/etc/rc.d/rc` script. The following sections describe run-level scripts and what you can do with them.

Starting run-level scripts

As previously mentioned, the `/etc/rc.d/rc` script is a script that is integral to the concept of run levels. Any change of run level causes the script to be executed, with the new run level as an argument. Here's a quick run-down of what the `/etc/rc.d/rc` script does:

- **Checks that run level scripts are correct.** The `rc` script checks to find each run-level script that exists and excludes those that represent backup scripts left by `rpm` updates.

- **Determines current and previous run levels.** Determines the current and previous run levels to know which run-level scripts to stop (previous level) and start (current level).

- **Decides whether to enter interactive startup.** If the confirm option is passed to the boot loader at boot time, all server processes must be confirmed at the system console before starting.

- **Kills and starts run-level scripts.** Stops run-level scripts from the previous level, then starts run-level scripts from the current level.

In Fedora, most of the services that are provided to users and computers on the network are started from run-level scripts.

Understanding run-level scripts

A software package that has a service to start at boot time (or when the system changes run levels) can add a script to the `/etc/init.d` directory. That script can then be linked to an appropriate run-level directory and either be started or stopped (to start or stop the service).

Table 12-5 lists many of the typical run-level scripts that are found in `/etc/init.d` and explains their function. Depending on the Fedora software packages you installed on your system, you may have dozens more run-level scripts than you see here. (Later, I describe how these files are linked into particular run-level directories.)

Table 12-5: Run-Level Scripts Contained in /etc/init.d

Run-Level Scripts	What Does It Do?
apmd	Controls the Advanced Power Management daemon, which monitors battery status, and which can safely suspend or shut down all or part of a machine that supports it.
atd	Starts or stops the at daemon to receive, queue, and run jobs submitted via the at or batch commands. (The anacron run-level script runs at and batch jobs that were not run because the computer was down.)
autofs	Starts and stops the automount daemon, for automatically mounting file systems (so, for example, a CD can be automatically mounted when it is inserted).
crond	Starts or stops the cron daemon to periodically run routine commands.
cups-lpd	Controls the printer daemon that handles spooling printing requests.
dhcpd	Starts or stops the dhcpd daemon, which automatically assigns IP addresses to computers on a LAN.
gpm	Controls the gpm daemon, which allows the mouse to interact with console- and text-based applications.
halt	Terminates all processes, writes out accounting records, removes swap space, unmounts all file systems, and either shuts down or reboots the machine (depending on how the command was called).
httpd	Starts the httpd daemon, which allows your computer to act as an HTTP server (that is, to serve Web pages).
iptables	Starts the iptables firewall daemon, which manages any iptables-style firewall rules set up for your computer.
keytable	Loads the predefined keyboard map.
killall	Shuts down any subsystems that may still be running prior to a shutdown or reboot.
kudzu	Detects and configures new hardware at boot time.
netfs	Mounts or unmounts network (NFS, SMB, and NCP) file systems.
network	Starts or stops all configured network interfaces and initializes the TCP/IP and IPX protocols.

Run-Level Scripts	What Does It Do?
nfs	Starts or stops the NFS-related daemons (`rpc.nfsd`, `rpc.mountd`, `rpc.statd`, and `rcp.rquotad`) and exports shared file systems.
pcmcia	Loads or unloads modules, drivers, and programs (including the `cardmgr` daemon) to support PCMCIA cards (Ethernet adapters, modems, memory cards, and so on) in laptop computers.
portmap	Starts or stops the `portmap` daemon, which manages programs and protocols that utilize the Remote Procedure Call (RPC) mechanism.
random	Loads or saves the current state of the machine's random number generator's random seed to ensure more random randomness.
routed	Starts or stops the `routed` daemon, which controls dynamic-routing table updates via the Router Information Protocol (RIP).
rwhod	Starts or stops the `rwhod` daemon, which enables others on the network to obtain a list of all currently logged-in users.
sendmail	Controls the `sendmail` daemon, which handles incoming and outgoing SMTP (Simple Mail Transport Protocol) mail messages.
single	Terminates all running processes and enters run level 1 (single-user mode).
smb	Starts or stops the `smbd` and `nmbd` daemons for allowing access to Samba file and print services.
snmpd	Starts or stops the `snmpd` (Simple Network Management Protocol) daemon, which enables others to view machine-configuration information.
squid	Starts or stops the `squid` services, which enables proxy service to clients on your network.
syslog	Starts or stops the `klogd` and `syslogd` daemons that handle logging events from the kernel and other processes, respectively.
xfs	Starts or stops `xfs`, the X Window font server daemon.
xinetd	Sets the machine's host name, establishes network routes, and controls `xinetd`, the network services daemon which listens for incoming TCP/IP connections to the machine.
ypbind	Binds to an NIS (Network Information Service) master server (if NIS is configured), and starts or stops the `ypbind` process, which communicates with the master server.

Each script representing a service that you want to start or stop is linked to a file in each of the run-level directories. For each run level, a script beginning with K stops the service, whereas a script beginning with S starts the service.

The two digits following the K or S in the filename provide a mechanism to select the priority in which the programs are run. For example, S12syslog is run before S90crond. However, while humans can readily see that 85 is less than 110, the file S110my_daemon is run before S85gpm. This is because the "ASCII collating sequence orders the files," which simply means that one positional character is compared to another. Therefore, a script beginning with the characters S110 is executed between S10network and S15netfs in run level 3.

All of the programs within the /etc/rcX.d directories (where X is replaced by a run-level number) are symbolic links, usually to a file in /etc/init.d. The /etc/rcX.d directories include the following:

- /etc/rc0.d: Run level 0 directory
- /etc/rc1.d: Run level 1 directory
- /etc/rc2.d: Run level 2 directory
- /etc/rc3.d: Run level 3 directory
- /etc/rc4.d: Run level 4 directory
- /etc/rc5.d: Run level 5 directory
- /etc/rc6.d: Run level 6 directory

In this manner, /etc/rc0.d/K05atd, /etc/rc1.d/K05atd, /etc/rc2.d/K05atd, /etc/rc3.d/S95atd, /etc/rc4.d/S95atd, /etc/rc5.d/S95atd, and /etc/rc6.d/K05atd are all symbolic links to /etc/init.d/atd. Using this simple, consistent mechanism, you can customize which programs are started at boot time.

Understanding what startup scripts do

Despite all the complicated rcXs, Ss, and Ks, the form of each startup script is really quite simple. Because they are in plain text, you can just open one with a text editor to take a look at what it does. For the most part, a run-level script can be run with a start option, a stop option, and possibly a restart option. For example, the following lines are part of the contents of the smb script that defines what happens when the script is run with different options to start or stop the Samba file and print service:

```
#!/bin/sh
#
# chkconfig: - 91 35
# description: Starts and stops the Samba smbd and nmbd daemons \
#              used to provide SMB network services.

      .
      .
      .
start() {
        KIND="SMB"
        echo -n $"Starting $KIND services: "
```

```
        daemon smbd $SMBDOPTIONS
        RETVAL=$?
        echo
        KIND="NMB"
        echo -n $"Starting $KIND services: "
        daemon nmbd $NMBDOPTIONS
        RETVAL2=$?
        echo
        [ $RETVAL -eq 0 -a $RETVAL2 -eq 0 ] && touch /var/lock/subsys/smb || \
            RETVAL=1
        return $RETVAL
}

stop() {
        KIND="SMB"
        echo -n $"Shutting down $KIND services: "
        killproc smbd
        RETVAL=$?
        echo
        KIND="NMB"
        echo -n $"Shutting down $KIND services: "
        killproc nmbd
        RETVAL2=$?
        [ $RETVAL -eq 0 -a $RETVAL2 -eq 0 ] && rm -f /var/lock/subsys/smb
        echo ""
        return $RETVAL
}

restart() {
        stop
        start
}
        .
        .
        .
```

To illustrate what this script essentially does, I skipped some of the beginning and end of the script (where it checked if the network was up and running and set some values). Here are the actions smb takes when it is run with start or stop:

- **start** — This part of the script starts the smbd and nmbd servers when the script is run with the start option.

- **stop** — When run with the stop option, the /etc/init.d/smb script stops the smbd and nmbd servers.

The restart option runs the script with a stop option followed by a start option. If you want to start the smb service yourself, you can type the following command (as root user):

```
# service smb start
```

```
Starting SMB services:                    [ OK ]
Starting NMB services:                    [ OK ]
```

To stop the service, you could type the following command:

```
# service smb stop
Shutting down SMB services:               [ OK ]
Shutting down NMB services:               [ OK ]
```

The smb run-level script is different from other run-level scripts in that it supports several other options than start and stop. For example, this script has options (not shown in the example) that allow you to reload the smb.conf configuration file (reload) and check the status of the service (rhstatus).

Changing run-level script behavior

Modifying the startup behavior of any such script merely involves opening the file in a text editor. For example, the atd daemon queues jobs submitted from the at and batch commands. Jobs submitted via batch are executed only if the system load is below a particular value, which can be set with a command-line option to the atd command. The default value of 0.8 is based on the assumption that a single-processor machine with less than 80 percent CPU utilization could handle the additional load of the batch job. However, if you were to add another CPU to your machine, the default threshold value would be too low and the batch jobs would not be sufficiently restricted.

You can change the system load threshold value from 0.8 to 1.6 to accommodate the increased processing capacity. To do this, simply modify the following line (in the start section) of the /etc/init.d/atd script:

```
daemon /usr/sbin/atd
```

Replace it with this line, using the -l argument to specify the new minimum system load value:

```
daemon /usr/sbin/atd -l 1.6
```

After saving the file and exiting the editor, you can reboot the machine or just run any of the following three commands to begin using the new batch threshold value:

```
service atd reload
service atd restart
service atd stop ; service atd start
```

> **NOTE:** Always make a copy of a run-level script before you change it. Also, keep track of changes you make to run-level scripts before you upgrade the packages they come from. You need to make those changes again after the upgrade.

If you are uncomfortable editing startup scripts and you simply want to add options to the daemon process run by the script, there may be a way of entering these changes without editing the startup script directly. Check the `/etc/sysconfig` directory and see if there is a file by the same name as the script you want to modify. If there is, that file probably provides values that you can set to pass options to the startup script. Sysconfig files exist for `amd`, `arpwatch`, `dhcpd`, `kudzu`, `ntpd`, `samba`, `squid`, and others.

Reorganizing or removing run-level scripts

There are several ways to deal with removing programs from the system startup directories, adding them to particular run levels, or changing when they are executed. From a Terminal window, you can use the `chkconfig` command. From a GUI, use the Service Configuration window.

> **CAUTION:** You should never remove the run-level file from the `/etc/init.d` directory. Because no scripts are run from the `/etc/init.d` directory automatically, it is okay to keep them there. Scripts in `/etc/init.d` are only accessed as links from the `/etc/rcX.d` directories. Keep scripts in the `init.d` directory so you can add them later by re-linking them to the appropriate run-level directory.

To reorganize or remove run-level scripts from the GUI, use the Service Configuration window. Either select System Settings → Server Settings → Services or log in as root user and type the following command in a Terminal window:

```
# serviceconf &
```

Figure 12-1 shows an example of the Service Configuration window.

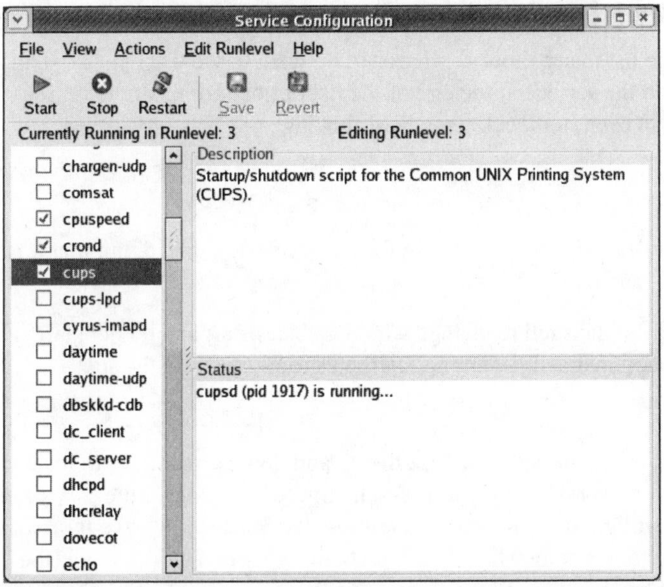

Figure 12-1: Reorganize, add, and remove run-level scripts from the Service Configuration window.

The Service Configuration window lets you reconfigure services for run levels 3, 4, and 5. The run levels that you are currently running and currently editing are displayed near the top of the screen. Services that are available for the run level appear in the middle of the frame, with check marks next to the ones configured to start at that level. Here is what you can do from this window:

- **Add** — Click the box next to each service you want to start automatically at that run level so that a check mark appears in the box.

- **Remove** — Click the run-level script that you want to remove for a particular run level to remove the check mark.

- **Save** — Click File, then Save Changes on the window to save any changes you have made to the run-level scripts.

- **Refresh** — Click View, then Refresh Service List to refresh the list of services.

- **Start, Stop, or Restart** — Click a service on the list. Select Actions, then either Start, Stop, or Restart Service. The selected service immediately starts, stops, or restarts.

Some administrators prefer text-based commands for managing run-level scripts and for managing other system services that start automatically. The chkconfig command can be used to list whether services that run-level scripts start, as well as services the xinetd daemon starts, are on or off. To see a list of all system services, with indications that they are on or off, type the following:

```
# chkconfig --list | less
```

You can then page through the list to see those services. If you want to view the status of an individual service, you can add the service at the end of the list option. For example, to see whether the nfs service starts in each run level, type the following:

```
# chkconfig --list nfs
nfs       0:off   1:off   2:off   3:on   4:on   5:on   6:off
```

This example shows that the nfs service is set to be on for run levels 3, 4, and 5, but that it is set to off for run levels 0, 1, 2, and 6.

Another tool that can be run from the shell to change which services start and do not start at various levels is the ntsysv command. Type the following as root user from the shell:

```
# ntsysv
```

A screen appears with a list of available services. Use the up and down arrow keys to locate the service you want. With the cursor on a service, press the Spacebar to toggle the service on or off. Press the Tab key to highlight the OK button, and press the Spacebar to save the change and exit. The ntsysv tool is somewhat clever; it checks your default run level (the initdefault set in the /etc/inittab file) and turns on the service so it starts at that run level.

Adding run-level scripts

Suppose you want to create and configure your own run-level script. For example, after installing the binaries for the fictitious my_daemon program, it needs to be configured to start up in run levels 3, 4, and 5, and terminated in any other run level. You can add the script to the /etc/init.d directory, then use the chkconfig command to configure it.

To use chkconfig, ensure that the following lines are included in the /etc/init.d/my_daemon script:

```
# chkconfig: 345 82 28
# description: Does something pretty cool - you really \
#    have to see it to believe it!
# processname: my_daemon
```

> **NOTE**: The line chkconfig: 345 82 28 sets the script to start in runlevels 3, 4, and 5. It sets start scripts to be set to 82 for those runlevels. It sets stop scripts to be set to 28 in all other levels.

With those lines in place, simply run the following command:

```
# chkconfig --add my_daemon
```

Appropriate links are created automatically. This can be verified with the following command:

```
# chkconfig --list my_daemon
```

The resulting output should look like this:

```
my_daemon 0:off 1:off 2:off 3:on 4:on 5:on 6:off
```

The script names that are created by chkconfig to make this all work are:

```
/etc/rc0.d/K28my_daemon
/etc/rc1.d/K28my_daemon
/etc/rc2.d/K28my_daemon
/etc/rc3.d/S82my_daemon
/etc/rc4.d/S82my_daemon
/etc/rc5.d/S82my_daemon
/etc/rc6.d/K28my_daemon
```

Managing xinetd services

There are a bunch of services, particularly Internet services, that are not handled by separate run-level scripts. Instead, a single run-level script called xinetd (formerly inetd) is run to handle incoming requests for these services. For that reason, xinetd is sometimes referred to as the *super-server*. The xinetd run-level script (along with the xinetd daemon that it runs) offers the following advantages:

- **Fewer daemon processes.** Instead of one (or more) daemon processes running on your computer to monitor incoming requests for each service, the xinetd daemon can listen for requests for many different services. As a result, when you type ps -ax to see what processes are running, dozens of fewer daemon processes will be running than there would be if each service had its own daemon.

- **Access control and logging.** By using xinetd to oversee the management of services, consistent methods of access control (such as PAM) and consistent logging methods (such as the /var/log/messages file) can be used across all of the services.

When a request comes into your computer for a service that xinetd is monitoring, xinetd uses the /etc/xinetd.conf file to read configuration files contained in the /etc/xinetd.d directory. Then, based on the contents of the xinetd.d file for the requested service, a server program is launched to handle the service request (provided that the service is not disabled).

Each server process is one of two types: single-thread or multithread. A single-thread server will handle only the current request, whereas a multithread server will handle all incoming requests for the service as long as there is still a client holding the process open. Then the multithread server will close and xinetd will begin monitoring that service again.

The following are a few examples of services that are monitored by xinetd. The daemon process that is started up to handle each service is also listed.

- **comsat** (/usr/sbin/in.comsat) — Alerts the biff client that new mail has arrived.
- **eklogin** (/usr/kerberos/sbin/klogind) — Kerberos-related login daemon.
- **finger** (/usr/sbin/in.fingerd) — Handles incoming finger requests for information from remote users about local users.
- **gssftp** (/usr/kerberos/sbin/ftpd) — Kerberos-related daemon for handling file transfer requests (FTP).
- **ntalk** (/usr/sbin/in.ntalkd) — Daemon for handling requests to set up chats between a remote user and a local one (using the talk command).
- **rlogin** (/usr/sbin/in.rlogind) — Daemon for responding to remote login requests (from a remote rlogin command).
- **rsh** (/usr/sbin/in.rshd) — Handles requests from a remote client to run a command on the local computer.

Other services that can be launched by requests that come to xinetd include services for remote telnet requests, Samba configuration requests (swat), and amanda network backups. A short description of each service is included in its /etc/xinetd.d file.

Manipulating run levels

Aside from the run level chosen at boot time (usually 3 or 5) and the shutdown or reboot levels (0 and 6, respectively), you can change the run level at any time while you're logged in (as root user). The telinit command (really just a symbolic link to init) enables you to specify a desired run level, causing the termination of all system processes that shouldn't exist in that run level, and starting all processes that should be running.

> **NOTE:** The `telinit` command is also used to instruct `init` to reload its configuration file, `/etc/inittab`. This is accomplished with either the `telinit q` or the `telinit Q` commands.

For example, if you encountered a problem with your hard disk on startup, you may be placed in single-user mode (run level 1) to perform system maintenance. After the machine is stable, you can just execute the command as follows:

```
# telinit 5
```

The `init` command handles terminating and starting all processes necessary to present you with a graphical login window.

Determining the current run level

You can determine the machine's current run level with the aptly named `runlevel` command. Using the previous example of booting into single-user mode and then manually changing the run level, the output of the `runlevel` command would be:

```
# runlevel
S 5
```

This means that the previous run level was S (for single-user mode) and the current run level is 5. If the machine had booted properly, the previous run level would be listed as N to indicate that there really wasn't a previous run level.

Changing to a shutdown run level

Shutting down the machine is simply a change in run level. With that in mind, other ways to change the run level include the `reboot`, `halt`, `poweroff`, and `shutdown` commands. The `reboot` command, which is a symbolic link to the `halt` command, executes a `shutdown -r now`, terminating all processes and rebooting the machine. The `halt` command executes `shutdown -h now`, terminating all processes and leaving the machine in an idle state (but still powered on). Similarly, the `poweroff` command, which is also a link to the `halt` command, executes a change to run level 0, but if the machine's BIOS supports Advanced Power Management (APM), it will switch off the power to the machine.

> **NOTE:** A time must be given to the `shutdown` command, either specified as +m (representing the number of minutes to delay before beginning shutdown) or as hh:mm (an absolute time value, where hh is the hour and mm is the minute that you would like the shutdown to begin). Alternatively, now is commonly used to initiate the shutdown immediately.

Scheduling System Tasks

Frequently, you need to run a process unattended or at off-hours. The at facility is designed to run such jobs at specific times. Jobs you submit are spooled in the directory /var/spool/at, awaiting execution by the at daemon atd. The jobs are executed using the current directory and environment that was active when the job was submitted. Any output or error messages that haven't been redirected elsewhere are e-mailed to the user who submitted the job.

The following sections describe how to use the at, batch, and cron facilities to schedule tasks to run at specific times. These descriptions also include ways of viewing which tasks are scheduled and deleting scheduled tasks that you don't want to run anymore.

Using at.allow and at.deny

There are two access control files designed to limit which users can use the at facility. The file /etc/at.allow contains a list of users who are granted access, and the file /etc/at.deny contains a similar list of those who may not submit at jobs. If neither file exists, only the superuser is granted access to at. If a blank /etc/at.deny file exists (as in the default configuration), all users are allowed to utilize the at facility to run their own at jobs.

Specifying when jobs are run

There are many different ways to specify the time at which an at job should run (most of which look like spoken commands). Table 12-6 has a few examples. These are not complete commands — they only provide an example of how to specify the time that a job should run.

Table 12-6: Samples for Specifying Times in an at Job

Command Line	When the Command Is Run
at now	The job is run immediately.
at now + 2 minutes	The job will start 2 minutes from the current time.
at now + 1 hour	The job will start one hour from the current time.
at now + 5 days	The job will start five days from the current time.
at now + 4 weeks	The job will start four weeks from the current time.
at now next minute	The job will start in exactly 60 seconds.
at now next hour	The job will start in exactly 60 minutes.
at now next day	The job will start at the same time tomorrow.

Command Line	When the Command Is Run
at now next month	The job will start on the same day and at the same time next month.
at now next year	The job will start on the same date and at the same time next year.
at now next fri	The job will start at the same time next Friday.
at teatime	The job will run at 4 p.m. They keywords noon and midnight can also be used.
at 16:00 today	The job will run at 4 p.m. today.
at 16:00 tomorrow	The job will run at 4 p.m. tomorrow.
at 2:45pm	The job will run at 2:45 p.m. on the current day.
at 14:45	The job will run at 2:45 p.m. on the current day.
at 5:00 Apr 14 2004	The job will begin at 5 a.m. on April14, 2004.
at 5:00 4/14/04	The job will begin at 5 a.m. on April 14, 2004.

Submitting scheduled jobs

The at facility offers a lot of flexibility in how you can submit scheduled jobs. There are three ways to submit a job to the at facility:

- **Piped in from standard input**. For example, the following command will attempt to build the Perl distribution from source in the early morning hours while the machine is likely to be less busy:

```
echo "cd /tmp/perl; make ; ls -al" | at 2am tomorrow
```

  An ancillary benefit to this procedure is that a full log of the compilation process will be e-mailed to the user who submitted the job.

- **Read as standard input.** If no command is specified, at will prompt you to enter commands at the special at> prompt, as shown in the following example. You must indicate the end of the commands by pressing Ctrl+D, which signals an End of Transmission (<EOT>) to at.

```
$ at 23:40
at> cd /tmp/perl
at> make
at> ls -al
at> <Ctrl-d>
```

- **Read from a file.** When the -f command-line option is followed by a valid filename, the contents of that file are used as the commands to be executed, as in the following example:

```
$ at -f /root/bin/runme now + 5 hours
```

This runs the commands stored in /root/bin/runme in five hours. The file can either be a simple list of commands or a shell script to be run in its own subshell (that is, the file begins with #!/bin/bash or the name of another shell).

Viewing scheduled jobs

You can use the atq command (effectively the same as at -l) to view a list of your pending jobs in the at queue, showing each job's sequence number, the date and time the job is scheduled to run, and the queue in which the job is being run.

The two most common queue names are a (which represents the at queue) and b (which represents the batch queue). All other letters (upper- and lowercase) can be used to specify queues with lower priority levels. If the atq command lists a queue name as =, it indicates that the job is currently running. Here is an example of output from the atq command:

```
# atq
2       2003-09-02 00:51 a
3       2003-09-02 00:52 a
4       2003-09-05 23:52 a
```

Here you can see that there are three at jobs pending (job numbers 2, 3, and 4, all indicated as a). After the job number, the output shows the date and hour each job is scheduled to run.

Deleting scheduled jobs

If you decide that you'd like to cancel a particular job, you can use the atrm command (equivalent to at -d) with the job number (or more than one) as reported by the atq command. For example, using the following output from atq:

```
# atq
18      2003-09-01 03:00 a
19      2003-09-29 05:27 a
20      2003-09-30 05:27 a
21      2003-09-14 00:01 a
22      2003-09-01 03:00 a
```

you can remove the jobs scheduled to run at 5:27 a.m. on September 29 and September 30 from the queue with the command atrm 19 20.

Using the batch command

If system resources are at a premium on your machine, or if the job you submit can run at a priority lower than normal, the batch command (equivalent to at -q b) may be useful. It is controlled by the same `atd` daemon, and it allows job submissions in the same format as `at` submissions (although the time specification is optional).

However, to prevent your job from usurping already scarce processing time, the job will run only if the system load average is below a particular value. The default value is 0.8, but specifying a command-line option to `atd` can modify this. This was used as an example in the earlier section describing startup and shutdown. Here is an example of the `batch` command:

```
$ batch
at> du -h /home > /tmp/duhome
at> <Ctrl-d>
```

In this example, after I type the `batch` command, the `at` facility is invoked to enable me to enter the command(s) I want to run. Typing the `du -h /home > /tmp/duhome` command line has the disk usages for everything in the `/home` directory structure output to the `/tmp/duhome` file. On the next line, pressing Ctrl+D ends the batch job. As soon as the load average is low enough, the command is run. (Run the `top` command to view the current load average.)

Using the cron facility

Another way to run commands unattended is via the `cron` facility. Part of the vixie-cron RPM package, `cron` addresses the need to run commands periodically or routinely (at least, more often than you'd care to manually enter them) and allows lots of flexibility in automating the execution of the command. As with the `at` facility, any output or error messages that haven't been redirected elsewhere are e-mailed to the user who submitted the job.

Also like the `at` facility, `cron` includes two access control files designed to limit which users can use it. The file `/etc/cron.allow` contains a list of users who are granted access, and the file `/etc/cron.deny` contains a similar list of those who may not submit `cron` jobs. If neither file exists, all users are granted access to `cron`.

There are four places where a job can be submitted for execution by the `cron` daemon `crond`:

- **The `/var/spool/cron/username` file.** This method, where each individual user (indicated by *username*) controls his or her own separate file, is the method used on UNIX System V systems.

- **The `/etc/crontab` file.** This is referred to as the *system crontab file*, and was the original crontab file from BSD UNIX and its derivatives. Only root has permission to modify this file.

- **The `/etc/cron.d` directory.** Files placed in this directory have the same format as the `/etc/crontab` file. Only root is permitted to create or modify files in this directory.

- **The /etc/cron.hourly, /etc/cron.daily, /etc/cron.weekly, and /etc/cron.monthly directories.** Each file in these directories is a shell script that runs at the times specified in the /etc/crontab file (by default, at one minute after the hour; at 4:02 a.m. every day; Sunday at 4:22 a.m.; and 4:42 a.m. on the first day of the month, respectively). Only root is allowed to create or modify files in these directories.

The standard format of an entry in the /var/spool/cron/*username* file consists of five fields specifying when the command should run: minute, hour, day of the month, month, and day of the week. The sixth field is the actual command to be run.

The files in the /etc/cron.d directory and the /etc/crontab file use the same first five fields to determine when the command should run. However, the sixth field represents the name of the user submitting the job (because it cannot be inferred by the name of the file as in a /var/spool/cron/*username* directory), and the seventh field is the command to be run. Table 12-7 lists the valid values for each field common to both types of files.

Table 12-7: Valid /etc/crontab Field Values

Field Number	Field	Acceptable Values
1	minute	Any integer between 0 and 59
2	hour	Any integer between 0 and 23
3	day of the month	Any integer between 0 and 31
4	month	Any integer between 0 and 12, or an abbreviation for the name of the month (Jan, Feb, Mar, Apr, May, Jun, Jul, Aug, Sep, Oct, Nov, Dec)
5	day of the week	Any integer between 0 and 7 (where both 0 and 7 can represent Sunday), or abbreviation for the day (Sun, Mon, Tue, Wed, Thu, Fri, Sat)

An asterisk (*) in any field indicates all possible values for that field. For example, an asterisk in the second column is equivalent to 0,1,2 . . . 22,23, and an asterisk in the fourth column means Jan,Feb,Mar . . . Nov,Dec. In addition, lists of values, ranges of values, and increments can be used. For example, to specify the days Monday, Wednesday, and Friday, the fifth field could be represented as the list Mon,Wed,Fri. To represent the normal working hours in a day, the range 9–5 could be specified in the second field. Another option is to use an increment, as in specifying 0–31/3 in the third field to represent every third day of the month, or */5 in the first field to denote every five minutes.

Lines beginning with a # character in any of the crontab-format files are comments, which can be very helpful in explaining what task each command is designed to perform. It is also possible to specify environment variables (in Bourne shell syntax, for example, NAME="value") within the crontab file. Any variable can be specified to fine-tune the environment in which the job will run, but one that may be particularly useful is MAILTO. The following line will send the results of the cron job to a user other than the one who submitted the job:

```
MAILTO=otheruser
```

If the following line appears in a crontab file, all output and error messages that haven't already been redirected will be discarded:

```
MAILTO=
```

Modifying scheduled tasks with crontab

The files in /var/spool/cron should not be edited directly. They should only be accessed via the crontab command. To list the current contents of your own personal crontab file, type the following command:

```
$ crontab -l
```

All crontab entries can be removed with the following command:

```
$ crontab -r
```

Even if your personal crontab file doesn't exist, you can use the following command to begin editing it:

```
$ crontab -e
```

The file automatically opens in the text editor that is defined in your EDITOR or VISUAL environment variables, with vi as the default. When you're done, simply exit the editor. Provided there were no syntax errors, your crontab file will be installed. For example, if your user name is jsmith, you have just created the file /var/spool/cron/jsmith. If you add a line (with a descriptive comment, of course) to remove any old core files from your source code directories, that file may look similar to this:

```
# Find and remove core files from /home/jsmith/src
5 1 * * Sun,Wed find /home/jsmith/src -name core.[0-9]* -exec rm {} \; > /dev/null 2>&1
```

Because core files in Fedora consist of the word core, followed by a dot (.) and process ID, this example will match all file beginning with core. and followed by a number. The root user can access any user's individual crontab file by using the -u username option to the crontab command.

Understanding cron files

There are separate `cron` directories set up to contain `cron` jobs that run hourly, daily, weekly, and monthly. These `cron` jobs are all set up to run from the `/etc/crontab` file. The default `/etc/crontab` file looks like this:

```
SHELL=/bin/bash
PATH=/sbin:/bin:/usr/sbin:/usr/bin
MAILTO=root
HOME=/

# run-parts
01 * * * * root run-parts /etc/cron.hourly
02 4 * * * root run-parts /etc/cron.daily
22 4 * * 0 root run-parts /etc/cron.weekly
42 4 1 * * root run-parts /etc/cron.monthly
```

The first four lines initialize the run-time environment for all subsequent jobs (the subshell in which jobs will run, the executable program search path, the recipient of output and error messages, and that user's home directory). The next five lines execute (as the user root) the `run-parts` program that controls programs that you may want to run periodically.

`run-parts` is a shell script that takes a directory as a command-line argument. It then sequentially runs every program within that directory (shell scripts are most common, but binary executables and links are also evaluated). The default configuration executes programs in `/etc/cron.hourly` at one minute after every hour of every day; `/etc/cron.daily` at 4:02 a.m. every day; `/etc/cron.weekly` at 4:22 a.m. on Sundays; and `/etc/cron.monthly` at 4:42 a.m. on the first day of each month.

Here are examples of files that are installed in `cron` directories for different software packages:

- **`/etc/cron.daily/logrotate.cron`** — Automates rotating, compressing, and manipulating system logfiles.

- **`/etc/cron.daily/makewhatis.cron`** — Updates the `whatis` database (contains descriptions of man pages), which is used by the `man -k`, `apropos`, and `whatis` commands to find man pages related to a particular word.

- **`/etc/cron.daily/slocate.cron`** — Updates the `/var/lib/slocate/slocate.db` database (using the `updatedb` command), which contains a searchable list of files on the machine.

- **`/etc/cron.daily/tmpwatch`** — Removes files from `/tmp`, `/var/tmp`, and `/var/catman` that haven't been accessed in ten days.

- **`/etc/cron.hourly/diskcheck`** — Checks available disk space on your hard drive each hour. Responds to low disk space based on settings in `/etc/diskcheck.conf`.

The `makewhatis.cron` script installed in `/etc/cron.weekly` is similar to the one in `/etc/cron.daily`, but it completely rebuilds the `whatis` database, rather than just updating the existing database.

Finally, in the `/etc/cron.d` directory are files that have the same format as `/etc/crontab` files.

> **NOTE:** If you are not comfortable working with cron from the command line, there is a KCron Task Scheduler window that comes with the KDE desktop for managing cron tasks. To launch KCron, type **kcron** from a Terminal window.

Summary

Shell scripts are an integral part of the Fedora system for configuring, booting, administering, and customizing Fedora. They are used to eliminate typing repetitive commands. They are frequently executed from the scheduling facilities within Fedora, allowing much flexibility in determining when and how often a process should run. And they control the startup of most daemons and server processes at boot time.

The `init` daemon and its configuration file, `/etc/inittab`, also factor heavily in the initial startup of your Fedora system. They implement the concept of run levels that is carried out by the shell scripts in `/etc/rc.d/init.d`, and they provide a means by which the machine can be shut down or rebooted in an orderly manner.

To have shell scripts configured to run on an ongoing basis, you can use the `cron` facility. Cron jobs can be added by editing `cron` files directly or by running commands such as `at` and `batch` to enter the commands to be run.

Chapter 13

Backing Up and Restoring Files

In This Chapter

- Doing a simple backup
- Selecting a backup strategy
- Selecting a backup medium
- Backing up to a hard drive
- Backing up files with dump
- Automating backup with cron
- Restoring backed-up files
- Backing up over the network
- Performing network backups with multiple computers
- Using the pax archiving utility

If you've ever suffered a hard drive crash, you know just how aggravating it can be. Irreplaceable data can be lost. Countless hours may be spent reinstalling your operating system and applications. It is not a fun experience. It need happen only once for you to learn the importance of making regular backups of your critical data.

Today, larger and faster backup media can simplify the process of backing up your data. Fedora supports many different types of media — such as writable CD (such as CD-R) , DVD (DVD+RW and DVD-RW), and magnetic tape — for creating backups. Using tools such as cron, you can configure backups to run unattended at scheduled times.

This chapter describes how to create a backup strategy and how to select media for backing up data on your Fedora system. It tells you how to do automated backups and backups over a network. It also describes how to restore individual files, or entire file systems, using tools such as the `restore` command.

Doing a Simple Backup with rsync

Cheap hard disk space, fast networks and some really neat new tools have given Linux users some nice backup alternatives to the old reliable removable media (such as tapes and CDs). To back up your personal data or the data from a small office computer, the examples in this section provide fairly simple ways of creating usable backups of your data.

To do this procedure, you need to have hard disk space on a computer that is at least slightly larger than the hard disk you are backing up. That hard disk space could be on:

- **A different partition** — By backing up to a separate disk partition, you are protected in case the partition you are backing up becomes corrupted. However, you are not protected if your hard disk goes bad.

- **A different hard disk** — Backing up to a separate hard disk can protect from a corrupted disk, but won't help you if your computer is hit by lightning, a flood, or other acts of God.

- **A different computer** — By backing up over the network, you can back up to another computer that is as far away from the souce of your data as makes you feel comfortable. You can back up to the computer down the hall or across the country.

To do the actual backup, the procedure uses the `rsync` command. The `rsync` command is like a remote copy command (similar to `rcp`) on steroids. In essence, `rsync` lets you copy files from one location to another. However, it also has some nice extra features that let you:

- **Only transfer differences** — If you transfer a file that was transferred during an earlier backup, `rsync` uses a checksum-search algorithm to determine the differences between the old file and the new one. Then it only sends the data needed to account for the differences between the two files.

- **Transfer data securely** — rsync combines with ssh (or another remote shell) to encrypt the data, so it can travel securely across a network.

- **Maintain ownership** — The transferred files can keep their same permissions, ownership, and group designations. (Because ownership is based on numeric UID and GID, matching user and group accounts must be set up between machines for the files to appear to be owned by the same users and groups after the files are copied.)

The following sections show examples of the `rsync` command at work.

Backing up files locally

The first example shows a simple backup of a user's personal files. Here I'm copying the `/home/chris` directory (including all its files and subdirectories) to another directory on the local computer. That directory (`/mnt/backup/homes`) could be on a separate partition (see Chapter 2 for creating separate partitions), hard disk (see Chapter 10 to add a hard disk), or a remote NFS file system (see Chapter 18 to mount an NFS file system):

```
# rsync -av /home/chris/ /mnt/backup/homes/
```

In this example, the entire contents of the `/home/chris` directory structure are added to the `/mnt/backup/homes/chris` directory. All files, subdirectories, links, devices and other file types are copied. By using the archive option (-a), all ownership, permissions, and creation times are maintained on the copied files.

If /mnt/backup/homes is on a separate disk, you now have your entire /home/chris directory copied in two places on the same machine. If the /mnt/backup/homes directory is an NFS shared directory (with write permission on), the files are now backed up to another machine.

Since our example is a backup of my personal files that don't change too often, after a few days of changes to the files, I might want to run the exact same command again:

```
# rsync -av /home/chris/ /mnt/backup/homes/
```

This time any new files are copied to the target directory and the changes to any files I modified are applied to the original backup files. Any files I deleted from my home directory will still be in the target directory (rsync doesn't remove deleted files unless you specifically tell it to). The result is, again, a complete copy of the /home/chris directory at the moment the rsync command is run, plus any files that have been deleted from any /home/chris directories.

Backing up files remotely

While the previous example was a quick, informal backup method, with more critical data, you will want to make sure that the data are being backed up to another computer and that the backup is done at regular intervals. This can be accomplished by using rsync in concert with ssh and cron.

Having ssh as the transport mechanism insures that data will be encrypted when it is transferred. Also, because the ssh service (sshd) is enabled by default on many Fedora and Red Hat Linux systems, you need only a user name and password to the remote system to do the backup. (As long as you can use ssh to connect to the remote machine and rsync is installed remotely, you can use the rsync command to transfer file there.) Here's an example:

```
# rsync -azv -e ssh /home/chris/ duck:/mnt/backup/homes/
root@duck's password: *******
building file list ... done
```

Here, I identify the remote computer (named duck in this case) by putting it before the remote directory name, separated with a colon. I use some different options as well. To the archive (-a) and verbose (-v) options, I add the -z option to compress the data (making it more efficient to transfer). I also use the -e ssh option to have rsync use an ssh remote shell to transfer data. The password prompt you see is the ssh login prompt.

You can repeat this command each time you want to back up your files. However, the more efficient way to do this is to set up this command to run as a cron job so that the backups happen automatically at set intervals.

To have rsync run automatically, you can't have it prompt you for a password. To have the `rsync` command run without prompting for a password, follow this procedure:

1. Set up ssh to do no-password logins for the user who is going to perform the backup (see Chapter 14 for information on how to do this).

2. Decide how often you want the backup to run. For example, if you want to run the `rsync` command once each day, as root user you could create a file called `/etc/cron.daily/mybackup`.

3. Set permissions to be executable:

    ```
    # chmod 755 /etc/cron.daily/mybackup
    ```

4. Add the command line to the `mybackup` file that you want to use:

    ```
    rsync -azv -e ssh /home/chris/ chris@duck:/mnt/backup/homes/
    ```

    Notice that I added the user name `chris` as the log-in user name on the remote computer (`duck`). For you, this will be the name of the person for which you set up a no-password login in step 1.

At this point, a backup will be done once each day to the machine specified.

> **NOTE:** With the simple backup command just shown, you can build on more complex features. In particular, you might want to think about building in a snapshot feature. Snapshots allow you to go back to a particular date and time to restore a backed-up file. Mike Rubel has an excellent procedure for doing rsync snapshots at his `www.mikerubel.org/computers/rsync_snapshots`) entitled "Easy Automated Snapshot-Style Backups with Linux and Rsync."

Selecting a Backup Strategy

While it is tempting to do the quick-and-easy backup, backing up important data requires more planning and forethought. There are several approaches you can take to backing up your data. You need to ask yourself a few questions to decide which approach is best for you. Some things that you should consider are:

- In the event of a crash, how much downtime can I tolerate?
- Will I need to recover older versions of my files or is the most recent revision sufficient?
- Do I need to back up files for just one computer or for many computers on a network?

Your answers to these questions will help you decide how often to do full backups and how often to do incremental backups. If the data is particularly critical, you may even decide that you need to have your data duplicated constantly, using a technique called *disk mirroring*. The following sections describe different backup methods.

Full backup

A full backup is one that stores every file on a particular disk or partition. If that disk should ever crash, you can rebuild your system by restoring the entire backup to a new disk. Whatever backup strategy you decide on, some sort of full backup should be part of it. You may perform full backups every night or perhaps only once every week; it depends on how often you add or modify files on your system, as well as the capacity of your backup equipment.

Incremental backup

An incremental backup is one that contains only those files that have been added or modified since the last time a more complete backup was performed. You may choose to do incremental backups to conserve your backup media. Incremental backups also take less time to complete, because they only backup data that has changed since the most recent backup (full or incremental). Incremental and other partial backup types can be important when systems are in high use during the work week and running a full backup would degrade system performance. Full backups can be reserved for the weekend when the system is not in use.

Disk mirroring

Full and incremental backups can take time to restore, and sometimes you just can't afford that downtime. By duplicating your operating system and data on an additional hard drive, you can greatly increase the speed with which you can recover from a server crash.

With disk mirroring, it is usually common for the system to continuously update the duplicate drive with the most current information. In fact, with a type of mirroring called RAID 1 (described in Chapter 10), the duplicate drive is written to at the same time as the original, and if the main drive fails, the duplicate can immediately take over. This is called *fault-tolerant* behavior, which is a must if you are running a mission-critical server of some kind.

Network backup

All of the preceding backup strategies can be performed over a network. This is good because you can share a single backup device with many computers on a network. This is much cheaper and more convenient than installing a tape drive or other backup device in every system on your network. If you have many computers, however, your backup device will require a lot of capacity. In such a case, you might want to consider a mechanical tape loader, DVD-RW drive or CD jukebox (which is capable of recording multiple CDs without operator intervention).

It is even possible to do a form of disk mirroring over the network. For example, a Web server may store a duplicate copy of its data on another server. If the first server crashes, a simple TCP/IP host name change can redirect the Web traffic to the second server. When the original server is rebuilt, it can recover all of its data from the backup server and be back in business.

Selecting a Backup Medium

Armed with a backup strategy in mind, it is time to select a backup medium. Several types of backup hardware and media are available for use with Fedora Core. Each type has its advantages and disadvantages.

The type of medium to choose depends largely on the amount of data you need to archive, how long you will store backups, how often you expect to recover data from your backups, and how much you can afford to spend. Table 13-1 compares the most common backup media.

Table 13-1: Comparison of Common Backup Media

Backup Medium	Advantage	Disadvantage
Magnetic tape	High capacity, low cost for archiving massive amounts of data.	Sequential access medium, so recovery of individual files can be slow.
Writable CDs	Random access medium, so recovery of individual files is easier. Backups can be restored from any CD-ROM drive.	Limited storage space (up to 700MB per CD).
Writable DVDs	Random access medium (like CDs). Large capacity (4.7GB, although the actual capacity you can achieve might be less).	DVD-RW drives and DVD-R disks are relatively expensive (though coming down in price). Less common than CD-ROM drives.
Additional hard drive	Allows faster and more frequent backups. Fast recovery from crashes. No media to load. Data can be located and recovered more quickly. You can configure the second disk to be a virtual clone of the first disk, so that you can boot off of the second disk if the first disk crashes.	Data cannot be stored offsite, thus there is risk of data loss if the entire server is destroyed. This method is not well suited to keeping historical archives of the many revisions of your files. The hard drive will eventually fill up.

The following sections describe how to use magnetic tape, writable DVDs, and writable CDs as backup media. How to use additional hard drives as backup media is described later in this chapter.

Magnetic tape

Magnetic tape was for years the most common medium used for backing up large amounts of computer data. Tapes provide a low-cost, convenient way to archive your files. Today's high-capacity tape drives can back up many gigabytes of data on an amazingly small tape, allowing vast amounts of information to be safely stored.

The primary disadvantage of magnetic tape is that it is a sequential access medium. This means that tapes are read or written from beginning to end, and searching for a particular file can be time-consuming. For this reason, tape is a good choice for backing up and restoring entire file systems, but not the ideal choice to recover individual files on a regular basis.

Fedora can use a wide variety of tape drives. Most SCSI tape drives will work with the generic Linux kernel. Even many IDE tape drives are supported via a "SCSI emulation" mode. Some drives, however, require installation of additional software.

> **NOTE:** As of this writing, the driver used to support SCSI tape drives (ide-scsi) is broken. If you need to use tape drives in Linux, check back with a Fedora mailing list to find out whether it has been fixed.

Using ftape tools for magnetic tape

If your tape drive is attached to an IDE floppy controller cable, you will need to use the ftape driver to access it. Fortunately, the ftape loadable module is bundled with the Linux 2.6 kernel. When your Linux system boots, it should autodetect the tape drive and load the ftape driver. To verify that your system loaded the tape driver, type the following command shortly after you boot your computer:

```
dmesg | grep ftape
```

This searches the most recent kernel messages for lines containing the word ftape. If the ftape module was loaded, you should see something like this:

```
ftape v3.04d 25/11/97
[000] ftape-init.c (ftape_init) - installing QIC-117 floppy tape
hardware drive... .
[001] ftape-init.c (ftape_init) - ftape_init @ 0xd08b0060.
[002] ftape-buffer.c (add_one_buffer) - buffer nr #1 @ c1503914, dma
area @ c02c0000.
[003] ftape-buffer.c (add_one_buffer) - buffer nr #2 @ c1503c44, dma
area @ c0298000.
[004] ftape-buffer.c (add_one_buffer) - buffer nr #3 @ c50abaac, dma
area @ c0328000.
[005] ftape-calibr.c (time_inb) - inb() duration: 1109 nsec.
[006] ftape-calibr.c (ftape_calibrate) - TC for `ftape_udelay()' = 310
nsec (at 20479 counts).
[007] ftape-calibr.c (ftape_calibrate) - TC for `fdc_wait()' = 2208 nsec
(at 2559 counts).
```

If the module was not loaded, then you should check if your kernel is compiled with support for the ftape module and your particular tape drive. It should be available and ready to include as a loadable module.

In most cases, an ftape device can be accessed just like a SCSI device. The primary difference is that an ftape device file contains the letters qft (for QIK Floppy Tape) where a SCSI tape contains st. For example, the device file for the first SCSI tape on your system will probably be /dev/st0; the device file for the first floppy tape will likely be /dev/qft0.

All of the standard tape- and archiving-related programs should work fine with both types of hardware. Nevertheless, there are a few extra programs that you might find useful when working with a floppy tape drive. These programs can be found in the ftape-tools package located at ftp://metalab.unc.edu/pub/Linux/kernel/tapes/. Download the file named ftape-tools-1.09.tar.gz. If a version higher than 1.09 is available, download that instead. Extract the ftape package using the tar command:

```
$ tar -xzvf ftape-tools-1.09.tar.gz
```

This extracts the package into an ftape-tools-1.09 directory. Use the cd command to go to that directory and to run the ./configure script to prepare the package's makefiles. Next, compile the package by typing the make command:

```
$ ./configure
$ make
```

Finally, assume root privilege using the su command and type make install to install the ftape-tools programs and online man pages to the appropriate directories:

```
# make install
```

Testing the magnetic tape drive

You should now be ready to test your tape drive. Insert a blank tape into the tape drive and type the following command:

```
$ mt -f /dev/qft0 rewind
```

You should hear the tape spin as the system rewinds the tape. This will be a very short process if the tape is already rewound. The mt command provided with ftape-tools is used to scan, rewind, and eject magnetic tapes in a floppy controller tape drive. It is very similar in operation to the st command, which is used to perform the same functions on SCSI tapes.

Formatting magnetic tapes

The ftape-tools package also includes a tool for formatting tapes as well. Most tapes now come preformatted. In the event that you have an older floppy controller tape drive that uses unformatted tapes, use the ftformat command to format them:

```
$ /usr/local/bin/ftformat -f /dev/qft0
```

Usually, the -f parameter with the device name is the only parameter that you need to supply. Nevertheless, you are encouraged to read the online man page for ftformat to learn more about its options and capabilities.

Writable CD drives

Another backup medium that is gaining popularity is the writable CD drive. Writable CD drives have several advantages over tape, the primary one being that CDs are a random access medium. This means that the CD drive can quickly locate a particular file on the CD without sequentially scanning through the entire disc. This is useful when you need to keep a revision history of frequently changing data files (such as source code for a software project or drafts of legal documents).

Another advantage is the extremely long life span of CDs. If you want to archive your backups for a very long time, a writable CD drive is a good choice. If your backups are intended for short-term storage, you should probably consider a rewritable or CD-RW CD drive. A rewritable CD (unlike plain writable CDs) can be reformatted and used to store new backups.

The biggest drawback is that a CD can store at most about 700MB of data. In contrast, DVDs can store 4.7GB of data and many tape drives can store multiple gigabytes of data. For example, DAT DDS-3 tapes can hold up to 24GB of compressed data, while 8mm AIT-2 tapes can hold up to 100GB of compressed data.

Getting cdrecord for writable CDs

To write CDs with Fedora Core you need to install the cdrecord package. This package contains components such as the `cdrecord`, `devdump`, `isodump`, `isoinfo`, `isovfy`, and `readcd` commands. The cdrecord package is included with the Fedora Core distribution.

> **NOTE:** The cdrecord package used to require that you use a SCSI CD drive. If you have an IDE/ATAPI CD drive, you no longer need to configure that drive to do SCSI emulation. In earlier versions of Fedora and Red Hat Linux, however, SCSI emulation is usually enabled automatically.

Writing to CDs

Because the data written to a CD becomes permanent once it is written, you need to format the CD and copy files to it all in one step. If you formatted it first, you would end up with an empty file system on a CD that can no longer be written to.

The first step is to create an image of the CD file system as a file on your computer. You do this with the `mkisofs` command. As an example, imagine that you want to back up the home directory for user `mary`. You would invoke the `mkisofs` command and pass it the name of the file system image file to create, followed by the directory to base it on:

```
$ mkisofs -R -o /var/tmp/mary.iso /home/mary
```

This creates an ISO9660 file system image in a file named `mary.iso` located in the `/var/tmp` directory. The `-R` option causes Linux-specific file ownership and long file names to be used. If your `/var` partition does not have enough room for the image, choose a different location.

> **TIP:** By default, `mkisofs` preserves the ownership and access rights of files and directories when it creates the file system image. This is appropriate when you are making a backup, but not when you are creating a software distribution CD. In such a case, add the `-r` option instead of `-R` as the first parameter to `mkisofs`. It will then store all files as publicly readable and, where appropriate, executable.

If you have an ATAPI CD drive, you no longer need a SCSI ID for that drive to be able to record to it. You could enter the device name instead of the SCSI ID (such as `dev=/dev/cdrom`). However, if you have a SCSI CD drive, before you can write the image file to a CD, you must first discover the SCSI bus number, device ID number, and Logical Unit Number (LUN) of the CD drive. Unless you have an actual SCSI bus in your computer, the emulated SCSI bus is probably numbered zero. You can find out which SCSI device ID the CD drive is using. Invoke the `cdrecord` command with the single parameter `-scanbus`:

```
# cdrecord -scanbus
```

You should see a response similar to the following:

```
Cdrecord 2.0 (i686-pc-linux-gnu) Copyright (C) 1995-2002 Jörg Schilling
Linux sg driver version: 3.1.25
Using libscg version 'schily-0.7'
scsibus0:
        0,0,0     0) 'IDE-CD ' 'R/RW 4x4x24  ' '1.04' Removable CD-ROM
        0,0,1     1) *
        0,0,2     2) *
        0,0,3     3) *
        0,0,4     4) *
        0,0,5     5) *
        0,0,6     6) *
        0,0,7     7) *
```

This tells you that the CD drive is using SCSI ID zero. The Logical Unit Number in this case should always be zero, so you now have all three numbers. You supply them to `cdrecord` as part of the `dev` parameter.

The SCSI bus number is listed first; it is followed by the ID number, and then by the LUN. The entire command should look similar to this:

```
# cdrecord -v speed=2 dev=0,0,0 -data /var/tmp/mary.iso
```

For an ATAPI CD drive, with the CD drive as `/dev/cdrom`, your command line might appear as follows instead:

```
# cdrecord -v speed=2 dev=/dev/cdrom -data /var/tmp/mary.iso
```

Several additional parameters are included in the command. The `-v` parameter tells `cdrecord` to supply verbose output to the screen. The `speed` parameter tells `cdrecord` what speed to record at (in this case X2). (You might choose to leave off `speed=2` and let `cdrecord` autodetect the record speed of your CD burner.) The `-data` parameter tells cdrecord that the next parameter is the name of the file system image to write to the CD. (You can add the -eject parameter to eject the CD when it is done.) As it works, cdrecord should display status messages that look similar to the following:

```
cdrecord: No write mode specified.
cdrecord: Asuming -tao mode.
cdrecord: Future versions of cdrecord may have drive dependent defaults.
cdrecord: Continuing in 5 seconds...
Cdrecord-Clone 2.01a27-dvd (i686-pc-linux-gnu) Copyright (C) 1995-2004
Jörg Schilling
TOC Type: 1 = CD-ROM
scsidev: '/dev/cdrom'
devname: '/dev/cdrom'
scsibus: -2 target: -2 lun: -2
Warning: Open by 'devname' is unintentional and not supported.
Linux sg driver version: 3.5.27
Using libscg version 'schily-0.8'.
cdrecord: Warning: using inofficial libscg transport code version
(schily - Red Hat-scsi-linux-sg.c-1.80-RH '@(#)scsi-linux-sg.c
1.80 04/03/08 Copyright 1997 J. Schilling').
SCSI buffer size: 64512
atapi: 1
Device type    : Removable CD-ROM
Version        : 0
Response Format: 1
Vendor_info    : 'IDE-CD '
Identifikation : 'R/RW 4x4x24      '
Revision       : '1.04'
Device seems to be: Generic mmc CD-RW.
Using generic SCSI-3/mmc   CD-R/CD-RW driver (mmc_cdr).
Driver flags   : MMC SWABAUDIO
Supported modes: TAO PACKET RAW/R16
Drive buf size : 1572864 = 1536 KB
FIFO size      : 4194304 = 4096 KB
Track 01: data    0 MB
Total size:       0 MB (00:04.02) = 302 sectors
Lout start:       1 MB (00:06/02) = 302 sectors
Current Secsize: 2048
ATIP info from disk:
  Indicated writing power: 5
  Is not unrestricted
  Is not erasable
  Disk sub type: Medium Type B, low Beta category (B-) (4)
  ATIP start of lead in:  -12369 (97:17/06)
  ATIP start of lead out: 359849 (79:59/74)
Disk type:    Short strategy type (Phthalocyanine or similar)
Manuf. index: 69
Manufacturer: Moser Baer India Limited
Manufacturer is guessed because of the orange forum embargo.
```

```
The orange forum likes to get money for recent information.
The information for this media may not be correct.
Blocks total: 359849 Blocks current: 359849 Blocks remaining: 359547
Starting to write CD/DVD at speed 4 in real TAO mode for single session.
Last chance to quit, starting real write    0 seconds. Operation starts.
Waiting for reader process to fill input buffer ... input buffer ready.
trackno=0
Performing OPC...
Starting new track at sector: 0
Track 01:   322 of   322 MB written (fifo 100%)  [buf  99%]   2.0x.
Track 01: Total bytes read/written: 338395136/338395136 (165232
sectors).
Writing  time:  1110.710s
Average write speed   2.0x.
Fixating...
Fixating time:  126.108s
cdrecord: fifo had 5331 puts and 5331 gets.
cdrecord: fifo was 0 times empty and 5262 times full, min fill was 96%.
```

After cdrecord finishes writing the CD and your shell prompt returns, delete the file system image file /var/tmp/mary.iso. Label the CD appropriately and store it in a safe place.

If you need any files that were copied to the CD, just return the CD to the CD drive. If it doesn't automatically open a window displaying the contents of the CD, type: mount /mnt/cdrom. Open /mnt/cdrom in a folder window and copy the files you want.

CROSS-REFERENCE: See Chapter 8 for more information on cdrecord. You can also learn more about installing and troubleshooting writable CD drives from the CD-Writing-HOWTO. Although it hasn't been updated yet to suit the 2.6 kernel, the author says he will update that HOWTO soon. Look for it here: wx.xpilot.org.

Writable DVD drives

Using a writable DVD drive and the dvdrecord command, you can back up your data to DVD-R disks. The procedure is almost identical to backing up data onto a CD disk, with the following exceptions:

- You use the dvdrecord command instead of cdrecord (although they both have nearly identical interfaces).
- Each backup disk can hold a lot more data (4.7GB compared to 700MB).
- Both the DVD writer and medium are more expensive than the CD counterparts.

NOTE: When manufacturers say 4.7GB, they are talking about 1000MB per GB, not 1024MB. Therefore, you can really only store up to about 4.4GB of data on a DVD.

The dvdrecord command should allow you to burn DVDs on any DVD burner that is compliant with the Multimedia Command (MMC) standard. Development of the dvdrecord command was done on a Pioneer DVR-A03 DVD writer.

Follow the procedure in the "Writable CD drives" section to create a file system image file (using mkisofs) and determine the location of your DVD-R driver. Then use the dvdrecord command to actually burn the DVD. Here is an example of a dvdrecord command line that burns a file system image called bigimage.cd:

```
# dvdrecord -v speed=2 dev=/dev/cdrom -data bigimage.cd
```

Backing Up to a Hard Drive

As noted in the simple backup procedure in the beginning of this chapter, removable media such as tapes, DVDs, and CDs are not the only choice for backing up your data. You may find it useful to install a second hard drive in your system and use that drive for backups. This has several advantages over other backup media:

- Data can be backed up quickly and throughout the day; thus, backed-up data will be more current in the event of a crash.

- There's no medium to load. Data can be located and recovered more quickly.

- You can configure the second disk to be a virtual clone of the first one. If the first disk crashes, you can simply boot off of the second disk rather than installing new hardware. With disk mirroring software, this process can even be automated.

- With new, cost-effective removable hard drives (including those connected via USB and Firewire), you have the convenience of removable media with what was once usually thought of as non-removable media.

There are, however, a few disadvantages to backing up to a hard drive. For example, the hard drive backup method is not well suited to keeping historical archives of the many revisions of your files, because the hard drive will eventually fill up. This problem can be reduced substantially, however, by using rsync snapshots, which store changes that are applied to modified files.

The simplest form of second-hard-drive backup is to simply copy important files to the other drive using the cp or tar command. The most sophisticated method is to provide fault-tolerant disk mirroring using RAID software. If you don't need the high level of protection from data loss that RAID disk mirroring provides, but you still like the idea of having a complete duplicate of your data on-hand and ready for use, there is an alternative—mirrordir.

Getting and installing mirrordir to clone directories

The mirrordir package is a way of doing hard-drive mirroring. Mirrordir is a powerful tool that enables you to make and maintain an exact copy of a hierarchy of directories. You can find the official mirrordir Web site at `http://mirrordir.sourceforge.net`. To download the package, click the Download RPM button.

After downloading the file, install it in the same way you install any rpm. For example, if you have downloaded the rpm file to `/tmp`, you can type:

```
# rpm -Uhv /tmp/mirrordir*rpm
```

Cloning a directory with mirrordir

Now that you have mirrordir installed, you can use it to clone a directory. Suppose you have a second hard drive with a partition large enough to hold a copy of your `/home` partition. Your first step is to create a directory to mount the partition on, and then mount it. Log in as root and type the following:

```
# mkdir -p /mirror/home
# mount /dev/hdb5 /mirror/home
```

In this example, you are mounting the fifth partition (5) of the second hard drive (hdb), hence the device name `/dev/hdb5`. The b refers to the second disk, and the 5 refers to the partition number. You may use a different drive or partition. If so, adjust the device name accordingly. Assuming the `mount` command successfully mounted the drive, you are ready to copy your `/home` partition. Enter the following command:

```
# mirrordir /home /mirror/home
```

This command causes the contents of the `/home` directory to be exactly duplicated in the `/mirror/home` directory.

> **CAUTION:** It is very important that you get the order of these parameters correct. If you reverse them, the entire contents of your `/home` directory will be deleted! You will, in essence, be copying an empty directory back to your `/home` directory.

You now have a backup of your entire `/home` partition. You can run `mirrordir` again in the future, and it will again make the `/mirror/home` directory an exact duplicate of `/home`. It will copy to `/mirror/home` only those files that have been added or modified since the previous run of `mirrordir`. Also, it will delete any files from `/mirror/home` that are no longer on `/home`. Thus, the mirror is kept current without copying the entire `/home` partition each time. If the disk with the `/home` partition should ever crash, you can replace the disk and then copy the file system back by issuing the `mirrordir` command with the parameters reversed:

```
# mirrordir /mirror/home /home
```

Furthermore, you can be up and running even faster by simply turning the mirrored partition into the actual home partition. Just edit the `/etc/fstab` file and change the device name for `/home` so that it matches the mirrored directory. Now unmount and remount the `/home` partition (or reboot the computer), and the mirrored directory will be mounted to `/home`. Your users will never be the wiser. You may even consider mirroring every partition on your main disk. Then, even a complete disk crash can be recovered from quickly. Simply turn the secondary disk into the primary disk, and you are up and running again.

Automating mirroring

To automate the mirroring process, I suggest creating a small script that mounts the mirror partition, runs the `mirrordir` command, and then unmounts the partition. Leaving the partition unmounted when not in use reduces the chance of data being accidentally deleted from it. Create a script named `mirror.sh` and place it in the `/usr/local/sbin` directory. Something similar to the following should do the trick:

```
#!/bin/sh
#
#  mirror.sh:  Mirror the /home partition to a second hard drive
#
/bin/mount /dev/hdb5 /mirror/home
mirrordir /home /mirror/home
/bin/umount /mirror/home
```

Now tell `cron` to periodically run this script. Invoke the `cron` command with the `-e` option. This brings up an editor containing root's `cron` jobs. Add a line similar to the following at the end of the list:

```
0 * * * * /usr/local/sbin/mirror.sh
```

Save and exit the editor. This cron entry causes the `mirror.sh` script to run once an hour. If you decide to mirror other partitions, you can do it quite easily by creating appropriate mount points in `/mirror` and then adding matching sections to the `mirror.sh` script.

Backing Up Files with dump

The `dump` command was historically one of the most commonly used tool for performing backups on UNIX systems. This command traces its history back to the early days of UNIX and thus is a standard part of nearly every version of UNIX. Likewise, the dump package is included in Fedora and Red Hat Linux. If it was not installed by default when you first set up your Linux system, you can install it from the `dump` RPM file located on the Fedora Linux installation CD #1.

NOTE: The dump and restore commands, while widely used for many years, are not considered to be particularly reliable or robust backup and restore tools these days. Descriptions of those tools are included here to support those with legacy backup media and automated scripts that still use those commands.

The dump package actually consists of several commands. You can read online man pages for more information about them. Table 13-2 provides a short description of the programs.

Table 13-2: Programs in the dump Package

Command	Description
dump	Creates backup archives of whole disk partitions or selected directories.
restore	Can be used to restore an entire archive or individual files from an archive to the hard drive.
rmt	A program used by the dump and restore commands to copy files across the network. You should never need to use this command directly.

Creating a backup with dump

When making a file system backup using the dump command, you must supply parameters specifying the dump level, the backup media, and the file system to back up. You can also supply optional parameters to specify the size of the backup media, the method for requesting the next tape, and the recording of file system dump times and status.

The first parameter to dump is always a list of single-letter option codes. This is followed by a space-separated list of any arguments needed by those options. The arguments appear in the same order as the options that require them. The final parameter is always the file system or directory being backed up.

```
# dump options arguments filesystem
```

Table 13-3 lists the various one-letter option codes for the dump command.

Table 13-3: Options to dump

Dump Options	Description
0-9	The dump level. Selecting a dump level of 0 backs up all files (a full dump). A higher number backs up only those files modified since the last dump of an equal or lower number (in essence, an incremental dump). The default dump level is 9.
-B records	The number of dump records per volume. Basically, the amount of data you can fit on a tape. This option takes a numeric argument.
-b kbperdump	The number of kilobytes per dump record. Useful in combination with the -B option. This option takes a numeric argument.
-h level	Files can be marked with a nodump attribute. This option specifies the dump level at or above which the nodump attribute is honored. This option takes a numeric argument of 1-9.
-f file	The name of the file or device to write the dump to. This can even be a file or device on a remote machine.
-d density	Sets the tape density. The default is 1600 bits per inch. This option takes a numeric argument.

Dump Options	Description
-n	When a dump needs attention (such as to change a tape), dump will send a message to all of the users in the operator group. This option takes no arguments.
-s *feet*	Specifies the length in feet of the dump tape. This calculation is dependent on tape density (option d) and the dump record (options B and b). This option takes a numeric argument.
-u	Record this backup in the /etc/dumpdates file. It is a good idea to use this option, especially if you create incremental backups.
-t *date*	Specify a date and time on which to base incremental backups. Any files modified or added after that time will be backed up. This option causes dump to ignore the /etc/dumpdates file. It takes a single argument, a date in the format specified by the ctime man page.
-W	This option causes dump to list the file systems that need to be backed up. It does this by looking at the /etc/dumpdates file and the /etc/fstab file.
-w	This works like the W option but lists the individual files that should be backed up.

Thus, a typical dump command may look similar to the following:

```
# dump 0uBf 500000 /dev/qft0 /dev/hda6
```

This command results in dump performing a level zero (full) backup of the /dev/hda6 file system, storing the backup on the tape drive /dev/qft0, and recording the results in /etc/dumpdates. The B option is used to increase the expected tape block count to 500000; otherwise, dump would prompt for a new tape far earlier than required. The dump command prints status messages to the screen, letting you know how far along the backup has progressed and estimating how much time it will take to complete. The output looks similar to this:

```
DUMP: Date of this level 0 dump: Sat Aug 23 23:33:37 2003
DUMP: Dumping /dev/hda6 (/home) to /dev/qft0
DUMP: Exclude ext3 journal inode 8
DUMP: Label: /home
DUMP: mapping (Pass I) [regular files]
DUMP: mapping (Pass II) [directories]
DUMP: estimated 93303 tape blocks on 0.19 tape(s).
DUMP: Volume 1 started with block 1 at: Sat Aug 23 23:33:47
DUMP: dumping (Pass III) [directories]
DUMP: dumping (Pass IV) [regular files]
DUMP: Closing /dev/qft0
DUMP: Volume 1 completed at: Sat Aug 23 23:35:35 2003
DUMP: Volume 1 94360 tape blocks (92.15MB)
DUMP: Volume 1 took 0:01:48
DUMP: Volume 1 transfer rate: 873 kB/s
```

```
DUMP: 94360 tape blocks (92.15MB) on 1 volume(s)
DUMP: finished in 108 seconds, throughput 873 kBytes/sec
DUMP: Date of this level 0 dump: Sat Aug 23  23:33:37 2003
DUMP: Date this dump completed: Sat Aug 23  23:35:35 2003
DUMP: Average transfer rate: 873 kB/s
DUMP: DUMP IS DONE
```

Understanding dump levels

The dump command can back up all files on a file system, or it can selectively back up only those files that have changed recently. The dump level parameter is used to specify this behavior. A dump level of 0 results in a full backup of all files on the file system. Specifying a higher number (1-9) backs up only those files that have been changed or added since the most recent dump of the same or lower dump level. I recommend you use dump levels to implement a full and incremental backup schedule similar to the one shown in Table 13-4.

Table 13-4: Recommended dump Schedule

Day of Week	Dump Level
Sunday	Level 0 (full dump). Eject the tape when done.
Monday	Level 9 (incremental dump).
Tuesday	Level 8 (incremental dump).
Wednesday	Level 7 (incremental dump).
Thursday	Level 6 (incremental dump).
Friday	Level 5 (incremental dump).
Saturday	Level 4 (incremental dump).

Note that after the full backup on Sunday, a level 9 incremental dump is done the next day, and a successively lower dump level is done each day after that. This results in all the files that have changed since Sunday being backed up on every single incremental backup. Each incremental backup is thus larger than the previous one; the backup contains all of the files from the previous incremental backup plus any files that have changed since then. This may seem wasteful of storage space on the backup tape, but it will save a lot of time and effort should there be a need to restore the file system.

For example, imagine that your hard drive crashed on Friday. After replacing the hard drive, you can restore the entire file system in two steps: restore the full backup from the prior Sunday, and then the most recent incremental backup from Thursday. You can do this because Thursday's backup contains all of the files from Monday, Tuesday, and Wednesday's tape as well as the files that changed after that. If the dump levels had progressed in positive order (level 1 for Monday, level 2 for Tuesday, and so on), *all* of the incremental backups would have to be restored in order to restore the file system to its most current state.

Automating Backups with cron

You can automate most of your backups with shell scripts and the cron daemon. Use the su command to become root, and then cd to the /usr/local/bin directory. Use any text editor to create a shell script called backups.sh that looks similar to the following:

```sh
#!/bin/sh
#
# backups.sh - A simple backup script, by Thad Phetteplace
#
# This script takes one parameter, the dump level.
# If the dump level is not provided, it is
# automatically set to zero. For level zero (full)
# dumps, rewind and eject the tape when done.
#

if [ $1 ]; then
        level=$1
else
        #
        # No dump level was provided, so set it
        # to zero
        #
        level="0"
fi

/sbin/dump $level'uf' /dev/nrft0 /
/sbin/dump $level'uf' /dev/nrft0 /home
/sbin/dump $level'uf' /dev/nrft0 /var
/sbin/dump $level'uf' /dev/nrft0 /usr


#
# If we are doing a full dump, rewind and eject
# the tape when done.
#
if [ $level = "0" ]; then
        #
        # Note: We should replace this with the /bin/st command
        # instead if we ever switch to a SCSI tape drive.
        #
        /bin/mt -f /dev/nrft0 rewind
        /bin/mt -f /dev/nrft0 offline
fi
```

You might have to change the partitions being backed up to match your set up, but this script should otherwise work quite well for you. After saving and exiting the editor, change the permissions on the file so that it is executable only by root:

```
# chmod 700 backups.sh
```

You can now back up your entire system by running the `backups.sh` script when logged in as root. The script accepts the dump level as its only parameter. If you leave the parameter off, it will automatically assume a level zero dump. Thus, the following two commands are equivalent:

```
# backups.sh
# backups.sh 0
```

You may need to customize this script for your situation. For example, I am using the tape device `/dev/nrft0`. You might be using a different tape device. Whatever device you use, you should probably use the version of its device name that begins with a the letter *n*. That tells the system that after it finishes copying data to the tape, it should *not* rewind the tape. For example, I used `/dev/nrft0` instead of `/dev/rst0` in the preceding script. If I had used `/dev/rst0`, each successive incremental backup would have overwritten the previous one.

Other things that you may change in this script include the partitions being backed up and the dump level at which the tape is ejected. It is not uncommon to eject the tape after the last incremental backup just before performing a full backup.

The most useful thing about this script is that you can easily configure your system to run it automatically. Simply add a few lines to the root `crontab` file, and the cron daemon will invoke the script on the days and times specified. While logged in as root, enter the `crontab` command with the `-e` option:

```
# crontab -e
```

This opens the root `crontab` file in an editor. Add the following lines at the end of the file:

```
0 22 * * 0 /usr/local/bin/backup.sh 0
0 22 * * 1 /usr/local/bin/backup.sh 9
0 22 * * 2 /usr/local/bin/backup.sh 8
0 22 * * 3 /usr/local/bin/backup.sh 7
0 22 * * 4 /usr/local/bin/backup.sh 6
0 22 * * 4 /usr/local/bin/backup.sh 5
0 22 * * 5 /usr/local/bin/backup.sh 4
```

Save and exit the file. The cron daemon will now run the backup script at 10:00 p.m. (22:00 in military time) every day of the week. This example implements the dump schedule outlined earlier. A full dump is performed on Sunday, and the tape is ejected when it is done. A new tape should be loaded on Monday, and then incremental backups will be written to that same tape for the rest of the week. The next full dump will be written to the end of that tape, unless someone is around on Sunday to eject and replace the tape before 10:00 p.m.

Restoring Backed Up Files

The `restore` command is used to retrieve files from a backup tape or other medium that was created by `dump`. You can use `restore` to recover an entire file system or to interactively select individual files. It recovers files from the specified media and copies them into the current directory (the one you ran the recover command in), re-creating subdirectories as needed. Much as with the dump command, the first parameter passed to the restore command is a list of single character option codes, as shown in Table 13-5.

Table 13-5: Restore Command Options

Restore Options	Description
-r	Restore the entire dump archive.
-C	Compare the contents of the dump file with the files on the disk. This is used to check the success of a restore.
-R	Start the restore from a particular tape of a multitape backup. This is useful for restarting an interrupted restore.
-X *filelist*	Extract only specific files or directories from the archive. This option takes one argument, a list of files or directories to extract.
-T *file*	List the contents of the dump archive. If a file or directory is given as an argument, list only the occurrence of that file, directory, or anything within the directory.
-i	Restore files in interactive mode.
-b *blocksize*	Specify the block size of the dump in kilobytes. This option takes a numeric argument.
-D *filesystem*	Specify the name of the file system to be compared when using the -C option. The file system name is passed as an argument.
-F *script*	Specify the name of the dump archive to restore from. This option takes an alphanumeric argument.
-h	If this option is specified, restore re-creates directories marked for extraction but will not extract their contents.
-m	Files are extracted by inode number instead of name. This is generally not very useful.
-N	Instead of extracting files, print their names.
-s *file#*	Specify the dump file to start with on a multiple file tape. This takes a numeric argument.
-T *directory*	Tells restore where to write any temporary files. This is useful if you booted from a floppy disk (which has no space for temporary files).
-v	Run in verbose mode. This causes restore to print information about each file as it restores it.
-y	The restore command will always continue when it encounters a bad block, rather than asking you if you want to continue.

Restoring an entire file system

Let's return to our earlier example of the Friday disk crash. You installed a shiny new hard drive and your backup tapes are in hand. It is time to restore the files. For the purpose of this example, I assume that the crashed drive contained only the /home partition and that the Fedora Linux operating system is still intact. If the crashed drive had contained the Fedora Linux operating system, you would first have to reinstall Fedora Linux before restoring the backup.

Before any files can be recovered to your new hard drive, an empty file system must be created on it. You will use the mkfs command to do this. The mkfs command can accept a variety of parameters, but usually you only need to supply the name of the device to create the file system on. Thus, to prepare the new hard drive type:

```
# mkfs /dev/hda6
```

Alternatively, because your /home drive is listed in the /etc/fstab file, you can simply specify the /home mountpoint and mkfs will figure out the correct device. Thus, the preceding command could be replaced with this:

```
# mkfs /home
```

> **CAUTION:** You should, of course, exercise extreme caution when using the mkfs command. If you specify the wrong device name, you could unintentionally wipe out all data on an existing file system.

After creating a file system on your new disk, mount the partition to a temporary mount point.

```
# mkdir /mnt/test
# mount /dev/hda6 /mnt/test
```

This connects the new file system to the /mnt/test directory. Now change into the directory (cd /mnt/test) and use the restore command to recover the entire file system off of your backup tape. Of course, it is assumed that you have loaded the tape into the tape drive.

```
# cd /mnt/test
# restore rf /dev/nrft0
```

When the restore is finished, you can unmount the partition and remount it to the appropriate mount point. If you have restored the file system to a different physical partition than it was originally on, be sure to modify the /etc/fstab file appropriately so that the correct partition is mounted next time the system is rebooted.

Recovering individual files

The restore command can also be used to recover individual files and directories. By using restore in interactive mode, you can type a series of restore commands to selectively restore files. To run restore in interactive mode, use the i parameter instead of r:

```
# restore if /dev/nrst0
```

The `restore` command will then read the file index from the backup tape and present you with a restore prompt. At this prompt, you can type the commands that enable you to select which directories and files to recover. You can navigate the directory structure of the backup index much the same way that you navigate an actual file system using a shell prompt. The interactive `restore` command even has its own version of the familiar `cd` and `ls` commands, as shown in Table 13-6.

Table 13-6: Interactive restore Commands

Command	Description
add	Add a file or directory to the list of files to be extracted. If a directory is marked for extraction, all of the directories and files within it will also be extracted.
cd	Change the current directory being viewed within the dump archive. Works similar to the `cd` command used at a shell prompt.
delete	Delete a file or directory from the list of files to be extracted. Deleting a directory from the list results in all of the files and directories within it also being deleted.
extract	Extract all of the marked files and directories from the archive and write them back to the file system.
help	List the available commands.
ls	List the contents of the current directory. If a directory name is provided as an argument, list the contents of that directory. Files or directories marked for extraction have a * character in front of them.
pwd	Print the full path name of the current directory of the dump archive.
quit	Exit the interactive restore program.
setmodes	Do not restore the files; instead, set the modes of already existing files on the target disk to match the modes recorded in the dump file. This is useful for recovering from a restore that was prematurely aborted.
verbose	Toggles verbose output versus quiet output during the restore process. Verbose output mode will echo information to the screen for every file that is restored.

As an example, pretend that the user `joe` has accidentally deleted his Mail subdirectory from his home directory. Joe happens to be your boss, so it is urgent that you recover his files. Here is how you may go about it.

Load the appropriate tape into the tape drive and log in as root. Use the `cd` command to go to the top of the `/home` partition, and then run the `restore` program in interactive mode:

```
# cd /home
# restore if /dev/nrft0
```

Verify that you have the backup tape for the /home partition by entering the ls command. You should see something like the following list of directories, representing users who have home directories in /home:

```
restore > ls
.:
bob/         jane/        joe/        lost+found/ mary/        thad/
```

Yes, this is the home partition. Now change the current directory to Joe's home directory using the cd command. Type **ls** again to view the contents of his home directory.

```
restore > cd joe
restore > ls
./joe:
.mozilla/              Desktop/              report.html
.tcshrc                Mail/                 letter.txt
.xinitrc               News/                 www/
```

Now mark the Mail directory for extraction using the add command:

```
restore > add Mail
```

If you use the ls command again, you see that the Mail directory is preceded with an asterisk (*) character, which means it has been marked for extraction.

```
restore > ls
./joe:
.mozilla/              Desktop/              report.html
.tcshrc                *Mail/                letter.txt
.xinitrc               News/                 www/
```

Now use the extract command to begin the extraction process. restore will prompt you for the number of the tape to start with. This is a single tape backup, so just enter the number **1**. When it prompts you to "set owner/mode for '.'?," answer yes by typing **y** and pressing Enter. restore will then restore the file permissions (if necessary) of the directory it is restoring to. This isn't critical when extracting individual files like this, but you should always answer yes to this prompt when doing a full restore. Anyway, your screen should now contain the following:

```
restore > extract
You have not read any tapes yet.
Unless you know which volume your file(s) are on you
should start with the last volume and work toward the first.
Specify next volume #: 1
set owner/mode for '.'? [yn] y
restore >
```

At this point, the files have been recovered and you can exit the restore program by issuing the quit command. That's all there is to it. You now know the basics of using the dump and restore commands.

Configuring Amanda for network backups

Using Amanda (the Advanced Maryland Automatic Network Disk Archiver), you can use a single large-capacity tape drive on a server to back up files from multiple computers over a network. The Amanda package includes a variety of commands. The online man page for Amanda describes the commands as shown in Table 13-7.

Table 13-7: Backup Commands Used with Amanda

Command	Description
amdump	Do automatic Amanda backups. This command is normally run by cron on a computer called the tape server host and requests backups of file systems located on backup clients. amdump backs up all disks in the disklist file to tape or, if there is a problem, to a special holding disk. After all backups are done, amdump sends mail reporting failures and successes.
amflush	Flush backups from the holding disk to tape. amflush is used after amdump has reported it could not write backups to tape. When this happens, backups stay in the holding disk. After the tape problem is corrected, run amflush to write backups from the holding disk to the tape.
amcleanup	Clean up after an interrupted amdump. This command is only needed if amdump was unable to complete for some reason, usually because the tape server host crashed while amdump was running.
amrecover	Provide an interactive interface to browse the Amanda index files and select which tapes to recover files from. amrecover can also run amrestore and the system restore program (such as tar) sometimes.
amrestore	Read an Amanda tape, searching for requested backups. amrestore is suitable for everything from interactive restores of single files to a full restore of all partitions on a failed disk.
amlabel	Write an Amanda format label onto a tape. All Amanda tapes must be labeled with amlabel. amdump and amflush will not write to an unlabeled tape.
amcheck	Verify the correct tape is in the tape drive and that all file systems on all backup client systems are ready to be backed up. Can optionally be run by cron before amdump, so someone will get mail warning that backups will fail unless corrective action is taken.
amadmin	Take care of administrative tasks, such as finding out which tapes are needed to restore a file system, forcing hosts to do full backups of selected disks, and looking at schedule balance information.
amtape	Take care of tape changer control operations, such as loading particular tapes, ejecting tapes, and scanning the tape rack.
amverify	Check Amanda backup tapes for errors (GNU tar format backups only).
amrmtape	Delete a tape from the tape list and from the Amanda database.
amstatus	Give the status of a running amdump.

The `amdump` command is the one that you will use the most, but before you can get started, you need to configure a few things on both the backup server (the system with the tape drive) and the backup clients (the systems being backed up).

Creating Amanda directories

You need to create some directories to hold the Amanda configuration files and to provide a location to write Amanda log files. The configuration files go in the `/etc/amanda` directory, and the log files go in `/var/lib/amanda`. In both cases, you should log in as the amanda user and create subdirectories within those directories, one subdirectory for each backup schedule that you intend to run and an index file, as shown in the following example.

> **NOTE:** For security reasons, you should do all amanda administration as the amanda user. To do this, the root user can create a password for amanda by typing `passwd amanda` and entering the new password. A better alternative, however, might be to leave amanda without a password, then simply type **su - amanda** (as shown below) to do amanda tasks as root user without an extra password. The rest of this procedure assumes that you are logged in as the amanda user.

```
# su - amanda
$ mkdir -p /var/lib/amanda/normal/index
$ mkdir -p /etc/amanda/normal
```

For the purpose of this example, I have created only a `normal` backup configuration that backs up the data drives on several machines. You may also decide to create an upgrade backup configuration that backs up the operating system partitions. You could then run that backup before you perform any operating system upgrades.

You also need to specify a holding disk that Amanda can use to temporarily spool backups before it writes them to disk. This directory should have a lot of free space. I have a large `/home` partition on my server, so I created an Amanda directory there to use as a holding disk:

```
# mkdir /home/amanda
# chmod 700 /home/amanda
# chown amanda /home/amanda
# chgrp disk /home/amanda
```

Creating the amanda.conf file

Next, as the amanda user, you must create two configuration files for Amanda and store them in the `/etc/amanda/normal` directory: `amanda.conf` and `disklist`. You can start by copying samples of these files from the `/etc/amanda/DailySet1` directory as follows:

```
$ cd /etc/amanda/DailySet1
$ cp amanda.conf disklist /etc/amanda/normal
```

The `amanda.conf` file sets a variety of general configuration values, and the `disklist` file defines which machines and partitions to back up. The `amanda.conf` file can be rather complicated, but, fortunately, most of its values can be left at their default values. Here is a simplified amanda.conf file with some comments embedded in it to help explain things:

```
#
# amanda.conf - sample Amanda configuration file. This started life as
#               the actual config file in use at CS.UMD.EDU.

org "GLACI"         # your organization name for reports
mailto "amanda"     # space separated list of operators at your site
dumpuser "amanda"   # the user to run dumps under

# Specify tape device and/or tape changer. If you don't have a tape
# changer, and you don't want to use more than one tape per run of
# amdump, just comment out the definition of tpchanger.

runtapes 1                  # number of tapes to be used in a single
                            # run of amdump
tapedev "/dev/nrft0"        # the no-rewind tape device to be used
rawtapedev "/dev/rft0"      # the raw device to be used (ftape only)

tapetype HP-DAT    # what kind of tape it is
          # (see tapetypes below)
labelstr "^normal[0-9][0-9]*$"    # label constraint all
                                  # tapes must match

# Specify holding disks. These are used as a temporary
# staging area for dumps before they are written to tape and
# are recommended for most sites.

holdingdisk hd1 {
    comment "main holding disk"
    directory "/home/amanda"    # where the holding disk is
    use 290 Mb                  # how much space can we use on it
    chunksize -1                # size of chunk
    }

# Note that, although the keyword below is infofile, it is
# only so for historic reasons, since now it is supposed to
# be a directory (unless you have selected some database
# format other than the 'text' default)

infofile "/usr/adm/amanda/normal/curinfo"   # database DIRECTORY
logdir   "/usr/sdm/amanda/normal"       # log directory
indexdir "/usr/adm/amanda/normal/index"   # index directory

# tapetypes

# Define the type of tape you use here, and use it in "tapetype"
# above. Some typical types of tapes are included here. The
```

```
# tapetype tells amanda how many MB will fit on the tape, how
# big the filemarks are, and how fast the tape device is.

define tapetype HP-DAT {
    comment "DAT tape drives"
    # data provided by Rob Browning <rlb@cs.utexas.edu>
    length 1930 mbytes
    filemark 111 kbytes
    speed 468 kbytes
}

# dumptypes
#
# These are referred to by the disklist file.

define dumptype global {
    comment "Global definitions"
    # This is quite useful for setting global parameters, so you
    # don't have to type them everywhere.
}

define dumptype always-full {
    global
    comment "Full dump of this filesystem always"
    compress none
    priority high
    dumpcycle 0
}
```

This example amanda.conf file was trimmed down from a larger example I copied from the /etc/amanda/DailySet1 directory. The example amanda.conf file provides additional information on the available configuration options. Also, the online man page for Amanda should be helpful (type **man amanda** to read it). You can find more instructions in the /usr/share/doc/amanda-server* directory. Generally, you have to do the following:

- Modify the org name for reports.
- Change the device names set for tapedev and rawtapedev to match your tape device.
- Select a tape type entry that is appropriate for your tape drive.
- Change the name of the directory specified in the holding disk section to match the directory you created earlier.

Creating a disklist file

You also must create a disklist file in the /etc/amanda/normal directory. This simply contains a list of the systems and disk partitions to back up. The qualifier always-full is included on each entry to tell Amanda what type of backup to perform. It means to use full, rather than incremental, backups.

```
# sample Amanda2 disklist file
#
# File format is:
#
#         hostname diskdev dumptype [spindle [interface]]
#
# where the dumptypes are defined by you in amanda.conf.

dexter hda5 always-full
dexter hda6 always-full
dexter hda7 always-full
dexter hda8 always-full

daffy hda5 always-full
daffy hda6 always-full
daffy hda7 always-full
daffy hdb1 always-full
daffy hdb2 always-full
```

This example file backs up two systems, `dexter` and `daffy`. The order of the systems and the partitions is selected so that the most important data is backed up first. This way, if a tape drive becomes full, you have still managed to back up the most important data.

Adding Amanda network services

Amanda is designed to perform backups over a network. The following `amanda` services are defined in the `/etc/services` file:

```
amanda          10080/udp
amanda          10080/tcp
amandaidx       10082/tcp
amidxtape       10083/tcp
```

On the amanda server

To offer these services to the network in Red Hat Linux, you need to configure the xinetd daemon to listen for those services. You do this by enabling the `amandaidx` and `amidxtape` services by typing the following (as root user):

```
# chkconfig amidxtape on
# chkconfig amandaidx on
```

This enables Amanda to accept requests from the client system and to start the backup process without any user intervention. You need to tell the `xinetd` daemon to reload the `/etc/xinetd.d` files before this change takes place. You can do this by typing the following as root user:

```
# /etc/init.d/xinetd reload
```

On each amanda client

Next you need to configure the `.amandahosts` file in the `/var/lib/amanda` directory on each computer (client) that the amanda server will back up from. This file should contain the fully qualified host and domain name of any backup servers that will connect to this client. When you begin, only your localhost is defined in this file as your backup server. To add another computer as a backup server, you could type the following (replacing *amandahost* with the name of the backup server, while you are logged in as the `amanda` user):

```
$ echo amandahost >> /var/lib/amanda/.amandahosts
```

You also need to make sure that the amanda client daemon is configured to run on the client. You do this by enabling the `amanda` service by typing the following (as root user) :

```
# chkconfig amanda on
```

This enables the amanda client to communicate with the amanda server. You need to tell the `xinetd` daemon to reload the `/etc/xinetd.d` files before this change takes place. You can do this by typing the following as root user:

```
# /etc/init.d/xinetd reload
```

Performing an Amanda backup

Now that everything is configured, you are ready to perform an Amanda backup. While logged in as root, type the following command:

```
# /usr/sbin/amdump normal
```

This runs the `amdump` command and tells it to read the configuration files it finds in the `/etc/amanda/normal` directory created earlier. It then works its way down the list of systems and partitions in the `disklist` file, backing up each partition in the order it occurs. The results of the amdump are written to the `/var/lib/amanda/normal` directory. Read the files you find there to check on the results of the backup. (See the previous section on how to create a `disklist` file to understand the process that `amdump` goes through.)

You can, of course, automate this process with `cron`. To create an `amdump` schedule similar to the regular dump schedule discussed in an earlier section, do the following. While logged in as root, enter the `crontab` command with the `-e` option:

```
# crontab -e
```

This opens the root `crontab` file in an editor. Add the following lines to the end of the file:

```
0 22 * * 0 /usr/sbin/amdump normal
0 22 * * 1 /usr/sbin/amdump incremental
0 22 * * 2 /usr/sbin/amdump incremental
0 22 * * 3 /usr/sbin/amdump incremental
```

```
0 22 * * 4 /usr/sbin/amdump incremental
0 22 * * 5 /usr/sbin/amdump incremental
0 22 * * 6 /usr/sbin/amdump incremental
```

Save and exit the file. The cron daemon will now run `amdump` at 10:00 p.m. (22:00 in military time) every day of the week. This example assumes that a second incremental configuration has been created. You can do this by creating a subdirectory named `incremental` under `/etc/amanda` and populating it with appropriately modified `amanda.conf` and `disklist` files. You must also create a subdirectory named `incremental` under `/usr/adm/amanda` so that `amanda` has somewhere to write the logfiles for this configuration.

It may be a bit of work to get it all in place, but when you do, Amanda can make your network backups much easier to manage. It may be overkill for a small office, but in a large enterprise network situation, it enables Fedora Core to act as a powerful backup server.

Using the pax Archiving Tool

Over the years, a variety of UNIX operating systems have arisen, resulting in a variety of similar but incompatible file archiving formats. Even tools that go by the same name may use slightly different storage formats on different systems. This can lead to big problems when trying to archive and retrieve data in a multiplatform environment. Fortunately, there is a solution.

The pax program is a POSIX standard utility that can read and write a wide variety of archive formats. An RPM package for pax is included with Fedora Core. If it is not already installed, copy the `pax-*` RPM file from your distribution media (CD #1), or download it from a Fedora download site, and then use the `rpm` command to install it.

```
# rpm -Uhv pax-*
```

Remember you need to be logged in as root when installing software with the `rpm` command.

Pax takes a variety of command-line options. The last parameter is usually the file or directory to archive. You may use wildcard characters such as `*` or `?` to specify multiple files or directories. The options you will use most often include the `-r` and `-w` parameters for specifying when you are reading or writing an archive. These are usually used in conjunction with the `-f` parameter, which is used to specify the name of the archive file.

By using `pax` parameters in different combinations, it is possible to extract an archive, create an archive, list the contents of an archive, or even copy an entire directory hierarchy from one location to another. Table 13-8 shows a few examples of the `pax` command in action.

Table 13-8: Examples of pax Use

Pax Command	Description
pax -f *myfiles*	List the contents of the archive named myfiles.
pax -r -f *myfiles*	Extract the contents of the archive named myfiles.
pax -w -f *myfiles* /etc	Create an archive named myfiles containing everything within the /etc directory.
pax -w -f *myfiles* *.txt	Archive all of the files in the current directory that have a .txt file extension.
pax -r -w */olddir /newdir*	Copy the entire contents of the directory /oldir into a new directory called /newdir.
pax -w -B 1440000 -f /dev/fd0 *	Archive the contents of the current directory onto multiple floppy disks.
pax -w -x cpio -f *myfiles* *	Archive the contents of the current directory into an archive file named myfiles using the cpio format.
pax -r -U mary -f *backups*	Extract all of the files owned by user mary from the archive named backups.

Note that by leaving off both the -r and -w options, you cause pax to simply list the contents of the archive. If you specify both the -r and -w options, then you should leave off the -f option and supply source and destination directories instead. This will cause the source directory to be completely cloned in the specified destination directory.

You can use additional parameters to further modify the pax command's behavior. For example, you can use the -x option in conjunction with the -w option to specify the specific archive type to create, or you can use the -B option to specify the number of bytes to write to each volume of a multivolume archive.

Table 13-9 describes the many optional parameters to the pax command.

Table 13-9: Options to pax

Pax Options	Description
-r	Read files from an archive.
-w	Write files to an archive.
-a	Append files to a previously created archive.
-b *blocksize*	Specify the archive's data block size. It must be a multiple of 512.

Pax Options	Description
`-c pattern`	Match all files except those that match the specified pattern.
`-d`	Match filename wildcards against file or directory names only, not the complete path.
`-f archive`	Specify the name of the archive.
`-i`	Interactively rename files when archiving.
`-k`	Do not overwrite existing files.
`-l`	Link files with hard links when in copy mode (`-r -w`).
`-n pattern`	Match only the first file that matches the supplied pattern.
`-o options`	Extra options specific to the archiving format used.
`-p string`	Specify the file characteristics to retain when archiving or copying. Read the pax man page for more information on this option.
`-s replstr`	Modify the archived filenames using the supplied regular expression.
`-t`	Preserve the access times of archived files.
`-u`	Do not overwrite files with older versions.
`-v`	Provide verbose output when running.
`-x format`	Specify the format of the archive. Valid formats include `cpio`, `bcpio`, `sv4cpio`, `sv4crc`, `tar`, and `ustar`. The default is to use `ustar` when creating an archive. Pax will automatically determine the correct file type when reading an archive.
`-z`	Indicates that `gzip` should be used to compress and decompress the archive.
`-B bytes`	Specify the number of bytes per archive volume. Use this option to create multivolume archives on removable media.
`-D`	Do not overwrite existing files with files that have an older inode modification time.
`-E limit`	Limit the number of times `pax` will retry on encountering a read or write error.
`-G group`	Select files based on a group name or GID. To select by GID, place a # sign in front of the group number.
`-H`	Follow only command-line symbolic links while performing a physical file system traversal.
`-L`	Follow all symbolic links when traversing a directory hierarchy.
`-P`	Do not follow symbolic links. This is the default.

Pax Options	Description
-T *time*	Select files based on their modification time. Read the `pax` man page for complete discussion of this parameter's syntax.
-U *user*	Select files based on the owner's user name, or by UID with a # sign in front of it.
-X	Do not traverse into directories that reside on a different device.
-Y	This option is the same as the -D option, except that the inode change time is checked using the pathname created after all the filename modifications have completed.
-Z	This option is the same as the -u option, except that the modification time is checked using the pathname created after all the filename modifications have completed.

As you can see, `pax` is a very flexible and powerful archiving tool. It can be particularly helpful in migrating data from older legacy systems to your new Linux system. When you are faced with the task of recovering archived data from an antiquated or even nonfunctioning UNIX system, the multiple file format support of `pax` can be a literal lifesaver.

Summary

I hope that you never experience a major hard drive crash, but if you ever do, the effort of making backups will repay itself many times over. A variety of low-cost backup hardware is available to use with your Fedora system. The traditional tape drive is an excellent choice for backing up large amounts of data. If long-term archiving of data is needed, a writable DVD or CD drive is a good choice. If minimizing downtime is your main concern, mirroring data to a second hard drive is another smart choice. As for the tools you choose to do your backups, the `dump` and `restore` commands are old favorites, dating back to the early UNIX days (although they are considered somewhat unreliable these days). The Amanda backup facility is excellent for network backups. If you are dealing with backups in several different formats, the `pax` command might be helpful.

Chapter 14

Computer Security Issues

In This Chapter

- Defining hacker and cracker
- Protecting against denial-of-service attacks
- Protecting against break-ins
- Protecting your network with iptables firewalls
- Detecting intrustions from log files
- Monitoring log files with LogSentry
- Using password protection
- Using encryption techniques
- Guarding your computer with PortSentry

With the growth of the Internet, computer and network security has become more important than ever. Assaults on your Fedora or Red Hat Linux system can come in many forms, such as denial-of-service attacks, break-in attempts, or hijacking your machine as a spam relay, to name a few.

In many cases, good practices for setting and protecting passwords, monitoring log files and creating good firewalls will keep out many would-be intruders. Sometimes, more proactive approaches are needed to respond to break-ins. This chapter will familiarize you, as a Linux administrator, with the dangers that exist and the tools necessary to protect your system.

Hacker versus Cracker

In short, a hacker is someone who programs creatively and usually for the pure enjoyment of it (most programmers who work on Linux are hackers in this sense). The correct term for someone who breaks into computer systems is a cracker.

There are many types of crackers, ranging from professional computer criminals to the hobbyist types who break into computers for the thrill. The growth of the cracker problem has kept pace with the growth of the Internet. A new, younger generation of crackers is emerging. These teenage pseudo-crackers do not have all the knowledge and skill of their true cracker counterparts, but they have access to a growing number of cracker tools that automate the breaking of a system's security.

By using programs and scripts created by more advanced crackers, youngsters can often break into systems without really knowing the details of how it is done. Because they are usually young and mostly dependent on tools provided by others, they are sometimes referred to as "scriptkiddies." Make no mistake, if your system is not properly secured, scriptkiddies can do just as much damage as any other cracker.

Whatever you call them, crackers pose a serious risk to anyone connecting a computer to the Internet. Their reasons for breaking into systems are varied; some hope to steal financial information, others wish to gain bragging rights among their peers.

Often, a system is broken into solely for use as a jumping-off point to launch further attacks on other systems. In some cases, the damage may be as little as an altered Web page, the Internet equivalent of graffiti. In other cases, the cracker may wipe out your entire hard drive to cover his or her tracks. Fortunately, there are ways to protect yourself.

Understanding Attack Techniques

Attacks on computing systems take on different forms, depending on the goal and resources of the attacker. Some attackers want to be disruptive, while others want to infiltrate your machines and utilize the resources for their own nefarious purposes. Still others are targeting your data for financial gain or blackmail. Here are three major categories of attacks:

- **Denial of Service (DOS)** — The easiest attacks to perpetrate are Denial of Service attacks. The primary purpose of these attacks is to disrupt the activities of a remote site by overloading it with irrelevant data. DOS attacks can be as simple as sending thousands of page requests per second at a Web site. These types of attacks are easy to perpetrate and easy to protect against. Once you have a handle on where the attack is coming from, a simple phone call to the perpetrator's ISP will get the problem solved.

- **Distributed Denial of Service (DDOS)** — More advanced DOS attacks are called Distributed Denial of Service attacks. DDOS attacks are much harder to perpetrate and nearly impossible to stop. In this form of attack, an attacker takes control of hundreds or even thousands of weakly secured Internet connected computers. The attacker then directs them in unison to send a stream of irrelevant data to a single Internet host. The result is that the power of one attacker is magnified thousands of times. Instead of an attack coming from one direction, as is the case in a normal DOS, it comes from thousands of directions at once. The best defense against a DDOS attack is to contact your ISP to see if it can filter traffic at its border routers.

Many people use the excuse, "I have nothing on my machine anyone would want" to avoid having to consider security. The problem with this argument is that attackers have a lot of reasons to use your machine. The attacker can turn your machine into an agent for later use in a DDOS attack. More than once, authorities have shown up at the door of a dumbfounded computer user asking questions about threats originating from their computer. By ignoring security, the owners have opened themselves up to a great deal of liability.

- **Intrusion attacks** — To remotely use the resources of a target machine, attackers must first look for an opening to exploit. In the absence of inside information such as passwords or encryption keys, they must scan the target machine to see what services are offered. Perhaps one of the services is weakly secured and the attacker can use some known exploit to finagle his or her way in.

  A tool called nmap is generally considered the best way to scan a host for services (note that nmap is a tool that can be used for good and bad). Once the attacker has a list of the available services running on his target, he needs to find a way to trick one of those services into letting him have privileged access to the system. Usually, this is done with a program called an *exploit*.

While DOS attacks are disruptive, intrusion type attacks are the most damaging. The reasons are varied, but the result is always the same. An uninvited guest is now taking up residence on your machine and is using it in a way you have no control over.

Protecting Against Denial-of-Service Attacks

As explained earlier, a denial-of-service attack attempts to crash your computer or at least degrade its performance to an unusable level. There are a variety of denial-of-service exploits. Most try to overload some system resource, such as your available disk space or your Internet connection. Some common attacks and defenses are discussed in the following sections.

Mailbombing

Mailbombing is the practice of sending so much e-mail to a particular user or system that the computer's hard drive becomes full. There are several ways to protect yourself from mailbombing. You can use the Procmail e-mail-filtering tool or configure your sendmail daemon.

CROSS-REFERENCE: See Chapter 19 for a more complete description of sendmail.

Blocking mail with Procmail

The Procmail e-mail-filtering tool is installed by default with Fedora Linux and is tightly integrated with the sendmail e-mail daemon; thus, it can be used to selectively block or filter out specific types of e-mail. You can learn more about Procmail at the Procmail Web site www.procmail.org.

To enable Procmail for your user account, create a .procmailrc file in your home directory. The file should be mode 0600 (readable by you but nobody else). Type the following, replacing *evilmailer* with the actual e-mail address that is mailbombing you.

```
# Delete mail from evilmailer
:0
* ^From.*evilmailer
/dev/null
```

The Procmail recipe looks for the From line at the start of each e-mail to see if it includes the string evilmailer. If it does, the message is sent to /dev/null (effectively throwing it away).

Blocking mail with sendmail

The Procmail e-mail tool works quite well when only one user is being mailbombed. If, however, the mailbombing affects many users, you should probably configure your sendmail daemon to block all e-mail from the mailbomber. Do this by adding the mailbomber's e-mail address or system name to the access file located in the /etc/mail directory.

Each line of the access file contains an e-mail address, host name, domain, or IP address followed by a tab and then a keyword specifying what action to take when that entity sends you a message. Valid keywords are OK, RELAY, REJECT, DISCARD, and ERROR. Using the REJECT keyword will cause a sender's e-mail to be bounced back with an error message. The keyword DISCARD will cause the message to be silently dropped without sending an error back. You can even return a custom error message by using the ERROR keyword.

Thus, an example /etc/mail/access file may look similar to this:

```
# Check the /usr/share/doc/sendmail/README.cf file for a description
# of the format of this file. (search for access_db in that file)
# The /usr/share/doc/sendmail/README.cf is part of the sendmail-doc
# package.
#
# by default we allow relaying from localhost...
localhost.localdomain          RELAY
localhost                      RELAY
127.0.0.1                      RELAY
#
# Senders we want to Block
#
evilmailer@yahoo.com    REJECT
stimpy.glaci.com        REJECT
cyberpromo.com          DISCARD
199.170.176.99          ERROR:"550 Die Spammer Scum!"
199.170.177             ERROR:"550 Email Refused"
```

As with most Linux configuration files, lines that begin with a # pound sign are comments. Our list of blocked spammers is at the end of this example file. Note that the address to block can be a complete e-mail address, a full host name, a domain only, an IP address, or a subnet.

To block a particular e-mail address or host from mailbombing you, log in to your system as root, edit the `/etc/mail/access` file, and add a line to `DISCARD` mail from the offending sender.

After saving the file and exiting the editor, you must convert the access file into a hash indexed database called access.db. The database is updated automatically the next time sendmail starts. Or you can convert the database immediately, as follows:

```
# cd /etc/mail
# make
```

Sendmail should now discard e-mail from the addresses you added.

Spam relaying

Another way in which your e-mail services can be abused is by having your system used as a spam relay. *Spam* refers to the unsolicited junk e-mail that has become a common occurrence on the Internet. Spammers often deliver their annoying messages from a normal dial-up Internet account. They need some kind of high-capacity e-mail server to accept and buffer the payload of messages. They deliver the spam to the server all in one huge batch and then log off, letting the server do the work of delivering the messages to the many victims.

Naturally, no self-respecting Internet Service Provider will cooperate with this action, so spammers resort to hijacking servers at another ISP to do the dirty work. Having your mailserver hijacked to act as a spam relay can have a devastating effect on your system and your reputation. Fortunately, open mail relaying is deactivated by default on Fedora and Red Hat Linux installations. Open mail relaying is one security issue that you will not have to worry about.

You can allow specific hosts or domains to relay mail through your system by adding those senders to your `/etc/mail/access` file with keyword RELAY. By default, relaying is only allowed from the local host. Refer to Chapter 19, as well as the sendmail documentation, for more information.

> **TIP:** One package you might consider using to filter out spam on your mail server is spamassassin. Spamassassin examines the text of incoming mail messages and attempts to filter out messages that are determined to be spam. Spamassassin is described in Chapter 19.

Smurf amplification attack

Smurfing refers to a particular type of denial-of-service attack aimed at flooding your Internet connection. It can be a difficult attack to defend against, because it is not easy to trace the attack to the attacker. Here is how smurfing works.

The attack makes use of the ICMP protocol, a service intended for checking the speed and availability of network connections. Using the `ping` command, you can send a network packet from your computer to another computer on the Internet. The remote computer will recognize the packet as an ICMP request and echo a reply packet to your computer. Your computer can then print a message revealing that the remote system is up and telling you how long it took to reply to the ping.

A smurfing attack uses a malformed ICMP request to bury your computer in network traffic. The attacker does this by bouncing a ping request off an unwitting third party in such a way that the reply is duplicated dozens or even hundreds of times. An organization with a fast Internet connection and a large number of computers is used as the relay. The destination address of the ping is set to an entire subnet instead of a single host. The return address is forged to be your machine's address instead of the actual sender. When the ICMP packet arrives at the unwitting relay's network, every host on that subnet replies to the ping! Furthermore, they reply to your computer instead of to the actual sender. If the relay's network has hundreds of computers, your Internet connection can be quickly flooded.

The best fix is to contact the organization being used as a relay and inform them of the abuse. Usually, they need only to reconfigure their Internet router to stop any future attacks. If the organization is uncooperative, you can minimize the effect of the attack by blocking the ICMP protocol on your router. This will at least keep the traffic off your internal network. If you can convince your ISP to block ICMP packets aimed at your network, it will help even more.

Protecting Against Distributed DOS Attacks

DDOS attacks are much harder to initiate and nearly impossible to stop. A DDOS attack begins with the penetration of hundreds or even thousands of weakly secured machines. These machines can then be directed to attack a single host based on the whims of the attacker.

With the advent of DSL and cable modem, millions of people are enjoying Internet access with virtually no speed restrictions. In their rush to get online, many of those people neglect even the most basic security. Since the vast majority of these people run Microsoft operating systems, they tend to get hit with worms and viruses rather quickly. After the machine has been infiltrated, quite often the worm or virus installs a program on the victim's machine that instructs it to quietly *call home* and announce that it is now ready to do *the master's bidding*.

At the whim of the master, the infected machines can now be used to focus a concentrated stream of garbage data at a selected host. In concert with thousands of other infected machines, a *scriptkiddie* now has the power to take down nearly any site on the Internet.

Detecting a DDOS is similar to detecting a DOS attack. One or more of the following signs are likely to be present:

- Sustained saturated data link
- No reduction in link saturation during off-peak hours
- Hundreds or even thousands of simultaneous network connections
- Extremely slow system performance

To determine if your data link is saturated, the act of pinging an outside host can tell much of the story. Much higher than usual latency is a dead giveaway. Normal ping latency (that is, the time it takes for a ping response to come back from a remote host) looks like the following:

```
# ping www.example.com
PING www.example.com (192.0.34.166) from 10.0.0.11: 56(84) bytes of data
64 bytes from 192.0.34.166: icmp_seq=1 ttl=49 time=40.1 ms
64 bytes from 192.0.34.166: icmp_seq=2 ttl=49 time=42.5 ms
64 bytes from 192.0.34.166: icmp_seq=3 ttl=49 time=39.5 ms
64 bytes from 192.0.34.166: icmp_seq=4 ttl=49 time=38.4 ms
64 bytes from 192.0.34.166: icmp_seq=5 ttl=49 time=39.0 ms

--- www.example.com ping statistics ---
5 packets transmitted, 5 received, 0% loss, time 4035ms
rtt min/avg/max/mdev = 38.472/39.971/42.584/1.432 ms
```

In the preceding example, the average time for a ping packet to make the round trip was about 39 thousandths of a second.

A ping to a nearly saturated link will look like the following:

```
# ping www.example.com
PING www.example.com (192.0.34.166): from 10.0.0.11: 56(84)bytes of data
64 bytes from 192.0.34.166: icmp_seq=1 ttl=62 time=1252 ms
64 bytes from 192.0.34.166: icmp_seq=2 ttl=62 time=1218 ms
64 bytes from 192.0.34.166: icmp_seq=3 ttl=62 time=1290 ms
64 bytes from 192.0.34.166: icmp_seq=4 ttl=62 time=1288 ms
64 bytes from 192.0.34.166: icmp_seq=5 ttl=62 time=1241 ms

--- www.example.com ping statistics ---
6 packets transmitted, 5 received, 0% loss, time 5032ms
rtt min/avg/max/mdev = 1218.059/1258.384/1290.861/28.000 ms
```

In this example, a ping packet took, on average, 1.3 seconds to make the round trip. From the first example to the second example, latency increased by a factor of 31! A data link that goes from working normally to slowing down by a factor of 31 is a clear sign that link utilization should be investigated.

For a more accurate measure of data throughput, a tool such as ttcp can be used. To test your connection with ttcp you must have installed the ttcp RPM package on machines inside *and* outside of your network. (The ttcp package comes on CD #3 included with this book.) If you are not sure if the package is installed, simply type **ttcp** at a command prompt. You should see something like the following:

```
# ttcp
Usage: ttcp -t [-options] host [ < in ]
       ttcp -r [-options > out]
```

```
Common options:
 -l ## length of bufs read from or written to network (default 8192)
 -u use UDP instead of TCP
 -p ## port number to send to or listen at (default 5001)
 -s -t: source a pattern to network
  -r: sink (discard) all data from network
 -A align the start of buffers to this modulus (default 16384)
 -O start buffers at this offset from the modulus (default 0)
 -v verbose: print more statistics
 -d set SO_DEBUG socket option
 -b ## set socket buffer size (if supported)
 -f X format for rate: k,K = kilo{bit,byte}; m,M = mega; g,G = giga
Options specific to -t:
 -n## number of source bufs written to network (default 2048)
 -D don't buffer TCP writes (sets TCP_NODELAY socket option)
Options specific to -r:
 -B for -s, only output full blocks as specified by -l (for TAR)
 -T "touch": access each byte as it's read
```

The first step is to start up a receiver process on the server machine:

```
# ttcp -rs
ttcp-r: buflen=8192, nbuf=2048, align=16384/0, port=5001  tcp
ttcp-r: socket
```

The −r flag denotes that the server machine will be the receiver. The −s flag, in conjunction with the −r flag, tells ttcp that we want to ignore any received data.

The next step is to have someone outside of your data link, with a network link close to the same speed as yours, set up a ttcp sending process:

```
# ttcp -ts server.example.com
ttcp-t: buflen=8192, nbuf=2048, align=16384/0, port=5001  tcp  ->
server.example.com
ttcp-t: socket
ttcp-t: connect
```

Let the process run for a few minutes and then press Ctrl+C on the transmitting side to stop the testing. The receiving side will then take a moment to calculate and present the results:

```
# ttcp -rs
ttcp-r: buflen=8192, nbuf=2048, align=16384/0, port=5001  tcp
ttcp-r: socket
ttcp-r: accept from 64.223.17.21
ttcp-r: 2102496 bytes in 70.02 real seconds = 29.32 KB/sec +++
ttcp-r: 1226 I/O calls, msec/call = 58.49, calls/sec = 17.51
ttcp-r: 0.0user 0.0sys 1:10real 0% 0i+0d 0maxrss 0+2pf 0+0csw
```

In this example, the average bandwidth between the two hosts was 29.32 kilobytes per second. On a link suffering from a DDOS, this number would be a mere fraction of the actual bandwidth the data link is rated for.

If the data link is indeed saturated, the next step is to determine where the connections are coming from. A very effective way of doing this is with the `netstat` command, which is included as part of the base Fedora installation. Type the following to see connection information:

```
# netstat -tupn
```

Table 14-1 describes each of the `netstat` parameters used here.

Table 14-1: netstat Parameters

Parameter	Description
-t, --tcp	Show TCP socket connections.
-u, --udp	Show UDP socket connections.
-p, --program	Show the PID and name of the program to which each socket belongs.
-n, --numeric	Show numerical address instead of trying to determine symbolic host, port, or user names.

The following is an example of what the output might look like:

```
Active Internet connections (w/o servers)
Proto Recv-Q Send-Q Local Address      Foreign Address       State       PID/Program name
tcp        0      0 65.213.7.96:22     13.29.132.19:12545    ESTABLISHED 32376/sshd
tcp        0    224 65.213.7.96:22     13.29.210.13:29250    ESTABLISHED 13858/sshd
tcp        0      0 65.213.7.96:6667   13.29.194.190:33452   ESTABLISHED 1870/ircd
tcp        0      0 65.213.7.96:6667   216.39.144.152:42709  ESTABLISHED 1870/ircd
tcp        0      0 65.213.7.96:42352  67.113.1.99:53        TIME_WAIT   -
tcp        0      0 65.213.7.96:42354  83.152.6.9:113        TIME_WAIT   -
tcp        0      0 65.213.7.96:42351  83.152.6.9:113        TIME_WAIT   -
tcp        0      0 127.0.0.1:42355    127.0.0.1:783         TIME_WAIT   -
tcp        0      0 127.0.0.1:783      127.0.0.1:42353       TIME_WAIT   -
tcp        0      0 65.213.7.96:42348  19.15.11.1:25         TIME_WAIT   -
```

The output is organized into columns defined as follows:

- **Proto** — Protocol used by the socket.
- **Recv-Q** — The number of bytes not yet copied by the user program attached to this socket.
- **Send-Q** — The number of bytes not acknowledged by the host.

- **Local Address** — Address and port number of the local end of the socket.
- **Foreign Address** — Address and port number of the remote end of the socket.
- **State** — Current state of the socket. Table 14-2 provides a list of socket states.
- **PID/Program name** — Process ID and program name of the process that owns the socket.

Table 14-2: Socket States

State	Description
ESTABLISHED	Socket has an established connection.
SYN_SENT	Socket actively trying to establish a connection.
SYN_RECV	Connection request received from the network.
FIN_WAIT1	Socket closed and shutting down.
FIN_WAIT2	Socket is waiting for remote end to shut down.
TIME_WAIT	Socket is waiting after closing to handle packets still in the network.
CLOSED	Socket is not being used.
CLOSE_WAIT	The remote end has shut down, waiting for the socket to close.
LAST_ACK	The remote end has shut down, and the socket is closed, waiting for acknowledgement.
LISTEN	Socket is waiting for an incoming connection.
CLOSING	Both sides of the connection are shut down, but not all of your data has been sent.
UNKNOWN	The state of the socket is unknown.

During a DOS attack, the foreign address is usually the same for each connection. In this case, it is a simple matter of typing the foreign IP address into the search form at www.arin.net/whois/ so you can alert your ISP.

During a DDOS attack, the foreign address will likely be different for each connection. In this case, it is impossible to track down all of the offenders, because there will likely be thousands of them. The best way to defend yourself is to contact your ISP and see if it can filter the traffic at its border routers.

Protecting Against Intrusion Attacks

Crackers have a wide variety of tools and techniques to assist them in breaking into your computer. Intrusion attacks focus on exploiting weaknesses in your security, so the crackers can take more control of your system (and potentially do more damage) than they could from the outside.

Fortunately, there are many tools and techniques for combating intrusion attacks. This section discusses the most common break-in methods and the tools available to protect your system. Though the examples shown are specific to Fedora and other Red Hat Linux systems, the tools and techniques are generally applicable to any other Linux or UNIX-like operating system.

> **CROSS-REFERENCE:** The tripwire package, which was recently dropped from the Fedora distribution, was a good tool for detecting whether intrusion attacks have taken place. The description of tripwire is not in this edition. However, if you are interested in installing the package on your own, you can find the description of tripwire at www.wiley.com/legacy/compbooks/negus.

Evaluating access to network services

Fedora, Red Hat Linux, and its UNIX kin provide many network services, and with them many avenues for cracker attacks. You should know these services and how to limit access to them.

So what do I mean by a network service? Basically, I am referring to any task that the computer performs that requires it to send and receive information over the network using some predefined set of rules. Routing e-mail is a network service. So is serving Web pages. Your Linux box has the potential to provide thousands of services. Many of them are listed in the /etc/services file. Look at a snippet of that file:

```
# /etc/services:
# service-name   port/protocol   [aliases ...]    [# comment]
chargen          19/tcp          ttytst source
chargen          19/udp          ttytst source
ftp-data         20/tcp
ftp-data         20/udp
# 21 is registered to ftp, but also used by fsp
ftp              21/tcp
ftp              21/udp          fsp fspd
ssh              22/tcp                      # SSH Remote Login Protocol
ssh              22/udp                      # SSH Remote Login Protocol
telnet           23/tcp
telnet           23/udp
# 24 - private mail system
smtp             25/tcp          mail
```

After comment lines, you will notice three columns of information. The left column contains the name of each service. The middle column defines the port number and protocol type used for that service. The rightmost field contains an optional alias or list of aliases for the service.

As an example, let us examine the last entry in the above file snippet. It describes the SMTP (Simple Mail Transfer Protocol) service, which is the service used for delivering e-mail over the Internet. The middle column contains the text 25/tcp, which tells us that the SMTP protocol uses port 25 and uses the Transmission Control Protocol (TCP) as its protocol type.

So, what exactly is a port number? It is a unique number that has been set aside for a particular network service. It allows network connections to be properly routed to the software that handles that service. For example, when an e-mail message is delivered from some other computer to your Linux box, the remote system must first establish a network connection with your system. Your computer receives the connection request, examines it, sees it labeled for port 25, and thus knows that the connection should be handed to the program that handles e-mail (which happens to be sendmail).

> **NOTE:** A program that runs quietly in the background handling service requests (such as sendmail) is called a daemon. Usually, daemons are started automatically when your system boots up, and they keep running until your system is shut down. Daemons may also be started on an as-needed basis by xinetd, a special daemon that listens on a large number of port numbers, then launches the requested process.

I mentioned that SMTP uses the TCP protocol. Some services use UDP, the User Datagram Protocol. All you really need to know about TCP and UDP (for the purpose of this security discussion) is that they provide different ways of packaging the information sent over a network connection. A TCP connection provides error detection and retransmission of lost data. UDP doesn't check to ensure that the data arrived complete and intact; it is meant as a fast way to send non-critical information.

Disabling network services

Although there are hundreds of services (listed in /etc/services) that potentially could be available and subject to attack on your Fedora or Red Hat Linux system, in reality only a few dozen services are installed and only a handful of those are on by default. Most network services are started by either the xinetd process or by a start-up script in the /etc/init.d directory.

xinetd is a daemon that listens on a great number of network port numbers. When a connection is made to a particular port number, xinetd automatically starts the appropriate program for that service and hands the connection to it.

The configuration file /etc/xinetd.conf is used to provide default settings for the xinetd server. The directory /etc/xinetd.d contains files telling xinetd what ports to listen on and what programs to start. Each file contains configuration information for a single service, and the file is usually named after the service it configures. For example, to enable the rsync service, edit the `rsync` file in the `/etc/xinetd.d` directory and look for a section similar to the following:

```
service rsync
{
    disable = yes
    socket_type        = stream
    wait               = no
    user               = root
    server             = /usr/bin/rsync
    server_args        = --daemon
    log_on_failure     += USERID
}
```

Note that the first line of this example identifies the service as `rsync`. This exactly matches the service name listed in the `/etc/services` file, causing the service to listen on port 873 for TCP and UDP protocols. You can see that the service is off by default (`disable = yes`). To enable the rsync services, change the line to read `disable = no` instead. Thus, the preceding example with rsync services enabled would look like this:

```
service rsync
{
    disable = no
    socket_type        = stream
    wait               = no
    user               = root
    server             = /usr/bin/rsync
    server_args        = --daemon
    log_on_failure     += USERID
}
```

> **TIP:** The rsync service is a nice one to turn on if your machine is an FTP server. It allows people to use an rsync client (which includes a checksum-search algorithm) to download files from your server. With that feature, users can restart a disrupted download without having to start from the beginning.

Because most services are disabled by default, your computer is only as insecure as you make it. You can double-check that insecure services, such as rlogin and rsh (which are included in the rsh-server package), are also disabled by making sure that `disabled = yes` is set in the `/etc/xinetd.d/rlogin` and rsh files.

> **TIP:** You can make the remote login service active but disable the use of the `/etc/host.equiv` and `.rhosts` files, requiring `rlogin` to always prompt for a password. Rather than disabling the service, locate the server line in the rsh file (`server = /usr/sbin/in.rshd`) and add a space followed by `-L` at the end.

You now need to send a signal to the xinetd process to tell it to reload its configuration file. The quickest way to do that is to restart the xinetd service. As the root user, type the following from a shell:

```
# service xinetd restart
Stopping xinetd:             [ OK ]
Starting xinetd:             [ OK ]
```

That's it — you have enabled the ipop3 service. Provided that you have properly configured your mail server (see Chapter 19), clients should now be able to get their mail from your computer.

Using TCP wrappers

Completely disabling an unused service is fine, but what about the services that you really need? How can you selectively grant and deny access to these services? In previous versions of Red Hat Linux, the TCP wrapper daemon (tcpd) was used to facilitate this sort of selective access. In the current version of Fedora, TCP wrapper support has been integrated into xinetd. xinetd will look at the files /etc/hosts.allow and /etc/hosts.deny to determine when a particular connection should be granted or refused for services such as rlogin, rsh, telnet, finger, and talk. TCP wrappers are also enabled by default for other services, such as a vsftpd FTP server (with tcp_wrappers=YES to your vsftpd.conf file)

When a service is requested that relies on TCP wrappers, the hosts.allow and hosts.deny files are scanned and checked for an entry that matches the IP address of the connecting machine. These checks are made when connection attempts occur:

- If the address is listed in the hosts.allow file, the connection is allowed and hosts.deny is not checked.

- Otherwise, if the address is in hosts.deny, the connection is denied.

- Finally, if the address is in neither file, the connection is allowed.

It is not necessary (or even possible) to list every single address that may connect to your computer. The hosts.allow and hosts.deny files enable you to specify entire subnets and groups of addresses. You can even use the keyword ALL to specify all possible addresses. You can also restrict specific entries in these files so they only apply to specific network services. Let's look at an example of a typical pair of hosts.allow and hosts.deny files. Here's the /etc/hosts.allow file:

```
#
# hosts.allow    This file describes the names of the hosts are
#                allowed to use the local INET services, as decided
#                by the '/usr/sbin/tcpd' server.
#

cups-lpd: 199.170.177.
in.telnetd: 199.170.177., .linuxtoys.net
vsftpd: ALL
```

Here's the /etc/hosts.deny file:

```
#
# hosts.deny    This file describes the names of the hosts which are
#               *not* allowed to use the local INET services, as
#               decided by the '/usr/sbin/tcpd' server.
#

ALL: ALL
```

The preceding example is a rather restrictive configuration. It allows connections to the cups-lpd and telnet services from certain hosts, but then denies all other connections. It also allows connections to the FTP service (vsftp) to all hosts. Let's examine the files in detail.

As usual, lines beginning with a # character are comments and are ignored by xinetd when it parses the file. Each noncomment line consists of a comma-separated list of daemons followed by a colon (:) character and then a comma-separated list of client addresses to check. In this context, a client is any computer that attempts to access a network service on your system.

A client entry can be a numeric IP address (such as 199.170.177.25) or a host name (such as jukebox.linuxtoys.net) but is more often a wildcard variation that specifies an entire range of addresses. A client entry can take four different forms. The online manual page for the hosts.allow file describes them as follows:

- A string that begins with a dot (.) character. A host name is matched if the last components of its name match the specified pattern. For example, the pattern .tue.nl matches the host name wzv.win.tue.nl.

- A string that ends with a dot (.) character. A host address is matched if its first numeric fields match the given string. For example, the pattern 131.155. matches the address of (almost) every host on the Eindhoven University network (131.155.x.x).

- A string that begins with an at (@) sign is treated as an NIS (formerly YP) netgroup name. A host name is matched if it is a host member of the specified netgroup. Netgroup matches are not supported for daemon process names or for client user names.

- An expression of the form *n.n.n.n/m.m.m.m* is interpreted as a *net/mask* pair. A host address is matched if *net* is equal to the bitwise *and* of the address and the mask. For example, the net/mask pattern 131.155.72.0/255.255.254.0 matches every address in the range 131.155.72.0 through 131.155.73.255.

The example host.allow contains the first two types of client specification. The entry 199.170.177. will match any IP address that begins with that string, such as 199.170.177.25. The client entry .linuxtoys.net will match host names such as jukebox.linuxtoys.net or picframe.linuxtoys.net.

Let's examine what happens when a host named jukebox.linuxtoys.net (with IP address 199.170.179.18) connects to your Fedora system using the Telnet protocol:

1. xinetd receives the connection request.

2. xinetd begins comparing the address and name of jukebox.linuxtoys.net to the rules listed in /etc/hosts.allow. It starts at the top of the file and works its way down the file until finding a match. Both the daemon (the program handling the network service on your Fedora box) and the connecting client's IP address or name must match the information in the hosts.allow file. In this case, the second rule that is encountered matches the request:

```
in.telnetd: 199.170.177., .linuxtoys.net
```

3. Daffy is not in the 199.170.177 subnet, but it is in the linuxtoys.net domain. xinetd stops searching the file as soon as it finds this match.

How about if Daffy connects to your box using the IMAP protocol? In this case, it matches none of the rules in hosts.allow; the only line that refers to the imapd daemon does not refer to the 199.170.179 subnet or to the linuxtoys.net domain. xinetd continues on to the hosts.deny file. The entry ALL: ALL matches anything, so tcpd denies the connection.

The ALL wildcard was also used in the hosts.allow file. In this case, we are telling xinetd to permit absolutely any host to connect to the FTP service on the Linux box. This is appropriate for running an anonymous FTP server that anyone on the Internet can access. If you are not running an anonymous FTP site, you probably should not use the ALL flag.

A good rule of thumb is to make your hosts.allow and hosts.deny files as restrictive as possible and then explicitly enable only those services that you really need. Also, grant access only to those systems that really need access. Using the ALL flag to grant universal access to a particular service may be easier than typing in a long list of subnets or domains, but better a few minutes spent on proper security measures than many hours recovering from a break-in.

> **TIP:** You can further restrict access to services using various options within the /etc/xinetd.conf file, even to the point of limiting access to certain services to specific times of the day. Read the manual page for xinetd (by typing **man xinetd** at a command prompt) to learn more about these options.

Protecting Your Network with Firewalls

What is a firewall? In the non-computer world, a firewall is a physical barrier that keeps a fire from spreading. Computer firewalls serve a similar purpose, but the "fires" that they attempt to block are attacks from crackers on the Internet. In this context, a firewall, also known as a *packet filter*, is a physical piece of computer hardware that sits between your network and the Internet, regulating and controlling the flow of information.

The most common types of firewalls used today are filtering firewalls. A filtering firewall filters the traffic flowing between your network and the Internet, blocking certain things that may put your network at risk. It can limit access to and from the Internet to only specific computers on your network. It can also limit the type of communication, selectively permitting or denying various Internet services.

For Fedora to act as a filtering firewall, you can use the iptables features. The iptables feature replaced ipchains as the default Red Hat Linux firewall several releases ago. For Fedora Core 2, ipchains has been dropped altogether. The iptables facility is described in this chapter.

> **NOTE:** You can read about differences between ipchains and iptables in the Iptables HOWTO, at `http://netfilter.samba.org/unreliable-guides/packet-filtering-HOWTO/packet-filtering-HOWTO.linuxdoc-7.html`.

Configuring an iptables firewall

The iptables firewall feature (also referred to as netfilter) is the default firewall software when you install Fedora. The ipchains firewall facility, once available with Red Hat Linux and Fedora Core 1, is no longer available with Fedora Core 2.

If you currently use ipchains on your Red Hat Linux system (for example, if you just upgraded to Fedora Core 2) and you want to convert to iptables, you need to disable ipchains before you can use iptables. In fact, if you try to use the iptables script (`/etc/init.d/iptables`) to start iptables while the ipchains module is loaded, the iptables startup script silently fails and exits.

While iptables is generally considered to be more complex than ipchains to work with, it is also considered to be more powerful and flexible. Because development is not continuing for ipchains, the few broken ipchains features that exist will probably stay broken.

This section describes how to turn on iptables and set up firewall rules for several different types of situations. It also tells how to turn on features related to firewalls that allow your iptables firewall to do Network Address Translation (NAT), IP masquerading, port forwarding, and transparent proxies.

> **NOTE:** The Fedora startup scripts will "punch a hole" through your firewall if you use certain services, and will therefore work even if they are not explicitly enabled in your `iptables` configuration. For example, NTP (which sets your system time from a network time server) and DNS resolution (which lets you contact a DNS server to resolve addresses) both open the ports they need in your firewall.

Turning on iptables

The following procedure describes how to get `iptables` going on your Fedora system.

> **TIP:** During the time that you turn off ipchains, turn on iptables, and configure the filtering rules for iptables, your computer may be unprotected from the network. You should test your firewall rules on non-critical computers, and then perform the switch on critical computers either quickly or by temporarily shutting down your network interfaces.

1. Stop the ipchains script from starting automatically at boot time:

```
# chkconfig ipchains off
```

2. Set the iptables script to start automatically at boot time:

```
# chkconfig iptables on
```

3. Now you can either reboot Fedora, or stop ipchains and unload the ipchains module, as follows:

```
# service ipchains stop
# modprobe -r ipchains
```

4. Before you can start iptables you must have a working set of rules that have been placed in your /etc/sysconfig/iptables file. To create those rules, refer to the examples in the following sections. (Without the configuration file in place, iptables fails silently.)

> **TIP:** If you are new to iptables, you can start with a workable set of default values by configuring your firewall during Fedora installation. I recommend selecting a Medium security firewall and configuring a few services to be allowed. The resulting /etc/sysconfig/iptables file will let you study how Fedora creates its firewalls rules.

5. If you are doing NAT or IP Masquerading, turn on IP packet forwarding. One way to allow this is to change the value of net.ipv4.ip_forward to 1 in the /etc/sysctl.conf file. Open that file as root user with any text editor and change the line to appear as follows:

```
net.ipv4.ip_forward = 1
```

6. Restart your network interfaces to have IP packet forwarding take effect.

```
# /etc/init.d/network restart
```

7. Once the rules file is in place, start up iptables:

```
# /etc/init.d/iptables start
```

8. At this point, iptables is installed as your firewall. You can check to see that the modules used by iptables are loaded by using the lsmod command, as follows:

```
# lsmod |grep ip
ipt_REJECT              4736    1
ipt_state               1536    7
ip_conntrack           24368    1  ipt_state
iptable_filter          2176    1
ip_tables              13568    3  ipt_REJECT,ipt_state,iptable_filter
```

9. If you want to allow passive FTP or IRC connections from computers on your LAN, you may need to load those modules by adding them to the /etc/modules.conf file. The

basic connection tracking module, ip_conntrack, should be loaded by default already. (See the description of passive FTP and IRC after the firewall-example sections.)

If your iptables service didn't start, make sure that:

- An ipchains module is not loaded. (Unload it with `modprobe -r` as shown previously.)
- The `/etc/sysconfig/iptables` file exists. (You need to create one if one was not already created for you when you installed Fedora.)

> **TIP:** As you add iptables rules, more modules will have to be loaded. Appropriate modules should be loaded automatically when a new rule is entered. Run `lsmod | grep ip` again after you have added a few rules to see which modules were added. Note that these modules will not be unloaded if you decide to stop iptables. They will stay loaded until the next reboot or until you remove them (`modprobe -r`).

The following sections contain examples of iptables firewall rules.

Creating iptables firewall rules

One way to configure iptables is to start by adding and deleting rules to your kernel from the command line. Then when you get a set of rules that you like, you save the rules that are currently running on your system. The tools you use to create your firewall rules and then make them permanent are as follows:

- **iptables** — Use this command to append (`-A`), delete (`-D`), replace (`-R`) or insert (`-I`) a rule. Use the `-L` option to list all current rules.
- **iptables-save -c** — Use this command to save the rules from the kernel and install them in the configuration file.
- **/etc/sysconfig/iptables** — This is the configuration file that contains the rules that were saved from the `iptables-save` command.
- **/etc/sysconfig/iptable-config** — You can add settings for managing your iptables rules to the `iptable-config` file. For example, any iptables modules, such as ip_conntrack and others described later in this chapter, can be added to the `IPTABLES_MODULES` line to be loaded automatically. You can also set whether the iptables table in your running kernel is saved to a file when iptables stops.
- **/etc/init.d/iptables** — This is the iptables start-up script that must run automatically each time Fedora reboots. When it starts, it clears all iptables rules and counters and installs the new rules from the `/etc/sysconfig/iptables` file. You can also use this script with different options from the command line to check the status of iptables (`status`) or to run `iptables-save` for you to save the current rules (`save`).

To get you started with iptables, I'm providing a sample set of iptables rules along with descriptions of how you might change those rules for different situations. Here's how you could load and save any of the sets of rules described in the following example:

1. If you are currently running ipchains, complete the procedure in the previous "Turning on iptables" section.

2. Stop iptables and clear all existing rules:

   ```
   # /etc/init.d/iptables stop
   ```

3. Add the rules shown in the following example to a file, using any text editor. Modify the rules to suit your situation and save the file.

4. As root user, run the file as a shell script. For example, if you named the file firescript, you could run it as follows:

   ```
   # sh firescript
   ```

5. See how the rules were loaded into the kernel:

   ```
   # iptables -L
   ```

6. If everything looks okay, save the rules that are now in the kernel into the /etc/sysconfig/iptables file:

   ```
   # cp /etc/sysconfig/iptables /etc/sysconfig/iptables-old
   # iptables-save > /etc/sysconfig/iptables
   ```

From now on the rules will be read each time you reboot or restart iptables. Save a copy of the script you used to create the rules, in case you ever need it again.

Example 1: Firewall for shared Internet connection (plus servers)

This example features a home or small-office LAN with a Fedora system acting as an iptables firewall between the LAN and the Internet. The firewall computer also acts as a Web server, FTP server, and DNS server. Figure 14-1 shows this configuration.

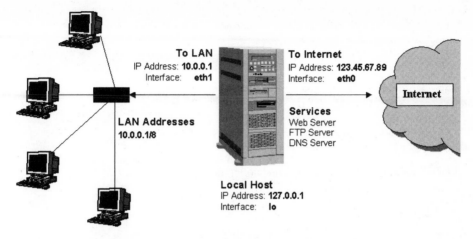

To LAN
IP Address: **10.0.0.1**
Interface: **eth1**

To Internet
IP Address: **123.45.67.89**
Interface: **eth0**

Internet

LAN Addresses
10.0.0.1/8

Services
Web Server
FTP Server
DNS Server

Local Host
IP Address: **127.0.0.1**
Interface: **lo**

Figure 14-1: Using iptables as a firewall between the Internet and a LAN.

If you want to use the sample firewall script that follows, you must change the following information to match your configuration:

Firewall computer — The firewall computer is set up as follows:

- **Local host** — 127.0.0.1 (IP address) and lo (interface). You shouldn't need to change these.

- **Connection to the Internet** — 123.45.67.89 (IP address) and eth0 (interface). Replace them with the static IP address and interface name associated with your connection to the Internet, respectively.

- **Connection to the LAN** — 10.0.0.1 (IP address) and eth1 (interface). Replace 10.0.0.1 and eth1 with the static IP address and interface name associated with your connection to your LAN, respectively.

Computers on the LAN — Each computer on the LAN in the example has an IP address between 10.0.0.2 to 10.0.0.254. Change 10.0.0.255 to a number that matches your LAN's range of addresses.

Here is an example of a script to load firewall rules that could be used for the configuration shown in Figure 14-1:

```
# (1) Policies (default)
iptables -P INPUT DROP
iptables -P OUTPUT DROP
iptables -P FORWARD DROP

# (2) User-defined chain for ACCEPTed TCP packets
iptables -N okay
```

```
iptables -A okay -p TCP --syn -j ACCEPT
iptables -A okay -p TCP -m state --state ESTABLISHED,RELATED -j ACCEPT
iptables -A okay -p TCP -j DROP


# (3) INPUT chain rules

# Rules for incoming packets from LAN
iptables -A INPUT -p ALL -i eth1 -s 10.0.0.0/24 -j ACCEPT
iptables -A INPUT -p ALL -i lo -s 127.0.0.1 -j ACCEPT
iptables -A INPUT -p ALL -i lo -s 10.0.0.1 -j ACCEPT
iptables -A INPUT -p ALL -i lo -s 123.45.67.89 -j ACCEPT
iptables -A INPUT -p ALL -i eth1 -d 10.0.0.255 -j ACCEPT


# Rules for incoming packets from the Internet

# Packets for established connections
iptables -A INPUT -p ALL -d 123.45.67.89 -m state --state
ESTABLISHED,RELATED -j ACCEPT

# TCP rules
iptables -A INPUT -p TCP -i eth0 -s 0/0 --destination-port 21 -j okay
iptables -A INPUT -p TCP -i eth0 -s 0/0 --destination-port 22 -j okay
iptables -A INPUT -p TCP -i eth0 -s 0/0 --destination-port 80 -j okay
iptables -A INPUT -p TCP -i eth0 -s 0/0 --destination-port 113 -j okay

# UDP rules
iptables -A INPUT -p UDP -i eth0 -s 0/0 --destination-port 53 -j ACCEPT
iptables -A INPUT -p UDP -i eth0 -s 0/0 --destination-port 2074 -j ACCEPT
iptables -A INPUT -p UDP -i eth0 -s 0/0 --destination-port 4000 -j ACCEPT

# ICMP rules
iptables -A INPUT -p ICMP -i eth0 -s 0/0 --icmp-type 8 -j ACCEPT
iptables -A INPUT -p ICMP -i eth0 -s 0/0 --icmp-type 11 -j ACCEPT

# (4) FORWARD chain rules
# Accept the packets we want to forward
iptables -A FORWARD -i eth1 -j ACCEPT
iptables -A FORWARD -m state --state ESTABLISHED,RELATED -j ACCEPT

# (5) OUTPUT chain rules
# Only output packets with local addresses (no spoofing)
iptables -A OUTPUT -p ALL -s 127.0.0.1 -j ACCEPT
iptables -A OUTPUT -p ALL -s 10.0.0.1 -j ACCEPT
iptables -A OUTPUT -p ALL -s 123.45.67.89 -j ACCEPT

# (6) POSTROUTING chain rules
iptables -t nat -A POSTROUTING -o eth0 -j SNAT --to-source 123.45.67.89
```

I divided the commands in the preceding script into six sections. The following text describes each of those sections.

(1) Policies — The `iptables -P` commands set the default policies for INPUT, OUTPUT, and FORWARD chains. By assigning each of those policies to DROP, any packet that isn't matched is discarded. In other words, for a packet to get through, it has to be specifically matched and ACCEPTed by one of the other rules in the script.

(2) User-defined chain — A user-defined chain I call `okay` is created to do a few more checks on packets requesting certain TCP services that I'm going to allow through (Web, FTP, and DNS services). The `-N okay` option creates the `okay` chain. The next line says that a SYN packet (`--syn`), which requests a new connection, is fine to let through. The next line allows through packets associated with an ESTABLISHED connection (one that has already had traffic pass through the interface) or a RELATED connection (one that is starting a new connection related to an already established connection). The final line in this set tells iptables to DROP packets that don't meet one of those checks.

(3) INPUT chain rules — The bulk of the packet filtering is done in the INPUT chain. The first sets of input rules indicates to iptables when to always accept packets from the Internet and from the LAN. The next three sets determine which requests for specific protocols (TCP, UDP, and ICMP) are accepted.

- **Packets from LAN** — Because you want the users on your LAN and the firewall computer itself to be able to use the Internet, this set of rules lets through packets that are initiated from those computers. The first line tells iptables to accept packets for ALL protocols for which the source is an acceptable addresses on your LAN (`-s 10.0.0.0/24`, which represents IP numbers `10.0.0.1` through `10.0.0.254`). The next three lines allow packets that come from all valid IP addresses on the firewall computer itself (`-s 127.0.0.1`, `10.0.0.1` and `123.45.67.89`). The last line accepts broadcast packets (`-d 10.0.0.255`) on the LAN.

- **Packets from Internet (already connected)** — This line is split in two (I just used the backslash to join the lines because the page wasn't wide enough to show it as one line). It ACCEPTs packets that are both associated with connections that are already established (`--state ESTABLISHED,RELATED`) and are requested directly to the firewall's IP address (`123.45.67.89`).

- **TCP rules (new connections)** — Here is where you open up the ports for the TCP services you want to provide to anyone from the Internet. In these lines you open ports for FTP service (`--destination-port 21`), secure shell service (`22`), Web service (`80`), and IDENTD authentication (`113`), the last of which might be necessary for protocols such as IRC. Instead of accepting these requests immediately, you jump to the `okay` chain you defined to further check that the packets was formed properly.

CAUTION: You want to ensure that the services on the ports to which you are allowing access are properly configured before you allow packets to be accepted to them.

- **UDP rules (new connections)** — These lines define the ports where connection packets are accepted from the Internet for UDP services. In this example I chose to accept requests for DNS service (`--destination-port 53`) because the computer is set up as a DNS server. The example also illustrates lines that accept requests for a couple of other optional ports. Port 2074 is needed by some multimedia applications the users on your LAN might want to use, and port 4000 is used by the ICQ protocol (for online chats).

- **ICMP rules** — ICMP messages are really more for reporting conditions of the server than for actually providing services. Packets from the Internet that are accepted for ICMP protocol requests in our example are those for ICMP types 8 and 11. Type 8 service, which allows your computer to accept *echo reply messages*, makes it possible for people to ping your computer to see if it is available. Type 11 service relates to packets whose *time to live* (TTL) was exceeded in transit, and for which you are accepting a Time Exceeded message that is being returned to us. (You need to accept Type 11 messages to use the `traceroute` command to find broken routes to hosts you want to reach.)

(4) FORWARD chain rules — Because this firewall is also acting as a router, FORWARD rules are needed to limit what the firewall will and will not pass between the two networks (Internet and local LAN). The first line forwards everything from the local LAN (`-A FORWARD -i eth1`). The second line forwards anything from the Internet that is associated with an established connection (`--state ESTABLISHED,RELATED`).

(5) OUTPUT chain rules — These rules basically exist to prevent anyone from your local computer from *spoofing* IP addresses (that is, from saying packets are coming from somewhere that they are not). According to these three rules, each packet output from your firewall must have as its source address one of the addresses from the firewall computer's interfaces (`127.0.0.1`, `10.0.0.0.1`, or `123.45.67.89`).

(6) POSTROUTING chain rules — The POSTROUTING chain defines rules for packets that have been accepted, but need additional processing. This is where the actual network-address translation (NAT) work takes place. For the NAT table (`-t nat`), in the POSTROUTING chain, all packets that go out to the Internet have their addresses translated to that of the firewall's external interface (`--to-source 123.45.67.89`). In this case I used the Source Network Address Translation (SNAT) chain because I have a static IP address (`123.45.67.89`) associated with my Internet connection. If I were using a dynamic IP address (via DHCP), I would use MASQUERADE instead of SNAT. I would also have to change any references to `-d 123.45.67.89` to `-i eth0`. (Of course, you would be using a different IP address and possibly a different Ethernet interface.)

Example 2: Firewall for shared Internet connection (no servers)

In this scenario, the firewall is protecting a Linux system (firewall) and several systems on the LAN that only want to connect to the Internet. No servers are behind this firewall, so you want to prevent people from the Internet from requesting services.

You could use the same script shown in Example 1, but not use lines that request TCP services. So you could drop the user-defined chain in section 2 and drop the TCP rules from section 3. You could also remove the ICMP rules, if you don't want your firewall to be visible to `ping` requests (Type 8) and if you don't care about receiving messages when your packets exceed their time to live values (Type 11), such as when a packet runs into a broken router.

Example 3: Firewall for single Linux system with Internet connection

In this example, there is one network interface, connecting your Fedora system to the Internet. You are not sharing that connection with other computers and you are not offering any services from your computer.

In this case, you could cut sections 2, 4, and 6. From section 3, you could cut all rules relating to incoming requests from the LAN and all TCP services. As I mentioned in Example 2, you could also remove the Type 8 ICMP rule to make your firewall invisible to `ping` requests from the Internet and the Type 11 ICMP rule to not accept messages about failed time-to-live packets.

Understanding iptables

Now that you've seen something about what iptables rules look like and how you can get them going, step back a bit and see how iptables works.

The iptables feature works by having IP packets (that is, network data) that enter or leave the firewall computer, traverse a set of chains that define what is done with the packet. Each rule that you add essentially does both of the following:

- Checks if a particular criterion is met (such as that a packet requests a particular service or comes from a particular address)

- Takes an action (such as dropping, accepting, or further processing a packet)

Different sets of rules are implemented for different types of tables. For example, tables exist for filtering (`filter`), network address translation (`nat`), and changing packet headers (`mangle`). Depending on the packet's source and destination, it traverses different chains. Most of the rules you create will relate to the `filter` table (which is implied if no other table is given).

The chains associated with the filter table are INPUT, OUTPUT, and FORWARD. You can add user-defined chains as well. You will probably be most interested in adding or removing particular TCP and UDP services using the basic rules shown in the previous example. Assign ACCEPT to packets you want to go through and DROP to those you want to discard. You can also assign REJECT to drop a packet but return a message to the sender, or LOG to neither drop nor accept the message, but to log information about the packet.

A lot of great features are built into iptables. The following descriptions tell you about some cool things you can do with iptables and give you some tips on using it.

Allowing FTP and IRC services through an iptables firewall

With passive FTP, the FTP client sends its IP address and the port number on which it will listen for data to the server. If that client is on a computer that is behind your firewall, for which you are doing NAT, that information must be translated as well or the FTP server will not be able to communicate with the client.

iptables uses connection-tracking modules to track connections. Using this feature, it can look inside the FTP data themselves (that is, not in the IP packet header), to get the information it needs to do NAT (remember that computers from the Internet can't talk directly to your private IP addresses). To do FTP connection tracking (to allow passive FTP connections to the clients on your LAN), you need to have the following modules loaded:

- `ip_conntrack`
- `ip_conntrack_ftp`
- `ip_nat_ftp`

The same is true for chats (IRC) and DCC sends. Addresses and port numbers are stored within the IRC protocol packets, so those packets must be translated too. To allow clients on your LAN to use IRC services, you need to load the following modules:

- `ip_conntrack_irc`
- `ip_nat_irc`

The default port for IRC connections is 6667. If you don't want to use the default you can add different port numbers when you load the connection-tracking modules:

```
insmod ip_conntrack_irc.o ports=6668,6669
```

Using iptables to do NAT or IP Masquerading

As noted in the iptables example, you can use Source Network Address Translation (SNAT) or IP Masquerading (MASQUERADE) to allow computers on your LAN with private IP addresses to access the Internet through your iptables firewall. Choose SNAT if you have a static IP address for your Internet connection and MASQUERADE if the IP address is assigned dynamically.

When you create the MASQUERADE or SNAT rule, it is added to the NAT table and the POSTROUTING chain. For MASQUERADE you must provide the name of the interface (such as eth0, ppp0, or slip0) to identify the route to the Internet or other outside network. For SNAT you must also identify the actual IP address of the interface. Here is an example of a MASQUERADE rule:

```
# iptables -t nat -A POSTROUTING -o eth0 -j MASQUERADE
```

Here is an example of a SNAT rule:

```
# iptables -t nat -A POSTROUTING -o eth0 -j SNAT --to-source 12.12.12.12
```

You can add several source addresses if you have multiple addresses that provide a route to the Internet (for example, `--to-source 12.12.12.12.1-12.12.12.12.254`). Although `MASQUERADE` uses some additional overhead, you probably need to use it instead of `SNAT` if you have a dial-up connection to the Internet for which the IP address changes on each connection.

Remember that you need to make sure that IP forwarding is turned on in the kernel. (It is off by default.) To turn it on permanently, edit the `/etc/sysctl.conf` file as described earlier. To turn it on temporarily, you can do the following:

```
# echo 1 > /proc/sys/net/ipv4/ip_forward
```

If you require dynamic IP addressing, turn on that service:

```
# echo 1 > /proc/sys/net/ipv4/ip_dynaddr
```

Using iptables as a transparent proxy

With the `REDIRECT` target you can cause traffic for a specific port on the firewall computer to be directed to a different one. Using this feature you can direct host computers on your local LAN to a proxy service on your firewall computer without those hosts knowing it.

The following is an example of a set of command-line options to the `iptables` command that causes a request for Web service (port 80) to be directed to a proxy service (port 3128):

```
-t nat -A PREROUTING -p tcp --dport 80 -j REDIRECT --to-ports 3128
```

You can only use `REDIRECT` targets in `PREROUTING` and `OUTPUT` chains within a `nat` table. You can also give a range of port numbers to spread the redirection across multiple port numbers.

Using iptables to do port forwarding

What if you have only one static IP address, but you want to use a computer other than your firewall computer to provide Web, FTP, DNS, or some other service? You can use the Dynamic Network Address Translation (`DNAT`) feature to direct traffic for a particular port on your firewall to another computer.

For example, if you wanted all requests for Web service (port 80) that were directed to the firewall computer (`-d 15.15.15.15`) to be directed to another computer on your LAN (such as `10.0.0.25`), you could use the following `iptables` command:

```
# iptables -t nat -A PREROUTING -p tcp -d 15.15.15.15 --dport 80 \
        -j DNAT --to-destination 10.0.0.25
```

(Note that the preceding example should actually appear on one line. The backslash indicates continuation on the next line.)

You can also spread the load for the service you are forwarding by providing a range of IP addresses (for example, `--to-destination 10.0.0.1-10.0.0.25`). Likewise, you can direct the request to a range of ports as well.

Using logging with iptables

Using the LOG target you can log information about packets that meet the criteria you choose. In particular you might want to use this feature to log packets that seem like they might be improper in some way. In other words, if you don't want to drop a packet for some reason, you can just log its activity and decide later if something needs to be corrected.

The LOG target directs log information to the standard tools used to do logging in Fedora: dmesg and syslogd. Here is an example of a rule using a LOG target:

```
-A FORWARD -p tcp -j LOG --log-level info
```

Instead of info, you could use any of the following log levels available with syslog: emerg, alert, crit, err, warning, notice, info, or debug. Using the --log-prefix option as follows, you could also add information to the front of all messages produced from this logging action:

```
-A FORWARD -p tcp -j LOG --log-level info --log-prefix "Forward INFO "
```

Enhancing your iptables firewall

You can modify or expand on the iptables examples given in this chapter in many ways. iptables is tremendously flexible.

When you actually create your own iptables firewall, you should refer to the iptables man page (type **man iptables**) for detailed descriptions of options, ways of matching, ways of entering addresses, and other details. I also recommend an excellent iptables Tutorial by Oskar Andreasson (http://iptables-tutorial.frozentux.net).

Here are a few tips for using iptables features:

- **Reduce rules** — Try to improve performance by reducing the number of rules. Using subchains can keep a packet from seeing rules that don't apply to it.

- **Deal with fragments** — Use the -f option to refer to the second and subsequent packets of a packet that was split into fragments. In general, it is safe to not drop second and third fragments for which you don't have a first packet fragment because they won't be reassembled. If you use NAT the fragments are assembled before filtering, so you shouldn't have problems with unfiltered fragments being sent through.

- **Opposite** — To make a rule its opposite, use an exclamation mark (!).

- **All interfaces** — To match all interfaces of a type, use a plus sign (+), as in eth+.

- **Blocking connections** — Use the --syn option to block SYN packets (that is, those packets requesting connections). This option only applies to TCP packets.

- **Limiting** — Use the --limit option to restrict the rate of matches that result in log messages. This option allows matches to only produce messages a limited number of times per second (the default is three per hour with burst of five).

- **DOS Attacks** — You can use the `--limit` option to reduce the impact of DOS attacks, but it still won't stop them altogether. As long as the traffic is directed at your server, your network bandwidth is being leeched away, and the machine still utilizes resources to ignore the data.

- **Table types** — The default table type is `filter`. The other types of tables are `nat` (for IP Masquerading) and `mangle` (for altering packets). To use a table other than `filter` you must add a `-t table_type` option, where `table_tape` is either `nat` or `mangle`.

Detecting Intrusions from Log Files

Preparing your system for a cracker attack is only part of the battle. You must also recognize a cracker attack when it is occurring. Understanding the various log files in which Fedora records important events is critical to this goal. The log files for your Fedora system can be found in the `/var/log` directory.

Fedora comes with a System Logs window (`system-logviewer` command) that you can use to view and search critical system log files from the GUI. To open the System Logs window, from the main desktop menu, select System Tools → System Logs. Figure 14-2 shows an example of the System Logs window.

To view a particular log file, click the log name in the left column. If you are looking for a particular message or problem, type a keyword into the Filter for"box, and click Filter. Only lines containing that word are displayed. Case matters, so searching for "Mem" won't find "mem" when you use the filter. Click Reset to display the whole file again.

Table 14-3 contains a listing of log files displayed on the System Logs window, along with other files in the `/var/log` directory that may interest you. (* Indicates a log file that is not contained in the System Logs window. Access these files directly from `/var/log`.)

Figure 14-2: Display system log files in the System Logs window.

Table 14-3: Log Files in the /var/log Directory

System Logs Name	Filename	Description
Boot Log	boot.log	Contains messages indicating which systems services have started and shut down successfully and which (if any) have failed to start or stop.
Cron Log	cron	Contains status messages from the crond, a daemon that periodically runs scheduled jobs, such as backups and log file rotation.
Kernel Startup Log	dmesg	A recording of messages printed by the kernel when the system boots.
FTP Log	xferlog	Contains information about files transferred using the wu-ftpd FTP service.
Apache Access Log	httpd/access_log	Logs requests for information from your Apache Web server.
Apache Error Log	httpd/error_log	Logs errors encountered from clients trying to access data on your Apache Web server.
Mail Log	maillog	Contains information about addresses to which and from which e-mail was sent. Useful for detecting spamming.

System Logs Name	Filename	Description
MySQL Server Log	mysqld.log	Includes information related to activities of the MySQL database server (mysqld).
News Log	spooler	Directory containing logs of messages from the Usenet News server, if you are running one.
RPM Packages	rpmpkgs	Contains a listing of RPM packages that are installed on your system.
Security Log	secure	Records the date, time, and duration of login attempts and sessions.
System Log	messages	A general-purpose log file to which many programs record messages.
Update Agent Log	up2date	Contains messages resulting from actions by the Red Hat Update Agent.
X Log	Xorg.0.log	Includes messages output by the X.Org X server.
*	gdm/:0.log	Holds messages related to the login screen (GNOME display manager).
*	samba/log.smbd	Shows messages from the Samba SMB file service daemon.
*	squid/access.log	Contains messages related to the squid proxy/caching server.
*	vsftpd.log	Contains messages relating to transfers made using the vsFTPd daemon (FTP server).
*	sendmail	Shows error messages recorded by the sendmail daemon.
*	uucp	Shows status messages from the Unix to Unix Copy Protocol daemon.

The role of syslogd

Most of the files in the /var/log directory are maintained by the syslogd service. The syslogd daemon is the System Logging Daemon. It accepts log messages from a variety of other programs and writes them to the appropriate log files. This is better than having every program write directly to its own log file because it allows you to centrally manage how log files are handled. It is possible to configure syslogd to record varying levels of detail in the log files. It can be told to ignore all but the most critical message, or it can record every detail.

The `syslogd` daemon can even accept messages from other computers on your network. This is particularly handy because it enables you to centralize the management and reviewing of the log files from many systems on your network. There is also a major security benefit to this practice. If a system on your network is broken into, the cracker cannot delete or modify the log files because those files are stored on a separate computer. It is important to remember, though, that those log messages are not, by default, encrypted. Anyone tapping into your local network will be able to eavesdrop on those messages as they pass from one machine to another. Also, though the cracker may not be able to change old log messages, he will be able to affect the system such that any new log messages should not be trusted.

It is not uncommon to run a dedicated loghost, a computer that serves no other purpose than to record log messages from other computers on the network. Because this system runs no other services, it is unlikely that it will be broken into. This makes it nearly impossible for a cracker to erase his or her tracks. It does not, however, mean that all of the log messages are accurate after a cracker has broken into a machine on your network.

Redirecting logs to a loghost with syslogd

To redirect your computer's log files to another computer's syslogd, you must make some changes to your local syslogd's configuration file. The file that you need to work with is `/etc/syslog.conf`. Become root using the `su -` command and then load the `/etc/syslog.conf` file in a text editor (such as vi). You should see something similar to this:

```
# Log all kernel messages to the console.
# Logging much else clutters up the screen.
#kern.*                                 /dev/console

# Log anything (except mail) of level info or higher.
# Don't log private authentication messages!
*.info;mail.none;news.none;authpriv.none;cron.none   /var/log/messages

# The authpriv file has restricted access.
authpriv.*                              /var/log/secure

# Log all the mail messages in one place.
mail.*                                  /var/log/maillog

# Log cron stuff
cron.*                                  /var/log/cron

# Everybody gets emergency messages
*.emerg                                          *

# Save news errors of level crit and higher in a special file.
uucp,news.crit                          /var/log/spooler
```

```
# Save boot messages also to boot.log
local7.*                                /var/log/boot.log


#
# INN
#
news.=crit                              /var/log/news/news.crit
news.=err                               /var/log/news/news.err
news.notice                             /var/log/news/news.notice
```

The lines beginning with a # character are comments. Other lines contain two columns of information, separated by colons (spaces won't work). The left field is a semicolon-separated list of message types and message priorities. The right field is the log file to which those messages should be written. To send the messages to another computer (the loghost) instead of a file, simply replace the log file name with the @ character followed by the name of the loghost. For example, to redirect the output normally sent to the messages, secure, and maillog log files, make these changes to the previous file:

```
# Log anything (except mail) of level info or higher.
# Don't log private authentication messages!
*.info;mail.none;news.none;authpriv.none;cron.none   @loghost

# The authpriv file has restricted access.
authpriv.*                              @loghost

# Log all the mail messages in one place.
mail.*                                  @loghost
```

The messages will now be sent to the syslogd running on the computer named loghost. The name loghost was not an arbitrary choice. It is customary to create such a host name and make it an alias to the actual system acting as the loghost. That way, if you ever need to switch the loghost duties to a different machine, you only need to change the loghost alias; you do not need to reedit the syslog.conf file on every computer.

Understanding the messages logfile

Because of the many programs and services that record information to the messages logfile, it is important that you understand the format of this file. Examining this file will often give you a good early warning of problems developing on your system. Each line in the file is a single message recorded by some program or service. Here is a snippet of an actual messages log file:

```
Feb 25 11:04:32 toys network: Bringing up loopback interface:  succeeded
Feb 25 11:04:35 toys network: Bringing up interface eth0:  succeeded
Feb 25 13:01:14 toys vsftpd(pam_unix)[10565]: authentication failure;
     logname= uid=0 euid=0 tty= ruser= rhost=10.0.0.5  user=chris
Feb 25 14:44:24 toys su(pam_unix)[11439]: session opened for
     user root by chris(uid=500)
```

This is really very simple when you know what to look for. Each message is divided into five main parts. From left to right they are:

- The date and time that the message was logged

- The name of the computer that the message came from

- The program or service name that the message pertains to

- The process number (enclosed in square brackets) of the program sending the message

- The actual text message itself

Let's examine the previous file snippet. In the first two lines, you can see that I restarted the network. The next line shows that I tried to log in as the user named chris to get to the FTP server on this system from a computer at address 10.0.0.5 (I typed the wrong password and authentication failed). The last line shows that I used the su command to become root user.

By occasionally reviewing the messages file and the secure file, it is possible to catch a cracking attempt before it is successful. If you see an excessive number of connection attempts for a particular service, especially if they are coming from systems on the Internet, you may be under attack.

> **CROSS REFERENCE:** The logsentry package provides a simpler way to manage your log files and not miss critical messages. Refer to "Monitoring Log Files with LogSentry" next.

Monitoring Log Files with LogSentry

Fedora has the ability to monitor and log nearly every activity that can occur on your computer. On a busy system, massive amounts of informational and error messages are produced and placed in log files. For the administrator, the hard part of monitoring log files isn't detecting or logging security problems; the hard part is remembering to check the log files and sift out those messages that pose a threat from all the other stuff that gets logged. This section describes how to monitor log files with the LogSentry package.

The LogSentry package is a handy tool that you can use to easily manage your system log files. Because you're more likely to glance through an e-mail than you are to remember to check log files, LogSentry puts information in front of you that may otherwise go unnoticed.

LogSentry checks log files produced by the standard Linux syslog facility, attempts to filter out messages that don't represent any security threat, and then categorizes messages that could represent a threat and e-mails those messages to the system administrator. By default, LogSentry will check messages in the messages, secure, and mail log files in the /var/log directory. By changing the LogSentry configuration files, you can change which log files are checked, how messages are filtered, and how often log-summary e-mail messages are sent. You may also want to change which features the syslog facility monitors and the level of syslog monitoring if you are interested in debugging a particular system feature.

> **NOTE:** Fedora includes the logwatch package in its distribution. Logwatch is configured to run once each day to monitor your log files. While logwatch is not as comprehensive a tool as LogSentry, you can expect to see a logwatch e-mail message produced daily that highlights any dangerous system activity that it detects. That e-mail is sent to your computer's system administrator.

Downloading and installing LogSentry

You can find the `logsentry` package at `rpmfind.net` and several FTP sites on the Internet. After `logsentry` is downloaded, to install the package, simply run the following command from the directory you downloaded it to:

```
# rpm -Uhv logsentry*
```

The LogSentry package consists of four configuration files (in the `/etc/logsentry` directory), the `cron` file that runs `logcheck.sh` (in `/etc/cron.d/logsentry.cron`), and the `logcheck.sh` and `logtail` commands (in `/usr/sbin`). There are also README files in the `/usr/share/doc/logcheck*` directory.

> **NOTE:** Because there are different versions of LogSentry floating around on the Web, including older versions named logcheck, the locations of commands and instructions for using LogSentry may be different from what I describe here. For example, the original logcheck package may include a `logcheck.sh` script in `/usr/bin` for running logcheck. The logsentry package used here is logsentry-1.1.1-1.i686.rpm.

Setting up LogSentry

You don't have to do anything to get LogSentry working. After LogSentry is installed, it runs once a day at midnight. The results are then e-mailed to the root user on the local host computer. There are several things you can do, however, to tailor LogSentry to suit your particular needs. See the "Configuring LogSentry to suit your needs" section, later in this chapter, for more information.

Running LogSentry

When you install the logsentry package, a script named `logsentry.cron` is placed in the `/etc/cron.d` directory. In this case, the `/etc/cron.d/logsentry.cron` script simply runs the `/usr/sbin/logcheck.sh` script.

Because the `logsentry.cron` script runs hourly, this means that you (or the administrator) will receive 24 e-mail messages each day, each containing the filtered log messages. You can create your own `cron` script to have the `logcheck.sh` launched on any schedule you like.

> **NOTE:** The `/usr/sbin/logcheck.sh` script uses the `/usr/sbin/logtail` command to gather only those log messages that you haven't already seen. The `logtail` command does this by creating a `.offset` file for each log file that Logcheck monitors. The next time Logcheck is run, only log messages that have arrived since the previous run are checked.

Using LogSentry

After LogSentry has been set up and run, to begin using LogSentry you start by simply reading the e-mail that LogSentry sends you. By default, the `root` user on your Fedora system will receive an e-mail message from LogSentry each hour. Log messages that are matched, and not excluded, are sorted under one of the following three headings in each e-mail message:

- **Active System Attack Alerts** — Represents messages that may represent an attack on your system.

- **Security Violations** — Includes failures and violations that may indicate a problem, but not necessarily an attack on your system.

- **Unusual System Events** — Includes all log messages that are neither matched nor excluded.

The following is an example of a LogSentry e-mail message.

```
Return-Path: <root@localhost.localdomain>
Received: (from root@localhost)
Subject: maple 04/06/04:19.01 ACTIVE SYSTEM ATTACK!
Status: R

Active System Attack Alerts
=-=-=-=-=-=-=-=-=-=-=-=
Apr  6 18:02:28 maple portsentry[1102]: attackalert: Possible stealth
scan from unknown host to TCP port: 111 (accept failed)
Apr  6 18:33:26 maple sendmail[1863]: f371XJw01863: "wiz" command from
duck.handsonhistory.com [10.0.0.28] (127.0.0.1)
Apr  6 18:33:29 maple sendmail[1863]: f371XJw01863: "debug" command from
duck.handsonhistory.com [10.0.0.28] (127.0.0.1)

Security Violations
=-=-=-=-=-=-=-=-=-=
Apr  6 18:02:28 maple portsentry[1102]: attackalert: Possible stealth
scan from unknown host to TCP port: 111 (accept failed)
Apr  6 18:39:14 maple  -- root[1121]: ROOT LOGIN ON tty1

Unusual System Events
=-=-=-=-=-=-=-=-=-=-=
Apr  6 18:01:35 maple last message repeated 291877 times
Apr  6 18:14:10 maple last message repeated 297510 times
Apr  6 18:20:58 maple kernel: SB 4.16 detected OK (220)
Apr  6 18:20:58 maple kernel: SB16: Bad or missing 16 bit DMA channel
Apr  6 18:20:58 maple kernel: sb: 1 Soundblaster PnP card(s) found.
Apr  6 18:38:37 maple syslog: syslogd startup succeeded
Apr  6 18:38:37 maple kernel: klogd 1.4-0, log source = /proc/kmsg
started.
Apr  6 18:38:37 maple kernel: Inspecting /boot/System.map-2.4.2-0.1.49
```

In the preceding e-mail, under the `Active System Attack Alerts` heading, you can see that a scan of port 111 (portmapper service) was detected by the PortSentry service. The next two messages indicate that a user from the host `duck.handsonhistory.com` tried to scan `sendmail` to see if `debug` and `wiz` services could be accessed. Under the `Security Violations` heading, the possible stealth scan appeared again. A normal login by the `root` user was also detected (although it represented no particular threat in this case).

Under the `Unusual System Events` heading, as noted earlier, are included all messages not matched (specifically added to another category) or excluded (specifically ignored) by any of the filter files. A lot of normal system-activity messages appear here. Over time, you may want to explicitly include or exclude messages that you see all the time or that catch your eye as a potential problem you need to watch. For example, the preceding lines that say `last message repeated 291877 times` indicate a potential denial-of-service attack. You may want to add the keywords "message repeated" to your `logcheck.hacking` list. Likewise, the words "Soundblaster PnP card(s) found" could be added to the `logcheck.ignore` file, because that message reflects normal processing.

In general, you want to react to attacks that you detect by preventing an attacker from gaining access to your system. If an attacker does get in, you want to get that attacker out of your system and clean up the damage as best you can. An excellent tool for detecting, logging, and denying access to your system by attackers is the PortSentry package discussed later in this chapter.

Configuring LogSentry to suit your needs

After LogSentry is installed, it will run without requiring any configuration. However, to better suit your needs, there are several configuration files you can modify. The following section describes those files.

Editing the logcheck script

The `/usr/sbin/logcheck.sh` script scans your log files and sorts the log messages that are e-mailed. You can change much of the behavior of the `logcheck.sh` script by changing the values of the variables within the script. To change the behavior of the `logcheck.sh` script, follow these steps:

1. Make a copy of the `/usr/sbin/logcheck.sh` file. For example:

   ```
   # cp /usr/sbin/logcheck.sh /usr/sbin/logcheck.sh.old
   ```

2. Open the script in any text editor while logged in as the `root` user and make any changes to the script. The following bullet list describes values that you may want to change.

   - **SYSADMIN** — This variable defines the `root` user as the one to receive the e-mail messages resulting from running Logcheck. You can change `root` to anyone you want to receive the LogSentry messages. This can be either local users or users on other computers (that is, *user@hostname*).

```
SYSADMIN=root
```

- **TMPDIR** — Sets where LogSentry writes its temporary files during processing. The directory is created when LogSentry starts and is removed before Logcheck finishes. You can change the location by modifying the following entry:

```
TMPDIR=/tmp/logcheck$$-$RANDOM
```

- **GREP** — The logcheck.sh script relies on a grep command that supports the -i, -v, and -f options to search the log files. By default, the egrep command is used for this purpose. You could change the value to grep or another command by modifying the following variable:

```
GREP=egrep
```

- **MAIL** — E-mail is sent by LogSentry using the mail command. To have LogSentry use a command other than the mail command to send e-mail messages to the administrator, change the following mail variable:

```
MAIL=mail
```

- **Filter files** — There are four filter files defined by LogSentry. The files each contain keywords that are either used to find messages or exclude messages that contain those keywords. The following variables are set to indicate the location of the four LogSentry filter files:

```
HACKING_FILE=/etc/logsentry/logcheck.hacking
VIOLATIONS_FILE=/etc/logsentry/logcheck.violations
VIOLATIONS_IGNORE_FILE=/etc/logsentry/logcheck.violations.ignore
IGNORE_FILE=/etc/logsentry/logcheck.ignore
```

For more information on filter files, see the "Changing LogSentry filter files" section, later in this chapter.

- **Log files** — The last entries in the /usr/sbin/logcheck.sh script that you may want to change designate which log files are monitored by the logcheck.sh script. By default, the script runs the logtail command to check the messages, secure, and maillog files (in /var/log). The following lines define which log files are checked and determine where the output of logtail is temporarily written.

```
$LOGTAIL /var/log/messages > $TMPDIR/check.$$
$LOGTAIL /var/log/secure >> $TMPDIR/check.$$
$LOGTAIL /var/log/maillog >> $TMPDIR/check.$$
```

> **TIP:** If you like, you can have more log files checked by adding more lines like the preceding ones. Just make sure that the first line includes a single arrow (to overwrite a previous check file) and that all subsequent lines contain double arrows (to append to the current check file).

Changing LogSentry filter files

The /etc/logsentry directory contains four filter files that define which messages are matched and e-mailed to the administrator. The contents of these files are simply keywords. Log files are searched (or *grepped*) for these keywords and sorted or discarded based on the results of the search.

Some keyword filter files are intended to uncover words or phrases that would appear in a log message in the event of a system break-in or misuse. Other keyword files are intended to find messages that pose no security threat (so that the messages can be excluded from the e-mailed log messages). Messages that match neither the included or excluded keywords are appended to the Unusual System Events heading of the e-mail summary output.

You can use filter files as they are. However, over time, you may want to modify these files for several reasons. If you are receiving repetitive, non-threatening messages in the LogSentry e-mails, you can add keywords that can filter out those messages. Also, you can add keywords later as you learn about new types of security breaches that you may want to look for.

Besides including alphanumeric characters, keywords can also include wildcard characters. For example, you could use an asterisk (*) to match any string of characters, a question mark (?) to match any single character, or a dollar sign ($) to match a keyword that appears at the end of a line.

> **CAUTION:** Use wildcards carefully. A mistaken wildcard character can result in too many or too few messages being included or excluded.

The four LogSentry filter files in the /etc/logsentry directory are:

- **logcheck.hacking** — Contains keywords that appear in log messages that represent known hacking attacks.
- **logcheck.ignore** — Contains keywords that represent messages that should always be ignored.
- **logcheck.violations** — Contains keywords that represent negative activities that may or may not represent real intrusions on your system.
- **logcheck.violations.ignore** — Contains keywords that represent messages that should be ignored from those found as part of the violations check.

Each of these files is described in the following sections.

> **NOTE:** It is important to note that messages that are neither explicitly matched (from `logcheck.hacking` and `logcheck.violations`) nor explicitly excluded (from `logcheck.ignore` and `logcheck.violations.ignore`) are included in the e-mail sent by Logcheck to the administrator. Those messages are displayed under the catchall heading `Unusual System Events`.

logcheck.hacking

Keywords from the `/etc/logsentry/logcheck.hacking` file are meant to uncover log messages representing attacks on your system. Log messages that are matched by keywords in this file are output in e-mail messages to your system administrator under the `logcheck.hacking` heading.

Messages that appear under this heading are the first messages to appear in the e-mail message. You can add other keywords to this file as you learn about messages that represent different types of attacks on your system.

Following are some examples of keywords that appear in the `logcheck.hacking` file:

```
"wiz"
"WIZ"
"debug"
"DEBUG"
ATTACK
nested
VRFY bbs
VRFY decode
VRFY uudecode
rlogind.*: Connection from .* on illegal port
rshd.*: Connection from .* on illegal port
sendmail.*: user .* attempted to run daemon
uucico.*: refused connect from .*
tftpd.*: refused connect from .*
login.*: .*LOGIN FAILURE.* FROM .*root
login.*: .*LOGIN FAILURE.* FROM .*guest
```

Most of the messages in this file are used to match log messages that result from someone probing your system with the Internet Security Scanner (ISS). ISS is a tool that can scan a set of IP addresses for potential security weaknesses. Though most of the security holes ISS checks for have been plugged over time, these log messages alert you to the fact that someone is checking the security of your system.

The `debug` and `wiz` keywords shown in the previous file will catch attempts by ISS to access `wiz` and `debug` services from the `sendmail` service. Likewise, `VRFY` is a command that ISS sends to requests of the `sendmail` service to ask for different user names. Other keyword phrases shown in the previous example match failed attempts to connect using different Linux network services (such as rlogind, rshd, sendmail, uucico, and so on).

logcheck.ignore

Keywords in the `/etc/logsentry/logcheck.ignore` file are used to find log messages that should be excluded (that is, ignored) by LogSentry and will therefore not appear in e-mail summaries. The keywords in this file reduce the number of log messages that are e-mailed to the administrator, making it easier to find the real problems. The following are some examples of keywords from the `logcheck.ignore` file.

```
cron.*CMD
cron.*RELOAD
cron.*STARTUP
ftp-gw.*: exit host
ftp-gw.*: permit host
ftpd.*ANONYMOUS FTP LOGIN
http-gw.*: exit host
http-gw.*: permit host
identd.*Successful lookup
identd.*from:
named.*Response from
```

Most of the entries in this file are used to match messages that represent the normal operation of various system services. The keywords shown in the previous example represent normal processing of `cron`, `ftp`, `http`, `identd`, and `named` features.

Notice that all of the keyword phrases shown in the preceding example include an asterisk (*) wildcard. If you add your own keywords to this file, using asterisks and other wildcards can help you be specific about the log messages you exclude.

logcheck.violations

There are certain words that imply negative behavior occurring on your computer. Though these words may not be associated with any particular attack, LogSentry notes messages containing these words and displays them under the following heading and e-mails them to the system administrator:

```
Security Violations
=-=-=-=-=-=-=-=-=-=
```

The following is an example of some of the keywords that appear in the `logcheck.violations` file:

```
ATTACK
BAD
DEBUG
FAILURE
ILLEGAL
REFUSED
denied
failed
unapproved
```

```
attackalert
```

Adding your own keywords to the file can help flag log messages that may be of particular concern for your computer. For example, you can add keywords that represent improper use of services that are not standard Linux features but can be accessed from the network.

logcheck.violations.ignore

Use the `logcheck.violations.ignore` file to exclude messages that were matched from the `logcheck.violations` file, but are known to not represent security problems. By default, only the following entry is contained in this file:

```
stat=Deferred
```

The previous keyword causes LogSentry to ignore log messages from `sendmail` that represent e-mail messages that haven't been sent because the receiving server was temporarily unavailable. As you use LogSentry, you are likely to repeatedly encounter certain log messages that represent no security threat. Add keywords here (specifically as possible) to exclude those messages from appearing continuously in e-mail messages from LogSentry.

Modifying syslog

The syslog service gathers the log messages of system activity that are used by LogSentry. Fedora, as well as most other Linux and UNIX systems, comes with `syslog` installed and operational by default. You can modify the `/etc/syslog.conf` file to tailor the behavior of `syslog` to best suit the way you use your system.

The syslog service is part of the `sysklogd` software package. To make sure that `sysklogd` is installed, type the following at a shell prompt:

```
# rpm -q sysklogd
```

The syslogd service is started automatically from the `/etc/init.d/syslog` start-up script. After that script has been run on your system, two daemon processes should be active on your system: `syslogd` and `klogd`. To see if they are running, type the following:

```
# ps -ax | grep log
```

The `/etc/syslog.conf` file contains information that defines which activities are logged, and from which system. LogSentry monitors three of the log files created by syslog (in the `/var/log` directory): `messages`, `secure`, and `maillog`. The following lines in the `/etc/syslog.conf` file instruct syslog to create those log files:

```
*.info;mail.none;news.none;authpriv.none;cron.none    /var/log/messages
authpriv.*                                             /var/log/secure
mail.*                                                 /var/log/maillog
```

Services on your Fedora system produce messages of different levels. Message levels, from most critical to least critical, are listed in Table 14-4.

Table 14-4: Message Levels

Level	What It Means
alert	Immediate action needed
crit	Critical
debug	Detailed processing information
emerg	System unusable
err	Error condition
info	Purely informational
notice	Important, but not an error
warning	Potential error

The line shown in the example indicates that all messages from the info level (*.info) and above are logged to the /var/log/messages file. However, messages of types mail, news, authpriv, and cron are excluded because they are sent to other log files. All authpriv (authpriv.*) messages are logged to the /var/log/secure file. mail messages (mail.*) are all logged to the /var/log/maillog file.

With this default configuration of syslog, LogSentry should catch all major security related activities. There are a few situations, however, where you may want to modify the /etc/syslog.conf file. For example, if you are receiving a lot of log messages for a particular type of service (such as ppp if you are having trouble with a dial-up connection), you may consider directing messages for that service to its own log file. Then, if LogSentry uncovers a problem, it's easier to go through only that log file for those messages relating to the problem service.

Another temporary change you may consider is if you need to debug a problem with your system. Changing *.info to *.debug temporarily can give you more details on a problem. (Make sure to change it back later, or syslog will chew up too much system resources.)

Using Password Protection

Passwords are the most fundamental security tool of any modern operating system and consequently, the most commonly attacked security feature. It is natural to want to choose a password that is easy to remember, but very often this means choosing a password that is also easy to guess. Crackers know that on any system with more than a few users, at least one person is likely to have an easily guessed password.

By using the "brute force" method of attempting to log in to every account on the system and trying the most common passwords on each of these accounts, a persistent cracker has a good shot of finding a way in. Remember that a cracker will automate this attack, so thousands of login attempts are not out of the question. Obviously, choosing good passwords is the first and most important step to having a secure system.

Here are some things to avoid when choosing a password:

- Do not use any variation of your login name or your full name. Even if you use varied case, append or prepend numbers or punctuation, or type it backwards, this will still be an easily guessed password.

- Do not use a dictionary word, even if you add numbers or punctuation to it.

- Do not use proper names of any kind.

- Do not use any contiguous line of letters or numbers on the keyboard (such as "qwerty" or "asdfg").

Choosing good passwords

A good way to choose a strong password is to take the first letter from each word of an easily remembered sentence. The password can be made even better by adding numbers, punctuation, and varied case. The sentence you choose should have meaning only to you, and should not be publicly available (choosing a sentence on your personal Web page is a bad idea). Table 14-5 lists examples of strong passwords and the tricks used to remember them.

Table 14-5: Ideas for Good Passwords

Password	How to Remember it
Mrci7yo!	My rusty car is 7 years old!
2emBp1ib	2 elephants make BAD pets, 1 is better
ItMc?Gib	Is that MY coat? Give it back

The passwords look like gibberish, but are actually rather easy to remember. As you can see, I can place emphasis on words that stand for capital letters in the password. You set your password using the passwd command. Type the passwd command within a command shell, and it will enable you to change your password. First, it will prompt you to enter your old password. To protect against someone "shoulder surfing" and learning your password, the password will not be displayed as you type.

Assuming you type your old password correctly, the passwd command will prompt you for the new password. When you type in your new password, the passwd command checks the password against cracklib to determine if it is a *good* or *bad* password. Non-root users will be required to try a different password if the one they have chosen is not a good password. The root user is the only user who is permitted to assign *bad* passwords. Once the password has been accepted by cracklib, the passwd command will ask you to enter the new password a second time to make sure there are no typos (which are hard to detect when you can't see what you are typing). When running as root, it is possible to change a user's password by supplying that user's login name as a parameter to the passwd command. Typing this:

```
# passwd joe
```

results in the passwd command prompting you for joe's new password. It does not prompt you for his old password in this case. This allows root to reset a user's password when that user has forgotten it (an event that happens all too often).

Using a shadow password file

In early versions of UNIX, all user account and password information was stored in a file that all users could read (although only root could write to it). This was generally not a problem because the password information was encrypted. The password was encrypted using a *trapdoor algorithm*, meaning the non-encoded password could be encoded into a scrambled string of characters, but the string could not be translated back to the non-encoded password.

How does the system check your password in this case? When you log in, the system encodes the password you entered, compares the resulting scrambled string with the scrambled string that is stored in the password file, and grants you access only if the two match. Have you ever asked a system administrator what the password on your account is only to hear, "I don't know" in response? If so, this is why: The administrator really doesn't have the password, only the encrypted version. The non-encoded password exists only at the moment you type it.

Breaking encrypted passwords

There is a problem with people being able to see encrypted passwords, however. Although it may be difficult (or even impossible) to reverse the encryption of a trapdoor algorithm, it is very easy to encode a large number of password guesses and compare them to the encoded passwords in the password file. This is, in orders of magnitude, more efficient than trying actual login attempts for each user name and password. If a cracker can get a copy of your password file, the cracker has a much better chance of breaking into your system.

Fortunately, Linux and all modern UNIX systems support a shadow password file by default. The shadow file is a special version of the passwd file that only root can read. It contains the encrypted password information, so passwords can be left out of the passwd file, which any user on the system can read. Linux supports the older, single password file method as well as the newer shadow password file. You should always use the shadow password file (it is used by default).

Checking for the shadow password file

The password file is named passwd and can be found in the /etc directory. The shadow password file is named shadow and is also located in /etc. If your /etc/shadow file is missing, then it is likely that your Linux system is storing the password information in the /etc/passwd file instead. Verify this by displaying the file with the less command.

```
# less /etc/passwd
```

Something similar to the following should be displayed:

```
root:DkkS6Uke799fQ:0:0:root:/root:/bin/bash
bin:*:1:1:bin:/bin:
daemon:*:2:2:daemon:/sbin:
   .
   .
   .
mary:KpRUp2ozmY5TA:500:100:Mary Smith:/home/mary:/bin/sh
joe:0sXrzvKnQaksI:501:100:Joe Johnson:/home/joe:/bin/sh
jane:ptNoiueYEjwX.:502:100:Jane Anderson:/home/jane:/bin/sh
bob:Ju2vY7A0X6Kzw:503:100:Bob Renolds:/home/bob:/bin/sh
```

Each line in this listing corresponds to a single user account on the Linux system. Each line is made up of seven fields separated by colon (:) characters. From left to right the fields are the login name, the encrypted password, the user ID, the group ID, the description, the home directory, and the default shell. Looking at the first line, you see that it is for the root account and has an encrypted password of DkkS6Uke799fQ. We can also see that root has a user ID of zero, a group ID of zero, and a home directory of /root, and root's default shell is /bin/sh.

All of these values are quite normal for a root account, but seeing that encrypted password should set off alarm bells in your head. It confirms that your system is not using the shadow password file. At this point, you should immediately convert your password file so that it uses /etc/shadow to store the password information. You do this by using the pwconv command. Simply log in as root (or use the su command to become root) and enter the pwconv command at a prompt. It will print no messages, but when your shell prompt returns, you should have a /etc/shadow file and your /etc/passwd file should now look like this:

```
root:x:0:0:root:/root:/bin/bash
bin:x:1:1:bin:/bin:
daemon:x:2:2:daemon:/sbin:
   .
   .
mary:x:500:100:Mary Smith:/home/mary:/bin/sh
joe:x:501:100:Joe Johnson:/home/joe:/bin/sh
jane:x:502:100:Jane Anderson:/home/jane:/bin/sh
bob:x:503:100:Bob Renolds:/home/bob:/bin/sh
```

Encrypted password data is replaced with an x. Password data moved to /etc/shadow.

There is also a screen-oriented command called authconfig that you can use to manage shadow passwords and other system authentication information. This tool also has features that let you work with MD5 passwords, LDAP authentication, or Kerberos 5 authentication as well. Type authconfig and step through the screens to use it.

To work with passwords for groups, you can use the `grpconv` command to convert passwords in `/etc/groups` to shadowed group passwords in `/etc/gshadow`. If you change `passwd` or group passwords and something breaks (you are unable to log in to the accounts), you can use the `pwunconv` and `grpunconv` commands, respectively, to reverse password conversion.

So, now you are using the shadow password file and picking good passwords. You have made a great start toward securing your system. You may also have noticed by now that security is not just a one-time job. It is an ongoing process, as much about policies as programs. Keep reading to learn more.

Using Encryption Techniques

The previous sections told you how to lock the doors to your Fedora system to deny access to crackers. The best dead bolt lock, however, is useless if you are mugged in your own driveway and have your keys stolen. Likewise, the best computer security can be for naught if you are sending passwords and other critical data unprotected across the Internet.

A savvy cracker can use a tool called a protocol analyzer or a network sniffer to peek at the data flowing across a network and pick out passwords, credit card data, and other juicy bits of information. The cracker does this by breaking into a poorly protected system on the same network and running software, or by gaining physical access to the same network and plugging in his or her own equipment.

You can combat this sort of theft by using encryption. The two main types of encryption in use today are symmetric cryptography and public-key cryptography.

Symmetric cryptography

Symmetric cryptography, also called private-key cryptography, uses a single key to both encrypt and decrypt a message. This method is generally inappropriate for securing data that will be used by a third party, due to the complexity of secure key exchange. Symmetric cryptography is generally useful for encrypting data for one's own purposes.

A classic use of symmetric cryptography is for a personal password vault. Anyone who has been using the Internet for any amount of time has accumulated a quantity of user names and passwords for accessing various sites and resources. A personal password vault lets you store this access information in an encrypted form. The end result is that you only have to remember one password to unlock all of your access information.

Until recently, the United States government was standardized on a symmetric encryption algorithm called DES (Data Encryption Standard) to secure important information. Because there is no direct way to crack DES encrypted data, to decrypt DES encrypted data without a password you would have to use an unimaginable amount of computing power to try to guess the password. This is also known as the *brute force* method of decryption.

As personal computing power has increased nearly exponentially, the DES algorithm has had to be retired. In its place, after a very long and interesting search, the United States. government has accepted the Rijndael algorithm as what it calls the AES (Advanced Encryption Standard). Although the AES algorithm is also subject to brute force attacks, it requires significantly more computing power to crack than the DES algorithm does.

For more information on AES, including a command line implementation of the algorithm, you can visit `http://aescrypt.sourceforge.net/`.

Public-key cryptography

Public-key cryptography does not suffer from key distribution problems, and that is why it is the preferred encryption method for secure Internet communication. This method uses two keys, one to encrypt the message and another to decrypt the message. The key used to encrypt the message is called the public key because it is made available for all to see. The key used to decrypt the message is the private key and is kept hidden. The entire process works like this:

Imagine that you want to send me a secure message using public-key encryption. Here is what we need:

1. I must have a public and private key pair. Depending on the circumstances, I may generate the keys myself (using special software) or obtain the keys from a key authority.

2. You want to send me a message, so you first look up my public key (or more accurately, the software you are using looks it up).

3. You encrypt the message with the public key. At this point, the message can only be decrypted with the private key (the public key cannot be used to decrypt the message).

4. I receive the message and use my private key to decrypt it.

Secure Socket Layer

A classic implementation of public-key cryptography is with SSL (secure socket layer) communication. This is the technology that enables you to securely submit your credit card information to an online merchant. The elements of an SSL encrypted session are as follows:

- SSL-enabled Web browser (Mozilla, Internet Explorer, Opera, Konquerer, etc.)
- SSL-enabled Web server (Apache)
- SSL certificate

To initiate an SSL session, a Web browser first makes contact with a Web server on port 443, also known as the HTTPS port (Hypertext Transport Protocol Secure). After a socket connection has been established between the two machines, the following occurs:

1. Server sends SSL certificate to browser.

2. Browser verifies identity of server through SSL certificate.

3. Browser generates symmetric encryption key.

4. Browser uses SSL certificate to encrypt symmetric encryption key.

5. Browser sends encrypted key to the server.

6. Server decrypts the symmetric key with its private key counterpart of the public SSL certificate.

7. Browser and server can now encrypt and decrypt traffic based on a common knowledge of the symmetric key.

Secure data interchange can now occur.

Creating SSL Certificates

In order to create your own SSL certificate for secure HTTP data interchange, you must first have an SSL-capable Web server. The Apache Web server (httpd package), which comes with Fedora, is SSL-capable. Once you have a server ready to go, you should familiarize yourself with the important server-side components of an SSL certificate:

```
# ls -l /etc/httpd/conf
-rw-r--r--  1 root       root        36010 Jul 14 15:45 httpd.conf
lrwxrwxrwx  1 root       root          37 Aug 12 23:45 Makefile ->
../../../usr/share/ssl/certs/Makefile
drwx------  2 root       root         4096 Aug 12 23:45 ssl.crl
drwx------  2 root       root         4096 Aug 12 23:45 ssl.crt
drwx------  2 root       root         4096 Jul 14 15:45 ssl.csr
drwx------  2 root       root         4096 Aug 12 23:45 ssl.key
drwx------  2 root       root         4096 Jul 14 15:45 ssl.prm

# ls -l /etc/httpd/conf.d/ssl.conf
-rw-r--r--  1 root       root        11140 Jul 14 15:45 ssl.conf
```

The /etc/httpd/conf and /etc/httpd/conf.d directories contains all of the components necessary to create your SSL certificate. Each component is defined as follows:

- **httpd.conf** — Web server configuration file.
- **Makefile** — Certificate building script.
- **ssl.crl** — Certificate revocation list directory.
- **ssl.crt** — SSL certificate directory.
- **ssl.csr** — Certificate service request directory.
- **ssl.key** — SSL certificate private key directory.
- **ssl.prm** — SSL certificate parameters.
- **ssl.conf** — Primary Web server SSL configuration file.

Now that you're familiar with the basic components, take a look at the tools used to create SSL certificates:

```
# cd /etc/httpd/conf
# make
This makefile allows you to create:
  o public/private key pairs
  o SSL certificate signing requests (CSRs)
  o self-signed SSL test certificates

To create a key pair, run "make SOMETHING.key".
To create a CSR, run "make SOMETHING.csr".
To create a test certificate, run "make SOMETHING.crt".
To create a key and a test certificate in one file, run "make
SOMETHING.pem".

To create a key for use with Apache, run "make genkey".
To create a CSR for use with Apache, run "make certreq".
To create a test certificate for use with Apache, run "make testcert".

Examples:
  make server.key
  make server.csr
  make server.crt
  make stunnel.pem
  make genkey
  make certreq
  make testcert
```

The make command utilizes the Makefile to create SSL certificates. Without any arguments the make command simply prints the information listed above. The following defines each argument you can give to make:

- **make server.key** — Creates generic public/private key pairs.

- **make server.csr** — Generates a generic SSL certificate service request.

- **make server.crt** — Generates a generic SSL test certificate.

- **make stunnel.pem** — Generates a generic SSL test certificate, but puts the private key in the same file as the SSL test certificate.

- **make genkey** — Same as `make server.key` except it places the key in the `ssl.key` directory.

- **make certreq** — Same as `make server.csr` except it places the certificate service request in the `ssl.csr` directory.

- **make testcert** — Same as `make server.crt` except it places the test certificate in the `ssl.crt` directory.

Using third-party certificate signers

In the real world, I know who you are because I recognize your face, your voice, and your mannerisms. On the Internet, I cannot see these things and must rely on a trusted third party to vouch for your identity. To ensure that a certificate is immutable, it has to be signed by a trusted third party when the certificate is issued and validated every time an end user taking advantage of your secure site loads it. The following is a list of the trusted third-party certificate signers:

- **GlobalSign** — `https://www.globalsign.net/`

- **Baltimore** — `https://www.baltimore.com/`

- **GeoTrust** — `https://www.geotrust.com/`

- **VeriSign** — `https://www.verisign.com/`

- **FreeSSL** — `http://www.freessl.com/`

- **Thawte** — `http://www.thawte.com/`

- **EnTrust** — `http://www.entrust.com/`

- **ipsCA** — `http://www.ipsca.com/`

- **COMODO Group** — `http://www.comodogroup.com/`

Each of these certificate authorities has gotten a chunk of cryptographic code embedded into nearly every Web browser in the world. This chunk of cryptographic code allows a Web browser to determine whether or not an SSL certificate is authentic. Without this validation, it would be trivial for crackers to generate their own certificates and dupe people into thinking they are giving sensitive information to a reputable source.

Certificates that are not validated are called *self-signed certificates*. If you come across a site that has not had its identity authenticated by a trusted third party, your Web browser will display a message similar to the one shown in Figure 14-3.

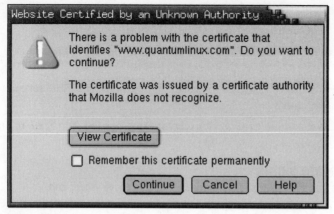

Figure 14-3: A pop-up window alerts you when a site is not authenticated.

This does not necessarily mean that you are encountering anything illegal, immoral, or fattening. Many sites opt to go with *self-signed* certificates, not because they are trying to pull a fast one on you, but because there may not be any reason to validate the true owner of the certificate and they do not want to pay the cost of getting a certificate validated. Some reasons for using a *self-signed* certificate include:

- **The Web site accepts no input** — In this case, you as the end user, have nothing to worry about. There is no one trying to steal your information because you aren't giving out any information. Most of the time this is done simply to secure the Web transmission from the server to you. The data in and of itself may not be sensitive, but, being a good netizen, the site has enabled you to secure the transmission to keep third parties from sniffing the traffic.

- **The Web site caters to a small clientele** — If you run a Web site that has a very limited set of customers, such as an Application Service Provider, you can simply inform your users that you have no certificate signer and that they can browse the certificate information and validate it with you over the phone or in person.

- **Testing** — It makes no sense to pay for an SSL certificate if you are only testing a new Web site or Web-based application. Use a *self-signed* certificate until you are ready to go live.

Creating a Certificate Service Request

To create a third-party validated SSL certificate, you must first start with a Certificate Service Request (CSR). To create a CSR, do the following on your Web server:

```
# cd /etc/httpd/conf
# make certreq
umask 77 ; \
/usr/bin/openssl genrsa -des3 1024 > /etc/httpd/conf/ssl.key/server.key
```

You will now be asked to enter a password to secure your private key. This password should be at least eight characters long, and should not be a dictionary word or contain numbers or punctuation. The characters you type will not appear on the screen, in order to prevent someone from shoulder surfing your password.

```
Enter pass phrase:
```

Enter the password once again to verify.

```
Verifying - Enter pass phrase:
```

The certificate generation process now begins.

At this point, it is time to start adding some identifying information to the certificate that the third-party source will later validate. Before you can do this, you must unlock the private key you just created. Do so by typing the password you typed above. Then enter information as you are prompted. An example of a session for adding information for your certificate is shown below:

```
Enter pass phrase for /etc/httpd/conf/ssl.key/server.key:
You are about to be asked to enter information that will be incorporated
into your certificate request.
What you are about to enter is what is called
a Distinguished Name or a DN.
There are quite a few fields but you can leave some blank
For some fields there will be a default value,
If you enter '.', the field will be left blank.
-----
Country Name (2 letter code) [GB]:US
State or Province Name (full name) [Berkshire]: Connecticut
Locality Name (eg, city) [Newbury]: Mystic
Organization Name (eg, company) [My Company Ltd]:Acme Marina, Inc.
Organizational Unit Name (eg, section) []:InfoTech
Common Name (eg, your name or your server's hostname)
[]:www.acmemarina.com
Email Address []: webmaster@acmemarina.com
```

To complete the process, you will be asked if you want to add any extra attributes to your certificate. Unless you have a reason to provide more information, you should simply press Enter at each of the following prompts to leave them blank.

```
Please enter the following 'extra' attributes
to be sent with your certificate request
A challenge password []:
An optional company name []:
```

Getting the CSR Signed

Once your CSR has been created, you now need to send it to a signing authority for validation. The first step in this process is to select a signing authority. Each signing authority has different deals, prices and products. Check out each of the signing authorities listed in the "Using third-party certificate signers" section earlier in this chapter to determine which works best for you. The following are areas where signing authorities differ:

- Credibility and stability
- Pricing
- Browser recognition
- Warranties
- Support
- Certificate strength

For good comparisons, studies and inside information to make the job of finding an SSL signer easier, go to www.whichssl.org.

After you have selected your certificate signer, you will have to go through some validation steps. Each signer has a different method of validating identity and certificate information. Some require that you fax articles of incorporation, while others require a company officer be made available to talk to a validation operator. At some point in the process you will be asked to copy and paste the contents of the CSR you created into the signer's Web form.

```
# cd /etc/httpd/conf/ssl.csr
# cat server.csr
-----BEGIN CERTIFICATE REQUEST-----
MIIB6jCCAVMCAQAwgakxCzAJBgNVBAYTAlVTMRQwEgYDVQQIEwtDb25uZWN0aWN1
dDEPMA0GA1UEBxMGTXlzdGljMRowGAYDVQQKExFBY211IE1hcmluYSwgSW5jLjER
MA8GA1UECxMISW5mb1RlY2gxGzAZBgNVBAMTEnd3dy5hY211bWFyaW5hLmNvbTEn
MCUGCSqGSIb3DQEJARYYd2VibWFzdGVyQGFjbWVtYXJpbmEuY29tMIGfMA0GCSqG
SIb3DQEBAQUAA4GNADCBiQKBgQDcYH4pjMxKMldyXRmcoz8uBVOvwlNZHyRWw8ZG
u2eCbvgi6w4wXuHwaDuxbuDBmw//Y9DMI2MXg4wDq4xmPi35EsO1Ofw4ytZJn1yW
aU6cJVQro46OnXyaqXZOPiRCxUSnGRU+0nsqKGjf7LPpXv29S3QvMIBTYWzCkNnc
gWBwwwIDAQABoAAwDQYJKoZIhvcNAQEEBQADgYEANv6eJOaJZGzopNR5h2YkR9Wg
18oBl3mgoPH60Sccw3pWsoW4qbOWq7on8dS/++QOCZWZI1gefgaSQMInKZ1II7Fs
YIwYBgpoPTMC4bp0ZZtURCyQWrKIDXQBXw7BlU/3A25nvkRY7vgNL9Nq+7681EJ8
W9AJ3PX4vb2+ynttcBI=
-----END CERTIFICATE REQUEST-----
```

You can use your mouse to copy and paste the CSR into the signer's Web form.

After you have completed the information validation, paid for the signing, and answered all of the questions, you have completed most of the process. Within 48 to 72 hours you should receive an e-mail with your shiny new SSL certificate in it. The certificate will look similar to the following:

```
-----BEGIN CERTIFICATE-----
MIIEFjCCA3+gAwIBAgIQMI262Zd6njZgN97tJAVFODANBgkqhkiG9w0BAQQFADCB
ujEfMB0GA1UEChMWVmVyaVNpZ24gVHJ1c3QgTmV0d29yazEXMBUGA1UECxMOVmVy
aVNpZ24sIEluXy4xMzAxBgNVBAsTKlZlcmlTaWduIEludGVybmF0aW9uYWwgU2Vy
dmVyIENBIC0gZ2xhc3MgMzFJMEcG10rY2g0Dd3d3LnZlcmlzaWduLmNvbS9DUFMg
SW5jb3JwLmJ51FJlZi4gTElBQk1SVRIExURC4oYyk5NyBWZXJpU2lnbjAeFw0w
MzAxMTUwMDAwMDBaFw0wNDAxMTUyMzU5NTlaMIGuMQswCQYDVQQGEwJVUzETMBEG
A1UECBMKV2FzaG1uZ3RvbiThErE371UEBxQLRmVkZXJhbCBXYXkxGzAZBgNVBAoU
EklETSBTZXJ2aWNlcywgSW5jLjEMMAoGA1UECxQDd3d3MTMwMQYDVQQLFCpUZXJt
cyBvZiB1c2UgYXQgd3d3LnZlcmlzawduLmNvbS9ycGGgKGMpMDAxFDASBgNVBAMU
C21kbXNlcnYuY29tMIGfMA0GCSqGS1b3DQEBAQUAA4GNADCBiQKBgQDaHSk+uzOf
7jjDFEnqT8UBa1L3yFILXFjhj3XpMXLGWzLmkDmdJjXsa4x7AhEpr1ubuVNhJVI0
FnLDopsx4pyr4n+P8FyS4M5grbcQzy2YnkM2jyqVF/7yOW2pD130t4eacYYaz4Qg
q9pTxhUzjEG4twvKCAFWfuhEoGu1CMV2qQ1DAQABo4IBJTCCASEwCQYDVR0TBAIw
ADBEBgNVHSAEPTA7MDkGC2CGSAGG+EUBBxcDMCOwKAYIKwYBBQUHAgEWHGh0dHBz
Oi8vd3d3LnZlcmlzaWduLmNvbS9ycGEwCwYDVRRPBAQDAgWgMCgGA1UdJQQhMB8G
CWCGSAGG+EIEM00c0wIYBQUHAwEGCCsGAQUFBwmCMDQGCCsGAQUFBwEBBCgwJjAk
BggrBgEFBQcwAYYYaHR0cDovL29jc2AudmVyaXNpZ24uY29tMEYGA1UdHwQ/MD0w
O6A5oDeGNWh0dHA6Ly9jcmwudmVyaXNpZ24uY29tL0NsYXNzM0ludGVybmF0aW9u
YWxTZXJ2ZXIuY3JsMBkGCmCGSAgG+E+f4Nfc3zYJODA5NzMwMTEyMA0GCSqGSIb3
DQEBBAUAA4GBAJ/PsVttmlDkQai5nLeudLceb1F4isXP17B68wXLkIeRu4Novu13
81LZXnaR+acHuCkW01b3rQPjgv2y1mwjkPmC1WjoeYfdxH7+Mbg/6fomnK9auWAT
WF0iFW/+a8OWRYQJLMA2VQOVhX4znjpGcVNY9AQSHm1UiESJy7vtd1iX
-----END CERTIFICATE-----
```

Copy and paste this certificate into an empty file called `server.crt`, which must reside in the `/etc/httpd/conf/ssl.crt` directory, and restart your Web server:

```
# service httpd restart
```

Assuming your Web site was previously working fine, you can now view it in a secure fashion by placing an "s" after the http in the Web address. So if you previously viewed your Web site at `http://www.acmemarina.com`, you can now view it in a secure fashion by going to `https://www.acmemarina.com`.

Creating Self-Signed Certificates

Generating and running a self-signed SSL certificate is much easier than having a signed certificate. To generate a self-signed SSL certificate, do the following:

1. Remove the key and certificate that currently exist:

   ```
   # cd /etc/httpd/conf
   # rm ssl.key/server.key ssl.crt/server.crt
   ```

2. Create your own server key:

   ```
   # /usr/bin/openssl genrsa 1024 > ssl.key/server.key
   ```

3. Make the server.key file readable and writable only by root:

```
# chmod 600 ssl.key/server.key
```

4. Create the self-signed certificate by typing the following:

```
# make testcert
umask 77 ; \
/usr/bin/openssl req -new -key /etc/httpd/conf/ssl.key/server.key
    -x509 -days 365 -out /etc/httpd/conf/ssl.key/server.crt
```

At this point, it is time to start adding some identifying information to the certificate that the third-party source will later validate. Before you can do this, you must unlock the private key you just created. Do so by typing the password you typed earlier. Then follow this sample procedure:

```
You are about to be asked to enter information that will be
  incorporated into your certificate request.
What you are about to enter is what is called
a Distinguished Name or a DN.
There are quite a few fields but you can leave some blank
For some fields there will be a default value,
If you enter '.', the field will be left blank.
-----
Country Name (2 letter code) [GB]:US
State or Province Name (full name) [Berkshire]: Ohio
Locality Name (eg, city) [Newbury]: Cincinnati
Organization Name (eg, company) [My Company Ltd]:Industrial Press, Inc.
Organizational Unit Name (eg, section) []:IT
Common Name (eg, your name or your server's hostname)
[]:www.industrialpressinc.com
Email Address []: webmaster@industrialpressinc.com
```

The generation process above places all files in the proper place. All you need to do is restart your Web server and add `https` instead of `http` in front of your URL. Don't forget, you'll get a certificate validation message from your Web browser, which you can safely ignore.

Restarting your Web server

By now you've probably noticed that your Web server requires you to enter your certificate password every time it is started. This is to prevent someone from breaking into your server and stealing your private key. Should this happen, you are safe in the knowledge that the private key is a jumbled mess. The cracker will not be able to make use of it. Without such protection, a cracker could get your private key and easily masquerade as you, appearing to be legitimate in all cases.

If you just cannot stand having to enter a password every time your Web server starts, and are willing to accept the increased risk, you can remove the password encryption on your private key. Simply do the following:

```
# cd /etc/httpd/conf/ssl.key
# /usr/bin/openssl rsa -in server.key -out  server.key
```

Troubleshooting your certificates

The following tips should help if you are having problems with your SSL certificate.

- Only one SSL certificate per IP address is allowed. If you want to add more than one SSL-enabled Web site to your server, you must bind another IP address to the network interface.

- Make sure the permission mask on the /etc/httpd/conf/ssl.* directories and their contents is 700 (rwx------).

- Make sure you aren't blocking port 443 on your Web server. All https requests come in on port 443. If you are blocking it, you will not be able to get secure pages.

- The certificate only lasts for one year. When that year is up, you have to renew your certificate with your certificate authority. Each certificate authority has a different procedure for doing this; check the authority's Web site for more details.

- Make sure you have the mod_ssl package installed. If it is not installed, you will not be able to serve any SSL enabled traffic.

Exporting encryption technology

Before describing how to use the various encryption tools, I need to warn you about an unusual policy of the United States government. For many years, the United States government treated encryption technology like munitions. As a result, anyone wanting to export encryption technology had to get an export license from the Commerce Department. This applied not only to encryption software developed within the United States, but also to software obtained from other countries and then re-exported to another country (or even to the same country you got it from). Thus, if you installed encryption technology on your Linux system and then transported it out of the country, you were violating federal law! Furthermore, if you e-mailed encryption software to a friend in another country or let him or her download it from your server, you violated the law.

In January 2000, U.S. export laws relating to encryption software were relaxed considerably. However, often the U.S. Commerce Department's Bureau of Export Administration requires a review of encryption products before they can be exported. U.S. companies are also still not allowed to export encryption technology to countries classified as supporting terrorism.

Using the Secure Shell package

The Secure Shell package (SSH) is a package that provides shell services similar to the rsh, rcp, and rlogin commands, but encrypts the network traffic. It uses Private-Key Cryptography, so it is ideal for use with Internet-connected computers. The Fedora distribution contains the following client and server software packages for SSH: openssh, openssh-client, and openssh-server packages.

Starting the SSH service

If you have installed the openssh-server software package, the SSH server is automatically configured to start. The SSH daemon is started from the /etc/init.d/sshd start-up script. To make sure the service is set up to start automatically, type the following (as root user):

```
# chkconfig --list sshd
sshd       0:off  1:off  2:on  3:on  4:on  5:on  6:off
```

This shows that the sshd service is set to run in system states 2, 3, 4, and 5 (normal bootup states) and set to be off in all other states. You can turn on the SSH service, if it is off, for your default run state, by typing the following as root user:

```
# chkconfig sshd on
```

This line turns on the SSH service when you enter run levels 2, 3, 4, or 5. To start the service immediately, type the following:

```
# /etc/init.d/sshd start
```

Using the ssh, sftp, and scp commands

Three commands you can use with the SSH service are ssh, sftp, and scp. Remote users use the ssh command to login to your system securely. The scp command lets remote users copy files to and from a system. The sftp command provides a safe way to access FTP sites.

Like the normal remote shell services, secure shell looks in the /etc/hosts.equiv file and in a user's .rhost file to determine whether it should allow a connection. It also looks in the ssh-specific files /etc/shosts.equiv and .shosts. Using the shosts.equiv and the .shosts files is preferable because it avoids granting access to the nonencrypted remote shell services. The /etc/shosts.equiv and .shosts files are functionally equivalent to the traditional hosts.equiv and .rhosts files, so the same instructions and rules apply.

Now you are ready to test the SSH service. From another computer on which SSH has been installed (or even from the same computer if another is not available), type the ssh command followed by a space and the name of the system you are connecting to. For example, to connect to the system ratbert.glaci.com, type:

```
# ssh ratbert.glaci.com
```

If this is the first time ever you have logged in to that system using the ssh command, it will ask you to confirm that you really want to connect. Type **yes** and press Enter when it asks this:

```
Host key not found from the list of known hosts.
Are you sure you want to continue connecting (yes/no)?
```

It should then prompt you for a user name and password in the normal way. The connection will then function like a normal telnet connection. The only difference is that the information is encrypted as it travels over the network. You should now also be able to use the ssh command to run remote commands from a shell on the remote system.

The scp command is similar to the rcp command for copying files to and from Linux systems. Here is an example of using the scp command to copy a file called memo from the home directory of the user named jake to the /tmp directory on a computer called maple:

```
$ scp /home/jake/memo maple:/tmp
passwd: ********
memo          100%|***************|   153    0:00
```

Enter the password for your user name (if a password is requested). If the password is accepted, the remote system indicates that the file has been copied successfully.

Similarly, the sftp command starts an interactive FTP session with an FTP server that supports SSH connections. Many security-conscious people prefer sftp to other ftp clients because it provides a secure connection between you and the remote host. Here's an example:

```
$ sftp ftp.handsonhistory.com
Connecting to ftp.handsonhistory.com
passwd: ********
sftp>
```

At this point you can begin an interactive FTP session. You can use get and put commands on files as you would using any FTP client, but with the comfort of knowing that you are working on a secure connection.

> **TIP:** The sftp command, as with ssh and scp, requires that the SSH service be running on the server. If you can't connect to a FTP server using sftp, the SSH service may not be available.

Using ssh, scp and sftp without passwords

For machines that you use a great deal, it is often helpful to set them up so that you do not have to use a password to log in. The following procedure shows you how to do that.

These steps will take you through setting up password-less authentication from one machine to another. In this example, the local user is named chuckw on a computer named host1. The remote user is also chuckw on a computer named host2.

1. Log in to the local computer (in this example, I log in as chuckw to host1).

> **NOTE:** Only run step 2 once as local user on your local workstation. Do not run it again unless you lose your ssh keys. When configuring subsequent remote servers, skip right to step 3.

2. Type the following to generate the ssh key:

   ```
   $ ssh-keygen -t dsa
   ```

3. Accept the defaults by pressing Enter at each request.

4. Type the following to copy the key to the remote server (replace chuckw with the remote user name and host2 with the remote host name):

   ```
   $ cd ~/.ssh
   $ scp id_dsa.pub chuckw@host2:/tmp
   chuckw@host2's password: *******
   ```

5. Type the following to add the ssh key to the remote-user's authorization keys (the code should be on one line, not wrapped):

   ```
   $ ssh chuck2@host2 'cat /tmp/id_dsa.pub >> /home/chuckw/.ssh/
   authorized_keys2'
   ```

> **NOTE:** The previous two steps will ask for passwords. This is okay.

6. Type the following to remove the key from the temporary directory:

   ```
   $ ssh chuckw@host2 /bin/rm /tmp/id_dsa.pub
   ```

> **NOTE:** The previous step should not ask for a password.

It is important to note that once you have this working, it will work regardless of how many times the IP address changes on your local computer. IP address has nothing to do with this form of authentication.

Guarding Your Computer with PortSentry

While LogSentry gathers and sorts log messages that may represent attempts to break into your computer system, the PortSentry takes a more active approach to protecting your system from network intrusions. PortSentry can be installed and configured on a Fedora system to monitor selected TCP and UDP ports, and can then react to attempts to access these ports (presumably by people trying to break in) in ways that you choose.

PortSentry acts as a nice complement to LogSentry by actively looking for intrusion behavior on network ports. When PortSentry perceives an attack, it reacts to the attack (in ways that you choose) and produces log messages about the activity that can be forwarded to the system administrator by LogSentry.

PortSentry operates in several different modes. Each of these modes can be applied to monitoring of TCP and UDP ports. The PortSentry modes include:

- **Basic** — This is the mode PortSentry uses by default. Selected UDP and TCP ports in this mode are bound by PortSentry, giving the monitored ports the appearance of offering a service to the network.

- **Stealth** — In this mode, PortSentry listens to the ports at the socket level instead of binding the ports. This mode can detect a variety of scan techniques (strobe-style, SYN, FIN, NULL, XMAS and UDP scans), but because it is more sensitive than basic mode, it is likely to produce more false alarms.

- **Advanced Stealth** — This mode offers the same detection method as the regular stealth mode, but instead of monitoring only the selected ports, it monitors all ports below a selected number (port number 1023, by default). You can then exclude monitoring of particular ports. This mode is even more sensitive than Stealth mode and is, therefore, more likely to cause false alarms than regular stealth mode.

> **NOTE:** When a port is "bound" by PortSentry or any other network service daemon process, all requests that come to that port from the network are handled by the binding process. For example, when the httpd daemon binds to port 80, requests for Web services from the network are processed by httpd.

Besides selecting the PortSentry mode and the ports that are monitored, you can also choose the response to your computer being scanned. By default, PortSentry can log intrusion attempts and block access to the intruder. PortSentry also offers ways of using other tools to respond to intrusions, including firewall rules, route changes, and host denial configuration.

Downloading and installing PortSentry

The portsentry package is not included in any Fedora or Red Hat Linux distribution. You can download the package from any Red Hat Linux FTP mirror site or from the rpmfind.net site. The portsentry package used in this chapter is portsentry-1.0-11.i386.rpm (the last version published by Red Hat as part of the 7.1 PowerTools). After downloading PortSentry, run the following command from the directory you downloaded it to:

```
# rpm -Uhv portsentry*
```

The installed portsentry package consists of several configuration files (in the /etc/portsentry directory), the portsentry start-up script (/etc/init.d/portsentry), and the portsentry command (in /usr/sbin). There are also README files of interest in the /usr/share/doc/portsentry* directory.

Using PortSentry as is

As with LogSentry, you don't need to do anything to get PortSentry to work after it is installed. By default, here is what PortSentry does when you install the portsentry package:

- The /etc/init.d/portsentry start-up script runs automatically when you boot to run levels 3, 4, or 5 (levels 3 and 5 are most commonly used).

- The following port numbers are configured to be monitored by PortSentry in basic mode:

  TCP: 1, 11, 15, 143, 540, 635, 1080, 1524, 2000, 5742, 6667, 12345, 12346, 20034, 31337, 32771, 32772, 32773, 32774, 40421, 49724, 54320

  UDP: 1, 513, 635, 640, 641, 700, 32770, 32771, 32772, 32773, 32774, 31337, 54321

- In response to attacks (represented by scans of the ports being monitored), all further attempts to connect to any services for the protocol (TCP or UDP) will be blocked.

The computers that are blocked from accessing your system are listed in either the portsentry.blocked.tcp or portsentry.blocked.udp files (in the /var/portsentry directory), depending on which protocol was scanned (TCP or UPD). Removing entries from these files to restore access to blocked computers.

Configuring PortSentry

Chances are that you will want to make some changes to the way that PortSentry runs. To change how PortSentry behaves, modify the /etc/portsentry/portsentry.conf file. In that file, you can choose which ports to monitor, the mode in which to monitor, and the responses to take when a scan is detected. The responses can include:

- Blocking access by the remote computer

- Rerouting messages from the remote computer to a dead host

- Adding a firewall rule to drop packets from the remote computer

The other file you may want to change is /etc/portsentry/portsentry.modes. The portsentry.modes file simply contains the modes that PortSentry can be run in.

Changing the portsentry.conf file

To edit the portsentry.conf file, as root user, open the /etc/portsentry/portsentry.conf file using any text editor. The following sections describe the information that can be changed in that file.

Selecting ports

The portsentry.conf file defines which ports are monitored in basic and stealth modes. By default, only basic TCP and UDP modes are active, so only those ports are monitored (unless you change to one of the stealth modes). The TCP_PORTS and UDP_PORTS options define which ports are monitored. Here is how they appear in the portsentry.conf file:

```
TCP_PORTS="1,11,15,143,540,635,1080,1524,2000,5742,6667,12345,12346,200
  34,31337,32771,32772,32773,32774,40421,49724,54320"
UDP_PORTS="1,513,635,640,641,700,32770,32771,32772,32773,32774,31337,
  54321"
```

Unless you are a TCP/IP expert, you're probably wondering what services these ports represent. The Internet Assigned Numbers Authority (IANA) assigns services to UDP and TCP ports. You can see these assignments at the following Web address:

```
www.iana.org/assignments/port-numbers
```

Network services in Fedora (as well as other Linux/UNIX systems) obtain port number assignments from the /etc/services file. So, in general, you can simply check the /etc/services file to find out most of the services that are assigned to ports being scanned.

Ports assigned for monitoring are chosen based on a couple of different criteria. Lower port numbers (1, 11, 15, and so on) are chosen to catch port scanners that begin at port 1 and scan through a few hundred ports. If the scanner is blocked after accessing port 1, it won't be able to get information about any other ports that might be open on your computer. Another criterion is to include ports that are checked specifically by intruders because those services might be vulnerable to attack. They include the systat (port 11) and netstat (port 15) services.

You will want to remove ports from the list in the portsentry.conf file if you are actually running the service assigned to that port. On the other hand, you might want to add ports to the list if you are paranoid about attacks and you want a bit more coverage. The portsentry.conf file contains some examples that you can uncomment (remove the # sign) so that more ports are monitored.

If you change from basic to stealth scans (as described in the "Changing the portsentry.modes file" section later in this chapter), the ports that are monitored are those defined by the ADVANCED_PORTS_TCP and ADVANCED_PORTS_UDP options. Here is how those two options are set by default:

```
ADVANCED_PORTS_TCP="1023"
ADVANCED_PORTS_UDP="1023"
```

The two preceding entries indicate that all ports from 1 to 1023 are monitored. Monitoring higher port numbers can result in many more false alarms, so this practice is not recommended. If you find that PortSentry is being tripped accidentally, you might want to exclude the ports being tripped by using the ADVANCED_EXCLUDE_TCP and ADVANCED_EXCLUDE_UDP options. The following example shows how these two values are set by default:

```
ADVANCED_EXCLUDE_TCP="111,113,139"
ADVANCED_EXCLUDE_UDP="520,138,137,67"
```

By default, ident and NetBIOS services for TCP (ports 111, 113, and 139) and route, NetBIOS, and Bootp broadcasts for UDP (ports 520, 138, 127, and 67) are excluded from the advanced scan. (The exclusion is because a remote computer might hit these ports without representing any misuse.) If you are running in stealth mode, you should likewise exclude any services that you are running on your system by adding their port numbers to this list.

Identifying configuration files

Besides the `portsentry.conf` file, there are several other configuration files used by PortSentry. You can identify the locations of these other files within the `portsentry.conf` file. Here are how those files are defined:

```
# Hosts to ignore
IGNORE_FILE="/etc/portsentry/portsentry.ignore"
# Hosts that have been denied (running history)
HISTORY_FILE="/var/portsentry/portsentry.history"
# Hosts denied this session only (temporary until next restart)
BLOCKED_FILE="/var/portsentry/portsentry.blocked"
```

Chances are that you will not want to move the location of these configuration files. Here are some descriptions of what these files are used for:

- The `portsentry.ignore` file contains a list of all IP addresses that you do not want blocked (even if they improperly try to access ports on your computer). By default, all IP addresses assigned to the local computer are added to this file. You can add IP addresses of trusted computers, if you like.

- The `portsentry.history` file contains a list of IP addresses for computers that have been blocked from accessing your computer.

- The `portsentry.blocked.*` files contain a list of computers that have been blocked from accessing your computer during the current session. The `portsentry.blocked.tcp` file contains IP addresses of computers that have improperly scanned TCP ports on your computer. Addresses of computers that have been blocked after scanning UDP ports are contained in the `portsentry.blocked.udp` file.

  Access to ports on your computer is only blocked during the current session (that is, until the next reboot or restart of PortSentry). So, to more permanently exclude remote computers, you should impose other restrictions (such as by using the `/etc/hosts.deny` file, a firewall command, or a reroute to a dead host). These methods are described later in this chapter.

Choosing responses

Someone scanning a port can be compared to someone checking a door in your house to see if it is locked. In most cases, it indicates that someone is checking your system for weaknesses. That is why, when another computer scans your ports, the default response from PortSentry is to block further access from the other computer to your computer for the duration of the current session. No action is taken to permanently block access from that computer. The `BLOCK_UDP` and `BLOCK_TCP` options in the `portsentry.conf` file set which type of automatic response is taken when ports are scanned. Here is how these options are set by default:

```
BLOCK_UDP="2"
BLOCK_TCP="2"
```

The value in quotation marks determines how PortSentry reacts to a scan of your ports by another computer. The following list describes each of these values.

- A value of `"2"` (the default value) causes access to be temporarily blocked to services for the scanned protocol (TCP or UDP) and for the action to be logged. Also, if any commands were defined to be run by a `KILL_RUN_CMD` option, that command is then run. (This option is not configured by default.)
- A value of `"0"` causes port scans to be logged, but not blocked.
- A value of `"1"` causes the `KILL_ROUTE` and `KILL_HOSTS_DENY` options to be run. (See the following list for descriptions of these options.) By default, further requests from the remote computer will be rerouted to a dead host, and the remote host's IP address will be added to the `/etc/hosts.deny` file, thereby denying access to network services.

Following are some suggestions on options you can use to change the responses to your ports being scanned:

- **KILL_ROUTE** — This option runs the `/sbin/route` command to reroute requests from the remote computer to a dead host. By default, this option is set to the following value, which effectively drops the request from the remote computer:

```
KILL_ROUTE="/sbin/route add -host $TARGET$ gw 127.0.0.1"
```

> **NOTE:** Instead of rerouting IP packets from the remote host, you can use firewall rules to deny access. If you use `ipchains` firewalls, uncomment the following line to deny access from the remote host. If you are using iptables, change ipchains to iptables and create an appropriate iptables response.

```
KILL_ROUTE="/sbin/ipchains -I input -s $TARGET$ -j DENY -l"
```

This `ipchains` rule would deny (in other words, drop) all packets from the remote computer. To make this action permanent, you could add the `ipchains` options (from the `-I` to the end of the line) to the `/etc/sysconfig/ipchains` file, replacing the `$TARGET$` with the actual IP address of the computer you want to deny access to.

- **KILL_HOSTS_DENY** — This option is used to deny requests for any network services that are protected by TCP wrappers. This option is set by default as follows:

```
KILL_HOSTS_DENY="ALL: $TARGET$"
```

With the preceding option set, $TARGET$ is replaced by the IP address of the intruding remote computer and the line in quotes is added to the `/etc/hosts.deny` file. For example, if the remote computer's IP address were `10.0.0.59`, the line that appears in `/etc/hosts.deny` would be:

```
ALL: 10.0.0.59
```

- **KILL_RUN_CMD** — Instead of using firewalls, rerouting, or TCP wrappers to deny an intruding computer from accessing your computer, you can choose any command you like in response. With the `BLOCK_TCP` and `BLOCK_UDP` options set to `"2"`, the value of `KILL_RUN_CMD` is run in response to a scan of your monitored ports.

  The value of `KILL_RUN_CMD` should be the full path to the script you want to run, plus any options. To include the IP address of the remote computer or the port number that was scanned, you could include the $TARGET$ or $PORT$ variables, respectively. Here is how the example appears that you would want to modify:

```
KILL_RUN_CMD="/some/path/here/script $TARGET$ $PORT$"
```

> **CAUTION:** Do not use any `KILL_RUN_CMD` to retaliate against the intruding remote host. Firstly, it is quite possible that the computer that is scanning your ports has itself been cracked and is thus not a valid target for retaliations, and secondly, retaliation may simply incite the cracker into further attacks on you.

- **PORT_BANNER** — You can send a message to the person who sets off the PortSentry monitor by setting the `PORT_BANNER` option. By default, no message is defined. However, you can uncomment the following line to use that message. (An abusive message is not recommended.)

```
PORT_BANNER="** UNAUTHORIZED ACCESS PROHIBITED ***
    YOUR CONNECTION ATTEMPT HAS BEEN LOGGED. GO AWAY."
```

The number of scans from an intruding computer that PortSentry will accept before setting off the responses described above can be set by using the `SCAN_TRIGGER` option. By default, that option is set as follows:

```
SCAN_TRIGGER="0"
```

The `"0"` value means that you won't accept any scans from an intruding system. In other words, the first scan will trip the PortSentry monitor. You can increase this value to be tolerant of one or more errant scans (though you probably won't want to).

Changing the portsentry.modes file

The `/etc/portsentry/portsentry.modes` file defines the modes in which the PortSentry command is run at boot time. Here is how that file appears by default:

```
tcp
udp
```

```
#stcp
#sudp
#atcp
#audp
```

The `tcp` and `udp` options are the basic PortSentry modes for the TCP and UDP services, respectively. Your other choices of options include *stealth TCP* (`stcp`) and *advanced stealth TCP* (`atcp`) and *stealth UDP* (`sudp`) and *advanced stealth UDP* (`audp`). Only run one TCP service and one UDP service. So, if you uncomment a stealth or advanced stealth service, be sure to add a comment in front of the appropriate basic service.

To activate the new services, you would then execute the following command:

```
# /etc/init.d/portsentry restart
```

The new PortSentry modes will take effect immediately. Those new modes will also be in effect when your computer reboots.

Testing PortSentry

You can test that your ports are properly protected in different ways. What you want to do is run a program that a potential intruder would run and see if it trips the appropriate response from PortSentry. For example, you could use a port scanner to see how your ports appear to the outside world. You could also use a command, such as `telnet`, to try and set off a particular port to see if PortSentry catches it.

`nmap` is a popular tool for scanning TCP and UDP ports. You can give the `nmap` command a host name or IP address, and it will scan about 1500 ports on computer to see which ports are open (and presumably offering services that could potentially be cracked).

An RPM of `nmap` is also available. You can download the nmap-frontend package, which contains a simple graphical interface to `nmap` called `xnmap`. I suggest that you install the packages on the system running PortSentry as well as on another system on your LAN (if one is available). Then run the following procedure on the PortSentry system to test it:

1. If PortSentry is running, shut it down by typing the following:

   ```
   # /etc/init.d/portsentry stop
   ```

2. Type the following `nmap` commands to see which ports are open on the local system:

   ```
   # nmap -sS -O 127.0.0.1
   # nmap -sU -O 127.0.0.1
   ```

   The output shows you which ports are currently offering services on your computer for TCP and UDP protocols, respectively.

3. If there are any services that you don't want open, you should turn off those services by using `chkconfig service off` (replacing *service* with the service name), by editing

the configuration file in the /etc/xinetd.d directory that represents the service and changing disable = no to disable = yes, or by changing your firewall setup.

4. If there are services that you want to be available from your computer, make sure that the port numbers representing those services are not being monitored by PortSentry. Remove the port number from the TCP_PORTS and/or UDP_PORTS options in the /etc/portsentry/portsentry.conf file, or PortSentry will report that there is a possible stealth scan on the port.

5. Restart PortSentry as follows:

```
# /etc/init.d/portsentry start
```

6. Run nmap again, as described previously. The ports offering legitimate services, as well as the ports being monitored by PortSentry, should all appear to be open.

7. Check the /var/log/messages file to make sure that PortSentry is not trying to monitor any ports on which you are offering services.

When you have determined that PortSentry is set up the way you would like it to be, run the nmap command from another computer on your network. This time, replace 127.0.0.1 with the name or IP address of the PortSentry computer. If everything is working, the first port that the remote computer scans on your PortSentry computer should block all subsequent scans.

Tracking PortSentry intrusions

Besides taking action against intruders, PortSentry logs its activities using the syslog utility. PortSentry's start-up, shutdown, and scan-detection activities are logged to your /var/log/messages file. The following are examples of PortSentry output in that file.

```
portsentry[13259]: adminalert: Psionic PortSentry 1.0 is starting.
portsentry[13260]: adminalert: Going into listen mode on TCP port: 1
portsentry[13260]: adminalert: Going into listen mode on TCP port: 11
           .
           .
           .
portsentry[13260]: adminalert: PortSentry is active and listening.
portsentry[]: attackalert:Connect from host:10.0.0.4 to TCP port: 31337
portsentry[]: attackalert: Connect from host: 10.0.0.4 to TCP port: 11
portsentry[]: attackalert: Host: 10.0.0.4 is already blocked. Ignoring
           .
           .
           .
portsentry[13371]: securityalert: Psionic PortSentry is shutting down
portsentry[13371]: adminalert: Psionic PortSentry is shutting down
```

The first part of the output shows PortSentry starting up. As PortSentry begins listening to each port, that port is noted in a separate log message. The next messages show the computer being scanned. Someone from host 10.0.0.4 ran nmap to scan the ports on the computer. PortSentry caught the scan of port 31337 and blocked attempts to scan other ports.

Finally, the last set of messages shows PortSentry being shut down. This is a security alert because someone besides you could shut down PortSentry to hide that they had broken in.

> **NOTE:** If you have been running the LogSentry package (described earlier), these messages show up in the e-mail messages you receive each hour from Logcheck.

Restoring access

If access was cut off to a computer that you wanted to have access, there are several things you can check to correct that problem:

- **/etc/hosts.deny** — See if the computer's IP address was mistakenly added to this file. This would cause network services to be denied to the host at that IP address.
- **/var/portsentry/portsentry.blocked** — Check that an entry for the computer's IP address wasn't added to the `portsentry.blocked.udp` or `portsentry.blocked.tcp` files.
- **route** — Run the `/sbin/route` command to see if messages from the computer are being rerouted to a dead host (probably the localhost).
- **iptables** — Run the `iptables -L` command to see if a new firewall was created to block access from the computer.

> **TIP:** To make sure that access isn't cut off again, you can add the IP address of the remote computer to the `/etc/portsentry/portsentry.ignore` file. Future improper scans or requests for services won't cause the remote computer to be blocked.

Summary

With the rise of the Internet, security has become a critical issue for nearly all computer users. Properly using passwords, securely configuring network services, and monitoring log files are critical ways of keeping your computer secure.

Using encryption keys you can help verify the authenticity of those you communicate with, as well as make the data you transmit more secure. With tools such as LogSentry and PortSentry, you can protect your Fedora system from intrusions.

Part IV
Fedora Network and Server Setup

Chapter 15

Setting Up a Local Area Network

In This Chapter

- Understanding local area networks
- Setting up a wired Ethernet LAN
- Setting up a wireless LAN
- Troubleshooting your LAN

In the home or in a small business, Fedora can help you connect to other Linux, Windows, and Macintosh computers so that you can share your computing equipment (files, printers, and devices). Add a connection to the Internet and routing among multiple LANs (described in Chapter 16), and Fedora can serve as a focal point for network computing in a larger enterprise.

This chapter helps you set up your own local area network (LAN). The procedures described here provide a foundation for sharing the computing resources in your home or organization. In particular, the chapter describes how to use Ethernet cards, wiring, and protocols to connect computers. It then tells you specifically how to configure your Fedora computer so that it can communicate with other computers.

Understanding Local Area Networks

Connecting the computers in your organization via a LAN can save you a lot of time and money. The amount of money you put into networking hardware, even in a small configuration (less than five or six users), can save you from buying multiple printers, backup media, and other hardware. Add a single, shared Internet connection and you no longer need multiple modems and Internet accounts.

With a LAN, you don't have to run down the hall anymore with your file on a disk to print it on your friend's printer. Information that had to wait for the mailroom to make the rounds can be sent in an instant to anyone (or everyone) on your LAN.

With a LAN, you begin to open the greatest potential of Linux — its ability to act as a server on a network. Because Fedora is more robust and feature-rich than other computing systems (certainly for the price), adding it to your LAN can provide a focal point to workstations that could use Linux as a file server, a mail server, a print server, or a boot server. (Those features are described later in this book.)

Creating and configuring a LAN consists of these steps:

1. **Setting up LAN hardware** — This entails choosing a network topology, purchasing the equipment you need, and installing it (adding cards and connecting wires or using wireless antennas).

2. **Configuring TCP/IP** — To use most of the networking applications and tools that come with Linux, you must have TCP/IP configured. TCP/IP lets you communicate not only with computers on your LAN, but to any computers that you can reach on your LAN, modem, or other network connection (particularly to the Internet).

Setting up LAN hardware

Even with a simple LAN, you must make some decisions about network topology (that is, how computers are connected). You must also make some decisions about network equipment (network interface cards, wires, hubs, and so on).

LAN topologies

Most small office and home LANs connect computers together in one of the following topologies:

- **Star topology** — The star topology is by far the most popular LAN topology. In this arrangement, each computer contains a Network Interface Card (NIC) that connects with a cable to a central hub. The cabling is typically Category 5 (twisted pair) wiring with RJ-45 connectors. Other equipment, such as printers and fax machines, can also be connected to the hub in a star topology. Figure 15-1 is an example of a star topology.

Star Topology

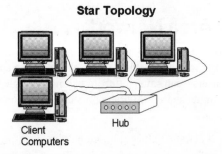

Client
Computers

Hub

Figure 15-1: In a star topology, machines on the network connect to a central hub.

- **Bus topology** — Instead of using hubs, the bus topology connects computers in a chain from one to the next. The cabling usually used is referred to as coaxial, or Thin Ethernet cable. A "T" connector attaches to each computer's NIC, then to two adjacent computers in the chain. At the two ends of the chain, the T connectors are terminated. Figure 15-2 illustrates an example of a bus topology.

Bus Topology

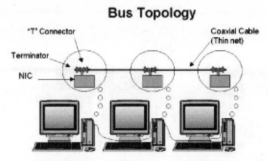

Figure 15-2: A bus topology chains computers together without using a hub.

- **Ring topology** — This is a less popular topology than star and bus topologies. In a ring topology, computers connect to a ring of wires on which tokens are taken and passed by computers that want to send information on the network. This type of topology typically uses IBM's token ring protocols.

You can configure a wireless Ethernet LAN in several different topologies, depending on how you want to use the LAN. With a wireless LAN, each computer broadcasts in the air rather than across wires. Here are some examples of wireless topologies:

- **Wireless peer-to-peer** — In this topology, frames of data are broadcast to all nodes within range, but are consumed only by the computers for which they are intended. This arrangement is useful if you are sharing file and print services among a group of client computers. Figure 15-3 shows an example of a peer-to-peer wireless LAN.

Figure 15-3: Wireless LANs can communicate as peers by broadcasting data.

- **Wireless access point** — A wireless interface can act as an access point for one or more wireless clients. Clients can be configured to communicate directly with the access point, instead of with every client that is within range. This arrangement is useful for point-to-point connections between two buildings, where the access point is acting as a gateway to the Internet or, for example, a campus intranet. Figure 15-4 depicts a point-to-point wireless LAN.

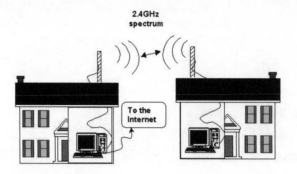

Figure 15-4: Wireless communication can go through an access point.

- **Multiple wireless access points and roaming** — Each wireless network can be configured as a separate cell. Multiple cells can be joined together in what is called a *Managed Wireless LAN*. In this arrangement, each cell's access point acts as a bridge (in fact, its actions are referred to as *bridging*) by passing all data from the cell to other cells without changing any node's MAC address. In other words, the managed wireless LAN makes the fact that there are multiple wireless cells invisible to the clients on those cells. This arrangement allows users to roam among cells as they come in and out of range without losing continuity of communication.

> **NOTE:** Although Linux does not support any wireless LAN cards that can act as a bridging wireless access point, you can have the Linux system act as a client to a bridging access point. Set your card to Managed mode and identify the MAC address for your wireless LAN's access point.

For our purposes, we focus on star (wired) and peer-to-peer (wireless) topologies. Common to both of these topologies is the protocol used to send data over those wired and wireless media — the Ethernet protocol.

LAN equipment

The equipment that you need to connect your LAN can include some or all of the following:

> **CROSS-REFERENCE:** For a complete description of wireless hardware, see the "Choosing wireless hardware" section later in this chapter.

- **Network Interface Card (NIC)** — Typically, one of these cards goes into a slot in each computer. For wired Ethernet networks, the cards can transmit data at 10 Mbps or 100 Mbps. Gigabit (1000 Mbps) NICs are also now available, but are quite a bit more expensive. An 802.11B wireless NIC card can operate at speeds of up to 11 Mbps, but is more expensive than a wired NIC card.

- **Cables** — For star topologies, cables are referred to as *twisted-pair*. Category 5e wiring, which contains four twisted-pair sets per wire, is the most common type of wiring used for LANs today. A connector at each end of the cable is an RJ-45 plug, similar to those used on telephone cables. Ethernet interfaces are either 10Base-T (10 Mbps speeds) or 100Base-TX (100 Mbps speeds). These cables plug into the computer's NIC at one end and the hub at the other.

  Figure 15-5 shows an example of a twisted-pair cable with an RJ-45 connector used for star topologies.

Figure 15-5: A star topology's twisted-pair cables have RJ-45 connectors (similar to telephone-cable connectors).

- **Hubs** — With the star topology, a hub is typically used to connect the computers. Sometimes hubs are also referred to as repeaters or concentrators because they receive signals from the nodes connected to them and send the signals on to other nodes.

  The questions you need to answer when choosing a hub are how many ports you need and how fast you want your network to go. If you need to expand in the future, hubs can be connected together. Most low-end hubs you can purchase today handle both 10 Mbps and 100 Mbps speeds.

- **Switches** — A switch can be used instead of a hub. It lets you divide a LAN that is getting too large into segments that are more manageable. A switch can reduce network traffic by directing messages intended for a specific computer directly to that computer. This is as opposed to a hub, which broadcasts all data to all nodes. Because switches have come down so much in price, in most cases you should just pay a few extra dollars and get a switch instead of a hub.

One piece of equipment that I won't go into yet is a router. A router is used to direct information from the LAN to other LANs or the Internet.

CROSS-REFERENCE: Machines that carry out routing functions are described in Chapter 16.

LAN equipment setup

With an Ethernet NIC, appropriate cables, and a hub (or switch), you are ready to set up your wired Ethernet LAN. If you don't yet have an Ethernet card for your computer, refer to the sidebar "Choosing an Ethernet Card" for information on choosing a card that will work in Linux. The steps for setting up an Ethernet LAN are:

1. Power down each computer and physically install the NIC card (following the manufacturer's instructions).

2. Using cables appropriate for your NIC cards and hub, connect each NIC to the hub.

3. Power up each computer.

4. If Fedora is not installed yet, install the software and reboot (as instructed). Chapter 2 tells you how to configure your Ethernet card while installing Linux.

5. If Fedora is already installed, refer to the "Configuring TCP/IP for your LAN" section for information on configuring your Ethernet cards.

6. When the system comes up, your Ethernet card and interface (eth0) should be ready to use. See the section "Checking your Ethernet connection" later in this chapter to learn how to determine whether your Ethernet connection is working.

Choosing an Ethernet Card

There are several ways to find out about supported Ethernet cards for Linux. Here are some suggestions:

- The /usr/src/linux*/Documentation/networking directory contains files that describe Ethernet cards that are supported in the Linux kernel. You need the kernel-source package installed to see these files.

- For laptops, PCMCIA cards supported in Fedora are defined in the /etc/pcmcia/config file. More than 100 PCMCIA Ethernet cards are listed, a handful of wireless PCMCIA LAN drivers, and a couple of Token Ring PCMCIA cards.

- The Linux Ethernet-HOWTO (www.tldp.org/HOWTO/Ethernet-HOWTO.html) describes many older Ethernet cards that are supported.

Configuring TCP/IP for your LAN

When you install Fedora, you are given the opportunity to add your TCP/IP host name and IP address, as well as some other information, to your computer or choose to have that information automatically provided using DHCP, or Dynamic Host Configuration Protocol. You also can set up a way to reach other computers on your LAN. That's typically done by adding computer names and IP addresses to your /etc/hosts file (as described here) or (often with more than a few machines) by using a DNS server.

> **CROSS-REFERENCE:** DNS is discussed in Chapter 16. Configuring your own DNS server is described in Chapter 25.

If you did not configure your LAN connection during installation of Linux, you can do so at any time using the Network Configuration window (neat command). The IP address and host names can be assigned statically to an Ethernet interface or retrieved dynamically at boot time from a DHCP server.

> **NOTE:** A computer can have more than one IP address because it can have multiple network interfaces. Each network interface must have an IP address (even if the address is assigned temporarily). So, if you have two Ethernet cards (eth0 and eth1), each needs its own IP address. Also, the address 127.0.0.1 represents the local host, so users on the local computer can access services in loopback.

To define your IP address for your Ethernet interface, follow this procedure:

1. Start the Network Configuration. From the red hat menu, click System Settings → Network or, as root user from a Terminal window, type neat. (If prompted, type the root password.) The Network Configuration window appears.

2. Click the Devices tab. A listing of your existing network interfaces appears.

3. Double-click the eth0 interface (representing your first Ethernet card). A pop-up window appears, enabling you to configure your eth0 interface. Figure 15-6 shows the Network Configuration window and the pop-up Ethernet Device window configuring eth0.

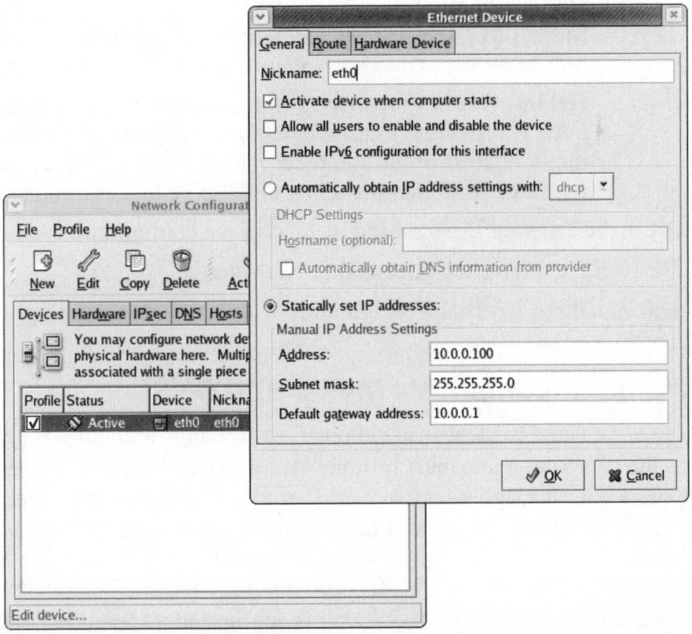

Figure 15-6: Configure your LAN interface using the Network Configuration window.

4. On the Ethernet Devices window that appears, you can enter the following information:

   • **Activate device when computer starts:** Check here to have eth0 start at boot time.

   • **Allow all users to enable and disable the device:** Check to **let** non-root users enable and disable the network interface.

   • **Enable IPv6 configuration for this interface:** Check here if **you** are connected to an IPV6 network. (Most networks are still IPV4.)

5. On the same window, you must choose whether to get your IP addresses from another computer at boot time or enter the adresses yourself:

   • **Automatically obtain IP address settings with:** Select this box if you have a DHCP or BOOTP server on the network from which you can obtain your computer's IP address, netmask, and gateway. DHCP is recommended if you **have** more than just a couple of computers on your LAN. (See Chapter 23 for how to set up a DHCP server.) You can, optionally, set your own host name, which can be just a name (such as jukebox) or a fully qualified domain name (such as jukebox.linuxtoys.net).

   • **Statically set IP addresses:** If there is no DHCP, or other boot server, on your LAN, you can add necessary IP address information statically by **selecting** this option and adding the following information:

     > **Address:** Type the IP address of this computer into the Address box. This number must be unique on your network. For your private LAN, you can use private IP addresses (see the section, "Understanding IP addresses" later in this chapter).

     > **Subnet Mask:** Enter the netmask to indicate what part of the IP address represents the network. (Netmask is described later in this chapter.)

     > **Default Gateway Address:** If a computer or router connected to your LAN is providing routing functions to the Internet or other network, type the IP address of the computer into this box. (Chapter 16 describes how to use NAT or IP masquerading and use Fedora as a router.)

6. Click OK in the Ethernet Device window to save the configuration and close the window.

7. Click File → Save to save the information you entered.

8. Click Activate in the Network Configuration window to start your connection to the LAN.

Identifying other computers (hosts and DNS)

Each time you use a name to identify a computer, as when browsing the Web or using an e-mail address, the computer name must be translated into an IP address. To resolve names to IP addresses, Fedora goes through a search order (based on the contents of three files in /etc: resolv.conf, nsswitch.conf, and host.conf). By default, it checks:

• Host names you add yourself (which end up in the /etc/hosts file).

• Hosts available via NIS (if an NIS server is configured as described in Chapter 23).

• Hosts names available via DNS.

You can use the Network Configuration window to add:

- **Host names and IP addresses.** You might do this to identify hosts on your LAN that are not configured on a DNS server.

- **DNS search path.** By adding domain names to a search path (such as linuxtoys.net), you can browse to a site by its host name (such as jukebox), and have Linux search the domains you added to the search path to find the host you are looking for (such as jukebox.linuxtoys.net).

- **DNS name servers.** A DNS server can resolve addresses for the domains it serves and contact other DNS servers to get addresses for all other DNS domains.

> **NOTE:** If you are configuring a DNS server, you can use that server to centrally store names and IP addresses for your LAN. This saves you the trouble of updating every computer's /etc/hosts file every time you add or change a computer on your LAN. Refer to Chapter 25 to learn how to set up a DNS server.

To add host names, IP addresses, search paths, and DNS servers, do the following:

1. Start the Network Configuration. As root user from a Terminal window, type neat& or from the red hat menu, click System Settings → Network. The Network Configuration window appears.

2. Click the Hosts tab. A list of IP addresses, host names, and aliases appears.

3. Click New. A pop-up window appears asking you to add the IP address, host name, and aliases for a host that you can reach on your network. Figure 15-7 shows the Network Configuration window and the pop-up window for adding a host.

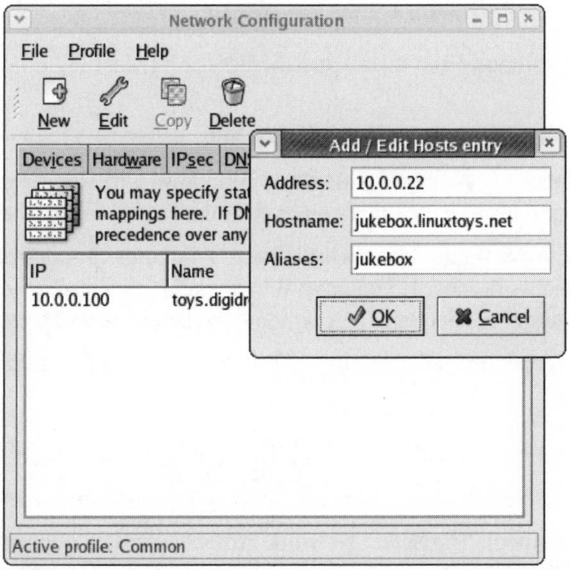

Figure 15-7: Add hosts to /etc/hosts using the Network Configuration window.

4. Type in the IP address number, host name, and, optionally, the host alias.

5. Click OK.

6. Repeat this process until you have added every computer on your LAN.

7. Click the DNS tab.

8. Type the IP address of the computers that serve as your Primary and Secondary DNS servers. You get these IP addresses from your ISP or, if you created your own DNS server, you can enter that server's IP address.

9. Type the name of the domain (probably the name of your local domain) to be searched for host names into the DNS Search Path box.

10. Click File → Save to save the changes.

11. Click File → Quit to exit.

Now, when you use programs such as ftp, ssh, or other TCP/IP utilities, you can use any host name that is identified on your local computer, exists in your search path domain, or can be resolved from the public Internet DNS servers. (Strictly speaking, you don't have to set up your /etc/hosts file. You could use IP addresses as arguments to TCP/IP commands. But names are easier to work with.)

Adding Windows computers to your LAN

It is likely that you have other types of computers on your LAN in addition to those running Linux systems (at least for a few more years). The following are general steps for adding your Windows computers to the Ethernet LAN we just created:

1. Power down your computer and install an Ethernet card. (Most PC Ethernet cards will run on Windows.)

2. Connect an Ethernet cable from the card to your hub.

3. Reboot your computer. If your card is detected, Windows will either automatically install a driver or ask you to insert a disk that comes with the card to install the driver.

4. Open the window to configure networking. (Start → Settings → Control Panel; then double-click the Network icon. If you have Windows XP, you also need to click "Set up or change your Internet connection."). A window to change network properties appears.

5. What you do next depends on the version of Windows you are running:

   For Windows 98:

   - Find the Ethernet card you have just installed in the list and select it.
   - Click Add. The Select Network Component Type pop-up window appears.
   - Double-click Protocol. The Select Network Protocol window appears.

- Click Microsoft, and then double-click TCP/IP. A new entry should appear in your Network window that looks similar to the following, depending on your card:

```
TCP/IP -> 3Com Etherlink III ISA
```

- Double-click on that new entry. The TCP/IP Properties window should appear, similar to the one in Figure 15-8 for Windows XP.

For Windows 2000 or XP:

- Click "Switch to classic view."
- Double-click the Network connections.
- Double-click Local Area Connection. The Local Area Connection Status window appears.
- Click Properties. The Local Area Connection Properties window appears.
- Select Internet Protocol (TCP/IP), and click the Properties button. The Internet Protocol (TCP/IP) Properties window appears as shown in Figure 15-8.

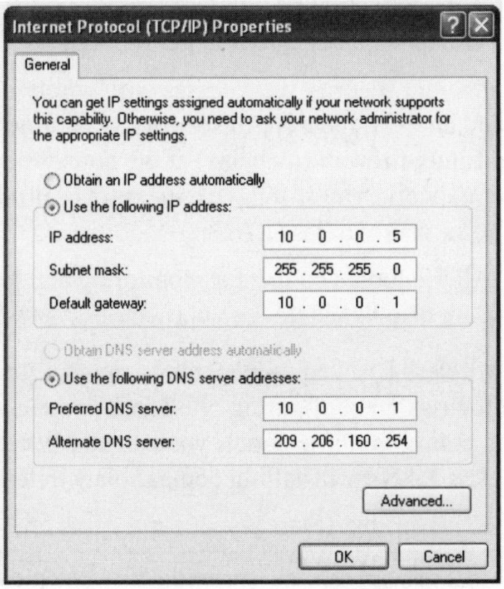

Figure 15-8: Configure TCP/IP on Windows XP for your Ethernet LAN.

6. Click either "Use the following IP address" or "Obtain an IP address."

NOTE: If you are using a DHCP server to assign IP addresses, click "Obtain an IP address automatically" instead. See Chapter 23 for information on setting up Linux as a DHCP server.

7. Add the IP address, Subnet mask, and Default Gateway for this computer.
8. Add the IP addresses of up to two DNS servers.

9. Click OK. You may need to reboot Windows for the settings to take effect.

At this point, your Windows computer knows to listen on the network (via its Ethernet card) for messages addressed to the IP address you have just entered.

Setting Up a Wireless LAN

Sometimes it's not convenient to run wires to all the computers on your network. Pulling Ethernet cables through existing walls can be a pain. Dragging wires into your garden so you can sit in a lounge chair and surf the Internet can ruin the ambiance. In many cases, a wireless LAN is an economical solution.

Although you can use wireless LAN cards with other computer systems, you may want to use Linux systems for one or more nodes in your wireless network. For example, the features in Linux can eliminate the need to buy other types of equipment. Some additional features that make Linux a valuable asset on a wireless LAN include:

- **Internet access** — You don't need a separate router or gateway machine to attach your wireless LAN to the Internet. Having wired and wireless Ethernet LAN cards on a Linux system enables your wireless clients to access the Internet through your Linux system.

- **Firewall** — Owing to some inherent security weaknesses with wireless encryption protocols, you may want to add an extra measure of security to your network by configuring firewalls. With a Linux firewall (ipchains) at the boundaries between your wireless LAN and your larger network, you still have a measure of protection for your larger network if someone cracks your wireless LAN.

- **Monitoring and logging** — All the tools you use for monitoring and logging activity on your wired networks in Linux are also available for your wireless network.

This chapter describes how to use wireless LAN equipment on computers running Fedora to create a wireless Ethernet LAN. It focuses on configuring two Linux systems for wireless communication; however, once you configure these nodes, you can add Windows, Linux, or other types of systems to your wireless LAN by installing compatible wireless cards on each system.

> **NOTE:** If you are having trouble with your wireless card, try running the `/sbin/dump_cis` command to view the card's data structures. If you see the message `open(): No such device`, it means that your card has not been detected and configured.

Understanding wireless networks

Wireless LANs are most appropriate in environments where wires are impractical. Despite some challenges such as security and interference, a wireless LAN provides these advantages:

- You don't have to run wires in places that are hard to reach. In many cases, a single wireless LAN can extend your network throughout a building or to another building without the need for wires between each node.

- For the price of a wireless card, you can save the expense of wires, hubs (the air is your hub), and wall repairs (to fix the holes from pulling wires through).

- You can freely move computers around within the transmission range that your environment allows (distances being limited by such variables as antenna power, obstacles, and rates of transmission).

Although several different wireless networking standards exist, this chapter focuses on the installation of relatively low-cost, standard IEEE 802.11b wireless-networking equipment. An 802.11b wireless network uses space in the spectrum available to the public (in other words, you use space in the air for which no special license is required). The 802.11b standard is often referred to as the *Wi-Fi,* or *Wireless Fidelity*, standard.

An 802.11b network is characterized by the following:

- It provides transmission rates of up to 11 Mbps. Transmission rates can also be set (or auto-detected) to 5.5, 2, and 1 Mbps.

- It uses the 2.4 GHz band of the spectrum. Microwave ovens and some high-end mobile phones also use this band. (Check local regulations if you are setting up an 802.11b network outside the United States.) To reduce congestion, 14 separate channels have been made available within the 2.4 GHz range.

- It allows transmission over distances as short as a desktop away to as long as several miles away (using special antennas). Greater distances can be gained at lower transmission speeds.

- Makes connections between multiple clients or clients and a base station (usually referred to as an *access point*). On the clients, the wireless LAN cards run in Ad-hoc mode, while the base station uses Managed mode.

NOTE: The Orinoco card, as well as other wireless-network cards supported in Linux, cannot act as an access point because it does not do bridging. Bridging allows a node to receive a frame from one node and forward it to another node without changing the first node's MAC address. (The MAC address uniquely identifies a network card.) A wireless LAN card in Linux, however, can communicate with an access point by running in Managed mode and indicating the MAC address of the access point.

Other 802.11 standards exist (such as 802.11a, which can operate at higher speeds), but for the most part wireless-equipment manufacturers have rallied around the 802.11b standard. Wireless cards and other equipment certified Wi-Fi (802.11b)–compatible by the Wireless Ethernet Compatibility Alliance (WECA) should be able to communicate with each other.

> **CROSS-REFERENCE:** To see a complete list of Wi-Fi–certified products, visit the WECA Web site (`www.wirelessethernet.org`, then click Wi-Fi Certified™ Products). Although these products should be able to communicate with each other, they do not all have drivers that are compatible with Linux.

After your wireless network has been configured, you can use the wireless connections as you would a regular wired Ethernet connection. For example, you can configure TCP/IP on top of your wireless network so that it acts as a gateway to your network's Internet connection. If you are using Linux as a wireless network client as well, you can take full advantage of firewall, masquerading, network proxy, or other networking features to protect and make full use of your wireless network.

Choosing wireless hardware

To get started with a wireless Linux LAN, you need at least two computers and two wireless LAN cards. The wireless LAN cards described in this chapter are PCMCIA-type cards that you insert into those credit-card–sized slots on laptop computers. If ISA or PCI slots alone are available on your computers, you will need to add an adapter card. You may also want (or need) to add indoor or outdoor antennas to your wireless network.

Selecting wireless cards

Not all wireless LAN cards that you can purchase today will work with Linux. When you select a card, make sure that a Linux driver has been created for the card. You will also want to look for several other features:

- **Card type** — Most wireless LAN cards are in PCMCIA (PC-card) form. To use these cards in desktop computers you will probably need an ISA or PCI adapter card.

- **Cost** — If you shop around, you can find wireless LAN cards that cost between $29 and $100 (and the prices will probably have gone down by the time you read this). More expensive cards may include external antennas or better encryption (128-bit as opposed to 64-bit).

- **External connector** — Different wireless LAN cards have different types of connectors, which can lock you into buying antennas from the manufacturer of the LAN card if you are communicating outside of a small area. People who know such things tell me that it is possible to take apart the cards and hack together your own antenna. However, because I don't want to be responsible for wrecking your card, and because there are legal issues related to antenna usage, I don't recommend this alternative.

- **Configurability** — If you really want to fine-tune your wireless LAN, find out how much control you have over configuring a card before you choose it. Descriptions of the `iwconfig` command later in this chapter will help you understand which wireless extensions you can manipulate. Refer to man pages for individual wireless-card drivers (for example, type `man wavelan`), for information on specific parameters that you can change.

I chose to use Orinoco wireless PC cards from Proxim Corporation to illustrate how to set up a wireless Linux LAN. Although other wireless cards are supported in Linux, Orinoco cards seem to have particularly good Linux drivers, and many people have reported success using them. The cards are also relatively inexpensive (about $60 to $90 at the time of this writing). Before Proxim acquired the Orinoco line from Agere Systems, Orinoco cards were referred to as *WaveLAN cards* and were produced by Lucent Technologies (as well as AT&T and NCR).

Other wireless cards supported in Fedora are listed in the PCMCIA Card Configuration Database file (`/etc/pcmcia/config`). Table 15-1 shows the wireless-network adapters listed in this file, along with the module required by each.

NOTE: Just because you don't see your wireless card listed in Table 15-1 doesn't mean that it won't work. The same technology is often referred to by different names. Rather than try to keep track of all the various acquisitions and name-changes in the wireless industry, I refer you to the Linux Wireless LAN HOWTO (`www.hpl.hp.com/personal/Jean_Tourrilhes/Linux`). The Drivers section provides more insight into which drivers work with which cards.

Table 15-1: Supported Wireless Network Adapters and Modules

Wireless Network Adapter	Module
350 Series Wireless LAN Adapter (Cisco Systems)	`airo_cs.ko`
Aironet PC4500 (Cisco Systems)	`airo_cs.ko`
Aironet PC4800 (Cisco Systems)	`airo_cs.ko`
AT&T WaveLAN Adapter	`wavelan_cs.ko`
Atmel AT76C50X wireless	`atmel_cs.ko`
Cabletron RoamAbout 802.11 DS	`wvlan_cs.ko`
Compaq WL100 11 Mbps Wireless Adapter	`orinoco_cs.ko`
Digital RoamAbout/DS	`wavelan_cs.ko`
ELSA AirLancer MC-11	`wvlan_cs.ko`
Lucent Technologies WaveLAN Adapter	`wavelan_cs.ko`
Intersil PRISM2 11 Mbps Wireless Adapter	`wvlan_cs.ko`
Lucent Technologies WaveLAN/IEEE Adapter	`orinoco_cs.ko`
MELCO WLI-PCM-L11	`orinoco_cs.ko`
MELCO WLI-PCM-L11G	`orinoco_cs.ko`
NCR WaveLAN Adapter	`wavelan_cs.ko`
Orinoco PC Cards	`orinoco_cs.ko`
PLANEX GeoWave/GW-CF110	`orinoco_cs.ko`

Wireless Network Adapter	Module
Planet WL3501	`wl3501_cs.ko`
Xircom CreditCard Netwave	`netwave_cs.ko`
ZCOMAX AirRunner/XI-300	`orinoco_cs.ko`

The Orinoco PC cards I purchased use the orinoco_cs.ko module. The cards come in two types: Gold Label, which offers 128-bit WEP RC4 encryption, and Silver Label, which offers only 64-bit WEP RC4 encryption. The two cards differ in cost by about $10. Both cards:

- offer compatibility with earlier WaveLAN/IEEE products.
- can communicate with other 802.11b wireless LAN equipment that has been Wi-Fi–certified by WECA.
- enable you to select transmission rates (11, 5.5, 2, or 1 Mbps), select channels (in the 2.4 GHz range), and use power-management features.

Because antennas are built into Orinoco PC cards, you may not need an additional antenna for indoor office environments. As with any wireless card, the distances you can achieve between your wireless nodes depend on transmission rate (lower speeds go farther), receiver sensitivity, and the amount and type of obstacles. At the maximum transmission rate (11 Mbps), the Orinoco card gives you an estimated range of between 80 feet (25 meters) in a closed area and 525 feet (160 meters) in an open area with no additional antenna.

Selecting adapter cards

If the computers on your wireless network are all laptops with PCMCIA slots, you only need to plug in your wireless cards to get started. However, if you are using a desktop computer with only ISA and PCI slots, you will also need an adapter card.

Before you purchase a wireless LAN card for your desktop computer, make sure that you can get a compatible adapter card. Proxim Corp. offers both ISA and PCI Orinoco adapter cards. If you have an ISA slot available, you should get an ISA adapter. The ISA card supports the following I/O addresses: 3E2-3E1 (default) and 3E2-3E3.

The PCI adapter works on computers that have the following features:

- PCI 2.2 (or higher) BIOS support
- PC99 compliance
- PCI slots only

The PCI adapter will not work on some older computers that don't meet the BIOS specifications. To use the PCI adapter in Linux, you may have to perform additional configuration in the operating system.

NOTE: Although using the Orinoco ISA and PCI adapters with a standard Type II PC is not specifically supported, many Type II PC cards (besides your wireless cards) will work in those adapters.

Selecting antennas

If you are setting up your wireless LAN among several computers in close proximity to each other, you may not need an additional antenna. To deal with obstructions and longer distances, however, you can add indoor or outdoor antennas to your wireless hardware.

Again, because I have been discussing Orinoco wireless PC cards, I will illustrate different types of indoor and outdoor antennas that are compatible with those cards.

Using indoor antennas

The antennas that are built into wireless LAN cards often work well enough to enable communication among computers in an open area. Additional indoor antennas are useful if the direct line of sight between the wireless LAN cards is blocked. A computer may be locked in a storage closet or stuck under a desk. A pile of papers might inhibit transmission, or a sheet of metal might stop it dead. A small antenna that draws the transmission away from the card might be the answer to these problems.

While most wireless LAN cards don't require a completely unobstructed line of sight, an obstacle can certainly slow reception. To get around this problem, an antenna such as the Orinoco IEEE range-extender can plug directly into an Orinoco Gold or Silver wireless LAN card. A 1.5-meter extension cable can bring the signal out from behind a closed door or out on top of a desk. When you set up the antenna, it is recommended that it be:

- placed in a central location.
- mounted vertically.
- located away from obstructions (metal surfaces in particular, and, to a lesser extent, solid objects such as concrete walls or stacks of papers).

Refer to the instructions that come with your antenna for specific guidelines regarding placing and mounting the antenna.

Using outdoor antennas

Choosing and setting up outdoor antennas for your wireless LAN can be more difficult and expensive than setting them up indoors. Once the outdoor antennas are in place, however, you can save money because you won't need multiple Internet access accounts (monthly fees, DSL/cable modems, and so on).

Although a complete description of the use of outside antennas with your wireless LAN is outside the scope of this chapter, here are some tips that will help you choose the best antennas for your wireless LAN.

- **Point-to-point versus multi-point** — If you are creating a point-to-point link between two outdoor locations (for example, to share an Internet connection between two buildings), a directional antenna can help you achieve greater distance and transmission speeds. However, if your antenna is providing multipoint access for several other outdoor antennas or wireless clients (such as students working from laptops on the campus lawn), an omnidirectional antenna may be more appropriate.

- **Clearance** — The clearer the line of sight between each outdoor antenna, the greater the distance and transmission speed you can achieve. Placing antennas at the highest possible points can prevent diminished performance caused by trees, cars, buildings, and other objects. The amount of distance between obstacles and the coverage area of your wireless transmission is referred to as the *clearance factor* (see Figure 15-9).

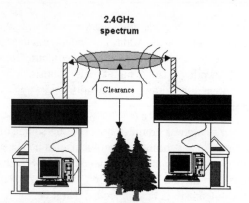

Figure 15-9: The distance of obstructive objects from the wireless signal is called the *clearance*.

- **Distance** — Although the actual distances over which antennas can send and receive data varies greatly based on different factors, you can achieve distances of many miles with outdoor antennas. For example, two Orinoco 24 dBi directional parabolic-grid antennas can theoretically achieve distances of up to 52 miles at an 11 Mbps transmission speed with a 180-meter clearance. Reduce that transmission rate to 1 Mbps and you can achieve distances of up to 149 miles with a 1200-meter clearance. Shorter distances are achieved with less expensive equipment, such as the Orinoco 14 dBi directional antenna which can achieve distances of up to 5.3 miles at 11 Mbps with a 13-meter clearance.

- **Cable factor** — The distances that transmissions travel on the cables between the wireless cards and the antennas can be a factor in choosing the right antenna. The shorter the cables, the greater the distance and speed you will get on your antenna.

The power of an antenna is rated in terms of *gain*. Gain is measured in decibels, based on a *theoretic isotropic radiator* (or *dBi*). Higher gains offer opportunities for reaching greater distances at greater speeds. However, the ability of the antenna to focus that power (directional versus omnidirectional), greatly affects the speeds and distances that can be achieved.

Installing wireless Linux software

If you did a personal desktop or Everything installation of Fedora on your computer, the software packages you need to create your wireless LAN may already be installed. Drivers and modules needed to support PCMCIA cards and wireless cards should be in your system.

Besides the wireless drivers, the following software packages contain tools for configuring and working with your wireless LAN cards in Fedora:

- **pcmcia-cs** — Contains commands and configuration files to support PCMCIA cards.

- **wireless-tools** — Contains commands for setting extensions for your wireless LAN interface. Commands include `iwconfig` (for configuring your wireless interface) and `iwlist` (for listing wireless statistics).

After you have established a wireless LAN interface, you can use a variety of Linux software to monitor and control access to that interface. You will need to install the appropriate software packages as well.

Configuring the wireless LAN

Before you begin testing the distances you can achieve with your wireless Linux LAN, I recommend that you configure wireless cards on two computers within a few feet of each other. After the two computers are communicating, you can change wireless settings to tune the connection and begin experimenting with transmission distances.

The following sections describe the steps you need to take to set up a wireless LAN between two Linux systems. Although only two nodes are described, you can add more computers to your wireless LAN once you know how. This procedure describes how to operate your wireless Linux LAN in two different modes:

- **Ad hoc** — All the computers in your wireless LAN are gathered into a single virtual network made up of only one cell. A single cell means that you cannot roam among different groups of wireless nodes and continue your communication invisibly. To do that requires a managed network.

- **Managed** — As I noted earlier, many wireless cards supported in Linux cannot operate as access points. A Linux wireless card, however, can operate as a node in a managed network. The wireless-configuration tools that come with Fedora let you identify the access point for Linux to use by indicating the access point's MAC address.

Choosing equipment

Start with two computers. (You can add more computers later, once you understand how to get your wireless interfaces working.) For this procedure, I used computers that had the following characteristics (you can use different computers and cards, if you like):

- **Computers** — One computer was a laptop with an available PCMCIA slot; the other was a desktop system with only PCI slots.

- **Wireless cards** — As I mentioned earlier, I purchased two Proxim (Lucent Technologies) Orinoco wireless LAN cards: one Gold Label and one Silver Label. For the desktop computer, I purchased a PCI adapter card because it had no PCMCIA slot. Both cards come with built-in antennas, so I had no need for additional antennas while setting up the two computers (in the same room) for wireless communication.

> **NOTE:** The only difference between the Gold and Silver Label cards is that the Gold card offers support for more secure encryption, so there was no reason for me to choose two different types of cards. If I had it to do over again, I would have used two Silver cards and saved a few dollars.

- **Fedora** — I installed Fedora on both machines, selecting a personal desktop install for the laptop and an Everything install for the desktop computer. (The Everything install was not strictly necessary, but I wanted to be able to use the GUI and various server features.)

Because I was using the desktop computer as a gateway to the Internet, that computer also had a wired Ethernet card that was connected to my DSL modem to provide a route to the Internet for any computers on my wired or wireless networks.

Inserting wireless cards

To physically install the wireless cards, follow the directions that come with the cards. For my laptop, I simply inserted one Orinoco card into a PCMCIA slot. For the desktop computer, I powered down, inserted the PCI adapter into a vacant slot, powered up, and inserted the other Orinoco PCMCIA card into the adapter.

Loading the modules

The cardmgr daemon monitors the PCMCIA slots on computers that have them. If a card is recognized and listed in the PCMCIA database when the card is inserted, the appropriate module is loaded. You should also hear two beeps indicating that the card has been recognized.

On my laptop, my Orinoco wireless card was recognized and its modules loaded. On my desktop computer (with the PCI adapter), the card was not recognized, so I had to do some extra configuration.

PCMCIA only

To see what modules are loaded after a card is inserted on a computer that has only PCMCIA slots, type the **lsmod** command (as root user). In my case, because the Orinoco card uses the orinoco and orinoco_cs modules (along with the hermes helper module), output from the lsmod command included the following lines:

```
# lsmod
Module              Size Used by
orinoco_cs          5640 1
orinoco            34368 0  [orinoco_cs]
hermes              5344 0  [orinoco_cs orinoco]
ds                  8608 1  [orinoco_cs]
yenta_socket       12384 1
pcmcia_core        50752 0  [orinoco_cs ds yenta_socket]
```

You can see that the orinoco_cs module was loaded and that the referring modules included the orinoco module, the hermes module, the ds (PC Card Driver Services) module, and the pcmcia_core module. If you are using a different card, you may instead see one of the following modules: airo_cs, wavelan_cs, wvlan_cs, ray_cs, or netwave_cs.

PCMCIA with adapter card

If your computer has only ISA or PCI slots, you will need an adapter to use your PCMCIA wireless LAN card. Fedora detected my adapter card and added the following lines to the /etc/sysconfig/pcmcia file so that the PCI adapter card would be recognized and the PCMCIA service would start automatically at boot time:

```
PCMCIA=yes
PCIC=yenta_socket
```

The yenta_socket driver is a PCMCIA controller driver that includes the Yenta register specification. Yenta is used for CardBus bridges made by Cirrus Logic for a variety of manufacturers (Texas Instruments, IBM, Toshiba, and others). The Orinoco PCI adapter was detected as a device using the yenta_socket driver.

Figure 15-10 shows an example of an Orinoco Silver Card using a PCI adapter.

Figure 15-10: The Orinoco Silver wireless LAN card can be used with a PCI adapter (shown here).

Checking that the cards are working

If the modules have been loaded properly, the cardmgr should recognize each card and start up the Ethernet interface for it. To check that this has happened, restart the interface as follows:

```
# /etc/init.d/pcmcia restart
Shutting down PCMCIA services: cardmgr modules.
Starting PCMCIA services: modules cardmgr.
```

You should hear a single beep when the card service stops, then two beeps when the adapter and wireless card are properly detected. Check the /var/log/messages file. You should see some messages at or near the end of this file, describing what happened when the PCMCIA interface was shut down and restarted. If the card is detected, you should see modules loaded successfully and a network interface started for the wireless card. Here are some examples:

```
Feb  9 17:26:33 toys kernel: Linux Kernel Card Services 3.1.22
Feb  9 17:26:33 toys kernel:  options:  [pci] [cardbus] [pm]
Feb  9 17:26:33 toys kernel: PCI: Found IRQ 5 for device 01:09.0
Feb  9 17:26:33 toys kernel: PCI: Sharing IRQ 5 with 00:1f.3
Feb  9 17:26:33 toys kernel: Yenta IRQ list 0000, PCI irq5
Feb  9 17:26:33 toys kernel: Socket status: 10000011
Feb  9 17:26:34 toys cardmgr[2571]: starting, version is 3.1.31
      .
      .
      .
Feb  9 17:26:34 toys kernel: cs: IO port probe 0x0c00-0x0cff: clean.
Feb  9 17:26:34 toys kernel: cs: IO port probe 0x0100-0x04ff: excluding
0x400-0x47f 0x4d0-0x4d7
Feb  9 17:26:34 toys kernel: cs: IO port probe 0x0a00-0x0aff: clean.
Feb  9 17:26:34 toys kernel: cs: memory probe 0xa0000000-0xa0ffffff:
clean.
Feb  9 17:26:34 toys cardmgr[2571]: socket 0: Lucent Technologies
WaveLAN/IEEE Adapter
Feb  9 17:26:34 toys cardmgr[2571]: executing: 'modprobe hermes'
Feb  9 17:26:34 toys cardmgr[2571]: executing: 'modprobe orinoco'
Feb  9 17:26:34 toys cardmgr[2571]: executing: 'modprobe orinoco_cs'
Feb  9 17:26:34 toys cardmgr[2571]: executing: './network start eth1'
Feb  9 17:26:34 toys /etc/hotplug/net.agent: invoke ifup eth1
```

The preceding code shows that the kernel recognizes the PCI card (at IRQ 5). The cardmgr identifies the Orinoco card as a WaveLAN/IEEE adapter in socket 0. The network script starts an Ethernet interface (eth1).

If the wireless LAN interface started properly, you should be able to see the new interface by using the iwconfig command. The following is an example of output from the iwconfig command:

```
eth1   IEEE 802.11-DS  ESSID:""  Nickname:"HERMES I"
       Mode:Managed  Frequency:2.457GHz  Access Point: 00:00:00:00:00:00
       Bit Rate:11Mb/s   Tx-Power=15 dBm   Sensitivity:1/3
       Retry limit:4   RTS thr:off   Fragment thr:off
       Encryption key:off
       Power Management:off
```

If your wireless LAN interface does not appear to be working, refer to the section "Troubleshooting a wireless LAN" later in this chapter. If the interface does seem to be working, you are ready to tune your wireless LAN card interface and set up TCP/IP to be able to use the interface.

Configuring the wireless interface

The Network Configuration window (neat command) can be used to configure wireless Ethernet card interfaces, as well as regular wired Ethernet cards. The following procedure describes how to configure a wireless Ethernet card using the Network Configuration window.

1. Start the Network Configuration. From the red hat menu, click System Settings → Network, or, as root user from a Terminal window, type **neat**. The Network Configuration window appears.

2. Click the New button. The Select Device Type window appears.

3. Click Wireless connection and Forward. The Select Wireless Device window appears.

4. Select your wireless card from the list of cards shown, and click Forward. The Configure Wireless Connection window appears, as shown in Figure 15-11.

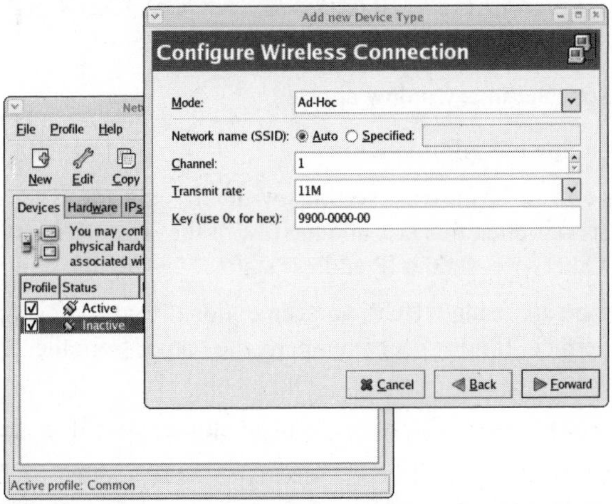

Figure 15-11: Add a wireless interface using the Network Configuration window.

5. Add the following information and click Forward:

   • **Mode** — Indicates the mode of operation for the wireless LAN card. Because I am setting up a wireless LAN consisting of only one cell (in other words, with no roaming to cells set up in other areas), I could set the mode to Ad hoc. Ad hoc mode allows the card to communicate directly with each of its peers. You can use Managed mode if you have multiple cells, requiring your card to communicate directly to an access point. You can also use Managed mode for a point-to-point network, such as when you use the wireless LAN to extend a network from one building to another.

- **Network Name (SSID)** — The network name (or Network ID) that identifies cells that are part of the same network. If you have a group of cells (which might include multiple nodes and repeaters among which a client could roam), this name can identify all of those cells as falling under one virtual network. Choose any name you like and then use that name for all computers in your virtual network. (SSID stands for Service Set ID.)

- **Channel** — Choose a channel between 1 and 14. You can begin with channel 1; if you get interference on that channel, try changing to other channels.

- **Transmit Rate** — Choose the rate of transmission from the following rates: 11M, 5.5M, 2M, 1M, or Auto. Choosing Auto allows the interface to automatically ramp down to lower speeds as needed. Lower speeds allow the interface to transmit over greater distances and deal with noisy channels.

- **Key** — You need the same encryption key for all wireless LAN cards that are communicating with each other. It is critical to get this value right. This key is used to encrypt all data transmitted and decrypt all data received on the wireless interface. You can enter the number (up to 10 digits) as XXXXXXXXXX or XXXX-XXXX-XX (where each X is a number), for example, 1234-5678-90.

A Configure Network Settings window appears.

6. You can enter the following information:

- **Automatically obtain IP address settings with:** If you want to get your IP address from a DHCP server, click this box and the rest of the information is obtained automatically. Otherwise, set the IP address statically using the other options.

- **Host name:** If you are using DHCP, you can optionally add a host name to identify this network interface. If none is entered here, the output from the /bin/hostname command is used.

- **Statically set IP addresses:** Click here to manually set your IP addresses.

- **Address:** If you selected static IP addresses, type the IP address of this computer into the Address box. This number must be unique on your wireless network.

- **Subnet Mask:** Enter the netmask to indicate what part of the IP address represents the network. (Netmask is described later in this chapter.)

- **Default Gateway Address:** If a computer on your wireless LAN is providing routing to the Internet or other network, type the IP address of the computer here.

7. Click Forward to see a listing of the information you just entered.

8. Click Apply to complete the new wireless network interface.

9. Click File → Save (on the main window) to save the interface.

This procedure creates an interface configuration file in your /etc/sysconfig/network-scripts directory. The name of the configuration file is ifcfg- followed by the interface name (such as eth0, eth1, and so on). So, if your wireless card is providing your only network interface, it would be called ifcfg-eth0.

Using any text editor, open the ifcfg-eth? file as root user. The following is an example of an ifcfg-eth1 file:

```
# Please read /usr/share/doc/initscripts-*/sysconfig.txt
# for the documentation of these parameters.
USERCTL=no
PEERDNS=no
GATEWAY=10.0.0.1
TYPE=Wireless
DEVICE=eth1
HWADDR=00:02:2d:2e:8c:a8
BOOTPROTO=none
NETMASK=255.255.255.0
ONBOOT=no
IPADDR=10.0.1.1
NAME=
DOMAIN=
ESSID=
CHANNEL=1
MODE=Ad-Hoc
KEY=9900-0000-00
RATE=11Mb/s
NETWORK=10.0.1.0
BROADCAST=10.0.1.255
```

In this example, the wireless card's hardware (MAC) address is automatically set to 00:02:2d:2e:8c:a8. (Your MAC address will be different.) The interface is not yet set to come up at boot time (ONBOOT=no). The interface device is eth1 (which matches the interface filename ifcfg-eth1), because this particular computer has another Ethernet card on the eth0 interface. The interface type is set to Wireless.

Other information in the file sets standard TCP/IP address information. The NETMASK is set to 255.255.255.0 and the IP address for the card is set to 10.0.1.1. The broadcast address is 10.0.1.255.

You can also set many options that are specific to your wireless network in this file. The following list explains some additional options that you might want to set:

- **NWID** — Identifies the name of this particular computer on the network. The computer's host name (determined from the uname -n command) is used by default if you don't set it with NWID.

- **FREQ** — You can choose a particular frequency in which to transmit. No value is required, because selecting a channel implies a certain frequency. If you do enter a frequency, the value must be a number followed by a k (kilohertz), M (megahertz), or G (gigahertz). The default values for the channels you select range from 2.412G (channel 1) to 2.484G (channel 14), with other channels occurring at increments of .005G. The default is 2.422G.

- **SENS** —You can select the sensitivity level of the access point. SENS can be set to 1 (low density), 2 (medium density), 3 (high density). The default is 1. The sensitivity threshold has an impact on roaming.

> **CAUTION:** The encryption algorithm used with 802.11 networks is the Wired Equivalent Privacy (WEP) algorithm. Though using the encryption key is more secure than not using it, some experts feel that WEP has some inherent flaws that might allow a drive-by hacker to decrypt your wireless LAN traffic. For that reason, I strongly recommend using additional techniques to protect your wireless LANs, such as firewalls and diligent log-checking. See the "Wireless Security" sidebar for further information.

Besides those options just shown, you can also pass any valid options to the iwconfig command (which actually interprets these values), by adding an IWCONFIG option to the configuration file. Display the iwconfig man page (man iwconfig) to see all wireless options. Also view the /etc/sysconfig/network-scripts/ifup-wireless script to see how the options you just added are processed.

> **NOTE:** On the computer that is acting as a gateway from your wireless network to the Internet, you need to turn on IP packet forwarding. Change the value of net.ipv4.ip_forward to 1 in /etc/sysctl.conf. Open that file as the root user with a text editor and change the line as follows:
>
> ```
> net.ipv4.ip_forward = 1
> ```

Repeat this procedure for each wireless Fedora computer on your LAN. At this point, your wireless network should be ready to go. Restart your network, as described in the following steps, to make sure that it is working.

Activating the wireless interfaces

To immediately activate the wireless interface you just configured, select the Wireless entry on the Network Configuration window and click the Activate button. After a few seconds, the Status should appear as Active.

To have the interface start when you reboot your computer, click the wireless interface from the Network Configuration window and select Edit. From the Wireless Device Configuration window that appears, click the box next to "Activate device when computer starts."

If you want to explicitly enter a Network Name (SSID), click the Wireless Settings tab on the Wireless Device Configuration window. From there, select Specified, type the network name (any name you choose to match others on your wireless network), and click OK.

Be sure to save your changes on the Network Configuration window by clicking File → Save.

Checking your wireless connection

Your wireless LAN interface should be operating at this point. If another wireless computer is available on your wireless network, try communicating with it using the ping command and its IP address (as described in the "Can you reach another computer on the LAN?" section later in this chapter).

If you are not able to communicate with other wireless nodes or if transmission is slow, you may have more work to do. For example, if you see messages that say "Destination Host Unreachable," instead of the output shown earlier, refer to the section on "Troubleshooting a wireless LAN" for help. If you want to fine-tune your wireless interface, refer to the "Manually configuring wireless cards" section later in this chapter.

Wireless Security

The Wireless Ethernet Compatibility Alliance (WECA) has recommended changes in response to security concerns about wireless networks. They did this because, unlike wired networks, which can often be physically protected within a building, wireless networks often extend beyond physical boundaries that can be protected.

The Wireless Equivalent Privacy (WEP) standard adds encryption to the 802.11 wireless standard. WECA refers to WEP as its way of providing "walls" that make wireless Ethernet as secure as wired Ethernet. However, you need to implement WEP, as well as other security methods that would apply to any computer network, in order to make your wireless network secure. Here are WECA's suggestions:

- Change the default WEP encryption key on a regular basis (possibly weekly or even daily). This prevents casual drive-by hackers from reading your encrypted transmissions.

- Use password protection on your drives and folders.

- Change the default Network Name (SSID).

- Use session keys, if available in your product (session keys are not supported in current Linux wireless drivers).

- Use MAC address filtering (supported in a limited way in Linux).

- Use a VPN (Virtual Private Network) system, which can add another layer of encryption beyond that which is available on your wireless network.

For larger organizations requiring greater security, WECA suggests such features as firewalls and user-verification schemes (such as Kerberos). As I mentioned earlier in this chapter, features for protecting from intrusions and restricting services are already built into Fedora. Refer to the descriptions of security tools in Chapters 14, 15, and 16 for methods of securing your network, its computers, and their services. In particular, you could consider adding a VPN such as CIPE (described in Chapter 16) to further secure all data sent on your wireless LAN.

Testing out distances

Although you may be thrilled to have a wireless LAN working between two computers, you will probably want these computers to be located some distance from each other to make the LAN useful. Getting your wireless LAN to work at the desired distances can be quite a challenge. See the section "Selecting antennas" earlier in this chapter for suggestions on selecting and using antennas to configure the type of wireless LAN you are interested in.

Setting wireless extensions

After the wireless module is loaded, you can change wireless extensions using the iwconfig command. The iwconfig command is the command that is actually used to set the options added to the ifcfg configuration script (for example, for the eth1 interface, the script would be /etc/sysconfig/network-scripts/eth1).

Some of the same options that you set when the module was loaded can be reset using the iwconfig command. The iwconfig command can be useful for testing different settings on an active wireless LAN. The syntax of the iwconfig command is as follows:

```
# iwconfig interface parameter value
```

The *interface* is the name of the wireless interface you want to change, such as eth1 or wvlan0. The *parameter* is the name of the option, and the *value* is replaced by its value. For example, to set your network name (ESSID) to Homelan, you could type the following as root user:

```
# iwconfig eth0 essid "Homelan"
```

Table 15-2 contains a list of available options for the iwconfig command. Refer to the "Configuring the Wireless Interface" section for further details on these options.

Table 15-2: Options for the iwconfig Command

Option	Description
essid *name*	Indicates the network name.
ap *address*	Indicates that the access point is at a particular MAC address. For low-quality connections, the client driver may return to trying to automatically detect the access point. This setting is only useful in Managed mode.
channel #	Picks the channel number to operate on.
frag *frag_size*	Sets the fragmentation threshold for splitting up packets before they are transmitted.
freq 2.4??G	Sets the frequency of the channel to communicate on.
key *xxxx-xxxx-xx*	Sets the key used for WEP encryption.

Option	*Description*
`mode` *option*	Sets the mode used for communications to Ad-hoc, Managed, Master, Repeater, Secondary, or Auto.
`nick` *name*	Sets the station name to define this particular computer.
`rate` *XX*M	Defines the transmission rate to use.
`rts` *number*	Sets the RTS/CTS threshold for packet transmission.
`retry` *number*	For cards that support MAC retransmissions, you can use this option to determine how many retries are made before the transmission fails. The value can be a number (indicating number of seconds allotted for retries), or a number followed by an `m` (for milliseconds) or `u` (for microseconds). Instead of a number, you can set a number of retries using the limit parameter. For example: `retry limit 100` indicates that the transmission can retry up to 100 times.
`sens` number	Sets the lowest possible sensitivity threshold for which the wireless interface will try to receive a packet. Raising this level can help block out interference from other wireless LANs that might weakly encroach on your transmission area.

The best place to add `iwconfig` options permanently in Fedora is the configuration file for your wireless interface in the `/etc/sysconfig/network-scripts` directory.

Options to `iwconfig` are added to the wireless interface file (such as `ifcfg-eth0` or `ifcfg-eth1`) using the `IWCONFIG` parameter. For example, to add an encryption-key value of 1234-1234-12 for your wireless LAN card, you could add the following line to your wireless-interface file:

```
IWCONFIG="key 1234-1234-12"
```

Understanding IP Addresses

Whether you are using a wired or a wireless network, each computer you communicate with (including yours) must have a unique address on the network. In TCP/IP, each computer must be assigned an IP address. This section gives you some background in IP addresses.

There are two basic ways to assign a host name and IP address to a network interface in Linux:

- **Static addresses** — With static IP addresses, each computer has an IP address that doesn't change each time the computer reboots or restarts its network interface. Its IP address can be entered manually, since it's not assigned on the fly. You can do this at Fedora installation time, or later using the Network Configuration window.

- **Dynamic addresses** — With dynamic addresses, a client computer gets its IP address assigned from a server on the network when the client boots. The most popular protocol for providing dynamic addresses is called Dynamic Host Configuration Protocol (DHCP). With this method, a client computer may not have the same IP address each time it boots.

> **TIP:** If you expect to add and remove computers regularly from your LAN or if you have a limited number of IP addresses, you should use DHCP to assign IP addresses. Chapter 23 describes how to set up a DHCP server.

An IP address is a four-part number, with each part represented by a number from 0 to 255 (256 numbers total). Part of that IP address represents the network the computer exists on, while the remainder identifies the specific host on that network. Here is an example of an IP address:

```
192.168.35.121
```

Originally, IP addresses were grouped together and assigned to an organization that needed IP addresses, based on IP address classes. These days, a more efficient method, referred to as Classless Inter-Domain Routing (CIDR), is used to improve routing and waste fewer IP addresses. These two IP address methods are described in the following sections.

IP address classes

Unfortunately, it's not so easy to understand which part of an IP address represents the network and which represents the host without explaining how IP addresses are structured. IP addresses are assigned in the following manner. A network administrator is given a pool of addresses. The administrator can then assign specific host addresses within that pool as new computers are added to the organization's local network. There were originally three basic classes of IP addresses, each representing a different size network.

- **Class A** — Each Class A address has a number between 0 and 127 as its first part. Host numbers within a Class A network are represented by any combination of numbers in the next three parts. A Class A network therefore contains millions of host numbers (approximately 256 x 256 x 256, with a few special numbers being invalid). A valid Class A network number is:

```
24.
```

- **Class B** — A Class B IP address has a number between 128 and 191 in its first part. With a Class B network, however, the second part also represents the network. This enables a Class B network to have more than 64,000 host addresses (256 x 256). A valid Class B network number is:

```
135.84
```

- **Class C** — A Class C IP address begins with a number between 192 and 223 in its first part. With a Class C network, the first three parts of an IP address represent the network, while only the last part represents a specific host. Thus, each Class C network can have 254 numbers (the numbers 0 and 254 can't be assigned to hosts). Here is an example of a Class C network number:

```
194.122.56
```

To tell your computer which part of a network address is the network and which is the host, you must enter a number that masks the network number. That number is referred to as the netmask.

Understanding netmasks

Suppose you are assigned the Class B address 135.84, but you are only given the pool of numbers available to the address 135.84.118. How do you tell your network that every address beginning with 135.84.118 represents a host on your network, but that other addresses beginning with 135.84 should be routed to another network? You can do it with a netmask.

The netmask essentially identifies the network number for a network. When you assign the IP address that is associated with your computer's interface to the LAN (eth0), you are asked for a netmask. By default, your computer fills in a number that masks the part of your IP address that represents the class of your network. For example, the default netmasks for Class A, B, and C networks are the following:

- Class A netmask: 255.0.0.0
- Class B netmask: 255.255.0.0
- Class C netmask: 255.255.255.0

Now, if your network was assigned the network number 135.84.118, to tell your computer that 135.84.118 is the network number and not 135.84 (as it normally would be for a Class B address), add a netmask of 255.255.255.0. So you could use host numbers from 1 to 254 (which would go into the fourth part of the number).

To further confuse the issue, you could mask only one or more bits that are part of the IP address. Instead of using the number 255, you could use any other number from 1 to 254 to mask only part of the numbers in that part of the address. (The numbers that you can use for each network get rather strange when you do this.)

Classless Inter-Domain Routing

The class method of allocating IP addresses had several major drawbacks. First, few organizations fell neatly into one class or another. For most organizations, a Class C address (up to 256 IP addresses) was too small, and a Class B address (up to 65,534 IP addresses) was too big. The result was a lot of wasted numbers in a world where IP addresses were running short. Second, IP classes resulted in too many routing table entries. As a result, routers were becoming overloaded with information.

The Classless Inter-Domain Routing addressing scheme set out to deal with these problems. The scheme is similar to IP address classes, but offers much more flexibility in assigning how much of the 32-bit IP address is the network identifier. Instead of the first 8, 16, or 32 bits identifying the network, 13 to 27 bits could identify the network. As a result, groups of assigned IP addresses could contain from 32 to about 524,000 host addresses.

To indicate the network identifier, a CIDR IP address is followed by a slash (/) and then a number from 13 to 27. A smaller number indicates a network containing more hosts. Here is an example of an IP address that uses the CIDR notation:

```
128.8.27.18/16
```

In this example, the first 16 bits (128.8) represent the network number, and the remainder (27.18) represents the specific host number. This network number can contain up to 65,536 hosts (the same as a class B address). The following list shows how many hosts can be represented in networks using different numbers to identify the network:

```
/13       524,288 hosts
/14       262,144 hosts
/15       131,072 hosts
/16        65,536 hosts
/17        32,768 hosts
/18        16,382 hosts
/19         8,192 hosts
/20         4,096 hosts
/21         2,048 hosts
/22         1,024 hosts
/23           512 hosts
/24           256 hosts
/25           128 hosts
/26            64 hosts
/27            32 hosts
```

The CIDR addressing scheme also helps reduce the routing overload problem by having a single, high-level route represent many lower-level routes. For example, an Internet Service Provider could be assigned a single /13 IP network and assign the 500,000-plus addresses to its customers. Routers outside the ISP would only need to know how to reach the ISP for those half-million addresses. The ISP would then be responsible for maintaining routing information for all of the host routes with that network address.

Getting IP addresses

So, what is the impact of assigning IP addresses for the computers on your LAN? How you choose which IP addresses to use depends on your situation. If you are part of a large organization, you should get addresses from your network administrator. Even if you don't connect to other LANs in your organization at the moment, having unique addresses can make it easier to connect to them in the future.

If you are setting up a network for yourself (with no other networks to consider in your organization), you can use private addresses. However, if you need to connect computers to the Internet as servers, apply for your own domain name (from an Internet domain registrar) and IP addresses (from your Internet Service Provider).

> **CROSS-REFERENCE:** Refer to Chapter 25 for information about getting the IP addresses and domain names you need to configure a public server on the Internet.

If you don't need to have your LAN accessible from the Internet, choose IP addresses from the set of available general-purpose IP addresses. Using these private IP addresses, you can still access the Internet from your LAN for such things as Web browsing and e-mail by using IP masquerading or Network Address Translation (NAT), as described in Chapter 16. Table 15-3 lists the private IP addresses not used on any public part of the Internet.

Table 15-3: Private IP Addresses

Network Class	Network Numbers	Addresses per Network Number
Class A	10.0.0.0	167,777,216
Class B	172.16.0.0 to 172.31.0.0	65,536
Class C	192.168.0.0 to 192.168.255.255	256

So, for a small private LAN, the following numbers are examples of IP addresses that could be assigned to the host computers on your network. (You could use any of the network numbers, plus host numbers, from the table. These are just examples.)

- 192.168.1.1
- 192.168.1.2
- 192.168.1.3
- 192.168.1.4
- 192.168.1.5

You could continue that numbering up to 192.168.1.254 on this network, and you could use a network mask of 255.255.255.0.

Troubleshooting Your LAN

After your LAN has been set up, your Ethernet cards installed, and host names and addresses added, there are several methods you can use to check that everything is up and working. Some troubleshooting techniques are shown in the following sections.

Did Linux find your Ethernet driver at boot time?

Type the following right after you boot your computer to verify whether Linux found your card and installed the Ethernet interface properly:

```
dmesg | grep eth
```

The dmesg command lists all the messages that were output by Linux at boot time. The grep eth command causes only those lines that contain the word *eth* to be printed. The first message shown below appeared on my laptop computer with the Netgear card. The second example is from my computer with the EtherExpress Pro/100 card:

```
eth0: NE2000 Compatible: port 0x300, irq3, hw_addr 00:80:C8:8C:8E:49
eth0: OEM i82557/i82558 10/100 Ethernet at 0xccc0, 00:90:27:4E:67:35, IRQ 17.
```

The message in the first example shows that a card was found at IRQ3 with a port address of 0x300 and an Ethernet hardware address of 00:80:C8:8C:8E:49. In the second example, the card is at IRQ 17, the port address is 0xccc0, and the Ethernet address is 00:90:27:4E:67:35.

> **NOTE:** If the eth0 interface is not found, but you know that you have a supported Ethernet card, check that your Ethernet card is properly seated in its slot.

Can you reach another computer on the LAN?

Try communicating with another computer on the LAN. The ping command can be used to send a packet to another computer and to ask for a packet in return. You could give ping either a host name (pine) or an IP address (10.0.0.10). For example, to ping a computer on the network called pine, type the following command:

```
# ping pine
```

If the computer can be reached, the output will look similar to the following:

```
PING pine (10.0.0.10): 56(84) data bytes
64 bytes from pine (10.0.0.10): icmp_seq=1 ttl=255 time=0.351 ms
64 bytes from pine (10.0.0.10): icmp_seq=2 ttl=255 time=0.445 ms
64 bytes from pine (10.0.0.10): icmp_seq=3 ttl=255 time=0.409 ms
64 bytes from pine (10.0.0.10): icmp_seq=4 ttl=255 time=0.457 ms
64 bytes from pine (10.0.0.10): icmp_seq=5 ttl=255 time=0.401 ms
64 bytes from pine (10.0.0.10): icmp_seq=6 ttl=255 time=0.405 ms
64 bytes from pine (10.0.0.10): icmp_seq=7 ttl=255 time=0.443 ms
64 bytes from pine (10.0.0.10): icmp_seq=8 ttl=255 time=0.384 ms
64 bytes from pine (10.0.0.10): icmp_seq=9 ttl=255 time=0.365 ms
64 bytes from pine (10.0.0.10): icmp_seq=10 ttl=255 time=0.367 ms

--- pine ping statistics ---
10 packets transmitted, 10 packets received, 0% packet loss, time 9011ms
rtt min/avg/max/mdev = 0.351/0.402/0.457/0.042 ms
```

A line of output is printed each time a packet is sent and received in return. It shows how much data was sent and how long it took for each package to be received. After you have watched this for a while, type Ctrl+C to stop ping. At that point, you will see statistics on how many packets were transmitted, received, and lost.

If you don't see output that shows packets have been received, it means you are not contacting the other computer. Try to verify that the names and addresses of the computers that you want to reach are in your `/etc/hosts` file or that your DNS server is accessible. Next, confirm that the names and IP addresses you have for the other computers you are trying to reach are correct (the IP addresses are the most critical).

Is your Ethernet connection up?

Using the `ifconfig` command, you can determine whether your Ethernet (and other network interfaces) are up and running. Type the following command:

```
# ifconfig
```

The output that appears is similar to the following:

```
eth0 Link encap:Ethernet HWaddr 00:90:27:4E:67:35
     inet addr:10.0.0.10 Bcast:10.0.0.255 Mask:255.255.255.0
     UP BROADCAST RUNNING MULTICAST MTU:1500 Metric:1
     RX packets:156 errors:0 dropped:0 overruns:0 frame:0
     TX packets:104 errors:0 dropped:0 overruns:0 carrier:0
     collisions:0 txqueuelen:100
     RX bytes:20179 (19.7 Kb)   TX bytes:19960 (19.4 Kb)
     Interrupt:11 Base address:0xe000 Memory:ff8ff000-ff8ff038

lo   Link encap:Local Loopback
     inet addr:127.0.0.1 Mask:255.0.0.0
     UP LOOPBACK RUNNING MTU:3924 Metric:1
     RX packets:56 errors:0 dropped:0 overruns:0 frame:0
     TX packets:56 errors:0 dropped:0 overruns:0 carrier:0
     collisions:0 txqueuelen:0
     RX bytes:3148 (3.0 Kb)  TX bytes:3148 (3.0Kb)
```

In this example, two network interfaces are up on the current computer. The first section shows your Ethernet interface (`eth0`), and its Ethernet hardware address, IP address (`inet addr`), broadcast address, and network mask. The next lines provide information on packets that have been sent, along with the number of errors and collisions that have occurred.

> **NOTE:** The `lo` entry is for loopback. This enables you to run TCP/IP commands on your local system without having a physical network up and running.

If your `eth0` interface does not appear, it may still be configured properly, but not running at the moment. Try to start the `eth0` interface by typing the following:

```
# ifconfig eth0 up
```

After this, type **ifconfig** again to see if eth0 is now running. If it is, it may be that eth0 is simply not configured to start automatically at boot time. You can change it so Ethernet starts at boot time (which I recommend), using the Network Configuration window described earlier in this chapter.

> **TIP:** If your network interfaces are not running at all, you can try to start them from the network initialization script. This interface reads parameters and basically runs ifconfig for all network interfaces on your computer. Type the following to restart your network:
>
> # /etc/init.d/network restart

Another way to see statistics for your Ethernet driver is to list the contents of the process pseudo file system for network devices. To do that, type the following:

```
# cat /proc/net/dev
```

The output should look like this:

```
Inter-|  Receive                                                |Transmit
face  |bytes packets errs drop fifo frame compressed multicast|bytes
    lo: 5362    64  0   0    0     0      0    5362      64  0   0    0
  sit0:    0     0  0   0    0     0      0       0       0  0   0    0
  eth0: 3083    35  0   0    0     0      0    3876      31  0   0    0
```

The output is a bit hard to read (this book isn't wide enough to show it without wrapping around, so the output was truncated at the right). With this output, you can see Receive and Transmit statistics for each interface. This output also shows you how many Receive and Transmit errors occurred in communication. (Transmit information is cut off in this example.)

For a more detailed look at your network, you can use the Ethereal window. Ethereal is described in the "Watching LAN traffic with Ethereal" section later in this chapter.

> **NOTE:** The sit0 network interface (which stands for Simple Internet Transition) can be used to encapsulate IPv6 packets into an IPv4 network. This allows IPv6 network communications to be routed across IPv4 networks. You would only use this interface if you have IPv6 networking enabled.

Troubleshooting a wireless LAN

If you set up your two (or more) wireless LAN cards to enable Fedora systems to communicate, and they are not communicating, you can troubleshoot the problem in several different ways.

Checking wireless settings

You can use the `iwlist` and `iwconfig` commands to check your wireless settings. The `iwconfig` command provides a quick overview of your wireless settings, while the `iwlist` command shows you information about parameters that you specify.

Use the `iwconfig` command, along with the name of the wireless LAN interface, to see information about that interface. For example, if the wireless interface were `eth1`, you could type the following:

```
# iwconfig eth1
eth0     IEEE 802.11-DS  ESSID:"Homelan"  Nickname:"pine"
         Mode:Ad-Hoc  Frequency:2.412GHz  Cell: 02:02:2D:2D:3B:30
         Bit Rate=11Mb/s   Tx-Power=15 dBm   Sensitivity:1/3
         RTS thr:off   Fragment thr:off
         Encryption key:7365-6375-31
         Power Management:off
         Link Quality:0/92  Signal level:-102 dBm  Noise level:-102 dBm
         Rx invalid nwid:0  invalid crypt:0  invalid misc:0
```

With `iwconfig`, you can see details about the wireless aspects of the Ethernet interface. In this example, the network name (`ESSID`) is `Homelan`, and the station name (`Nickname`) is `pine`. The interface is operating in Ad hoc mode on channel 1 (frequency of 2.412 GHz). Transmission rates are at the maximum speed of 11 Mbps. The encryption key that must be used by every node the card connects with is `7365-6375-31`. Other settings describe the link and signal quality.

The `iwlist` command lets you request specific information about the wireless LAN interface. The syntax is to follow the `iwlist` command with the interface name and the information you are interested in. For example:

```
# iwlist eth0 freq
eth 0     14 channels in total; available frequencies :
          Channel 01 : 2.412 GHz
          Channel 02 : 2.417 GHz
          Channel 03 : 2.422 GHz
          Channel 04 : 2.427 GHz
          Channel 05 : 2.432 GHz
          Channel 06 : 2.437 GHz
          Channel 07 : 2.442 GHz
          Channel 08 : 2.447 GHz
          Channel 09 : 2.452 GHz
          Channel 10 : 2.457 GHz
          Channel 11 : 2.462 GHz
```

The `freq` parameter displays the available frequencies (and channels) available for communication. Note that all the available frequencies are in the 2.4 GHz range.

```
# iwlist eth0 rate
```

```
eth0        4 available bit-rates :
            1 Mb/s
            2 Mb/s
            5.5 Mb/s
            11 Mb/s
```

The preceding `rate` parameter displays the transmission rates available for the wireless interface. You can see that 1, 2, 5.5, and 11 Mbps rates are available for the current interface.

```
# iwlist eth0 keys
eth0        2 key sizes : 40, 104bits
            4 keys available :
                    [1] 7365-6375-31 (40 bits)
                    [2] off
                    [3] off
                    [4] off
            Current Transmit Key: [1]
```

The `keys` parameter lets you see the encryption keys available with the interface. It also shows the key sizes currently available. Because the card reflected in the preceding example supports 64- and 128-bit encryption, the key sizes available are 40 and 104 bits. (The encryption algorithm automatically generates the last 24 bits of each key.)

If you are troubleshooting your wireless LAN connection, some settings are more likely than others to cause problems. It is important to set the following wireless LAN settings properly — if you don't, they may keep your network from working:

- **Network ID (ESSID)** — You may not be able to communicate among peer computers if the Network ID (ESSID) doesn't match on each of them. Network IDs are case sensitive — for example, Mylan is not the same as MyLAN.

- **Encryption key** — Having encryption keys that don't match is like trying to log in to Linux with the wrong password. Check that all nodes are using the same key.

- **Mode** — If you are communicating through an access point, your mode should be set to Managed and you must provide the MAC address for that access point. In most single-cell networks, you should set all nodes to Ad hoc. The Ad hoc mode allows all nodes to communicate directly to each other as peers.

- **Channel or frequency** — The channel and frequency options are just two different means of setting the same value. For example, setting the channel to 1 is the same as setting the frequency to 2.412G (GHz). Make sure that the nodes on your network are able to communicate on the same frequency.

Checking TCP/IP

To ensure that your wireless LAN is communicating with its peers, use the `ping` command (as described earlier in this chapter). If you believe that your cards are working properly, but the `ping` command continues to give you a Network Unreachable message, you may have a problem with your TCP/IP configuration. Here are some items you can check from the Network Configuration window:

- **IP address** — Know the correct IP address of the peer you are trying to reach.

- **Host name** — If you ping the peer computer by name, make sure that your computer can properly resolve that name into the correct IP address, or have the peer's host name and IP address properly listed in the /etc/hosts file locally. The former option will probably require that you have one or more DNS servers identified to resolve the name.

If you can reach another computer on the wireless LAN, but not computers outside of that LAN (such as Internet addresses), check that you have properly identified the location of your gateway. If the gateway address is correct, and you can reach that gateway, it may be that the gateway itself is not configured to allow packet forwarding.

If you found that any of the preceding information needed to be changed and you changed it, you should restart the wireless LAN interface. One way to do that is to restart the PCMCIA interface and the network interfaces as follows:

```
# /etc/init.d/pcmcia restart
# /etc/init.d/network restart
```

Adapting to poor reception

Your wireless LAN might be working fine while your two wireless computers are sitting on the same desk. But if performance degrades when you separate the computers, you may need to identify any potential obstructions. Then you must decide how to get around them. For desktop systems, a small indoor antenna can bring the signal out from under a desk or out of a closet. For adjacent buildings, a roof antenna might be the answer.

In cities or other congested areas, many people and pieces of equipment can be competing for the 2.4 GHz range. You may want to move a microwave oven or high-end remote phone that may be interfering with your wireless LAN. These settings might help adapt to poor reception:

- **Reduce transmission rate** — Instead of using 11 Mbps, you can explicitly ramp down to 5.5, 2, or 1 Mbps. Slower rates can mean more efficient operation in noisy places.

- **Use smaller fragment sizes** — Though there is more total overhead to transmitting packets broken up into smaller fragments, they can often provide better overall performance in noisy environments. Change the frag parameter to reduce fragment sizes.

- **Use different frequencies** — By specifically requesting that certain frequencies (or channels) be used for transmission, you can avoid congested channels.

Use debugging tools

Because most wireless LAN cards were created for Windows systems, debugging tools from the manufacturers are available only on those systems. If your computer is a dual-boot system (Windows and Linux), try booting in Windows to test the quality of your wireless network.

In Fedora, you can use many of the tools you use for wired Ethernet networks and other TCP/IP network interfaces. Here are a couple of examples:

- **Ethereal** — The Ethereal window (type **ethereal** as the root user from a Terminal window) lets you watch Ethernet frames being sent and received by your wireless LAN interface. For example, the output of Ethereal can tell you whether a failed connection reflects a lack of reception or rejected requests. (Ethereal is described in the next section.)

- **/var/log/messages** — When the wireless LAN interface starts up, messages related to that startup are sent to the `/var/log/messages` file. In some cases, these messages will reflect improper options being set for the wireless LAN module.

Watching LAN Traffic with Ethereal

If you really want to understand the coming and going of information on your LAN, you need a tool that analyzes network traffic. Ethereal is a graphical tool for capturing and displaying the packets being sent across your network interfaces. Using filters to select particular hosts, protocols, or direction of data, you can monitor activities and track problems on your network.

In addition to reading Ethernet packet data gathered by Ethereal, the Ethereal window can be used to display captured files from LanAlyzer, Sniffer, Microsoft Network Monitor, Snoop, and a variety of other tools. These files can be read from their native formats or after being compressed with gzip (`.gz`).

Ethereal can track more than 100 packet types (representing different protocols). It can also display specific fields related to each protocol, such as various data sizes, source and destination addresses, port numbers, and other values.

Starting Ethereal

To start Ethereal, type the following (as root user) from a Terminal window:

```
# ethereal &
```

The Ethereal window, shown in Figure 15-12, appears. (If the `ethereal` command is not found, the package is probably not installed. You can install the ethereal and ethereal-gnome packages from installation CD #3.)

The primary function of Ethereal is to take a snapshot of the packets coming across your network interfaces and display that data in the Ethereal window. You can filter the data based on a variety of filter primitives. When the capture is done, you can step through and sort the data based on the values in different columns. Optionally, you can save the captured data to a file to study the data at a later time.

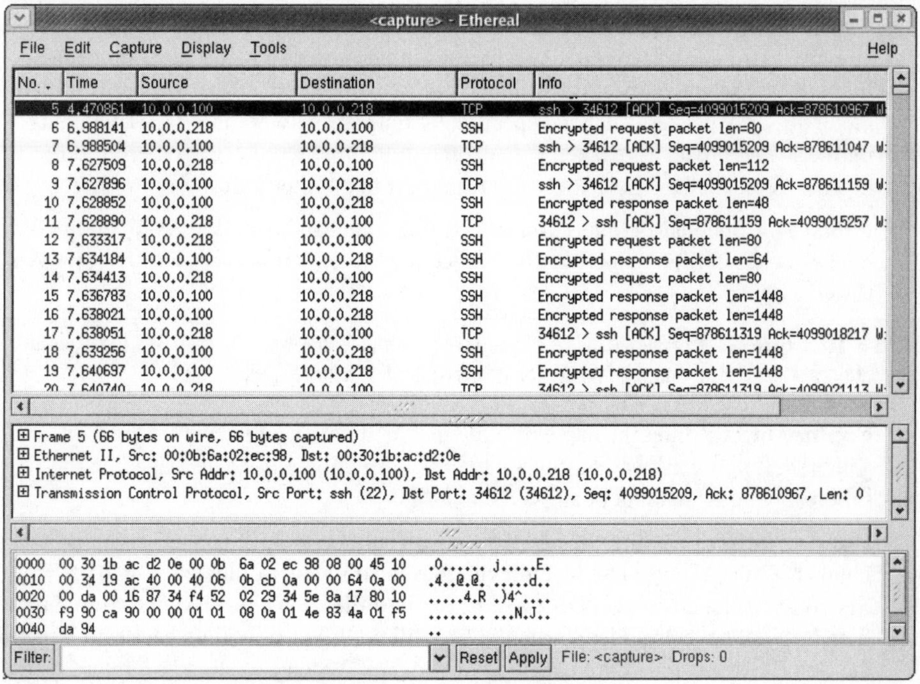

Figure 15-12: Configure your Ethernet card for TCP/IP during installation.

TIP: If you can't use Ethereal because you don't have a GUI available, you can use the `tcpdump` command from the shell. It is not as friendly as Ethereal, but it supports the same filtering syntax. Because `tcpdump` can produce a lot of output, you will probably want to use some form of filtering and/or direct the output of the command to a file. (Type **man tcpdump** for information on filter options.)

Capturing Ethernet data

With the Ethereal window displayed, you can capture data relating to packet activities on any of your Ethernet network interfaces by doing the following:

1. Click Capture.

2. Click Start. An Ethereal Capture Options window appears.

3. Click the down arrow next to the Interface box, to see what interfaces are available, and select one. If you have only one Ethernet card installed, select eth0 to choose to capture data for packets being sent across that card. You can also choose to monitor the lo interface, to watch the loopback driver. (By choosing lo, you can see requests from local users for local TCP/IP services).

4. Choose other options relating to what data is captured:

- **Limit each packet to:** Limits the size of each packet to a maximum number of bytes.

- **Capture packets in promiscuous mode:** Any computer on a LAN can see all packets that traverse the LAN, except those packets intended for switched portions of the LAN. With this on, all packets seen by your network interface are captured. With this mode off, only packets intended specifically for your network interface (including multicast and broadcast packets) are captured. In other words, turn on promiscuous mode to monitor the whole LAN and turn it off to monitor only your interface.

- **Filter:** This optional field lets you enter a filter that can be used to filter capture data. You can type in filters individually or click the Filter button to use a filter you have stored earlier.

> **CROSS-REFERENCE:** Filtering is one of the most powerful features of Ethereal. See the sidebar "Using Ethereal Filters" for further information on how to enter filters into the Filter field.

- **Capture file(s):** Enter the name of a file in which you want to capture the data gathered. If you don't enter a filename, the information will be displayed on the Ethereal window without being saved to a file.

- **Use ring buffer (Number of files):** Select this option to have packets captured in a set number of files. To use this feature, you must also specify a filename (such as /tmp/abc) and a file size. Data will be put into files you chose, named from the root filename you have provided. Once the files fill up, Ethereal will go back and write to the first file again and continue filling up the files. When you stop the capture, you are left with the number of capture files you chose, containing the most recent data.

- **Update list of packets in real time:** Select this option to have packet information appear in the Ethereal window as each packet crosses the interface. With this option off, the information is displayed after you stop capturing it.

- **Automatic scrolling in live capture:** If you are updating packets in real time, select this option to have packet information scroll up after the screen fills. With this off, you just see the first screen of packets and have to scroll down manually to see the rest.

- **Stop capture after X packets captured:** By default, Ethereal will capture data from the moment you click OK until you click Stop (with this value set to 0). Or, click here and type a number to capture only that number of packets. Other fields let you request to capture a certain number of kilobytes of data or ask to capture data for a set number of seconds. Once the limit is reached, capture stops and the file is stored in /tmp/etherXXXX???????, where ??????? is replaced by a string of characters.

- **Enable MAC/network/transport name resolution:** With any of these three options on, names are displayed instead of addresses (if possible). For example, for transport names, Source and Destination IP addresses are displayed as host names (if they can be resolved from /etc/hosts or DNS). With this option off, IP addresses appear in the Source and Destination columns.

5. Click OK. Ethereal begins gathering data on packets encountered by the interface.

   The Ethereal Capture window displays information on how many incoming and outgoing packets have crossed the interface since the capture began. The number of packets that are associated with each protocol Ethereal monitors is displayed, along with the percentage of total packets associated with each protocol.

6. Click Stop (or the capture might stop automatically, if it has reached a size or time limit set by you). The snapshot of data you just took will appear on the Ethereal window. Packets are displayed in the order in which they traversed the interface.

7. You can choose to save the data to your hard disk by selecting File → Save As.

At this point, you can start interpreting the data.

Interpreting captured Ethernet data

With the captured data displayed in your Ethereal window, you can get a detailed view of the network traffic that your computer is exposed to. The Ethereal window is divided into three parts. The top part contains a scrollable list of packets. The protocol tree for the current packet appears in the middle part of the display. A hexadecimal dump of the entire contents of the packet appears in the bottom part.

You can sort data in different ways from the top part of the window by clicking on the column headings. To see more details relating to different items in the protocol tree for the current packet, you can click the plus sign next to the protocol information that interests you.

The following are some tips that will help you interpret what the data means:

- The Source and Destination columns show where each packet came from and where it went. If the Enable name resolution option is on (which is recommended), the host name associated with IP packets is displayed. This makes it much easier to see which computer is communicating with you.

- To see all activity associated with a particular location, click the Source or Destination column. Packets will be sorted alphabetically, making it easier for you to scroll through the activity list for the location that interests you.

- If you are trying to debug a particular feature, click the Protocol column to gather activities based on protocol. For example, if you were trying to get Samba to work (for Windows file or printer sharing), sorting by protocol would enable you to see all NetBIOS and NBNS (NetBIOS name server) requests that came to your computer.

- To mark a packet of interest to you, click the middle mouse button. This will highlight the packet, making it easier to find later. (If you only have a two-button mouse, and you indicated during installation that it should emulate a three-button mouse, you can click both mouse buttons together to emulate the middle mouse button.)

Using Ethereal Filters

If you are monitoring a busy server or a busy network, Ethereal can gather so much data that it can become almost unusable. If you know what you are looking for, however, you can filter what packets are captured based on values you enter.

Filters in Ethereal are implemented using the pcap library (type **man pcap** to read about it). The filter expressions you can use with Ethereal are described on the `tcpdump` man page. Here are some examples of filters that you could enter into the Filter box when you capture Ethernet data with Ethereal:

```
host 10.0.0.15
```

The host primitive lets you only capture packets that are either to or from a particular host computer (by IP address or host name). By preceding host with `src` or `des`, you can indicate that you only want packages sent from a particular source or to a particular destination host.

```
tcp port 80
```

You can enter a protocol name (such as `tcp`, `ether`, `udp`, or `ip`) to limit captured packets to those that are assigned to that protocol. As shown in the previous example, with `tcp` you could also indicate a port number (such as 80, to monitor traffic to and from your Web server).

You can filter for certain special activities on the network, using the `gateway`, `broadcast`, or `multicast` primitives. Entering `gateway host` lets you find packets sent to a gateway host that is neither a Source nor Destination for the packet (which is determined because the Ethernet address doesn't match either of those IP addresses). Enter `ether broadcast` to monitor broadcast packets on your Ethernet network, such as announcements from name servers announcing availability. Likewise, you could filter for multicast packets on ether or ip protocols (`ether multicast`).

The Info column gives you details about the intention of the packet. For example, you can see the type of service that was requested (such as http for Web service or FTP for file transfer). You can see what information is being broadcast and determine when attempts to find particular host computers are failing. If you believe someone is using your network improperly, you can see which sites they are visiting and the services they are requesting.

Another handy option is one that lets you follow the stream of TCP information. Click Tools → Follow TCP Stream. The Contents of TCP stream window that appears lets you see the total output of the HTTP, SMTP, or other protocol being used.

Summary

Linux is at its best when it is connected to a network. Configuring a LAN enables you to share resources with other computers in your home or organization. These resources can include files, printers, CD-ROM drives, and backup media.

This chapter describes how to create a LAN with a Fedora system being used on one of the computers on that LAN. It helps you determine the kind of equipment you need to obtain, and the layout (topology) of the network.

If something isn't working with your network interface to the LAN, you can use utilities such as `ifconfig` to check that your Ethernet interface is configured and running properly. You can also check that Linux found and installed the proper driver for your Ethernet card. After an Ethernet interface is working, you can use the Ethereal window to monitor the packets coming and going across the interface between your computer and the network.

If a wired network in not possible or convenient, Linux includes support for wireless LAN cards. A wireless LAN can be an effective means of extending your network to areas that are difficult or expensive to reach with wired connections.

Chapter 16

Connecting to the Internet

In This Chapter

- Understanding how the Internet is structured
- Using dial-up connections to the Internet
- Connecting your LAN to the Internet
- Setting up Linux as a router
- Configuring a virtual private network
- Setting up Linux as a proxy server
- Setting up proxy clients

This chapter demonstrates how to connect Fedora to any TCP/IP-based network, such as the Internet, a private LAN, or a company WAN. The differences in how you connect have more to do with the network medium you use (that is, telephone lines, LAN router, and so on) than they do with whether you are connecting to the public Internet or a company's private network.

Connections to the Internet described in this chapter include a simple dial-up connection from your own Fedora system. The most popular protocol for making dial-up connections to the Internet is Point-to-Point Protocol (PPP). It also builds on the procedures in Chapter 15 for creating your own Local Area Network (LAN) by teaching you how to connect your LAN to the Internet.

This chapter first provides an overview of the structure of the Internet, including descriptions of domains, routing, and proxy service. It then discusses how to connect your Fedora system to the Internet using PPP dial-up connections. For those who want to connect a LAN to the Internet, it describes how to use Fedora as a router and set it up to do IP masquerading (to protect your private LAN addresses). Finally, it describes how to configure Fedora as a proxy server, including how to configure client applications such as Mozilla and Microsoft Internet Explorer.

Understanding How the Internet Is Structured

In order to operate, the Internet relies on maintaining a unique set of names and numbers. The names are domain names and host names, which enable the computers connected to the Internet to be identified in a hierarchy. The numbers are Internet Protocol (IP) addresses and port numbers, which enable computers to be grouped together into interconnected sets of subnetworks, yet remain uniquely addressable by the Internet.

An Internet Service Provider (ISP) will give you the information you need to set up a connection to the Internet. You plug that information into the programs used to create that connection, such as scripts to create a Point-to-Point Protocol (PPP) connection over telephone lines. See the section later in this chapter on outgoing dial-up connections for descriptions of the information needed from your ISP and the procedures for configuring PPP to connect to the Internet.

The following list describes the basic Internet structure in more detail:

- **IP addresses** — These are the numbers that uniquely define each computer known to the Internet. Internet authorities assign pools of IP addresses (along with network masks, or netmasks) so that network administrators can assign addresses to each individual computer that they control. An alternative to assigned addresses is to use a reserved set of private IP addresses.

> **CROSS-REFERENCE:** See Chapter 15 for a description of IP addresses.

- **Port numbers** — Port numbers provide access points to particular services. A server computer will listen on the network for packets that are addressed to its IP address, along with one or more port numbers. For example, a Web server listens to port 80 to respond to requests for HTTP content.

- **Domain names** — On the Internet, computer names are organized in a hierarchy of domain names and host names. If you want to have and maintain your own Internet domain, you need to be assigned one that fits into one of the top-level domains (domains such as .com, .org, .net, .edu, .us, and so on).

- **Host names** — If a domain name is assigned to your organization, you are free to create your own host names within that domain. This is a way of associating a name (host name) with an address (IP address). When you use the Internet, you use a *fully qualified domain name* to identify a host computer. For example, in the domain `handsonhistory.com`, a host computer named `baskets` would have a fully qualified domain name of `baskets.handsonhistory.com`.

  Within an organization, you should choose a host-naming scheme that makes sense to you. For example, for `handsonhistory.com`, you could have host names dedicated to different crafts (`baskets`, `decoys`, `weaving`, and so on). Some organizations use the names from Norse mythology such as thor, odin, and loki, or beer brands such as summit, jamespage, guinness, and so on.

> **TIP:** For a list of naming schemes, see c2.com/cgi/wiki?NamesGivenToComputers.

- **Routers**— If you have a LAN or other type of network in your home or organization that you want to connect to the Internet, you can share an Internet connection. You do this by setting up a router. The router connects to both your network and the Internet, providing a route for data to pass between your network and the Internet. This is especially useful if you connect to the Internet over a dial-up or broadband connection, since your Linux box can act as a router and you can share the connection among all your computers.

- **Firewalls and IP masquerading** — To keep your private network somewhat secure, yet still allow some data to pass between it and the Internet, you can set up a firewall. The firewall restricts the kind of data packets or services that can pass through the boundary between the private and public networks. If your network uses private addresses, or if you just want to protect the addresses of computers behind your firewall, you can use techniques such as Network Address Translation (NAT) orIP masquerading.

> **NOTE:** Although you can set up a firewall to filter packets on any computer on your private network, firewalls are typically configured most stringently on the machine that routes packets between the public and private networks. In this way, intruders can be stopped before they get on your private network and security can be relaxed somewhat between your computers behind the firewall.

- **Proxies** — You can bypass some of the configuration required to allow the computers on your LAN to communicate directly with the Internet by configuring a proxy server. With a proxy server, a computer on your LAN can run Internet applications (such as a Web browser) and have them appear to the Internet as if they are actually running on the proxy server.

> **CROSS-REFERENCE:** You can read about firewalls in Chapter 14. IP masquerading and proxy servers are described in the "Enable forwarding and masquerading" and "Setting up Linux as a Proxy Server" sections later in this chapter.

Internet domains

You can't read a magazine, watch a TV commercial, or open a cereal box these days without coming across a "something.com." When a company, organization, or person wants you to connect to them on the Internet, it relies on the uniqueness of its particular domain name. However, within that domain name, the company or organization to which it has been assigned can arrange its content however it chooses.

Internet domains are organized in a structure called the *domain name system* (DNS). At the top of that structure is a set of *top-level domains* (or TLDs). Some of the top-level domains are used commonly in the United States, although they are available for worldwide use. TLDs such as edu (for colleges and universities), gov (for United States government), and mil (for

United States military sites) were among the most used TLDs in the early Internet. In more recent years, `com` (for commercial sites) has experienced the most growth.

The `us` domain was added to include U.S. institutions, such as local governments and elementary schools, as well as to individuals within a geographical region of the United States. Recently, new domains such as `info` (for information-gathering sites) `biz` (an alternative to `com` for businesses), and `ws` (an all-purpose Web-site domain) have been added.

To facilitate the entry of other countries to the Internet, the International Organization for Standardization (ISO) has defined a set of two-letter codes that are assigned to each country. Within each country are naming authorities responsible for organizing the subdomains. Some subdomains are organized by categories, while others are structured by geographic location.

> **TIP:** Several RFCs (Request for Comments) define the domain name system. RFC 1034 covers domain name concepts and facilities. RFC 1035 is a technical description of how DNS works. RFC 1480 describes the `us` domain. For a more general description of DNS, there is RFC 1591. You can view RFCs at the RFC Database (`www.rfc-editor.org/rfc.html`).

Common top-level domain names

Of the generic TLDs in use today, several are used throughout the world, while two are available only in the United States. Here are descriptions of common TLDs:

- **com** — Businesses, corporations, and other commercial organizations fall into this TLD. As the Internet has grown into an important tool for commerce, domains in this TLD have grown at a dramatic rate.

- **edu** — Colleges and universities fall under this TLD. Although it was originally intended for all educational institutions, two-year colleges, high schools, and elementary schools are now organized by location under country codes (such as US in the United States).

- **gov** — This TLD is used primarily for U.S. federal government locations. Although most local government sites are expected to fall under the us domain, some states (including Washington state) are making the .gov TLD available to local cities and counties.

- **int** — This domain includes international databases and organizations created by international treaties such as NATO.

- **mil** — U.S. military organizations fall under this domain.

- **net** — Computer network providers fall under this domain.

- **org** — A variety of organizations that are neither governmental nor commercial in nature fall under this catchall TLD.

As noted earlier, other TLDs have been added recently to relieve some of the drain on `.com` names. In particular, those doing business on the Internet can get a `.biz` name. If you want to create a gathering point for information on a subject, you might choose a domain name from the `info` TLD. If yours is a general catch-all site, you can use the ws TLD.

Domain-name formation

As noted earlier, domain names are hierarchical, which means there can be subdomains beneath second-level domains, as well as host computers. (Second-level domains are the names directly below the TLDs that are assigned to individual people and organizations.) Each subdomain is separated by a dot (.), starting with the top-level domain on the right and with the second-level domain and each subsequent subdomain appearing to the left. Here is an example of a fully qualified domain name for a host:

```
baskets.crafts.handsonhistory.com
```

In this example, the top-level domain is .com. The second-level domain name assigned to the organization that controls the domain is handsonhistory. Within that domain is a subdomain called crafts. The last name (baskets) refers to a particular computer within that second-level domain. From other hosts in the second-level domain, the host can be referred to simply as baskets. From the Internet, you would refer to it as baskets.crafts.handsonhistory.com.

> **CROSS-REFERENCE:** For more details on how the domain-name system is structured, and for information on how to set up your own DNS server in Fedora, see Chapter 25.

Host names and IP addresses

In the early days of the Internet, every known host computer name and address was collected into a file called HOSTS.TXT and distributed throughout the Internet. This quickly became cumbersome because of the size of the list and the constant changes being made to it. The solution was to distribute the responsibility for resolving host names into IP addresses to many DNS servers throughout the Internet.

To make the domain names friendly, the names contain no network addresses, routes, or other information needed to deliver messages. Instead, each computer must rely on some method to translate domain names and host names into IP addresses. The DNS server is the primary means of resolving the names to addresses. If you request a service from a computer using a fully qualified domain name (including all domains and subdomains), the request will go to a DNS server to resolve that name into an IP address. It will gather that information either directly from the DNS server that owns that information or, which is more likely, from another DNS server along the way that has gathered that information.

If you have a private LAN or other network, you can keep your own list of host names and IP addresses. For the computers you work with all the time, it's easier to type baskets than baskets.crafts.handsonhistory.com. There are a couple of ways (besides DNS) that your computer can resolve the IP address for computers for which you give only the host name:

- **Check the /etc/hosts file.** In your computer's /etc/hosts file, you can place the names and IP addresses for the computers on your local network. In this way, your computer doesn't need to query the DNS server to get the address (which may not be there anyway if you are on a private network and don't have your own DNS server).

- **Check specified domains.** You can specify that if the host name requested doesn't include a fully qualified domain name and the host name is not in your /etc/hosts file, then your computer should check certain specified domain names.

On your Fedora system, when you make a request to resolve a host name into an IP address, the contents of the /etc/resolv.conf file will most likely determine where your computer searches for that information. That file can specify your local domain, an alternative list of domains, and the location of one or more DNS servers. Here is an example of an /etc/resolv.conf file:

```
domain crafts.handsonhistory.com
search crafts.handsonhistory.com handsonhistory.com
nameserver 10.0.0.10
nameserver 10.0.0.12
```

In this example, the local domain is crafts.handsonhistory.com. If you try to contact a host by giving only its host name (with no domain name), your computer can check in both crafts.handsonhistory.com and handsonhistory.com domains to find the host. If you give the fully qualified domain name, it can contact the name servers (first 10.0.0.10 and then 10.0.0.12) to resolve the address. (You can specify up to six name servers that your computer will query in order until the address is resolved. The total search line is limited to 256 characters, however.)

If your system uses DHCP, where another server on your network assigns your Linux system an IP address, your /etc/resolv.conf file can look more like the following:

```
; generated by /sbin/dhclient-script
search ce1.client2.big_isp.com
nameserver 10.0.0.10
nameserver 10.0.0.12
```

In this example, the /etc/resolv.conf file was created by the DHCP client code, based on information from the DHCP server. Note that big_isp.com is an alias for a large communications company.

> **TIP:** Your resolver knows to check your /etc/hosts file first because of the contents of the /etc/host.conf and /etc/nsswitch.conf files. By default, the nsswitch.conf file has your resolver check local files first, followed by DNS to resolve addresses. The host.conf file indicates that local files (hosts) be checked first for the address, followed the DNS system (bind). You can change that behavior by modifying those files. See the resolv.conf man page for further information.

Routing

Knowing the IP address of the computer you want to reach is one thing; being able to reach that IP address is another. Even if you connect your computers on a LAN, to have full connectivity to the Internet there must be at least one node (that is, a computer or dedicated device) through which you can route messages that are destined for locations outside your LAN. That is the job of a *router*.

A router is a device that has interfaces to at least two networks and is able to route network traffic between the two networks. In my example of a small business that has a LAN that it wants to connect to the Internet, the router would have a connection and IP address on the LAN, as well as a connection and IP address to a network that provides access to the Internet.

A computer running Linux can act as a router between any two TCP/IP interfaces, for example, if the computer has two LAN cards or if it has a network interface card and a modem (for a dial-up connection to the Internet). Alternatively, you can purchase a dedicated router, such as Cisco ADSL routers, that can exclusively perform routing between your LAN and the Internet or network service provider.

> **TIP:** Unlike regular dial-up modems, xDSL modems have several different standards that are not all compatible. Before purchasing an xDSL modem, check with your ISP. If your ISP supports xDSL, it can tell you the exact models of xDSL modems you can use to get xDSL service.

Proxies

Instead of having direct access to the Internet (as you do with routing), you can have indirect access via the computers on your LAN by setting up a *proxy server*. With a proxy server, you don't have to configure and secure every computer on the LAN for Internet access. When, for example, a client computer tries to access the Internet from a Web browser, the request goes to the proxy server. The proxy server then makes that request to the Internet. Using a proxy server, Internet access is fairly easy to set up and quite secure to use. Fedora can be configured as a proxy server (as described later in this chapter).

Using Dial-up Connections to the Internet

Many individuals and even some small businesses that need to connect to the Internet still do so using modems and telephone lines. Your modem connects to a serial port (COM1, COM2, and so on) on your computer and then into a telephone wall jack. Then your computer dials a modem at your Internet service provider or business that has a connection to the Internet.

The most common protocol for making dial-up connections to the Internet (or other TCP/IP network) is Point-to-Point Protocol (PPP). This section describes how to use PPP protocol to connect to the Internet.

Getting information

To establish a PPP connection, you need to get some information from the administrator of the network that you are connecting to. This is either your Internet service provider (ISP) when you sign up for Internet service, or the person in your workplace who wears a pocket protector and walks around carrying cables, two or more cellular phone, and a couple of beepers. (When a network goes down, these people are in demand!) Here is the kind of information you need to set up your PPP connection:

- **Telephone number** — This telephone number gives you access to the modem (or pool of modems) at the ISP. If it is a national ISP, make sure that you get a local or toll-free telephone number (otherwise, you will rack up long distance fees on top of your ISP fees).

- **Account name and password** — This information is used to verify that you have an Internet account with the ISP. This is referred to as an *account name* when you connect to Linux or other UNIX system. (When connecting to an NT server, the account name may be referred to as a *system name*.)

- **An IP number** — Most ISPs use Dynamic IP numbers, which means that you are assigned an IP number temporarily when you are connected. Your ISP assigns a permanent IP number if it uses Static IP addresses. If your computer or all the computers on your LAN need to have a more permanent presence on the network, you may be given one Static IP number or a set of Static IP addresses to use.

- **DNS Server IP addresses** — Your computer translates Internet host names to IP addresses by querying a Domain Name System (DNS) server. Your ISP should give you at least one IP address for a preferred (and possibly alternate) DNS server.

- **PAP or CHAP secrets** — You may need a PAP id or CHAP id and a secret, instead of a login and password when connecting to a Windows NT system. These features are used with authentication on Microsoft operating systems, as well as other systems. Linux and other UNIX servers don't typically use this type of authentication, although they support PAP and CHAP on the client side.

Besides providing an Internet connection, your ISP typically also provides services for use with your Internet connection. Although you don't need this information to create your connection, you will need it soon afterward to configure these useful services. Here is some information you should acquire:

- **Mail server** — If your ISP is providing you with an e-mail account, you must know the address of the mail server, the type of mail service (such as Post Office Protocol or POP3), and the authentication password for the mail server in order to get your e-mail.

- **News server** — To enable you to participate in newsgroups, the ISP may provide the name of a news server. If the server requires you to log on, you will also need a password.

After you have gathered this information, you are ready to set up your connection to the Internet. To configure Fedora to connect to your ISP, follow the PPP procedure described below.

Setting up dial-up PPP

Point-to-Point Protocol (PPP) is used to create Internet Protocol (IP) connections over serial lines. Most often, the serial connection is established over a modem; however, it will also work over serial cables (null modem cables) or digital lines (including ISDN and DSL).

Although one side must dial out while the other side must receive the call to create a PPP connection over a modem, after the connection is established, information can flow in both directions. For the sake of clarity, however, I refer to the computer placing the call as the client and the computer receiving the call as the server.

To simplify the process of configuring PPP (and other network interfaces), Fedora lets you configure dial-up by using either the Internet Configuration Wizard or another tool, such as kppp:

- **Internet Configuration Wizard** — From the main desktop menu, choose System Tools → Internet Configuration Wizard. The Select Device Type window that appears lets you configure and test your dial-up PPP connection.

- **KPPP Window** — From the KDE desktop, select Internet → KPPP, or from a Terminal window run the kppp command. From the KPPP window you can set up a PPP dial-up connection and launch it.

Before you begin either of the two dial-up procedures, physically connect your modem to your computer, plug it in, and connect it to your telephone line. If you have an internal modem, you will probably see a telephone port on the back of your computer that you need to connect. If your modem isn't detected, you can reboot your computer or run wvdialconf create (as described later in this chapter) to have it detected.

Creating a dial-up connection with the Internet Configuration Wizard

Use the Internet Configuration Wizard to set up dial-up networking. To start it, choose System Tools → Internet Configuration Wizard from the main menu. (Type the root password, if prompted.) A Select Device Type window appears to help you select the device for your Internet connection (a dial-up modem, in this case), as shown in Figure 16-1.

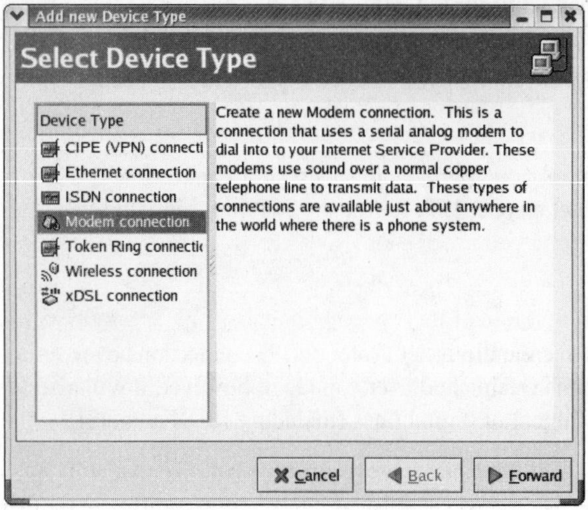

Figure 16-1: The Internet Configuration Wizard helps you set up a PPP Internet connection.

Follow the procedure below from the first Select Device Type window.

1. From the Select Device Type window that appears, select Modem connection and click Forward. The wizard searches for a modem and the Select Modem window appears.

2. Select the following modem properties and click Forward:

   - **Modem Device** — If the modem is connected to your first serial port (COM1) you can select /dev/ttyS0; for the second serial port (COM2) choose /dev/ttyS1. (By convention, the device is often linked to /dev/modem. Type **ls –l /dev/modem** to see if it is linked to a tty device.)

   - **Baud Rate** — This is the rate at which the computer talks to the modem (which is typically considerably faster than the modem can talk over the phone lines). The default is 115200. For dial-up connections, the value of 57600 is probably fine.

   - **Flow Control** — Check the modem documentation to see if the modem supports hardware flow control (CRTSCTS). If it doesn't, select software flow control (XON/XOFF).

   - **Modem Volume** — This is off by default, because the modem noise can be annoying. However, I usually select medium while I am setting up the modem. Then I turn it off once everything is working. The sound can give you can get a sense of where things are stopping if you can't get a connection.

   - **Use touch tone dialing** — Leave this check box on in most cases. If for some reason your phone system doesn't support touch-tone dialing, you can turn it off.

The Select Provider window appears.

3. Enter the following provider information and click Forward:

    - **Internet Provider** — If you are using Internet service in any of the countries shown in the Internet Provider window, select the plus sign next to that country name. If your Internet provider appears under the National list, select it. Information is automatically filled in for that provider. Otherwise, you need to fill in the rest of the dialog window. Click Forward.

    - **Phone Number** — Enter the telephone number of the ISP you want to dial into. (An optional prefix is available in case you need to dial 9 or some other number to get an outside dial tone.)

    - **Provider Name** — The name of the Internet service provider. In the current release of Fedora, there is a bug that causes the dial-up to fail if you use any provider name other than ppp0. If that has not been fixed, please use ppp0 here as the provider name. (For multiple dial-up accounts, use ppp1, ppp2, and so on.)

    - **Login Name** — The login name assigned to you from the ISP. The ISP may have called the login name a login ID or something similar.

    - **Password** — The password associated with the login name.

    After clicking Forward, the IP Settings window appears.

4. With a dial-up connection, you would typically select Automatically obtain IP address settings. However, if the ISP has assigned a static IP address that you can use, click the Statically set IP addresses check box, and then enter your IP address, Subnet Mask, and Default Gateway Address. Then click Forward to continue.

    The Create Dialup Connection window appears, displaying information you just entered.

5. If all the information looks correct, click Apply (otherwise, click the Back button to change any information). The window closes.

6. The Network Configuration window appears, ideally with a new PPP connection of modem type appearing in the window. (If it doesn't appear, select System Settings → Network.)

7. Click the new dial-up entry so it is highlighted.

8. Click File → Save to save the new dial-up configuration you just created.

9. Click the ppp device name and click the Activate button. The Internet dialer starts up and dials your ISP. (If you have sound turned on, you should hear your modem dialing out.)

If everything is working properly, you should see your login and password accepted and the PPP connection completed. Try opening Mozilla or other Web browser and see if you can access a Web site on the Internet. If this doesn't work the first time, don't be discouraged. There are many things to check to get your dial-up PPP connection working. Skip ahead to the "Checking your PPP connection" section.

Launching your PPP connection

Although your dial-up connection should now be configured (as described in the previous section), it is not set to connect automatically. One way to start the connection is to set it up to launch from the desktop panel. Here's how:

From the GNOME desktop:

1. Right-click the Panel and then choose Add to Panel → Launcher from Menu → System Settings → Network from the main menu. An icon appears on the panel that you can click to open the Network configuration window.

2. Select the new icon from the panel. A Network Configuration window appears.

3. Select the dial-up interface you added (probably ppp0) and click Activate to connect.

From the KDE desktop:

1. Right-click the panel and then choose Add → Application Button → System Settings → Network from the main menu.

2. Select the new icon from the panel (type the root password, if prompted). A Network Configuration window appears.

3. Select the dial-up interface you added (probably ppp0) and click Activate to connect.

From this point forward, icons will appear on your desktop that you can select to immediately connect to your ISP over the dial-up connection you configured.

Launching your PPP connection on demand

Instead of starting a dial-up PPP connection manually each time you want to contact the Internet, you can set your dial-up connection to start automatically when an application (such as a Web browser or e-mail program) tries to use the connection. On-demand dialing is particularly useful if:

- The dial-up connection on your Linux system is acting as the gateway for other computers in your home or office. You don't have to run over to your Linux box to start the connection when another computer needs the dial-up connection.

- You run programs at off hours that require an Internet connection (like remote backups).

- You don't want to be bothered clicking an extra icon when you just want to browse the Web a bit.

The risk of on-demand dialing is that dial-up connections can start up when you don't want them to, since the connection starts automatically. (Some people get worried when their computer starts dialing by itself in the middle of the night.)

Here is an example of settings you can add to your dial-up configuration file (probably `/etc/sysconfig/network-scripts/ifcfg-ppp0`) to configure on-demand dialing:

```
ONBOOT=yes
DEMAND=yes
IDLETIMEOUT=600
RETRYTIMEOUT=30
```

The ONBOOT=yes starts the pppd daemon (but doesn't immediately begin dialing because DEMAND is set to yes). Also, because DEMAND=yes, a dial-up connection attempt is made anytime traffic tries to use your dial-up connection. With IDLETIMEOUT set to 600, the connection is dropped after 600 seconds (10 minutes) with no traffic on the connection. With RETRYTIMEOUT set to 30, a dropped connection is retried after 30 seconds (unless the connection was dropped by an idle timeout, in which case there is no retry). You can change the timeout values as it suits you.

> **NOTE:** Because it can take a bit of time for dial-up connections to be established, operations may fail while dialing occurs. In particular, DNS requests can time out in 30 seconds, which may not be long enough to establish a dial-up connection. If you have three DNS servers configured for each client, you have a 90-second timeout period. As a result, the modem connection may be running before the request fails.

Checking your PPP connection

To debug your PPP connection or simply to better understand how it works, you can run through the steps below. They will help you understand where information is being stored and how tools can be used to track this information.

Checking that your modem was detected

It is possible that your modem is not supported under Linux. If that is the case, your PPP connection might be failing because the modem was not detected at all. To scan your serial ports to see where your modem might be, type the following (as root user):

```
$ wvdialconf create
```

The wvdialconf command is really made to build a configuration file (the /etc/wvdial.conf file) that is used by the dialer command (wvdial). Its first action, however, is to scan the serial ports on your computer and report where it finds modems. If it tells you that "no modem was detected," it's likely that either your modem isn't connected properly or no driver is available to support the modem.

If the modem wasn't detected, you should determine whether or not it is a modem supported in Linux. You can do this by finding out what type of chip set is used in the modem. This is even more important than finding out the manufacturer of the modem, since the same manufacturer can use chips from different companies. (This applies primarily to internal modems, since most external serial modems and many USB modems are supported in Linux.)

After you have determined the chip set being used, check the Web site linmodems.org. This site contains information on so-called Win-modems, which have only recently begun to be supported in Linux. Search for the chip set on your modem from this site. It will tell you if there is a driver available for your modem.

Checking that your PPP interface is working

One way to do this is with the `ping` command. From the Terminal window, type **ping** along with any Internet address you know. For example:

```
$ ping www.handsonhistory.com
PING handsonhistory.com (198.60.22.8) from 192.168.0.43 : 56(84)
bytes of data.
64 bytes from handsonhistory.com (198.60.22.8): icmp_seq=0
ttl=240 time=120 msec
64 bytes from handsonhistory.com (198.60.22.8): icmp_seq=1
ttl=240 time=116 msec
64 bytes from handsonhistory.com (198.60.22.8): icmp_seq=2
ttl=240 time=120 msec

--- www.handsonhistory.com ping statistics ---
4 packets transmitted, 3 packets received, 25% packet loss
round-trip min/avg/max/mdev = 116.816/119.277/120.807/1.779 ms
```

Press Ctrl+C to end the `ping` command. The previous lines show the responses from `www.handsonhistory.com`. It sent back packets from the IP address `198.60.22.8` in response to each one it received. You can see the sequence of packets (`icmp_seq`) and the time it took for each response (in milliseconds). If you receive packets in return, you will know two things: first, that your connection is working, and second, that your name to address translation (from the DNS addresses in `/etc/resolv.conf`) is working.

Checking the default route

After starting a dial-up connection, check that the default route is set using `route -n`, as shown in the following example:

```
# /sbin/route -n
Kernel IP routing table
Destination    Gateway       Genmask           Flags Metric Ref Use Iface
198.62.1.1     0.0.0.0       255.255.255.255   UH    0      0   0 ppp0
10.0.0.0       0.0.0.0       255.0.0.0         U     0      0   0 eth0
127.0.0.0      0.0.0.0       255.0.0.0         U     0      0   0 lo
0.0.0.0        198.62.1.1    0.0.0.0           UG    0      0   0 ppp0
```

This shows that the gateway was set to the remote PPP server (`198.62.1.1`), as well as showing the other interfaces running on my computer. There are two `ppp0` entries. The first shows the destination as a host (`UH`). The second shows the destination as a gateway (`UG`). All addresses that can't be resolved on the local LAN are directed to the gateway address.

Checking that the name servers are set

If you are able to ping a remote computer by IP address, but are not able to resolve any addresses, your DNS servers may not be set correctly. As root user from a Terminal window, open the /etc/resolv.conf file and check that there are lines identifying one or more DNS servers in this file. These should be supplied to you by your ISP (unless you run your own DNS server). Here are some examples (the numbers are fictitious):

```
nameserver 111.11.11.111
nameserver 222.22.22.222
```

Try using the ping command to make sure that the name servers are live.

Checking the chap-secrets or pap-secrets file

PPP supports two authentication protocols in Fedora: Challenge Handshake Authentication Protocol (CHAP) and Password Authentication Protocol (PAP). Here is what each protocol does to authenticate:

- **CHAP** — The server sends the client a challenge packet (which includes the server name). The client sends back a response that includes its name and a value that combines the secret and the challenge. The client name and secret are stored in your /etc/ppp/chap-secrets file.

- **PAP** — The client sends its name and a password (clear text) for authentication. The client name and secret are stored in your /etc/ppp/pap-secrets file.

By default, PPP in Fedora will authenticate if the server requests it, unless it has no secrets to share. If it has no secrets, PPP (or, more specifically, the PPP daemon pppd) will refuse authentication. It is likely that you will find the user names and passwords you provided when you set up your PPP connection in both of these files (Fedora assumes that you may be using CHAP or PAP authentication).

The chap-secrets and pap-secrets formats are the same. Each authentication line can contain the client name, the server name, and the secret. The server name can be represented by an * (to allow this secret to be used to authenticate any server). This is useful if you don't know what the server name will be. Also, remember that case is significant (that is, Myserver is not the same as myserver).

> **TIP:** For more about PAP and CHAP in PPP for Linux, see the pppd man page (type **man pppd**).

In any case, here's an example of what a chap-secrets file may look like:

```
# Secrets for authentication using CHAP
# client              server        secret                     IP addresses
####### redhat-config-network will overwrite this part!!! (begin) ######
"abcusername"         "ppp0"        "MySecretPassword"
```

> **CAUTION:** The pap-secrets and chap-secrets files should not be accessible by anyone but the root user. Anyone gaining this information could use it to access your Internet account. By default, permissions are closed to all but the root user. (To close permission, type **chmod 600 /etc/ppp/*-secrets**.)

Looking at the ifcfg-ppp0 file

The `ifcg-ppp0` file (`/etc/sysconfig/network-scripts/ifcfg-ppp0`) contains options that are passed to the pppd daemon for features that are negotiated with the remote PPP server. Most of the problems that can occur with your PPP connection result from getting some of the options wrong (particularly asking for features the server can't or won't provide).

Here is an example of the `ifcfg-ppp0` file used to connect to a Windows NT PPP server:

```
DEVICE=ppp0
NAME=Acme_Internet_Service
MODEMPORT=/dev/ttyS0
LINESPEED=115200
PAPNAME=guest
ONBOOT=yes
DEFROUTE=yes
DEMAND=yes
IDLETIMEOUT=600
```

The device name is `ppp0` (which is associated with the configuration file `ifcfg-ppp0`). `NAME` is the name you assigned to the connection. `MODEMPORT` is the device name associated with the port the modem is connected to (in this case, COM1). `LINESPEED` sets the speed, in bps, between the computer and the modem (not the dial-up speed, which is typically slower). `PAPNAME` is the user name that you log in with, assuming you are using PAP authentication.

`ONBOOT` is set to `yes` to start the `pppd` daemon at boot time (but not dial out yet, since `DEMAND=yes` is set). `DEFROUTE=yes` sets the default route to be this PPP connection. `DEMAND=yes` causes the link to be initiated only when traffic is present. `IDLETIMEOUT=600` causes your connection to time out after 600 seconds of being idle.

> **TIP:** If you want to see the exact options set by each of these parameters, look at the contents of the `/etc/sysconfig/network-scripts/ifup-ppp` script. For example, if `DEFROUTE=yes`, then the option defaultroute is sent to the pppd daemon. See the pppd man page for a description of each option (type **man pppd**).

You can add a `PPPOPTIONS` line to set any additional options you want passed to the pppd daemon process. There are some cases where the ISP will require other values that are not included here. Likewise, there are some options that you should not put in this file when connecting to certain types of servers. Here are some suggestions of values that either should not be in this file or should be (in some cases) for some Windows NT servers. For descriptions of these options, see the pppd man page:

- **remotename=*remotename*** — You may need this value for PAP authentication, but it should not be entered for CHAP authentication. (For CHAP, the remote PPP server sends you its name.)

- **require-chap, require-pap, auth, noauth** — It's a nice idea to ask a Windows NT server to authenticate itself (which is what `require-chap` and `require-pap` do for their respective protocols). The `auth` value requires the server to authenticate itself before packets can be sent or received. However, I'm told on good authority that Windows NT will not let you do any of this. Authentication will fail and you will not get a connection. You may need to indicate explicitly that the server is not required to authenticate itself by entering the `noauth` option.

- **default-asyncmap** — PAP can fail to authenticate because of "link transparency problems." If authentication fails and you are sure you have the authentication information correct, try adding this value.

- **ipcp-accept-local, ipcp-accept remote** — Sometimes a server will request your local IP address, even if it wants to assign one itself. The same is true of the remote address. Try adding these lines to the options file:

```
192.168.0.1:192.168.0.2
ipcp-accept-local
ipcp-accept-remote
demand
```

This gives temporary local and remote addresses and tells the remote server that it can replace those values. Instead of using private IP addresses (as shown here), you could use `0.0.0.0` instead.

- **bsdcomp, deflate** — Certain kinds of compression are not supported with Windows NT PPP servers. So, you should not request BSD compression (`bsdcomp`) or Deflate compression (`deflate`). In some cases, you may want to prohibit those types of compression: `nobsdcomp`, `nodeflate`, and `noccp` (for no compression control protocol).

As noted earlier, the best place for descriptions of `pppd` options is the pppd man page. For a sample options file, look in `/usr/share/doc/ppp*/sample`.

Running debugging

If your modem is working, but you are not getting connected at all, the first thing to do is turn on logging for PPP. This will help you track down the problem. If you are still stumped after looking at the logging output, take the log file and have an expert review it. Make sure that debugging is turned on by setting `DEBUG=yes` in the `ifcfg-ppp0` file.

> **TIP:** I recommend posting your failed PPP output to the comp.protocol.ppp newsgroup, where some very smart PPP experts can help answer your questions. Before you post, however, read a few days' worth of messages from the group. Chances are that someone has already run into the same problem and has a solution. Also, post only the parts of the log file that are relevant. You can also ask your local Linux user group for help.

To have debugging directed to a separate log file for PPP, add these lines to the `/etc/syslog.conf` file:

```
daemon.*        /var/log/pppmsg
local2.*        /var/log/pppmsg
```

After this, restart the syslogd daemon process as follows:

```
# service syslog restart
```

It's best to try to do this debugging process from the desktop because it helps to have several Terminal windows open (I would suggest at least three). From the first window, start a command that lists the contents of the log file we just defined above (`pppmsg`) as debug messages come in:

```
# tail -f /var/log/pppmsg
```

In the next window, start the PPP interface. Assuming it is the `ppp0` interface, use the following command as root user:

```
# ifup ppp0
```

Here is a partial listing of the output:

```
Sep  6 20:43:51 maple pppd[2077]: pppd 2.4.1 started by root, uid 0
Sep  6 20:43:51 maple ifup-ppp: pppd started for ppp0 on /dev/modem at 115200
Sep  6 20:43:52 maple chat[2079]: abort on (BUSY)
Sep  6 20:43:52 maple chat[2079]: abort on (ERROR)
Sep  6 20:43:52 maple chat[2079]: abort on (NO CARRIER)
Sep  6 20:43:52 maple chat[2079]: abort on (NO DIALTONE)
Sep  6 20:43:52 maple chat[2079]: abort on (Invalid Login)
Sep  6 20:43:52 maple chat[2079]: abort on (Login incorrect)
Sep  6 20:43:52 maple chat[2079]: send (ATZ^M)
Sep  6 20:43:52 maple chat[2079]: expect (OK)
Sep  6 20:43:53 maple chat[2079]: ATZ^M^M
Sep  6 20:43:53 maple chat[2079]: OK
Sep  6 20:43:53 maple chat[2079]:  -- got it
Sep  6 20:43:53 maple chat[2079]: send (ATDT5551212^M)
Sep  6 20:43:53 maple chat[2079]: expect (CONNECT)
Sep  6 20:43:53 maple chat[2079]: ^M
Sep  6 20:44:10 maple chat[2079]: ATDT5551212^M^M
Sep  6 20:44:10 maple chat[2079]: CONNECT
Sep  6 20:44:10 maple chat[2079]:  -- got it
Sep  6 20:44:10 maple chat[2079]: send (\d)
```

```
Sep  6 20:44:14 maple pppd[2077]: Serial connection established.
Sep  6 20:44:14 maple pppd[2077]: Using interface ppp0
Sep  6 20:44:14 maple pppd[2077]: Connect: ppp0 <--> /dev/modem
           .
           .
           .
Sep  6 20:44:17 maple pppd[2077]: local  IP address 222.62.137.121
Sep  6 20:44:17 maple pppd[2077]: remote IP address 222.62.1.105
Sep  6 20:44:17 maple pppd[2077]: primary   DNS address 111.222.111.253
Sep  6 20:44:17 maple pppd[2077]: secondary DNS address 111.222.111.254
```

This output shows starting the PPP connection on /dev/modem. After verifying that the modem is working, the chat script sends the telephone number. The connection is made, and the PPP interface is started. After some parameter negotiations, the server assigns IP addresses to both sides of the communication, and the connection is ready to use.

If you do get connected, but none of your applications (Web browser, FTP, and so on) seem to work, check that your PPP interface is noted as the default route (/sbin/route -n). If it is, check that you have the DNS servers specified correctly in your /etc/resolv.conf file. Use the ping command on those DNS servers' IP addresses to make sure you can get through.

Connecting Your LAN to the Internet

The users on your LAN are happy that you made it so that they can share files and printers with each other. However, if they want to get out to the Internet they may need to use their own modem, telephone line, and Internet account to get there. With your users already connected on a LAN, you can set up a connection to the Internet in Linux that everyone can share. The advantages of doing this are as follows:

- **Save on modems** — Instead of each computer having its own modem, you can have one high-speed device (such as a DSL router or cable modem) that routes all traffic to the Internet.

- **Save on telephone lines** — Instead of using a telephone line for each person who wants to get to the Internet, you can use one line to your ISP. (In the case of DSL, the telephone company will even let you use the same telephone line for both analog voice and high-speed digital data.)

- **Central maintenance** — If information related to your Internet connection changes (such as your dial-out number or name server addresses), you can administrate those changes in one location instead of having to change it on every computer.

- **Central security** — You can better control the Internet traffic that comes in to and goes out of your network.

The procedures in this section assume that you have already set up a LAN, as described in Chapter 15. It is also assumed that you have an outgoing connection from your Fedora system to the Internet that all traffic between the computers on your LAN and the Internet can pass through. That outgoing connection may be dial-up or may come through another LAN card connected (to a DSL router) or other LAN. This section describes two ways to set up your Fedora system so clients on the LAN can access the Internet:

- **As a router** — By configuring Fedora as a router, it can route IP packets from clients on the LAN to the Internet through the dial-up connection.

- **As a proxy server** — You can configure Fedora as a proxy server. In this way, client computers on your LAN can access the Internet as though the connection were coming from the Linux computer.

Setting up Fedora as a Router

There are several different ways to set up routing from your LAN to the Internet. You can have a dedicated router or you can have a computer already connected to your LAN that will act as a router. This section describes how to use your Fedora system as a router.

A computer may have several network interfaces, such as a loopback, an Ethernet LAN, a direct line to another computer, or a dial-up interface. For a client computer to use a router to reach the Internet, it may have a private IP address assigned to it on the LAN. A connection to a routing computer would act as the gateway to all other addresses.

Here's an example of Fedora being used as a router between a LAN and the Internet:

- The Fedora system has at least two network interfaces: one to the office LAN and one to the Internet. The interface to the Internet may be a dial-up PPP connection or a higher-speed DSL or cable modem connection.

- Packets on the LAN that are not addressed to a known computer on the LAN are forwarded to the router (that is, the Fedora system acting as a router). So, each client identifies that Fedora system as the gateway system.

- The Fedora "router" firewall is set up to receive packets from the local LAN, then forwards those packets to its other interface (possibly a PPP connection to the Internet). If the LAN uses private IP addresses, the firewall is also configured to use IP masquerading or Network Address Translation.

The following sections describe how to set up the Fedora router, as well as the client computers from your LAN (Fedora and MS Windows clients) that will use this router. Using Fedora as a router also provides an excellent opportunity to improve the security of your Internet connection by setting up a firewall to filter traffic and hide the identity of the computers on your LAN (IP masquerading).

Configuring the Linux router

To configure your Fedora computer as a router, you need to have a few things in place. Here's what you need to do before you set up routing:

- **Connect to your LAN.** Add a network card and optionally set up the addresses in `/etc/hosts` to the computers on your LAN (as described in Chapter 15) or using DHCP (as described in Chapter 23).

- **Connect to the Internet.** Set up a dial-up or other type of connection from your Fedora computer to your ISP. This is described earlier in this chapter in the section on setting up outgoing PPP connections.

- **Configure your Fedora computer as a router.** See the rest of this section.

The type of IP addresses you are using on your LAN will have an impact on a couple of steps in this procedure. Here are the differences:

- **Private IP addresses** — If the computers on your LAN use private IP addresses (described in Chapter 15), you need to set up Linux as a firewall to do IP masquerading or NAT (as described in Chapter 14). Because those numbers are private, they must be hidden from the Internet when the Fedora router forwards their requests. Packets forwarded with masquerading or NAT look to the outside world as though they came from the Fedora computer forwarding the packets.

- **Valid IP addresses** — If your LAN uses addresses that were officially assigned by your ISP or other registration authority, you don't need to do IP masquerading or NAT. (Actually, for any machine you want to expose to the world, such as a public server, you will want to have a valid, public IP address.)

Enable forwarding and masquerading

With your Fedora computer's LAN and Internet interfaces in place, follow the procedure below to set up Linux as a router. After this procedure is completed, any client computer on your LAN can identify your Fedora computer as its gateway so it can use Fedora to get to the Internet.

1. Open the `/etc/sysconfig/network` file in a text editor as the root user. Then add either a default gateway or default gateway device as described below.

   Your default gateway is where traffic destined for networks outside of your own is sent. This is where you would identify your Internet connection. Here is how you choose which one to enter:

   - **Default Gateway** — If there is a static IP address you use to reach the Internet, enter that IP address here. For example, if your Internet connection went through a DSL modem connected to your NIC card at address `192.168.0.1`, you would enter that address as follows:

   ```
   GATEWAY=192.168.0.1
   ```

   - **Default Gateway Device** — If you reach the Internet using a dynamic address that is assigned when you connect to a particular interface, you would enter that interface here. For example, if you had a dial-up interface to the Internet on the first PPP device, you would enter **ppp0** as the default gateway device as follows:

```
GATEWAYDEV=ppp0
```

When you are done, the contents of this file should look similar to the following:

```
NETWORKING=yes
HOSTNAME='maple.handsonhistory.com'
DOMAINNAME='handsonhistory.com'
#GATEWAY=
GATEWAYDEV=ppp0
```

In this case, the computer is configured to route packets over a dial-up connection to the Internet (ppp0).

2. Turn on IP packet forwarding. One way to do this is to change the value of net.ipv4.ip_forward to 1 in the /etc/sysctl.conf file. Open that file as root user with any text editor and change the line to appear as follows:

```
net.ipv4.ip_forward = 1
```

NOTE: You need to reboot for this change to take effect. To have the change take place immediately without rebooting, you can type: **echo 1 > /proc/sys/net/ipv4**

3. If the computers on your LAN have valid IP addresses, skip ahead to the section on configuring Fedora routing clients. If your computers have private IP addresses, continue with this procedure.

CAUTION: The lines shown below for configuring your iptables firewall to do IP masquerading should be used in addition to your other firewall rules. They do not, in themselves, represent a secure firewall, but merely describe how to add masquerading to your firewall. See Chapter 14 for details about how to configure a more complete firewall and when to use NAT versus IP masquerading.

4. To get IP masquerading going on your Fedora router, you need to define which addresses will be masqueraded and forwarded. The procedure is different, depending on whether you are using ipchains or iptables for your firewall.

TIP: If you are not sure which, if any, firewall is configured for your computer, type **iptables -L** and **ipchains -L**. The resulting output will display firewall rules for the one that is working and an "Incompatible with this kernel" message for the one that is not. In the current Fedora version, iptables is the default firewall. Unless you have upgraded from a much older Red Hat Linux system, you will probably be using iptables.

The following examples assume that you are masquerading all computers on your private LAN 10.0.0 (that is, 10.0.0.1, 10.0.0.2, and so on) and routing packets from that LAN to the Internet over your dial-up (ppp0) interface.

- **For iptables**, type the following as root user:

```
# iptables -t nat -A POSTROUTING -o ppp0 -j MASQUERADE
# iptables -A FORWARD -s 10.0.0.0/24 -j ACCEPT
# iptables -A FORWARD -d 10.0.0.0/24 -j ACCEPT
# iptables -A FORWARD -s ! 10.0.0.0/24 -j DROP
```

The previous commands turn on masquerading in the NAT table by appending a POSTROUTING rule (`-A POSTROUTING`) for all outgoing packets on the first dial-up PPP interface (`-o ppp0`). The next two lines accept forwarding for all packets from (`-s`) and to (`-d`) the 10.0.0 network (`10.0.0.0/24`). The last line drops packets that don't come from the 10.0.0 network.

The previous lines add rules to your running iptables firewall in the Linux kernel. To make the current rules permanent, save the current rules as follows:

```
# service iptables save
```

This copies all the current rules to the `/etc/sysconfig/iptables` file, from which the rules are read each time you reboot your system. If the new rules don't work, just copy the `iptables.save` file back to the original `iptables` file.

- **For ipchains**, add these lines to `/etc/sysconfig/ipchains` file (key lines in bold):

```
:input ACCEPT
:forward ACCEPT
-P forward DENY
-A forward -i ppp0 -s 10.0.0.0/255.255.255.0 -j MASQ
:output ACCEPT
```

5. At this point, you may want to restart your network as follows:

```
# /etc/init.d/network restart
```

6. Then, depending on which type of firewall you are using, type one of the following:

```
# /etc/init.d/iptables restart
```

or

```
# /etc/init.d/ipchains restart
```

7. To see if your new rules have gone into effect, type **iptables -L** or **ipchains -L** (again, depending on which firewall you are using). All current rules are displayed.

If the route to the Internet from Linux is being provided by a dial-up connection, you probably want to turn on on-demand dialing (as described earlier in this chapter).

Configuring network clients

In this example, there are a variety of Linux and Windows operating system clients on a LAN. One Fedora computer has a connection to the Internet and is set up to act as a router between the Internet and the other computers on the LAN (as described previously). To be able to reach computers on the Internet, each client must be able to do the following:

- Resolve the names it requests (for example, www.redhat.com) into IP addresses.
- Find a route from the local system to the remote system, using its network interfaces.

Each Linux client computer knows how to find another computer's address based on the contents of the /etc/host.conf, /etc/hosts, and /etc/resolv.conf files. The contents of the host.conf file, by default, is the following:

```
order hosts,bind
```

This tells your system to check for any host names (hosts) that you request by first checking the contents of the /etc/hosts file and then checking with name servers that are identified in the /etc/resolv.conf file. In our case, we will put the addresses of the few hosts we know about on our private network (whether on the LAN, direct connection, or other network interface) in the /etc/hosts file. Then, the system knows to resolve addresses using a DNS server (bind) based on addresses of name servers we add to the /etc/resolv.conf file.

Next, each client machine must know how to get to the Internet. Do this by adding a default route (sometimes called a *gateway*) to each client. To permanently add a default route on the client Fedora system, do the following:

1. Set the default route to point to the router. This entails setting the GATEWAY or GATEWAYDEV value in the /etc/sysconfig/network file as described in the previous procedure. (This time, the address will point to the LAN interface of the router.)

2. Restart your network interfaces by typing the following as root user:

```
# /etc/init.d/network restart
```

3. When the computer comes back up, type the following:

```
# netstat -r
Kernel IP routing table
Destination  Gateway    Genmask        Flags  MSS Window  irtt Iface
10.0.0.0     *          255.255.255.0  U      0 0            0 eth0
127.0.0.0    *          255.0.0.0      U      0 0            0 lo
default      10.0.0.1 0.0.0.0          UG     0 0            0 eth0
```

You can see that the default gateway was set to the host at the IP address 10.0.0.1 on the eth0 Ethernet interface. Assuming that router is ready to route your packets to the Internet, your Fedora client is now ready to use that router to find all IP addresses that you request that you do not already know where to find. (The netstat -r command provides the same output as the /sbin/route command.)

Configuring Windows network clients

If you have some Microsoft systems on your LAN, you need to configure them so that they can connect to the Internet through your router. To set up the Windows operating system computers on your private network to access the Internet through your routing computer, you can either set up a DHCP server or add a few pieces of information to each Windows system. Here's how to do this from Windows ME and most other Windows systems:

1. Choose Start → Settings → Control Panel.

2. Open the Network icon in the Control Panel.

3. Double-click the interface shown that supports connecting to the Linux router. (For a LAN, it may look like this: TCP/IP → 3Com EtherLink III.)

4. Click the IP address tab, and then either leave the Obtain an IP address automatically button selected (if you are using DHCP to get the IP address, as described in Chapter 23) or select the Specify an IP address button (if you intend to add a static IP address). In the second case, you then need to type in the IP address and subnet mask for the host computer.

5. Click the Gateway tab, type the IP address of your Linux router, and then click Add.

6. Click the DNS Configuration tab, type in the number of the DNS server that you use to resolve addresses on the Internet, and then click Add. Repeat this step if you have multiple DNS servers.

7. Click OK.

8. You may need to reboot your computer at this point, if Windows requires you to do so.

At this point, try accessing a Web site from your Internet browser on the Windows computer. If the Internet connection is up on your Fedora computer, you should be able to connect to the Internet through your LAN connection to the Fedora computer.

Configuring a Virtual Private Network Connection

Sometimes the people and offices that have to work closely together are not physically close together. For example, you may have:

- Two branch offices that need to constantly share sales databases, or

- An employee who needs to access office computers, printers, and files from home.

Rather than purchase expensive leased lines from a phone company, you want to use an inexpensive network medium, like the Internet, to let the two sides communicate. The problem is that you don't want to open up access to file sharing, print sharing, and other private services to the Internet. You also don't want communication between these sites to be exposed to anyone who is watching Internet traffic. One solution is to set up a virtual private network.

A virtual private network (VPN) provides a way to set up secure communications over an otherwise insecure network. With a VPN connection in place, the two sides of a connection can communicate as safely as they do on the same corporate LAN. To do this, a VPN usually offers the following features:

- **Authentication** — Using passwords or other techniques, two ends of a communication can prove that they are who they say they are before accepting a connection. After the connection is in place, communications can flow in both directions across it.

- **Encryption** — By encrypting all data being sent between the two points on the public network, you can be assured that even if someone could see the packets you send, they couldn't read them. Creating a connection between two public network addresses to use for exchanging encrypted data is known as *tunneling*.

There are several ways of going about setting up VPN connections in Linux:

- **Internet Protocol SECurity (IPSEC)** — IPSEC is a standard developed by the Internet Engineering Task Force (IETF) as the required method of encryption when the IP version 6 becomes the standard Internet protocol (right now IPv4 is the standard in North America and Europe). There are several implementations of IPSEC over IPV4 in Linux these days. Fedora includes IPSEC support by including the Linux 2.6 kernel and offering an administrative interface for configuring it (via the ipsec-tools package).

- **PPP over OpenSSH** — With this method, using software that is already in Fedora, you can configure a PPP interface (as you would a regular dial-up connection) to use SSH to encrypt all data that goes across the PPP interface. While this method is not too difficult to configure, it can provide poor performance. To see how to create a PPP over OpenSSH VPN, refer to the VPN PPP-SSH HOW-TO (search www.tldp.org).

- **Crypto IP Encapsulation (CIPE)** — Using this method, IP packets are routed across selected IP interfaces as encrypted UDP packets. CIPE is easy to set up and carries less overhead than PPP over OpenSSH, so you should get better performance. One drawback is that, because it is not a standard VPN, CIPE is not available on all platforms.

In this chapter, I provide an overview of the features and tools in IPSEC in Fedora Core 2. For CIPE, I provide a step-by-step procedure for setting up a CIPE VPN between two Fedora and/or Red Hat Linux systems. For us, CIPE is a good choice because an easy CIPE interface is included on the Network Configuration window and it's tuned to perform well between Linux systems.

Understanding IPSEC

To provide more secure transmission of TCP/IP data in the new Internet Protocol version 6 (IPv6) standard, developers of that standard created the Internet Protocol Security (IPSEC) architecture. With IPSEC, encrypted communication is possible right at the Internet Protocol (IP) level and methods for providing access control, data integrity, authentication and traffic flow confidentiality are standardized as well.

In practical terms, organizations that have computers that need to communicate on public networks in ways that are secure and private can create virtual private networks (VPNs) with IPSEC. Unlike other VPN implementations (such as CIPE, described later), which require a manual exchange of keys to work, IPSEC offers an automated way of creating security associations between communications endpoints and managing keys.

With slow adoption of IPv6 in the United States and other places, IPSEC has been included (backported) into the IPv4 protocol, which is still the most common IP version used on the Internet. That backport was added into the IP protocol included with the Linux 2.6 kernel that comes with Fedora Core 2. The Internet standard RFC2401 document describes the IPSEC architecture.

Using IPSEC protocols

IPSEC consists of two primary protocols: Authentication Header (AH) and Encapsulated Security Payload (ESP). Look in the `/etc/protocols` file and you'll see that AH is assigned to protocol number 50 and ESP is assigned to protocol number 51.

To authenticate peer computers and exchange symmetric keys, IPSEC uses the Internet Key Exchange (IKE) protocol. At the beginning of communication between two host computers using IPSEC, IKE does the following:

- Authenticates that the peer computers are who they say they are.
- Negotiates security associations.
- Chooses secret symmetric keys (using Diffie-Hellmann key exchange).

The security associations established by IKE are stored in a security association database (SAD). A security association holds information about the communications endpoints (possibly public Internet IP addresses), whether Authentication Header (AH) or Encapsulater (ESP) protocols are being used with IPSEC, and the secret key/algorithm being used.

IPSEC itself has two possible modes of operation: tunnel mode and transport mode.

- **Tunnel mode** — The entire IP datagram is encapsulated into the new IP datagram by IPSEC. This protects both the data and the control information from being seen by anyone except the communications endpoint that is allowed to decrypt the communication.
- **Transport mode** — Only the data (the payload intended for the client receiving the data) is encrypted. To do this, IPSEC inserts its own header between the Internet Protocol header and the protocol header for the upper layer.

Included in the protocol header of each packet transmitted is information referred to as Hash Message Authentication Codes (HMAC). Including these codes with transmitted data in IPSEC offers the following advantages:

- **Data integrity** — By using a hash algorithm to create a hash from a secret key and the data in the IP datagram, the resulting HMAC is added to the IPSEC protocol header. The receiver can then check that the HMAC is correct using its own copy of that secret key. Supported authentication algorithms include MD5, SHA1, and SHA2 (256, 384, and 512).

- **Data privacy** — By using symmetric encryption algorithms (such as DES, NULL, AES, 3DES, and Blowfish), datagrams are encrypted so their contents cannot be seen by outsiders.

By recording a sequence of packets during data communications, an intruder can attempt denial-of-service attacks by replaying that sequence of packets. IPSEC combats that type of attack by accepting packets that are within a "sliding window" of sequence numbers or higher. Packets using older sequence numbers are dropped.

Using IPSEC in Fedora

Using IPSEC in Fedora Core 2, you can configure virtual private networks (VPN) between Fedora and other systems that support IPSEC. It is important that hosts at both ends of the IPSEC VPN are configured in the same way. In fact, you may have the best results by using the same operating system version and IPSEC software (in the case of Fedora, ipsec-tools package and IP protocol drivers that come with the 2.6 kernel).

By default, the necessary modules to use IPSEC are already available in Fedora 2. The tools you use to configure IPSEC are contained in the ipsec-tools packages. You set up IPSEC in the kernel in much the same way that you set up firewalls with iptables: you run commands that load settings into the kernel, either from command line options (standard input) or from a file containing your preconfigured options.

The commands you use to set up a VPN with IPSEC include the following:

- **setkey** — Use this command to load the data about your VPN connections into the kernel. It can add, change, flush or dump information in the Security Association Database (SAD) and the Security Policy Database (SPD) for your IPSEC VPN. Typically, you would create a configuration file in the format described on the setkey man page, then run `setkey -f filename` to load that data into the kernel.

- **racoon** — Use this command to create IKE security associations between host computers communicating together over an IPSEC VPN. Security data are loaded into racoon from the `/etc/racoon.conf` file (unless that file is overridden from the `racoon` command line using the `-f` option).

Sample configuration files to use with setkey are available from the IPSEC-HOWTO (`www.ipsec-howto.org`). A sample `racoon.conf` file is included with the ipsec-tools package (in the `/usr/share/doc/ipsec-tools-*` directory). For an in-depth description of the tools used with IPSEC, refer to the Kame Project Web site (`www.kame.net`).

Understanding CIPE

The job of CIPE is to set up a secure link between two communications end points. Using CIPE, the link can be authenticated and the data can be encrypted.

Compared to VPN protocols such as IPSEC, CIPE is fairly easy to set up. Both sides of the link (such as computers at two branch offices) have to have public network connections (probably public Internet addresses), be running CIPE, and use the same link key. The link key, which is known only to the two link ends, is used to authenticate the connection and encrypt the data between the two sites. You can create this key during CIPE setup. Both sides of the link need that same key for CIPE to work.

CIPE passes data between its two end points using the UDP protocol. Because CIPE is a network layer protocol, data from any application programs that communicate over that link are encrypted. This makes is safe from anyone on the public network that might be trying to intercept your communications.

When you set up a CIPE link, you identify the IP addresses and port numbers used for the communication. To allow CIPE to work properly, you need to open your firewalls to allow the ports you select to accept UDP traffic. To allow multiple CIPE connections to the same computer, you can configure separate CIPE interfaces, each using different UDP port numbers.

The cipe package was removed from Fedora Core in version 2. However, the Network Configuration window in Fedora still supports cipe, so you can configure cipe in Fedora Core 2 by getting the Fedora Core 1 cipe package from a Fedora software repository and configuring it as described in this chapter. You can install the cipe RPM for Fedora Core directly from the Internet, using the following command:

```
# rpm -U //ayo.freshrpms.net/fedora/linux/1/i386/RPMS.os/cipe-1.4.5-
18.i386.rpm
```

Alternatively, you could download the RPM from any software repository that has it and install it from that directory (instead of over the Internet).

Setting up a CIPE VPN

For this example, two computers, each running the current version of Fedora, are configured at two locations, each with a connection to the Internet. I start with the following assumptions:

- Each of the two computers has a connection to the Internet, with at least one of the two having a static IP address.

- Both computers are running the current Fedora Core operating system. (Although this is not required, because you need only the cipe package for the connection to work, I am using the Fedora GUI in the procedure to configure the connection.)

- Although the two sides of a CIPE connection are referred to as peers, Peer 1 of the CIPE connection operates in server mode while Peer 2 acts as a client to initiate the CIPE connection.

- Peer 1 will create the CIPE key and transmit that key (securely) to Peer 2 before Peer 2 begins configuring its CIPE configuration.

Figure 16-2 illustrates a simple example of a CIPE VPN that connects Linux computers between two offices over the Internet.

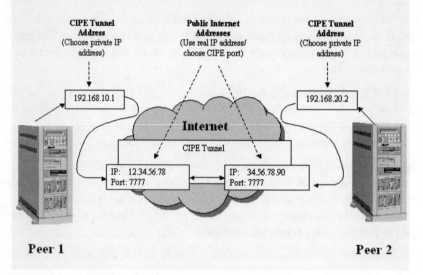

Figure 16-2: A CIPE VPN is configured between two Linux systems over the Internet.

Configuring CIPE Peer 1

To begin, you can use the Network Configuration window (the `neat` command) to create the CIPE configuration. Here's how:

1. Open the Network Configuration window by selecting System Settings → Network (or type **neat&** from a Terminal window).

2. Click New to add a new network interface.

3. Click CIPE (VPN) connection and click Forward.

4. Add the following information to the Configure Tunnel window and click Forward when you are done:

- **Device** — The name of the CIPE interface on the local computer. The default, which is fine for your first CIPE interface, is `cipcb0`. (If you intend to have multiple CIPE connections to this computer, they are named `cipcb1`, `cipcb2`, and so on.)

- **Tunnel Through Device** — This is the name of the IP interface through which the CIPE connection is made. Click the down arrow to see which interfaces are available (eth0, ppp0, and so on). You can either choose a particular interface or simply leave the None - Server Mode item elected. This allows CIPE connections on any interface on which a request comes in for the "Local Port" set in the next field.

- **Local Port** — This defines the port number on which CIPE listens for connection requests from the remote CIPE clients. The default is 7777, but you can use any unused port number (as long as the CIPE client knows which one to ask for).

- **Remote Peer Address** — As a CIPE server, this can be set to Server Mode (auto). The remote client address is determined at the time the remote client tries to set up the CIPE connection.

- **Remote Peer Port** — As with "Remote Peer Address," the Remote Peer Port can be determined when the remote client tries to set up the CIPE connection.

- **Remote Virtual Address** — This is where you set the remote IP address for the CIPE client that is connecting to you on the virtual network you are creating. Choose IP addresses from private network addresses that you haven't used for any of your other local networks. These are the IP addresses used by your CIPE tunnel.

- **Local Virtual Address** — This is the local IP address for the virtual network connection you are setting up for your CIPE server. It cannot be the same IP address as the address representing your regular connection to the Internet (in other words, the IP address of your eth0 or ppp0 connection).

- **Secret Key** — Type a string of characters as your secret key or click the Generate button to generate a secret key. This exact key must also be used on the remote computer that connects to you to create the VPN. A 128-bit key is used.

Notice that the box at the bottom of the screen contains the setting you will use to configure the remote side of your CIPE connection. Write down these settings or copy and paste them into a file for later reference.

5. Click Forward. The screen asks you to review and accept the CIPE connection you created.

6. Click Apply. You are now back to the main Network Configuration window.

7. Click Apply to apply your new CIPE interface.

8. With the new CIPE interface selected, click Activate to start the CIPE interface.

> **NOTE:** If you want to start the CIPE interface at boot time, select the interface and click Edit. In the window that appears, select the "Activate device when computer starts" check box and click OK. Then click Apply again in the main Network Configuration window to save the changes.

9. Click Close to close the Network Configuration window.

At this point, the new CIPE interface (probably cipeb0) should be in place. The following is an example of the `/etc/sysconfig/network-scripts/ifcfg-cipcb0` file containing settings for the interface you just created:

```
TYPE=CIPE
DEVICE=cipcb0
ONBOOT=yes
IPADDR=192.168.20.2
MYPORT=7777
ME=34.56.78.90:7777
PTPADDR=192.168.10.1
PEER=12.34.57.78:7777
```

The settings above show that the connection type is `CIPE` and the interface name is `cipcb0`. The interface is started at boot time (`ONBOOT=yes`). The IP addresses for the CIPE tunnel you create are `192.168.20.2` (on your side) and `192.168.10.1` (on the remote side). Notice that these are private IP addresses representing different networks (`192.168.20` and `192.168.10`). (Don't use public IP addresses for `IPADDR` or `PTADDR`!)

The `PEER` value indicates that the remote peer will connect to you from IP address `12.34.56.78` on port number `7777`. The `ME` value identifies the IP address of your real connection to the Internet. Replace `12.34.56.78` and `34.56.78.90` with the real, public IP address of the remote peer and your local computer, respectively! The port numbers can be any unused UDP ports you choose. They don't have to be the same (although they are here), but each side does need to know which ports the other side is using.

Although once the other side is up, you should be able to ping each other across the connection, to make the connection useful, you may need to do some additional work:

- **Turn on IP forwarding.** If you want the remote CIPE to forward requests to other interfaces on your computer (permanently), add this to the `/etc/sysctl.conf` file:

```
net.ipv4.ip_forward = 1
```

  To have IP forwarding take effect immediately, type the following as root user:

```
# echo 1 > /proc/sys/net/ipv4
```

- **Open your firewall for CIPE.** At the very least, you need to allow the remote CIPE peer to connect to your UDP port. In our case, we need to open port 7777 on your external LAN interface (for this example, I used 34.56.78.90, although yours will be different).

- **Add routes.** Edit the `/etc/cipe/ip-up` script to include the routes to connect the subnetworks on each side of the connection. For our example, I added the following route so that I could address any computer on the remote LAN (`192.168.10.0`) from my local CIPE connection:

```
route add -net 192.168.10.0 netmask 255.255.255.0 gw $5
```

- **Add other ciped options.** You can add options to the /etc/cipe/options.cipcb0 file to pass to the ciped-cb daemon. To see the available options, type **info cipe**. Then scroll down and select Parameter List to see a list of all parameters you can set for the daemon. (The options.cipcb0 file is where the link key is stored, so to use a new key you can change it here. Be sure to keep it protected from access by anyone but root!)

> **TIP:** If you want to create multiple VPNs to the same public IP address, you can create multiple CIPE interfaces and assign each one to a different UDP port number.

Configuring CIPE Peer 2

Repeat the configuration you did for Peer 1 on Peer 2. Much of the information, however, will be reversed. Here's an example of /etc/sysconfig/network-scripts/ifcfg-cipcb0 on Peer 2:

```
TYPE=CIPE
DEVICE=cipcb0
ONBOOT=yes
IPADDR=192.168.10.1
MYPORT=7777
ME=12.34.57.78:7777
PTPADDR=192.168.20.2
PEER=34.56.78.90:7777
```

Again, be sure to replace the values of ME and PTPADDR with real IP addresses for your locations. The same issues also apply to changing IP forwarding, opening your firewall, adding routes, and adding other ciped options. Remember, you have basically just set up a tunnel between two computers on the Internet. What the packets that cross that interface can do once they arrive at the remote computer is up to you.

Checking your CIPE VPN

If you set your CIPE interfaces to boot automatically, they will be started the next time you reboot the computer. (Or, start them now by typing /etc/init.d/network restart.) If your connections to the Internet are up on both sides, the CIPE tunnel should start and connect across your Internet interfaces.

To check that the CIPE tunnel is active, simply use the ping command. For example, in this sample you could type from Peer 1 to Peer 2:

```
# ping 192.168.20.1
```

If the ping is successful, you can use the ethereal window to check that the tunnel is actually working properly. For example, if your tunnel were communicating over the eth0 interface on

Peer 1, capturing packets on that interface with ethereal while you were pinging the remote CIPE would result in lines that look like the following:

```
34.56.78.90    12.34.56.78   UDP Source port: 7777 Destination port: 7777
12.34.56.78    34.56.78.90   UDP Source port: 7777 Destination port: 7777
```

Because the ping requests are encrypted, all you see traveling across the interface are UDP packets between ports 7777 on the two IP addresses representing the Internet interfaces being used by the CIPE tunnel.

If you need to communicate across the peer to another computer, make sure that you have set up the routes to do that. In particular, if you are creating a CIPE connection over a PPP dial-up connection directly to your company, and are routing from there to the Internet, make sure that the remote CIPE computer knows to route data back to your CIPE interface.

Setting up Linux as a Proxy Server Red Hat

You have a LAN set up, and your Fedora computer has both a connection to the LAN and a connection to the Internet. One way to provide Web-browsing services to the computers on the LAN without setting up routing is to configure Fedora as a proxy server.

The Squid proxy caching server software package comes with Fedora. In a basic configuration, you can get the software going very quickly. However, the package is full of features that let you adapt it to your needs. You can control which hosts have access to proxy services, how memory is used to cache data, how logging is done, and a variety of other features. Here are the basic proxy services available with Squid:

- **HTTP** — Allowing HTTP proxy services is the primary reason to use Squid. This is what lets client computers access Web pages on the Internet from their browsers (through your Fedora computer). In other words, HTTP proxy services will find and return the content to you for addresses that look similar to this: www.ab.com.

- **FTP** — This represents File Transfer Protocol (FTP) proxy services. When you enable HTTP for a client, you enable FTP automatically (for example, ftp://ftp.ab.com).

- **Gopher** — The gopher protocol proxy service was one of the first mechanisms for organizing and searching for documents on the Internet (it predates the Web by more than a decade). Nobody uses gopher anymore. However, gopher is automatically supported when you enable HTTP for a client.

Besides allowing proxy services, Squid can also be part of an Internet cache hierarchy. Internet caching occurs when Internet content is taken from the original server and copied to a caching server that is closer to you. When you, or someone else in the caching hierarchy, requests that content again, it can be taken from the caching server instead of from the original server.

You don't have to cache Internet content for other computers to participate in caching with Squid. If you know of a parent caching-computer that will allow you access, you can identify that computer in Squid and potentially speed your Web browsing significantly.

Caching services in Squid are provided through your Linux system's ICP port. Besides ICP services, you can also enable Simple Network Management Protocol (SNMP) services. SNMP lets your computer provide statistics and status information about itself to SNMP agents on the network. SNMP is a feature for monitoring and maintaining computer resources on a network.

> **CAUTION:** SNMP poses a potential security risk if it is not configured properly. Use caution when configuring SNMP with Squid.

The squid daemon process (`/usr/sbin/squid`) can be started automatically at system boot time. After it is set up, most of the configuration for Squid is done in the `/etc/squid/squid.conf` file. The `squid.conf` file contains lots of information about how to configure Squid (the file contains more than 3200 lines of comments and examples, although there are only 32 lines of active settings).

For further information about the Squid proxy server, refer to the Squid Web Proxy Cache home page (`www.squid-cache.org`).

Starting the squid daemon

When you install Fedora, you have an opportunity to install Squid (squid package). If you are not sure whether or not Squid was installed, type the following:

```
# rpm -q squid
squid-2.5.STABLE5-2
```

If squid is not installed, you can install it from CD #1 that comes with this book. Next you can check whether or not squid is configured to run. To do that, type the following:

```
# chkconfig --list squid
squid          0:off  1:off  2:off  3:off  4:off  5:off  6:off
```

If the squid service is off for run levels 3, 4, and 5 (it's off at all run levels by default), you can set it to start automatically at boot time. To set up the squid daemon to start at boot time, type the following:

```
# chkconfig squid on
```

At this point, the squid daemon should start automatically when your system boots. By default, the squid daemon will run with the `-D` option. The `-D` option enables Squid to start without having an active Internet connection. If you want to add other options to the squid daemon, you can edit the `/etc/sysconfig/squid` configuration file. Look for the line that looks similar to the following:

```
SQUID_OPTS="-D"
```

You can add any options, along with the `-D` option, between the quotes. Most of these options are useful for debugging Squid:

- **-a** *port#* — Substitute for `port#` a port number that will be used instead of the default port number (3128) for servicing HTTP proxy requests. This is useful for temporarily trying out an alternative port.

- **-f** **squidfile** — Use this option to specify an alternative `squid.conf` file (other than `/etc/squid/squid.conf`). Replace *squidfile* with the name of the alternative `squid.conf` file. This is a good way to try out a new `squid.conf` file before you replace the old one.

- **-d** *level* — Change the debugging level to a number indicated by *level*. This also causes debugging messages to be sent to `stderr`.

- **-X** — Use this option to check that the values are set properly in your `squid.conf` file. It turns on full debugging while the `squid.conf` file is being interpreted.

You can restart the Squid service by typing `/etc/init.d/squid restart`. While the squid daemon is running, there are several ways you can run the `squid` command to change how the daemon works, using these options:

- **squid -k reconfigure** — Causes Squid to again read its configuration file.

- **squid -k shutdown** — Causes Squid to exit after waiting briefly for current connections to exit.

- **squid -k interrupt** — Shuts down Squid immediately, without waiting for connections to close.

- **squid -k kill** — Kills Squid immediately, without closing connections or log files. (Use this option only if other methods don't work.)

With the squid daemon ready to run, you need to set up the `squid.conf` configuration file.

Using a simple squid.conf file

You can use the `/etc/squid/squid.conf` file that comes with squid to get started. Though the file contains lots of comments, the actual settings in that file are quite manageable. The following paragraphs describe the contents of the default `squid.conf` file:

```
hierarchy_stoplist cgi-bin ?
```

The `hierarchy_stoplist` tag indicates that when a certain string of characters appears in a URL, the content should be obtained from the original server and not from a cache peer. In this example, requests for the string `cgi-bin` and the question mark character (?) are all forwarded to the originating server.

```
acl QUERY urlpath_regex cgi-bin \?
no_cache deny QUERY
```

The preceding two lines can be used to cause URLs containing certain characters to never be cached. These go along with the previous line by not caching URLs containing the same strings (`cgi-bin` and ?) that are always sought from the original server.

```
acl all src 0.0.0.0/0.0.0.0
acl manager proto cache_object
acl localhost src 127.0.0.1/255.255.255.255
```

The `acl` tags are used to create access control lists. The first line above creates an access control list called `all` that includes all IP addresses. The next `acl` line assigns the manager `acl` to handle the `cache_object` protocol. The `localhost` source is assigned to the IP address of `127.0.0.1`.

The next several entries define how particular ports are handled and how access is assigned to HTTP and ICP services.

```
acl SSL_ports port 443 563
acl Safe_ports port 80          # http
acl Safe_ports port 21          # ftp
acl Safe_ports port 443 563     # https, snews
acl Safe_ports port 70          # gopher
acl Safe_ports port 210         # wais
acl Safe_ports port 1025-65535  # unregistered ports
acl Safe_ports port 280         # http-mgmt
acl Safe_ports port 488         # gss-http
acl Safe_ports port 591         # filemaker
acl Safe_ports port 777         # multiling http
acl CONNECT method CONNECT
http_access allow manager localhost
http_access deny manager
http_access deny !Safe_ports
http_access deny CONNECT !SSL_ports
http_access allow localhost
http_access deny all
http_reply_access allow all
icp_access allow all
```

The following sections describe these settings in more detail, as well as other tags you might want to set in your `squid.conf` file. By default, no clients can use the squid proxy server, so you at least want to define which computers can access proxy services.

To make sure that this simple Squid configuration is working, follow this procedure:

1. On the Squid server, restart the squid daemon. To do this, type **/etc/init.d/squid restart**. (If Squid isn't running, use start instead of restart.)

2. On the Squid server, start your connection to the Internet (if it is not already up).

3. On a client computer on your network, set up Mozilla (or another Web browser) to use the Squid server as a proxy server (described later in this chapter). (In Mozilla, select Edit → Preferences → Advanced → Proxies, then choose Manual proxy configuration and add the Squid server's computer name and, by default, port 3128 to each protocol.)

4. On the client computer, try to open any Web page on the Internet with the browser you just configured.

If the Web page doesn't appear, see the Squid debugging section for how to fix the problem.

Modifying the Squid configuration file

If you want to set up a more complex set of access permissions for Squid, you should start with the default `squid.conf` configuration file (described earlier).

To begin, open the `/etc/squid/squid.conf` file (as the root user). You will see a lot of information describing the values that you can set in this file. Most of the tags that you need to configure Squid are used to set up cache and provide host access to your proxy server.

> **TIP:** Don't change the `squid.conf.default` file! If you really mess up your `squid.conf` file, you can start again by making another copy of this file to `squid.conf`. If you want to recall exactly what change you have made so far, type the following from the `/etc/squid` directory:
>
> # **diff squid.conf squid.conf.default | less**
>
> This will show you the differences between your actual `squid.conf` and the version you started with.

Configuring access control in squid.conf

To protect your computing resources from being used by anyone, Squid requires that you define which host computers have access to your HTTP (Web) services. By default, all hosts are denied access to Squid HTTP services except for the local host. With the `acl` tag, you can create access lists. Then, with the `http_access` tag, you can authorize access to HTTP (Web) services for the access lists you create.

The form of the access control list tag (`acl`) is:

```
acl   name   type   string
acl   name   type   file
```

The `name` is any name you want to assign to the list. A `string` is a string of text, and `file` is a file of information that applies to the particular `type` of acl. Valid acl types include `dst`, `src`, `dstdomain`, `srcdomain`, `url_path_pattern`, `url_pattern`, `time`, `port`, `proto`, `method`, `browser`, and `user`.

Several access control lists are set up by default. You can use these assigned acl names to assign permissions to HTTP or ICP services. You can also create your own acl names to assign to those services. Here are the default acl names from the `/etc/squid/squid.conf` file that you can use or change:

```
acl all src 0.0.0.0/0.0.0.0
acl manager proto cache_object
acl localhost src 127.0.0.1/255.255.255.255
acl SSL_ports port 443 563
acl Safe_ports port 80          # http
```

```
acl Safe_ports port 21              # ftp
acl Safe_ports port 443 563         # https, snews
acl Safe_ports port 70              # gopher
acl Safe_ports port 210             # wais
acl Safe_ports port 1025-65535      # unregistered ports
acl Safe_ports port 280             # http-mgmt
acl Safe_ports port 488             # gss-http
acl Safe_ports port 591             # filemaker
acl Safe_ports port 777             # multiling http
acl CONNECT method CONNECT
```

When Squid tries to determine which class a particular computer falls in, it goes from top to bottom. In the first line, all host computers (address/netmask are all zeros) are added to the acl group all. In the second line, you create a manager group called manager that has access to your cache_object (the capability to get content from your cache). The group localhost is assigned to your loopback address. Secure socket layer (SSL) ports are assigned to the numbers 443 and 563, whereas Safe_ports are assigned to the numbers shown above. The last line defines a group called CONNECT (which you can use to allow access to SSL ports).

To deny or enable access to HTTP services on the Squid computer, the following definitions are set up:

```
http_access allow manager localhost
http_access deny manager
http_access deny !Safe_ports
http_access deny CONNECT !SSL_ports
http_access allow localhost
http_access deny all
```

These definitions are quite restrictive. The first line allows someone requesting cache objects (manager) from the local host to do so, but the second line denies anyone else making such a request. Access is not denied to ports defined as safe ports. Also, secure socket connections via the proxy are denied on all ports, except for SSL ports (!SSL_ports). HTTP access is permitted only from the local host and is denied to all other hosts.

To allow the client computers on your network access to your HTTP service, you need to create your own http_access entries. You probably want to do something more restrictive than simply saying http_access allow all. Here is an example of a more restrictive acl group and how to assign that group to HTTP access:

```
acl ourlan src 10.0.0.1-10.0.0.100/255.255.255.0
http_access allow ourlan
```

In the previous example, all computers at IP addresses 10.0.0.1 through 10.0.0.100 are assigned to the ourlan group (the netmask is 255.255.255.0, indicating that the network address is 10.0.0.0). Access is then allowed for ourlan with the http_access line.

Configuring caching in squid.conf

Caching, as it relates to a proxy server, is the process of storing data on an intermediate system between the Web server that sent the data and the client that received it. The assumption is that later requests for the same data can be serviced more quickly by not having to go all the way back to the original server. Instead, the proxy server can simply send you the content from its copy in cache. Another benefit of caching is that it reduces demands on network resources and on the information servers.

You can arrange caching with other caching proxy servers to form a cache hierarchy. The idea is to have a *parent cache* exist close to an entry to the Internet backbone. When a *child cache* requests an object, if the parent doesn't have it, the parent goes out and gets the object, sends a copy to the child, and keeps a copy itself. That way, if another request for the data comes to the parent, it can probably service that request without making another request to the original server. This hierarchy also supports *sibling caches*, which can, in effect, create a pool of caching servers on the same level.

> **CAUTION:** Caching can consume a lot of your hard disk space if you let it. If you have separate partitions on your system, make sure that you have enough space in /var to handle the added load.

Here are some cache-related tags that you should consider setting:

- **cache_peer** — If there is a cache parent whose resources you can use, you can add the parent cache using this tag. You would need to obtain the parent cache's host name, the type of cache (parent), proxy port (probably 3128), and ICP port (probably 3130) from the administrator of the parent cache. (If you have no parent cache, you don't have to set this value.) Here's an example of a cache_peer entry:

```
cache_peer parent.handsonhistory.com parent 3128 3130
```

  You can also add options to the end of the line, such as proxy-only (so that what you get from the parent isn't stored locally) and weight=n (where n is replaced by a number above 1 to indicate that the parent should be used above other parents). Add default if the parent is used as a last resort (when all other parents don't have the requested data).

- **cache_mem** — Specifies the amount of cache memory (RAM) used to store in-transit objects (ones that are currently being used), hot objects (ones that are used often), and negative-cached objects (recent failed requests). The default is 8MB, though you can raise that value. To set cache_mem to 16MB, enter the following:

```
cache_mem  16 MB
```

> **NOTE:** Because Squid will probably use a total of three times the amount of space you give it for all its processing, Squid documentation recommends that you use a cache_mem size one-third the size of the space that you actually have available for Squid.

- **cache_dir** — Specifies the directory (or directories if you want to distribute cache across multiple disks or partitions) in which cache swap files are stored. The default is the `/var/spool/squid` directory. You can also specify how much disk space to use for cache in megabytes (100 is the default), the number of first-level directories to create (16 is the default), and the number of second-level directories (256 is the default). Here is an example:

```
cache_dir  /var/spool/squid 100 16 256
```

> **NOTE:** The cache directory must exist. Squid won't create it for you. It will, however, create the first- and second-level directories.

- **cache_mgr** — Add the e-mail address of the user who should receive e-mail if the cache daemon dies. By default, e-mail is sent to the local Webmaster. To change that value to the root user, use the following:

```
cache_mgr  root
```

- **cache_effective_user** — After the squid daemon process is started as root, subsequent processes are run as `squid` user and group (by default). To change that subsequent user to a different name (for example, to `nobody`) set the `cache_effective_user` as follows:

```
cache_effective_user  nobody
```

> **NOTE:** When I changed the `cache_effective_user` name so that a user other than `squid` ran the `squid` daemon, the messages log recorded several failed attempts to initialize the Squid cache before the process exited. When I changed the user name back to `squid`, the process started properly. To use the `cache_effective_user` feature effectively, you must identify which files are not allowing access.

Configuring port numbers in squid.conf

When you configure client computers to use your Squid proxy services, the clients need to know your computer's name (or IP address) and the port numbers associated with the services. For a client wanting to use your proxy to access the Web, the HTTP port is the needed number. Here are the tags that you use to set port values in Squid for different services, along with their default values:

- **http_port 3128** — The `http_port` is set to 3128 by default. Client workstations need to know this number (or the number you change this value to) to access your proxy server for HTTP services (that is, Web browsing).

- **icp_port 3130** — ICP requests are sent to and from neighboring caches through port 3130 by default.

- **htcp_port 4827** — ICP sends HTCP requests to and from neighboring caches on port 4827 by default.

Debugging Squid

If Squid isn't working properly when you set it up, or if you just want to monitor Squid activities, there are several tools and log files to help you.

Checking the squid.conf file

By running the squid daemon with the -X option (described earlier), you can check what is being set from the squid.conf file. You can add an -X option to the SQUID_OPTS line in the /etc/init.d/squid file. Then run /etc/init.d/squid restart. A whole lot of information is output, which details what is being set from squid.conf. If there are syntax errors in the file, they appear here.

Checking Squid log files

Squid log files (in Fedora) are stored in the /var/log/squid directory by default. The following are the log files created there, descriptions of what they contain, and descriptions of how they might help you debug potential problems:

- **access.log** — Contains entries that describe each time the cache has been hit or missed when a client requests HTTP content. Along with that information is the identity of the host making the request (IP address) and the content they are requesting. Use this information to find out when content is being used from cache and when the remote server must be accessed to obtain the content. Here is what some of the access result codes mean:

  - **TCP_DENIED** — Squid denied access for the request.
  - **TCP_HIT** — Cache contained a valid copy of the object.
  - **TCP_IMS_HIT** — A fresh version of the requested object was still in cache when the client asked if the content had changed.
  - **TCP_IMS_MISS** — An If-Modified-Since request was issued by the client for a stale object.
  - **TCP_MEM_HIT** — Memory contained a valid copy of the object.
  - **TCP_MISS** — Cache did not contain the object.
  - **TCP_NEGATIVE_HIT** — The object was negatively cached, meaning that an error was returned (such as the file not being found) when the object was requested.
  - **TCP_REF_FAIL_HIT** — A stale object was returned from cache because of a failed request to validate the object.

- **TCP_REFRESH_HIT** — A stale copy of the object was in cache, but a request to the server returned information that the object had not been modified.

- **TCP_REFRESH_MISS** — A stale cache object was replaced by new, updated content.

- **TCP_SWAPFAIL** — An object could not be accessed from cache, despite the belief that the object should have been there.

- **cache.log** — Contains valuable information about your Squid configuration when the squid daemon starts up. You can see how much memory is available (Max Mem), how much swap space (Max Swap), the location of the cache directory (`/var/spool/squid`), the types of connections being accepted (HTTP, ICP, and SNMP), and the port on which connections are being accepted. You can also see a lot of information about cached objects (such as how many are loaded, expired, or canceled).

- **store.log** — Contains entries that show when content is being swapped out from memory to the cache (SWAPOUT), swapped back into memory from cache (SWAPIN), or released from cache (RELEASE). You can see where the content comes from originally and where it is being placed in the cache. Time is logged in this file in raw UNIX time (in milliseconds).

You might also be interested in another log file: `/var/log/messages`. This file contains entries describing the startup and exit status of the squid daemon.

Using the top command

Run the `top` command to see information about running processes, including the Squid process. If you are concerned about performance hits from too much Squid activity, type **M** from within the top window. The M option displays information about running processes, sorted by the percent of memory each process is using. If you find that Squid is consuming too large a percentage of your system memory, you can reduce the memory usage by resetting the `cache_mem` value in your `squid.conf` file.

Setting up Proxy Clients

For your Fedora proxy server to provide Web-browsing access (HTTP) to the Windows and Fedora client computers on your network, each client needs to do a bit of set-up within the Web browser. The beauty of using proxy servers is in what your client computers don't need to know, such as the following:

- Addresses of DNS servers
- Telephone numbers of ISPs
- Chat scripts to connect to the ISP

There are probably other things that clients don't need to know, but you get the idea. After the proxy server has a connection to the Internet and has allowed a client computer on the LAN access to that service, all the client needs to know is the following:

- **Host name** — The name or IP address of the proxy server. (This assumes that the client can reach the proxy over the company's LAN or other IP-based network.)
- **Port numbers** — The port number of the HTTP service (3128 by default). That same port number can be used for FTP and gopher services as well.

How you go about setting up proxy service on the client has more to do with the browser you are using than with the operating system you are using. Follow the procedures outlined in the following sections for setting up Mozilla, Microsoft Internet Explorer, Mosaic, or Lynx browsers.

Configuring Mozilla to use a proxy

Normally, you would set up Mozilla to browse the Web over a TCP/IP connection to the Internet (over telephone lines or via a router on your LAN). Follow this procedure to change Mozilla to access the Web through your proxy server:

1. Open Mozilla.
2. Choose Edit → Preferences. The Preferences window appears.
3. Next to the Advanced category, click the plus sign and select Proxies.
4. Click Manual proxy configuration to open the Proxies window (see Figure 16-3).
5. Type the proxy server's name or IPaddress in the address boxes for HTTP, FTP, and Gopher services.
6. Type the port number for HTTP services on your proxy server (probably 3128) in the Port boxes for HTTP, FTP, and Gopher services.
7. Click OK.

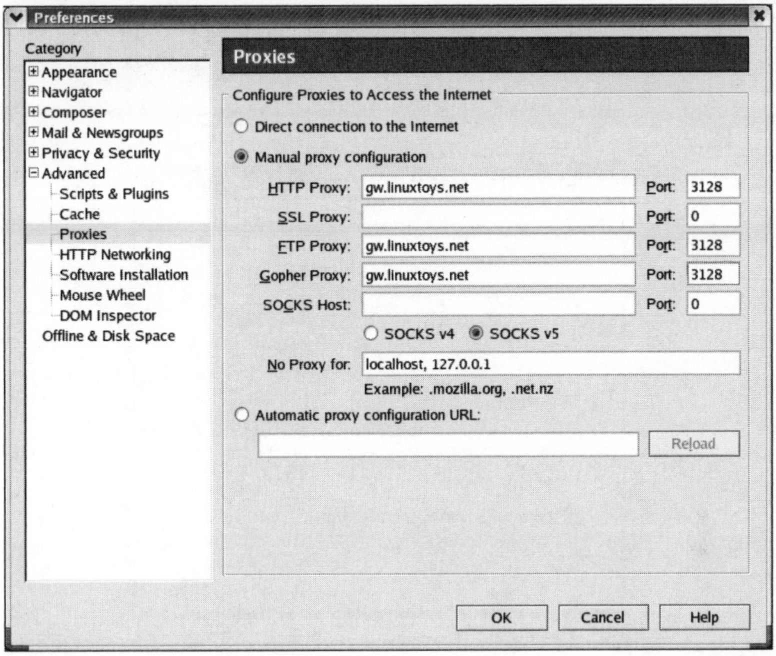

Figure 16-3: The Preferences window identifies proxy servers and port numbers in Mozilla.

The next time you request a Web address from Mozilla, it will contact the proxy server to try to obtain the content.

Configuring Internet Explorer to use a proxy

If you have Microsoft Windows clients on your network, you can configure them to use your Linux proxy server as well. To configure Internet Explorer to use your Linux proxy server to get to the Web, you need to change a few Internet options. Follow this procedure:

1. Open the Internet Explorer window.

2. Choose View (or Tools) → Internet Options. The Internet Options window appears.

3. Click the Connections tab.

4. Assuming you have a LAN already configured, click Local Area Network and then click LAN Settings. The Local Area Network Settings window should appear, as shown in Figure 16-4.

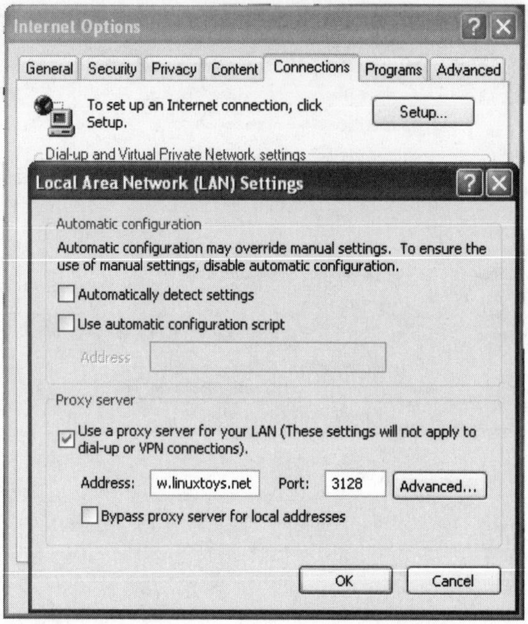

Figure 16-4: The Local Area Network Settings window lets you add proxies to Internet Options in Internet Explorer.

5.   Click the Use a proxy server box so a check mark appears.

6.   Type the address of the proxy server and the port number for HTTP services (probably 3128).

> **TIP:** Microsoft Internet Explorer assumes that the same ports are used for HTTP, Gopher, and FTP services. If this is not true, click Advanced and change the port numbers for each service accordingly.

7.   Click OK (in the Local Area Network Settings window) and OK again (in the Internet Options window).

The next time you try to access the Web from Internet Explorer, it will try to do so through the proxy server you defined.

Configuring other browsers to use a proxy

There are different methods for indicating a proxy server to other browsers available with Linux. To have a Mosaic or lynx browser use a proxy server to access the Internet, add an environment variable to the shell where the browser will run. Here's how you would set the environment variables for HTTP, Gopher, and FTP proxy services to a proxy computer named maple using a csh or tcsh shell:

```
setenv http_proxy http://maple:3128/
setenv gopher_proxy http://maple:3128/
setenv ftp_proxy http://maple:3128/
```

If you are using a ksh or bash shell, type the following:

```
export http_proxy=http://maple:3128
export gopher_proxy=http://maple:3128
export ftp_proxy=http://maple:3128
```

You can add any of these values to your start-up scripts. Or, to make them available on a system-wide basis, you could add them to a system configuration file, such as /etc/profile or /etc/skel/.bash_profile.

For the elinks and links browsers, you can indicate to use a proxy server in the /etc/elinks.conf file. For example, here are the lines you would add to the /etc/elinks.conf file to have elinks and links use the computer named maple act as a proxy for FTPand HTTP services:

```
protocol.ftp.proxy.host maple:3128
protocol.http.proxy.host maple:3128
```

Summary

Connecting to the Internet opens a whole world of possibilities for your Fedora computer. Using Fedora as a public Web server, mail server, or FTP server depends on Fedora's capability to connect to the Internet. Likewise, if your computers are already connected in a LAN, adding an Internet connection can provide Internet access to everyone on the LAN in one stroke.

Descriptions of how Internet domains are organized built on the coverage of IP addresses in the previous chapter. Creating dial-up connections to the Internet focused on descriptions of PPP. This chapter also discusses several different techniques for connecting your LAN to the Internet. You can set up your Fedora computer as a router or as a Squid proxy server.

To use your Internet connection to transport sensitive data to another location in your company's private network, you can configure a VPN. This chapter describes how to use IPSEC in Fedora to create a VPN connection between two locations.

## Chapter 17

Setting Up a Print Server

In This Chapter

- Understanding printing in Linux
- Setting up printers
- Using printing commands
- Managing document printing
- Sharing printers

Sharing printers is a good way to save money and make your printing more efficient. Very few people need to print all the time, but when they do want to print something, they usually need it quickly. Setting up a print server can save money by eliminating the need for a printer at every workstation. Some of those savings can be used to buy printers that can output more pages per minute or have higher-quality output.

You can attach printers to your Fedora Linux system to make them available to users of that system or to other computers on the network. You can configure your Fedora Linux printer as a remote CUPS printer, a Samba printer, or a NetWare printer. With Samba and NetWare, you are emulating Windows and NetWare servers.

This chapter describes configuring and using printers in Fedora Linux. It focuses on Common UNIX Printing Service (CUPS), which is the recommended print service for the current version of Fedora Linux. To configure CUPS printers, this chapter focuses on the Fedora Printer Configuration window (`system-config-printer` command).

Once a local printer is configured, print commands (such as `lpr`) are available for carrying out the actual printing. Commands also exist for querying print queues (`lpq`), manipulating print queues (`lpc`), and removing print queues (`lprm`). A local printer can also be shared as a print server to users on other computers on your network.

Choosing CUPS or LPRng Print Services

In earlier releases of Red Hat Linux, there were two major printing services offered with Red Hat Linux: CUPS and LPRng. Although LPRng has been dropped from the distribution, the

LPRng package is still available and still can be used with Fedora Linux. The following sections discuss some of the characteristics of those two services.

Common UNIX Printing Service

CUPS has become the standard for printing from Linux and other UNIX-like operating systems. Instead of being based on older, text-based line printing technology, CUPS was designed to meet today's needs for standardized printer definitions and sharing on IP-based networks (as most computer networks are today). Here are some features of CUPS:

- **IPP** — At its heart, CUPS is based on the Internet Printing Protocol (www.pwg.org/ipp), a standard that was created to simplify how printers can be shared over IP networks. In the IPP model, printer servers and clients who want to print can exchange information about the model and features of a printer using HTTP (that is, Web content) protocol. A server could also broadcast the availability of a printer, so a printing client can easily find a list of locally available printers.

- **Drivers** — CUPS also standardized how printer drivers are created. The idea was to have a common format that could be used by printer manufacturers that could work across all different types of UNIX systems. That way, a manufacturer only had to create the driver once to work for Linux, Mac OS X, and a variety of UNIX derivatives.

- **Printer classes** — Using printer classes, you can create multiple print server entries that point to the same printer or one print server entry that points to multiple printers. In the first case, multiple entries could each allow different options (such as pointing to a particular paper tray or printing with certain character sizes or margins). In the second case, you could have a pool of printers so that printing is distributed. This would decrease the occurrence of congested print jobs, caused by a malfunctioning printer or a printer that is dealing with very large documents.

- **UNIX print commands** — To integrate into Linux and other UNIX environments, CUPS offers versions of standard commands for printing and managing printers that have been traditionally offered with UNIX systems. (See the "Switching printing service" section for information on how to have CUPS take over these standard commands.)

The Printer configuration window (system-config-printer command) lets you configure printers that use the CUPS facility. However, CUPS also offers a Web-based interface for adding and managing printers. Configuration files for CUPS are contained in the /etc/cups directory. In particular, you might be interested in the cupsd.conf file (which identifies permission, authentication, and other information for the printer daemon) and printers.conf (which identifies addresses and options for configured printers).

Line Printer New Generation

The LPRng print service is an extended version of the old Berkeley UNIX LPR print spooler facility. It was designed to work in a networked computing environment, where multiple printers and queues needed to be managed. While still supporting older printing commands (lpr, lpq, lprm, and others), it added many administrative and security features (such as support for Kerberos and PGP authentication).

If you have used LPRng in previous releases of Fedora or Red Hat Linux, you should consider switching to CUPS. By default, the procedures in this chapter use CUPS as the underlying print service.

Switching printing service

CUPS is the preferred alternative to LPRng in Fedora Linux. CUPS is based on the Internet Printing Protocol, whose purpose is to standardize printing services across all UNIX platforms (including Linux).

CUPS supports many of the same interfaces that are in LPRng. Thus, if you decide to replace LPRng with CUPS, you can still use the following commands to print and manage documents:

- **cancel or lprm** — Cancels a print job.
- **lp or lpr** — Prints a document.
- **lpc** — Controls print service operation. (Although in CUPS it only lists printer status.)
- **lpq** — Views print queues.
- **lpstat** — Views the status of the print service.

In other words, after you replace the underlying print service, you and the others who print on your Fedora Linux system should still be able to use the print service as you did before. (Most of these basic printing commands are described later in this chapter.)

> **NOTE:** To use CUPS, you must install the htmlview and cups packages from CD #1.

You can switch to CUPS easily by using the alternatives feature. In previous versions of Red Hat Linux, the alternatives system linked the printing commands into the new service via the Printer Switcher window. Because the Printer Switcher window is no longer available with Fedora, you have to change the service manually. Then, all you have to do is start up the CUPS daemon instead of the LPRng daemon for CUPS to take over. (Chapter 10 shows you how to use the alternatives system to switch to CUPS. Switching service to CUPS enables new printing commands, stops the lpd daemon, and starts the cupsd daemon.)

Although switching LPRng for CUPS isn't too difficult, you must still do some work to configure CUPS. The following sections provide an overview of configuring CUPS as your printing service.

Setting Up Printers

To install a printer from your desktop, use the Printer Configuration window (`printconf-gui` command). This tool enables you to add printers, delete printers, and edit printer properties. It also lets you send test pages to those printers to make sure they are working properly.

The key here is that you are configuring printers that are managed by your print daemon (`cupsd` for the CUPS service). After a printer is configured, users on your local system can use it. After that, you can refer to the "Configuring Print Servers" section to learn how to make the server available to users from other computers on your network.

The printers that you set up can be connected directly to your computer (as on a parallel port) or to another computer on the network (for example, from another UNIX system, Windows system, or NetWare server).

Configuring local printers

Add a local printer (in other words, a printer connected directly to your computer) with the Printer configuration window using the following procedure. (See the "Choosing a Printer" sidebar if you don't yet have a printer.) Go to Edit a Printer to change the settings for an existing printer.

> **TIP:** You should connect your printer before starting this procedure. This enables the printer software to autodetect the printer's location and to immediately test the printer when you have finished adding it.

Choosing a Printer

If you are choosing a new printer to use with your Fedora Linux system, look for one that is PostScript-compatible. The PostScript language is the preferred format for Linux and UNIX printing and has been for many years. Every major word processing product that runs on Fedora, Red Hat Linux, and UNIX systems supports PostScript printing.

If you get a PostScript printer and it is not explicitly shown in the list of supported printers, simply select the PostScript filter when you install the printer locally. No special drivers are needed. Your next best choice is to choose a printer that supports PCL. In either case, make sure that the PostScript or PCL are implemented in the printer hardware and not in the Windows driver.

When selecting a printer, avoid those that are referred to as *Winprinters*. These printers use nonstandard printing interfaces (those other than PostScript or PCL). Support for these low-end printers is hit-or-miss. For example, some low-end HP DeskJet printers use the pnm2ppa driver to print documents in Printing Performance Architecture (PPA) format. Some Lexmark printers use the pbm217k driver to print.

Although drivers are available for many of these Winprinters, many of them are not fully supported.

Ghostscript may also support your printer; if it does, you can use that tool to do your printing. Ghostscript (found at `www.ghostscript.com`) is a free PostScript-interpreter program. It can convert PostScript content to output that can be interpreted by a variety of printers.

You'll find an excellent list of printers supported in Linux at `www.linuxprinting.org`. I strongly recommend that you visit that site before you purchase a printer to work with Linux. Besides showing supported printers, the site also has a page describing how to choose a printer for use with Linux (`www.linuxprinting.org/suggested.html`).

Adding a local printer

To add a local printer, follow these steps:

1. To open the Printer Configuration, either select System Settings → Printing from the main menu or type the following as root user from a Terminal window:

   ```
   # printconf-gui &
   ```

   The Printer Configuration window appears.

2. Click New. An Add a New Print Queue window appears.

3. Click Forward. The window that appears asks you to add a printer name and short description for the printer, as shown in Figure 17-1.

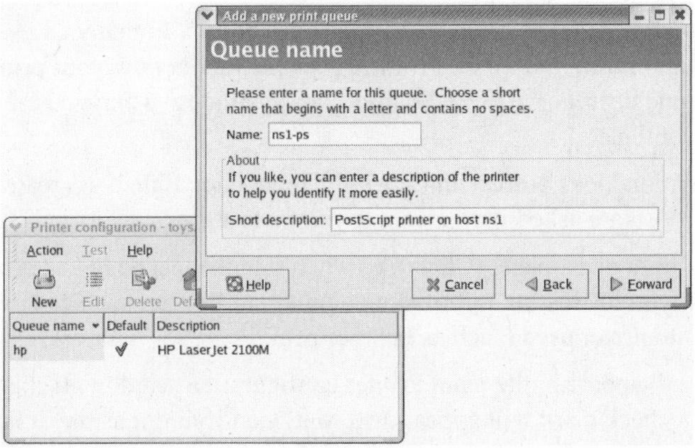

Figure 17-1: Add printers connected locally or remotely with the Printer configuration window.

4. Add the following information; then click Forward:

   - **Name:** Add the name you want to give to identify the printer. The name must begin with a letter, but after the initial letter, it can contain a combination of letters, numbers, dashes (-), and underscores (_). For example, an HP printer on a computer named `maple` could be named `hp-maple`.

- **Description:** Add a few words describing the printer, such as its features (an HP LaserJet 2100M with PCL and PS support) or its location (in Room 205 under the coffee pot).

The Queue type window appears.

5. Select Locally-connected, choose the device to which the printer is connected (`/dev/lp0`, `/dev/usb/lp0`, and `/dev/ttyS0` are the first parallel, usb, and serial ports, respectively), and click Forward. (Type **lpinfo -v | less** to see all available ports.) Alternatively, you could do one of the following:

   - If your printer is not on the list because you have not yet connected it, you can connect it now and select Rescan Devices to have your computer try again to detect the printer.

   - If you intend to connect your printer later, or for some reason it's not being scanned, click Custom Device and specify the device name where the printer will be found.

The Printer Model window appears.

6. Click the arrow on the select manufacturer box, then choose the manufacturer of your printer. From the list that appears, select the printer model you have.

> **TIP:** If your printer doesn't appear on the list but supports PCL (which is HP's Printer Control Language), you can try selecting one of the HP printers (such as HP LaserJet). If your printer supports PostScript, you can select PostScript printer from the list. Selecting Raw Print Queue enables you to send documents to the printer that are already formatted for that printer type.

7. With your printer model selected, click the Notes button. In many cases, you will see good information from the Linux Printing Database about how your printer is configured and how to tune it further. (Close the information window when you are done.) Click Forward to continue.

8. If the information looks correct, click Apply; then click Finish to create the entry for your printer. You are asked if you want to print a test page.

9. Click Yes to print a test page. (Click Yes when told the test page has printed.) This test page will tell you interesting information about your printer, such as the resolution and the type of interpreter used (such as PostScript).

The printer will appear in the main Printer configuration window. If it is the only printer configured, a check mark will appear next to it, identifying it as the default printer. As you add other printers, you can change the default printer by selecting the one you want and clicking the Default button.

10. Choose Apply to save the changes (if necessary).

11. If you would like to try other test pages, click Test and select one of the following:

- **US Letter PostScript test page** — Sends a letter-sized (8.5" x 11") page to the printer in PostScript format. If you have a color printer, the page appears in color.

- **A4 PostScript test page** — Sends an A4 PostScript-formatted page to the printer.

- **ASCII text test page** — Sends plain text to the named printer.

- **Duplex test** — Sends a test page to see if the printer is in half or full duplex.

- **JPEG test** — Sends a JPEG image to the printer.

Printing should be working at this point. (If you want to share this printer with other computers on your network, refer to the "Configuring Print Servers" section of this chapter.)

Editing a local printer

After you have created a printer queue, you can edit the printer queue definitions to change how the printer behaves. From the Printer configuration window, do the following:

1. **Edit** — With your printer selected, click Edit. The Edit a Print Queue page appears. The following steps describe how to change options besides those you added originally.

2. **Queue options** — Click the Queue options tab. From this tab, you can:

   - Add banner pages at the beginning and/or end of a job. This is good practice for a printer that is shared by many people. The banner page helps you sort who gets which print job. The standard banner page shows the ID of the print job, the title of the file, the user that requested the print job, and any billing information associated with it.

   - Change the imageable area by setting all four side margins. The default is 36 points (one inch) on all four margins. You can adjust any of the four margins.

   - Add or remove filter options. These options define attributes of printing to the selected printer. Click the Add button to see queue options you can add. Options are stored in the /etc/cups/lpoptions file for each printer. Options that you might want to change include cpi (print text documents 10, 12, or 17 characters per inch) or lpi (print text documents 6 or 8 lines per inch). For descriptions of other options, look at the CUPS Internet Printing Protocol page (/usr/share/doc/cups-*/ipp.html).

3. **Driver options** — Click Driver options to set defaults for options related to the printer driver. Many of these options can be overridden when someone prints a document. Here are a few of the options you might want to set:

   - **Media Source** — For multitray printers, you can select which tray to use by default.

   - **Page Size** — The default is U.S. letter size, but you can also ask the printer to print legal size, envelopes, or ISO A4 standard pages.

   - **Resolution** — Select the default printing resolution (such as 300, 600, or 1,200 dots per inch). Higher resolutions result in better quality, but take longer to print.

   - **Printing Mode** — Choose to print in grayscale or color.

Click OK when you are satisfied with the changes you made to the local printer.

Configuring remote printers

To use a printer that is available on your network, you must identify that printer to your Fedora Linux system. Supported remote printer connections include Networked CUPS (IPP) printers, Networked UNIX (LPD) printers, Networked Windows (SMB) printers, NetWare printers and JetDirect printers. (Of course, both CUPS and UNIX print servers can be run from Linux systems, as well as other UNIX systems.)

In each case, you need a network connection from your Fedora Linux system that enables you to reach the servers to which those printers are connected. To use a remote printer, of course, requires that someone set up that printer on the remote server computer. See the section "Configuring Print Servers" later in this chapter for information on how to do that in Fedora Linux.

You can use the Printer configuration window to configure each of the remote printer types:

1. From the Red Hat menu, select System Settings → Printing.
2. Click New. The Add a New Printer Queue window appears.
3. Click Forward. The Queue Name window appears.
4. Type a short name and description of the printer and click Forward.
5. Click the Select a Queue Type box and select one of the following:
   - Networked CUPS (IPP)
   - Networked UNIX (LPD)
   - Networked Windows (SMB)
   - Networked Novell (NCP)
   - Networked JetDirect

   Click Forward.
6. Next, continue following the steps in whichever of the following sections is appropriate.

Adding a remote CUPS printer

After choosing to add a CUPS printer from the Printer configuration window, you must add the following information to the window that appears:

- **Server** — The host of the computer to which the printer is attached (or otherwise accessible). This can be an IP address or TCP/IP host name for the computer (the TCP/IP name is accessible from your /etc/hosts file or through a DNS name server).
- **Path** — The printer name on the remote CUPS print server. CUPS supports the concept of printer instances, which allows each printer to have several sets of options. So, if the remote CUPS printer is configured this way, you might be able to choose a particular

path to a printer, such as hp/300dpi or hp/1200dpi. A slash character separates the print queue name from the printer instance.

Complete the rest of the procedure as you would for a local printer.

Adding a remote UNIX printer

After you have selected to add a UNIX printer from the Printer configuration window, you must add the following information to the window that appears:

- **Server** — The host name of the computer to which the printer is attached (or otherwise accessible). This is the IP address or TCP/IP name for the computer (the TCP/IP name is accessible from your /etc/hosts file or through a DNS name server).

- **Queue** — The printer name on the remote UNIX computer.

Complete the configuration as you would for a local printer.

> **TIP:** If the print job is rejected when you send it to test the printer, the print server computer may not have allowed you access to the printer. Ask the remote computer's administrator to add your host name to the /etc/lpd.perms file. (Type **lpq -P***printer* to see the status of your print job.)

Adding a Windows (SMB) printer

Enabling your computer to access an SMB printer (the Windows printing service) involves adding an entry for the printer in the Printer configuration window.

After you have selected to add a Windows printer to the Printer configuration window (described previously), you are presented with a list of computers on your network that have been detected as offering SMB services (file and/or printing service). You can:

- Select the server (click the arrow next to its name so that it points down).

- Select the printer from the list of available printers shown.

- When prompted, fill in the user name and password needed to access the SMB printer. (You may also fill in the Workgroup information, if required.) Click OK to continue.

Alternatively, you could identify a server that does not appear on the list of servers. Click the Specify button and input the following information in the appropriate fields:

- **Workgroup** — The workgroup name assigned to the SMB server. Filling in the workgroup name isn't necessary in all cases.

> **TIP:** If you are printing to a Windows 95/98 printer, you can find the Workgroup and Hostname of Print Server entries in the Network window. From Windows 95/98, choose Start → Settings → Control Panel. Open the Network window, and then click its Identification tab, which will display the computer name and workgroup. If there is no Identification tab, you may need to install the Client for Microsoft Networks client in the Network window.

- **Server** — The server name is the NetBIOS name or IP address for the computer, which may or may not be the same as its TCP/IP name. To translate this name into the address needed to reach the SMB host, Samba checks several places where the name may be assigned to an IP address. Samba checks the following (in the order shown) until it finds a match: the local /etc/hosts file, the local /etc/lmhosts file, a WINS server on the network, or responses to broadcasts on each local network interface to resolve the name.

- **Share** — The share name is the name under which the printer is shared with the remote computer. It may be different from the name by which local users of the SMB printer know the printer.

> **TIP:** To find a remote printer name on most Windows systems, first go to the Printers folder (Start → Settings → Printers), and double-click the printer being shared. From the printer queue window that appears, choose Printer → Properties, and then select the Sharing tab. The Sharing tab indicates whether the printer is shared and, if so, the name under which it is shared.

- **User** — The user name is the name required by the SMB server system to give you access to the SMB printer. A user name is not necessary if you are authenticating the printer based on share-level, rather than user-level, access control. With share-level access, you can add a password for each shared printer or file system.

- **Password** — The password associated with the SMB user name or the shared resource, depending on the kind of access control being used.

> **CAUTION:** When you enter a User and Password for SMB, that information is stored unencrypted in the /etc/cups/printers.conf file. Be sure that the file remains readable only by root.

Complete the configuration as you would for a local printer.

The result is new entries in the /etc/cups/cupsd.conf and printers.conf files. This /etc/cups/printers.conf entry shows the printer entry we just created:

```
<Printer NS1-PS>
Info Created by redhat-config-Eprinter 0.6.x
DeviceURI smb://jjones:my9passswd@FSTREET/NS1/hp
Location HP on ns1
State Idle
Accepting Yes
JobSheets none none
QuotaPeriod 0
PageLimit 0
KLimit 0
</Printer>
```

The DeviceURI is the key information. A lot of information is packed into the DeviceURI line. It identifies the location as a smb object. The user name is jjones, with a password of my9passswd. The workgroup is FSTREET, the server is NS1, and the printer queue name is hp.

The contents of the cupsd.conf file define who you will allow to use this printer.

```
<Location /printers/NS1-PS>
Order Deny,Allow
Deny From All
Allow From 127.0.0.1
AuthType None
</Location>
```

Based on the information just shown, only users from the local host (127.0.0.1) are allowed to use the printer. No authentication is necessary for them to use it.

If everything is set up properly, you should be able to use the standard lpr command to print the file to the printer. With this example, you could use the following form for printing:

```
$ cat file1.ps | lpr -P NS1-PS
```

> **TIP:** If you are receiving failure messages, make sure that the computer to which you are printing is accessible. For the example above, you could type **smbclient -L NS1 -U jjones**. Type the password (my9passswd, in this case). If you get a positive name query response after you enter a password, you should see a list of shared printers and files from that server. Check the names, and try printing again.

Adding a NetWare printer

With this procedure, you set up your Fedora Linux system to use a printer that is connected to (or otherwise managed by) a NetWare file and print server. As with SMB printing, you must gather the information about the server, queue, user, and password.

Select to add a Novell printer (Novell created NetWare) from the Printer configuration window (described previously), and then fill in the following information:

- **Server** — The host name of the computer to which the printer is attached (or otherwise accessible). This is the NetWare Server name for the computer.

- **Queue** — The name of the print queue on the NetWare server.

- **User** — The user name required by the NetWare server system to enable access to the NetWare printer.

- **Password** — The password associated with the user name.

Complete the configuration as you would for a local printer.

Working with CUPS Printing

The Printer configuration window effectively hides the underlying CUPS facility. There may be times, however, when you want to work directly with the tools and configuration files that come with CUPS. The following sections describe how to use some special CUPS features.

Using Web-based CUPS administration

Although the preferred way to configure CUPS printing in Fedora Linux is with the Printer configuration window, CUPS offers its own Web-based administrative tool. CUPS listens on port 631 to provide access to the CUPS Web-based administrative interface. On the local computer, type the following into your Web browser's location box:

```
http://localhost:631/admin
```

You will be prompted for a valid login name and password. Type the root login name and the root user's password. A screen similar to the one shown in Figure 17-2 appears.

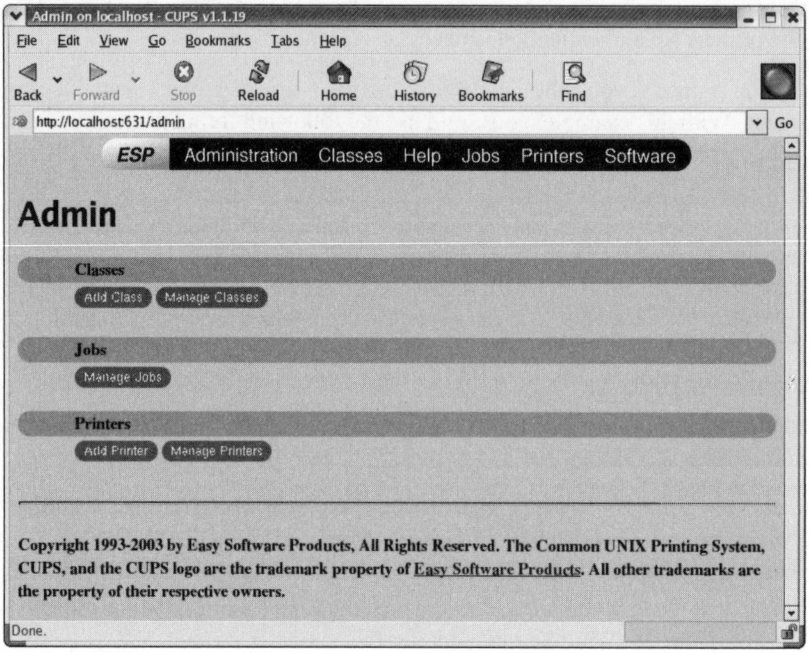

Figure 17-2: CUPS enables Web-based administration via port 631.

By default, Web-based CUPS administration is only available from the localhost. To access Web-based CUPS administration from another computer, you must change the /admin section in the /etc/cups/cupsd.conf file. As recommended in the text of this file, you should limit access to CUPS administration from the Web. In the following example, I added an Allow line to allow access from a host from IP address 10.0.0.5 (you must also change the Listen 127.0.0.1:631 line to listen outside of your local host, as described a bit later).

```
<Location /admin>
AuthType Basic
AuthClass System
Order Deny, Allow
```

```
Deny from All
Allow From 127.0.0.1
Allow From 10.0.0.5
</Location>
```

From the computer at address 10.0.0.5, I typed the same line shown above in my Web browser (substituting the CUPS server's name or IP address for localhost). When prompted, I entered the root user name and password.

Although the Fedora project doesn't recommend adding or modifying printers through this interface, you can safely:

- **List print jobs** — Click Jobs to see what print jobs are currently active from any of the printers configured for this server. Click Show Completed Jobs to see information about jobs that are already printed.

- **Create a printer class** — Click Classes; then click Add Class and identify a name and location for a printer class. Click Continue. Then, from the list of printers configured on your server, select which ones will go into this class.

- **View printers** — Without changing printer configurations, you can click Printers and view the printers you have configured. For each printer that appears, you can click Stop Printer (to stop the printer from printing, but still accept print jobs for the queue), Reject Jobs (to not accept any further print jobs for the moment), or Print Test Page (to print a page). Figure 17-3 shows the Printers page.

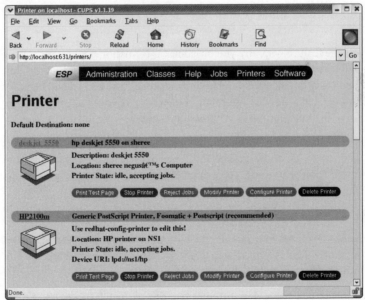

Figure 17-3: Temporarily stop printing or print test pages from the Printers page.

Configuring the CUPS server (cupsd.conf)

The `cupsd` daemon process listens for requests to your CUPS print server and responds to those requests based on settings in the `/etc/cups/cupsd.conf` file. The configuration variables in `cupsd.conf` file are in the same form as those of the Apache configuration file (`httpd.conf`).

The Printer configuration window adds access information to the `cupsd.conf` file. You can step through the `cupsd.conf` file to further tune your CUPS server. Here are a few suggestions:

```
Classification topsecret
```

With the classification set to `topsecret`, you can have Top Secret displayed on all pages that go through the print server. Other classifications you can substitute for `topsecret` include: `classified`, `confidential`, `secret`, and `unclassified`.

```
ServerCertificate /etc/cups/ssl/server.crt
ServerKey /etc/cups/ssl/server.key
```

The `ServerCertificate` and `ServerKey` lines can be set up to indicate where the certificate and key are stored, respectively. Activate these two lines if you want to do encrypted connections. Then add your certificate and key to the files noted.

```
Browsing On
BrowseProtocols cups
BrowseAddress 255.255.255.255
Listen 127.0.0.1:631
```

Browsing is the feature whereby you broadcast information about your printer on your local network and listen for other print servers' information. Browsing is on by default. Browsing information is also broadcast, by default, on address `255.255.255.255`. You can allow or deny incoming CUPS browser information (`BrowseAllow` and `BrowseDeny`) for selected addresses. All incoming browser information is allowed, by default.

To allow Web-based CUPS administration, the `cupsd` daemon listens on port 631 of the local host (`127.0.0.1`). To allow anyone to access this service from your network (if he or she has the proper login and password), you can change the Listen line shown previously to `Listen *:631`.

```
BrowseRelay source-address destination-address
```

With `BrowseRelay` on, you can allow CUPS to browse information to be passed among two or more networks. This is a good way to allow users on several connected LANs to discover and use printers on other nearby LANs.

You can allow or deny access to different features of the CUPS server. An access definition for a CUPS printer (created from the Printer configuration window) might appear as follows:

```
<Location /printers/ns1-hp1>
Order Deny,Allow
Deny From All
Allow From 127.0.0.1
AuthType None
</Location>
```

Here, printing to the ns1-hp1 printer is only allowed for users on the local host (127.0.0.1). No password is needed (AuthType None). To allow access to the administration tool requires the CUPS be configured to prompt for a password (AuthType Basic).

If you change any of the settings in the cupsd.conf file, you must restart the CUPS service to have the changes take effect. As root user, type **chkconfig cupsd restart**.

Configuring CUPS printer options

When a new printer is created from the Printer configuration window, that printer is defined in the /etc/cups/printers.conf file. Here is an example of a printer definition in printers.conf:

```
</Printer hp>
<DefaultPrinter printer>
Info Created by system-config-printer 0.6.x
DeviceURI parallel:/dev/lp0
Location HP LaserJet 2100M in hall closet
State Idle
Accepting Yes
JobSheets none none
QuotaPeriod 0
PageLimit 0
KLimit 0
</Printer>
```

This is an example of a local printer that serves as the default printer for the local system. The most interesting information relates to the DeviceURI, which shows us that the printer is connected to parallel port /dev/lp0. The State is Idle (ready to accept printer jobs) and the Accepting value is Yes (the printer is accepting print jobs by default).

The DeviceURI has several ways to identify the device name of a printer, reflecting where the printer is connected. Here are some examples listed in the printers.conf file:

```
DeviceURI parallel:/dev/plp
DeviceURI serial:/dev/ttyd1?baud=38400+size=8+parity=none+flow=soft
DeviceURI scsi:/dev/scsi/sc1d6l0
DeviceURI socket://hostname:port
DeviceURI tftp://hostname/path
DeviceURI ftp://hostname/path
DeviceURI http://hostname[:port]/path
DeviceURI ipp://hostname/path
DeviceURI smb://hostname/printer
```

The first three examples show the form for local printers (parallel, serial, and scsi). The other examples are for remote hosts. In each case, *hostname* can be the host's name or IP address. Port numbers or paths identify the locations of each printer on the host.

> **TIP:** If you find that you are not able to print because a particular printer driver is not supported in CUPS, you can set up your printer to accept jobs in raw mode. This can work well if you are printing from WIndows clients that have the correct print drivers installed on those clients. To allow raw printing in CUPS, uncomment the following line from the `/etc/cups/mime.types` file in Fedora Linux:
>
> ```
> application/octet-stream
> ```
>
> And uncomment the following line from the `/etc/cups/mime.convs` file:
>
> ```
> application/octet-stream   application/vnd.cups-raw   0   -
> ```
>
> After that, you can print files as raw data to your printers without using the `-oraw` option to print commands.

Managing Printing

To monitor your printing, Fedora Linux provides a Print Manager icon right on the desktop panel. Click it (or type **gnome-print-manager**) to see the GNOME Print Manager. Figure 17-4 shows an example of this window.

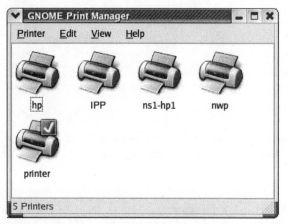

Figure 17-4: Display queues for your active printers.

A checkmark indicates the default printer. Select a printer and click Printer → Open. A window opens, displaying any print jobs that are queued for the selected printer.

At the moment, there doesn't appear to be any GUI tool for enabling and disabling the print queues or stopping and starting printing. Inside the `/etc/cups/printers.conf` file, each printer's definition describes whether it is stopped or active (`State` set to `Idle` or `Stopped`) and whether or not the queue is accepting print jobs (`Accepting Yes` or `No`). If you manually change any of those settings, you must restart the print server (type **service cups restart**).

Using Printing Commands

To remain backward compatible with older UNIX and Linux printing facilities, CUPS supports many of the old commands for working with printing. Most command-line printing with CUPS can be performed with the `lpr` command. Word processing applications, such as StarOffice, OpenOffice, and AbiWord, are set up to use this facility for printing.

With the Printer configuration window, you can define the filters needed for each printer so that the text can be formatted properly. Options to the `lpr` command can add filters to properly process the text. Other commands for managing printed documents include `lpq` (for viewing the contents of print queues), `lprm` (for removing print jobs from the queue), and `lpc` (for controlling printers).

> **CROSS-REFERENCE:** Chapter 6 provides examples of how to format and print documents in several different formats, including `troff` and TeX.

Using lpr to print

With the `lpr` command, you can print documents to both local and remote printers. Document files can be either added to the end of the `lpr` command line or directed to the `lpr` command using a pipe (`|`). Here is an example of a simple `lpr` command:

```
$ lpr doc1.ps
```

When you just specify a document file with `lpr`, output is directed to the default printer. As an individual user, you can change the default printer by setting the value of the PRINTER variable. Typically, you would add the PRINTER variable to one of your startup files, such as $HOME/.bashrc. Here is a line to add to your .bashrc file to set your default printer to lp3:

```
export PRINTER=lp3
```

To override the default printer, specify a particular printer on the `lpr` command line. The following example uses the `-P` option to select a different printer:

```
$ lpr -P canyonps doc1.ps
```

The `lpr` command has a variety of options that enable `lpr` to interpret and format several different types of documents. These include `-# num`, where num is replaced by the number of copies to print (from 1 to 100) and `-l` (which causes a document to be sent in raw mode, presuming that the document has already been formatted).

Listing status with lpc

The `lpc` command in CUPS has limited features. You can use `lpc` to list the status of your printers. Here is an example:

```
$ lpc status
hp:
```

```
                    printer is on device 'parallel' speed -1
                    queuing is enabled
                    printing is disabled
                    no entries
                    daemon present
deskjet_5550:

                    printer is on device '/dev/null' speed -1
                    queuing is enabled
                    printing is disabled
                    no entries
                    daemon present
```

This output shows two active printers. The first (hp) is connected to your parallel port. The second (deskjet_5550) is a network printer (shown as /dev/null). The hp printer is currently disabled (offline), although the queue is enabled so people can continue to send jobs to the printer.

Removing print jobs with lprm

Users can remove their own print jobs from the queue with the lprm command. Used alone on the command line, lprm removes all the user's print jobs from the default printer. To remove jobs from a specific printer, use the -P option, as follows:

```
$ lprm -P lp0
```

To remove all print jobs for the current user, type the following:

```
$ lprm -
```

The root user can remove all the print jobs for a specific user by indicating that user on the lprm command line. For example, to remove all print jobs for the user named mike, the root user would type the following:

```
$ lprm mike
```

To remove an individual print job from the queue, indicate the job number of that print job on the lprm command line. To find the job number, type the lpq command. Here's what the output of that command may look like:

```
$ lpq
printer is ready and printing
Rank    Owner            Job Files              Total Size Time
active  root             133 /home/jake/pr1        467
2       root             197 /home/jake/mydoc    23948
```

The output shows two printable jobs waiting in the queue. (In this case, they're not printing because the printer is off.) Under the Job column, you can see the job number associated with each document. To remove the first print job, type the following:

```
# lprm 133
```

Configuring Print Servers

You've configured a printer so that you and the other users on your computer can print to it. Now you want to share that printer with other people in your home, school, or office. Basically, that means configuring that printer as a print server.

The printers that are configured on your Linux system can be shared in different ways with other computers on your network. Not only can your computer act as a Linux print server (CUPS or LPRng), it can also look to client computers like a NetWare or SMB print server. After a local printer is attached to your Fedora Linux system, and your computer is connected to your local network, you can use the procedures in this section to share it with client computers using a Linux (UNIX), NetWare, or SMB interface.

> **CROSS-REFERENCE:** See Chapter 26 for information on configuring Linux as an AppleTalk server using the netatalk package.

Configuring a shared CUPS printer

After a local printer is added to your Fedora Linux computer, making it available to other computers on your network is fairly easy. If a TCP/IP network connection exists between the computers sharing the printer, then you must simply grant permission to individual hosts or users from remote hosts to access your computer's printing service. The procedures for setting up local printers are discussed earlier in this chapter.

To share a local printer as a print server to other computers on your network, do the following:

1. From the main Red Hat menu, select System Settings → Printing. The Printer configuration window appears.

2. Click the name of the printer you want to share. (If the printer is not yet configured, refer to the "Setting Up Printers" section earlier in this chapter.)

3. Select Action → Sharing. The Sharing properties window appears.

4. On the Queue tab, click the check box next to "This queue is available to other computers." The words "All hosts" should appear in the Allowed Hosts box, indicating that all computers that can access your computer from the network can access the selected printer.

5. If you only want selected hosts to access your printer, click Remove (to remove the All Hosts line), then click Add. You can share your printer in one of the following ways:

   - **All hosts** — This is the default, where any computer can print on the printer.

   - **Network devices** — If you have a LAN connection, you can select Network Devices and click the interface (such as eth0) to allow computers on the LAN to access your printer. This is a good choice if, for example, your computer is acting as a router. You could allow computers on your LAN to access your printer, but not allow computers from the Internet to use the printer.

- **Network address** — You can restrict access to your printer to a select set of network addresses. The address pool can be indicated with a CIDR address (see Chapter 16 for a description of how to form CIDR addresses).

- **Single IP address** — You can indicate that a particular IP address can access your printer. Repeat this step to add more than a single IP address.

   Click OK to continue.

6. From the Sharing properties window, click OK.

7. From the Printer configuration window, click Apply to apply the changes.

At this point, you can configure other computers to use your printer. If you try to print from another computer and it doesn't work, here are a few things to try:

- **Open your firewall** — If you have a restrictive firewall, it may not permit printing. You must allow access to port 513 (UDP and TCP) to allow access to printing on your computer. See Chapter 14 for information on configuring your firewall.

- **Enable LPD-style printing** — Certain applications may require an older LPD-style printing service in order to print on your shared printer. To enable LPD-style printing on your CUPS server, you must turn on the cups-lpd service. As root user, type **chkconfig cups-lpd on**. Then restart the xinetd daemon (`service xinetd restart`).

- **Check names and addresses** — Make sure that you entered your computer's name and print queue properly when you configured it on the other computer. Try using the IP address instead of the host name (if that worked, it would indicate a DNS name resolution problem). Running a tool such as ethereal can let you watch where the transaction fails.

Access changes to your shared printer are made in the `/etc/cups/cupsd.conf` file.

Configuring a shared NetWare printer

NetWare server functions delivered with Fedora Linux can be offered using the mars_nwe package. This package enables you to do file and printer sharing from Fedora Linux as though the resources being shared were coming from a NetWare server. Although not all NetWare features are offered, the mars_nwe package does well with basic NetWare file and printer sharing. Although mars_nwe is no longer part of the Fedora Linux distribution, you can get the mars_nwe package for Fedora from `http://rpmfind.net`, as well as from various yum repositories.

> **CROSS-REFERENCE:** See Chapter 18 for information on setting up the mars_nwe package to share NetWare resources. The mars_nwe service must be running to share your printer as a NetWare print server.

You can make your Fedora Linux printers available as NetWare printers by adding entries to the `/etc/nwserv.conf` file. This file is used for configuring most mars_nwe information.

Of particular interest for adding printers is the Print Queues section (section 21). Fedora Linux printers are identified as NetWare print queues by indicating each line as a section 21 entry. Here is an example:

```
21 PSPRINT  SYS:/PRINT/PSPRINT lpr -Ppsprint
```

The number 21 identifies the entry as a NetWare print queue. PSPRINT is the name of the queue (you can name the queue anything you like). The queue directory is identified as SYS:/PRINT/PSPRINT. Note that the queue directory is different from the lpd spool directory. Finally, the last part of the entry is the lpr command line, used to print documents submitted to this print queue.

Assuming you have done your basic NetWare server configuration, as described in Chapter 18, use this procedure to check that you can print to the NetWare print server you just set up in Linux:

1. Restart the mars_nwe service to incorporate the changes you just made to nwserv.conf by typing the following:

   ```
   # service mars-nwe restart
   ```

2. Type the slist command to ensure that the NetWare server you configured is available:

   ```
   # slist
   Known NetWare File Servers          Network   Node Address
   ------------------------------------------------------------
   PINE                                7F000001  000000000001
   ```

   In this example, the NetWare server name (of the NetWare server running on Linux) is PINE. Your server name will be different.

3. Use the nprint command to print to your NetWare print server in Linux. Type the following commands:

   ```
   $ cd /usr/share/printconf/tests
   $ nprint -S PINE -U GUEST -q PSPRINT testpage.asc
   Logging into PINE as GUEST
   Password:
   ```

   In the previous example, the NetWare server name is PINE, the user name is GUEST, and the print queue name is PSPRINT. By default, the guest account has no password, so you can simply press Enter at the Password prompt.

> **NOTE:** You don't need to change to the tests directory in the previous example. I did because I know that the tests directory contains several test print pages in different formats. The textpage.asc is a plain-text file. You can also try printing testpage.ps (a PostScript file) or testpage-a4.ps (an A4 PostScript page).

Configuring a shared Samba printer

Your Fedora Linux printers can be configured as shared SMB printers. To share your printer as though it were a Samba (SMB) printer, all you need to do is configure basic Samba server settings as described in Chapter 18. All your printers should be shared on your local network by default. The next section shows what the resulting settings look like and how you might want to change them.

Understanding smb.conf for printing

When you configure Samba, as described in Chapter 18, the /etc/samba/smb.conf file is configured to allow all your configured printers to be shared. Here are a few lines from the smb.conf file that relate to printer sharing:

```
printcap name = /etc/printcap
load printers = yes
printing = cups
encrypt passwords = yes
smb passwd file = /etc/samba/smbpasswd
unix password sync = Yes
[printers]
        comment = All Printers
        path = /var/spool/samba
        browseable = no
        writeable = no
        printable = yes
```

The settings shown resulted from configuring Samba from the Samba Server Configuration window. In this case, I selected to use encrypted passwords. The lines show that printers from /etc/printcap were loaded and that the CUPS service is being used. Password encryption is on and the /etc/samba/smbpasswd file stores the encrypted passwords. Because password sync is on, each user's Samba password is synchronized with the local UNIX password for the user.

The last few lines are the actual printers definition. It shows that users can print to all printers (printable = yes).

Setting up SMB clients

Chances are good that if you are configuring a Samba printer on your Fedora Linux computer, you will want to share it with Windows clients. If Samba is set up properly on your computer, and the client computers can reach you over the network, finding and using your printer should be fairly straightforward.

The first place a client computer should look for your shared Samba printer is in Network Neighborhood (or My Network Places, for Windows 2000). From the Windows 9x desktop, double-click the Network Neighborhood icon. (From Windows 2000, double-click the My

Network Places icon.) The name of your host computer (the NetBIOS name, which is probably also your TCP/IP name) should appear on the screen or within a workgroup folder on the screen. Open the icon that represents your computer. The window that opens should show your shared printers and folders.

If your computer's icon doesn't appear in Network Neighborhood or My Network Places, try using the Search window. From Windows XP, choose Start → Search → Computer or People. Type your computer's name into the Named box and click Search. If the Search window finds your computer, double-click it. A window displaying the shared printers and folders from your computer appears. Figure 17-5 shows the results of a search for a computer in Windows XP.

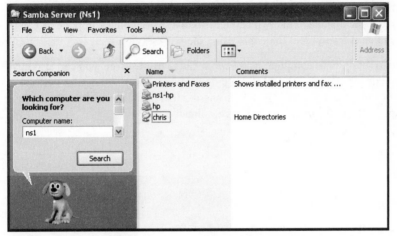

Figure 17-5: Find and display your Samba printer from Find: Computer.

After your shared printer appears in the window, the client can configure a pointer to that printer by opening (double-clicking) the printer icon. You should see a message telling you that you must set up the printer before you can use it. Click Yes to proceed to configure the printer for local use. The Add Printer Wizard appears. Answer the questions that ask you how you intend to use the printer, and add the appropriate drivers. When you are done, the printer will appear in your printer window. It can now be selected as the printer for any application program in Windows 9x.

Another way to configure an SMB printer from a Windows operating system is to go to Start → Settings → Printers. Open the Add Printer icon, and then select Network Printer from the first window. Open the Add Printer icon. Then, follow the instructions to add a printer from the network.

Summary

Sharing printers is an economical and efficient way to use your organization's printing resources. A centrally located printer can make it easier to maintain a printer, while still allowing everyone to get his or her printing jobs done.

You configure your printer with the Printer configuration window. A variety of filters make it possible to print to different kinds of printers, as well as to printers that are connected to computers on the network.

The default printing service in Fedora Linux is the Common UNIX Printing Service (CUPS). You can replace the older LPRng service with CUPS using the alternatives feature. Alternatives lets you switch between the two services so that overlapping components can be exchanged in a way that is transparent to people using the print service.

Besides being able to set up your computer as a Fedora Linux print server, you can also have your computer emulate a NetWare or an SMB (Windows) print server. After your network is configured properly and a local printer is installed, sharing that printer over the network as a UNIX, NetWare, or SMB print server is not very complicated.

Chapter 18

Setting Up a File Server

In This Chapter

- Setting up an NFS file server in Linux
- Setting up a Samba file server in Linux
- Setting up a NetWare file server in Linux

When groups of people need to work together on projects, they usually need to share documents. Likewise, it can be efficient for groups of people on a computer network to share common applications and directories of information needed to do their jobs. A common way to files store centrally and share them on a network is by setting up a file server.

Fedora and other Red Hat Linux systems include support for each of the most common file server protocols in use today. The Network File System (NFS) has always been the file-sharing protocol of choice for Linux and other UNIX systems. Networks with many Windows and OS/2 computers tend to use Samba (SMB protocol). Prior to SMB, NetWare was the most prominent file-server software used on local area networks (LANs).

This chapter describes how to set up file servers and clients associated with NFS, Samba, and NetWare file servers set up in Linux.

> **CROSS-REFERENCE:** Two other types of file servers are also described in this book: FTP (using vsftpd) and AppleTalk (using netatalk). To set up public FTP file servers, refer to Chapter 20. Chapter 26 describes how to set up a netatalk server for file sharing with Apple computers.

Goals of Setting Up a File Server

By centralizing data and applications on a *file server*, you can accomplish several goals:

- **Centralized distribution** — You can add documents or applications to one location and make them accessible to any authorized computer or user. In this way, you don't have to be responsible for placing necessary files on every computer.
- **Transparency** — Using protocols such as NFS, clients of your file server (Windows, Linux, or UNIX systems) can connect your file systems to their local file systems as if

your file systems existed locally. (In other words, no drive letters. Just change to the remote system's mount point and you are there.)

Setting Up an NFS File Server

Instead of representing storage devices as drive letters (A, B, C, and so on), as they are in Microsoft operating systems, Fedora and Red Hat Linux systems connect file systems from multiple hard disks, floppy disks, CD-ROMs, and other local devices invisibly to form a single Linux file system. The Network File System (NFS) facility lets you extend your Linux file system in the same way, to connect file systems on other computers to your local directory structure as well.

> **CROSS-REFERENCE:** See Chapter 10 for a description of how to mount local devices on your Linux file system. The same command (`mount`) is used to mount both local devices and NFS file systems.

Creating an NFS file server is an easy way to share large amounts of data among the users and computers in an organization. An administrator of a Linux system that is configured to share its file systems using NFS has to perform the following tasks to set up NFS:

1. **Set up the network** — If a LAN or other network connection is already connecting the computers on which you want to use NFS (using TCP/IP as the network transport), you already have the network you need.

2. **On the server, choose what to share** — Decide which file systems on your Linux NFS server to make available to other computers. You can choose any point in the file system to make all files and directories below that point accessible to other computers.

3. **On the server, set up security** — You can use several different security features to suit the level of security with which you are comfortable. Mount-level security lets you restrict the computers that can mount a resource and, for those allowed to mount it, lets you specify whether it can be mounted read/write or read-only. With user-level security, you map users from the client systems to users on the NFS server. In this way, users can rely on standard Linux read/write/execute permissions, file ownership, and group permissions to access and protect files.

4. **On the client, mount the file system** — Each client computer that is allowed access to the server's NFS shared file system can mount it anywhere the client chooses. For example, you may mount a file system from a computer called maple on the `/mnt/maple` directory in your local file system. After it is mounted, you can view the contents of that directory by typing **ls /mnt/maple**. Then you can use the `cd` command below the `/mnt/maple` mount point to see the files and directories it contains.

Figure 18-1 illustrates a Linux file server using NFS to share (export) a file system and a client computer mounting the file system to make it available to its local users.

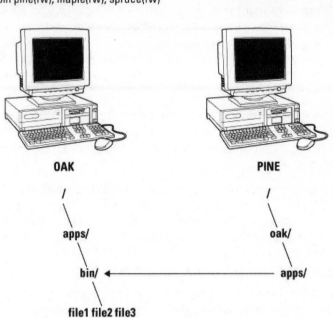

/etc/exports File
/apps/bin pine(rw), maple(rw), spruce(rw)

 # mount oak:/apps/bin apps/bin

OAK

PINE

/

apps/

bin/ ◄────────────────────────

file1 file2 file3

/

oak/

apps/

Figure 18-1: NFS can make selected file systems available to other computers.

In this example, a computer named oak makes its /apps/bin directory available to clients on the network (pine, maple, and spruce) by adding an entry to the /etc/exports file. The client computer (pine) sees that the resource is available, then mounts the resource on its local file system at the mount point /oak/apps. At this point, any files, directories, or subdirectories from /apps/bin on oak are available to users on pine (given proper permissions).

Although it is often used as a file server (or other type of server), Linux is a general-purpose operating system. So, any Fedora or Red Hat Linux system can share file systems (export) as a server or use another computer's file systems (mount) as a client. Contrast this with dedicated file servers, such as NetWare, which can only share files with client computers (such as Windows workstations) and will never act as a client.

Many people use the term *file system* rather loosely. A file system is usually a structure of files and directories that exists on a single device (such as a hard disk partition or CD-ROM). When I talk about the Linux file system, however, I am referring to the entire directory structure (which may include file systems from several disks or NFS resources), beginning from root (/) on a single computer. A shared directory in NFS may represent all or part of a computer's file system, which can be attached (from the shared directory down the directory tree) to another computer's file system.

Sharing NFS file systems

To share an NFS file system from your Linux system, you need to export it from the server system. Exporting is done in Fedora and Red Hat Linux by adding entries into the /etc/exports file. Each entry identifies the directory in your local file system that you want to share with other computers. The entry identifies the other computers that can share the resource (or opens it to all computers) and includes other options that reflect permissions associated with the directory.

Remember that when you share a directory, you are sharing all files and subdirectories below that directory as well (by default). So, you need to be sure that you want to share everything in that directory structure. There are still ways to restrict access within that directory structure (those methods are described later).

Fedora Linux provides a graphical tool for configuring NFS called the NFS Server Configuration window (system-config-nfs command). The following sections describe how to use the NFS Server Configuration window to share directories with other computers, and then describes the underlying configuration files that are changed to make that happen.

Using the NFS Server Configuration window

The NFS Server Configuration window (system-config-nfs command) allows you to share your NFS directories using a graphical interface. Start this window from the main red hat menu by clicking System Settings → Server Settings → NFS.

To share a directory with the NFS Server Configuration window, do the following:

1. From the NFS Server Configuration window, click File → Add Share. The Add NFS Share window appears, as shown in Figure 18-2.

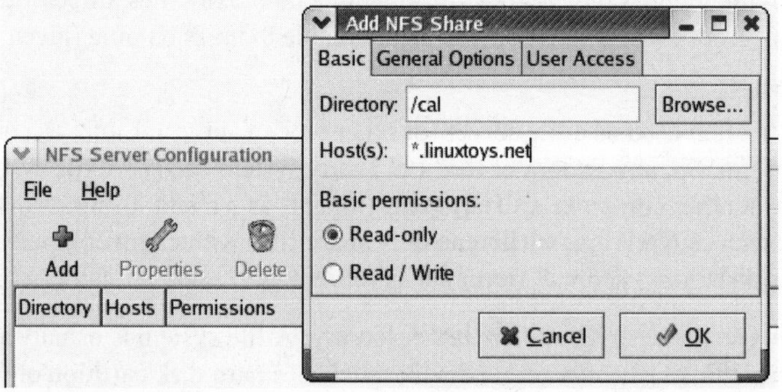

Figure 18-2: Identify a directory to share and access permissions with the NFS Server Configuration window.

2. In the Add NFS Share window Basic tab, enter the following information:

- **Directory** — Type the name of the directory you want to share. (The directory must exist before you can add it.)

- **Host(s)** — Enter one or more host names to indicate which hosts can access the shared directory. Host names, domain names, and IP addresses are allowed here. Separate each name with a space. (See the "Host names in /etc/exports" section later in this chapter for valid host names.) Add an asterisk (*) to place no restrictions on which hosts can access this directory.

NOTE: Although I've just described how it should work, adding multiple host names does not work properly at the moment. If you are adding more than a single host, domain name, or IP address, you may need to either create separate shares for each one you share to, or edit the `/etc/exports` file by hand, as described in the following sections.

- **Basic permissions** — Click Read-only or Read/Write to let remote computers mount the shared directory with read access only or read/write access, respectively.

3. Click the General Options tab. This tab lets you add options that define how the shared directory behaves when a remote host connects to it (mounts it):

- **Allow connections from ports 1024 and higher** — Normally, an NFS client will request the NFS service from a port number under 1024. Select this option if you need to allow a client to connect to you from a higher port number. (This sets the `insecure` option.) To allow a Mac OS X computer to mount a shared NFS directory, you must have the `insecure` option set for the shared directory.

- **Allow insecure file locking** — If checked, NFS will not authenticate any locking requests from remote users of this shared directory. Older NFS clients may not deliver their credentials when they ask for a file lock. (This sets the `insecure_locks` option.)

- **Disable subtree checking** — By selecting this option, NFS won't verify that the requested file is actually in the shared directory (only that it's in the correct file system). You can disable subtree checking if an entire file system is being shared. (This sets the `no_subtree_check` option.)

- **Sync write operations on request** — This is on by default, which forces a write operation from a remote client to be synced on your local disk when the client requests it. (This sets the `sync` option.)

- **Force sync of write operations immediately** — If keeping the shared data immediately up-to-date is critical, select this option to force the immediate synchronization of writes to your hard disk. (This sets the `no_wdelay` option.)

4. Click the User Access tab, then select any of the following options:

- **Treat the remote root user as local root** — If this option is on, it enables the remote root user host accessing your shared directory to save and modify files as though he or she were the local root user. Having this on is a security risk, since the remote user can potentially modify critical files. (This sets the `no_root_squash` option.)

- **Treat all client users as anonymous users** — When this option is on, you can indicate that particular user and group IDs be assigned to every user accessing the shared directory from a remote computer. Enter the user ID and group ID you want assigned to all remote users. (This sets the `anonuid` and `anongid` options to the numbers you choose.)

5. Click OK. The new shared directory appears in the NFS Server Configuration window.

At this point, the configuration file (`/etc/exports`) should have the shared directory entry created in it. To turn on the NFS service and make the shared directory available, type the following from a Terminal window as root user:

1. To immediately turn on NFS, type:

```
# service nfs start
```

2. To permanently turn on the NFS service, type:

```
# chkconfig nfs on
```

3. If you have a firewall configured, you must ensure that UDP ports 111 and 2049 are accepting requests. (See Chapter 14 for information on configuring your firewall.)

The next few sections describe the `/etc/exports` file you just created. At this point, a client can only use your shared directory if he mounts it on his local file system. Refer to the "Using NFS file systems" section later in this chapter.

Configuring the /etc/exports file

The shared directory information you entered into the NFS Server Configuration window is added to the `/etc/exports` file. As root user, you can use any text editor to configure the `/etc/exports` file to modify shared directory entries or add new ones. Here is an example of an `/etc/exports` file, including some entries that it could include:

```
/cal    *.linuxtoys.net(rw)              # Company events
/pub    (ro,insecure,all_squash)         # Public dir
/home   maple(rw,squash uids=0-99) spruce(rw,squash uids=0-99)
```

The following text describes those entries:

- **/cal** — Represents a directory that contains information about events related to the company. It is made accessible to everyone with accounts to any computers in the company's domain (`*.linuxtoys.net`). Users can write files to the directory as well as read them (indicated by the `rw` option). The comment (`# Company events`) simply serves to remind you of what the directory contains.

- **/pub** — Represents a public directory. It allows any computer and user to read files from the directory (indicated by the `ro` option), but not to write files. The `insecure` option enables any computer, even one that doesn't use a secure NFS port, to access the directory. The `all_squash` option causes all users (UIDs) and groups (GIDs) to be mapped to the `nfsnobody` user, giving them minimal permission to files and directories.

- **/home** — This entry enables a set of users to have the same `/home` directory on different computers. Say, for example, that you are sharing `/home` from a computer named oak. The computers named maple and spruce could each mount that directory on their own `/home` directory. If you gave all users the same user name/UIDs on all machines, you could have the same `/home/user` directory available for each user, regardless of which computer they logged into. The `uids=0-99` is used to exclude any administrative login from another computer from changing any files in the shared directory.

Of course, you can share any directories that you choose (these were just examples), including the entire file system (`/`). There are security implications of sharing the whole file system or sensitive parts of it (such as `/etc`). Security options that you can add to your `/etc/exports` file are described throughout the sections that follow.

The format of the `/etc/exports` file is:

```
Directory    Host(Options)    # Comments
```

`Directory` is the name of the directory that you want to share. `Host` indicates the host computer that the sharing of this directory is restricted to. `Options` can include a variety of options to define the security measures attached to the shared directory for the host. (You can repeat Host/Option pairs.) `Comments` are any optional comments you want to add (following the # sign).

Host names in /etc/exports

You can indicate in the `/etc/exports` file which host computers can have access to your shared directory. Be sure to have a space between each host name. Here are ways to identify hosts:

- **Individual host** — You can enter one or more TCP/IP host names or IP addresses. If the host is in your local domain, you can simply indicate the host name. Otherwise, you can use the full host.domain format. These are valid ways of indicating individual host computers:

```
maple
maple.handsonhistory.com
10.0.0.11
```

- **IP network** — To allow access to all hosts from a particular network address, indicate a network number and its netmask, separated by a slash (/). These are valid ways of indicating network numbers:

```
10.0.0.0/255.0.0.0
172.16.0.0/255.255.0.0
192.168.18.0/255.255.255.0
```

- **TCP/IP domain** — Using wildcards, you can include all or some host computers from a particular domain level. Here are some valid uses of the asterisk and question mark wildcards:

```
*.handsonhistory.com
*craft.handsonhistory.com
???.handsonhistory.com
```

The first example matches all hosts in the `handsonhistory.com` domain. The second example matches `woodcraft`, `basketcraft`, or any other host names ending in `craft` in the `handsonhistory.com` domain. The final example matches any three-letter host names in the domain.

> **NOTE:** Using an asterisk doesn't match subdomains. For example, `*.handsonhistory.com` would *not* cause the host name `mallard.duck.handsonhistory.com` to be included in the access list. Also, separate multiple host names with spaces, but if you add options after each host name, leave no spaces between the host name and the parentheses. For example:
>
> `*.handsonhistory.com(rw) *.example.net(ro)`

- **NIS groups** — You can allow access to hosts contained in an NIS group. To indicate an NIS group, precede the group name with an at (@) sign (for example, `@group`).

Access options in /etc/exports

You don't have to just give away your files and directories when you export a directory with NFS. In the options part of each entry in `/etc/exports`, you can add options that allow or limit access by setting read/write permission. These options, which are passed to NFS, are as follows:

- **ro** — Only allow the client to mount this exported file system read-only. The default is to mount the file system read/write.

- **rw** — Explicitly ask that a shared directory be shared with read/write permissions. (If the client chooses, it can still mount the directory read-only.)

User mapping options in /etc/exports

Besides options that define how permissions are handled generally, you can also use options to set the permissions that specific users have to NFS shared file systems.

One method that simplifies this process is to have each user with multiple user accounts have the same user name and UID on each machine. This makes it easier to map users so that they have the same permission on a mounted file system as they do on files stored on their local hard disk. If that method is not convenient, user IDs can be mapped in many other ways. Here are some methods of setting user permissions and the /etc/exports option that you use for each method:

- **root user** — Normally, the client's root user is mapped into the nfsnobody user name (UID 65534). This prevents the root user from a client computer from being able to change all files and directories in the shared file system. If you want the client's root user to have root permission on the server, use the no_root_squash option.

> **TIP:** There may be other administrative users, in addition to root, that you want to squash. I recommend squashing UIDs 0–99 as follows: squash_uids=0-99.

- **nfsnobody user/group** — By using nfsnobody user name and group name, you essentially create a user/group whose permissions will not allow access to files that belong to any real users on the server (unless those users open permission to everyone). However, files created by the nfsnobody user or group will be available to anyone assigned as the nfsnobody user or group. To set all remote users to the nfsnobody user/group, use the all_squash option.

  The nfsnobody user is assigned to UIDs and GIDs of 65534. This prevents the ID from running into a valid user or group ID. Using anonuid or anongid options, you can change the nfsnobody user or group, respectively. For example, anonuid=175 sets all anonymous users to UID 175 and anongid=300 sets the GID to 300. (Only the number is displayed when you list file permission, however, unless you add entries with names to /etc/password and /etc/group for the new UIDs and GIDs.)

- **User mapping** — If the same users have login accounts for a set of computers (and they have the same IDs), NFS, by default, will map those IDs. This means that if the user named mike (UID 110) on maple has an account on pine (mike, UID 110), from either computer he could use his own remotely mounted files from the other computer.

  If a client user who is not set up on the server creates a file on the mounted NFS directory, the file is assigned to the remote client's UID and GID. (An ls -l on the server would show the UID of the owner.) You can identify a file that contains user mappings using the map_static option.

> **TIP:** The exports man page describes the map_static option, which should let you create a file that contains new ID mappings. These mappings should let you remap client IDs into different IDs on the server.

Exporting the shared file systems

After you have added entries to your /etc/exports file, you can actually export the directories listed using the exportfs command. If you reboot your computer or restart the

NFS service, the `exportfs` command is run automatically to export your directories. However, if you want to export them immediately, you can do so by running `exportfs` from the command line (as root).

> **TIP:** It's a good idea to run the `exportfs` command after you change the exports file. If any errors are in the file, `exportfs` will identify those errors for you.

Here's an example of the `exportfs` command:

```
# /usr/sbin/exportfs -a -v
exporting maple:/pub
exporting spruce:/pub
exporting maple:/home
exporting spruce:/home
exporting *:/mnt/win
```

The `-a` option indicates that all directories listed in `/etc/exports` should be exported. The `-v` option says to print verbose output. In this example, the `/pub` and `/home` directories from the local server are immediately available for mounting by those client computers that are named (maple and spruce). The `/mnt/win` directory is available to all client computers.

Running the `exportfs` command temporarily makes your exported NFS directories available. To have your NFS directories available on an ongoing basis (that is, every time your system reboots), you need to set your `nfs` start-up scripts to run at boot time. This is described in the next section.

Starting the nfs daemons

For security purposes, the NFS service is turned off by default on your Fedora system. You can use the `chkconfig` command to turn on the NFS service so that your files are exported and the `nfsd` daemons are running when your system boots.

There are two start-up scripts you want to turn on for the NFS service to work properly. The `nfs` service exports file systems (from `/etc/exports`) and starts the `nfsd` daemon that listens for service requests. The `nfslock` service starts the `lockd` daemon, which helps allow file locking to prevent multiple simultaneous use of critical files over the network.

You can use the `chkconfig` command to turn on the nfs service by typing the following commands (as root user):

```
# chkconfig nfs on
# chkconfig nfslock on
```

The next time you start your computer, the NFS service will start automatically and your exported directories will be available. If you want to start the service immediately, without waiting for a reboot, you can type the following:

```
# /etc/init.d/nfs start
# /etc/init.d/nfslock start
```

The NFS service should now be running and ready to share directories with other computers on your network.

Using NFS file systems

After a server exports a directory over the network using NFS, a client computer connects that directory to its own file system using the mount command. The mount command is the same one used to mount file systems from local hard disks, CDs, and floppies. Only the options to give to mount are slightly different.

Mount can automatically mount NFS directories that are added to the /etc/fstab file, just as it does with local disks. NFS directories can also be added to the /etc/fstab file in such a way that they are not automatically mounted. With a noauto option, an NFS directory listed in /etc/fstab is inactive until the mount command is used, after the system is up and running, to mount the file system.

Manually mounting an NFS file system

If you know that the directory from a computer on your network has been exported (that is, made available for mounting), you can mount that directory manually using the mount command. This is a good way to make sure that it is available and working before you set it up to mount permanently. Here is an example of mounting the /tmp directory from a computer named maple on your local computer:

```
# mkdir /mnt/maple
# mount maple:/tmp /mnt/maple
```

The first command (mkdir) creates the mount point directory (/mnt is a common place to put temporarily mounted disks and NFS file systems). The mount command then identifies the remote computer and shared file system separated by a colon (maple:/tmp). Then, the local mount point directory follows (/mnt/maple).

> **NOTE:** If the mount failed, make sure the NFS service is running on the server and that the server's firewall rules don't deny access to the service. From the server, type **ps ax | nfsd**. You should see a list of nfsd server processes. If you don't, try to start your NFS daemons as described in the previous section. To view your firewall rules, type **iptables -L** (see Chapter 14 for a description of firewalls). By default, the nfsd daemon listens for NFS requests on port number 2049. Your firewall must accept udp requests on ports 2049 (nfs) and 111 (rpc).

To ensure that the mount occurred, type **mount**. This command lists all mounted disks and NFS file systems. Here is an example of the mount command and its output:

```
# mount
/dev/hda3 on / type ext3 (rw)
```

```
none on /proc type proc (rw)
none on /sys type sysfs (rw)
none on /dev/pts type devpts (rw,gid=5,mode=620)usbdevfs on
/proc/bus/usb type usbdevfs (rw)
/dev/hda1 on /boot type ext3 (rw)
none on /dev/shm type tmpfs (rw)
maple:/tmp on /mnt/maple type nfs (rw,addr=10.0.0.11)
```

The output from the `mount` command shows your mounted disk partitions, special file systems, and NFS file systems. The first output line shows your hard disk (`/dev/hda3`), mounted on the root file system (`/`), with read/write permission (`rw`), with a file system type of `ext3` (the standard Linux file system type). The small `/boot` file system is also of type ext3. The `/proc`, `/sys`, `/dev/shm`, `/dev/pts`, and `usbdevfs` mount points represent special file system types. The just-mounted NFS file system is the `/tmp` directory from maple (`maple:/tmp`). It is mounted on `/mnt/maple` and its mount type is `nfs`. The file system was mounted read/write (`rw`) and the IP address of maple is `10.0.0.11` (`addr=10.0.0.11`).

What I just showed is a simple case of using mount with NFS. The mount is temporary and is not remounted when you reboot your computer. You can also add options to the `mount` command line for NFS mounts:

- **-a** — Mount all file systems in `/etc/fstab` (except those indicated as `noauto`).
- **-f** — This goes through the motions of (fakes) mounting the file systems on the command line (or in `/etc/fstab`). Used with the `-v` option, `-f` is useful for seeing what mount would do before it actually does it.
- **-r** — Mounts the file system as read-only.
- **-w** — Mounts the file system as read/write. (For this to work, the shared file system must have been exported with read/write permission.)

The next section describes how to make the mount more permanent (using the `/etc/fstab` file) and how to select various options for NFS mounts.

Automatically mounting an NFS file system

To set up an NFS file system to mount automatically each time you start your Fedora system, you need to add an entry for that NFS file system to the `/etc/fstab` file. The `/etc/fstab` file contains information about all different kinds of mounted (and available to be mounted) file systems for your Fedora system.

The format for adding an NFS file system to your local system is the following:

```
host:directory    mountpoint    nfs    options    0    0
```

The first item (`host:directory`) identifies the NFS server computer and shared directory. `mountpoint` is the local mount point on which the NFS directory is mounted, followed by the file system type (nfs). Any options related to the mount appear next in a comma-separated list. (The last two zeros just tell Fedora not to dump the contents of the file system and not to run fsck on the file system.)

The following are two examples of NFS entries in /etc/fstab:

```
maple:/tmp    /mnt/maple nfs    rsize=8192,wsize=8192  0 0
oak:/apps     /oak/apps  nfs    noauto,ro              0 0
```

In the first example, the remote directory /tmp from the computer named maple (maple:/tmp) is mounted on the local directory /mnt/maple (the local directory must already exist). The file system type is nfs, and read (rsize) and write (wsize) buffer sizes are set at 8192 to speed data transfer associated with this connection. In the second example, the remote directory is /apps on the computer named oak. It is set up as an NFS file system (nfs) that can be mounted on the /oak/apps directory locally. This file system is not mounted automatically (noauto), however, and can be mounted only as read only (ro) using the mount command after the system is already running.

> **TIP:** The default is to mount an NFS file system as read/write. However, the default for exporting a file system is read-only. If you are unable to write to an NFS file system, check that it was exported as read/write from the server.

Mounting noauto file systems

In your /etc/fstab file are devices for other file systems that are not mounted automatically (probably /dev/cdrom and /dev/fd0, for your CD-ROM and floppy disk devices, respectively). A noauto file system can be mounted manually. The advantage is that when you type the mount command, you can type less information and have the rest filled in by the contents of the /etc/fstab file. So, for example, you could type:

```
# mount /oak/apps
```

With this command, mount knows to check the /etc/fstab file to get the file system to mount (oak:/apps), the file system type (nfs), and the options to use with the mount (in this case ro for read-only). Instead of typing the local mount point (/oak/apps), you could have typed the remote file system name (oak:/apps) instead, and had other information filled in.

> **TIP:** When naming mount points, including the name of the remote NFS server in that name can help you remember where the files are actually being stored. This may not be possible if you are sharing home directories (/home) or mail directories (/var/spool/mail).

Using mount options

You can add several mount options to the /etc/fstab file (or to a mount command line itself) to impact how the file system is mounted. When you add options to /etc/fstab, they must be separated by commas. The following are some options that are valuable for mounting NFS file systems:

- **hard** — With this option on, if the NFS server disconnects or goes down while a process is waiting to access it, the process will hang until the server comes back up. This option is helpful if it is critical that the data you are working with not get out of sync with the programs that are accessing it. (This is the default behavior.)

- **soft** — If the NFS server disconnects or goes down, a process trying to access data from the server will time out after a set period of time when this is on.

- **rsize** — The number of bytes of data read at a time from an NFS server. The default is 1024. Using a larger number (such as 8192) will get you better performance on a network that is fast (such as a LAN) and is relatively error-free (that is, one that doesn't have a lot of noise or collisions).

- **wsize** — The number of bytes of data written at a time to an NFS server. The default is 1024. Performance issues are the same as with the `rsize` option.

- **timeo=#** — Sets the time after an RPC timeout occurs that a second transmission is made, where # represents a number in tenths of a second. The default value is seven-tenths of a second. Each successive timeout causes the timeout value to be doubled (up to 60 seconds maximum). You should increase this value if you believe that timeouts are occurring because of slow response from the server or a slow network.

- **retrans=#** — Sets the number of minor retransmission timeouts that occur before a major timeout. When a major timeout occurs, the process is either aborted (soft mount) or a Server Not Responding message appears on your console.

- **retry=#** — Sets how many minutes to continue to retry failed mount requests, where # is replaced by the number of minutes to retry. The default is 10,000 minutes (which is about one week).

- **bg** — If the first mount attempt times out, try all subsequent mounts in the background. This option is very valuable if you are mounting a slow or sporadically available NFS file system. By placing mount requests in the background, Fedora can continue to mount other file systems instead of waiting for the current one to complete.

NOTE: If a nested mount point is missing, a timeout to allow for the needed mount point to be added occurs. For example, if you mount `/usr/trip` and `/usr/trip/extra` as NFS file systems, if `/usr/trip` is not yet mounted when `/usr/trip/extra` tries to mount, `/usr/trip/extra` will time out. Hopefully, `/usr/trip` will come up and `/usr/trip/extra` will mount on the next retry.

- **fg** — If the first mount attempt times out, try subsequent mounts in the foreground. This is the default behavior. Use this option if it is imperative that the mount be successful before continuing (for example, if you were mounting `/usr`).

Any of the values that don't require a value can have no appended to it to have the opposite effect. For example, nobg indicates that the mount should not be done in the background.

Using autofs to mount NFS file systems on demand

With the autofs facility configured and turned on, you can cause any NFS shared directories to mount on demand. If you know the host name and directory being shared by another host computer, you can simple change (cd) to the autofs mount directory (/net by default) and have the shared resource automatically mount and be accessible to you.

The following steps explain how to turn on the autofs facility:

1. As root user from a Terminal window, open the /etc/auto.master file and uncomment the last line, so it appears as follows:

   ```
   /net    /etc/auto.net
   ```

   This causes the /net directory to act as the mount point for the NFS shared directories you want to access on the network.

2. Start the autofs service by typing the following as root user:

   ```
   # service autofs start
   ```

3. Set up the autofs service to restart every time you boot your system:

   ```
   # chkconfig autofs on
   ```

Believe it or not, that's all you have to do. Provided that you have a network connection to the NFS servers from which you want to share directories, you can try to access a shared NFS directory. For example, if you know that the /usr/local/share directory is being shared from the computer on your network named shuttle, do the following:

1. Type the following:

   ```
   $ cd /net/shuttle
   ```

   If the computer named shuttle has any shared directories that are available to you, you will be able to successfully change to that directory.

2. Type the following:

   ```
   $ ls
   usr
   ```

   You should be able to see that the usr directory is part of the path to a shared directory. If there were shared directories from other top-level directories, you would see those as well (such as /var or /tmp). Of course, seeing any of those directories is dependent on how security is set up on the server.

3. Next, you could try going straight to the shared directory. For example:

```
$ cd /net/shuttle/usr/local/share
$ ls
info man music television
```

At this point, the `ls` should reveal the contents of the `/usr/local/share` directory on the computer named shuttle. What you can do with that content depends on how that content was configured for sharing by the server.

Unmounting NFS file systems

After an NFS file system is mounted, unmounting it is simple. You use the `umount` command with either the local mount point or the remote file system name. For example, here are two ways you could unmount `maple:/tmp` from the local directory `/mnt/maple`.

```
# umount maple:/tmp
# umount /mnt/maple
```

Either form will work. If `maple:/tmp` is mounted automatically (from a listing in `/etc/fstab`), the directory will be remounted the next time you boot Fedora. If it was a temporary mount (or listed as `noauto` in `/etc/fstab`), it will not be remounted at boot time.

> **TIP**: The command is not `unmount`, it is `umount`. This is easy to get wrong.

If you get the message "device is busy" when you try to unmount a file system, it means the unmount fails because the file system is being accessed. Most likely, one of the directories in the NFS file system is the current directory for your shell (or the shell of someone else on your system). The other possibility is that a command is holding a file open in the NFS file system (such as a text editor). Check your Terminal windows and other shells, and `cd` out of the directory if you are in it, or just close the Terminal windows.

If an NFS file system won't unmount, you can force unmount it (`umount -f /mnt/maple`) or unmount and clean up later (`umount -l /mnt/maple`). The `-l` option is usually the better choice, because a force unmount can disrupt a file modification that is in progress.

Other cool things to do with NFS

You can share some directories to make it consistent for a user to work from any of several different Linux computers on your network. Some examples of useful directories to share are:

- **/var/spool/mail** — By sharing this directory from your mail server, and mounting it on the same directory on other computers on your network, users can access their mail from any of those other computers. This saves users from having to download messages to their current computers or from having to log in to the server just to get mail. There is only one mailbox for each user, no matter from where it is accessed.

- **/home** — This is a similar concept to sharing mail, except that all users have access to their home directories from any of the NFS clients. Again, you would mount /home on the same mount point on each client computer. When the user logs in, that user has access to all the user's start-up files and data files contained in the /home/user directory.

> **TIP:** If your users rely on a shared /home directory, you should make sure that the NFS server that exports the directory is fairly reliable. If /home isn't available, the user may not have the start-up files to log in correctly, or any of the data files needed to get work done. One workaround is to have a minimal set of start-up files (.bashrc, .Xdefaults, and so on) available in the user's home directory when the NFS directory is not mounted. Doing so allows the user to log in properly at those times.

- **/project** — Although you don't have to use this name, a common practice among users on a project is to share a directory structure containing files that people on the project need to share. This way everyone can work on original files and keep copies of the latest versions in one place. (Of course a better way to manage a project is with CVS or some other version control-type software, but this is a poor person's way to do it.)

- **/var/log** — An administrator can keep track of log files from several different computers by mounting the /var/log file on the administrator's computer. (Each server may need to export the directory to allow root to be mapped between the computers for this to work.) If there are problems with a computer, the administrator can then easily view the shared log files live.

If you are working exclusively with Fedora, Red Hat Linux, and other UNIX systems, NFS is probably your best choice for sharing file systems. If your network consists primarily of Microsoft Windows computers or a combination of systems, you may want to look into using Samba for file sharing.

Setting Up a Samba File Server

Samba is a software package that comes with Fedora and Red Hat Linux systems. Samba enables you to share file systems and printers on a network with computers that use the Session Message Block (SMB) protocol. SMB is the protocol that is delivered with Windows operating systems for sharing files and printers. Although you can't always count on NFS being installed on Windows clients (unless you install it yourself), SMB is always available (with a bit of setup).

On Fedora, the Samba software package contains a variety of daemon processes, administrative tools, user tools, and configuration files. To do basic Samba configuration, you can start with the Samba Server Configuration window. This window provides a graphical interface for configuring the server and setting directories to share.

Most of the Samba configuration you do ends up in the /etc/samba/smb.conf file. If you need to access features that are not available through the Samba Server Configuration window, you can edit /etc/samba/smb.conf by hand or use SWAT, a Web-based interface to configure Samba.

Daemon processes consist of smbd (the SMB daemon) and nmbd (the NetBIOS name server). The smbd daemon makes the file sharing and printing services you add to your Linux system available to Windows client computers. The client computers this package supports include:

- Windows 9*x*
- Windows 2000
- Windows NT
- Windows ME
- Windows XP
- Windows for Workgroups
- MS Client 3.0 for DOS
- OS/2
- Dave for Macintosh Computers
- Samba for Linux

As for administrative tools for Samba, you have several shell commands at your disposal. You can check your configuration file using the testparm and testprns commands. The smbstatus command tells you which computers are currently connected to your shared resources. Using the nmblookup command, you can query for NetBIOS names (the names used to identify host computers in Samba).

Although Samba uses the NetBIOS service to share resources with SMB clients, the underlying network must be configured for TCP/IP. Although other SMB hosts can use TCP/IP, NetBEUI, and IPX/SPX to transport data, Samba for Linux supports only TCP/IP. Messages are carried between host computers with TCP/IP and are then handled by NetBIOS.

Getting and installing Samba

To see if Samba is installed on your Fedora system, type the following:

```
# rpm -qa | grep samba
samba-*
system-config-samba
samba-swat-*
samba-common-*
samba-client-*
```

You should see the name of each of the five packages above, followed by the version number (I represented version numbers with an asterisk). Although not installed with all installation groups in Fedora, the packages that make up Samba are spread across Fedora CD #1 and CD #4. To install Samba, mount the first CD and run the following:

```
# mount /mnt/cdrom
# cd /mnt/cdrom/Fedora/RPMS
# rpm -Uhv samba*
# cd ; umount /mnt/cdrom
```

Repeat the above procedure for the other CD. Before you start trying to configure Samba, read the README file (located in `/usr/share/doc/samba*`). It provides a good overview of the SMB protocol and Samba.

Configuring a simple Samba server

The Samba Server Configuration window enables you to do a basic Samba configuration and then identify which directories you want to share. To make this procedure useful, I'm setting up a particular type of shared environment (which you can modify later if you prefer). Here are the characteristics:

- **A single local area network:** Contains multiple Windows and Linux machines.
- **User-level security:** Any user who wants to get to the shared Samba files must have a valid login and password on the Linux Samba server.
- **Encrypted passwords:** Many clients use encrypted passwords with Samba (SMB) by default. I'll describe how to turn on encrypted passwords for clients that don't use encrypted passwords.
- **A guest user account:** The guest user account will be useful later, so you can set up Samba to let users without special accounts use the server's printers via Samba.

The following procedure describes how to configure Samba and create a shared directory in Samba:

1. To open the Samba Server Configuration window, click System Settings → Server Settings → Samba. The Samba Server Configuration window opens. (You will likely need to enter the root password.)
2. Click Preferences → Server Settings. The Server Settings window appears, as shown in Figure 18-3.
3. Type the workgroup name (to match that of other computers with which you want to share files) and a short description.

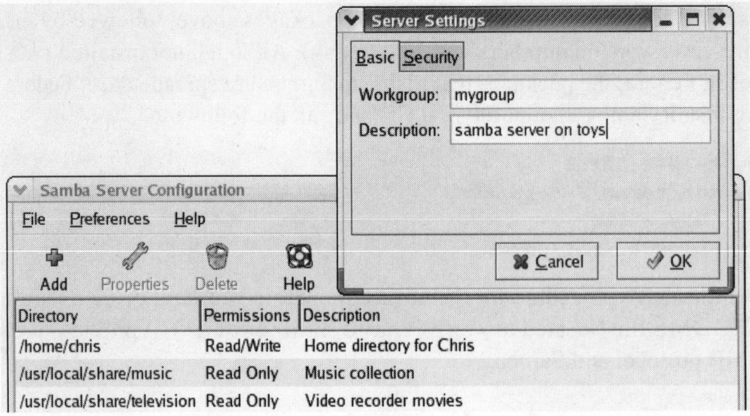

Figure 18-3: Define the workgroup and description for your Samba server.

4. Click the Security tab. A window appears like the one shown in Figure 18-4.

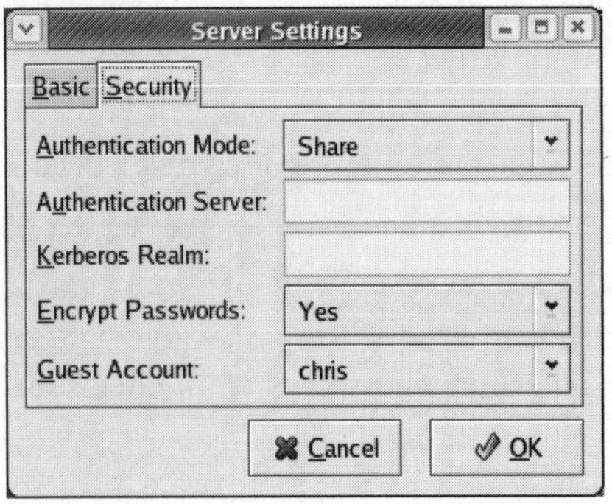

Figure 18-4: Fill in Basic and Security information for your Samba server.

5. Provide the following information for the fields on the Security tab and click OK:

   • **Authentication Mode** — Select User, Share, Server, ADS, or Domain. For this example, I selected User. (See the "Security options" section later in this chapter for details on each of the authentication modes.)

   • **Authentication Server** — This field is only valid if your Samba server is configured to use Server or Domain security. It identifies the server (NetBios name) that will be used to authenticate the user name and password the Samba client enters to gain access to this Samba server. With user authentication, passwords are checked on the Samba server (in this example, therefore, this field is blank.)

   • **Encrypt Passwords** — Select Yes (to expect clients to send encrypted passwords) or No (to expect clear-text password). See the section on Samba clients later in this chapter to determine how to configure clients to use encrypted passwords.

- **Guest Account** — Set this field to a user name that you want assigned to requests from anonymous users. Even with User mode security set globally, you can assign guest access to particular Samba shares (such as printers).

With User mode security (which is being used in this example), any user who wants to access a Samba share must have a regular user account on the Linux system. (Refer to Chapter 11 for information on adding user accounts.)

6. To add a user as a Samba user (that is, one who can access your Samba server), select Preferences → Samba Users. The Samba Users window appears.

7. Click Add User. The Create New Samba User window appears.

8. Provide information for the following fields in the Create New Samba User window and click OK:

   - **Unix Username** — Click this box, then select the Linux user name to which you want to give access to the Samba server.

   - **Windows Username** — This is the user name provided by the user when he or she requests the shared directory. (Often, it is the same as the Unix username.)

   - **Samba Password** — Type the Samba password, then retype it into the Confirm Samba Password field.

9. Repeat the previous step for each user you want to access the Samba shared directory.

10. Now that you have configured the default values for your Samba server, add a directory to share by clicking File → Add Share. The Create Samba Share window appears.

11. Fill in the following fields shown in the Create Samba Share window:

    - **Directory** — Type the name of the directory you want to share. For example, you might want to share a user's home directory, such as /home/chris.

    - **Description** — Type any description you like of the Shared directory.

    - **Basic Permissions** — Select either Read-only or Read/Write. For Read-only, files can be viewed, but not changed, on the shared directory. For Read/Write, the user is free to add, change, or delete files, provided he or she has Linux file access to the particular file.

12. Click the Access tab, select one of the following choices for access to the share, and then click OK:

    - **Only allow access to specific users** — Click here, then choose which users will be allowed to access the shared directory. For example, if you are sharing a user's directory (such as /home/chris), you probably want to restrict access to that directory to the directory's owner (for example, chris). Read and write access to particular files and directories are determined by the Linux ownership and group assigned to them.

- **Allow access to everyone** — Choose this option if you want to allow anyone to access this directory. (All users will have privileges assigned to the guest user when accessing the directory.)

   After you click OK, Samba is started and the new directory is immediately available. You can close the Samba Server Configuration window.

13. Although Samba should be running at this point, you probably need to set Samba to start automatically every time you reboot Linux. To do that, type the following as root user in a Terminal window:

```
# chkconfig smb on
```

You can repeat the steps for adding a Samba shared directory for every directory you want to make available on your network. At this point, you can either:

- Go through your Samba server settings in more detail (as described in the "Configuring Samba with SWAT" section) to understand how you might want to further tune your Samba server.

- Try accessing the shared directories you just created from a client computer on your network.

If you cannot open the shared directory you just configured from a Windows computer or other Linux computer on your LAN, you are probably experiencing one of the following problems:

- The client isn't supplying a valid user name and password.

- The client isn't supplying an encrypted password.

The quick way around these problems is to use only share-level security (which, of course, throws your security right out the window). The other solution is to get passwords up-to-date and make sure that clients are using encrypted passwords (as described in the "Setting up Samba clients" section later in this chapter).

Configuring Samba with SWAT

The Samba Web Administration Tool (SWAT) is a Web-based interface for configuring Samba. While it's not quite as easy to use as the Samba Server Configuration window, it does offer more options for tuning Samba and Help descriptions for each option.

> **CAUTION:** Both SWAT and the Samba Server Configuration window configure Samba by modifying the `/etc/samba/smb.conf` file. Different GUI tools can overwrite each other's settings, sometimes in a way that causes the other tool not to work.
>
> In general, it's best to make a backup copy of your files before switching GUI tools. Eventually, you should choose one tool and stick with it.

Turning on the SWAT service

Before you can use SWAT, you must do some configuration. To set up SWAT to run from your browser, follow these steps:

1. To turn on the swat service, type the following, as root user, from a Terminal window:

    ```
    # chkconfig swat on
    ```

2. To pick up the change to the swat service, restart the xinetd start-up script as follows:

    ```
    # service xinetd restart
    ```

When you have finished this procedure, use the SWAT program, described in the next section, to configure Samba.

Starting with SWAT

You can run the SWAT program by typing the following URL in your local browser:

```
http://localhost:901/
```

At this point, the browser will prompt you for a user name and password. Enter the root user name and password. The SWAT window should appear, as shown in Figure 18-5.

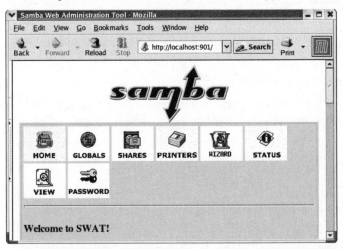

Figure 18-5: Use SWAT from your browser to manage your Samba configuration.

> **TIP:** Instead of running SWAT from your local browser, you can run it from another computer on the network by substituting the server computer's name for `localhost`. (To allow computers besides `localhost` to access the swat service, you must change or remove the `only_from = 127.0.0.1` line from the `/etc/xinetd.d/swat` file and restart the xinetd service.)

The rest of this section describes how to use SWAT to create your configuration entries (in /etc/samba/smb.conf) and to work with that configuration.

> **CAUTION:** Any time you use a GUI to change a plain-text configuration file (as you do with SWAT), you may lose some of the information that you put in by hand. In this case, SWAT deletes comment lines and rearranges other entries. To protect changes you have made manually, make a backup copy of your /etc/samba/smb.conf file before you edit it with SWAT.

Creating global Samba settings in SWAT

A group of global settings affects how file and print sharing are generally accomplished on a Samba server. They appear under the [global] heading in the /etc/samba/smb.conf file. To edit global variables, click the GLOBALS button on the SWAT window.

Seven option types are available: Base options, security options, logging options, tuning, printing options, browse options, and WINs options. To view and modify your global Samba server settings, click the GLOBALS button. Then add the following options.

> **NOTE:** Each option shown relates to the exact parameters used in the /etc/samba/smb.conf file. You can refer to the smb.conf man page (type **man smb.conf**) to get more information on these parameters.

Base options
The following options relate to basic information associated with your Samba server:

- **workgroup** — The name of the workgroup associated with the group of SMB hosts. By default, the value for this field is WORKGROUP.

- **relm** — If you are using kerberos authentication, this value indicates the kerberos relm to use. Typically, that is reflected by the host name of the server providing the service.

- **netbios name** — The name assigned to this Samba server. You can use the same name as your DNS host name or leave it blank, in which case the DNS host name is used automatically.

- **netbios alias** —This enables you to set a way of referring to a host computer (an alias) that is different from the host's TCP/IP DNS name.

- **server string** — A string of text identifying the server. This name appears in places such as the printer comment box. By default, it says Samba and the version number.

- **interfaces** — Lets you set up more than one network interface. This enables Samba to browse several different subnetworks. The form of this field can be *IP Address/Subnetwork Mask*. Or, you could identify a network interface (such as eth0 for the first Ethernet card on your computer). For example, a Class C network address may appear as:

  ```
  192.168.24.11/255.255.255.0
  ```

Security options

Of the security options settings, the first option (security) is the most important one to get right. It defines the type of security used to give access to the shared file systems and printers to the client computers. (To see some of the fields described here, you need to click the Advanced view.)

- **security** — Sets how password and user information is transferred to the Samba server from the client computer. As noted earlier, it's important to get this value right. The default value for security (security=user) is different than the default value for security (security=share) in pre-2.0 versions of Samba. If you are coming from an earlier version of Samba and clients are failing to access your server, this setting is a good place to start. Here are your options:

  - **user** — The most common type of security used to share files and printers to Windows 95/98/2000 and Windows NT clients. It is the default set with Samba in the current release. This setting is appropriate if users are doing a lot of file sharing (as opposed to a Samba server used mostly as a print server). It requires that a user provide a user name/password before using the server.

    The easiest way to get this method working is to give a Fedora user account to every client user who will use the Fedora Samba server. This provides basically the same file permissions to a user account through Samba as the same user would get if he or she were logged in directly to Linux.

> **CAUTION:** Apparently, there is a bug in Windows for Workgroups that causes the password that the user types in to be ignored from a "connect drive" dialog box. Instead, Windows uses the user name and password in effect for the user's current Windows login session. One way around this problem, although it is clumsy from a security standpoint, is to assign the same user name/password combination for each user on the Fedora computer that they use in Windows.

  - **share** — The share value for security works best for just print sharing or for providing file access that is more public (guest sharing). A client doesn't need to provide a valid user name and password to access the server. However, the user will typically have a "guest" level of permission to access and change files. See the sidebar describing guest accounts for further information.

  - **server** — The security option that, from the client's point of view, is the same as user security, in that the client still has to provide a valid user name/password combination to use the Samba server at all. The difference is on the server side. With server security, the user name/password is sent to another SMB server for validation. If this fails, Samba will try to validate the client using `user` security.

  - **domain** — This security option also, from the client's point of view, looks the same as *user* security. This setting is used only if the Samba server has been added to a Windows NT domain (using the `smbpasswd` command). When a client tries to connect to the Samba server in this mode, its user name and password are sent to a

Windows NT Primary or Backup Domain controller. This is accomplished the same way that a Windows NT server would perform validation. Valid Linux user accounts must still be set up.

- **encrypt passwords** — Controls whether encrypted passwords can be negotiated with the client. This is on (Yes) by default. For *domain* security, this value must be Yes. Later versions of Windows NT (4.0 SP3 or later) and Windows 98 and Windows 2000 expect encrypted passwords to be on. (See the "Setting up Samba clients" section for information on getting clients to use encrypted passwords.)

- **update encrypted** — Allows users who log in with a plain-text password to automatically have their passwords updated to an encrypted password when they log in. Normally, this option is off. It can be turned on when you want an installation using plain-text passwords to have everyone updated to encrypted password authentication. It saves users the trouble of running the smbpasswd command directly from the server. After everyone is updated, this feature can be turned off. When this option is on, the encrypt passwords option should be set to no.

- **obey pam restrictions** — Turn this on (Yes) if you want to use PAM for account and session management. Even if activated, PAM is not used if the encrypted passwords feature is turned on (encrypt passwords = yes).

- **pam password change** — Indicates to use the PAM password change control flag for Samba. If this is on (Yes), SMB clients will use PAM instead of the program listed in the Password Program value for changing SMB passwords.

- **passwd program** — Indicates which password program to use to change Linux user passwords. By default, /usr/bin/passwd is used, with the current user name (%u) inserted.

- **passwd chat** — Sets the chat that goes on between the Samba daemon (smbd) and the Linux password program (/usr/bin/passwd by default) when smbd tries to synchronize SMB passwords with Linux user passwords.

- **username map** — This sets the file used to map Samba user names. By default, this file is /etc/samba/smbusers.

- **unix password sync** — With this on (Yes), Samba tries to update a user's Linux user password with his or her SMB password when the SMB password is changed. To do this, SMB runs the passwd command as the root user. This is on by default.

- **guest account** — Specifies the user name for the guest account. When a service is specified as Guest OK, the user name entered here will be used to access that service. The account is usually the *nobody* user name.

> **TIP:** Make sure that the guest account is a valid user. (The default of *nobody* should already be set up to work.) With an invalid user as the guest account, the IPC$ connection that lists the shared resources fails.

- **hosts allow** — Contains a list of one or more hosts that are allowed to use your computer's Samba services. By default, users from any computer can connect to the Samba server (of course, they still have to provide valid user names and passwords). Usually, you use this option to allow connections from specific computers (such as 10.0.0.1) or computer networks (such as 10.0.0.) that are excluded by the hosts deny option.

- **hosts deny** — Contains a list of one or more hosts from which users are not allowed to use your computer's Samba services. You can make this option fairly restrictive, and then add the specific hosts and networks you want to use the Samba server. By default, no hosts are denied.

Logging options

The following options help define how logging is done on your Samba server:

- **log level** — Sets the debug level used when logging Samba activity. Raise the level from the default (0) to log more Samba activity.

- **log file** — Defines the location of the Samba smb log file. By default, Samba log files are contained in `/var/log/samba` (with file names `log.nmbd`, `log.smbd`, and `smb.log`). In this option, the %m is replaced by smb to set the smb log file as `/var/log/samba/smb.log`.

- **max log size** — Sets the maximum amount of space, in kilobytes, that the log files can consume. By default, the value is set to 0 (no limit).

Assigning Guest Accounts

Samba always assigns the permissions level of a valid user on the Linux system to clients who use the server. In the case of share security, the user is assigned a guest account (the *nobody* user account by default).

If the guest account value isn't set, Samba goes through a fairly complex set of rules to determine which user account to use. The result is that it can be hard to assure which user permissions will be assigned in each case. This is why it is recommended to use *user* security if you want to provide more specific user access to your Samba server.

Tuning options

The Socket Options option lets you pass options to the protocols Samba uses to communicate. The following options are set by default: `TCP_NODELAY`, `SO_RCVBUF=8192`, and `SO_SNDBUF=8192`. The first option disables Nagle's algorithm, which is used to manage the transmission of TCP/IP packets. The other two options set the maximum size of the sockets receive buffer and send buffer to 8192, respectively. These options are set to improve performance (reportedly up to 10 times faster than without setting these options). In general, you shouldn't change these options.

Printing options

The printing option is used to define how printer status information is presented. For Fedora, the value is typically cups. You can use printing styles from other types of operating systems, such as UNIX System V (sysv), AIX (aix), HP UNIX (hpux), and Berkeley UNIX (bsd), to name a few. LPRng (lprng), offered by many UNIX systems, is also included.

Browse options

A browse list is a list of computers that are available on the network to SMB services. Clients use this list to find computers that are not only on their own LAN, but also computers in their workgroups that may be on other reachable networks.

In Samba, browsing is configured by options described below and implemented by the nmbd daemon. If you are using Samba for a workgroup within a single LAN, you probably don't need to concern yourself with the browsing options. If, however, you are using Samba to provide services across several physical subnetworks, you might want to consider configuring Samba as a domain master browser. Here are some points to think about:

- Samba can be configured as a master browser. This allows it to gather lists of computers from local browse masters to form a wide-area server list.

- If Samba is acting as a domain master browser, Samba should use a WINS server to help browse clients resolve the names from this list.

- Samba can be used as a WINS server, although it can also rely on other types of operating systems to provide that service.

- There should be only one domain master browser for each workgroup. Don't use Samba as a domain master for a workgroup with the same name as an NT domain.

If you are working in an environment that has a mix of Samba and Windows NT servers, you should use an NT server as your WINS server. If Samba is your only file server, you should choose a single Samba server (nmbd daemon) to supply the WINS services.

> **NOTE:** A WINS server is basically a name server for NetBIOS names. It provides the same service that a DNS server does with TCP/IP domain names: it can translate names into addresses. A WINS server is particularly useful for allowing computers to communicate with SMB across multiple subnetworks where information is not being broadcast across the subnetworks' boundaries.

To configure the browsing feature in Samba, you must have the workgroup named properly (described earlier in this section). Here are the global options related to SMB browsing.

> **NOTE:** If browsing isn't working, check the nmbd log file (`/var/log/samba/log.nmbd`). To get more detail, increase the debug information level to 2 or 3 (described earlier in this section) and restart Samba. The log can tell you if your Samba server is the master browser and, if so, which computers are on its list.

- **os level** — Set a value to control whether your Samba server (nmbd daemon) may become the local master browser for your workgroup. Raising this setting increases the Samba server's chance to control the browser list for the workgroup in the local broadcast area.

  If the value is 0, a Windows machine will probably be selected. A value of 60 will probably ensure that the Samba server is chosen over an NT server. The default is 20.

- **preferred master** — Set this to Yes if you want to force selection of a master browser. By setting this to Yes, the Samba server also has a better chance of being selected. (Setting Domain Master to Yes along with this option should ensure that the Samba server will be selected.) This is set to Auto by default, which causes Samba to try to detect the current master browser before taking that responsibility.

- **local master** — Set this to Yes if you want the Samba server to become the local browser master. (This is not a guarantee, but gives it a chance.) Set the value to No if you do not want your Samba server selected as the local master. Local Master is Auto by default.

- **domain master** — Set this to Yes if you want the Samba server (nmbd daemon) to identify itself as the domain master browser for its workgroup. This list will then allow client computers assigned to the workgroup to use SMB-shared files and printers from subnetworks that are outside of their own subnetwork. This is set to No by default.

WINS options

Use the WINS options if you want to have a particular WINS server provide the name-to-address translation of NetBIOS names used by SMB clients. As noted earlier, you probably don't need to use a WINS server if all of the clients and servers in your SMB workgroup are on the same subnetwork. That's because NetBIOS names can be obtained through addresses that are broadcast. It is possible to have your Samba server provide WINS services.

- **wins server** — If there is a WINS server on your network that you want to use to resolve the NetBIOS names for your workgroup, you can enter the IP address of that server here. Again, you will probably want to use a WINS server if your workgroup extends outside of the local subnetwork.

- **wins support** — Set this value to Yes if you want your Samba server to act as a WINS server. (It's No by default.) Again, this is not needed if all the computers in your workgroup are on the same subnetwork. Only one computer on your network should be assigned as the WINS server.

Besides the values described here, you can access dozens more options by clicking the Advanced View button. When you have filled in all the fields you need, click Commit Changes on the screen to have the changes written to the `/etc/samba/smb.conf` file.

Configuring shared directories with SWAT

To make your shared directory available to others, you can add an entry to the SWAT window. To use SWAT to set up Samba to share directories, do the following:

> **NOTE:** You may see one or more security warnings during the course of this procedure. These messages warn you that someone can potentially view the data you are sending to SWAT. If you are working on your local host or on a private LAN, the risk is minimal.

1. From the main SWAT window, click the SHARES button.

2. Type the name of the directory that you want to share in the Create Share box, then click Create Share.

3. Add any of these options:

   - **comment** — A few words to describe the shared directory (optional).

   - **path** — The path name of the directory you are sharing.

   - **guest account** — If Guest OK is selected, then the user name that is defined here is assigned to users accessing the file system. No password will be required to access the share. The nobody user account (used only by users who access your computer remotely) is the default name used. (The FTP user is also a recommended value.)

   - **read only** — If Yes, then files can only be read from this file system, but no remote user can save or modify files on the file system. Select No if you want users to be allowed to save files to this directory over the network.

   - **guest ok** — Select Yes to enable anyone access to this directory without requiring a password.

   - **hosts allow** — Add the names of the computers that will be allowed to access this file system. You can separate host names by commas, spaces, or tabs. Here are some valid ways of entering host names:

     localhost — Allow access to the local host.

     192.168.74.18 — IP address. Enter an individual IP address.

     192.168.74. — Enter a network address to include all hosts on a network. (Be sure to put a dot at the end of the network number or it won't work!)

     maple, pine — Enable access to individual hosts by name.

     EXCEPT *host* — If you are allowing access to a group of hosts (such as by entering a network address), use EXCEPT to specifically deny access from one host from that group.

- **hosts deny** — Deny access to specific computers by placing their names here. By default, no particular computers are excluded. Enter host names in the same forms you used for Hosts Allow.

- **browseable** — Indicates whether you can view this directory on the list of shared directories. This is on (Yes) by default.

- **available** — Enables you to leave this entry intact, but turns off the service. This is useful if you want to close access to a directory temporarily. This is on (Yes) by default. Select No to turn it off.

4. Select Commit Changes.

At this point, the shared file systems should be available to the Samba client computers (Windows 9x, Windows NT, Windows 2000, OS/2, Linux, and so on) that have access to your Linux Samba server. Before you try that, however, you can check a few things about your Samba configuration.

Checking your Samba setup with SWAT

From the SWAT window, select the STATUS button.

From this window, you can restart your smbd and nmbd processes. Likewise, you can see lists of active connections, active shares, and open files. (The preferred way to start the smbd and nmbd daemons is to set up the smb service to start automatically. Type **chkconfig smb on** to set the service to start at boot time.)

Working with Samba files and commands

Although you can set up Samba through the Samba Server Configuration window or SWAT, many administrators prefer to edit the /etc/samba/smb.conf directly. As root user, you can view the contents of this file and make needed changes. If you selected *user* security (as recommended), you will also be interested in the smbusers and smbpasswd file (also in the /etc/samba directory). These files, as well as commands such as testparm and smbstatus, are described in the following sections.

Editing the smb.conf file

Changes you make using the Samba Server Configuration window or SWAT Web interface are reflected in your /etc/samba/smb.conf file. Here's an example of an smb.conf file (with comments removed):

```
[global]
workgroup = ESTREET
server string = Samba Server on Maple
hosts allow = 192.168.0.
printcap name = /etc/printcap
load printers = yes
```

```
printing = cups
log file = /var/log/samba/%m.log
max log size = 0
smb passwd file = /etc/samba/smbpasswd
security = user
encrypt passwords = Yes
unix password sync = Yes
passwd program = /usr/bin/passwd %u
passwd chat = *New*password* %n\n *Retype*new*password* %n\n *passwd:
         *all*authentication*tokens*updated*successfully*
pam password change = yes
obey pam restrictions = yes
socket options = TCP_NODELAY SO_RCVBUF=8192 SO_SNDBUF=8192
username map = /etc/samba/smbusers
dns proxy = no

[homes]
comment = Home Directories
browseable = no
writable = yes
valid users = %S
create mode = 0664
directory mode = 0775

[printers]
comment = All Printers
path = /var/spool/samba
browseable = no
guest ok = no
writable = no
printable = yes
```

In the [global] section, the workgroup is set to ESTREET, the server is identified as the Samba Server on Maple, and only computers that are on the local network (192.168.0.) are allowed access to the Samba service. You must change the local network to match your network.

Definitions for the local printers that will be shared are taken from the /etc/printcap file, the printers are loaded (yes), and the cups printing service (which is the default print service used by Fedora) is used.

Separate log files for each host trying to use the service are created in /var/log/samba/%m.log (with %m automatically replaced with each host name). There is no limit to log file size (0).

In this case, we are using user-level security (security = user). This allows a user to log in once and then easily access the printers and the user's home directory on the Linux system. Password encryption is on (encrypt passwords = yes) because most Windows systems have password encryption on by default. Passwords are stored in the `/etc/samba/smbpasswd` file on your Linux system.

The `dns proxy = no` option prevents Linux from looking up system names on the DNS server (used for TCP/IP lookups).

The `[homes]` section allows each user to be able to access his or her Linux home directory from a Windows system on the LAN. The user will be able to write to the home directory. However, other users will not be able see or share this directory. The `[printers]` section allows all users to print to any printer that is configured on the local Linux system.

Adding Samba users

Doing user-style Samba security means assigning a Linux user account to each person using the Linux file systems and printers from his or her Windows workstation. (You could assign users to a guest account instead, but in this example, all users have their own accounts.) Then you need to add SMB passwords for each user. For example, here is how you would add a user whose Windows 98 workstation login is `chuckp`:

1. Type the following as root user from a Terminal window to add a Linux user account:

```
# useradd -m chuckp
```

2. Add a Linux password for the new user as follows:

```
# passwd chuckp
Changing password for user chuckp
New UNIX password: ********
Retype new UNIX password: ********
```

3. Repeat the previous steps to add user accounts for all users from Windows workstations on your LAN that you want to give access to your Linux system to.

4. Type the following command to create the Samba password file (`smbpasswd`):

```
# cat /etc/passwd | /usr/bin/mksmbpasswd.sh > /etc/samba/smbpasswd
```

5. Add an SMB password for the user as follows:

```
# smbpasswd chuckp
New SMB password: **********
Retype new SMB password: **********
```

Repeat this step for each user. Later, each user can log in to Linux and rerun the `passwd` and `smbpasswd` commands to set private passwords.

> **NOTE:** In the most recent version of Samba, options are available in the `smb.conf` file that cause SMB and Linux passwords to be synchronized automatically. See descriptions of the passwd program, passwd phat, and UNIX password sync options in the SWAT section of this chapter.

Starting the Samba service

To start the Samba SMB and NMB daemons, you can run the /etc/init.d/smb start-up script by typing the following as the root user:

```
# service smb start
```

This runs the Samba service during the current session. To set up Samba to start automatically when your Linux system starts, type the following:

```
# chkconfig smb on
```

This turns on the Samba service to start automatically in run levels 3, 4, or 5. You can now check SMB clients on the network to see if they can access your Samba server.

Testing your Samba permissions

You can run several commands from a shell to work with Samba. One is the testparm command, which you can use to check the access permissions you have set up. It lists global parameters that are set, along with any shared directories or printers.

Checking the status of shared directories

The smbstatus command can view who is currently using Samba shared resources offered from your Linux system. The following is an example of the output from smbstatus:

```
Samba version 3.0.3-4
PID       Username      Group        Machine
------------------------------------------------------------------

Service       pid     machine       Connected at
-------------------------------------------------------

IPC$          10865   shuttle       Thu May 13 15:12:13 2004
tmp           10866   shuttle       Thu May 13 15:12:14 2004
tmp           10874   10.0.0.218    Thu May 13 15:18:01 2004

Locked files:
Pid    DenyMode   Access R/W   Oplock Name
-------------------------------------------------------

10874 DENY_FCB  0x3     RDWR NONE   /tmp/.m.swp Thu May 13 15:18:20 2004
10874 DENY_NONE 0x1     RDWR NONE   /tmp/m      Thu May 13 15:18:30 2004
```

This output shows that from your Linux Samba server, the tmp service (which is a share of the /tmp directory) is currently open by the computer named shuttle. PID 10874 is the process number of the smbd daemon on the Linux server that is handling the service. The files open are the /tmp/m and /tmp/.m.swap, which happen to be opened by a vi command. Both have read/write access.

Setting up Samba clients

Once you have configured your Samba server, you can try using the shared directories from a client computer on your network. The following sections describe how to use your Samba server from another Linux system or from various Windows systems.

Using Samba shared directories from Linux

There are several methods of connecting to shared directories from your Samba client. The following sections address these methods.

Using Samba from Nautilus

To connect to a Samba share from a Nautilus, use the Open Location box by clicking File → Open Location. Then type **smb:** into your Nautilus file manager Open Location box.

A list of SMB workgroups on your network appears in the window. You can select a workgroup, choose a server, and then select a resource to use. This should work for shares requiring no password.

The Nautilus interface seems to be a bit buggy when you need to enter passwords. Also, it requires you to either send clear-text passwords or type the user and password into your location box. For example, to get to my home directory (/home/chris) through Nautilus, I can type my user name, password, server name, and share name as follows:

```
smb://chris:my72mgb@toys/chris
```

Mounting Samba directories in Linux

Linux can view your Samba shared directories as it does any other medium (hard disk, NFS shares, CD-ROM, and so on). Using the mount command, you can mount a Samba shared file system so that it is permanently connected to your Linux file system.

The following example of the mount command shows how I would mount my home directory (/home/chris) from a computer named toys on a local directory (/mnt/toys). As root user, from a Terminal window, type:

```
# mkdir /mnt/toys
# mount -t smbfs -o username=chris,password=a72mg //toys/chris /mnt/toys
```

The file system type for a Samba share is smbfs (-t smbfs). I pass the username (chris) and password (a72mg) as options (-o). The remote share of my home directory on toys is //toys/chris. The local mount point is /mnt/toys. At this point, you can access the contents of /home/chris on toys as you would any file or directory locally. You will have the same permission to access and change the contents of that directory (and its subdirectories) as you would if you were the user chris using those contents directly from toys.

To mount the Samba shared directory permanently, you can add an entry to your `/etc/fstab` file. For the example just described, you could add the following line (as root user):

```
//toys/chris   /mnt/toys    smbfs    username=chris,password=a72mg
```

Using Samba shared directories from Windows

Sharing Samba file systems from your Linux system over your network with users on Windows client computers requires some configuration of those clients. On Windows 95/98 and similar systems, most of the configuration is performed from the Network window. To open the Network window, do the following from Windows 95/98:

1. Choose Start → Settings → Control Panel.

2. From the Control Panel, double-click the Network icon.

On the Network window, you can see the network components (protocols, clients, adapters, and services). Samba relies on a working TCP/IP network, so you should have already set up TCP/IP on your LAN (as described in Chapter 15). To use Samba file systems, you also need to have at least the following network components configured:

- **Client for Microsoft Networks** — The client that allows print and file sharing. If it is not listed, you can add it by choosing Add → Client → Add → Microsoft → Client for Microsoft Networks → OK.

- **NetBEUI protocol** — The protocol used to carry out file and print sharing among older Microsoft Windows (and other) systems. If it is not listed, add it by choosing Add → Protocol → Add → Microsoft → NetBEUI → OK. You don't need this protocol for Windows XP. (NetBEUI is a raw NetBIOS protocol. If your computer lets you run NetBIOS over TCP and bypass NetBEUI, you should do so.)

- **A Network Adapter** — Represents the networking medium that actually connects the computer together. Chances are this represents a LAN card, such as an Ethernet card.

- **TCP/IP protocol** — If TCP/IP is not yet added for your network adapter, choose Add → Protocol → Add → Microsoft →TCP/IP. Then click OK. Click the TCP/IP entry for your network adapter; then click Properties. From the Bindings tab, make sure that Client for Microsoft Networks is checked. From the WINS Configuration tab, click Enable WINS Resolution, type the IP address for your Linux server, and click Add. Then click OK.

> **TIP:** If you want to allow the client to share its own files and printers, you can click File and Print Sharing. Then you can select to turn on file access and/or printer access from the pop-up window that appears.

Other information that you need to add relates to the client computer's identity and access. On the Network window, click the Identification tab. On that tab, enter a name for the client computer, the name of the workgroup and a description of the computer. Next, click the Access Control tab. From there, select either User-level or Share-level access control (to match the type of control set up on the server). Click OK when you are done. (At this point, you may need to reboot Windows.)

To see the file and print services available from your Linux Samba server (as well as from other computers on the network), open the Network Neighborhood window. To open the window, double-click the Network Neighborhood icon on the Windows 95 desktop. Figure 18-6 shows an example of the Network Neighborhood window for a small LAN.

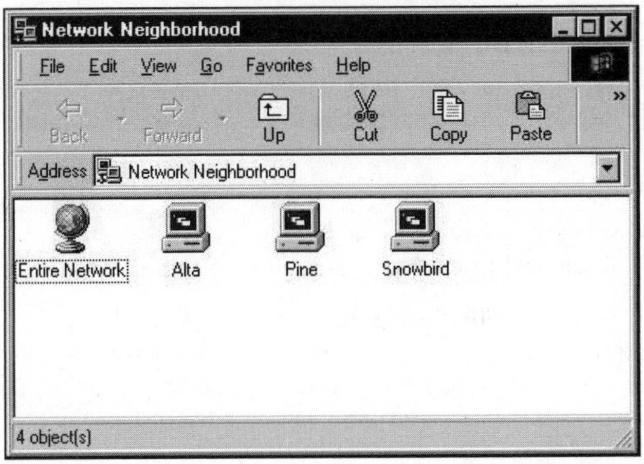

Figure 18-6: View your Linux Samba server from the Network Neighborhood window.

The Network Neighborhood window shows the computers that Windows found on your network. If your server appears on the screen (in my case, the server's name is pine), double-click it. Otherwise, you may need to double-click Entire Network, then open the workgroup that your server is a part of to find your server. The server should show two kinds of resources:

- **Printers** — A name and a printer icon should represent each printer shared from the server. To access a printer, double-click it. Windows will have you set up the printer for your computer. After that, you can print with it as you would any local printer.

- **Directories** — A name and folder icon should represent shared directories from the server. Open the directory to see the files and folders in that directory.

Double-click a folder to view the contents of that folder. At this point, you may receive a request to enter a password. Type the password and click OK. You should be able to view the contents of the folder, and its subfolders, at this time.

TIP: If you plan to use the directory often, you may want to assign a drive letter to it. Right-click the folder icon, then select Map Network Drive. Select a drive from the list and, if you like, choose Reconnect at logon to have it available when you log on. Then click OK.

If the file server that you are looking for does not appear in your Network Neighborhood, you can try to search for it. Choose Start → Find → Computer. Type the name of the computer to search for, and then select Find Now. If the computer name appears, double-click it. A window should open, displaying the shared directories and printers from the server.

Alternatively, you can also create an lmhosts file to help your Windows 95 computer find your Linux Samba server. Copy the sample C:\windows\lmhosts.sam file to C:\windows\lmhosts. Then edit the file to add the host names and IP addresses of the SMB servers on your network.

Troubleshooting your Samba server

A lot can go wrong with a Samba server. If your Samba server isn't working properly, the descriptions in this section should help you pinpoint the problem.

Basic networking in place?

Before computers can share directories and printers from Samba, they must be able to communicate on your LAN. Refer to Chapter 15 for information on setting up a LAN.

In Samba, your Samba server can use the TCP/IP name as the NetBIOS name (used by Window networks for file and printer sharing), or a separate NetBIOS name can be set in the smb.conf file. It is critical, however, that the broadcast address be the same as those for all clients communicating with your Samba server. To see your broadcast address, type the following (as root user):

```
# ifconfig -a
eth0       Link encap:Ethernet  HWadd 00:D1:B3:75:A5:1B
           inet addr:10.0.0.1  Bcast:10.0.0.255  Mask:255.255.255.0
```

The important information is the broadcast address (Bcast: 10.0.0.255). This is determined by the netmask (Mask:255.255.255.0). If the broadcast address isn't the same for the Samba server and the clients on the LAN, the clients cannot see that the Samba server has directories or printers to share.

Samba service running?

First, try the smbclient command from your Linux system to check that everything is running and being shared as you expect it to be. The smbclient command is a great tool for getting information about a Samba server and even accessing shared directories from both Linux and Windows computers. While logged in as root or any user who has access to your Samba server, type the following:

```
$ smbclient -L localhost
Password: **********
Domain=[ESTREET] OS=[Unix] Server=[Samba 3.0.3-4]
```

```
Sharename         Type        Comment
---------         ----        -------
homes             Disk        Home Directories
IPC$              IPC         IPC Service (Samba Server)
ADMIN$            Disk        IPC Service (Samba Server)
hp-ns1            Printer
Domain=[ESTREET] OS=[Unix] Server=[Samba 3.0.3-4]

Server                  Comment
---------               -------
PINE                    Samba Server
MAPLE                   Windows XP
NS1                     Samba Server

Workgroup               Master
---------               -------
ESTREET                 PINE
```

This shows that the Samba server is running on the local computer. Shared directories and printers, as well as servers in the workgroup, appear here. If the Samba server is not running, you will see "Connection refused" messages. You need to start the Samba service as described in the "Starting the Samba service" section earlier in this chapter.

Firewall open?

If the Samba server is running, it should begin broadcasting its availability on your LAN. If you try to access the server from a Windows or Linux client on your LAN, but get a "Connection refused" error, the problem may be that the firewall on your Linux Samba server is denying access to the NetBIOS service. If you have a secure LAN, you can type the following (as root user) to flush your firewall rules temporarily:

```
# iptables -F
```

Then, try to connect to the Samba Server from a Windows or Linux client. If you find that you can connect to the server, turn the firewall back on:

```
# service iptables restart
```

You then need to open access to ports 137, 138, and 139 in your firewall so that the Samba server will be able to accept connections for services. (See Chapter 14 for information on modifying your firewalls.)

User passwords working?

Try accessing a shared Samba directory as a particular user (from the local host or other Linux system on your LAN). You can use the smbclient command to do this. Here is an example:

```
# smbclient //localhost/tmp -U chris
added interface ip=10.0.0.1 bcast=10.0.0.255 nmask=255.255.255.0
```

```
Password: *******
Domain=[ESTREET] OS=[Unix] Server=[Samba 2.2.7a]
smb: \>
```

In this example, smbclient connects to the directory share named tmp as the Samba user named chris. If the password is accepted, you should see information about the server and a smb: \> prompt. If you cannot, then access the same shared directory from a Windows client, it's quite possible that the client is passing an improper user name and password. Part of the problem may be that the Windows client is not providing encrypted passwords.

For certain Windows clients, using encrypted passwords requires that you change a Windows registry for the machine. One way to change the registry is with the Windows regedit command. Registry changes required for different Windows systems are contained within the /usr/share/doc/samba-*/docs/Registry directory.

> **TIP:** The smbclient command, used here to list server information and test passwords, can also be used to browse the shared directory and copy files after you are connected. After you see the smb: \> prompt, type **help** to see the available commands. The interface is similar to any ftp client, such as sftp.

Setting Up a NetWare File Server in Linux

NetWare (from Novell, Inc.) used to be the most popular software for sharing files and printers among PCs connected in LANs. NetWare is referred to as a network operating system. That means that NetWare takes control of the whole computer and manages its resources. Although NetWare is not like client operating systems (such as Windows 2000 or XP) that you could keep on your desk at work to do word processing, it is a highly efficient file and print server.

Linux provides software for emulating a NetWare server from your Linux system. One package that used to ship with Fedora Linux is the Martin Stovers NetWare Emulator (mars-nwe package). Although this package is no longer distributed with Fedora, you can still obtain the mars-nwe packages from various Internet RPM repositories.

Though mars-nwe doesn't do everything a NetWare server can do, it does a good job as a basic file-and-print server. Here are features that mars-nwe includes:

- **File Services** — You can share directory structures (referred to as volumes) from Linux using the NetWare Emulator.

- **Print Services** — You can share printers associated with NetWare services using the NetWare Emulator.

- **RIP/SAP daemon** — This daemon allows your Linux computer to function as an IPX router. (IPX is the native protocol used to communicate among NetWare systems.)

On the client side, the ncpfs package is an additional package that you would need to install if you want your Fedora system to take advantage of services from NetWare servers (it's on CD #3). This package offers a full range of client commands for accessing NetWare services.

These commands enable you to mount NetWare volumes, display information about available services, and work with NetWare bindery objects.

Creating the NetWare file server

To share NetWare services from your Linux server, you need to use the IPX protocol to communicate with NetWare clients over your physical network. A common situation is to use IPX over an Ethernet LAN (which is what is described in this section).

> **CROSS-REFERENCE:** See Chapter 15 for information on setting up an Ethernet LAN.

Most of the configuration of your NetWare server in Linux is done in the /etc/nwserv.conf file. The nwserv.conf file that is delivered with mars-nwe contains a lot of commented information that describes what you need to do to configure NetWare services in Linux. Refer to the commented text in the nwserv.conf file for more details on different ways of configuring NetWare servers in Fedora Linux.

Configuring /etc/nwserv.conf

Information that you need to add to your /etc/nwserv.conf file is organized in sections. Each entry in a section begins with the number of that section. Here are some of the sections that you may need to modify for your NetWare server in Linux. (The number assigned to each section is shown in parentheses.)

- **Volumes** (1) — The names of volumes (Linux directories) you want to share.
- **Server Name** (2) — The identity of your server.
- **Internal Network Number** (3) — A number that uniquely identifies your server. The address either must be a hexadecimal number or must include the word *auto* to use your current IP address as your internal network number.
- **IPX Devices** (4) — Contains information used by the IPX network. It includes the IP network number, the network interface's device name (such as eth0), the frame type (ethernet_ii, 802.2, 802.3, or SNAP), and the number of ticks (a tick is a 1/18 of a second increment that is used to determine the time it takes packets to travel over a particular interface). You don't need to do this if your IPX network is already set up.
- **Password Handling** (7) — Defines whether (and how) passwords are encrypted from clients. (The default is 0, which enforces encryption of all client passwords.)
- **Minimal UID/GID Rights** (10) — Assigns the minimal user rights to the shared volumes from your Linux server. By default, the *nobody* user rights (UID=99) are assigned. Also by default, the *nobody* group rights (GID=99) are assigned.
- **Supervisor Login** (12) — Assigns the NetWare supervisor login to a particular login on your Linux system. It is recommended that you assign a special login instead of using root (to limit the security implications). By default, the supervisor login is assigned to

the Linux root login (UID=0). This entry is read only once, the first time the server is started. The entry should also include an initial password for the login.

- **User Logins** (13) — Maps regular Linux logins on your computer into Linux NetWare server logins. You can also add a default password, although none is required.

- **Automatic Login Mapping** (15) — Defines whether to map your Linux user logins (those in /etc/passwd) automatically into your Linux NetWare server. For commonly mapped logins, the same password is assigned. By default, logins are reread from /etc/passwd and assigned the password top-secret.

- **Startup Tests** (16) — Runs sanity checks at start-up with this value set to 1 (the default).

You can find information about a few other values that are used to set printing, debugging, and timing by reading the descriptions in the /etc/nwserv.conf file. Here is an example of the values I set to share a NetWare volume from a Linux system. Some of these values are defaults that are set in the nwserv.conf file. (These entries are spread throughout the /etc/nwserv.conf file.)

```
1       SYS            /var/mars_nwe/sys      rk 711 600
1       CDROM          /mnt/cdrom             kr   auto    1
2       maple1
4       0x0            eth0      802.3        1
7       1
10      99
11      99
12      SUPERVISOR     root      secret
15      99             top-secret
```

In this sample, the SYS (/var/mars_nwe/sys directory) and CDROM (/mnt/cdrom) volumes are being shared. The server's name is assigned as maple1. The address is selected automatically (auto) from the IP address of the local computer. By using 0x0 the Linux kernel can choose a network number for you. The network interface is eth0 (the first Ethernet network on the computer) and the frame type used is 802.3. Minimal user and group permissions are assigned to UID 99 (user nobody). SUPERVISOR permissions are assigned to root user (with an initial password of secret). The password for UID 99 is top-secret.

Starting the NetWare server daemon

At this point, all you have to do is start your NetWare server process. You can do that by typing **nwserv**. Your other option, which is better in the long term, is to start the server from a system init script. The mars-nwe package delivers such a script, but it is probably not configured to start automatically on your system. To set the script to start the NetWare server process automatically, type the following:

```
# chkconfig mars-nwe on
```

This command sets up mars-nwe to start at run levels 3, 4, and 5. The next time you reboot your Linux system, the `nwserv` daemon will start providing your NetWare services. Or, you could start the service immediately by typing the following:

```
# service mars-nwe start
```

Using NetWare client commands

The ncpfs software package comes with a set of utilities that work with NetWare file and print services. Here are a few of those commands.

- **nsend** — Sends a message to a user's workstation. The `nsend` command looks for information about the file server, user name and, optionally, a password, in the `.nwclient` file in your home directory. For example, to send a message to the system administrator, you could type **nsend supervisor 'Hello, how is your day?'.**

- **nwauth** — Authenticates to a NetWare server. You can specify the server (`-S` *servername*) and user (`-U` *username*) you want to authenticate. Otherwise, nwauth will look in your $HOME/.nwclient file for that information. If you run this command from the shell, the server will prompt you for a password.

- **nwbols** — Lists the NetWare bindery objects that you specify.

- **nwboprops** — Lists properties associated with a specified NetWare bindery object.

- **nwbpset** — Sets NetWare bindery properties value or creates a bindery property.

- **nwfsinfo** — Displays information about a file server without requiring you to log in to the server.

- **nwpasswd** — Changes your password on a NetWare server.

- **nwpurge** — Purges a directory of files that were previously erased.

- **nwrights** — Displays the NetWare rights associated with a particular file or directory.

- **nwsfind** — Searches for a NetWare server and displays a route (network address) to the server.

- **nwtrustee** — Displays a lot of trustee directory assignments associated with an object.

- **nwuserlist** — Displays a list of users that are currently logged in to a NetWare server.

- **nwvolinfo** — Shows information about a NetWare server volume.

- **slist** — Shows a list of all available NetWare servers.

- **ncpmount** — Mounts volumes from a NetWare file server.

- **ncpumount** — Unmounts volumes from a NetWare file server.

- **nwbocreate** — Creates a bindery object for a NetWare file server.

- **nwborm** — Deletes a bindery object for a NetWare file server.

- **nwfsctrl** — Runs a command on the NetWare file server.

- **nwgrant** — Adds a bindery object and its associated trustee rights to a directory.

- **nwmsg** — Sends a NetWare user broadcast message.

- **nwrevoke** — Revokes a directory's trustee rights.

Many NetWare commands can draw on configuration information in your $HOME/.nwclient file. When you run a NetWare command without specifying a server name, user name, or password, that information can be obtained from the .nwclient file. This file must have secure permissions (0600) because it can contain passwords and other private information. Entries in a .nwclient file may look similar to the following:

```
nwfs1/mike mypasswd
remserv/guest -
```

The first line is a listing for a file server named nwfs1 and a user named mike, followed by the password for that account, mypasswd. On the next line, the server's name is remserv and the user account is guest. No password is required for this account (indicated by the -).

Summary

By providing centralized file servers, an organization can efficiently share information and applications with people within the organization, with customers, or with anyone around the world. Several different technologies are available in Fedora Linux to enable you to make your Fedora Linux computer a file server.

The Network File System (NFS) protocol was one of the first file server technologies available. It is particularly well suited for sharing file systems among Fedora Linux and other UNIX systems. NFS uses standard mount and umount commands to connect file systems to the directory structures of client computers.

The Samba software package that comes with Fedora Linux contains protocols and utilities for sharing files and printers among Windows and OS/2 operating systems. It uses SMB protocols that are included with all Microsoft Windows systems, and therefore provides a convenient method of sharing resources on LANs containing many Windows systems.

NetWare used to be the dominant network operating system for LANs. It provided file- and printer-sharing services for networked PCs, although in recent years it has branched out to offer a variety of network services. With the mars-nwe package, you can provide basic NetWare file and print services from your Fedora computer. With the ncpfs package, you can also use many NetWare client services to query NetWare servers and use NetWare file systems and printers.

Chapter 19

Setting Up a Mail Server

In This Chapter

- Introducing SMTP and Sendmail
- Installing and running Sendmail
- Configuring sendmail
- Introducing Postfix
- Stopping spam with SpamAssassin
- Getting mail from the server (IMAP and POP3)
- Configuring SquirrelMail
- Administering a mailman mailing list

Today, electronic messaging is part of the communication backbone, the core of information dissemination within companies of all sizes. Everyone uses e-mail, from the mailroom to the laboratories to the CEO's office. And if you're in charge of an organization's mail server, you'll be notified (incessantly) when it stops working.

This chapter explains how to set up a mail server in Fedora to send and receive messages. In particular, it focuses on configuring a Sendmail mail server, but also tells how to configure a Postfix mail server (which is also in the Fedora Linux distribution). Once the mail server is configured, Fedora provides your mail server's users with different ways of getting their e-mail from your server, such as downloading it to their mail client (with IMAP or POP3) or reading it from a Web browser (using SquirrelMail).

Mailing list configuration and administration (using the mailman software package) are also discussed in this chapter, detailing how mailing list management software integrates and interfaces with the mail server.

> **NOTE:** Although the primary aspects of mail server configuration are discussed in this chapter, many configuration aspects are beyond its scope and thus are not addressed. Because security is an important concern when you're connected to the Internet, it is given considerable focus here.

Introducing SMTP and sendmail

Even with multimedia attachments and HTML encoding prevalent in e-mail messages today, the technology behind message transfer hasn't changed significantly since the early 1980s. The framework for the Simple Mail Transfer Protocol (SMTP) was initially described in RFC 821 in 1982. The protocol itself was extended in 1993 (RFC 1425), yielding the Extended Simple Mail Transfer Protocol (ESMTP), which provides more commands and new delivery modes.

The three parts to message transfer are the Mail Transfer Agent (MTA), the Mail Delivery Agent (MDA), and the Mail User Agent (MUA). The MTA, commonly referred to as the mail server (of which sendmail and postfix are examples), actually handles distributing outgoing mail and listening for incoming mail from the Internet. The MDA accepts messages from the MTA and copies the message into a user's mailbox. Fedora uses `procmail` as the default MDA, as specified in the sendmail configuration file (`sendmail.conf`). End users, for whom the mail is ultimately intended, use MUAs to get mail from the server and read it from their desktops. Most MUAs support Post Office Protocol (POP3) and Internet Message Access Protocol (IMAP) features for getting mail from the server so it can be read and managed from the user's desktop computer.

> **CROSS-REFERENCE:** See Chapter 9 for details on Mail User Agents available with Fedora Linux.

This chapter focuses on the sendmail MTA, the most common mail server on the Internet. Nearly 70 percent of all e-mail messages on the Internet are delivered by sendmail. With the growing Internet population, billions of e-mail messages are sent and received each day. As an alternative to sendmail, this chapter also includes a short description of postfix.

For getting mail from the server, this chapter describes the dovecot software package, which include POP3 and IMAP server software. As an alternative, for allowing users to read and manage e-mail from a Web broswer, this chapter describes how to configure SquirrelMail.

There have been three major releases of sendmail. The original sendmail (sendmail version 5) was written in 1983 by Eric Allman, a student at the University of California at Berkeley. He maintained the code until 1987, when Lennart Lövstrand enhanced the program and developed IDA sendmail. Eric Allman returned to Berkeley in 1991 and embarked on a major code revision, releasing sendmail V8 in 1993, which incorporated the extensions from IDA sendmail. The current version (8.12.9) is based on this "version 8" code.

Installing and Running sendmail

In Fedora, the sendmail distribution consists of three RPM packages: sendmail, sendmail-cf, and sendmail-doc. Only the first package is truly necessary to send and receive mail on your machine. The second package includes configuration macros and other files that can help you reconfigure your site's sendmail installation if the defaults are insufficient. The third package contains documentation files that help to explain some of the details of the current version.

The sendmail binary packages are included in the Fedora distribution. The sendmail package is on CD #1, while the sendmail-cf package is on CD #3and the sendmail-doc package is on CD #4. From the Fedora RPMS directory on each CD-ROM, the following command installs the packages:

```
# rpm -Uhv sendmail*
```

Starting sendmail

Once installed, the sendmail service is turned on by default. To start sendmail immediately, you can either reboot the machine or just run `service sendmail start` to start the server. The procedure for starting and stopping sendmail is no different from that of any other server process.

Other Mail Servers for Fedora or Red Hat Linux

The open-source version of sendmail is not the only mail server available for Fedora and other Red Hat Linux systems, but it is definitely the most common. The following list describes other servers and provides URLs for further information:

- **Postfix** — Like Sendmail, the Postfix MTA is also included with Fedora. Written by Wietse Venema (of tcp_wrappers fame), this free mail server was designed with security in mind and executes most functions as an unprivileged user in a restricted chroot environment. The server encompasses more than a dozen small programs (each performing a simple, distinct task) and several single-purpose queues. You can find more information and source code at `www.postfix.org`.

- **Exim** — The Exim MTA is a free mail server (under GPL) that runs on Linux and other UNIX systems. Exim was added to Fedora in Fedora Core 2. This MTA includes flexible features for checking and routing mail. Find out more about Exim from the Exim Home Page (`www.exim.org`).

- **Qmail** — Also conceived with security as a high priority, this mail server (written by Daniel J. Bernstein) offers secure and reliable message transfer, mailbox quotas, virtual domains, and antispam features. More information is available from `www.qmail.org/top.html`.

- **Sendmail (commercial version)** — Sendmail, Inc. (`www.sendmail.com`) offers products based on the same source code as open-source sendmail, aimed at enterprise e-mail installations. Products include Mailstream Manager (which includes support for enterprise-wide, high-volume mail service with anti-spam and anti-virus features), Mailcenter (offering IMAP/POP, Webmail and intelligent inboxes) and Workforce Mail (scalable, policy-based email service for the enterprise).

- **Smail** — Smail offers many of the same features as sendmail but is somewhat easier to configure and requires less memory. Smail is most appropriate for small

> to medium size mail servers. The Smail project page is available at
> `www.weird.com/~woods/projects/smail.html`. The source code can be
> downloaded from `ftp://ftp.planix.com/pub/Smail/`.

By default, incoming messages received by sendmail are processed and stored in the
`/var/spool/mail` directory. Each file in this directory represents a valid user name on the
local machine. The file is created automatically when you add a user. People with login
accounts use this directory and their user account name as their incoming mailboxes (for
example, `/var/spool/mail/johnq`).

Outgoing messages go in the `/var/spool/mqueue` directory while waiting to be sent.
Filenames in this directory follow a consistent naming scheme. The first two characters
indicate what type of data is stored in the file (see Table 19-1). Subsequent characters form a
unique random identifier based on the PID of the sendmail process that is handling that
message.

Table 19-1: File Prefixes in /var/spool/mqueue

Filename Prefix	Type of Data Stored
df	The data that constitutes the body of an e-mail message.
qf	The queue control file that contains the message headers and other administrative details.
tf	A temporary copy of the qf file, created if delivery errors occur.
xf	Any error messages generated while trying to send the message.

Other programs

Several other executable programs are included in the distribution. These are described in
Table 19-2.

Table 19-2: Other Related Sendmail Programs

Program	Description
mailq	Displays a summary of the messages awaiting processing in the mail queue (the command is equivalent to `sendmail -bp`).
mailstats	Displays message quantity and byte count statistics.
makemap	Translates text files (`/etc/mail/virtusertable`) to hashed Berkeley databases (`/etc/mail/virtusertable.db`). This command runs each time the sendmail script starts.
newaliases	Translates the plain-text `/etc/aliases` file into the hashed Berkeley database file `/etc/aliases.db` (the command is equivalent to `sendmail -bi`).
praliases	Prints out all aliases defined in `/etc/aliases`.

Program	Description
procmail	Not included with the sendmail package, but is used as an MDA for sendmail. (It is included in Red Hat Linux in the procmail package.)
purgestat	Clears the directory where host status information is stored. The command is equal to `sendmail -bH`, which is disabled by default.
rmail	Handles incoming mail via UUCP.
smrsh	Implements a restricted shell for running programs from sendmail.

Logging performed by sendmail

The amount of logging performed by sendmail is configurable in the `sendmail.mc` file, but the default level provides good coverage of informational notices and error messages. By default, the syslog facility configuration file (`/etc/syslog.conf`) tells syslog to store logging information from sendmail in the `/var/log/maillog` file. A few examples from this file are shown in this section.

An informational message similar to the following is written in the `/var/log/maillog` file each time the daemon starts (which also causes the hashed alias database to be regenerated):

```
May 16 12:52:40 toys sendmail[1758]: alias database /etc/aliases
     rebuilt by root
May 16 12:52:40 toys sendmail[1758]: /etc/aliases: 63 aliases, longest
     10 bytes, 625 bytes total
May 16 12:52:40 toys sendmail[1787]: starting daemon (8.12.8):
     SMTP+queueing@01:00:00
```

Each time a message is sent or received, a log file entry is created:

```
May 16 12:54:34 toys sendmail[1120]: OAA01120: from=root, size=161,
  class=0, pri=3 0161, nrcpts=1,
  msgid=<199907191254.OAA01120@toys.linuxtoys.net>, relay=root@localhost
May 16 12:54:35 toys sendmail[1127]: OAA01120: to=jkpat, ctladdr=root
  (0/0), delay=00:00:01, xdelay=00:00:00, mailer=local, stat=Sent
```

Besides showing normal mail server activities, the logs also show when people attempt to break into your mail server. The `wiz` and `debug` commands were implemented in earlier versions of sendmail and were found to be a huge security problem. You may see log file entries, such as those shown in the following code examples, as people with malicious intent check to make sure that you're not running a vulnerable sendmail daemon. Also, the `expn` and `vrfy` commands (which can be disabled via a configuration option) could give out more information than you'd care to distribute.

```
May 16 13:03:27 toys sendmail[699]: NOQUEUE: "wiz" command from
localhost
    [127.0.0 .1] (127.0.0.1)
May 16 13:03:29 toys sendmail[699]: NOQUEUE: "debug" command from
    localhost [127.0 .0.1] (127.0.0.1)
```

```
May 16 13:03:37 toys sendmail[701]: NOQUEUE: localhost [127.0.0.1]:
    expn oracle
May 16 13:03:43 toys sendmail[702]: NOQUEUE: localhost [127.0.0.1]:
    vrfy oracle
```

Configuring sendmail

To configure the sendmail facility, you edit configuration files in /etc/mail and /etc that are then used to by the sendmail start-up script to generate database files. Those database files are, in turn, used by the sendmail daemon to control the behavior of your sendmail server. Once sendmail is configured, you can begin adding user accounts to have mailboxes on your server. The general steps I describe in this section for configuring sendmail are:

1. **Getting a domain name** — You need a unique Internet domain name to assign to your mail server. You can purchase an Internet domain name from one of many different places, and then have DNS MX records for your domain point to the mail server you are creating.

2. **Configuring basic sendmail settings** — In this step, you edit the /etc/mail/sendmail.mc file. That file defines such things as the locations of other configuration and log files, as well as letting you configure some behavior of the sendmail daemon.

3. **Defining outgoing mail access** —The most critical security issue associated with your mail server is which mail messages it will accept to relay to other mail servers. By editing the /etc/mail/access file, you can indicate the hosts and users from which your server will accept mail for local delivery or relay.

4. **Configuring virtual servers** — By default, sendmail assumes that you are setting up the mail server for the domain of which the server is a member. To have sendmail on a single computer be the mail server for multiple domains (referred to as virtual servers), you need to define each domain name in the /etc/mail/local-host-names file.

5. **Configuring virtual users** — Using the /etc/mail/virtusertable configuration file, you can instruct the sendmail daemon what to do with the mail it receives for the users and domains it's configured to handle. This file give you a lot of flexibility to take mail addressed to a particular user and direct it to a particular mail box, forward it to a different mail address, or reject that mail in various ways.

6. **Adding user accounts** — You need to add a user account for every user that has a mailbox on your mail server.

7. **Starting sendmail and generating database files.** Starting sendmail runs the sendmail server daemon, but also compiles your configuration files into database files that can be used by sendmail. If the server is already running, you can simply compile the configuration files and have any new settings take effect without restarting the server.

The following subsections provide details on each of these steps.

Getting a domain name

For people to be able to send mail to the users on your mail server, you must have your own domain name. Chapter 25 describes how to get your own domain names and set up a DNS server. The critical issue for your mail server is to make sure that the MX record for your domain on the DNS server points to the address of your mail server.

Configuring basic sendmail settings (sendmail.mc)

Much of the configuration of your sendmail server comes from information in your /etc/mail/sendmail.mc file. Because this file sets sendmail default values that can be used in most cases, you may not have to do much with sendmail.mc. However, I recommend you step through this section so you understand how your mail server is configured.

Changes you make to the sendmail.mc file do not immediately take effect. First you must compile the sendmail.mc settings to generate the /etc/mail/sendmail.cf file. I describe how to do that in the "Starting sendmail and generating database files" section.

The resulting /etc/mail/sendmail.cf file contains over 1,700 lines of settings and comments that are used to direct the behavior of your sendmail daemon. The m4 macros you use in the sendmail.mc file are different from the resulting settings in the sendmail.cf file.

To find out which macros to use for a setting you find in the sendmail.cf file, refer to the /usr/share/doc/sendmail/README.cf file. If you are interested in details on the contents of your sendmail.cfm file, I have included an exhaustive description of sendmail.cf at the *Red Hat Linux Bible* Web site: (www.wiley.com/compbooks/negus).

> **CAUTION:** Because of the way sendmail is configured in Fedora, you should not directly modify the sendmail.cf file. The sendmail.cf file is regenerated automatically when sendmail restarts if sendmail.mc changes. As a result, any modifications made directly to sendmail.cf will be lost.

The following code samples are from the /etc/mail/sendmail.mc file that accompanies the Fedora version of sendmail.

> **NOTE:** Lines that begin with dnl (delete to new line) in the sendmail.mc file are comment lines. In most cases, I have left them out in the examples shown.

```
divert(-1)dnl
include(`/usr/share/sendmail-cf/m4/cf.m4')dnl
VERSIONID(`setup for Red Hat Linux')dnl
OSTYPE(`linux')dnl
```

The first few lines of the sendmail.mc file do some housekeeping. The divert line removes extra output when the configuration file is generated. The include line causes rule sets needed by sendmail to be included. The VERSIONID line identifies the configuration file as being for Red Hat Linux systems, such as Fedora (though this setting is not checked, so it could be anything you like). The OSTYPE, however, must be set to linux to get the proper location of files needed by sendmail.

```
dnl define(`SMART_HOST', `smtp.your.provider')
```

By default, the sendmail daemon tries to send your outgoing e-mails directly to the mail server to which they are addressed. If you want all e-mail to be relayed through a particular mail server instead, you can remove the comment (dnl, which stands for "delete to new line") from the SMART_HOST line above. Then, change smtp.your.provider to the fully qualified domain name of the mail server you want to use.

```
define(`confDEF_USER_ID', ``8:12'')dnl
define(`confTRUSTED_USER', `smmsp')dnl
```

Instead of running as the root user, the daemon runs as the mail user (UID 8) and mail group (GID 12), based on the confDEF_USER_ID line set previously. This is a good policy, since it prevents someone who might compromise your mail server from gaining root access to your machine. The confTRUSTED_USER line adds smmsp to the list of users that are trusted by sendmail. Other trusted users are root, uucp, and daemon. (The smmsp user is assigned ownership to some sendmail spool directories and mail database files.)

```
dnl define(`confAUTO_REBUILD')dnl
define(`confTO_CONNECT', `1m')dnl
```

If you remove dnl, the confAUTO_REBUILD line will tell sendmail to automatically rebuild the aliases database, if necessary. The confTO_CONNECT line sets the time sendmail will wait for an initial connection to complete to one minute (1m).

```
define(`confTRY_NULL_MX_LIST',true)dnl
define(`confDONT_PROBE_INTERFACES',true)dnl
```

With confTRY_NULL_MX_LIST true, if a receiving server is the best mail exchange (MX) for a host, try connecting to that host directly. If confDONT_PROBE_INTERFACES is true, the sendmail daemon will not insert local network interfaces into the list of known equivalent addresses.

```
define(`PROCMAIL_MAILER_PATH', `/usr/bin/procmail')dnl
define(`ALIAS_FILE', `/etc/aliases')dnl
dnl define(`STATUS_FILE', `/var/log/mail/statistics')dnl
```

The next three lines (PROCMAIL_MAILER_PATH, ALIAS_FILE, and STATUS_FILE) set locations for the program that distributes incoming mail (procmail, by default), the mail aliases file, and the mail statistics file, respectively.

```
define(`UUCP_MAILER_MAX', `2000000')dnl
define(`confUSERDB_SPEC', `/etc/mail/userdb.db')dnl
define(`confPRIVACY_FLAGS', `authwarnings,novrfy,noexpn,restrictqrun')dnl
define(`confAUTH_OPTIONS', `A')dnl
```

The UUCP_MAILER_MAX line sets the maximum size (in bytes) for messages received by the UUCP mailer. The confUSERDB_SPEC line sets the location of the user database (where you can override the default mail server for specific users). The confPRIVACY_FLAGS line causes sendmail to insist on certain mail protocols. For example, authwarnings causes X-Authentication-Warning headers to be used and noted in log files. The novrfy and noexpn settings prevent those services from being requested. The restrictqrun option prevents the -q option to sendmail.

```
dnl define(`confAUTH_OPTIONS', `A p')dnl
dnl TRUST_AUTH_MECH(`EXTERNAL DIGEST-MD5 CRAM-MD5 LOGIN PLAIN')dnl
dnl define(`confAUTH_MECHANISMS', `EXTERNAL GSSAPI DIGEST-MD5 CRAM-MD5
     LOGIN PLAIN')dnl
define ('CERT_DIR','/etc/mail/certs')define(`CERT_DIR','`/etc/mail/certs')
define(`confCACERT_PATH', `CERT_DIR')
define(`confCACERT', `CERT_DIR/cacert.pem')
define(`confSERVER_CERT', `CERT_DIR/cert.pem')
define(`confSERVER_KEY', `CERT_DIR/key.pem')
define(`confCLIENT_CERT', `CERT_DIR/cert.pem')
define(`confCLIENT_KEY', `CERT_DIR/key.pem')
dnl define(`confDONT_BLAME_SENDMAIL',`groupreadablekeyfile')dnl
```

Some of the group of lines just shown that begin with dnl (so they are commented out) can be uncommented (remove the initial dnl) to provide certain features. Others are set explicitly. The confAUTH_OPTIONS line can be used to set options used with SMTP authentication. This example (with A and p options) would allow authenticated users with plain text logins to send mail. The TRUST_AUTH_MECH line would cause sendmail to allow authentication mechanisms other than plain passwords (if dnl were removed). The confAUTH_MECHANISMS line can configure the types of authentication mechanisms that can be used (if dnl were removed). The next few lines above set the location of the certificates directory for sendmail to /etc/mail/certs, then identify different files in that directory that hold the certificates and keys needed for authentication. The confDONT_BLAME_SENDMAIL line should be uncommented if the key file needs to be readable by applications other than sendmail. (Normally, you would not want the file to be readable by everyone.)

```
dnl define(`confTO_QUEUEWARN', `4h')dnl
dnl define(`confTO_QUEUERETURN', `5d')dnl
dnl define(`confQUEUE_LA', `12')dnl
dnl define(`confREFUSE_LA', `18')dnl
define(`confTO_IDENT', `0')dnl
```

The commented lines above actually show the default values set for certain timeout conditions. You can remove comments and change these values if you like. The confTO_QUEUEWARN option sets how long after delivery of a message has been deferred to send a warning message to the sender. Four hours (4h) is the default. The confTO_QUEUERETURN option sets how long before an undeliverable message is returned. The confQUEUE_LA and confREFUSE_LA options set the system load average levels at which mail received is queued or refused, respectively. The confTO_IDENT option sets the timeout when waiting for a response to an IDENT query to be received (by default it is 0, which means no timeout).

```
FEATURE(`smrsh',`/usr/sbin/smrsh')dnl
FEATURE(`mailertable',`hash -o /etc/mail/mailertable.db')dnl
FEATURE(`virtusertable',`hash -o /etc/mail/virtusertable.db')dnl
FEATURE(redirect)dnl
FEATURE(always_add_domain)dnl
FEATURE(use_cw_file)dnl
FEATURE(use_ct_file)dnl
FEATURE(local_procmail,`',`procmail -t -Y -a $h -d $u')dnl
FEATURE(`access_db',`hash -T<TMPF> -o /etc/mail/access.db')dnl
FEATURE(`blacklist_recipients')dnl
```

The FEATURE macro is used to set some special sendmail features. The smrsh feature defines /usr/sbin/smrsh as the simple shell used by sendmail to receive commands. The mailertable and virtusertable options set the locations of the mailertable and virtusertable databases. The redirect option allows you to reject mail for users who have moved and provide new addresses. The always_add_domain option causes the local domain name to be added to the host name on all delivered mail. The use_cw_file and use_ct_file options tell sendmail to use the file /etc/mail/local-host-names for alternative host names for this mail server and /etc/mail/trusted-users for trusted user names, respectively. (A trusted user can send mail as another user without resulting in a warning message.)

The local_procmail option sets the command used to deliver local mail (procmail), as well as options to that command (including the $h hostname and $u user name). The access_db option sets the location of the access database, which identifies which hosts and users are allowed to relay mail through the server. The blacklist_recipients option turns on the ability of the server to block incoming mail for selected users, hosts, or addresses. (The access_db and blacklist_recipients features are useful for blocking spam.)

```
DAEMON_OPTIONS(`Port=smtp,Addr=127.0.0.1, Name=MTA')dnl
```

As it stands, the DAEMON_OPTIONS line allows only incoming mail created by the local host to be accepted. Be sure to comment this line out if you want to allow incoming mail from the Internet or other network interface (such as the local LAN).

```
FEATURE(`accept_unresolvable_domains')dnl
```

The accept_unresolvable_domains option is on, causing you to accept mail from host computers that don't have resolvable domain names. If you have client computers (such as dial-up computers) that need to use your mail server, leave this option on. Turning it off, however, can help eliminate spam.

```
LOCAL_DOMAIN(`localhost.localdomain')dnl
MAILER(smtp)dnl
MAILER(procmail)dnl
```

The LOCAL_DOMAIN option here causes the name localhost.localdomain to be accepted as a name for your local computer. The last lines in your sendmail.mc file define the mailers to use on your server. The /usr/share/sendmail-cf/mailer directory contains definitions for smtp, procmail, and other mailers. After you have made the changes you want to the sendmail.mc file, you can regenerate the sendmail.cf file as described in the "Starting sendmail and generating database files" section.

Defining outgoing mail access

Every time an e-mail message intended for outgoing mail is received by your sendmail server, the server needs to decide if it will accept or reject relaying of that message. Policies that are too restrictive might prevent legitimate mail from getting out. Policies that are too loose can leave your server open to spammers.

With e-mail abuse the way it is these days, you cannot run an open relay (where your server simply relays all messages it receives to the requested mail servers). Spammers can use software referred to as spiders to look for open relays. If you leave your mail server open, they will find you quickly and use your machine to relay their spam. The result of a spammer using your machine can be:

- You could end up on blacklists. Some e-mail blacklist maintainers look for open relays themselves and block them before abuse is even reported. Servers that use those blacklists will block all mail from you, even legitimate e-mail.

- People will hate you. Your mail server will be identified as the one sending the spam. As a result, people may retaliate against your server, or at the very least really wish you would stop sending them ads to help them get out of debt or enhance themselves in some way.

This section describes how to set up the sendmail access file (/etc/mail/access) to include a sensible set of rules defining for whom your server will relay mail. Using the access file, sendmail can make decisions about whether or not to relay a message based on the sender's host/domain name, IP address, or e-mail address. You can further refine the match by checking for those addresses in Connect, From, or To data associated with the message.

There are then four basic actions you can have the server take on a match:

- **RELAY** — Your mail server could simply send the message on to the mail server requested in the mail message.

- **REJECT** — The message is rejected (not relayed) and the sender is told it was rejected.

- **DISCARD** — The message is silently discarded and the sender is not told.

- **ERROR:** *text you choose* — You can add some informative text here, to give the sender some reason why the relay did not occur.

The `/etc/mail/access` file, by default, only relays messages from users who are directly logged into the mail server (localhost). Without being explicitly allowed, users from all other machines are not allowed to relay messages. Here's how the access file is set up by default:

```
localhost.localdomain     RELAY
localhost                 RELAY
127.0.0.1                 RELAY
```

With these defaults set, only mail sent from the local machine is relayed. So, if the only outgoing mail you send is done while you are logged in directly to the server, you don't need to change this file. The following examples illustrate how you can selectively choose to relay or reject mail received by your sendmail server:

```
Connect:192.168                 RELAY
Connect:linuxtoys.net           RELAY
Connect:spammer-domain.com      REJECT

From:chris@linuxtoys.net        RELAY
To:spidermaker.com              RELAY
To:former-user@linuxtoys.net    ERROR: User no longer works here
```

On the `Connect:192.168` line, the network address (presumably the first part of the IP addresses used on your LAN) is allowed to relay mail. This is a good way to allow everyone sending mail from a machine on the local LAN to have their mail relayed. On the next line (`Connect:linuxtoys.net`), essentially mail coming from any machine in the named domain is allowed to be relayed. The third line represents a domain that you know to be a spam relay, so you reject messages originating from that domain.

The next three lines indicate how to treat mail received for relaying, based on the From and To names associated with the message. As you can see, the first example allows relay of any messages from chris@linuxtoys.net. In the last example, mail being forwarded to a particular person (former-user@linuxtoys.net) is rejected and a custom error message (in this case "User no longer works here") is sent back to the sender.

> **NOTE:** Use some caution when you are creating relay rules based on user e-mail address. Because those values are reported by the users themselves, they are vulnerable to being spoofed.

Once you have adjusted this file to suit you, you must rebuild the access database (`access.db` file) for the changes to take effect. See "Starting sendmail and generating database files" for information on this topic.

Configuring virtual servers

If you have set up a sendmail mail server for one domain, it's quite possible that you will someday want to have multiple domains served from that same computer. To create virtual servers on the same computer, you must add the name of every domain being served to the `/etc/mail/local-host-names` file.

For example, if your sendmail server were handling e-mail accounts for `linuxtoys.net`, `example.com` and `example.net` domains, the `local-host-names` file would appear as follows:

```
# local-host-names - include all aliases for your machine here.
linuxtoys.net
example.com
example.net
```

Even if you are only serving one domain with your mail server, it is a good idea to identify that domain in this file. When messages come to the server for the domains listed here, sendmail knows to try to deliver the messages locally. Messages for domains not listed here sendmail interprets as needing to be relayed.

> **NOTE:** If you want to off-load the processing of mail for a particular domain that is currently being directed to your sendmail server, you can use the `/etc/mail/mailertable` file. After setting up a DNS MX record to point to your sendmail server for this domain, and listing that domain name in the `mailertable` file, you can identify another computer that sendmail will forward all the traffic to for that domain. For example:
>
> ```
> example.com        smtp:mx1.linuxtoys.net
> ```
>
> This example shows that all messages destined for example.com that are received by your sendmail server are forwarded to the server named `mx1.linuxtoys.net`. The smtp indicates that the server supports Simple Mail Transfer Protocol.

Configuring virtual users

Incoming mail to your sendmail server will be directed to your machine with a request to deliver the message to a particular person at a particular domain name. For each domain that the sendmail server supports, you can identify how e-mail to mail recipients of that domain is treated.

With sendmail, you set up virtual user definitions in the `/etc/mail/virtusertable` file. Essentially, you are telling sendmail to redirect messages addressed to particular user names and/or domain names based on definitions you set up.

Configuring the `virtusertable` file is particularly important if your server is handling mail for multiple domains. That's because, by default, mail for the same user name (regardless of the domain name) will be stored in the same mailbox. For example, if your server handles mail for `example.com` and `linuxtoys.net` domains, mail for `chris@example.com` and `chris@linuxtoys.net`, would all be directed to `/var/spool/mail/chris` mailbox. With the `virtusertable` file, you can change that behavior in a lot of ways.

The `virtusertable` file is empty by default. The following are some examples that illustrate how incoming messages can be directed in different ways based on `virtusertable` definitions.

```
chris@linuxtoys.net            chris
cnegus@linuxtoys.net           chris
francois@linuxtoys.net         francois@spidermaker.com
info@linuxtoys.net             info-list
bogus@linuxtoys.net            error:nouser No such user here
@example.net                   example-catchall
@example.com                   %1@linuxtoys.net
```

In the first two lines, incoming mail destined for `chris` or `cnegus` at `linuxtoys.net` is directed to the mailbox for the local mail server user named `chris`. In the next line, any e-mail directed to francois in the same domain goes to `francois@spidermaker.com`. After that, e-mail sent to the info user name is saved to the local `info-list` mail account.

The line beginning with bogus@linuxtoys.net illustrates an error condition. Here, e-mail destined for the user named `bogus` will be rejected with the error message `No such user here` being directed back to the sender. Besides creating custom error messages, you can also use any Enhanced Mail System Status codes that are compliant with RFC 1893.

The last two lines (beginning with `@example.net` and `@example.com`) illustrate how e-mail for all recipients for a given domain can all be directed to the same place. In the first case, all example.net messages go into the mailbox for the user named example-catchall. The last line shows how the users from a particular domain can all be mapped into their same user name (`%1`) on a selected domain name.

Once you have made changes to this file to suit you, you must rebuild the virtusertable database (`virtusertable.db` file) for the changes to take effect. See "Starting sendmail and generating database files" for information on this topic.

Adding user accounts

Ultimately the e-mail received by your mail server is placed in a user's mailbox, where the user can pick it up and read it at his or her leisure. Each of those user names must be added as as real users on your Fedora system. For example, to add the user chris to your Fedora sendmail server, you could type (as root user):# **useradd -s /sbin/nologin chris**This action creates a user account named chris in the `/etc/passwd` file, sets the shell to `/sbin/nologin`, and creates a mail box for that user in `/var/spool/mail/chris`. The `/sbin/nologin` shell prevents the user from logging in to a shell (which is a good security practice when you only want a user to have mail or FTP access, for example). Now, sendmail can direct e-mail to that user's mail box.

Starting sendmail and generating database files

None of the configuration that you just did to your `sendmail.mc`, `virtusertable`, `access`, `domaintable`, and `mailertable` configuration files take effect until they are regenerated into database (.db) files. There are a few different ways you can go about loading your configuration files into database files:

- **Restarting sendmail** — Each time you reboot your computer or restart the sendmail daemon (`service sendmail restart`), all sendmail configuration files (including `sendmail.mc`)are compiled into database files that are ready to be used by the sendmail server. You can also just rebuild the databases without stopping the sendmail daemon (including the `/etc/aliases.db` file) using the sendmail startup script. To simply rebuild the database type:

```
# /etc/init.d/sendmail reload
```

This command rebuilds all the database files, including the `/etc/aliases` file.

- **Making the configuration files** — Using the `make` command, you can have some or all of the configuration files made into database files, so they become immediately usable by the sendmail daemon. To do that, change to the `/etc/mail` directory, then type either **make all** or **make** with the target database file you are creating. For example:

```
# cd /etc/mail
# make virtusertable.db
```

You can replace virtusertable.db with `access.db`, `domaintable.db`, `mailertable.db`, or `sendmail.db`. (Note that you use the .db target name and not the name of the original configuration file.) As mentioned, you can also use the `make all` command to rebuild all database file.

At this point, your sendmail server should be up and running. You can test your server by sending mail to it and checking log files to see how the server reacted. Make sure that your firewall allows requests on TCP and UDP ports 25. Then check that your mail server is responding to requests by typing the following:

```
# telnet localhost 25
Trying 127.0.0.1...
Connected to localhost.localdomain (127.0.0.1).
Escape character is '^]'.
220 toys.linuxtoys.net ESMTP Sendmail 8.12.11/8.12.11;
    Sun, 23 May 2004 03:34:02-07--
```

You can see that the sendmail daemon is running and responding to port number 25. Try typing HELO. When you are done, type Ctrl+V, Ctrl-] to exit.

> **NOTE:** For more information on troubleshooting your mail server, refer to the *Linux Troubleshooting Bible*, from Wiley Publishing.

Redirecting mail

At times, your e-mail users may want to redirect mail to some place other than their own mailboxes on the local server. Each user can redirect his or her mail using the `.forward` file. System-wide, you as the administrator can set aliases to redirect mail in the `/etc/aliases` file.

The .forward file

One way for users to redirect their own mail is through the use of the `.forward` file, as described in the previously listed `sendmail.cf` file. The format of a plain-text `.forward` file is a comma-separated list of mail recipients. Common uses of the `.forward` file include:

- Piping mail to a program to filter the mailbox contents:

```
"| /usr/bin/procmail"
```

- Sending mail destined for one user (for example, jkpat) to another (for example, cht09, on a different machine in this case):

```
cht09@other.mybox.com
```

- Delivering mail to the local user (jkpat again) *and* sending it to two others (cht09 and brannigan):

```
\jkpat, cht09@other.mybox.com, \brannigan
```

> **TIP:** You are not allowed to have a `.forward` file in a directory that can be read by all users. If you leave permissions open on a `.forward` file, sendmail will ignore that file and not forward mail as you want. To allow `.forward` files with open permissions to be used by sendmail, you can remove the `dnl` from the `confDONT_BLAME_SENDMAIL` line in the `sendmail.mc` file.

The aliases file

A more flexible method of handling mail delivery (system-wide rather than being specific to one particular user) involves the `/etc/aliases` file, which is also a plain-text file. The aliases file contains a name followed by a colon, and then a user name, another alias, a list of addresses, a file, or a program to which mail will be delivered. The name on the left side of the colon (which can be a valid user name or just an alias) can then be used as an e-mail recipient on the local machine or on a remote machine.

Some aliases are already set by default in `/etc/aliases`. For example, because there are a lot of administrative users defined in Fedora (bin, adm, lp, etc.), instead of having separate mailboxes for each one, messages for all of them are directed to the root user's mailbox as follows:

```
bin:          root
daemon:       root
adm:          root
lp:           root
```

Using the aliases file for mail-aliasing allows for several extensions to normal mail-handling behavior:

- You can use the aliases file yourself to create mini-mailing lists. Here's an example:

```
info-list:  chris, tweeks, francois@spidermaker.com
```

In this example, any messages sent to info-list are distributed to chris, tweeks, and francois@spidermaker.com. Notice that the user list can be a combination of local users and outside mail addresses.

- One account can receive mail under several different names:

```
patterson: jkpat
```

This indicates that any mail addressed to patterson@mybox.com (just an alias) will arrive in the mailbox of jkpat (an actual user account).

- Mail can be received under a name that isn't a valid (or reasonable) user name:

```
Charlie.Jackson.II@mybox.com: jackson
```

He wouldn't really want to type Charlie.Jackson.II as a user name, but that doesn't mean he can't receive mail as such.

- Messages intended for one user can be redirected to another account (or to several accounts):

```
oldemployee: bradford
consultant: bradford, jackson, patterson
users: :include:/root/mail/lists/users
```

Here, any message for oldemployee@mybox.com would be delivered to the mailbox of user bradford. Also, the users bradford, jackson, and patterson would receive any mail addressed to consultant. The third line indicates that the recipients of the "users" alias are specified in the file /root/mail/lists/users.

- Mail can be sent directly to a file on the local machine:

```
acsp-bugs: /dev/null
trouble-ticket: /var/spool/trouble/incoming
```

In the first line, because the fictional ACSP program is no longer used on the machine, there's no need to track its errors, so the mail is effectively ignored. The second line stores incoming trouble tickets in the /var/spool/trouble/incoming file. Remember that if you enable this, anyone anywhere can send you a sufficiently large message to fill up the partition on which that directory resides. This is a security risk and should be carefully evaluated before being implemented.

When you are done adding new aliases, type the following to have those changes take effect:

```
# newaliases
```

> **TIP:** When resolving addresses, sendmail doesn't actually use the /etc/aliases text file. For faster access, the text file is turned into a Berkeley database file, /etc/aliases.db, which resolves aliased addresses. For this reason, the newaliases command (equivalent to sendmail -bi) must be run to rebuild the database file each time the /etc/aliases text file is modified.

Introducing Postfix

Postfix is a mail-transfer agent that you can use in place of Sendmail to handle mail service on your Red Hat Linux system. Postfix is meant to be easier to administer and be more secure.

Although many of the configuration files and other components are different from those in Sendmail, some are meant to replace Sendmail components. To help you make the transition from Postfix to Sendmail, Fedora Linux has configured the two packages to use the alternatives system. Chapter 10 describes how to use the Mail Transport Agent Switcher to change from one transport to the other.

When you switch to Postfix and start the Postfix daemon, as described in Chapter 10, Postfix takes over as the MTA, replaces Sendmail components with Postfix components, and uses some of the same locations for mailboxes and log files. Postfix takes over mail transport based on configuration files set in the `/etc/postfix` directory. The following is an overview of the default locations used by the Postfix service:

- **Mail configuration** (`/etc/postfix/main.cf`) — The primary configuration file for Postfix. Identifies the locations of Postfix queues, commands, and aliases, as well as defining the host and domain names that Postfix is serving. If you do not add a fully-qualified domain name to this file, Postfix will use your local host name as the name of the mail service it represents.

- **Mailboxes** (`/var/spool/mail`) — Directory containing incoming mail files, with each user's mailbox represented by a file of the user's name. (This is the same default spool directory used by Sendmail.)

- **Mail Queue** (`/var/spool/postfix`) — Location of directories where mail messages are queued for delivery.

- **Mail Log** (`/var/log/maillog`) — Location of mail-log files.

Although most options you need for Postfix are described in the `/etc/postfix/main.cf` file, you can see many more available options in the `main.cf.default` file in the same directory. Based on the default configuration in the `main.cf` file, here is how Postfix will handle outbound and incoming mail:

- **Outbound Mail** — The local host name is added as the sending host for the mail posted from this computer. You might want to change it to the local domain name (set `myorigin = $mydomain`).

- **Incoming Mail** — Only mail destined for the local host name is kept on the local server by default. Other mail is forwarded. To have all mail for your domain kept on the local server, add `$mydomain` to the `mydestination` line.

For complete information on configuring Postfix, refer to `www.postfix.org/docs.html`.

Stopping Spam with SpamAssassin

Despite the fact that it is rude and antisocial, there are people who send out thousands of unsolicited e-mail messages (referred to as spam), hoping to get a few responses. Using a tool called SpamAssassin, you can configure your incoming mail service to tag messages it believes to be spam so you and your users can deal with those messages as you choose.

There are several methods that SpamAssassin uses to identify spam:

- **Checking mail headers** — Examining the headers of your incoming mail to look for well-known tricks used to make the e-mail look valid.

- **Checking mail text** — Looking for text style, content, and disclaimers in message bodies that are commonly used in spam.

- **Checking blacklists** — Checking `mail-abuse.org`, `ordb.org`, and other blacklists to find e-mail sent from sites known before to relay spam.

- **Checking spam signatures** — Comparing e-mail signatures. Since spam often consists of the exact same message sent thousands of times, taking signatures of spam messages lets SpamAssassin compare your message to a database of known spam messages. SpamAssassin uses Vipul's Razor (see `http://razor.sourceforge.net`).

Although there are many different ways to deal with spam (or rather, e-mail that *might* be spam), most of the experts I have consulted like to configure SpamAssassin to simply tag incoming e-mail messages that appear to be spam. Then they encourage each user of the e-mail server to create his own rules for filtering the spam.

> **NOTE:** Although the procedure here describes how to use SpamAssassin from the RPM package that comes with the latest version of Fedora, many people get their version of SpamAssassin directly from the `SpamAssassin.org` Web site. Because anti-spam software is evolving so quickly (to keep ahead of spammers), some people like to make sure they have the very latest software.

Setting up SpamAssassin on your mail server

Here's a quick procedure for enabling SpamAssassin and having your users choose what to do with spam messages that are encountered:

1. Configure your mail transport agent (sendmail or postfix) to use the procmail command as its mailer. For sendmail, it is already configured as the default mailer, based on the following line in the `/etc/mail/sendmail.mc` file:

   ```
   FEATURE(local_procmail,` ',`procmail -t -Y -a $h -d $u')dnl
   ```

2. Make sure that the SpamAssassin `spamd` daemon is running (it should already be on for run levels 2-5), and if it isn't, start it by typing the following (as root user):

```
# chkconfig --list spamassassin
spamassassin   0:off   1: off    2:on   3:on   4:on   5:on   6:off
# chkconfig spamassassin on
```

3. Create an `/etc/procmailrc` file (using any text editor, as root user). This procmailrc file example pipes all mail messages received by procmail through `spamc` (which is the client side of the `spamd` daemon turned on in the previous step):

```
:0fw
| /usr/bin/spamc
```

If you like, you can do a lot more in the `procmailrc` file to deal with spam on a system-wide basis. You could, for example, create procmail recipes that take reported spam e-mail messages and sorts them into a system-wide spam folder or deletes them completely. Likewise, each user can create an individual `$HOME/.procmailrc` file to create personal procmail recipes. (Type **man procmailex** for examples of rules in a `procmailrc` file.)

4. Check the `/etc/mail/spamassassin/local.cf` file. This file contains rules that are used system-wide by SpamAssassin, unless they are overridden by a user's individual `$HOME/.spamassassin/user_prefs` file. Here are the contents of the `local.cf` file:

```
required_hits 5
rewrite_subject 1
subject_tag [SPAM]
report_safe 0
```

In SpamAssassin, a scoring system is used to guess at whether a particular message is spam or not. The `required_hits` line shows that a score of 5 is needed to flag the message as spam. You should set that higher for a public mail server (such as 8 or 10). Setting `rewrite_subject` to 1 allows SpamAssassin to change the Subject line of a message. The `subject_tag [SPAM]` line has SpamAssassin add the text "[SPAM]" to the Subject line of spam it finds. The `report_safe 0` line ensures that only the message header is changed, while the content is intact. (Type **man Mail::SpamAssassin::Conf** to see other settings you can use in the `local.cf` file.)

Because there will almost certainly be some false-positives, you risk preventing your users from seeing an e-mail they need if you do system-wide filtering. To avoid this problem, the approach shown here lets the user decide what to do with e-mail tagged as spam. Users can even adjust their own threshold for when a message is believed to be spam.

Next, you should have the users of that mail server set up their own user preferences in their home directories. The preferences set in each user's `$HOME/.spamassassin/user_prefs` file help tell SpamAssassin how to behave for that user's e-mail. Here are examples of lines a user might want to have in that file:

```
required_hits          3
whitelist_from         jsmith@example.com bjones@example.net
blacklist_from         *.example.org
```

The `required_hits` line (which is on by default) sets the number of hits needed to consider the message to be spam. Hits are based on scores for matching or not matching criteria in the tests SpamAssassin performs. (See `http://spamassassin.org/tests.html`.)

The `whitelist_from` and `blacklist_from` lines let you set addresses for people, individual hosts, or entire domains that should not be considered as spam (`whitelist_from`) or should always be considered as spam (`blacklist_from`). For other ways to modify SpamAssassin behavior, type the following command:

```
man Mail::SpamAssassin::Conf
```

At this point, SpamAssassin should be running and identifying spam based on input from you and the people using your e-mail server. Next, each user needs to decide what to do with the messages that are marked as spam, as described in the following section.

> **TIP:** Techniques you can use along with SpamAssassin include services like RealTime Blackhole Lists (RBL) and SpamCop. With RBL (`http://mail-abuse.org/rbl`), you can block spam messages before they even reach your server. SpamCop (`www.spamcop.net`) provides a service that allows you to enter spam messages you receive into a database that helps others block the same spam messages.

Setting e-mail readers to filter spam

Each user can turn on filtering in his e-mail reader to decide what to do with each message tagged as spam from SpamAssassin. A common practice is to direct e-mail marked as spam to a separate folder. Because some real mail can occasionally be mistakenly marked as spam, you could check the spam folder every week or two, just to make sure you didn't miss anything.

Here's an example of how to add a filter rule from Evolution Email:

1. Create a folder labeled SPAM under your incoming mailbox.
2. Click Tools → Filters.
3. From the Filters window, click Add. An Add Rule window appears.
4. Identify a rule name (such as Spam) that adds a criterion that looks for a specific header (X-Spam-Flag) containing specific text (YES). Then under Add Action, select an action (Move to Folder) and identify the folder to contain the spam messages (SPAM).

When you ask to receive mail from your mail server, all messages with the X-Spam-Flag set to `yes` will be sorted into your SPAM folder. As an alternative, you could check for the text [SPAM] to appear in the subject line as the criterion for sorting the spam messages.

Other mail readers (Mozilla mail, pine, Netscape mail, and others) also include features for filtering and sorting e-mail based on criteria you enter.

Getting Mail from the Server (POP3 or IMAP)

After you have set up your mail server, you will want to let users access their e-mail from that server. That means either having each user log in to the mail server to read his or her e-mail or, more likely, configuring Post Office Protocol (POP3) or IMAP to let users access their mail from their workstations. Here are descriptions of POP3 and IMAP:

- **POP3** — With POP3, users download and manage their e-mail messages on their local workstations. POP3 is simpler and requires fewer server resources.

- **IMAP** — With IMAP, messages stay on the server, although you can manipulate those messages from the mail client. Because the messages stay on the server, an IMAP server requires more disk space and uses more CPU. However, you do have the advantage of logging in to different workstations to read your mail and having the mail and folders you have set up appear the same.

Fedora comes with two software packages that are able to provide POP3 and IMAP service. The dovecot package is primarily an IMAP server that also contains a small POP3 server. It supports mail in both maildir (where each mail account can contain multiple folders on the server) and mbox (where all messages are in a single file) formats.

The cyrus-imapd package was built to scale up to enterprise-level mail server technology. Many security features are built into cyrus-imapd, including the ability to run on sealed servers where mailbox storage and user access are tightly controlled by the server.

This section describes how to use POP3 to allow the users of your mail server to download their mail messages from your server over the network. POP3 is the more common and simpler of the two protocols for accessing mailboxes over networks.

Accessing mailboxes in Linux

When e-mail messages are received on your sendmail or postfix mail server, they are sorted to separate files, each of which represents a user's mailbox. The default location of mailbox files is the `/var/spool/mail` directory. So the login account jsmith would have a mailbox:

```
/var/spool/mail/jsmith
```

While logged into the mail server, jsmith could simply type **mail** from a Terminal window to read his e-mail (using the simple, text-based `mail` command). However, because most people prefer to get their e-mail from the comfort of their own desktop computer, you can set up either Post Office Protocol (POP3) or Internet Message Access Protocol (IMAP).

POP3 and IMAP servers listen on the network for requests for a user's e-mail, then either download the entire contents of the mailbox to the user's mail reader (as with POP3) or let the user manage the messages while the messages stay on the server (as with IMAP).

Typically, your mail server will be configured to use either POP3 or IMAP to provide e-mail messages to your users (though it is possible to have both running on the same machine).

The next section tells how to set up an IMAP or POP3 service to allow access to e-mail accounts.

> **TIP:** At times, you may want to check your e-mail on a computer that is not your regular computer, but be able to save messages later. In that case, most mail readers let you choose a setting that copies the e-mail messages without deleting them from your POP3 server. That way, when you get back to your regular computer, you can copy the messages again. IMAP avoids that problem by always keeping the mail messages on the server and letting the user create and work with additional folders on the server.

Configuring IMAP and POP3 with dovecot

When a user is added to Fedora, a mailbox is configured under that user name in the /var/spool/mail directory (such as /var/spool/mail/chris). The format of that file, by default, is the traditional mbox format, with all messages and attachments stored in that one file. By configuring the POP3 service on your mail server, users will be able to download their e-mail messages from e-mail clients on other machines. By configuring IMAP, users can work with messages and folders directly on the server.

In Fedora Core 2, the dovecot or cyrus-imapd packages can be used in place of the Washington University imap package (that was dropped from the last version of Fedora) to provide POP and IMAP servers. The following procedure describes how to configure the IMAP or POP3 service in Fedora using dovecot.

1. Review the values set in the /etc/dovecot.conf file. For this example, I assume the defaults, which include:

   - **mbox** — All mail is stored in one file. For IMAP servers, the Maildir style is used. Maildir stores each message in a separate file.

   - **protocols** — This sets which protocols to listen for. By default imap and imaps are on. You can add pop3 and pop3s, so that the line appears as follows:

     ```
     protocols = imap imaps pop3 pop3s
     ```

   - **auth_userdb = passwd** — Although it is possible to use different authentication methods, the default is to simply authenticate the user's name and password from the /etc/passwd file. The authentication method used is pam and passwords are used in plain text format. See /usr/share/doc/dovecot*/auth.txt for information on authentication types.

2. Turn on the dovecot service by typing the following (as root user):

   ```
   # chkconfig dovecot on
   ```

3. Start the POP service immediately by starting up the dovecot service as follows:

   ```
   # /etc/init.d/dovecot start
   ```

All users who have user accounts on your mail server are configured, by default, to accept e-mail. For example, if e-mail comes in to the `mail.handsonhistory.com` server for a user named jsmith, the message is copied to the `/var/spool/mail/jsmith` file on the server. Continuing the example, from jsmith's computer, he could set up his mail reader as follows:

- **Mail server:** mail.handsonhistory.com
- **User name:** jsmith
- **Password:** *theuserspassword*
- **Protocol:** POP3

After the mail reader is configured, when jsmith clicks Send & Receive from his mail reader, all e-mail messages in the `/var/spool/mail/jsmith` file are downloaded to his local mail reader. The messages are then erased from the server.

> **NOTE:** If none of your users are able to download messages from your mail server, verify that your firewall (iptables) is configured to allow access to the POP service. By default, pop3 listens on port 110 and pop3 with ssl support listens on port 995.

Getting mail from your browser with Squirrelmail

Once your mail server is up and running, you can configure Squirrelmail to allow the users of your mail server to get their mail from their Web browsers. To use Squirrelmail, you must install the squirrelmail package from CD #3 of the Fedora installation set.

Squirrelmail has a very intuitive, menu-based administrative interface. That interface includes a variety of plugins you can add to Squirrelmail to use features such as spell checking, calendar, password changing, and fetching mail from a POP3 server. You can get more plugins from squirrelmail.org as well.

To configure Squirrelmail, type the following as root user from a Terminal window:

```
# /usr/share/squirrelmail/config/conf.pl
```

Features you might want to consider tuning include: Organization preferences (such as the organization's name and logo to put into the Squirrelmail interface), Themes (more than two dozen are available), and Plugins (just check whether any of those that are available to install are interesting).

Also, by default, mail can only be accessed from a browser on the local host, so you will probably want to change Server Settings. For example, change the Domain name to the name of the domain from which you will allow users to access their mail.

For a user to get to mail using squirrelmail, he simply needs to type the following address into the location box of his Web browser (replacing *server* with `localhost` or the name of the computer, if you are running this outside of the localhost):

```
http://server/webmail
```

Figure 19-1 shows an example of the webmail browser interface with the webmail logo replaced with the logo from my organization (in this case, LinuxToys.net).

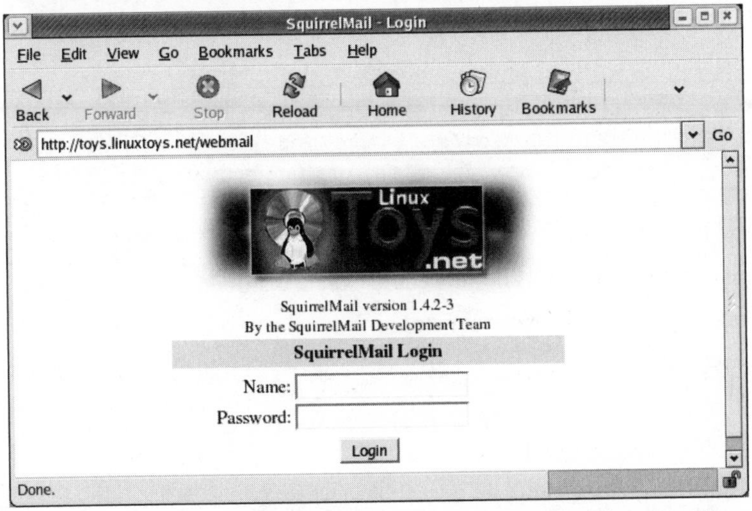

Figure 19-1: Add a logo to SquirrelMail and let users login from the Web to get mail.

Type your username and password. Your mailbox should appear, as illustrated in Figure 19-2:

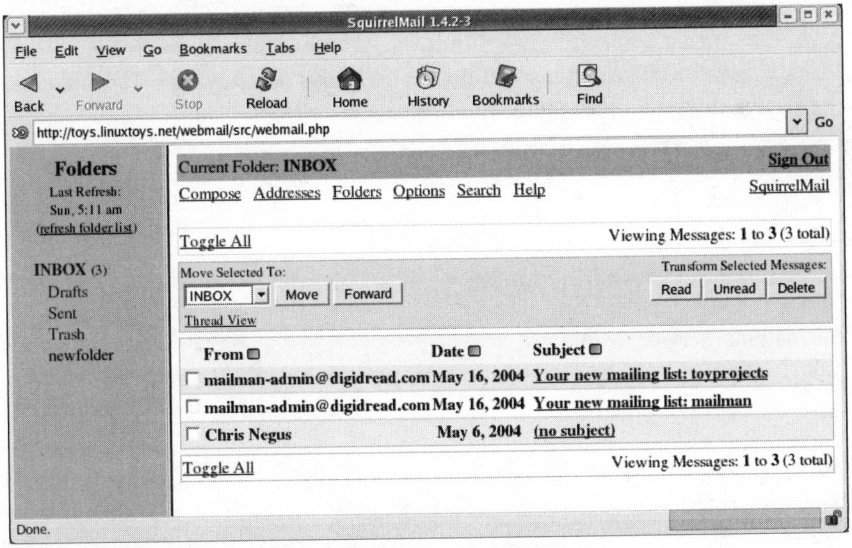

Figure 19-2: Manage your mail from multiple folders in SquirrelMail.

Administering a Mailing List with mailman

Mailman is a popular open source package for managing e-mail discussion lists. Besides offering flexible administrative interfaces for setting up and managing lists, it also has Web-based interfaces that make it easy for people to join lists, access discussion list archives, and tune their own preferences.

> **NOTE:** If you find that you need more information about configuring mailman, there are plenty of places to go. Check the mailman Web site at `www.gnu.org/software/mailman/mailman.html`. You can also view README files in `/usr/share/doc/mailman-*` and `/var/mailman`.

The following is a brief procedure for configuring a discussion list using mailman:

1. Install the mailman RPM from CD #3 of the Fedora Core 2 distribution.

2. Start your Web server (if it isn't already running) as follows:

   ```
   # service httpd start
   # chkconfig httpd on
   ```

3. Create a password for your site as follows:

   ```
   # /var/mailman/bin/mmsitepass
   New site password: *****
   Again to confirm password: *****
   ```

4. Edit the `/var/mailman/Mailman/mm_cfg.py` file and change the `DEFAULT_URL_HOST` and `DEFAULT_EMAIL_HOST` values. For example, the host name of the computer I'm configuring my mailing list on is toys.linuxtoys.net. The default e-mail host is linuxtoys.net. The values would appear as follows:

   ```
   DEFAULT_EMAIL_HOST    = 'toys.linuxtoys.net'
   DEFAULT_URL_HOST DEF  = 'linuxtoys.net'
   ```

5. To create a mailman mailing list, type the following:

   ```
   # /var/mailman/bin/newlist mailman
   ```

6. Start the mailman service as follows:

   ```
   # service mailman start
   # chkconfig mailman on
   ```

7. Create a new mailing list, using the `newlist` command as follows:

   ```
   # /var/mailman/bin/newlist
   Enter the name of the list: projectlist
   Enter the email of the person running the list: chris@linuxtoys.net
   Initial projectlist password: *****
   To finish creating your mailing list, you must edit /etc/aliases (or
   ```

```
equivalent) file by adding the following lines, and running the
`newaliases' program:

## projectlist mailing list
projectlist:              "|/var/mailman/mail/mailman post projectlist"
projectlist-admin:        "|/var/mailman/mail/mailman admin projectlist"
projectlist-bounces:      "|/var/mailman/mail/mailman bounces projectlist"
projectlist-confirm:      "|/var/mailman/mail/mailman confirm projectlist"
projectlist-join:         "|/var/mailman/mail/mailman join projectlist"
projectlist-leave:        "|/var/mailman/mail/mailman leave projectlist"
projectlist-owner:        "|/var/mailman/mail/mailman owner projectlist"
projectlist-request:      "|/var/mailman/mail/mailman request projectlist"
projectlist-subscribe:    "|/var/mailman/mail/mailman subscribe projectlist"
projectlist-unsubscribe:  "|/var/mailman/mail/mailman unsubscribe
projectlist"
```

 8. Copy and past the text just shown (starting from the line `## projectlist mailing list`) into the end of your `/etc/aliases` file.

 9. Run the `newaliases` command. At this point you should be able to view the new mailing list from your Web browser. From a Web browser on the local system, type the following name in the address box:

```
http://localhost/mailman/listinfo
```

 10. If everything appears to be working, begin adding more mailing lists. In my example, I created a mailing list called Toyprojects. The name of that project appears on the list shown in Figure 19-3.

 11. Next, select that project name (click on it). The Info page should appear for the project.

 12. Scroll to the bottom of that page and click on the project administrative interface link.

 13. When prompted, type in the List Administrator Password. Now you can configure the look, feel and behavior of your mailing list. Important information you will want to consider includes:

 • Privacy options — Do you want the list to be public or private (as in, just within your organization)? Who do you want to allow to see your member list?

 • Send filters — Who can post messages to the list? Is the list moderated or unmoderated? Might the list just go in one direction, for example, as a way to contact customers?

 • Membership management — Can your members see other member information? What are your policies for adding and removing members?

 14. When you are finished configuring the options, be sure to submit your changes.

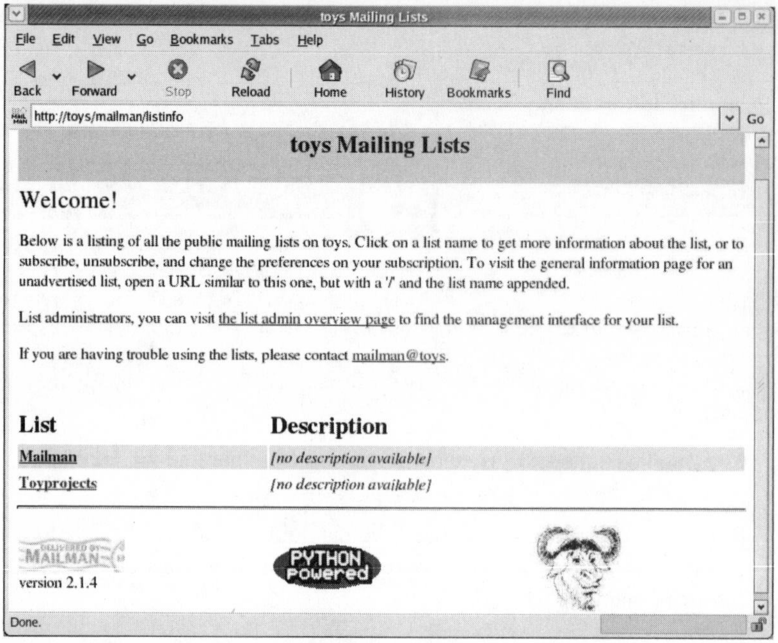

Figure 19-3: Create multiple mailing lists in mailman.

At this point, you can allow users to join the list. Encourage them to explore and set their own user preferences.

If you encounter problems configuring mailman, refer to the INSTALL.REDHAT and README files in the /usr/share/doc/mailman-* directory.

Summary

Fedora includes a full range of tools for configuring and managing mail servers. For mail transfer agents, Fedora includes the Sendmail and Postfix software packages. Both are considered to be excellent, professional quality mail servers.

To allow users to access their mailboxes from the server, Fedora includes the dovecot and cyrus-imapd packages. Those packages implement POP3 and IMAP protocols to allow e-mail to be downloaded or manimpulated on the server. You can also configure SquirrelMail to allow users to access their mail through a Web-based interface.

To set up mailing lists in Fedora, you can use the mailman package. Besides including some very flexible configuration tools, mailman also provides simple Web-based access to mailing list preferences and archives.

Chapter 20

Setting Up an FTP Server

In This Chapter

- Understanding FTP servers
- Using the vsFTPd FTP server
- Getting more information about FTP servers

File Transfer Protocol (FTP) has been the standard method for sharing files over the Internet for many years. Even with the popularity of the Web, which made document database services such as Gopher and WAIS almost obsolete, FTP servers are still the most common way to make directories of documents and software available to the public over the Internet.

File-sharing applications, such as NFS and Samba, are excellent tools for sharing files and directories over a private network. For organizations that need to share large numbers of files over public networks, however, FTP server software provides more robust tools for sharing files and protecting your computer systems. Also, FTP client software (for accessing FTP servers) is available for any type of computer that can access a network.

This chapter describes how to set up and maintain an FTP server using the Very Secure FTP Server package (vsFTPd).

> **CAUTION:** Configuring your FTP server to share private files or to allow users to upload files to your server involves more risks than just allowing downloads. See the end of this chapter for references to documents from CERT that provide FTP security tips.

Understanding FTP Servers

The first implementations of FTP date back to 1971, predating the Web by more than a decade. FTP was created at a time when most computing was done on large mainframe computers and minicomputers. The predominant platforms using FTP were UNIX systems.

FTP set out to solve the need to publish documents and software so that people could get them easily from other computer systems. On the FTP server, files were organized in a directory structure; users could connect to the server over the network (usually the Internet), move up and down the directory structure to find the files that interested them, and download files from (and possibly upload files to) the server.

Originally, one drawback with FTP servers was that when people looked for a file or a document on the Internet, they had to know which FTP server held the file they were looking for. Tools such as Gopher and WAIS helped in searches. With the advent of the Web, however, users can now rely on a variety of search engines and links from Web pages to help identify FTP servers that have the files they want. In fact, when you download files by clicking a link from a Web page, you may not even be aware that the file is being downloaded from an FTP server.

Attributes of FTP servers

That FTP was implemented on large, multiuser UNIX systems accounts for many of the design decisions that remain a part of FTP today. FTP servers in Linux draw on FTP features that have resulted from years of testing and experience gained from other UNIX versions of FTP. Some attributes of FTP servers follow:

- Because FTP was originally used on multiuser systems, only limited parts of the file system in Fedora are devoted to public FTP access. Those who access FTP from a public user account (by default, the `anonymous` user name) are automatically given an FTP directory (often `/var/ftp`) as their root directory. From there, the anonymous user can access only files and directories below that point in the file system.

- Access to the FTP server relies on a login process that uses standard UNIX login names (that is, those user names found in `/etc/passwd`). Although strangers to the system could log in using `anonymous` as a user name, users with their own accounts on the system could log in with their own user names through FTP and most likely have access to a greater part of the file system (in particular, their own private files and directories).

- The `lftp` command and other FTP client programs let you log in and then operate from a command interpreter (similar to a very simple shell). Many of the commands that you use from that command interpreter are familiar UNIX commands. You change directories with `cd`, list files with `ls`, change permissions with `chmod`, and check your location with `pwd` (to name a few). When you find where you want to be, you use the `get` command to download a file or the `put` command to upload one.

As an administrator of an FTP server, it is your responsibility to make sure that you share your files in a way that gives people access to the information that you want them to have without compromising the security of your system. This means implementing a strong security policy and relentlessly monitoring the system to prevent abuse.

CROSS-REFERENCE: See Chapter 14 for information on computer security issues.

FTP user types

Several different types of users can log in to and use an FTP server. *Real users* represent the category of users who have login accounts to the Fedora system that contains your FTP server (that is, you know them and have given them permission for other uses besides FTP). A *guest user* is similar to a real user account, except that guest user access to the computer's file system is more restricted. The user name anonymous is the most common for providing public access.

The vsFTPd server also supports the concept of virtual users. The recommended method for creating virtual users for vsFTPd is to configure PAM (pluggable authentication modules) to point to per-user configuration files. A tutorial to configure vsFTPd to allow virtual users is available at www.linux-corner.net/linux/services/ftp.html.

> **NOTE:** Although vsFTPd is the only full-blown FTP server software in Fedora, the WU-FTPD FTP server sofware, which was once part of Red Hat Linux, is still available on the Web. At this point, you must decide if you want to run the vsFTPd server on your Fedora system or download WU-FTPD (wu-ftpd package) and install it instead. The one you choose will take over the full functions of FTP service on your computer. Descriptions for setting up WU-FTPD from a previous edition of the *Red Hat Linux Bible* are available online from the companion Web site to this book: www.wiley.com/compbooks/negus.

Using the Very Secure FTP Server

The Very Secure FTP Server (vsFTPd) is the only FTP server software included in the Fedora distribution. vsFTPd is becoming the FTP server of choice for sites that need to support thousands of concurrent downloads. It was also designed to secure your systems against most common attacks.

Red Hat, Inc. itself uses vsFTPd on its own FTP servers (ftp.redhat.com). Other organizations in the Linux/GNU world have also made the switch to vsFTPd, including Debian Linux (ftp.debian.org) and the GNU Project (ftp.gnu.org).

Besides security and scalability, vsFTPd was designed for simplicity. Therefore, fewer options exist for configuring vsFTPd than you find in WU-FTPD, an older FTP server package which is still commonly used, so you are expected to rely on standard Linux file and directory permissions to provide refined access to your server. Getting started with vsFTPd, or using it to replace WU-FTPD, is fairly straightforward.

Quick-starting vsFTPd

By enabling the vsFTPd service, you can almost instantly have an FTP service running with the default values (set in the /etc/vsftpd/vsftpd.conf file). The following is a quick procedure for getting your vsFTPd server up and running.

> **NOTE:** If you have been using the WU-FTP server on your computer and you are switching to vsFTPd, you need to turn off WU-FTP. To do that, change disable=no to disable=yes in the /etc/xinetd.d/wu-ftpd file. Then, once you have completed the following procedure, vsFTPd will take control of the default FTP configuration, allowing access to the /var/ftp directory and listening on the default FTP port. Because the two packages have some different default settings, however, you may want to do additional tuning to get vsFTPd to perform as you would like it to.

1. To use the vsFTPd server, you must make sure that the vsFTPd software package is installed.

    ```
    # rpm -q vsftpd
    ```

2. Enable the vsFTPd server by typing the following line (as root user):

    ```
    # chkconfig vsftpd on
    ```

3. Start the vsFTPd server as follows:

    ```
    # service vsftpd start
    ```

4. Try to log in to the FTP server as anonymous (using any e-mail address as the password) (if you are connecting over a network, use the more-secure `sftp` command instead):

    ```
    $ ftp localhost
    Connected to yourhost
    220 (vsFTPd 1.2.1)
    530 Please login with USER and PASS
    Name (localhost:chris): anonymous
    331 Please specify the password.
    Pasword: ******
    230 Login successful.
    Remote system type is UNIX.
    Using binary mode to transfer files.
    ftp>
    ```

If you saw messages similar to the preceding, your vsFTPd server is now up and running. Next, try to access the server from another computer on the network to be sure that it is accessible.

> **NOTE:** If your FTP server is not accessible to the outside world, you may need to ensure that your network is configured properly and that your firewall allows access to port 21. Refer to Appendix C for information on getting your network services working.

The next section explains the `/etc/vsftpd/vsftpd.conf` configuration file.

Configuring vsFTPd

Most of the configuration of vsFTPd is done in the `/etc/vsftpd/vsftpd.conf` file. Although many values are not set explicitly in `vsftpd.conf`, you can override the defaults by setting *option=value* statements in this file. You can set such things as which users have access to your vsFTPd server, how logging is done, and how timeouts are set.

Go through the following section for more information about how vsFTPd is configured by default and how you can further configure your vsFTPd server.

User accounts

Users who can access your vsFTPd server are, by default, the anonymous user and any users with real-user accounts on your system. (A *guest* user is simply a real user account that is restricted to its own home directory.) The following lines set these user access features:

```
anonymous_enable=YES
local_enable=YES
```

The anonymous_enable line lets users log in anonymously using either the anonymous or ftp user name. Any users with local accounts (in /etc/passwd) can log into the FTP server with local_enable set to YES. An exception to this rule is that, by default, all user accounts listed in the /etc/vsftpd.user_list file are denied access.

> **NOTE:** If you want to disable access by anonymous users, don't just comment out anonymous_enable. Anonymous access is on by default, so you must set anonymous_enable=NO to disable it.

Check the vsftpd.user_list file to see which users are denied access to the vsFTPd server. Note that root and other administrative logins are excluded. You can add other users to this list or change the location of the list by setting the userlist_file parameter to the file you want. To add a user to the vsftpd.user_list or use the userlist_file parameter to create a new list, you must also have userlist_enable set to YES (as it is by default). For example:

```
userlist_file=/etc/vsftpd.user_list_local
userlist_enable=YES
```

If you like, you can change the meaning of the /etc/vsftpd.user_list file so that only the users in that list are allowed to use the vsFTPd service. Set userlist_deny=NO and change the /etc/vsftpd.user_list to include only names of users to whom you want to grant access to the server. (All other users, including anonymous and ftp, will be denied access.)

Setting FTP access

The vsFTPd server software provides a simple and seemingly secure approach to access permissions. Instead of using settings in the FTP service to selectively prevent downloads and uploads of particular directories (as FTP servers such as WU-FTPD do), you can use standard Linux file and directory permissions to limit access. There are, however, the following general settings in the /etc/vsftpd/vsftpd.conf file to let users get files from and put files onto your vsFTPd server.

Downloading files

Any users with valid logins (anonymous or real users, excluding some administrative logins) can download files from the vsFTPd server, by default. The ability to download a particular file or a file from a particular directory is governed by the following basic Linux features:

- **File and directory permissions** — Standard file and directory permissions apply as a means of limiting access to particular files, even in accessible file systems. So, if the root user puts a file with 600 permission (read/write to root only) in the /var/ftp directory, an anonymous user is not able to download that file.

- **Root directory** — The root directory (chroot) for anonymous users is /var/ftp. The root directory for regular users is the entire computer's root directory (/), although their current directory after connecting to FTP is /home/*user*, where *user* is the user name. So an anonymous user is restricted to downloads from the /var/ftp directory structure, while a regular user potentially has access to the whole file system. Another possibility is to create *guest* accounts by restricting some or all users to their home directories.

You can use the chroot_local_user option to change the root directory for regular users so that they are restricted to their home directory. In general you will not want to do this, because using the same user name and password for general Linux logins doesn't place such restrictions on your users. To restrict all regular users to their home directory when using vsFTPd, add this line to the vsftpd.conf file:

```
chroot_local_user=YES
```

To enable the concept of *guest* users, you can choose to limit only selected users to their home directories. You do this by setting chroot_list_enable to YES, then adding a list of guest users to a file noted with the chroot_list_file option. The following example lets you add such a list (one user name per line) to the /etc/vsftpd.chroot_list file:

```
chroot_list_enable=YES
chroot_list_file=/etc/vsftpd.chroot_list
```

> **TIP**: To restrict a user to FTP access only, set the user's shell to /sbin/nologin in the /etc/passwd file.

You can add a setting to the vsftpd.conf file to affect how files are downloaded. To enable ASCII downloads, you can enable that feature as follows:

```
ascii_download_enable=YES
```

Without making that change, all downloads are done in binary mode. Although vsFTPd will seem to allow the user to change to ascii mode, ascii mode will not work if this setting is NO.

Uploading (writing) files from local users

Two values set in the `vsftpd.conf` file allow the uploading of files during a vsFTPd session. The following defaults allow any users with regular, local user accounts to upload files:

```
write_enable=YES
local_umask=022
```

The `write_enable` value must be `YES` if you intend to allow any users the ability to write to the FTP server. The `umask=022` value sets the default file permission used when a local user creates a file on the server. (The 022 value causes files created to have 644 permission, allowing the user read and write permission and everyone else only read permission.)

As with downloading, uploading in `ascii` mode is prohibited by default. Though `ascii` downloads create a potential security hole for draining resources from your server, `ascii` uploads are apparently not as dangerous and can be useful for uploading text files. To allow `ascii` uploads, add the following line:

```
ascii_upload_enable=YES
```

Uploading (writing) files from anonymous users

The ability to upload files is turned off for anonymous FTP users. If you want to turn it on, add the following line to the `vsftpd.conf` file:

```
anon_upload_enable=YES
```

You must also make sure that the `/var/ftp` directory contains one or more directories with write permissions open to anonymous users. For example, you might want to create an `incoming` directory and open its permissions (`chmod 777 /var/ftp/incoming`).

Files uploaded by anonymous users will be created with 600 permission by default (read/write permission for the `ftp` user, not accessible to any other users so that even the user who uploaded the files can't remove them). To allow 644 permission, for example, you can add the following line:

```
anon_umask=022
```

When you allow the anonymous user to upload files, you can grant limited ability to change the files he or she uploads. By adding the following line, you can allow anonymous users to rename or delete any files owned by anonymous users (provided that the files are in directories for which the users have write permission):

```
anon_other_write_enable=YES
```

If you also want to allow anonymous users to create their own directories, add the following:

```
anon_mkdir_write_enable=YES
```

By default, the `ftp` user is given ownership of uploaded files from anonymous users. If you want to indicate that anonymous uploads be owned by a different user (of your choice), you can use the `chown_uploads` and `chown_username` options. For example, if you have a user account named `mynewuser`, you can set these options as follows:

```
chown_uploads=YES
chown_username=mynewuser
```

Of course, you can create and use any user name you want. However, for security reasons you should not use the root login or any other administrative login for this purpose.

Adding message files

Although vsFTPd doesn't support the arrangement of README and welcome files FTP servers such as WU-FTP support, you can add `.message` files to any accessible directory on your vsFTPd server. Then, if you use the default `dirmessage_enable` option as follows, the text from the `.message` file will be displayed when the user enters the directory:

```
dirmessage_enable=YES
```

You will probably at least want to add a `.message` file to the root directory of the FTP server for anonymous users. By default, that location is `/var/ftp/.message`. If you want to use files other than `.message` files, you can set the `message_file` option. For example, to have text from the `.mymessage` file displayed when you enter a directory, you can add the following line:

```
message_file=.mymessage
```

You can also set a one-line message to appear before the login prompt. You can do this by entering the following line, replacing the text with anything you want to say:

```
ftpd_banner=Welcome to My FTP service.
```

Logging vsFTPd activities

Logging is enabled in vsFTPd by default, and the activities of your vsFTPd site are written to the `/var/log/xferlog` file. The following options enable logging and change the log file to `/var/log/vsftpd.log`:

```
xferlog_enable=YES
xferlog_file=/var/log/vsftpd.log
```

You can turn off logging if you like by changing YES to NO. (Note, however, that logging enables you to watch for potential break-ins, so turning it off is not recommended.) Or you can change the location of the log file by changing the value of the `xferlog_file` option.

If you want to be able to use tools that generate transfer statistics, you can have vsFTPd log data written in the standard xferlog format that is used by WU-FTPD and other FTP servers. To store your transfer data in xferlog format, set the following option:

```
xferlog_std_format=YES
```

Setting timeouts

The following timeouts are set by default in vsFTPd (these values are built in, so you don't have to make any changes to the /etc/vsftpd/vsftpd.conf file for them to take effect):

```
accept_timeout=60
connect_timeout=60
idle_session_timeout=600
data_connection_timeout=120
```

The accept_timeout=60 and connect_timeout=60 values determine how long the client has to establish a PASV or PORT style connection, respectively, before the connection times out. Both are set to 60 seconds. (Note that these two lines are not automatically included in the configuration file; you can add them by hand if you want to change their values.) The idle_session_timeout=600 option causes the FTP session to be dropped if the user has been inactive for more than 10 minutes (600 seconds). The data_connection_timeout value sets the amount of time, during which no progress occurs, that the server will wait before dropping the connection (the default here is 120 seconds).

Navigating a vsFTPd site

Most shell wildcard characters that a user might expect to use, such as question marks and brackets, are supported by vsFTPd. There is one particularly useful wildcard character you can use with the ls command, and one option you can turn on. The asterisk (*) wildcard can be used with the ls command. Multiple asterisks in the same line are supported. You can add support for the -R option of ls so that a user can recursively list the contents of the current directory and all subdirectories. To turn on this feature, which is off by default, you can add the following line to the vsftpd.conf file:

```
ls_recurse_enable=YES
```

Getting More Information about FTP Servers

There are plenty of resources for gaining more information about FTP servers. Here are some of your options:

- **FAQ** — To check out the vsFTPd FAQ, go to /usr/share/doc/vsftpd*/FAQ.

- **RFCs** — Requests for comments are the documents that define standard protocols used with the Internet. The main RFC for FTP is RFC959. You can obtain RFCs from a variety of locations on the Internet, including the Internet RFC/FYI/STD/BCP Archives: www.faqs.org/rfcs.

- **CERT** — This organization provides useful documents for setting up FTP servers. Anonymous FTP Abuses describes how to respond to and recover from FTP server abuse. It also tells how to deal with software piracy issues. Anonymous FTP

Configuration Guidelines provide general guidance in setting up your FTP area, as well as specific challenges of setting up a writable FTP area. Both of those documents are available from the CERT Tech Tips page (`www.cert.org/tech_tips`).

> **TIP:** I strongly recommend reading the FTP documents from CERT. The tips in these documents will help keep your FTP server secure, while enabling you to offer the services that you want to share.

Summary

The FTP service is the primary method of offering archives of document and software files to users over the Internet. The only FTP server package delivered with Fedora is the Very Secure FTP (vsFTPd) server. The vsFTPd server relies on standard Linux file and user permissions to provide a simple, yet secure, FTP environment to run in Fedora.

Chapter 21

Setting Up a Web Server

In This Chapter

- Introduction to Web servers
- Quick starting the Apache Web server
- Configuring the Apache Web server
- Starting and stopping the server
- Monitoring server activities

The World Wide Web is the fastest growing segment of the Internet. According to Netcraft (`www.netcraft.com`), there were more than 50 million Web sites on the Internet in May 2004.Electronic commerce has provided a new virtual storefront for businesses trying to stay on the cutting edge of technology.

The Web has also been a boon to organizations seeking an inexpensive means to publish and distribute information. And with increasing computing power, decreasing prices, free operating systems such as Linux, and free Web servers such as Apache and TUX, it's getting even easier for anyone to establish a presence on the Web.

This chapter shows you how to install and configure the Apache Web server. Each of the server's configuration files is described and explained in detail. You learn about various options for starting and stopping the server, as well as how to monitor the activity of a Web server. Security is an issue addressed throughout the chapter in the descriptions and examples.

> **NOTE:** The current version of Fedora Linux comes with Apache version 2.0. Apache 2.0 includes support for a new Apache application programming interface, UNIX threading (for multi-processing), Internet Protocol version 6 (IPv6), and multiple protocols. A handful of new modules have also been added. With version 2.0, the package names apache and apache-manual changed to httpd and httpd-manual.

Introduction to Web Servers

The World Wide Web, as it is known today, began as a project of Tim Berners-Lee at the European Center for Particle Physics (CERN). The original goal was to provide one consistent interface for geographically dispersed researchers and scientists who needed access to information in a variety of formats. From this idea came the concept of using one client (the Web browser) to access data (text, images, sounds, video, and binary files) from several types of servers (HTTP, FTP, SMTP, Gopher, NNTP, WAIS, Finger, and streaming-media servers).

The Web server usually has a simpler job: to accept HyperText Transfer Protocol (HTTP) requests and send a response to the client. However, this job can get much more complex (as the server can also), executing functions such as:

- Performing access control based on file permissions, user name/password pairs, and host name/IP address restrictions.

- Parsing a document (substituting appropriate values for any conditional fields within the document) before sending it to the client.

- Spawning a Common Gateway Interface (CGI) script or custom Application Programming Interface (API) program to evaluate the contents of a submitted form, presenting a dynamically created document, or accessing a database.

- Sending a Java applet to the client.

- Logging any successful accesses, failures, and errors.

The Apache Web server

The Apache Web server was originally based on HTTPd, a free server from the National Center for Supercomputing Applications (NCSA). At the time, HTTPd was the first and only Web server on the Internet. Unfortunately, the development of the server wasn't keeping up with the needs of Webmasters, and several security problems had been discovered. Many Webmasters had been independently applying their own features and fixes to the NCSA source code. In early 1995, a group of these developers pooled their efforts and created "a patchy server," initially just a collection of patches to the HTTPd code. Since then, the Apache Group has largely rewritten the code and created a stable, multiplatform Web server daemon.

Apache is also the base for several other Web servers, most of which use Apache's freely available source code and add improved security features such as Secure Sockets Layer (SSL) for encrypted data transfer or advanced authentication modules.

The main features of the Apache Web server include:

- The stability and rapid development cycle associated with a large group of cooperative volunteer programmers.

- Full source code, downloadable at no charge.

- Ease of configuration using plain-text files.

- Access control based on client host name/IP address or user name/password combinations.

- Support for server-side scripting as well as CGI scripts.

- A custom API that enables external modules (for example, for extended logging capabilities, improved authentication, caching, connection tracking, and so on) to be used by the server daemon.

Apache is not the only Web server available for Fedora and other Red Hat Linux systems, but it is the one most commonly used with Linux, and is the most popular server used on the Internet according to recent Netcraft surveys (`http://news.netcraft.com/archives/web_server_survey.html`). In addition to Apache, Fedora comes with the TUX Web server.

The TUX Web server

The TUX Web server (also referred to as the Red Hat Content Accelerator) is a high-performance, kernel-based Web server that is part of Fedora and Red Hat Linux distributions. By operating within the Linux kernel, TUX can very efficiently serve static content (such as images) while integrating with another Web server's daemon to handle dynamic content that is not supported in TUX's kernel drivers (such as various scripting languages that TUX doesn't know about).

> **NOTE:** The status of TUX has been somewhat up in the air regarding support in the 2.6 kernel. If you are interested in TUX, I suggest you subscribe to the TUX mailing list for the latest information on its availability. Go to `www.redhat.com/mailing-lists` and subscribe to `tux-list@redhat.com`.

On a computer where it is being used, the TUX server typically takes over the primary Web server port (port 80). (An Apache Web server would listen on 8080 or some other port.) The TUX service launches from the `/etc/init.d/tux` init script and runs based on kernel parameters that you set in `/proc/net/tux`.

At a minimum you need to set the serverport (for TUX), the clientport (for Apache), and the `DOCROOT` kernel parameters for the location of the Web-server content. That location (typically `/var/www/html`) must be the same for both the TUX and Apache servers. TUX processes some of the data types that it supports with kernel drivers and others with loadable modules. As more of these modules become available, more data types will be able to run in the kernel, and will not have to be handed off to slower, user-level processes.

Special features in TUX include *mass virtual hosting*, which allows multiple domains to be supported on one Web server (referred to as virtual hosting), and FTP support, which allows you to configure TUX as an anonymous FTP server. Also, because TUX doesn't start a process for each client, thousands of client connections can be active at one time without excessive demands being made on memory allocation.

For more information on TUX, install the tux package that comes with Fedora Linux. Then refer to the documentation starting with `/usr/share/doc/tux-*/tux/index.html`, using a browser.

Other Web servers available for Fedora

Some other Web servers that can run on Fedora and other Red Hat Linux distributions are described in the following list, with URLs that provide more detailed information.

- **Stronghold 4** — This Apache-based Web server from Red Hat features 128-bit SSL encryption and a digital certificate. According to Netcraft (www.netcraft.com), Stronghold is the top commercial SSL Web server for UNIX systems. For details, see Red Hat's Stronghold page at www.redhat.com/software/stronghold.

- **Zope** — In addition to being able to serve Web content, Zope includes features for adding news, membership information, and search capabilities. Originally created by Zope Corporation (www.zope.org), Zope is now available as an open source project covered under the GPL. Zope is not included with Fedora, but can be obtained from the Zope development site (zope.sourceforge.net). Zope is python-based.

- **AOLserver 3.5** — Originally called NaviPress, this server features Web-based administration, access-control, SSL encryption, and SQL database drivers. More information and downloadable source code can be found at aolserver .sourceforge.net.

- **Boa 0.94** — Designed to be fast and simple and not laden with features, Boa requires less system resources than other servers and is ideal for older hardware. Boa is also popular for use on embedded systems. It can be downloaded from www.boa.org.

- **CERN (W3C) Jigsaw 2.2** — The latest HTTP/1.1 reference server, written completely in Java and freely available, can be found at www.w3.org/Jigsaw. It features extensive caching, an improved mechanism for executing external programs (although CGI is also supported), and a graphical administration tool.

- **Servertec iServer 1.1** — Written in Java, this relatively small server provides load balancing and fault tolerance in a clustered environment and can be easily coupled with application and database servers. Further details are available at www.servertec .com/products/iws/iws.html.

Quick Starting the Apache Web Server

If Apache wasn't installed during the Fedora installation, you can install it later from the CD-ROMs that come with this book. You will need the httpd package and optionally the httpd-manual package (named apache and apache-manual in earlier versions).

> **NOTE:** It is possible for a new version of Apache to be released before an equivalent Fedora package is available. Or perhaps you'd prefer to customize the server's compile-time options and build Apache directly from the Apache source code (SRPMS) that come with Fedora.

Here's a quick way to get your Apache Web server going. From here, you'll want to customize it to match your needs and your environment (as described in the section that follows).

1. Make sure that Apache is installed by typing the following from a Terminal window:

```
$ rpm -qa | grep httpd
system-config-httpd-1.2.0-1.1
httpd-devel-2.0.48-18
httpd-2.0.48-18
httpd-manual-2.0.48-18
```

   The version number you see may be different. You need only the httpd package to get started. I recommend httpd-manual because it has excellent information on the whole Apache setup. The httpd-devel package includes the apxs tool for building and installing extension modules. The system-config-httpd package contains a GUI-based Apache Configuration tool.

2. A valid host name is recommended for your Apache server (for example, abc.handsonhistory.com). If you don't have a real, fully qualified domain name, you can edit the /etc/httpd/conf/httpd.conf file and define the ServerName as your computer's IP address. Open the httpd.conf file (as the root user) in any text editor, search for the line containing ServerName new.host.name:80, and uncomment it. It should appear as follows:

```
ServerName new.host.name:80
```

   To make the Web server available to your LAN, you can use your IP address instead of new.host.name (for example, ServerName 10.0.0.1). The :80 represents the port number (which is the default). For a public Web server, get a real DNS host name.

3. Add an administrative e-mail address where someone can contact you in case an error is encountered with your server. In the /etc/httpd/conf/httpd.conf file, the default administrative address appears as follows:

```
ServerAdmin root@localhost
```

   Change root@localhost to the e-mail address of your Apache administrator.

4. Start the httpd server. As root user, type the following:

```
# service httpd start
```

   If all goes well, this message should appear: Starting httpd: [OK]. Now you're ready to go.

5. To have httpd start every time you boot your system, run the command as root user.

```
# chkconfig httpd on
```

6. To make sure that the Web server is working, open Mozilla (or another Web browser) and type the following into the location box and press Enter:

```
http://localhost/
```

7. You should see the Test Page for the Apache Web server, as shown in Figure 21-1. To access this page from another computer, you will need to enter your Apache server's host name or IP address.

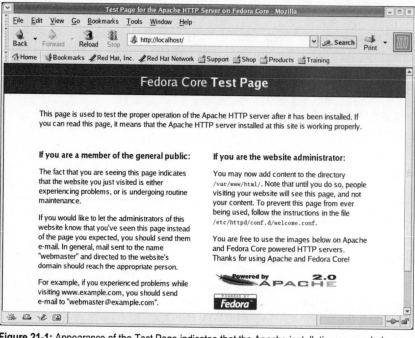

Figure 21-1: Appearance of the Test Page indicates that the Apache installation succeeded.

> **TIP:** It is not necessary to be connected to a network (or even to have a network connection) just to test the server or to view the files on your machine. Rather than specify the server's real name in the URL, just use "localhost" (that is, `http://localhost/`) from a browser on the same computer. In fact, it's best to fully test the configuration before making the server accessible on an unprotected network.

8. The Test Page is actually an error condition, indicating that you haven't added any content to your Web site yet. To get started, you should add an `index.html` file that contains your own home page content in the `/var/www/html` directory. Then you can continue to add your own content to that directory structure.

Now that your Web server is working (or at least, I hope it is), you should step through the next section. It helps you understand how to set up more complex Web server arrangements and protect your server from misuse. Stepping through that section will also help you troubleshoot your Web server, in case it isn't working.

> **TIP:** If your Web server is accessible from your local host, but not available to others from your LAN or the Internet, you may need to change your firewall rules to allow greater access. Appendix C explains how to make your Web or other server accessible. In particular, you need to open tcp port 80.

Configuring the Apache Server

The primary file for configuring your Apache Web server is `httpd.conf` (located in the `/etc/httpd/conf` directory). A few years ago, the Apache project began recommending not using additional configuration files, such as `srm.conf` and `access.conf`, and simply put everything in `httpd.conf`. In recent releases, however, there has been a trend toward having modules and other components used with Apache have their own configuration files (usually located in the `/etc/httpd/conf.d` directory).

All Apache configuration files are plain-text files and can be edited with your favorite text editor. The `/etc/httpd/conf/httpd.conf` file is reproduced in its entirety in the following section, with explanations inserted after related blocks of options (intended to supplement the comments provided with each file).

Some individual modules, scripts and other services related to Apache, such as perl, php, ssl, webalizer, and mysql, have individual configuration files that may interest you. Those files are contained in the `/etc/httpd/conf.d` directory. The "Configuring modules (`/etc/httpd/conf.d/*.conf`)" section later in this chapter discusses modules and related features.

> **CROSS-REFERENCE:** More information on Apache can be obtained on your own Web server, from `http://localhost/manual/` (if the httpd-manual package is installed).

Configuring the Web server (httpd.conf)

The `httpd.conf` file is the primary configuration file for the Apache Web server. It contains options that pertain to the general operation of the server. The default filename (`/etc/httpd/conf/httpd.conf`) can be overridden by the `-f filename` command-line argument to the httpd daemon or the `ServerConfigFile` directive. The following sections list the contents of the `httpd.conf` file and describe how to use the file.

The first section contains comments about the `httpd.conf` file:

```
#
# Based on the NCSA server configuration files originally by Rob McCool
#
#
# This is the main Apache server configuration file. It contains the
# configuration directives that give the server its instructions.
# See <URL:http://httpd.apache.org/docs-2.0/> for detailed information
# about the directives.
#
# Do NOT simply read the instructions in here without understanding
# what they do.  They're here only as hints or reminders.  If you are
# unsure consult the online docs. You have been warned.
#
# The configuration directives are grouped into three basic sections:
```

```
#  1. Directives that control the operation of the Apache server
#     process as a whole (the 'global environment').
#  2. Directives that define parameters of the main or default server,
#     which responds to requests that aren't handled by a virtual host.
#     These directives also provide default values for the settings
#     of all virtual hosts.
#  3. Settings for virtual hosts, which allow Web requests to be sent
#     to different IP addresses or hostnames and have them handled by
#     the same Apache server process.
#
# Configuration and logfile names: If the filenames you specify for
# many of the server's control files begin with "/" (or "drive:/" for
# Win32), the server will use that explicit path.  If the filenames do
# *not* begin with "/", the value of ServerRoot is prepended -- so
# "logs/foo.log"with ServerRoot set to "/usr/local/apache" will be
# interpreted by the server as "/usr/local/apache/logs/foo.log".
#
```

This section consists entirely of comments. It basically tells you how information is grouped together in this file and how the httpd daemon accesses this file. By default, log files are in the /var/log/httpd directory.

Setting the global environment

In "Section 1: Global Environment" of the httpd.conf file, you set directives that affect the general workings of the Apache server. Here is what the different directives are for:

```
### Section 1: Global Environment
#
# The directives in this section affect overall operation of Apache,
# such as the number of concurrent requests it can handle or where it
# can find its configuration files.
#
```

Revealing subcomponents

The ServerTokens directive lets you prevent remote computers from finding out what subcomponents you are running on your Apache server. Comment out this directive if you don't mind exposing this information. To prevent exposure, ServerTokens is set as follows:

```
#
# Don't give away too much information about all the subcomponents
# we are running.  Comment out this line if you don't mind remote sites
# finding out what major optional modules you are running
ServerTokens OS
```

Setting the server root directory

The `ServerRoot` directive specifies the directory that contains the configuration files, a link to the log file directory, and a link to the module directory. An alternative `ServerRoot` path name can be specified using the `-d` command-line argument to `httpd`.

```
# ServerRoot: The top of the directory tree under which the server's
# configuration, error, and log files are kept.
#
# NOTE! If you intend to place this on an NFS (or other network) mounted
# filesystem then please read the LockFile documentation (available
# at <URL:http://httpd.apache.org/docs-2.0/mod/core.html#lockfile>);
# you will save yourself a lot of trouble.
#
# Do NOT add a slash at the end of the directory path.
#
ServerRoot "/etc/httpd"
```

Storing the server's ScoreBoard file

On some systems, a `ScoreBoard` file is created to store internal server process information. Fedora Linux does not need to use the `ScoreBoardFile`, because the status information usually saved in that file is stored in memory instead.

Storing the server's PID file

The Apache Web server keeps track of the PID for the running server process. You can change the locations of this file using the entry described next:

```
#
# PidFile: The file in which the server should record its process
# identification number when it starts.
#
PidFile run/httpd.pid
```

Apache uses the `PidFile` to store the process ID of the first (root-owned) master daemon process. This information is used by the `/etc/init.d/httpd` script when shutting down the server and also by the server-status handler (as described later).

Configuring timeout values

You can set several values that relate to timeout. Some of these values are described in the text following the code:

```
#
# Timeout: The number of seconds before receives and sends time out.
#
Timeout 300

#
# KeepAlive: Whether or not to allow persistent connections (more than
# one request per connection). Set to "Off" to deactivate.
```

```
#
KeepAlive Off

#
# MaxKeepAliveRequests: The maximum number of requests to allow
# during a persistent connection. Set to 0 to allow unlimited amount.
# We recommend you leave this number high, for maximum performance.
#
MaxKeepAliveRequests 100

#
# KeepAliveTimeout: Number of seconds to wait for the next request from
# the same client on the same connection.
#
KeepAliveTimeout 15
```

The Timeout directive determines the number of seconds that Apache will hold a connection open between the receipt of packets, between the receipt of acknowledgments on sent responses, or while receiving an incoming request. The default of five minutes (300 seconds) can certainly be lowered if you find an excessive number of open, idle connections on your machine.

The KeepAlive directive instructs Apache to hold a connection open for a period of time after a request has been handled. This enables subsequent requests from the same client to be processed faster, as a new connection doesn't need to be created for each request.

The MaxKeepAliveRequests directive sets a limit on the number of requests that can be handled with one open connection. The default value is certainly reasonable because most connections will hit the KeepAliveTimeout before MaxKeepAliveRequests.

The KeepAliveTimeout directive specifies the number of seconds to hold the connection while awaiting another request. You might want to increase the default (15 seconds). Reasons for having a longer timeout could be to allow all the images on the page to be downloaded on the same connection or to take into account how long it may take a client to peruse your average page and select a link from it. The Web application you are using may also need a longer persistent connection. (Of course, a longer KeepAliveTimeout prevents each server from moving on to another client during this time period, so you may find that you need to add more request processes to account for that.)

Setting the number of server processes

To operate efficiently, a Web server has to be able to handle lots of incoming requests for content simultaneously. To be ready for requests for Web content, Apache (as it is set up in Fedora) has multiple server processes (httpd daemons) running and listening to service requests. Those servers can, in turn, direct requests to multiple threads to service the content requests.

With the Multi-Processing Module (MPM) feature (introduced in Apache 2.0), support for threads was added to Apache. On an operating system that supports Native POSIX Thread Libraries (which Fedora Core 2 does), threading allows Apache to improve performance by needing fewer process slots and less memory for the number of servers it needs. Adding threads consumes fewer resources than adding processes.

For a low-volume Web server, you can probably leave the parameters alone that support the MPM feature. You will probably have enough processes to handle your incoming requests, but not so many that they will be a drain on your server. However, if your server needs to serve up lots of content consistently, or needs to respond occasionally to large spikes of requests, you should consider tuning the MPM-related parameters in the `httpd.conf` file.

Here are a few issues to consider if you want to change any of the MPM-related parameters:

- **RAM is critical** — Every process and thread that is active consumes some amount of memory. If the number of active processes and threads goes beyond the amount of RAM you have, your computer will begin to use swap space and performance will degrade quickly. Make sure this is enough RAM on your system to handle the maximum number of server processes and threads you expect to run on your Apache Web server.

- **Configure for maximum load** — Apache is able to create new server processes and threads as they are needed. You don't need to have the maximum number of processes and threads available at all times. Instead, you can configure the maximum number of servers and threads that Apache can dynamically add as demand on the server requires.

- **Configure for performance** — Performance degrades when Apache has to start a new thread (small amount), start a server process (greater amount), or use swap space (greatest amount). In the perfect world, the exact number of servers you need should be the default number of servers running, with a few spares to handle reasonable spikes. If response is critical, you might opt to have more servers running than you need so that performance isn't hurt when spikes come.

When Apache starts up, it launches a set number of httpd server processes (one parent and multiple child httpd processes) to handle incoming requests for content for the Web server. Parameters for defining how many httpd server processes are available include those that set:

- How many child server processes should be started by the parent httpd server (`StartServers`)
- The minimum number of server processes kept spare (`MinSpareServers`)
- The maximum number of server processes kept spare (`MaxSpareServers`)
- The maximum number of server processes allowed to start (`MaxClients`)
- The maximum number of requests a process can serve (`MaxRequestsPerChild`)

Parameters for defining how many threads are available for each httpd server process include those that set:

- The minimum number of spare threads that should always be available, after which more will be created (`MinSpareThreads`)

- The maximum number for spare threads, after which active threads will be deleted to get back to the number of threads per child (`MaxSpareThreads`)

- The number of threads always available to each child process (`ThreadsPerChild`)

The following code example shows how MPM-specific parameters in the `httpd.conf` file are set for the `prefork.c` module (non-threaded module for managing servers processes) and `worker.c` (multi-thread, multi-process Web server module).

```
##
## Server-Pool Size Regulation (MPM specific)
##
<IfModule prefork.c>
StartServers         8
MinSpareServers      5
MaxSpareServers     20
MaxClients          150
MaxRequestsPerChild  4000
</IfModule>

<IfModule worker.c>
StartServers          2
MaxClients          150
MinSpareThreads      25
MaxSpareThreads      75
ThreadsPerChild      25
MaxRequestsPerChild   0
</IfModule>
```

Apache starts a master daemon process owned by root that binds to the appropriate port, then switches to a nonprivileged user. More servers (equivalent to the value of the `StartServers` directive in `prefork.c`) will then be started as the same nonprivileged user (the apache user in this case).

Apache attempts to intelligently start and kill servers based on the current load. If the amount of traffic decreases and there are too many idle servers, some will be killed (down to the number of servers noted in `MinSpareServers`). Similarly, if many requests arrive in close proximity and there are too few servers waiting for new connections, more servers will be started (up to the number of servers noted in `MaxClients`).

> **NOTE:** Getting the value of `MaxClients` right is critical, because it puts a lid on the total number of simultaneous client connections that can be active at a time. If the number of `MaxClients` servers are in use, no more will be created and subsequent requests to the server will fail.

Using the values specified above, when the daemon is started, the parent and eight child server processes will run, waiting for connections (as defined by StartServers). As more requests arrive, Apache will ensure that at least five server processes are ready to answer requests. When requests have been fulfilled and no new connections arrive, Apache will begin killing processes until the number of idle Web server processes is below 20. The value of StartServers should always be somewhere between MinSpareServers and MaxSpareServers.

Apache limits the total number of simultaneous threads with the MaxClients directive. The default value is 150, which should be sufficiently high. However, if you find that you frequently have nearly that many threads running, remember that any connection beyond the 150th will be rejected. In such cases, if your hardware is sufficiently powerful (and if your network connection can handle the load), you should increase the value of MaxClients.

> **NOTE:** You can see the state of your Apache server processes and get a feel for the server's activity by viewing the server-status page for your server, as described later in this chapter.

To minimize the effect of possible memory leaks (and to keep the server pool "fresh"), each server process is limited in the number of requests that it can handle (equal to the value of MaxRequestsPerChild). After servicing 4000 requests (the value specified above), the process will be killed. It is even more accurate to say that each process can service 4000 *connections* because all KeepAlive requests (occurring prior to encountering a KeepAliveTimeout) are calculated as just one request.

In a multiprocessor environment, setting thread values described previously can both limit the number of threads that servers can consume and supply as many threads as you will allow to handle server processing. MinSpareThreads and MaxSpareThreads control the number of threads available that are not being used. More are added if available threads fall below MinSpareThreads. If spare threads go above MaxSpareThreads, some are dropped.

Binding to specific addresses

You can bind to specific IP addresses using the Listen directive. Listen directives can be used to add to the default bindings you already have:

```
# Listen: Allows you to bind Apache to specific IP addresses and/or
# ports, in addition to the default. See also the <VirtualHost>
# directive.
#
# Change this to Listen on specific IP addresses as shown below to
# prevent Apache from glomming onto all bound IP addresses (0.0.0.0)
#Listen 12.34.56.78:80
Listen 80
```

The Listen directive is more flexible than the BindAddress and Port directives. Multiple Listen commands can be specified, enabling you to specify several IP address/port number combinations. It can also be used to specify just IP addresses (in which case the Port directive is still necessary) or just port numbers. By default, Apache listens to port 80 (for standard http services) and port 443 (for secure https services) on all interfaces on the local computer (which is where Web browsers expect to find Web content).

Including module-specific configuration files

The following lines cause Apache to load configuration files from the /etc/httpd/conf.d directory. This directory contains configuration files associated with specific modules.

```
#
# Load config files from the config directory "/etc/httpd/conf.d".
#
Include conf.d/*.conf
```

> **CROSS-REFERENCE:** The "Configuring modules (/etc/httpd/conf.d/*.conf)" section, later in this
> chapter, describes some of the configuration files in the conf.d directory that may interest you.

Selecting modules in httpd.conf

During the compilation process, individual Apache modules can be selected for dynamic linking. Dynamically linked modules are not loaded into memory with the httpd server process unless LoadModule directives explicitly identify those modules to be loaded. The blocks of code that follow select several modules to be loaded into memory by using the LoadModule directive with the module name and the path to the module (relative to ServerRoot). The following text shows a partial listing of these modules:

```
#
# Dynamic Shared Object (DSO) Support
# Example:
# LoadModule foo_module modules/mod_foo.so
#
LoadModule access_module modules/mod_access.so
LoadModule auth_module modules/mod_auth.so
LoadModule auth_anon_module modules/mod_auth_anon.so
LoadModule auth_dbm_module modules/mod_auth_dbm.so
LoadModule auth_digest_module modules/mod_auth_digest.so
LoadModule include_module modules/mod_include.so
LoadModule log_config_module modules/mod_log_config.so
LoadModule env_module modules/mod_env.so
LoadModule mime_magic_module modules/mod_mime_magic.so
        .
        .
        .
LoadModule actions_module modules/mod_actions.so
LoadModule speling_module modules/mod_speling.so
LoadModule userdir_module modules/mod_userdir.so
LoadModule alias_module modules/mod_alias.so
```

```
LoadModule rewrite_module modules/mod_rewrite.so
```

Apache modules are included in the list of active modules via the `LoadModule` directive. The `ClearModuleList` directive removes all entries from the current list of active modules. Each of the standard modules that come with Apache is described in Table 21-1.

If a particular module contains features that are not necessary, it can easily be commented out of the above list. Similarly, you might want to add the features or functionality of a third-party module (for example, `mod_perl`, which integrates the Perl runtime library for faster Perl script execution, or `mod_php`, which provides a scripting language embedded within HTML documents) by including those modules in the lists above.

Table 21-1: Dynamic Shared Object (DSO) Modules

Module	*Description*
mod_access	Provides access control based on originating host name/IP address.
mod_actions	Conditionally executes CGI scripts based on the file's MIME type or the request method.
mod_alias	Allows for redirection and mapping parts of the physical file system into logical entities accessible through the Web server.
mod_asis	Enables files to be transferred without adding any HTTP headers (for example, the Status, Location, and Content-type header fields).
mod_auth	Provides access-control based on user name/password pairs. The authentication information is stored in a plain-text file, although the password is encrypted using the `crypt()` system call.
mod_auth_anon	Similar to anonymous FTP, this module enables predefined user names access to authenticated areas by using a valid e-mail address as a password.
mod_auth_dbm	Provides access control based on user name/password pairs. The authentication information is stored in a DBM binary database file, with encrypted passwords.
mod_auth_digest	Provides MD5 Digest user authentication.
mod_auth_ldap	Lets you use an LDAP directory to store the HTTP Basic authentication database.
mod_autoindex	Implements automatically generated directory indexes.
mod_cache	Allows local or proxied Web content to be cached. Used with the `mod_disk_cache` or `mod_file_cache` modules.

Module	Description
mod_cern_-meta	Offers a method of emulating CERN HTTPD meta file semantics.
mod_cgi	Controls the execution of files that are parsed by the "cgi-script" handler or that have a MIME type of x-httpd-cgi. ScriptAlias sets the default directory.
mod_dav	Provides Web-based Distributed Authoring and Versioning (WebDAV) to upload Web content using copy, create, move, and delete resources.
mod_dav_fs	Used to provide file system features to the mod_dav module.
mod_deflate	Includes the DEFLATE output filter, to compress data before it is sent to the client.
Mod_dir	Sets the list of filenames that may be used if no explicit filename is selected in a URL that references a directory.
mod_disk_cache	Enables a disk-based storage manager to use with mod_proxy.
mod_env	Controls environment variables passed to CGI scripts.
mod_expires	Implements time limits on cached documents by using the Expires HTTP header.
mod_file_cache	Allows caching of frequently requested static files.
mod_headers	Enables the creation and generation of custom HTTP headers.
mod_imap	Controls inline image map files, which have a MIME type of x-httpd-imap or that are parsed by the imap handler.
mod_include	Implements Server-Side Includes (SSI), which are HTML documents that include conditional statements parsed by the server prior to being sent to a client. This module also has the ability to include files one into another.
mod_info	Provides a detailed summary of the server's configuration, including a list of actively loaded modules and the current settings of every directive defined within each module.
mod_ldap	Used to speed performance of Web sites using LDAP servers.
mod_log_config	Enables a customized format for information contained within the log files.
mod_mem_cache	Used with mod_cache to provide memory-based storage.
mod_mime	Alters the handling of documents based on predefined values or the MIME type of the file.

Module	Description
mod_mime_magic	Similar to the UNIX file command, this module attempts to determine the MIME type of a file based on a few bytes of the file's contents.
mod_negotiation	Provides for the conditional display of documents based on the Content-Encoding, Content-Language, Content-Length, and Content-Type HTTP header fields.
mod_proxy	Implements an HTTP 1.1 proxy/gateway server.
mod_proxy_connect	Entension to mod_proxy to handle CONNECT requests.
mod_proxy_ftp	Extension to mod_proxy to handle FTP requests.
mod_proxy_http	Extension to mod_proxy to handle HTTP requests.
mod_rewrite	Provides a flexible and extensible method for redirecting client requests and mapping incoming URLs to other locations in the file system.
mod_setenvif	Conditionally sets environment variables based on the contents of various HTTP header fields.
mod_speling	Attempts to automatically correct misspellings in requested URLs.
mod_ssl	Implements cryptography using SSL and TLS protocols.
mod_status	Provides a summary of the activities of each individual httpd server process, including CPU and bandwidth usage levels.
mod_suexec	Lets CGI scripts run with permission of a particular user or group.
mod_userdir	Specifies locations that can contain individual users' HTML documents.
mod_usertrack	Uses cookies to track the progress of users through a Web site.
mod_vhost_alias	Contains support for dynamically configured mass virtual hosting.

More information about each module (and the directives that can be defined within it) can be found on your server at http://localhost/manual/mod/.

Setting the main server's configuration

The second section of the http.conf file relates to directives handled by your main server. In other words, these values are used in all cases except when they are changed in virtual host definitions. To change the same directives for particular virtual hosts, add them within virtual host containers.

Choosing the server's user and group

The `httpd` daemon doesn't have to run as the root user; in fact, your system is more secure if it doesn't. By setting `User` and `Group` entries, you can have the `httpd` daemon run using the permissions associated with a different user and group:

```
# If you wish httpd to run as a different user or group, you must run
# httpd as root initially and it will switch.
#
# User/Group: The name (or #number) of the user/group to run httpd as.
#  . On SCO (ODT 3) use "User nouser" and "Group nogroup".
#  . On HPUX you may not be able to use shared memory as nobody, and
#  the suggested workaround is to create a user www and use that user.
#  NOTE that some kernels refuse to setgid(Group) or semctl(IPC_SET)
#  when the value of (unsigned)Group is above 60000;
#  don't use Group #-1 on these systems!
#
User apache
Group apache
```

By default, apache is defined as both the user and group for the server. If you change the `User` and `Group` directives, you should specify a nonprivileged entity. This minimizes the risk of damage if your site is compromised. The first daemon process that is started runs as root. This is necessary to bind the server to a low-numbered port and to switch to the user and group specified by the `User` and `Group` directives. All other processes run under the user ID (UID) and group ID (GID) defined by those directives.

Choosing the HTTP port number

Apache listens on particular ports for HTTP requests. The port that is used is set by the `Port` entry as follows:

```
#
# Port: The port to which the standalone server listens. For
# ports < 1023, you will need httpd to be run as root initially.
#
Port 80
```

Port 80 is the default for HTTP traffic, which is why `http://www.apache.org:80/` is the same as `http://www.apache.org/`. If the server is bound to a different port, the port number must be specified in the URL. Most Web servers run on port 80, although they can accept connections on any port (up to 65536) that is not already bound to a particular service (see the `/etc/services` file for a list of common services and protocols and the ports they use). Only root can run programs that listen for connections on privileged ports (those below 1024).

Setting an e-mail address

You can identify an address where users can send e-mail if there is a problem with your server. This is done with the `ServerAdmin` directive:

```
#
# ServerAdmin: Your address, where problems with the server should be
# e-mailed.  This address appears on some server-generated pages, such
# as error documents. e.g. admin@your-domain.com
#
ServerAdmin you@your.address
```

The `ServerAdmin` directive can be set to any valid e-mail address. The default is
`root@localhost`.

Setting the server name

If your server name is anything but your exact registered host or domain name, you should
identify your server name here. As the comments point out, the `ServerName` directive can be
set to a value other than the actual host name of your machine. However, this other name
should still point to your machine in DNS if the server is to be a public Internet server.
Frequently, www is just an alias for the real name of the machine (for example, a machine may
respond to `www.linuxtoys.net`, but its real name may be `al.linuxtoys.net`).

```
ServerName jukebox.linuxtoys.net
```

Apache tries to use your host name as the `ServerName` if you don't enter a valid server name.
It is recommended that you explicitly enter a `ServerName` here.

Setting canonical names

Use the `UseCanonicalName` directive to create a self-referencing URL, as follows:

```
## UseCanonicalName: Determines how Apache constructs self-referencing
# URLs and the SERVER_NAME and SERVER_PORT variables.
# When set "Off", Apache will use the Hostname and Port supplied
# by the client.  When set "On", Apache will use the value of the
# ServerName directive.
#
UseCanonicalName Off
```

The `UseCanonicalName` directive provides a form of naming consistency. When it is set to
on, Apache uses the `ServerName` and `Port` directives to create a URL that references a file
on the same machine (for example, `http://www.linuxtoys.net/docs/`). When
`UseCanonicalName` is `Off`, the URL consists of whatever the client specified (for example,
the URL could be `http://al.linuxtoys.net/docs/` or `http://al/docs/` if the
client is within the same domain).

This can be problematic, particularly when access-control rules require user name and
password authentication: if the client is authenticated for the host `al.linuxtoys.net` but a
link sends him or her to `www.linuxtoys.net` (physically the same machine), the client will
be prompted to enter a user name and password again. It is recommended that
`UseCanonicalName` be set to `On`. In the preceding situation, the authentication would not

need to be repeated, because any reference to the same server would always be interpreted as
`www.linuxtoys.net`.

Identifying HTTP content directories

There are several directives for determining the location of your server's Web content. The
main location for your Web content is set to `/var/www/html` by the `DocumentRoot`
directive. (Note that this location has changed from versions of Red Hat Linux prior to Red
Hat Linux 7. The location was formerly in `/home/http`.)

```
# DocumentRoot: The directory out of which you will serve your
# documents. By default, all requests are taken from the directory, but
# symbolic links and aliases may be used to point to other locations.
DocumentRoot "/var/www/html"
```

Setting access options and overrides

You can set individual access permissions for each directory in the Web server's directory
structure. The default is fairly restrictive. Here is the default:

```
<Directory />
    Options FollowSymLinks
    AllowOverride None
</Directory>
```

This segment sets up a default block of permissions for the `Options` and `AllowOverride`
directives. The `<Directory />...</Directory>` tags enclose the directives that are to
be applied to the / directory (which is `/var/www/html` by default, as defined by
DocumentRoot).

The `Options FollowSymLinks` directive instructs the server that symbolic links within the
directory can be followed to allow content that resides in other locations on the computer.
None of the other special server features will be active in the / directory, or in any directory
below that, without being explicitly specified later. Next, the following access options are
specifically set for the root of your Web server (`/var/www/html`). (I removed the comments
here for clarity.)

```
<Directory "/var/www/html">
    Options Indexes FollowSymLinks
    AllowOverride None
    Order allow,deny
    Allow from all
</Directory>
```

If you have changed the value of `DocumentRoot` earlier in this file, you need to change the
`/var/www/html` to match that value. The `Options` set for the directory are `Indexes` and
`FollowSymLinks`. Those and other special server features are described in Table 21-2. The
`AllowOverride None` directive instructs the server that an `.htaccess` file (or the value

of `AccessFileName`) cannot override any of the special access features. You can replace `None` with any of the special access features described in Table 21-3.

> **NOTE:** Remember that unless you specifically enable a feature described in Tables 21-2 and 21-3, that feature is not enabled for your server (with the exceptions of `Indexes` and `FollowSymLinks`).

Table 21-2: Special Server Features for the Options Directive

Feature	Description
ExecCGI	The execution of CGI scripts is permitted.
FollowSymLinks	The server will traverse symbolic links.
Includes	Server-Side Includes are permitted.
IncludesNOEXEC	Server-Side Includes are permitted, except the #exec element.
Indexes	If none of the files specified in the `DirectoryIndex` directive exists, a directory index will be generated by mod_autoindex.
MultiViews	The server allows content negotiation based on preferences from the user's browser, such as preferred language, character set, and media type.
SymLinksIfOwnerMatch	The server will traverse symbolic links only if the owner of the target is the same as the owner of the link.
None	None of the features above are enabled.
All	All the features above are enabled, with the exception of `MultiViews`. This must be explicitly enabled.

Table 21-3: Special Access Features for the AllowOverride Directive

Feature	Description
AuthConfig	Enables authentication-related directives (`AuthName`, `AuthType`, `AuthUserFile`, `AuthGroupFile`, `Require`, and so on).
FileInfo	Enables MIME-related directives (`AddType`, `AddEncoding`, `AddLanguage`, `LanguagePriority`, and so on).

Feature	Description
Indexes	Enables directives related to directory indexing (FancyIndexing, DirectoryIndex, IndexOptions, IndexIgnore, HeaderName, ReadmeName, AddIcon, AddDescription, and so on).
Limit	Enables directives controlling host access (Allow, Deny, and Order).
Options	Enables the Options directive (as described in Table 21-5).
None	None of the access features above can be overridden.
All	All the access features above can be overridden.

Disabling indexes in root directory

The following directives disable indexing for the root directory (probably /var/www/html), so that your index.html, or the default one put there by the Fedora Project, is displayed when that directory is requested. (The default way of listing the contents of directories on your Apache Web server is defined in the "Defining Indexing" section later in this chapter).

```
#
# Disable autoindex for the root directory, and present a
# default Welcome page if no other index page is present.
#
<LocationMatch "^/$>
    Options -Indexes
    ErrorDocument 403 /error/noindex.html
</LocationMatch>
```

Identifying user directories

If you have multiple users on your server and you want each to be able to publish their own Web content, it is common practice to identify a directory name that users can create in their own home directories to store that content. When you identify the name that is appended to a user's home directory, that directory is used to respond to requests to the server for the user's name(~user). This directory name used to be set to public_html by default; however, it is now turned off by default.

To allow access to your users' personal Web pages, add a comment character (#) to the UserDir disable line. Then remove the # from the UserDir public_html line to make users' personal public_html directories accessible through the Web server. After removing extra comment lines, the following text shows what the enabled section looks like:

```
# UserDir: The name of the directory which is appended onto a user's
# home directory if a ~user request is received.
```

```
<ifModule mod_userdir.c>
#  UserDir disable
UserDir public_html
</IfModule>
```

Besides uncommenting the UserDir public_html line shown in the previous example, you must make both the user's home directory and public_html directory executable by everyone in order for the UserDir directive to allow access to a particular user's public_html directory. For example, the user cjb could type the following to make those directories accessible.

```
$ chmod 711 /home/cjb
$ mkdir /home/cjb/public_html
$ chmod 755 /home/cjb/public_html
```

For UserDir to work, the mod_userdir module must also be loaded (which it is by default).

There are two ways in which the UserDir directive can handle an incoming request that includes a user name (for example, ~cjb). One possible format identifies the physical path name of the individual users' publicly accessible directories. The other can specify a URL to which the request is redirected. A few examples are presented in Table 21-4, using the URL http://www.mybox.com/~cjb/proj/c004.html as a sample request.

Table 21-4: UserDir Path Name and URL Examples

UserDir Directive	*Referenced Path or URL*
UserDir public_html	~cjb/public_html/proj/c004.html
UserDir /public/*/WWW	/public/cjb/WWW/proj/c004.html
UserDir /usr/local/web	/usr/local/web/cjb/proj/c004.html
UserDir http://www.mybox.com/users	http://www.mybox.com/users/cjb/proj/c004.html
UserDir http://www.mybox.com/~*	http://www.mybox.com/~cjb/proj/c004.html
UserDir http://www.mybox.com/*/html	http://www.mybox.com/cjb/html/proj/c004.html

The UserDir directive can also be used to explicitly allow or deny URL-to-path name translation for particular users. For example, it is a good idea to include the following line to avoid publishing data that shouldn't be made public:

```
UserDir disable root
```

Alternatively, use the following lines to disable the translations for all but a few users:

```
UserDir disable
UserDir enable wilhelm cjb jsmith
```

The `DirectoryIndex` directive establishes a list of files that is used when an incoming request specifies a directory rather than a file. For example, a client requests the URL `http://www.mybox.com/~jsmith`. Because it's a directory, it is automatically translated to `http://www.mybox.com/~jsmith/`. Now that directory is searched for any of the files listed in the `DirectoryIndex` directive. The first match (from the default list of `index.html` and `index.html.var`) is used as the default document in that directory. If none of the files exist and the Indexes option (as in the `httpd.conf` file) is selected, the server will automatically generate an index of the files in the directory.

```
# DirectoryIndex: sets the file that Apache will serve if a directory
# is requested.
#
# The index.html.var file (a type-map) is used to deliver content-
# negotiated documents.  The MultiViews Option can be used for the
# same purpose, but it is much slower.
#
DirectoryIndex index.html index.html.var
```

Setting directory-access control

You and your users can add an access file to each directory to control access to that directory. By default, the `AccessFileName` directive sets `.htaccess` as the file containing this information. The following lines set this filename and prevent the contents of that file from being viewed by visitors to the Web site. If you change the file to a name other than `.htaccess`, be sure to change the line below ("`\.ht`") that denies access to that file.

```
#
# AccessFileName: The name of the file to look for in each directory
# for access control information.
#
AccessFileName .htaccess

<Files ~ "^\.ht">
    Order allow,deny
    Deny from all
</Files>
```

You can add the same access directives to a `.htaccess` file as you do to the `httpd.conf` file. In general, it is more efficient to use a `<Directory>` directive in the `httpd.conf` file than it is to create a `.htaccess` file. With a `<Directory>` directive, you can specifically identify the access associated with that directory alone. Because directives you put in `.htaccess` apply to all directives below the current directory, any time you add a `.htaccess` file to a directory, Apache must search all directories above that point (for example, /, /var, /var/www. and so on) to include settings from possible `.htaccess` files in those directories as well.

Setting MIME-type defaults

The location of the MIME type definitions file is defined by the `TypesConfig` directive. The `DefaultType` directive sets the MIME type:

```
# TypesConfig describes where the mime.types file (or equivalent) is
# to be found.
#
TypesConfig /etc/mime.types


#
# DefaultType is the default MIME type the server will use for a
# document if it cannot otherwise determine one, such as from filename.
# extensions If your server contains mostly text or HTML documents,
# "text/plain" is a good value.  If most of the content is binary, such
# as applications or images, you may want to use "application/octet-
# stream" instead to keep browsers from trying to display binary files
# as though they are text.
#
DefaultType text/plain
```

Using the `mod_mime_magic` module, a server can look for hints to help figure out what type of file is being requested. You must make sure this module is loaded to Apache for it to be used (it is loaded by default). The module can use hints from the `/usr/share/magic.mime` (off by default) and `/etc/httpd/conf/magic` (on by default) files to determine the contents of a requested file. Here are the directives that cause that module to be used:

```
<IfModule mod_mime_magic.c>
#    MIMEMagicFile /usr/share/magic.mime
     MIMEMagicFile conf/magic
</IfModule>
```

Setting host name lookups

With the Apache Web server, you can have the server look up addresses for incoming client requests. Turning on the `HostnameLookups` entry can do this:

```
# HostnameLookups: Log the names of clients or just their IP addresses
HostnameLookups Off
```

If the `HostnameLookups` directive is turned on, every incoming connection will generate a DNS lookup to translate the client's IP address into a host name. If your site receives many requests, the server's response time could be adversely affected. The `HostnameLookups` should be turned off unless you use a log file analysis program or statistics package that requires fully qualified domain names and cannot perform the lookups on its own. The `logresolve` program that is installed with the Apache distribution can be scheduled to edit log files by performing host name lookups during off-peak hours.

Configuring HTTP logging

You can set several values related to logging of Apache information. When a relative path name is shown, the directory set by ServerRoot (/etc/httpd/ by default) is appended (for example, /etc/httpd/logs/error_log). As shown in the following example, you can set the location of error logs, the level of log warnings, and some log nicknames:

```
#
# ErrorLog: The location of the error log file.
# If you do not specify an ErrorLog directive within a <VirtualHost>
# container, error messages relating to that virtual host will be
# logged here.  If you *do* define an error logfile for a <VirtualHost>
# container, that host's errors will be logged there and not here.
#
ErrorLog logs/error_log


#
# LogLevel: Control the number of messages logged to the error_log.
# Possible values include: debug, info, notice, warn, error, crit,
# alert, emerg.
#
LogLevel warn


#
# The following directives define some format nicknames for use with
# a CustomLog directive (see below).
#
LogFormat "%h %l %u %t \"%r\" %>s %b \"%{Referer}i\"\"%{User-
    Agent}i\""combined
LogFormat "%h %l %u %t \"%r\" %>s %b" common
LogFormat "%{Referer}i -> %U" referer
LogFormat "%{User-agent}i" agent


#
# Location and format of the access logfile (Common Logfile Format).
# If you do not define any access logfiles within a <VirtualHost>
# container, they will be logged here.  Contrariwise, if you *do*
# define per-<VirtualHost> access logfiles, transactions will be
# logged therein and *not* in this file.
#
# CustomLog /var/log/httpd/access_log common
CustomLog logs/access_log combined

# If you would like to have agent and referer logfiles, uncomment the
# following directives.
#
#CustomLog /var/log/httpd/referer_log referer
#CustomLog /var/log/httpd/agent_log agent
```

```
#
# If you prefer a single logfile with access, agent, and referer info
# (Combined Logfile Format) you can use the following directive.
#
#CustomLog logs/httpd/access_log combined
```

The previous several lines deal with how server errors, client tracking information, and incoming requests are logged. The ErrorLog directive, which can specify an absolute path name or a path name relative to the ServerRoot (which is /etc/httpd by default), indicates where the server should store error messages. In this case the specified file is logs/error_log, which expands to /etc/httpd/logs/error_log (which in reality is a symlink to the error_log file in the /var/log/httpd directory).

The LogLevel directive controls the severity and quantity of messages that appear in the error log. Messages can range from the particularly verbose debug log level to the particularly silent emerg log level. With debug, a message is logged anytime the configuration files are read, when an access-control mechanism is used, or if the number of active servers has changed. With emerg, only critical system-level failure creates a panic condition for the server.

The level specified by the LogLevel directive indicates the least-severe message that will be logged — all messages at that severity and above are recorded. For example, if LogLevel is set to warn, the error log will contain messages at the warn, error, crit, alert, and emerg levels. The default value of warn is a good choice for normal use (it will log only significant events that may eventually require operator intervention), but info and debug are perfect for testing a server's configuration or tracking down the exact location of errors.

The four LogFormat lines define (for later use) four types of log file formats: combined, common, referer, and agent. The tokens available within the LogFormat directive are described in Table 21-5. The LogFormat definitions can be modified to your own personal preference, and other custom formats can be created as needed.

Table 21-5: Available Tokens within LogFormat

Token	Description
%a	The IP address of the client machine.
%b	The number of bytes sent to the client (excluding header information).
%{VAR}e	The contents of the environment variable VAR.
%f	The filename referenced by the requested URL.
%h	The host name of the client machine.
%{Header}i	The contents of the specified header line in the HTTP request.

Token	Description
%l	As reported by the identd daemon (if available), the user on the client machine who initiated the request.
%{Note}n	The contents of the message Note from a different module.
%{Header}o	The contents of the specified header line in the HTTP response.
%p	The port number on which the request was received.
%P	The PID of the server process that handled the request.
%r	The actual HTTP request from the client.
%s	The server response code generated by the request.
%t	The current local time and date. The time format can be altered using %{Format}t, where Format is described in the strftime(3) man page.
%T	The number of seconds required to fulfill the client request.
%u	If access-control rules require user name and password authentication, this represents the user name supplied by the client.
%U	The URL requested by the client.
%v	The host name and domain name of the server according to the Domain Name System (DNS).
%V	The host name and domain name of the server handling the request according to the ServerName directive.

The common format includes the client host's name or IP address, the user name as reported by the ident daemon and the server's authentication method (if applicable), the local time at which the request was made, the actual HTTP request, the server response code, and the number of bytes transferred. This format is a de facto standard among Web servers (and lately even among FTP servers). The more popular format is combined.

For the purpose of connection tracking, the referer format stores the URL (from the same site or an external server) that linked to the document just delivered (relative to the ServerRoot). For example, if the page http://www.redhat.com/corp/about_us.html contained a link to your home page at http://www.mybox.com/linuxguy/bio.html, when a client accessed that link, the referer log on www.mybox.com would look like:

```
http://www.redhat.com/corp/about_us.html -> /linuxguy/bio.html
```

This information can be used to determine which path each client took to reach your site.

The agent format stores the contents of the User-agent: HTTP header for each incoming connection. This field typically indicates the browser name and version, the language, and the operating system or architecture on which the browser was run. On a Pentium II running Fedora, Mozilla will produce the following entry:

```
Mozilla/5.0 (X11; U; Linux i686; en-US; rv:1.6)
```

The combined format includes all the information from the other three log file formats into one line. This format is useful for storing all connection-related log entries in one centralized file.

The CustomLog directives assign one of the defined LogFormat formats to a filename (again, specified as an absolute path name or a path name relative to the ServerRoot). The only uncommented definition assigns combined format to the /etc/httpd/logs/access_log file. To retain the agent or referer information separately, uncomment the definitions. Also, you could choose to comment out the CustomLog /etc/httpd/logs/access_log combined line and use the definition for the combined format instead.

Adding a signature

Any page that is generated by the Apache server can have a signature line added to the bottom of the page. Examples of server-generated pages include a directory listing, error page, a status page, or an info page. The ServerSignature directive can be set to On, Off, or EMail. Here is how ServerSignature appears by default:

```
# Optionally add a line containing the server version and virtual
# host name to server-generated pages (error documents, FTP directory
# listings, mod_status and mod_info output etc., but not CGI generated
# documents).
# Set to "EMail" to also include a mailto: link to the ServerAdmin.
# Set to one of:  On | Off | EMail
#
ServerSignature On
```

With ServerSignature On, this line appears at the bottom of server-generated pages:

```
Apache/2.0.48 (Fedora) Server at toys.linuxtoys.net Port 80
```

With ServerSignature set to EMail, a link to the Web page's administrative e-mail account is added to the signature line (the server name becomes the link). If the directive is set to Off, the line doesn't appear at all.

Aliasing relocated content

There are various ways to define alias content. These include the Alias and the ScriptAlias directives. Here are alias-related settings in httpd.conf (with comments removed):

```
#
# Aliases: Add here as many aliases as you need (with no limit). The
format is
```

```
# Alias fakename realname
#
Alias /icons/ "/var/www/icons/"

<Directory "/var/www/icons">
    Options Indexes MultiViews
    AllowOverride None
    Order allow,deny
    Allow from all
</Directory>

Alias /manual "/var/www/manual"

<Directory "/var/www/manual">
    Options Indexes
    AllowOverride None
    Order allow,deny
    Allow from all
</Directory>

# ScriptAlias: This controls which directories contain server scripts.
ScriptAlias /cgi-bin/ "/var/www/cgi-bin/"

# "/var/www/cgi-bin" should be changed to whatever your ScriptAliased
# CGI directory exists, if you have that configured.
#
<Directory "/var/www/cgi-bin">
    AllowOverride None
    Options None
    Order allow,deny
    Allow from all
</Directory>
```

The Alias directive points to a file system location (not necessarily within the
DocumentRoot). For example, with the following line in place, requests for documents in
/bigjob (http://www.mybox.com/bigjob/index.html) would result in the
retrieval of /home/newguy/proj/index.html.

```
Alias /bigjob /home/newguy/proj
```

The manual and icons aliases allow access to the Apache manuals and icons used by the
Web server, respectively, from your Web site. The manuals and icons directories are
accessible from the /var/www directory.

The ScriptAlias directive performs a related function, but directories that it aliases contain
executable code (most likely CGI scripts). The syntax is the same as for the Alias directive.
Pay special attention whenever you use ScriptAlias.

Redirecting requests for old content

As content changes on your Web server, some content will become obsolete while other content may move to a different place in the file system or to a different server. Using the `Redirect` directive, you can redirect requests for old content to new locations.

By default, there are no `Redirect` directives set for your Apache server. However, you can uncomment the following example and tailor it to your needs:

```
# Redirect permanent /foo http://www.example.com/bar
```

`Redirect` can be used to instruct clients that the document they seek has moved elsewhere (to the same server or to an external location) by simply indicating the old and new locations. If the previous `Redirect` option were in place, a client's attempt to access `http://www.mybox.com/foo` would redirect to `http://www.example.com/bar`.

Besides using `permanent` as the service for Redirect (which results in a redirect status 301), you could instead use `temp` (a redirect status of 302), `seeother` (a replaced status of 303), or `gone` (a permanently removed status of 401). You could also give any status code between 300 and 399 as the service, which represent different error responses. (These numbers are HTTP error codes.)

Defining indexing

It's possible to have your Apache server show different icons for different types of files. To use this feature, `IndexOptions` should be set to `FancyIndexing`, and `AddIconByEncoding`, `AddIconByType`, and `AddIcon` directives should be used:

```
# Directives controlling display of server-generated directory listings.

# FancyIndexing is if you want fancy directory indexing or standard.
# VersionSort is whether files containing version numbers should be
# compared in the natural way, so that `apache-1.3.9.tar' is placed
# before `apache-1.3.12.tar'.
#
IndexOptions FancyIndexing VersionSort NameWidth=*
#
# AddIcon* directives tell the server which icon to show for different
# files or filename extensions.  These are only displayed for
# FancyIndexed directories.
#
AddIconByEncoding (CMP,/icons/compressed.gif) x-compress x-gzip

AddIconByType (TXT,/icons/text.gif) text/*
AddIconByType (IMG,/icons/image2.gif) image/*
AddIconByType (SND,/icons/sound2.gif) audio/*
AddIconByType (VID,/icons/movie.gif) video/*

AddIcon /icons/binary.gif .bin .exe
```

```
AddIcon /icons/binhex.gif .hqx
AddIcon /icons/tar.gif .tar
AddIcon /icons/world2.gif .wrl .wrl.gz .vrml .vrm .iv
AddIcon /icons/compressed.gif .Z .z .tgz .gz .zip
AddIcon /icons/a.gif .ps .ai .eps
AddIcon /icons/layout.gif .html .shtml .htm .pdf
AddIcon /icons/text.gif .txt
AddIcon /icons/c.gif .c
AddIcon /icons/p.gif .pl .py
AddIcon /icons/f.gif .for
AddIcon /icons/dvi.gif .dvi
AddIcon /icons/uuencoded.gif .uu
AddIcon /icons/script.gif .conf .sh .shar .csh .ksh .tcl
AddIcon /icons/tex.gif .tex
AddIcon /icons/bomb.gif core

AddIcon /icons/back.gif ..
AddIcon /icons/hand.right.gif README
AddIcon /icons/folder.gif ^^DIRECTORY^^
AddIcon /icons/blank.gif ^^BLANKICON^^

#
# DefaultIcon: which icon to show for files which do not have an icon
# explicitly set.
#
DefaultIcon /icons/unknown.gif

#
# AddDescription: allows you to place short description after a file in
# server-generated indexes.  These are only displayed for FancyIndexed
# directories.
# Format: AddDescription "description" filename
#
#AddDescription "GZIP compressed document" .gz
#AddDescription "tar archive" .tar
#AddDescription "GZIP compressed tar archive" .tgz

#
# ReadmeName: the name of the README file the server will look for by
# default, and append to directory listings.
#
# HeaderName is the name of a file which should be prepended to
# directory indexes.
#
ReadmeName README.html
HeaderName HEADER.html

#
# IndexIgnore is a set of filenames which directory indexing should
```

```
# ignore and not include in the listing.  Shell-style wildcarding is
# permitted.
#
IndexIgnore .??* *~ *# HEADER* README* RCS CVS *,v *,t
```

The previous block of options deals with how server-generated directory indexes are handled. The IndexOptions FancyIndexing VersionSort NameWidth=* directive enables an autogenerated directory index to include several bits of information about each file or directory, including an icon representing the file type, the filename, the last modification time for the file, the file's size, and a description of the file. Figure 21-2 shows an example of a directory using default FancyIndexing settings.

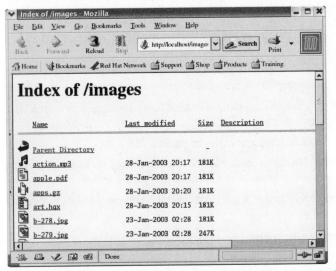

Figure 21-2: Change how directories are displayed from Apache using IndexOptions.

The VersionSort option allows files that include version numbers to be sorted as would be most natural (so, for example, version-2 would come before version-10 with this option on). The NameWidth=* option allows filenames of any length to be displayed. You change the asterisk to a number representing the maximum number of characters that can be displayed in the Name column. If IndexOptions is not set to FancyIndexing, the index only lists the file's name.

The AddIconByEncoding directive is used to configure the output of FancyIndexing. It causes a particular icon to be displayed for files matching a particular MIME encoding. In the AddIconByEncoding line in the previous example, compressed.gif (with an alternative image tag of "CMP" for browsers that don't load images) will be displayed for files with a MIME encoding of x-compress and x-gzip. The AddIconByType directive has the same syntax but matches files based on their MIME type.

The `AddIcon` directive performs a similar function, but the icons are displayed based on a pattern in the filename. In the lines above, for example, `bomb.gif` will be displayed for files ending with `core`, and `binary.gif` will be displayed for files ending in `.bin` and `.exe`. The `folder.gif` icon represents a subdirectory.

If there is a conflict between the `AddIcon`, `AddIconByEncoding`, or `AddIconByType` directives, the `AddIcon` directive has precedence. The `DefaultIcon` directive specifies the image to be displayed (`unknown.gif`, according to the line above) if no previous directive has associated an icon with a particular file.

The `HeaderName` and `ReadmeName` directives specify files that will be inserted at the top and bottom of the autogenerated directory index, if they exist. Using the default values, the server first looks for `HEADER.html`, then `HEADER`, to include at the top of the "fancy index." At the end of the index, `README.html` or `README` (whichever is located first) is inserted.

The `IndexIgnore` directive specifies files that should not appear in an autogenerated directory index. The line above excludes:

- Any filename starting with a dot and containing at least two additional characters.
- Any filename ending with a tilde (~) or what is commonly called a hash mark (#) (typically used by text editors as temporary files or backup files).
- Filenames beginning with `HEADER` or `README` (the files displayed at the top and bottom of the directory listing, according to the `HeaderName` and `ReadmeName` directives).
- The RCS (Revision Control System) or CVS (Concurrent Versions System) directories.

Defining encoding and language

The `AddEncoding` directive lets you set compression definitions that can be used by browsers to encode data as it arrives. The `AddLanguage` directive lets you indicate the language of a document, based on its file suffix.

```
#
# AddEncoding: allows you to have certain browsers (Mosaic/X 2.1+)
# uncompress information on fly. Note: Not all browsers support this.
# Despite name similarity, the following Add* directives have nothing
# to do with the FancyIndexing customization directives above.
#
AddEncoding x-compress Z
AddEncoding x-gzip gz tgz


#
# DefaultLanguage and AddLanguage allows you to specify the language of
# a document. You can then use content negotiation to give a browser a
# file in a language it can understand.
    .

    .
```

```
            .
# Spanish (es) - Swedish (sv) - Catalan (ca) - Czech(cz)
# Polish (pl) - Brazilian Portuguese (pt-br) - Japanese (ja)
# Russian (ru)
#
AddLanguage da .dk
AddLanguage nl .nl
AddLanguage en .en
AddLanguage et .ee
AddLanguage fr .fr
            .
            .
            .
# LanguagePriority: allows you to give precedence to some languages
# in case of a tie during content negotiation.
#
# Just list the languages in decreasing order of preference. We have
# more or less alphabetized them. You probably want to change this.
#
LanguagePriority en da nl et fr de el it ja ko no pl pt pt-br ru ltz ca
        es sv tw
```

The AddEncoding directive supplements or overrides mappings provided by the TypesConfig file (/etc/mime.types by default). Knowledge of the MIME type/encoding may allow certain browsers to automatically manipulate files as they are being downloaded or retrieved.

The AddLanguage directive performs similar mappings, associating a MIME language definition with a filename extension. The LanguagePriority directive determines the precedence if a particular file exists in several languages (and if the client does not specify a preference). Using the preceding definition, if the file index.html were requested from a directory that contained the files index.html.de, index.html.en, index.html.fr, and index.html.it, the index.html.en file would be sent to the client.

Using LanguagePriority, you can set which language is used in case a decision on what language to use can't be made during content negotiation. If you are expecting multilanguage use of your Web content, you should check (and probably change) the priority here.

Choosing character sets

The default character set to use and character sets to use for files with particular file extensions are set using the AddDefaultCharset an AddCharset directives, respectively. Although UTF-8 is the default character set, it is recommended to set it here specifically (as shown). Other standard ISO fonts, as well as some nonstandard fonts, are set using AddCharset directives.

```
AddDefaultCharset UTF-8
#
AddCharset ISO-8859-1   .iso8859-1   .latin1
```

```
AddCharset ISO-8859-2    .iso8859-2    .latin2 .cen
AddCharset ISO-8859-3    .iso8859-3    .latin3
AddCharset ISO-8859-4    .iso8859-4    .latin4
AddCharset ISO-8859-5    .iso8859-5    .latin5 .cyr .iso-ru
AddCharset ISO-8859-6    .iso8859-6    .latin6 .arb
       .
       .
       .
```

You can retrieve an official list character sets and the file extensions that are assigned to them at www.iana.org/assignments/character-sets.

Adding MIME types and handlers

With the AddType directive, you can enhance the MIME types assigned for your Apache Web server without editing the /etc/mime.types file. With the AddHandler directive, you can map selected file extensions to handlers (that result in certain actions being taken):

```
# AddType allows you to add to or override the MIME configuration
# file mime.types for specific file types.

AddType application/x-tar .tgz

#
# For server-parsed imagemap files:
#
AddHandler imap-file map

#
# For type maps (negotiated resources):
# (This is enabled by default to allow the Apache "It Worked" page
#  to be distributed in multiple languages.)
#
AddHandler type-map var
```

Defining actions and headers

Some types of media can be set to execute a script when they are opened. Likewise, certain handler names, when opened, can be set to perform specified scripts. The Action directive can be used to configure these scripts:

```
# Action lets you define media types that execute a script whenever
# a matching file is called. This eliminates the need for repeated URL
# pathnames for oft-used CGI file processors.
# Format: Action media/type /cgi-script/location
# Format: Action handler-name /cgi-script/location
```

The Action directive maps a CGI script to a handler or a MIME type, whereas the Script directive maps a CGI script to a particular HTTP request method (GET, POST, PUT, or

DELETE). These options allow scripts to be executed whenever a file of the appropriate MIME type is requested, a handler is called, or a request method is invoked.

Customizing error responses

For different error conditions that occur, you can define specific responses. The responses can be in plain text, redirects to pages on the local server, or redirects to external pages:

```
#
# Customizable error responses come in three flavors:
# 1) plain text 2) local redirects 3) external redirects
#
# Some examples:
#ErrorDocument 500 "The server made a boo boo."
#ErrorDocument 404 /missing.html
#ErrorDocument 404 "/cgi-bin/missing_handler.pl"
#ErrorDocument 402 http://www.example.com/subscription_info.html
#
```

As the comments suggest, the ErrorDocument directive can customize any server response code, redirecting it to an external page, a local file or CGI script, or to a simple text sentence. Table 21-6 lists the most common server response codes and their meanings.

Table 21-6: HTTP Response Codes

Response Code	Meaning
200 OK	The request was successfully processed.
201 Created	Using the POST request method, a new file was successfully stored on the server.
202 Accepted	The request has been received and is currently being processed.
204 No Content	The request was successful, but there is no change in the current page displayed to the client.
301 Moved Permanently	The requested page has been permanently moved, and future references to that page should use the new URL that is displayed.
302 Moved Temporarily	The requested page has been temporarily relocated. Future references should continue to use the same URL, but the current connection is being redirected.
304 Not Modified	A cached version of the page is identical to the requested page.
400 Bad Request	The client's request contains invalid syntax.
401 Unauthorized	The client specified an invalid user name/password combination.
402 Payment Required	The client must provide a means to complete a monetary transaction.

Response Code	Meaning
403 Forbidden	Access-control mechanisms deny the client's request.
404 Not Found	The requested page does not exist on the server.
500 Internal Server Error	Usually encountered when running a CGI program, this response code indicates that the program or script contains invalid code or was given input that it cannot handle.
501 Not Implemented	The request method (for example, GET, POST, PUT, DELETE, HEAD) is not understood by the server.
502 Bad Gateway	Using the Web server as a proxy, an error was encountered in fulfilling the request to an external host.
503 Service Unavailable	The server is currently processing too many requests.
505 HTTP Version Not Supported	The request version (for example, HTTP/1.0, HTTP/1.1) is not understood by the server.

To make it easier to internationalize error messages and standardize how these messages are presented, the latest version of Apache includes what are referred to as variant pages (ending in a .var suffix). These variant pages, which offer variable output based on language, are stored in the /var/www/error directory.

```
Alias /error/ "/var/www/error/"

<IfModule mod_negotiation.c>
<IfModule mod_include.c>
    <Directory "/var/www/error">
        AllowOverride None
        Options IncludesNoExec
        AddOutputFilter Includes html
        AddHandler type-map var
        Order allow,deny
        Allow from all
        LanguagePriority en es de fr
        ForceLanguagePriority Prefer Fallback
    </Directory>

    ErrorDocument 400 /error/HTTP_BAD_REQUEST.html.var
    ErrorDocument 401 /error/HTTP_UNAUTHORIZED.html.var
    ErrorDocument 403 /error/HTTP_FORBIDDEN.html.var
    ErrorDocument 404 /error/HTTP_NOT_FOUND.html.var
    ErrorDocument 405 /error/HTTP_METHOD_NOT_ALLOWED.html.var
        .
        .
        .
```

The `ErrorDocument` directive associates a particular error code number with a particular `.var` file that contains multiple possible responses based on language.

Setting responses to browsers

If file extensions are not enough to determine a file's MIME type, you can define hints with the `MimeMagicFile` directive. With the `BrowserMatch` directive, you can set responses to conditions based on particular browser types:

```
#
# The following directives modify normal HTTP response behavior to
# handle known problems with browser implementations.
#
BrowserMatch "Mozilla/2" nokeepalive
BrowserMatch "MSIE 4\.0b2;" nokeepalive downgrade-1.0 force-response-1.0
BrowserMatch "RealPlayer 4\.0" force-response-1.0
BrowserMatch "Java/1\.0" force-response-1.0
BrowserMatch "JDK/1\.0" force-response-1.0


#
# The following directive disables redirects on non-GET requests for
# a directory that does not include the trailing slash.  This fixes a
# problem with Microsoft WebFolders which does not appropriately handle
# redirects for folders with DAV methods.
# Same deal with Apple's DAV filesystem and Gnome VFS support for DAV.
#
BrowserMatch "Microsoft Data Access Internet Publishing Provider"
    redirect-carefully
BrowserMatch "^WebDrive" redirect-carefully
BrowserMatch "^WebDAVFS/1.[012]" redirect-carefully
BrowserMatch "^gnome-vfs" redirect-carefully
```

The `BrowserMatch` directive enables you to set environment variables based on the contents of the User-agent: header field. The `force-response-1.0` variable causes a HTTP/1.0 response, indicating that Apache will respond to the browser in basic HTTP 1.0 operations.

> **NOTE:** If you are following the `httpd.conf` file, you notice that we are skipping descriptions of the server-status lines and server-info lines. They are described in the "Monitoring Server Activities" section later in this chapter.

Enabling proxy and caching services

Proxy and caching services are turned off by default. You can turn them on by uncommenting the following directives:

```
#
# Proxy Server directives. Uncomment the following lines to
# enable the proxy server:
```

```
#
#<IfModule mod_proxy.c>
#      ProxyRequests On
#
#<Proxy:*>
#      Order deny,allow
#      Deny from all
#      Allow from .example.com
#</Proxy>

#
# Enable/disable the handling of HTTP/1.1 "Via:" headers.
# ("Full" adds server version; "Block" removes outgoing Via: headers)
# Set to one of: Off | On | Full | Block
#
#ProxyVia On

# To enable a cache of proxied content, uncomment the following lines.
# See http:/httpd.apache.org/docs-2.0/mod/mod_cache.html for more
details.
#
#<IfModule mod_disk_cache.c>
# CacheEnable disk /
# CacheRoot "/var/cache/mod_proxy"
# CacheSize 500
#</IfModule>

#</IfModule>
# End of proxy directives.
```

Apache can function as a proxy server, a caching server, or a combination of the two. If ProxyRequests is set to off, the server will simply cache files without acting as a proxy. If CacheRoot (which specifies the directory used to contain the cache files) is undefined, no caching will be performed. Both proxy and caching services are off (commented out) by default.

If you turn on caching, the CacheRoot should exist on a file system with enough free space to accommodate the cache, which is limited by the CacheSize directive. However, you should have 20 to 40 percent more space available in the file system because cache cleanup (to maintain the CacheSize, in kilobytes) occurs only periodically (which you can set using the CacheGcInterval directive).

You can add other directives to this example to enable other caching features. The CacheMaxExpire directive can indicate the maximum number of hours that a document will exist in the cache without checking the original document for modifications. The CacheLastModifiedFactor applies to documents that do not have an expiration time, even though the protocol would support one. To formulate an expiration date, the factor (a floating-point number) is multiplied by the number of hours since the document's last

modification. For example, if the document were modified three days ago and the
`CacheLastModifiedFactor` were 0.25, the document would expire from the cache in 18
hours (as long as this value is still below the value of `CacheMaxExpire`).

The `CacheDefaultExpire` directive (specifying the number of hours before a document
expires) applies to documents received via protocols that do not support expiration times. The
`NoCache` directive contains a space-separated list of IP addresses, host names, or keywords in
host names that should not have documents cached.

Here's how the caching server behaves if you uncomment the previous `Cache` lines:

- The cached files would exist in `/var/cache/mod_proxy`.
- Cache size is limited to 500 Kbytes.

You might want to allow a much larger `CacheSize`, and possibly set a short
`CacheGcInterval`, but otherwise the supplied values are reasonable. The
`CacheGcInterval` value can be a floating-point number (for example, 1.25 indicates 75
minutes).

Configuring virtual hosting

If you have one Web server computer, but more than one domain that you want to serve with
that computer, you can set up Apache to do virtual hosting. With name-based virtual hosting, a
single IP address can be the access point for multiple domain names on the same computer.
With IP-based virtual hosting, you have a different IP address for each virtual host.

With virtual hosting, when a request comes into your Apache server from a Web browser
through a particular IP address on your computer, Apache checks the domain name being
requested and displays the content associated with that domain name. As an administrator of a
Web server that supports virtual hosting, you must make sure that everything that needs to be
configured for that virtual server is set up properly (you must define such things as locations
for the Web content, log files, administrative contact, and so on).

Virtual hosting is defined with the `VirtualHost` tags. Information related to virtual hosts in
the `/etc/httpd/conf/httpd.conf` file is shown in the following code:

```
### Section 3: Virtual Hosts
#
# VirtualHost: If you want to maintain multiple domains/hostnames on
# your machine you can setup VirtualHost containers for them. Most
# configurations use only name-based virtual hosts so the server
# doesn't need to worry about IP addresses. This is indicated by the
# asterisks in the directives below.
#
# Please see the documentation at
# <URL:http://httpd.apache.org/docs-2.0/vhosts/>
# for further details before you try to setup virtual hosts.
```

```
#
# You may use the command line option '-S' to verify your virtual host
# configuration.
#
# Use name-based virtual hosting.
#
#NameVirtualHost *

#
# VirtualHost example:
# Almost any Apache directive may go into a VirtualHost container.
# The first VirtualHost section is used for requests without a known
# server name.
#
#<VirtualHost *>
#     ServerAdmin webmaster@dummy-host.example.com
#     DocumentRoot /www/docs/dummy-host.example.com
#     ServerName dummy-host.example.com
#     ErrorLog logs/dummy-host.example.com-error_log
#     CustomLog logs/dummy-host.example.com-access_log common
#</VirtualHost>
```

The following example lists virtual host directives that would allow you to host the domains
handsonhistory.com and linuxtoys.net on the same computer:

```
NameVirtualHost *

<VirtualHost *>
     DocumentRoot /var/www/handsonhistory
     ServerName www.handsonhistory.com
     ServerAlias handsonhistory.com
     ServerAdmin webmaster@handsonhistory.com
     ErrorLog logs/handsonhistory.com-error_log
     CustomLog logs/handsonhistory.com-access_log common
</VirtualHost>

<VirtualHost *>
     DocumentRoot /var/www/linuxtoys
     ServerName www.linuxtoys.net
     ServerAlias linuxtoys.net
     ServerAdmin webmaster@linuxtoys.net
     ErrorLog logs/linuxtoys.net-error_log
     CustomLog logs/linuxtoys.net-access_log common
</VirtualHost>
```

Configuring modules and related services (/etc/httpd/conf.d/*.conf)

Any module that requires special configuration will typically have a configuration file (`.conf` file) in the `/etc/httpd/conf.d` directory. Here are modular configuration files that are contained in that directory, along with some ways of using those files:

- **auth_mysql.conf** — Configure authentication based on data you add to a MySQL database. Comments in the file describe how to set up the database and then use it to do user or group authentication before allowing a client to access your Web content.

- **auth_pgsql.conf** — Configure authentication based on data in a PostgreSQL database.

- **htdig.conf** — Identify the location of the htdig search content that can be used on your Web site (`/usr/share/htdig` is the default location). To see the htdig search screen from a Web browser, type **http://localhost/htdig**. (The htdig system lets you set up tools for indexing and searching your Web site or company intranet. It is optional for your Web server)

- **mailman.conf** — Set up mailman list server software to allow features such as making mailing-list archives available from Apache.

- **original.ssl.conf** — Configure SSL support so that Apache knows how to serve pages requested over a secure connection (https).

- **perl.conf** — Identifies and loads the `mod_perl` module so that your Web pages can include Perl code.

- **php.conf** — Identifies and loads the libphp4 module so that your Web pages can include PHP scripting language. There is also a `DirectoryIndex` setting that allows an `index.php` file you add to a directory to be served as a directory index.

- **python.conf** — Identifies and loads the `mod_python` module so Web pages can include Apache handlers written in Python.

- **squirrelmail.conf** — Identifies the location of the SquirrelMail Web-based mail interface so that it can be incorporated into your Apache Web server. To see the SquirrelMail login screen, type **http://localhost/webmail** into a browser window.

- **subversion.conf** — Loads the `mod_dav_svn` and `mod_authz_svn` modules to let you access a Subversion repository from Apache. By uncommenting lines in this file, you can set `/home/svnroot` as the location where you hold authorization files.

- **webalizer.conf** — Lets you identify who can access the webalizer data (statistics about your Web site).

- **wordtrans.conf** — Identifies the location of the WordTrans language translation window so that it can be incorporated into your Apache Web server. To see the WordTrans login screen, type **http://localhost/wordtrans** into a browser window.

These configuration files are read when the httpd server starts. The information in these files could have been added to `httpd.conf`. However, files are put here so that different packages can add their own configuration settings without having the RPM software package incorporate some automated method of adding their configuration information to the `httpd.conf` file.

Starting and Stopping the Server

The procedure for starting and stopping the Apache Web server is no different from that of many other daemons. You can use the `chkconfig` command to set the httpd service to start at boot time.

> **CROSS-REFERENCE:** See Chapter 12 for detailed information on the inner workings of the shell scripts that control starting and stopping daemons and server processes.

The `/etc/init.d/httpd` shell script accepts any of a handful of command-line arguments. If it is called with the argument `start`, the `httpd` script will run one master daemon process (owned by `root`), which will spawn other daemon processes (equal to the number specified by the `StartServers` directive) owned by the user `apache` (from the `User` and `Group` directives). These processes are responsible for responding to incoming HTTP requests. If called with `stop`, the server will be shut down as all `httpd` processes are terminated.

If given a command-line argument of `restart`, the script will simply execute `stop` and `start` procedures in sequence. Using `reload` as the argument will send the hangup signal (`-HUP`) to the master `httpd` daemon, which causes it to reread its configuration files and restart all the other `httpd` daemon processes. The shell script also supports an argument of `status`, which will report if the daemon is running and, if it is, the PIDs of the running processes. All other command-line arguments result in an error and cause a usage message to be printed.

The actual binary for Apache, `/usr/sbin/httpd`, supports several command-line arguments, although the default values are typically used. The possible command-line arguments are listed in Table 21-7.

Table 21-7: Command-Line Arguments to httpd

Argument	Description
-c *directive*	Read the configuration files and then process the *directive*. This may supersede a definition for the directive within the configuration files.
-C *directive*	Process the *directive* and then read the configuration files. The directive may alter the evaluation of the configuration file, but it may also be superseded by another definition within the configuration file.
-d *directory*	Use *directory* as the ServerRoot directive, specifying where the module, configuration, and log file directories are located.
-D *parameter*	Define *parameter* to be used for conditional evaluation within the IfDefine directive.
-f *file*	Use *file* as the ServerConfigFile directive, rather than the default of /etc/httpd/conf/httpd.conf.
-h	Display a list of possible command-line arguments.
-l	List the modules linked into the executable at compile time.
-L	Print a verbose list of directives that can be used in the configuration files, along with a short description and the module that contains each directive.
-S	List the configured settings for virtual hosts.
-t	Perform a syntax check on the configuration files. The results will either be: Syntax OK or an error notification, for example: Syntax error on line 118 of /etc/httpd/conf/httpd.conf
-T	Same as -t, except that there is no check of the DocumentRoot value.
-v	Print the version information: Server version: Apache/2.0.48 Server built: March 17 2004 11:23:11

Argument	Description
-V	List the version information and any values defined during compilation:
	`Server version: Apache/2.0.48`
	`Server built: March 17 2004 11:23:11`
	`Server's Module Magic Number: 20020903:5`
	`Architecture:      32-bit`
	`Server compiled with....`
	`-D APACHE_MPM_DIR="server/mpm/prefork"`
	`-D APR_HAS_MMAP`
	`-D APR_HAVE_IPV6 (IPV4-mapped addresses enabled)`
	.
	.
	.
	`-D SERVER_CONFIG_FILE="conf/httpd.conf"`
-X	Only the single master daemon process is started, and no other httpd processes will be spawned. This should be used only for testing purposes directly from the command line.

Monitoring Server Activities

Apache provides two unique built-in methods to check the performance of your Web server. The server-status handler can be configured to show information about server processes. The server-info handler can be configured to display a detailed summary of the Web server's configuration. You can activate these services by adding the following lines to the /etc/httpd/conf/httpd.conf file, respectively:

```
<Location /server-status>
    SetHandler server-status
    Order deny,allow
    Deny from all
    Allow from .handsonhistory.com
</Location>

<Location /server-info>
    SetHandler server-info
    Order deny,allow
    Deny from all
    Allow from .handsonhistory.com
</Location>
```

In this example, all computers in the `handsonhistory.com` domain can display the server-info and server-status pages. You can change `handsonhistory.com` to the name of any domain or host that your Apache server is hosting.

Displaying server information

The Server Information (server-info) page contains the server version information and various general configuration parameters and breaks up the rest of the data by module. Each loaded module is listed, with information about all directives supported by that module, and the current value of any defined directives from that module.

The Server Information is usually quite verbose and contains much more information than can be displayed in Figure 21-3, which shows only the links to each module's section and the general Server Settings section.

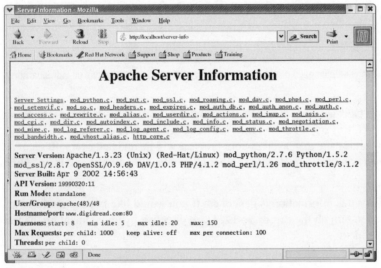

Figure 21-3: The server-info page displays server and module information.

Displaying server status

The contents of the server-status page include version information for the server, the current time, a timestamp of when the server was last started, and the server's uptime. The page also details the status of each server process, choosing from several possible states (waiting for a connection, just starting up, reading a request, sending a reply, waiting to read a request before reaching the number of seconds defined in the `KeepAliveTimeout`, performing a DNS lookup, logging a transaction, or gracefully exiting).

The bottom of the server-status page lists each server by process ID (PID) and indicates its state, using the same possible values. Figure 21-4 shows an example of this page.

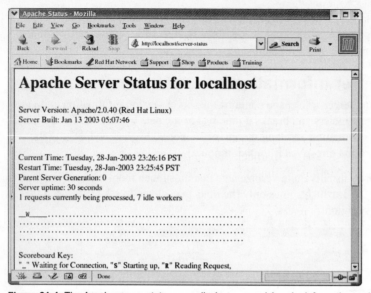

Figure 21-4: The Apache server-status page displays general Apache information and reports on individual server process activities.

The server-status page can also perform automatic updates to provide even closer monitoring of the server. If the URL `http://localhost/server-status?refresh=40` is specified, the server-status page displayed in your browser will be updated every 40 seconds. This enables a browser window to be devoted entirely to continually monitoring the activities of the Web server.

By default, only basic status information is generated. If you would like to generate full status information, you need to turn on the `ExtendedStatus` directive by uncommenting the last line in the following code:

```
#
# ExtendedStatus: controls whether Apache will generate "full" status
# information (ExtendedStatus On) or basic information (ExtendedStatus
# Off) when the "server-status" handler is called. The default is Off.
#
#ExtendedStatus On
```

Further security of server-info and server-status

Because both the server-info and server-status pages contain private information that should not be accessible to just anyone on the network, there are a few extra ways you can secure that information. You can restrict that information only to the local host; however, in some environments that may not be practical.

If you must allow other machines or networks access to such detailed configuration information, allow only as many machines as is necessary, and preferably only those machines on your local network. Also, be aware that, in the wrong hands, the information displayed by the server-info and server-status pages can make it much easier for the security of your entire machine to be compromised.

It may also be beneficial to change the URL used to reference both of the aforementioned pages. This is an example of "security through obscurity," which should not be relied on but which can make it just a little more difficult for unauthorized individuals to obtain information about your Web server's configuration (particularly if you cannot restrict such connections to the local network). To accomplish this, simply change the filename in the Location directive, as in the following lines:

```
<Location /server.information.page>
```

and:

```
<Location /server.status.page>
```

Logging errors

The error log contains messages generated by the server that describe various error conditions. The ErrorLog and LogLevel directives in the httpd.conf file (as described in the section on configuring the server) can modify the filename and the amount of information that is logged. The default file is /etc/httpd/logs/error_log (which is a link to /var/log/httpd/error_log). Here are a few sample lines from the error log:

```
[Thu Apr 15 10:29:13 2004] [notice] Apache/2.0.48 (Fedora)
     configured -- resuming normal operations
[Thu Apr 15 10:43:07 2004] [error] [client 127.0.0.1] client denied by
     server configuration: /var/www/html/server-status
[Thu Apr 15 10:06:42 2004] [error] [client 127.0.0.1] File
     does not exist: /var/www/html/newfile.html
[Thu Apr 15 01:12:28 2004 [notice] caught SIGTERM, shutting down
```

The first line indicates that the server has just been started and will be logged regardless of the LogLevel directive. The second line indicates an error that was logged to demonstrate a denied request. The third line shows an error, which represents a request for a file that does not exist. The fourth line, also logged regardless of the LogLevel directive, indicates that the server is shutting down. The error log should also be monitored periodically because it will contain the error messages from CGI scripts that might need repair.

Logging hits

Every incoming HTTP request generates an entry in the transfer log (by default, /etc/httpd/logs/access_log, which is a link to /var/log/httpd/access_log). Statistics packages and log file analysis programs typically use this file because manually reading through it can be a rather tedious exercise. (See the information on LogSentry in Chapter 14.)

The format of the transfer log can be altered by the `LogFormat` and `CustomLog` directives in the `httpd.conf` file (as described in the "Configuring the Server" section). If you attempted to access `http://localhost/` following the installation procedure (from Figure 21-1), the following lines (in the "common" format) would be written to the `access_log`:

```
127.0.0.1 - - [15/Jun/2004:23:32:28 -0400] "GET / HTTP/1.1" 200 1945
127.0.0.1 - - [15/Jun/2004:23:32:36 -0400] "GET /powered_by.gif
    HTTP/1.1" 200 1817
127.0.0.1 - - [15/Jun/2004:23:32:36 -0400] "GET /icons/apache_pb.gif
    HTTP/1.1" 200 2326
```

Viewing the server-info and server-status pages (as shown in Figures 21-3 and 21-4, respectively) generated the following entries:

```
127.0.0.1 - - [15/Jun/2004:23:40:41 -0400] "GET /server-info HTTP/1.1"
    200 42632
127.0.0.1 - - [15/Feb/2003:23:41:49 -0400] "GET /server-status
    HTTP/1.1" 200 1504
```

The denied attempt to access the server-status page logged the following line (note the 403 server response code):

```
127.0.0.1 - - [15/Jun/2004:23:43:07 -0400] "GET /server-status
    HTTP/1.1" 403 211
```

Analyzing Web-server traffic

The `webalizer` package can take Apache log files and produce usage reports for your server. Those reports are created in HTML format so you can display the information graphically. Information is produced in both table and graph form.

To use the `webalizer` command, the webalizer package must be installed. You can run `webalizer` with no options and have it take the values in the `/etc/webalizer.conf` files to get the information it needs. As an alternative, you can use command-line options to override settings in the `webalizer.conf` file. To use the defaults, simply run the following:

```
# webalizer
```

If all goes well, the command should run for a few moments and exit silently. Based on the information in the `/etc/webalizer.conf` file, the `/var/log/httpd/access_log` log file is read and an `index.html` file is copied to the `/var/www/html/usage/` directory. You can view the output by opening the file in any browser window. For example, you could type the following:

```
# mozilla /var/www/html/usage/index.html
```

The output report shows a 12-month summary of Web server activity. On the bar chart, for each month a green bar represents the number of hits on the Web site, the dark blue bar shows the number of different files hit, and the light blue bar shows the number of pages opened. It also shows data for the number of visits and the number of sites that visited in the right column. The amount of data transferred, in kilobytes, is displayed as well.

Figure 21-5 shows an example of a `webalizer` output file for a Web server that has been running for several months.

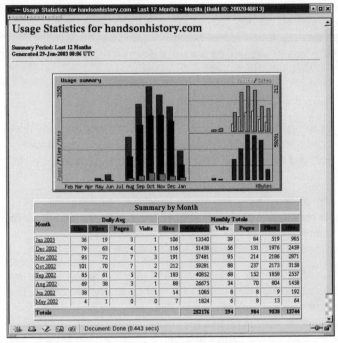

Figure 21-5: Webalizer displays Web data in chart and column formats.

Below the chart, a table shows daily and monthly summaries for activity during each month. Users can click the name of a month to see detailed activity.

> **TIP:** Because webalizer supports both common log format (CLF) and combined log format, it can be used to display information for log files other than those produced for Apache. For example, you could display statistics for your FTP server or Squid server.

Several other software tools are available for analyzing transfer statistics. The accompanying sidebar on statistics packages available for Fedora and other Red Hat Linux systemsdescribes some of these tools.

Statistics Packages Available for Fedora Linux

Analyzing the transfer log by hand isn't much fun. Several packages have been written to automate this task, including the following two:

- **Analog** — This free log-file analyzer is very fast and easily configurable, and it produces very detailed output (including bar graphs and hypertext links). More information can be found at `www.analog.cx`.

- **AWStats** — The Advanced Web Statistics tool (`awstats.sourceforge.net`) produces graphical statistics representing Web-server access. AWStats can work with log files in the Apache common log format, as well as log files from sendmail, FTP and other network servers. It can report statistics, such as the number of people who have visited, visits made per person, the domain and country of each visitor, and the number of visits made by robots.

Summary

Web servers are responsible for storing and delivering the vast amount of content available on the World Wide Web to clients all over the world. Although several Web-server software packages are available for Fedora and systems, the most popular is by far the Apache Web server.

This chapter describes how to install, configure, and run an Apache server in Fedora. The `httpd` daemon process handles requests for Web content (HTTP). Configuration files define what content is made available and how it can be accessed. In particular, the `/etc/httpd/conf/httpd.conf` file is used to configure the server.

The apache package also includes facilities for logging error and transfer messages. You can look for the `access_log` and `error_log` files in the `/etc/httpd/logs` directory. The `access_log` file contains information on content requests that have been serviced by the server. The `error_log` file lists error conditions that have occurred and times when service has been denied. You can use tools such as webalizer to simplify the viewing of Apache log data.

Chapter 22

Setting Up an LDAP Address Book Server

In This Chapter

- Understanding LDAP
- Using OpenLDAP
- Configuring an LDAP server
- Creating an LDAP address book
- Using Mozilla Mail to access the address book

Sometimes an organization needs a convenient way to gather, store, and distribute information for access by the applications that need it. The Lightweight Directory Access Protocol (LDAP) simplifies the process of creating and using directories of information by network-ready applications.

The intention of LDAP is to simplify the overhead needed to provide directory services described in the X.500 specification. LDAP is actually a subset of X.500 features. By standardizing the structure of database information, LDAP can get around proprietary storage formats to allow many different applications to share the same data.

> **NOTE:** X.500 is a CCITT specification that has become part of the Open Systems Interconnection (OSI) standards that define a layered framework for interconnecting networks and related services. With the dominance of TCP/IP networks (such as the Internet) in the world, OSI never became the predominent network framework that some expected it to be. Despite that, the seven-layer OSI reference model is often used in classrooms to teach networking theory. Likewise some ot these specifications, such as X.500, have been adopted (and sometimes adapted) where standard, cross-platform features are required.

Fedora Core systems include OpenLDAP software packages to implement LDAP server and client services. To illustrate how to configure and use an LDAP server with OpenLDAP, and make it accessible to user applications, this chapter goes through the process of setting up a shared address book on your Fedora Core system. It also describes how to use e-mail clients that can access the LDAP address book.

Understanding LDAP

LDAP lets people create directories of information that can be shared among client applications over a network. It is particularly geared toward applications that are used to look up information that is fairly stable over and over again (in other words, information that's being looked at more than it's being changed). That's why LDAP is popular for uses like storing information about people, addresses, and other kinds of data that may require high access with relatively few changes.

Because of LDAP's extraordinarily flexible design, as an LDAP developer or administrator you have a lot of control over:

- How the information in the directories is organized.
- How and by whom information can be accessed.
- The scale, local to global, by which information is distributed. (Information can be replicated to other servers at any scale you choose and synced up automatically.)

Despite its flexibility, however, you don't have to begin designing each directory you create from scratch. LDAP has many predefined structures of information you can rely on to build your LDAP directories. Those data structures are defined in several different standards documents referred to as RFCs (Request for Comments). (There are RFCs for almost every aspect of the Internet protocols and related application services.) Important RFCs for LDAP definitions include:

- **RFC 2252** — Defines the framework for LDAP.
- **RFC 2256** — Defines the X.500 user schema for LDAPv3.
- **RFCs 1274, 2079, 2247, 2307, 2587, 2589** — Define specifications for including user attributes, Uniform Resource Identifiers, domain names, NIS data, public key infrastructure (PKI), and dynamic directory services in LDAP directories.

The documents on which these RFCs are based include the CCITT X.500 standard and the related ISO IS95494 directory services standards. In particular, X.521 and X.520 define some of the most basic object classes and attribute types.

Keep in mind, however, that these standards provide guidelines. When you put together your own LDAP directory, your OpenLDAP server will have to deal directly with the schemas that implement those standards on the OpenLDAP server.

Defining information in schemas

The elements that make up LDAP directories are organized into what are called schemas. When you create or use an LDAP directory, the types of information in the schemas you will be working include the following types of items:

- **Object classes** — An object provides a name under which you would group together a bunch of attributes. So, with an address book, you might include the `inetOrgPerson` object class, under which you could store attributes associated with a person.

- **Attributes** — As its name implies, an attribute holds a piece of information associated with an object class. For example, the `inetOrgPerson` object class could have attributes such as telephone number, e-mail address, and so on.

> **NOTE:** If you are familiar with databases, the LDAP directory terminology might seem a bit different to you. You can think of attributes as fields and object classes as tables.

Examples of object classes include `country`, `locality`, `organization`, and many others. For each object class, there may be required attributes and a list of optional attributes. You can see the definitions for many standard object classes and attributes in the schema files that come with any LDAP server.

In OpenLDAP, several default schemas are included in the `/etc/openldap/schema` directory. The example e-mail address book I show you how to create in this chapter relies entirely on schemas provided with OpenLDAP. You don't have to create any schema files yourself to do the examples in this chapter. If you need more objects and attributes than are provided by default, you can get schemas from other places or create your own.

> **CROSS-REFERENCE:** For information on schemas included with OpenLDAP, refer to the OpenLDAP Schema Specification page (`www.openldap.org/doc/admin22/schema.html`). That page also describes how you can go about extending those schemas. Check those schemas, as well as the schema definitions in RFCs described earlier, before you create your own object classes or attributes.

As you begin dealing with your LDAP directory, you will access the object classes and attributes as names. To the LDAP server, however, each of those items is represented by a unique string of numbers and dots. Each string is referred to as an Object Identifier (OID). If you are not creating your own object classes or attributes, you don't need to deal with OIDs. To understand what OIDs are and when you might want to get your own OID assignment, refer to the "Understanding OIDs" sidebar.

Understanding OIDs

If you look into a schema file (`/etc/openldap/schemas/*`), you will see that every LDAP object class and attribute is mapped into a dot-separated number. That number is a hierarchical string that is referred to as an Object Identifier (OID).

Because LDAP is intended to be a global directory (where all entries can be unique), if you want to create a directory that can be accessed globally, you should try to use items that have existing OIDs assigned whenever possible. However, if you find that you need to create object classes or attributes that are not already defined, you can consider getting an Object Identifier (OID) for your organization. The alternative is to make up your own attribute name and OID, in which case you should either never expect that data to be globally accessible or try not to conflict with existing OIDs.

Like a domain name, an OID assignment enables you to create branches under that OID as you need them. If your organization has its own OID assigned, you are guaranteed of having every item you create under that number be globally unique (as long as you maintain those assignments properly yourself).

To give you some examples of OIDs, private enterprise numbers used primarily for companies using SNMP are stored under the OID number 1.3.6.4.1. Companies represented under that OID include IBM (1.3.6.4.1.2), Cisco Systems (1.3.6.4.1.9), and Hewlett Packard (1.3.6.4.1.11).

If you break down each number into its component parts, you see that they start with the top-level OID 1 (for ISO-assigned OIDs), then 3 (ISO identified Organizations), then 6 (US Department of Defense), then 4 (Internet), then 1 (private). After that is the number representing each company.

You can see the complete list of enterprise numbers on the Private Enterprise Numbers list: `www.iana.org/assignments/enterprise-numbers`. Search for OID assignments (from the top node) from: `www.alvestrand.no/objectid/top.html`. You can request your OID from the Internet Assigned Numbers Authority (`www.iana.org`).

Structuring your LDAP directories

While standards documents are used to keep the object classes, attributes, and other elements of LDAP directories unique, you are free to put together those elements into your own LDAP directories however you want. The structure you use to create your directories is the LDAP Data Interchange Format (LDIF).

Every piece of information you store in your LDAP directory must fall under a base distinguished name (or *base dn*). Because many organizations these days can be represented by a unique Internet domain name, the domain name is a popular way to identify your LDAP base dn. In fact, for the examples in this chapter, the base distinguished name I use is linuxtoys.net. If you are creating an LDAP directory for an organization that can be represented by a domain name you can replace linuxtoys.net with your domain name.

If you are creating an LDAP directory structure for a larger organization (in other words, more than just a single address book as I am doing here), you need to think hard about how you want the directory structured. You may want to add country codes (us, de, it, and so on) under your base distinguished name for a multinational company.

Setting Up the OpenLDAP Server

All the software packages you need to set up an OpenLDAP server are included on the CDs that come with Fedora distributions. With those packages installed, you can start configuring your OpenLDAP server.

Installing OpenLDAP packages

To configure your OpenLDAP server, you should start by installing all the openldap packages from your Fedora distribution. First, check which openldap packages are installed:

```
# rpm -qa "openldap*"
openldap-2.1.25-5.1
openldap-servers-2.1.25-5.1
openldap-devel-2.1.25-5.1
openldap-clients-2.1.25-5.1
```

You only need the openldap-devel package if you are developing LDAP applications. Otherwise, you can install the openldap package from CD #1 and the openldap-clients and openldap-servers packages from CD #3 of the Fedora CDs that come with this book.

Configuring the OpenLDAP server (slapd.conf)

You configure the access and use of your OpenLDAP databases in the configuration file, `/etc/openldap/slapd.conf`.

> **NOTE:** For a more complete description on features you can use in your `slapd.conf` file, refer to the `slapd.conf` man page.

1. **Edit `slapd.conf`.** Open the `/etc/openldap/slapd.conf` file as root user, using any text editor. The following steps tell you some of the information you might want to change.

2. **Review the schemas.** In the `slapd.conf` file, schemas are included from the `/etc/openldap/schema` directory that are generally useful for creating LDAP directories. Other schemas you might use will often rely on these schemas being included. So, unless you know you don't need them, don't delete any of these schemas:

```
include       /etc/openldap/schema/core.schema
include       /etc/openldap/schema/cosine.schema
include       /etc/openldap/schema/inetorgperson.schema
include       /etc/openldap/schema/nis.schema
include       /etc/openldap/schema/redhat/autofs.schema
```

The `core.schema` file is required for all LDAP directories. The `cosine.schema` and `inetorgperson.schema` files are particularly useful (and needed for this procedure). The `nis.schema` file is used to provide Network Information System data in an LDAP directory.

> **TIP:** The LDAP Schema Viewer (`http://ldap.akbkhome.com`) enables you to view object classes, attributes, syntaxes, and matching rules for common schemas for LDAP. Definitions also point to RFCs that more fully define each object class.

3. **Add backend database definitions.** In the `slapd.conf` file, you need to define some backend database definitions. Each set of backend definitions applies to a group of databases of the same type.

   Here's an example of how the backend database definitions would appear for a computer in the domain named `linuxtoys.net` (of course, you would replace `linuxtoys` and `net` with those of your own domain):

   ```
   ##################################################
   # ldbm and/or bdb database definitions
   ##################################################

   database        ldbm
   suffix          "dc=linuxtoys,dc=net"
   directory       /var/lib/ldap
   rootdn          "cn=manager,dc=linuxtoys,dc=net"
   access to * by users read
   ```

   This `database` is of the type `ldbm` (Lightweight Directory Access Protocol Proxy backend), which defines how that data for this database are stored. The `bdb` (Berkeley DB transactional backend) is another common backend database type you could use. The suffix specifies that queries to this `slapd` server for `linuxtoys.net` are directed to this database. The directory line identifies the `/var/lib/ldap` directory as the location for this LDAP directory.

   The `rootdn` line indicates that root access can be granted to change data in databases associated with the `linuxtoys.net` distinguished name (provided the password is supplied with `rootpw`, as described in the next step). Access control and other restrictions you may put on the database do not apply to this user. However, access control is applied to all other users, who are given read-only permission.

4. **Add a password.** In the `slapd.conf` file, you need to enter the password that is required to modify your OpenLDAP backend database. By default, the `rootpw` line defines a clear-text string that is your password. The password will give you full control of the backend database. It will look something like the following:

   ```
   rootpw          mysecret
   ```

> **NOTE:** If you are going to use a clear-text password, you should make sure that your `slapd.conf` file has read permissions closed to the world (`chmod 640 /etc/openldap/slapd.conf`). See the "Creating an encrypted password" sidebar for information on creating an encrypted password to access your OpenLDAP backend database.

Creating an encrypted password

To create an encrypted password for the administrator of the OpenLDAP database you can use the `slappasswd` command. You can create the password using Crypt, SSHA, SMD5, MD5, or SSH encryption. Here's an example of creating a password for OpenLDAP using MD5 encryption:

```
# slappasswd -h {md5} > /tmp/myslap
New password: ********
Re-enter new password: ********
# cat /tmp/myslap
{MD5}uBoM+LOQg5GHHJ2Z4NLu9A==
```

Enter a password (twice) to create an encrypted MD5 password. This example directs the encrypted password into the `/tmp/myslap` file, you can read into the `slapd.conf` file later. (I had you "cat" the file right now so you could see what the encrypted password looks like. Your password will be different.) Here's what the rwpasswd line will look like with an encrypted, rather than a clear-text password:

```
rootwp      {MD5}uBoM+LOQg5GHHJ2Z4NLu9A==
```

5. **Save slapd.conf.** Save your changes to the `slapd.conf` file and close it.

6. **Check slapd.conf.** You can check for syntax errors in your `slapd.conf` file by running the `slapd` daemon with the `-t` option, as follows:

```
# slapd -t
config check succeeded
```

If there were something wrong with the syntax of the file (for example, if you left off a quote or misplaced a comma), the message would say `config check failed` instead. Try to correct the problem and check the file again.

At this point, you can try starting the OpenLDAP service.

Starting the OpenLDAP service

You start the OpenLDAP as you do most services in Fedora Core and other Red Hat Linux systems, using the `service` and `chkconfig` commands. The service name for OpenLDAP is ldap. To start the service immediately, type the following:

```
# service ldap start
Starting slapd:          [ OK ]
```

To set the ldap service to start each time the system is rebooted, type the following:

```
# chkconfig ldap on
```

By default, the ldap service will have read permissions open to everyone.

Setting up the Address Book

When I set up the structure of the address book database, I base the distinguished name (dn) for the database on the organization's domain name (in our example, linuxtoys.net).

With the suffix set to linuxtoys.net (`suffix "dc=linuxtoys,dc=net"`) in the `slapd.conf` file (yours will be different), the backend database is set up to handle queries to the distinguished name (dn) linuxtoys.net. Next, we can create the structure for the address book for that organization under that distinguished name.

> **NOTE:** The `dc=` stands for Domain Component. When you include a domain name as your distinguished name, the order in which you put the parts of that domain name places the part closest to the DNS root last. So, in our example, the `dc=linuxtoys` comes before `dc=net`. See RFC 2247 if you are interested in the specification for including domain names in LDAP directories.

We want to create the address book file in a format that can be loaded into the OpenLDAP database. The format we need is referred to as the LDAP Data Interchange Format (LDIF). Information you enter in this format can be used to both build the database and load a lot of data into the directory at once from a file.

The following steps explain how to create an LDIF file containing the definitions of your address book for the `linuxtoys.net` directory (distinguished name), and then load that file into your LDAP server.

1. **Create an ldif file.** As root user, using any text editor, create a file to hold your LDAP directory entry. In my example, I used the file `/etc/openldap/toypeople.ldif`.

> **NOTE:** When you create your ldif file, be sure to leave a blank line before each new distinguished (`dn:`) line. The blank line tells ldapadd to start a new entry. Without the blank line, LDAP will not think that you are starting a new distinguished name.

2. **Define the organization.** You need to define the directory that you will be loading into the LDAP server. So, for my example, I added information defining the organization as Linux Toys under the distinguished name linuxtoys.net (`dc=linuxtoys,dc=net`), by adding the following information to my `toypeople.ldif` file.

```
dn:              dc=linuxtoys,dc=net
objectClass:     top
objectClass:     dcObject
objectClass:     organization
dc:              linuxtoys
o:               Linux Toys
```

3. **Add an organizational role.** I identified the role of administrator of the address book by adding the following lines to the `toypeople.ldif` file.

```
dn:            cn=manager,dc=linuxtoys,dc=net
objectClass:   organizationalRole
cn:            Manager
description:   LinuxToys Address Book Administrator
```

4. **Add an organizational unit.** Because in this example the address book basically consists of names and addresses of members of the organization, I call the organizational unit (`ou`) members.

```
dn:            ou=members,dc=linuxtoys,dc=net
objectClass:   top
objectClass:   organizationalUnit
ou:            members
```

NOTE: Although in my example I am creating an address book that is at the top of my directory structure, if you are in a large company chances are that you will want a more complex directory structure. For example, instead of having one address book at the top of your directory structure, you may create additional organizational units for countries, locations, or departments. Then, each of those units might have their own address books. You also might want to support multiple directories under each unit. For example, there may be a separate directory for keeping track of computer equipment or company vehicles.

5. **Add people.** With the directory structure in place, and with a `members` unit under the linuxtoys.net distinguished name, I can begin adding people to the directory. I define each person as `organizationalPerson` and `inetOrgPerson` object classes. There are a lot of different attributes I could add to each person's information. However, most of the attributes I've chosen are ones that will be read by the Mozilla Mail client (which I will show later in this chapter). Here are the two entries:

```
dn:            cn=John Jones,ou=members,dc=linuxtoys,dc=net
objectClass:   organizationalPerson
objectClass:   inetOrgPerson
cn:            John Jones
mail:          jwjones@linuxtoys.net
givenname:     John
sn:            Jones
uid:           jwjones
o:             Linux Toys
telephoneNumber: 800-555-1212
homePhone:     800-555-1313
mobile:        800-555-1414
pager:         800-555-1515
facsimileTelephoneNumber: 800-555-1414
title:         Account Executive
homePostalAddress: 1515 Broadway$New York NY 99999
```

```
dn:              cn=Sheree Glass,ou=members,dc=linuxtoys,dc=net
objectClass:     top
objectClass:     organizationalPerson
objectClass:     inetOrgPerson
ou:              members
cn:              Sheree Glass
mail:            sheree@linuxtoys.net
givenname:       Sheree
sn:              Glass
uid:             slglass
o:               Linux Toys
telephoneNumber: 800-555-2893
homePhone:       800-555-4329
mobile:          800-555-8458
pager:           800-555-4955
facsimileTelephoneNumber: 800-555-3838
title:           Interior Decorator
homePostalAddress: 167 E Street$Salt Lake UT 99999
```

As you can see here, the two people listed in the address book directory (called members) are each associated with a common name (cn), John Jones and Sheree Glass, which fall under the linuxtoys.net domain components. You can add as many people as you want to this file by repeating this structure.

> **NOTE:** You may find that you don't need all of the attributes shown here or may want to add others. Refer to the schema files to see a list of attributes that are available with organizationalPerson, inetOrgPerson, and other object classes you might want to use with your address book.

6. **Save the ldif file.** Save the changes to your ldif file (in my case the file is called /etc/openldap/toypeople.ldif).

7. **Add the information to the LDAP server.** You can use the ldapadd command to add the entire contents of the ldif file you created to your LDAP directory. Here is the command I used to add the contents of my ldif file (called toypeople.ldif) to my LDAP directory:

```
# ldapadd -x -D "cn=manager,dc=linuxtoys,dc=net" -W -f toypeople.ldif
Enter LDAP Password: mysecret
adding new entry "dc=linuxtoys,dc=net"

adding new entry "cn=manager,dc=linuxtoys,dc=net"

adding new entry "ou=members,dc=linuxtoys,dc=net"

adding new entry "cn=John Jones,ou=members,dc=linuxtoys,dc=net"

adding new entry "cn=Sheree Glass,ou=members,dc=linuxtoys,dc=net"
```

The password shown here (which will not display as you type it) is the one you added to your `slapd.conf` file. In the example, I used `mysecret` as the password. The `-x` says to use simple authentication (no SASL). The `-D` says to use the distinguished name defined earlier in the slapd.conf file (`cn=manager,dc=linuxtoys,dc=net`). The `-W` says to prompt for the password, instead of entering it on the command line. The `-f` indicates the file to load (in our example, `toypeople.ldif`).

As the `ldapadd` command successfully adds each entry, it lists the distinguished name (`dn`) associated with each one.

8. **Restart the server.** You can restart the server at this point by typing the following:

```
# /etc/init.d/ldap restart
```

9. **Search the directory.** To make sure that everything was properly inserted into the directory, you can run the following search command:

```
# ldapsearch -x -W -D 'cn=Manager,dc=linuxtoys,dc=net' '(objectClass=*)'
# extended LDIF
#
# LDAPv3
# base <dc=linuxtoys,dc=net> with scope sub
# filter: (objectClass=*)
# requesting: ALL
#

# linuxtoys.net
dn: dc=linuxtoys,dc=net
objectClass: top
objectClass: dcObject
objectClass: organization
dc: linuxtoys
o: Linux Toys

# manager, linuxtoys.net
dn: cn=manager,dc=linuxtoys,dc=net
objectClass: organizationalRole
cn: Manager
description: LinuxToys Address Book Administrator

# members, linuxtoys.net
dn: ou=members,dc=linuxtoys,dc=net
objectClass: top
objectClass: organizationalUnit
ou: members

# John Jones, members, linuxtoys.net
dn: cn=John Jones,ou=members,dc=linuxtoys,dc=net
objectClass: organizationalPerson
```

```
objectClass: inetOrgPerson
cn: John Jones
mail: jwjones@linuxtoys.net
givenName: John
sn: Jones
uid: jwjones
o: Linux Toys
     .
     .
     .

# Sheree Glass, members, linuxtoys.net
dn: cn=Sheree Glass,ou=members,dc=linuxtoys,dc=net
objectClass: top
objectClass: organizationalPerson
objectClass: inetOrgPerson
ou: members
cn: Sheree Glass
mail: sheree@linuxtoys.net
     .
     .
     .
```

In this example, I asked to use simple authentication (clear-text passwords with the `-x` option), start at the base (`-b`) of the linuxtoys.net directory to begin the search, and list all object classes (`objectClass=*`). If you like, you can pipe the output to `less` so you can page through it.

10. **Debug your directory.** Don't expect your ldif file to load the first time without any errors. While you debug your address book directory, I recommend that you use a non-production machine and just clear out the database files after each failed attempt to load your directory. Assuming that you kept your LDAP directory files in `/var/lib/ldap` and that it's okay to erase the whole database while you debug your entries, you can do the following:

> **CAUTION:** You're about to erase the LDAP directory files you created. Don't do this step if you have information in your LDAP directory files that is not in your ldif file. Don't erase your ldif file, because you need it to recreate your directory files.

```
# rm /var/lib/ldap/*
# /etc/init.d/ldap restart
# ldapadd -x -D "cn=manager,dc=linuxtoys,dc=net" -W -f toypeople.ldif
```

Repeat this process until you feel that your ldif file, and all the information it contains, has been properly loaded into your LDAP directory files.

At this point, you can decide if you need to further tune your LDAP directory (as described in the "More ways to configure LDAP" section). After that, I recommend that you check that your LDAP address book directory is working properly by trying to access it from Mozilla Mail (as described later in this chapter).

More ways to configure LDAP

If you plan to scale up your LDAP directory to be used by more than just a small office or home e-mail server, there are some additional configuration options you might want to consider. Here are a few suggestions:

- **Replicate the LDAP directory** — You can make your LDAP directory accessible from multiple LDAP servers and have updates to your directory be disseminated to those servers. See the man page for the slurpd daemon (which handles update replication) and the OpenLDAP Administrator's Guide for information on setting up LDAP directory replication.

- **Add certificates** — Transport Layer Security is built into the OpenLDAP server. For information on defining certificates and ciphers that will be accepted by the slapd daemon, refer to the slapd.conf man page.

- **Change log levels** — You can specify the level of debugging that is done by the slapd daemon. By adding the loglevel *<integer>* option to the slapd.conf file, you can have slapd do the following types of logging:

  - 1   Trace function calls
  - 2   Debug packet handling
  - 4   Heavy trace debugging
  - 8   Connection management
  - 16   Print out packets sent and received
  - 32   Search filter processing
  - 64   Configuration file processing
  - 128   Access control list processing
  - 256   Stats log connections/operations/results
  - 512   Stats log entries sent
  - 1024   Print communication with shell backends
  - 2048   Entry parsing

  By default, the loglevel is 256. To log everything, set the loglevel to 256. To get combinations of loglevel features, simply add the numbers you want together. For example, for trace function calls, heavy trace debugging and connection management, use the number 13 (as in 1 + 4 + 8).

- **Limit searches** — You can limit the number of entries that can be returned by a search (sizelimit 500, by default) and the amount of time slapd will take to answer a search request in seconds (timelimit 3600). Add new values that you want for your LDAP directory to your slapd.conf file.

- **Add access control policy** — In the `slapd.conf` file, the default database access is set to allow read access by anyone who can access the database. If you want to change that behavior, you can add access lines to selectively decide who can read and write to your database. For this example, I want to allow everyone to be able to read from the database, but only allow people to change their own information. Refer to the `slapd.conf` man page for further information.

Accessing Your Address Book from Mozilla Mail

With your LDAP address book configured and running, you should be able to use it to get e-mail addresses from any e-mail client that supports LDAP directories. Assuming your LDAP directory is up and running, the following example shows how to use Mozilla Mail (which comes with Fedora Core distributions) to search your LDAP directory for e-mail addresses.

1. From Mozilla Mail or Web browser, select the address book. (That can be done by either selecting Window → Address Book or by clicking the address book icon in the lower-left corner of the window.)

2. From the Address Book window, select File → New → LDAP Directory. The Directory Server Properties window appears, as shown in Figure 22-1.

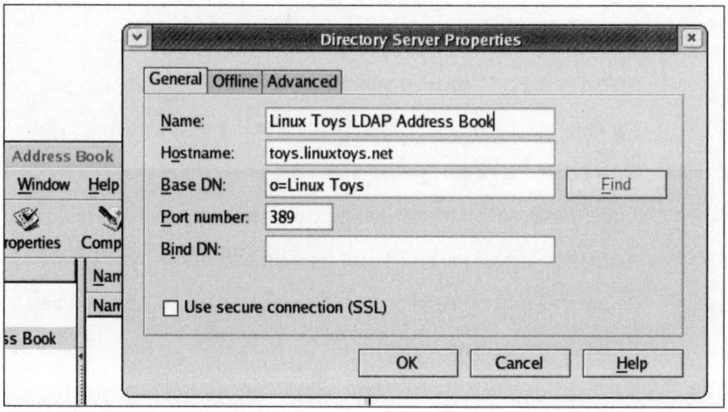

Figure 22-1: Enter information about your LDAP directory server to search for addresses from Mozilla Mail.

3. Enter the following information into the Directory Server properties window:

- **Name** — Choose any name you like to identify the LDAP directory server.

- **Hostname** — Add the host name or IP address of the computer running the LDAP server.

- **Base DN** — This identifies the point in the directory hierarchy where you are going to begin your search. For this example, I chose to use the organization name (Linux Toys) and the base distinguished name for beginning the search.

- **Port number** — By default, LDAP service is available on port number 389. You would only change this if you knew the server were configured to listen on a different port number.

- **Bind DN** — When the LDAP connection is made, you can ask to bind to a distinguished name other than the base dn by entering it here.

Click OK to save the configuration.

4. If you want to simply search the directory for an e-mail address, click Tools → Search Addresses. The Advanced Address Book Search window appears. In the Search In drop-down list box, select the LDAP directory you just configured. Then add a search string and click Search. Figure 22-2 shows the two entries that were added during the example of setting up the LDAP directory:

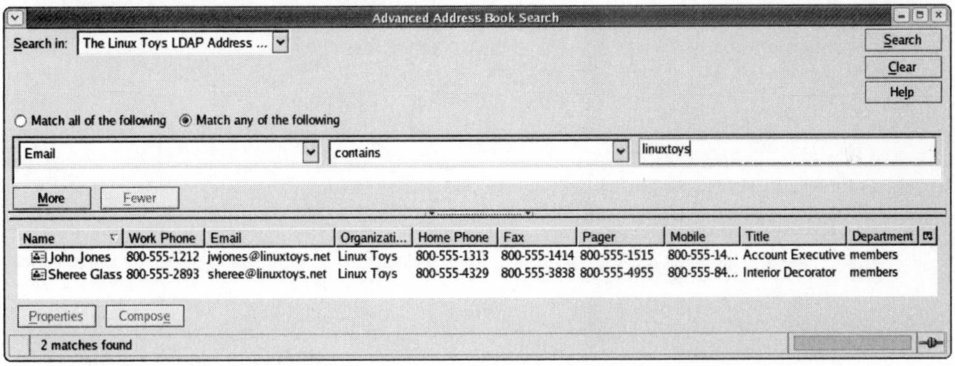

Figure 22-2: Search an LDAP address book directory by name, e-mail address, or other information.

As you can see from Figure 22-2, many of the attributes that were added to the LDAP directory can be displayed in the Mozilla Mail Address Book Search window. After an entry is found, you can:

- Double-click the entry to see an address book card with as much information as is available for the person displayed.

- Click on an entry, and then click the Compose button to open a compose window, ready to send an e-mail to the person selected.

If your LDAP directory is not accessible from the Mozilla Mail client, run Mozilla Mail on the LDAP server. If you are able to access the LDAP directory from the local server, it means that for some reason requests are being rejected from the server to outside hosts. Verify that the firewall on the server has port 389 open (which is used by default to access LDAP services). Next, check how access permissions are being set in the `slapd.conf` file

Summary

Lightweight Directory Access Protocol (LDAP) is a popular tool for creating directories of information that need to be accessed by a variety of different network-ready applications. LDAP is based on the CCITT X.500 standard, but provides a more workable subset of those features for creating directories of information that needs to be highly accessible.

In Fedora Core systems, OpenLDAP is included for you to use if you want to offer LDAP services from your computer. To configure an LDAP server, you need to set up the slapd.conf file (to configure the slapd daemon) and create entries that are then loaded into your LDAP directory files. Those entries are typically added to a file in LDIF format and loaded into files in the /var/lib/ldap directory by the ldapadd command.

Chapter 23

Setting Up Boot Servers: DHCP and NIS

In This Chapter

- Using Dynamic Host Configuration Protocol (DHCP)
- Setting up a DHCP server
- Setting up a DHCP client
- Using Network Information Service
- Setting up Linux as an NIS client
- Setting up Linux as an NIS master server
- Setting up Linux as an NIS slave server

If your business, organization, or home network has more than a few computers, administering each computer individually can be difficult. Renaming your domain or getting a new pool of IP addresses can result in your having to change configuration files on every computer on the network. A new member in your organization could mean adding a new user account to multiple computers.

Fedora offers several mechanisms for centrally configuring and distributing critical information associated with your network, its servers, and the people who use your computing resources. DHCP provides a means of dynamically configuring the IP addresses, network numbers, and server locations for the computers on your local network. NIS offers a means of distributing a variety of configuration files (containing such information as user accounts, passwords, and network addresses) to other Linux and UNIX systems on your network.

This chapter describes how to set up Fedora as a DHCP or NIS server. It then explains how to verify that those services are working and how to set up client computers to use those services.

Using Dynamic Host Configuration Protocol

Setting up a Dynamic Host Configuration Protocol (DHCP) server enables you to centrally manage the addresses and other network information for client computers on your private network. With DHCP configured on your network, a client computer can simply indicate that it wants to use DHCP and the DHCP server can provide its IP address, network mask, DNS server, NetBIOS server, router (gateway), and other information needed to get up and running on the network.

With DHCP, you can greatly simplify the initial network configuration that each client computer on your network needs to do. Later, as your network evolves, you can easily update that information, having changes automatically picked up by clients when they restart their network interfaces.

Setting Up a DHCP Server

Assuming you have already set up the physical connections between your DHCP server and the client computers on your network (presumably an Ethernet LAN), the minimum tools you need to get the DHCP server working are:

- A firewall that allows DHCP access
- A configured /etc/dhcpd.conf file
- A running dhcpd server daemon (which can be started at boot time)

After the DHCP server is running, it broadcasts its availability as a DHCP server to the LAN. A client simply boots up (with an Ethernet network interface turned on and DHCP identified as its method of getting network addresses), and the information it needs to get up and running on the network is fed to it from the server.

> **NOTE:** The dhcpd.conf file can serve a wide range of configuration information to DHCP clients. To see the full set of options and parameters you can set in that file, refer to the dhcp-options and dhcpd.conf man pages (type **man dhcp-options**).

Opening your firewall for DHCP

The firewall on your DHCP server must be configured to allow access to UDP ports 67 and 68. If you are using iptables (and you did not open ports 67 and 68 during installation), you can add a new rule to iptables and then save the changes permanently. Type the following as root user:

```
# iptables -I INPUT -i eth0 -p udp --sport 67:68 --dport 67:68 -j ACCEPT
```

In this example, requests are allowed to and from ports 67 and 68 on the eth0 interface (which is your first Ethernet card). If your DHCP server is also a routing firewall for your network, you want to make sure that you are only offering DHCP services to your LAN and not to the Internet. (You need to figure out if eth0, eth1, or some other card is connected to your LAN.)

If the rule was accepted (type **iptables -L** to make sure), you can save your entire firewall configuration so that the new rule is included permanently. To do that, type the following (as root user):

```
# iptables-save > /etc/sysconfig/iptables
```

This updates your `/etc/sysconfig/iptables` file so that all the current rules (including the one you just added) are included the next time iptables is restarted.

Configuring the dhcpd.conf file

Suppose you have a single pool of IP addresses that you want to distribute to a set of computers that are all on the same subnetwork. In other words, all the computers are connected to one hub (or a set of daisy-chained hubs). Here is an example of a simple `dhcpd.conf` file:

```
ddns-update-style interim;
ignore client-updates;


subnet 10.0.0.0 netmask 255.0.0.0 {

  option routers                  10.0.0.1;
  option domain-name-servers      10.0.0.1;
  option subnet-mask              255.0.0.0;
  option domain-name              "handsonhistory.com";

  range dynamic-bootp 10.0.0.150 10.0.0.225;
  default-lease-time 21600;
  max-lease-time 43200;

  # Set name server to appear at a fixed address
  host ns {
    next-server ns1.handsonhistory.com;
    hardware ethernet 00:D0:B3:79:B5:35;
    fixed-address 10.0.0.1;
  }
}
```

In this example, this DHCP server is providing IP addresses for client computers on a small LAN. The first two lines tell the DHCP server not to update DNS records for the local domain based on the IP addresses it assigns.

The DHCP server is serving a single LAN: `10.0.0.0` network with a `255.0.0.0` netmask. Other data in this file define what information the DHCP server will hand out to clients on this LAN.

A single server at address `10.0.0.1` is used as the router (or gateway) and DNS server for the LAN. To ensure that this server always gets the fixed address of `10.0.0.1`, a host entry is set to the hardware address (`00:D0:B3:79:B5:35`) for the Ethernet card on the host named ns.

The pool of addresses handed out by this DHCP server is 10.0.0.150 to 10.0.0.225, as set by the `range dynamic-bootp` line. (Using `dynamic-bootp` allows bootp and dhcp clients to get addresses.) Along with the IP address that each client is assigned, the client is also given the associated subnet-mask and domain name.

The IP addresses that the DHCP server hands out are leased to each client for a particular time. The default-lease-time (set to 21,600 seconds here, or 6 hours) is the time assigned if the client doesn't request a particular lease period. The max-lease-time (43,200 seconds here, or 12 hours) is the highest amount of time the server will assign, if the client requests it. Clients can renew leases, so they don't have to lose the IP address while they are still using it.

Expanding the dhcpd.conf file

As I noted earlier, this is a very simple example that works well for a single network of client computers. Below are some examples of ways that you can expand your `dhcpd.conf` file.

- If you have multiple ranges of addresses on the same subnetwork, you can add multiple range options to a subnet declaration. Here is an example:

```
subnet 10.0.0.0 netmask 255.0.0.0 {
   range 10.0.0.10 10.0.0.100;
   range 10.0.0.200 10.0.0.250;
}
```

This example causes the DHCP server to assign IP addresses between the ranges of 0.0.10 and 0.0.100 and between 0.0.200 and 0.0.250 on network number 10.

- You can set fixed addresses for particular host computers. In particular, you would want to do this for your server computers so that their addresses don't change. One way to do this is based on the Ethernet hardware address of the server's Ethernet card. All information for that computer can be contained in a host definition, such as the following:

```
host pine {
   hardware ethernet 00:04:5A:4F:8E:47;
   fixed-address 10.0.0.254;
}
```

Here, when the DHCP server encounters the Ethernet address, the `fixed-address` (10.0.0.254) is assigned to it. Type **ifconfig -a** on the server computer to see the address of its Ethernet hardware (while the interface is up). Within this host definition, you can add other options as well. For example, you could set the location of different routes (`routers` option).

- Many of the options enable you to define the locations of various server types. These options can be set globally or within particular host or subnet definitions. For example:

```
option netbios-name-servers 10.0.0.252;
option time-servers 10.0.0.253;
```

In these examples, the `netbios-name-servers` option defines the location of the WINS server (if you are doing Windows file and print server sharing using Samba). The `time-servers` option sets the location of a time server on your network.

- The DHCP server can be used to provide the information an X Terminal or diskless workstation could use to boot up on the network. The following is an example of a definition you could use to start such a computer on your network:

```
host maple {
     filename "/dwboot/maple.nb";
     hardware ethernet 00:04:5A:4F:8E:47;
     fixed-address 10.0.0.150;
          }
```

In the previous example, the boot file used by the diskless workstation from the DHCP server is located at /dwboot/maple.nb. The `hardware ethernet` value identifies the address of the Ethernet card on the client. The client's IP address is set to 10.0.0.150. All of those lines are contained within a host definition, where the host name is defined as maple. (See the Thin Clients heading in Table 23-2 for other options that may be useful for configuring thin clients.)

Adding options

There are dozens of options you can use in the /etc/dhcpd.conf file to pass information from the DHCP server to DHCP clients. Table 23-1 describes data types you can use for different options. Table 23-2 describes options that are available.

Table 23-1: Data Types

Data Types	Description
ip-address	Enter *ip-address* as either an IP address number (11.111.111.11) or a fully qualified domain name (comp1.handsonhistory.com). To use a domain name, the name must be resolvable to an IP address number.
int32, int16, int8, uint32, uint16, uint8	Used to represent signed and unsigned 32-, 16-, and 8-bit integers.
"string"	Enter a string of characters, surrounded by double quotes.
Boolean	Enter true or false when a boolean value is required.
data-string	Enter a string of characters in quotes ("client1") or a hexadecimal series of octets (00:04:5A:4F:8E:47).

Options contain values that are passed from the DHCP server to clients. Although Table 23-2 lists valid options, the client computer will not be able to use every value you could potentially pass to it. In other words, not all options are appropriate in all cases.

Table 23-2 is divided into the following categories:

- **Names, Addresses, and Time** — These options set values that are used by clients to have their host name, domain name, network numbers, and time (offset from GMT) defined.

- **Servers and Routers** — These options are used to tell DHCP clients where on the network to find routers and servers. Though more than a dozen server types are listed, most often you will just indicate the address of the router and the DNS servers the client will use.

- **Routing** — These options indicate whether or not the client routes packets.

- **Thin Clients** — These options are useful if DHCP is being used as a boot server for thin clients. A thin client may be an X Terminal or diskless workstation that has processing power, but no disk (or a very small disk) so it can't store a boot image and a file system itself.

Table 23-2: DHCP Options

Options	Descriptions
Names, Addresses, and Time	
option host-name *string*;	Indicates the name that the client computer can use to identify itself. It can either be a simple host name (for example, `pine`) or a fully qualified domain name (for example, `pine.handsonhistory.com`). You may use this in a `host` declaration, where a host computer is identified by an Ethernet address.
option domain-name *string*;	Identifies the default domain name the client should use to resolve DNS host names.
option *subnet-mask ip-address*;	Associates a subnetwork mask with an IP address. For example, `option 255.0.0.0 10.0.0.1;`.
option time-offset *int32*;	Indicates the offset (in seconds) from the Universal Time Coordinate (UTC). For example, a six-hour UTC offset is set as follows: `option time-offset 21600;`.

Servers and Routers	
option routers *ip-address* [, *ip-address*...];	Lists, in order of preference, one or more routers connected to the local subnetwork. The client may refer to this value as the gateway.
option domain-name-servers *ip-address* [, *ip-address*...];	Lists one or more Domain Name System (DNS) servers that the client can use to resolve names into IP addresses. List servers in the order in which they should be tried.
option time-servers *ip-address* [, *ip-address*...];	Lists, in order of preference, one or more time servers that can be used by the DHCP client.
option ien116-name-servers *ip-address* [, *ip-address*...];	Lists, in order of preference, one or more IEN 116 name servers that can be used by the client. (IEN 116 name servers predate modern DNS servers and are considered obsolete.)
option log-servers *ip-address* [, *ip-address*...];	Lists one or more MIT-LCS UDP log servers. List servers in the order in which they should be tried.
option cookie-servers *ip-address* [, *ip-address*...];	Lists one or more Quote of the Day (cookie) servers (see RFC 865). List servers in the order in which they should be tried.
option lpr-servers *ip-address* [, *ip-address*...];	Lists one or more line printer servers that are available. List servers in the order in which they should be tried.
option impress-servers *ip-address* [, *ip-address*...];	Lists one or more Imagen Impress image servers. List servers in the order in which they should be tried.
option resource-location-servers *ip-address* [, *ip-address*...];	Lists one or more Resource Location servers (RFC 887). List servers in the order in which they should be tried.
option nis-domain *string*;	Indicates the name of the NIS domain, if an NIS server is available to the client.
option nis-servers *ip-address* [, *ip-address*...];	Lists addresses of NIS servers available to the client, in order of preference.
option ntp-servers *ip-address* [, *ip-address*...];	Lists addresses of network time protocol servers, in order of preference.

option netbios-name-servers *ip-address* [, *ip-address*...];	Lists the addresses of WINS servers, used for NetBIOS name resolution (for Windows file and print sharing).
option netbios-dd-server *ip-address* [, *ip-address*...];	Lists the addresses of NetBIOS datagram distribution (NBDD) servers, in preference order.
option netbios-node-type *uint8*;	Contains a number (a single octet) that indicates how NetBIOS names are determined (used with NetBIOS over TCP/IP). Acceptable values include: 1 (broadcast: no WINS), 2 (peer: WINS only), 4 (mixed: broadcast, then WINS), 8 (hybrid: WINS, then broadcast).
option font-servers *ip-address* [, *ip-address*...];	Indicates the location of one or more X Window font servers that can be used by the client, listed in preference order.
option nisplus-domain *string*;	Indicates the NIS domain name for the NIS+ domain.
option nisplus-servers *ip-address* [, *ip-address*...];	Lists addresses of NIS+ servers available to the client, in order of preference.
option smtp-server *ip-address* [, *ip-address*...];	Lists addresses of SMTP servers available to the client, in order of preference.
option pop-server *ip-address* [, *ip-address*...];	Lists addresses of POP3 servers available to the client, in order of preference.
option nntp-server *ip-address* [, *ip-address*...];	Lists addresses of NNTP servers available to the client, in order of preference.
option www-server *ip-address* [, *ip-address*...];	Lists addresses of WWW servers available to the client, in order of preference.
option finger-server *ip-address* [, *ip-address*...];	Lists addresses of Finger servers available to the client, in order of preference.
option irc-server *ip-address* [, *ip-address*...];	Lists addresses of IRC servers available to the client, in order of preference.

Routing	
option ip-forwarding *flag*;	Indicates whether the client should allow (1) or not allow (0) IP forwarding. This would be allowed if the client were acting as a router.
option non-local-source-routing *flag*;	Indicates whether or not the client should allow (1) or disallow (0) datagrams with nonlocal source routes to be forwarded.
option static-routes *ip-address ip-address* [, *ip-address ip-address*...];	Specifies static routes that the client should use to reach specific hosts. (List multiple routes to the same location in descending priority order.)
option router-discovery *flag*;	Indicates whether the client should try to discover routers (1) or not (0) using the router discovery mechanism.
option router-solicitation-address *ip-address*;	Indicates an address the client should use to transmit router solicitation requests.
Thin Clients	
option boot-size *uint16*;	Indicates the size of the default boot image (in 512-octet blocks) that the client computer uses to boot.
option merit-dump *string*;	Indicates where the core image should be dumped if the client crashes.
option swap-server *ip-address*;	Indicates where the client computer's swap server is located.
option root-path *string*;	Indicates the location (path name) of the root disk used by the client.
option tftp-server-name *string*;	Indicates the name of the TFTP server that the client should use to transfer the boot image. Used more often with DHCP clients than with BOOTP clients.
option bootfile-name *string*;	Indicates the location of the bootstrap file that is used to boot the client. Used more often with DHCP clients than with BOOTP clients.
option x-display-manager *ip-address* [, *ip-address*...];	Indicates the locations of X Window System Display Manager servers that the client can use, in order of preference.

Starting the DHCP server

After the /etc/dhcpd.conf file is configured, you can start the DHCP server immediately. As root user from a Terminal window, type the following:

```
# service dhcpd start
```

Your DHCP server should now be available to distribute information to the computers on your LAN. If there are client computers on your LAN waiting on your DHCP server, their network interfaces should now be active.

If everything is working properly, you can have your DHCP server start automatically each time your computer boots by turning on the dhcpd service as follows:

```
# chkconfig dhcpd on
```

There are a few ways you can verify that your DHCP server is working:

- Check the /var/lib/dhcp/dhcpd.leases file. If a client has successfully been assigned addresses from the DHCP server, a lease line should appear in that file. There should be one set of information that looks like the following for each client that has leased an IP address:

```
lease 10.0.0.225 {
        starts 2 2002/05/04 03:48:12;
        ends 2 2002/05/04 15:48:12;
        hardware ethernet 00:50:ba:d8:03:9e;
        client-hostname "pine:;
}
```

- Turn on the Ethereal window (type ethereal& from a Terminal window) and start capturing data (in promiscuous mode). Restart the DHCP server and restart the network interface on the client. You should see a series of DHCP packets that show a sequence that looks like the following: DHCP Offer, DHCP Discover, DHCP Offer, DHCP Request, and DHCP ACK.

- From the client computer, you should be able to start communicating on the network. If the client is a Linux system, type the **ifconfig -a** command. Your Ethernet interface (probably eth0) should appear, with the IP address set to the address assigned by the DHCP server.

When the server is running properly, you can continue to add DHCP clients to your network to draw on the pool of addresses you assign.

Setting Up a DHCP Client

Configuring a network client to get addresses from your DHCP server is fairly easy. Different types of operating systems, however, have different ways of using DHCP. Here are examples for setting up Windows and Linux DHCP clients.

Windows:

1. From most Windows operating systems (Windows 95, 98, 2000, ME, and so on), you open the Network window from the Control Panel (Start → Settings → Control Panel).

2. From the Configuration tab, click the TCP/IP interface associated with your Ethernet card (something like TCP/IP → 3Com EtherLink III).

3. Click Properties. The Properties window appears.

4. Click the IP Address tab and then select the Obtain an IP Address Automatically check box.

5. Click OK and reboot the computer so the client can use the new IP address.

Linux:

1. While you are initially installing Linux, click Configure using DHCP on the Network Configuration screen. Your network client should automatically pick up its IP address from your DHCP server when it starts up.

2. To set up DHCP after installation, open the Network Configuration window (`neat` command).

3. From the Network Configuration window:

   a. Click the Devices tab (on by default).

   b. Click your Ethernet device (probably eth0).

   c. Click Edit.

   d. Click the General tab.

   e. Click "Automatically obtain IP address settings with" and select dhcp.

   f. Click OK.

   g. Click Apply.

4. Then, from a Terminal window, type:

```
# service network restart
```

By default, a Fedora client will not accept all information passed to it from the DHCP server. The way that the Fedora client handles DHCP server input is based on settings in the `/etc/sysconfig/network-scripts/ifup` script. If the client has DHCP turned on, when the system starts up networking, the `ifup` script runs the `dhclient` command. You can adjust the behavior of dhclient by creating the /etc/dhclient.conf file. (Type **man dhclient.conf** to find out how you can set your dhclient.conf file.)

Understanding Network Information Service

Network Information Service (NIS) was created by Sun Microsystems as a way of managing information that is shared among a group of host computers on a network. Using NIS, computers can share a common set of user accounts, user groups, and TCP/IP host names, as well as other information.

> **NOTE:** NIS was originally called Yellow Pages, but Sun had to change this name because it was trademarked. Some people still refer to NIS as YP, and many of the NIS commands (and even NIS package names) begin with the letters "yp." To use NIS as a client, you need to have the ypbind and yp-tools packages installed. To configure an NIS server, you need the ypserv package installed as well.

The information you share with NIS comes from files that are used with UNIX systems and, therefore, compatible with other UNIX-like systems, such as Fedora or Red Hat Linux. The group of computers that the master NIS server supports is referred to as an *NIS domain*. This domain is a defined set of host computers that may or may not be the same group of computers contained in a TCP/IP domain.

With NIS, an administrator creates information databases called *maps* from common UNIX (or Linux) system files. The NIS maps are created on the master NIS server and are accessible to other host computers from that server. Just in case the master server is down or inaccessible, one or more slave servers can be defined. The NIS slave servers contain copies of the NIS maps and can provide that information to client computers when the master is unavailable. However, NIS slave servers are not used to create the maps.

When the maps have been shared among the computers in the NIS domain, the main result is that all the computers share a common set of users and network configuration. The following is a list of files that are available for sharing by NIS (not all of them are set up for sharing by default).

- **/etc/group** — Defines the groups to which users on the computer belong.
- **/etc/passwd** — Defines the users who have accounts set up on the computer.
- **/etc/shadow** — Contains encrypted passwords for the users set up in the /etc/passwd file.
- **/etc/gshadow** — Contains encrypted passwords associated with groups contained in the /etc/groups file. (This file is optional and is usually not used.)
- **/etc/passwd.adjunct** — Secures password entries if your system doesn't use shadow passwords. (This file is used with SunOS systems.)

- **/etc/aliases** — Contains user aliases used with e-mail. It allows mail that is sent to a particular user name to be directed to a different user (or set of users). On some systems, this file may be `/etc/mailaliases` instead.

- **/etc/ethers** — Used by the RARP to map Ethernet addresses into IP numbers. This file is optional. (By default, RARP support is not configured in Fedora.)

- **/etc/bootparams** — Contains entries needed to start diskless workstations (typically used to boot Sun Microsystems diskless workstations).

- **/etc/hosts** — Contains the names and IP addresses of computers that can be reached on TCP/IP networks. (Often used to contain all the addresses for a private LAN, while Internet addresses would be determined from a DNS server.)

- **/etc/networks** — Used to attach a name to a network. In this way, you can refer to networks by name rather than by number.

- **/etc/printcap** — Contains printer definitions.

- **/etc/protocols** — Identifies numbers that are assigned to different Internet network protocols (such as IP, TCP, UDP, and others).

- **/etc/publickey** — Used on some UNIX systems to contain user names and associated public and private keys for secure networking in NFS and related features.

- **/etc/rpc** — Contains listings of supported Remote Procedure Call (rpc) protocols. These protocols are used with Sun Microsystems UNIX systems to allow requests for network services, such as NIS and others.

- **/etc/services** — Contains listings that identify port number and protocols for supported network services that are used with Internet protocols.

- **/etc/netgroup** — Used to define users (from particular hosts and domains) for permission-checking associated with remote mounts, remote shells, and remote logins.

- **/etc/netid** — Contains information that maps RPC network names to UNIX credentials.

NOTE: Some of the files just shown may not be applicable to your Fedora system. Don't worry if some of these files don't exist. In the course of setting up your system (adding users, configuring networks, and so on), you will set up the files you need.

Although these files are created in the `/etc` directory, the NIS administrator can copy these files to a different location and change them, so as not to share the master NIS server's original configuration files. Files can also be added to this list or removed from the list as the NIS administrator chooses. When an NIS client computer is configured, this configuration information can be obtained from the NIS master server.

Setting Up Fedora as an NIS Client

If your network uses NIS centrally to administer users, groups, network addresses, and other information, you can set up your Fedora system to use that information as an NIS client. To configure Fedora as an NIS client, you need to get the following information from your NIS administrator:

- **NIS Domain Name** — This is a keyword used to describe the group of hosts that use the common set of NIS files. Domain name is an unfortunate way of referring to this keyword, because it doesn't have anything to do with the TCP/IP domain name. Its only similarity is that it refers to a group of computers.

- **NIS Master Server Name** — This is the name of the computer on your network that maintains the NIS databases and responds to requests from the network for that information.

- **NIS Slave Server Names** — An NIS domain may have more than one NIS server that can handle requests for information from the domain's NIS database. An NIS slave server keeps copies of the NIS maps so that it can respond to requests if the master NIS server goes down. (NIS slave servers are optional.)

When you installed Fedora, if you knew that your network used NIS, you could have selected NIS as the way to handle user names and passwords on your computer. If you have not already configured NIS for your computer, the procedures that follow will describe how to do that. The procedures consist of defining your NIS domain name, setting up the `/etc/yp.conf` file, and configuring NIS client daemons (`ypbind` and `ypwhich`) to start when you boot your system.

Defining an NIS domain name

You can set your Fedora computer's NIS domain name using the `domainname` command. For example, if your NIS domain name were `trident`, you could set it by typing the following as the root user from the shell:

```
# domainname trident
```

To verify that your NIS domain name is set, simply type `domainname` and you will see the name. Unfortunately, you're not done yet. Running `domainname` doesn't set the NIS domain name permanently. As soon as you reboot the computer, it is gone. (You can verify this by typing **domainname** again after a reboot.)

To make the NIS domain name permanent, you need to have the `domainname` command run automatically each time your system boots. There are many ways to do this. What I did was add the command line (`domainname trident`) to a run-level script that runs before the `ypbind` daemon is started. I edited the `/etc/init.d/network` file and added the following lines just after the first set of comment lines (about line number 9).

```
# Set the NIS domain name.
domainname trident
```

This caused my NIS domain name to be set each time my Fedora system booted. When you add this entry, make sure you spell the NIS domain name properly (including upper- and lowercase letters). If you get it slightly wrong, you will see `ypbind` failure messages when you boot.

> **CAUTION:** Be very careful editing a run-level script. Make a copy before you edit it. If you make a mistake editing one of these files, you could find yourself with a network or other essential service that doesn't work. You also risk losing this information when you upgrade your system at a later date.

Setting up the /etc/yp.conf file

The `ypbind` daemon needs information about your NIS domain and NIS servers for it to work. That information is set up in your `/etc/yp.conf` file. The first entries define your NIS domain name and NIS servers. For example, if you had an NIS domain called *trident* and a master server called *maple*, you would have the following entry in your `/etc/yp.conf` file:

```
domain trident server maple
```

If you had other slave NIS servers named *oak* and *pine*, for example, you could also have the following entries:

```
domain trident server oak
domain trident server pine
```

You can also set your computer to broadcast to the local network for your NIS server. If your domain were named *trident*, for example, you would use the domain/broadcast option as follows:

```
domain trident broadcast
```

If the address of your NIS server is contained in your `/etc/hosts` file, you can specify that `ypbind` look in that file to find the server's IP address. For example, if your NIS master server is named *maple*, you would add the following entry:

```
ypserver maple
```

When `ypbind` starts, all the information in this file is read. It is then used to contact the appropriate NIS server.

Configuring NIS client daemons

After your NIS client information is all set up, all you need to do to run NIS as a client is start the `ypbind` and `ypwhich` daemons. The `ypbind` daemon runs continuously as two processes: The master `ypbind` process handles requests for information from your NIS server, and the slave `ypbind` process checks the bindings from time to time. The `ypwhich` daemon finds your NIS master server.

Getting these daemons running is pretty easy. You can set up an existing run-level script called `ypbind` to start automatically at boot time. To do this, you can run the following command (as root user from a Terminal window):

```
# chkconfig ypbind on
```

To start the `ypbind` daemon immediately, type:

```
# /etc/init.d/ypbind start
```

> **CROSS-REFERENCE:** For more information on run-level scripts, refer to Chapter 12.

Checking that NIS is working

To check that your NIS client is communicating with your NIS master server, follow the instructions in this section.

> **NOTE:** If your NIS server isn't configured yet, refer to the "Setting Up Fedora as an NIS Master Server" section later in this chapter to configure your NIS server. Then return to this procedure to make sure that everything is working properly.

From the NIS client computer, type the following command to make sure that you are communicating with the NIS server:

```
# ypwhich
maple
```

The output shown here indicates that the NIS client is bound to the NIS server named *maple*. Next, check that the maps are being shared using the `ypcat` command. (To see what files are being shared from the NIS server, look in the server's `/var/yp/nisdomain` directory, where *nisdomain* is replaced by your NIS domain name.) Type one of the files shown in that directory along with the `ypcat` command. Here's an example:

```
# ypcat hosts
10.0.0.45     ash
10.0.0.46     pine
10.0.0.47     maple
```

If you are communicating with the NIS server and able to access map files, you can now define which maps the NIS client uses of those shared map files.

Using NIS maps

For the information being distributed by the NIS server to be used by the NIS client, you must configure the `/etc/nsswitch.conf` file to include `nis` in the search path for each file you want to use.

The following is a listing from the `/etc/nsswitch.conf` file showing valid values that can be in the search paths for accessing different configuration files.

```
# Legal entries are:
#
#    nisplus or nis+     Use NIS+ (NIS version 3)
#    nis or yp           Use NIS (NIS version 2), also called YP
#    dns                 Use DNS (Domain Name Service)
#    files               Use the local files
#    db                  Use the local database (.db) files
#    compat              Use NIS on compat mode
#    hesiod              Use Hesiod for user lookups
#    [NOTFOUND=return]   Stop searching if not found so far
#
```

For the purposes of this example, I want to add `nis` in the paths for the files I want to distribute from my NIS server to this NIS client. In most cases, only the local files are checked (`files`). The following are examples of how some entries appear:

```
passwd:       files
shadow:       files
group:        files
hosts:        files dns
```

For each of these entries, the original files are checked first (`/etc/passwd`, `/etc/shadow`, and so on). For host names, the DNS server is checked after the local hosts file. For this example, you can add `nis` to access the maps being shared from the NIS server. (Linux NIS servers only implement `nis` and not `nisplus`.) The lines would then appear as follows:

```
passwd:       files nis
shadow:       files nis
group:        files nis
hosts:        files nis dns
```

As soon as the `/etc/nsswitch` file is changed, the data from the NIS maps are accessible. No need to restart the NIS service. You can go through and change any of the files listed in the `/etc/nsswitch` file so that it is configured to let your system access the NIS maps being shared.

Setting Up Fedora as an NIS Master Server

To configure your Fedora system as an NIS master server, you should first configure it as an NIS client (that is, set the NIS domain name, set up `/etc/yp.conf`, and configure client daemons as described earlier). Then you can create the NIS maps and configure the NIS master server daemon processes (ypserv and rpc.yppasswdd). The following subsections describe these procedures.

> **NOTE:** If there is a firewall on your NIS server, you must make UDP port 111 (sunrpc) available or NIS clients won't be able to connect to your NIS service. If the computer is also a router, if possible, block access to port 111 outside of your local network.

Creating NIS maps

To create NIS maps so that your Fedora system can be an NIS master server, start from the /var/yp directory from a Terminal window as root user. In that directory, a Makefile enables you to configure which files are being shared with NIS. The files that are shared by default are listed near the beginning of this chapter and within the Makefile itself.

Choosing files to map

If you don't want to share any file that is set up in the Makefile, you can prevent that file from being built. Do this by finding the following line in the Makefile and simply deleting the file you want excluded:

```
all: passwd group hosts rpc services netid protocols mail \
        # netgrp shadow publickey networks ethers bootparams printcap \
        # amd.home auto.master auto.home auto.local passwd.adjunct \
        # timezone locale netmasks
```

You may notice that not all the names in the all: line represent the exact filename. For example, netgrp is for the /etc/netgroup file. The files that each name represents are listed a few lines below the all: line in the Makefile. You may also notice that many of the files are already commented out, including the shadow file.

> **TIP:** The NIS-HOWTO document suggests that using shadow passwords with NIS is "always a bad idea." Options in the Makefile (described in the next section) enable you to automatically merge the shadow and gshadow files into the passwd and group files, respectively.

Choosing mapping options

Several options are set in the Makefile. You can choose to change these options or leave them as they are. Here are the options:

- **B=** — You can use the B= option to allow NIS to use the domain name resolver to find hosts that are not in the current domain. By default, B= is not set. To turn on this feature, set it to -b (B=-b).

- **NOPUSH=true** — When set to true (the default), the NOPUSH option prevents the maps from being pushed to a slave server. This implies that the NIS master server is the only server for the NIS domain. Set this to false, and place the host names of slave servers

into the `/var/yp/ypservers` file if you do not want the NIS master to be the only
server for the domain.

- **MINUID=500** — To prevent password entries from being distributed for administrative
  users, the `MINUID` is set to 500. This assumes that all regular user accounts on the
  system that you want to share have UIDs that are 500 or above.

- **MINGID=500** — To prevent password entries from being distributed for administrative
  groups, the `MINGID` is set to `500`. This assumes that all regular groups that you want to
  share have GIDs that are 500 or above.

> **NOTE:** Tools for adding users and groups to Fedora always begin with the number 500. Some UNIX and
> Linux systems, however, may use lower UIDs and GIDs for regular users. In those cases, you may need to
> lower MINUID and MINGID to below 500, but not below 100 (which always represent administrative logins).

- **MERGE_PASSWD=true** — Keep this option set to `true` if you want each user's
  password to be merged from the shadow file back into the `passwd` file that is shared by NIS.

- **MERGE_GROUP=true** — Keep this option set to `true` if you want each group's
  password to be merged from the `gshadow` file back into the group file that is shared by NIS.

To build the NIS maps, your system must have the `awk`, `make`, and `umask` commands. In the
Makefile, the locations of these commands are `/usr/bin/gawk`, `/usr/bin/gmake`, and
`umask`, respectively. (The `umask` command is a shell built-in command, so you don't have to
look for its location.) You can use comparable commands in different locations by changing
the values of the `AWK`, `MAKE`, and `UMASK` variables in the Makefile.

Besides the options just mentioned, there are several variables you can set to change the
location of NIS files. For example, the locations of password files (YPPWDDIR) and other
source files (YPSRCDIR) are both set to `/etc` by default. The location of YP commands
(YPBINDIR) is set to `/usr/lib/yp`. If you want to change the values of these or other
variables, you can do so in the Makefile.

Defining NIS client access

Add the IP addresses of the client computers that are allowed access to your NIS maps to the
`/var/yp/securenets` file. By default, any computer on any network that can reach your
NIS master can have access to your maps (which is not a secure situation). So, it is important
that you configure this file. IP numbers can be given in the form of netmask/network pairs. For
example:

```
255.255.255.0           10.0.0.0
```

This example enables access to your NIS master server maps from all computers on network
number 10.0.0.

> **CROSS-REFERENCE:** See Chapter 15 for descriptions of IP addresses and netmasks.

Configuring access to maps

In the /etc/ypserv.conf file, you can define rules regarding which client host computers have access to which maps. You can also set several related options. Access rules in the ypserv.conf file have the following format:

```
host:map:security:mangle[:field]
```

Asterisks can replace *host* and *map* fields to create rules that match any host or map, respectively. The *host* field is the IP address for the network or particular host for which the rule applies. The *map* field is the name of the map for which you are defining access. The *security* field is replaced by none (to always allow access), port (to allow access from a port less than port number 1024), deny (to deny access to this map), or des (to require DES authentication).

The *mangle* field is replaced by yes or no (to indicate whether a field in the map should be replaced by an x if a request comes from an unprivileged host). If the *mangle* field is set to yes, *field* is replaced by the name of the field that should be mangled (the second field is used by default).

The following options can be set in the ypserv.conf file:

- **dns** — If yes (dns: yes), NIS will query the TCP/IP name server for host names when host names are not found in maps. By default, dns:no is set.
- **xfr_check_port** — If yes (xfr_check_port:yes), the NIS master server must run on a port that is less than port number 1024. If no, any port number may be used. By default, this is set to yes.

If you make changes to the /etc/ypserv.conf file, the ypserv daemon will pick up those changes the next time your system reboots (or the ypserv service restarts). Alternatively, you can have ypserv read the contents of the file immediately by sending the ypserv process a SIGHUP signal. Removing the comment character (#) from the following line in /etc/ypserv.conf allows all hosts access to all maps:

```
* : * : * : none
```

Generating the NIS map database

To install and build the NIS database, run the ypinit command. To start the ypinit program, type the following:

```
# /usr/lib/yp/ypinit -m
   next host to add:  maple
   next host to add:
```

The ypinit command should automatically choose your host name to use as an NIS server. After that, it asks you to add slave servers. Add one at a time; then press Ctrl+D after you have entered your last slave server. Verify that the list of NIS servers is correct (type **y**). (Remember that slave servers are not required.)

The database is built at this point. A new directory that has the name of your NIS domain is created in /var/yp. For example, if your NIS domain name is trident, the directory is /var/yp/trident. All maps built are then placed in that directory.

Adding NIS slave servers

In Fedora, NIS is configured by default to have a master NIS server and no slave NIS servers. You can allow your NIS maps to be pushed to one or more slave servers by setting NOPUSH=false in the /var/yp/Makefile file. After that, you need to add the names of the slave servers to your /var/yp/ypservers file. You can either add the host names manually or have them added automatically when you run the ypinit command later.

Configuring NIS server daemons

The NIS server must be running several daemon processes to be an NIS server. Fedora supplies run-level scripts that you can configure to start NIS server daemon processes. These scripts, located in the /etc/init.d directory, include the following:

- **ypserv** — This script starts the ypserv (/usr/sbin/ypserv) daemon. It reads information from the /etc/ypserv.conf file to determine what to do. Then it listens for requests from NIS client computers on the network.

- **yppasswdd** — This script starts the rpc.yppasswdd (/usr/sbin/rpc.yppasswdd) daemon. This daemon handles requests from users on NIS client computers who want to change their user passwords.

Unless you requested that these scripts be configured to start at boot time when you installed Fedora, they will not start automatically. You can use the following chkconfig command to set ypserv and yppasswdd scripts to start automatically at boot time.

```
# chkconfig ypserv on
# chkconfig yppasswdd on
```

If you want to start the services immediately, you can type the following:

```
# /etc/init.d/ypserv start
# /etc/init.d/yppasswdd start
```

The NIS master server should be up and running. If there are any NIS slave servers, you should configure them now.

Setting Up Fedora as an NIS Slave Server

To set up an NIS slave server, you must configure it as you do an NIS master server, but with one exception: Instead of creating the NIS maps, you run the ypinit command so that the NIS maps can be copied from the server. The option that you give to ypinit is the -s *master* option, where *master* is replaced by the name of your NIS master server. Here is an example of running `ypinit` where the NIS master server is named maple:

```
# /usr/lib/yp/ypinit -s maple
```

As long as the NIS slave server is allowed access, the maps should be copied to your computer from the NIS master server. If the NIS master server goes down, this slave computer should be able to handle NIS requests from the network.

At this point, you can return to the section on setting up NIS as a client to make sure that your NIS server is running properly and distributing the maps to its clients.

Summary

DHCP and NIS both provide mechanisms for centrally administering computers on your network. DHCP can provide information that helps client computers get up and running quickly on the network. NIS enables you to distribute a wide range of configuration information among Linux and UNIX systems.

DHCP is used to provide information about your network to Windows, Linux, Mac, or other client computers on your network. IP addresses can be assigned dynamically, meaning they are distributed from a pool of IP addresses. Or specific addresses can be assigned to clients, based on specific Ethernet hardware addresses.

You can configure Fedora as an NIS client, an NIS master server, or an NIS slave server. An NIS client can take advantage of shared information from an NIS server. The NIS master server builds the databases of information (called maps) and enables access to those maps from the network. Optional NIS slave servers can be used to maintain copies of the NIS maps, enabling NIS service to continue on the network in the event that the NIS master server goes down.

## Chapter 24

Setting Up a MySQL Database Server

In This Chapter

- Finding MySQL packages
- Configuring the MySQL server
- Working with MySQL databases
- Displaying MySQL databases
- Making changes to tables and records
- Adding and removing user access
- Checking and fixing databases

MySQL is a popular structured query language (SQL) database server. Like other SQL servers, MySQL provides the means of accessing and managing SQL databases. However, MySQL also provides tools for creating database structures, as well as for adding, modifying, and removing data from those structures. Because MySQL is a relational database, data can be stored and controlled in small, manageable tables. Those tables can be used in combination to create flexible yet complex data structures.

A Swedish company called MySQL AB is responsible for developing MySQL (www.mysql.com). MySQL AB has released MySQL as an open-source product, gaining revenue by offering a variety of MySQL support packages. The company also supports several application programming interfaces (APIs) to help application developers and Web content creators to access MySQL content.

Because MySQL is an open-source product, it has been ported to several different operating systems (primarily UNIX and Linux systems, though there are Windows versions and now even a Mac OS X version as well). As you may have guessed, these include binary versions of MySQL that run on Fedora. This chapter contains descriptions of and procedures for the version of MySQL that is contained in the Fedora distribution.

> **NOTE:** The version of MySQL that comes with this version of Fedora is 3.23. If you want to explore later versions of MySQL, go to `www.mysql.com`. As of this writing, you can download production versions of MySQL 4.0 and development versions of MySQL 4.1 and 5.0.

Finding MySQL Packages

You need at least the mysql and mysql-server packages installed to set up MySQL using the procedures described in this chapter. The following MySQL packages come with the Fedora distribution:

- **mysql** — This software package contains a lot of MySQL client programs (in `/usr/bin`), several client shared libraries, the default MySQL configuration file (`/etc/my.cnf`), a few sample configuration files, files to support different languages, and documentation.

- **mysql-server** — This software package contains the MySQL server daemon (`mysqld`) and the `mysqld` start-up script (`/etc/init.d/mysqld`). The package also creates various administrative files and directories needed to set up the MySQL databases.

- **mysql-devel** — This software package contains libraries and header files required for developing MySQL applications.

- **php-mysql** — This software package contains a shared library that allows PHP applications to access MySQL databases. This basically allows you to add PHP scripts to your Web pages that can access your MySQL database.

In the current version of Fedora, all mysql software packages are contained on CDs #1 and #3. If they are not installed, you can install the mysql packages using the `rpm` command or the system-config-packages window (as described in Chapter 5).

Configuring the MySQL Server

Like most server software in Fedora, the MySQL server relies on a start-up script and a configuration file to provide the service. Server activities are logged to the `mysqld.log` file in the `/var/log` directory. There are also `mysql` user and group accounts for managing MySQL activities. The following sections describe how these components all work together.

> **TIP:** For many of the steps described in this section, the MySQL server daemon must be running. Starting the server is described in detail later in this chapter. For the moment, you can start the server temporarily by typing the following (as root user): **service mysqld start**

Using mysql user/group accounts

When the MySQL software is installed, it automatically creates a `mysql` user account and a `mysql` group account. These user and group accounts are assigned to MySQL files and activities. In this way, someone can manage the MySQL server without needing to have root permission.

The `mysql` user entry appears in the `/etc/password` file as follows:

```
mysql:x:27:27:MySQL Server:/var/lib/mysql:/bin/bash
```

The `mysql` entry just shown indicates that the UID and GID for the `mysql` user is 27. The text string identifying this user account is `MySQL Server`. The home directory is `/var/lib/mysql` and the default shell is `/bin/bash`. The home directory identified will contain directories that hold each table of data you define for the MySQL server.

The group entry for `mysql` is even simpler. The following entry in the `/etc/group` file indicates that the `mysql` group has a group ID (GID) of 27.

```
mysql:x:27:
```

If you care to check the ownership of files associated with MySQL, you will see that most of these files have `mysql` assigned as the user account and group account that own each file. This allows daemon processes that are run by the `mysql` user to access the database files.

Adding administrative users

To administer MySQL, you need to have at least one administrative account. By default, the root user has full access to your MySQL server database and no password assigned. You can assign a password to the root user using the `mysqladmin` command. To add the root user as a MySQL administrator, log in as the root user and type the following from a Terminal window (substituting your own password in place of `my47gmc`):

```
# mysqladmin -u root password my47gmc
```

After this command is run, the root user can run any MySQL administrative commands using the password.

If you happen to be logged in as another user when you want to use administrative privilege for a MySQL command, you can do that without re-logging in. Simply add the `-u root` argument to the command line of the MySQL command you are running. In other words, the Linux root user account has no connection to the MySQL root user account after the MySQL account is created. You would typically use different passwords for the two accounts.

> **TIP:** To save yourself the trouble of typing in the password each time you run a MySQL client command, you can add a password option under the `[client]` group in one of the option files. The most secure way to do that is to create a `.my.cnf` file in the root user's home directory that contains the following lines (substituting your password for the last argument shown).
>
> ```
>     [client]
>     password=my47gmc
> ```

Setting MySQL options

You can set options that affect how the MySQL applications behave by using options files or command-line arguments. The MySQL server (as well as other administrative tools) reads the following options files when it starts up (if those files exist):

- `/etc/my.cnf` — Contains global options read by `mysqld` (server daemon) and `mysql.server` (script to start the server daemon).

- `/var/lib/mysql/my.cnf` — Contains options primarily for the `mysqld` daemon.

- `-defaults-extra-file` — You can identify a file on the command line that contains options to be used by the server. For example, the following command would cause the file `/home/jim/my.cnf` to be read for options after the global options and before the user-specific options:

  > # **mysqld --defaults-extra-file=/home/jim/my.cnf**

- `$HOME/.my.cnf` — Contains user-specific options. (The `$HOME` refers to the user's home directory, such as `/home/susyq`.)

Table 24-1 shows the MySQL commands that read the options files (in the order shown in the previous bullet list) and use those options in their processing. Options are contained within groups that are identified by single words within brackets. Group names that are read by each command are also shown in the table.

Table 24-1: Option Groups Associated with MySQL Commands

Command	Description	Group names
`mysqld` (in `/usr/libexec`)	The MySQL server daemon.	[mysqld] [server]
`safe_mysqld`	Run by the `mysql` start-up script to start the MySQL server.	[mysql] [server] [mysql.server]
`mysql`	Offers a text-based interface for displaying and working with MySQL databases.	[mysql] [client]
`mysqladmin`	Used to create and maintain MySQL databases.	[mysqladmin] [client]
`isamchk`	Used to check, fix, and optimize ISAM databases (.ism suffix).	[isamchk]
`myisamchk`	Used to check, fix, and optimize MyISAM databases (.myi suffix).	[myisamchk]

Command	Description	Group names
`pack_isam`	Used to pack ISAM databases (.ism suffix).	[pack_isam]
`myisampack`	Used to compress MyISAM database tables.	[myisampack]
`mysqldump`	Offers a text-based interface for backing up MySQL databases.	[mysqldump] [client]
`mysqlimport`	Loads plain-text data files into MySQL databases.	[mysqlimport] [client]
`mysqlshow`	Shows MySQL databases and tables you select.	[mysqlshow] [client]

Though you can use any of the options files to set your MySQL options, begin by configuring the /etc/my.cnf file. Later, if you want to override any of the values set in that file you can do so using the other options files or command-line arguments.

Creating the my.cnf configuration file

Global options that affect how the MySQL server and related client programs run are defined in the /etc/my.cnf file. The default my.cnf file contains only a few settings needed to get a small MySQL configuration going. The following is an example of the /etc/my.cnf file that comes with MySQL:

```
[mysqld]
datadir=/var/lib/mysql
socket=/var/lib/mysql/mysql.sock

[mysql.server]
user=mysql
basedir=/var/lib

[safe_mysqld]
err-log=/var/log/mysqld.log
pid-file=/var/run/mysqld/mysqld.pid
```

Most of the settings in the default my.cnf file define the locations of files and directories needed by the mysqld server. Each option is associated with a particular group, with each group identified by a name in square brackets. The previous options are associated with the mysqld daemon ([mysqld]), the MySQL server ([mysql.server]), and the safe_mysqld script that starts the mysqld daemon ([safe_mysqld]). (See Table 24-1 for a list of these clients.)

The default `datadir` value indicates that `/var/lib/mysql` is the directory that stores the mysql databases you create. The `socket` option identifies `/var/lib/mysql/mysql.sock` as the socket that is used to create the MySQL communications end-point associated with the mysqld server. The `basedir` option identifies `/var/lib` as the base directory in which the mysql software is installed. The `user` option identifies `mysql` as the user account that has permission to do administration of the MySQL service.

The `err-log` and `pid-file` options tell the `safe_mysqld` script the locations of the error log (`/var/log/mysqld.log`) and the file that stores the process ID of the `mysqld` daemon when it is running (`/var/run/mysqld/mysqld.pid`). The `safe_mysqld` script actually starts the `mysqld` daemon from the `mysqld` start-up script.

> **NOTE:** Each option that follows a group name is assigned to that group. Group assignments end when a new group begins or when the end of file is reached.

Choosing options

There are many values that are used by the MySQL server that are not explicitly defined in the `my.cnf` file. The easiest way to see which options are available for MySQL server and clients is to run each command with the `--help` option. For example, to view the available `mysqld` options (as well as other information) type the following from a Terminal window:

```
# /usr/libexec/mysqld --help | less
```

Then press the Spacebar to step through the information one screen at a time. (An example of this output is shown in the next section.)

Another way to find which options are available is with the `man` command. For example, to see which options are available to set for the `mysqld` daemon, type the following:

```
man mysqld
```

It's quite likely that you can try out your MySQL database server without changing any options at all. However, after you set up your MySQL database server in a production environment, you will almost surely want to tune the server to match the way the server is used. For example, if it is a dedicated MySQL server, you will want to allow MySQL to consume more of the system resources than it would by default.

The following list shows a few examples of additional options that you might want to set for MySQL:

- **password =** *yourpwd* — Adding this option to a [client] group in a user's $HOME/.my.cnf file allows the user to run MySQL client commands without having to enter a password each time. (Replace *yourpwd* with the user's password.)

- **port = #** — Defines the port number to which the MySQL service listens for MySQL requests. (Replace # with the port number you want to use.) By default, MySQL listens to port number 3306 on TCP and UDP protocols.

- **safe-mode** — Tells the server to skip some optimization steps when the server starts.

- **tmpdir =** *path* — Identifies a directory, other than the default /tmp, for MySQL to use for writing temporary files. (Substitute a full path name for *path*.)

In addition to the options you can set, MySQL clients also have a lot of variables that you can set. Variables set such things as buffer sizes, timeout values, and acceptable packet lengths. These variables are also listed on the --help output. To change a variable value, you can use the --set-variable option, followed by the variable name and value. For example, to set the sort_buffer variable to 10MB, you could add the following option under your [mysqld] group:

```
[mysqld]
set-variable = sort_buffer=10M
```

The following is a list of other variables you could set for your server. In general, raising the values of these variables improves performance, but also consumes more system resources. So you need to be careful raising these values on machines that are not dedicated to MySQL or that have limited memory resources.

> **NOTE:** For variables that require you to enter a size, indicate Megabytes using an M (for example, 10M) or Kilobytes using a K (for example, 256K).

- **key_buffer_size =** *size* — Sets the buffer size that is used for holding index blocks that are used by all threads. This is a key value to raise to improve MySQL performance.

- **max_allowed_packet =** *size* — Limits the maximum size of a single packet. Raise this limit if you require processing of very large columns.

- **myisam_sort_buffer_size =** *size* — Sets the buffer size used for sorting while repairing an index, creating an index, or altering a table.

- **record_buffer =** *size* — Sets the buffer size used for threads doing sequential scans. Each process doing a sequential scan allocates a buffer of the size set here.

- **sort_buffer =** *size* — Defines how much buffer size is allocated for each thread that needs to do a sort. Raising this value makes sorting threads go faster.

- **table_cache = #** — Limits the total number of tables that can be open at the same time for all threads. The number of this variable represents the total number of file descriptors that MySQL can have open at the same time.

- **thread_cache =** *size* — Sets the number of threads that are kept in cache, awaiting use by MySQL. When a thread is done being used, it is placed back in the cache. If all the threads are used, new threads must be created to service requests.

Checking options

In addition to seeing how options and variables are set in the options files, you can also view how all variables are set on your current system. You can view both the defaults and the current values being used by the MySQL server.

The --help command-line argument lets you see the options and variables as they are set for the server and for each MySQL client. Here is an example of the output showing this information for the mysqld server daemon:

```
# /usr/libexec/mysqld --help | less
        .
        .
        .


The default values (after parsing the command line arguments) are:

basedir:        /usr/
datadir:        /var/lib/mysql/
tmpdir:         /tmp/
language:       /usr/share/mysql/english/
pid file:       /var/lib/mysql/maple.pid
TCP port:       3306
Unix socket: /var/lib/mysql/mysql.sock


system locking is not in use

Possible variables for option --set-variable (-O) are:
back_log                current value: 50
bdb_cache_size          current value: 8388600
bdb_log_buffer_size     current value: 0
bdb_max_lock            current value: 10000
bdb_lock_max            current value: 10000
binlog_cache_size       current value: 32768
connect_timeout         current value: 5
        .
        .
        .


table_cache             current value: 64
thread_concurrency      current value: 10
thread_cache_size       current value: 0
tmp_table_size          current value: 33554432
thread_stack            current value: 65536
wait_timeout            current value: 28800
```

After the server is started, you can see the values that are actually in use by running the mysqladmin command with the variables option. (Pipe the output to the less command so you can page through the information.) Here is an example (if you haven't stored your password, you will be prompted to enter it here):

```
# mysqladmin variables | less
+------------------------+----------------------------------------------|
| Variable_name          | Value                                        |
+------------------------+----------------------------------------------|
| back_log               | 50                                           |
| basedir                | /usr/                                        |
| bdb_cache_size         | 8388600                                      |
| bdb_log_buffer_size    | 32768                                        |
| bdb_home               | /var/lib/mysql/                              |
| bdb_max_lock           | 10000                                        |
| bdb_logdir             |                                              |
| bdb_shared_data        | OFF                                          |
| bdb_tmpdir             | /tmp/                                        |
                           .
                           .
                           .
| tmp_table_size         | 33554432                                     |
| tmpdir                 | /tmp/                                        |
| version                | 3.23.58                                      |
| wait_timeout           | 28800                                        |
+------------------------+----------------------------------------------+
```

If you decide that the option and variable settings that come with the default MySQL system don't exactly suit you, you don't have to start from scratch. Sample my.cnf files that come with the mysql package let you begin with a set of options and variables that are closer to the ones you need.

Using sample my.cnf files

Sample my.cnf files are available in the /usr/share/doc/mysql-server* directory. To use one of these files, do the following:

1. Keep a copy of the old my.cnf file:

    # **mv /etc/my.cnf /etc/my.cnf.old**

2. Copy the sample my.cnf file you want to the /etc/my.cnf file. For example, to use the my-medium.cnf file, type the following:

    # **cp /usr/share/doc/mysql-server*/my-medium.cnf /etc/my.cnf**

3. Edit the new /etc/my.cnf file (as root user) using any text editor to further tune your MySQL variables and options.

The following subsections describe each of the sample my.cnf files.

my-small.cnf

This options file is recommended for computer systems that have less than 64MB of memory and are only used occasionally for MySQL. With this options file, MySQL won't be able to handle a lot of usage but it won't be a drag on the performance of your computer.

For the mysqld server, buffer sizes are set low — only 64K for the sort_buffer and 16K for the key_buffer. The thread_stack is only set to 64K and net_buffer_length is only 2K. The table_cache is set to 4.

my-medium.cnf

As with the small options file, the my-medium.cnf file is intended for systems where MySQL is not the only important application running. This system also has a small amount of total memory available — between 32MB and 64MB — however more consistent MySQL use is expected.

The key_buffer size is set to 16M in this file, while the sort_buffer value is raised to 512K for the mysqld server. The table_cache is set to 64 (allowing more simultaneous threads to be active). The net_buffer_length is raised to 8K.

my-large.cnf

The my-large.cnf sample file is intended for computers that are dedicated primarily to MySQL service. It assumes about 512M of available memory.

Server buffers allow more active threads and better sorting performance. Half of the system's assumed 512M of memory is assigned to the key_buffer variable (256M). The sort_buffer size is raised to 1M. The table_cache allows more simultaneous users (up to 256 active threads).

my-huge.cnf

As with the my-large.cnf file, the my-huge.cnf file expects the computer to be used primarily for MySQL. However, the system for which it is intended offers much more total memory (between 1G and 2G of memory).

Sort buffer size (sort_buffer) is raised to 2M while the key_buffer is set to consume 384M of memory. The table_cache size is doubled to allow up to 512 active threads.

Starting the MySQL Server

For Fedora, the MySQL server is off by default. To turn it on, however, is fairly simple. The /etc/init.d/mysqld start-up script is delivered with the mysql-server package. To start the server, you can run the mysqld start-up script to have it start immediately, then set it to start each time your system boots.

To start the MySQL server immediately, type the following from a Terminal window as root user:

```
# service mysqld start
```

To set the MySQL server to start each time the computer reboots, type the following (as root):

```
# chkconfig mysqld on
```

This sets mysqld to start during most multiuser run states (levels 3, 4, and 5). To check that the service is turned on for those levels, type **chkconfig --list mysqld** from a Terminal window.

Checking That MySQL Server Is Working

You can use the mysqladmin or mysqlshow commands to check that the MySQL server is up and running. Here's an example of how to check information about the MySQL server using the mysqladmin command.

```
# mysqladmin -u root -p version proc
Enter password: ********
mysqladmin  Ver 8.23 Distrib 3.23.58, for redhat-linux-gnu on i386
Copyright (C) 2000 MySQL AB & MySQL Finland AB & TCX DataKonsult AB
This software comes with ABSOLUTELY NO WARRANTY. This is free software,
and you are welcome to modify and redistribute it under the GPL license

Server version       3.23.58
Protocol version     10
Connection           Localhost via UNIX socket
UNIX socket          /var/lib/mysql/mysql.sock
Uptime:              2 days 10 hours 47 min 35 sec

Threads: 1  Questions: 184  Slow queries: 0  Opens: 1  Flush tables: 3
Open tables: 1 Queries per second avg: 0.001

+----+------+----------+------+-------+------+-----+------------------+
| Id | User | Host     | db   |Command| Time |State| Info             |
+----+------+----------+------+-------+------+-----+------------------+
| 52 | root | localhost|      | Query | 0    |     | show processlist |
+--------+----------+-----------------+----------+----------+-----------+---
-----+----------------------------+
```

Each of the two options to mysqladmin shown here provides useful information. The version information shows the mysqladmin version is 8.23 and the number assigned to this distribution of the mysql server is 3.23.58. The binary package was created for PC versions of Linux/GNU on the i686 processor. The connection to the server is through a UNIX socket (mysql.sock) on the local host. The server has been up for 2 days, 10 hours, 47 minutes, and

35 seconds. Statistics show that there is one thread (connection to the server) currently active. There have been 184 requests to the server.

The `proc` option shows that one client is currently connected to the server. That client is logged into MySQL as the root user on the `localhost`. The client that has an Id of 52 (which you could use, as the server's administrator, if you wanted to disconnect the user) is currently querying the MySQL database.

If the server were not running at the moment, the `mysqladmin` command shown in the previous example would result in a failure message:

```
mysqladmin: connect to server at 'localhost' failed.
```

Recommended remedies are to try to restart the server (by typing `service mysqld restart`) or to make sure that the socket exists (`/var/lib/mysql/mysql.sock`).

Working with MySQL Databases

The first time you start the MySQL server (using the start-up script described previously), the system creates the initial grant tables for the MySQL database. It does this by running the `mysql_install_db` command.

The `mysql_install_db` command starts you off with two databases: `mysql` and `test`. As you create data for these databases, that information is stored in the `/var/lib/mysql/mysql` and `/var/lib/mysql/test` directories, respectively.

Starting the mysql command

To get started creating databases and tables, you can use the `mysql` command. From any Terminal window, open the `mysql` database on your computer by typing the following:

```
# mysql -u root -p mysql
Enter password: ********

Welcome to the MySQL monitor. Commands end with ; or \g.
Your MySQL connection id is 39 to server version: 3.23.58
Type 'help;' or '\h' for help. Type '\c' to clear the buffer

mysql>
```

Type in the root user's MySQL password as prompted. (If no password has been set, you can skip the `-p` option.) The `mysql>` prompt appears, ready to accept commands for working with the mysql default database on the localhost. If you are connecting to the MySQL server from another host computer, add `-h hostname` to the command line (where *hostname* is the name or IP address of the computer on which the MySQL server is running). Remember, you can also log in as any valid mysql login you created, regardless of which Linux login account you are currently logged in under.

As the MySQL monitor welcome text notes, be sure to end each command that you type with a semicolon (;) or \g. If you type a command and it appears to be waiting for more input, it's probably because you forgot to put a semicolon at the end.

Before you begin using the mysql interface to create databases, try checking the status of the MySQL server using the status command. The following is an example of output from the status command:

```
mysql> status
--------------
mysql  Ver 11.18 Distrib 3.23.58, for pc-linux-gnu (i686)

Connection id:          43
Current database:       mysql
Current user:           root@localhost
Current pager:          stdout
Using outfile:          ''
Server version:         3.23.58
Protocol version:       10
Connection:             Localhost via UNIX socket
Client characterset:    latin1
Server characterset:    latin1
UNIX socket:            /var/lib/mysql/mysql.sock
Uptime:                 1 day 2 hours 57 min 19 sec

Threads: 1  Questions: 136  Slow queries: 0  Opens: 12
Flush tables: 1  Open tables: 6 Queries per second avg: 0.001
--------------
```

The status information tells you about the version of the MySQL server (11.18) and the distribution (3.23.58). The output also reminds you of the current database (mysql) and your user name (root@localhost). You can see how long the server has been up (Uptime). You can also see how many threads are currently active and how many commands have been run to query this server (Questions).

Creating a database with mysql

Within an interactive mysql session, you can create and modify databases and tables. If you are not already connected to a mysql session, type the following command (assuming the mysql user name of root):

```
# mysql -u root -p
Enter password: *******
mysql>
```

The general steps for creating a MySQL database include creating the database name, identifying the new database as the current database, creating tables, and adding data to the tables. While you are connected to a mysql session, you can run the following procedure to create a sample database.

1. To create a new database name, use the CREATE DATABASE command at the mysql> prompt. For example, to create a database named allusers, type the following:

```
mysql> CREATE DATABASE allusers;
```

This action creates a database called allusers in the /var/lib/mysql directory. (While you don't have to use capitals for the commands just shown, it makes it easier to distinguish the commands from the database entries.)

> **NOTE:** Alternatively, you could create a database from the command line using the mysqladmin command. For example, to create the database named allusers with mysqladmin, you could type the following: **mysqladmin -u root -p create allusers**

2. To see what databases are available for your mysql server, type the following at the mysql> command prompt:

```
mysql> SHOW DATABASES;
+----------+
| Database |
+----------+
| allusers |
| mysql    |
| test     |
+----------+
  3 rows in set (0.00 sec)
```

The databases shown here are named allusers, mysql, and test. The allusers database is the one created in the previous step. The mysql database contains user access data. The test database is created automatically for creating test mysql databases.

3. To work with the database you just created (allusers), you need to make allusers your current database. To do that, type the following at the mysql> command prompt:

```
mysql> USE allusers;
Database changed
```

4. Creating a table for your database requires some planning and understanding of table syntax. You can type in the following commands and column information to try out creating a table. For more detailed information on creating tables and using different data types, refer to the section "Understanding MySQL Tables" later in this chapter.

To create a table called names, use the following CREATE TABLE command at the mysql> prompt:

```
mysql> CREATE TABLE names (
-> firstname       varchar(20)       not null,
```

```
-> lastname          varchar(20)      not null,
-> streetaddr        varchar(30)      not null,
-> city              varchar(20)      not null,
-> state             varchar(20)      not null,
-> zipcode           varchar(10)      not null
-> );
Query OK, 0 rows affected (0.00 sec)
```

You have now created a table called names for a database named allusers. It contains columns called firstname, lastname, streetaddr, city, state, and zipcode. Each column allows record lengths of between 10 and 30 characters. Although MySQL supports several different database formats, because none is specified here, the default MyISAM database type is used.

With a database and one table created, you can now add data to the table.

Adding data to a MySQL database table

After the database is created and the structure of a database table is in place, you can begin working with the database. You can add data to your MySQL database by manually entering each record during a mysql session or by adding the data into a plain-text file and loading that file into the database.

Manually entering data

To do the procedure in this section, I assume you have an open interactive mysql session and that you have created a database and table as described in the previous section. If you are not already connected to a mysql session, type the following command (assuming the mysql user name of root):

```
# mysql -u root -p
Enter password: *******
mysql>
```

To add data to an existing MySQL database, the following procedure describes how to view the available tables and load data into those tables manually. The next section describes how to create a plain-text file containing database data and how to load that file into your database.

1. To make the database you want to use your current database (in this case, allusers), type the following command from the mysql> prompt:

   ```
   mysql> USE allusers;
   Database changed
   ```

2. To see the tables that are associated with the current database, type the following command from the mysql> prompt:

   ```
   mysql> SHOW tables;
   +--------------------+
   ```

```
| Tables_in_allusers |
+--------------------+
| names              |
+--------------------+
1 row in set (0.00 sec)
```

You can see that the only table defined so far for the allusers database is the one called names.

3. To display the format of the names table, type the following command at the mysql> prompt:

```
mysql> DESCRIBE names;
+-----------+-------------+------+-----+---------+-------+
| Field     | Type        | Null | Key | Default | Extra |
+-----------+-------------+------+-----+---------+-------+
| firstname | varchar(20) |      |     |         |       |
| lastname  | varchar(20) |      |     |         |       |
| streetaddr| varchar(30) |      |     |         |       |
| city      | varchar(20) |      |     |         |       |
| state     | varchar(20) |      |     |         |       |
| zipcode   | varchar(10) |      |     |         |       |
+-----------+-------------+------+-----+---------+-------+
```

4. To add data to the new table, you can use the INSERT INTO command from the mysql> prompt. Here is an example of how to add a person's name and address to the new table:

```
mysql> INSERT INTO names
-> VALUES ('Jerry','Wingnut','167 E Street',
-> 'Roy','UT','84103');
```

In this example, the INSERT INTO command identifies the names table. Then it indicates that values for a record in that table include the name Jerry Wingnut at the address 167 E Street, Roy, UT 84103.

5. To check that the data has been properly entered into the new table, type the following command from the mysql> prompt:

```
mysql> SELECT * FROM names;
+-----------+----------+--------------+------+-------+---------+
| firstname | lastname | streetaddr   | city | state | zipcode |
+-----------+----------+--------------+------+-------+---------+
| Jerry     | Wingnut  | 167 E Street | Roy  | UT    | 84103   |
+-----------+----------+--------------+------+-------+---------+
```

The resulting output shows the data you just entered, displayed in the columns you defined for the names table. If you like, you can continue adding data in this way.

Typing each data item individually can be tedious. As an alternative, you can add your data to a plain-text file and load it into your MySQL database, as described in the following section.

Loading data from a file

Using the LOAD DATA command during a mysql session, you can load a file containing database records into your MySQL database. Here are a few things you need to know about creating a data file to be loaded into MySQL.

- You can create the file using any Linux text editor.
- Each record, consisting of all the columns in the table, must be on its own line. (A line feed indicates the start of the next record.)
- Separate each column by a Tab character.
- You can leave a column blank for a particular record by placing a \N in that column.
- Any blank lines you leave in the file result in blank lines in the database table.

In this example, the following text is added into a plain-text file. The text is in a format that can be loaded into the names table created earlier in this chapter. To try it out, type the following text into a file. Make sure that you insert a Tab character between each value.

Chris	Smith	175 Harrison Street	Gig Harbor	WA	98999
John	Jones	18 Talbot Road NW	Coventry	NJ	54889
Howard	Manty	1515 Broadway	New York	NY	10028

When you are done entering the data, save the text to any accessible filename (for example, /tmp/name.txt). Remember the filename so that you can use it later. If you are not already connected to a mysql session, type the following command (assuming mysql is the user name root):

```
# mysql -u root -p
Enter password: ******
mysql>
```

Next, identify the database (allusers in this example) as the current database by typing the following:

```
mysql> USE allusers;
Database changed
```

To actually load the file into the names table in the allusers database, type the following command to load the file (in this case, /tmp/name.txt) from the mysql> prompt.

> **NOTE:** Either enter the full path to the file or have it in the directory where the mysql command starts. In the latter case, you can type the filename without indicating its full path.

```
mysql> LOAD DATA INFILE "/tmp/name.txt" INTO TABLE names;
Query OK, 3 rows affected (0.02 sec)
```

```
Records: 3  Deleted: 0 Skipped: 0 Warnings: 0
```

Type the following at the `mysql>` prompt to make sure that the records have been added correctly:

```
mysql> SELECT * FROM names;
+----------+----------+---------------------+------------+-------+-------+
| firstname| lastname | streetaddr          | city       | state |zipcode|
+----------+----------+---------------------+------------+-------+-------+
| Chris    | Smith    | 175 Harrison Street | Gig Harbor | WA    | 98999 |
| John     | Jones    | 18 Talbot Road NW   | Coventry   | NJ    | 54889 |
| Howard   | Manty    | 1515 Broadway       | New York   | NY    | 10028 |
+----------+----------+---------------------+------------+-------+-------+
```

Understanding MySQL Tables

You have a lot of flexibility when it comes to setting up MySQL tables. To have your MySQL database operate as efficiently as possible, you want to have the columns be assigned to the most appropriate size and data type to hold the data you need to store.

Use the following tables as a reference to the different data types that can be assigned to your columns. Data types available for use in MySQL fall into these categories: numbers, time and date, and character strings. Here are a few things you need to know as you read these tables:

- The maximum display size for a column is 255 characters. An M data type option sets the number of characters that are displayed and, in most cases, stored for the column.

- There can be up to 30 digits following the decimal point for floating-point data types. A D option to a data type indicates the number of digits allowed for a floating-point number following the decimal point. (The value should be no more than two digits less than the value of the display size being used.)

- The UNSIGNED option (shown in braces) indicates that only positive numbers are allowed in the column. This allows the column to hold larger positive numbers.

- The ZEROFILL option (shown in braces) indicates that the data in the column will be padded with zeros. For example, the number 25 in a column with a data type of INTEGER(7) ZEROFILL would appear as 0000025. (Any ZEROFILL column automatically becomes UNSIGNED.)

- All values shown in braces are optional.

- The parentheses shown around the (M) and (D) values are necessary if you enter either of those values. In other words, don't type the braces, but do type the parentheses.

Table 24-2 shows numeric data types that you can use with MYSQL.

Table 24-2: Numeric Data Types for Columns

Data Type	Description	Space Needed
BIGINT[(M)] [UNSIGNED] [ZEROFILL]	Can contain large integers with the following allowable values: -9223372036854775808 to 9223372036854775807 (unsigned) 0 to 18446744073709551615 (signed)	Uses 8 bytes.
DECIMAL[(M[,D])] [ZEROFILL]	Contains an unpacked floating-point number (signed only). Each digit is stored as a single character. When you choose the display value (M), decimal points and minus signs are not counted in that value. The value of (M) is 10 by default. Setting D to zero (which is the default) causes only whole numbers to be used.	Uses M+2 bytes if D is greater than 0. Uses M+1 bytes if D is equal to 0.
DOUBLE[(M,D)] [ZEROFILL]	Contains a double-precision, floating-point number of an average size. Values that are allowed include: -1.7976931348623157E+308 to -2.2250738585072014E-308 0 2.2250738585072014E-308 to 1.7976931348623157E+308.	Uses 8 bytes.
DOUBLE PRECISION	Same as DOUBLE.	Same as DOUBLE.
FLOAT(X) [ZEROFILL]	Contains a floating-point number. For a single-precision floating-point number X can be less than or equal to 24. For a double-precision floating-point number, X can be between 25 and 53. The display size and number of decimals are undefined.	Uses 4 bytes.

Data Type	Description	Space Needed
FLOAT[(M,D)] [ZEROFILL]	Contains a single-precision floating-point number. Values that are allowed include: -3.402823466E+38 to -1.175494351E-38 0 1.175494351E-38 to 3.402823466E+38. If the display value (M) is less than or equal to 24, the number is a single-precision floating-point number.	Uses 4 bytes if X is less than or equal to 24. Uses 8 bytes if X is greater than or equal to 25 and less than or equal to 53.
INT[(M)] [UNSIGNED] [ZEROFILL]	Contains an integer of normal size. The range is -2147483648 to 2147483647 if it's signed and 0 to 4294967295 if unsigned.	Uses 4 bytes.
INTEGER[(M)] [UNSIGNED] [ZEROFILL]	Same as INT.	Same as INT.
MEDIUMINT[(M)] [UNSIGNED] [ZEROFILL]	Contains an integer of medium size. The range is -8388608 to 8388607 if it's signed and 0 to 16777215 if unsigned.	Uses 3 bytes.
NUMERIC(M,D) [ZEROFILL]	Same as DECIMAL.	Same as DECIMAL.
REAL	Same as DOUBLE.	Same as DOUBLE.
SMALLINT[(M)] [UNSIGNED] [ZEROFILL]	Contains an integer of small size. The range is -32768 to 32767 if it's signed and 0 to 65535 if it's unsigned.	Uses 2 bytes.
TINYINT[(M)] [UNSIGNED] [ZEROFILL]	A very small integer, with a signed range of -128 to 127 and a 0 to 255 unsigned range.	Uses 1 byte.

The default format of dates in MySQL is YYYY-MM-DD, which stands for the year, month, and day. Any improperly formatted date or time values will be converted to zeros. Table 24-3 shows time and date data types that you can use with MYSQL.

Table 24-3: Time/Date Data Types for Columns

Data Type	Description	Space Needed
DATE	Contains a date between the range of January 1, 1000 (1000-01-01) and December 31, 9999 (9999-12-31).	Uses 3 bytes.
DATETIME	Contains a combination of date and time between zero hour of January 1, 1000 (1000-01-01 00:00:00) and the last second of December 31, 9999 (9999-12-31 23:59:59).	Uses 8 bytes.
TIMESTAMP[(M)]	Contains a timestamp from between zero hour of January 1, 1970 (1970-01-01 00:00:00) and a time in the year 2037. It is stored in the form: YYYYMMDDHHMMSS. Using (M), you can reduce the size of the TIMESTAMP displayed to less than the full 14 characters (though the full 4-byte TIMESTAMP is still stored).	Uses 4 bytes.
TIME	Contains a time between -838:59:59 and 838:59:59. The format of the field is in hours, minutes, and seconds (HH:MM:SS).	Uses 3 bytes.
YEAR[(2|4)]	Contains a year, represented by either two or four digits. For a four-digit year, YEAR mean 1901–2155 (0000 is also allowed). For a two-digit year, the digits 70-69 can .represent 1970-2069	Uses 1 byte.

Table 24-4 shows string data types that you can use with MYSQL.

Table 24-4: String Data Types for Columns

Data Type	Description	Space Needed
BLOB	Contains a binary large object (BLOB) that varies in size, based on the actual value of the data, rather than on the maximum allowable size. Searches on a BLOB column are case-sensitive.	Uses up to L+2 bytes, where L is less than or equal to 65535.

Data Type	Description	Space Needed
[NATIONAL] CHAR(M) [BINARY]	Contains a character string of fixed length, with spaces padded to the right to meet the length. To display the value, the spaces are deleted. The value of (M) determines the number of characters (from 1 to 255). If the BINARY keyword is used, sorting of values is case-sensitive (it is case-insensitive by default). The NATIONAL keyword indicates that the default CHARACTER set should be used.	Uses between 1 and 255 bytes, based on the value of (M).
ENUM('val1','val2',...)	Contains enumerated strings that are typically chosen from a list of values indicated when you create the column. For example, you set a column definition to ENUM("dog","cat","mouse"). Then, if you set the value of that column to "1" the value displayed would be "dog", "2" would be "cat" and "3" would be mouse. It lets you take a number as input and have a string as output. Up to 65535 values are allowed.	Uses either 1 byte (for up to about 255 values) or 2 bytes, (for up to 65535 values).
LONGBLOB	Contains a binary large object (BLOB) that varies in size, based on the actual value of the data, rather than on the maximum allowable size. LONGBLOB allows larger values than MEDIUMBLOB. Searches on a LONGBLOB column are case-sensitive.	Uses up to L+4 bytes, where L is less than or equal to 4294967295.
LONGTEXT	Same as LONGBLOB, except that searching is done on these columns in case-insensitive style.	Uses up to L+4 bytes, where L is less than or equal to 4294967295.
MEDIUMBLOB	Contains a binary large object (BLOB) that varies in size, based on the actual value of the data, rather than on the maximum allowable size. MEDIUMBLOB allows larger values than BLOB. Searches on a MEDIUMBLOB column are case-sensitive.	Uses up to L+3 bytes, where L is less than or equal to 16777215.

Data Type	Description	Space Needed
MEDIUMTEXT	Same as MEDIUMBLOB, except that searching is done on these columns in case-insensitive style.	Uses up to L+3 bytes, where L is less than or equal to 16777215.
SET('val1','val2',...)	Contains a set of values. A SET column can display zero or more values from the list of values contained in the SET column definition. Up to 64 members are allowed.	Uses 1, 2, 3, 4 or 8 bytes, varying based on how many of the up to 64 set members are used.
TEXT	Same as BLOB, except that searching is done on these columns in case-insensitive style.	Uses up to L+2 bytes, where L is less than or equal to 65535.
TINYBLOB	Contains a binary large object (BLOB) that varies in size, based on the actual value of the data, rather than on the maximum allowable size. TINYBLOB allows smaller values than BLOB. Searches on a TINYBLOB column are case-sensitive.	Uses up to L+1 bytes, where L is less than or equal to 255.
TINYTEXT	Same as TINYBLOB, except that searching is done on these columns in case-insensitive style.	Uses up to L+1 bytes, where L is less than or equal to 255.
[NATIONAL] VARCHAR(M) [BINARY]	Contains a character string of variable length, with no padded spaces added. The value of (M) determines the number of characters (from 1 to 255). If the BINARY keyword is used, sorting of values is case-sensitive (it is case-insensitive by default). The NATIONAL keyword indicates that the default CHARACTER set should be used.	Uses L+1 bytes, where L is less than or equal to M and M is from 1 to 255 characters.

Displaying MySQL Databases

There are many different ways of sorting and displaying database records during a mysql session. If you are not already connected to a mysql session, type the following command (assuming the mysql user name of root):

```
# mysql -u root -p
Enter password: *******
mysql>
```

When you are in your `mysql` session (and have chosen a database), you can display all or selected table records, choose which columns are displayed, or choose how records are sorted.

Displaying all or selected records

Assuming that the current database is `allusers` (as shown in the previous examples), type the following command to choose (SELECT) all records (*) from the `names` table and display them in the order in which they were entered into the database.

```
mysql> SELECT * FROM names;
+-----------+----------+--------------------+-------------+--------+---------+
| firstname |lastname  |streetaddr          | city        | state  | zipcode |
+-----------+----------+--------------------+-------------+--------+---------+
| Chris     |Smith     |175 Harrison Street | Gig Harbor  | WA     | 98999   |
| John      |Jones     |18 Talbot Road NW   | Coventry    | NJ     | 54889   |
| Howard    |Manty     |1515 Broadway       | New York    | NY     | 10028   |
+-----------+----------+--------------------+-------------+--------+---------+
```

The following command displays all records from the `names` table that have the lastname column set to Jones. Instead of using lastname, you could search for a value from any column name used in the table.

```
mysql> SELECT * FROM names WHERE lastname = "Jones";
+-----------+----------+--------------------+-------------+--------+---------+
| firstname |lastname  |streetaddr          | city        | state  | zipcode |
+-----------+----------+--------------------+-------------+--------+---------+
| John      |Jones     |18 Talbot Road NW   | Coventry    | NJ     | 54889   |
+-----------+----------+--------------------+-------------+--------+---------+
```

Using the OR operator, you can select records that match several different values. In the following command, records that have either Chris or Howard as the firstname are matched and displayed.

```
mysql> SELECT * FROM names WHERE firstname = "Chris" OR firstname = "Howard";
+-----------+----------+--------------------+-------------+--------+---------+
| firstname | lastname | streetaddr         | city        | state  | zipcode |
+-----------+----------+--------------------+-------------+--------+---------+
| Chris     | Smith    | 175 Harrison Street| Gig Harbor  | WA     | 98999   |
| Howard    | Manty    | 1515 Broadway      | New York    | NY     | 10028   |
+-----------+----------+--------------------+-------------+--------+---------+
```

To match and display a record based on the value of two columns in a record, you can use the AND operator. In the following command, any record that has Chris as the firstname and Smith as the lastname is matched.

```
mysql> SELECT * FROM names WHERE firstname = "Chris" AND lastname = "Smith";
+-----------+----------+--------------------+-------------+--------+---------+
| firstname | lastname | streetaddr         | city        | state  | zipcode |
+-----------+----------+--------------------+-------------+--------+---------+
```

```
| Chris     | Smith    | 175 Harrison Street | Gig Harbor  | WA     | 98999   |
+-----------+----------+---------------------+-------------+--------+---------+
```

Displaying selected columns

You don't need to display every column of data. Instead of using the asterisk (*) shown in the previous examples to match all columns, you can enter a comma-separated list of column names. The following command displays the firstname, lastname, and zipcode records for all of the records in the names table:

```
mysql> SELECT firstname,lastname,zipcode FROM names;
+-----------+----------+---------+
| firstname | lastname | zipcode |
+-----------+----------+---------+
| Chris     | Smith    | 98999   |
| John      | Jones    | 54889   |
| Howard    | Manty    | 10028   |
+-----------+----------+---------+
```

Likewise, you can sort columns in any order you choose. Type the following command to show the same three columns with the zipcode column displayed first:

```
mysql> SELECT zipcode,firstname,lastname FROM names;
+---------+-----------+----------+
| zipcode | firstname | lastname |
+---------+-----------+----------+
| 98999   | Chris     | Smith    |
| 54889   | John      | Jones    |
| 10028   | Howard    | Manty    |
+---------+-----------+----------+
```

You can also mix column selection with record selection as shown in the following example:

```
mysql> SELECT firstname,lastname,city FROM names WHERE firstname = "Chris";
+-----------+----------+------------+
| firstname | lastname | city       |
+-----------+----------+------------+
| Chris     | Smith    | Gig Harbor |
+-----------+----------+------------+
```

Sorting data

You can sort records based on the values in any column you choose. For example, using the ORDER BY operator, you can display the records based on the lastname column:

```
mysql> SELECT * FROM names ORDER BY lastname;
+-----------+----------+--------------------+------------+--------+---------+
| firstname | lastname | streetaddr         | city       | state  | zipcode |
+-----------+----------+--------------------+------------+--------+---------+
| John      | Jones    | 18 Talbot Road NW  | Coventry   | NJ     | 54889   |
```

```
| Howard   |Manty    |1515 Broadway       | New York    | NY     | 10028   |
| Chris    |Smith    |167 Small Road      | Gig Harbor  | WA     | 98999   |
+----------+---------+--------------------+-------------+--------+---------+
```

To sort records based on city name, you could use the following command:

```
mysql> SELECT * FROM names ORDER BY city;
+----------+---------+--------------------+-------------+--------+---------+
| firstname |lastname |streetaddr         | city        | state  | zipcode|
+----------+---------+--------------------+-------------+--------+---------+
| John     |Jones    |18 Talbot Road NW   | Coventry    | NJ     | 54889   |
| Chris    |Smith    |167 Small Road      | Gig Harbor  | WA     | 98999   |
| Howard   |Manty    |1515 Broadway       | New York    | NY     | 10028   |
+----------+---------+--------------------+-------------+--------+---------+
```

Now that you have entered and displayed the database records, you may find that you need to change some of them. The following section describes how to update database records during a mysql session.

Making Changes to Tables and Records

As you begin to use your MySQL database, you will find that you need to make changes to both the structure and content of the database tables. The following section describes how you can alter the structure of your MySQL tables and change the content of MySQL records. If you are not already connected to a mysql session, type the following command (assuming the mysql user name of root):

```
# mysql -u root -p
Enter password: ******
mysql>
```

To use the examples shown in the following sections, identify the database (allusers in this example) as the current database by typing the following:

```
mysql> USE allusers;
Database changed
```

Altering MySQL tables

After you have created your database tables, there will inevitably be changes you want to make to them. This section describes how to use the ALTER command during a mysql session for the following tasks: adding a column, deleting a column, renaming a column, and changing the data type for a column.

To add a column to the end of your table that displays the current date, type the following:

```
mysql> ALTER TABLE names ADD curdate TIMESTAMP;
```

The previous line tells `mysql` to change the table in the current database called `names` (`ALTER TABLE names`), add a column named `curdate` (`ADD curdate`), and assign the value of that column to display the current date (`TIMESTAMP` data type). If you decide later that you want to remove that column, you can remove it by typing the following:

```
mysql> ALTER TABLE names DROP COLUMN curdate;
```

If you want to change the name of an existing column, you can do so using the `CHANGE` option to `ALTER`. Here is an example:

```
mysql> ALTER TABLE names CHANGE city town varchar(20);
```

In the previous example, the names table is chosen (`ALTER TABLE names`) to change the name of the city column to town (`CHANGE city town`). The data type of the column must be entered as well (`varchar(20)`), even if you are not changing it. In fact, if you just want to change the data type of a column, you would use the same syntax as the previous example but simply repeat the column name twice. Here's an example:

```
mysql> ALTER TABLE names CHANGE zipcode zipcode INTEGER;
```

The previous example changes the data type of the zipcode column from its previous type (`varchar`) to the `INTEGER` type.

Updating and deleting MySQL records

You can select records based on any value you choose and update any values in those records. When you are in your `mysql` session, you can use `UPDATE` to change the values in a selected table. Here is an example:

```
mysql> UPDATE names SET streetaddr = "933 3rd Avenue" WHERE firstname = "Chris";
Query OK, 1 row affected (0.00 sec)
Rows matched: 1 Changed: 1 Warnings: 0
```

The previous example attempts to update the names table (`UPDATE names`). In this example, each record that has the firstname column set to `"Chris"` will have the value of the streetaddr column for that record changed to `"933 3rd Avenue"` instead. Note that the query found one (1) row that matched. That one row matched was also changed, with no error warnings necessary. You can use any combination of values to match records (using `WHERE`) and change column values (using `SET`) that you would like. After you have made a change, it is a good idea to display the results to make sure that the change was made as you expected.

To remove an entire row (that is, one record), you can use the `DELETE` command. For example, if you wanted to delete any row where the value of the firstname column is `"Chris"`, you would type the following:

```
mysql> DELETE FROM names WHERE firstname = "Chris";
Query OK, 1 row affected (0.00 sec)
```

The next time you show the table, there should be no records with the first name Chris.

Adding and Removing User Access

There are several different methods you can use to control user access to your MySQL databases. To begin with, assign a user name and password to every user who accesses your MySQL databases. Then you can use the GRANT and REVOKE commands of mysql to specifically indicate the databases and tables users and host computers can access, as well as the rights they have to those databases and tables.

> **CAUTION:** Database servers are common targets of attacks from crackers. While this chapter gives some direction for granting access to your MySQL server, you need to provide much more stringent protection for the server if you are allowing Internet access. Refer to the General Security Issues section of the MySQL manual (`/usr/share/doc/mysql*/manual.html`) for further information on securing your MySQL server.

Adding users and granting access

Although you have a user account defined to create databases (the root user, in this example), to make a database useful, you might want to allow access to other users as well. The following procedure describes how to grant privileges for your MySQL database to other users.

> **NOTE:** If you are upgrading your MySQL from a version previous to 3.22, run the `mysql_fix_privilege_tables` script. This script adds new GRANT features to your databases. If you don't run the script, you will be denied access to the databases.

In this example, I am adding a user named bobby who can log in to the MySQL server from the localhost. The password for bobby is i8yer2shuz. (Remember that there does not have to be a Fedora user account named bobby. So any user on the localhost with the password for bobby can log in to that MySQL account.)

1. If you are not already connected to a `mysql` session, type the following command (assuming the `mysql` user name of root):

    ```
    # mysql -u root -p
    Enter password: *******
    mysql>
    ```

2. To create the user named `bobby` and a password `i8yer2shuz`, use the GRANT command as follows:

    ```
    mysql> GRANT USAGE ON *.*
        -> TO bobby@localhost IDENTIFIED BY "i8yer2shuz";
    ```

    At this point, someone could log in from the localhost using the name bobby and i8yer2shuz password (`mysql -u bobby -p`). But the user would have no privilege to work with any of the databases. Next you need to grant privileges.

3. To grant bobby privileges to work with the database called `allusers`, type the following:

```
mysql> GRANT DELETE,INSERT,SELECT,UPDATE ON allusers.*
    -> TO bobby@localhost;
```

In this example, the user named bobby is allowed to log in to the MySQL server on the localhost and access all tables from the `allusers` database (`USE allusers`). For that database, bobby can use the `DELETE`, `INSERT`, `SELECT`, and `UPDATE` commands.

4. To see the privileges that you just granted, select mysql as your current database, then select the `db` table as follows:

```
mysql> USE mysql;
Database changed
mysql> SELECT * FROM db WHERE db="allusers";
+---------------+-----------+--------+---------------+-------------+--
---------------+----------------
|Host           |Db         |User    |Select_priv    |Insert_priv
|Update_priv |Delete_priv
+---------------+-----------+--------+---------------+-------------+--
---------------+----------------
|localhost      |allusers   |bobby | Y              | Y            |
Y             | Y
+---------------+-----------+--------+---------------+-------------+--
---------------+----------------
```

The output here shows all users who are specifically granted privileges to the `allusers` database. Only part of the output is shown here because it is very long. You can make a very wide Terminal window to view the output if you don't like reading wrapped text. Other privileges on the line will be set to N (no access).

Revoking access

You can revoke privileges you grant using the `REVOKE` command. To revoke all privileges for a user to a particular database, use the following procedure:

1. If you are not already connected to a `mysql` session, type the following command (assuming the `mysql` user name of root):

```
# mysql -u root -p
Enter password: ******
mysql>
```

2. To revoke all privileges of a user named bobby to use a database named `allusers` on your MySQL server, type the following:

```
mysql> REVOKE ALL PRIVILEGES ON allusers.*
    -> FROM bobby@localhost;
```

At this point, bobby has no privileges to use any of the tables in the `allusers` databases.

3. To see the privileges that you just granted, select `mysql` as your current database, then select the `db` table as follows:

```
mysql> USE mysql;
Database changed
mysql> SELECT * FROM db WHERE db="allusers";
```

The output should show that the user named bobby is no longer listed as having access to the `allusers` database. (The results might just say `Empty set.`)

Checking and Fixing Databases

Over time, databases can become corrupted or store information inefficiently. MySQL comes with commands that you can use to check and repair your databases. The `myisamchk` and `isamchk` commands are available to check MyISAM and ISAM database tables, respectively.

MyISAM tables are used by default with MySQL. The tables are stored in the directory `/var/lib/mysql/`*dbname* by default, where *dbname* is replaced by the name of the database you are using. For each table, there are three files in this directory. Each file begins with the table name and ends with one of the following three suffixes:

.frm   Contains the definition (or form) or the table

.MYI   Contains the table's index.

.MYD   Contains the table's data.

The following procedure describes how to use the `myisamchk` command to check your MyISAM tables. (The procedure is the same for checking ISAM tables, except that you use the `isamchk` command instead.)

> **CAUTION:** Do a backup of your database tables before running a repair with `myisamchk`. Although `myisamchk` is unlikely to damage your data, backups are still a good precaution.

1. Stop MySQL temporarily by typing the following from a Terminal window as root user:

```
# /etc/init.d/mysqld stop
```

2. You can check all or some of your database tables at once. The first example shows how to check a table called `names` in the `allusers` database.

```
# myisamchk /var/lib/mysql/allusers/names.MYI
Checking MyISAM file: /var/lib/mysql/allusers/names.MYI
Data records:        5   Deleted blocks:        0
- check file-size
- check key delete-chain
- check record delete-chain
```

```
- check index reference
- check record links
```

You could also check tables for all your databases at once as follows:

```
# myisamchk /var/lib/mysql/*/*.MYI
```

The preceding example shows a simple, five-record database where no errors were encountered. If instead of the output shown in the previous example, you see output like the following, you may need to repair the database:

```
Checking MyISAM file: names.MYI
Data records:        5   Deleted blocks:        0
- check file-size
myisamchk: warning: Size of datafile is: 89 Should be: 204
- check key delete-chain
- check record delete-chain
- check index reference
- check record links
myisamchk: error: Found wrong record at 0
MyISAM-table 'names.MYI' is corrupted
Fix it using switch "-r" or "-o"
```

3. To fix a corrupted database, you could run the following command:

```
# myisamchk -r /var/lib/mysql/allusers/names.MYI
- recovering (with keycache) MyISAM-table 'names.MYI'
Data records: 5
Found wrong stored record at 0
Data records: 4
```

4. If for some reason the -r options doesn't work, you can try running the myisamchk command with the -o option. This is a slower, older method of repair, but it can handle a few problems that the -r option cannot. Here is an example:

```
# myisamchk -o /var/lib/mysql/allusers/names.MYI
```

If your computer has a lot of memory, you can raise the key buffer size value on the myisamchk command line, which will lessen the time it takes to check the databases. For example, you could use the following command line:

```
myisamchk -r -O --key_buffer_size=64M *.MYI
```

This would set the key buffer size to 64MB.

Summary

MySQL is a structured query language (SQL) server that runs on Fedora Linux, as well as other operating systems. Using a start-up script (/etc/init.d/mysqld) and a configuration file (/etc/my.cnf), you can quickly get a MySQL server up and running.

With tools such as the mysqladmin and mysql commands, you can administer the MySQL server and create databases and tables that are as simple or complex as you need. During mysql sessions, you can modify the structure of your database tables or add, update, and delete database records. You have a variety of options for querying data and sorting the output. You also have a lot of control over who can access your database tables and what privileges users have to modify, add to, or delete from the databases you control.

Chapter 25

Making Servers Public with DNS

In This Chapter

- Determining goals for your server
- Connecting a public server
- Configuring a public server
- Setting up a DNS server

In previous chapters you built Web, mail, and FTP servers in Linux. Now you want to expose those servers to the outside world. Options range from handing them to a hosting company and saying, "Take care of it," to managing the servers yourself out of your own home or office.

The following are some cases where you may want to consider some level of self-hosting:

- You're willing to provide the level of support that your organization needs in its servers.
- You just want an inexpensive way to publish some documents on the Web or maintain a public mail server for a few people, and 24/7 support isn't critical.
- You think self-hosting is cool and you want to try it.

The first goal of this chapter is to help you decide how much server support you want to maintain or provide to someone else. The second goal is to suggest how to set up your own public servers, including possibly configuring your own Domain Name System (DNS) server.

The descriptions of setting up your LAN (see Chapter 15) and connecting it to the Internet (see Chapter 16) focus on how to share information locally and let local users share an outgoing Internet connection, respectively. Building on that information, this chapter explains how to set up a DNS server, as well as other issues that relate to securing and maintaining public servers.

CAUTION: After you open your server to Internet traffic, break-in attempts will occur. Most will come from automated scripts, sent from infected computers on the Internet. Because Red Hat Linux comes with good built-in security features, many attacks bounce off harmlessly (after logging messages). Allowing incoming connections, however, creates vulnerabilities that aren't there with an outgoing-only Internet connection. I recommend you use security tools, described in Chapter 14, to protect your servers.

Determining Goals for Your Server

Before you open up that server sitting in your back office to the Internet, stop for a moment and think about your goals. Here are a few questions that you may want to ask yourself:

- How critical is this server for supporting your business?
- How much traffic do you expect on your server?
- Do you need to support the server 24 hours per day, 365 days per year?
- Do you know enough to maintain and secure your server?
- Can you get the connection speed that you require at a reasonable cost for your location?
- Do you need special equipment to keep the server running, such as an uninterruptible power supply?

What I'm getting at here is that maintaining a public server requires some resources. If the server is critical to your business and in high demand, you may not have the time or expertise to support this server yourself. Also, if no high-speed Internet access is available to your location, even a well-configured server may not have the bandwidth to support your clients.

Using a hosting service

Tons of places are ready and willing to host your Web content. The number gets a bit smaller, however, if you need to find a place that can help you maintain your Red Hat Linux server. In that case, you want to find a company that offers dedicated hosting (that is, gives you control of an entire server) or permits you to co-locate your server on its premises. In either case, you want to make sure that your server:

- Is physically secure.
- Can access enough Internet bandwidth.
- Has someone there if the server goes down.

You can use such a hosting provider in these ways and still use Fedora or Red Hat Linux as your server:

- Co-locate your server at a hosting provider or ISP. In this arrangement, you can get lots of bandwidth and retain your root privileges so that you can still maintain the server yourself. The downside is that the provider probably isn't expected to fix your server if a hardware failure occurs.
- "Rent" a server (at a place such as Rackspace.com), where you get the bandwidth and someone to fix the hardware (which that organization often puts together and maintains) if something goes wrong.

Although this setup probably costs more money, the added support and security may prove well worth it. In either of the preceding cases, where the server resides at the hosting provider, you can also expect that service to include such extras as the use of its DNS service. (In other words, after you register a domain name and sign up with the hosting service, you can probably skip the rest of this chapter.)

Connecting a Public Server

If your organization's Internet service is currently used for outgoing connections, you must consider different security issues if you intend to allow incoming connections. The following are some differences:

- **Outgoing connection** — By providing outgoing Internet access, you need only enable your users to connect to the Internet and gain access to other computers' services. You don't need a domain name, and you don't need your own static IP address. (Chapter 16 describes how to set up a LAN to share an Internet service used primarily for outgoing service.) The focus of your network is on outgoing requests for services.

- **Incoming connection** — If you're setting up a public server, you want people from the Internet to find you and access services that you offer. The focus is on incoming requests for your computer's services, which means that you probably want a public host/domain name for the server and one or more static, public IP addresses for the server.

You have many different ways to connect your Fedora or Red Hat Linux server to the Internet and offer its services to the public. In the following sections, I describe what you need to get your server up and running on the Internet.

Choosing an ISP

Although every ISP expects to see outgoing traffic on your Internet connection, not all of them expect incoming traffic (that is, traffic that someone initiates from outside your network). So although your ISP — which may be your local phone company, your cable TV company, or an independent ISP — may expect you to download files from remote servers, it may not expect people to download large files from you.

Assuming that you're going to house the server in your place of work or residence, you need to obtain the following information from a potential ISP:

- Does its Terms of Service agreement enable you to offer services over its connection?
- Does it have static IP addresses that it's willing to assign to you?
- Does it provide connections robust enough to handle the traffic demands on your server?

Checking Terms of Service

Any ISP that handles more than a few users has a document that describes what you can do with the Internet connection that it provides you. That document probably carries a name such as "Terms of Service" or "User Agreement." If you can't find it on the ISP's Web site, you will almost certainly see it after you click a link to sign up for an account.

Typically, an ISP requires you to sign up for a business account if you want to do any kind of business on your Internet service. Here are some excerpts from agreements for several ISPs:

". . .you are not permitted to use your Internet connection to sell or advertise goods or services. This is permitted only to those who have purchased a business account or a virtual server."

"Dialup clients are not to use their dialup connection for active or constantly connected Web/FTP/mail or other server services."

"Anyone wanting to promote a business or sell a product must use a business account."

Internet access is the volume business for most ISPs, and they consider business accounts for those who want to manage their own Web presence as premium services. So although you can technically use a personal account to set up a server (TCP/IP doesn't care what goes across the wire), the ISP's Terms of Service or Acceptable Use Policy may not permit you to do so. Although your DSL connection may easily handle a handful of hits a day on your Web server, offering that service can result in the termination of your account by the ISP. Check into what the ISP considers acceptable use before you use any Internet account to set up a public server.

Getting static IP addresses

Most dialup and DSL Internet-access accounts use dynamic IP addresses. So whenever you connect to your Internet service, the provider assigns the IP address to that connection. After you disconnect, the ISP can reclaim that IP address to assign to someone else. The next time you connect, you're likely to get a different IP address.

For a server to have constant, reliable presence on the Internet, it will typically have one or more *static IP addresses*. Most ISPs charge an additional fee for static IP addresses. Each static IP address typically costs between $5 and $20 per month.

> **NOTE:** You can assign a public DNS host name to a server without a static IP address using Dynamic DNS. Dynamic DNS adds software to your server that alerts the provider if its IP address changes. You can find a good description of how Dynamic DNS works at www.webwatchmen.com/how.html.

The number of static IP addresses that you need varies, depending on how you configure your servers. Most likely, you want at least two static IP addresses, one for each of two DNS servers (if you're configuring DNS). In a small organization, those same servers may also offer your Web server, mail server, and other services as well. In general, you want one static IP address for each computer that you make publicly accessible to the Internet.

> **TIP:** You can do some tricks with services such as port forwarding (iptables in Chapter 14) and virtual hosting (Apache Web server in Chapter 21) that enable multiple physical computers to offer services or give the appearance of having multiple computers on a single static IP address. These tricks can reduce the number of IP addresses you need to buy. (To simplify the discussion here, however, I'm assuming that each public server has its own static, public IP address.)

Choosing a connection speed

Another difficulty with keeping your servers in your own home or business is choosing how fast an Internet connection you need. Although most data centers at ISPs offer more than enough bandwidth for your needs, high-speed Internet connections may not be available to your location — or may prove prohibitively expensive.

Although it's technically possible, using a dialup connection (up to 56 Kbps) to support an Internet server is generally considered unacceptable. "Always-on" connection services that you may want to consider include the following:

- **Digital Subscriber Line (DSL)** — DSL service is becoming widely available these days. Using only the standard telephone wiring in your home, you can maintain an always-on Internet connection and telephone service on the same wires. Speeds of between 256 Kbps and 7 Mbps are available with DSL service (although the actual speeds that you attain are typically slower than those in the advertisements).

- **Integrated Services Digital Network (ISDN)** — ISDN has been around longer than DSL to offer high-speed network services, and it's comparable to DSL in the speeds that it can offer. However, ISDN is typically more expensive to implement than DSL at comparable speeds.

- **Frame relay** — This service is a packet-switching protocol that runs across wide-area networks. Although it can prove much more expensive than either DSL or ISDN, it can achieve much higher rates of speed. Speeds can range from 56 Kbps to 1.544 Mbps, or even as much as 45 Mbps. Frame relay can operate across a variety of network media. A primary advantage is that it uses virtual circuits that offer a fixed rate of speed, because the circuit between you and the ISP isn't shared with other ISP customers.

If your business can afford it, you might want dedicated T-1 or T-3 lines for your business. A *T-1 connection* can operate at data rates of 1.444 Mbps. A *T-3 line* can support rates of 43 Mbps. Check with your local ISPs for available connection types and pricing.

Getting a domain name

Domain names are available from dozens of different domain registrars these days. You can check the availability of domain names from any of these registrar's Web sites, such as GoDaddy (`godaddy.com`) or Network Solutions (`networksolutions.com`). Or you can use the `whois` command that comes with Red Hat Linux.

The *top-level domain* (TLD) in which you register your own domain should reflect the type of business or organization that you represent. Commercial businesses typically use the `.com` TLD. Newer TLDs, however, such as `.biz` and `.info`, are now available for domains that represent a business community or for information about businesses and individuals. A new `.ws` domain is also available for domains dedicated to Web sites.

Other common TLDs are .net (for network services companies) and .org (for organizations). Institutions of higher education in the United States use the .edu TLD. A TLD that has recently become available for public use is the .us TLD, for organizations within the United States. Countries outside of the U.S. each already have their own TLD.

Checking domain name availability

With an active Internet connection, you can use the whois command in Red Hat Linux to check if a domain name is available in the .com, .net, .org, or .edu domains. Following is an example of using whois to check the availability of the domain handsonhistory.com:

```
$ whois handsonhistory.com
[Querying whois.internic.net]
  .
            .
            .

Registrant:
Hands-On-History (HANDSONHISTORY-DOM)
   PO Box 943
   Port Angeles, NJ 98221
   US

   Domain Name: HANDSONHISTORY.COM
       .
       .
       .

   Technical Contact:
       Support  (SU1012-ORG)   domains@XMISSION.COM
       Xmission Domain (XDS)
       51 East 400 South, Suite #200
       Salt Lake City , UT 84111
       US
       801-539-0852

   Record expires on 17-May-2012.
   Record created on 25-Sep-1998.
   Database last updated on 13-Apr-2004 01:21:40 EST.

   Domain servers in listed order:

   NS.XMISSION.COM              198.60.22.2
   NS1.XMISSION.COM             198.60.22.22
```

If the name were available, you'd see the message No match for HANDSONHISTORY.COM. Because the name isn't available, you can see information about the domain name registrar, name servers containing address records for the domain, and a variety of contact information.

Reserving a domain name

At one point, Network Solutions was the only company from which you could get a domain name in the most popular U.S. domains (`.com`, `.net`, and `.org`). Now, there are new TLDs and dozens of domain registrars from which you can select a domain name.

You can have your ISP obtain your domain name for you, or you can go to one of the domain registrars yourself and register online to get your domain name.

> **NOTE:** Because prices and services can vary so widely, I recommend that you shop around for a domain registrar. The Internet Corporation for Assigned Names and Numbers (ICANN) maintains a list of accredited registrars at `www.icann.org/registrars/accredited-list.html`. The list contains links to registrar sites and a list of the TLDs that they support.

Although each registrar offers different domain and hosting-related services, the following list describes the information that you want to collect before you register your domain (and if you don't have all this information at the moment, don't worry — you can go back and fill in most of it later):

- **Domain name** — If you haven't already chosen a domain name by using the `whois` command, each registrar offers a search tool at its Web site that enables you to check the availability of any name that interests you.

- **Term of registration** — You must decide how many years of use you want to pay for on the domain name. You can typically pay in one-year increments, with the cost per year usually less the more years for which you reserve the name. Before the domain name expires, you can reregister it.

- **Contact information** — Provide the name, e-mail address, street address, company name, and phone numbers for the person in charge of the domain-name registration (probably you). You fill in separate sets of information for the registrant, technical contact, administrative contact, and billing contact.

> **NOTE:** If you don't fill in the other contact information, the registrar uses the registrant contact information for each of those categories. If someone else is managing your server, you are the registrant and the hosting company provides a technical contact.

- **Hosting options** — If you're providing your own hosting in Fedora or Red Hat Linux, you want to decline the Web-hosting service offer that you're given as you register the domain. Along with hosting, the registrar is likely to offer you other hosting options (such as support for ASP pages and FrontPage extensions). It may also offer you e-mail service.

- **Domain Name System Servers** — The registrar asks you to supply the primary DNS server and one or more secondary DNS servers. If your ISP is providing your DNS service, you can add that information now. If you're getting set up on DNS later, you can usually "park" the domain at the domain registrar and then come back after you obtain DNS to identify the DNS servers with the registrar.

To pay for the domain name, the service expects you to provide a credit card number. Some registrars accept other forms of payment, although credit cards are the most popular means.

Configuring Your Public Server

With a domain name, a suitable Internet connection, and one or more static IP addresses, you need to prepare your server to share it on the Internet. In addition to choosing the types of services you want to offer, you must be more thoughtful about the security of your servers.

Configuring networking

Whether you're configuring your computer for browsing the Web or offering up a server, procedures for creating network interfaces are very similar. See Chapters 15 and 16 for information on configuring TCP/IP for your computer. Following is a quick review of what you need to do to get a live connection to the Internet that's suitable for your server:

- **Add network interfaces** — Depending on what type of network connection you have, you must configure TCP/IP to work across that connection. Most likely, that connection requires that you configure an Ethernet, PPP, or ISDN interface. If you didn't already configure the connection when you installed Red Hat Linux, you can do so at any time by using the Red Hat Network Configuration window (via the `neat` command).

> **NOTE:** One major difference between configuring a server for connection to the Internet and a computer that you use primarily for Internet access is in how you set your IP address. You quite likely got the IP address for your Internet connection by using DHCP. Now you will probably enter the IP address that you got from your ISP as a static IP address.

- **Add DNS server information** — Although the server IP addresses that you enter for DNS servers are probably ones that your ISP configured, you may want to add your own DNS servers. If so, make sure that your server points to your master and slave DNS servers for IP address resolution. You can also have the other computers on your LAN point to your DNS servers to resolve domain names to IP addresses. (The `/etc/resolv.conf` file is where you identify your DNS servers.) After you add your own DNS server, all your clients should change their `/etc/resolv.conf` files to include the new domain name and DNS server information.

- **Add host name** — As soon as you have a real domain name, you can name your computer within the structure of that domain name. If you haven't installed Fedora or Red Hat Linux, you can enter this host name during installation. For example, to add a host called `duck` at `handsonhistory.com`, you'd enter `duck.handsonhistory.com` as you install Red Hat. Later, you can change the name in the `/etc/sysconfig/network` file.

> **NOTE:** Changing your host name after you install Red Hat Linux can sometimes cause problems. Services such as printing and the X server (for your graphical desktop) sometimes fail after you change your host name. Check to make sure that printing and other network services are still working after you change your host name. Sometimes restarting the network interface can solve the problem.

After you set up your network interfaces and related information for your server, test the Internet connection by using the `ping` command, as I describe in Chapter 16. Next, if DNS is already configured for your domain, try to `ping` your server by name to see whether those in the outside world can reach you by name. Make sure that the static IP address that appears in response matches the static IP address that you were assigned.

Configuring servers

Some services are more appropriate for public exposure than others. You probably don't want to offer your print server, for example, to anyone on the Internet. Similarly, file sharing with Samba or NFS isn't appropriate to share publicly across the Internet.

If you're creating your first public server, you may want to consider setting up at least the following basic types of servers:

- **Web server** — This type of server, of course, provides the most common way to publish text, images, and a variety of other content to the Internet. Refer to Chapter 21 for information on configuring an Apache Web server.

- **FTP server** — This type of server provides the most common way of sharing directories of documents, images, application programs, and other content that users can download from your site. See Chapter 20 for information on setting up an FTP server.

- **Mail server** — Presumably, if you have a domain name that you like and a Linux server up and running, you may very well want to get a mail server running too. That way, you can create one or more e-mail addresses that look like `chris@linuxtoys.net`. See Chapter 19 for information on configuring a mail server.

Of course, you can share any type of server that you choose. Web, FTP, and mail servers, however, are designed for sharing publicly. The basic configuration for these types of servers isn't that difficult. Securing and monitoring these — or any — public servers, however, requires special effort, as the following sections describe.

Managing security

Before you set up your Red Hat Linux system as a server, you can use it simply to make outgoing connections to the Internet. You can use your firewall (iptables) to close off the ports on your interface to the Internet (making your computer quite secure). Now, however, you need to open some of the ports on that interface to accept incoming requests. With more ports open, you must also become more consistent in monitoring those ports.

Opening your firewall

Making your server public doesn't mean leaving your computer wide open. By using firewall rules, you can set your computer to allow outsiders to open connections to certain ports and block requests on other ports. Assuming that you set up your firewall to block incoming connections, here's a list of services (and the associated port numbers) that you may want to consider accepting through your firewall from your external interface to the Internet:

- Web server — Port 80
- Mail server — Port 25
- FTP server — Port 21
- DNS server — Port 53 (if you're supporting your own DNS)
- SSH server — Port 22 (allows secure login service to administer the computer remotely or remote users to add Web content or other server content to the server)

To see which ports are assigned to which services by default, refer to the /etc/services file. In most cases, a configuration file for a service indicates the default port number the service listens on. One way of making a service more private is to change the port number that a service listens on. Then the user must know to ask for the service at that particular port.

Chapter 14 describes how to change your firewall to accept requests for these services. I start with the iptables example in that chapter when I create the DNS example later in this chapter. You can use that description as a model for setting up a firewall to go with DNS. In the DNS example, you have separate computers for mail, FTP, and Web services. For a low-volume server, however, you can have them all on the same computer.

Checking logs and system files

By making your servers public, you also make them more open to attacks. Although firewalls are a good first line of defense, you still need to watch the activity on those ports that you leave open. A consistent program of monitoring traffic and checking changes to your server, therefore, becomes more critical. The following are a few techniques that you can use to help secure your servers:

- **General security** — Make sure that you protect all your user accounts by using good passwords and the correct file permissions settings.
- **Tripwire** — Use tripwire to take a snapshot of your critical system files so that you can check later whether anyone's altered those files.
- **Logcheck** — Use logcheck to screen log files and e-mail suspicious messages to you.

I describe these and other security techniques in Chapter 14.

Keeping up with updates

You can expect to find and correct security breaches continuously. You must keep up with software updates that are published to plug security holes. Although some of these updates address theoretical security problems, others are created in response to real break-ins or denial-of-service attacks that are known to exploit weaknesses in the components that come with your operating system.

For Red Hat Enterprise Linux systems, using the Red Hat Network (and its up2date facility) is the best way of getting security updates on a timely basis that are tailored for Red Hat Linux. For Fedora Linux, you can use up2date or yum to download and install updates from Fedora mirror sites that carry those updates (see Chapter 5 for information on using yum). You should also check CERT and other organizations (which I describe in Chapter 14) for security alerts.

After your server is secure and correctly configured, your last step is to start the server on the Internet with a domain name that points to it. Either ask your service provider to configure DNS for you, or set up your own DNS server, as I describe in the following section.

Setting Up a Domain Name System Server

The *Domain Name System* (*DNS*) is essentially a distributed database that translates host names into IP addresses (and IP addresses back to host names). That database also contains information related to each domain, such as how the domain is organized into zones, where to route mail for that domain, and who to contact with questions associated with the domain.

By setting up a DNS server, you become part of a hierarchy of DNS servers that make up the Internet. At the top of this hierarchy is the root server, represented by a dot (.). Below the root server are the Top Level Domains, or TLDs (such as .com, .org, and so on). Domains that individual organizations own and maintain lie below the TLDs. That's where you come in.

As someone who's setting up a DNS server, you're responsible for managing the host names and IP addresses for the computers in the domain (or domains) for which you're responsible. Keeping your DNS information correct means that people can access the services that you want to share, and the Internet as a whole works that much better as a result.

Besides using your DNS server to help people from the Internet find the public servers in your domain, you can also use DNS to provide name and IP address mapping for computers on your private network. The example in the "DNS name server example" section later in this chapter describes how to configure both private and public name and IP address records for a domain.

> **CAUTION:** Setting up a DNS server can be a complex and (these days) potentially dangerous undertaking. A compromised DNS server can cause requests for host addresses to be directed to a cracker's server. The sample DNS server in this section is one created as an example of a DNS server for a home or small office environment. For information on the many different ways to set up a DNS server, go to the BIND 9 Administrator Reference manualat `/usr/share/doc/bind-9.2.3/arm/Bv9ARM.html`.

Understanding DNS

The basic function of a *name server* is to answer queries by providing the information that those queries request. A DNS name server primarily translates domain and host names into IP addresses. Each domain is typically represented by at least two DNS servers.

- **Primary (master) name server** — This name server contains authoritative information about the domains that it serves. In response to queries for information about its domains, this server provides that information marked as being authoritative. The primary is the ultimate source for data about the domain. The secondary name server only carries the same authority in that it has received and loaded a complete set of domain information from the primary.

- **Secondary (slave) name server** — This name server gets all information for the domain from the primary name server. As is the case for the primary server, DNS considers the secondary's information about the domain that it serves authoritative. (You set secondary servers in the NS RR records for the zone in the `named.conf` file on the primary.)

NS records in the parent zone for a domain list the primary and one or more secondary name servers. This *delegation* of servers defines the servers that have authority for the zone.

Because zone records change as you add, remove, or reconfigure the computers in the zone, you assign expiration times for information about your zone. You set the expiration time in the time to live (TTL) field, in the `named.conf` file (which I describe later).

Other specialized types of DNS servers are possible as well. Although these types of servers don't have authority for any zones, they can prove useful for special purposes:

- **Caching name server** — This type of server simply caches the information it receives about the locations of hosts and domains. It holds information that it obtains from other authoritative servers and reuses that information until the information expires (as set by the TTL fields).

- **Forwarding name server** — Creating a server that's not authoritative for a zone but that can forward name server requests to other name servers may prove efficient. This server is essentially a caching name server, but is useful in cases where computers lie behind a firewall and in which only one computer can make DNS queries outside that firewall on behalf of all the internal computers.

Understanding authoritative zones

As an administrator of a DNS server, you need to configure several zones. Each zone represents part of the DNS namespace as you view it from your DNS server. Besides the one or more zones representing your domain, you have a zone that identifies your local host and possibly your local, private LAN.

If you configure a server as authoritative for a zone, that server has the last word on resolving addresses for that zone. Your master name server is authoritative for the domain you learned how to configure in the "DNS name server example" section but not for domains outside your domain.

Remember that the DNS server that you configure is the ultimate authority for your zone. Other zones don't know how you configure your host names and IP addresses unless you properly set up your DNS server to distribute that information across the Internet.

The definitive data that you set up for your domain exists in the form of *resource records*. Resource records consist of the data associated with all names below the authoritative point in the tree structure. When the DNS server uses these records to reply to queries, it sets the *authoritative answer* (*AA*) bit in the packet that includes the reply. The AA bit indicates that your name server has the best and most current information available about your domain.

Understanding BIND

In Fedora, Red Hat Linux, and most other Linux and UNIX systems, you implement DNS services by using the *Berkeley Internet Name Domain* (*BIND*) software. The Internet Software Consortium maintains BIND (at `www.isc.org/products/BIND`). The particular version of BIND that I describe in this chapter is BIND 9.

The basic components of BIND include the following:

- **DNS server daemon** (`/usr/sbin/named`) — The `named` daemon listens on a port (port number 53 by default) for DNS service requests and then fulfills those requests based on information in the configuration files that you create. Mostly, `named` receives requests to resolve the host names in your domain to IP addresses.

> **NOTE:** The `named` daemon actually launches from the `/etc/init.d/named` startup script. You need to set that script to start automatically after your DNS server is ready to go. You can also use the `named` startup script to check the status of the `named` daemon.

- **DNS configuration files** (`named.conf` and `/var/named/*`) — The `/etc/named.conf` file is where you add most of the general configuration information that you need to define the DNS services for your domain. Separate files in the `/var/named` directory contain specific zone information.

- **DNS lookup tools** — You can use several tools to check that your DNS server is resolving host names properly. These include commands such as `host`, `dig`, and `nslookup` (which are part of the bind-utils software package).

To maintain your DNS server correctly, you can also perform the following configuration tasks with your DNS server:

- **Logging** — You can indicate what you want to log and where log files reside.
- **Remote server options** — You can set options for specific DNS servers to perform such tasks as blocking information from a bad server, setting encryption keys to use with a server, or defining transfer methods.

You don't need to give out DNS information to everyone who requests it. You can restrict access to those who request it based on the following:

- **Access control list (acl)** — This list can contain those hosts, domains, or IP addresses that you want to group together and apply the same level of access to your DNS server. You create acl records to group those addresses, then indicate what domain information the locations in that acl can or can't access.
- **Listen-on ports** — By default, your name server accepts only name server requests that come to port 53 on your name server. You can add more port numbers if you want your name server to accept name service queries on different ports.
- **Authentication** — To verify the identities of hosts that are requesting services from your DNS server, you can use keys for authentication and authorization. (The `key` and `trusted-keys` statements are used for authentication.)

> **CROSS-REFERENCE:** You should already know what domain names and IP addresses are. Refer to Chapters 15, for IP addresses, and 16, for DNS information, if you need to refresh your memory.

DNS name server example

To get an idea of what you need to set up your DNS server, the following sections step you through an example of a DNS server for a domain called *yourdomain.com*. In the example, you're creating a DNS server for a small office network that includes the following:

- A private, local network that resides behind a firewall.
- A server providing DNS service and acting as a firewall between the LAN and the Internet.

In this office, other computers on the LAN are using the same Internet connection for outgoing communications. So the firewall on the server does network address translation (NAT) to enable the client computers to use the firewall as a router to the Internet. Figure 25-1 shows the configuration of the example *yourdomain.com* domain.

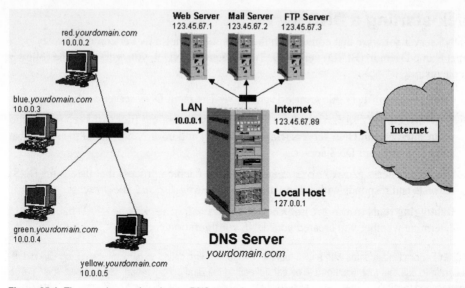

Figure 25-1: The sample *yourdomain.com* DNS server has a combination of public servers and private client computers.

Figure 25-1 illustrates a small office network that's sharing a single Internet connection. The DNS, Web, mail, and FTP servers all have public IP addresses. (These addresses are fictitious, so please don't try to use them.) Behind the DNS server (which is also operating as a firewall) are four client computers that have private IP addresses. (You can reuse these addresses and other private addresses that I describe in Chapter 15.)

The job of the DNS server, in this configuration, is to map the names of the public servers (www.`yourdomain.com`, mail.`yourdomain.com`, ftp.`yourdomain.com`, and ns1.`yourdomain.com`) into the static IP addresses that the ISP assigns (`123.45.67.1` through `123.45.67.4`). The DNS server also provides DNS service from the private addresses on the LAN, so each computer can reach the others on the LAN without needing to store all computer names in their own /etc/hosts file.

A key feature to this example is that it divides the view of this domain between what the outside world can see and what the computers on the private network can see. Using the view feature of BIND, I create an *outside* view that lets queries from the Internet find only public servers (Web, Mail, and FTP) in the domain. Then I create an *inside* view that lets queries from the local LAN find both the public servers and private computers (red, blue, green and yellow) in the domain.

The sections that follow describe how to set up a DNS server for the example in Figure 25-1.

Quick-starting a DNS server

The DNS server software that comes with the current Fedora Linux version is Berkeley Internet Name Daemon (BIND) version 9. To configure BIND 9, you work with the following components:

- **Configuration file** (`/etc/named.conf`) — The main DNS server configuration file.
- **Zone directory** (`/var/named`) — The directory containing files that keep information about Internet root DNS servers (`named.ca` file) and information about the zones that you create for your DNS server.
- **Daemon process** (`/usr/sbin/named`) — The daemon process that listens for DNS requests and responds with information that the `named.conf` file presents.
- **Debugging tools** (`named-checkconf`, and `named-checkzone`) — What you use to determine whether you created your DNS configuration correctly.

> **NOTE:** Fedora Linux comes with a GUI tool for configuring Bind called `system-config-bind`. If you decide to use that tool, you need to be careful editing the Bind configuration files by hand. It is recommended that if there are changes you want to make to the `named.conf` file that are not supported by the `system-config-bind` window, you should put those changes in the `/etc/named.custom` file instead.

BIND 9 also includes tools for creating DNSSEC secured zones. By using these tools, you can create and generate keys to provide authentication and secure address resolution. The example illustrated in these sections doesn't include DNSSEC configuration.

The basic steps in creating a DNS server for your example are as follows:

- Identifying your DNS servers
- Creating DNS Configuration files (`named.conf` and `/var/names/*`)
- Starting the named daemon
- Monitoring named activities

In the example configuration, you set up a primary master DNS server and a slave DNS server. The primary server holds the authoritative records for the domain. The secondary server is there to share requests for information about the domain, particularly in case the primary goes down.

Identifying your DNS servers

If you didn't have your DNS servers set up at the time that you purchased your domain name with a registration authority, you might have just "parked" the domain name there until you configured your DNS servers. Whenever you're ready to set up your DNS servers, return to that registration authority and provide the following information about your DNS servers:

- DNS server IP addresses (the static IP addresses of your DNS servers, probably primary and slave)

- DNS server host names (often `ns1.yourdomain.com`, where you replace *yourdomain.com* with your domain name for the primary; the slave host name is `ns2.yourdomain.com`)

You should register both the primary and slave DNS servers. After you update this record, that information typically takes a day or two to propagate throughout the Internet. Once your DNS servers are registered, you also need to tell the registration authority to use those DNS servers as the authority for addresses in your domain. The registration authority probably offers an online form you can fill out to identify your DNS servers.

Creating DNS configuration files (named.conf and /var/names/*)

In configuring a DNS server, you're actually creating definitions that apply to a particular *zone* in the public DNS tree, as well as several local zones that apply to your computer and local network. To create a useful DNS server for your example small-office environment, you have the following zones:

- **Public DNS server zone** — The DNS server is authoritative for the domain that you're serving. This zone serves the names and IP addresses for your public servers. In the example `named.conf` file shown in the next section, you need to replace the name *yourdomain.com* with the domain that you're creating. These records become accessible to everyone on the Internet.

- **Private DNS server zone** — So each computer on the private network doesn't need to know the IP addresses for other computers on your private network, a zone is added in the example `named.conf` file to let the DNS server resolve these addresses. The names and IP addresses (which are private) are available only to computers on your LAN.

Note that by creating different views of these zones, different information will be returned to queries, depending on where the queries come from. For example, when someone from the Internet requests the address of the DNS server (`ns1.yourdomain.com`), they will get the address 123.45.67.89. However, when a query for `ns1.yourdomain.com` comes from inside the LAN, the address 10.0.0.1 is returned. Also, any queries from the Internet for addresses of private computers (`red.yourdomain.com`, `blue.yourdomain.com`, and so on) are rejected.

Editing /etc/named.conf

To begin, you configure the `/etc/named.conf` file on the primary master DNS server representing your example *yourdomain*.com domain. This example starts from the `/etc/named.conf` file that comes with the caching-nameserver package in Fedora Linux. (Make sure that you install the caching-nameserver and bind packages before you continue.) Following are a few tips relating to editing the `named.conf` file:

- If a statement contains substatements, make sure that you end the last substatement with a semicolon.
- Comments can appear in the same formats that popular programming languages use. These languages include C (begin with /* and end with */), C++ (begin with // and go to the end of the physical line), and shell or Perl styles (begin from a # and go to the end of the physical line).
- A leading exclamation mark (!) negates an element. Putting !123.45.67.89 in a statement causes the IP address 123.45.67.89 not to match the element. (Just make sure that the negation occurs before a positive match or the positive match takes precedence.)

The edited version of the /etc/named.conf file is as follows:

```
options {
 directory "/var/named";
};

acl "mylan" {
    127/8; 10.0.0.0/24;
};

view "inside" {
    match-clients { "mylan"; };
    recursion yes;

    zone "." IN {
    type hint;
    file "named.ca";
    };

    zone "0.0.10.in-addr.arpa" IN {
    type master;
    file "yourlan.db";
    };

    zone "yourdomain.com" {
    type master;
    file "db.yourdomain.com.inside";
    allow-transfer { 10.0.0.2; };
      };
};

view "outside" {
    match-clients { any; };
    recursion no;

    zone "." IN {
    type hint;
    file "named.ca";
```

```
    };

    zone "yourdomain.com" {
    type master;
    file "db.yourdomain.com.outside";
    allow-transfer { 123.45.67.2; };
      };
};

include "/etc/rndc.key";
```

The `options` definition lies at the beginning of the `/etc/named.conf` file and identifies the `/var/named` directory as the location where the zone files reside. The `acl` lines define the `mylan` access-control list, which consists of host computers on the 10.0.0.0 local private network and the localhost (127/8). (You use this definition in the `0.0.10.in-addr.arpa` zone to enable only users on the LAN to perform reverse lookups of names of computers on the LAN.)

The DNS server is broken up into two views: inside and outside. The `inside` view defines how IP addresses are resolved for requests that come from the private LAN and localhost (as defined in `mylan`). By having recursion on (`recursion yes`), the `named` daemon will allow name server queries from any computer on the LAN. The `outside` view defines how queries coming from all other places (presumably, the Internet) are handled. With recursion off (`recursion no`), only queries from other name servers are honored. (Turning recursion off can help eliminate a common attack, where a cracker causes your server to seek information from a DNS server controlled by the cracker.)

Each zone entry in the `/etc/named.conf` file describes the type of server this computer is for the zone (master in all cases here, except the root zone), the database file (in `/var/named`) that contains records for the zone, and other options relating to the zone records. The `named.ca` file is set up for you by default. It identifies the locations of the Internet root servers.

I made the other zones (`yourlan.db`, `db.yourdomain.com.inside`, `db.yourdomain.com.outside` and `0.0.10.in-addr.arpa`) for this example. For the "inside" view, the `yourlan.db` file lets the computers on your LAN do reverse address lookups (getting the names for IP address queries). The `db.yourdomain.com.inside` file contains names and addresses for all computers in your domain (including those on the local LAN). The DNS slave server for the inside view of this domain is at 10.0.0.2. (Clients in your LAN would use 10.0.0.1 and 10.0.0.2 as DNS servers in /etc/resolv.conf.)

For the "outside" view, the `db.yourdomain.com.outside` file contains names and IP addresses for any computers in your domain you want to make public (computers on your private LAN are excluded). The DNS slave server for the outside view of this domain is 123.45.67.2.

Notice that each zone points to a zone file in the `/var/named` directory. Table 25-1 shows which file in the `/var/named` directory each zone points to.

Table 25-1: Zones and Related Zone Files in DNS Example

Zone	Zone File (in /var/named directory)
. (a single dot representing Internet root servers)	`named.ca`
0.0.10.in-addr.arpa	`yourlan.db`
yourdomain.com (inside view)	`db.yourdomain.com.inside`
yourdomain.com (outside view)	`db.yourdomain.com.outside`

Be very careful editing the `/etc/named.conf` file. Forgetting a semicolon is all too easy, resulting in the entire file not loading. To ensure that the `/etc/named.conf` file doesn't contain any syntax errors, you can run the following command (as root user):

```
# named-checkconf
```

If a syntax error is present, a message identifies the problematic line and informs you what seems to be wrong with it. If the syntax is correct, continue to create the zone files in the `/var/named` directory.

Setting up the zone files

The `/var/named` directory contains the zone files that the `/etc/named.conf` file names. For the example, you need to create only three zone files from scratch. You can (and should) leave the `named.ca` file alone.

The zone files are where most of the real work of the domain name server occurs. In the example, the `db.yourdomain.com.inside` file contains the basic records for the *yourdomain*.com domain, including all private names and addresses. The following is an example of that file:

```
$TTL       86400
@          IN        SOA        yourdomain.com. hostmaster.yourdomain.com.
(
                                            2003040701   ; Serial
                                            28800        ; Refresh
                                            14400        ; Retry
                                            3600000      ; Expire
                                            86400 )      ; Minimum
; Name servers
           IN        NS         ns1.yourdomain.com.
           IN        NS         ns2.yourdomain.com.

; Mail server for domain
```

```
                  IN    MX   10      mail.yourdomain.com.

; Public servers
ns1               IN    A            10.0.0.1
ns2               IN    A            10.0.0.2
mail              IN    A            123.45.67.2
www               IN    A            123.45.67.3
ftp               IN    A            123.45.67.4

; Private clients on the LAN
red               IN    A            10.0.0.2
blue              IN    A            10.0.0.3
green             IN    A            10.0.0.4
yellow            IN    A            10.0.0.5

; EOF
```

The zone file for your "inside" yourdomain.com contains resource records that include information about the zone. Your DNS server uses the TTL (time-to-live) record to tell name servers that store the information that you provide for this domain how long they can keep the information before they need to throw it out and get fresh information. The first value is the default for the entire zone, and the time is in seconds. So a value of 86,400 seconds indicates that a client that is using the information should obtain fresh records about this domain every 24 hours.

The SOA line identifies the start of authority for the domain. The at (@) sign represents the yourdomain.com. name. The dot (.) must appear at the end of the domain name. The dot represents the root server of the Internet. If you leave the dot off, your DNS server appends the domain name, so the DNS server will use the name yourdomain.com.yourdomain.com. The hostmaster.yourdomain.com string indicates the e-mail address of the person who is to receive e-mail regarding the domain. (The first dot changes to an @ sign, resulting in hostmaster@yourdomain.com). Other information regarding the SOA record is as follows:

- **Serial** — Start with any number here. If the zone records change, increase the serial number to alert other servers that they need to get fresh data about your domain.

> **CAUTION:** If you forget to increase the serial number after changing zone records, other servers that cache this data never pick up your changes. To help remember, use the date in the serial number. The number 2004042701 would be for April 27, 2004. The 01 represents the first change made on that day.

- **Refresh** — Defines how often the slave DNS server for the zone checks for changes. (Here, 28,800 seconds represents 8 hours.)

- **Retry** — If the slave can't reach the master, it tries again after this retry interval. (Here, 14,400 seconds represents 4 hours.)

- **Expire** — If the slave can't contact the master within the expire time (here, 3,600,000 seconds, or 1,000 hours), the slave discards the data.

- **Minimum** — Defines the cache time to live for negative answers. (Here, it's 86,400 seconds, or 24 hours.)

The name server (NS) records define the name servers that represent this zone. In this case, NS records define hosts with the names ns1 and ns2 in *yourdomain.com*. The MX record indicates the location of the mail server for the domain, so that the DNS server can direct e-mail to users in *yourdomain.com*. The rest of the file defines IP addresses for the private clients and public servers that are associated with the domain. Notice that the server at address 10.0.0.2 serves as a client on the LAN and a slave DNS server.

For the "outside" *yourdomain.com* zone we made a db.*yourdomain.com*.outside file using the same information from the "inside" file, with the following exceptions:

- Removed all references to private clients on the LAN. That way, someone poking around from the Internet can't get information about your private computers.

- Changed the addresses of the primary and slave DNS servers (ns1 and ns2) to 123.45.67.1 and 123.45.67.2, respectively. In that way, only public addresses for name servers are seen by the public.

The other new file in the example is the yourlan.db file, which contains the information necessary to perform reverse IP lookups for the computers on your LAN. Here's an example:

```
$TTL     86400
@        IN      SOA      0.0.0.10.in-addr.arpa. hostmaster.yourdomain.com. (
                                   2004042701  ; Serial
                                   28800       ; Refresh
                                   14400       ; Retry
                                   3600000     ; Expire
                                   86400 )     ; Minimum
         IN      NS       0.0.0.10.in-addr.arpa.
1        IN      PTR      yourdomain.com.
2        IN      PTR      red.yourdomain.com.
3        IN      PTR      blue.yourdomain.com.
4        IN      PTR      green.yourdomain.com.
5        IN      PTR      yellow.yourdomain.com.

; EOF
```

The SOA record identifies 0.0.0.10.in-addr.arpa. as the start of authority for the zone. The NS line defines 0.0.0.10.in-addr.arpa. as the name server for the zone. Other records are pointers to host names that reverse-map on the 10.0.0. network. The records represent the address for the DNS server (*yourdomain.com*) and each of the clients on the LAN (red, blue, green, and yellow).

After you finish creating your own zone files, you can use the named-checkzone command to make sure that each zone file is correctly formed. Here is how you'd run the named-checkzone command (as root user) to check the two *yourdomain.com* zone files:

```
# named-checkzone yourdomain.com /var/named/db.yourdomain.com.inside
zone yourdomain.com/IN: loaded serial 2004042701
OK
# named-checkzone yourdomain.com /var/named/db.yourdomain.com.outside
zone yourdomain.com/IN: loaded serial 2004042701
OK
```

The output indicates that both files are okay and that named-checkzone command is able to load the new serial numbers. In this case, the serial number represents the first serial number (01) on April 27, 2004 (2004042701).

Starting the named (DNS) daemon

To start the named daemon and see whether it's working, type the following (as root user):

```
# /etc/init.d/named start
```

If the named daemon starts successfully, clients of your DNS server should start getting information about your domain. To set the named daemon to start each time that the system boots up, type the following:

```
# chkconfig named on
```

Remember that, whenever you make changes to the named.conf or any of the zone files, you must increase the serial number for anyone checking your domain records to pick up those changes. After that, you should restart the named service too (as root user) as follows:

```
# /etc/init.d/named restart
```

If you see the Starting named message, your DNS server is probably up and running. If you want to make sure that your server is correctly resolving addresses, the following section describes some tools that you can use to check your DNS name server.

Checking that DNS is working

The best way to verify whether your DNS server is working correctly is to watch it in action. Here are a few commands you can use to check out your DNS server. The first example uses the host command to get the IP address for the host computer named blue in the local domain:

```
# host blue
blue.yourdomain.com has address 10.0.0.3
```

Instead of using the simple host name to get the computer's IP address, you can enter an IP address (instead of the name) or a fully qualified host name. In the following example, the dig command is used with a domain name to get information about the addresses for a domain:

```
# dig yourdomain.com
; <<>> DiG 9.2.1 <<>> yourdomain.com
;; global options:  printcmd
;; Got answer:
;; ->>HEADER<<- opcode: QUERY, status: NOERROR, id: 43728
;; flags: qr aa rd ra; QUERY: 1, ANSWER: 1, AUTHORITY: 2, ADDITIONAL: 0

;; QUESTION SECTION:
;yourdomain.com.                    IN      A

;; AUTHORITY SECTION:
yourdomain.com.            604800 IN       NS      ns1.yourdomain.com.
yourdomain.com.            604800 IN       NS      ns2.yourdomain.com.

;; Query time: 24 msec
;; SERVER: 10.0.0.1#53(10.0.0.1)
;; WHEN: Mon Apr   5  02:12:32 2004
;; MSG SIZE  rcvd: 129
```

Sections in the output from dig include a question section and an authority section. The results show name server assignments and addresses associated with the domain you're querying about. The nslookup command is another tool you can use to look up domain information. In the following example, nslookup looks up the server that is resolving ftp.*yourdomain.com*:

```
# nslookup -sil ftp.yourdomain.com
Server:        123.45.67.1
Address:       123.45.67.1#53

Name:    ftp.yourdomain.com
Address: 123.45.67.3
```

The output from the nslookup command includes the name of the computer fulfilling the request and its IP address, along with the name and address of the computer you're asking for. (The -sil option prevents a message that nslookup might soon be removed from Fedora Linux.) Try nslookup with an IP address (such as 10.0.0.1) to make sure reverse lookup works.

To check the status of the named server that is running on your local system, use the same script that starts named. Type the following to check the status of your DNS server daemon:

```
# /etc/init.d/named status
number of zones: 5
debug level: 0
xfers running: 0
xfers deferred: 0
soa queries in progress: 0
query logging is OFF
server is up and running
```

If you can't reach the computers that your DNS server is serving by name or IP address, you should make sure that each client's address records are correct. You can also try to `ping` each client and server computer using the full host name or IP address.

Getting More Information about BIND

For details on many other BIND options that I don't describe in this chapter, you can refer to several places, as the following list relates:

- **/usr/share/doc/bind-*/arm** — Contains HTML and XML versions of the BIND 9 Administrator Reference Manual.

- **Man pages** — Type the `man` command, following it by `named` or `named.conf`. These man pages contain terse descriptions of options and variables that relate to the `named` daemon and `named.conf` file, respectively.

- **Internet Software Consortium** (`www.isc.org/products/BIND`) — The ISC Web site contains information and downloads related to BIND. On this site, find links to BIND mailing lists, security advisories relating to BIND, and BIND history.

Summary

The choice to connect your Fedora or Red Hat Linux server to the Internet isn't one to make lightly. If the server is critical to your business and support for the server is too much for you to handle, you should consider handing your server over to a hosting provider.

If you do decide to expose your Fedora or Red Hat Linux server to the Internet to offer Web, FTP, mail, or other types of services, you should carefully consider the security implications and prepare for them. By using Linux features that I describe in other parts of this book, you can create firewalls, monitor log files, and track changes to system files to protect your computers.

One way of controlling the public exposure of your servers is to obtain a domain name and configure your own Domain Name System (DNS) server. You can set up your DNS server to resolve host names to IP addresses for clients that request the information from the Internet, as well as to the users on your local, private LAN.

Chapter 26

Using Linux Servers from a Mac

In This Chapter

- Inside Mac OS X
- Using Mac OS X network services
- Accessing Samba servers
- Accessing AppleTalk (netatalk) servers
- Configuring an AppleTalk (netatalk) server in Linux

In the old days (like, a couple of years ago), you had to make Linux look like a file and printer server on an AppleTalk network in order to use a Linux server from an Apple Mac. While that is still true with an older Mac (OS 8 or 9), if you have a new iMac with OS X the whole world changes. That's because Mac OS X is a lot like Linux on the inside.

This chapter is for people who have (or want to have) Macs on their desktops and Linux as their servers. It covers a variety of server types that you can set up in Linux, then access from a Mac OS 8, OS 9, or OS X operating system. In particular:

- **For Mac desktop users** — The chapter describes how users can access shared resources from their Linux servers.
- **For system administrators** — The chapter explains how to set up an AppleTalk server in Linux using the netatalk software package. (Chapters 17 through 25 describe how to configure other types of native Linux servers that you can access from your Mac computers.)

I wrote this chapter in response to several readers of earlier editions of this book who wanted to replace their Windows servers with Linux servers. I hope this chapter will help start them, and you, on the road to taking full advantage of powerful networked Linux features from your easy-to-use Mac desktops.

Looking Inside Mac OS X

Inside new Apple computers is an operating system referred to as *Mac OS X*. You might also hear Mac OS X referred to as *Jaguar* (OS X 10.2.*x*) or *Panther* (OS X 10.3.*x*). Like Linux, OS X has a free UNIX-like operating system at its core that, in this case, has been turned into a commercial product. That core, instead of being a Linux kernel, is based on an open source project called Darwin (`www.opendarwin.org`).

Although Mac OS X and Linux are very different on the surface, there are many striking similarities. If you open a Terminal (shell) window on your Mac, you'll find that you can use many of the same basic commands that you can use from Linux. In addition, many of the same open source projects are included in both operating systems. These include:

- Samba (Windows file/printer server)
- Apache (Web server)
- CUPS (Linux print service)
- Sendmail (mail transport agent)
- BIND (DNS server)

- There are also a few differences:Fedora is primarily covered under the General Public License, while OS X is based partly on an Open Source license and partly on a proprietary license. In August, 2003, APSL 2.0 was released (`www.opensource.apple.com/apsl`) and is now certified as a Free Software License from the Free Software Foundation.

- Fedora uses the Linux kernel; Mac OS X is based on the FreeBSD kernel.

- Most Linux configuration is done using system-config windows, which often create text-based configuration files (mostly in the `/etc` directory) from command-line or GUI applications; Mac OS X stores the configuration file in its own NetInfo database, which is manipulated primarily by GUI tools as well as by the `niutil` command.

- Fedora requires root permission for many administrative operations; OS X discourages overuse of the root login and encourages user accounts that are granted administrative privileges.

For the examples in this chapter, I used an iMac running Mac OS X 10.2.6. Because there were big improvements made between 10.1 and 10.2, I recommend that you upgrade your software if you are using the former. To see what version is installed on your Mac, open the Apple System Profiler from your Mac computer.

Using Network Services from Mac OS X

You can easily connect your Mac OS X computer to your LAN by configuring the Network window. If Fedora is configured as a DHCP server (see Chapter 23), your Mac OS X client can detect that. Or, you can configure your LAN interfaces manually, as follows:

1. From the Dock bar, click System Preferences and select Network. This opens the Network window, which enables you to configure your network interfaces (see Figure 26-1).

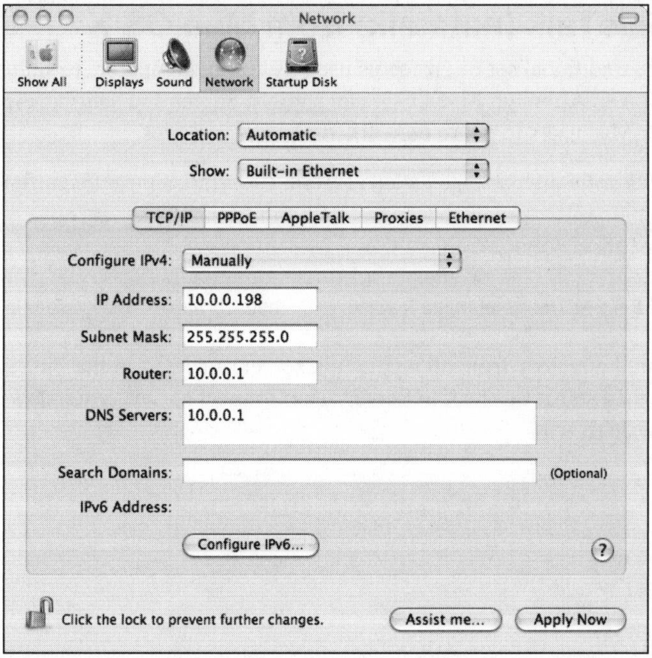

Figure 26-1: Configure your Mac OS X network interface to connect to Linux servers.

2. If you are connecting to your Linux servers from a LAN, click the Show field and select Built-in Ethernet.

3. Click the TCP/IP tab. Then select either DHCP or Manually in the Configure Ipv4 field. If you select Manually, you can add the IP address of your computer, its netmask, the location of the router, the location of the DNS servers, and the domains to search. (For a home or small business, you might have a single Linux server serving as your router and DNS server. In this example, 10.0.0.1 is serving both of those functions.)

4. Click the AppleTalk tab. If you have configured your Linux server as an AppleTalk file and printer server (using netatalk), select the check box to turn on AppleTalk network protocols.

5. Click the Proxies tab. If you need to use a proxy server to access the Internet or other wide area network, use this tab to identify the proxies you are using.

The latest iMac computers have built-in Ethernet jacks that you can use to plug into your network hub. Plug your iMac into your LAN hub and you should be ready to use your Linux servers from Mac OS X.

Using AppleTalk (netatalk) from Mac OS X

AppleTalk is the traditional set of protocols used by Apple computers to share files and printers over a LAN. Although Mac OS X can support Samba file sharing, AppleTalk is still a familiar way for Mac users to get to networked printers and files.

Inside Fedora is a software package called netatalk that you can use to configure Fedora as an AppleTalk file and printer server. To a Mac client, the netatalk server looks no different than any other AppleTalk server.

CROSS-REFERENCE: Refer to the "Setting up the netatalk server" section later in this chapter.

To access a shared directory from an AppleTalk server, click Go in the Finder bar at the top of the screen, and then select Connect to Server. The Connect to Server window appears, as shown in Figure 26-2.

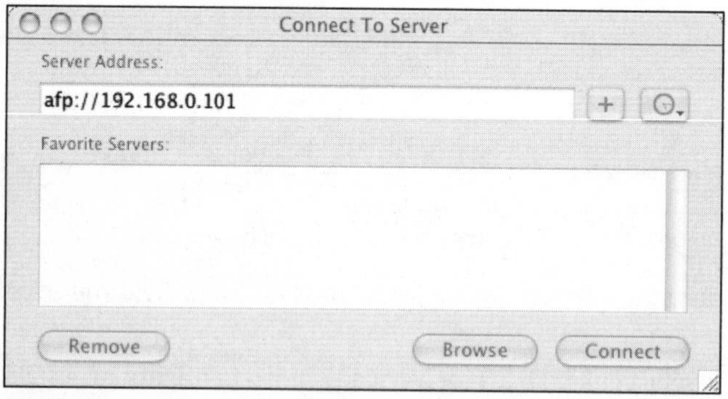

Figure 26-2: In Mac OS X, see Samba and AppleTalk shares from the Connect to Server window.

Enter the address, as shown in Figure 26-2, or click the Browse button to see a list of available servers.

After you click Connect, a pop-up window appears, prompting for a user name and password. Use the Options window to set up your preferences for logging on to the server. You can have the password added to your keychain so you don't have to type it in each time you access the server. You can also select to send the password in clear text (which is the default) and be warned that you are doing that. The server determines whether you need to enter a clear-text or encrypted password. You can also request a secure connection over SSH for your login (which is a good idea to prevent someone from sniffing out your password from the network).

Figure 26-3 shows the Options window for selecting password options as just described.

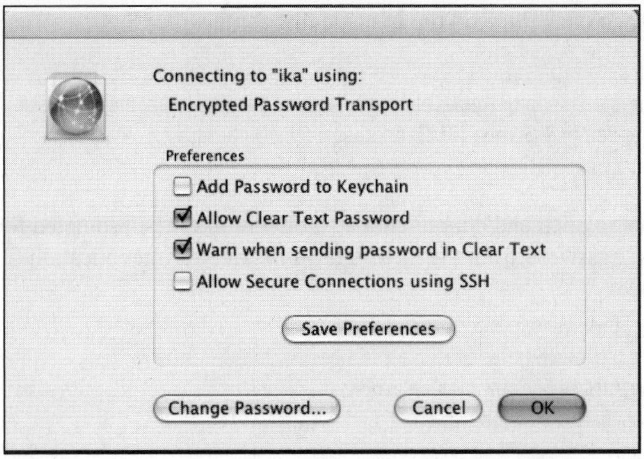

Figure 26-3: Select authentication options when you connect to your AppleTalk (netatalk) server.

After the user name and password are accepted, an icon representing the AppleTalk share appears on your desktop. Double-click to open the shared directory. You can change the contents of that directory in any way that your login will allow.

Using AppleTalk from Mac OS 8 or OS 9

Prior to Mac OS X, Mac clients accessed AppleTalk shares from the Chooser window. The procedure for accessing a netatalk (or other AppleTalk) server went something like this:

1. Click the Apple menu and select Chooser. The Chooser window appears.

2. Click AppleShare. The file servers available on the local network appear in the Select a File Server window.

3. Click the file server you want to access and click OK. You are prompted for a user name and password (or just presented with a guest login).

4. Add the requested information and click OK. An icon representing the server appears on the desktop.

At this point, you can open the icon representing the shared directories and begin using the files and subfolders contained within.

Using Windows and Linux servers (Samba)

The procedure for accessing Samba servers from your Mac OS X system is similar to the AppleTalk procedure. As with the AppleTalk procedure, you open the Go menu from the Finder bar and select Connect to Server. From the Connect to Server window, do the following:

1. Click the Browse button, then click the workgroup name that contains the Samba server that you want.

> **TIP:** If you're not sure if the server is a Samba or AppleTalk server, look at the address at the bottom of the window after you click the server name. A Samba (SMB) address begins with `smb:/`, while an AppleTalk server begins with `afp:/`.

2. Choose the server you want to open and double-click it. You will likely be prompted for your Samba user name and password from the SMB/CIFS Filesystem Authentication window (see Figure 26-4).

Figure 26-4: After requesting a Samba share, you must authenticate to the server.

3. Type the user name and password (and optionally, you can click the Add to Keychain box). The keychain lets you store your user name and password, so you don't have to type it again the next time you access this Samba share. An icon representing the Samba share should appear on your desktop.

If the Samba server doesn't appear on the Connect to Server window, you can type the name or IP address of the server, followed by the share name you want in the address box on the bottom of the window. Here's an example of an address for accessing a Samba share from the Connect to Server window:

```
smb://192.168.0.3/toyprojects
```

In this example, smb tells Mac OS X that it is looking for a Samba share. The Samba server in this example is located at IP address 192.168.0.3 (you could have used a NetBIOS name instead of an IP address here as well). The name of the share is `toyprojects`. You could also add the workgroup and user name to the command line. Here's an example that asks for a share named `toyprojects` on a server named `toys`, in the `ESTREET` workgroup, as the user named `chris`:

```
smb://ESTREET;chris@toys/toyprojects
```

Here are a few things you should know about accessing Samba shares from Mac OS X:

- When authenticating your password (see Figure 26-4), Mac OS X sends your password in clear text. Unlike when authenticating an AppleTalk share, there is no way to select to send encrypted passwords from this window.

- The example of setting up Linux Samba shares in Chapter 18 shows how to set up Samba to ask for encrypted passwords (and therefore will fail authentication from Mac OS X). To get around the problem (on a secure network), you can create a share that either accepts clear-text passwords or have the share be available to guest users.

> **NOTE:** To configure a particular Samba share to work from a Mac OS X client, you can edit the `/etc/samba/smb.conf` file (as root user). In a shared directory definition, add the line `guest ok = yes` (to allow guest users access to the share) or `encrypt passwords = no` to accept clear-text passwords.

Sharing X applications

Most UNIX-like computer systems rely on the *X Window System* (also referred to as *X11* or simply *X*) to display graphically based windows over a network. Sharing applications over the network with X requires little more than having X running and making it accessible to displays that are directed to your display (see Chapter 3 for information on launching X applications).

Although the default graphical interface for Mac OS X is a facility called Aqua, there is now an X11 for Mac OS X available for Mac users. The latest version of Mac OS X, nicknamed *Panther*, includes a native X installation. You must choose a Custom install or upgrade when you install Panther to get the X packages on your system. For further information on the state of the X Window System in Mac OS X, or to download your own copy of X11 for Mac OS X, go to `www.apple.com/macosx/features/x11`.

With X11 installed and running on your Mac OS X, you can launch X applications from your Linux system and have them appear on your Mac OS X desktop.

Configuring an AppleTalk Server in Linux

If you have a mixture of older Macs (such as a Power Macintosh with Mac OS 8.1) and newer Macs (such as an iMac with Mac OS X) on the same LAN, an AppleTalk server could be the best way to share files and printers among them. With the netatalk package installed on your Fedora server, netatalk can be configured to act as that AppleTalk server.

Using netatalk, you can allow multiple Mac clients to use the following features from a computer running Fedora:

- **AppleShare file server** — Files and directories you share from your AppleTalk server (via netatalk) are stored with features and permissions that a Mac user would expect.

- **AppleTalk printer server** — Printers configured on your Linux server can be shared as though they were AppleTalk printers.
- **AppleTalk router** — Your Linux system can act as a router between multiple AppleTalk networks.

The netatalk project site is located at `http://netatalk.sourceforge.net`. There, you can find documentation (including an FAQ), as well as links to helpful netatalk Web sites.

To use netatalk in its most basic configuration, all you need to do is:

- Create a LAN connecting your Linux netatalk server and Mac client computers. (You can configure netatalk as a router to connect multiple LANs.)
- Start netatalk as described in the "Starting netatalk" section. This enables any users with user logins to your Linux computer to access their home directories from a Mac (using Linux logins and passwords). You can also add printers and other directories to share.

Before you fire up netatalk, however, I recommend that you check out the following section.

Before you start using netatalk

Know that when you are creating an AppleTalk server on a Linux file system, you are creating a hybrid-type file system. Strange issues can arise because the two types of servers handle ownership, access, and file attributes (such as what applications launch a file) differently.

On the netatalk shared directory structure (referred to as a *volume* or *share*), special directories exist to hold attributes (file type and creator), trash, temporary items, and find content. If you change files or directories on AppleTalk volumes from Linux without taking special precautions, you'll delete a file and leave its attributes around or create a file that has no attributes (so a Mac doesn't know how to launch it). You can't even move a whole directory structure from one Linux partition to another without losing the connection between the files and their attributes.

Here are a few tips to think about before you start using netatalk:

- Use Mac clients to create, move, and copy files on the Mac volume whenever possible. This is the best way to keep your volumes clean and working properly.
- If you must move netatalk files and folders from a Linux shell, use the `apple_mv`, `apple_cp`, and `apple_rm` commands (described later in this chapter).
- You can share the same volumes with both your Mac clients (using netatalk) and Windows clients (using Samba), but this involves certain risks and caveats as well. See the "Sharing files with netatalk and Samba" section later in this chapter for ways to avoid trouble.
- Mac users expect permission on files and directories to be more open than many Linux administrators are comfortable with. Check the "Securing netatalk volumes" section for information on the best ways to securely provide the necessary access.

- Tools for tracking down network services and troubleshooting problems for AppleTalk networks are different than those used for pure TCP/IP networks. Refer to the "Troubleshooting netatalk" section for information on the tools you can use for tracking down network problems.

Setting up the netatalk server

The following steps provide a high-level overview of how to set up your netatalk server. (The sections that follow contain details on how to do these steps.)

1. **Start netatalk** — Like most Linux network services, netatalk can be set to start automatically from a start-up script, in this case `/etc/init.d/atalk`. (You can do some limited file sharing with the default configuration, as described in the next section.)

2. **Configure general settings (`/etc/atalk/netatalk.conf` file)** — Use the `netatalk.conf` file to add your own general netatalk server settings. The default settings for the general netatalk configuration are:

   - **Clients** — Up to 20 Mac clients can connect to your server at a time.

   - **AppleTalk host name** — Your computer's host name (type **hostname -s** to see it) is used as your computer's AppleTalk server host name.

   - **Authentication** — Netatalk will allow users to connect using a guest login (*nobody* user) with no password, a clear-text password, or an encrypted password (Diffie-Hellman style authentication).

   - **Guest user** — A guest user can connect without entering a password and access shared volumes that are open to the world. This guest user is assigned to the Linux *nobody* user name. (By default, no guest shares are set up.)

   - **Daemon processes** — Netatalk starts daemon processes to manage your AppleTalk network interface (`atalkd` daemon), start the AppleTalk print sharing service (`papd` daemon), and start the AppleTalk filing protocol (`afpd` daemon) for sharing volumes.

3. **Configure server settings (`/etc/atalk/afpd.conf` file)** — Configuring `afpd.conf` lets you set up specific settings for your netatalk server (you can even have multiple, virtual servers configured that each look different to the outside world). The contents of the `afpd.conf` file affect how the AppleTalk filing protocol daemon (`afpd`) shares its volumes with Mac clients.

4. **Set up users** — The netatalk server can rely on the Linux users you add to the computer (using clear-text passwords), then limit access to your shared volumes based on those permissions. Or, you can configure netatalk to use encrypted passwords to validate users.

5. **Share volumes (`/etc/atalk/AppleVolumes.default` file)** — When netatalk starts, each user with a valid Linux login to your computer can, by default, access his or her own home directory as an AppleTalk share from a Mac client. You can (and probably

will) have more shared volumes by configuring them in the `AppleVolumes.default` file.

6. **Securing shared volumes** — Netatalk can take advantage of Linux security features to protect shared volumes. You can secure volumes at the host, user, and file and directory level.

7. **Share printers (`/etc/atalk/papd.conf` file)** — Netatalk can share any printer you have connected to Linux (or otherwise configured locally) by adding a definition to the `papd.conf` file. No printers are shared until you add them.

As you work with your shared volumes and printers, you will find that maintenance issues arise from time to time. In particular, you should refer to the following sections: "File- and directory-level security" (for dealing with hidden attribute files and directories), "Sharing files with netatalk and Samba" (to share the same directories from netatalk and Samba), and "Troubleshooting netatalk" (for general troubleshooting tips).

Starting netatalk

Start up netatalk as you would most Linux network services: from a start-up script. The netatalk script is called `atalk` (`/etc/init.d/atalk`). To turn it on, type the following as root user:

```
# chkconfig atalk on
```

The previous command causes netatalk to start the next time you reboot. To start it now, type:

```
# service atalk start
```

Here's what happens when you start the AppleTalk service:

- The AppleTalk daemon (`atalkd`) starts from the contents of the `/etc/atalk/atalkd.conf` file.

- The `papd` daemon registers print services using the contents of the `/etc/atalk/papd.conf` file.

- The `afpd` daemon registers volumes from the contents of the `/etc/atalk/AppleVolumes.default` file (using settings from the `AppleVolumes.system` file).

To check that the netatalk service started properly, as root user type the following from any Linux system on the network (the output may take a minute or two to appear):

```
# nbplkup
toys:AFPServer             65280.115:128
toys:netatalk              65280.115:4
toys:Workstation           65280.115:4
```

To check if your netatalk server is available from a Mac client, go to the Mac client and perform the appropriate procedure:

- **For a pre–Mac OS X client** — Click the Apple Chooser. From the Chooser window, click AppleShare. The netatalk server should appear in the Select a file server pane. Click on it and click OK, then use any valid user login and password from Linux to open that user's home directory.

- **For a Mac OS X client** — From the Finder bar, click Go, then Connect to server. Type the URL of the netatalk shared directory. For example, for the home directory on the computer named `toys` for the user named `chris`, you could type the following:

```
afp://toys/chris
```

If you can't find and open the netatalk server from your Mac, see the "Troubleshooting netatalk" section in this chapter for some suggestions.

Defining general AppleTalk server settings

Settings in the `/etc/atalk/netatalk.conf` file define information related to the general operation of your netatalk server. Step 2 of "Setting up the netatalk server" describes the default settings in this file. The following code lines illustrate a few things you might want to change (as root user).

```
AFPD_MAX_CLIENTS=100
```

Instead of limiting the number of Mac clients who can simultaneously use your netatalk server to 20, you can use any number you like (I used 100 in the previous example). To change the zone and server name, you could change the following settings:

```
ATALK_ZONE=GSTREET
ATALK_NAME="History 101"
```

This example sets the zone name to `GSTREET` and the server name to `History 101`. To change how authentication is performed, you could use one of the following two `AFPD_UAMLIST` examples:

```
AFPD_UAMLIST="-U uams_guest.so"
AFPD_UAMLIST="-U uams_clrtxt.so"
```

The first example makes netatalk a guest-only server. The second line allows only valid users from the Linux system using clear-text passwords. The following line enables you to change the guest user account:

```
AFPD_GUEST=nobody
```

You could change `nobody` to any valid user account on Linux, and that account will be used as your guest user. Other settings in the `netatalk.conf` file let you set which daemons run.

Defining specific AppleTalk servers settings

Your netatalk server can appear as multiple file servers, each with different attributes. You can set up these "virtual" servers in the /etc/atalk/afpd.conf file. Within each file server entry, you name the server, and then assign a variety of options to set how it is accessed. A few examples of how to do this are shown as comments in the afpd.conf file itself:

```
"Guest Volume" -uamlist uams_guest.so -loginmesg "Welcome guest!"
"User Volume" -uamlist uams_clrtxt.so -port 12000
```

The "Guest Volume" example causes a "Welcome guest!" message to appear when a user logs into the server. Because it is a guest server (uams_guest.so), no password is required. In the "User Volume" example, clear-text passwords and valid user accounts are needed for the volume. The service is provided on port number 12000. Guest Volume and User Volume appear as the names of the two servers, respectively, in the Mac's chooser window.

If your Linux computer is a router, with one or more network interfaces connected to public networks, you should use the -ipaddr *IPaddress* option. With that option, you can restrict access to the netatalk server from a particular network interface (probably one that only allows access from your local LAN). There are more than 30 options listed in afpd.conf that you can consider.

Setting up users

As mentioned earlier, the netatalk server (by default) allows users with valid user names and passwords to log in to the server with clear-text (unencrypted) passwords and gain access to (at least) their own home directories. See the "Securing netatalk volumes" section later in this chapter to see how to set up the server to use encrypted passwords.

Sharing netatalk volumes

You use the AppleVolumes.default file to indicate which volumes from the netatalk server are made available to your Mac clients. This file is located in /etc/atalk/AppleVolumes.default.

> **NOTE:** See the "File- and directory-level security" section for detailed information on hidden files and directories, as well as user and group permissions issues related to sharing volumes.

Look at the last line in the AppleVolumes.default file. The single tilde (~) on a line by itself tells the AppleTalk daemon to make all Linux home directories (usually in the /home directory) available as AppleTalk shared directories. When a user logs into the netatalk server, the user's own home directory appears as an available shared directory. A user who chooses to open that directory has the same rights to change, add, and delete files that he has when logged in directly to Linux.

A common practice is to add the text `"Home Directory"` to the line that contains the single tilde (~) so that it appears as follows:

```
~    "Home Directory"
```

Sharing additional directories can be done by simply adding a full path name to the directory you want to share and the volume name you want to assign to it. For example:

```
/var/toyprojects "Linux Toys"
```

As you can see in this example, `/var/toysprojects` is shared under the name `"Linux Toys"`. The path name is limited to 27 characters. In this simple case, access permissions to the volume are determined by the user, host, and folder-level security that is set up for the volume (see the "Securing netatalk volumes" section for more information).

You can also add options directly to each listing in the `AppleVolumes.default` file. On the same line, after the path (`/var/toyprojects`) and volume name (`"Linux Toys"`) options as shown in the previous example, you can add some options. Here are a few options that might interest you (look inside the `AppleVolumes.default` file for others):

- **casefold:***option* — Normally, when a shared volume appears on the Mac client's screen, file and directory names appear in upper- and lowercase as they exist on the Linux system. By replacing *option* in the casefold option with `tolower` or `toupper`, you can have lowercase or uppercase apear in both directions, respectively. Or, you could have case translated (`xlatelower` or `xlateupper`) to set what the client sees.

- **allow:***users/@groups* or **deny:***users/@groups* — You could add specific users or groups to an `allow` or `deny` option to have those users or groups allowed or denied access to the shared *volume*. (Separate each with a comma; indicate a group with an @ sign.)

- **password:***pwd* — Replace *pwd* with a password (up to eight characters) to define a password that is specific to the volume.

- **rolist:***users/@groups* or **rwlist:***users/@groups* — Use `rolist` or `rwlist` options to allow read-only or read/write access, respectively, to the users or groups you add to the list. (Separate each with a comma; indicate a group with an @ sign.)

By opening these shared volumes and creating files and folders in them, Mac clients automatically create some files and folders that are invisible to the Mac client. These files and folders hold resource fork information and other features that would not normally be in a Linux file system. The "File- and directory-level security" section describes these files and folders.

> **NOTE:** Although most of the files and folders described in the following section are invisible to Mac clients, if you share the same directories using Samba or some Linux file-sharing feature (such as NFS), they will be visible. You can use the veto feature of Samba to hide these files from Windows users.

Securing netatalk volumes

Some Linux and netatalk features can be used to secure your volumes from unwanted access or misuse. The following sections describe how to protect your netatalk servers at the user, host, and file and directory levels.

User-level security

When you create a shared volume (in `AppleVolumes.default`), you can indicate which users can access that volume. Users can be authenticated using clear-text passwords (to log in to their basic Linux user accounts) or by setting up a special encrypted password file using netatalk.

Users can be assigned to particular volumes when you define those volumes in the `AppleVolumes.default` file as described earlier. Here's an example where the users `mike` and `jojo` and anyone in the group `wheel` are allowed access to a volume:

```
/var/homework "History homework" allow:mike,jojo,@wheel
```

To use the default clear-text passwords, you need only set up user accounts as you normally would in Linux (see Chapter 11). However, to use encrypted passwords for users (on a server configured to use encrypted passwords in the `afpd.conf` file as described earlier), you must create an AppleTalk password file (`/etc/atalk/afppasswd`). As root, type the following:

```
# afppasswd -c
```

This command gathers all regular users (UID 500 and above) and the guest user (*nobody*) and adds them to the `afppasswd` file. After you create `afppasswd` initially, you can later add individual users manually to that file (provided they also have valid Linux accounts).

Next, you need to add proper passwords for each of the users that will be allowed access to your netatalk shares. For example:

```
# afppasswd -a jake
Enter NEW AFP password: *******
Enter NEW AFP password again: *******
```

Issues related to choosing a good password (see Chapter 14) are true for setting AppleTalk passwords as well. If the passwords match, the user will be able to log in using the assigned user name and password when he tries to mount the AppleTalk volume from the netatalk server, provided the netatalk service is using encrypted authentication (`uams_dxh.so`).

Host-level security

You can restrict which computers on your network have access to your netatalk services using the `/etc/hosts.allow` and `/etc/hosts.deny` files. These files are described in the "Using TCP wrappers" section of Chapter 14. These are the same files you use to allow or restrict access to other Linux networking services.

The following is an example of an entry in the `hosts.allow` file.

```
ALL: .linuxtoys.com EXCEPT abc.linuxtoys.com
```

This example allows access to netatalk (and all other services) from all computers in the `linuxtoys.com` domain except for the computer named `abc.linuxtoys.com`. See Chapter 14 for details about other ways to indicate services (instead of ALL) and hosts.

File- and directory-level security

Netatalk creates hidden files and directories to handle Mac features that are not in Linux. Understanding those files and directories and working with standard Linux ownership and permissions are the best ways to refine access to the AppleTalk volumes you share.

Understanding hidden Mac files and directories

Netatalk creates special files and directories that you can't see from the Mac Finder. Because these files begin with a dot (.), they are hidden from normal directory listings (`ls`) in Linux as well. The following descriptions should help you understand these files and directories.

> **NOTE:** To see hidden files from a folder window (from the GNOME desktop), click Edit → Preferences. Then from the Views tab, select the "Show hidden and backup files" check box. Type **ls -a** to see them from a Terminal window.

- **.AppleDouble** — Every directory within your shared AppleTalk (netatalk) volume contains a `.AppleDouble` directory. This directory is created automatically as soon as you create a file or directory from a Mac client on the netatalk server. Within this directory are separate files representing attributes of each file in the associated directory. For example, creating a text file in `/var/toyprojects` called `mytext.txt` would create a file called `/var/toyprojects/.AppleDouble/mytext.txt` that contained attributes about that file.

  You can create an Icon directory to `.AppleDouble`, enabling you to add custom icons to the shared volume. Icons in the directory (named *file.icon* after the file type) should be readable by everyone who can see the icon and writable to those allowed to change it.

- **.AppleDouble/.Parent** — This directory within each .AppleDouble directory contains information about the shared directory.

- **.AppleDesktop** — For each shared volume, this directory is located in the top-level directory. This directory contains information about the applications that created the data stored on the volumes and the icons used to represent that data.

- **Network Trash Folder** — This folder, in the top-level shared directory, holds deleted files from the client. (Note spaces in the directory name, which must be preceded with a backspace to access the folder from the Linux shell.)

- **Temporary Items** — Some applications need this folder (located in the top-level directory) to create temporary files.

Other directories may also appear, because applications that work on files in a volume need special directories to get their work done.

Setting file and directory permissions

Permissions on shared netatalk volumes tend to be more wide open than would typically be the case on shared Linux directories in order to match the expectations that Mac users generally have about permissions.

In particular, the set UID (user) or GID (group) bit is often turned on for directories. By using the set UID or GID feature, any file or directory created in the directory with set UID or GID turned on would be owned by the associated user or group. For example, follow these steps as root user from the shell (creating any directory name you want to share):

```
# mkdir /var/toyprojects
# chown chris /var/toyprojects
# chgrp toygroup /var/toyprojects
# chmod 2775 /var/toyprojects
# ls -ld /var/toyprojects
drwxrwsr-x      2      chris      toygroup      4096  Mar 16 13:32
/var/toyprojects
```

In this example, I prepared a directory to be shared by netatalk called /var/toyprojects. I made the owner of the directory the user chris (use your own user name). I created a group (see Chapter 11 for creating groups) and called it toygroup. Then I set the permission to 2775 on the directory, which means that the group set-GID bit is on (2), the owner (chris) has full read/write/execute permission (7), the group (toygroup) has full read/write/execute permission (7), and other has only read and execute permissions (5). (Instead of 2, 4 sets the set-UID bit to be on.)

Turning on the group set-GID bit causes all files and directories created in /var/toyprojects (and its subdirectories) to be assigned to the toygroup group, regardless of who created it. Because I set group permissions wide open (7), anything created in /var/toyprojects and its subdirectories will be under the complete control of anyone assigned to toygroup. This is a nice technique for sharing files in a group project.

> **CAUTION:** Setting the set-UID and GID bits can be dangerous, especially if execute permissions gets turned on by the root user. Anyone who can run an application from Linux with the set-UID or GID bits turned on will have the full permissions of the associated user or group to do what they could do with that application. That could include overwriting critical system files.

After the top-level directory is created, netatalk will create the files and directories it needs (such as .AppleDouble and Network Trash Folder) as the Mac clients add files and folders. Netatalk should also propagate the correct permissions to those items.

Here are some tips about setting permissions:

- A user must have write permission to the .AppleDesktop directory (and subdirectories) to create an application in a shared directory.

- Make permissions to the Network Trash Folder writable by everyone who has access to the shared volume or their files will always be permanently deleted instead of put here.

- Open permissions to the Temporary Items directory or applications (such as Photoshop) will fail to work with files from the shared volume.

- Turn off write permissions to programs (executable files) to protect them from being exploited.

Setting Appletalk file and folder type and creator

To check type and creator attributes on Mac files, use the `afile` command as follows:

```
# afile file
```

In this form, you can see attributes for files and directories of known types. To see all files (even those without associated attributes stored in the .AppleDouble directory), use the -a option to `afile`.

Use the `achfile` command to change the type (-t) and creator (-c) of the Macintosh file. Creator and file type pairs are defined in the /etc/atalk/AppleVolumes.system file. You can change these entries to cause different applications to be used for selected file types.

Moving, copying, and deleting netatalk files

When you access files on your netatalk volumes from a Mac client computer, file attributes are maintained or removed properly. Linux commands don't deal with Mac file attributes, however, so you need to run special commands from Linux to move these files and maintain their attributes, instead of the regular Linux commands (mv, cp, rm, and so on).

> **NOTE:** Before you use the `apple_cp` and related commands to add files to your Appletalk volume, open the volume from a Mac client and create a file there. This will cause the appropriate directories and files (.AppleDouble and so on) to be created so they are available to add attributes from Linux apple_* commands.

The commands for copying, moving, and removing files from a shell in Linux on your netatalk server volumes are apple_cp, apple_mv, and apple_rm. For example:

```
# apple_cp memo1.doc /var/av1/memos/
```

This command copied my memo1.doc file from my current directory to the /var/av2/memos/ directory (presumably on the same netatalk volume). This action also copies the resource forks associated with the file to the .AppleDouble directory to the directory you are moving to. Here are examples of move and remove commands:

```
# apple_mv memo1.doc /var/av1/memos/oldmemos/
# apple_rm memo1.doc
```

The `apple_mv` command moves the `memo1.doc` file from the current directory to the `oldmemos` directory (moving attribute information from .AppleDouble to the new .AppleDouble directory). The `apple_rm` command deletes `memo1.doc` and removes its attribute information.

Sharing files with netatalk and Samba

A common practice if you have both Mac and Windows clients on the same network that need to share the same files is to have both Samba and netatalk configured to share the same volume (that is, set of directories). Before you do that, however, be aware of the following:

- By default, creating files from Mac clients (on netatalk volumes) will make the files you create easiest to work with from the Mac.

- You can hide files from Samba users with the `veto` option in `AppleVolumes.default` (From Linux, see the `/usr/share/doc/netatalk*/doc/README.veto` file.)

- If you don't care about Mac attributes, you can set the `noadouble` option in the `AppleVolumes.default` file to create files without them.

- Avoiding certain characters in your file and directory names can make it easier for you to share those items among different types of clients. When possible, avoid characters such as slash (/), backslash (\) and colon (:) when naming files. Also, wildcard characters such as asterisks (*) and pound signs (#) can cause problems.

- The `veto` option for Samba (in `smb.conf`) can be used to hide Mac files (such as .AppleDouble directories) from Samba users.

Here's an example of a veto line you might want to add to your `/etc/samba/smb.conf` file. It prevents Samba users from accessing hidden netatalk-specific directories:

```
veto files = /.AppleDouble/.AppleDesktop/Network Trash
Folder/TheVolume/SettingsFolder
```

Here's a veto line you can add to your `/etc/atalk/atalkd.conf` file to keep netatalk users from accessing directories used by Samba:

```
veto: recycled/desktop.ini/Folder.htt/Folder Settings/
```

Here are a few issues related to `veto` options:

- Get the upper- and lowercase letters right (the option is case-sensitive).

- Type veto names completely. The veto feature doesn't support asterisks (*), brackets ([) and other wildcard characters to match multiple file names.

Printer Sharing

You can set up printer sharing using netatalk so that Mac clients using the standard AppleTalk print service (called *Printer Access Protocol*, or *PAP*) can print to your Linux computer. To do that, you must:

- Configure a local Linux printer (see Chapter 17).
- Set up the /etc/atalk/papd.conf file to point to that printer.
- Restart the atalk service (or, more specifically, the papd daemon).

When a Mac client prints to a Linux printer configured in this way, the print job is handed to the standard Linux lpd daemon and put into a spool file for printing, along with Linux print jobs for the printer.

> **NOTE:** Mac OS X computers can print directly to Linux print services (CUPS or LPRng) without requiring netalk printing. Older Mac OS 9 clients, however, might need to see an AppleTalk printer that you set up in this way with netatalk.

The papd.conf file follows the same basic format as the /etc/printcap file (traditionally used for Linux printing). Here's an example of a printer configured in the papd.conf file:

```
LaserJet2100M:\
                :pr=| /usr/bin/lpr -P hp01:\
                :pd=/etc/atalk/laserjet.ppd:\
                :op=root:\
                :am:uams_guest.so:
```

The printer in this example is named LaserJet2100M. To print the file from the Mac client, it takes the output file and pipes it to the lpr -P hp01 command (hp01 is the name of the local printer). The ppd file is /etc/atalk/laserjet.ppd. The root user is the operator, and guests are allowed to print to the printer (no password is needed).

The printer definition file (ppd) must be installed on both the netatalk server (at the location noted in the papd.conf file) and on the Mac client.

To test that the interface to your AppleTalk printer is working, use the pap command:

```
# pap -p LaserJet2100M /etc/hosts
```

The -p option identifies your netatalk printer. It this example, it prints a copy of your /etc/hosts file. Or, you can just check the status of the printer:

```
# papstatus -p LaserJet2100M
```

Troubleshooting netatalk

Several tools are available that enable you to see the status of your AppleTalk network. The aecho command can test whether a particular AppleTalk host computer is alive. The nbplkup command can be used to check out the services that are currently available on your AppleTalk network.

> **NOTE:** In general, AppleTalk should be used on trusted networks. If you are running a firewall on your netatalk server, however, you must open access to several ports for netatalk to work. In particular, you may need to open ports 548 (AFP over TCP/IP), 201 (AppleTalk routing), 202 (AppleTalk name binding), 204 (AppleTalk echo), and 206 (AppleTalk zones).

Use the aecho command (similar to the TCP/IP ping command) to check whether an AppleTalk host computer is alive. The aecho command sends an Apple Echo Protocol (aep) packet to the host you want to check. Here's an example:

```
# aecho toys
14 bytes from 65280.115: aep_seq=0. time=0, ms
14 bytes from 65280.115: aep_seq=1. time=0, ms

----65280.115 AEP Statistics----
2 packets sent, 2 packets received, 0% packet loss
round-trip (ms)  min/avg/max = 0/0/0
```

If the AppleTalk server is up and running, you can use the nbplkup command to see what printers and volumes are currently available. For large networks, you can limit the output of nbplkup by adding a share name or printer name (such as :hpjet), or by entering a host name (for example, toys). Here's an example:

```
# nbplkup :AFPServer
duck:AFPServer              65280.115:130
User Volume:AFPServer       65280.21:129
Guest Volume:AFPServer      65280.21:130
```

By querying for :AFPServer, nbplkup listed all AppleTalk file servers on the local network. The first one shown is from the host named duck. The second and third line were from the same computer (at address 65280.21), but were registered as separate servers.

After restarting your netatalk server, you can check that the daemons all started properly. The following are lines from the /var/log/messages file.

```
Mar 14 17:44:23 toys atalkd[2013]: zip_getnetinfo for eth0
Mar 14 17:44:33 toys atalkd[2013]: zip_getnetinfo for eth0
Mar 14 17:44:43 toys atalkd[2013]: config for no router
Mar 14 17:44:44 toys atalkd[2013]: ready 0/0/0
Mar 14 17:44:44 toys atalk: atalkd startup succeeded
Mar 14 17:44:57 toys atalk: papd startup succeeded
Mar 14 17:44:57 toys papd[2070]: restart (1.5.5)
Mar 14 17:44:57 toys atalk: afpd startup succeeded
Mar 14 17:45:03 toys afpd[2074]: toys:AFPServer@* started on
65280.96:128 (1.5.5)
```

```
Mar 14 17:45:03 toys afpd[2074]: ASIP started on 10.0.0.100:548(1)
(1.5.5)
Mar 14 17:45:03 toys afpd[2074]: uam: uams_clrtxt.so loaded
Mar 14 17:45:03 toys afpd[2074]: uam: uams_dhx.so loaded
Mar 14 17:45:03 toys afpd[2074]: uam: "DHCAST128" available
Mar 14 17:45:03 toys afpd[2074]: uam: "Cleartxt Passwrd" available
```

In the previous example, you can see that the atalk start-up script successfully started up the `atalkd`, `papd`, and `afpd` daemons. The `atalkd` daemon looks for AppleTalk network information on the first Ethernet interface (eth0). The `papd` daemon started, but had no printers to register. The `afpd` daemon started an AppleTalk file server on the server (`toys:AFPServer`). It then identified the user authentication methods (`uams`) that are available (both clear-text and encrypted passwords are available here).

Accessing NFS Servers from the Mac

For many years, Network File System (NFS) has been the preferred method for sharing files among Linux and other UNIX-like computer systems. Although Mac OS X does support NFS connections from its Connect to Server window, you need to do a little trick on the Linux server for that server to accept connections from the Mac OS X computer.

The following procedure describes how to use the Connect to Server window from a Mac OS X client to access files and directories from a shared Linux NFS server. You can then use the files and directories (also called folders) that reside on the Linux NFS server as though they existed on your Mac OS X computer.

As I've mentioned, the procedure relies on being able to make a small change to how the Linux NFS server offers the shared directory. If you don't have access to the Linux server, you either need to ask the administrator of the Linux server to make the change or connect your Mac to the Linux NFS server manually. (I describe the manual procedure at the end of this section.)

Connecting to NFS from the Connect to Server window

To create an NFS shared directory in Linux and connect to it from a Mac client, do the following:

1. On the Linux server, export a shared directory using the NFS facility as described in Chapter 18. To be able to use the shared directory from Mac OS X, however, you must be sure to add the `insecure` option. For example, to share the `/var/music` directory from the Linux server named `jukebox.linuxtoys.net`, you can add the following line to the `/etc/exports` file on that server:

    ```
    /var/music    *(rw,insecure)
    ```

    This example allows the `/var/music` directory to be shared with all computers (*) and provides read and write permission (rw). The `insecure` option lets clients that request the exported directory make the request from an insecure port (ports above 1024). This is important because the Mac OS X Connect to Server window makes its request to mount the shared directory from a port above 1024, and fails without the option.

2. On the Linux server, verify that the NFS service is running and re-export the shared directory by typing the following (as root user):

```
# exportfs -a -v
```

3. On the Mac OS X client, select Go in the Finder bar at the top of the screen, and then select Connect to Server. The Connect to Server window appears.

4. On the Mac OS X client, type the address of the share directory into the Address box. For example, to connect to the shared NFS (nfs://) directory called /var/music from the computer named jukebox.linuxtoys.net, you can type the address: **nfs://jukebox.linuxtoys.net/var/music** (see Figure 26-5).

If everything is working properly, an icon representing the server should appear on your Mac OS X desktop. Open that icon to see the contents of the shared directory. You can use the shared files and directories as though they were on your Mac (if permissions on the server permits you to do so). Drop the icon in the trash when you are done.

> **NOTE:** If you are unable to connect to the shared directory, go through the NFS procedures in Chapter 18 more carefully. In particular, make sure that firewall ports are open on the server and that the user and host permissions are set to allow the level of access that you require.

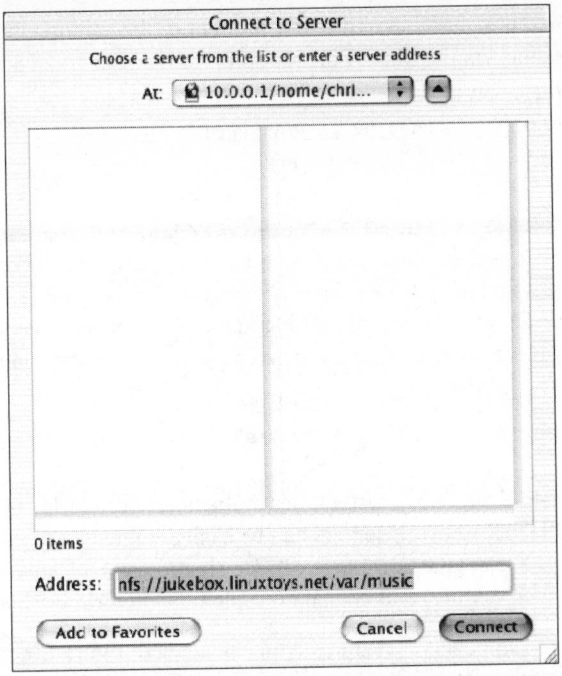

Figure 26-5: Connect to an NFS server from the Connect to Server window.

Connecting to NFS from the command line

You might very well not have any control over how the Linux NFS server is configured. So if the insecure option isn't set, you will fail to mount an NFS directory from the Mac's Connect to Server window. A possible workaround is to manually mount the NFS directory from Mac OS X and use a secure port. Here's how:

1. On the Mac OS X computer, gain access to the root user account as follows:

   a. With the Folder icon selected, click Go → Applications. The Applications folder appears.

   b. Open the Utilities folder, then the Netinfo Manager utility.

   c. Click on the lock icon on the Netinfo Manager window so that it unlocks.

   d. Click Security → Enable Root User. (If you see a Netinfo error, click OK.)

   e. Type in and verify the new root user password, then click Verify. (Remember that password!)

   f. Click the open lock icon to close it and prevent further changes.

2. On the Mac OS X computer, click the Terminal icon to open a shell and log in as root:

```
# su -
Password: *******
```

3. Create a directory that is accessible to the user account of the person who wants to use the shared NFS directory on the Mac. For example, for the user chris you might type:

```
# mkdir /Users/chris/music
# chown chris /Users/chris/music
```

4. Mount the NFS shared directory on the directory you just created. For example:

```
# mount -o "-P" jukebox.linuxtoys.net:/var/music /Users/chris/music
```

The -P says to use a priviledged port. Replace jukebox.linuxtoys.net and /var/music with the server's name and the shared directory, respectively. The user can now access /var/music from the /Users/chris/music directory on the Mac OS X client.

Summary

Because Darwin, a UNIX-like operating system, lies at the heart of the Mac OS X operating system, native Linux and UNIX network servers can be easily connected to these new Macs in a variety of ways. Mac OS X can take advantage of files shared from a Linux server over Samba (Windows file/printer sharing) and netatalk (AppleTalk file/printer sharing).

Instead of just using native Linux server features, you can also configure Linux to act like an AppleTalk file server using the netatalk package. With netatalk, you can set up multiple file servers and protect the volumes (directories) they share with various password and permissions techniques.

Part V
New Technology

Chapter 27

Adopting the Linux 2.6 Kernel

In This Chapter

- Getting to know the 2.6 kernel
- Improvements to desktop performance
- Improvements in laptop support
- Improvements to server performance
- Improvements in hardware support
- Using the 2.6 kernel beyond Fedora Core 2

When the Linux kernel is working well, it should be almost invisible to the people using Linux. External devices should be detected and configured automatically. Applications should be able to read and write data from storage devices, communications cards or any other types of supported hardware. By most accounts, the new 2.6 kernel included with Fedora Core 2 does those jobs well and provides a solid foundation for continued growth of Linux.

The focus of this chapter is on improvements in the 2.6 kernel that relate to how you might use it in Fedora Core 2. For that reason, I've broken down descriptions of the 2.6 kernel in much the same way I divided up the book: desktop, server, and administrative features (in this case, represented by a section on supported hardware drivers). After that, I describe features in the 2.6 kernel that relate to how it can be used outside of Fedora Core 2.

Familiarizing Yourself with the Kernel

The Linux kernel is the software the allows application programs to communicate with the computer hardware and coexist with other running applications on the same system. To do that, the kernel must:

- **Know about the hardware drivers on the computer** — In Linux, the code that lets applications communicate with each piece of computer hardware can either be built into the kernel as drivers or added to the kernel after it is running, using what are called loadable modules.
- **Be able to manage applications** — By performing scheduling functions, the kernel can decide which running processes have access to the computer's processor and for what

duration. Processes are assigned priorities that can slow or speed the completions of those processes requests.

- **Understand file systems** — Because the kernel is responsible for letting processes read, write, and execute files that are stored in different types of file systems, the kernel must know about how those file systems are structured. It must also know the permissions each user has to access those files.

There are many other things that a kernel does as well. However, these three are some of the most obvious functions of the kernel to someone using a Linux system.

Checking your current kernel

If you want to know what kernel your Linux system is currently running, you can type the `uname -a` command as follows:

```
# uname -a
Linux jukebox.linuxtoys.net 2.6.5-1.358 #1 Thu May 20 12:32:44 EDT 2004
   i686 i686 i386 GNU/Linux
```

This example shows the current kernel as 2.6.5-1.358. Because you can have multiple kernels available on your hard disk, each of which may require drivers and modules that are specific to that kernel, the kernel version number is used to store the compatible components. For example, you can look for directories named for your kernel version in:

- **/lib/modules** — Modules that can be loaded as needed to support hardware connected to your computer are stored under the `/lib/modules` directory. One way that modules for the 2.6 kernel are different from the 2.4 kernel counterparts is that they end with a .ko extension (as opposed to a .o for 2.4 kernel modules). You can use the basename of the modules you find in kernel and unsupported subdirectories with the `modinfo` command to display descriptions of what hardware each driver supports.

- **/usr/src** — If you install the kernel-source package, a subdirectory of `/usr/src` that is named `linux-2.6.*` (where the asterisk is replaced by the revision level of the kernel), contains source code and documentation for your kernel. The `Documentation` subdirectory of that directory contains a wealth of information about the drivers and components that make up your kernel.

When you get the kernel with Fedora Core 2, it has already been built for you and stored in the `/boot` directory under the name `vmlinuz-2.6.*` (again, replacing the asterisk with the kernel revision level). Red Hat had to make some decisions about what drivers to include in the bootable kernel itself. Drivers that are needed for your particular hardware configuration can be detected after you boot Linux and can be added in the form of loadable modules.

Because there are some inefficiencies from using a kernel that includes drivers you don't need, and must load drivers you do need, some Linux experts prefer to build their own kernels. In most cases, however, the performance gains are negligible, so most people simply take the small performance hits to load the modules they need a boot time.

If you do need to work with modules on your Linux system, you can use tools such as insmod (to install a module), modprobe (to install/remove a module along with any dependent modules), lsmod (to see what modules are installed), rmmod (to remove a module), or modinfo (to view information about a module). Those tools are described in Chapter 10.

Because, as I mentioned earlier, if the kernel is working well it should be nearly invisible to you, it helps to know what to look for to understand what you are gaining from the 2.6 kernel. The sections in this chapter break down Linux 2.6 kernel features by desktop, server, and other systems.

Using the /sys directory

For the 2.6 kernel, many tunable features are available in the new /sys directory structure. For example, if you want to see how values for the new anticipatory scheduler are set for your first ide hard disk (/dev/hda), you could do the following:

> **NOTE:** The anticipatory scheduler in the 2.6 kernel is currently disabled in Fedora Core 2. The reason is that it has had some errors relating to handling swap space and was, therefore, considered to be unsuitable for desktop systems (which is how many Fedora systems are used).

```
# cd /sys/block/hda/queue/iosched
# ls
fifo_batch front_merges read_expire write_expire writes_starved
# cat *
16
1
500
5000
2
```

Here you can see the values of fifo_batch (16), front_merges (1), read_expire (500), write_expire (5000) and writes_starved (2). If you are working on a non-production system and you want to play around with your tunables, you can do so by simply echoing new values to the files representing each parameter.

> **CAUTION:** Changing kernel parameters can have a drastic effect, either positive or negative, on the performance of your system. While a reboot will put back most values to their original states, you should be careful changing parameters on a system that contains important data.

Check the kernel Documentation directory (or do an online search) to read about the definitions of kernel parameters. For example, you can read more about the scheduler options just shown in the as-iosched.txt file (in /usr/src/linux*/Documentation). You can change any of these parameters on the fly by simply echoing a new value to a file. For example:

```
# echo 32 > /sys/block/hda/queue/iosched/fifo_batch
```

In this example, the `fifo_batch` parameter (default 16) is raised to 32. This parameter defines how many contiguous requests can be in a set of requests. The idea of `fifo_batch` is to avoid a whole bunch of individual seeks going to the dispatch queue, so a higher number will perform better on a system that is always seeking large files. However, this could harm performance on systems that do many small seeks, as the kernel will pause where it doesn't need to in anticipation of more similar seeks to come.

To see how your system performs with different `fifo_batch` values, you can try copying large files from your hard disk with the time command (`time cp whatever /tmp`), changing the value of the `fifo_batch`, then timing the copy again. You will begin to get a flavor for how the different values affect the performance of your system.

Improvements to Desktop Performance

As the first Linux systems leaned toward being primarily server operating systems, kernel features were not originally best focused on providing a comfortable desktop experience. Activities done on the desktop (such as moving windows around or launching applications) were not given priority over, say, system maintenance tasks that may have been kicked off to run in the background.

Several new features were added to the Linux 2.6 kernel that were specifically aimed at improving the experience of desktop users with Linux. Because some of these features still exhibit unreliable behavior, they have been disabled in Fedora Core 2. The following bullet items describe some of the desktop-related features in the 2.6 kernel and note those that are not yet enabled in Fedora Core 2:

- **Anticipatory scheduler** — By anticipating what the user will want to do next, the kernel can look ahead, guess what the user might want next, and begin preparing to respond to that request. The anticipatory scheduler in the 2.6 kernel tries to anticipate read requests that it thinks processes will make next. It does this by maintaining per-process statistics to help it guess if there will be another dependent read soon after one just requested. In that way, the kernel can wait before returning the requested information and do several similar reads one after the other. This can result in great performance improvements.

  There are several tunable parameters associated with the anticipatory scheduler that are available to advanced users. Check out `/sys/block/*/queue/iosched` (where the asterisk is replaced by the name of the disk you are tuning, such as `hda` for your first hda hard disk). There should be tunable parameters available for your hard disks, floppy disks, and loop devices.

The anticipatory scheduler is currently disabled in Fedora Core 2.

- **Improved threading support** — Native POSIX Thread Library (NPTL) can result in significantly improved desktop performance. Threads can improve performance by allowing small pieces of code to run independently, without incurring the overhead required to start and stop each piece of code as an independent process. Particular improvements have been seen in desktop performance and on multiprocessor systems.

> **NOTE:** Red Hat, Inc. sponsored the NPTL development, and back-ported this feature into the 2.4 kernel. So, Red Hat Linux 9 and Fedora Core 1 already had NPTL support built in, without having to upgrade to the full 2.6 kernel.

- **Preemptible kernel** — Having a kernel that can be preempted (in other words, allow it to give attention to a user-level task while it is waiting on a kernel-level task) has the potential for significantly improving desktop performance. With kernel preemption enabled, a kernel activity that is taking a long time to complete will no longer keep all other activities from gaining access to the processor. This can result in actions that a desktop user expects to happen immediately (such as moving a window or opening a menu) to not be stopped by some background kernel activity. Likewise, applications that require smooth performance (such as audio and video playing) are more likely to not be interrupted by a demanding kernel process.

The preemptible kernel feature is not enabled in Fedora Core 2. The feature is still considered to be unstable.

- **More devices** — For desktop users, there have been dramatic improvements to support for many of today's popular external devices. These include USB, firewire, PC cards, and Hot Plug devices, so you'll have a better chance of getting your external modem, Webcam, digital camera, and other devices working properly with the 2.6 kernel. (See the "Improvements in Hardware Support" section later in this chapter.)

- **Multimedia enhancements** — You should get better and more consistent performance with your sound system with the addition of the Advanced Linux Sound Architecture (ALSA) to the 2.6 kernel. For gaming, there is improved support for joysticks that includes analog joystick support in ALSA drivers and an I-Force joystick driver that supportes force feedback. Likewise, as mentioned earlier, general improvements to the kernel will make playback of multimedia content to go more smoothly with the 2.6 kernel.

Improvements to Laptop Support

Besides those features that improve the 2.6 kernel's graphical interface support, the most striking improvement to laptop support relates to power management. With the improved and simplified device driver model in the 2.6 kernel, a more effective power management model is also possible.

The 2.6 kernel supports Advanced Configuration and Power Interface (ACPI). While ACPI was included to some extent in the 2.4 kernel delivered with Fedora Core 1, it has been greatly improved in the latest kernel. In this new power management model, the kernel can communicate with all ACPI-compatible devices about their power states. Then, using ACPI tools, an systems administrator or advanced user can create rules that tell the devices how to react when different events occur. For example, you could have a Webcam turn off or the hard disk spin down when you ask to go into sleep mode.

Improvements to Server Performance

While Linux has always been a strong contender as a server operating system, it has not always scaled up well to high-end computer systems. With the 2.6 kernel, more support has been added to allow Linux to make use of more processing power.

- **More processing power** — While the ability to use multiple processors on the same computer has been supported in Linux for some time, the 2.6 kernel has added support for more than 16 CPUs on a single computer.

- **Multiple memory pools** — Former limitations resulting from having a single pool of memory being shared by multiple processors have been adressed by the Non-Uniform Memory Acccess (NUMA) feature in the 2.6 kernel. With NUMA, the kernel allows for support of multiprocessor computers that can take advantage of the most appropriate available memory resources.

- **More devices** — In the 2.4 kernel, there were only 255 allowable major devices and 255 subdevices. With the 2.6 kernel, many more devices can be defined. The 2.6 kernel allows 4095 major devices, while allowing over one million subdevices for each type.

- **Larger file systems** — On 32-bit hardware, the 2.6 kernel allows file systems that can store up to 16 terabytes of data. This is an eight-fold improvement over what the 2.4 kernel could support.

- **Support for high-bandwidth networks** — With support for TCP Segmentation Offloading (TSO) enabled in the 2.6 kernel along with high-speed Intel PRO/1000 network driver (e1000) enabled, transfer rates for two-way communication can be significantly increased. TSO offloads the task of dividing large packets into smaller packets to the network interface card.

Improvements in Hardware Support

The Linux 2.6 kernel represents the first kernel version where all hardware devices are unified under a single device model. This model makes it easier for the kernel to manage and keep track of all the hardware connected to the computer.

The physical representation of how the kernel views the computer hardware is connected to the /sys file system. So, as you go up and down the /sys directory structure, you see the device structure that the kernel sees. For example, I connected a Webcam to a USB port on my computer's motherboard. The directory /sys/bus/usb/drivers/Philips webcam/ appeared, with a subdirectory containing links to information about the state of the Webcam.

Speaking of USB, hot pluggable devices such as those that connect to USB ports, Firewire ports, and PCMCIA slots represent some of the major enhancements to hardware support by the 2.6 kernel. Those and other hardware devices now supported by the 2.6 kernel are described in the following section.

> **NOTE:** Firewire is currently disabled in Fedora Core 2. This is due to some bugs that could cause Fedora installation to fail on a computer where a Firewire device is connected. There have been some indicattions that a fix might be available soon, so if Firewire devices are important to you, look for Fedora kernel updates in the near future.

Supporting USB devices

The 2.6 kernel is a must for computer hardware that includes USB 2.0 devices. While some support for USB 2.0 devices has been backported to the 2.4 kernel, you can expect more solid support in the 2.6 kernel. USB 1.1 offered speeds of 1.5Mbps (low speed) and 12Mbps (full speed). Alternatively, USB 2.0 devices operating at their full potential (high speed) run at 480Mpbs. This makes them appropriate for:

- High-quality Webcams
- Ethernet adapters running at 100BaseT
- External disk drives, used to provide portable storage in many applications, such as playing music, video, or other types of content

There have been compatibility problems with some USB 2.0 devices. Devices that are certified as USB 2.0 that will work with the Linux 2.6 kernel should display the red, white, and blue "Certified Hi-Speed USB" logo.

For the 2.6 kernel, there are generic USB drivers to handle sound (audio.ko), modems and ISDN adapters (cdc-acm.ko), printers (usblp.ko), and MIDI devices (usb-midi.ko). There are specific drivers to support Bluetooth devices, scanners, tablets, touch screens, digital cameras, FM radio devices, serial port boards, and mass storage devices.

For further information about USB 2.0 devices that are supported in the 2.6 Linux kernel, refer to the Linux USB site (http://linux-usb.org).

Running older hardware

Support for legacy hardware that has not been in previous Linux kernels has been added to the 2.6 Linux kernel. For example, plug-and-play extensions for Industry Standard Architecture (ISA) busses are included in the 2.6 kernel. Although MCA and EISA busses have been included in earlier Linux kernels, support for those architectures have been added to the new 2.6 kernel device database, also helping those architectures to support full plug-and-play extensions. In other words, more legacy hardware should be detected, configured, and managed automatically in the 2.6 kernel.

Using the 2.6 Kernel Beyond Fedora Core

Although the first Linux kernel was created so that Linux Torvalds could have his home PC work like the UNIX operating systems he used at school, the latest 2.6 Linux kernel can stretch well outside the boundaries of the average PC.

The 2.6 kernel can now run on multiple computer architectures. It has also recently included significant improvements to allow it to run better on small, embedded Linux devices, as well as scale up to large, multiprocessor, high-throughput enterprise servers.

Running the 2.6 kernel on embedded systems

Today, you can find Linux running on all kinds of devices, from TIVO personal video recorders to hand-held computers. With improvements to the 2.6 kernel to support embedded systems, you can expect that trend to continue. The skills you learn with Linux today will help you work with all kinds of devices now and in the future.

Code from the uClinux project (`www.uclinux.org`) has been merged into the 2.6 kernel. The uClinux project ported the Linux kernel to run on microprocessors without a Memory Management Unit (MMU). Removing MMU allows uCLinux to run without the hardware overhead required for multitasking applications. uCLinux was first ported to the Motorola MC68328 microprocessor and run on a PalmPilot.

With the inclusion of the uClinux code, the 2.6 kernel becomes ready to be ported to run on many new, inexpensive specialty processors. Besides the Motorola m68k processors, the Linux 2.6 kernel will support the NEC v850 processor and Hitachi H8/300 series of processors. Other processors to which uClinux has been ported are listed on the uClinux Ports page (`www.uclinux.org/ports`).

Linux 2.6 kernel ports for other architectures

The Fedora CDs that come with this book are built to run on Pentium class and above PCs. Ports of the Linux 2.6 kernel, however, are available to run on many other different processor types. You can find ports of Linux to dozens of different computer architectures on the Ports of Linux page (`http://perso.wanadoo.es/xose/linux/linux_ports.html`).

While this trend to port Linux to many different architectures is expected to continue with the 2.6 kernel, a new subarchitecture feature of the 2.6 kernel adds a new dimension to possible future ports. The subarchitecture feature separates processor types and hardware types. This feature opens the possibility to support architectures such as the NCR Voyager architecture and PC-9800 architecture (both of which supported x86 processors on nonstandard hardware). The subarchitecture feature opens the gates for the 2.6 kernel to be ported to other computer hardware that uses industry standard Pentium-class processors with specialized hardware.

> **NOTE:** Although the Fedora Core 2 distribution included with this book runs on 32-bit Intel x86 architecture PCs, there is an AMD64 version of Fedora Core 2 available as well. You can download a copy of that distribution from `http://fedora.redhat.com/download`. Most of the software descriptions in this book will work with that distribution as well.

Summary

The Linux 2.6 kernel that is included with Fedora Core 2 represents some significant improvements in performance and hardware support for Fedora Core desktop and server systems. Fedora Core desktop systems can expect significant improvements both in performance and in availability of desktop hardware, including a variety of hot-pluggable USB devices. For servers, the 2.6 kernel can support more enterprise-ready servers, by allowing larger hard disks, more processors, and higher network throughput. Skills that you learn using the 2.6 kernel in Fedora might also help you work with a variety of embedded devices that might someday be running Linux systems that include 2.6 kernel technology.

Chapter 28

Implementing
Security Enhanced Linux

The Security Enhanced Linux (SELinux) feature is new to Fedora in Fedora Core 2. SELinux definitely falls into the category of cutting edge Linux technology. In other words, it is potentially very powerful, but it doesn't work so well yet. While SELinux is not quite ready for prime-time use, its inclusion in Fedora Core 2 provides an opportunity to try out and get to know this important security technology while it is still being developed.

SELinux represents a new security model that can be applied to Linux systems. Instead of the all-or-nothing, either-you-have-root-privilege-or-you-don't approach to security in traditional Linux and UNIX system, SELinux allows much finer granularity in how permissions to run and alter components on the computer are handed out.

This chapter sets out to give you an understanding of what SELinux is. It describes how to turn on SELinux in Fedora Core 2 (it's off by default). Then it gives you some ideas about what the pieces of SELinux are and what you can do with them.

Understanding Security Enhanced Linux

With traditional UNIX and Linux systems, when a user got root access to your computer, he owned the machine. The root user (or whomever took over as root user) could override ownership, read/write/execute permissions, and processor scheduling priorities. This security model made Linux and UNIX systems unacceptable for highly secure environments, where the risk of one exploit taking down the whole operating system was unacceptable.

Organizations such as the United States National Security Agency (NSA) recognized the need to have operating systems in secure environments be able to separate information in terms of confidentiality and data integrity. The mechanism that NSA recommended to accomplish that is referred to as *Mandatory Access Control* (MAC).

The Security Enhanced Linux (SELinux) project aims at providing MAC functionality into the Linux kernel. By implementing rules for what all operating system components can and can't do, an application that has security flaws or has been taken over for malicious intent can be contained. In other words, gaining control of one component of a system doesn't allow a cracker to take over the entire computer.

The mechanisms for implementing these security rules in SELinux are referred to as *policies*. Using policy configuration files, SELinux implements two different security models: *Type Enforcement* (TE) and *Role-Based Access Control* (RBAC).

- **Type Enforcement** — Under the TE model, every object in the operating system is bound to a security attribute called a *type*. Every process is bound to a security attribute called a *domain*. This approach allows for very tight control of every object in the operating system. Every user is allowed to access objects in the operating system based on the domain in which he or she is allowed to operate.

- **Role-Based Access Control** — Using the RBAC model, SELinux lets each user operate in a specific role. The roles are arranged in a hierarchy, with specific permissions associated with each role provided by type enforcement.

In traditional Linux, a user is assigned a specific user ID (UID) and group ID (GID), which affords that user certain access to system resources. For instance, it gives the user certain rights to read, write, or execute files and directories based on whether that user owns the file or directory or is part of a group assigned to that file or directory.

In SELinux, a data file, directory, or application can have many more attributes associated with it. Those attributes might actually give more permissions to access the component than were available in traditional Linux security. At the same time, having access to the component wouldn't necessarily give that user control of that component in a way that could be exploited beyond what the security policies allow the user to do.

Users in SELinux

The model that SELinux uses to define the rights that users have on an SELinux-enabled system can co-exist with the existing Linux user model, rather than replace it. With SELinux enabled, Linux user still have their accounts defined through definitions in the `/etc/passwd` file. A user that is also assigned a role in SELinux is referred to as a *Defined User*.

Special users in SELinux include the system_u (which is the user assigned to system processes) and user_u (which is the optional assignment used to indicate if general users are allowed to use the feature in question).

When a user logs in, that user can choose the context in which to operate. In particular, the root user can choose to operate under a staff_r:staff_t context (which prevents the user from doing some system administration) or choose a sysadm_r::sysadm_t context that will allow more system administration activities.

Policies in SELinux

In the policies set by default for SELinux in Fedora Core 2 (when SELinux is enabled), there are definitions that apply to users, software programs, file system objects, devices, file types, and many other components. You can review the policies for your SELinux installation in the `/etc/security/selinux/src/policy` directory.

I recommend that you go through the procedure for getting started with SELinux and run the `sepcut` command to start the SE Linux Policy Customization Tool. You can use that tool to browse the policy directories and read the policy contents defined there.

Using SELinux in Fedora Core 2

Support for SELinux in Fedora Core is built into the Linux 2.6 kernel as well as the following software packages:

- **checkpolicy** — Contains the SELinux policy compiler named `checkpolicy`. You only need this package if you want to build policies for SELinux. Using `checkpolicy`, you create binary policy files from policy configurations and parameters in a `policy.conf` file. (Type **man checkpolicy** to read about `checkpolicy`. A `policy.conf` file is available in `/etc/security/selinux/src/policy/policy.conf`)

- **policy** — Contains sample SELinux policy configurations. These configurations are contained in the `/etc/security` and `/etc/security/selinux` directories.

- **policycoreutils** —Contains basic utilities needed to operate an SELinux system. Commands include `fixfiles` (to check and possibly correct security attributes on file systems), `restorecon` (to set security attributes for selected files), `audit2allow` (to translate messages from `/var/log/messages` to rules that SELinux can use), `newrole` (open a shell in a new role), `load_policy` (to load a policy file), `run_init` (to run an init script using the correct context), `sestatus` (to check whether SELinux is currently enabled), and `setfiles` (to set the security contexts of files).

- **selinux-doc** — Contains a lot of SELinux documentation that is stored in the `/usr/share/SELinux` directory.

- **setools** — Contains tools for managing parts of a running policy that define what access users have to parts of the Linux system. Tools include seinfo (which prints policy statistics), sepcut (a graphical policy customization tool), sesearch (to search type enforcement rules in SELinux policies), seuser (to work with users and roles associated with a policy), seuseradd (adds SELinux features to the useradd tool for adding Linux users), seusermod (adds SELinux features to the usermod tool for modifying Linux user accounts), seuserdel (adds SELinux features to the userdel tool for deleting Linux user accounts), and seaudit (graphical audit tool for analyzing log files for SELinux).

Getting Started with SELinux

SELinux is installed but disabled by default with Fedora Core 2. If you are dedicating a computer to trying out SELinux, you can enable SELinux when you install Fedora Core 2. However, be prepared to see lots of warning messages and expect things that you used to be able to do as root to fail if you don't change contexts (as described later).

> **NOTE:** Remember, SELinux is still in early development stages and requires a change of mindset from traditional Linux or UNIX system administrator. Before you begin, go through the Fedora Core 2 SELinux FAQ for the latest information on running SELinux in Fedora. (See `http://people.redhat.com/kwade/fedora-docs/selinux-faq-en`.)

Here's a quick procedure for doing a bit of exploring of SELinux features in Fedora Core 2.

> **CAUTION:** I strongly recommend against enabling SELinux on any sort of production machine. Even during normal operations, SELinux in Fedora Core 2 constantly spews error messages that can be difficult to decipher. All the SELinux activity can make it hard to see real error conditions that are occurring.
>
> As an alternative, you can install Fedora Core 2 with SELinux off (which is the default). After that, you can still look at policy files, try some of the commands, and read included documentation, as described in this chapter, to learn about SELinux.

1. Insert CD #1 from the Fedora Core 2 installation set into the CD drive and reboot the computer.

2. You can choose to install Fedora Core 2 with SELinux disabled or enabled:

    *   **disabled** — Just install Fedora Core as you would normally (as described in Chapter 2). By default, it will be disabled. You can still run SELinux commands and view policy files as described in this procedure.

    *   **enabled** — To enable SELinux in the Fedora Core 2 kernel, type `selinux` at the boot prompt as follows:

    ```
    boot: selinux
    ```

3. Install Fedora Core 2 as you would normally. The only SELinux-specific feature you are asked to enable during installation is to make Security Enhanced Linux Extensions active when you configure your firewall.

4. Select any type of installation that you want to have on your computer. However, you should be sure to install the SELinux packages described in the previous section, so you can start playing around with the tools available with SELinux.

5. Log in as the root user.

> **NOTE:** There seems to be a bug in SELinux that prevents the root user from logging in through the GUI with SELinux enabled. If the GUI fails to start for you, press Ctrl+Alt+F2, log in as root, and type the following command:
>
> ```
> # setfiles /etc/security/selinux/file_contexts /root
> ```
>
> You may need to reboot your computer (or at least change runlevels) so you can try to log in to the GUI again as root user.

6. In order to be able to do some of the administrative tasks that you associate with the root user, you will need to change your context after you login as root. Here is how you are prompted to change context after you login as root:

```
Your default context is root:staff_r:staff_t.
Do you want to choose a different one? [n] y
[2] root:sysadm_r:sysadm_t
Enter number of choice: 2
```

7. As shown, you are given the chance to change contexts by typing **y**. After that, type **2** to choose the new context.

8. After Fedora is running and you have successfully logged in, check the state of SELinux on the system. In the /etc/sysconfig/selinux file, check the value of SELINUX. It can be set to one of the following states:

   - **enforcing** — SELinux policies are being enforced.

   - **permissive** — SELinux policies are being checked, but policy issues result in warnings instead of enforcement.

   - **disabled** — SELinux policies are not being enforced.

   Because you turned on SELinux when you installed Fedora Core 2, SELINUX should be set to enforcing on your system.

9. To find out about the policies in force on your SELinux system, type the following command:

```
# seinfo
Statistics for policy file:
/etc/security/selinux/src/policy/policy.conf
    Classes:          30    Permissions:     128
    Types:          1244    Attributes:       68
    Users:             5    Roles:             7
    Allow:         26671    Neverallow:       54
    Auditallow:        4    Dontaudit:      2700
    Type_trans:     1271    Type_change:      17
    Role allow:        8    Role trans:      105
    Initial SIDs:     26
```

Here you can see the location of the `policy.conf` file that is in effect. You can also see statistics associated with that policy.

10. A good way to review the policies that are currently in effect in your SELinux system is to use the SePCuT: SE Linux Policy Customization Tool (`sepcut` command). With the setools package installed, you can start `sepcut` from a Terminal window by typing

```
# sepcut &
```

To display the policies delivered with Fedora Core 2, click Policy → Choose Policy Directory. Then select the following directory and click OK to view your policy:

```
/etc/security/selinux/src/policy
```

Figure 28-1 shows an example of the SePCuT window:

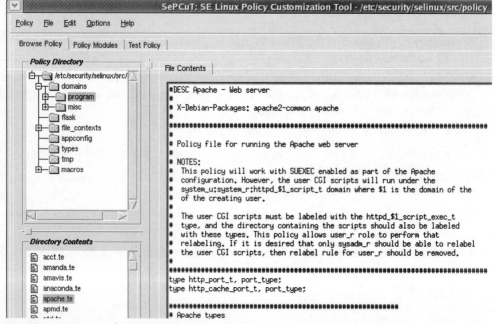

Figure 28-1: View SELinux policies in the SePCuT window.

Using the SePCuT window, you can browse the policy files to see what policies are set for your system. For example, in the Policy Directory pane select domains → programs. The list of files that appear in the Directory Contents pane show how policies are set for individual software projects (such as apache, automount, and bluetooth).

11. Check out log files in `/var/log`. If you have SELinux enabled, you will find lots of error messages, complaining about different components trying to do operations they are not permitted to do. With a lot of activity, the `dmesg` and `messages` files will be flooded with SELinux warning messages.

If you are finished testing SELinux, you can disable SELinux by `adding selinux=0` to the end of the kernel line on the GRUB screen for your kernel when you reboot your computer. Alternatively, you can change the value of `SELINUX` in the `/etc/sysconfig/selinux` file to `SELINUX=disabled`.

Learning More about SELinux

To dig deeper into SELinux, there are a variety of technical reports, FAQs, and component documents available. Here are a few places you can try:

- **FC2 SELinux FAQ** (`people.redhat.com/kwade/fedora-docs/selinux-faq-en`) — Provides information specific to the SELinux implementation in Fedora Core 2.

- **Getting Started with SE Linux HOWTO** (`www.lurking-grue.org/GettingStartedWithNewSELinucHOWTO.pdf`) — Provides helpful hints for getting started with SELinux.

- **SELinux Documentation** (`www.nsa.gov/selinux/info/docs.cfm`) — This site provides links to published papers, technical reports and presentations related to SELinux.

Summary

While SELinux is still in early stages of development, it is an important technology for allowing Linux to operate in highly secure environments. Although SELinux and several software packages of related tools are included with Fedora Core 2, SELinux is disabled by default. You can enable SELinux when you install Fedora Core 2 and later disable it if you choose to do so.

Appendix A

About the CD-ROMs

The CD-ROMs that accompany this book consist of the complete set of four installation CDs from the Red Hat–sponsored Fedora Project called Fedora Core 2. To install the installation CDs:

- Follow the instructions provided in Chapter 2 and on the CD-ROMs.
- Refer to Appendix B for a complete list of the Fedora Core 2 software packages.

If for some reason you don't have your CDs handy, you can find information on how to download any of these packages from the Fedora Project Web site at `fedora.redhat.com/download`.

Web sites such as `Freshrpms.net`, `rpm.livna.org`, and `RPMfind.net` can help you find extra, useful software packages that are not in Fedora (or any other Red Hat distribution) or that were once included with the Red Hat Linux PowerTools CD. Some of these sites act as repositories that allow you to download sets of dependent packages (see the description of `yum` in Chapter 5).

Fedora Source Code CDs

From time to time, you may want to recompile the Linux kernel. Doing so requires the kernel source code, which you can find in the kernel-source package included on this book's companion CD #3. The source code for all other packages in Fedora is available in the following ways:

- For the cost of shipping and handling, you can obtain the set of Fedora Core 2 source code CDs from Wiley Publishing, Inc. See the coupon in the back of the book for details. Changing this source code requires some knowledge of programming and software compilation tools.
- As with the installation CDs, you can download the source code CDs for Fedora Core 2 from the Fedora Project Web site (`fedora.redhat.com/download`).

Fedora Rescue CD

Late in the process, the Fedora Project added a ninth CD to the Fedora Core 2 software set. The Fedora Core 2 Rescue CD contains those features needed to rescue your Fedora system if, for example, the system failed to boot because of a corrupted file system. As with the other Fedora Core 2 CDs, you can download this CD from `fedora.redhat.com/download`.

To use the Fedora Core 2 Rescue CD, do the following:

1. Insert the Rescue CD into the CD drive.

2. Reboot your computer. You will see the Fedora Core 2 Rescue CD welcome screen with the `boot:` prompt at the bottom.

3. Press Enter to begin rescue mode. (You could also type **linux** to begin a Fedora Core install with this CD, or press the F2 function key to see other options.) The rescue CD asks you to choose a language.

4. Choose a language and select OK. You are asked to choose a keyboard type.

5. Choose a keyboard type and select OK. You are asked if you want to start network interfaces.

6. Choose Yes (to start a network interface, if you have a network interface card installed) or No (to continue booting without a network interface).

7. If you said Yes, choose DHCP, or type in a static IP address and Netmask for your computer. Also, identify your gateway (the machine that connects you to the Internet) and one or more DNS servers you need for address resolution.

8. When you enter the rescue environment. you need to choose whether or not to mount your Linux installation (under `/mnt/sysimage` directory) by selecting Continue, to mount it as read-only (select Read-Only), or to not mount it (select Skip).

If everything went well, you should receive the message: `Your system is mounted under the /mnt/sysimage directory`. You will see a shell prompt. Now you can:

- Try to fix any errors in your Linux configuration, beginning at `/mnt/sysimage` to find your normal root (/) directory.

- Backup or transfer files from your computer to other media or computers, if your system remains unbootable, so you can save any critical files.

When you are done, remove the CD and reboot your computer.

> **NOTE:** Everything you do with the rescue CD you can also do with the first CD in your Fedora Core 2 installation set. The rescue CD is just more convenient in some cases because it is smaller to copy (only 76MB as compared with 633 for CD #1) and quicker to boot up. It will also fit on a medium that is smaller than a full-size CD.

Appendix B

Fedora Core 2 RPMs

More than 1,600 RPM Package Manager (RPM) software packages make up the Linux distribution referred to as Fedora Core 2. This appendix contains an alphabetical listing and descriptions of those Fedora Core 2 software packages.

Packages are distributed across the four CDs that come with this book. Descriptions in this appendix help you determine the contents of those packages. You typically install the bulk of those packages when you install Fedora as described in Chapter 2. Later, you can add other packages using the Package Management window (Chapter 2) or the rpm command (Chapter 5).

Comparing Fedora and Enterprise Packages

The Fedora Project was set up as a proving ground for developing technology that can be used by Red Hat, Inc. to include in its Red Hat Enterprise Linux products. You can look at Fedora Core 2 as a way of getting a jump on technology that is slated to be included in Red Hat Enterprise Linux and related Linux distributions.

Although the timing of the releases of Fedora Core 2 and the next release of Red Hat Enterprise Linux (presumably version 4) may make some version numbers different, there are hundreds of software packages that will probably be the same in the two distributions.

Removed Packages

If you can't seem to find a software package you relied on in previous Red Hat Linux or Fedora Core distributions, you might be interested in the following list. It shows packages from Fedora Core 1 that are not in the Fedora Core 2 distribution:

- **cipe:** VPN daemon and kernel modules for Crypto IP Encapsulation (CIPE).
- **gtoaster:** A compact disc recording package that supports both audio and data files.
- **imap:** IMAP and POP protocol daemons for handling client mail transport.
- **imap-devel:** IMAP development tools for interfacing with IMAP mail servers.
- **ipchains:** Components for implementing firewalls and IP masquerading on IP networks.
- **kernel-BOOT:** A trimmed-down version of the Linux kernel for placing on a boot disk.

- **kernel-pcmcia-cs:** Software that supports PCMCIA devices (typically for laptops).
- **losetup:** Linux loop device tools for mapping regular files to virtual block devices.
- **mars-nwe:** NetWare file and print server emulation components.
- **mrproject:** A GNOME-based project management system.
- **nmh:** The nmh e-mail system, which can be used as a replacement for MH mail.
- **redhat-config-*:** Red Hat utilities for configuring aspects of a Linux system. (The applications are all still included with Fedora, but the names were changed to begin with `system-config-*`.)
- **redhat-switch-mail:** Mail transport agent switcher.
- **redhat-switch-mail-gnome:** GNOME-based mail transport agent switcher.
- **sndconfig:** A sound configuration utility.
- **switchdesk-gnome:** The GNOME look-and-feel version of the desktop switcher utility.
- **switchdesk-kde:** The KDE look-and-feel version of the desktop switcher utility.
- **xawtv:** A simple TV application for video4linux-compliant devices.
- **xawtv-tv-fonts:** Bitmap fonts for xawtv.
- **xcpustate:** An X Window-based CPU usage monitor.
- **XFree86:** Set of software packages associated with the XFree86 implementation of the X Window System. It has been replaced by the X.org X server software.
- **xtraceroute:** An X and GTK+–based graphical display of traceroute's output.

Red Hat Linux Packages on the CDs

The packages contained on the installation CD-ROMs are as follows:

- **4Suite:** Python programming tools for manipulating XML content and object databases.
- **a2ps:** Tools for converting text and other types of files into PostScript for printing.
- **abiword:** The AbiWord word processing application.
- **ac-archive:** The Autoconf Macro Archive providing macros for the autoconf tool.
- **acl:** Utilities needed for manipulating access control lists.
- **acpid:** Dispatches ACPI events to user-space programs.
- **adjtimex:** The `adjtimex` command for regulating the system clock.
- **alchemist:** Back-end XML-based application configuration architecture.
- **alchemist-devel:** Files needed for developing programs that use alchemist.
- **alsa-lib:** Advanced Linux Sound Architecture (ALSA) library.
- **alsa-lib-devel:** Advanced Linux Sound Architecture (ALSA) header files.
- **alsa-utils:** Advanced Linux Sound Architecture (ALSA) utilities.
- **amanda:** The amanda network-capable machine backup application.
- **amanda-client:** Client components for amanda network backup.
- **amanda-devel:** Libraries and docs needed to develop amanda applications.
- **amanda-server:** Server components for running amanda network backups.

- **am-utils:** Utilities for automounting file systems. Includes the amd daemon.
- **anaconda:** The Red Hat Linux installation program.
- **anaconda-help:** Help information used in the anaconda installer.
- **anaconda-images:** Graphical images used in the anaconda installer.
- **anaconda-runtime:** Used to build Red Hat media sets.
- **anacron:** Periodic command scheduler for machines that do not run 24 hours per day.
- **ant**: Tools for building platform-independent Java applications for Apache Jakarta and XML.
- **ant-core**: Core classes needed for Ant applications.
- **ant-devel**: Headers needed for CNI extensions to Ant applications.
- **ant-optional**: Headers needed for optional Ant tasks.
- **apel:** A portable emacs library for customizing emacs.
- **apel-xemacs:** A portable emacs library.
- **apmd:** The advanced power management software for monitoring battery power.
- **apr:** Apache portable runtime library.
- **apr-devel:** APR library development tools.
- **apr-util:** APR utility library.
- **apr-util-devel:** APR utility library development tools.
- **arpwatch:** The arpwatch utility for tracking Ethernet/IP address pairings.
- **arts:** The analog real-time synthesizer software used with the KDE 3 sound system.
- **arts-devel:** Libraries and documentation needed to develop programs using arts.
- **ash:** A lightweight shell, similar to the UNIX System V sh (Bourne) shell.
- **asp2php:** Tools for converting active server pages to PHP format.
- **asp2php-gtk:** A gtk+ front-end interface for the asp2php application.
- **aspell*:** A set of packages for spell checking in a variety of languages.
- **aspell-devel:** Libraries and documentation needed to develop applications using aspell.
- **at:** The at and batch commands facilitate one-shot, time-oriented job control.
- **atk:** A set of interfaces for adding accessibility support to applications.
- **atk-devel:** The libraries, header files, and documentation for atk.
- **at-spi:** Allows screen readers, magnifiers, or scripts to interact with GUI controls.
- **at-spi-devel:** Libraries and header files for compiling at-spi.
- **attr:** Tools for manipulating extended filesystem attributes.
- **audiofile:** Utilities that implement the SGI Audio File library for processing audio files.
- **audiofile-devel:** Development tools associated with audio software development.
- **aumix:** The aumix program for adjusting audio mixing device (/dev/mixer) settings.
- **authconfig:** Tools for configuring system authorization resources.
- **authconfig-gtk:** A graphical tool for configuring system-authorization resources.
- **autoconf:** Tools to create scripts to make portable, configurable source-code packages.

- **autoconf213:** An older version of autoconf.
- **autoconvert:** Autoconverter tools for converting Chinese HZ/GB/BIG5 encodings.
- **autoconvert-xchat:** Autoconvert-xchat plugins.
- **autofs:** Automatically mounts and unmounts file systems through the automount daemon.
- **automake:** The automake makefile generator.
- **automake14:** Included for projects not updated to work with newer automake.
- **automake15:** Included for projects not updated to work with newer automake.
- **automake16:** Included for projects not updated to work with newer automake.
- **automake17:** Included for projects not updated to work with newer automake.
- **autorun:** Software that automatically detects and mounts CD-ROMs.
- **awesfx:** Utilities for controlling the AWE32 sound driver.
- **balsa:** The balsa e-mail reader (which is part of the GNOME desktop).
- **basesystem:** Part of the base Red Hat Linux system.
- **bash:** Version 2.05b of the GNU Bash shell (Bourne Again SHell).
- **bc:** The bc precision-calculator command-line utility and language.
- **bcel**: Byte Code Engineering Library (BCEL) for working with Java class files.
- **bcel-devel**: Byte Code Engineering Library (BCEL) development tools.
- **beecrypt:** General purpose cryptography library.
- **beecrypt-devel:** Files needed to develop applications with beecrypt.
- **beecrypt-python:** Python bindings for developing applications with beecrypt.
- **bg5ps:** A tool that converts BIG5 encoded Chinese into printable PostScript.
- **bind:** Berkeley Internet Name Domain implentation of the DNS protocols.
- **bind-chroot:** A chrooted implementation of the BIND name server.
- **bind-devel:** Header files needed for BIND 9.x.x DNS software development.
- **bind-libs:** Runtime libraries needed for the BIND packages.
- **bind-utils:** The dig, dnsquery, nslookup, nsupdate, and other DNS utilities.
- **binutils:** GNU command-line tools, such as `ar`, `as`, `ld`, `nm`, `size`, and others.
- **bison:** The GNU bison parser generator (replacement for `yacc`).
- **bitmap-fonts:** Bitmap fonts from the Xfree86 package designed for use on terminals.
- **bitmap-fonts-cjk:** Bitmap fonts selected from Xfree86 for use by anaconda.
- **bitstream-vera-fonts:** High-quality Latin fonts donated by Vera.
- **blas:** Basic Linear Algebra Subprograms (BLAS) libraries for basic linear algebra.
- **bluez-bluefw:** Bluetooth firmware loader.
- **bluez-hcidump:** A Bluetooth protocol analyzer.
- **bluez-libs:** Libraries for Bluetooth applications.
- **bluez-libs-devel:** Development libraries for Bluetooth applications.
- **bluez-pan:** Bluetooth personal area networking tools.

- **bluez-pin:** Bluetooth software to ask users for PIN to pair Bluetooth devices.
- **bluez-sdp:** Bluetooth service discovery protocol libraries.
- **bluez-sdp-devel:** Bluetooth service discovery protocol library tools.
- **bluez-utils:** Bluetooth utilities.
- **bogl:** Small graphics library for Linux's frame buffers.
- **bogl-bterm:** Terminal emulator that displays to a frame buffer.
- **bogl-devel:** Development libraries for Ben's Own Graphics Library.
- **bonobo:** A CORBA-based system utilized by the GNOME desktop environment.
- **bonobo-devel:** Libraries for developing bonobo document model applications.
- **boost:** Boost peer reviewed C++ libraries.
- **boost-devel:** Boost C++ library development tools.
- **bootparamd:** The `bootparamd` boot parameter server to boot diskless workstations.
- **booty:** Python library for anaconda and up2date bootloader configuration.
- **bridge-utils:** Utilities for bridging multiple Ethernet LANs.
- **bridge-utils-devel:** Programming interface to the Linux Ethernet bridge.
- **brltty:** Braille display driver.
- **bug-buddy:** A graphical bug-reporting tool.
- **busybox:** A single binary providing simplified versions of common Linux commands.
- **busybox-anaconda:** A version of busybox for use with anaconda.
- **byacc:** The Berkeley `yacc` parser generator.
- **bzip2:** The bzip2 and bzcat utilities for compressing and uncompressing files.
- **bzip2-devel:** Programming tools associated with the bzip and bzcat utilities.
- **bzip2-libs:** Libraries for applications using bzip2.
- **caching-nameserver:** Configuration files used for caching-only name servers.
- **cadaver:** A command-line WebDAV client.
- **Canna:** A unified Japanese character input system.
- **Canna-devel:** Developments tools associated with Canna.
- **Canna-libs:** Runtime library for the Canna Japanese input system.
- **cdda2wav:** Coverts CD audio files into WAV sound files.
- **cdecl:** Composes C and C++ type declarations from english or vice versa.
- **cdicconf:** Maintenance tools for the Canna dictionary.
- **cdlabelgen:** Generates frontcards and traycards for compact disc cases.
- **cdp:** Textmode utility for playing music CDs.
- **cdparanoia:** Compact disk digital audio extraction tool.
- **cdparanoia-devel:** Development tools for digital audio extraction.
- **cdparanoia-libs:** Libraries for cdparanoia.
- **cdrdao:** A tool for writing audio CD-ROMs in disc-at-once mode.

- **cdrecord:** Software for writing data to writable CD-ROMs.
- **cdrecord-devel:** Development tools for writing data to writable CD-ROMs.
- **checkpolicy:** SELinux policy compiler.
- **chkconfig:** Changes system service run-level information.
- **chkfontpath:** Command-line interface for managing the X server font path.
- **chromium:** An arcade-style shooting game.
- **ckermit:** Cross-platform serial and network communications software.
- **cleanfeed:** Filters spam from incoming USENET news feeds.
- **commons-*:** A set of packages for developing reusable JAVA components under the Apache Jakarta Commons project (`http://jakarta.apache.org/commons`).
- **compat-db:** Legacy releases of the Berkeley Database.
- **compat-gcc:** Compatibility compiler for building binaries for Red Hat 7.3 and older.
- **compat-gcc-c++:** Generates C++ binaries for older Red Hat Linux systems.
- **compat-gcc-g77:** Generates Fortran 77 binaries for older Red Hat Linux systems.
- **compat-gcc-java:** Generates Java binaries for older Red Hat Linux systems.
- **compat-gcc-objc:** Generates Objective-C binaries for older Red Hat Linux Systems.
- **compat-libgcj:** Java runtime library for the Red Hat Linux 7.3 Java compiler (gcj)
- **compat-libgcj-devel:** Libraries for compiling with the gcc java compiler.
- **compat-libstdc++:** Snapshot implementation of the GCC Standard C++ library.
- **compat-libstdc++-devel:** Libraries for the Red Hat C++ compatibility compiler.
- **compat-pwdb:** Library for managing the Linux's PAM interface to user authentication.
- **compat-slang:** Programming library for the S-Lang extension language.
- **comps:** Comps file and header lists for Red Hat Linux.
- **comps-extras:** Tools and images for working on the comps file.
- **comsat:** Asynchronous mail notification client and server.
- **control-center:** GNOME desktop configuration tool.
- **coreutils:** A set of GNU tools commonly used in shell scripts.
- **cpio:** Copying files to or from a number of archive formats into files, disk, or tape.
- **cpp:** The cpp (C preprocessor) macro processing utility, for preprocessing C code.
- **cproto:** Creates function prototypes and variable declarations from C source code.
- **cracklib:** Library for applications that need to test the "strength" of a password.
- **cracklib-dicts:** Dictionaries that are used by CrackLib when testing password security.
- **crontabs:** The root crontabs files, used by the `cron` daemon to schedule tasks.
- **cryptsetup:** The cryptsetup utility for creating encrypted filesystems.
- **ctags:** The ctags tool for generating tag files of objects from C source code.
- **cup:** Java parser generator.
- **cups:** The Common Unix Printing System.

- **cups-devel:** Development environment for CUPS.
- **cups-libs:** Libraries allowing applications to use CUPS natively.
- **curl:** A feature-packed utility for retrieving files using various Internet protocols.
- **curl-devel:** The files needed for building applications that use curl functionality.
- **cvs:** Maintains a history of file changes.
- **cyrus-imapd*:** Set of packages to support high-performance IMAP and POP3 environments that can run on sealed servers.
- **cyrus-sasl:** The Cyrus version of the Simple Authentication and Security Layer (SASL).
- **cyrus-sasl-devel:** The files needed for developing applications that use cyrus-sasl.
- **cyrus-sasl-gssapi:** Plugins for cyrus-sasl that support GSSAPI authentication.
- **cyrus-sasl-md5:** Cyrus-sasl plugins for CRAM-MD5 and DIGEST-MD5 authentication.
- **cyrus-sasl-plain:** Cyrus-sasl plugins for PLAIN and LOGIN authentication schemes.
- **db4:** C library for revision 4 of the Berkeley Database.
- **db4-devel:** Header files and libraries for db4 development.
- **db4-tcl:** Development files for using the Berkeley DB (version 4) with tcl.
- **db4-utils:** Command-line tools for managing a revision 4 Berkeley database.
- **dbh:** Disk-based hash library.
- **dbh-devel:** Header files for disk-based hash library.
- **dbus:** Systemwide message bus service.
- **dbus-devel:** Development tools for systemwide message bus service.
- **dbus-glib:** GLIB library for using D-BUS.
- **dbus-x11:** Xlib tools required by DBUS, so X doesn't have to be installed.
- **ddd:** The Data Display Debugger, a GUI that interacts with command-line debuggers.
- **ddskk:** A simple Kana to Kanji conversion tool for emacs.
- **ddskk-xemacs:** Simple Kana to Kanji conversion tool for XEmacs.
- **ddskkd-cdb:** A dictionary server for the SKK Japanese input method.
- **dejagnu:** An Expect/Tcl framework for testing programs.
- **desktop-backgrounds-basic:** A selection of images to use as screen backgrounds.
- **desktop-backgrounds-extra:** Supplements desktop-backgrounds-basic.
- **desktop-file-utils:** Creates and validates .desktop files.
- **desktop-printing:** Desktop icon and code to support drag-n-drop printing.
- **dev:** Commonly used Linux device files.
- **dev86:** An x86 assembler and linker.
- **devhelp:** An API document browser for GNOME 2.
- **device-mapper:** Userspace support for the device-mapper.
- **devlabel**: Consistent storage device access facilitated by symlinking.
- **dhclient:** DHCP client application.

- **dhcp:** Dynamic Host Configuration Protocol (DHCP) server and relay agent.
- **dhcp-devel:** Libraries for interfacing with the ISC DHCP server.
- **dia:** Visio-like diagramming and drawing program.
- **dialog:** The dialog utility for showing dialog boxes in text mode interfaces.
- **dictd:** The ict client, used to access to dictionary definitions from a DICT server.
- **dietlibc:** A small implementation of libc.
- **diffstat:** Generates statistics from the output of the `diff` command.
- **diffutils:** Contains the `diff`, `cmp`, `diff3`, and `sdiff` utilities for comparing files.
- **diskcheck:** A utility that monitors the remaining free space on a hard drive.
- **distcache:** Distributed SSL session cache.
- **distcache-devel:** Development tools for distcache distributed session cache.
- **dmalloc:** A drop-in replacement for memory management routines.
- **docbook-*:** A set of packages containing DocBook SGML DTDs and style sheets.
- **dos2unix:** Converts text files from DOS to UNIX format.
- **dosfstools:** Tools for creating and working with DOS file systems.
- **dovecot:** Dovecot secure imap server.
- **doxygen:** Creates documents from C or C++ source code.
- **doxygen-doxywizard:** A GUI front-end to create and edit doxygen configuration files.
- **dtach:** A simple program that emulates the detach feature of screen.
- **dump:** Utilities for backing up and restoring ext2/3 file systems.
- **dvdrecord:** A command-line CD/DVD recording program.
- **dvd+rw-tools:** Tools for mastering DVD+RW/+R media.
- **dvgrab:** Captures digital video from a firewire connected device.
- **e2fsprogs:** Programs for finding and fixing inconsistencies in ext2 file systems.
- **e2fsprogs-devel:** Libraries and header files to develop programs for the ext2 file system.
- **ed:** A line-oriented text editor (which was the original UNIX text editor).
- **eel2:** The Eazel Extensions Library, a collection of widgets and functions for GNOME.
- **eel2-devel:** Libraries and include files for developing with eel.
- **efax:** Sends and receives faxes using any Class 1, 2, or 2.0 fax modem.
- **eject:** Ejects CDs, floppies, Jazz disks, or other media.
- **ElectricFence:** Detects memory allocation violations.
- **elfutils:** Collection of utilities for handling compiled objects.
- **elfutils-devel:** Development utilities for handling compiled objects.
- **elfutils-libelf:** Provides a DSO that facilitates the reading and writing of ELF files.
- **elinks:** A text-mode Web browser with support for frames.
- **emacs:** Libraries needed to run the emacs editor.
- **emacs-common:** The libraries needed to run the GNU Emacs text editor.

- **emacs-el:** The emacs-elisp sources of elisp programs used with the emacs text editor.
- **emacs-leim:** The Emacs Lisp code used with international character scripts.
- **emacs-nox:** The Emacs text editor without support for the X Window System.
- **emacspeak:** A speech interface that allows visually impaired users to use the computer.
- **enscript:** Print filter for formatting ASCII text into PostScript output.
- **eog:** Eye of GNOME image viewer.
- **epic:** Enhanced ircii chat client.
- **epiphany:** A GNOME Web browser based on Mozilla.
- **eruby:** A Ruby interpreter for Ruby code embedded in text files.
- **eruby-devel:** Header files and libraries allowing an application to use eRuby.
- **eruby-libs:** Libraries required for eRuby.
- **esound:** Allows multiple programs to share a sound card.
- **esound-devel:** Libraries and include files for developing EsounD applications.
- **ethereal:** A tool for analyzing network traffic on UNIX –ish operating systems.
- **ethereal-gnome:** GNOME desktop environment integration for ethereal.
- **ethtool:** Displays and changes Ethernet card settings.
- **evolution:** GNOME's groupware suite of integrated information-management tools.
- **exim:** The exim mail transfer agent.
- **exim-doc:** Exim documentation.
- **exim-mon:** X11 monitor application for exim.
- **exim-sa:** Exim SpamAssassin at SMPT time – d/l plugin.
- **expat:** C library for stream-oriented XML parsing.
- **expat-devel:** Documentation and libraries for developing XML applications with expat.
- **expect:** A tcl extension for automating interactive utilities such as FTP, fsck, and telnet.
- **expect-devel:** Expect development libraries.
- **expectk:** A program-script interaction and testing utility.
- **fam:** Tracks file system changes through a daemon and API.
- **fam-devel:** Libraries and header files for fam.
- **fbset**: Used to change video modes on fbcon consoles.
- **fedora-logos:** Red Hat-related icons and pictures.
- **fedora-release:** Fedora Core release file.
- **festival:** A free multilingual speech synthesizer.
- **festival-devel:** Header files and libraries allowing applications to use festival.
- **fetchmail:** Retrieves and forwards mail over SLIP and PPP links.
- **file:** Identifies file type based on file contents.
- **file-roller:** Manages archives such as tar files.
- **filesystem:** The basic directory level layout of the Red Hat Linux system.

- **findutils:** GNU versions of the find and xargs utilities.
- **finger:** Client for displaying information about system users.
- **finger-server:** Server for providing the finger service to network clients.
- **firstboot:** Runs after installation to facilitate easier configuration of the system.
- **flac:** An encoder/decoder for the Free Lossless Audio Codec.
- **flac-devel:** Static libraries and header files from FLAC.
- **flex:** Generates C source code for recognition of lexical patterns in text.
- **flim:** A library that provides basic features for message encoding in emacs.
- **flim-xemacs:** A library that provides basic features for message encoding in XEmacs.
- **fontconfig:** Locates and sets fonts based on requirements set by applications.
- **fontconfig-devel:** Headers and documentation for developing fontconfig applications.
- **fonta-arabic:** Arabic fonts from the King Abdulaziz City for Science and Technology.
- **fonts-bengali:** Fonts for Bengali.
- **fonts-hebrew:** Hebrew fonts from the Culmus project.
- **fonts-ISO8859-2*:** Various Central European– and Greek-language fonts.
- **fonts-ja:** Japanese bitmap fonts.
- **fonts-KOI8-R*:** Various Russian- and Ukranian-language fonts.
- **foomatic:** A spooler-independent database of printers and printer drivers.
- **freeciv:** The freeciv clone of the Civilization II strategy game.
- **freeglut:** A free implementation of the GLUT library.
- **freeglut-devel:** Development tools for freeGLUT.
- **freeradius:** Highly configurable RADIUS server.
- **freeradius-mysql:** MySQL bindings for freeradius.
- **freeradius-postgresql:** PostgreSQL bindings for freeradius.
- **freeradius-unixODBC:** unixODBC bindings for freeradius.
- **freetype:** A free and portable font rendering engine for TrueType fonts.
- **freetype-demos:** A collection of freetype demos.
- **freetype-devel:** Components for using the FreeType font rendering engine.
- **freetype-utils:** Several utilities for managing fonts.
- **FreeWnn:** Converts Japanese Kana characters to Kanji characters and vice versa.
- **FreeWnn-common:** Common files needed for Wnn Kana to Kanji conversion.
- **FreeWnn-devel:** Tools for developing applications for FreeWnn.
- **FreeWnn-libs:** Runtime libraries for running FreeWnn applications.
- **fribidi:** A free implementation of the Unicode BiDi algorithm.
- **fribidi-devel:** Development tools for the Unicode BiDi algorithm.
- **fsh:** The `fsh` command for creating secure network tunnels.
- **ftp:** Generic client for the File Transfer Protocol.

- **ftpcopy:** Tools to facilitate mirroring of FTP sites
- **g-wrap:** A tool for creating Scheme interfaces to C libraries.
- **g-wrap-devel:** Include files and libraries needed for g-wrap development.
- **gail:** Implements the ATK accessibility interfaces for packages such as at-spi.
- **gail-devel:** Files required to compile applications that use GAIL.
- **gaim:** Open source clone of the popular AOL instant messager client.
- **gal:** The GNOME Applications Library (GAL), including GNOME utilities and widgets.
- **gal-devel:** Development tools associated with the GNOME Applications Library.
- **gawk:** The gawk (GNU awk) text processing utility.
- **gcc*:** This set of packages contains GNU C language compilers and related tools.
- **GConf:** The GNOME configuration database system.
- **GConf2:** A configuration database API used to store user preferences.
- **GConf-devel:** Library files required for developing with GConf.
- **GConf2-devel:** Library files required for developing with GConf2.
- **gconf-editor:** Editor and admin tool for GConf configuration sources.
- **gd:** A graphics library for creating JPEG and PNG image files.
- **gdb:** A command-driven debugger.
- **gdbm:** The Gdbm database indexing library.
- **gdbm-devel:** Components to develop applications to use the GNU database system.
- **gd-devel:** Components to develop applications that use the gd graphics library.
- **gdk-pixbuf:** The GDK Pixbuf image loading libraries.
- **gdk-pixbuf-devel:** Development tools associated with GDK Pixbuf.
- **gdk-pixbuf-gnome:** GNOME Canvas support for displaying images.
- **gdm:** The GNOME display manager, maintains an X-based graphical login.
- **gd-progs:** Utility programs associated with the gd graphics library.
- **gedit:** A compact, GNOME-based text editor.
- **gedit-devel:** The files needed for developing plug-ins for the gEdit editor.
- **genromfs:** Utilities for building romfs file systems for initial RAM disks.
- **gettext:** Tools and utilities for creating multilingual messages.
- **gftp:** A multithreaded graphical ftp program.
- **ggv:** A Ghostscript front-end, adding panning and persistent user settings to Ghostscript.
- **ghostscript:** Displays and prints PostScript files.
- **ghostscript-devel:** Header files for developing Ghostscript-enabled applications.
- **ghostscript-fonts:** A set of type fonts used with the Ghostscript program.
- **ghostscript-gtk:** A GTK-enabled PostScript interpreter and renderer.
- **giftrans:** Converts GIF87 files to GIF89 format.
- **gimp:** GNU Image Manipulation Program.

- **gimp-data-extras:** Patterns, gradients, and other graphical elements to use with GIMP.
- **gimp-devel:** Libraries needed to develop GIMP plug-ins and extensions.
- **gimp-gap**: Plug-ins to create and edit animations in GIMP.
- **gimp-help**: User manual for GIMP.
- **gimp-print:** Drivers that provide enhanced printing during demanding tasks.
- **gimp-print-cups:** Native drivers for Canon, Epson, and compatible printers.
- **gimp-print-devel:** Libraries, and documentation to the GIMP printing interface.
- **gimp-print-plugin:** GIMP plug-in for gimp-print.
- **gimp-print-utils:** Utility programs from gimp-print.
- **gkrellm:** Monitoring software that charts CPU use, disk activity, and network traffic.
- **gkrellm-daemon:** Server side of gkrellm.
- **gkrellm-devel:** Header files for gkrellm.
- **gkrellm-wireless:** Plug-in to monitor wireless LAN cards with gkrellm.
- **glade:** Software for developing quick user interfaces for the GTK+ toolkit.
- **glade2:** A version of glade for GTK+ 2.0.
- **glib:** Glib version 1.2 library of common functions used to improve portability.
- **glib2:** Glib version 2 library of common functions used to improve portability.
- **glib2-devel:** Static libraries and header files used with the glib2 development package.
- **glibc:** Standard libraries used by a multitude of programs.
- **glibc-common:** Common binaries, locale support, and time zone databases.
- **glibc-devel:** Standard header and object files to develop most C language programs.
- **glibc-headers:** Header files for development using standard C libraries.
- **glibc-kernheaders:** Header files for the Linux kernel for use by glibc.
- **glibc-profile:** The libraries needed to create programs being profiled with gprof.
- **glibc-utils:** Various tools useful during program debugging.
- **glib-devel:** Static libraries and header files to support the GIMP Xlibrary.
- **Glide3:** A programming interface to 3DfxVoodoo graphics cards.
- **Glide3-devel:** Interface for using 3D accelators in 3Dfx Interactive Voodoo cards.
- **gmp:** The MP library for handling arithmetic and floating-point number functions.
- **gmp-devel:** Components to develop GNU MP arbitrary precision applications.
- **gnome-applets:** Applets (tiny graphical applications) used on the GNOME desktop.
- **gnome-audio:** A set of sounds that you can use with your GNOME environment.
- **gnome-audio-extra:** Sound files that can be used with the GNOME desktop.
- **gnome-bluetooth:** Simple GUI to control Bluetooth devices.
- **gnome-desktop:** Code shared among GNOME components.
- **gnome-desktop-devel:** Libraries for compiling GNOME-desktop components.
- **gnome-games:** GNOME games such as solitaire, gnothello, and tetris.

- **gnome-icon-theme:** Base GNOME desktop environment icons.
- **gnome-kerberos:** The krb5 tools for managing Kerberos 5 tickets.
- **gnome-keyring:** Keyring and password manager for the GNOME desktop.
- **gnome-keyring-devel:** Development libraries and header files for gnome-keyring.
- **gnome-libs:** Libraries needed by the GNOME desktop environment and applications.
- **gnome-libs-devel:** Libraries needed to create applications to run on a GNOME desktop.
- **gnome-mag**: GNOME magnifying library for AT-SPI applications.
- **gnome-mag-devel**: Development tooks for the GNOME AT-SPI magnifying library.
- **gnome-media:** The GNOME CD player and other multimedia tools.
- **gnomemeeting:** An H323 teleconferencing tool compatible with Microsoft NetMeeting.
- **gnome-mime-data:** The file-type recognition data files for GNOME-VFS.
- **gnome-netstatus:** Network interface monitoring applet for GNOME panel.
- **gnome-panel:** Provides desktop management utilities.
- **gnome-pilot:** Files needed to integrate GNOME and PalmOS devices like Palm Pilots.
- **gnome-pilot-conduits:** Additional conduits for gnome-pilot.
- **gnome-pilot-devel:** Libraries needed to enable applications to use gnome-pilot.
- **gnome-print:** Fonts and tools needed by GNOME applications to print from GNOME.
- **gnome-print-devel:** Software development tools associated with printing in GNOME.
- **gnome-python2-*:** Wrappers that allow GNOME components to be written in Python.
- **gnome-session:** Handles startup and shutdown of core GNOME components.
- **gnome-speech:** GNOME text-to-speech tools.
- **gnome-speech-devel:** Development tools for GNOME text-to-speech features.
- **gnome-spell:** A bonobo component for spell checking.
- **gnome-system-monitor:** A simple process and system monitor.
- **gnome-terminal:** A GNOME terminal emulator.
- **gnome-themes:** Themes collection for GNOME.
- **gnome-user-docs:** A glossary, introduction, and other documentation for GNOME.
- **gnome-utils:** Several useful GNOME utilities, such as a calculator and a calendar.
- **gnome-vfs:** The GNOME virtual file system libraries.
- **gnome-vfs-devel:** Libraries and header files to develop GNOME-VFS2 applications.
- **gnome-vfs-extras:** GNOME-VFS modules including a Samba smb network browser.
- **gnome-vfs2:** Revision 2.0 of the GNOME virtual file system libraries.
- **gnome-vfs2-devel:** Libraries and header files to develop GNOME-VFS2 applications.
- **gnome-vfs2-smb:** Windows fileshare support for gnome-vfs.
- **gnopernicus:** The gnopernicus screen magnifier.
- **gnucash:** A personal finance tracker.
- **gnucash-backend-postgres:** Backend for storing GnuCash data in PostgreSQL.

- **gnuchess:** The GNU chess program and related utilities.
- **gnumeric:** The GNOME-based gnumeric spreadsheet program.
- **gnumeric-devel:** Development tools for the gnumeric spreadsheet application.
- **gnupg:** GNU Privacy Guard, used for secure communication and data storage.
- **gnuplot:** Utilities, used to plot scientific and other types of data.
- **gob2:** Preprocessor for making GObject objects.
- **gok:** GNOME onscreen keyboard.
- **gpdf:** Viewer for Portable Document Format (PDF) files for GNOME.
- **gperf:** C++ hash function generator.
- **gphoto2:** Manage and access images from digital cameras.
- **gphoto2-devel:** Header files needed to create applications that use gphoto2.
- **gpm:** Console-based mouse server.
- **gpm-devel:** Libraries for developing text-mode programs with mouse functionality.
- **gqview:** Feature rich image viewer.
- **grep:** Utilities for finding string patterns in files.
- **grip:** A graphical front-end for various compact disc rippers and MP3 encoders.
- **groff:** Console-based text formatting utilities.
- **groff-gxditview:** GUI-based `groff` text output viewer.
- **groff-perl:** Utilities for working with groff documents that require Perl.
- **grub:** Grand Unified Boot Loader, used for booting operating systems such as Linux.
- **gsl:** GNU Scientific Library for numerical analysis and high-level mathematics.
- **gsl-devel:** Header and library files needed to create applications that use gsl.
- **gstreamer:** Streaming media framework.
- **gstreamer-devel:** Development libraries for streaming media framework.
- **gstreamer-plugins:** Plug-ins for the streaming media framework.
- **gstreamer-plugins-devel:** Development libraries for the streaming media framework.
- **gstreamer-tools:** Basic command line tools used with the streaming media framework.
- **gthumb:** An application for viewing, editing, and organizing collections of images.
- **gtk+:** GIMP graphical toolkit for building X-based graphical user interfaces.
- **gtk+-devel:** gtk+ development tools to create applications that need GIMP.
- **gtk2:** A toolkit used to create graphical user interfaces (GUIs).
- **gtk2-devel:** Header files and developer documentation for the GTK+ toolkit.
- **gtk2-engines:** Theme engines for GTK+ 2.0
- **gtkam:** A GTK-based interface to gphoto2.
- **gtkam-gimp:** A GIMP plug-in to allow digital-camera access through gphoto2.
- **gtk-doc:** Tools that generate documentation for GTK+, GNOME, and Glib components.
- **gtk-engines:** GTK+ toolkit themes (including Notif, Redmond95, and Metal).

- **gtkglarea:** An OpenGL widget for the GTK+ GUI library.
- **gtkhtml:** A lightweight HTML renderer/printing/editing engine.
- **gtkhtml-devel:** Libraries needed to develop applications that use gtkhtml.
- **gtkhtml2:** An HTML display widget for GTK+ 2.0
- **gtkhtml2-devel:** Libraries needed to create gtkhtml2 applications.
- **gtkhtml3:** The gtkhtml library.
- **gtkhtml3-devel:** Libraries needed to create gtkhtml3 applications.
- **Gtk-Perl:** Perl extensions for gtk+ that facilitate GUI creation using Perl.
- **gtksourceview:** Library for viewing source code files.
- **gtksourceview-devel:** Tools for compiling applications with gtksourceview libraries.
- **gtkspell:** On-the-fly spell checking for GtkTextView widgets.
- **gtkspell-devel:** Development tools for gtkspell.
- **guile:** A library implementation of the Scheme programming language.
- **guile-devel:** Libraries and headers needed to link programs with the GUILE library.
- **Guppi:** A GNOME-based data analysis and visualization system.
- **Guppi-devel:** Header files and libraries needed to develop applications that use Guppi.
- **gv:** A lightweight front-end tool for viewing PostScript and PDF documents in X.
- **gzip:** A data compression utility.
- **h2ps:** Converts Korean Hangul from text to PostScript.
- **hdparm:** Utility for setting and viewing hard drive parameters.
- **hesiod:** Utilities and libraries for viewing hesiod databases.
- **hesiod-devel:** Libraries and headers for applications that use hesiod databases.
- **hexedit:** A hexadecimal file viewer and editor.
- **hfsutils*:** Set of packages that offer support for Macintosh hierarchical file systems.
- **hicolor-icon-theme:** Basic requirement for icon themes.
- **hotplug:** Hotplug utilities for loading modules needed when a USB device is connected.
- **hpijs:** A collection of optimized HP-printer drivers.
- **hpoj:** HP OfficeJet low-level driver infrastructure.
- **hpoj-devel:** Development libraries for HP OfficeJet low-level driver infrastructure.
- **htdig:** The htdig Web indexing and search system.
- **htdig-web:** CGI scripts and HTML code used by htdig.
- **htmlview:** Used by applications to display their HTML-based help pages.
- **httpd:** The Apache Web server configuration files, documentation, and daemons.
- **httpd-devel:** Apache Web server header files and apxs tool for extension modules.
- **httpd-manual:** The Apache manual (in HTML format).
- **hwbrowser:** A browser for the current system hardware configuration.
- **hwcrypto:** Libraries for interfacing with hardware crypto accelerators under Linux.

- **hwdata:** Identification and configuration data for system hardware.
- **icon-slicer:** Tool for greating icon themes.
- **iiimf*:** Intranet/Internet Input Method Framework packages.
- **ImageMagick:** A feature-rich graphical display and editing tool.
- **ImageMagick-c++:** C++ bindings for applications that use ImageMagick functionality.
- **ImageMagick-c++-devel:** C++ libraries used with ImageMagick graphics library.
- **ImageMagick-devel:** Libraries needed to implement ImageMagick APIs.
- **ImageMagick-perl:** Perl bindings to ImageMagick.
- **imlib:** Image loading and rendering library used with the X Window System.
- **imlib-cfgeditor:** The imlib_conf program, used to control how imlib renders images.
- **imlib-devel:** Components to develop programs with Imlib image and rendering library.
- **indent:** The indent utility for beautifying C programming code.
- **inews:** Posts Usenet news articles to a local news server.
- **info:** A text-based browser for displaying texinfo (pronounced "tech-info") files.
- **initscripts:** Boot time and runlevel initialization scripts.
- **inn:** The InterNetNews server for creating and maintaining a news server in Linux.
- **inn-devel:** Components to develop applications that use the InterNetNews system.
- **intltool:** A utility for internationalizing various data files.
- **iproute:** The `ip` command and related utilities used for routing IP traffic.
- **ipsec-tools:** Tools for configuring and using IPSEC.
- **iptables:** Advanced packet filtering tools.
- **iptables-devel:** Development package for iptables.
- **iptables-ipv6:** Advanced packet filtering tools for IPv6 networks.
- **iptraf:** A console-based network monitoring tool.
- **iptstate**: The iptstate utility to display the state of an iptables firewall.
- **iputils:** Various network-monitoring utilities, including `ping` and `rdisc`.
- **ipvsadm**: Utility to administer kernel IP virtual server table.
- **ipxutils:** A set of utilities for configuring and working with Novell IPX networks.
- **irb:** Interactive Ruby, a terminal-based Ruby expression evaluator.
- **irda-utils:** The IrDA utilities, used to communicate with infrared devices.
- **iscsi:** The iSCSI daemon and utility programs.
- **isdn4k-utils:** Tools for configuring ISDN subsystem.
- **isdn4k-utils-devel:** Library and header files needed to develop capi applications.
- **isdn4k-utils-vboxgetty:** The vboxgetty and vboxputty tools used with ISDN voice box.
- **isicom:** Utilities for loading Multitech Intelligent Serial Internal data files.
- **jadetex:** The `jadetex` and `pdfjadetex` commands to work with DSSSL documents.
- **jaf**: Files to support JavaBeans Activation Framework (JAF).

- **jaf-devel**: Development tools related to JavaBeans Activation Framework (JAF).
- **jcode.pl:** A perl library for Japanese character code conversion.
- **jed:** The jed text editor, based on the slang screen library.
- **jfsutils:** Utilities for managing a JFS file system.
- **jisksp14:** 14 dots jis auxiliary kanji font.
- **jisksp16:** 16 dots jis auxiliary kanji font.
- **joe:** The joe modeless text editor that uses Borland WordStar keybindings.
- **joystick:** Utilities for attaching and configuring a joystick.
- **jpilot:** A desktop organizer application for the Palm Pilot.
- **junit**: Framework for unit testing in Java.
- **junit-devel**: Headers needed by CNI extensions to junit.
- **jwhois:** Whois client for whois and finger-style queries.
- **k3b**: KDE graphical utility for burning CDs and DVDs.
- **kakasi:** Japanese character converter that sets Kanji to Hiragana, Katakana, or Romaji.
- **kakasi-devel:** The header and library files for developing applications that use Kakasi.
- **kakasi-dict:** The base Kakasi dictionary.
- **kappa20:** Japanese fonts in 20pt.
- **kbd:** Utilities for configuring the system console.
- **kcc:** A Kanji code converter.
- **kdbg:** The KDE graphical front-end for the GNU debugger (gdb).
- **kdeaddons:** K Desktop plug-ins Konquerer, noatun, and Kate.
- **kdeaddons-atlantikdesigner:** Game board designer for Atlantik.
- **kdeadmin:** Tape backup, user administration, and other system tools for KDE.
- **kdeartwork:** Additional artwork (themes, sound themes, and so on) for KDE.
- **kdeartwork-icons:** Icon themes (kdeclassic, slick, and so on) for KDE.
- **kdebase:** Basic KDE tools such as kwm, kfm file manager, and konsole.
- **kdebase-devel:** Header files for developing applications using kdebase.
- **kdebindings:** KDE bindings to non-C++ languages.
- **kdebindings-devel:** Development files for kdebindings.
- **kdeedu:** Edutainment applications for KDE.
- **kdeedu-devel:** Development libraries for KDE edutainment applications.
- **kdegames:** KDE games such as kasteroids, kblackbox, and ksmiletris.
- **kdegames-devel:** Libraries enabling the creation of games for KDE.
- **kdegraphics:** Graphical applications for the K desktop environment.
- **kdegraphics-devel:** Development tools for KDE application development.
- **kde-i18n*:** A set of packages providing support for various human languages.
- **kdelibs:** Libraries needed by the K desktop Environment.

- **kdelibs-devel:** Tools and documentation for developing KDE desktop applications.
- **kdemultimedia:** KDE multimedia applications.
- **kdemultimedia-devel:** KDE multimedia application development libraries.
- **kdenetwork:** Networking applications for the K Desktop environment.
- **kdenetwork-devel:** Libraries to develop KDE networking applications.
- **kdepim:** A set of personal information management (PIM) tools for the KDE desktop.
- **kdepim-devel:** Libraries needed to develop applications that use kdepim.
- **kdesdk:** KDE software development kit.
- **kdesdk-devel:** Development libraries for the KDE software development kit.
- **kdetoys:** Utilities, such as kmoon (moon phases) and kworldwatch (watch timezones).
- **kdeutils:** K desktop utilities.
- **kdeutils-devel:** KDE utility development libraries.
- **kdevelop:** Development tools to create applications with consistent KDE interfaces.
- **kernel-2.6.*:** The Linux kernel for various types of CPU.
- **kernel-doc:** Documentation files that come with parts of the Linux kernel source code.
- **kernel-smp-*:** The symmetric multiprocessing Linux kernel version for various CPUs.
- **kernel-source:** The source code files that are used to build the Red Hat Linux kernel.
- **kernel-utils:** Several utilities to control the Linux kernel or the computer's hardware.
- **kinput2-canna-wnn6:** Server for X programs needing Canna or Wnn6 Japanese-text.
- **knm_new:** A Kaname-cho font.
- **koffice:** A set of office productivity applications.
- **koffice-devel:** Files needed to develop plug-ins for KOffice.
- **koffice-i18n:** Internationalization support for KOffice.
- **kon2:** A Kanji emulator for the console.
- **kon2-fonts:** Fonts for kon.
- **krb5*:** Packages used to provide support for Kerberos authentication methods.
- **krbafs*:** The krbafs library, with support for AFS tokens with Kerberos 5 credentials.
- **kudzu:** The kudzu hardware autodetection and configuration utilities.
- **kudzu-devel:** Header files used to create kudzu applications.
- **lam:** Local Area Management (LAM) tools for managing clusters of network computers.
- **lapack:** The Linear Algebra Package (LAPACK) to solve simultaneous linear equations.
- **less:** Text browser, similar to more, but better.
- **lesstif:** A free version of OSF/Motif, providing a set of widgets to develop applications.
- **lesstif-devel:** Library and header files to develop Motif-1.2–based programs for LessTif.
- **lftp:** A sophisticated ftp/http file transfer program.
- **lha:** An archiving and compression utility for LHarc format archives.
- **libacl:** Dynamic library for access control list support.

- **libacl-devel:** Static libraries and headers for developing applications that use ACLs.
- **libaio:** A Linux-native asynchronous I/O-access library.
- **libaio-devel:** Development files creating applications that support libaio.
- **libao:** A cross-platform audio output library.
- **libao-devel:** Header files and documentation needed to develop applications with libao.
- **libart_lgpl:** Graphic routine library used by libgnomecanvas.
- **libart_lgpl-devel:** Libraries and headers needed to compile libart_lgpl.
- **libattr:** Dynamic library for filesystem extended attributes.
- **libattr-devel:** Libraries for developing programs that use extended filesystem attributes.
- **libacv1394:** Firewire control library.
- **libacv1394-devel:** Libraries required to build applications that use firewire devices.
- **libbtctl:** Library for the GNOME Bluetooth Subsystem.
- **libbonobo:** Corba-based component system for the GNOME desktop.
- **libbonobo-devel:** Development libraries and headers for building bonobo applications.
- **libbonoboui:** User interface components for bonobo applications.
- **libbonoboui-devel:** Header files needed to compile applications that use libbonoboui.
- **libcap:** A library for getting and setting POSIX.1e capabilities.
- **libcap-devel:** Headers and libraries needed for developing applications that use libcap.
- **libcapplet0:** GNOME 1 control center library compatibility package.
- **libcapplet0-devel:** Header files for GNOME 1 control center library compatibility.
- **libcroco:** A CSS2 parsing library.
- **libdbi:** The C independent abstraction layer allowing multiple database connections.
- **libdbi-dbd-*:** Libdbi support for various databases.
- **libdbi-devel:** Development files needed to create applications that use libdbi.
- **libesmtp:** A library that manages the posting of e-mail using SMTP.
- **libesmtp-devel:** Development tools needed to develop applications using libesmtp.
- **libexif:** EXIF image tag library.
- **libexif-devel:** The files needed for libexif application development.
- **libf2c:** Fortran 77 runtime libraries.
- **libfortran-ssa:** GCC Fortran support.
- **libfortran-ssa-devel:** GCC Fortran support libraries.
- **libgail-gnome:** GAIL accessibility implementation for GTK+ and GNOME.
- **libgal2*:** A variety of GNOME widget functions and utilities.
- **libgcc:** GCC version 3.2 exception handling library.
- **libgcc-ssa:** GCC version 3.0 shared support library.
- **libgcj:** The Java runtime library for gcc.
- **libgcj-devel:** Development tools associated with the Java runtime library for gcc.

- **libgcj-ssa:** Java runtime library for GCC.
- **libgcj-ssa-devel:** Libraries for Java development using GCC version 3.
- **libgcj34:** Java runtime library for GCC version 3.4.
- **libjcg34-devel:** Libraries for java development using GCC.
- **libgcrypt:** General-purpose crypto library based on GPG.
- **libgcrypt-devel:** Development tools for libgcrypt.
- **libghttp:** GNOME http client library for making HTTP 1.1 requests.
- **libghttp-devel:** Library and header files for libghttp development.
- **libglade:** Libraries that can be used to create GLADE user interface applications.
- **libglade-devel:** Tools and documentation for developing GLADE applications.
- **libglade2:** The libglade library for loading user interfaces from XML descriptions.
- **libglade2-devel:** Tiles needed to develop applications that use libglade.
- **libgnat:** GNU Ada 95 runtime shared libraries.
- **libgnome:** GNU Object Model Environment (GNOME) base libraries.
- **libgnomecups:** GNOME library for CUPS integration.
- **libgnomecups-devel:** GNOME library for CUPS integration (development files).
- **libgnome-devel:** Libraries and headers for libgnome development.
- **libgnomecanvas:** Library for creating custom displays using common widgets.
- **libgnomecanvas-devel:** Libraries and headers for libgnomecanvas development.
- **libgnomeprint:** GNOME printing library.
- **libgnomeprint-devel:** Libraries for developing printing in GNOME applications.
- **libgnomeprint15:** Components needed to support GNOME printing.
- **libgnomeprint22:** GNOME printing library.
- **libgnomeprint-devel22:** Libraries for developing printing in GNOME applications.
- **libgnomeprintui:** GUI support for libgnome print.
- **libgnomeprintui-devel:** Libraries for compiling libgnomeprintui applications.
- **libgnomeprintui22:** GUI support for libgnome print.
- **libgnomeprintui22-devel:** Libraries for compiling libgnomeprintui applications.
- **libgnomeui:** GNOME-based GUI library.
- **libgnomeui-devel:** Libraries and headers for compiling libgnomeui applications.
- **libgsf:** A library for reading and writing structured files.
- **libgsf-devel:** Development libraries for reading and writing structured files.
- **libgtop2:** A library that gets information about system usage.
- **libgtop2-devel:** Components needed to develop applications to monitor system usage.
- **libIDL:** Library for parsing Interface Definition Language.
- **libIDL-devel:** Development libraries and headers for libIDL.
- **libieee1284:** A library for interfacing IEEE 1284-compatible devices.

- **libieee1284-devel:** Files for developing applications that use libieee1284.
- **libjpeg:** The libjpeg library for manipulating JPEG images.
- **libjpeg-devel:** Header files and libraries for creating programs that use JPEG images.
- **libmng:** Library for working with images in MNG and JNG formats.
- **libmng-devel:** Header files related to the libmng library.
- **libmng-static:** Statically linked versions of the libmng library.
- **libmusicbrainz:** Software library for accessing MusicBrainz servers.
- **libmusicbrainz-devel:** Headers for developing programs that will use libmusicbrainz.
- **libobjc:** Objective C runtime libraries.
- **libofx:** Tools to support Open Financial Exchange (OFX) applications.
- **libofx-devel:** Development components to support OFX.
- **libogg:** Ogg bitstream format libraries.
- **libogg-devel:** Documentation and header files for developing ogg applications.
- **libole2:** Structured storage OLE2 (Object Linking and Embedding) library.
- **libole2-devel:** Header files to develop applications for OLE2-structured storage files.
- **libpcap:** User level hooks for monitoring low-level network traffic.
- **libpng10:** An old version of the libpng library for working with PNG image files.
- **libpng10-devel:** Libraries and headers for developing programs that use PNG images.
- **libpng:** The libpng library for working with PNG image files.
- **libpng-devel:** Libraries and headers needed to develop programs that use PNG images.
- **libraw1394:** Library providing low-level firewire access.
- **libraw1394-devel:** Development libraries for using libraw1394 functionality.
- **librep:** Tools and documentation associated with the librep Lisp dialect.
- **librep-devel:** Header files and tools associated with the libred Lisp dialect.
- **librsvg2:** An SVG library based on libart.
- **librsvg-devel2:** Development files required to develop applications using librsvg.
- **libsane-hopj:** SANE scanner drivers for HP's multi-function devices.
- **libselinux:** SELinux library and simple utilities.
- **libselinux-devel:** Header files and development documentation.
- **libsoup:** Library for enabling GNOME libraries to access HTTP servers.
- **libsoup-devel:** Development tools for libsoup.
- **libstdc++:** The EGCS libraries needed to run C++ applications.
- **libstdc++-devel:** Standard C++ development libraries.
- **libstdc++-ssa:** GNU Standard C++ Library Version 3.
- **libstdc++-ssa-devel:** Header files and libraries for C++ development.
- **libstdc++34:** GNU Standard C++ Library version 3.4.
- **libstdc++34-devel:** Header files and libraries for C++ development.

- **libtabe:** Chinese lexicon libraries for xcin input method.
- **libtabe-devel:** Header files and libraries required to develop applications to use libtabe.
- **libtermcap:** Libraries to access the termcap database to manage character displays.
- **libtermcap-devel:** Components to develop programs that access the termcap database.
- **libtiff:** Libraries for using and saving TIFF image files.
- **libtiff-devel:** Development tools used to work with TIFF image files in applications.
- **libtool:** The libtool shell scripts, used to build generic shared libraries.
- **libtool-libs:** Runtime libraries for libtool utilities (to build generic shared libraries).
- **libtool-libs13:** Compatibility libraries for the shared libraries in libtool-1.3.
- **libungif:** Library functions needed to use and save GIF image files.
- **libungif-devel:** Development tools to create applications to load and save GIF images.
- **libungif-progs:** Several utilities for working with GIF images.
- **libusb:** A library that facilitates access to USB devices.
- **libusb-devel:** Development files needed to create applications that use libusb.
- **libuser:** A standardized interface for administration of user accounts.
- **libuser-devel:** Header files and static libraries to develop applications that use libuser.
- **libvorbis:** The Ogg Vorbis open audio compression codec and runtime libraries.
- **libvorbis-devel:** Header files and documentation to develop applications using libvorbis.
- **libwnck:** Library for implementing pagers and tasklists.
- **libwnck-devel:** Development files for applications that use libwnck.
- **libwpd:** Library for handling WordPerfect documents.
- **libwpd-devel:** Development tools for handling WordPerfect documents.
- **libwpd-tools:** Tools for transforming WordPerfect documents.
- **libwvstreams:** A network programming library written in C++.
- **libwvstreams-devel:** Development files for applications that use libwvstreams.
- **libxfce4*:** Packages for XFce descktop.
- **libxklavier:** Library providing high-level API for X Keyboard Extension.
- **libxklavier-devel:** Header files to develop libxklavier applications.
- **libxml:** A library of functions for working with XML files.
- **libxml-devel:** Contains tools for developing applications that use the libxml library.
- **libxml2:** A library to work with XML and HTML files, including DTD support.
- **libxml2-devel:** Development files for applications using libxml2.
- **libxml2-python:** Python bindings for the libxml2 library.
- **libxslt:** Tools to translate XML to structures using the XSLT transformation mechanism.
- **libxslt-devel:** Libraries and include files required to develop applications using libxslt.
- **libxslt-python:** Python bindings for the libxslt library.
- **licq:** The licq ICQ chat utility.

- **licq-gnome:** A GNOME front-end for licq.
- **licq-kde:** A KDE front-end for licq.
- **licq-qt:** A Qt front-end for licq.
- **licq-text:** A text mode front-end for licq.
- **lilo:** The LILO (LInux LOader) program for booting Linux or other operating systems.
- **linc:** A library for simplified writing of network programs.
- **linc-devel:** Development files for applications that use linc functionality.
- **linuxdoc-tools:** A text-formatting package based on SGML.
- **lm_sensors:** Modules for interfacing with sensors that monitor computer hardware.
- **lm_sensors-devel:** Software tools for interfacing with hardware monitors.
- **lockdev:** The liblockdev library for locking devices.
- **lockdev-devel:** Static library versions and headers for the liblockdev library.
- **logrotate:** Rotate growing log files.
- **logwatch:** A customizable log file analysis program.
- **lrzsz:** The lrz and lsz utilities, which are used to provide Zmodem functions in Linux.
- **lslk:** A utility for listing lock files.
- **lsof:** A utility for listing information about open files.
- **ltrace:** A tool for running and tracing the activities of a running command.
- **lv:** The lv multilingual file viewer and related utilities.
- **lvm:** Logical Volume Manager tools to manage physical hard disk volumes.
- **lvm2:** The new version of Logical Volume Manager for Linux.
- **lynx:** A text-based Internet Web browser.
- **m2crypto:** Support for OpenSSL in Python scripts.
- **m4:** An implementation of the UNIX m4 macro processor.
- **macutils:** Utilities for working with files that are often used with Macintosh computers.
- **Maelstrom:** The Maelstrom (shoot-the-asteroids) game.
- **magicdev:** The magicdev daemon for detecting and playing audio CDs.
- **MagicPoint:** An X11-based presentation tool.
- **mailcap:** A configuration file for defining how special data types are handled.
- **mailman:** A Web-oriented mailing list manager.
- **mailx:** A small utility for easily sending plain text e-mail messages.
- **make:** A utility for building and installing software from source code.
- **MAKEDEV:** A program to create and maintain files in the /dev directory.
- **man:** A facility for displaying system manual pages.
- **man-pages*:** A set of packages containing manual pages in different languages.
- **mc:** The Midnight Commander visual shell for managing a variety of file interfaces.
- **mdam:** Software RAID array control utility.

- **memprof:** A tool for memory profiling and leak detection.
- **memtest86:** A thorough stand-alone memory tester for x86 architecture computers.
- **metacity:** The metacity window manager.
- **mew:** Messaging functions for Emacs.
- **mew-common:** Functions used in mew and mew-xemacs.
- **mew-xemacs:** Messaging functions for XEmacs.
- **mgetty:** The mgetty implementation of getty for allowing logins over serial lines.
- **mgetty-sendfax:** The sendfax program for sending faxes with the mgetty program.
- **mgetty-viewfax:** The viewfax utility to show faxes that were received by mgetty.
- **mgetty-voice:** The vgetty utilities for supporting voice communications with mgetty.
- **mikmod:** The MikMod music file player for playing a variety of audio formats.
- **mingetty:** A small implementation of getty for terminal logins.
- **miniChinput:** A smaller version of Chinput, a Chinese XIM server.
- **minicom:** A text-based modem control utility for communicating over serial lines.
- **mkbootdisk:** A bootable floppy disk creation utility.
- **mkinitrd:** A utility for creating initial RAM disk images.
- **mkisofs:** A tool for creating ISO9660 (CD-ROM) file systems.
- **mktemp:** A scripting utility for safely creating /tmp files.
- **mod_auth_mysql:** Basic authentication for the Apache Web server using MySQL.
- **mod_auth_pgsql:** Basic authentication for the Apache Web server using PostgresQL.
- **mod_dav_svn:** Apache server module for Subversion software source repository.
- **mod_perl:** A Perl interpreter used with Apache to allow it to interpret Perl code.
- **mod_perl-devel:** Tools for building XS modules that use mod_perl.
- **mod_python:** An embedded Python interpreter for the Apache Web server.
- **mod_ssl:** An Apache module to provide secure cryptography using SSL and TLS.
- **modutils:** Utilities for managing kernel modules (loading, unloading, and so on).
- **mozilla*:** The Mozilla Web browser and related utilities and programming libraries.
- **mpage:** Facilitates printing several pages of PostScript output on a single page.
- **mrtg:** The Multi Router Traffic Grapher tool creates charts of network traffic.
- **mtools:** Utilities for managing MS-DOS formatted disks.
- **mtr:** A network diagnostic tool that combines ping and traceroute features.
- **mtr-gtk:** A GTK interface to the mtr network diagnostic tool.
- **mt-st:** The mt (magnetic tape) and st (SCSI tape) programs for managing tape drives.
- **mtx:** A utility for working with tape libraries and autoloaders.
- **mutt:** A text mode e-mail mail user agent.
- **mx-2:** A collection of Python software tools.
- **mx4j:** Libraries to support Java Management Extenstions (JMX).

- **mx4j-devel:** Headers required to support Java Management Extensions (JMX).
- **mx4j-tools:** Tools to use with Java Management Extensions (JMX).
- **MyODBC:** An ODBC driver for MySQL.
- **mysql*:** This set of packages contains the MySQL database application and tools.
- **MySQL-Python:** Python modules to support MySQL.
- **nabi:** Simple Hangul X Input Method.
- **namazu:** A full-text search engine.
- **namazu-cgi:** CGI interface to namazu.
- **namazu-devel:** Libraries that allow applications to use namazu.
- **nano:** A small text editor.
- **nasm:** The nasm Netwide Assembler.
- **nasm-doc:** Documentation for the nasm Netwide Assembler.
- **nasm-rdoff:** Tools for the RDOFF binary format, which can be used with nasm.
- **nautilus:** A network user window that integrates file, application, and Internet resources.
- **nautilus-cd-burner:** CD burning front-end for GNOME and Nautilus.
- **nautilus-media:** Audio viewer for GStreamer.
- **nc:** The Netcat (nc) utility for reading and writing data across TCP/IP connections.
- **ncftp:** A feature-packed FTP client program, including session resumption.
- **ncompress:** Fast compression and decompression utilities.
- **ncpfs:** Components needed to use the Novell NetWare ncpfs file systems.
- **ncurses:** A character-based screen GUI library.
- **ncurses-devel:** Components to create applications to use the ncurses screen handling.
- **ncurses-c++-devel:** C++ bindings to ncurses.
- **nedit:** A GUI text editor for XWindows and Motif.
- **neon:** An HTTP and WebDAV client library.
- **neon-devel:** Development tools for neon.
- **netatalk:** AppleTalk transport protocol implementation.
- **netatalk-devel:** Development libraries that allow applications to use netatalk.
- **netconfig:** A text-based tool for configuring network interfaces.
- **netdump:** Tools that write kernel messages and crash dumps to a remote system.
- **netdump-server:** A program that listens for kernel messages across a network.
- **netpbm:** Tools for working with various graphic formats.
- **netpbm-devel:** Static libraries and headers for the netpbm interface.
- **netpbm-progs:** Scripts for working with graphical images.
- **net-snmp:** A collection of SNMP tools and libraries.
- **net-snmp-devel:** Development environment for the NET-SNMP project.
- **net-snmp-perl:** The perl NET-SMNP module and the mib2c tool.

- **net-snmp-utils:** Network management utilities using SNMP.
- **net-tools:** Basic networking tools such as ifconfig, netstat and route.
- **newt:** A library for creating color, text-based, and widget-based user interfaces.
- **newt-devel:** Header files and libraries to develop Newt-based text-mode applications.
- **nfs-utils:** Network File System (NFS) tools to share files and directories on a network.
- **nhpf:** A utility for creating PostScript files in the Korean Hangul font.
- **njamd:** An advanced debugger for detecting memory allocation errors.
- **nkf:** The nkf network Kanji code conversion filter.
- **nmap:** A network exploration tool and security scanner.
- **nmap-frontend:** A Gtk+ front-end for nmap.
- **nptl-devel:** Development libraries for using the NPTL libraries.
- **nscd:** The nscd daemon for caching name services requests from NIS and DNS.
- **nss_db:** Libraries to let programs access basic system information from BSD databases.
- **nss_db-compat:** Libraries that provide access to older versions of BSD databases.
- **nss_ldap:** The NSS library and PAM modules to support LDAP clients.
- **ntp:** The Network Time Protocol daemon. Synchronizes system time from ntp servers.
- **ntsysv:** A utility for configuring services at different run levels.
- **nut:** Software tools for monitoring uninterruptible power supply (UPS) systems.
- **nut-cgi:** CGI scripts for monitoring UPS systems.
- **nut-client:** Client utilities for monitoring UPS systems over a network.
- **nvi-m17n:** Nvi text editor files for encoding Japanese, Korean, and Chinese.
- **nvi-ml17n-canna:** The nvi multilingual text editor with support for canna input.
- **nvi-ml17n-nocanna:** The nvi multilingual text editor without support for canna input.
- **oaf:** An object activation framework for GNOME.
- **oaf-devel:** Libraries and include files for developing applications that use oaf.
- **octave:** The GNU octave tools for performing numerical computations.
- **Omni:** Printer-driver support using Ghostscript.
- **Omni-foomatic:** Foomatic data for the Omni printer-driver system.
- **open:** Utility for using virtual consoles to run programs.
- **openh323:** A library implementation of the H323 teleconferencing protocol.
- **openh323-devel:** Libraries and headers needed to develop using openh323.
- **openhbci*:** Client-side tools for Home Banking Computer Interface (HBCI) support.
- **openjade:** Uutilities for parsing DSSSL SGML content.
- **openjade-devel:** Development tools for openjade.
- **openldap:** Components needed to run OpenLDAP programs.
- **openldap-clients:** Client programs used to work with OpenLDAP directories.
- **openldap-devel:** Tools and documentation needed to create LDAP client programs.

- **openldap-servers:** Server programs used to make OpenLDAP directories available.
- **openmotif:** The OpenMotif libraries and programs.
- **openmotif21:** Compatibility libraries for OpenMotif 2.1.
- **openmotif-devel:** Development libraries that enable the creation of Motif applications.
- **openobex:** Open OBEX shared C library.
- **openobex-apps:** Applications for using OBEX.
- **openobex-devel:** Development tools for OpenOBEX.
- **openoffice:** The OpenOffice.org comprehensive office suite.
- **openoffice-i18n:** Internationalization for the OpenOffice office suite.
- **openoffice-libs:** OpenOffice shared libraries.
- **openssh*:** Components needed by OpenSSH client and server processes.
- **openssl*:** Components needed to provide Secure Socket Layer (SSL) services.
- **oprofile:** System-wide profiler for x86 processors.
- **oprofile-devel:** Header files and libraries for developing apps that use oprofile.
- **ORBit*:** Components used with the ORBit CORBA (Common Object Request Broker Architecture) ORB (Object Request Broker).
- **ots:** Text summarization tool.
- **ots-devel:** Tools for developing ots programs.
- **pam:** Pluggable Authentication Modules libraries to select authentication mechanisms.
- **pam_krb5:** A PAM library for use with Kerberos 5 authentication.
- **pam_smb:** A PAM module for authenticating against external SMB servers.
- **pam-devel:** Static libraries and header files needed for PAM applications.
- **pan:** A graphical USENET news reader.
- **pango:** Pango software for rendering international text.
- **pango-devel:** Development tools for Pango software that render international text.
- **parted:** A utility for creating and resizing disk partitions.
- **parted-devel:** The GNU parted library for manipulating disk partitions.
- **passivetex:** TeX macros that process XSL formatting objects.
- **passwd:** The `passwd` command for adding or changing user passwords.
- **patch:** GNU Patch utility for modifying and upgrading files.
- **patchutils:** Programs that manipulate patch files.
- **pax:** The pax utility for creating and reading archive files.
- **pccts:** Software tools that help implement compilers and other translation systems.
- **pciutils:** Utilities to view and configure information for devices connected to a PCI bus.
- **pciutils-devel:** Header files associated with PCI utilities.
- **pcmcia-cs:** Utilities for handling PCMCIA devices.
- **pcre:** A Perl-compatible, regular expression library.

- **pcre-devel:** Headers and libraries needed for developing applications with pcre.
- **pdksh:** The pdksh implementation of the David Korn's Korn shell.
- **perl*:** Perl high-level programming language and components.
- **php*:** PHP embedded scripting language and components.
- **pidentd:** The pidentd daemon for returning identity information.
- **pilot-link:** Tools for synchronizing a USR Palm Pilot with a Red Hat Linux system.
- **pilot-link095-compat:** Compatibility libraries for pilot-link095.
- **pilot-link-devel:** Components needed to build the pilot-link application.
- **pinfo:** A manual and info page viewer
- **pkgconfig:** The pkg-config utility for entering package compilation options.
- **planner**: The Planner visual project management application.
- **plugger:** The generic Netscape plug-in for use with standard Linux programs.
- **pmake:** The BSD 4.4 version of make.
- **pnm2ppa:** Drivers for printing to HP PNA printers.
- **policy*:** Packages for SELinux policy core utilities.
- **popt:** A C language library for parsing command-line parameters.
- **portmap:** A utility for managing RPC connections for NFS and NIS.
- **postfix:** A mail transport agent (MTA).
- **postgresql*:** A set of packages to create and maintain a PostgreSQL database server.
- **ppp:** The Point-to-Point Protocol daemon for managing serial line TCP/IP connections.
- **prelink:** An ELF prelinking utility.
- **printman:** GNOME print monitoring tool.
- **privoxy:** Privacy proxy. Useful on individual workstations for enhancing Web privacy.
- **procinfo:** A utility for displaying kernel information from /proc.
- **procmail:** A local e-mail delivery management tool.
- **procps:** Utilities, such as ps, free, and top, for displaying system information.
- **psacct:** Process accounting utilities, such as ac, lastcomm, accton, and sa.
- **psgml:** PSGML software that allows GNU Emacs to edit SGML and XML documents.
- **psmisc:** Utilities, such as pstree, killall, and fuser, for managing processes.
- **pstack:** A program that displays stack traces of running processes.
- **psutils:** Utilities for manipulating PostScript documents.
- **pump-devel:** Software development libraries to interface with the pump facility.
- **pvm:** The pvmd daemon and related utilities for coordinating several virtual machines.
- **pvm-gui:** The X-based xpvm tools for graphically managing a virtual machine.
- **pwlib:** Portable Windows library to produce programs to run on Windows and UNIX.
- **pwlib-devel:** Development libraries for creating applications that use pwlib.
- **pychecker:** A Python source code checking tool.

- **pydict:** An English/Chinese dictionary written in Python.
- **pygtk2:** The modules that enable you to use gtk features in Python.
- **pygtk2-devel:** Files to build wrappers to let GTK+ libraries interoperate with pygtk2.
- **pygtk2-libglade:** The libglade module; provides a wrapper for the libglade library.
- **pyOpenSSL:** Python wrapper around the OpenSSL library.
- **pyorbit:** Python bindings for accessing the ORBit2 CORBA ORB.
- **pyorbit-devel:** Development libraries for building ORBit2 add-on library wrappers.
- **PyQt:** Contains the Python bindings for Qt.
- **PyQt-devel:** Files needed to build bindings for C++ classes based on any Qt class.
- **PyQt-examples:** Sample code demonstrating how to use the Python bindings for Qt.
- **python:** The Python interpreter, an object-oriented scripting language.
- **python-devel:** Header files and libraries to add dynamically loaded Python extensions.
- **python-docs:** Documentation for the Python programming language (text and LaTeX).
- **python-optik:** Python bindings for the Optik comand line parsing library.
- **python-tools:** Tools to provide a Tkinter-based IDE for Python.
- **pyxf86config:** Python wrappers for the XFree86 configuration files.
- **PyXML:** Xml libraries for Python.
- **qmkbootdisk:** Graphical front-end for creating boot disks.
- **qt:** The shared library for the Qt GUI toolkit.
- **qt-designer:** User interface development tools for the Qt toolkit.
- **qt-devel:** Components needed to develop Qt applications.
- **qt-MySQL:** MySQL drivers for Qt's SQL classes.
- **qt-ODBC:** ODBC drivers for Qt's SQL classes.
- **qt-PostgreSQL:** Postgres drivers for Qt's SQL classes.
- **quagga:** Tools for managing TCP/IP routing protocol.
- **quagga-contrib:** Third-party tools to use with quagga.
- **quagga-devel:** Tools for developing quagga applications.
- **quanta:** An HTML editor for the KDE environment.
- **quota:** The quota, quotacheck, and quotaon tools for managing disk space.
- **radvd:** The router advertisement daemon for IPv6.
- **raidtools:** Several raid utilities for configuring raid file system devices.
- **rarpd:** Reverse Address Resolution Protocol daemon.
- **rcs:** The Revision Control System. Manages multiple versions of files.
- **rdate:** Retrieves and sets date and time from network time servers.
- **rdesktop:** Open source Windows Terminal Server client. Requires no server extensions.
- **rdist:** Maintains exact copies of files on multiple computers.
- **readline:** Allows programs to edit text lines with emacs keys.

- **readline-devel:** Components for developing applications that use the readline library.
- **recode:** Converts between character sets.
- **recode-devel:** Development files that allow applications to use recode.
- **redhat-artwork:** Artwork that makes up the Red Hat standard look and feel.
- **redhat-lsb:** Linux Standards Base (LSB) support for Red Hat Linux.
- **redhat-menus:** XML-based configuration and data files for desktop menus.
- **redhat-rpm-config:** Red Hat–specific RPM configuration files.
- **reiserfs-utils:** Utilities for checking and repairing ReiserFS file systems.
- **rep-gtk:** The rep-gtk binding of GTK+ for the rep Lisp interpreter.
- **rhdb-utils:** Miscellaneous utilities for PostgreSQL (Red Hat Edition).
- **rhgb:** RedHat graphical boot.
- **rhn-applet:** A panel applet that indicates that newer Red Hat packages are available.
- **rhnlib:** Python libraries for the Red Hat Network project.
- **rhpl:** Library of Python code used by programs in Red Hat Linux.
- **rhythmbox:** Tool for ripping audio CDs, managing music, and burning CD-ROMs.
- **rmt:** Remote tape device access utility.
- **rootfiles:** The default user configuration files provided to the root user.
- **routed:** A daemon that handles routing traffic and maintains routing tables.
- **rpm:** A utility for installing and managing RPM (.rpm) software packages.
- **rpm-build:** Development tools for creating RPM packages.
- **rpmdb-redhat:** The database for the entire Red Hat Linux distribution.
- **rpm-devel:** Components to create applications that manipulate RPM packages.
- **rpm-python:** Native Python bindings to the RPM API.
- **rp-pppoe:** PPP over Ethernet software, for connecting to an ISP over xDSL.
- **rsh:** The rsh, rcp, rlogin remote access utilities.
- **rsh-server:** Server-side daemon for the rsh remote access utilities.
- **rsync:** A network file synchronization utility.
- **ruby*:** This set of packages contains an object-oriented scripting language called Ruby.
- **rusers:** Displays users who are logged in to machines on a local network.
- **rusers-server:** Server-side daemon for the rusers utility.
- **rwall:** A tool for sending messages to all who are currently logged in to a particular host.
- **rwall-server:** Server-side daemon for the rwall utility.
- **rwho:** Enables a user to determine who is logged into a given host.
- **samba:** The Samba server software for sharing Windows files, folders, and printers.
- **samba-client:** Samba utilities needed to provide file and print sharing with Windows.
- **samba-common:** Samba configuration files and utilities for configuring a Samba server.
- **samba-swat:** A Web-based samba configuration utility.

- **sane-backends:** Scanner Access Now Easy utilities for using and managing scanners.
- **sane-backends-devel:** Programming libraries for interfacing with scanners.
- **sane-frontends:** Graphical front-end to SANE.
- **sash:** A statically linked shell with simplified versions of some built-in commands.
- **sawfish:** The sawfish X11 window manager.
- **schedutils:** Utilities for working with process scheduler attributes.
- **screen:** A utility for managing multiple logins on a single terminal.
- **scrollkeeper:** A cataloging system for documentation on open systems.
- **SDL:** Simple DirectMedia Layer for fast access to frame buffer and audio devices.
- **SDL-devel:** Simple DirectMedia Layer application programming interface.
- **SDL_image:** A sample image loading utility for SDL.
- **SDL_image-devel:** A library for loading images for SDL applications.
- **SDL_mixer:** Simple DirectMedia Layer (SDL) sound mixing tools.
- **SDL_mixer-devel:** SDL sound mixing application development tools.
- **SDL_net:** A portable network library for use with SDL.
- **SDL_net-devel:** Libraries and include files to develop SDL networked applications.
- **sed:** A text stream editor.
- **selinux-doc:** SELinux documentation.
- **sendmail:** The sendmail mail transport agent.
- **sendmail-cf:** Utilities and files for generating a sendmail configuration file.
- **sendmail-devel:** Development files for sendmail add-ons.
- **sendmail-doc:** Sendmail documentation (PostScript and troff formats).
- **setarch:** Tells the kernel to report a different architecture from the current one.
- **setools:** SELinux tools for managing policy.
- **setools-gui:** Graphical tools for handling SETools.
- **setserial:** A utility for setting and viewing serial port information.
- **setup:** Default versions of basic system configuration files located in /etc.
- **setuptool:** A utility for accessing text mode configuration tools.
- **sgml-common:** Catalog and DTD files used with SGML.
- **shadow-utils:** Utilities for using shadow passwords and related user/group information.
- **shapecfg:** Configures network bandwidth parameters.
- **shared-mime-info:** Shared MIME information database.
- **sharutils:** Utilities for encoding and decoding shell archives.
- **sip:** Generates bindings for C++ classes for use by Python.
- **sip-devel:** Files needed to generate Python bindings for any C++ class library.
- **skkdic:** A dictionary for a simple Kana-Kanji conversion program.
- **skkinput:** A Kana to Kanji converter with multiple input protocols.

- **slang:** The S-Lang language extension libraries and related components.
- **slang-devel:** Components needed to develop S-Lang–based applications.
- **slocate:** Utility for locating files based on a centralized database updated nightly.
- **slrn:** The slrn threaded Internet news reader.
- **slrn-pull:** Spools news for offline news reading.
- **sound-juicer:** CD ripping tool for GStreamer.
- **sox:** A general-purpose sound configuration utility.
- **sox-devel:** Libraries needed to develop SoX applications.
- **spamassassin:** An e-mail spam filter based on an evolved genetic algorithm.
- **specspo:** Object catalogues for internationalizing Red Hat packages.
- **speex:** Voice compression format (codec).
- **speex-devel:** Development package for speex.
- **splint:** A C program error checker.
- **squid:** A proxy caching server for HTTP, FTP, and gopher.
- **squirrelmail:** The SquirrelMail Webmail client.
- **star:** An archiving tool with ACL support.
- **stardict:** An English-to-Chinese dictionary.
- **startup-notification:** A library for tracking application startup.
- **startup-notification-devel:** Header files and static libraries for libstartup-notification.
- **statserial:** Displays signals on 9- and 25-pin serial ports.
- **strace:** Traces system calls performed by a selected program.
- **struts**: Framework for building Java Web applications.
- **struts-webapps**: Sample Web applications using Struts.
- **stunnel:** Adds secure SSL services to non-SSL applications.
- **subversion:** A concurrent version control system.
- **subversion-devel:** Development libraries for subversion applications.
- **subversion-perl:** Perl libraries for subversion applications.
- **sudo:** Enables administrative access to privileged commands on a limited basis.
- **swig:** Connects C/C++/Objective C to other high-level languages.
- **switchdesk:** The desktop switcher utility for changing window managers.
- **sylpheed:** A GTK+-based e-mail and news client.
- **symlinks:** Checks and corrects broken symbolic links.
- **sysklogd:** The syslogd and klogd daemon processes, for logging system messages.
- **syslinux:** A simple boot loader that can boot from a DOS (FAT) file system.
- **sysreport:** Manages system checks for hardware problems.
- **sysstat:** The sar and iostat system monitoring tools.

- **system-config-*:** Red Hat utilities for configuring aspects of a Linux system. In previous versions of Fedora and Red Hat Linux, these utilities began with `redhat-config`.
- **system-logviewer:** Graphical interface for viewing and searching log files.
- **system-switch-mail:** Mail transport agent switcher.
- **system-switch-mail-gnome:** GNOME-based mail transport agent switcher.
- **SysVinit:** Basic Linux boot and startup programs.
- **taipeifonts:** Chinese Big5 fonts.
- **talk:** Talk client for one-on-one Internet chatting.
- **talk-server:** A daemon process that facilitates one-on-one Internet chatting.
- **tar:** Archival and restoration utility.
- **tcl:** The TCL scripting language environment.
- **tcl-devel:** TCL scripting language development tools.
- **tcl-html:** HTML manuals for TCL.
- **tclx:** TCL extensions designed to make Linux programming tasks easier to implement.
- **tclx-devel:** Development components associated with TCL extensions.
- **tclx-doc:** Documentation associated with TCL extensions.
- **tcp_wrappers:** Small daemon programs that monitor insecure server processes.
- **tcpdump:** A command-line utility for monitoring network traffic.
- **tcsh:** A `csh`-like command shell interpreter.
- **telnet:** The client program for the telnet remote login protocol.
- **telnet-server:** The server side of the telnet remote login protocol.
- **termcap:** Information for text terminal oriented applications.
- **tetex:** Tools for creating TeTeX documents.
- **tetex-afm:** The afm2tfm utility for converting PostScript font metric files.
- **tetex-doc:** Documentation that describes how to produce TeX formatted documents.
- **tetex-dvips:** The dvips utility for converting TeX files to PostScript format.
- **tetex-fonts:** Fonts for use with TeX documents.
- **tetex-latex:** LaTeX front-end utilities for producing TeX documents.
- **tetex-xdvi:** The xdvi program to preview TeX output files in the X Window System.
- **texinfo:** The texinfo system to develop online and printed documents.
- **tftp:** The Trivial File Transfer Protocol. Used to boot diskless workstations.
- **tftp-server:** Server side of the tftp protocol.
- **time:** A utility for monitoring processing time of a selected program.
- **timidity++:** The Timidity++ MIDI player and converter.
- **tix:** The Tix (Tk Interface Extension) add-on to the Tk widget set.
- **tix-devel:** Tix header files and development documentation.
- **tix-doc:** Tk Interface eXtension documentation.

- **tk:** The Tk X Window System widget set, designed to work with tcl scripting.
- **tk-devel:** Tk graphical toolkit for Tcl.
- **tkinter:** The Tkinter graphical interface for the Python scripting language.
- **tmake:** Creates and maintains project makefiles.
- **tmpwatch:** Removes temporary files that have not been used for a set interval of time.
- **tomcat**: Components that make up the Java Servlet and JavaServer Pages reference technology.
- **tomcat-devel**: Development tools associated with Java Servlet and JavaServer Pages.
- **tomcat-libs**: Libraries associated with Java Servlet and JavaServer Pages.
- **tomcat-test**: Test suite for Tomcat technology.
- **tora:** A GUI-based database development tool.
- **traceroute:** Traces the route of IP packets across a network.
- **transfig:** Translates FIG or PIC figures to other formats.
- **tree:** Displays the contents of directories in a tree format.
- **tsclient:** Client for VNC and Windows Terminal Server.
- **ttcp:** A tool for testing the throughput of TCP connections.
- **ttfonts-ja:** Japanese True Type fonts.
- **ttfonts-ko:** Baekmuk Korean True Type fonts.
- **ttfonts-zh_CN:** Chinese True Type fonts.
- **ttfonts-zh_TW:** Chinese True Type fonts.
- **ttfprint:** A utility that converts a Chinese text file to PostScript.
- **ttmkfdir:** A utility for creating `fonts.scale` files.
- **tux:** A kernel-based threaded HTTP server.
- **tuxracer:** A 3d racing game featuring Tux, the Linux mascot.
- **tvtime:** A high-quality TV viewer.
- **tzdata:** Time zone data.
- **udev:** A userspace implementation of devfs.
- **umb-scheme:** An implementation of the Scheme programming language.
- **unarj:** A utility for uncompressing .arj compressed archives.
- **units:** Converts units from one type of measurement to another.
- **unix2dos:** Converts Linux/UNIX files to DOS files.
- **unixODBC*:** This set of packages contains tools for the ODBC driver manager.
- **unzip:** A utility for testing, listing, and extracting files from .zip archives.
- **up2date:** The Red Hat Linux update agent.
- **up2date-gnome:** The GNOME interface to the `up2date` command.
- **urw-fonts:** A free version of the 35 standard PostScript fonts.
- **usbutils:** Utilities for inspecting USB devices.
- **usbview:** The usbview utility for viewing USB devices.

- **usermode:** Utilities, such as userinfo and userpasswd, for managing user data.
- **usermode-gtk:** Graphical tools for a variety of user account management tasks.
- **utempter:** The libutempter shared library and `utempter` command.
- **util-linux:** Many basic Linux utilities for users and system administrators.
- **uucp:** The classic uucp utilities for transferring files among remote host computers.
- **vconfig:** Configures and adjusts 802.1q VLAN parameters.
- **VFlib2*:** This set of packages contains tools for converting vector fonts to bitmaps.
- **vim-common:** Support files for the vim editor.
- **vim-enhanced:** Enhancements to the vim editor, including Python and Perl interpreters.
- **vim-minimal:** A minimal version of the vim editor.
- **vim-X11:** X Window-based implementation of the vim editor.
- **vixie-cron:** Vixie implementation of the cron utility, adding some security features.
- **vlock:** The vlock utility for locking console sessions.
- **vnc:** A robust application for viewing desktops from remote computers over a network.
- **vnc-doc:** Documentation related to the vnc server and vncviewer applications.
- **vnc-server:** Server daemon for the `vnc` desktop viewer.
- **vorbis-tools:** Runtime library and utilities related to Vorbis audio format.
- **vsftpd:** The Very Secure FTP daemon.
- **vte:** Experimental terminal emulator widget for use with GTK+ 2.0.
- **vte-devel:** Files needed for developing applications with vte.
- **w3c-libwww:** The libwww Web API, a C interface for Linux, UNIX, and Windows.
- **w3c-libwww-apps:** The `w3c` and `webbot` commands.
- **w3c-libwww-devel:** Libraries and header files to create w3c-libwww applications.
- **w3m:** A text file viewer that can also be used as a text-mode Web browser.
- **w3m-el:** The w3m interface for emacs.
- **w3m-el-common:** Common files used by w3m-el and w3m-el-xemacs.
- **w3m-el-xemacs:** The w3m interface for XEmacs.
- **w3m-img**: Inline helper application for displaying images in the w3m text-based Web browser.
- **webalizer:** A flexible Web server log file analysis program.
- **wget:** A simple HTTP or FTP file retrieval utility.
- **which:** Shows the full path of a selected program.
- **wireless-tools:** Tools for configuring communication to wireless Ethernet equipment.
- **wl:** The Wanderlust IMAP4, POP, and NNTP client for GNU emacs.
- **wl-common:** Common files for wl and wl-xemacs.
- **wl-xemacs:** The Wanderlust IMAP4, POP, and NNTP client for XEmacs.
- **Wnn6-SDK:** The Wnn6 client runtime library.
- **Wnn6-SDK-devel:** Library and header files for Wnn6 client development.

- **words:** A dictionary of English words that exists in the /usr/dict directory.
- **wordtrans*:** A multilanguage word translator and front-end for Qt, KDE, and WWW.
- **wvdial:** The wvdial intelligent dialer for PPP.
- **x3270:** Software for emulating an IBM 3270 terminal.
- **x3270-text:** A text mode IBM 3270 terminal emulator.
- **x3270-x11:** An X Window IBM 3270 terminal emulator.
- **xalan-j*:** Set of packages for transforming XML documents into HTML.
- **Xaw3d:** The Xaw3d libraries needed to run programs make use of MIT Athena widgets.
- **Xaw3d-devel:** Xaw3d development tools (enhanced MIT Athena widgets for X).
- **xboard:** A graphical, X-based interface to GNU chess.
- **xcdroast:** Utilities for burning your own music and data CD-ROMs.
- **xchat:** A feature packed X Window-based IRC chat utility.
- **xcin:** An X-input method server for Chinese characters.
- **xdelta:** A binary file delta generator and an RCS replacement library.
- **xdelta-devel:** Static library and header files for the Xdelta environment.
- **xemacs:** The libraries needed to run the emacs text editor.
- **xemacs-el:** A variety of elisp programs for use with the emacs text editor.
- **xemacs-info:** The info documentation for the emacs text editor.
- **xemacs-sumo-*:** Xemacs Lisp sump packages.
- **xfce*:** Lightweight desktop environment.
- **xfdesktop:** Desktop manager for the XFce Desktop Environment.
- **xferstats:** Compiles information about file transfers from logfiles.
- **xffm:** Next generation file manager and XMB network navigator for XFce4.
- **xffm-icons:** Icons for xffm file manager.
- **xfig:** A utility for creating vector graphics that can be saved in a number of formats.
- **xfsprogs:** Utilities for managing the XFS file system.
- **xfsprogs-devel:** XFS file system–specific static libraries and headers.
- **xfwm4:** Next generation window manager for xfce.
- **xfwm4-themes:** Additional themes for xfwm4.
- **xhtml1-dtds:** XML document type definition for XHTML 1.0.
- **xinetd:** A secure replacement for the inetd super server.
- **xinitrc:** A utility for configuring X Window System startup.
- **xisdnload:** A graphical tool for displaying load activity on ISDN network connections.
- **xloadimage:** An image display and manipulation utility.
- **xml-common:** A collection of XML entities and DTDs.
- **xmlsec1:** Library providing support for XML Signature and XML Encryption standards.

- **xmlsec1-devel:** Libraries, includes, and so on, to develop applications with XML Digital Signatures and XML Encryption support.
- **xmlsec1-openssl:** OpenSSL crypto plugin for XML Security Library.
- **xmlsec1-openssl-devel:** OpenSSL crypto plugin for XML Security Library.
- **xmltex:** A namespace-aware XML parser written in TeX.
- **xmlto:** A tool that converts XML to various formats using XSL.
- **xmms:** A versatile multimedia player.
- **xmms-devel:** Header files needed by the Xmms multimedia player.
- **xmms-flac:** X MultiMedia System plugin to play FLAC files.
- **xmms-skins:** Skins for the Xmms media player.
- **xojpanel:** A graphical tool for displaying LCD contents on HP printers.
- **xorg-x11*:** Set of package containing the X.Org X server and related utilities, fonts and documentation.
- **xosview:** A utility for graphically showing system load and CPU usage.
- **xpdf:** An open-source PDF file viewer.
- **xrestop**: Utility to monitor applications' use of X server resources.
- **xsane:** An X interface to the Sane scanner and digital camera framework.
- **xsane-gimp:** A Gimp library interface to the xsane scanner and digital camera interface.
- **xscreensaver:** A large set of screensaver programs.
- **xsnow:** An X WindowSystem-based dose of Christmas cheer.
- **xsri:** Displays images on the background of your X display.
- **xterm:** The xterm terminal emulator command for the X Window System.
- **yelp:** The GNOME 2 centralized help and documentation browser.
- **ypbind:** The ypbind daemon process for binding NIS clients to an NIS domain.
- **ypserv:** The ypserv components for setting up a Linux NIS server.
- **yp-tools:** Tools for NIS based on the FreeBSD version of YP.
- **ytalk:** A multiuser chat program.
- **yum:** Tools for downloading and installing packages in RPM format.
- **zip:** A compression and decompression utility.
- **zisof-tools:** Utilities that create compressed CD-ROM file systems.
- **zlib:** A general-purpose, patent-free, loss-less data compression library.
- **zlib-devel:** Libraries for developing applications that require zlib compression.
- **zsh:** A shell/command-line interpreter similar to an enhanced ksh.
- **zsh-html:** Zsh shell manual in html format.

Appendix C

Running Network Services

Because Fedora can provide so many different kinds of services (serving Web pages, printers, files, and other resources), it's easy to lose track of them. Let's say you install all server software packages with Fedora. How do you know which servers will start up automatically and which will need special configuration to work? Where do you start to look for configuration files, start-up scripts, and daemon processes? How do you know if your firewall configuration is blocking access to the services?

This appendix provides a quick reference to the network services that come with Fedora. It offers an overview of the services described in detail in other chapters. You can use this appendix to help you remember how to get services working or as a guide to help you debug a service that needs fixing.

> **CAUTION:** Any services your computer offers to users who can reach it over a network pose a potential security threat. Refer to Chapter 14 for information on security, as well as the sections in the book that describe configuration of each feature in detail.

Checklist for Running Networking Services

As computer security issues increase with the rising onslaught of computer crackers and viruses, operating systems (such as Fedora or Red Hat Linux) are moving toward more security rather than more ease-of-use. Simply installing server software isn't enough to get the service up and running.

If a service isn't working, check the following items to hunt down the problem:

1. **Is the software package(s) installed?** Each network service is represented by one or more software packages. Use the command rpm -qc *packagename* to find configuration files, and the command rpm -qd *packagename* to find documentation. If you did a personal desktop or workstation install, most network server software may not be installed on your computer at all. Check Table C-1 to see which package(s) is needed for a service to work. (There might be other package dependencies as well, to which you will be alerted when you try to install the package.) Then use the rpm command to install the software from one of the installation CDs.

2. **Does the firewall permit access to the service?** The Fedora Linux installation procedure lets you configure a firewall. If you choose the default (Medium security) firewall, most services will not be available outside your local computer. Refer to Chapter 14 for information on how to change your firewall configuration to open ports that provide the different services.

3. **Is the start-up script set up to automatically launch the service?** Most network services are launched from start-up scripts that cause daemon processes to continuously listen to the network for requests for the service. See the "Networking Service Daemons" section for information on how to find start-up scripts and have them launch automatically.

4. **Is the configuration file created for the service?** Even if the daemon process is listening for requests for a network service, one or more configuration files associated with the service must probably be set up before requests will be accepted. Table C-1 lists important configuration files for each type of server.

5. **Does the configuration file permit proper access to the service?** Within the configuration file for a service, there might be several levels of permissions that a user must go through to get permission to the service. For example, a configuration file might allow access to the service from a particular host computer, but deny access to a particular user.

6. **Are there other restrictions to the service being shared?** Some standard Linux security measures might block access to a service that is otherwise open to being shared. For example, you can share a Linux directory using NFS or FTP servers, but local file permissions might block access to the directory or files within the shared directory.

The rest of this appendix provides an overview of the daemon processes, start-up scripts, configuration files, and software packages that are associated with the networking services that come with Fedora Linux.

Networking Service Daemons

This section provides a quick review of how networking services (as well as other services) are started in Fedora Linux. The two main directories containing files that define how services are started are /etc/xinetd.d and /etc/init.d.

- **/etc/xinetd.d** contains configuration files used by the xinetd daemon.
- **/etc/init.d** contains start-up scripts that are linked to /etc/rc?.d directories so they can be started at different run levels.

Each of these methods for handling network services is described in the following sections.

> **NOTE:** Some Fedora Linux configuration tools also store configuration information in the `/etc/sysconfig` directory. For example, there are configuration files for `iptables` and `sendmail` in `/etc/sysconfig`. If you search the scripts in the `/etc/init.d` directory for the word `sysconfig`, you will see just how many services look in that directory for configuration information.

The xinetd super-server

The `xinetd` daemon is referred to as the *super-server*. It listens for incoming requests for services based on information in separate files in the `/etc/xinetd.d` directory. When a request for a service is received by the `xinetd` daemon (for a particular network port number), `xinetd` typically launches a different daemon to handle the request. So instead of having separate daemons running for every network service, only the `xinetd` daemon needs to run — plus an additional daemon process for each service currently in use.

To see if a particular service handled by `xinetd` is on or off, go to the `/etc/xinetd.d` directory and open the file representing that service with a text editor. A `default` line at the top of the file indicates whether or not the service is on or off by default. The `disable` line actually sets whether or not the service is currently disabled. The following example is an excerpt from the `/etc/xinetd.d/tftp` file:

```
service tftp
{

        socket_type       = dgram
        protocol          = udp
        wait              = yes
        user              = root
        server            = /usr/sbin/in.tftpd
        server_args       = -s /tftpboot
        disable           = yes
        per_source        = 11
        cps               = 100 2
        flags             = IPv4
}
```

In this example, the `tftp` configuration file represents the Trivial File Transfer Protocol (TFTP) service. By default, the service is turned off. When the service is on, a request to the `xinetd` server daemon for a tftp service from the network is handed to the `/usr/sbin/in.tftpd` daemon. The `in.tftpd` daemon, in turn, handles the remote user's request for file transfer service from this Linux system that is acting as a TFTP server. Other entries in this file contain options that are passed to the TFTP daemon.

To enable a service in an `/etc/xinetd.d` file, edit the file using any text editor as the root user. Turning on the service is as easy as changing the `disable` option from yes to no and restarting the `xinetd` daemon. For example, you could change the line in the `/etc/xinetd.d/tftp` so that it appears as follows:

```
disable    =  no
```

Then you could restart the xinetd daemon (without turning off the daemon itself):

```
# service xinetd restart
```

> **NOTE:** Although not all services support this, the xinetd services lets you use the reload instead of the restart option with the service command just shown. With xinitd already running, a reload can occur faster and with less interruption to system services by not completely shutting down xinetd.

In this case, you could look in the /etc/services file and see that tftp services are (by default) received on port number 69 for TCP/IP and UDP networks. So, any request that comes into your computer for port 69 is first directed to the xinetd daemon, then handled by the tftpd daemon. If authentication is correct, the requested file transfer can take place.

> **CROSS-REFERENCE:** The xinetd super-server is described in Chapter 12.

The init.d start-up scripts

Network services that are not available via the xinetd daemon are typically handled by scripts in the /etc/init.d directory. For a script in the /etc/init.d directory to activate a service, it must be linked to a file in one of the run-level directories (/etc/rc?.d) that begins with the letter *S* followed by a two-digit number.

For example, the script for starting the print service daemon (/etc/init.d/lpd) is linked to the file S60lpd in the /etc/rc2.d, /etc/rc3.d, /etc/rc4.d, and /etc/rc5.d directories. In that way, the print service is started when Fedora Linux is running in initialization states 2, 3, 4, or 5.

> **CROSS-REFERENCE:** See Chapter 12 for more details on run levels and start-up scripts.

For the most part, system administrators are not expected to modify these start-up scripts. However, to have a service turned on or off for a particular run level, change the script to a filename that begins with an *S* (start) to one that begins with a *K* (kill). You can easily do this with the chkconfig command or the Service Configuration window. To start that window, type **serviceconf** from a Terminal window while you are logged in as the root user.

Start-up scripts typically start one or more daemon processes that represent a particular service. To add options to a particular daemon, you typically don't have to edit the start-up script directly. Instead, look for configuration files in the /etc/sysconfig directory. For example, daemons options representing the DNS (named), Samba (smbd and nmbd), and system logging (syslogd) services have options files in the /etc/sysconfig directory.

Choosing Alternatives

Some services in Fedora Linux can be implemented by several different software packages. Although you can, you probably don't want to run multiple mail and print servers on the same computer. At the very least, you should set the software you want to use by default.

In Fedora Linux, an "alternatives" feature is packaged into the operating system. Alternatives is an implementation of the Debian GNU/Linux alternatives feature. In essence, alternatives links the software you choose (or leave by default) into the common locations where the service being implemented is launched or made available.

> **CROSS-REFERENCE:** See the "Choosing Software Alternatives" section in Chapter 10 for more information on the alternatives feature.

The first services to be implemented under alternatives in Fedora Linux are print and mail server packages. However, when LPRng was dropped from Fedora, it left only mail as the service that's supported by the alternatives feature.

To switch your mail service from the main Red Hat menu, select System Tools → Mail Transport Agent Switcher (or type **system-switch-mail** from a Terminal window). The window that appears enables you to choose between the Sendmail (default), Postfix, and Exim mail-transport agents.

Figure C-1 shows an example of the system-switch-mail window.

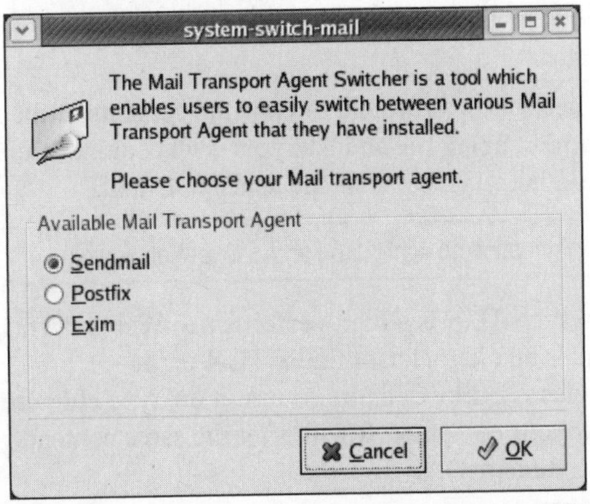

Figure C-1: Change your default mail-transport agent with system-switch-mail.

Referencing Network Services

This section contains the quick reference information related to Fedora Linux network services. The table listing these services (Table C-1) contains the following information:

- **Feature:** What type of service is it?
- **Package names:** What software packages must be installed to use the service?
- **Start-up scripts:** Which start-up scripts launch the service?
- **Daemon:** What daemon process is running to provide the service?
- **Configuration files:** What configuration files can you modify to tailor the service to your specific needs?

The descriptions following the table provide additional information about the service. That information includes whether or not the service is started by default and where you can find more information about the service.

> **NOTE:** When the `xinetd` daemon is noted as the start-up script, the daemon process to which the service is handed off is also noted.

The following sections provide some additional information about the services described in Table C-1.

Web server

In most cases, you use the apache software package to create a Web server in Fedora Linux. If apache is installed, you must turn on the service to use it (as root user, type **chkconfig httpd on**). Start-up will fail unless you have a valid name (and IP address) for your Web server. To define a server name, add a `ServerName` entry to the `httpd.conf` file and restart the service.

Users who can access your system from the network will be able to view the contents of the `/var/www/html` directory. Replace the `index.html` file and add your own content. If the httpd-manual package is installed, `/var/www/manual` contains the apache manual.

> **CROSS-REFERENCE:** See Chapter 21 for information on configuring an Apache Web server.

An alternative to apache is the TUX HTTP server. TUX is a high-performance Web server. The entire protocol stack for TUX runs in the Linux kernel. Configure TUX in the `/etc/sysconfig/tux` file. The TUX service is off by default. To turn it on, type **chkconfig tux on** and it will start the next time you start your computer. It will offer the same content that apache does (from the `/var/www/html` directory).

File servers

File services in Fedora Linux can be provided using FTP servers, Samba (Windows) servers, Network File System (NFS) servers, and NetWare servers. The following sections describe each of these.

FTP servers

The Very Secure FTP daemon (`vsftpd`) package was designed from scratch to be very scalable and fast. It is geared toward FTP sites that require support for lots of simultaneous users. Configure `vsftpd` by editing the `/etc/vsftpd.conf` and `/etc/vsftpd.user_list` files. The vsftpd package shares the `/var/ftp` directory structure and listens on port 21 for service requests.

To turn on FTP service, type the following (as root user):

```
# service vsftpd start
# chkconfig vsftpd on
```

CROSS-REFERENCE: See Chapter 20 for information on how to configure the `vsftpd` FTP server.

NOTE: An FTP server with Kerberos 5 support is also included with Fedora Linux. The `krb5-workstation` package contains the `ftpd` daemon that includes Kerberos 5 support. The wu-ftp FTP server software is no longer in the Fedora Linux distribution.

Samba server

The Samba server software supports the Server Message Block (SMB) file- and printer-sharing protocol. SMB is most often used to share resources on local networks consisting of computers running Microsoft Windows. You would not typically share SMB files and printers over a public network, such as the Internet.

Samba services are off by default in Fedora Linux. To have Samba start automatically when you boot your computer, simply type **chkconfig smb on** as the root user.

In order for Samba to be useful, edit the Samba configuration file, `/etc/samba/smb.conf`. An easy way to configure this file is with the Samba Server Configuration window (described in Chapter 18).

CROSS-REFERENCE: For more information about configuring Samba, see Chapters 17 and 18.

Netatalk server

The Netatalk server software lets Linux act as an AppleTalk server for Macintosh computers. To use netatalk, you must install the netatalk package and turn on the service by typing **chkconfig atalk on**. Configuration is done from files in the `/etc/atalk` directory.

CROSS-REFERENCE: See Chapter 26 for information on setting up netatalk.

NetWare server

NetWare is an operating system from Novell, Inc. that provides dedicated file and print services to network users. The mars-nwe package lets you set up your computer to emulate a NetWare file server. Although mars-nwe is no longer distributed with Fedora Linux, the package is available from various software repositories.

> **CROSS-REFERENCE:** Information on setting up NetWare services in Fedora Linux is provided in Chapter 18.

If you install mars-nwe, by default, NetWare file and print services are off. To turn them on, type **chkconfig mars_nwe on**. To make the service usable, you must edit the /etc/nwserv.conf file.

Login servers

A variety of login servers are available for use with Fedora Linux. Both telnet and rlogin services can be used to allow users from other computers to log in to Fedora Linux from the network. These days, however, ssh is the preferred login service. For most of these services, you need to remember to allow access to that service from your firewall.

If the telnet-server package is installed, the telnet service is off by default. If telnet is enabled, the xinetd daemon passes all requests for telnet service (by default, port 23) to the in.telnetd daemon to present the telnet login prompt. Once it is on, only users with real logins to the computer can log in to the computer — anonymous users are not supported. Users who log in using telnet are presented with a shell interface for accessing the computer.

Fedora Linux also includes login daemons that provide Kerberos 5 support. Kerberos 5 provides a higher level of security than is available with other login servers. Kerberos 5–enabled login servers include Klogin (Kerberos 5) and EKlogin (Kerberos 5 with encryption).

The rlogin service has been available for UNIX systems for a long time, though it is generally less secure than the other login services described here. The rlogin service is off by default on your Fedora Linux system.

A newer addition to the login servers available with Fedora Linux is the OpenSSH server. This service is on by default. To access this service, use applications that come with the openssh-client software package, such as the ssh, sftp, and slogin remote login commands. Many Linux administrators use OpenSSH tools, as opposed to older remote login tools such as rlogin and telnet because OpenSSH is believed to be more secure.

> **CAUTION:** Not only is the SSH service on by default, but unlike other login services, it will allow root login over the network. If you are uncomfortable with that, you should change the PermitRootLogin yes line in the /etc/ssh/sshd_config file as follows:
>
> ```
> PermitRootLogin no
> ```

E-mail servers

The most common protocols used to download e-mail from a mail server to a client workstation are Post Office Protocol (POP) and Internet Message Protocol (IMAP). If you configure Fedora Linux as your mail server, you can configure the dovecot package to provide POP and IMAP services.

Dovecot is an IMAP/POP3 mail server that works with both maildir and mbox formats. You use IMAP or POP3 if your users get their mail from their own desktop instead of by running their mail clients on the mail server. By default, all POP or IMAP services are off. Choose the POP or IMAP server you would like to use from those provided in the e-mail reader servers listing in Table C-1.

The default mail-transfer agent that comes with Fedora Linux is called sendmail. If sendmail software is installed, the sendmail service is started automatically. However, you must configure various files in the /etc/mail directory for the service to work beyond the localhost.

Postfix is an alternative to sendmail, as is the Exim mail transport agent. Using the alternatives feature (described earlier in this appendix and in Chapter 10), you can easily make any of those packages your default mail-transfer agent. Configuration files for postfix are located in the /etc/postfix directory, while exim configuration files are in the /etc/exim directory. Also make sure that you turn sendmail off (chkconfig sendmail off) and turn postfix or exim on (chkconfig postfix on or chkconfig exim on).

> **CROSS-REFERENCE:** Chapter 19 contains details on how to configure sendmail and postfix.

The comsat service can be turned on to check when e-mail arrives in users' mailboxes in Fedora Linux. Though comsat is off by default, if you turn it on you can use the biff or xbiff commands to alert users when e-mail arrives in their mailboxes. To turn comsat on, simply edit the comsat file in /etc/xinetd.d to change the disable = yes entry to disable = no.

News server

Fedora Linux comes with the Internet Network News Server (INN) software to let you set up a Fedora Linux system as a news server. INN can provide your users access to thousands of Internet newsgroups.

By default, INN service is off in Fedora Linux. To turn it on, type **chkconfig inn on**. To make the service usable, you must edit files in the /etc/news directory.

> **CAUTION:** Because a news server can potentially consume huge amounts of system resources, you must think carefully about how you configure it. Details about how to configure an INN news server are available from the *Red Hat Fedora Linux 2 Bible* Web site:
> www.wiley.com/legacy/compbooks/negus.

Print servers

The Common UNIX Printing System (CUPS) print server software is included as the default printer software for the current release of Fedora Linux. As an alternative, the LPR New Generation (LPRng) software is still available but is no longer provided with Fedora Linux.

> **CROSS-REFERENCE:** Information on setting up printers can be found in Chapter 17.

The Common UNIX Printing System (CUPS) is a recently developed alternative to LPRng and other printing interfaces that were built on facilities originally designed for line printers in the 1970s. CUPS is based on the Internet Printing Protocol (RFC 2616). Although it is compatible with other UNIX/Linux print facilities, CUPS is intended to make it easier to support new printers, protocols, and other devices as they become available.

The CUPS server (cupsd) is set up to run by default. Because CUPS is configured to be used as the printing service by default, you should run the system-switch-printer command if you want LPRng as the default print service for your computer. Configuration files for CUPS are located in the /etc/cups directory.

Network administration servers

Some network servers offer services that monitor or configure network configurations. Several of these services, listed in Table C-1, are described in the following sections.

Network Time Protocol server

The Network Time Protocol (NTP) Server synchronizes time among computers on a network.

The Fedora Linux firstboot process lets you turn on the NTP service. To further tune ntp, you must edit the /etc/ntp.conf file. The /etc/ntp.conf file contains information that identifies the addresses of synchronization sources and modes of operation. The /etc/ntp/keys file can be used to turn on authentication.

Portmap server

The portmap server translates Remote Procedure Call (RPC) numbers to TCP/IP and UDP port numbers. Certain network services, such as NFS (nfs) and Wall (rwalld), only work properly if this server is running. RPC numbers are stored in the /etc/rpc file.

SWAT

The Samba Web Administration Tool (SWAT) provides a Web-based interface for configuring Samba file and print services. When properly configured, a Web browser can access the SWAT service (with a root user password). Although this is a well-tested interface, the Samba Server Configuration window is the preferred tool for configuring Samba in Fedora Linux.

By default, the SWAT service is off in Fedora Linux. To turn the service on, edit the
/etc/xinetd.d/swat file and change the disable = yes entry to disable = no. This
makes the service available to a Web browser on the local host that asks for port number 901
(for example, http://localhost:901). You can remove the line only_from =
127.0.0.1 to allow a Web browser from any computer that has access to your computer on
the network to use SWAT. (Of course, a remote user would also need to know your root
password.)

Arpwatch server

The Arpwatch service can be turned on to monitor Ethernet/IP activities on your network. Any
potential problems (such as two different computers using the same IP address) are logged to
the syslog facility (usually to the /var/log/messages file).

By default, the Arpwatch service is turned off. To turn it on, type **chkconfig arpwatch on**.
You can check the /var/log/messages file to see if the Arpwatch services started
successfully and watch for changes on your network.

Simple Network Management Protocol server

The Simple Network Management Protocol (SNMP) server lets your Fedora Linux system
listen for SNMP requests from the network. With this server running, other computers using
SNMP tools can monitor the activities of your computer (based on configuration files set up on
your system).

By default, SNMP is turned off. To turn it on, type **chkconfig snmpd on** and **chkconfig
snmptrapd on**. SNMP configuration can be quite complex. Start by referring to the
snmpd.conf man page (type **man snmpd.conf**). Pay special attention to security issues with
SNMP. Refer to the net-snmp project site (http://net-snmp.sourceforge.net) for a
tutorial and more information.

Information servers

By distributing such information as host names, user account information, and network
addresses, an administrator can more easily manage groups of networked computers. Popular
types of servers for managing network information include Network Information System
(NIS), Dynamic Host Configuration Protocol (DHCP), and Lightweight Directory Access
Protocol (LDAP).

Network Information System servers

Network Information System (NIS) is a software feature developed by Sun Microsystems to
manage information needed to configure a group of UNIX (and now Linux) computers on a
network. Using NIS, a group of computers can share common passwd, groups, hosts, and
other configuration files.

By default, NIS services are off. You can turn on NIS services for your Linux computer as either an NIS client (using shared information) or an NIS server (distributing shared information). NIS client computers need to start the /etc/init.d/ypbind script and identify the NIS servers in the /etc/yp.conf file.

To use Fedora Linux as an NIS server, you must gather up the configuration files you want to share, then start the /etc/init.d/ypserv script. The script runs the /usr/sbin/ypserv daemon, which takes care of the distribution of information to the NIS client computers.

> **CROSS-REFERENCE:** Chapter 23 describes the NIS client and server software.

Dynamic Host Configuration Protocol server

Instead of going to each computer on your local network and adding all the TCP/IP information they need in order to work (IP address, netmasks, gateways, and so on), you can configure Fedora Linux as a Dynamic Host Configuration Protocol (DHCP) server to distribute that information. The client computer simply identifies the IP address of the DHCP server so that when the client starts up its network connection, the DHCP server automatically assigns its network address.

By default, DHCP is turned off. To turn it on, type **chkconfig dhcpd on**. Besides starting the service, you must also configure the /etc/dhcpd.conf file.

> **CROSS-REFERENCE:** Chapter 23 describes how to set up a DHCP server.

Lightweight Directory Access Protocol server

If your organization uses Lightweight Directory Access Protocol (LDAP) databases of information, running the LDAP server that comes with Fedora Linux enables you to access those databases. Likewise, the LDAP server enables you to use LDAP-enabled applications, such as Netscape Roaming Access and sendmail 8.

By default, the LDAP service is turned off. To turn it on, type **chkconfig ldap on**. In addition to running the start-up script, you must configure files in the /etc/ldap/ directory.

> **CROSS-REFERENCE:** Chapter 22 shows an example of how to set up an e-mail address book using LDAP.

Domain Name System server

A Domain Name System (DNS) server is set up to translate host names to IP addresses on a TCP/IP network. Fedora Linux can be configured as a DNS server using the named daemon.

By default, the DNS server is not configured to start automatically in Fedora Linux. To start a DNS server, type **chkconfig named on**. In addition to starting the service, you must configure the /etc/named.conf file and configure zone files (in the /var/named directory).

Reverse Address Resolution Protocol server

The Reverse Address Resolution Protocol (RARP) daemon responds to requests from RARP clients that must obtain their own IP addresses. Today, RARP is not used very often.

By default, the RARP service is off. To start an RARP server, type **chkconfig rarpd on**. When requests come in for addresses, the /usr/sbin/rarpd daemon checks the /etc/ethers or NIS+ databases for addresses.

Database services

Database servers provide tools for accessing and managing databases of information. The Postgresql service uses the postmaster daemon to handle requests for its services. The MySQL server runs the mysqld daemon to handle access to its databases. These daemons are started from start-up scripts in /etc/init.d: postgresql and mysqld scripts, respectively.

> **CROSS-REFERENCE:** Chapter 24 describes how to set up a MySQL database server.

User services

Fedora Linux can provide end users with a variety of network services. These services let users run remote programs, send messages in real time, and get information on active users.

Remote execution servers

Remote execution servers respond to requests from other computers to run commands on the local computer. This can be a security issue, so be careful in configuring these services. Three remote execution service daemons are available with Fedora Linux: Rsh, Rexec, and Kshell.

- The Rsh service (/usr/sbin/in.rshd) accepts requests for remote execution requests that were initiated by the rsh command (from other Linux or UNIX systems). By default, the service is off. The host or user (or both) must be allowed access before remote execution is permitted. Access is configured in the /etc/hosts.equiv file or in the .rhosts file in each user's home directory.

- The Rexec service (/usr/sbin/in.rexecd) accepts remote execution requests from the rexec command (from other Linux or UNIX systems). By default, the service is off. To allow remote execution, the user making the request must provide a valid user name and password.

- The Kshell service (/usr/kerberos/sbin/kshd) receives remote execution requests from the rsh command. It uses Kerberos authentication and encryption, making it more secure than the alternative in.rshd daemon. By default, the service is off. However, if you turn it on (by editing the `/etc/xinetd.d/kshell` file and changing the `disable = yes` entry to `disable = no`), it takes precedence over the `in.rshd` daemon.

The OpenSSH service (using the sshd daemon) described earlier can also be used for remote execution. OpenSSH is actually considered to be a more secure way to do remote execution than the other methods just described.

> **CROSS-REFERENCE:** Login commands for using login services are described in Chapter 16.

Talk server

Use the `in.talk` or `in.ntalk` servers to allow users to communicate using the `talk` command. The `talk` command enables users to type messages back and forth in real time. The `talk` daemon handles requests on port 517, and the `ntalk` daemon handles requests on port 518.

Both services are turned off by default. To turn on either service, edit the `/etc/xinetd.d/talk` and/or `/etc/xinetd.d/ntalk` files and change the `disable = yes` entry to `disable = no`.

Finger server

The finger (`/usr/sbin/in.fingerd`) server lets people use the `finger` command to request information about active users on Linux or UNIX systems locally or over a network. This service is off by default. If the `in.fingerd` server accepts a request from a `finger` command, the output to the user who made the request looks something like the following:

```
[maple]
Login: jake                    Name: Jake W. Jones
Directory: /home/jake          Shell: /bin/bash
Last login Mon Oct 14 13:34 (PDT) on pts/2 from maple
Mail last read Mon Oct 14 12:10 2000 (PDT)
```

The output shows the user's login name, real name, home directory, and shell. It also shows when the user last logged in and accessed his or her e-mail.

Remote user identification

The rusers server (`/usr/sbin/rpc.rusersd`) enables users to query the system from a remote computer to list who is currently logged in to the Fedora Linux system. The `rusers` command can be used to query the `rpc.rusersd` server.

By default, the rusers service is off. To start the server, type **chkconfig rusersd on**.

Write-to-All server

The Write-to-All (rwall) server (/user/sbin/rpc.rwalld) accepts requests to broadcast a text message to the screens of all users currently logged in to the Fedora Linux or other UNIX system. The request is made with the rwall command. By default, the rwall service is off. To start an rwall server, type **chkconfig on rwalld**.

Security services

Fedora Linux provides some services to protect your local network from outside attacks. These services include system logging, virtual private network servers, and caching servers. The following sections describe those services.

System logging

Though not specifically a network service, the system-logging facility (sysklogd package) logs information and error messages from most of the network services (and other services) on your computer. The system-logging daemon (/sbin/syslogd) should be running at all times.

The syslogd daemon is, by default, started at all multi-user run levels (2, 3, 4, and 5). You can change what messages are logged or have logging messages directed to different files by reconfiguring the /etc/syslog.conf file. You can change options used by the syslogd daemon by editing the /etc/sysconfig/syslog file.

Virtual private network servers

By encrypting data that travels across public networks, a virtual private network (VPN) can provide a secure way for users to access your local network from remote locations. Fedora Core 1 came with the Crypto IP Encapsulation (CIPE) virtual private network software. In Fedora Core 2, the IPSEC virtual private network service is included.

> **CROSS-REFERENCE**: See Chapter 16 for more information on IPSEC.

Proxy/caching server

The Squid server (/usr/sbin/squid) can be used as both a proxy server and a caching server. A proxy server can allow computers on your local network to communicate with the Internet by passing all requests through the proxy server. A caching server stores Web content that has been accessed by a local user on a computer that is physically closer to the user than the originating computer.

By default, the Squid server is off. To start the Squid server, type **chkconfig squid on**. You must also set up the /etc/squid/squid.conf file to identify who has access to the server and what services they can access.

> **CROSS-REFERENCE**: Chapter 16 provides details for configuring Squid.

Table C-1: Quick Reference to Network Services

Feature	Package Names	Startup Script(s)	Daemon	Configuration File(s)
Web Server				
Web-Servers (Apache)	httpd httpd-manual httpd-devel	/etc/init.d/httpd	/usr/sbin/httpd	/etc/httpd/conf/ httpd.conf
(Tux)	tux	/etc/init.d/tux	/usr/sbin/tux	/etc/sysconfig/tux
File Servers				
FTP Servers (Vs-ftpd)	vsftpd	/etc/init.d/vsftpd	/usr/sbin/vsftpd	/etc/vsftpd.conf /etc/vsftpd.user_list
FTP Server with Kerberos Support (Gss-FTP)	krb5-workstation	/etc/init.d/xinetd (/etc/xinetd.d/gssftp)	/usr/sbin/xinetd (/usr/kerberos/sbin/ftpd)	/etc/krb5.conf
Samba Windows File and Printers (SMB)	samba samba-common samba-client samba-swat system-config-samba	/etc/init.d/smb /etc/init.d/winbind	/usr/sbin/smbd /usr/sbin/nmbd /usr/sbin/winbindd	/etc/samba/smb.conf
UNIX Network File System (NFS)	nfs-utils system-config-nfs	/etc/init.d/nfs /etc/init.d/nfslock	/usr/sbin/rpc.nfsd /usr/sbin/rpc.mountd /sbin/rpc.statd	/etc/exports
AppleTalk File and Print Server (Netatalk)	netatalk	/etc/init.d/atalk	/usr/sbin/atalkd	/etc/atalk/*
NetWare Server (Mars-Nwe)	mars-nwe (no longer in Fedora, but available)	/etc/init.d/mars-nwe	/usr/sbin/nwserv /usr/sbin/ncpserv /usr/sbin/nwbind	/etc/nwserv.conf

Table C-1: *(continued)*

Feature	Package Names	Startup Script(s)	Daemon	Configuration File(s)
Login Servers				
Telnet	telnet-server	/etc/init.d/xinetd (/etc/xinetd.d/telnet)	/usr/sbin/xinetd (/usr/sbin/in.telnetd)	/etc/issue.net
Telnet with Kerberos Support (Krb5-telnet)	krb5-workstation	/etc/init.d/xinetd (/etc/xinetd.d/krb5-telnet)	/usr/sbin/xinetd (/usr/kerberos/sbin/telnetd)	/etc/krb5.conf
Open Secure Shell (Openssh)	openssh-server	/etc/init.d/sshd	/usr/sbin/sshd	/etc/ssh/*
Remote Login (Rlogin)	rsh-server	/etc/init.d/xinetd (/etc/xinetd.d/rlogin)	/usr/sbin/xinetd (/usr/sbin/in.rlogind)	/etc/hosts.equiv $HOME/.rhosts
Remote Login with Kerberos Support (Eklogin)	krb5-workstation	/etc/init.d/xinetd (/etc/xinetd.d/eklogin)	/usr/sbin/xinetd (/usr/kerberos/sbin/klogind)	/etc/krb5.conf $HOME/.k5login $HOME/.klogin
(Klogin)	krb5-workstation	/etc/init.d/xinetd (/etc/xinetd.d/klogin)	/usr/sbin/xinetd (/usr/kerberos/sbin/klogind)	/etc/krb5.conf $HOME/.k5login $HOME/.klogin
E-mail Servers				
Remote Mail Access Servers (IMAP)	cyrus-imapd	/etc/init.d/cyrus-imapd	/usr/lib/cyrus-imapd/cyrus-master (imapd)	/etc/imapd.conf /etc/cyrus.conf
(LMTP)	cyrus-imapd	/etc/init.d/cyrus-imapd	/usr/lib/cyrus-imapd/cyrus-master (lmtpd)	/etc/imapd.conf /etc/cyrus.conf
(POP3)	cyrus-imapd	/etc/init.d/cyrus-imapd	/usr/lib/cyrus-imapd/cyrus-master (pop3d)	/etc/cyrus.conf

Table C-1: (continued)

Feature	Package Names	Startup Script(s)	Daemon	Configuration File(s)
(Postfix)	postfix	/etc/init.d/postfix	/usr/sbin/postfix	/etc/postfix/*
(Exim)	exim	/etc/init.d/exim	/usr/sbin/exim	
E-mail Notice Server (comsat)	comsat	/etc/init.d/xinetd (/etc/xinetd.d/comsat)	/usr/sbin/xinetd (/usr/sbin/in.comsat)	
News Server				
Internet Network News (INN)	inn	/etc/init.d/innd	/usr/bin/innd	/usr/lib/news/bin/innd
Print Servers				
LPR New Generation (LPRng)	LPRng	/etc/init.d/lpd	/usr/sbin/lpd	/etc/printcap /etc/printcap.local /etc/lpd.conf /etc/lpd.perms
Common UNIX Printing System (CUPS)	cups cups-drivers cups-libs cups-drivers-hpijs	/etc/init.d/cups	/usr/sbin/cupsd	/etc/cups/*
Network Administration Servers				
Network Time Protocol Server (NTP)	ntp	/etc/init.d/ntpd	/usr/sbin/ntpd	/etc/ntp.conf /etc/ntp/keys /etc/ntp/ntpservers
Network Portmap (RPC to DARPA)	portmap	/etc/init.d/portmap	/sbin/portmap	/etc/rpc
Samba Administration (SWAT)	samba-swat	/etc/init.d/xinetd (/etc/xinetd.d/swat)	/usr/sbin/xinetd (/usr/sbin/swat)	/etc/smb.conf

Table C-1: *(continued)*

Feature	Package Names	Startup Script(s)	Daemon	Configuration File(s)
Network Management (arpwatch)	arpwatch	/etc/init.d/arpwatch	/usr/sbin/arpwatch	/etc/sysconfig/arpwatch
Simple Network Management Protocol (SNMP)	net-snmp	/etc/init.d/snmpd /etc/init.d/snmptrapd	/usr/sbin/snmpd	/etc/snmp/snmpd.conf
Information Servers				
Network Information Server (Ypbind)	ypbind	/etc/init.d/ypbind	/sbin/ypbind	/etc/yp.conf
(Yppasswdd)	ypserv	/etc/init.d/yppasswdd	/usr/sbin/rpc. yppasswd	/etc/passwd /etc/shadow
(Ypserv)	ypserv	/etc/init.d/ypserv	/usr/sbin/ypserv	/etc/ypserv.conf
Dynamic Host Configuration Protocol Server (DHCP)	dhcp	/etc/init.d/dhcpd	/usr/sbin/dhcpd	/etc/dhcpd.conf
Lightweight Directory Access Protocol (LDAP)	openldap-servers	/etc/init.d/ldap	/usr/sbin/slapd /usr/sbin/slurpd	/etc/openldap/slapd.conf
Domain Name System Server (DNS)	bind bind-utils	/etc/init.d/named	/usr/sbin/named	/etc/named.conf /var/named/*

Table C-1: (continued)

Feature	Package Names	Startup Script(s)	Daemon	Configuration File(s)
Reverse Address Resolution Protocol Server (RARP)	rarpd	/etc/init.d/rarpd	/usr/sbin/rarpd	/etc/ethers
Database Services				
MySQL Database	mysql mysql-server	/etc/init.d/mysqld	/usr/libexec/mysqld	/etc/my.cnf
Postgresql	postgresql-libs postgresql postgresql-server	/etc/init.d/postgresql	/usr/bin/postmaster	/var/lib/pgsql/data
User Services				
Remote Execution Servers (Rsh)	rsh-server	/etc/init.d/xinetd (/etc/xinetd.d/rsh)	/usr/sbin/xinetd (/usr/sbin/in.rshd)	/etc/hosts.equiv $HOME/.rhosts
(Rexec)	rsh-server	/etc/init.d/xinetd (/etc/xinetd.d/rexec)	/usr/sbin/xinetd (/usr/sbin/in.rexecd)	/etc/passwd
(Kshell)	krb5-workstation	/etc/init.d/xinetd (/etc/xinetd.d/kshell)	/usr/sbin/xinetd (/usr/kerberos/sbin/kshd)	/etc/krb5.conf
Talk Server (ntalk) (talk)	talk-server talk-server	/etc/init.d/xinetd (/etc/xinetd.d/ntalk) /etc/init.d/xinetd (/etc/xinetd.d/talk)	/usr/sbin/xinetd (/usr/sbin/in.ntalkd) /usr/sbin/xinetd (/usr/sbin/in.talkd)	

Table C-1: (continued)

Feature	Package Names	Startup Script(s)	Daemon	Configuration File(s)
Finger Server (Finger)	finger-server	/etc/init.d/xinetd (/etc/xinetd.d/finger)	/usr/sbin/xinetd (/usr/sbin/in.fingerd)	
Identify Users (Rusers)	rusers-server	/etc/init.d/rusersd	/usr/sbin/rpc.rusersd	
Write All Users (Rwall)	rwall-server	/etc/init.d/rwalld	/usr/sbin/rpc.rwalld	
Security Services				
System Logging (syslog)	syslogd	/etc/init.d/syslog	/sbin/syslogd	/etc/syslog.conf
Caching Server (Squid)	squid	/etc/init.d/squid	/usr/sbin/squid	/etc/squid/squid.conf

Index

GNU General Public License

Version 2, June 1991

Copyright © 1989, 1991 Free Software Foundation, Inc.

59 Temple Place - Suite 330, Boston, MA 02111-1307, USA

Everyone is permitted to copy and distribute verbatim copies of this license document, but changing it is not allowed.

Preamble

The licenses for most software are designed to take away your freedom to share and change it. By contrast, the GNU General Public License is intended to guarantee your freedom to share and change free software — to make sure the software is free for all its users. This General Public License applies to most of the Free Software Foundation's software and to any other program whose authors commit to using it. (Some other Free Software Foundation software is covered by the GNU Library General Public License instead.) You can apply it to your programs, too.

When we speak of free software, we are referring to freedom, not price. Our General Public Licenses are designed to make sure that you have the freedom to distribute copies of free software (and charge for this service if you wish), that you receive source code or can get it if you want it, that you can change the software or use pieces of it in new free programs; and that you know you can do these things.

To protect your rights, we need to make restrictions that forbid anyone to deny you these rights or to ask you to surrender the rights. These restrictions translate to certain responsibilities for you if you distribute copies of the software, or if you modify it.

For example, if you distribute copies of such a program, whether gratis or for a fee, you must give the recipients all the rights that you have. You must make sure that they, too, receive or can get the source code. And you must show them these terms so they know their rights.

We protect your rights with two steps: (1) copyright the software, and (2) offer you this license which gives you legal permission to copy, distribute and/or modify the software.

Also, for each author's protection and ours, we want to make certain that everyone understands that there is no warranty for this free software. If the software is modified by someone else and passed on, we want its recipients to know that what they have is not the original, so that any problems introduced by others will not reflect on the original authors' reputations.

Finally, any free program is threatened constantly by software patents. We wish to avoid the danger that redistributors of a free program will individually obtain patent licenses, in effect making the program proprietary. To prevent this, we have made it clear that any patent must be licensed for everyone's free use or not licensed at all.

The precise terms and conditions for copying, distribution and modification follow.

Terms and Conditions for Copying, Distribution and Modification

0. This License applies to any program or other work which contains a notice placed by the copyright holder saying it may be distributed under the terms of this General Public License. The "Program", below, refers to any such program or work, and a "work based on the Program" means either the Program or any derivative work under copyright law: that is to say, a work containing the Program or a portion of it, either verbatim or with modifications and/or translated into another language. (Hereinafter, translation is included without limitation in the term "modification".) Each licensee is addressed as "you".

   Activities other than copying, distribution and modification are not covered by this License; they are outside its scope. The act of running the Program is not restricted, and the output from the Program is covered only if its contents constitute a work based on the Program (independent of having been made by running the Program). Whether that is true depends on what the Program does.

1. You may copy and distribute verbatim copies of the Program's source code as you receive it, in any medium, provided that you conspicuously and appropriately publish on each copy an appropriate copyright notice and disclaimer of warranty; keep intact all the notices that refer to this License and to the absence of any warranty; and give any other recipients of the Program a copy of this License along with the Program.

   You may charge a fee for the physical act of transferring a copy, and you may at your option offer warranty protection in exchange for a fee.

2. You may modify your copy or copies of the Program or any portion of it, thus forming a work based on the Program, and copy and distribute such modifications or work under the terms of Section 1 above, provided that you also meet all of these conditions:

a) You must cause the modified files to carry prominent notices stating that you changed the files and the date of any change.

b) You must cause any work that you distribute or publish, that in whole or in part contains or is derived from the Program or any part thereof, to be licensed as a whole at no charge to all third parties under the terms of this License.

c) If the modified program normally reads commands interactively when run, you must cause it, when started running for such interactive use in the most ordinary way, to print or display an announcement including an appropriate copyright notice and a notice that there is no warranty (or else, saying that you provide a warranty) and that users may redistribute the program under these conditions, and telling the user how to view a copy of this License. (Exception: if the Program itself is interactive but does not normally print such an announcement, your work based on the Program is not required to print an announcement.)

These requirements apply to the modified work as a whole. If identifiable sections of that work are not derived from the Program, and can be reasonably considered independent and separate works in themselves, then this License, and its terms, do not apply to those sections when you distribute them as separate works. But when you distribute the same sections as part of a whole which is a work based on the Program, the distribution of the whole must be on the terms of this License, whose permissions for other licensees extend to the entire whole, and thus to each and every part regardless of who wrote it.

Thus, it is not the intent of this section to claim rights or contest your rights to work written entirely by you; rather, the intent is to exercise the right to control the distribution of derivative or collective works based on the Program.

In addition, mere aggregation of another work not based on the Program with the Program (or with a work based on the Program) on a volume of a storage or distribution medium does not bring the other work under the scope of this License.

3. You may copy and distribute the Program (or a work based on it, under Section 2) in object code or executable form under the terms of Sections 1 and 2 above provided that you also do one of the following:

a) Accompany it with the complete corresponding machine-readable source code, which must be distributed under the terms of Sections 1 and 2 above on a medium customarily used for software interchange; or,

b) Accompany it with a written offer, valid for at least three years, to give any third party, for a charge no more than your cost of physically performing source distribution, a complete machine-readable copy of the corresponding source code, to be distributed under the terms of Sections 1 and 2 above on a medium customarily used for software interchange; or,

c) Accompany it with the information you received as to the offer to distribute corresponding source code. (This alternative is allowed only for noncommercial distribution and only if you received the program in object code or executable form with such an offer, in accord with Subsection b above.)

The source code for a work means the preferred form of the work for making modifications to it. For an executable work, complete source code means all the source code for all modules it contains, plus any associated interface definition files, plus the scripts used to control compilation and installation of the executable. However, as a special exception, the source code distributed need not include anything that is normally distributed (in either source or binary form) with the major components (compiler, kernel, and so on) of the operating system on which the executable runs, unless that component itself accompanies the executable.

If distribution of executable or object code is made by offering access to copy from a designated place, then offering equivalent access to copy the source code from the same place counts as distribution of the source code, even though third parties are not compelled to copy the source along with the object code.

4. You may not copy, modify, sublicense, or distribute the Program except as expressly provided under this License. Any attempt otherwise to copy, modify, sublicense or distribute the Program is void, and will automatically terminate your rights under this License. However, parties who have received copies, or rights, from you under this License will not have their licenses terminated so long as such parties remain in full compliance.

5. You are not required to accept this License, since you have not signed it. However, nothing else grants you permission to modify or distribute the Program or its derivative works. These actions are prohibited by law if you do not accept this License. Therefore, by modifying or distributing the Program (or any work based on the Program), you indicate your acceptance of this License to do so, and all its terms and conditions for copying, distributing or modifying the Program or works based on it.

6. Each time you redistribute the Program (or any work based on the Program), the recipient automatically receives a license from the original licensor to copy, distribute or modify the Program subject to these terms and conditions. You may not impose any further restrictions on the recipients' exercise of the rights granted herein. You are not responsible for enforcing compliance by third parties to this License.

7. If, as a consequence of a court judgment or allegation of patent infringement or for any other reason (not limited to patent issues), conditions are imposed on you (whether by court order, agreement or otherwise) that contradict the conditions of this License, they do not excuse you from the conditions of this License. If you cannot distribute so as to satisfy simultaneously your obligations under this License and any other pertinent obligations, then as a consequence you may not distribute the Program at all. For example, if a patent

license would not permit royalty-free redistribution of the Program by all those who receive copies directly or indirectly through you, then the only way you could satisfy both it and this License would be to refrain entirely from distribution of the Program.

If any portion of this section is held invalid or unenforceable under any particular circumstance, the balance of the section is intended to apply and the section as a whole is intended to apply in other circumstances.

It is not the purpose of this section to induce you to infringe any patents or other property right claims or to contest validity of any such claims; this section has the sole purpose of protecting the integrity of the free software distribution system, which is implemented by public license practices. Many people have made generous contributions to the wide range of software distributed through that system in reliance on consistent application of that system; it is up to the author/donor to decide if he or she is willing to distribute software through any other system and a licensee cannot impose that choice.

This section is intended to make thoroughly clear what is believed to be a consequence of the rest of this License.

8. If the distribution and/or use of the Program is restricted in certain countries either by patents or by copyrighted interfaces, the original copyright holder who places the Program under this License may add an explicit geographical distribution limitation excluding those countries, so that distribution is permitted only in or among countries not thus excluded. In such case, this License incorporates the limitation as if written in the body of this License.

9. The Free Software Foundation may publish revised and/or new versions of the General Public License from time to time. Such new versions will be similar in spirit to the present version, but may differ in detail to address new problems or concerns.

   Each version is given a distinguishing version number. If the Program specifies a version number of this License which applies to it and "any later version", you have the option of following the terms and conditions either of that version or of any later version published by the Free Software Foundation. If the Program does not specify a version number of this License, you may choose any version ever published by the Free Software Foundation.

10. If you wish to incorporate parts of the Program into other free programs whose distribution conditions are different, write to the author to ask for permission. For software which is copyrighted by the Free Software Foundation, write to the Free Software Foundation; we sometimes make exceptions for this. Our decision will be guided by the two goals of preserving the free status of all derivatives of our free software and of promoting the sharing and reuse of software generally.

NO WARRANTY

11. BECAUSE THE PROGRAM IS LICENSED FREE OF CHARGE, THERE IS NO WARRANTY FOR THE PROGRAM, TO THE EXTENT PERMITTED BY APPLICABLE LAW. EXCEPT WHEN OTHERWISE STATED IN WRITING THE COPYRIGHT HOLDERS AND/OR OTHER PARTIES PROVIDE THE PROGRAM "AS IS" WITHOUT WARRANTY OF ANY KIND, EITHER EXPRESSED OR IMPLIED, INCLUDING, BUT NOT LIMITED TO, THE IMPLIED WARRANTIES OF MERCHANTABILITY AND FITNESS FOR A PARTICULAR PURPOSE. THE ENTIRE RISK AS TO THE QUALITY AND PERFORMANCE OF THE PROGRAM IS WITH YOU. SHOULD THE PROGRAM PROVE DEFECTIVE, YOU ASSUME THE COST OF ALL NECESSARY SERVICING, REPAIR OR CORRECTION.

12. IN NO EVENT UNLESS REQUIRED BY APPLICABLE LAW OR AGREED TO IN WRITING WILL ANY COPYRIGHT HOLDER, OR ANY OTHER PARTY WHO MAY MODIFY AND/OR REDISTRIBUTE THE PROGRAM AS PERMITTED ABOVE, BE LIABLE TO YOU FOR DAMAGES, INCLUDING ANY GENERAL, SPECIAL, INCIDENTAL OR CONSEQUENTIAL DAMAGES ARISING OUT OF THE USE OR INABILITY TO USE THE PROGRAM (INCLUDING BUT NOT LIMITED TO LOSS OF DATA OR DATA BEING RENDERED INACCURATE OR LOSSES SUSTAINED BY YOU OR THIRD PARTIES OR A FAILURE OF THE PROGRAM TO OPERATE WITH ANY OTHER PROGRAMS), EVEN IF SUCH HOLDER OR OTHER PARTY HAS BEEN ADVISED OF THE POSSIBILITY OF SUCH DAMAGES.

END OF TERMS AND CONDITIONS